CHRISTIAN WRITERS' MARKET GUIDE 2010

2010
Christian Writers' Market Guide

THE ESSENTIAL
REFERENCE TOOL
FOR THE
CHRISTIAN WRITER

Sally E. Stuart

Tyndale House Publishers, Inc.
CAROL STREAM, ILLINOIS

Visit Tyndale's exciting Web site at www.tyndale.com.

Visit Sally Stuart's Web site at www.stuartmarket.com.

TYNDALE and Tyndale's quill logo are registered trademarks of Tyndale House Publishers, Inc.

Christian Writers' Market Guide 2010

Copyright © 2010 by Sally E. Stuart. All rights reserved.

Cover photo copyright © by Mark Swallow/iStockphoto. All rights reserved.

Designed by Ron Kaufmann

Edited by Susan Taylor

Published in association with the literary agency of Books & Such, Janet Kobobel Grant, 52 Mission Circle, Suite 122 PMB 170, Santa Rosa, CA 95409.

ISSN 1080-3955

ISBN 978-1-4143-3425-7

Printed in the United States of America

16	15	14	13	12	11	10
7	6	5	4	3	2	1

CONTENTS

PART 2: PERIODICAL PUBLISHERS

PART 3: SPECIALTY MARKETS

PART 4: HELPS FOR WRITERS

INTRODUCTION

I can't believe this is actually the twenty-fifth annual edition of this guide. But as I look back, I can't help but reflect on all the publishers who have come and gone and all the changes that have happened—and are continuing to happen—on an almost-daily basis. Some changes are good, and some are bad, but all have helped define this industry.

Again this year I've been observing the changes and trying to determine what they mean for you. Certainly the economy is responsible for publishers and publications pulling back, downsizing, or shutting down entirely, but the most outstanding change seems to be a result of the expansion of technology.

For years I have been teaching classes on how to submit material for publication and stressing how important it is to address your submission to a specific editor by name. However, even that seems to be changing. At one point we went from sending mailed submissions to an overwhelming preference for e-mail contact, but that, too, is changing. Because editors are being overwhelmed with spam, many are moving to an online submission form.

As I've prepared this guide, I couldn't help but notice how many markets are no longer even naming an editor for submissions. Many are identified only by a generic e-mail address or title. We seem to be losing that initial connection to an actual editor—making it impossible to target a specific editor as I've recommended in the past. Of course, once your piece is accepted, you do make that connection to an actual editor.

And speaking of change, one of the biggest changes for the Guide is that we have a new publisher. Tyndale House has published this edition and will continue to do so going forward. Of course, a new publisher inevitably means changes—but changes we trust will take us into the future and keep up with the advancements in technology. Over the next five years we will be moving toward making the guide fully available online. Although the details are still in the planning stage, it is likely that the book will get smaller each year as more of the material goes online. Of course, that means the price of the book will be falling as well. More details on all this will be given as they become available. Although Tyndale House does not plan to continue to produce the CD, you will still be able to get the CD from me.

Now, back to the content of this year's Guide. Another thing you will notice in this edition is how many publishers are no longer listing a mailing address, phone or fax number, or even that e-mail address. You will find that more include their submission guidelines on their Websites, but often they don't provide a lot of information—which is why I try to fill in the blanks with the contents of this guide. Much of what you find here is not included even by those who do put guidelines on their sites. Last year I mentioned that blogs weren't catching on too quickly with publishers, but by now many have proven me wrong. Often the companies' Websites will connect you to their blogs if they have them.

With all the changes in the economy and within the industry, I wasn't sure how the total numbers of publishers listed in this year's Guide would be changing, so I was eager to do the final tallies. I wasn't surprised with the results. This edition lists 384 book publishers, 32 fewer than last year (including 22 new); and 636 periodicals, 18 fewer than last year (including 45 new). As usual, a few new topics appear in the book and periodical lists. Note that one new topic in the book section is "Music/Musicals" for those who need to find markets for the music they write.

As we see more and more periodicals going online or adding an online version, I thought it a good idea to add a code to identify them. An @ sign in front of a listing in the periodical section identifies an e-zine or online version. It's interesting to note that over 30 percent of the publications listed now fall into this category

In the book publishers' section, I wanted to identify those publishers who also produce e-books, so you'll find that same sign (@) in front of those listings.

The "Resources for Writers" section, which continues to be available only on the CD, includes about 100 new entries and two new subsections: Social Networking and an expanded "Blogs & Blogging" section. I encourage you to spend some time in that section, identifying those listings that will help you do your job better and more easily.

You will also find the Glossary of Terms back in the print edition.

This year I want to remind you again not to rely entirely on the topical listings for potential markets. Many good markets never fill out their list of topics, so you are likely to miss opportunities if you look only at that list.

Since a number of periodical publishers are now accepting assignments only, it is even more important that you establish a reputation in your areas of interest and expertise. Once you have acquired a number of credits in a given field, write to some of those assignment-only editors, giving your credits, and ask for an assignment. In general, you will be better off striving to get an assignment than hoping to fill one of the few slots left for unsolicited material.

Although agents continue to come and go, this year the list has dropped to fewer than seventy-five—which is a reflection of my decision to tighten up my qualifications for appropriate agents. It is still crucial that you carefully check out agents before signing a contract or committing to work with them. See the introduction to the agent section for some tips on how to do that. Because contacting agents has become more important in a writer's quest for publication, I indicate which conferences have agents, as well as editors, on staff. Attending conferences is becoming one of the best ways to make contact with agents as well as publishers.

If you are new to this Guide or only want to find specific markets for your work, you'll want to check out the supplementary lists that appear throughout the book. Read through the glossary and spend a few minutes learning terms you are not familiar with. Review the lists of writers' groups and conferences, and mark those you might be interested in pursuing. The denominational and corporate-family listings will help you start connecting periodicals and book publishers with their different denominations or publishing groups. With so many publishers being bought out or merging, this will help keep you up-to-date on the new members of these growing families.

Also be sure to study the "How to Use This Book" section. It will save you time trying to understand the meanings of the notations in the primary listings, and it's full of helpful hints. Remember to send for a catalog and guidelines or sample copies from any of the publishers or periodicals you are not familiar with. Study those carefully before submitting anything to that publisher or periodical. Also realize that publishers who make their guidelines available on their Websites do sometimes include more or different information online than you get in the usual guidelines sheet.

One of the most common complaints I've received from publishers over the years is that the material they receive is often not appropriate for their needs. Editors tell me repeatedly that they are looking for writers who understand their periodical or publishing house and its unique approach to the marketplace. With a little time and effort, you can meet an editor's expectations, distinguish yourself as a professional, and sell what you write.

Please also note that I have started a marketing blog (see next page) where you can find all kinds of information about the industry and keep your market guide up-to-date during the year. I make entries almost every day.

Finally, my special thanks to Donna Schlachter for producing the "Resources for Writers" section this year—always a daunting project. I also want to thank her husband, Patrick, for developing and overseeing the database I use to produce the guide each year. I couldn't do it without his professional help.

As always, I wish you well as you travel this exciting road to publication, whether for the first time or as a longtime veteran. And as I remind you every year, each of you has been given a specific mission in the field of writing. You and I often feel inadequate for the task, but I learned a long time ago that the writing assignments God has given me could not be written quite as well by anyone else.

Sally E. Stuart
1647 S.W. Pheasant Dr.
Aloha OR 97006
(503) 642-9844 (Please call after 9:00 a.m. Pacific time.)
Fax (503) 848-3658
E-mail: stuartcwmg@aol.com
Website: www.stuartmarket.com
Blog: www.stuartmarket.blogspot.com

- Please contact me for information on how to receive the *Christian Writers' Market Guide* automatically every year and freeze the price at $24.99, plus postage, for future editions (no matter how much the price goes up), or for information on getting the guide at a discounted group rate or getting books on consignment for your next seminar or conference.

- For a list of more than 60 additional books or pamphlets to help you with your specific writing needs, visit the bookstore on my Website.

- For information on editorial services (including book proposals and book contract evaluations), see my listing in the "Editorial Services" section under "Oregon."

- I also have a limited number of dates available to speak at writers' conferences. Contact me for availability.

HOW TO USE THIS BOOK

The purpose of this market guide is to make your marketing job easier and more targeted. It will serve you well, however, only if you use it as a springboard for becoming an expert on those publishers best suited to your writing topics and style. The following explanations and guidelines will help you become an expert on marketing yourself.

1. Spend time getting acquainted with the setup of this resource book. You cannot make the best use of it until you know exactly what it has to offer. Study the table of contents, where you will find comprehensive listings of periodical and book topics.

2. When looking at the topical sections, be sure to check topics related to your primary subject. Some cross-referencing may be helpful. For example, if you have a novel that deals with doctor-assisted suicide, you might look at the list for adult fiction and the list for controversial issues and see which publishers are on both lists. Those would be good potential markets. In the topical sections you will find a letter *R* following both book and periodical publishers that accept reprints (pieces that have been printed by other publishers/publications but for which you retain the rights). You will find a dollar sign ($) in front of the periodicals that are paying markets. That will help you find those quickly when getting paid is your primary goal for a particular piece. There is an *A* in front of the names of book publishers that require the use of an agent.

3. In each book-publisher listing you will find the following information (as available) in this format:

(a) Name of publisher
(b) Address, phone and fax numbers, e-mail address, Website
(c) Denomination or affiliation
(d) Name of editor—This may include the senior editor's name, followed by the name of another editor to whom submissions should be sent. In a few cases, several editors are named with the types of books each is responsible for. Address any correspondence to the appropriate editor.
(e) Statement of purpose
(f) List of imprint names
(g) Number of inspirational/religious titles published per year, followed by formats of books published (hardcover, trade paperbacks, mass-market paperbacks, coffee-table books). Note that coffee-table books have a listing in the topical listings for books.
(h) Number of submissions received annually
(i) Percentage of books from first-time authors
(j) (Usually) whether the publisher accepts, prefers, requires, or doesn't accept manuscripts through agents
(k) Percentage of books from freelance authors they subsidy publish (if any). This does not refer to percentage paid by author. If percentage of subsidy is over 50 percent, the publisher will be listed in a separate section under "Subsidy Publishers."
(l) Whether they reprint out-of-print books from other publishers
(m) Preferred manuscript length in words or pages; "pages" refers to double-spaced manuscript pages.
(n) Average amount of royalty, if provided. If royalty is a percentage of wholesale or net, it is based on price paid by bookstores or distributors. If it is on retail price, it is based on cover price of the book.
(o) Average amount paid for advances. Whether publishers pay an advance or not is noted in the listing; if they did not answer the question, there is no mention of it.

(p) Whether they pay flat fees (in these cases the author receives no royalties)

(q) Average first printing (number of books usually printed for a first-time author)

(r) Average length of time between acceptance of a manuscript and publication of the work

(s) Whether they consider simultaneous submissions. This means you can send a query or complete manuscript simultaneously to more than one publisher, as long as you advise everyone involved that you are doing so.

(t) Length of time it should take them to respond to a query/proposal or to a complete manuscript (when two lengths of time are given, the first refers to a query and the latter to a complete manuscript). Give them a one-month grace period beyond that, and then send a polite follow-up letter if you haven't heard from them.

(u) Whether a publisher "accepts," "prefers," or "requires" the submission of an accepted manuscript on disk. (Do not send your unsolicited manuscripts/submissions on disk.) Most publishers now do accept or require that books be sent on a computer disk (usually along with a hard copy) or by e-mail, but since each publisher's needs are different, that information will be supplied to you by the individual publisher when the time comes. This section also indicates whether publishers accept submissions by e-mail and whether they want one sent as an attachment or copied into the message.

(v) Which Bible version the publisher may prefer

(w) Whether they do print-on-demand publishing

(x) Availability and cost of writer's guidelines and book catalogs. If the listing says "Guidelines," it means guidelines are available for a #10 (business size) SASE with a first-class stamp. The cost of the catalog (if any), the size of envelope, and amount of postage are given, if specified (affix stamps to envelope; don't send them loose). Tip: If postage required would be more than $2.38, I suggest you put $2.38 in postage on the envelope and clearly mark it "Media Mail." (That is enough for up to one pound.) If the listing says "free catalog," it means you need only request it; they do not ask for payment or an SASE. Note: If sending for both guidelines and catalog, it is not necessary to send two envelopes; guidelines will be sent with the catalog. The listing will also indicate whether guidelines are available by e-mail or on the Website.

(y) Nonfiction and Fiction sections indicate preference for query letter, book proposal, or complete manuscript, and whether they accept phone, fax, or e-queries. (If it does not say they accept them, assume they do not; this reference applies to fiction as well as nonfiction.) If they want a query letter, send just a letter describing your project. If they want a query letter/proposal, you can add a chapter-by-chapter synopsis and sample chapters. If not specified, send from one to three chapters. This data is often followed by a quote from the publishers about their needs or what they don't want to see.

(z) Special Needs—If a publisher has specific needs, especially those that are not included in the subject listings, they are indicated here.

(aa) Ethnic Books—Usually specifies which ethnic groups they target

(bb) Also Does—Indicates which publishers also publish booklets, pamphlets, tracts, or e-books

(cc) Photos/Artwork—Indicates whether they accept freelance photos for book covers. If interested, contact them for details or photography guidelines. This year I have also added information on whether publishers will accept queries about artwork from freelancers.

(dd) Tips—Specific tips provided by the editor/publisher

Note: At the end of some listings you will find an indication that the publisher receives mailings of book proposals from The Writer's Edge (see "Editorial Services/Illinois" for an explanation of that service) and/or ChristianManuscriptSubmissions.com (see Website or index).

4. In each periodical listing you will find the following information (as available) in this format:

(a) Name of periodical

(b) Address, phone and fax numbers, e-mail address, Website

(c) Denomination or affiliation

(d) Name of senior editor and editor to submit to (if different)

(e) Theme of publication

(f) Format of publication, frequency of publication, number of pages, and size of circulation. Format refers to whether it is a magazine, newsletter, journal, tabloid, newspaper, or take-home paper. Frequency of publication and number of pages are both indicators of how much material the publishers can use. Circulation indicates the amount of exposure your material will receive and often indicates how well the publishers might pay or the probability that they will stay in business.

(g) Subscription rate—Amount given is for a one-year subscription in the country of origin. I suggest you subscribe to at least one of your primary markets every year to become better acquainted with its specific focus.

(h) Date established—Included only if 2007 or later

(i) Openness to freelance work; percentage of freelance written. This indicates the percentage of unsolicited freelance versus assigned articles. Since not all publishers have responded to this question, some will still give the two percentages combined or indicate only the unsolicited number. If they buy only a small percentage, it often means they are open but receive little material that is appropriate. When you have a choice, choose those with the higher percentage of freelance-written work, but only if you have done your homework and know they are an appropriate market for your material.

(j) Preference for query or complete manuscript also tells whether they want a cover letter with complete manuscripts and whether they accept phone, fax, or e-mail queries. If it does not mention cover letters or phone, fax, or e-mail queries, assume they do not accept them.

(k) Payment schedule, payment on acceptance (they pay when the piece is accepted) or on publication (they pay when it is published), and rights purchased. (See glossary for definitions of different rights.)

(l) If a publication does not pay or pays in copies or subscription, that is indicated in bold capital letters.

(m) If a publication is not copyrighted, you should ask for your copyright notice to appear on your published piece so your rights will be protected.

(n) Preferred word lengths and average number of manuscripts purchased per year (in parentheses)

(o) Response time—The time they usually take to respond to your query or manuscript submission. (Add at least two weeks for mail delays.)

(p) Seasonal material (also refers to holiday)—Holiday or seasonal material should reach them by at least the specified length of time in advance.

(q) Acceptance of simultaneous submissions and reprints—If they accept simultaneous submissions, it means they will look at submissions (usually a timely topic or holiday material) sent simultaneously to several publishers. It's best to send to nonoverlapping markets such as denominational), and be sure to indicate that it is a simultaneous submission. Reprints are pieces you have sold previously but to which you hold the rights (which means you sold only first or onetime rights to the original publisher and the rights reverted to you as soon as they were published).

(r) Whether they accept, prefer, or require submissions on disk or by e-mail. Many now prefer an e-mail submission rather than on disk. Most will want a query or hard copy first.

If it does not say they prefer or require disks, you should wait to see if they ask for them. If they accept an e-mail submission, it will indicate whether they want it as an attached file or copied into the message. If it says they accept e-mail submissions but doesn't indicate a reference, it usually means they will take them either way.

(s) Average kill-fee amount (see glossary for definition), if they pay one

(t) Whether or not they use sidebars (see glossary for definition) and whether they do so regularly or occasionally

(u) Their preferred Bible version—The version most frequently listed is the NIV (New International Version). If no version is indicated, they usually have no preference. See glossary for "Bible Versions" list.

(v) Whether they accept submissions from children or teens. A list of the publishers open to submissions from young writers is in the topical listings under "Young-Writer Markets."

(w) Availability and cost for writer's guidelines, theme lists, and sample copies—If the listing says "Guidelines," it means they are available for a #10 SASE (business size) with a first-class stamp. Many more now have guidelines available by e-mail or Website, and the listing will indicate that. The cost for a sample copy, the size of envelope, and number of stamps required are given, if specified (affix stamps to envelope; don't send them loose). Tips: (1) If postage required is more than $2.38, I suggest you put $2.38 in postage on the envelope and clearly mark it "Media Mail." (That is enough for up to one pound.) If the listing says "free sample copy," it means you need only to request it; they do not ask for payment or an SASE. (2) If you're sending for both guidelines and sample copy, it is not necessary to send two envelopes; guidelines will be sent with sample copy. If a listing doesn't mention guidelines or sample copy, they probably don't have them.

(x) "Not in topical listings" means the publisher has not supplied a list of topics they are interested in. Send for their guidelines or study sample copies to determine topics used.

(y) Poetry—Name of poetry editor (if different). Average number of poems bought each year. Types of poetry. Number of lines. Payment rate. Maximum number of poems you may submit at one time.

(z) Fillers—Name of fillers editor (if different). Types of fillers accepted; word length. Payment rate.

(aa) Columns/Departments—Name of column editor (if different). Names of columns in the periodical (information in parentheses gives focus of column); word-length requirements. Payment rate. Be sure to see sample before sending ms or query. Most columns require a query.

(bb) Special Issues or Needs—Indicates topics of special issues they have planned for the year or unique topics not included in regular subject listings

(cc) Ethnic—Any involvement they have in the ethnic market

(dd) Contest—Information on contests they sponsor or how to obtain that information. See "Contest" section at back of book for full list of contests.

(ee) Tips—Tips from the editor on how to break into this market or how to be successful as an author

(ff) At the end of some listings you will find a notation about where that particular periodical placed in the Top 50+ Christian Periodicals list in 2009 and/or their place in previous years. This list is compiled annually to indicate the most writer-friendly publications. To receive a complete listing, plus a prepared analysis sheet and writer's guidelines for the top 50 of those markets, send $25 (includes postage) to Sally Stuart, 1647 S.W. Pheasant Dr., Aloha OR 97006, or order from www.stuartmarket.com.

(gg) Some listings also include EPA winners. These awards are made annually by the Evangelical Press Association (a trade organization for Christian periodicals). This section also indicates the top-ten best-selling magazines in Christian retail stores.

5. It is important that you adhere closely to the guidelines set out in these listings. If a publisher asks for a query only, do not send a complete manuscript. Following these guidelines will mark you as a professional.

6. If your manuscript is completed, select the proper topical listing and target audience, and make up a list of possible publishers. Check first to see which ones will accept a complete manuscript (if you want to send it to those that require a query, you will have to write a query letter or book proposal to send first). Please do not assume that your manuscript will be appropriate for all those on the list. Read the primary listing for each, and if you are not familiar with a publisher, read their writer's guidelines and study one or more sample copies or the book catalog. (The primary listings tell how to get these.) Be sure the slant of your manuscript fits the slant of the publisher.

7. If you have an idea for an article, short story, or book but you have not written it yet, reading the appropriate topical listing will help you decide on a possible slant or approach. Select some publishers to whom you might send a query about your idea. If your idea is for an article, do not overlook the possibility of writing on the same topic for a number of different periodicals listed under that topic, either with the same target audience or another from the list. For example, you could write on money management for a general adult magazine, a teen magazine, a women's publication, or a magazine for pastors. Each would require a different slant, but you would get a lot more mileage from that idea.

8. If you do not have an idea, simply start reading through the topical listings or the primary listings. They are sure to trigger any number of book or magazine article ideas you could go to work on.

9. If you run into words or terms you are not familiar with, check the glossary at the back of the book for definitions.

10. If you need someone to look at your material to evaluate it or to give it a thorough editing, look up the section on "Editorial Services," and find someone to send it to for such help. That often will make the difference between success or failure in publishing.

11. If you are a published author with other books to your credit, you may be interested in finding an agent. Some agents will consider unpublished authors (their listing will indicate that), but many require an author to have a completed manuscript before being considered (see agent list). Christian agents are at a premium, so it can be hard to find an agent unless you have had some success in book writing. The agent list also includes secular agents who handle religious/inspirational material.

12. Check the "Group" list to find a group to join in your area. Go to the "Conference" list to find a conference you might attend this year. Attending a conference every year or two is almost essential to your success as a writer, especially when you get into book writing.

13. Send an SASE with every query or manuscript. If you do not want your manuscript returned, indicate that in your cover letter, and send a #10 SASE for their acceptance or rejection letter.

14. Do not rely solely on the information provided in this guide! It is just that—a guide—and is not intended to be complete by itself. It is important to your success as a freelance writer that you learn how to use writer's guidelines and study book catalogs or sample copies before submitting to any publisher.

PART 1

Book Publishers

1

Topical Listings of Book Publishers

One of the most difficult aspects of marketing yourself is determining which publishers might be interested in your book. This topical listing is designed to help you do just that.

First, look up your topic of interest in the following lists. If you don't find the specific topic, check the list of topics in the table of contents, and pursue any related topics.

Once you have discovered which publishers are interested in a particular topic, the next step is to secure writer's guidelines and book catalogs from those publishers. Just because a particular publisher is listed under your topic, don't assume that it would automatically be interested in your book. It is your job to determine whether your approach to the subject will fit within the unique scope of that publisher's catalog. It is also helpful to visit a Christian bookstore to see some of the books produced by each publisher you are interested in pursuing.

Note, too, that the primary listings for each publisher indicate what the publisher prefers to see in the initial contact—a query, a book proposal, or a complete manuscript.

An *A* in parentheses (A) before a listing indicates the publisher accepts submissions through agents only. This year these appear at the top of each topical list.

An *S* in parentheses (S) before a listing indicates that the publisher is listed in the "Subsidy Publishers" section and does at least 50 percent subsidy publishing or print-on-demand. Please note that some of these publishers do some royalty publishing as well (check their listings), so if you aren't interested in a subsidy deal, you can contact them and indicate that you are interested only in a royalty contract.

An *R* in parentheses (R) after a listing indicates which publishers reprint out-of-print books from other publishers.

An asterisk [*] following a topic/category name indicates it is a new topic this year.

AFRICAN AMERICAN MARKETS
(A) Doubleday Religion (R)
(A) One World/Ballantine

(S) American Binding (R)
(S) Booklocker.com (R)
Branden Publishing (R)
Cambridge Scholars Pub.
Charisma Kids
CLC Publications (R)
Fortress Press
Forward Movement
(S) IMD Press (R)
InterVarsity Press (R)
Judson Press (R)
Lift Every Voice (R)
Moody Publishers
National Black Theatre
New Hope (R)
Pilgrim Press (R)

St. Anthony Mess. Press (R)
(S) Tate Publishing (R)
UMI Publishing (R)
Walk Worthy (R)

APOLOGETICS
(A) FaithWords
(A) Harvest House
(A) Nelson, Thomas
(A) Regal

Aadeon Publishing (R)
Aaron Book Publishing (R)
Abingdon Press
(S) ACW Press (R)
Ambassador-Emerald (R)
(S) American Binding (R)
AMG Publishers (R)
Baylor Univ. Press
Bethany House (R)
(S) Black Forest (R)

Blue Dolphin
BMH Books (R)
(S) Booklocker.com (R)
(S) Bookstand Publishing (R)
Bridge-Logos (R)
(S) Brown Books
Cambridge Scholars Pub.
Canticle Books (R)
Catholic Answers (R)
Chalice Press
ChapterTwo (R)
Christian Family (R)
Christian Heritage (R)
College Press (R)
Continuum Intl. (R)
(S) Creation House (R)
Crossway Books
CSS Publishing
Deo Volente
Discovery House (R)
Eerdmans Pub., Wm. B. (R)

(S) Elderberry Press
Emmaus Road
(S) Essence (R)
Evangelical Press
Fair Havens (R)
(S) Fairway Press (R)
Father's Press
Forever Books (R)
Forward Movement
GRQ (R)
Guardian Angel
Hendrickson (R)
Hensley Publishing
Hidden Brook Press (R)
(S) Holy Fire Publishing (R)
Hope Publishing (R)
Howard Books
(S) IMD Press (R)
(S) Insight Publishing (R)
InterVarsity Press (R)
Kregel (R)
Lighthouse Publishing (R)
Lighthouse Trails (R)
Lion and Lamb
Lutheran Univ. Press
Magnus Press (R)
Master Books
Messianic Jewish Publishers (R)
Millennium III (R)
Monarch Books
NavPress Th1nk (R)
New Leaf
New Seeds (R)
(S) One World (R)
Our Sunday Visitor (R)
P & R Publishing (R)
Parson Place (R)
(S) Pleasant Word (R)
Power Publishing (R)
(S) Providence Pub. (R)
Randall House
Reformation Trust
Rose Publishing
(S) Sage Press (R)
Salt-Works (R)
Samaritan Press (R)
Scepter Publishers (R)
St. Anthony Mess. Press (R)
(S) Star Bible Publications
Strang Book Group (R)

(S) Tate Publishing (R)
(S) Trafford Publishing (R)
VBC Publishing
Whitaker House
(S) WinePress (R)
(S) Word Alive

ARCHAEOLOGY
(A) Doubleday Religion (R)
(A) HarperOne

Aaron Book Publishing (R)
Abingdon Press
(S) ACW Press (R)
(S) American Binding (R)
Baker Academic
Baker Books
(S) Black Forest (R)
Blue Dolphin
BMH Books (R)
(S) Booklocker.com (R)
Boyds Mills Press (R)
(S) Brentwood (R)
(S) Brown Books
Cambridge Scholars Pub.
ChapterTwo (R)
Christian Writer's Ebook (R)
Comfort Publishing (R)
Conciliar Press (R)
Dover Publications (R)
Eerdmans Pub., Wm. B. (R)
(S) Elderberry Press
(S) Essence (R)
Facts On File
(S) Fairway Press (R)
FaithWalk
Fordham Univ. Press (R)
Forever Books (R)
Gollehon Press
Hendrickson (R)
Hidden Brook Press (R)
(S) Holy Fire Publishing (R)
(S) Insight Publishing (R)
Kregel (R)
Lighthouse Publishing (R)
Lion and Lamb
Lutterworth Press (R)
Master Books
Monarch Books
New Leaf

New Seeds (R)
(S) One World (R)
Pacific Press
(S) Pleasant Word (R)
Power Publishing (R)
(S) Providence Pub. (R)
Rose Publishing
(S) Tate Publishing (R)
(S) TEACH Services (R)
Third World Press (R)
(S) Trafford Publishing (R)
Univ. Press of America (R)
VBC Publishing
(S) WinePress (R)
(S) Word Alive
Yale Univ. Press (R)

ART, FREELANCE
Aadeon Publishing (R)
Aaron Book Publishing (R)
Abingdon Press
Ambassador Books
Ambassador-Emerald (R)
AMG Publishers (R)
Anglicans United (R)
(S) Black Forest (R)
Blue Dolphin
(S) Booklocker.com (R)
Cambridge Scholars Pub.
Carson-Dellosa
Chelsea House (R)
Christian Ed. Pub.
Comfort Publishing (R)
Dawn Publications
Dove Inspirational (R)
Editorial Portavoz
Eerdmans/Young Readers
E.F.S. Online Pub.
Fair Havens (R)
Faith Alive
FamilyLife (books) (R)
Focus on the Family (R)
Forever Books (R)
Group Publishing
Guardian Angel
(S) Holy Fire Publishing (R)
(S) IMD Press (R)
Jebaire Publishing
Journey Forth/BJU (R)
Judson Press (R)

Knight George Pub. House
Legacy Press (R)
Lighthouse Publishing (R)
Lighthouse Trails (R)
Lion and Lamb
Liturgy Training (R)
Marcher Lord Press
Messianic Jewish Publishers (R)
Mission City Press
Monarch Books
Parson Place (R)
Parsons Publishing (R)
Pauline Kids (R)
Pelican Publishing (R)
Players Press (R)
(S) Pleasant Word (R)
Power Publishing (R)
(S) Providence Pub. (R)
Quintessential Books (R)
Rainbow Publishers (R)
Randall House
Ravenhawk Books (R)
Rose Publishing
Salt-Works (R)
Samaritan Press (R)
Sheed & Ward
Starik Publishing
(S) TEACH Services (R)
Treble Heart Books (R)
VBC Publishing
Warner Press
White Stone Books (R)
Wilshire Book (R)
(S) WinePress (R)

AUTOBIOGRAPHY
(A) Doubleday Religion (R)
(A) FaithWords
(A) HarperOne
(A) Nelson, Thomas
(A) WaterBrook Press (R)

Aaron Book Publishing (R)
(S) ACW Press (R)
Ambassador-Emerald (R)
(S) American Binding (R)
Baker Books
Believe Books
(S) Black Forest (R)
Blue Dolphin

(S) Book Publishers (R)
(S) Booklocker.com (R)
(S) Bookstand Publishing (R)
Boyds Mills Press (R)
Branden Publishing (R)
(S) Brentwood (R)
Bridge-Logos (R)
(S) Brown Books
Carey Library, Wm. (R)
ChapterTwo (R)
Christian Heritage (R)
Christian Writer's Ebook (R)
CLC Publications (R)
Comfort Publishing (R)
Continuum Intl. (R)
(S) Creation House (R)
CrossLink Publishing
(S) Dean Press, Robbie (R)
E.F.S. Online Pub.
(S) Elderberry Press
(S) Essence (R)
Evergreen Press
(S) Fairway Press (R)
Father's Press
Forever Books (R)
Friends United Press
Georgetown Univ. Press
Hidden Brook Press (R)
His Work Christian Pub. (R)
(S) Holy Fire Publishing (R)
(S) IMD Press (R)
(S) Insight Publishing (R)
Kirk House
KNB Publications
Life Changing Media
(S) LifeVest Publishing
Lighthouse Publishing (R)
Lighthouse Trails (R)
Lion and Lamb
Lutterworth Press (R)
(S) McDougal Publishing (R)
Monarch Books
New Seeds (R)
(S) One World (R)
Pacific Press
Parson Place (R)
Parsons Publishing (R)
(S) Pleasant Word (R)
Power Publishing (R)
(S) Providence Pub. (R)

Quiet Waters (R)
(S) Sage Press (R)
(S) Selah Publishing (R)
(S) Southern Baptist Press (R)
Still Waters Revival (R)
Strang Book Group (R)
(S) Tate Publishing (R)
(S) TEACH Services (R)
(S) Trafford Publishing (R)
Univ. Press of America (R)
(S) VMI Publishers
(S) WinePress (R)
(S) Word Alive
(S) Zoë Life Publishing

**BIBLE/BIBLICAL
STUDIES**
(A) Cook, David C.
(A) Doubleday Religion (R)
(A) Regal
(A) WaterBrook Press (R)

Aadeon Publishing (R)
Aaron Book Publishing (R)
Abingdon Press
ACTA Publications
(S) ACW Press (R)
Ambassador Books
Ambassador-Emerald (R)
(S) American Binding (R)
AMG Publishers (R)
Anglicans United (R)
Baker Academic
Baker Books
Baylor Univ. Press
Bethany House (R)
Blue Dolphin
BMH Books (R)
(S) Booklocker.com (R)
(S) Bookstand Publishing (R)
(S) Brentwood (R)
Bridge-Logos (R)
(S) Brown Books
Cambridge Scholars Pub.
Canticle Books (R)
Carey Library, Wm. (R)
Catholic Answers (R)
Chalice Press
ChapterTwo (R)
Christian Ed. Pub.

Christian Family (R)
Christian Focus (R)
Christian Liberty Press
Christian Writer's Ebook (R)
Clarke & Co., James (R)
College Press (R)
Conciliar Press (R)
Concordia Academic
Congregational Life
Contemporary Drama
Continuum Intl. (R)
CrossLink Publishing
CSS Publishing
(S) DCTS Publishing
(S) Dean Press, Robbie (R)
Deo Volente
Discovery House (R)
Editorial Portavoz
Eerdmans Pub., Wm. B. (R)
(S) Elderberry Press
Emmaus Road
(S) Essence (R)
Evangelical Press
Evergreen Press
Fair Havens (R)
(S) Fairway Press (R)
Faith Alive
FaithWalk
Father's Press
First Fruits of Zion
Forever Books (R)
Fortress Press
Foursquare Media
Good Book (R)
Gospel Publishing
Group Publishing
Grupo Nelson
Hannibal Books
Harcourt Religion
Harrison House
Hendrickson (R)
Hensley Publishing
Hidden Brook Press (R)
(S) Holy Fire Publishing (R)
(S) IMD Press (R)
Inkling Books (R)
(S) Insight Publishing (R)
InterVarsity Press (R)
Jebaire Publishing
Journey Forth/BJU (R)

Jubilant Press (R)
(S) Kindred Books (R)
Kregel (R)
Libros Liguori
Lift Every Voice (R)
Lighthouse Publishing (R)
Lion and Lamb
Lutheran Univ. Press
Lutterworth Press (R)
Magnus Press (R)
(S) McDougal Publishing (R)
Mercer Univ. Press (R)
Messianic Jewish Publishers (R)
Monarch Books
Morehouse
NavPress
NavPress Th1nk (R)
New Hope (R)
New Leaf
New York Univ. Press
(S) One World (R)
Our Sunday Visitor (R)
P & R Publishing (R)
Pacific Press
Paradise Research (R)
Parson Place (R)
Parsons Publishing (R)
Pauline Kids (R)
Paulist Press
Pflaum Publishing
Pilgrim Press (R)
(S) Pleasant Word (R)
Power Publishing (R)
(S) Providence Pub. (R)
Quill Driver Books
Randall House Digital
Revival Nation
Rose Publishing
Salt-Works (R)
Samaritan Press (R)
Sheed & Ward
Smyth & Helwys
(S) Southern Baptist Press (R)
SparrowCrowne Press (R)
St. Anthony Mess. Press (R)
St. Bede's Publications (R)
St. Pauls/Alba House (R)
(S) Star Bible Publications
(S) Tate Publishing (R)
(S) TEACH Services (R)

(S) Trafford Publishing (R)
Tyndale House Publishers
UMI Publishing (R)
Univ. Press of America (R)
VBC Publishing
(S) VMI Publishers
Walk Worthy (R)
Wesleyan Publishing
Westminster John Knox
Whitaker House
(S) WinePress (R)
(S) Word Alive
Yale Univ. Press (R)
Youth Specialties
(S) Zoë Life Publishing
Zondervan

BIBLE COMMENTARY

(A) Cook, David C.
(A) Doubleday Religion (R)
(A) Tyndale House (R)

Aaron Book Publishing (R)
Abingdon Press
(S) ACW Press (R)
Ambassador Books
Ambassador-Emerald (R)
(S) American Binding (R)
AMG Publishers (R)
Anglicans United (R)
B & H Publishing
Baker Books
(S) Black Forest (R)
Blue Dolphin
BMH Books (R)
(S) Booklocker.com (R)
(S) Bookstand Publishing (R)
Bridge-Logos (R)
(S) Brown Books
Cambridge Scholars Pub.
Carey Library, Wm. (R)
Catholic Answers (R)
Chalice Press
ChapterTwo (R)
Christian Family (R)
Christian Focus (R)
Christian Writer's Ebook (R)
Clarke & Co., James (R)
College Press (R)
Conciliar Press (R)
Continuum Intl. (R)

CrossLink Publishing
CSS Publishing
Discovery House (R)
Editorial Portavoz
Eerdmans Pub., Wm. B. (R)
(S) Elderberry Press
Emmaus Road
(S) Essence (R)
Evangelical Press
(S) Fairway Press (R)
Father's Press
Fifth-Estate (R)
Forever Books (R)
Grupo Nelson
Harrison House
Hendrickson (R)
Hidden Brook Press (R)
(S) Holy Fire Publishing (R)
(S) IMD Press (R)
Inkling Books (R)
(S) Insight Publishing (R)
InterVarsity Press (R)
Intl. Awakening (R)
Kregel (R)
Libros Liguori
Lighthouse Publishing (R)
Lutheran Univ. Press
Lutterworth Press (R)
Messianic Jewish
    Publishers (R)
Monarch Books
New Canaan (R)
New Leaf
New Seeds (R)
(S) One World (R)
Our Sunday Visitor (R)
P & R Publishing (R)
Paulist Press
(S) Pleasant Word (R)
Power Publishing (R)
(S) Providence Pub. (R)
Reformation Trust
Rose Publishing
(S) Sage Press (R)
Scepter Publishers (R)
Sheed & Ward
St. Anthony Mess. Press (R)
St. Bede's Publications (R)
St. Pauls/Alba House (R)
(S) Star Bible Publications

(S) Tate Publishing (R)
(S) TEACH Services (R)
(S) Trafford Publishing (R)
UMI Publishing (R)
VBC Publishing
Westminster John Knox
(S) WinePress (R)
Wipf and Stock
(S) Word Alive
Yale Univ. Press (R)
(S) Zoë Life Publishing
Zondervan

BIOGRAPHY
(A) Ballantine
(A) Doubleday Religion (R)
(A) HarperOne
(A) Nelson, Thomas
(A) One World/Ballantine
(A) WaterBrook Press (R)
(A) W Publishing

Aaron Book Publishing (R)
(S) ACW Press (R)
Ambassador-Emerald (R)
(S) American Binding (R)
Baker Books
Believe Books
(S) Black Forest (R)
Blue Dolphin
(S) Book Publishers (R)
(S) Booklocker.com (R)
Boyds Mills Press (R)
Branden Publishing (R)
(S) Brentwood (R)
Bridge-Logos (R)
(S) Brown Books
Carey Library, Wm. (R)
Catholic Answers (R)
Chalice Press
ChapterTwo (R)
Charisma Kids
Christian Family (R)
Christian Focus (R)
Christian Heritage (R)
Christian Liberty Press
Christian Writer's Ebook (R)
Cistercian (R)
Clarke & Co., James (R)
CLC Publications (R)
College Press (R)

Comfort Publishing (R)
Conciliar Press (R)
Continuum Intl. (R)
(S) Creation House (R)
CrossLink Publishing
(S) Dean Press, Robbie (R)
Discovery House (R)
Eerdmans Pub., Wm. B. (R)
E.F.S. Online Pub.
(S) Elderberry Press
(S) Essence (R)
Evangelical Press
Facts On File
Fair Havens (R)
(S) Fairway Press (R)
FaithWalk
Fordham Univ. Press (R)
Forever Books (R)
Friends United Press
Gentle Path Press
Georgetown Univ. Press
Guideposts Books
Hannibal Books
Hidden Brook Press (R)
His Work Christian Pub. (R)
(S) Holy Fire Publishing (R)
Hope Publishing (R)
Inkling Books (R)
(S) Insight Publishing (R)
Intl. Awakening (R)
Jossey-Bass
Kaleidoscope Press (R)
Kirk House
KNB Publications
(S) LifeVest Publishing
Lighthouse Publishing (R)
Lighthouse Trails (R)
Lion and Lamb
Lutterworth Press (R)
(S) McDougal Publishing (R)
Mercer Univ. Press (R)
Mission City Press
Monarch Books
New Leaf
New Seeds (R)
(S) One World (R)
Pacific Press
Parson Place (R)
Parsons Publishing (R)
(S) Path Publishing (R)

Pauline Books (R)
Pauline Kids (R)
(S) Pleasant Word (R)
Power Publishing (R)
(S) Providence Pub. (R)
Quill Driver Books
Quintessential Books (R)
Ravenhawk Books (R)
Reformation Trust
(S) Sage Press (R)
Scepter Publishers (R)
(S) Selah Publishing (R)
Sheed & Ward
(S) Southern Baptist Press (R)
Still Waters Revival (R)
Strang Book Group (R)
(S) Tate Publishing (R)
(S) TEACH Services (R)
(S) Trafford Publishing (R)
Univ. of AR Press (R)
Univ. Press of America (R)
(S) VMI Publishers
Whitaker House
(S) WinePress (R)
(S) Word Alive
Yale Univ. Press (R)
(S) Zoë Life Publishing

BOOKLETS

(A) Harvest House

Aaron Book Publishing (R)
(S) American Binding (R)
Catholic Answers (R)
Chalice Press
ChapterTwo (R)
Christian Writer's Ebook (R)
Concordia
(S) Creation House (R)
(S) Dean Press, Robbie (R)
Emmaus Road
(S) Essence (R)
Evergreen Press
Fair Havens (R)
Family Life (books) (R)
Forward Movement
(S) Fruitbearer Pub.
Good Book (R)
(S) Holy Fire Publishing (R)
(S) Insight Publishing (R)
InterVarsity Press (R)

Intl. Awakening (R)
Libros Liguori
Life Cycle Books (R)
Lighthouse Trails (R)
Liguori Public. (R)
Liturgy Training (R)
Lutterworth Press (R)
(S) One World (R)
Our Sunday Visitor (R)
P & R Publishing (R)
Pacific Press
(S) Path Pub. in Christ (R)
Paulist Press
Power Publishing (R)
(S) Providence Pub. (R)
Randall House
Rose Publishing
(S) Sage Press (R)
Salt-Works (R)
(S) Star Bible Publications
Strang Book Group (R)
(S) Tate Publishing (R)
Trinity Foundation (R)
(S) WinePress (R)
(S) Word Alive
(S) Xulon Press (R)

CANADIAN/FOREIGN

Ambassador-Emerald (R)
Cambridge Scholars Pub.
Canadian Inst. for Law (R)
ChapterTwo (R)
Christian Focus (R)
Clarke & Co., James (R)
Congregational Life
(S) Essence (R)
Forever Books (R)
Guernica Editions (R)
Hidden Brook Press (R)
(S) Kindred Books (R)
Kingsley Pub., Jessica (R)
Lutterworth Press (R)
Monarch Books
(S) One World (R)
Ponder Publishing
Revival Nation
St. Michael's Abbey
Still Waters Revival (R)
(S) Trafford Publishing (R)
(S) Word Alive

CELEBRITY PROFILES

(A) FaithWords
(A) Nelson, Thomas

Aaron Book Publishing (R)
(S) ACW Press (R)
(S) American Binding (R)
Baker Books
Blue Dolphin
(S) Booklocker.com (R)
(S) Brown Books
Christian Writer's Ebook (R)
Comfort Publishing (R)
(S) Elderberry Press
(S) Essence (R)
(S) Fairway Press (R)
FaithWalk
Forever Books (R)
Hay House
Hidden Brook Press (R)
(S) Holy Fire Publishing (R)
Howard Books
(S) Insight Publishing (R)
Life Changing Media
Lighthouse Publishing (R)
Monarch Books
(S) One World (R)
(S) Path Pub. in Christ (R)
(S) Pleasant Word (R)
Power Publishing (R)
(S) Providence Pub. (R)
Quill Driver Books
Ravenhawk Books (R)
(S) Sage Press (R)
(S) Selah Publishing (R)
Strang Book Group (R)
(S) Tate Publishing (R)
(S) Trafford Publishing (R)
(S) VMI Publishers
Whitaker House
(S) WinePress (R)
(S) Word Alive

CHARISMATIC

(A) Nelson, Thomas
(A) Regal

Aaron Book Publishing (R)
(S) ACW Press (R)
(S) American Binding (R)

Anglicans United (R)
(S) Black Forest (R)
Blue Dolphin
(S) Booklocker.com (R)
Bridge-Logos (R)
Canticle Books (R)
Charisma Kids
Chosen Books
Comfort Publishing (R)
(S) Creation House (R)
CSS Publishing
Destiny Image (books) (R)
Eerdmans Pub., Wm. B. (R)
(S) Elderberry Press
(S) Essence (R)
(S) Fairway Press (R)
Forever Books (R)
(S) Fruitbearer Pub.
Gospel Publishing
Harrison House
Hidden Brook Press (R)
(S) Holy Fire Publishing (R)
(S) IMD Press (R)
Life Changing Media
Lighthouse Publishing (R)
Lutheran Univ. Press
Magnus Press (R)
Monarch Books
(S) One World (R)
Parsons Publishing (R)
(S) Path Pub. in Christ (R)
(S) Pleasant Word (R)
Power Publishing (R)
(S) Providence Pub. (R)
Revival Nation
(S) Sage Press (R)
(S) Salvation Publisher (R)
Strang Book Group (R)
(S) Tate Publishing (R)
(S) Trafford Publishing (R)
Whitaker House
(S) WinePress (R)
(S) Word Alive
(S) Zoë Life Publishing

CHILDREN'S BOARD BOOKS
Ambassador Books
Candy Cane Press
Carson-Dellosa

Eerdmans/Young Readers
(S) Elderberry Press
Knight George Pub.
Messianic Jewish Publishers (R)
New Leaf
(S) One World (R)
Pauline Kids (R)
Standard Publishing
(S) Tate Publishing (R)
(S) Trafford Publishing (R)
(S) WinePress (R)
(S) Word Alive

CHILDREN'S DEVOTIONALS*
(S) Brown Books
Carson-Dellosa
Group Publishing
Guardian Angel
Lighthouse Trails (R)
Pauline Kids (R)
(S) Sage Press (R)
Warner Press

CHILDREN'S EASY READERS
(A) Cook, David C.
(A) Tyndale House (R)

Aaron Book Publishing (R)
Ambassador Books
Atheneum/Young Readers
Baker Books
(S) Booklocker.com (R)
(S) Bookstand Publishing (R)
Boyds Mills Press (R)
(S) Brown Books
Carson-Dellosa
Charisma Kids
Conciliar Press (R)
(S) Creation House (R)
Dawn Publications
(S) Dean Press, Robbie (R)
E.F.S. Online Pub.
(S) Elderberry Press
(S) Essence (R)
Evergreen Press
(S) Fairway Press (R)
Father's Press
Guardian Angel
Harvest Day

Hidden Brook Press (R)
His Work Christian Pub. (R)
(S) Holy Fire Publishing (R)
(S) IMD Press (R)
Inkling Books (R)
Journey Forth/BJU (R)
Journey Stone (R)
Knight George Pub.
Legacy Press (R)
Lift Every Voice (R)
Lighthouse Publishing (R)
Lion and Lamb
Master Books
McRuffy Press
New Leaf
(S) One World (R)
Our Sunday Visitor (R)
Pacific Press
Pauline Kids (R)
Paulist Press
Pelican Publishing (R)
(S) Providence Pub. (R)
Salty's Books (R)
Samaritan Press (R)
Standard Publishing
Strang Book Group (R)
(S) Tate Publishing (R)
(S) Trafford Publishing (R)
VBC Publishing
(S) VMI Publishers
Warner Press
(S) Word Alive
(S) Zoë Life Publishing

CHILDREN'S PICTURE BOOKS
(A) Cook, David C.
(A) Tyndale House (R)
(A) WaterBrook Press (R)

Aadeon Publishing (R)
Aaron Book Publishing (R)
Abingdon Press
Ambassador Books
Atheneum/Young Readers
Baker Books
Bethany House (R)
(S) Black Forest (R)
(S) Booklocker.com (R)
(S) Book Publishers (R)
(S) Bookstand Publishing (R)

Boyds Mills Press (R)
Bridge-Logos (R)
(S) Brown Books
Candy Cane Press
Christian Focus (R)
Conciliar Press (R)
(S) Creation House (R)
(S) CrossHouse (R)
Dove Inspirational (R)
Editorial Portavoz
Eerdmans Pub., Wm. B. (R)
Eerdmans/Young Readers
(S) Elderberry Press
(S) Essence (R)
Evergreen Press
Extreme Diva
Faith Communications
Father's Press
Fifth-Estate (R)
Forever Books (R)
(S) Fruitbearer Pub.
Gentle Path Press
Grupo Nelson
Guardian Angel
Harvest Day
His Work Christian Pub. (R)
(S) Holy Fire Publishing (R)
(S) IMD Press (R)
Journey Stone (R)
Kaleidoscope Press (R)
Knight George Pub.
Kregel (R)
Legacy Press (R)
(S) LifeVest Publishing
Lighthouse Publishing (R)
Lighthouse Trails (R)
Lion and Lamb
Master Books
Messianic Jewish Publishers (R)
Monarch Books
New Leaf
(S) One World (R)
P & R Publishing (R)
Pauline Kids (R)
Pelican Publishing (R)
(S) Pleasant Word (R)
(S) Providence Pub. (R)
Putnam/Young Readers
Revival Nation
Salt-Works (R)

Salty's Books (R)
Samaritan Press (R)
(S) Selah Publishing (R)
Standard Publishing
(S) Tate Publishing (R)
(S) TEACH Services (R)
Third World Press (R)
(S) Trafford Publishing (R)
Warner Press
White Stone Books (R)
(S) WinePress (R)
(S) Zoë Life Publishing

CHRIST

(A) Cook, David C.
(A) Doubleday Religion (R)
(A) Nelson, Thomas

Aaron Book Publishing (R)
(S) ACW Press (R)
Ambassador-Emerald (R)
(S) American Binding (R)
Atheneum/Young Readers
Barbour
Bethany House (R)
(S) Black Forest (R)
Blue Dolphin
BMH Books (R)
(S) Booklocker.com (R)
(S) Bookstand Publishing (R)
(S) Brown Books
Canticle Books (R)
Catholic Answers (R)
Charisma Kids
Christian Family (R)
Christian Focus (R)
Christian Heritage (R)
Christian Writer's Ebook (R)
CLC Publications (R)
Continuum Intl. (R)
(S) Creation House (R)
CrossLink Publishing
CSS Publishing
Discovery House (R)
Eerdmans Pub., Wm. B. (R)
E.F.S. Online Pub.
(S) Elderberry Press
Eldridge Plays
Emmaus Road
(S) Essence (R)

Evangelical Press
(S) Fairway Press (R)
Father's Press
Forever Books (R)
Gollehon Press
GRQ (R)
Guardian Angel
Guideposts Books
Hendrickson (R)
Hidden Brook Press (R)
(S) Holy Fire Publishing (R)
(S) IMD Press (R)
(S) Insight Publishing (R)
Journey Forth/BJU (R)
Lift Every Voice (R)
Lighthouse Publishing (R)
Lillenas
Lion and Lamb
Lutheran Univ. Press
Magnus Press (R)
Monarch Books
NavPress Th1nk (R)
New Leaf
New Seeds (R)
(S) One World (R)
Our Sunday Visitor (R)
P & R Publishing (R)
Paradise Research (R)
Parson Place (R)
Pauline Kids (R)
Pilgrim Press (R)
(S) Pleasant Word (R)
Power Publishing (R)
(S) Providence Pub. (R)
Quintessential Books (R)
Reformation Trust
Rose Publishing
Salt-Works (R)
SparrowCrowne Press (R)
St. Anthony Mess. Press (R)
St. Bede's Publications (R)
(S) Star Bible Publications
Strang Book Group (R)
(S) Tate Publishing (R)
(S) TEACH Services (R)
Torch Legacy
(S) Trafford Publishing (R)
VBC Publishing
(S) VMI Publishers
(S) WinePress (R)

(S) Word Alive
Yale Univ. Press (R)
(S) Zoë Life Publishing

CHRISTIAN BUSINESS
(A) Cook, David C.
(A) Doubleday Religion (R)
(A) Nelson, Thomas
(A) WaterBrook Press (R)

Aaron Book Publishing (R)
(S) ACW Press (R)
Ambassador-Emerald (R)
(S) American Binding (R)
Anglicans United (R)
(S) Black Forest (R)
Blue Dolphin
BMH Books (R)
(S) Booklocker.com (R)
(S) Bookstand Publishing (R)
(S) Brown Books
Chalice Press
Christian Family (R)
Christian Writer's Ebook (R)
Cladach Publishing
(S) Creation House (R)
CSS Publishing
Eerdmans Pub., Wm. B. (R)
E.F.S. Online Pub.
(S) Elderberry Press
(S) Essence (R)
Evergreen Press
(S) Fairway Press (R)
Father's Press
Forever Books (R)
Forward Movement
Grupo Nelson
Hannibal Books
Hidden Brook Press (R)
(S) Holy Fire Publishing (R)
Howard Books
(S) IMD Press (R)
(S) Insight Publishing (R)
InterVarsity Press (R)
Jebaire Publishing
Journey Forth/BJU (R)
Jubilant Press (R)
Kirk House
Lift Every Voice (R)
Lighthouse Publishing (R)

Lion and Lamb
Lutheran Univ. Press
Millennium III (R)
Monarch Books
New Leaf
(S) One World (R)
(S) Path Pub. in Christ (R)
Pilgrim Press (R)
(S) Pleasant Word (R)
Power Publishing (R)
PREP Publishing (R)
(S) Providence Pub. (R)
Quintessential Books (R)
Ravenhawk Books (R)
(S) Sage Press (R)
(S) Salvation Publisher (R)
St. Anthony Mess. Press (R)
(S) Star Bible Publications
Starik Publishing
Strang Book Group (R)
(S) Tate Publishing (R)
(S) TEACH Services (R)
(S) Trafford Publishing (R)
Treble Heart Books (R)
Trinity Foundation (R)
VBC Publishing
(S) VMI Publishers
Westminster John Knox
Whitaker House
(S) WinePress (R)
(S) Word Alive
(S) Zoë Life Publishing

CHRISTIAN EDUCATION
(A) Cook, David C.
(A) Doubleday Religion (R)

Aaron Book Publishing (R)
(S) ACW Press (R)
(S) American Binding (R)
Baker Academic
Baker Books
Blue Dolphin
(S) Booklocker.com (R)
(S) Bookstand Publishing (R)
(S) Brentwood (R)
(S) Brown Books
Carson-Dellosa
Chalice Press
Christian Ed. Pub.

Christian Family (R)
Christian Heritage (R)
Christian Liberty Press
Christian Writer's Ebook (R)
Church Growth Inst.
College Press (R)
Congregational Life
Contemporary Drama
CSS Publishing
(S) DCTS Publishing
(S) Dean Press, Robbie (R)
Eerdmans Pub., Wm. B. (R)
E.F.S. Online Pub.
(S) Elderberry Press
Eldridge Plays
(S) Essence (R)
ETC Publications
Evangelical Press
(S) Fairway Press (R)
Faith Alive
Father's Press
Forever Books (R)
Gospel Publishing
Group Publishing
Harcourt Religion
Harvest Day
Hensley Publishing
Hidden Brook Press (R)
(S) Holy Fire Publishing (R)
(S) IMD Press (R)
(S) Insight Publishing (R)
InterVarsity Press (R)
Judson Press (R)
Kingsley Pub., Jessica (R)
Kirk House
Knight George Pub.
Kregel (R)
Lift Every Voice (R)
Lighthouse Publishing (R)
Lion and Lamb
Liturgical Press
Lutheran Univ. Press
Lutterworth Press (R)
Master Books
Meriwether
Millennium III (R)
Monarch Books
New Canaan (R)
New Leaf
Northwestern

(S) One World (R)
Our Sunday Visitor (R)
Pacific Press
(S) Path Pub. in Christ (R)
Pilgrim Press (R)
(S) Pleasant Word (R)
Power Publishing (R)
(S) Providence Pub. (R)
Quintessential Books (R)
Rainbow Publishers (R)
Randall House
Reference Service
Rose Publishing
(S) Sage Press (R)
(S) Salvation Publisher (R)
Samaritan Press (R)
Smyth & Helwys
(S) Southern Baptist Press (R)
Standard Publishing
(S) Star Bible Publications
Starik Publishing
Still Waters Revival (R)
(S) Tate Publishing (R)
(S) TEACH Services (R)
Torch Legacy
(S) Trafford Publishing (R)
Treble Heart Books (R)
Trinity Foundation (R)
UMI Publishing (R)
Univ. Press of America (R)
VBC Publishing
(S) WinePress (R)
(S) Word Alive
(S) Zoë Life Publishing

CHRISTIAN HOMESCHOOLING

Aaron Book Publishing (R)
(S) ACW Press (R)
(S) American Binding (R)
Baker Books
Blue Dolphin
BMH Books (R)
(S) Booklocker.com (R)
(S) Bookstand Publishing (R)
(S) Brentwood (R)
(S) Brown Books
Carson-Dellosa
Chalice Press
Christian Family (R)

Christian Focus (R)
Christian Writer's Ebook (R)
(S) CrossHouse (R)
CSS Publishing
(S) Dean Press, Robbie (R)
Eerdmans Pub., Wm. B. (R)
(S) Elderberry Press
(S) Essence (R)
ETC Publications
Evangelical Press
(S) Fairway Press (R)
Father's Press
Forever Books (R)
(S) Fruitbearer Pub.
Hannibal Books
Harcourt Religion
Hidden Brook Press (R)
(S) Holy Fire Publishing (R)
(S) IMD Press (R)
Inkling Books (R)
(S) Insight Publishing (R)
Jesus Filled Day (books)
Jubilant Press (R)
Kaleidoscope Press (R)
Lift Every Voice (R)
Lighthouse Publishing (R)
Lion and Lamb
Little Lauren Books
Master Books
Mission City Press
Monarch Books
New Leaf
(S) One World (R)
Pacific Press
Parsons Publishing (R)
(S) Path Pub. in Christ (R)
(S) Pleasant Word (R)
Power Publishing (R)
(S) Providence Pub. (R)
Rose Publishing
Standard Publishing
(S) Star Bible Publications
Starik Publishing
Still Waters Revival (R)
(S) Tate Publishing (R)
(S) TEACH Services (R)
(S) Trafford Publishing (R)
(S) WinePress (R)
(S) Word Alive
(S) Zoë Life Publishing

CHRISTIAN LIVING

(A) Cook, David C.
(A) Doubleday Religion (R)
(A) FaithWords
(A) HarperOne
(A) Harvest House
(A) Nelson, Thomas
(A) Regal
(A) Revell
(A) Tyndale House (R)
(A) WaterBrook Press (R)
(A) W Publishing

Aadeon Publishing (R)
Aaron Book Publishing (R)
Abingdon Press
ACTA Publications
(S) ACW Press (R)
Ambassador Books
Ambassador-Emerald (R)
(S) American Binding (R)
B & H Publishing
Baker Books
Barbour
Beacon Hill Press (R)
Bethany House (R)
(S) Black Forest (R)
Blue Dolphin
(S) Booklocker.com (R)
(S) Bookstand Publishing (R)
(S) Brentwood (R)
(S) Brown Books
Canticle Books (R)
Chalice Press
Christian Family (R)
Christian Focus (R)
Christian Writer's Ebook (R)
Cladach Publishing
CLC Publications (R)
(S) Creation House (R)
CrossLink Publishing
Crossroad Publishing (R)
Crossway Books
CSS Publishing
(S) DCTS Publishing
Destiny Image (books) (R)
Dimensions for Living
Discovery House (R)
Editorial Portavoz
Eerdmans Pub., Wm. B. (R)

E.F.S. Online Pub.
(S) Elderberry Press
Elijah Press
Emmaus Road
(S) Essence (R)
Evangelical Press
Evergreen Press
Fair Havens (R)
(S) Fairway Press (R)
FaithWalk
Father's Press
Forever Books (R)
Forward Movement
Fresh Air Books
Good News Pub.
GRQ (R)
Guideposts Books
Harvest Day
HeartSpring Pub. (R)
Hendrickson (R)
Hidden Brook Press (R)
His Work Christian Pub. (R)
(S) Holy Fire Publishing (R)
Hope Publishing (R)
Howard Books
(S) IMD Press (R)
(S) Impact Christian (R)
(S) Insight Publishing (R)
InterVarsity Press (R)
Jebaire Publishing
Jesus Filled Day (books)
Jossey-Bass
Journey Forth/BJU (R)
Judson Press (R)
(S) Kindred Books (R)
Kingsley Pub., Jessica (R)
Life Changing Media
Life Cycle Books (R)
Lift Every Voice (R)
Lighthouse Publishing (R)
Lighthouse Trails (R)
Lillenas
Lion and Lamb
Liturgical Press
Lutheran Univ. Press
Lutheran Voices
Lutterworth Press (R)
Magnus Press (R)
(S) McDougal Publishing (R)
Monarch Books

Moody Publishers
Multnomah
NavPress
NavPress Th1nk (R)
New Hope (R)
(S) One World (R)
Our Sunday Visitor (R)
Parsons Publishing (R)
(S) Path Pub. in Christ (R)
Pauline Books (R)
Pauline Kids (R)
Pilgrim Press (R)
(S) Pleasant Word (R)
Port Hole Publications
Power Publishing (R)
(S) Providence Pub. (R)
Quill Driver Books
Quintessential Books (R)
Ragged Edge (R)
Randall House
Reformation Trust
Rose Publishing
(S) Sage Press (R)
(S) Salvation Publisher (R)
Samaritan Press (R)
(S) Selah Publishing (R)
Smyth & Helwys
SparrowCrowne Press (R)
St. Anthony Mess. Press (R)
Standard Publishing
(S) Star Bible Publications
Starik Publishing
Still Waters Revival (R)
Strang Book Group (R)
(S) Tate Publishing (R)
Tau Publishing (R)
(S) TEACH Services (R)
Torch Legacy
(S) Trafford Publishing (R)
Treble Heart Books (R)
UMI Publishing (R)
Univ. Press of America (R)
VBC Publishing
(S) VMI Publishers
Wesleyan Publishing
Westminster John Knox
White Stone Books (R)
(S) WinePress (R)
(S) Word Alive
(S) Zoë Life Publishing

CHRISTIAN SCHOOL BOOKS

Aaron Book Publishing (R)
(S) ACW Press (R)
(S) American Binding (R)
Baker Books
Blue Dolphin
(S) Booklocker.com (R)
(S) Bookstand Publishing (R)
Carson-Dellosa
Christian Liberty Press
Christian Writer's Ebook (R)
CrossLink Publishing
CSS Publishing
(S) Dean Press, Robbie (R)
Eerdmans Pub., Wm. B. (R)
E.F.S. Online Pub.
(S) Elderberry Press
(S) Essence (R)
ETC Publications
Facts On File
(S) Fairway Press (R)
Father's Press
Forever Books (R)
Heart of Wisdom
Hidden Brook Press (R)
(S) Holy Fire Publishing (R)
(S) IMD Press (R)
Inkling Books (R)
(S) Insight Publishing (R)
Journey Forth/BJU (R)
Kaleidoscope Press (R)
Kingsley Pub., Jessica (R)
Knight George Pub.
Lighthouse Publishing (R)
Lion and Lamb
Mason Crest Publishers
Master Books
McRuffy Press
Monarch Books
New Canaan (R)
New Leaf
(S) One World (R)
Our Sunday Visitor (R)
Pacific Press
Pauline Kids (R)
(S) Pleasant Word (R)
Power Publishing (R)
(S) Providence Pub. (R)
Rose Publishing

(S) Southern Baptist Press (R)
(S) Star Bible Publications
Starik Publishing
(S) Tate Publishing (R)
(S) Trafford Publishing (R)
Trinity Foundation (R)
(S) WinePress (R)
(S) Word Alive
(S) Zoë Life Publishing

CHRISTMAS BOOKS*
(S) American Binding (R)
(S) Black Forest (R)
(S) Brown Books
Cladach Publishing
CLC Publications (R)
Crossroad Publishing (R)
Eldridge Plays (play)
Forever Books (R)
(S) Fruitbearer Pub.
(S) Holy Fire Publishing (R)
Howard Books
Judson Press (R)
Lighthouse Publishing (R)
Meriwether
Pauline Kids (R)
(S) Trafford Publishing (R)
Warner Press
White Stone Books (R)
(S) WinePress (R)

CHURCH HISTORY
(A) Doubleday Religion (R)
(A) HarperOne

Aaron Book Publishing (R)
Abingdon Press
ACTA Publications
(S) ACW Press (R)
Ambassador-Emerald (R)
(S) American Binding (R)
Anglicans United (R)
B & H Publishing
Baker Books
Baylor Univ. Press
(S) Black Forest (R)
Blue Dolphin
(S) Booklocker.com (R)
(S) Bookstand Publishing (R)
Boyds Mills Press (R)
Branden Publishing (R)

Canticle Books (R)
Carey Library, Wm. (R)
Catholic Answers (R)
Chalice Press
ChapterTwo (R)
Christian Family (R)
Christian Focus (R)
Christian Heritage (R)
Christian Writer's Ebook (R)
Cistercian (R)
Clarke & Co., James (R)
College Press (R)
Continuum Intl. (R)
(S) Creation House (R)
(S) CrossHouse (R)
CrossLink Publishing
Crossroad Publishing (R)
Crossway Books
CSS Publishing
Editorial Portavoz
Eerdmans Pub., Wm. B. (R)
E.F.S. Online Pub.
(S) Elderberry Press
Elijah Press
Emmaus Road
(S) Essence (R)
Evangelical Press
(S) Fairway Press (R)
FaithWalk
Father's Press
Forever Books (R)
Fortress Press
Forward Movement
Founders Press
Gollehon Press
Hannibal Books
Hendrickson (R)
Hidden Brook Press (R)
(S) Holy Fire Publishing (R)
(S) IMD Press (R)
(S) Insight Publishing (R)
InterVarsity Press (R)
Intl. Awakening (R)
Kirk House
Kregel (R)
Libros Liguori
Lighthouse Publishing (R)
Lion and Lamb
Loyola Press
Lutheran Univ. Press

Lutterworth Press (R)
Messianic Jewish Publishers (R)
Millennium III (R)
Monarch Books
NavPress Th1nk (R)
New Canaan (R)
New Leaf
New Seeds (R)
New York Univ. Press
(S) One World (R)
Our Sunday Visitor (R)
Pacific Press
(S) Path Pub. in Christ (R)
Paulist Press
(S) Pleasant Word (R)
Power Publishing (R)
(S) Providence Pub. (R)
Quintessential Books (R)
Randall House
Reformation Trust
Rose Publishing
(S) Sage Press (R)
Scepter Publishers (R)
(S) Selah Publishing (R)
Sheed & Ward
Smyth & Helwys
St. Anthony Mess. Press (R)
St. Bede's Publications (R)
(S) Star Bible Publications
(S) Tate Publishing (R)
(S) Trafford Publishing (R)
Trinity Foundation (R)
Univ. of AR Press (R)
Univ. Press of America (R)
Westminster John Knox
(S) WinePress (R)
Wipf and Stock
(S) Word Alive
Yale Univ. Press (R)
(S) Zoë Life Publishing
Zondervan

CHURCH LIFE
(A) Doubleday Religion (R)
(A) HarperOne
(A) Nelson, Thomas
(A) W Publishing

Aaron Book Publishing (R)
Abingdon Press
(S) ACW Press (R)

Ambassador-Emerald (R)
(S) American Binding (R)
Baker Books
Bethany House (R)
(S) Black Forest (R)
Blue Dolphin
(S) Booklocker.com (R)
(S) Brentwood (R)
Chalice Press
ChapterTwo (R)
Charisma Kids
Christian Writer's Ebook (R)
Clarke & Co., James (R)
CLC Publications (R)
Continuum Intl. (R)
(S) Creation House (R)
Crossway Books
CSS Publishing
(S) DCTS Publishing
Destiny Image (R)
Discovery House (R)
Editorial Unilit
Eerdmans Pub., Wm. B. (R)
E.F.S. Online Pub.
(S) Elderberry Press
Emmaus Road
(S) Essence (R)
Evangelical Press
(S) Fairway Press (R)
FaithWalk
Father's Press
Forever Books (R)
Forward Movement
Hannibal Books
Harrison House
Hendrickson (R)
Hidden Brook Press (R)
(S) Holy Fire Publishing (R)
Hope Publishing (R)
Howard Books
(S) IMD Press (R)
(S) Impact Christian (R)
(S) Insight Publishing (R)
InterVarsity Press (R)
Jubilant Press (R)
Judson Press (R)
Kirk House
Kregel (R)
Libros Liguori
Lift Every Voice (R)

Lighthouse Publishing (R)
Lillenas
Lion and Lamb
Lutheran Univ. Press
Lutterworth Press (R)
Monarch Books
NavPress
NavPress Th1nk (R)
New Hope (R)
New Leaf
(S) One World (R)
P & R Publishing (R)
Pacific Press
(S) Path Pub. in Christ (R)
Pauline Kids (R)
Pilgrim Press (R)
(S) Pleasant Word (R)
Power Publishing (R)
(S) Providence Pub. (R)
Quintessential Books (R)
Randall House
Reformation Trust
Resource Publications
Revival Nation
(S) Sage Press (R)
(S) Selah Publishing (R)
Smyth & Helwys
St. Anthony Mess. Press (R)
(S) Star Bible Publications
Strang Book Group (R)
(S) Tate Publishing (R)
(S) TEACH Services (R)
Torch Legacy
Touch Publications (R)
(S) Trafford Publishing (R)
(S) VMI Publishers
Wesleyan Publishing
Westminster John Knox
(S) WinePress (R)
(S) Word Alive
Youth Specialties
(S) Zoë Life Publishing

CHURCH MANAGEMENT
(A) Doubleday Religion (R)

Aaron Book Publishing (R)
Abingdon Press
(S) ACW Press (R)
Ambassador-Emerald (R)
(S) American Binding (R)

B & H Publishing
(S) Black Forest (R)
Blue Dolphin
BMH Books (R)
(S) Booklocker.com (R)
Chalice Press
Christian Heritage (R)
CLC Publications (R)
(S) Creation House (R)
CSS Publishing
Eerdmans Pub., Wm. B. (R)
(S) Elderberry Press
(S) Essence (R)
Evangelical Press
(S) Fairway Press (R)
Father's Press
Forever Books (R)
Group Publishing
Hannibal Books
Harrison House
Hidden Brook Press (R)
(S) Holy Fire Publishing (R)
Hope Publishing (R)
(S) IMD Press (R)
(S) Insight Publishing (R)
Journey Forth/BJU (R)
Judson Press (R)
Kirk House
Kregel (R)
Lighthouse Publishing (R)
Lion and Lamb
Lutheran Univ. Press
Monarch Books
New Leaf
(S) One World (R)
Our Sunday Visitor (R)
(S) Path Pub. in Christ (R)
(S) Pleasant Word (R)
Power Publishing (R)
(S) Providence Pub. (R)
(S) Sage Press (R)
St. Anthony Mess. Press (R)
(S) Star Bible Publications
Strang Book Group (R)
(S) Tate Publishing (R)
(S) TEACH Services (R)
(S) Trafford Publishing (R)
Wesleyan Publishing
(S) WinePress (R)
(S) Word Alive

CHURCH RENEWAL

(A) Doubleday Religion (R)
(A) HarperOne

Aaron Book Publishing (R)
Abingdon Press
(S) ACW Press (R)
(S) American Binding (R)
Baker Books
Blue Dolphin
BMH Books (R)
(S) Booklocker.com (R)
(S) Brentwood (R)
Bridge-Logos (R)
Canticle Books (R)
Carey Library, Wm. (R)
Chalice Press
Charisma Kids
Christian Focus (R)
Christian Writer's Ebook (R)
Church Growth Inst.
CLC Publications (R)
(S) Creation House (R)
CSS Publishing
Destiny Image (R)
Destiny Image (books) (R)
Eerdmans Pub., Wm. B. (R)
(S) Elderberry Press
Emmaus Road
(S) Essence (R)
Evangelical Press
(S) Fairway Press (R)
FaithWalk
Father's Press
Forever Books (R)
Forward Movement
Hannibal Books
Hidden Brook Press (R)
(S) Holy Fire Publishing (R)
Hope Publishing (R)
Howard Books
(S) IMD Press (R)
(S) Impact Christian (R)
(S) Insight Publishing (R)
InterVarsity Press (R)
Intl. Awakening (R)
Judson Press (R)
Kregel (R)
Libros Liguori
Lighthouse Publishing (R)

Lillenas
Lion and Lamb
Lutheran Univ. Press
(S) McDougal Publishing (R)
Monarch Books
NavPress Th1nk (R)
(S) One World (R)
Pacific Press
Parson Place (R)
(S) Path Pub. in Christ (R)
Pilgrim Press (R)
(S) Pleasant Word (R)
Power Publishing (R)
(S) Providence Pub. (R)
Quintessential Books (R)
Resource Publications
Revival Nation
(S) Sage Press (R)
(S) Salvation Publisher (R)
(S) Selah Publishing (R)
(S) Sermon Select Press
Smyth & Helwys
(S) Southern Baptist Press (R)
St. Anthony Mess. Press (R)
(S) Star Bible Publications
(S) Tate Publishing (R)
(S) TEACH Services (R)
(S) Trafford Publishing (R)
(S) VMI Publishers
Wesleyan Publishing
Westminster John Knox
(S) WinePress (R)
(S) Word Alive

CHURCH TRADITIONS

(A) Doubleday Religion (R)
(A) Nelson, Thomas

Aaron Book Publishing (R)
Abingdon Press
(S) ACW Press (R)
Ambassador-Emerald (R)
(S) American Binding (R)
Anglicans United (R)
Atheneum/Young Readers
Baker Books
(S) Black Forest (R)
Blue Dolphin
(S) Booklocker.com (R)
Boyds Mills Press (R)
Carey Library, Wm. (R)

Catholic Answers (R)
Chalice Press
Christian Family (R)
Christian Heritage (R)
Christian Writer's Ebook (R)
Cistercian (R)
Clarke & Co., James (R)
Conciliar Press (R)
Continuum Intl. (R)
(S) Creation House (R)
CSS Publishing
Eerdmans Pub., Wm. B. (R)
E.F.S. Online Pub.
(S) Elderberry Press
Emmaus Road
(S) Essence (R)
(S) Fairway Press (R)
FaithWalk
Father's Press
Forever Books (R)
Forward Movement
Founders Press
Hidden Brook Press (R)
(S) Holy Fire Publishing (R)
Howard Books
(S) IMD Press (R)
Inkling Books (R)
(S) Insight Publishing (R)
InterVarsity Press (R)
Kregel (R)
Libros Liguori
Lighthouse Publishing (R)
Lion and Lamb
Lutheran Univ. Press
Monarch Books
NavPress Th1nk (R)
New York Univ. Press
(S) One World (R)
Our Sunday Visitor (R)
Pacific Press
(S) Path Pub. in Christ (R)
Pauline Kids (R)
(S) Pleasant Word (R)
Power Publishing (R)
Praeger Publishers
(S) Providence Pub. (R)
Randall House
Rose Publishing
(S) Sage Press (R)
St. Anthony Mess. Press (R)

St. Bede's Publications (R)
St. Pauls/Alba House (R)
(S) Star Bible Publications
(S) Tate Publishing (R)
(S) Trafford Publishing (R)
(S) VMI Publishers
(S) WinePress (R)
(S) Word Alive

COFFEE-TABLE BOOKS
(A) Harvest House

Aaron Book Publishing (R)
ACTA Publications
(S) ACW Press (R)
Ambassador-Emerald (R)
(S) Black Forest (R)
(S) Brown Books
Cistercian (R)
(S) Creation House (R)
Father's Press
Forever Books (R)
GRQ (R)
Hidden Brook Press (R)
(S) IMD Press (R)
Kirk House
Liturgy Training (R)
Lutheran Univ. Press
Monarch Books
New Leaf
Players Press (R)
(S) Pleasant Word (R)
(S) Providence Pub. (R)
(S) Sage Press (R)
Salt-Works (R)
(S) Trafford Publishing (R)
(S) VMI Publishers
(S) WinePress (R)
(S) Zoë Life Publishing

COMPILATIONS
(A) Doubleday Religion (R)
(A) WaterBrook Press (R)

Aaron Book Publishing (R)
(S) ACW Press (R)
(S) American Binding (R)
Barbour
(S) Black Forest (R)
(S) Booklocker.com (R)
(S) Bookstand Publishing (R)

(S) Brentwood (R)
Christian Heritage (R)
Christian Writer's Ebook (R)
CLC Publications (R)
(S) Creation House (R)
Eerdmans Pub., Wm. B. (R)
(S) Elderberry Press
(S) Essence (R)
(S) Fairway Press (R)
Father's Press
Forever Books (R)
Group Publishing
GRQ (R)
Hidden Brook Press (R)
(S) Holy Fire Publishing (R)
InterVarsity Press (R)
Lighthouse Publishing (R)
Monarch Books
(S) One World (R)
(S) Pleasant Word (R)
(S) Providence Pub. (R)
(S) Sage Press (R)
Salt-Works (R)
Strang Book Group (R)
(S) Tate Publishing (R)
(S) Trafford Publishing (R)
Treble Heart Books (R)
Univ. Press of America (R)
(S) VMI Publishers
(S) WinePress (R)
(S) Word Alive

CONTROVERSIAL ISSUES
(A) Doubleday Religion (R)
(A) FaithWords
(A) HarperOne
(A) Harvest House

Aadeon Publishing (R)
Aaron Book Publishing (R)
(S) ACW Press (R)
(S) American Binding (R)
AMG Publishers (R)
Atheneum/Young Readers
Baker Books
(S) Black Forest (R)
Blue Dolphin
(S) Booklocker.com (R)
(S) Bookstand Publishing (R)
(S) Brentwood (R)

Bridge-Logos (R)
Canadian Inst. for Law (R)
Canticle Books (R)
Catholic Answers (R)
Chalice Press
ChapterTwo (R)
Christian Family (R)
Christian Writer's Ebook (R)
Conciliar Press (R)
Continuum Intl. (R)
(S) Creation House (R)
(S) Dean Press, Robbie (R)
Destiny Image (R)
Destiny Image (books) (R)
Eerdmans Pub., Wm. B. (R)
E.F.S. Online Pub.
(S) Elderberry Press
Emmaus Road
(S) Essence (R)
Evangelical Press
(S) Fairway Press (R)
FaithWalk
Father's Press
Fifth-Estate (R)
Forever Books (R)
Gentle Path Press
Gollehon Press
Hannibal Books
Hay House
Hidden Brook Press (R)
(S) Holy Fire Publishing (R)
Hope Publishing (R)
Howard Books
Inkling Books (R)
(S) Insight Publishing (R)
InterVarsity Press (R)
Jossey-Bass
Judson Press (R)
Kingsley Pub., Jessica (R)
Kregel (R)
Life Cycle Books (R)
Lighthouse Publishing (R)
Lighthouse Trails (R)
Little Lauren Books
Lutterworth Press (R)
Magnus Press (R)
Monarch Books
Mountain View
NavPress Th1nk (R)
New Leaf

(S) One World (R)
Pilgrim Press (R)
(S) Pleasant Word (R)
Power Publishing (R)
(S) Providence Pub. (R)
Ravenhawk Books (R)
Resource Publications
Revival Nation
Rose Publishing
(S) Sage Press (R)
Salt-Works (R)
(S) Selah Publishing (R)
Still Waters Revival (R)
Strang Book Group (R)
(S) Tate Publishing (R)
(S) Trafford Publishing (R)
(S) VMI Publishers
(S) WinePress (R)
(S) Word Alive
(S) Zoë Life Publishing

COOKBOOKS

(A) Ballantine
(A) Countryman, J.
(A) Harvest House
(A) Nelson, Thomas
(A) One World/Ballantine

Aaron Book Publishing (R)
Adams Media
(S) American Binding (R)
Barbour
(S) Black Forest (R)
(S) Book Publishers (R)
(S) Booklocker.com (R)
(S) Bookstand Publishing (R)
(S) Brentwood (R)
Bridge-Logos (R)
(S) Brown Books
Christian Writer's Ebook (R)
(S) CrossHouse (R)
DiskUs Publishing
Dove Inspirational (R)
Dover Publications (R)
(S) Elderberry Press
(S) Essence (R)
Evergreen Press
Extreme Diva
(S) Fairway Press (R)
Guardian Angel
Hannibal Books

Health Communications
Hidden Brook Press (R)
His Work Christian Pub. (R)
(S) Holy Fire Publishing (R)
(S) IMD Press (R)
Journey Stone (R)
(S) LifeVest Publishing
Monarch Books
(S) One World (R)
Pacific Press
Pelican Publishing (R)
(S) Pleasant Word (R)
Power Publishing (R)
(S) Providence Pub. (R)
(S) Sage Press (R)
Siloam
(S) Southern Baptist Press (R)
Strang Book Group (R)
(S) Tate Publishing (R)
(S) TEACH Services (R)
(S) Trafford Publishing (R)
(S) WinePress (R)
(S) Word Alive
Xyzzy Press
(S) Zoë Life Publishing

COUNSELING AIDS

(A) Nelson, Thomas

Aaron Book Publishing (R)
(S) ACW Press (R)
Ambassador-Emerald (R)
(S) American Binding (R)
Baker Books
(S) Black Forest (R)
Blue Dolphin
(S) Booklocker.com (R)
(S) Brentwood (R)
Bridge-Logos (R)
(S) Brown Books
CarePoint (R)
Chalice Press
Christian Family (R)
Christian Writer's Ebook (R)
CSS Publishing
(S) Dean Press, Robbie (R)
Editorial Portavoz
Eerdmans Pub., Wm. B. (R)
E.F.S. Online Pub.
(S) Elderberry Press
(S) Essence (R)

Evangelical Press
Evergreen Press
Fair Havens (R)
(S) Fairway Press (R)
FaithWalk
Father's Press
Forever Books (R)
Gentle Path Press
Good Book (R)
Harcourt Religion
Hidden Brook Press (R)
(S) Holy Fire Publishing (R)
(S) Insight Publishing (R)
InterVarsity Press (R)
Journey Forth/BJU (R)
Kaleidoscope Press (R)
Kingsley Pub., Jessica (R)
Kregel (R)
Langmarc
Life Cycle Books (R)
Lighthouse Publishing (R)
Lion and Lamb
(S) McDougal Publishing (R)
Monarch Books
(S) One World (R)
P & R Publishing (R)
Paradise Research (R)
Pilgrim Press (R)
(S) Pleasant Word (R)
Power Publishing (R)
(S) Providence Pub. (R)
Quill Driver Books
Quintessential Books (R)
Randall House
Reference Service
(S) Sage Press (R)
(S) Sermon Select Press
(S) Southern Baptist Press (R)
(S) Star Bible Publications
Strang Book Group (R)
(S) Tate Publishing (R)
(S) Trafford Publishing (R)
Treble Heart Books (R)
(S) VMI Publishers
(S) WinePress (R)
(S) Word Alive
Youth Specialties

CREATION SCIENCE

(A) Harvest House

Aaron Book Publishing (R)
(S) ACW Press (R)
(S) American Binding (R)
(S) Black Forest (R)
Blue Dolphin
BMH Books (R)
(S) Booklocker.com (R)
(S) Bookstand
    Publishing (R)
Bridge-Logos (R)
Cambridge Scholars Pub.
ChapterTwo (R)
Christian Family (R)
Christian Writer's Ebook (R)
Editorial Portavoz
Eerdmans Pub., Wm. B. (R)
(S) Elderberry Press
(S) Essence (R)
Evangelical Press
Fair Havens (R)
(S) Fairway Press (R)
Forever Books (R)
Hidden Brook Press (R)
(S) Holy Fire Publishing (R)
Hope Publishing (R)
Inkling Books (R)
(S) Insight Publishing (R)
Kaleidoscope Press (R)
Lighthouse Publishing (R)
Master Books
Monarch Books
NavPress Th1nk (R)
New Leaf
(S) One World (R)
Pacific Press
Parson Place (R)
(S) Pleasant Word (R)
Power Publishing (R)
(S) Providence Pub. (R)
(S) Sage Press (R)
Salt-Works (R)
(S) Star Bible Publications
Strang Book Group (R)
(S) Tate Publishing (R)
(S) TEACH Services (R)
(S) Trafford Publishing (R)
Whitaker House
(S) WinePress (R)
(S) Word Alive
(S) Zoë Life Publishing

CULTS/OCCULT

(A) HarperOne
(A) Harvest House

Aaron Book Publishing (R)
(S) ACW Press (R)
(S) American Binding (R)
Baker Books
(S) Black Forest (R)
(S) Booklocker.com (R)
Catholic Answers (R)
ChapterTwo (R)
Christian Writer's Ebook (R)
CLC Publications (R)
Conciliar Press (R)
Editorial Portavoz
Eerdmans Pub., Wm. B. (R)
(S) Elderberry Press
(S) Essence (R)
Evangelical Press
(S) Fairway Press (R)
Fifth-Estate (R)
Forever Books (R)
Hidden Brook Press (R)
(S) Holy Fire Publishing (R)
(S) Impact Christian (R)
(S) Insight Publishing (R)
Kregel (R)
Lighthouse Publishing (R)
Monarch Books
New York Univ. Press
(S) One World (R)
(S) Pleasant Word (R)
Power Publishing (R)
(S) Providence Pub. (R)
Ravenhawk Books (R)
Revival Nation
Rose Publishing
(S) Sage Press (R)
(S) Selah Publishing (R)
SparrowCrowne Press (R)
(S) Star Bible Publications
(S) Tate Publishing (R)
(S) Trafford Publishing (R)
Whitaker House
(S) WinePress (R)
(S) Word Alive

CURRENT/
SOCIAL ISSUES

(A) Doubleday Religion (R)

(A) FaithWords
(A) HarperOne
(A) Harvest House
(A) Nelson, Thomas
(A) Tyndale House (R)
(A) W Publishing

Aadeon Publishing (R)
Aaron Book Publishing (R)
(S) ACW Press (R)
(S) American Binding (R)
AMG Publishers (R)
Atheneum/Young Readers
B & H Publishing
Baker Academic
Baker Books
Beacon Hill Press (R)
Bethany House (R)
(S) Black Forest (R)
Blue Dolphin
(S) Booklocker.com (R)
(S) Bookstand Publishing (R)
Boyds Mills Press (R)
Branden Publishing (R)
(S) Brentwood (R)
Bridge-Logos (R)
(S) Brown Books
Canadian Inst. for Law (R)
Catholic Answers (R)
Chalice Press
Christian Family (R)
Christian Writer's Ebook (R)
Conari Press
Concordia Academic
(S) Creation House (R)
CrossLink Publishing
Crossroad Publishing (R)
(S) DCTS Publishing
Deo Volente
Destiny Image (R)
Editorial Portavoz
Eerdmans Pub., Wm. B. (R)
E.F.S. Online Pub.
(S) Elderberry Press
Eldridge Plays
(S) Essence (R)
Evangelical Press
(S) Fairway Press (R)
FaithWalk
Father's Press

Forever Books (R)
Forward Movement
Gentle Path Press
Georgetown Univ. Press
Gollehon Press
Good News Pub.
Hannibal Books
Health Communications
Hendrickson (R)
Hidden Brook Press (R)
(S) Holy Fire Publishing (R)
Howard Books
Inkling Books (R)
(S) Insight Publishing (R)
InterVarsity Press (R)
Jossey-Bass
Journey Forth/BJU (R)
Judson Press (R)
Kingsley Pub., Jessica (R)
Kregel (R)
Life Cycle Books (R)
Lighthouse Publishing (R)
Liguori Public. (R)
Lillenas
Loyola Press
Lutheran Univ. Press
Millennium III (R)
Monarch Books
NavPress Th1nk (R)
New Canaan (R)
New Hope (R)
New York Univ. Press
(S) One World (R)
Pilgrim Press (R)
(S) Pleasant Word (R)
Power Publishing (R)
(S) Providence Pub. (R)
Putnam/Young Readers
Quill Driver Books
Ravenhawk Books (R)
Rose Publishing
(S) Sage Press (R)
Salt-Works (R)
(S) Selah Publishing (R)
Sheed & Ward
Smyth & Helwys
(S) Star Bible Publications
Still Waters Revival (R)
Strang Book Group (R)
(S) Tate Publishing (R)

(S) Trafford Publishing (R)
Treble Heart Books (R)
VBC Publishing
(S) VMI Publishers
Whitaker House
(S) WinePress (R)
(S) Word Alive
Yale Univ. Press (R)
(S) Zoë Life Publishing

CURRICULUM
(A) Cook, David C.
(A) W Publishing

Aaron Book Publishing (R)
CarePoint (R)
Christian Ed. Pub.
Christian Liberty Press
College Press (R)
Concordia
Congregational Life
CrossLink Publishing
Eerdmans Pub., Wm. B. (R)
E.F.S. Online Pub.
(S) Elderberry Press
Facts On File
(S) Fairway Press (R)
Faith Alive
Forever Books (R)
Gospel Light
Gospel Publishing
Group Publishing
Hannibal Books
Harcourt Religion
Hidden Brook Press (R)
(S) Holy Fire Publishing (R)
(S) IMD Press (R)
Knight George Pub.
Lighthouse Publishing (R)
Lighthouse Trails (R)
Lion and Lamb
Mason Crest Publishers
Messianic Jewish
    Publishers (R)
Monarch Books
New Leaf
Northwestern
(S) One World (R)
Power Publishing (R)
(S) Providence Pub. (R)
Randall House Digital

Smyth & Helwys
Standard Publishing
Starik Publishing
(S) Tate Publishing (R)
(S) Trafford Publishing (R)
UMI Publishing (R)
Univ. Press of America (R)
(S) WinePress (R)
(S) Word Alive
Youth Specialties
(S) Zoë Life Publishing

DATING/SEX
(A) Ballantine
(A) Cook, David C.
(A) Doubleday Religion (R)
(A) FaithWords
(A) HarperOne
(A) Nelson, Thomas
(A) WaterBrook Press (R)

Aaron Book Publishing (R)
(S) ACW Press (R)
(S) American Binding (R)
Barbour
Bethany House (R)
Blue Dolphin
(S) Booklocker.com (R)
Bridge-Logos (R)
Catholic Answers (R)
ChapterTwo (R)
Christian Writer's Ebook (R)
Crossroad Publishing (R)
Destiny Image (books) (R)
Eerdmans Pub., Wm. B. (R)
E.F.S. Online Pub.
(S) Elderberry Press
Emmaus Road
(S) Essence (R)
Evangelical Press
Evergreen Press
(S) Fairway Press (R)
FaithWalk
FamilyLife (books) (R)
Forever Books (R)
Forward Movement
Frederick Fell (R)
Gentle Path Press
GRQ (R)
Health Communications
Hidden Brook Press (R)

(S) Holy Fire Publishing (R)
(S) Insight Publishing (R)
Kregel (R)
Lift Every Voice (R)
Lighthouse Publishing (R)
Lillenas
Little Lauren Books
Monarch Books
NavPress Th1nk (R)
(S) One World (R)
P & R Publishing (R)
Pauline Books (R)
(S) Pleasant Word (R)
Power Publishing (R)
(S) Providence Pub. (R)
Quill Driver Books
Randall House
Rose Publishing
(S) Sage Press (R)
Siloam
SparrowCrowne Press (R)
St. Anthony Mess. Press (R)
(S) Star Bible Publications
Strang Book Group (R)
(S) Tate Publishing (R)
(S) Trafford Publishing (R)
(S) VMI Publishers
Walk Worthy (R)
Whitaker House
(S) WinePress (R)
(S) Word Alive
Youth Specialties
(S) Zoë Life Publishing

DEATH/DYING

(A) Cook, David C.
(A) Doubleday Religion (R)
(A) HarperOne
(A) Nelson, Thomas
(A) WaterBrook Press (R)

Aaron Book Publishing (R)
Abingdon Press
ACTA Publications
(S) ACW Press (R)
(S) American Binding (R)
Baker Books
(S) Black Forest (R)
Blue Dolphin
(S) Book Publishers (R)

(S) Booklocker.com (R)
Bridge-Logos (R)
(S) Brown Books
Chalice Press
Christian Family (R)
Christian Writer's Ebook (R)
(S) Creation House (R)
Crossroad Publishing (R)
CSS Publishing
Discovery House (R)
Editorial Portavoz
Eerdmans Pub., Wm. B. (R)
E.F.S. Online Pub.
(S) Elderberry Press
Emmaus Road
(S) Essence (R)
Evangelical Press
Evergreen Press
(S) Fairway Press (R)
FaithWalk
Father's Press
Forever Books (R)
Forward Movement
Guardian Angel
Health Communications
Hidden Brook Press (R)
(S) Holy Fire Publishing (R)
Hope Publishing (R)
(S) Insight Publishing (R)
Kingsley Pub., Jessica (R)
Kregel (R)
Life Cycle Books (R)
Lift Every Voice (R)
Lighthouse Publishing (R)
Lillenas
Lion and Lamb
Loyola Press
Lutheran Univ. Press
Lutterworth Press (R)
Monarch Books
New Seeds (R)
(S) One World (R)
P & R Publishing (R)
Pacific Press
Pauline Books (R)
Paulist Press
Pilgrim Press (R)
(S) Pleasant Word (R)
Power Publishing (R)
(S) Providence Pub. (R)

Randall House
Rose Publishing
(S) Sage Press (R)
Sheed & Ward
Siloam
Smyth & Helwys
SparrowCrowne Press (R)
St. Anthony Mess. Press (R)
(S) Star Bible Publications
Strang Book Group (R)
(S) Tate Publishing (R)
(S) TEACH Services (R)
(S) Trafford Publishing (R)
(S) VMI Publishers
Whitaker House
(S) WinePress (R)
(S) Word Alive
(S) Zoë Life Publishing

DEVOTIONAL BOOKS

(A) Cook, David C.
(A) Countryman, J.
(A) Doubleday Religion (R)
(A) FaithWords
(A) HarperOne
(A) Harvest House
(A) Nelson, Thomas
(A) Regal
(A) Tyndale House (R)
(A) WaterBrook Press (R)
(A) W Publishing

Aaron Book Publishing (R)
Abingdon Press
(S) ACW Press (R)
Ambassador Books
Ambassador-Emerald (R)
(S) American Binding (R)
Baker Books
Barbour
Bethany House (R)
(S) Black Forest (R)
Blue Dolphin
(S) Booklocker.com (R)
(S) Bookstand Publishing (R)
(S) Brentwood (R)
(S) Brown Books
Canticle Books (R)
ChapterTwo (R)
Christian Family (R)

Christian Focus (R)
Christian Heritage (R)
Christian Writer's Ebook (R)
CLC Publications (R)
Concordia
Congregational Life
Contemporary Drama
Continuum Intl. (R)
(S) Creation House (R)
CrossLink Publishing
CSS Publishing
Dimensions for Living
Discovery House (R)
Editorial Portavoz
Eerdmans Pub., Wm. B. (R)
E.F.S. Online Pub.
(S) Elderberry Press
Emmaus Road
(S) Essence (R)
Evangelical Press
Evergreen Press
Extreme Diva
Fair Havens (R)
(S) Fairway Press (R)
FaithWalk
Forever Books (R)
Forward Movement
Founders Press
Friends United Press
(S) Fruitbearer Pub.
Gollehon Press
Group Publishing
GRQ (R)
Guideposts Books
Hannibal Books
Harrison House
Harvest Day
HeartSpring Pub. (R)
Hidden Brook Press (R)
(S) Holy Fire Publishing (R)
Howard Books
(S) IMD Press (R)
(S) Impact Christian (R)
Inkling Books (R)
(S) Insight Publishing (R)
Jebaire Publishing
Judson Press (R)
KNB Publications
Kregel (R)
Legacy Press (R)

Libros Liguori
Lift Every Voice (R)
Lighthouse Publishing (R)
Liguori Public. (R)
Lion and Lamb
Lutterworth Press (R)
Magnus Press (R)
(S) McDougal Publishing (R)
Messianic Jewish Publishers (R)
Mission City Press
Monarch Books
MOPS Intl.
Morehouse
New Hope (R)
New Seeds (R)
(S) One World (R)
P & R Publishing (R)
Parson Place (R)
Parsons Publishing (R)
(S) Path Pub. in Christ (R)
Pauline Books (R)
Pilgrim Press (R)
(S) Pleasant Word (R)
Power Publishing (R)
(S) Providence Pub. (R)
Quill Driver Books
Ragged Edge (R)
Randall House
Revival Nation
Rose Publishing
(S) Sage Press (R)
Salt-Works (R)
(S) Salvation Publisher (R)
Samaritan Press (R)
(S) Selah Publishing (R)
Smyth & Helwys
St. Anthony Mess. Press (R)
Standard Publishing
(S) Star Bible Publications
Strang Book Group (R)
(S) Tate Publishing (R)
(S) Trafford Publishing (R)
Treble Heart Books (R)
Tsaba House
VBC Publishing
(S) VMI Publishers
Wesleyan Publishing
White Stone Books (R)
(S) WinePress (R)
(S) Word Alive

Youth Specialties
(S) Zoë Life Publishing

DISCIPLESHIP

(A) Cook, David C.
(A) Doubleday Religion (R)
(A) HarperOne
(A) Nelson, Thomas
(A) Regal
(A) WaterBrook Press (R)
(A) W Publishing

Aadeon Publishing (R)
Aaron Book Publishing (R)
Abingdon Press
(S) ACW Press (R)
Ambassador-Emerald (R)
(S) American Binding (R)
Anglicans United (R)
B & H Publishing
Baker Books
Barbour
Beacon Hill Press (R)
Bethany House (R)
(S) Black Forest (R)
Blue Dolphin
BMH Books (R)
(S) Booklocker.com (R)
(S) Bookstand Publishing (R)
(S) Brentwood (R)
Bridge-Logos (R)
(S) Brown Books
Carey Library, Wm. (R)
Chalice Press
ChapterTwo (R)
Charisma Kids
Christian Family (R)
Christian Focus (R)
Christian Heritage (R)
Christian Writer's Ebook (R)
CLC Publications (R)
College Press (R)
Continuum Intl. (R)
(S) Creation House (R)
Crossway Books
CSS Publishing
(S) DCTS Publishing
Deo Volente
Destiny Image (books) (R)
Discovery House (R)
Editorial Portavoz

Eerdmans Pub., Wm. B. (R)
E.F.S. Online Pub.
(S) Elderberry Press
(S) Essence (R)
Evangelical Press
Evergreen Press
Fair Havens (R)
(S) Fairway Press (R)
FaithWalk
Father's Press
Forever Books (R)
Forward Movement
Founders Press
Foursquare Media
Gospel Publishing
Group Publishing
Harrison House
Hendrickson (R)
Hensley Publishing
Hidden Brook Press (R)
(S) Holy Fire Publishing (R)
Howard Books
(S) IMD Press (R)
Inkling Books (R)
(S) Insight Publishing (R)
InterVarsity Press (R)
Journey Forth/BJU (R)
Judson Press (R)
Kregel (R)
Lift Every Voice (R)
Lighthouse Publishing (R)
Lillenas
Lion and Lamb
Lutheran Univ. Press
(S) McDougal Publishing (R)
Messianic Jewish Publishers (R)
Mission City Press
Monarch Books
Moody Publishers
NavPress
NavPress Th1nk (R)
New Hope (R)
(S) One World (R)
P & R Publishing (R)
Pacific Press
Parson Place (R)
Pilgrim Press (R)
(S) Pleasant Word (R)
Power Publishing (R)
(S) Providence Pub. (R)

Quill Driver Books
Quintessential Books (R)
Randall House
Reformation Trust
Revival Nation
Rose Publishing
(S) Sage Press (R)
Salt-Works (R)
(S) Salvation Publisher (R)
Samaritan Press (R)
Smyth & Helwys
(S) Southern Baptist Press (R)
St. Anthony Mess. Press (R)
Standard Publishing
(S) Star Bible Publications
Strang Book Group (R)
(S) Tate Publishing (R)
(S) TEACH Services (R)
Touch Publications (R)
(S) Trafford Publishing (R)
(S) VMI Publishers
Whitaker House
(S) WinePress (R)
(S) Word Alive
Youth Specialties
(S) Zoë Life Publishing

DIVORCE
(A) Cook, David C.
(A) Nelson, Thomas
(A) WaterBrook Press (R)

Aaron Book Publishing (R)
(S) ACW Press (R)
Ambassador Books
(S) American Binding (R)
Baker Books
Bethany House (R)
(S) Black Forest (R)
Blue Dolphin
(S) Booklocker.com (R)
(S) Brentwood (R)
Bridge-Logos (R)
(S) Brown Books
Chalice Press
Christian Writer's Ebook (R)
College Press (R)
(S) Creation House (R)
CSS Publishing
(S) Dean Press, Robbie (R)
Editorial Portavoz

Eerdmans Pub., Wm. B. (R)
E.F.S. Online Pub.
(S) Elderberry Press
(S) Essence (R)
Evangelical Press
Fair Havens (R)
(S) Fairway Press (R)
FaithWalk
Forever Books (R)
Forward Movement
Gentle Path Press
Guideposts Books
Health Communications
Hidden Brook Press (R)
(S) Holy Fire Publishing (R)
(S) IMD Press (R)
(S) Insight Publishing (R)
InterVarsity Press (R)
Kregel (R)
Lighthouse Publishing (R)
Lillenas
Lion and Lamb
Messianic Jewish Publishers (R)
Monarch Books
(S) One World (R)
P & R Publishing (R)
Pacific Press
(S) Pleasant Word (R)
Power Publishing (R)
(S) Providence Pub. (R)
Randall House
Rose Publishing
(S) Sage Press (R)
Samaritan Press (R)
(S) Southern Baptist Press (R)
St. Anthony Mess. Press (R)
(S) Star Bible Publications
Strang Book Group (R)
(S) Tate Publishing (R)
(S) Trafford Publishing (R)
(S) VMI Publishers
(S) WinePress (R)
(S) Word Alive
(S) Zoë Life Publishing

DOCTRINAL
(A) Doubleday Religion (R)
(A) Tyndale House (R)

Aaron Book Publishing (R)
(S) ACW Press (R)

Ambassador-Emerald (R)
(S) American Binding (R)
Baker Books
Beacon Hill Press (R)
Bethany House (R)
(S) Black Forest (R)
Blue Dolphin
(S) Booklocker.com (R)
(S) Bookstand Publishing (R)
(S) Brentwood (R)
(S) Brown Books
Canticle Books (R)
Catholic Answers (R)
Chalice Press
ChapterTwo (R)
Christian Family (R)
Christian Focus (R)
Christian Heritage (R)
Christian Writer's Ebook (R)
Cistercian (R)
Clarke & Co., James (R)
CLC Publications (R)
College Press (R)
Concordia
Continuum Intl. (R)
(S) Creation House (R)
Crossway Books
(S) DCTS Publishing
Editorial Portavoz
Eerdmans Pub., Wm. B. (R)
(S) Elderberry Press
(S) Essence (R)
Evangelical Press
Fair Havens (R)
(S) Fairway Press (R)
Forever Books (R)
Forward Movement
Hidden Brook Press (R)
(S) Holy Fire Publishing (R)
(S) IMD Press (R)
(S) Impact Christian (R)
(S) Insight Publishing (R)
InterVarsity Press (R)
Kregel (R)
Libros Liguori
Lighthouse Publishing (R)
Liturgical Press
Lutheran Univ. Press
Messianic Jewish Publishers (R)
Monarch Books

(S) One World (R)
Pacific Press
(S) Pleasant Word (R)
Power Publishing (R)
(S) Providence Pub. (R)
Reformation Trust
Rose Publishing
(S) Sage Press (R)
Scepter Publishers (R)
(S) Southern Baptist Press (R)
St. Anthony Mess. Press (R)
(S) Star Bible Publications
Still Waters Revival (R)
(S) Tate Publishing (R)
(S) Trafford Publishing (R)
Trinity Foundation (R)
UMI Publishing (R)
VBC Publishing
(S) WinePress (R)
(S) Word Alive
(S) Zoë Life Publishing

DRAMA

Aaron Book Publishing (R)
(S) American Binding (R)
Baker's Plays (R)
(S) Black Forest (R)
(S) Brentwood (R)
Contemporary Drama
E.F.S. Online Pub.
(S) Elderberry Press
Eldridge Plays
Encore Performance
Fair Havens (R)
(S) Fairway Press (R)
Forever Books (R)
Guardian Angel
Guernica Editions (R)
Hidden Brook Press (R)
(S) Holy Fire Publishing (R)
Kregel (R)
Lighthouse Publishing (R)
Lillenas
Lion and Lamb
Meriwether
Monarch Books
National Black Theatre
National Drama
(S) One World (R)
Players Press (R)

(S) Pleasant Word (R)
Power Publishing (R)
(S) Providence Pub. (R)
Randall House
Ravenhawk Books (R)
(S) Sage Press (R)
Salt-Works (R)
Samaritan Press (R)
(S) Southern Baptist Press (R)
(S) Tate Publishing (R)
(S) Trafford Publishing (R)
Treble Heart Books (R)
Warner Press
(S) WinePress (R)
(S) Word Alive
Youth Specialties
(S) Zoë Life Publishing

E-BOOKS
(A) Harvest House
(A) Tyndale House (R)

Ambassador-Emerald (R)
Blue Dolphin
(S) Booklocker.com (R)
(S) Bookstand Publishing (R)
Christian Writer's Ebook (R)
College Press (R)
Comfort Publishing (R)
(S) Dean Press, Robbie (R)
DiskUs Publishing
Emmaus Road
Evangelical Press
Fair Havens (R)
Fifth-Estate (R)
Guardian Angel
InterVarsity Press (R)
Jubilant Press (R)
Life Changing Media
Lighthouse Publishing (R)
More Than Novellas
(S) One World (R)
Paradise Research (R)
(S) Path Pub. in Christ (R)
Power Publishing (R)
Randall House Digital
Resource Publications
(S) Sage Press (R)
Salt-Works (R)
Samaritan Press (R)
(S) Selah Publishing (R)

Smyth & Helwys
(S) Trafford Publishing (R)
Treble Heart Books (R)
White Rose (R)
White Stone Books (R)
(S) Word Alive
(S) Xulon Press (R)

ECONOMICS

Aaron Book Publishing (R)
(S) ACW Press (R)
Ambassador-Emerald (R)
(S) American Binding (R)
Baker Books
Baylor Univ. Press
Blue Dolphin
(S) Booklocker.com (R)
(S) Brentwood (R)
(S) Brown Books
Canadian Inst. for Law (R)
Christian Writer's Ebook (R)
(S) Creation House (R)
Eerdmans Pub., Wm. B. (R)
E.F.S. Online Pub.
(S) Elderberry Press
(S) Essence (R)
Evergreen Press
(S) Fairway Press (R)
FaithWalk
Father's Press
Forever Books (R)
Hidden Brook Press (R)
(S) Holy Fire Publishing (R)
(S) Insight Publishing (R)
Lighthouse Publishing (R)
Monarch Books
New Hope (R)
(S) One World (R)
(S) Path Pub. in Christ (R)
Pilgrim Press (R)
(S) Pleasant Word (R)
Power Publishing (R)
Praeger Publishers
(S) Providence Pub. (R)
Quintessential Books (R)
(S) Sage Press (R)
(S) Salvation Publisher (R)
Sheed & Ward
(S) Star Bible Publications
(S) Tate Publishing (R)

(S) TEACH Services (R)
(S) Trafford Publishing (R)
Trinity Foundation (R)
Univ. Press of America (R)
(S) VMI Publishers
(S) WinePress (R)
(S) Word Alive
(S) Zoë Life Publishing

ENCOURAGEMENT

(A) Doubleday Religion (R)
(A) WaterBrook Press (R)

Aaron Book Publishing (R)
(S) ACW Press (R)
Ambassador-Emerald (R)
(S) American Binding (R)
Barbour
(S) Black Forest (R)
Blue Dolphin
(S) Booklocker.com (R)
(S) Brown Books
CarePoint (R)
Christian Family (R)
Christian Focus (R)
CLC Publications (R)
(S) Creation House (R)
CSS Publishing
Discovery House (R)
Editorial Portavoz
Eerdmans Pub., Wm. B. (R)
E.F.S. Online Pub.
(S) Elderberry Press
(S) Essence (R)
Evangelical Press
Fair Havens (R)
(S) Fairway Press (R)
Father's Press
Forever Books (R)
Fresh Air Books
Guardian Angel
Hidden Brook Press (R)
(S) Holy Fire Publishing (R)
Howard Books
(S) IMD Press (R)
(S) Insight Publishing (R)
Jebaire Publishing
Journey Forth/BJU (R)
Life Changing Media
Lift Every Voice (R)

Lighthouse Publishing (R)
Lion and Lamb
Messianic Jewish
   Publishers (R)
Monarch Books
NavPress Th1nk (R)
New Hope (R)
(S) One World (R)
Parson Place (R)
(S) Path Pub. in Christ (R)
(S) Pleasant Word (R)
Port Hole Publications
Power Publishing (R)
(S) Providence Pub. (R)
Quill Driver Books
Quintessential Books (R)
Randall House
Revival Nation
(S) Sage Press (R)
(S) Salvation Publisher (R)
Samaritan Press (R)
SparrowCrowne Press (R)
(S) Star Bible Publications
Strang Book Group (R)
(S) Tate Publishing (R)
(S) Trafford Publishing (R)
VBC Publishing
White Stone Books (R)
(S) WinePress (R)
(S) Word Alive
(S) Zoë Life Publishing

ENVIRONMENTAL ISSUES

(A) Doubleday Religion (R)

Aaron Book Publishing (R)
ACTA Publications
(S) ACW Press (R)
(S) American Binding (R)
Baker Books
(S) Black Forest (R)
Blue Dolphin
(S) Booklocker.com (R)
Boyds Mills Press (R)
Christian Writer's Ebook (R)
Crossroad Publishing (R)
Dawn Publications
Eerdmans Pub., Wm. B. (R)
E.F.S. Online Pub.
(S) Elderberry Press

(S) Essence (R)
Evangelical Press
Facts On File
(S) Fairway Press (R)
FaithWalk
Forever Books (R)
Forward Movement
Georgetown Univ. Press
Grupo Nelson
Hendrickson (R)
Hidden Brook Press (R)
(S) Holy Fire Publishing (R)
(S) Insight Publishing (R)
InterVarsity Press (R)
Judson Press (R)
Lighthouse Publishing (R)
Lutterworth Press (R)
Monarch Books
Morehouse
New Leaf
(S) One World (R)
Pilgrim Press (R)
(S) Pleasant Word (R)
Power Publishing (R)
Praeger Publishers
(S) Providence Pub. (R)
Quintessential Books (R)
Ravenhawk Books (R)
(S) Sage Press (R)
Sheed & Ward
(S) Southern Baptist Press (R)
Tarcher, Jeremy P. (R)
(S) Tate Publishing (R)
(S) Trafford Publishing (R)
Univ. Press of America (R)
(S) VMI Publishers
(S) WinePress (R)
(S) Word Alive

ESCHATOLOGY

(A) Harvest House
(A) Nelson, Thomas

Aaron Book Publishing (R)
(S) ACW Press (R)
(S) American Binding (R)
Anglicans United (R)
Baker Books
(S) Black Forest (R)
Blue Dolphin

BMH Books (R)
(S) Booklocker.com (R)
(S) Bookstand Publishing (R)
Bridge-Logos (R)
Chalice Press
ChapterTwo (R)
Christian Family (R)
Christian Heritage (R)
Christian Writer's Ebook (R)
College Press (R)
Continuum Intl. (R)
(S) Creation House (R)
CSS Publishing
(S) DCTS Publishing
Eerdmans Pub., Wm. B. (R)
(S) Elderberry Press
Emmaus Road
(S) Essence (R)
Evangelical Press
(S) Fairway Press (R)
Fifth-Estate (R)
Forever Books (R)
Grupo Nelson
Hidden Brook Press (R)
(S) Holy Fire Publishing (R)
(S) IMD Press (R)
(S) Insight Publishing (R)
Kirk House
Kregel (R)
Lighthouse Publishing (R)
Lighthouse Trails (R)
Lutheran Univ. Press
Messianic Jewish Publishers (R)
Millennium III (R)
Monarch Books
New Leaf
New Seeds (R)
(S) One World (R)
Pacific Press
Parson Place (R)
Pauline Books (R)
(S) Pleasant Word (R)
Power Publishing (R)
(S) Providence Pub. (R)
Rose Publishing
(S) Sage Press (R)
(S) Selah Publishing (R)
St. Pauls/Alba House (R)
(S) Star Bible Publications
Strang Book Group (R)

(S) Strong Tower (R)
(S) Tate Publishing (R)
(S) TEACH Services (R)
(S) Trafford Publishing (R)
VBC Publishing
(S) WinePress (R)
(S) Word Alive
(S) Zoë Life Publishing

ETHICS

Aadeon Publishing (R)
Aaron Book Publishing (R)
(S) ACW Press (R)
(S) American Binding (R)
Baker Books
(S) Black Forest (R)
Blue Dolphin
(S) Booklocker.com (R)
(S) Bookstand Publishing (R)
(S) Brentwood (R)
Cambridge Scholars Pub.
Catholic Answers (R)
Chalice Press
Christian Heritage (R)
Christian Writer's Ebook (R)
Clarke & Co., James (R)
CLC Publications (R)
Conciliar Press (R)
Continuum Intl. (R)
(S) Creation House (R)
Crossroad Publishing (R)
Crossway Books
Dover Publications (R)
Eerdmans Pub., Wm. B. (R)
E.F.S. Online Pub.
(S) Elderberry Press
(S) Essence (R)
Evangelical Press
(S) Fairway Press (R)
FaithWalk
Father's Press
Forever Books (R)
Fortress Press
Forward Movement
Georgetown Univ. Press
Guardian Angel
Hannibal Books
Hendrickson (R)
Hidden Brook Press (R)
(S) Holy Fire Publishing (R)

Howard Books
(S) IMD Press (R)
Inkling Books (R)
(S) Insight Publishing (R)
InterVarsity Press (R)
Kingsley Pub., Jessica (R)
Kirk House
Kregel (R)
Libros Liguori
Life Cycle Books (R)
Lift Every Voice (R)
Lighthouse Publishing (R)
Lion and Lamb
Lutheran Univ. Press
Lutterworth Press (R)
Mercer Univ. Press (R)
Messianic Jewish
    Publishers (R)
Monarch Books
NavPress Th1nk (R)
(S) One World (R)
Our Sunday Visitor (R)
Pacific Press
Paragon House (R)
Pauline Books (R)
Paulist Press
Pilgrim Press (R)
(S) Pleasant Word (R)
Power Publishing (R)
(S) Providence Pub. (R)
Quintessential Books (R)
Ravenhawk Books (R)
(S) Sage Press (R)
Salt-Works (R)
Sheed & Ward
Smyth & Helwys
St. Anthony Mess. Press (R)
St. Pauls/Alba House (R)
(S) Star Bible Publications
Still Waters Revival (R)
(S) Tate Publishing (R)
(S) TEACH Services (R)
(S) Trafford Publishing (R)
Treble Heart Books (R)
Trinity Foundation (R)
Univ. Press of America (R)
(S) VMI Publishers
Walk Worthy (R)
Westminster John Knox
Whitaker House

(S) WinePress (R)
(S) Word Alive
Yale Univ. Press (R)

ETHNIC/CULTURAL
(A) Doubleday Religion (R)
(A) HarperOne
(A) One World/Ballantine

Aaron Book Publishing (R)
(S) ACW Press (R)
(S) American Binding (R)
Baker Books
(S) Black Forest (R)
Blue Dolphin
(S) Booklocker.com (R)
(S) Bookstand Publishing (R)
Boyds Mills Press (R)
Branden Publishing (R)
Cambridge Scholars Pub.
Carey Library, Wm. (R)
Chalice Press
Christian Writer's Ebook (R)
CLC Publications (R)
College Press (R)
Concordia
(S) Creation House (R)
(S) Dean Press, Robbie (R)
Eerdmans Pub., Wm. B. (R)
E.F.S. Online Pub.
(S) Elderberry Press
(S) Essence (R)
Evangelical Press
Facts On File
(S) Fairway Press (R)
FaithWalk
Forever Books (R)
Fortress Press
Forward Movement
Friends United Press
Georgetown Univ. Press
Grupo Nelson
Guardian Angel
Guernica Editions (R)
Hidden Brook Press (R)
(S) Holy Fire Publishing (R)
Howard Books
(S) IMD Press (R)
(S) Insight Publishing (R)
InterVarsity Press (R)
Judson Press (R)

Kaleidoscope Press (R)
Kirk House
Kregel (R)
Libros Liguori
Lift Every Voice (R)
Lighthouse Publishing (R)
Liguori Public. (R)
Lutheran Univ. Press
Millennium III (R)
Monarch Books
Moody Publishers
NavPress Th1nk (R)
New Hope (R)
New Seeds (R)
New York Univ. Press
(S) One World (R)
Oregon Catholic
Pacific Press
Paulist Press
Pilgrim Press (R)
(S) Pleasant Word (R)
Power Publishing (R)
(S) Providence Pub. (R)
(S) Sage Press (R)
St. Anthony Mess. Press (R)
Standard Publishing
(S) Tate Publishing (R)
Third World Press (R)
Torch Legacy
(S) Trafford Publishing (R)
UMI Publishing (R)
Univ. of AR Press (R)
Univ. Press of America (R)
(S) VMI Publishers
Walk Worthy (R)
Whitaker House
(S) WinePress (R)
(S) Word Alive
Yale Univ. Press (R)
(S) Zoë Life Publishing

EVANGELISM/
WITNESSING
(A) Cook, David C.
(A) Nelson, Thomas
(A) Tyndale House (R)
(A) W Publishing

Aaron Book Publishing (R)
(S) ACW Press (R)
Ambassador-Emerald (R)

(S) American Binding (R)
Anglicans United (R)
Baker Books
(S) Black Forest (R)
Blue Dolphin
BMH Books (R)
(S) Booklocker.com (R)
(S) Bookstand Publishing (R)
(S) Brentwood (R)
Bridge-Logos (R)
Carey Library, Wm. (R)
Catholic Answers (R)
Chalice Press
ChapterTwo (R)
Christian Family (R)
Christian Focus (R)
Christian Heritage (R)
Christian Writer's Ebook (R)
Church Growth Inst.
CLC Publications (R)
(S) Creation House (R)
(S) CrossHouse (R)
CrossLink Publishing
CSS Publishing
(S) DCTS Publishing
Deo Volente
Discovery House (R)
Editorial Portavoz
Eerdmans Pub., Wm. B. (R)
E.F.S. Online Pub.
(S) Elderberry Press
(S) Essence (R)
Evangelical Press
Evergreen Press
Fair Havens (R)
(S) Fairway Press (R)
Faith Alive
FaithWalk
Father's Press
Forever Books (R)
Founders Press
Gollehon Press
Good Book (R)
Good News Pub.
Gospel Publishing
Group Publishing
Harvest Day
Hidden Brook Press (R)
(S) Holy Fire Publishing (R)
(S) IMD Press (R)

(S) Impact Christian (R)
(S) Insight Publishing (R)
InterVarsity Press (R)
Judson Press (R)
Kregel (R)
Lift Every Voice (R)
Lighthouse Publishing (R)
Lillenas
Lion and Lamb
Lutheran Univ. Press
(S) McDougal Publishing (R)
Messianic Jewish Publishers (R)
Monarch Books
Moody Publishers
NavPress Th1nk (R)
New Hope (R)
(S) One World (R)
P & R Publishing (R)
Pacific Press
Paradise Research (R)
Parson Place (R)
Pilgrim Press (R)
(S) Pleasant Word (R)
Power Publishing (R)
(S) Providence Pub. (R)
Randall House
Revival Nation
Rose Publishing
Salt-Works (R)
Samaritan Press (R)
(S) Selah Publishing (R)
(S) Southern Baptist Press (R)
St. Anthony Mess. Press (R)
(S) Star Bible Publications
Still Waters Revival (R)
Strang Book Group (R)
(S) Tate Publishing (R)
(S) TEACH Services (R)
(S) Trafford Publishing (R)
VBC Publishing
(S) VMI Publishers
Wesleyan Publishing
(S) WinePress (R)
(S) Word Alive
Yale Univ. Press (R)
(S) Zoë Life Publishing

EXEGESIS

(A) Doubleday Religion (R)

Aaron Book Publishing (R)

Abingdon Press
(S) ACW Press (R)
(S) American Binding (R)
Baker Books
(S) Black Forest (R)
Blue Dolphin
BMH Books (R)
(S) Booklocker.com (R)
(S) Bookstand Publishing (R)
Catholic Answers (R)
ChapterTwo (R)
Christian Family (R)
Christian Focus (R)
Christian Writer's Ebook (R)
Cistercian (R)
CLC Publications (R)
College Press (R)
Continuum Intl. (R)
CSS Publishing
Eerdmans Pub., Wm. B. (R)
(S) Elderberry Press
(S) Essence (R)
Evangelical Press
(S) Fairway Press (R)
Forever Books (R)
Hendrickson (R)
Hidden Brook Press (R)
(S) Holy Fire Publishing (R)
(S) IMD Press (R)
(S) Insight Publishing (R)
InterVarsity Press (R)
Kregel (R)
Lighthouse Publishing (R)
Lutheran Univ. Press
(S) McDougal Publishing (R)
Monarch Books
New Leaf
(S) One World (R)
Paradise Research (R)
Paulist Press
(S) Pleasant Word (R)
Power Publishing (R)
(S) Providence Pub. (R)
Reformation Trust
Rose Publishing
Salt-Works (R)
St. Anthony Mess. Press (R)
St. Bede's Publications (R)
(S) Star Bible Publications
(S) Tate Publishing (R)

(S) Trafford Publishing (R)
VBC Publishing
(S) VMI Publishers
Westminster John Knox
(S) WinePress (R)
(S) Word Alive
Yale Univ. Press (R)
(S) Zoë Life Publishing

EXPOSÉS
Aaron Book Publishing (R)
(S) ACW Press (R)
Ambassador-Emerald (R)
(S) American Binding (R)
Baker Books
Blue Dolphin
(S) Booklocker.com (R)
(S) Brentwood (R)
ChapterTwo (R)
Christian Writer's Ebook (R)
Eerdmans Pub., Wm. B. (R)
E.F.S. Online Pub.
(S) Elderberry Press
(S) Fairway Press (R)
Forever Books (R)
Hidden Brook Press (R)
(S) Holy Fire Publishing (R)
(S) Insight Publishing (R)
Lighthouse Publishing (R)
Lighthouse Trails (R)
(S) One World (R)
Power Publishing (R)
(S) Providence Pub. (R)
Ravenhawk Books (R)
Salt-Works (R)
(S) Southern Baptist Press (R)
(S) Star Bible Publications
(S) Trafford Publishing (R)
(S) WinePress (R)
(S) Word Alive
(S) Zoë Life Publishing

FAITH
(A) Doubleday Religion (R)
(A) FaithWords
(A) HarperOne
(A) Nelson, Thomas
(A) Tyndale House (R)
(A) W Publishing
(A) WaterBrook Press (R)

Aadeon Publishing (R)
Aaron Book Publishing (R)
Abingdon Press
ACTA Publications
(S) ACW Press (R)
Ambassador Books
Ambassador-Emerald (R)
(S) American Binding (R)
B & H Publishing
Baker Books
Barbour
Bethany House (R)
(S) Black Forest (R)
Blue Dolphin
(S) Booklocker.com (R)
(S) Bookstand Publishing (R)
Bridge-Logos (R)
(S) Brown Books
Chalice Press
ChapterTwo (R)
Christian Family (R)
Christian Focus (R)
Christian Heritage (R)
Christian Writer's Ebook (R)
CLC Publications (R)
Comfort Publishing (R)
Congregational Life
Continuum Intl. (R)
(S) Creation House (R)
CrossLink Publishing
(S) DCTS Publishing
Destiny Image (R)
Destiny Image (books) (R)
Discovery House (R)
Eerdmans Pub., Wm. B. (R)
E.F.S. Online Pub.
(S) Elderberry Press
Eldridge Plays
Emmaus Road
(S) Essence (R)
Evangelical Press
Evergreen Press
(S) Fairway Press (R)
Faith Communications
FaithWalk
Father's Press
Forever Books (R)
Forward Movement
Fresh Air Books
Friends United Press

(S) Fruitbearer Pub.
Gollehon Press
Good Book (R)
Group Publishing
GRQ (R)
Grupo Nelson
Guardian Angel
Guideposts Books
Harrison House
Harvest Day
Hensley Publishing
Hidden Brook Press (R)
(S) Holy Fire Publishing (R)
Howard Books
(S) IMD Press (R)
(S) Insight Publishing (R)
InterVarsity Press (R)
Jebaire Publishing
Jossey-Bass
Journey Forth/BJU (R)
Judson Press (R)
Kregel (R)
Legacy Publishers
Life Changing Media
Lift Every Voice (R)
Lighthouse Publishing (R)
Liguori Public. (R)
Lillenas
Lion and Lamb
Loyola Press
Lutheran Univ. Press
Lutterworth Press (R)
Magnus Press (R)
(S) McDougal Publishing (R)
Messianic Jewish
    Publishers (R)
Mission City Press
Monarch Books
Morehouse
NavPress Th1nk (R)
New Hope (R)
New Seeds (R)
(S) One World (R)
Pacific Press
Paradise Research (R)
Parson Place (R)
Parsons Publishing (R)
(S) Path Pub. in Christ (R)
Pauline Books (R)
Pflaum Publishing

Pilgrim Press (R)
(S) Pleasant Word (R)
Power Publishing (R)
(S) Providence Pub. (R)
Quill Driver Books
Quintessential Books (R)
Randall House
Revival Nation
Rose Publishing
(S) Sage Press (R)
Salt-Works (R)
(S) Salvation Publisher (R)
Samaritan Press (R)
Scepter Publishers (R)
(S) Selah Publishing (R)
SparrowCrowne Press (R)
St. Anthony Mess. Press (R)
St. Bede's Publications (R)
St. Pauls/Alba House (R)
(S) Star Bible Publications
Strang Book Group (R)
(S) Tate Publishing (R)
(S) TEACH Services (R)
(S) Trafford Publishing (R)
Treble Heart Books (R)
UMI Publishing (R)
VBC Publishing
(S) VMI Publishers
Wesleyan Publishing
Whitaker House
White Stone Books (R)
(S) WinePress (R)
(S) Word Alive
Youth Specialties
(S) Zoë Life Publishing

FAMILY LIFE
(A) Cook, David C.
(A) FaithWords
(A) HarperOne
(A) Harvest House
(A) Nelson, Thomas
(A) Regal
(A) Tyndale House (R)
(A) W Publishing
(A) WaterBrook Press (R)

Aaron Book Publishing (R)
Abingdon Press
ACTA Publications

(S) ACW Press (R)
Ambassador Books
Ambassador-Emerald (R)
(S) American Binding (R)
B & H Publishing
Baker Books
Barbour
Beacon Hill Press (R)
Bethany House (R)
(S) Black Forest (R)
Blue Dolphin
(S) Booklocker.com (R)
(S) Bookstand Publishing (R)
Boyds Mills Press (R)
Branden Publishing (R)
(S) Brentwood (R)
Bridge-Logos (R)
(S) Brown Books
CarePoint (R)
Chalice Press
ChapterTwo (R)
Christian Family (R)
Christian Focus (R)
Christian Writer's Ebook (R)
College Press (R)
Comfort Publishing (R)
Conari Press
Concordia
(S) Creation House (R)
CrossLink Publishing
Crossroad Publishing (R)
Crossway Books
(S) DCTS Publishing
Destiny Image (R)
Destiny Image (books) (R)
Dimensions for Living
Discovery House (R)
Dove Inspirational (R)
Editorial Portavoz
Eerdmans Pub., Wm. B. (R)
E.F.S. Online Pub.
(S) Elderberry Press
Eldridge Plays
Emmaus Road
(S) Essence (R)
Evangelical Press
Evergreen Press
Extreme Diva
Fair Havens (R)
(S) Fairway Press (R)

Faith Communications
FaithWalk
FamilyLife (books) (R)
Father's Press
Focus on the Family (R)
Forever Books (R)
Forward Movement
Gentle Path Press
Grupo Nelson
Guardian Angel
Guideposts Books
Hannibal Books
Health Communications
Heart of Wisdom
Hensley Publishing
Hidden Brook Press (R)
(S) Holy Fire Publishing (R)
Hope Publishing (R)
Howard Books
(S) IMD Press (R)
(S) Insight Publishing (R)
InterVarsity Press (R)
Journey Forth/BJU (R)
Judson Press (R)
Kregel (R)
Langmarc
Legacy Press (R)
Life Changing Media
Life Cycle Books (R)
LifeSong Publishers
Lift Every Voice (R)
Lighthouse Publishing (R)
Liguori Public. (R)
Lillenas
Lion and Lamb
Loyola Press
Lutterworth Press (R)
(S) McDougal Publishing (R)
Millennium III (R)
Monarch Books
MOPS Intl.
Morehouse
Mountain View
New Hope (R)
(S) One World (R)
Our Sunday Visitor (R)
P & R Publishing (R)
Pacific Press
Pauline Books (R)
Pelican Publishing (R)

Pilgrim Press (R)
(S) Pleasant Word (R)
Port Hole Publications
Power Publishing (R)
(S) Providence Pub. (R)
Quiet Waters (R)
Quintessential Books (R)
Randall House
(S) Recovery Commun.
(S) Sage Press (R)
(S) Salvation Publisher (R)
Samaritan Press (R)
(S) Selah Publishing (R)
Sheed & Ward
(S) Southern Baptist Press (R)
St. Anthony Mess. Press (R)
(S) Star Bible Publications
Starik Publishing
Still Waters Revival (R)
Strang Book Group (R)
(S) Tate Publishing (R)
(S) TEACH Services (R)
Torch Legacy
(S) Trafford Publishing (R)
VBC Publishing
Vision Forum
(S) VMI Publishers
Whitaker House
White Stone Books (R)
(S) WinePress (R)
(S) Word Alive
(S) Zoë Life Publishing

FICTION: ADULT/ GENERAL

(A) Ballantine
(A) FaithWords
(A) HarperOne
(A) Nelson, Thomas, Fiction
(A) One World/Ballantine

Aaron Book Publishing (R)
Ambassador-Emerald (R)
(S) American Binding (R)
Blue Dolphin
(S) Book Publishers (R)
(S) Bookstand
    Publishing (R)
(S) Brown Books
Cladach Publishing

Comfort Publishing (R)
(S) Creation House (R)
E.F.S. Online Pub.
(S) Essence (R)
Fair Havens (R)
Frederick Fell (R)
Guernica Editions (R)
(S) Holy Fire Publishing (R)
Howard Books
(S) Infinity Publishing
Invisible College Press
Kregel (R)
LifeSong Publishers
(S) LifeVest Publishing
Lighthouse Publishing (R)
Lighthouse Trails (R)
Mountain View
Multnomah
Parson Place (R)
(S) Providence Pub. (R)
Quintessential Books (R)
Ravenhawk Books (R)
Revival Nation
(S) Sage Press (R)
Samaritan Press (R)
Steeple Hill
Strang Book Group (R)
(S) Trafford Publishing (R)
Treble Heart Books (R)
Virtual Tales (R)
Whitaker House
White Stone Books (R)
Xyzzy Press

FICTION: ADULT/ RELIGIOUS

(A) Ballantine
(A) Doubleday Religion (R)
(A) FaithWords
(A) HarperOne
(A) Harvest House
(A) Nelson, Thomas, Fiction
(A) One World/Ballantine
(A) Revell
(A) WaterBrook Press (R)

Aaron Book Publishing (R)
(S) ACW Press (R)
Adams Media
Ambassador Books

Ambassador-Emerald (R)
(S) American Binding (R)
B & H Publishing
Baker Books
Barbour
Bethany House (R)
(S) Black Forest (R)
(S) Book Publishers (R)
(S) Booklocker.com (R)
(S) Bookstand Publishing (R)
Branden Publishing (R)
Bridge-Logos (R)
(S) Brown Books
Christian Focus (R)
Christian Liberty Press
Christian Writer's Ebook (R)
Cladach Publishing
Comfort Publishing (R)
(S) Creation House (R)
(S) CrossHouse (R)
Deo Volente
Destiny Image (R)
Destiny Image (books) (R)
DiskUs Publishing
Eerdmans Pub., Wm. B. (R)
E.F.S. Online Pub.
(S) Elderberry Press
Elijah Press
(S) Essence (R)
Evergreen Press
(S) Fairway Press (R)
FaithWalk
Father's Press
Focus on the Family (R)
Forever Books (R)
(S) Fruitbearer Pub.
Gollehon Press
Guideposts Books
Hannibal Books
Heartsong Presents
HeartSpring Pub. (R)
Hidden Brook Press (R)
His Work Christian Pub. (R)
(S) Holy Fire Publishing (R)
Howard Books
(S) IMD Press (R)
(S) Infinity Publishing
(S) Insight Publishing (R)
Invisible College Press
KNB Publications

Kregel (R)
(S) LifeVest Publishing
Lift Every Voice (R)
Lighthouse Publishing (R)
Lighthouse Trails (R)
Lillenas
Lion and Lamb
Love Inspired
Love Inspired Historical
(S) McDougal Publishing (R)
Messianic Jewish Publishers (R)
Moody Publishers
Mountain View
Multnomah
NavPress
New Seeds (R)
OakTara Pub. (R)
(S) One World (R)
Pacific Press
Parson Place (R)
Parsons Publishing (R)
(S) Path Pub. in Christ (R)
(S) Pleasant Word (R)
Port Hole Publications
Power Publishing (R)
PREP Publishing (R)
(S) Providence Pub. (R)
Quiet Waters (R)
Quintessential Books (R)
Randall House
Resource Publications
(S) Sage Press (R)
Salt-Works (R)
Samaritan Press (R)
Scepter Publishers (R)
(S) Selah Publishing (R)
(S) Self Publish Press (R)
(S) Star Bible Publications
Starik Publishing
Steeple Hill
Strang Book Group (R)
(S) Tate Publishing (R)
(S) Trafford Publishing (R)
Treble Heart Books (R)
Tsaba House
Virtual Tales (R)
Vision Forum
(S) VMI Publishers
Walk Worthy (R)
Whitaker House

White Rose (R)
White Stone Books (R)
(S) WinePress (R)
(S) Word Alive
(S) Xulon Press (R)
Xyzzy Press

FICTION: ADVENTURE

(A) One World/Ballantine
(A) WaterBrook Press (R)

Aadeon Publishing (R)
Aaron Book Publishing (R)
(S) ACW Press (R)
Ambassador Books
Ambassador-Emerald (R)
(S) American Binding (R)
Atheneum/Young Readers
Baker Books
Barbour
(S) Black Forest (R)
(S) Book Publishers (R)
(S) Booklocker.com (R)
(S) Bookstand Publishing (R)
Boyds Mills Press (R)
(S) Brentwood (R)
Bridge-Logos (R)
(S) Brown Books
Christian Ed. Pub.
Christian Family (R)
Christian Writer's Ebook (R)
Cladach Publishing
(S) Creation House (R)
DiskUs Publishing
Eerdmans/Young Readers
E.F.S. Online Pub.
(S) Elderberry Press (R)
(S) Essence (R)
Evergreen Press
Fair Havens (R)
(S) Fairway Press (R)
FaithWalk
Forever Books (R)
Hidden Brook Press (R)
(S) Holy Fire Publishing (R)
Howard Books
(S) Infinity Publishing
(S) Insight Publishing (R)
Journey Forth/BJU (R)
Kaleidoscope Press (R)

Knight George Pub.
(S) LifeVest Publishing
Lift Every Voice (R)
Lighthouse Publishing (R)
Lion and Lamb
Messianic Jewish Publishers (R)
Mission City Press
Mountain View
Multnomah
(S) One World (R)
P & R Publishing (R)
Parson Place (R)
Parsons Publishing (R)
Pauline Kids (R)
(S) Pleasant Word (R)
Port Hole Publications
PREP Publishing (R)
Quintessential Books (R)
Randall House
Ravenhawk Books (R)
(S) Sage Press (R)
Salt-Works (R)
Samaritan Press (R)
(S) Selah Publishing (R)
(S) Self Publish Press (R)
(S) Southern Baptist Press (R)
Starik Publishing
Strang Book Group (R)
(S) Tate Publishing (R)
(S) Trafford Publishing (R)
Treble Heart Books (R)
(S) VMI Publishers
Warner Press
White Stone Books (R)
(S) WinePress (R)

FICTION: ALLEGORY

Aadeon Publishing (R)
Aaron Book Publishing (R)
(S) ACW Press (R)
(S) American Binding (R)
Atheneum/Young Readers
Baker Books
Barbour
(S) Black Forest (R)
(S) Booklocker.com (R)
(S) Bookstand Publishing (R)
Bridge-Logos (R)
(S) Brown Books
Christian Family (R)

Christian Writer's Ebook (R)
(S) Creation House (R)
Destiny Image (books) (R)
E.F.S. Online Pub.
(S) Elderberry Press
(S) Essence (R)
Evergreen Press
(S) Fairway Press (R)
Forever Books (R)
Hidden Brook Press (R)
(S) Holy Fire Publishing (R)
Howard Books
(S) Infinity Publishing
(S) Insight Publishing (R)
(S) LifeVest Publishing
Lighthouse Publishing (R)
Lion and Lamb
Multnomah
New Seeds (R)
OakTara Pub. (R)
(S) One World (R)
(S) Pleasant Word (R)
Port Hole Publications
Randall House
Realms
Reformation Trust
(S) Sage Press (R)
Salt-Works (R)
Samaritan Press (R)
(S) Selah Publishing (R)
Strang Book Group (R)
(S) Tate Publishing (R)
(S) TEACH Services (R)
(S) Trafford Publishing (R)
(S) VMI Publishers
White Stone Books (R)
Wilshire Book (R)
(S) WinePress (R)

FICTION: BIBLICAL

(A) Nelson, Thomas, Fiction
(A) WaterBrook Press (R)

Aadeon Publishing (R)
Aaron Book Publishing (R)
Abingdon Press
(S) ACW Press (R)
Ambassador-Emerald (R)
(S) American Binding (R)
Atheneum/Young Readers

Baker Books
(S) Black Forest (R)
(S) Booklocker.com (R)
(S) Bookstand Publishing (R)
(S) Brentwood (R)
Bridge-Logos (R)
(S) Brown Books
Charisma Kids
Christian Family (R)
Christian Writer's Ebook (R)
College Press (R)
(S) Creation House (R)
Destiny Image (R)
Destiny Image (books) (R)
Eerdmans Pub., Wm. B. (R)
Eerdmans/Young Readers
E.F.S. Online Pub.
(S) Elderberry Press
(S) Essence (R)
Evergreen Press
Fair Havens (R)
(S) Fairway Press (R)
Father's Press
Forever Books (R)
Guideposts Books
Hannibal Books
Hidden Brook Press (R)
(S) Holy Fire Publishing (R)
Howard Books
(S) IMD Press (R)
(S) Infinity Publishing
(S) Insight Publishing (R)
(S) Kindred Books (R)
LifeSong Publishers
(S) LifeVest Publishing
Lift Every Voice (R)
Lighthouse Publishing (R)
Lighthouse Trails (R)
Lillenas
Lion and Lamb
Love Inspired Historical
Messianic Jewish Publishers (R)
Mission City Press
Moody Publishers
Multnomah
NavPress
NavPress Th1nk (R)
New Seeds (R)
OakTara Pub. (R)
(S) One World (R)

P & R Publishing (R)
Pacific Press
Parsons Publishing (R)
(S) Pleasant Word (R)
Port Hole Publications
Power Publishing (R)
(S) Providence Pub. (R)
Quintessential Books (R)
Randall House
Realms
Reformation Trust
(S) Sage Press (R)
Salt-Works (R)
Samaritan Press (R)
(S) Self Publish Press (R)
(S) Southern Baptist Press (R)
Steeple Hill
Strang Book Group (R)
(S) Tate Publishing (R)
(S) Trafford Publishing (R)
(S) VMI Publishers
Walk Worthy (R)
Warner Press
White Stone Books (R)
(S) WinePress (R)

FICTION: CHICK LIT

(A) Nelson, Thomas, Fiction
(A) WaterBrook Press (R)

Aaron Book Publishing (R)
(S) ACW Press (R)
Ambassador Books
(S) American Binding (R)
Atheneum/Young Readers
(S) Booklocker.com (R)
(S) Bookstand Publishing (R)
(S) Brown Books
Christian Writer's Ebook (R)
(S) Creation House (R)
(S) Elderberry Press
(S) Essence (R)
Forever Books (R)
Hidden Brook Press (R)
(S) Holy Fire Publishing (R)
(S) Infinity Publishing
(S) Insight Publishing (R)
(S) LifeVest Publishing
Lighthouse Publishing (R)
Lion and Lamb

Little Lauren Books
Love Inspired Suspense
Multnomah
NavPress Th1nk (R)
(S) One World (R)
(S) Pleasant Word (R)
Port Hole Publications
Randall House
Ravenhawk Books (R)
(S) Sage Press (R)
Steeple Hill
Strang Book Group (R)
(S) Trafford Publishing (R)
(S) VMI Publishers
Whitaker House
White Stone Books (R)
(S) WinePress (R)

FICTION: CONTEMPORARY

(A) Ballantine
(A) FaithWords
(A) Nelson, Thomas, Fiction
(A) One World/Ballantine
(A) Revell
(A) Tyndale House (R)
(A) WaterBrook Press (R)

Aadeon Publishing (R)
Aaron Book Publishing (R)
(S) ACW Press (R)
Ambassador Books
Ambassador-Emerald (R)
(S) American Binding (R)
AMG Publishers (R)
Atheneum/Young Readers
Avon Inspire
B & H Publishing
Baker Books
Barbour
Bethany House (R)
(S) Black Forest (R)
(S) Booklocker.com (R)
(S) Bookstand Publishing (R)
Branden Publishing (R)
(S) Brentwood (R)
(S) Brown Books
Charisma Kids
Christian Ed. Pub.
Christian Writer's Ebook (R)

Cladach Publishing
(S) Creation House (R)
Destiny Image (R)
Destiny Image (books) (R)
DiskUs Publishing
Eerdmans/Young Readers
E.F.S. Online Pub.
(S) Elderberry Press
(S) Essence (R)
(S) Fairway Press (R)
FaithWalk
Focus on the Family (R)
Forever Books (R)
Frederick Fell (R)
Heartsong Presents
Hidden Brook Press (R)
(S) Holy Fire Publishing (R)
Howard Books
(S) Infinity Publishing
(S) Insight Publishing (R)
Invisible College Press
Journey Forth/BJU (R)
Kregel (R)
(S) LifeVest Publishing
Lift Every Voice (R)
Lighthouse Publishing (R)
Lillenas
Lion and Lamb
Love Inspired
(S) McDougal Publishing (R)
Mission City Press
Moody Publishers
Mountain View
Multnomah
NavPress
NavPress Th1nk (R)
OakTara Pub. (R)
(S) One World (R)
Parson Place (R)
Pauline Kids (R)
(S) Pleasant Word (R)
Port Hole Publications
Putnam/Young Readers
Randall House
Ravenhawk Books (R)
(S) Sage Press (R)
Salt-Works (R)
Samaritan Press (R)
(S) Self Publish Press (R)
(S) Southern Baptist Press (R)

Steeple Hill
Strang Book Group (R)
(S) Tate Publishing (R)
Third World Press (R)
(S) Trafford Publishing (R)
(S) VMI Publishers
Walk Worthy (R)
Whitaker House
White Stone Books (R)
(S) WinePress (R)

FICTION: COZY MYSTERIES

Aaron Book Publishing (R)
(S) ACW Press (R)
(S) American Binding (R)
(S) Bookstand Publishing (R)
(S) Brown Books
Comfort Publishing (R)
(S) Essence (R)
Forever Books (R)
Heartsong/Mysteries
Hidden Brook Press (R)
(S) Holy Fire Publishing (R)
(S) Infinity Publishing
(S) Insight Publishing (R)
Journey Forth/BJU (R)
Lighthouse Publishing (R)
Mountain View
Parson Place (R)
(S) Pleasant Word (R)
Port Hole Publications
(S) Sage Press (R)
Strang Book Group (R)
(S) Trafford Publishing (R)
Treble Heart Books (R)
(S) WinePress (R)

FICTION: ETHNIC

(A) Ballantine
(A) One World/Ballantine

Aaron Book Publishing (R)
(S) ACW Press (R)
(S) American Binding (R)
Atheneum/Young Readers
Baker Books
(S) Black Forest (R)
(S) Booklocker.com (R)
(S) Bookstand Publishing (R)
Boyds Mills Press (R)

Branden Publishing (R)
Christian Writer's Ebook (R)
Destiny Image (R)
DiskUs Publishing
E.F.S. Online Pub.
(S) Elderberry Press
(S) Essence (R)
Evergreen Press
(S) Fairway Press (R)
Focus on the Family (R)
Forever Books (R)
Guernica Editions (R)
Hidden Brook Press (R)
(S) Holy Fire Publishing (R)
(S) IMD Press (R)
(S) Infinity Publishing
(S) Insight Publishing (R)
Kaleidoscope Press (R)
(S) LifeVest Publishing
Lift Every Voice (R)
Lighthouse Publishing (R)
Multnomah
(S) One World (R)
(S) Pleasant Word (R)
Putnam/Young Readers
(S) Sage Press (R)
Samaritan Press (R)
Strang Book Group (R)
(S) Tate Publishing (R)
Third World Press (R)
(S) Trafford Publishing (R)
(S) VMI Publishers
Walk Worthy (R)
White Stone Books (R)
(S) WinePress (R)

FICTION: FABLES/ PARABLES
(A) HarperOne

Aadeon Publishing (R)
Aaron Book Publishing (R)
(S) ACW Press (R)
Ambassador-Emerald (R)
(S) American Binding (R)
(S) Black Forest (R)
Blue Dolphin
(S) Booklocker.com (R)
(S) Bookstand Publishing (R)
(S) Brown Books
E.F.S. Online Pub.

(S) Elderberry Press
(S) Essence (R)
Forever Books (R)
Hidden Brook Press (R)
(S) Holy Fire Publishing (R)
(S) Infinity Publishing
(S) Insight Publishing (R)
(S) LifeVest Publishing
Lighthouse Publishing (R)
(S) One World (R)
Parson Place (R)
(S) Pleasant Word (R)
Quintessential Books (R)
Randall House
Resource Publications
(S) Sage Press (R)
Salt-Works (R)
Samaritan Press (R)
(S) Tate Publishing (R)
(S) Trafford Publishing (R)
(S) VMI Publishers
(S) WinePress (R)

FICTION: FANTASY
(A) Ballantine
(A) WaterBrook Press (R)

Aaron Book Publishing (R)
(S) ACW Press (R)
(S) American Binding (R)
AMG Publishers (R)
Atheneum/Young Readers
Barbour
(S) Booklocker.com (R)
(S) Bookstand Publishing (R)
Christian Writer's Ebook (R)
Comfort Publishing (R)
(S) Creation House (R)
Destiny Image (R)
Destiny Image (books) (R)
DiskUs Publishing
Dover Publications (R)
Eerdmans Pub., Wm. B. (R)
E.F.S. Online Pub.
(S) Elderberry Press
(S) Essence (R)
Evergreen Press
(S) Fairway Press (R)
Forever Books (R)
Hidden Brook Press (R)
(S) Holy Fire Publishing (R)

(S) Infinity Publishing
(S) Insight Publishing (R)
Invisible College Press
(S) LifeVest Publishing
Lighthouse Publishing (R)
Marcher Lord Press
Mission City Press
Mountain View
Multnomah
NavPress Th1nk (R)
OakTara Pub. (R)
(S) One World (R)
P & R Publishing (R)
Parsons Publishing (R)
(S) Pleasant Word (R)
Port Hole Publications
Putnam/Young Readers
Ravenhawk Books (R)
Realms
(S) Sage Press (R)
Samaritan Press (R)
Starik Publishing
Strang Book Group (R)
(S) Tate Publishing (R)
(S) Trafford Publishing (R)
Treble Heart Books (R)
(S) VMI Publishers
Warner Press
Whitaker House
(S) WinePress (R)

FICTION: FRONTIER
(A) Harvest House
(A) Nelson, Thomas, Fiction

Aaron Book Publishing (R)
(S) ACW Press (R)
Ambassador-Emerald (R)
(S) American Binding (R)
AMG Publishers (R)
Atheneum/Young Readers
Baker Books
Bethany House (R)
(S) Black Forest (R)
(S) Booklocker.com (R)
(S) Bookstand Publishing (R)
(S) Brentwood (R)
(S) Brown Books
Christian Writer's Ebook (R)
Cladach Publishing

(S) Elderberry Press
(S) Essence (R)
(S) Fairway Press (R)
Forever Books (R)
Guardian Angel
Hidden Brook Press (R)
(S) Holy Fire Publishing (R)
(S) Infinity Publishing
(S) Insight Publishing (R)
Journey Forth/BJU (R)
Kaleidoscope Press (R)
(S) LifeVest Publishing
Lighthouse Publishing (R)
Lion and Lamb
Mission City Press
Mountain View
Multnomah
(S) One World (R)
Parson Place (R)
(S) Pleasant Word (R)
Port Hole Publications
Randall House
Ravenhawk Books (R)
(S) Sage Press (R)
Samaritan Press (R)
(S) Self Publish Press (R)
(S) Southern Baptist Press (R)
Strang Book Group (R)
(S) Tate Publishing (R)
(S) Trafford Publishing (R)
Treble Heart Books (R)
(S) VMI Publishers
Whitaker House
(S) WinePress (R)

FICTION: FRONTIER/ ROMANCE

(A) Harvest House
(A) Nelson, Thomas, Fiction

Aaron Book Publishing (R)
(S) ACW Press (R)
Ambassador-Emerald (R)
(S) American Binding (R)
AMG Publishers (R)
Baker Books
Barbour
Bethany House (R)
(S) Black Forest (R)
(S) Booklocker.com (R)

(S) Bookstand Publishing (R)
(S) Brentwood (R)
(S) Brown Books
Christian Writer's Ebook (R)
Cladach Publishing
(S) Elderberry Press
(S) Essence (R)
(S) Fairway Press (R)
Forever Books (R)
Heartsong Presents
Hidden Brook Press (R)
(S) Holy Fire Publishing (R)
(S) Infinity Publishing
(S) Insight Publishing (R)
(S) LifeVest Publishing
Lighthouse Publishing (R)
Love Inspired Historical
More Than Novellas
Mountain View
Multnomah
(S) One World (R)
Parson Place (R)
(S) Pleasant Word (R)
Port Hole Publications
Randall House
Ravenhawk Books (R)
(S) Sage Press (R)
Samaritan Press (R)
(S) Self Publish Press (R)
(S) Southern Baptist Press (R)
Steeple Hill
Strang Book Group (R)
(S) Tate Publishing (R)
(S) Trafford Publishing (R)
Treble Heart Books (R)
(S) VMI Publishers
Whitaker House
White Rose (R)
White Stone Books (R)
(S) WinePress (R)

FICTION: HISTORICAL

(A) Ballantine
(A) FaithWords
(A) Nelson, Thomas, Fiction
(A) One World/Ballantine
(A) Revell
(A) WaterBrook Press (R)

Aadeon Publishing (R)
Aaron Book Publishing (R)

Abingdon Press
(S) ACW Press (R)
Ambassador Books
Ambassador-Emerald (R)
(S) American Binding (R)
AMG Publishers (R)
Atheneum/Young Readers
Avon Inspire
B & H Publishing
Baker Books
Bethany House (R)
(S) Black Forest (R)
Blue Dolphin
(S) Book Publishers (R)
(S) Booklocker.com (R)
(S) Bookstand Publishing (R)
Boyds Mills Press (R)
Branden Publishing (R)
(S) Brentwood (R)
Bridge-Logos (R)
(S) Brown Books
Charisma Kids
Christian Family (R)
Christian Liberty Press
Christian Writer's Ebook (R)
Comfort Publishing (R)
Deo Volente
DiskUs Publishing
Eerdmans Pub., Wm. B. (R)
Eerdmans/Young Readers
(S) Elderberry Press
(S) Essence (R)
Fair Havens (R)
(S) Fairway Press (R)
Father's Press
Focus on the Family (R)
Forever Books (R)
Hannibal Books
Hidden Brook Press (R)
(S) Holy Fire Publishing (R)
Howard Books
(S) Infinity Publishing
(S) Insight Publishing (R)
Journey Forth/BJU (R)
Kregel (R)
(S) LifeVest Publishing
Lift Every Voice (R)
Lighthouse Publishing (R)
Mission City Press
Moody Publishers

Mountain View
Multnomah
NavPress
New Canaan (R)
OakTara Pub. (R)
(S) One World (R)
Parson Place (R)
Parsons Publishing (R)
Pauline Kids (R)
(S) Pleasant Word (R)
Port Hole Publications
(S) Providence Pub. (R)
Putnam/Young Readers
Quintessential Books (R)
Randall House
Ravenhawk Books (R)
Realms
Reformation Trust
(S) Sage Press (R)
Salt-Works (R)
Samaritan Press (R)
(S) Self Publish Press (R)
(S) Southern Baptist Press (R)
Strang Book Group (R)
(S) Tate Publishing (R)
(S) TEACH Services (R)
Third World Press (R)
(S) Trafford Publishing (R)
Treble Heart Books (R)
Vision Forum
(S) VMI Publishers
Whitaker House
White Stone Books (R)
(S) WinePress (R)

FICTION: HISTORICAL/ ROMANCE

(A) Harvest House
(A) Nelson, Thomas, Fiction
(A) Tyndale House (R)
(A) WaterBrook Press (R)

Aaron Book Publishing (R)
Abingdon Press
(S) ACW Press (R)
Ambassador-Emerald (R)
(S) American Binding (R)
AMG Publishers (R)
B & H Publishing
Baker Books
Barbour

Bethany House (R)
(S) Black Forest (R)
(S) Booklocker.com (R)
(S) Bookstand Publishing (R)
(S) Brentwood (R)
(S) Brown Books
Christian Writer's Ebook (R)
Comfort Publishing (R)
(S) Elderberry Press
(S) Essence (R)
(S) Fairway Press (R)
Forever Books (R)
Hannibal Books
Heartsong Presents
Hidden Brook Press (R)
(S) Holy Fire Publishing (R)
(S) Infinity Publishing
(S) Insight Publishing (R)
(S) LifeVest Publishing
Lift Every Voice (R)
Lighthouse Publishing (R)
Love Inspired Historical
More Than Novellas
Mountain View
Multnomah
(S) One World (R)
Parson Place (R)
(S) Pleasant Word (R)
Port Hole Publications
PREP Publishing (R)
Randall House
Ravenhawk Books (R)
(S) Sage Press (R)
(S) Self Publish Press (R)
(S) Southern Baptist Press (R)
Steeple Hill
Strang Book Group (R)
(S) Tate Publishing (R)
(S) Trafford Publishing (R)
Treble Heart Books (R)
(S) VMI Publishers
Whitaker House
White Rose (R)
White Stone Books (R)
(S) WinePress (R)

FICTION: HUMOR

(A) Ballantine
(A) FaithWords
(A) One World/Ballantine

Aadeon Publishing (R)
Aaron Book Publishing (R)
(S) ACW Press (R)
Ambassador Books
Ambassador-Emerald (R)
(S) American Binding (R)
Atheneum/Young Readers
Baker Books
(S) Black Forest (R)
(S) Booklocker.com (R)
(S) Bookstand Publishing (R)
Boyds Mills Press (R)
Christian Focus (R)
Christian Writer's Ebook (R)
(S) Creation House (R)
DiskUs Publishing
Eerdmans/Young Readers
(S) Elderberry Press
Encore Performance
(S) Essence (R)
Evergreen Press
(S) Fairway Press (R)
Forever Books (R)
Hidden Brook Press (R)
His Work Christian Pub. (R)
(S) Holy Fire Publishing (R)
(S) Infinity Publishing
(S) Insight Publishing (R)
Journey Forth/BJU (R)
Kaleidoscope Press (R)
(S) LifeVest Publishing
Lighthouse Publishing (R)
Lillenas
Lion and Lamb
Mountain View
Multnomah
NavPress Th1nk (R)
(S) One World (R)
Parson Place (R)
Parsons Publishing (R)
(S) Pleasant Word (R)
Port Hole Publications
PREP Publishing (R)
Putnam/Young Readers
Quintessential Books (R)
Randall House
Ravenhawk Books (R)
(S) Sage Press (R)
Salt-Works (R)
Samaritan Press (R)

(S) Selah Publishing (R)
Strang Book Group (R)
(S) Tate Publishing (R)
(S) Trafford Publishing (R)
Treble Heart Books (R)
(S) VMI Publishers
White Stone Books (R)
(S) WinePress (R)

FICTION: JUVENILE (AGES 8-12)

(A) Tyndale House (R)

Aadeon Publishing (R)
Aaron Book Publishing (R)
(S) ACW Press (R)
Ambassador Books
(S) American Binding (R)
AMG Publishers (R)
Atheneum/Young Readers
Avon Inspire
Baker Books
Barbour
(S) Black Forest (R)
Blue Dolphin
(S) Book Publishers (R)
(S) Booklocker.com (R)
(S) Bookstand Publishing (R)
Boyds Mills Press (R)
(S) Brown Books
Carson-Dellosa
Christian Ed. Pub.
Christian Focus (R)
(S) Creation House (R)
(S) CrossHouse (R)
(S) Dean Press, Robbie (R)
DiskUs Publishing
Dover Publications (R)
Eerdmans Pub., Wm. B. (R)
Eerdmans/Young Readers
E.F.S. Online Pub.
(S) Elderberry Press
(S) Essence (R)
Evergreen Press
Fair Havens (R)
(S) Fairway Press (R)
Forever Books (R)
(S) Fruitbearer Pub.
Guardian Angel
Hidden Brook Press (R)

His Work Christian Pub. (R)
(S) Holy Fire Publishing (R)
(S) Infinity Publishing
(S) Insight Publishing (R)
Journey Forth/BJU (R)
Kaleidoscope Press (R)
(S) Kindred Books (R)
Kregel (R)
LifeSong Publishers
(S) LifeVest Publishing
Lift Every Voice (R)
Lighthouse Publishing (R)
Lion and Lamb
Mission City Press
Moody Publishers
New Canaan (R)
(S) One World (R)
P & R Publishing (R)
Pacific Press
Parson Place (R)
Pauline Kids (R)
(S) Pleasant Word (R)
Port Hole Publications
Power Publishing (R)
(S) Providence Pub. (R)
Putnam/Young Readers
Quiet Waters (R)
Reformation Trust
Revival Nation
Salt-Works (R)
Salty's Books (R)
Samaritan Press (R)
(S) Selah Publishing (R)
(S) Self Publish Press (R)
Standard Publishing
Strang Book Group (R)
(S) Tate Publishing (R)
(S) TEACH Services (R)
Third World Press (R)
(S) Trafford Publishing (R)
(S) VMI Publishers
Walk Worthy (R)
Warner Press
White Stone Books (R)
(S) WinePress (R)
(S) Word Alive

FICTION: LITERARY

(A) Ballantine
(A) FaithWords

(A) HarperOne
(A) Nelson, Thomas, Fiction
(A) One World/Ballantine
(A) WaterBrook Press (R)

Aadeon Publishing (R)
Aaron Book Publishing (R)
(S) ACW Press (R)
Ambassador Books
(S) American Binding (R)
Atheneum/Young Readers
Baker Books
Bethany House (R)
(S) Black Forest (R)
(S) Booklocker.com (R)
(S) Bookstand Publishing (R)
Boyds Mills Press (R)
Branden Publishing (R)
(S) Brown Books
Christian Writer's Ebook (R)
Cladach Publishing
DiskUs Publishing
Dover Publications (R)
Eerdmans Pub., Wm. B. (R)
Eerdmans/Young Readers
E.F.S. Online Pub.
(S) Elderberry Press
(S) Essence (R)
(S) Fairway Press (R)
FaithWalk
Father's Press
Focus on the Family (R)
Forever Books (R)
Guernica Editions (R)
Hidden Brook Press (R)
(S) Holy Fire Publishing (R)
Hourglass Books (R)
(S) Infinity Publishing
(S) Insight Publishing (R)
Invisible College Press
Journey Forth/BJU (R)
(S) LifeVest Publishing
Lighthouse Publishing (R)
Moody Publishers
Multnomah
NavPress
(S) One World (R)
(S) Pleasant Word (R)
Port Hole Publications
(S) Providence Pub. (R)

Putnam/Young Readers
Quintessential Books (R)
Ravenhawk Books (R)
(S) Sage Press (R)
Salt-Works (R)
(S) Self Publish Press (R)
Strang Book Group (R)
(S) Tate Publishing (R)
Third World Press (R)
(S) Trafford Publishing (R)
(S) VMI Publishers
Walk Worthy (R)
White Stone Books (R)
(S) WinePress (R)

FICTION: MYSTERY/ ROMANCE

(A) Ballantine
(A) Nelson, Thomas, Fiction

Aaron Book Publishing (R)
(S) ACW Press (R)
(S) American Binding (R)
B & H Publishing
Baker Books
Barbour
Bethany House (R)
(S) Black Forest (R)
(S) Booklocker.com (R)
(S) Bookstand Publishing (R)
(S) Brentwood (R)
(S) Brown Books
Christian Writer's Ebook (R)
Comfort Publishing (R)
Destiny Image (R)
(S) Elderberry Press
(S) Essence (R)
(S) Fairway Press (R)
Forever Books (R)
Guideposts Books
Heartsong/Mysteries
Hidden Brook Press (R)
(S) Holy Fire Publishing (R)
Howard Books
(S) Infinity Publishing
(S) Insight Publishing (R)
Kregel (R)
(S) LifeVest Publishing
Lift Every Voice (R)
Lighthouse Publishing (R)
Little Lauren Books

Love Inspired Suspense
More Than Novellas
Mountain View
Multnomah
(S) One World (R)
Parson Place (R)
(S) Pleasant Word (R)
Port Hole Publications
PREP Publishing (R)
Randall House
(S) Sage Press (R)
(S) Selah Publishing (R)
(S) Self Publish Press (R)
(S) Southern Baptist
    Press (R)
Starik Publishing
Steeple Hill
Strang Book Group (R)
Summerside Press
(S) Tate Publishing (R)
(S) Trafford Publishing (R)
Treble Heart Books (R)
(S) VMI Publishers
White Rose (R)
White Stone Books (R)
(S) WinePress (R)

FICTION: MYSTERY/ SUSPENSE

(A) Ballantine
(A) One World/Ballantine
(A) Revell
(A) Tyndale House (R)

Aadeon Publishing (R)
Aaron Book Publishing (R)
(S) ACW Press (R)
Ambassador Books
(S) American Binding (R)
Avon Inspire
B & H Publishing
Baker Books
Bethany House (R)
(S) Black Forest (R)
Blue Dolphin
(S) Booklocker.com (R)
(S) Bookstand Publishing (R)
(S) Brown Books
Christian Ed. Pub.
Christian Focus (R)

Christian Writer's Ebook (R)
Comfort Publishing (R)
(S) Creation House (R)
Deo Volente
DiskUs Publishing
Eerdmans/Young Readers
E.F.S. Online Pub.
(S) Elderberry Press
(S) Essence (R)
(S) Fairway Press (R)
Father's Press
Focus on the Family (R)
Forever Books (R)
Gollehon Press
Guideposts Books
Heartsong/Mysteries
Hidden Brook Press (R)
His Work Christian Pub. (R)
(S) Holy Fire Publishing (R)
Howard Books
(S) Infinity Publishing
(S) Insight Publishing (R)
Invisible College Press
Journey Forth/BJU (R)
Kregel (R)
(S) LifeVest Publishing
Lift Every Voice (R)
Lighthouse Publishing (R)
Love Inspired Suspense
Mission City Press
Moody Publishers
Mountain View
Multnomah
OakTara Pub. (R)
(S) One World (R)
Parson Place (R)
Parsons Publishing (R)
Pauline Kids (R)
(S) Pleasant Word (R)
Port Hole Publications
PREP Publishing (R)
(S) Providence Pub. (R)
Putnam/Young Readers
Quintessential Books (R)
Ravenhawk Books (R)
(S) Sage Press (R)
Salt-Works (R)
(S) Selah Publishing (R)
(S) Self Publish Press (R)
Starik Publishing

Steeple Hill
Strang Book Group (R)
(S) Tate Publishing (R)
(S) Trafford Publishing (R)
Treble Heart Books (R)
(S) VMI Publishers
(S) WinePress (R)

FICTION: NOVELLAS
Aadeon Publishing (R)
Aaron Book Publishing (R)
(S) ACW Press (R)
(S) American Binding (R)
Atheneum/Young Readers
Baker Books
Barbour
(S) Booklocker.com (R)
(S) Bookstand Publishing (R)
Christian Writer's Ebook (R)
E.F.S. Online Pub.
(S) Elderberry Press
(S) Essence (R)
(S) Fairway Press (R)
Forever Books (R)
Guernica Editions (R)
Hidden Brook Press (R)
(S) Holy Fire Publishing (R)
(S) Infinity Publishing
(S) Insight Publishing (R)
Lighthouse Publishing (R)
Little Lauren Books
Mission City Press
More Than Novellas
Mountain View
(S) One World (R)
(S) Path Pub. in Christ (R)
(S) Pleasant Word (R)
Quintessential Books (R)
(S) Sage Press (R)
Salt-Works (R)
Samaritan Press (R)
(S) Trafford Publishing (R)
Treble Heart Books (R)
Virtual Tales (R)
White Stone Books (R)
(S) WinePress (R)

FICTION: PLAYS
Aadeon Publishing (R)
(S) American Binding (R)

Baker's Plays (R)
(S) Bookstand Publishing (R)
(S) Brentwood (R)
CSS Publishing
Dover Publications (R)
E.F.S. Online Pub.
Eldridge Plays
Encore Performance
(S) Essence (R)
(S) Fairway Press (R)
Forever Books (R)
Guardian Angel
Guernica Editions (R)
(S) Holy Fire Publishing (R)
(S) IMD Press (R)
Lillenas
Meriwether
Mission City Press
National Black Theatre
National Drama
(S) One World (R)
Players Press (R)
(S) Pleasant Word (R)
(S) Sage Press (R)
Salt-Works (R)
(S) Southern Baptist Press (R)
Third World Press (R)

FICTION: ROMANCE
(A) Ballantine
(A) Harvest House
(A) Nelson, Thomas, Fiction
(A) One World/Ballantine
(A) Tyndale House (R)
(A) WaterBrook Press (R)

Aaron Book Publishing (R)
(S) ACW Press (R)
(S) American Binding (R)
Baker Books
Barbour
Bethany House (R)
(S) Black Forest (R)
(S) Booklocker.com (R)
(S) Bookstand Publishing (R)
(S) Brown Books
Christian Writer's Ebook (R)
Comfort Publishing (R)
(S) Creation House (R)
DiskUs Publishing

(S) Elderberry Press
(S) Essence (R)
(S) Fairway Press (R)
Forever Books (R)
Hannibal Books
Heartsong Presents
Hidden Brook Press (R)
(S) Holy Fire Publishing (R)
(S) Infinity Publishing
(S) Insight Publishing (R)
(S) LifeVest Publishing
Lift Every Voice (R)
Lighthouse Publishing (R)
Little Lauren Books
Love Inspired
Love Inspired Suspense
More Than Novellas
Mountain View
Multnomah
OakTara Pub. (R)
(S) One World (R)
Parson Place (R)
(S) Pleasant Word (R)
Port Hole Publications
Randall House
(S) Sage Press (R)
(S) Selah Publishing (R)
Steeple Hill
Strang Book Group (R)
Summerside Press
(S) Tate Publishing (R)
(S) Trafford Publishing (R)
Treble Heart Books (R)
(S) VMI Publishers
Whitaker House
White Rose (R)
White Stone Books (R)
(S) WinePress (R)

FICTION: SCIENCE FICTION
(A) WaterBrook Press (R)

Aaron Book Publishing (R)
(S) ACW Press (R)
(S) American Binding (R)
Atheneum/Young Readers
(S) Booklocker.com (R)
(S) Bookstand Publishing (R)
Christian Focus (R)

Christian Writer's Ebook (R)
Comfort Publishing (R)
(S) Creation House (R)
Destiny Image (R)
DiskUs Publishing
Dover Publications (R)
(S) Elderberry Press
(S) Essence (R)
Evergreen Press
(S) Fairway Press (R)
Forever Books (R)
Gollehon Press
Hidden Brook Press (R)
(S) Holy Fire Publishing (R)
(S) Infinity Publishing
(S) Insight Publishing (R)
Invisible College Press
(S) LifeVest Publishing
Lighthouse Publishing (R)
Marcher Lord Press
Mountain View
OakTara Pub. (R)
(S) One World (R)
(S) Pleasant Word (R)
Port Hole Publications
PREP Publishing (R)
Putnam/Young Readers
Quintessential Books (R)
Realms
(S) Sage Press (R)
Starik Publishing
Strang Book Group (R)
(S) Tate Publishing (R)
(S) Trafford Publishing (R)
Treble Heart Books (R)
(S) VMI Publishers (R)
WinePress (R)

FICTION: SHORT STORY COLLECTIONS

(A) Ballantine

Aadeon Publishing (R)
Aaron Book Publishing (R)
(S) ACW Press (R)
(S) American Binding (R)
Atheneum/Young Readers
Baker Books
(S) Black Forest (R)
(S) Booklocker.com (R)

(S) Bookstand Publishing (R)
Branden Publishing (R)
Christian Writer's Ebook (R)
Comfort Publishing (R)
DiskUs Publishing
Eerdmans Pub., Wm. B. (R)
E.F.S. Online Pub.
(S) Elderberry Press
(S) Essence (R)
(S) Fairway Press (R)
Forever Books (R)
Hidden Brook Press (R)
His Work Christian Pub. (R)
(S) Holy Fire Publishing (R)
Hourglass Books (R)
(S) IMD Press (R)
(S) Insight Publishing (R)
Kaleidoscope Press (R)
Knight George Pub.
Mountain View
(S) One World (R)
Parson Place (R)
Pauline Kids (R)
(S) Pleasant Word (R)
Port Hole Publications
(S) Providence Pub. (R)
Quintessential Books (R)
Randall House
(S) Sage Press (R)
Salt-Works (R)
Samaritan Press (R)
(S) Tate Publishing (R)
Third World Press (R)
(S) Trafford Publishing (R)
Virtual Tales (R)
(S) VMI Publishers
Walk Worthy (R)
(S) WinePress (R)

FICTION: SKITS*

Encore Performance
Forever Books (R)
Lillenas
Merriwether Publishing

FICTION: SPECULATIVE

Aadeon Publishing (R)
Aaron Book Publishing (R)
(S) ACW Press (R)
(S) American Binding (R)

Baker Books
(S) Booklocker.com (R)
(S) Bookstand Publishing (R)
Christian Writer's Ebook (R)
(S) Elderberry Press
(S) Essence (R)
Forever Books (R)
Hidden Brook Press (R)
(S) Holy Fire Publishing (R)
(S) Infinity Publishing
(S) Insight Publishing (R)
(S) LifeVest Publishing
Lighthouse Publishing (R)
Marcher Lord Press
Mountain View
Multnomah
OakTara Pub. (R)
(S) One World (R)
(S) Pleasant Word (R)
Port Hole Publications
Realms
(S) Sage Press (R)
Salt-Works (R)
Strang Book Group (R)
(S) Tate Publishing (R)
(S) Trafford Publishing (R)
(S) VMI Publishers
(S) WinePress (R)

FICTION: TEEN/YOUNG ADULT

(A) FaithWords
(A) Nelson, Thomas, Fiction
(A) WaterBrook Press (R)

Aaron Book Publishing (R)
(S) ACW Press (R)
Ambassador Books
Ambassador-Emerald (R)
(S) American Binding (R)
AMG Publishers (R)
Atheneum/Young Readers
Baker Books
Barbour
Blue Dolphin
(S) Book Publishers (R)
(S) Booklocker.com (R)
(S) Bookstand Publishing (R)
Boyds Mills Press (R)
Christian Focus (R)

Christian Writer's Ebook (R)
Comfort Publishing (R)
(S) Creation House (R)
DiskUs Publishing
Eerdmans Pub., Wm. B. (R)
Eerdmans/Young Readers
E.F.S. Online Pub.
(S) Elderberry Press
(S) Essence (R)
Evergreen Press
(S) Fairway Press (R)
Faith Communications
Forever Books (R)
(S) Fruitbearer Pub.
Gollehon Press
Hidden Brook Press (R)
His Work Christian Pub. (R)
(S) Holy Fire Publishing (R)
(S) Infinity Publishing
(S) Insight Publishing (R)
Journey Forth/BJU (R)
Kirk House
Kregel (R)
Legacy Press (R)
(S) LifeVest Publishing
Lift Every Voice (R)
Lighthouse Publishing (R)
Lighthouse Trails (R)
Lion and Lamb
Little Lauren Books
Mission City Press
Moody Publishers
Mountain View
Multnomah
NavPress
NavPress Th1nk (R)
New Canaan (R)
(S) One World (R)
P & R Publishing (R)
Parson Place (R)
Parsons Publishing (R)
(S) Pleasant Word (R)
Power Publishing (R)
Putnam/Young Readers
Quiet Waters (R)
Randall House
Ravenhawk Books (R)
Revival Nation
(S) Sage Press (R)
Samaritan Press (R)

(S) Selah Publishing (R)
Starik Publishing
Strang Book Group (R)
(S) Tate Publishing (R)
(S) TEACH Services (R)
Third World Press (R)
(S) Trafford Publishing (R)
Treble Heart Books (R)
(S) VMI Publishers
Walk Worthy (R)
White Stone Books (R)
(S) WinePress (R)
(S) Word Alive

FICTION: WESTERNS
Aaron Book Publishing (R)
(S) ACW Press (R)
Ambassador-Emerald (R)
(S) American Binding (R)
Baker Books
(S) Black Forest (R)
(S) Booklocker.com (R)
(S) Bookstand
    Publishing (R)
(S) Brown Books
Christian Writer's Ebook (R)
Deo Volente
DiskUs Publishing
(S) Elderberry Press
(S) Essence (R)
(S) Fairway Press (R)
Forever Books (R)
Hidden Brook Press (R)
(S) Holy Fire Publishing (R)
(S) Infinity Publishing
(S) Insight Publishing (R)
Journey Forth/BJU (R)
(S) LifeVest Publishing
Lighthouse Publishing (R)
Mountain View
Multnomah
(S) One World (R)
Parson Place (R)
(S) Pleasant Word (R)
Quintessential Books (R)
Randall House
Ravenhawk Books (R)
(S) Sage Press (R)
Salt-Works (R)
Strang Book Group (R)

(S) Tate Publishing (R)
(S) Trafford Publishing (R)
Treble Heart Books (R)
(S) VMI Publishers
Whitaker House
White Stone Books (R)
(S) WinePress (R)

FORGIVENESS
(A) Doubleday Religion (R)
(A) FaithWords
(A) HarperOne
(A) Harvest House
(A) Nelson, Thomas
(A) Regal

Aaron Book Publishing (R)
Abingdon Press
ACTA Publications
(S) ACW Press (R)
Ambassador-Emerald (R)
(S) American Binding (R)
B & H Publishing
Barbour
(S) Black Forest (R)
Blue Dolphin
(S) Booklocker.com (R)
(S) Bookstand Publishing (R)
Bridge-Logos (R)
(S) Brown Books
Canticle Books (R)
CarePoint (R)
Chalice Press
ChapterTwo (R)
Christian Family (R)
Christian Focus (R)
Christian Writer's Ebook (R)
CLC Publications (R)
(S) Creation House (R)
CrossLink Publishing
CSS Publishing
(S) DCTS Publishing
Destiny Image (books) (R)
Discovery House (R)
Editorial Portavoz
Eerdmans Pub., Wm. B. (R)
E.F.S. Online Pub.
(S) Elderberry Press
Eldridge Plays
Emmaus Road

(S) Essence (R)
Evangelical Press
Evergreen Press
(S) Fairway Press (R)
FaithWalk
Father's Press
Forever Books (R)
Forward Movement
Gentle Path Press
Guardian Angel
Health Communications
Hensley Publishing
Hidden Brook Press (R)
(S) Holy Fire Publishing (R)
Howard Books
(S) IMD Press (R)
(S) Insight Publishing (R)
InterVarsity Press (R)
Jossey-Bass
Journey Forth/BJU (R)
Judson Press (R)
Kregel (R)
Lift Every Voice (R)
Lighthouse Publishing (R)
Lillenas
Lion and Lamb
Lutheran Univ. Press
Monarch Books
NavPress
NavPress Th1nk (R)
New Hope (R)
(S) One World (R)
Pacific Press
Parson Place (R)
Parsons Publishing (R)
(S) Path Pub. in Christ (R)
Pilgrim Press (R)
(S) Pleasant Word (R)
Power Publishing (R)
PREP Publishing (R)
(S) Providence Pub. (R)
Quill Driver Books
Randall House
Revival Nation
Rose Publishing
(S) Sage Press (R)
Salt-Works (R)
(S) Salvation Publisher (R)
Samaritan Press (R)
SparrowCrowne Press (R)

St. Anthony Mess. Press (R)
St. Pauls/Alba House (R)
(S) Star Bible Publications
Strang Book Group (R)
(S) Tate Publishing (R)
(S) TEACH Services (R)
Torch Legacy
(S) Trafford Publishing (R)
Treble Heart Books (R)
VBC Publishing
(S) VMI Publishers
White Stone Books (R)
(S) WinePress (R)
(S) Word Alive
(S) Zoë Life Publishing

GAMES/CRAFTS

Baker Books
(S) Booklocker.com (R)
(S) Bookstand Publishing (R)
Contemporary Drama
(S) Elderberry Press
(S) Essence (R)
(S) Fairway Press (R)
Group Publishing
Guardian Angel
Harcourt Religion
Hidden Brook Press (R)
(S) Holy Fire Publishing (R)
Jubilant Press (R)
Kaleidoscope Press (R)
Knight George Pub.
Legacy Press (R)
Lighthouse Publishing (R)
Lion and Lamb
Mission City Press
Monarch Books
Morehouse
(S) One World (R)
Players Press (R)
Rainbow Publishers (R)
Samaritan Press (R)
Standard Publishing
(S) Tate Publishing (R)
(S) Trafford Publishing (R)
Warner Press
(S) Zoë Life Publishing

GIFT BOOKS

(A) Harvest House

Aaron Book Publishing (R)
ACTA Publications
(S) Black Forest (R)
Blue Dolphin
(S) Book Publishers (R)
(S) Bookstand Publishing (R)
Bridge-Logos (R)
(S) Brown Books
(S) Creation House (R)
Dimensions for Living
Eerdmans Pub., Wm. B. (R)
(S) Essence (R)
Evangelical Press
Forever Books (R)
(S) Fruitbearer Pub.
GRQ (R) (S)
Holy Fire Publishing (R)
Howard Books
Lighthouse Publishing (R)
Lion and Lamb
(S) Path Pub. in Christ (R)
(S) Pleasant Word (R)
Power Publishing (R)
Ravenhawk Books (R)
Salt-Works (R)
Strang Book Group (R)
(S) Trafford Publishing (R)
(S) WinePress (R)

GRIEF

(A) Nelson, Thomas

Aaron Book Publishing (R)
Abingdon Press
ACTA Publications
(S) ACW Press (R)
Ambassador-Emerald (R)
(S) American Binding (R)
Anglicans United (R)
Bethany House (R)
(S) Black Forest (R)
Blue Dolphin
(S) Booklocker.com (R)
(S) Bookstand Publishing (R)
Bridge-Logos (R)
(S) Brown Books
Cambridge Scholars Pub.
CarePoint (R)
Chalice Press
CLC Publications (R)

(S) Creation House (R)
CrossLink Publishing
Crossroad Publishing (R)
Discovery House (R)
Eerdmans Pub., Wm. B. (R)
(S) Elderberry Press
(S) Essence (R)
Evangelical Press
Father's Press
Forever Books (R)
Gentle Path Press
GRQ (R)
Health Communications
(S) Holy Fire Publishing (R)
Howard Books
(S) IMD Press (R)
(S) Insight Publishing (R)
Kingsley Pub., Jessica (R)
Lighthouse Publishing (R)
Lillenas
Lion and Lamb
Lutterworth Press (R)
Monarch Books
New Hope (R)
Parson Place (R)
(S) Pleasant Word (R)
Power Publishing (R)
(S) Providence Pub. (R)
Randall House
Rose Publishing
(S) Sage Press (R)
(S) Salvation Publisher (R)
(S) Star Bible Publications
(S) TEACH Services (R)
(S) Trafford Publishing (R)
VBC Publishing
Whitaker House
(S) WinePress (R)

GROUP STUDY BOOKS
Aaron Book Publishing (R)
Abingdon Press
(S) ACW Press (R)
(S) American Binding (R)
AMG Publishers (R)
Baker Books
BMH Books (R)
(S) Booklocker.com (R)
(S) Bookstand Publishing (R)
(S) Brentwood (R)

Bridge-Logos (R)
CarePoint (R)
Carey Library, Wm. (R)
Chalice Press
Christian Writer's Ebook (R)
College Press (R)
Congregational Life
(S) CrossHouse (R)
CrossLink Publishing
CSS Publishing
Eerdmans Pub., Wm. B. (R)
E.F.S. Online Pub.
(S) Essence (R)
Evangelical Press
Evergreen Press
Fair Havens (R)
(S) Fairway Press (R)
Forever Books (R)
Founders Press
Foursquare Media
Good Book (R)
Gospel Publishing
Group Publishing
Hannibal Books
Hensley Publishing
Hidden Brook Press (R)
(S) Holy Fire Publishing (R)
(S) IMD Press (R)
InterVarsity Press (R)
Jesus Filled Day (books)
Jubilant Press (R)
Judson Press (R)
Lighthouse Publishing (R)
Lion and Lamb
Mission City Press
Monarch Books
NavPress Th1nk (R)
New Hope (R)
(S) One World (R)
Pacific Press
Paradise Research (R)
Parson Place (R)
Pilgrim Press (R)
(S) Pleasant Word (R)
Power Publishing (R)
(S) Providence Pub. (R)
Randall House
Rose Publishing
(S) Sage Press (R)
Salt-Works (R)

Smyth & Helwys
(S) Southern Baptist Press (R)
St. Anthony Mess. Press (R)
(S) Star Bible Publications
(S) Tate Publishing (R)
(S) Trafford Publishing (R)
UMI Publishing (R)
(S) VMI Publishers
(S) WinePress (R)
(S) Word Alive
(S) Zoë Life Publishing

HEALING
(A) Cook, David C.
(A) FaithWords
(A) Nelson, Thomas

Aaron Book Publishing (R)
ACTA Publications
(S) ACW Press (R)
(S) American Binding (R)
Baker Books
(S) Black Forest (R)
Blue Dolphin
(S) Book Publishers (R)
(S) Booklocker.com (R)
(S) Bookstand Publishing (R)
(S) Brentwood (R)
Bridge-Logos (R)
(S) Brown Books
Cambridge Scholars Pub.
Canticle Books (R)
CarePoint (R)
Chalice Press .
Christian Heritage (R)
Christian Writer's Ebook (R)
CLC Publications (R)
Comfort Publishing (R)
(S) Creation House (R)
Crossroad Publishing (R)
CSS Publishing
Destiny Image (R)
Destiny Image (books) (R)
Eerdmans Pub., Wm. B. (R)
E.F.S. Online Pub.
(S) Elderberry Press
(S) Essence (R)
(S) Fairway Press (R)
FaithWalk
Father's Press
Forever Books (R)

Forward Movement
Gentle Path Press
Good Book (R)
Harrison House
Hay House
Health Communications
Hidden Brook Press (R)
(S) Holy Fire Publishing (R)
Hope Publishing (R)
(S) Impact Christian (R)
(S) Insight Publishing (R)
Kingsley Pub., Jessica (R)
Life Changing Media
Lighthouse Publishing (R)
Lillenas
Lion and Lamb
Loyola Press
Lutheran Univ. Press
Lutterworth Press (R)
Magnus Press (R)
(S) McDougal Publishing (R)
Monarch Books
(S) One World (R)
Pacific Press
Paradise Research (R)
Parson Place (R)
Parsons Publishing (R)
(S) Path Pub. in Christ (R)
Pilgrim Press (R)
(S) Pleasant Word (R)
Power Publishing (R)
(S) Providence Pub. (R)
(S) Recovery Commun.
Revival Nation
(S) Sage Press (R)
(S) Salvation Publisher (R)
(S) Selah Publishing (R)
Siloam
(S) Southern Baptist Press (R)
SparrowCrowne Press (R)
(S) Star Bible Publications
Strang Book Group (R)
(S) Tate Publishing (R)
(S) TEACH Services (R)
(S) Trafford Publishing (R)
(S) VMI Publishers
Whitaker House
(S) WinePress (R)
(S) Word Alive
(S) Zoë Life Publishing

HEALTH

(A) Ballantine
(A) FaithWords
(A) Harvest House
(A) Nelson, Thomas

Aaron Book Publishing (R)
(S) ACW Press (R)
Ambassador Books
Ambassador-Emerald (R)
(S) American Binding (R)
Baker Books
Blue Dolphin
(S) Book Publishers (R)
(S) Booklocker.com (R)
(S) Bookstand Publishing (R)
(S) Brentwood (R)
(S) Brown Books
Cambridge Scholars Pub.
Chalice Press
Christian Writer's Ebook (R)
(S) Creation House (R)
Destiny Image (books) (R)
Eerdmans Pub., Wm. B. (R)
E.F.S. Online Pub.
(S) Elderberry Press
(S) Essence (R)
Evangelical Press
Evergreen Press
Facts On File
Fair Havens (R)
(S) Fairway Press (R)
Forever Books (R)
Forward Movement
Gentle Path Press
Good Book (R)
Grupo Nelson
Guardian Angel
Hay House
Health Communications
Hidden Brook Press (R)
His Work Christian Pub. (R)
(S) Holy Fire Publishing (R)
Hope Publishing (R)
(S) IMD Press (R)
(S) Insight Publishing (R)
Jebaire Publishing
Kaleidoscope Press (R)
Kingsley Pub., Jessica (R)
Langmarc

Legacy Publishers
Life Changing Media
Life Cycle Books (R)
Lighthouse Publishing (R)
Lion and Lamb
Loyola Press
Messianic Jewish Publishers (R)
Monarch Books
Morehouse
Mountain View
New Hope (R)
(S) One World (R)
Pacific Press
Paradise Research (R)
Parsons Publishing (R)
(S) Path Pub. in Christ (R)
(S) Pleasant Word (R)
Power Publishing (R)
(S) Providence Pub. (R)
Quintessential Books (R)
(S) Recovery Commun.
(S) Sage Press (R)
(S) Salvation Publisher (R)
Sheed & Ward
Siloam
(S) Southern Baptist Press (R)
(S) Star Bible Publications
Strang Book Group (R)
Tarcher, Jeremy P. (R)
(S) Tate Publishing (R)
(S) TEACH Services (R)
Third World Press (R)
(S) Trafford Publishing (R)
Treble Heart Books (R)
VBC Publishing
(S) VMI Publishers
(S) WinePress (R)
(S) Word Alive
Xyzzy Press
(S) Zoë Life Publishing

HISPANIC MARKETS
(A) Doubleday Religion (R)

(S) American Binding (R)
Anglicans United (R)
B & H Publishing
(S) Booklocker.com (R)
Cambridge Scholars Pub.
ChapterTwo (R)

Concordia
Editorial Portavoz
Editorial Unilit
Emmaus Road
Forever Books (R)
Forward Movement
Grupo Nelson
InterVarsity Press (R)
Judson Press (R)
Liturgy Training (R)
New Hope (R)
Oregon Catholic
Parsons Publishing (R)
Pilgrim Press (R)
St. Anthony Mess. Press (R)
Strang Book Group (R)
(S) Tate Publishing (R)
Tyndale House Publishers
Whitaker House

HISTORICAL
(A) Doubleday Religion (R)
(A) HarperOne
(A) Nelson, Thomas
(A) One World/Ballantine

Aadeon Publishing (R)
Aaron Book Publishing (R)
(S) ACW Press (R)
Ambassador Books
Ambassador-Emerald (R)
(S) American Binding (R)
AMG Publishers (R)
Anglicans United (R)
Atheneum/Young Readers
Baker Academic
Baker Books
(S) Black Forest (R)
Blue Dolphin
(S) Booklocker.com (R)
(S) Bookstand Publishing (R)
Boyds Mills Press (R)
(S) Brentwood (R)
Bridge-Logos (R)
(S) Brown Books
Cambridge Scholars Pub.
Canadian Inst. for Law (R)
Canticle Books (R)
Carey Library, Wm. (R)
Catholic Answers (R)

Chalice Press
ChapterTwo (R)
Christian Family (R)
Christian Heritage (R)
Christian Liberty Press
Christian Writer's Ebook (R)
Cistercian (R)
Clarke & Co., James (R)
College Press (R)
Comfort Publishing (R)
Conciliar Press (R)
Concordia Academic
Continuum Intl. (R)
(S) Creation House (R)
CrossLink Publishing
Custom Book
Eerdmans Pub., Wm. B. (R)
E.F.S. Online Pub.
(S) Elderberry Press
Elijah Press
(S) Essence (R)
ETC Publications
Evangelical Press
Facts On File
(S) Fairway Press (R)
FaithWalk
Fifth-Estate (R)
Fordham Univ. Press (R)
Forever Books (R)
Founders Press
Foursquare Media
Harvest Day
Heart of Wisdom
Hidden Brook Press (R)
His Work Christian Pub. (R)
(S) Holy Fire Publishing (R)
(S) IMD Press (R)
(S) Impact Christian (R)
Inkling Books (R)
(S) Insight Publishing (R)
InterVarsity Press (R)
Jossey-Bass
Kirk House
Kregel (R)
(S) LifeVest Publishing
Lift Every Voice (R)
Lighthouse Publishing (R)
Lion and Lamb
Loyola Press
Lutheran Univ. Press

Lutterworth Press (R)
Mercer Univ. Press (R)
Messianic Jewish Publishers (R)
Monarch Books
New Seeds (R)
New York Univ. Press
(S) One World (R)
Paradise Research (R)
(S) Path Pub. in Christ (R)
(S) Pleasant Word (R)
Power Publishing (R)
(S) Providence Pub. (R)
Quintessential Books (R)
Ragged Edge (R)
(S) Sage Press (R)
Salt-Works (R)
Scepter Publishers (R)
Sheed & Ward
(S) Southern Baptist Press (R)
St. Augustine's Press (R)
(S) Star Bible Publications
Still Waters Revival (R)
(S) Tate Publishing (R)
(S) TEACH Services (R)
Third World Press (R)
(S) Trafford Publishing (R)
Treble Heart Books (R)
Trinity Foundation (R)
Univ. of AR Press (R)
Univ. Press of America (R)
Vision Forum
(S) WinePress (R)
(S) Word Alive
Yale Univ. Press (R)

HOLIDAY/SEASONAL
(A) Cook, David C.
(A) FaithWords
(A) HarperOne

Aaron Book Publishing (R)
Abingdon Press
(S) ACW Press (R)
Ambassador Books
(S) American Binding (R)
Barbour
Blue Dolphin
(S) Booklocker.com (R)
Chalice Press
Christian Writer's Ebook (R)

CSS Publishing
Discovery House (R)
E.F.S. Online Pub.
(S) Elderberry Press
Eldridge Plays
Encore Performance
(S) Essence (R)
Evangelical Press
Evergreen Press
(S) Fairway Press (R)
FamilyLife (books) (R)
Forever Books (R)
Forward Movement
Good News Pub.
Guardian Angel
Guideposts Books
Hidden Brook Press (R)
(S) Holy Fire Publishing (R)
Howard Books
(S) IMD Press (R)
(S) Insight Publishing (R)
Judson Press (R)
Lighthouse Publishing (R)
Lion and Lamb
Meriwether
Messianic Jewish
    Publishers (R)
Monarch Books
New Hope (R)
(S) One World (R)
Pauline Books (R)
Pflaum Publishing
(S) Pleasant Word (R)
Power Publishing (R)
(S) Providence Pub. (R)
Putnam/Young Readers
Randall House
Ravenhawk Books (R)
(S) Sage Press (R)
Salt-Works (R)
St. Anthony Mess. Press (R)
Standard Publishing
Strang Book Group (R)
(S) Tate Publishing (R)
(S) Trafford Publishing (R)
(S) VMI Publishers
Warner Press
White Stone Books (R)
(S) WinePress (R)
(S) Word Alive

HOLINESS

Aaron Book Publishing (R)
(S) ACW Press (R)
Ambassador-Emerald (R)
(S) American Binding (R)
Bethany House (R)
(S) Black Forest (R)
Blue Dolphin
(S) Booklocker.com (R)
Bridge-Logos (R)
(S) Brown Books
Chalice Press
ChapterTwo (R)
Christian Family (R)
Christian Focus (R)
Christian Heritage (R)
CLC Publications (R)
(S) Creation House (R)
Eerdmans Pub., Wm. B. (R)
E.F.S. Online Pub.
(S) Elderberry Press
(S) Essence (R)
Evangelical Press
Father's Press
Forever Books (R)
Forward Movement
GRQ (R)
Hidden Brook Press (R)
(S) Holy Fire Publishing (R)
Howard Books
(S) IMD Press (R)
(S) Insight Publishing (R)
InterVarsity Press (R)
Lighthouse Publishing (R)
Lillenas
Monarch Books
NavPress Th1nk (R)
Parson Place (R)
Parsons Publishing (R)
(S) Pleasant Word (R)
Power Publishing (R)
(S) Providence Pub. (R)
Revival Nation
(S) Sage Press (R)
Salt-Works (R)
(S) Salvation Publisher (R)
St. Anthony Mess. Press (R)
St. Bede's Publications (R)
St. Pauls/Alba House (R)
(S) Star Bible Publications

Strang Book Group (R)
(S) Tate Publishing (R)
(S) TEACH Services (R)
(S) Trafford Publishing (R)
Wesleyan Publishing
(S) WinePress (R)
(S) Zoë Life Publishing

HOLY SPIRIT

(A) Nelson, Thomas
(A) Regal
Aaron Book Publishing (R)
(S) ACW Press (R)
(S) American Binding (R)
Baylor Univ. Press
(S) Black Forest (R)
Blue Dolphin
(S) Booklocker.com (R)
Bridge-Logos (R)
Canticle Books (R)
ChapterTwo Publications (R)
Christian Family (R)
Christian Focus (R)
Christian Heritage (R)
Christian Writer's Ebook (R)
CLC Publications (R)
Comfort Publishing (R)
(S) Creation House (R)
CSS Publishing
Destiny Image (R)
Destiny Image (books) (R)
Eerdmans Pub., Wm. B. (R)
E.F.S. Online Pub.
(S) Elderberry Press
(S) Essence (R)
Evangelical Press
(S) Fairway Press (R)
Father's Press
Forever Books (R)
Forward Movement
Gospel Publishing
Harrison House
Hidden Brook Press (R)
(S) Holy Fire Publishing (R)
(S) IMD Press (R)
(S) Insight Publishing (R)
InterVarsity Press (R)
Kregel (R)
Lift Every Voice (R)
Lighthouse Publishing (R)

Lillenas
Lion and Lamb
Lutheran Univ. Press
Monarch Books
NavPress Th1nk (R)
(S) One World (R)
Pacific Press
Parson Place (R)
Parsons Publishing (R)
(S) Path Pub. in Christ (R)
Pilgrim Press (R)
(S) Pleasant Word (R)
Power Publishing (R)
(S) Providence Pub. (R)
Revival Nation
Rose Publishing
(S) Sage Press (R)
(S) Salvation Publisher (R)
St. Anthony Mess. Press (R)
St. Bede's Publications (R)
St. Pauls/Alba House (R)
(S) Star Bible Publications
Strang Book Group (R)
(S) Tate Publishing (R)
(S) TEACH Services (R)
(S) Trafford Publishing (R)
VBC Publishing
(S) VMI Publishers
Westminster John Knox
Whitaker House
(S) WinePress (R)
(S) Word Alive
(S) Zoë Life Publishing

HOMESCHOOLING RESOURCES
Aaron Book Publishing (R)
(S) ACW Press (R)
(S) American Binding (R)
Baker Books
(S) Book Publishers (R)
(S) Booklocker.com (R)
(S) Bookstand Publishing (R)
(S) Brentwood (R)
ChapterTwo (R)
Christian Focus (R)
Christian Writer's Ebook (R)
(S) CrossHouse (R)
CrossLink Publishing
Eerdmans Pub., Wm. B. (R)

E.F.S. Online Pub.
(S) Elderberry Press
Eldridge Plays
Emmaus Road
(S) Essence (R)
ETC Publications
Evangelical Press
Fair Havens (R)
(S) Fairway Press (R)
Forever Books (R)
Guardian Angel
Hannibal Books
Heart of Wisdom
Hidden Brook Press (R)
(S) Holy Fire Publishing (R)
(S) IMD Press (R)
Journey Forth/BJU (R)
Lighthouse Publishing (R)
Lighthouse Trails (R)
Lion and Lamb
Little Lauren Books
Mason Crest Publishers
Master Books
McRuffy Press
Mission City Press
Monarch Books
New Canaan (R)
New Leaf
(S) One World (R)
(S) Path Pub. in Christ (R)
(S) Pleasant Word (R)
Power Publishing (R)
(S) Providence Pub. (R)
Rose Publishing
Salt-Works (R)
Samaritan Press (R)
Starik Publishing
(S) Tate Publishing (R)
(S) Trafford Publishing (R)
(S) WinePress (R)
(S) Word Alive
(S) Zoë Life Publishing

HOMILETICS
Aaron Book Publishing (R)
Abingdon Press
(S) ACW Press (R)
(S) American Binding (R)
Baker Books
(S) Black Forest (R)

(S) Booklocker.com (R)
Chalice Press
Christian Family (R)
Christian Focus (R)
Christian Writer's Ebook (R)
CSS Publishing
(S) DCTS Publishing
Eerdmans Pub., Wm. B. (R)
(S) Elderberry Press
Emmaus Road
(S) Essence (R)
Evangelical Press
(S) Fairway Press (R)
Forever Books (R)
Hidden Brook Press (R)
(S) Holy Fire Publishing (R)
(S) IMD Press (R)
(S) Insight Publishing (R)
Judson Press (R)
Kregel (R)
Lighthouse Publishing (R)
Lutheran Univ. Press
Monarch Books
Morehouse
(S) One World (R)
(S) Pleasant Word (R)
Power Publishing (R)
(S) Providence Pub. (R)
Resource Publications
Rose Publishing
Salt-Works (R)
St. Anthony Mess. Press (R)
St. Pauls/Alba House (R)
(S) Star Bible Publications
(S) Tate Publishing (R)
(S) Trafford Publishing (R)
VBC Publishing
(S) VMI Publishers
Westminster John Knox
(S) WinePress (R)
(S) Word Alive
(S) Zoë Life Publishing

HOW-TO
(A) Ballantine
(A) Harvest House
(A) Nelson, Thomas
(A) One World/Ballantine
(A) Perigee Books
(A) Revell

Aaron Book Publishing (R)
(S) ACW Press (R)
Adams Media
(S) American Binding (R)
Baker Books(S)
Black Forest (R)
Blue Dolphin
(S) Booklocker.com (R)
(S) Bookstand Publishing (R)
(S) Brentwood (R)
Bridge-Logos (R)
Christian Writer's Ebook (R)
Church Growth Inst.
Destiny Image (R)
DiskUs Publishing
E.F.S. Online Pub.
(S) Elderberry Press
Encore Performance
(S) Essence (R)
Evangelical Press
Evergreen Press
Fair Havens (R)
(S) Fairway Press (R)
FaithWalk
Forever Books (R)
Frederick Fell (R)
Gospel Light
GRQ (R)
Guardian Angel
Harcourt Religion
Hidden Brook Press (R)
His Work Christian Pub. (R)
(S) Holy Fire Publishing (R)
Howard Books
(S) IMD Press (R)
Inkling Books (R)
(S) Insight Publishing (R)
Kaleidoscope Press (R)
Kirk House
(S) LifeVest Publishing
Lighthouse Publishing (R)
Lion and Lamb
Meriwether
Monarch Books
Mountain View
(S) One World (R)
Our Sunday Visitor (R)
Pacific Press
Parson Place (R)
(S) Path Pub. in Christ (R)

(S) Path Publishing (R)
Pauline Books (R)
Players Press (R)
(S) Pleasant Word (R)
Power Publishing (R)
PREP Publishing (R)
(S) Providence Pub. (R)
Quintessential Books (R)
(S) Recovery Commun.
(S) Sage Press (R)
Salt-Works (R)
(S) Salvation Publisher (R)
(S) Southern Baptist Press (R)
Standard Publishing
Still Waters Revival (R)
Tarcher, Jeremy P. (R)
(S) Tate Publishing (R)
(S) Trafford Publishing (R)
Treble Heart Books (R)
VBC Publishing
(S) VMI Publishers
Walk Worthy (R)
Wilshire Book (R)
(S) WinePress (R)
(S) Word Alive
(S) Zoë Life Publishing

HUMOR

(A) Ballantine
(A) Cook, David C.
(A) Countryman, J.
(A) FaithWords
(A) Harvest House
(A) Nelson, Thomas
(A) One World/Ballantine

Aaron Book Publishing (R)
ACTA Publications
(S) ACW Press (R)
Ambassador Books
(S) American Binding (R)
Baker Books
Barbour
(S) Black Forest (R)
Blue Dolphin
(S) Booklocker.com (R)
(S) Bookstand Publishing (R)
Boyds Mills Press (R)
(S) Brentwood (R)
Bridge-Logos (R)

Christian Writer's Ebook (R)
(S) Creation House (R)
E.F.S. Online Pub.
(S) Elderberry Press
Eldridge Plays
(S) Essence (R)
Evergreen Press
(S) Fairway Press (R)
Forever Books (R)
Forward Movement
Guideposts Books
Health Communications
Hidden Brook Press (R)
(S) Holy Fire Publishing (R)
(S) Insight Publishing (R)
Kaleidoscope Press (R)
Kirk House
Lighthouse Publishing (R)
Lillenas
Lion and Lamb
Loyola Press
Meriwether
Monarch Books
MOPS Intl.
NavPress Th1nk (R)
(S) One World (R)
Pacific Press
Parson Place (R)
(S) Path Pub. in Christ (R)
(S) Path Publishing (R)
(S) Pleasant Word (R)
Power Publishing (R)
(S) Providence Pub. (R)
Putnam/Young Readers
Quill Driver Books
Quintessential Books (R)
(S) Sage Press (R)
Salt-Works (R)
(S) Salvation Publisher (R)
Samaritan Press (R)
(S) Selah Publishing (R)
(S) Southern Baptist Press (R)
(S) Tate Publishing (R)
(S) Trafford Publishing (R)
Treble Heart Books (R)
(S) VMI Publishers
Walk Worthy (R)
White Stone Books (R)
(S) WinePress (R)
(S) Word Alive

Xyzzy Press
(S) Zoë Life Publishing

INSPIRATIONAL
(A) Countryman, J.
(A) Doubleday Religion (R)
(A) FaithWords
(A) Harvest House
(A) Nelson, Thomas
(A) Perigee Books
(A) Tyndale House (R)
(A) WaterBrook Press (R)
(A) W Publishing

Aadeon Publishing (R)
Aaron Book Publishing (R)
Abingdon Press
(S) ACW Press (R)
Adams Media
Ambassador Books
Ambassador-Emerald (R)
(S) American Binding (R)
Baker Books
Barbour
Beacon Hill Press (R)
Believe Books
Bethany House (R)
(S) Black Forest (R)
Blue Dolphin
(S) Booklocker.com (R)
(S) Bookstand Publishing (R)
(S) Brentwood (R)
Bridge-Logos (R)
(S) Brown Books
Canticle Books (R)
Catholic Book
ChapterTwo (R)
Charisma Kids
Christian Family (R)
Christian Focus (R)
Christian Writer's Ebook (R)
CLC Publications (R)
Comfort Publishing (R)
Concordia
Continuum Intl. (R)
(S) Creation House (R)
(S) CrossHouse (R)
CrossLink Publishing
CSS Publishing
(S) DCTS Publishing

Destiny Image (R)
Destiny Image (books) (R)
Dimensions for Living
Discovery House (R)
Dove Inspirational (R)
E.F.S. Online Pub.
(S) Elderberry Press
Eldridge Plays
(S) Essence (R)
Evangelical Press
Evergreen Press
(S) Fairway Press (R)
Faith Communications
FaithWalk
Forever Books (R)
Forward Movement
Fresh Air Books
(S) Fruitbearer Pub.
Gollehon Press
GRQ (R)
Grupo Nelson
Guardian Angel
Harrison House
Hay House
Health Communications
HeartSpring Pub. (R)
Hidden Brook Press (R)
(S) Holy Fire Publishing (R)
Hope Publishing (R)
Howard Books
(S) IMD Press (R)
(S) Impact Christian (R)
(S) Insight Publishing (R)
Jebaire Publishing
Journey Forth/BJU (R)
Journey Stone (R)
Judson Press (R)
Kaleidoscope Press (R)
Kirk House
Langmarc
Life Changing Media
(S) LifeVest Publishing
Lighthouse Publishing (R)
Lillenas
Lion and Lamb
Loyola Press
Lutheran Univ. Press
Lutheran Voices
Magnus Press (R)
(S) McDougal Publishing (R)

Monarch Books
Mountain View
NavPress Th1nk (R)
New Seeds (R)
(S) One World (R)
Pacific Press
Paradise Research (R)
Parson Place (R)
Parsons Publishing (R)
(S) Path Pub. in Christ (R)
(S) Path Publishing (R)
Paulist Press
Pelican Publishing (R)
Pilgrim Press (R)
(S) Pleasant Word (R)
Port Hole Publications
Power Publishing (R)
(S) Providence Pub. (R)
Quill Driver Books
Quintessential Books (R)
Ragged Edge (R)
Ravenhawk Books (R)
Revival Nation
(S) Sage Press (R)
Salt-Works (R)
(S) Salvation Publisher (R)
Samaritan Press (R)
(S) Selah Publishing (R)
Smyth & Helwys
(S) Southern Baptist
   Press (R)
SparrowCrowne Press (R)
St. Anthony Mess. Press (R)
St. Pauls/Alba House (R)
(S) Star Bible Publications
Strang Book Group (R)
(S) Tate Publishing (R)
Tau Publishing (R)
(S) TEACH Services (R)
Torch Legacy
(S) Trafford Publishing (R)
Treble Heart Books (R)
VBC Publishing
(S) VMI Publishers
Wesleyan Publishing
Whitaker House
White Stone Books (R)
(S) WinePress (R)
(S) Word Alive
(S) Zoë Life Publishing

LAY COUNSELING
Aaron Book Publishing (R)
(S) ACW Press (R)
Ambassador-Emerald (R)
(S) American Binding (R)
(S) Bookstand Publishing (R)
Eerdmans Pub., Wm. B. (R)
E.F.S. Online Pub.
(S) Essence (R)
Evangelical Press
Forever Books (R)
(S) Holy Fire Publishing (R)
(S) Insight Publishing (R)
Kingsley Pub., Jessica (R)
Lighthouse Publishing (R)
Lion and Lamb
Paradise Research (R)
Parsons Publishing (R)
(S) Pleasant Word (R)
Power Publishing (R)
(S) Providence Pub. (R)
(S) Sage Press (R)
Samaritan Press (R)
(S) Trafford Publishing (R)
Treble Heart Books (R)
(S) WinePress (R)

LEADERSHIP
(A) Cook, David C.
(A) Nelson, Thomas
(A) Regal
(A) WaterBrook Press (R)

Aaron Book Publishing (R)
Abingdon Press
(S) ACW Press (R)
Ambassador-Emerald (R)
(S) American Binding (R)
B & H Publishing
Baker Books
Beacon Hill Press (R)
Bethany House (R)
(S) Black Forest (R)
Blue Dolphin
BMH Books (R)
(S) Booklocker.com (R)
(S) Bookstand Publishing (R)
Bridge-Logos (R)
Chalice Press
Christian Family (R)

Christian Focus (R)
Christian Writer's Ebook (R)
Church Growth Inst.
CLC Publications (R)
College Press (R)
(S) Creation House (R)
CrossLink Publishing
Crossroad Publishing (R)
Crossway Books
CSS Publishing
(S) DCTS Publishing
Destiny Image (R)
Editorial Portavoz
Eerdmans Pub., Wm. B. (R)
E.F.S. Online Pub.
(S) Elderberry Press
(S) Essence (R)
Evangelical Press
Evergreen Press
(S) Fairway Press (R)
Faith Alive
FaithWalk
Forever Books (R)
Gospel Publishing
Group Publishing
Grupo Nelson
Guardian Angel
Harrison House
Hidden Brook Press (R)
(S) Holy Fire Publishing (R)
(S) IMD Press (R)
(S) Insight Publishing (R)
InterVarsity Press (R)
Jossey-Bass
Jubilant Press (R)
Judson Press (R)
Kirk House
Kregel (R)
Lift Every Voice (R)
Lighthouse Publishing (R)
Lillenas
Lion and Lamb
Lutheran Univ. Press
(S) McDougal Publishing (R)
Monarch Books
Morehouse
NavPress
NavPress Th1nk (R)
Neibauer Press (R)
New Hope (R)

(S) One World (R)
Parson Place (R)
Parsons Publishing (R)
Pilgrim Press (R)
(S) Pleasant Word (R)
Ponder Publishing
Power Publishing (R)
(S) Providence Pub. (R)
Quintessential Books (R)
Randall House
Ravenhawk Books (R)
(S) Sage Press (R)
Salt-Works (R)
(S) Salvation Publisher (R)
(S) Selah Publishing (R)
Sheed & Ward
Standard Publishing
(S) Star Bible Publications
Strang Book Group (R)
(S) Tate Publishing (R)
(S) Trafford Publishing (R)
UMI Publishing (R)
Univ. Press of America (R)
VBC Publishing
(S) VMI Publishers
Wesleyan Publishing
Whitaker House
White Stone Books (R)
(S) WinePress (R)
(S) Word Alive
(S) Zoë Life Publishing

LIFESTYLE
(A) Harvest House

Aaron Book Publishing (R)
(S) ACW Press (R)
(S) American Binding (R)
Bethany House (R)
Blue Dolphin
BMH Books (R)
(S) Booklocker.com (R)
(S) Bookstand Publishing (R)
Chalice Press
Cladach Publishing
(S) Creation House (R)
CrossLink Publishing
Discovery House (R)
Eerdmans Pub., Wm. B. (R)
E.F.S. Online Pub.

(S) Elderberry Press
(S) Essence (R)
Evangelical Press
Fair Havens (R)
Forever Books (R)
Fresh Air Books
GRQ (R)
Health Communications
Heart of Wisdom
(S) Holy Fire Publishing (R)
Howard Books
(S) Insight Publishing (R)
Lift Every Voice (R)
Lighthouse Publishing (R)
Messianic Jewish Publishers (R)
Monarch Books
NavPress
NavPress Th1nk (R)
Pauline Books (R)
(S) Pleasant Word (R)
Port Hole Publications
Power Publishing (R)
(S) Providence Pub. (R)
Ravenhawk Books (R)
(S) Sage Press (R)
(S) Salvation Publisher (R)
Samaritan Press (R)
(S) Star Bible Publications
Strang Book Group (R)
(S) TEACH Services (R)
(S) Trafford Publishing (R)
(S) WinePress (R)
Xyzzy Press

LITURGICAL STUDIES
(A) Doubleday Religion (R)

Aaron Book Publishing (R)
(S) ACW Press (R)
(S) American Binding (R)
American Cath. Press (R)
Baker Books
(S) Booklocker.com (R)
(S) Bookstand Publishing (R)
(S) Brentwood (R)
Canticle Books (R)
Catholic Answers (R)
Catholic Book
Chalice Press
Christian Heritage (R)

Christian Writer's Ebook (R)
Cistercian (R)
Clarke & Co., James (R)
Conciliar Press (R)
Continuum Intl. (R)
CSS Publishing
Eerdmans Pub., Wm. B. (R)
E.F.S. Online Pub.
(S) Elderberry Press
Emmaus Road
(S) Fairway Press (R)
Forever Books (R)
Group Publishing
Hidden Brook Press (R)
(S) Holy Fire Publishing (R)
(S) Insight Publishing (R)
InterVarsity Press (R)
Lighthouse Publishing (R)
Liturgical Press
Liturgy Training (R)
Lutheran Univ. Press
Lutterworth Press (R)
Messianic Jewish Publishers (R)
Monarch Books
Morehouse
New Seeds (R)
(S) One World (R)
Oregon Catholic
Parson Place (R)
Paulist Press
Pilgrim Press (R)
(S) Pleasant Word (R)
Power Publishing (R)
(S) Providence Pub. (R)
Ravenhawk Books (R)
Resource Publications
Salt-Works (R)
(S) Southern Baptist Press (R)
St. Anthony Mess. Press (R)
St. Bede's Publications (R)
(S) Tate Publishing (R)
(S) Trafford Publishing (R)
Univ. Press of America (R)
(S) WinePress (R)
(S) Word Alive

MARRIAGE
(A) Cook, David C.
(A) Doubleday Religion (R)
(A) FaithWords

(A) HarperOne
(A) Nelson, Thomas
(A) Regal
(A) Revell
(A) Tyndale House (R)
(A) WaterBrook Press (R)
(A) W Publishing

Aaron Book Publishing (R)
ACTA Publications
(S) ACW Press (R)
Ambassador Books
(S) American Binding (R)
Anglicans United (R)
B & H Publishing
Baker Books
Barbour
Beacon Hill Press (R)
Bethany House (R)
(S) Black Forest (R)
Blue Dolphin
(S) Booklocker.com (R)
(S) Bookstand Publishing (R)
(S) Brentwood (R)
(S) Brown Books
Catholic Answers (R)
ChapterTwo (R)
Christian Family (R)
Christian Writer's Ebook (R)
College Press (R)
(S) Creation House (R)
(S) CrossHouse (R)
CrossLink Publishing
Crossroad Publishing (R)
Crossway Books
CSS Publishing
(S) Dean Press, Robbie (R)
Destiny Image (R)
Destiny Image (books) (R)
Dimensions for Living
Discovery House (R)
Editorial Portavoz
Eerdmans Pub., Wm. B. (R)
E.F.S. Online Pub.
(S) Elderberry Press
Emmaus Road
(S) Essence (R)
Evangelical Press
Evergreen Press
Fair Havens (R)

(S) Fairway Press (R)
FaithWalk
FamilyLife (books) (R)
Focus on the Family (R)
Forever Books (R)
Forward Movement
GRQ (R)
Guideposts Books
Hannibal Books
Health Communications
Hensley Publishing
Hidden Brook Press (R)
(S) Holy Fire Publishing (R)
Hope Publishing (R)
Howard Books
(S) IMD Press (R)
(S) Insight Publishing (R)
InterVarsity Press (R)
Journey Forth/BJU (R)
Judson Press (R)
Kregel (R)
Legacy Publishers
Life Changing Media
Lift Every Voice (R)
Lighthouse Publishing (R)
Lillenas
Lion and Lamb
Loyola Press
(S) McDougal Publishing (R)
Messianic Jewish Publishers (R)
Millennium III (R)
Monarch Books
MOPS Intl.
New Hope (R)
(S) One World (R)
Pacific Press
Parson Place (R)
Parsons Publishing (R)
Pauline Books (R)
Paulist Press
Pilgrim Press (R)
(S) Pleasant Word (R)
Power Publishing (R)
(S) Providence Pub. (R)
Quiet Waters (R)
Quintessential Books (R)
Randall House
(S) Sage Press (R)
Samaritan Press (R)
Scepter Publishers (R)

(S) Selah Publishing (R)
(S) Southern Baptist Press (R)
St. Anthony Mess. Press (R)
Standard Publishing
(S) Star Bible Publications
Still Waters Revival (R)
Strang Book Group (R)
(S) Tate Publishing (R)
(S) TEACH Services (R)
(S) Trafford Publishing (R)
VBC Publishing
(S) VMI Publishers
Whitaker House
(S) WinePress (R)
(S) Word Alive
(S) Zoë Life Publishing

MEMOIRS
(A) Ballantine
(A) Doubleday Religion (R)
(A) FaithWords
(A) HarperOne
(A) Nelson, Thomas
(A) One World/Ballantine

Aaron Book Publishing (R)
(S) ACW Press (R)
(S) American Binding (R)
Baker Books
(S) Black Forest (R)
(S) Booklocker.com (R)
(S) Book Publishers (R)
(S) Bookstand Publishing (R)
(S) Brown Books
Christian Heritage (R)
Christian Writer's Ebook (R)
Cistercian (R)
Cladach Publishing
(S) Creation House (R)
E.F.S. Online Pub.
(S) Elderberry Press
(S) Essence (R)
(S) Fairway Press (R)
FaithWalk
Forever Books (R)
Forward Movement
(S) Fruitbearer Pub.
Guideposts Books
Health Communications
Hidden Brook Press (R)

His Work Christian Pub. (R)
(S) Holy Fire Publishing (R)
(S) Insight Publishing (R)
(S) LifeVest Publishing
Lighthouse Publishing (R)
Lighthouse Trails (R)
Lutterworth Press (R)
Monarch Books
NavPress Th1nk (R)
(S) One World (R)
Pacific Press
(S) Pleasant Word (R)
Power Publishing (R)
(S) Providence Pub. (R)
Quill Driver Books
Quintessential Books (R)
Randall House
(S) Sage Press (R)
(S) Salvation Publisher (R)
Samaritan Press (R)
(S) Tate Publishing (R)
(S) TEACH Services (R)
(S) Trafford Publishing (R)
Univ. Press of America (R)
(S) VMI Publishers
(S) WinePress (R)
(S) Word Alive
(S) Zoë Life Publishing

MEN'S BOOKS
(A) Doubleday Religion (R)
(A) Harvest House
(A) Nelson, Thomas
(A) Regal
(A) WaterBrook Press (R)
(A) W Publishing

Aaron Book Publishing (R)
(S) ACW Press (R)
Ambassador Books
(S) American Binding (R)
AMG Publishers (R)
B & H Publishing
Baker Books
Barbour
Beacon Hill Press (R)
Bethany House (R)
(S) Black Forest (R)
Blue Dolphin
BMH Books (R)

(S) Booklocker.com (R)
(S) Bookstand Publishing (R)
Bridge-Logos (R)
Christian Writer's Ebook (R)
College Press (R)
(S) Creation House (R)
CrossLink Publishing
Crossroad Publishing (R)
Crossway Books
Dimensions for Living
Editorial Portavoz
Eerdmans Pub., Wm. B. (R)
E.F.S. Online Pub.
(S) Elderberry Press
Emmaus Road
(S) Essence (R)
Evangelical Press
Evergreen Press
Fair Havens (R)
(S) Fairway Press (R)
Faith Communications
FaithWalk
Forever Books (R)
Gentle Path Press
GRQ (R)
Hensley Publishing
Hidden Brook Press (R)
(S) Holy Fire Publishing (R)
Howard Books
(S) IMD Press (R)
Inkling Books (R)
(S) Insight Publishing (R)
InterVarsity Press (R)
Kregel (R)
Lift Every Voice (R)
Lighthouse Publishing (R)
Loyola Press
(S) McDougal Publishing (R)
Messianic Jewish Publishers (R)
Monarch Books
NavPress Th1nk (R)
(S) One World (R)
Pacific Press
Parson Place (R)
Pilgrim Press (R)
(S) Pleasant Word (R)
Power Publishing (R)
(S) Providence Pub. (R)
Quintessential Books (R)
Randall House

Ravenhawk Books (R)
(S) Sage Press (R)
Samaritan Press (R)
(S) Selah Publishing (R)
(S) Star Bible Publications
Strang Book Group (R)
(S) Tate Publishing (R)
(S) Trafford Publishing (R)
VBC Publishing
(S) VMI Publishers
Whitaker House
White Stone Books (R)
(S) WinePress (R)
(S) Word Alive
(S) Zoë Life Publishing

MINIBOOKS

(S) American Binding (R)
(S) Black Forest (R)
(S) Bookstand Publishing (R)
GRQ (R)
Harrison House
(S) Holy Fire Publishing (R)
(S) IMD Press (R)
Legacy Press (R)
Lighthouse Publishing (R)
Little Lauren Books
Monarch Books
(S) One World (R)
(S) Path Pub. in Christ (R)
Rose Publishing
Salt-Works (R)
Strang Book Group (R)
(S) Tate Publishing (R)
(S) Trafford Publishing (R)
Treble Heart Books (R)

MIRACLES

(A) HarperOne

Aaron Book Publishing (R)
(S) ACW Press (R)
(S) American Binding (R)
Baker Books
(S) Black Forest (R)
Blue Dolphin
(S) Booklocker.com (R)
(S) Brentwood (R)
Christian Heritage (R)
Christian Writer's Ebook (R)
(S) Creation House (R)

CrossLink Publishing
CSS Publishing
Destiny Image (books) (R)
E.F.S. Online Pub.
(S) Elderberry Press
(S) Essence (R)
Evangelical Press
Evergreen Press
(S) Fairway Press (R)
Forever Books (R)
Gollehon Press
Guideposts Books
Harrison House
Hidden Brook Press (R)
(S) Holy Fire Publishing (R)
(S) IMD Press (R)
(S) Impact Christian (R)
(S) Insight Publishing (R)
Lighthouse Publishing (R)
Lillenas
Lion and Lamb
Loyola Press
(S) McDougal Publishing (R)
Monarch Books
(S) One World (R)
Pacific Press
Paradise Research (R)
Parson Place (R)
Parsons Publishing (R)
(S) Path Pub. in Christ (R)
(S) Pleasant Word (R)
Power Publishing (R)
(S) Providence Pub. (R)
Quill Driver Books
Revival Nation
(S) Salvation Publisher (R)
Samaritan Press (R)
(S) Selah Publishing (R)
(S) Southern Baptist Press (R)
St. Anthony Mess. Press (R)
(S) Star Bible Publications
Strang Book Group (R)
(S) Tate Publishing (R)
(S) TEACH Services (R)
(S) Trafford Publishing (R)
(S) VMI Publishers
Whitaker House
(S) WinePress (R)
(S) Word Alive
(S) Zoë Life Publishing

MISSIONS/MISSIONARY
Aaron Book Publishing (R)
(S) ACW Press (R)
(S) American Binding (R)
(S) Ampelos Press
Baker Books
Believe Books
(S) Black Forest (R)
(S) Booklocker.com (R)
(S) Brentwood (R)
(S) Brown Books
Carey Library, Wm. (R)
ChapterTwo (R)
Christian Focus (R)
Christian Heritage (R)
Christian Writer's
    Ebook (R)
CLC Publications (R)
(S) Creation House (R)
(S) CrossHouse (R)
CSS Publishing
Discovery House (R)
Eerdmans Pub., Wm. B. (R)
E.F.S. Online Pub.
(S) Elderberry Press
(S) Essence (R)
Evangelical Press
Evergreen Press
Fair Havens (R)
(S) Fairway Press (R)
FaithWalk
Father's Press
Forever Books (R)
Forward Movement
Friends United Press
Hannibal Books
Harvest Day
Hidden Brook Press (R)
(S) Holy Fire Publishing (R)
Hope Publishing (R)
(S) IMD Press (R)
(S) Insight Publishing (R)
InterVarsity Press (R)
Lift Every Voice (R)
Lighthouse Publishing (R)
Lighthouse Trails (R)
Lillenas
Lion and Lamb
Lutheran Univ. Press
Lutterworth Press (R)

(S) McDougal Publishing (R)
Monarch Books
(S) One World (R)
P & R Publishing (R)
Pacific Press
Parson Place (R)
Parsons Publishing (R)
(S) Pleasant Word (R)
Power Publishing (R)
(S) Providence Pub. (R)
Quiet Waters (R)
Randall House
Rose Publishing
Salt-Works (R)
(S) Southern Baptist Press (R)
St. Anthony Mess. Press (R)
(S) Star Bible Publications
Strang Book Group (R)
(S) Tate Publishing (R)
(S) TEACH Services (R)
(S) Trafford Publishing (R)
VBC Publishing
(S) VMI Publishers
(S) WinePress (R)
(S) Word Alive
Yale Univ. Press (R)
(S) Zoë Life Publishing

MONEY MANAGEMENT
(A) Cook, David C.
(A) FaithWords
(A) Harvest House
(A) Nelson, Thomas
(A) WaterBrook Press (R)

Aaron Book Publishing (R)
(S) ACW Press (R)
Ambassador-Emerald (R)
(S) American Binding (R)
Baker Books
Barbour
Blue Dolphin
BMH Books (R)
(S) Booklocker.com (R)
(S) Brentwood (R)
Christian Writer's Ebook (R)
Comfort Publishing (R)
(S) Creation House (R)
Editorial Portavoz
Eerdmans Pub., Wm. B. (R)

E.F.S. Online Pub.
(S) Elderberry Press
(S) Essence (R)
Evangelical Press
Evergreen Press
(S) Fairway Press (R)
FaithWalk
Forever Books (R)
Forward Movement
Grupo Nelson
Hannibal Books
Health Communications
Hensley Publishing
Hidden Brook Press (R)
His Work Christian Pub. (R)
(S) Holy Fire Publishing (R)
(S) IMD Press (R)
(S) Insight Publishing (R)
Journey Forth/BJU (R)
Judson Press (R)
Legacy Publishers
Lift Every Voice (R)
Lighthouse Publishing (R)
Lion and Lamb
Millennium III (R)
Moody Publishers
Mountain View
New Hope (R)
(S) One World (R)
Pacific Press
Parson Place (R)
(S) Pleasant Word (R)
Power Publishing (R)
(S) Providence Pub. (R)
Quintessential Books (R)
Ravenhawk Books (R)
Reference Service
(S) Sage Press (R)
(S) Salvation Publisher (R)
Samaritan Press (R)
(S) Southern Baptist Press (R)
(S) Star Bible Publications
Strang Book Group (R)
(S) Tate Publishing (R)
(S) TEACH Services (R)
(S) Trafford Publishing (R)
VBC Publishing
(S) VMI Publishers
Walk Worthy (R)
(S) WinePress (R)

(S) Word Alive
Xyzzy Press
(S) Zoë Life Publishing

MUSIC/MUSICALS*
Abingdon Press
American Cath. Press (R)
Baker's Plays (R)
$ Cathedral Age (magazine)
Contemporary Drama
Eldridge Plays
Encore Performance
Gospel Communications
Lighthouse Publishing (R)
Lillenas
Lutheran Forum (magazine)
National Black Theatre
(S) Path Pub. in Christ (R)
Players Press (R)

MUSIC-RELATED BOOKS
(A) Countryman, J.

Aaron Book Publishing (R)
American Cath. Press (R)
Baker Books
Blue Dolphin
BMH Books (R)
(S) Booklocker.com (R)
Cambridge Scholars Pub.
Christian Writer's Ebook (R)
Contemporary Drama
Destiny Image (books) (R)
Eerdmans Pub., Wm. B. (R)
E.F.S. Online Pub.
Eldridge Plays
(S) Essence (R)
Evangelical Press
(S) Fairway Press (R)
FaithWalk
Forever Books (R)
Guardian Angel
Hidden Brook Press (R)
His Work Christian Pub. (R)
(S) Holy Fire Publishing (R)
(S) Insight Publishing (R)
Lighthouse Publishing (R)
Lion and Lamb
Lutheran Univ. Press
Monarch Books

(S) One World (R)
Players Press (R)
(S) Pleasant Word (R)
Power Publishing (R)
(S) Providence Pub. (R)
(S) Sage Press (R)
Samaritan Press (R)
Standard Publishing
(S) Star Bible Publications
(S) Tate Publishing (R)
(S) Trafford Publishing (R)
(S) VMI Publishers
(S) WinePress (R)
(S) Word Alive

NOVELTY BOOKS FOR KIDS
Atheneum/Young Readers
Baker Books
(S) Brown Books
E.F.S. Online Pub.
(S) Elderberry Press
(S) Fairway Press (R)
Forever Books (R)
Guardian Angel
(S) IMD Press (R)
Journey Stone (R)
Legacy Press (R)
Lift Every Voice (R)
Lion and Lamb
Monarch Books
(S) One World (R)
Salt-Works (R)
Samaritan Press (R)
Standard Publishing
(S) Tate Publishing (R)
(S) Trafford Publishing (R)
White Stone Books (R)
(S) Word Alive

PAMPHLETS
(A) Harvest House

Chalice Press
ChapterTwo (R)
Christian Writer's Ebook (R)
Concordia
Emmaus Road
(S) Essence (R)
Evangelical Press
Forever Books (R)

Forward Movement
Founders Press
(S) Fruitbearer Pub.
Good Book (R)
(S) IMD Press (R)
Intl. Awakening (R)
Libros Liguori
Lift Every Voice (R)
Liguori Public. (R)
Liturgy Training (R)
Neibauer Press (R)
(S) One World (R)
Our Sunday Visitor (R)
Paradise Research (R)
Paulist Press
Randall House
Rose Publishing
Salt-Works (R)
Trinity Foundation (R)

PARENTING
(A) Ballantine
(A) Cook, David C.
(A) FaithWords
(A) Nelson, Thomas
(A) Regal
(A) Revell
(A) Tyndale House (R)
(A) WaterBrook Press (R)
(A) W Publishing

Aaron Book Publishing (R)
(S) ACW Press (R)
Adams Media
Ambassador Books
Ambassador-Emerald (R)
(S) American Binding (R)
AMG Publishers (R)
B & H Publishing
Baker Books
Barbour
Beacon Hill Press (R)
Bethany House (R)
(S) Black Forest (R)
Blue Dolphin
(S) Booklocker.com (R)
(S) Book Publishers (R)
(S) Brentwood (R)
(S) Brown Books
Christian Family (R)
Christian Writer's Ebook (R)

College Press (R)
Conari Press
Conciliar Press (R)
Concordia
(S) Creation House (R)
CrossLink Publishing
Crossroad Publishing (R)
(S) Dean Press, Robbie (R)
Destiny Image (books) (R)
Dimensions for Living
Discovery House (R)
Editorial Portavoz
Eerdmans Pub., Wm. B. (R)
E.F.S. Online Pub.
(S) Elderberry Press
Emmaus Road
(S) Essence (R)
Evangelical Press
Evergreen Press
(S) Fairway Press (R)
Focus on the Family (R)
Forever Books (R)
Forward Movement
Grupo Nelson
Harrison House
Health Communications
Hensley Publishing
Hidden Brook Press (R)
His Work Christian Pub. (R)
(S) Holy Fire Publishing (R)
Howard Books
(S) IMD Press (R)
(S) Insight Publishing (R)
InterVarsity Press (R)
Journey Forth/BJU (R)
Kaleidoscope Press (R)
Kingsley Pub., Jessica (R)
Kregel (R)
Langmarc
Life Changing Media
Lift Every Voice (R)
Lighthouse Publishing (R)
Liguori Public. (R)
Lillenas
Lion and Lamb
(S) McDougal Publishing (R)
Messianic Jewish Publishers (R)
Millennium III (R)
Mission City Press
Monarch Books

MOPS Intl.
Morehouse
New Hope (R)
(S) One World (R)
Our Sunday Visitor (R)
P & R Publishing (R)
Pacific Press
Parsons Publishing (R)
Pauline Books (R)
(S) Pleasant Word (R)
Port Hole Publications
Power Publishing (R)
(S) Providence Pub. (R)
Quintessential Books (R)
Randall House
Rose Publishing
(S) Sage Press (R)
Salt-Works (R)
Scepter Publishers (R)
(S) Selah Publishing (R)
St. Anthony Mess. Press (R)
Standard Publishing
(S) Star Bible Publications
Starik Publishing
Still Waters Revival (R)
Strang Book Group (R)
Tarcher, Jeremy P. (R)
(S) Tate Publishing (R)
(S) TEACH Services (R)
Torch Legacy
(S) Trafford Publishing (R)
Treble Heart Books (R)
VBC Publishing
(S) VMI Publishers
Walk Worthy (R)
Whitaker House
(S) WinePress (R)
(S) Word Alive
(S) Zoë Life Publishing

PASTORS' HELPS
Aaron Book Publishing (R)
(S) ACW Press (R)
(S) American Binding (R)
B & H Publishing
Baker Academic
Baker Books
Beacon Hill Press (R)
Blue Dolphin
(S) Booklocker.com (R)

(S) Bookstand Publishing (R)
(S) Brentwood (R)
Bridge-Logos (R)
Chalice Press
Christian Focus (R)
Christian Writer's Ebook (R)
Church Growth Inst.
(S) Creation House (R)
CrossLink Publishing
CSS Publishing
(S) DCTS Publishing
Editorial Portavoz
Eerdmans Pub., Wm. B. (R)
E.F.S. Online Pub.
(S) Elderberry Press
(S) Essence (R)
Evangelical Press
(S) Fairway Press (R)
Fifth-Estate (R)
Forever Books (R)
Fortress Press
Gospel Publishing
Group Publishing
Harcourt Religion
Hidden Brook Press (R)
(S) Holy Fire Publishing (R)
(S) IMD Press (R)
(S) Insight Publishing (R)
(S) Kindred Books (R)
Kingsley Pub., Jessica (R)
Kregel (R)
Lighthouse Publishing (R)
Lion and Lamb
Liturgical Press
Liturgy Training (R)
Lutheran Univ. Press
Monarch Books
Neibauer Press (R)
(S) One World (R)
Pilgrim Press (R)
(S) Pleasant Word (R)
Power Publishing (R)
(S) Providence Pub. (R)
Randall House
(S) Sermon Select Press
(S) Southern Baptist Press (R)
St. Anthony Mess. Press (R)
Standard Publishing
(S) Star Bible Publications
(S) Tate Publishing (R)

(S) TEACH Services (R)
Torch Legacy
(S) Trafford Publishing (R)
Treble Heart Books (R)
VBC Publishing
(S) VMI Publishers
Wesleyan Publishing
(S) WinePress (R)
(S) Word Alive
(S) Zoë Life Publishing
Zondervan

PERSONAL EXPERIENCE

(A) HarperOne
(A) Nelson, Thomas
(A) W Publishing

Aaron Book Publishing (R)
(S) ACW Press (R)
Ambassador-Emerald (R)
(S) American Binding (R)
Baker Books
(S) Black Forest (R)
Blue Dolphin
(S) Booklocker.com (R)
(S) Bookstand Publishing (R)
(S) Brentwood (R)
Bridge-Logos (R)
Canticle Books (R)
CarePoint (R)
Chicken Soup
Christian Family (R)
Christian Writer's Ebook (R)
(S) Creation House (R)
CrossLink Publishing
Crossroad Publishing (R)
(S) DCTS Publishing
Destiny Image (R)
E.F.S. Online Pub.
(S) Elderberry Press
(S) Essence (R)
Evangelical Press
Fair Havens (R)
(S) Fairway Press (R)
FaithWalk
Forever Books (R)
Fresh Air Books
(S) Fruitbearer Pub.
Gentle Path Press
GRQ (R)

Guideposts Books
Hannibal Books
Hidden Brook Press (R)
(S) Holy Fire Publishing (R)
(S) IMD Press (R)
(S) Insight Publishing (R)
Jebaire Publishing
Jesus Filled Day (books)
Kregel (R)
Life Changing Media
Lighthouse Publishing (R)
Lighthouse Trails (R)
Lion and Lamb
(S) McDougal Publishing (R)
Monarch Books
NavPress Th1nk (R)
(S) One World (R)
Pacific Press
(S) Path Pub. in Christ (R)
(S) Pleasant Word (R)
Power Publishing (R)
(S) Providence Pub. (R)
Quill Driver Books
Randall House
Ravenhawk Books (R)
Revival Nation
(S) Sage Press (R)
(S) Salvation Publisher (R)
Samaritan Press (R)
(S) Southern Baptist
    Press (R)
(S) Star Bible Publications
Strang Book Group (R)
(S) Tate Publishing (R)
(S) TEACH Services (R)
(S) Trafford Publishing (R)
(S) VMI Publishers
(S) WinePress (R)
(S) Word Alive
(S) Zoë Life Publishing

PERSONAL GROWTH

(A) FaithWords
(A) HarperOne
(A) Nelson, Thomas
(A) Regal
(A) Tyndale House (R)
(A) WaterBrook Press (R)
(A) W Publishing

Aadeon Publishing (R)

Aaron Book Publishing (R)
(S) ACW Press (R)
Ambassador Books
Ambassador-Emerald (R)
(S) American Binding (R)
AMG Publishers (R)
B & H Publishing
Baker Books
Barbour
Bethany House (R)
(S) Black Forest (R)
Blue Dolphin
BMH Books (R)
(S) Booklocker.com (R)
(S) Book Publishers (R)
(S) Bookstand Publishing (R)
Bridge-Logos (R)
Canticle Books (R)
CarePoint (R)
Charisma Kids
Christian Family (R)
Christian Writer's Ebook (R)
CLC Publications (R)
Conari Press
(S) Creation House (R)
CrossLink Publishing
Crossroad Publishing (R)
(S) DCTS Publishing
Destiny Image (R)
Destiny Image (books) (R)
Discovery House (R)
E.F.S. Online Pub.
(S) Elderberry Press
(S) Essence (R)
Evangelical Press
Evergreen Press
(S) Fairway Press (R)
FaithWalk
Forever Books (R)
Forward Movement
Gentle Path Press
GRQ (R)
Guideposts Books
Hannibal Books
Hay House
Health Communications
Hensley Publishing
Hidden Brook Press (R)
(S) Holy Fire Publishing (R)
Howard Books

(S) IMD Press (R)
(S) Insight Publishing (R)
InterVarsity Press (R)
Jebaire Publishing
Jesus Filled Day (books)
Jossey-Bass
Journey Forth/BJU (R)
(S) Kindred Books (R)
Kregel (R)
Life Changing Media
Lift Every Voice (R)
Lighthouse Publishing (R)
Lillenas
Lion and Lamb
(S) McDougal Publishing (R)
Monarch Books
NavPress
NavPress Th1nk (R)
New Hope (R)
New Seeds (R)
(S) One World (R)
Pacific Press
Parson Place (R)
Parsons Publishing (R)
(S) Path Pub. in Christ (R)
(S) Path Publishing (R)
Pilgrim Press (R)
(S) Pleasant Word (R)
Power Publishing (R)
(S) Providence Pub. (R)
Quill Driver Books
Quintessential Books (R)
Randall House
Ravenhawk Books (R)
Resource Publications
Revival Nation
(S) Sage Press (R)
Samaritan Press (R)
(S) Star Bible Publications
Strang Book Group (R)
(S) Tate Publishing (R)
(S) TEACH Services (R)
(S) Trafford Publishing (R)
(S) VMI Publishers
White Stone Books (R)
(S) WinePress (R)
(S) Word Alive
Xyzzy Press
(S) Zoë Life Publishing

PERSONAL RENEWAL
(A) HarperOne
(A) Regal
(A) Tyndale House (R)

Aaron Book Publishing (R)
(S) ACW Press (R)
(S) American Binding (R)
Baker Books
Barbour
(S) Black Forest (R)
Blue Dolphin
BMH Books (R)
(S) Booklocker.com (R)
(S) Bookstand Publishing (R)
Bridge-Logos (R)
Canticle Books (R)
Charisma Kids
Christian Writer's Ebook (R)
CLC Publications (R)
Conari Press
(S) Creation House (R)
Crossroad Publishing (R)
(S) DCTS Publishing
Destiny Image (R)
Destiny Image (books) (R)
E.F.S. Online Pub.
(S) Elderberry Press
(S) Essence (R)
Evangelical Press
Evergreen Press
(S) Fairway Press (R)
FaithWalk
Forever Books (R)
Forward Movement
Fresh Air Books
Gentle Path Press
GRQ (R)
Hannibal Books
Health Communications
Hensley Publishing
Hidden Brook Press (R)
(S) Holy Fire Publishing (R)
Howard Books
(S) IMD Press (R)
(S) Impact Christian (R)
(S) Insight Publishing (R)
Intl. Awakening (R)
Kirk House
Kregel (R)

Life Changing Media
Lift Every Voice (R)
Lighthouse Publishing (R)
Lillenas
Lion and Lamb
(S) McDougal Publishing (R)
Monarch Books
NavPress
NavPress Th1nk (R)
New Hope (R)
New Seeds (R)
(S) One World (R)
Pacific Press
(S) Path Pub. in Christ (R)
(S) Path Publishing (R)
Pilgrim Press (R)
(S) Pleasant Word (R)
Power Publishing (R)
(S) Providence Pub. (R)
Quill Driver Books
Randall House
Ravenhawk Books (R)
Revival Nation
(S) Sage Press (R)
(S) Star Bible Publications
Strang Book Group (R)
(S) Tate Publishing (R)
(S) TEACH Services (R)
(S) Trafford Publishing (R)
(S) VMI Publishers
(S) WinePress (R)
(S) Word Alive
(S) Zoë Life Publishing

PHILOSOPHY
(A) Doubleday Religion (R)
(A) HarperOne
(A) One World/Ballantine

Aaron Book Publishing (R)
(S) ACW Press (R)
(S) American Binding (R)
Baker Books
Baylor Univ. Press
(S) Black Forest (R)
Blue Dolphin
(S) Booklocker.com (R)
(S) Bookstand Publishing (R)
Branden Publishing (R)
(S) Brentwood (R)

Cambridge Scholars Pub.
Cambridge Univ. Press
Christian Writer's Ebook (R)
Clarke & Co., James (R)
Continuum Intl. (R)
(S) Creation House (R)
Crossroad Publishing (R)
Dover Publications (R)
Eerdmans Pub., Wm. B. (R)
E.F.S. Online Pub.
(S) Elderberry Press
(S) Essence (R)
Evangelical Press
(S) Fairway Press (R)
FaithWalk
Fifth-Estate (R)
Fordham Univ. Press (R)
Forever Books (R)
Hidden Brook Press (R)
(S) Holy Fire Publishing (R)
(S) IMD Press (R)
Inkling Books (R)
(S) Insight Publishing (R)
InterVarsity Press (R)
Kregel (R)
Larson Publications (R)
Lighthouse Publishing (R)
Lutheran Univ. Press
Lutterworth Press (R)
Mercer Univ. Press (R)
Monarch Books
New Seeds (R)
(S) One World (R)
Paragon House (R)
(S) Pleasant Word (R)
Port Hole Publications
Power Publishing (R)
(S) Providence Pub. (R)
Quintessential Books (R)
(S) Sage Press (R)
Salt-Works (R)
St. Augustine's Press (R)
St. Pauls/Alba House (R)
(S) Star Bible Publications
Still Waters Revival (R)
Tarcher, Jeremy P. (R)
(S) Tate Publishing (R)
(S) TEACH Services (R)
Third World Press (R)
(S) Trafford Publishing (R)

Trinity Foundation (R)
Univ. Press of America (R)
(S) VMI Publishers
(S) WinePress (R)
Wipf and Stock
(S) Word Alive
Xyzzy Press

PHOTOGRAPHS (FOR COVERS)

Aadeon Publishing (R)
Abingdon Press
Ambassador Books
Ambassador-Emerald (R)
(S) American Binding (R)
(S) Black Forest (R)
Blue Dolphin
(S) Booklocker.com (R)
(S) Book Publishers (R)
(S) Bookstand Publishing (R)
(S) Brentwood (R)
Bridge-Logos (R)
Cambridge Scholars Pub.
Canadian Inst. for Law (R)
CarePoint (R)
Carey Library, Wm. (R)
Catholic Answers (R)
Catholic Univ. of Amer.
    Press
Christian Focus (R)
Church Growth Inst.
Cistercian (R)
Comfort Publishing (R)
Conciliar Press (R)
Continuum Intl. (R)
(S) Creation House (R)
(S) CrossHouse (R)
CrossLink Publishing
(S) Dean Press, Robbie (R)
Dove Inspirational (R)
(S) Essence (R)
ETC Publications
Fair Havens (R)
FaithWalk
FamilyLife (books) (R)
Father's Press
Forever Books (R)
(S) Fruitbearer Pub.
Georgetown Univ. Press
Guardian Angel

Guernica Editions (R)
Harcourt Religion
(S) IMD Press (R)
Intl. Awakening (R)
Jebaire Publishing
Journey Stone (R)
Jubilant Press (R)
Kingsley Pub., Jessica (R)
Knight George Pub.
Life Changing Media
Lift Every Voice (R)
Lighthouse Publishing (R)
Lion and Lamb
Liturgy Training (R)
Lutheran Univ. Press
Marcher Lord Press
Monarch Books
Mountain View
Neibauer Press (R)
New Canaan (R)
New Hope (R)
New Leaf
(S) One World (R)
Oregon Catholic
Our Sunday Visitor (R)
Parson Place (R)
(S) Path Pub. in Christ (R)
Pauline Kids (R)
Paulist Press
Pelican Publishing (R)
Pilgrim Press (R)
Players Press (R)
(S) Pleasant Word (R)
Power Publishing (R)
Quintessential Books (R)
Ravenhawk Books (R)
Samaritan Press (R)
(S) Selah Publishing (R)
Sheed & Ward
St. Anthony Mess. Press (R)
(S) Star Bible Publications
Strang Book Group (R)
(S) Tate Publishing (R)
Tau Publishing (R)
(S) TEACH Services (R)
Touch Publications (R)
(S) Trafford Publishing (R)
Treble Heart Books (R)
Trinity Foundation (R)
Troitsa Books

United Methodist
Univ. of AR Press (R)
Wilshire Book (R)
(S) WinePress (R)
(S) Xulon Press (R)
(S) Zoë Life Publishing

POETRY

Aaron Book Publishing (R)
(S) ACW Press (R)
(S) American Binding (R)
Atheneum/Young Readers
(S) Black Forest (R)
Blue Dolphin
(S) Booklocker.com (R)
(S) Bookstand Publishing (R)
Boyds Mills Press (R)
Branden Publishing (R)
(S) Brentwood (R)
Christian Writer's Ebook (R)
(S) Creation House (R)
(S) Dean Press, Robbie (R)
DiskUs Publishing
Eerdmans Pub., Wm. B. (R)
E.F.S. Online Pub.
(S) Elderberry Press
(S) Essence (R)
(S) Fairway Press (R)
Forever Books (R)
Guernica Editions (R)
Harvest Day
Hidden Brook Press (R)
(S) Holy Fire Publishing (R)
(S) Insight Publishing (R)
(S) LifeVest Publishing
Lighthouse Publishing (R)
More Than Novellas
New Seeds (R)
(S) One World (R)
(S) Path Pub. in Christ (R)
(S) Path Publishing (R)
(S) Pleasant Word (R)
(S) Poems By Me (R)
(S) Poet's Cove Press
Power Publishing (R)
(S) Providence Pub. (R)
(S) Sage Press (R)
(S) Selah Publishing (R)
(S) Southern Baptist Press (R)
(S) Tate Publishing (R)

(S) Trafford Publishing (R)
(S) WinePress (R)
(S) Word Alive
Xyzzy Press
(S) Zoë Life Publishing

POLITICS

(A) Doubleday Religion (R)
(A) HarperOne
(A) Harvest House
(A) Nelson, Thomas
(A) One World/Ballantine

Aadeon Publishing (R)
Aaron Book Publishing (R)
(S) ACW Press (R)
(S) American Binding (R)
AMG Publishers (R)
Baker Books
Baylor Univ. Press
(S) Black Forest (R)
Blue Dolphin
(S) Booklocker.com (R)
Branden Publishing (R)
(S) Brentwood (R)
Cambridge Scholars Pub.
Canadian Inst. for Law (R)
Carson-Dellosa
Christian Writer's Ebook (R)
(S) Creation House (R)
Crossroad Publishing (R)
Eerdmans Pub., Wm. B. (R)
E.F.S. Online Pub.
(S) Elderberry Press
(S) Essence (R)
(S) Fairway Press (R)
Fordham Univ. Press (R)
Forever Books (R)
Georgetown Univ. Press
Gollehon Press
Hidden Brook Press (R)
(S) Holy Fire Publishing (R)
Howard Books
Inkling Books (R)
(S) Insight Publishing (R)
Invisible College Press
Lighthouse Publishing (R)
Mercer Univ. Press (R)
Morehouse
New Canaan (R)
(S) One World (R)

(S) Path Publishing (R)
Pilgrim Press (R)
(S) Pleasant Word (R)
Power Publishing (R)
Praeger Publishers
(S) Providence Pub. (R)
Ravenhawk Books (R)
(S) Sage Press (R)
Salt-Works (R)
Still Waters Revival (R)
Strang Book Group (R)
(S) Tate Publishing (R)
Third World Press (R)
(S) Trafford Publishing (R)
Trinity Foundation (R)
Univ. Press of America (R)
(S) VMI Publishers
(S) WinePress (R)
(S) Word Alive
Yale Univ. Press (R)

POPULAR CULTURE

(A) FaithWords

Aaron Book Publishing (R)
(S) ACW Press (R)
(S) American Binding (R)
Bethany House (R)
Blue Dolphin
(S) Creation House (R)
Eerdmans Pub., Wm. B. (R)
E.F.S. Online Pub.
Eldridge Plays
(S) Essence (R)
Forever Books (R)
GRQ (R)
Health Communications
(S) Holy Fire
    Publishing (R)
Howard Books
(S) Insight Publishing (R)
InterVarsity Press (R)
Judson Press (R)
Kregel (R)
Lift Every Voice (R)
Lighthouse Publishing (R)
Lillenas
Lutterworth Press (R)
Millennium III (R)
Morehouse
Pauline Books (R)

(S) Pleasant Word (R)
Power Publishing (R)
Praeger Publishers
(S) Providence Pub. (R)
Quill Driver Books
Ravenhawk Books (R)
(S) Sage Press (R)
Salt-Works (R)
(S) Trafford Publishing (R)
(S) WinePress (R)
Yale Univ. Press (R)

POSTMODERNISM

(A) Nelson, Thomas

Aaron Book Publishing (R)
(S) ACW Press (R)
(S) American Binding (R)
(S) Booklocker.com (R)
Cambridge Scholars Pub.
Chalice Press
(S) Creation House (R)
Deo Volente
Eerdmans Pub., Wm. B. (R)
(S) Elderberry Press
(S) Essence (R)
Evangelical Press
Fair Havens (R)
Forever Books (R)
(S) Holy Fire Publishing (R)
Howard Books
(S) Insight Publishing (R)
InterVarsity Press (R)
Jossey-Bass
Kregel (R)
Lighthouse Publishing (R)
Monarch Books
Paragon House (R)
(S) Pleasant Word (R)
Power Publishing (R)
Praeger Publishers
(S) Providence Pub. (R)
Quill Driver Books
Resource Publications
(S) Sage Press (R)
Salt-Works (R)
(S) Star Bible Publications
Strang Book Group (R)
(S) Trafford Publishing (R)
(S) WinePress (R)

PRAISE*

E.F.S. Online Pub.
Lighthouse Publishing (R)
Port Hole Publications
(S) Sage Press (R)
(S) WinePress (R)

PRAYER

(A) Cook, David C.
(A) Doubleday Religion (R)
(A) FaithWords
(A) HarperOne
(A) Harvest House
(A) Nelson, Thomas
(A) Regal
(A) Tyndale House (R)
(A) WaterBrook Press (R)
(A) W Publishing

Aaron Book Publishing (R)
Abingdon Press
ACTA Publications
(S) ACW Press (R)
Ambassador Books
Ambassador-Emerald (R)
(S) American Binding (R)
Anglicans United (R)
Baker Books
Barbour
Beacon Hill Press (R)
Bethany House (R)
(S) Black Forest (R)
Blue Dolphin
BMH Books (R)
(S) Booklocker.com (R)
(S) Bookstand Publishing (R)
(S) Brentwood (R)
Bridge-Logos (R)
Catholic Book
Charisma Kids
Christian Family (R)
Christian Focus (R)
Christian Heritage (R)
Christian Writer's Ebook (R)
Cistercian (R)
CLC Publications (R)
College Press (R)
Continuum Intl. (R)
(S) Creation House (R)
(S) CrossHouse (R)

CrossLink Publishing
Crossroad Publishing (R)
CSS Publishing
(S) DCTS Publishing
Destiny Image (R)
Destiny Image (books) (R)
Discovery House (R)
Eerdmans Pub., Wm. B. (R)
E.F.S. Online Pub.
(S) Elderberry Press
Emmaus Road
(S) Essence (R)
Evangelical Press
Evergreen Press
Fair Havens (R)
(S) Fairway Press (R)
Faith Alive
FaithWalk
Father's Press
Forever Books (R)
Forward Movement
(S) Fruitbearer Pub.
Good Book (R)
Gospel Publishing
GRQ (R)
Guideposts Books
Harcourt Religion
Harrison House
Hensley Publishing
Hidden Brook Press (R)
(S) Holy Fire Publishing (R)
Hope Publishing (R)
Howard Books
(S) IMD Press (R)
(S) Impact Christian (R)
(S) Insight Publishing (R)
InterVarsity Press (R)
Intl. Awakening (R)
Jebaire Publishing
Jesus Filled Day (books)
Journey Forth/BJU (R)
Kregel (R)
Legacy Press (R)
Libros Liguori
Lift Every Voice (R)
Lighthouse Publishing (R)
Liguori Public. (R)
Lillenas
Lion and Lamb
Liturgy Training (R)

Loyola Press
Lutheran Univ. Press
Lutterworth Press (R)
(S) McDougal Publishing (R)
Messianic Jewish Publishers (R)
Monarch Books
Moody Publishers
Morehouse
NavPress Th1nk (R)
New Seeds (R)
(S) One World (R)
Our Sunday Visitor (R)
Pacific Press
Paradise Research (R)
(S) Path Pub. in Christ (R)
Pauline Books (R)
Pauline Kids (R)
Paulist Press
Pflaum Publishing
Pilgrim Press (R)
(S) Pleasant Word (R)
Port Hole Publications
Power Publishing (R)
(S) Providence Pub. (R)
Quill Driver Books
Quintessential Books (R)
Randall House
Revival Nation
Rose Publishing
(S) Sage Press (R)
(S) Salvation Publisher (R)
Samaritan Press (R)
Scepter Publishers (R)
(S) Selah Publishing (R)
Smyth & Helwys
(S) Southern Baptist Press (R)
SparrowCrowne Press (R)
St. Anthony Mess. Press (R)
St. Bede's Publications (R)
St. Pauls/Alba House (R)
Standard Publishing
(S) Star Bible Publications
Still Waters Revival (R)
Strang Book Group (R)
(S) Tate Publishing (R)
(S) TEACH Services (R)
(S) Trafford Publishing (R)
VBC Publishing
(S) VMI Publishers
Walk Worthy (R)

Wesleyan Publishing
Westminster John Knox
Whitaker House
White Stone Books (R)
(S) WinePress (R)
(S) Word Alive
(S) Zoë Life Publishing

PRINT-ON-DEMAND

Aadeon Publishing (R)
Aaron Book Publishing (R)
ABC Book Publishing
(S) ACW Press (R)
(S) American Binding (R)
(S) Black Forest (R)
Blue Dolphin
(S) Booklocker.com (R)
(S) Brentwood (R)
Bridge-Logos (R)
Christian Writer's Ebook (R)
Comfort Publishing (R)
Continuum Intl. (R)
CrossLink Publishing
Crossroad Publishing (R)
CSS Publishing
(S) Dean Press, Robbie (R)
Editorial Portavoz
(S) Elderberry Press
Encore Performance
Evangelical Press
Evergreen Press
Fifth-Estate (R)
Forever Books (R)
Georgetown Univ. Press
Hannibal Books
Hidden Brook Press (R)
(S) Holy Fire Publishing (R)
(S) Infinity Publishing
Inkling Books (R)
(S) Insight Publishing (R)
(S) Kindred Books (R)
Lighthouse Publishing (R)
Lion and Lamb
Little Lauren Books
Lutterworth Press (R)
OakTara Pub. (R)
(S) One World (R)
Players Press (R)
(S) Pleasant Word (R)
(S) Poems By Me (R)

Power Publishing (R)
Randall House Digital
Ravenhawk Books (R)
(S) Sage Press (R)
(S) Salvation Publisher (R)
(S) Self Publish Press (R)
Sheed & Ward
(S) Strong Tower (R)
(S) Trafford Publishing (R)
Univ. Press of America (R)
VBC Publishing
(S) Word Alive
(S) Xulon Press (R)

PROGRAM RESOURCES

Aaron Book Publishing (R)
Abingdon Press
Christian Ed. Pub.
Christian Liberty Press
Concordia
Congregational Life
CrossLink Publishing
Eerdmans Pub., Wm. B. (R)
E.F.S. Online Pub.
Eldridge Plays
(S) Essence (R)
Evangelical Press
FamilyLife (books) (R)
Forever Books (R)
Foursquare Media
Good Book (R)
Gospel Light
Gospel Publishing
Group Publishing
(S) Holy Fire Publishing (R)
Judson Press (R)
Lillenas
Lion and Lamb
Paradise Research (R)
Pflaum Publishing
Power Publishing (R)
Rose Publishing
Sheed & Ward
(S) Trafford Publishing (R)
(S) WinePress (R)

PROPHECY

(A) Harvest House
(A) W Publishing

Aaron Book Publishing (R)
(S) ACW Press (R)
(S) American Binding (R)
Baker Books
(S) Black Forest (R)
Blue Dolphin
BMH Books (R)
(S) Booklocker.com (R)
(S) Bookstand Publishing (R)
(S) Brentwood (R)
Bridge-Logos (R)
ChapterTwo (R)
Charisma Kids
Christian Writer's Ebook (R)
Comfort Publishing (R)
(S) Creation House (R)
CSS Publishing
Destiny Image (books) (R)
Eerdmans Pub., Wm. B. (R)
(S) Elderberry Press
(S) Essence (R)
Evangelical Press
Fair Havens (R)
(S) Fairway Press (R)
FaithWalk
Father's Press
Forever Books (R)
Harrison House
Hidden Brook Press (R)
(S) Holy Fire Publishing (R)
(S) IMD Press (R)
(S) Insight Publishing (R)
Kregel (R)
Lighthouse Publishing (R)
Lutheran Univ. Press
Lutterworth Press (R)
(S) McDougal Publishing (R)
Monarch Books
New Leaf
(S) One World (R)
Pacific Press
Parson Place (R)
Parsons Publishing (R)
(S) Path Pub. in Christ (R)
(S) Pleasant Word (R)
Power Publishing (R)
(S) Providence Pub. (R)
Randall House
Ravenhawk Books (R)
(S) Sage Press (R)

(S) Salvation Publisher (R)
Samaritan Press (R)
(S) Selah Publishing (R)
(S) Southern Baptist Press (R)
(S) Star Bible Publications
Still Waters Revival (R)
Strang Book Group (R)
(S) Tate Publishing (R)
(S) TEACH Services (R)
(S) Trafford Publishing (R)
(S) VMI Publishers
(S) WinePress (R)
(S) Word Alive
(S) Zoë Life Publishing

PSYCHOLOGY
(A) One World/Ballantine
(A) Tyndale House (R)

Aaron Book Publishing (R)
(S) ACW Press (R)
Adams Media
(S) American Binding (R)
Baker Academic
Blue Dolphin
(S) Book Publishers (R)
(S) Booklocker.com (R)
(S) Bookstand Publishing (R)
(S) Brentwood (R)
Cambridge Scholars Pub.
CarePoint (R)
Christian Writer's Ebook (R)
(S) Creation House (R)
Eerdmans Pub., Wm. B. (R)
E.F.S. Online Pub.
(S) Elderberry Press
(S) Essence (R)
Evangelical Press
Evergreen Press
(S) Fairway Press (R)
FaithWalk
Fifth-Estate (R)
Forever Books (R)
Gentle Path Press
GRQ (R)
Health Communications
Hidden Brook Press (R)
(S) Holy Fire Publishing (R)
Hope Publishing (R)
(S) IMD Press (R)

(S) Insight Publishing (R)
InterVarsity Press (R)
Kregel (R)
Larson Publications (R)
Life Changing Media
Lighthouse Publishing (R)
Lion and Lamb
Lutterworth Press (R)
Monarch Books
Mountain View
(S) One World (R)
Paragon House (R)
(S) Pleasant Word (R)
Power Publishing (R)
(S) Providence Pub. (R)
Quill Driver Books
Quintessential Books (R)
(S) Recovery Commun.
(S) Sage Press (R)
Samaritan Press (R)
Siloam
(S) Southern Baptist
    Press (R)
(S) Star Bible Publications
Tarcher, Jeremy P. (R)
(S) Tate Publishing (R)
(S) TEACH Services (R)
Third World Press (R)
(S) Trafford Publishing (R)
Treble Heart Books (R)
Univ. Press of America (R)
(S) VMI Publishers
Wilshire Book (R)
(S) WinePress (R)
(S) Word Alive

RACISM
Aaron Book Publishing (R)
(S) ACW Press (R)
(S) American Binding (R)
Atheneum/Young Readers
Baker Books
(S) Black Forest (R)
Blue Dolphin
(S) Book Publishers (R)
(S) Booklocker.com (R)
(S) Bookstand Publishing (R)
Cambridge Scholars Pub.
Chalice Press
Christian Writer's Ebook (R)

(S) DCTS Publishing
Destiny Image (R)
Eerdmans Pub., Wm. B. (R)
E.F.S. Online Pub.
(S) Elderberry Press
(S) Essence (R)
Evangelical Press
(S) Fairway Press (R)
FaithWalk
Forever Books (R)
Forward Movement
Guernica Editions (R)
Hidden Brook Press (R)
(S) Holy Fire Publishing (R)
Howard Books
(S) Insight Publishing (R)
InterVarsity Press (R)
Judson Press (R)
Kirk House
Lift Every Voice (R)
Lighthouse Publishing (R)
Monarch Books
New Hope (R)
(S) One World (R)
Pilgrim Press (R)
(S) Pleasant Word (R)
Power Publishing (R)
(S) Providence Pub. (R)
(S) Sage Press (R)
Salt-Works (R)
(S) Star Bible Publications
Strang Book Group (R)
(S) Tate Publishing (R)
(S) Trafford Publishing (R)
Univ. Press of America (R)
(S) VMI Publishers
(S) WinePress (R)
(S) Word Alive

RECOVERY
(A) HarperOne
(A) Tyndale House (R)
(A) WaterBrook Press (R)

Aaron Book Publishing (R)
(S) ACW Press (R)
Ambassador Books
(S) American Binding (R)
Baker Books
(S) Black Forest (R)

Blue Dolphin
(S) Book Publishers (R)
(S) Booklocker.com (R)
(S) Bookstand Publishing (R)
(S) Brown Books
CarePoint (R)
Chalice Press
Christian Writer's Ebook (R)
(S) Creation House (R)
CSS Publishing
Eerdmans Pub., Wm. B. (R)
E.F.S. Online Pub.
(S) Elderberry Press
(S) Essence (R)
Evangelical Press
Evergreen Press
(S) Fairway Press (R)
Faith Communications
FaithWalk
Forever Books (R)
Gentle Path Press
Good Book (R)
GRQ (R)
Hannibal Books
Health Communications
Hidden Brook Press (R)
(S) Holy Fire Publishing (R)
Hope Publishing (R)
Howard Books
(S) IMD Press (R)
(S) Insight Publishing (R)
Langmarc
Lighthouse Publishing (R)
Lion and Lamb
(S) McDougal Publishing (R)
Monarch Books
(S) One World (R)
Paradise Research (R)
Parsons Publishing (R)
(S) Pleasant Word (R)
Power Publishing (R)
Randall House
(S) Recovery Commun.
(S) Sage Press (R)
Siloam
SparrowCrowne Press (R)
(S) Star Bible Publications
Strang Book Group (R)
(S) Tate Publishing (R)
(S) Trafford Publishing (R)

VBC Publishing
(S) VMI Publishers
Wilshire Book (R)
(S) WinePress (R)
(S) Word Alive
(S) Zoë Life Publishing

REFERENCE
(A) Cook, David C.
(A) Doubleday Religion (R)
(A) HarperOne
(A) Tyndale House (R)

Aaron Book Publishing (R)
Abingdon Press
(S) ACW Press (R)
Ambassador-Emerald (R)
(S) American Binding (R)
AMG Publishers (R)
Baker Academic
Baker Books
Barbour
Bethany House (R)
BMH Books (R)
(S) Booklocker.com (R)
(S) Bookstand Publishing (R)
Branden Publishing (R)
(S) Brentwood (R)
Bridge-Logos (R)
Cambridge Scholars Pub.
Christian Heritage (R)
Christian Writer's Ebook (R)
Clarke & Co., James (R)
College Press (R)
(S) Creation House (R)
CrossLink Publishing
Crossroad Publishing (R)
Dover Publications (R)
Editorial Portavoz
Eerdmans Pub., Wm. B. (R)
E.F.S. Online Pub.
(S) Elderberry Press
(S) Essence (R)
Evangelical Press
Facts On File
(S) Fairway Press (R)
FaithWalk
Fifth-Estate (R)
Forever Books (R)
GRQ (R)

Grupo Nelson
Guardian Angel
Hendrickson (R)
Hidden Brook Press (R)
(S) Holy Fire Publishing (R)
(S) IMD Press (R)
(S) Impact Christian (R)
InterVarsity Press (R)
Intl. Awakening (R)
Invisible College Press
Kaleidoscope Press (R)
Kregel (R)
Life Cycle Books (R)
Lighthouse Publishing (R)
Lion and Lamb
Lutterworth Press (R)
Millennium III (R)
Monarch Books
New Leaf
(S) One World (R)
Our Sunday Visitor (R)
Paragon House (R)
Power Publishing (R)
(S) Providence Pub. (R)
Randall House
Reference Service
Rose Publishing
Sheed & Ward
(S) Southern Baptist
    Press (R)
(S) Star Bible Publications
Starik Publishing
Still Waters Revival (R)
(S) Tate Publishing (R)
(S) TEACH Services (R)
Third World Press (R)
(S) Trafford Publishing (R)
Univ. Press of America (R)
VBC Publishing
(S) WinePress (R)
(S) Word Alive
Zondervan

RELATIONSHIPS

(A) FaithWords
(A) Harvest House
(A) Nelson, Thomas
(A) Regal

Aaron Book Publishing (R)
(S) ACW Press (R)

Adams Media
Ambassador Books
Ambassador-Emerald (R)
(S) American Binding (R)
Barbour
Bethany House (R)
(S) Black Forest (R)
Blue Dolphin
(S) Booklocker.com (R)
(S) Bookstand Publishing (R)
Bridge-Logos (R)
(S) Brown Books
CarePoint (R)
Christian Focus (R)
Church Growth Inst.
Cladach Publishing
CLC Publications (R)
(S) Creation House (R)
(S) CrossHouse (R)
CrossLink Publishing
Crossroad Publishing (R)
Discovery House (R)
Eerdmans Pub., Wm. B. (R)
E.F.S. Online Pub.
(S) Elderberry Press
Emmaus Road
(S) Essence (R)
Evangelical Press
Evergreen Press
Extreme Diva
FamilyLife (books) (R)
Forever Books (R)
Forward Movement
Fresh Air Books
Gentle Path Press
Hannibal Books
Health Communications
Hensley Publishing
Hidden Brook Press (R)
(S) Holy Fire Publishing (R)
Howard Books
(S) IMD Press (R)
(S) Insight Publishing (R)
InterVarsity Press (R)
Judson Press (R)
Kregel (R)
Life Changing Media
Lift Every Voice (R)
Lighthouse Publishing (R)
Lillenas

Lion and Lamb
Little Lauren Books
Lutterworth Press (R)
Monarch Books
MOPS Intl.
NavPress
NavPress Th1nk (R)
New Hope (R)
P & R Publishing (R)
(S) Path Pub. in Christ (R)
Port Hole Publications
Power Publishing (R)
(S) Providence Pub. (R)
Quill Driver Books
Quintessential Books (R)
Ravenhawk Books (R)
(S) Sage Press (R)
Salt-Works (R)
Samaritan Press (R)
St. Anthony Mess. Press (R)
(S) Star Bible Publications
Strang Book Group (R)
(S) Tate Publishing (R)
(S) TEACH Services (R)
Torch Legacy
(S) Trafford Publishing (R)
Whitaker House
(S) WinePress (R)
(S) Zoë Life Publishing

RELIGION

(A) Ballantine
(A) Doubleday Religion (R)
(A) FaithWords
(A) HarperOne
(A) Nelson, Thomas
(A) Revell
(A) Tyndale House (R)
(A) WaterBrook Press (R)
(A) W Publishing

Aaron Book Publishing (R)
Abingdon Press
ACTA Publications
(S) ACW Press (R)
Ambassador Books
Ambassador-Emerald (R)
(S) American Binding (R)
American Cath. Press (R)
Atheneum/Young Readers

B & H Publishing
Baker Academic
Baker Books
Baylor Univ. Press
(S) Black Forest (R)
Blue Dolphin
(S) Booklocker.com (R)
(S) Bookstand Publishing (R)
Boyds Mills Press (R)
Branden Publishing (R)
(S) Brentwood (R)
Cambridge Scholars Pub.
Cambridge Univ. Press
Catholic Answers (R)
Catholic Univ. of Amer. Press
Chalice Press
ChapterTwo (R)
Chelsea House (R)
Christian Family (R)
Christian Heritage (R)
Christian Writer's Ebook (R)
Church Growth Inst.
Clarke & Co., James (R)
CLC Publications (R)
Comfort Publishing (R)
Concordia
Continuum Intl. (R)
(S) Creation House (R)
CrossLink Publishing
Crossroad Publishing (R)
CSS Publishing
Eerdmans Pub., Wm. B. (R)
E.F.S. Online Pub.
(S) Elderberry Press
Emmaus Road
(S) Essence (R)
Evangelical Press
Facts On File
(S) Fairway Press (R)
FaithWalk
Father's Press
Fifth-Estate (R)
Fordham Univ. Press (R)
Forever Books (R)
Fortress Press
Forward Movement
Georgetown Univ. Press
GRQ (R)
Harrison House
Hendrickson (R)

Hidden Brook Press (R)
His Work Christian Pub. (R)
(S) Holy Fire Publishing (R)
(S) Impact Christian (R)
(S) Insight Publishing (R)
InterVarsity Press (R)
Invisible College Press
Jossey-Bass
Kirk House
Larson Publications (R)
Libros Liguori
Life Changing Media
Life Cycle Books (R)
Lighthouse Publishing (R)
Lillenas
Lion and Lamb
Liturgy Training (R)
Loyola Press
Lutheran Univ. Press
Lutterworth Press (R)
(S) McDougal Publishing (R)
Mercer Univ. Press (R)
Monarch Books
Mountain Church Books (R)
NavPress Th1nk (R)
New Seeds (R)
New York Univ. Press
(S) One World (R)
Oregon Catholic
Our Sunday Visitor (R)
Pacific Press
Paradise Research (R)
Parsons Publishing (R)
(S) Path Pub. in Christ (R)
Paulist Press
Pflaum Publishing
Pilgrim Press (R)
(S) Pleasant Word (R)
Power Publishing (R)
Praeger Publishers
(S) Providence Pub. (R)
Quintessential Books (R)
Ragged Edge (R)
Rose Publishing
(S) Sage Press (R)
Salt-Works (R)
Sheed & Ward
Smyth & Helwys
(S) Southern Baptist Press (R)
St. Anthony Mess. Press (R)

St. Bede's Publications (R)
St. Pauls/Alba House (R)
(S) Star Bible Publications
Still Waters Revival (R)
Strang Book Group (R)
Tarcher, Jeremy P. (R)
(S) Tate Publishing (R)
Tau Publishing (R)
(S) TEACH Services (R)
Third World Press (R)
Torch Legacy
(S) Trafford Publishing (R)
Trinity Foundation (R)
Univ. of AR Press (R)
Univ. Press of America (R)
(S) VMI Publishers
Westminster John Knox
Whitaker House
(S) WinePress (R)
(S) Word Alive
Xyzzy Press
Yale Univ. Press (R)
(S) Zoë Life Publishing

RELIGIOUS TOLERANCE

(A) FaithWords

Aaron Book Publishing (R)
(S) ACW Press (R)
(S) American Binding (R)
Baker Books
Baylor Univ. Press
(S) Black Forest (R)
Blue Dolphin
(S) Booklocker.com (R)
Boyds Mills Press (R)
Cambridge Scholars Pub.
Chalice Press
Christian Writer's Ebook (R)
(S) Creation House (R)
Eerdmans Pub., Wm. B. (R)
E.F.S. Online Pub.
(S) Elderberry Press
(S) Essence (R)
Evangelical Press
(S) Fairway Press (R)
FaithWalk
Forever Books (R)
Forward Movement

Hidden Brook Press (R)
(S) Holy Fire Publishing (R)
Howard Books
(S) Insight Publishing (R)
Judson Press (R)
Lighthouse Publishing (R)
Lillenas
Lion and Lamb
Lutterworth Press (R)
Monarch Books
New Canaan (R)
New Seeds (R)
(S) One World (R)
Paragon House (R)
(S) Path Pub. in Christ (R)
(S) Pleasant Word (R)
Power Publishing (R)
(S) Providence Pub. (R)
Quill Driver Books
(S) Sage Press (R)
St. Anthony Mess. Press (R)
(S) Star Bible Publications
Strang Book Group (R)
(S) Tate Publishing (R)
(S) TEACH Services (R)
(S) Trafford Publishing (R)
(S) VMI Publishers
Westminster John Knox
(S) WinePress (R)
(S) Word Alive
Yale Univ. Press (R)

RETIREMENT

(A) Harvest House

Aaron Book Publishing (R)
(S) ACW Press (R)
(S) American Binding (R)
Baker Books
(S) Black Forest (R)
Blue Dolphin
(S) Booklocker.com (R)
Christian Writer's Ebook (R)
Cladach Publishing
College Press (R)
Eerdmans Pub., Wm. B. (R)
E.F.S. Online Pub.
(S) Elderberry Press
(S) Essence (R)
Evangelical Press

(S) Fairway Press (R)
Forever Books (R)
Forward Movement
Health Communications
Hidden Brook Press (R)
(S) Holy Fire Publishing (R)
(S) Insight Publishing (R)
Kirk House
Lighthouse Publishing (R)
Lillenas
Lion and Lamb
Monarch Books
(S) One World (R)
(S) Path Pub. in Christ (R)
(S) Pleasant Word (R)
Power Publishing (R)
(S) Providence Pub. (R)
(S) Sage Press (R)
(S) Southern Baptist Press (R)
(S) Star Bible Publications
Strang Book Group (R)
(S) Tate Publishing (R)
(S) TEACH Services (R)
(S) Trafford Publishing (R)
(S) WinePress (R)
(S) Word Alive
(S) Zoë Life Publishing

SCHOLARLY

(A) Cook, David C.
(A) Doubleday Religion (R)

Aaron Book Publishing (R)
Abingdon Press
(S) ACW Press (R)
(S) American Binding (R)
Baker Academic
Baker Books
Baylor Univ. Press
Blue Dolphin
(S) Booklocker.com (R)
Branden Publishing (R)
Cambridge Scholars Pub.
Cambridge Univ. Press
Chalice Press
Christian Heritage (R)
Christian Writer's Ebook (R)
Cistercian (R)
Clarke & Co., James (R)
Concordia

Concordia Academic
Continuum Intl. (R)
Crossroad Publishing (R)
Eerdmans Pub., Wm. B. (R)
E.F.S. Online Pub.
(S) Elderberry Press
(S) Essence (R)
ETC Publications
Evangelical Press
Facts On File
(S) Fairway Press (R)
Fifth-Estate (R)
Fordham Univ. Press (R)
Forever Books (R)
Fortress Press
Georgetown Univ. Press
Gollehon Press
Guardian Angel
Hendrickson (R)
Hidden Brook Press (R)
(S) Holy Fire Publishing (R)
(S) IMD Press (R)
(S) Impact Christian (R)
Inkling Books (R)
(S) Insight Publishing (R)
InterVarsity Press (R)
Intl. Awakening (R)
Kregel (R)
Life Cycle Books (R)
Lighthouse Publishing (R)
Lion and Lamb
Liturgy Training (R)
Lutheran Univ. Press
Master Books
Mercer Univ. Press (R)
New Leaf
New York Univ. Press
(S) One World (R)
Paragon House (R)
Pilgrim Press (R)
(S) Pleasant Word (R)
Power Publishing (R)
(S) Providence Pub. (R)
Quintessential Books (R)
(S) Sage Press (R)
Smyth & Helwys
(S) Star Bible Publications
St. Augustine's Press (R)
St. Bede's Publications (R)
(S) Tate Publishing (R)

(S) Trafford Publishing (R)
Trinity Foundation (R)
Univ. of AR Press (R)
Univ. Press of America (R)
VBC Publishing
(S) VMI Publishers
Westminster John Knox
(S) WinePress (R)
Wipf and Stock
(S) Word Alive
Yale Univ. Press (R)
Youth Specialties
(S) Zoë Life Publishing
Zondervan

SCIENCE

(A) Doubleday Religion (R)

Aaron Book Publishing (R)
(S) ACW Press (R)
(S) American Binding (R)
Baker Books
(S) Black Forest (R)
Blue Dolphin
(S) Booklocker.com (R)
Boyds Mills Press (R)
Cambridge Scholars Pub.
Christian Family (R)
Christian Writer's Ebook (R)
Eerdmans Pub., Wm. B. (R)
E.F.S. Online Pub.
(S) Elderberry Press
(S) Essence (R)
Evangelical Press
Facts On File
(S) Fairway Press (R)
Fordham Univ. Press (R)
Forever Books (R)
Forward Movement
Guardian Angel
Heart of Wisdom
Hidden Brook Press (R)
(S) Holy Fire Publishing (R)
Inkling Books (R)
(S) Insight Publishing (R)
InterVarsity Press (R)
Kaleidoscope Press (R)
Knight George Pub.
Lighthouse Publishing (R)
Lion and Lamb

Lutterworth Press (R)
Master Books
Monarch Books
New Leaf
(S) One World (R)
Parsons Publishing (R)
(S) Pleasant Word (R)
Power Publishing (R)
Quintessential Books (R)
(S) Sage Press (R)
Salt-Works (R)
(S) Star Bible Publications
(S) Tate Publishing (R)
(S) TEACH Services (R)
(S) Trafford Publishing (R)
Trinity Foundation (R)
Troitsa Books
(S) WinePress (R)
(S) Word Alive

SELF-HELP

(A) Ballantine
(A) HarperOne
(A) Harvest House
(A) Nelson, Thomas
(A) One World/Ballantine
(A) Perigee Books
(A) Revell
(A) Tyndale House (R)
(A) WaterBrook Press (R)

Aaron Book Publishing (R)
(S) ACW Press (R)
Adams Media
Ambassador Books
(S) American Binding (R)
Baker Books
(S) Black Forest (R)
Blue Dolphin
(S) Book Publishers (R)
(S) Booklocker.com (R)
(S) Bookstand
   Publishing (R)
Bridge-Logos (R)
CarePoint (R)
Christian Writer's Ebook (R)
CLC Publications (R)
Comfort Publishing (R)
(S) Creation House (R)
CrossLink Publishing

Crossroad Publishing (R)
(S) DCTS Publishing
(S) Dean Press, Robbie (R)
Destiny Image (R)
Dimensions for Living
E.F.S. Online Pub.
(S) Elderberry Press
(S) Essence (R)
Evangelical Press
Evergreen Press
Extreme Diva
Fair Havens (R)
(S) Fairway Press (R)
FaithWalk
Frederick Fell (R)
Forever Books (R)
Gentle Path Press
Gollehon Press
Good Book (R)
GRQ (R)
Grupo Nelson
Guideposts Books
Hay House
Health Communications
Hidden Brook Press (R)
His Work Christian Pub. (R)
(S) Holy Fire Publishing (R)
Howard Books
(S) IMD Press (R)
(S) Insight Publishing (R)
Langmarc
Life Changing Media
Lighthouse Publishing (R)
Lutterworth Press (R)
Monarch Books
Mountain View
(S) One World (R)
Paradise Research (R)
(S) Path Pub. in Christ (R)
(S) Path Publishing (R)
Pauline Books (R)
Pilgrim Press (R)
(S) Pleasant Word (R)
Power Publishing (R)
PREP Publishing (R)
(S) Providence Pub. (R)
Quill Driver Books
Quintessential Books (R)
Ragged Edge (R)
(S) Sage Press (R)

(S) Salvation Publisher (R)
(S) Selah Publishing (R)
SparrowCrowne Press (R)
(S) Star Bible Publications
Starik Publishing
Strang Book Group (R)
Tarcher, Jeremy P. (R)
(S) Tate Publishing (R)
Third World Press (R)
Torch Legacy
(S) Trafford Publishing (R)
Treble Heart Books (R)
Tsaba House
VBC Publishing
(S) VMI Publishers
Walk Worthy (R)
Wilshire Book (R)
(S) WinePress (R)
(S) Word Alive

SENIOR ADULT CONCERNS
(A) Cook, David C.
(A) Harvest House

Aaron Book Publishing (R)
(S) ACW Press (R)
(S) American Binding (R)
Baker Books
(S) Black Forest (R)
Blue Dolphin
(S) Booklocker.com (R)
Chalice Press
Christian Writer's Ebook (R)
Cladach Publishing
Discovery House (R)
Eerdmans Pub., Wm. B. (R)
E.F.S. Online Pub.
(S) Elderberry Press
(S) Essence (R)
Evangelical Press
Evergreen Press
Fair Havens (R)
(S) Fairway Press (R)
Focus on the Family (R)
Forever Books (R)
Gollehon Press
Hidden Brook Press (R)
(S) Holy Fire Publishing (R)
(S) IMD Press (R)

(S) Insight Publishing (R)
Langmarc
Lighthouse Publishing (R)
Lillenas
Lion and Lamb
Monarch Books
New Hope (R)
(S) One World (R)
(S) Pleasant Word (R)
Power Publishing (R)
(S) Providence Pub. (R)
(S) Sage Press (R)
Samaritan Press (R)
(S) Southern Baptist Press (R)
(S) Star Bible Publications
Strang Book Group (R)
(S) Tate Publishing (R)
(S) Trafford Publishing (R)
(S) VMI Publishers
(S) WinePress (R)
(S) Word Alive
(S) Zoë Life Publishing

SERMONS
Aaron Book Publishing (R)
Abingdon Press
(S) ACW Press (R)
Ambassador-Emerald (R)
(S) American Binding (R)
Baker Books
(S) Black Forest (R)
(S) Booklocker.com (R)
(S) Bookstand Publishing (R)
(S) Brentwood (R)
Chalice Press
ChapterTwo (R)
Christian Family (R)
Christian Focus (R)
Christian Writer's Ebook (R)
Church Growth Inst.
Continuum Intl. (R)
CrossLink Publishing
CSS Publishing
(S) DCTS Publishing
Editorial Portavoz
Eerdmans Pub., Wm. B. (R)
E.F.S. Online Pub.
(S) Elderberry Press
(S) Essence (R)
Evangelical Press

(S) Fairway Press (R)
Forever Books (R)
Group Publishing
Hidden Brook Press (R)
(S) Holy Fire Publishing (R)
(S) IMD Press (R)
(S) Insight Publishing (R)
Judson Press (R)
Kregel (R)
Lighthouse Publishing (R)
Lion and Lamb
Liturgical Press
Lutterworth Press (R)
(S) McDougal Publishing (R)
Monarch Books
Mountain View
(S) One World (R)
Pacific Press
(S) Pleasant Word (R)
Power Publishing (R)
(S) Providence Pub. (R)
Salt-Works (R)
(S) Salvation Publisher (R)
Samaritan Press (R)
(S) Southern Baptist Press (R)
(S) Sermon Select Press
St. Pauls/Alba House (R)
(S) Star Bible Publications
Still Waters Revival (R)
(S) Tate Publishing (R)
(S) TEACH Services (R)
Torch Legacy
(S) Trafford Publishing (R)
(S) VMI Publishers
(S) WinePress (R)
(S) Word Alive
(S) Zoë Life Publishing

SINGLES' ISSUES
(A) Cook, David C.
(A) FaithWords
(A) Harvest House
(A) Perigee Books

Aaron Book Publishing (R)
(S) ACW Press (R)
Ambassador Books
Ambassador-Emerald (R)
(S) American Binding (R)
Baker Books

Barbour
Bethany House (R)
(S) Black Forest (R)
Blue Dolphin
(S) Booklocker.com (R)
(S) Brentwood (R)
Christian Focus (R)
Christian Writer's Ebook (R)
(S) Creation House (R)
(S) Dean Press, Robbie (R)
Destiny Image (R)
Eerdmans Pub., Wm. B. (R)
E.F.S. Online Pub.
(S) Elderberry Press
(S) Essence (R)
Evangelical Press
Evergreen Press
Fair Havens (R)
(S) Fairway Press (R)
FaithWalk
Forever Books (R)
(S) Fruitbearer Pub.
Health Communications
Hensley Publishing
Hidden Brook Press (R)
(S) Holy Fire Publishing (R)
(S) IMD Press (R)
(S) Insight Publishing (R)
InterVarsity Press (R)
Judson Press (R)
Kregel (R)
Lift Every Voice (R)
Lighthouse Publishing (R)
Lillenas
Lion and Lamb
Little Lauren Books
(S) McDougal Publishing (R)
Messianic Jewish Publishers (R)
Monarch Books
NavPress Th1nk (R)
New Hope (R)
(S) One World (R)
P & R Publishing (R)
Pacific Press
Parsons Publishing (R)
(S) Pleasant Word (R)
Power Publishing (R)
(S) Providence Pub. (R)
Quill Driver Books
Quintessential Books (R)

(S) Sage Press (R)
Salt-Works (R)
Samaritan Press (R)
(S) Star Bible Publications
Strang Book Group (R)
(S) Tate Publishing (R)
(S) Trafford Publishing (R)
VBC Publishing
(S) VMI Publishers
Walk Worthy (R)
Whitaker House
(S) WinePress (R)
(S) Word Alive
(S) Zoë Life Publishing

SOCIAL JUSTICE ISSUES
(A) FaithWords
(A) HarperOne
(A) Nelson, Thomas

Aaron Book Publishing (R)
(S) ACW Press (R)
(S) American Binding (R)
Atheneum/Young Readers
Baker Books
(S) Black Forest (R)
Blue Dolphin
(S) Booklocker.com (R)
(S) Brentwood (R)
Canadian Inst. for Law (R)
Chalice Press
Christian Writer's Ebook (R)
(S) DCTS Publishing
Destiny Image (R)
Destiny Image (books) (R)
Eerdmans Pub., Wm. B. (R)
E.F.S. Online Pub.
(S) Elderberry Press
(S) Essence (R)
Evangelical Press
(S) Fairway Press (R)
Forever Books (R)
Forward Movement
Georgetown Univ. Press
Hendrickson (R)
Hidden Brook Press (R)
(S) Holy Fire Publishing (R)
Hope Publishing (R)
Howard Books
Inkling Books (R)

(S) Insight Publishing (R)
InterVarsity Press (R)
Jossey-Bass
Judson Press (R)
Kingsley Pub., Jessica (R)
Libros Liguori
Life Cycle Books (R)
Lift Every Voice (R)
Lighthouse Publishing (R)
Monarch Books
Morehouse
NavPress
NavPress Th1nk (R)
New Hope (R)
(S) One World (R)
Our Sunday Visitor (R)
Paulist Press
Pilgrim Press (R)
(S) Pleasant Word (R)
Power Publishing (R)
(S) Providence Pub. (R)
Quill Driver Books
Quintessential Books (R)
Ravenhawk Books (R)
(S) Sage Press (R)
Sheed & Ward
St. Anthony Mess. Press (R)
(S) Star Bible Publications
Still Waters Revival (R)
Strang Book Group (R)
(S) Tate Publishing (R)
(S) Trafford Publishing (R)
(S) VMI Publishers
(S) WinePress (R)
(S) Word Alive
Yale Univ. Press (R)
Youth Specialties

SOCIOLOGY
Aaron Book Publishing (R)
(S) ACW Press (R)
(S) American Binding (R)
Baker Books
(S) Black Forest (R)
Blue Dolphin
(S) Booklocker.com (R)
(S) Brentwood (R)
Cambridge Scholars Pub.
Carey Library, Wm. (R)
Christian Writer's Ebook (R)

Eerdmans Pub., Wm. B. (R)
E.F.S. Online Pub.
(S) Elderberry Press
(S) Essence (R)
Evangelical Press
(S) Fairway Press (R)
FaithWalk
Fordham Univ. Press (R)
Forever Books (R)
Hidden Brook Press (R)
(S) Holy Fire Publishing (R)
(S) IMD Press (R)
(S) Insight Publishing (R)
InterVarsity Press (R)
Life Cycle Books (R)
Lighthouse Publishing (R)
Lion and Lamb
(S) McDougal Publishing (R)
Monarch Books
New York Univ. Press
(S) One World (R)
(S) Pleasant Word (R)
Power Publishing (R)
(S) Providence Pub. (R)
Quill Driver Books
(S) Sage Press (R)
(S) Star Bible Publications
Still Waters Revival (R)
Strang Book Group (R)
(S) Tate Publishing (R)
Third World Press (R)
(S) Trafford Publishing (R)
Univ. Press of America (R)
(S) VMI Publishers
(S) WinePress (R)
(S) Word Alive

SPIRITUAL GIFTS
(A) Nelson, Thomas
(A) Regal
(A) W Publishing

Aaron Book Publishing (R)
(S) ACW Press (R)
Ambassador Books
(S) American Binding (R)
B & H Publishing
Baker Books
(S) Black Forest (R)
Blue Dolphin

(S) Booklocker.com (R)
Bridge-Logos (R)
(S) Brown Books
Canticle Books (R)
ChapterTwo (R)
Christian Writer's Ebook (R)
Church Growth Inst.
CLC Publications (R)
Comfort Publishing (R)
(S) Creation House (R)
(S) CrossHouse (R)
CrossLink Publishing
CSS Publishing
(S) Dean Press, Robbie (R)
Destiny Image (R)
Destiny Image (books) (R)
Eerdmans Pub., Wm. B. (R)
E.F.S. Online Pub.
(S) Elderberry Press
(S) Essence (R)
Evangelical Press
(S) Fairway Press (R)
FaithWalk
Father's Press
Forever Books (R)
Forward Movement
Gospel Publishing
Group Publishing
Grupo Nelson
Guardian Angel
Harrison House
Hensley Publishing
Hidden Brook Press (R)
(S) Holy Fire Publishing (R)
Howard Books
(S) IMD Press (R)
(S) Insight Publishing (R)
InterVarsity Press (R)
Kregel (R)
Lift Every Voice (R)
Lighthouse Publishing (R)
Lillenas
Lion and Lamb
Lutheran Univ. Press
Magnus Press (R)
Monarch Books
New Hope (R)
(S) One World (R)
Pacific Press
Parson Place (R)

Parsons Publishing (R)
(S) Path Pub. in Christ (R)
(S) Pleasant Word (R)
Power Publishing (R)
(S) Providence Pub. (R)
Revival Nation
Rose Publishing
(S) Salvation Publisher (R)
(S) Selah Publishing (R)
St. Anthony Mess. Press (R)
St. Bede's Publications (R)
(S) Star Bible Publications
Strang Book Group (R)
(S) Tate Publishing (R)
Tau Publishing (R)
(S) TEACH Services (R)
(S) Trafford Publishing (R)
(S) VMI Publishers
Whitaker House
(S) WinePress (R)
(S) Word Alive
(S) Zoë Life Publishing

SPIRITUALITY
(A) Ballantine
(A) Doubleday Religion (R)
(A) FaithWords
(A) HarperOne
(A) Nelson, Thomas
(A) Perigee Books
(A) Tyndale House (R)
(A) WaterBrook Press (R)
(A) W Publishing

Aaron Book Publishing (R)
Abingdon Press
ACTA Publications
(S) ACW Press (R)
Ambassador Books
(S) American Binding (R)
Baker Books
Bethany House (R)
(S) Black Forest (R)
Blue Dolphin
(S) Book Publishers (R)
(S) Booklocker.com (R)
(S) Bookstand
    Publishing (R)
(S) Brentwood (R)
Bridge-Logos (R)

(S) Brown Books
Cambridge Scholars Pub.
Canticle Books (R)
ChapterTwo (R)
Christian Heritage (R)
Christian Writer's Ebook (R)
Cistercian (R)
Cladach Publishing
Clarke & Co., James (R)
CLC Publications (R)
Conari Press
Continuum Intl. (R)
(S) Creation House (R)
CrossLink Publishing
Crossroad Publishing (R)
CSS Publishing
Destiny Image (R)
Destiny Image (books) (R)
Discovery House (R)
Eerdmans Pub., Wm. B. (R)
E.F.S. Online Pub.
(S) Elderberry Press
Emmaus Road
(S) Essence (R)
Evangelical Press
Evergreen Press
Fair Havens (R)
(S) Fairway Press (R)
Faith Communications
FaithWalk
Forever Books (R)
Forward Movement
Frederick Fell (R)
Gentle Path Press
Good Book (R)
GRQ (R)
Guardian Angel
Hay House
Hidden Brook Press (R)
(S) Holy Fire Publishing (R)
Howard Books
(S) IMD Press (R)
(S) Impact Christian (R)
(S) Insight Publishing (R)
InterVarsity Press (R)
Invisible College Press
Jossey-Bass
Kingsley Pub., Jessica (R)
Kirk House
Kregel (R)

Larson Publications (R)
Libros Liguori
Lighthouse Publishing (R)
Liguori Publications (R)
Lillenas
Lion and Lamb
Loyola Press
Lutheran Univ. Press
Lutterworth Press (R)
Magnus Press (R)
Monarch Books
Morehouse
NavPress Th1nk (R)
New Hope (R)
New Seeds (R)
(S) One World (R)
Pacific Press
Paradise Research (R)
Paragon House (R)
Parsons Publishing (R)
(S) Path Pub. in Christ (R)
Pauline Books (R)
Paulist Press
Pilgrim Press (R)
(S) Pleasant Word (R)
Power Publishing (R)
(S) Providence Pub. (R)
Quill Driver Books
Quintessential Books (R)
Ragged Edge (R)
Ravenhawk Books (R)
Resource Publications
Revival Nation
(S) Sage Press (R)
Salt-Works (R)
(S) Selah Publishing (R)
Sheed & Ward
Smyth & Helwys
(S) Southern Baptist Press (R)
SparrowCrowne Press (R)
St. Anthony Mess. Press (R)
(S) Star Bible Publications
St. Bede's Publications (R)
St. Pauls/Alba House (R)
Strang Book Group (R)
(S) Tate Publishing (R)
Tau Publishing (R)
(S) TEACH Services (R)
(S) Trafford Publishing (R)
Treble Heart Books (R)

(S) VMI Publishers
(S) WinePress (R)
(S) Word Alive
(S) Zoë Life Publishing

SPIRITUAL LIFE
(A) FaithWords
(A) HarperOne
(A) Nelson, Thomas
(A) Regal
(A) WaterBrook Press (R)

Aadeon Publishing (R)
Aaron Book Publishing (R)
Abingdon Press
ACTA Publications
(S) ACW Press (R)
Ambassador Books
(S) American Binding (R)
Anglicans United (R)
B & H Publishing
Barbour
Beacon Hill Press (R)
Bethany House (R)
(S) Black Forest (R)
Blue Dolphin
BMH Books (R)
(S) Booklocker.com (R)
(S) Bookstand Publishing (R)
Bridge-Logos (R)
(S) Brown Books
Canticle Books (R)
Chalice Press
ChapterTwo (R)
Christian Family (R)
Christian Focus (R)
Christian Writer's Ebook (R)
Church Growth Inst.
CLC Publications (R)
Comfort Publishing (R)
Congregational Life
Continuum Intl. (R)
(S) Creation House (R)
(S) CrossHouse (R)
CrossLink Publishing
CSS Publishing
Destiny Image (books) (R)
Eerdmans Pub., Wm. B. (R)
E.F.S. Online Pub.
(S) Elderberry Press

Eldridge Plays
Elijah Press
Emmaus Road
(S) Essence (R)
Evangelical Press
Evergreen Press
(S) Fairway Press (R)
FaithWalk
Father's Press
Fifth-Estate (R)
Forever Books (R)
Forward Movement
Gentle Path Press
GRQ (R)
Guardian Angel
Harrison House
Hidden Brook Press (R)
(S) Holy Fire Publishing (R)
Howard Books
(S) IMD Press (R)
(S) Insight Publishing (R)
InterVarsity Press (R)
Jossey-Bass
Journey Forth/BJU (R)
Judson Press (R)
Kregel (R)
Legacy Publishers
Life Changing Media
(S) LifeVest Publishing
Lift Every Voice (R)
Lighthouse Publishing (R)
Lillenas
Lion and Lamb
Lutterworth Press (R)
Magnus Press (R)
Monarch Books
Morehouse
NavPress
NavPress Th1nk (R)
New Hope (R)
New Seeds (R)
(S) One World (R)
Parsons Publishing (R)
(S) Path Pub. in Christ (R)
Paulist Press
Pilgrim Press (R)
(S) Pleasant Word (R)
Port Hole Publications
Power Publishing (R)
(S) Providence Pub. (R)

Quill Driver Books
Quintessential Books (R)
Randall House
Reformation Trust
Revival Nation
Rose Publishing
(S) Sage Press (R)
(S) Salvation Publisher (R)
Samaritan Press (R)
SparrowCrowne Press (R)
St. Anthony Mess. Press (R)
(S) Star Bible Publications
St. Bede's Publications (R)
Strang Book Group (R)
(S) Tate Publishing (R)
(S) TEACH Services (R)
(S) Trafford Publishing (R)
Treble Heart Books (R)
(S) VMI Publishers
Wesleyan Publishing
Whitaker House
(S) WinePress (R)
(S) Word Alive
(S) Zoë Life Publishing

SPIRITUAL WARFARE

(A) Nelson, Thomas
(A) Regal
(A) W Publishing

Aadeon Publishing (R)
Aaron Book Publishing (R)
(S) ACW Press (R)
(S) American Binding (R)
Anglicans United (R)
B & H Publishing
Baker Books
(S) Black Forest (R)
Blue Dolphin
(S) Booklocker.com (R)
(S) Bookstand Publishing (R)
Bridge-Logos (R)
(S) Brown Books
Carey Library, Wm. (R)
ChapterTwo (R)
Christian Family (R)
Christian Focus (R)
Christian Writer's Ebook (R)
CLC Publications (R)
Comfort Publishing (R)

(S) Creation House (R)
CrossLink Publishing
Destiny Image (R)
Destiny Image (books) (R)
Editorial Portavoz
Eerdmans Pub., Wm. B. (R)
E.F.S. Online Pub.
(S) Elderberry Press
(S) Essence (R)
Evangelical Press
Evergreen Press
(S) Fairway Press (R)
FaithWalk
Father's Press
Forever Books (R)
Grupo Nelson
Harrison House
Hensley Publishing
Hidden Brook Press (R)
(S) Holy Fire Publishing (R)
(S) IMD Press (R)
(S) Impact Christian (R)
(S) Insight Publishing (R)
Legacy Publishers
Lighthouse Publishing (R)
Lion and Lamb
(S) McDougal Publishing (R)
Messianic Jewish Publishers (R)
Monarch Books
NavPress Th1nk (R)
New Hope (R)
(S) One World (R)
Parson Place (R)
Parsons Publishing (R)
(S) Pleasant Word (R)
Power Publishing (R)
(S) Providence Pub. (R)
Quill Driver Books
Revival Nation
(S) Salvation Publisher (R)
Samaritan Press (R)
(S) Selah Publishing (R)
St. Anthony Mess. Press (R)
(S) Star Bible Publications
Strang Book Group (R)
(S) Tate Publishing (R)
(S) TEACH Services (R)
(S) Trafford Publishing (R)
Treble Heart Books (R)
VBC Publishing

Whitaker House
(S) WinePress (R)
(S) Word Alive
(S) Zoë Life Publishing

SPORTS/RECREATION
(A) Ballantine
(A) One World/Ballantine

Aaron Book Publishing (R)
ACTA Publications
(S) ACW Press (R)
Ambassador Books
(S) American Binding (R)
Baker Books
Blue Dolphin
(S) Booklocker.com (R)
(S) Bookstand Publishing (R)
Boyds Mills Press (R)
(S) Brown Books
Christian Writer's Ebook (R)
Comfort Publishing (R)
Cross Training
E.F.S. Online Pub.
(S) Elderberry Press
(S) Essence (R)
Evangelical Press
Evergreen Press
Facts On File
(S) Fairway Press (R)
Forever Books (R)
Guardian Angel
Hidden Brook Press (R)
His Work Christian Pub. (R)
(S) Holy Fire Publishing (R)
(S) Insight Publishing (R)
Judson Press (R)
Lighthouse Publishing (R)
Lion and Lamb
Lutterworth Press (R)
Monarch Books
(S) One World (R)
(S) Pleasant Word (R)
Power Publishing (R)
(S) Providence Pub. (R)
Ravenhawk Books (R)
Reference Service
(S) Sage Press (R)
Strang Book Group (R)
(S) Tate Publishing (R)

(S) Trafford Publishing (R)
(S) VMI Publishers
(S) WinePress (R)
(S) Word Alive
Xyzzy Press
(S) Zoë Life Publishing

STEWARDSHIP
Aaron Book Publishing (R)
(S) ACW Press (R)
(S) American Binding (R)
Anglicans United (R)
Baker Books
Bethany House (R)
(S) Black Forest (R)
Blue Dolphin
BMH Books (R)
(S) Booklocker.com (R)
(S) Brown Books
Christian Focus (R)
Christian Writer's Ebook (R)
Church Growth Inst.
CLC Publications (R)
College Press (R)
(S) Creation House (R)
CrossLink Publishing
CSS Publishing
Eerdmans Pub., Wm. B. (R)
E.F.S. Online Pub.
(S) Elderberry Press
(S) Essence (R)
Evangelical Press
Evergreen Press
(S) Fairway Press (R)
FaithWalk
Father's Press
Forever Books (R)
Forward Movement
Group Publishing
Hensley Publishing
Hidden Brook Press (R)
(S) Holy Fire Publishing (R)
Hope Publishing (R)
(S) IMD Press (R)
(S) Insight Publishing (R)
InterVarsity Press (R)
Judson Press (R)
Kirk House
Kregel (R)
Lift Every Voice (R)

Lighthouse Publishing (R)
Lillenas
Lion and Lamb
Lutheran Univ. Press
(S) McDougal Publishing (R)
Monarch Books
Neibauer Press (R)
New Hope (R)
(S) One World (R)
Our Sunday Visitor (R)
Pacific Press
Parson Place (R)
Parsons Publishing (R)
Pilgrim Press (R)
(S) Pleasant Word (R)
Power Publishing (R)
(S) Providence Pub. (R)
Quill Driver Books
Revival Nation
Rose Publishing
(S) Sage Press (R)
(S) Salvation Publisher (R)
St. Anthony Mess. Press (R)
(S) Star Bible Publications
(S) Tate Publishing (R)
(S) TEACH Services (R)
(S) Trafford Publishing (R)
VBC Publishing
(S) VMI Publishers
Westminster John Knox
(S) WinePress (R)
(S) Word Alive
(S) Zoë Life Publishing

THEOLOGY
(A) Cook, David C.
(A) Doubleday Religion (R)
(A) HarperOne
(A) Nelson, Thomas
(A) Tyndale House (R)

Aaron Book Publishing (R)
Abingdon Press
(S) ACW Press (R)
Ambassador-Emerald (R)
(S) American Binding (R)
American Cath. Press (R)
Baker Books
Bethany House (R)
Blue Dolphin

BMH Books (R)
(S) Booklocker.com (R)
(S) Bookstand Publishing (R)
(S) Brentwood (R)
(S) Brown Books
Canticle Books (R)
Catholic Answers (R)
Catholic Univ. of Amer. Press
Chalice Press
ChapterTwo (R)
Christian Family (R)
Christian Focus (R)
Christian Heritage (R)
Christian Writer's Ebook (R)
Cistercian (R)
Clarke & Co., James (R)
CLC Publications (R)
College Press (R)
Conciliar Press (R)
Concordia
Concordia Academic
Continuum Intl. (R)
(S) Creation House (R)
CrossLink Publishing
Crossroad Publishing (R)
Crossway Books
CSS Publishing
Deo Volente
Eerdmans Pub., Wm. B. (R)
E.F.S. Online Pub.
(S) Elderberry Press
Emmaus Road
(S) Essence (R)
Evangelical Press
(S) Fairway Press (R)
FaithWalk
Father's Press
Fifth-Estate (R)
First Fruits of Zion
Forever Books (R)
Fortress Press
Forward Movement
Founders Press
Georgetown Univ. Press
Gollehon Press
Hidden Brook Press (R)
(S) Holy Fire Publishing (R)
(S) IMD Press (R)
(S) Impact Christian (R)
Inkling Books (R)

(S) Insight Publishing (R)
InterVarsity Press (R)
Intl. Awakening (R)
Kingsley Pub., Jessica (R)
Kirk House
Kregel (R)
Lift Every Voice (R)
Lighthouse Publishing (R)
Lighthouse Trails (R)
Lion and Lamb
Liturgical Press
Lutheran Univ. Press
Lutheran Voices
Lutterworth Press (R)
Magnus Press (R)
Mercer Univ. Press (R)
Meriwether
Monarch Books
Morehouse
Multnomah
NavPress Th1nk (R)
(S) One World (R)
Pacific Press
Paulist Press
Pflaum Publishing
Pilgrim Press (R)
(S) Pleasant Word (R)
Power Publishing (R)
(S) Providence Pub. (R)
Randall House
Ravenhawk Books (R)
Reformation Trust
Resource Publications
Rose Publishing
(S) Sage Press (R)
Sheed & Ward
Smyth & Helwys
(S) Southern Baptist
    Press (R)
St. Anthony Mess. Press (R)
(S) Star Bible Publications
St. Augustine's Press (R)
St. Bede's Publications (R)
St. Pauls/Alba House (R)
Still Waters Revival (R)
(S) Tate Publishing (R)
(S) TEACH Services (R)
(S) Trafford Publishing (R)
Trinity Foundation (R)
UMI Publishing (R)

Univ. Press of America (R)
VBC Publishing
(S) VMI Publishers
Wesleyan Publishing
Westminster John Knox
(S) WinePress (R)
Wipf and Stock
(S) Word Alive
Yale Univ. Press (R)
(S) Zoë Life Publishing
Zondervan

TIME MANAGEMENT
(A) Cook, David C.
(A) Nelson, Thomas

Aaron Book Publishing (R)
(S) ACW Press (R)
(S) American Binding (R)
Baker Books
Barbour
(S) Black Forest (R)
Blue Dolphin
(S) Booklocker.com (R)
(S) Bookstand Publishing (R)
(S) Brown Books
Christian Writer's Ebook (R)
(S) CrossHouse (R)
Crossroad Publishing (R)
(S) DCTS Publishing
E.F.S. Online Pub.
(S) Elderberry Press
(S) Essence (R)
Evangelical Press
Evergreen Press
(S) Fairway Press (R)
Forever Books (R)
Forward Movement
GRQ (R)
Health Communications
Hensley Publishing
Hidden Brook Press (R)
(S) Holy Fire Publishing (R)
(S) IMD Press (R)
(S) Insight Publishing (R)
Judson Press (R)
Kirk House
Lighthouse Publishing (R)
Lillenas
Lion and Lamb

Monarch Books
New Hope (R)
(S) One World (R)
(S) Pleasant Word (R)
Power Publishing (R)
(S) Providence Pub. (R)
Quill Driver Books
(S) Sage Press (R)
(S) Salvation Publisher (R)
(S) Star Bible Publications
Strang Book Group (R)
(S) Tate Publishing (R)
(S) Trafford Publishing (R)
VBC Publishing
(S) VMI Publishers
Walk Worthy (R)
(S) WinePress (R)
(S) Word Alive
(S) Zoë Life Publishing

TRACTS
ChapterTwo (R)
Christian Writer's Ebook (R)
(S) Essence (R)
Evangelical Press
Forward Movement
(S) Fruitbearer Pub.
Good News Pub.
(S) Holy Fire Publishing (R)
(S) IMD Press (R)
Intl. Awakening (R)
Libros Liguori
Life Cycle Books (R)
Liguori Public. (R)
Lutterworth Press (R)
Neibauer Press (R)
(S) One World (R)
(S) Path Pub. in Christ (R)
Randall House
Rose Publishing
Tract League
Trinity Foundation (R)
(S) Word Alive

TRAVEL
(A) Ballantine
(A) One World/Ballantine

Aaron Book Publishing (R)
(S) ACW Press (R)

(S) American Binding (R)
Baker Books
(S) Book Publishers (R)
(S) Booklocker.com (R)
(S) Brentwood (R)
(S) Brown Books
Cambridge Scholars Pub.
ChapterTwo (R)
Christian Heritage (R)
Christian Writer's Ebook (R)
Cladach Publishing
Comfort Publishing (R)
E.F.S. Online Pub.
(S) Elderberry Press
(S) Essence (R)
(S) Fairway Press (R)
FaithWalk
Forever Books (R)
Hidden Brook Press (R)
(S) Holy Fire Publishing (R)
Hope Publishing (R)
(S) IMD Press (R)
(S) Insight Publishing (R)
(S) LifeVest Publishing
Lighthouse Publishing (R)
Liguori Public. (R)
Lion and Lamb
Lutterworth Press (R)
Monarch Books
(S) One World (R)
(S) Pleasant Word (R)
Power Publishing (R)
(S) Providence Pub. (R)
(S) Sage Press (R)
(S) Tate Publishing (R)
(S) Trafford Publishing (R)
(S) WinePress (R)
(S) Word Alive
Xyzzy Press

TWEEN BOOKS
Aaron Book Publishing (R)
(S) ACW Press (R)
Ambassador Books
Ambassador-Emerald (R)
(S) American Binding (R)
Atheneum/Young Readers
Barbour
(S) Black Forest (R)
(S) Booklocker.com (R)

(S) Bookstand Publishing (R)
Comfort Publishing (R)
Eerdmans Pub., Wm. B. (R)
E.F.S. Online Pub.
(S) Elderberry Press
Eldridge Plays
(S) Essence (R)
Forever Books (R)
(S) Fruitbearer Pub.
Hidden Brook Press (R)
(S) Holy Fire Publishing (R)
(S) Insight Publishing (R)
Journey Stone (R)
(S) Kindred Books (R)
Legacy Press (R)
Lighthouse Publishing (R)
Lion and Lamb
Little Lauren Books
Messianic Jewish Publishers (R)
Mission City Press
New Leaf
Parsons Publishing (R)
Power Publishing (R)
Putnam/Young Readers
(S) Sage Press (R)
(S) Tate Publishing (R)
(S) Trafford Publishing (R)
White Stone Books (R)
(S) WinePress (R)
(S) Zoë Life Publishing

WOMEN'S ISSUES
(A) Ballantine
(A) Cook, David C.
(A) Doubleday Religion (R)
(A) FaithWords
(A) HarperOne
(A) Harvest House
(A) Nelson, Thomas
(A) One World/Ballantine
(A) Perigee Books
(A) Regal
(A) W Publishing

Aaron Book Publishing (R)
ACTA Publications
(S) ACW Press (R)
Adams Media
Ambassador Books
Ambassador-Emerald (R)

(S) American Binding (R)
AMG Publishers (R)
B & H Publishing
Baker Academic
Baker Books
Barbour
Beacon Hill Press (R)
Bethany House (R)
(S) Black Forest (R)
Blue Dolphin
BMH Books (R)
(S) Book Publishers (R)
(S) Booklocker.com (R)
(S) Bookstand Publishing (R)
Branden Publishing (R)
Bridge-Logos (R)
Chalice Press
Christian Writer's Ebook (R)
College Press (R)
Comfort Publishing (R)
(S) Creation House (R)
(S) CrossHouse (R)
CrossLink Publishing
Crossway Books
(S) Dean Press, Robbie (R)
Destiny Image (R)
Discovery House (R)
Eerdmans Pub., Wm. B. (R)
E.F.S. Online Pub.
(S) Elderberry Press
Eldridge Plays
Emmaus Road
(S) Essence (R)
Evangelical Press
Evergreen Press
Facts On File
Fair Havens (R)
(S) Fairway Press (R)
Faith Communications
FaithWalk
FamilyLife (books) (R)
Focus on the Family (R)
Forever Books (R)
Fortress Press
(S) Fruitbearer Pub.
Gentle Path Press
GRQ (R)
Guernica Editions (R)
Health Communications
Hensley Publishing

Hidden Brook Press (R)
(S) Holy Fire Publishing (R)
Hope Publishing (R)
Howard Books
(S) IMD Press (R)
Inkling Books (R)
(S) Insight Publishing (R)
InterVarsity Press (R)
Journey Forth/BJU (R)
Jubilant Press (R)
Judson Press (R)
Kirk House
Kregel (R)
Langmarc
Legacy Publishers
Life Cycle Books (R)
Lift Every Voice (R)
Lighthouse Publishing (R)
Lion and Lamb
Little Lauren Books
Loyola Press
(S) McDougal Publishing (R)
Messianic Jewish Publishers (R)
Monarch Books
Moody Publishers
Morehouse
NavPress
NavPress Th1nk (R)
New Hope (R)
New York Univ. Press
(S) One World (R)
Parson Place (R)
Pauline Books (R)
Pilgrim Press (R)
(S) Pleasant Word (R)
Port Hole Publications
Power Publishing (R)
Praeger Publishers
(S) Providence Pub. (R)
Quill Driver Books
Randall House
Ravenhawk Books (R)
Reference Service
(S) Sage Press (R)
Samaritan Press (R)
(S) Selah Publishing (R)
Sheed & Ward
(S) Southern Baptist Press (R)
SparrowCrowne Press (R)
St. Anthony Mess. Press (R)

(S) Star Bible Publications
Still Waters Revival (R)
Strang Book Group (R)
Tarcher, Jeremy P. (R)
(S) Tate Publishing (R)
(S) TEACH Services (R)
Third World Press (R)
(S) Trafford Publishing (R)
Univ. of AR Press (R)
VBC Publishing
(S) VMI Publishers
Whitaker House
White Stone Books (R)
(S) WinePress (R)
(S) Word Alive
(S) Zoë Life Publishing

WORLD ISSUES

(A) Doubleday Religion (R)
(A) HarperOne
(A) Tyndale House (R)

Aadeon Publishing (R)
Aaron Book Publishing (R)
(S) ACW Press (R)
(S) American Binding (R)
AMG Publishers (R)
Baker Books
(S) Black Forest (R)
Blue Dolphin
(S) Booklocker.com (R)
Boyds Mills Press (R)
Branden Publishing (R)
Bridge-Logos (R)
Carey Library, Wm. (R)
Chalice Press
Christian Writer's Ebook (R)
(S) Creation House (R)
CrossLink Publishing
Eerdmans Pub., Wm. B. (R)
E.F.S. Online Pub.
(S) Elderberry Press
(S) Essence (R)
Evangelical Press
(S) Fairway Press (R)
FaithWalk
First Fruits of Zion
Forever Books (R)
Georgetown Univ. Press
Guernica Editions (R)

Hidden Brook Press (R)
(S) Holy Fire Publishing (R)
(S) Insight Publishing (R)
InterVarsity Press (R)
Kirk House
Kregel (R)
Lift Every Voice (R)
Lighthouse Publishing (R)
Lillenas
Lion and Lamb
Monarch Books
NavPress
NavPress Th1nk (R)
New Hope (R)
(S) One World (R)
Pilgrim Press (R)
(S) Pleasant Word (R)
Power Publishing (R)
(S) Providence Pub. (R)
Quintessential Books (R)
Ravenhawk Books (R)
(S) Sage Press (R)
Salt-Works (R)
(S) Selah Publishing (R)
(S) Star Bible Publications
Still Waters Revival (R)
Strang Book Group (R)
(S) Tate Publishing (R)
(S) Trafford Publishing (R)
VBC Publishing
(S) VMI Publishers
(S) WinePress (R)
(S) Word Alive
Yale Univ. Press (R)
(S) Zoë Life Publishing

WORSHIP

(A) Cook, David C.
(A) Nelson, Thomas
(A) Regal
(A) W Publishing

Aaron Book Publishing (R)
Abingdon Press
(S) ACW Press (R)
Ambassador-Emerald (R)
(S) American Binding (R)
B & H Publishing
Barbour
Bethany House (R)

(S) Black Forest (R)
BMH Books (R)
(S) Booklocker.com (R)
Bridge-Logos (R)
Chalice Press
ChapterTwo (R)
Charisma Kids
Christian Focus (R)
Christian Heritage (R)
Christian Writer's Ebook (R)
Clarke & Co., James (R)
CLC Publications (R)
College Press (R)
Continuum Intl. (R)
(S) Creation House (R)
CrossLink Publishing
CSS Publishing
Deo Volente
Destiny Image (R)
Eerdmans Pub., Wm. B. (R)
E.F.S. Online Pub.
(S) Elderberry Press
Eldridge Plays
Emmaus Road
(S) Essence (R)
Evangelical Press
(S) Fairway Press (R)
Faith Alive
FaithWalk
Father's Press
Forever Books (R)
Forward Movement
Founders Press
Group Publishing
GRQ (R)
Harrison House
Harvest Day
Hidden Brook Press (R)
(S) Holy Fire Publishing (R)
(S) IMD Press (R)
(S) Insight Publishing (R)
InterVarsity Press (R)
Journey Forth/BJU (R)
Judson Press (R)
Kregel (R)
Lift Every Voice (R)
Lighthouse Publishing (R)
Lillenas
Lion and Lamb
Liturgy Training (R)

Lutheran Univ. Press
Lutterworth Press (R)
Messianic Jewish Publishers (R)
Monarch Books
Morehouse
National Drama
NavPress Th1nk (R)
New Hope (R)
(S) One World (R)
Oregon Catholic
Pacific Press
Parsons Publishing (R)
Pilgrim Press (R)
(S) Pleasant Word (R)
Power Publishing (R)
(S) Providence Pub. (R)
Randall House
Reformation Trust
Resource Publications
Revival Nation
Rose Publishing
(S) Sage Press (R)
Salt-Works (R)
Samaritan Press (R)
(S) Selah Publishing (R)
St. Anthony Mess. Press (R)
(S) Star Bible Publications
Strang Book Group (R)
(S) Tate Publishing (R)
(S) TEACH Services (R)
(S) Trafford Publishing (R)
VBC Publishing
(S) VMI Publishers
Westminster John Knox
(S) WinePress (R)
(S) Word Alive

WORSHIP RESOURCES

Aaron Book Publishing (R)
Abingdon Press
(S) ACW Press (R)
Ambassador-Emerald (R)
(S) American Binding (R)
American Cath. Press (R)
B & H Publishing
Baker Books
(S) Black Forest (R)
(S) Booklocker.com (R)
(S) Bookstand Publishing (R)
Catholic Book

Chalice Press
Christian Writer's Ebook (R)
CSS Publishing
(S) DCTS Publishing
Eerdmans Pub., Wm. B. (R)
E.F.S. Online Pub.
(S) Elderberry Press
Eldridge Plays
(S) Essence (R)
Evangelical Press
(S) Fairway Press (R)
Faith Alive
FaithWalk
Forever Books (R)
Forward Movement
Founders Press
Group Publishing
Harvest Day
Hidden Brook Press (R)
(S) Holy Fire Publishing (R)
(S) IMD Press (R)
(S) Insight Publishing (R)
InterVarsity Press (R)
Judson Press (R)
Kregel (R)
Lighthouse Publishing (R)
Lillenas
Lion and Lamb
Liturgical Press
Liturgy Training (R)
Lutheran Univ. Press
Meriwether
Monarch Books
Morehouse
National Drama
(S) One World (R)
Our Sunday Visitor (R)
Parsons Publishing (R)
Pilgrim Press (R)
(S) Pleasant Word (R)
Power Publishing (R)
(S) Providence Pub. (R)
Randall House
Resource Publications
Salt-Works (R)
Smyth & Helwys
Standard Publishing
(S) Tate Publishing (R)
(S) TEACH Services (R)
(S) Trafford Publishing (R)

(S) VMI Publishers
Westminster John Knox
(S) WinePress (R)
(S) Word Alive
(S) Zoë Life Publishing

WRITING HOW-TO

Aaron Book Publishing (R)
(S) American Binding (R)
(S) Booklocker.com (R)
(S) Bookstand Publishing (R)
Christian Writer's Ebook (R)
E.F.S. Online Pub.
(S) Elderberry Press
(S) Essence (R)
Evergreen Press
Fair Havens (R)
(S) Fairway Press (R)
FaithWalk
Forever Books (R)
Hidden Brook Press (R)
(S) Holy Fire Publishing (R)
Jubilant Press (R)
Lighthouse Publishing (R)
Lion and Lamb
Little Lauren Books
Mission City Press
(S) One World (R)
Parson Place (R)
(S) Path Pub. in Christ (R)
(S) Pleasant Word (R)
Ponder Publishing
Power Publishing (R)
(S) Providence Pub. (R)
(S) Sage Press (R)
(S) Selah Publishing (R)
(S) Tate Publishing (R)
(S) Trafford Publishing (R)
Treble Heart Books (R)
(S) VMI Publishers
(S) WinePress (R)
(S) Word Alive
Write Now (R)

YOUTH BOOKS (NONFICTION)

Note: Listing denotes books for eight- to twelve-year-olds, junior high, or senior high age. If all three, it will say "all." If no age

group is listed, the publishers did not specify.

(A) WaterBrook Press (R) (All)
Aaron Book Publishing (R) (8-12/Jr. High)
(S) ACW Press (R) (All)
Ambassador Books (All)
(S) American Binding (R) (Jr./Sr. High)
Anglicans United (R) (8-12/Jr. High)
Atheneum/Young Readers (All)
Baker Books
Barbour (8-12/Jr. High)
(S) Black Forest (R) (All)
(S) Book Publishers (R) (All)
(S) Booklocker.com (R) (All)
(S) Bookstand Publishing (R) (All)
Boyds Mills Press (R) (All)
(S) Brown Books (All)
Carson-Dellosa (8-12)
Charisma Kids (8-12/Jr. High)
Chelsea House (R) (Jr./Sr. High)
Christian Ed. Pub.
Christian Focus (R) (All)
Christian Liberty Press (All)
Christian Writer's Ebook (R) (All)
Conciliar Press (R) (8-12)
Concordia (All)
Contemporary Drama
(S) Creation House (R) (All)
(S) CrossHouse (R) (All)
Dawn Publications (Jr. High)
Eerdmans Pub., Wm. B. (R) (All)
E.F.S. Online Pub. (All)
(S) Elderberry Press (All)
(S) Essence (R) (All)
Evergreen Press
Facts On File
Father's Press (All)
Focus on the Family (R) (Sr. High)
Forever Books (R) (All)
Grupo Nelson (Jr. High)
Guardian Angel (8-12)
Harcourt Religion (Sr. High)
Health Communications (Jr./Sr. High)

Hidden Brook Press (R)(All)
(S) Holy Fire Publishing (R)(All)
(S) IMD Press (R)(All)
(S) Insight Publishing (R)(All)
Journey Stone (R)
   (8-12/Jr. High)
(S) Kindred Books (R)(All)
Knight George Pub. (All)
Legacy Press (R)(8-12)
Life Cycle Books (R)(8-12)
Lift Every Voice (R)(All)
Lighthouse Publishing (R)(All)
Lighthouse Trails (R)(All)
Lion and Lamb (All)
Little Lauren Books (Jr./Sr. High)
Master Books (All)
McRuffy Press (8-12)
Meriwether (Jr./Sr. High)
Messianic Jewish Publishers (R)
Mission City Press (8-12)
Monarch Books (All)
Moody Publishers
NavPress (Sr. High)
NavPress Th1nk (R)(Sr. High)
New Canaan (R)(All)
New Leaf (All)
(S) One World (R)(All)
P & R Publishing (R)(All)
Pacific Press

Pauline Kids (R)(8-12)
Pflaum Publishing (All)
(S) Pleasant Word (R)(All)
Power Publishing (R)(All)
Putnam/Young Readers (All)
Quill Driver Books (Sr. High)
Randall House (All)
Ravenhawk Books (R)
   (Jr./Sr. High)
Starik Publishing (Sr. High)
(S) Tate Publishing (R)(All)
(S) Trafford Publishing (R)(All)
Treble Heart Books (R)
   (Jr./Sr. High)
(S) VMI Publishers (All)
Warner Press (8-12)
White Stone Books (R)(All)
(S) WinePress (R)(All)
(S) Word Alive (All)
Youth Specialties (Jr./Sr. High)
(S) Zoë Life Publishing

YOUTH PROGRAMS
(S) ACW Press (R)
(S) American Binding (R)
Baker Books
Carson-Dellosa
Christian Liberty Press
Christian Writer's Ebook (R)

Church Growth Inst.
Contemporary Drama
CrossLink Publishing
E.F.S. Online Pub.
Eldridge Plays
(S) Fairway Press (R)
Faith Alive
Forever Books (R)
Gospel Publishing
Group Publishing
Harcourt Religion
(S) Holy Fire Publishing (R)
(S) IMD Press (R)
(S) Insight Publishing (R)
Knight George Pub.
Kregel (R)
Lillenas
Lion and Lamb
Mission City Press
Monarch Books
NavPress Th1nk (R)
(S) One World (R)
Pilgrim Press (R)
Ponder Publishing
Power Publishing (R)
(S) Providence Pub. (R)
Randall House Digital
Standard Publishing
(S) Tate Publishing (R)

2

Alphabetical Listings of Book Publishers

If you do not find the publisher you are looking for below, check the "General Index." See the introduction to that index for the codes used to identify the current status of each unlisted publisher. If you do not understand all the terms or abbreviations used in these listings, read the "How to Use This Book" section. Remember to check out any publisher thoroughly before signing a contract.

+ A plus sign before a listing indicates the listing is new this year and was not included last year.
@ This sign indicates that the publisher produces e-books.

AADEON PUBLISHING COMPANY. PO Box 223, Hartford CT 06141. Fax (206) 666-5132. E-mail: submissions@aadeon.com. Website: www.aadeon.com. Submit to The Editor. Addresses spiritual, social, and cultural issues related to the United States of America. Must be insightful, historically and biblically accurate, and focused toward a Christian readership. Publishes 1 title/yr., trade paperback. Accepts mss through agents or authors. Does print-on-demand. Reprints books. Requires 160,000 words or more. Royalty 8 percent on net; no advance. Average first printing 100-5,000. Publication within 1 yr. Considers simultaneous submissions. Requires accepted ms on disk in Microsoft Word. Responds in 1-4 mos. Requires NKJV. Guidelines on Website; no catalog.
   Nonfiction: Proposal/3 chapters or complete ms; no phone/fax/e-query.
   Artwork: Open to queries from freelance artists.
   Tips: "We are particularly interested in manuscripts that challenge average people to confront and overcome the negative influences of an increasingly secular and godless society. Manuscripts must be well organized, professionally edited, easy to understand, biblically based, and scripturally supported (frequent quotations from the Bible—chapter and verse—to support writings). Manuscripts must clearly speak to both a Christian and non-Christian audience."

AARON BOOK PUBLISHING. 1093 Bristol Caverns Hwy., Bristol TN 37620. (423) 212-1208. E-mail: info@aaronbookpublishing.com. Website: www.aaronbookpublishing.com. Imprint of Black Forest Press. Tim Rouse, ed. Honesty, uniqueness, service. Publishes hardcover, mass-market, coffee-table books. Some subsidy; does print-on-demand. Reprints books. Any length. Royalty on retail. Considers simultaneous submissions. Prefers mss by e-mail. Prefers KJV. Guidelines by mail; catalog for 9 x 12 SAE/5 stamps.
   Nonfiction/Fiction: Query first; proposal/2-3 chapters; phone/e-query OK.
   Special Needs: Books of good content. Strong characters and a great story line.
   Artwork: Open to queries from freelance artists.
   Contest: Sponsors contests occasionally.
   Tips: Open to almost any topic.

ABC BOOK PUBLISHING LLC. 20609 N.E. Lakeside Dr., Fairview OR 97024. E-mail: info@abc bookpublishing.com. Website: www.abcbookpublishing.com. Rich Brott, pub. Publishes 20 titles/yr.; trade paperbacks. Does print-on-demand. Royalty 10 percent on net; no advance. Publication within 6 mos. Wants accepted mss by e-mail. Guidelines by e-mail; catalog online.
   Nonfiction: E-query.
   Tips: "We are a new publisher intent on providing a vehicle for worldwide distribution of nonfiction works."

ABINGDON PRESS. 201—8th Ave. S., PO Box 801, Nashville TN 37202. (615) 749-6000. Fax (615) 749-6512. E-mail: [first initial and last name] @umpublishing.org. Website: www.abingdon press.com. United Methodist Publishing House. Editors: Mary C. Dean, ed-in-chief; Ron Kidd, gen. interest bks.; Robert Ratcliff, professional and academic bks.; John Kutsko, dir. of acq.; Joseph A. Crowe, gen. interest bks.; Judith Pierson, children's bks. Books and church supplies directed primarily to a mainline religious market. Cokesbury. Publishes 120 titles/yr.; hardcover, trade paperbacks. Receives 3,000 submissions annually. Less than 5 percent of books from first-time authors. Accepts mss through agents or authors. No reprints. Prefers 144 pgs. Royalty 5-10 percent on retail; pays an advance. Average first printing 3,500-4,000. Publication within 18 mos. No simultaneous submissions. Requires requested ms on disk. Responds in 8-12 wks. Prefers NRSV or a variety of which NRSV is one. Guidelines on Website; free catalog.

Nonfiction: Proposal/2 chapters; no phone/fax/e-query.

Fiction: Solicited or agented material only.

Ethnic Books: African American, Hispanic, Native American, Korean.

Music: Submit to Gary Alan Smith, Music Resources Sr. Development Editor. Produces sacred choral and instrumental music, books, and supplies. See guidelines on Website.

Photos: Accepts freelance photos for book covers.

Tips: "We develop and produce materials to help more people in more places come to know and love God through Jesus Christ and to choose to serve God and neighbor."

**Note: This publisher serviced by ChristianManuscriptSubmissions.com.

ACTA PUBLICATIONS. 5559 W. Howard St., Skokie IL 60077-2621. Toll-free (800) 397-2282. (847) 676-2282. Toll-free fax (800) 397-0079. (847) 676-2287. E-mail: acta@actapublications .com. Website: www.actapublications.com. Catholic. Gregory F. Augustine Pierce, pres. & copub. Wants books that successfully integrate daily life and spirituality. Publishes 10 titles/yr.; hardcover, trade paperbacks, coffee-table books. Receives 100 submissions annually. 50 percent of books from first-time authors. Prefers 150-200 pgs. Royalty 10-12 percent of net; no advance. Average first printing 3,000. Publication within 1 yr. Responds in 2 mos. Prefers NRSV. Guidelines on Website; catalog for 9 x 12 SAE/2 stamps.

Nonfiction: Query or proposal/1 chapter; no phone/fax/e-query.

Tips: "Most open to books that are useful to a large number of average Christians. Read our catalog and one of our books first."

ADAMS MEDIA CORP. 57 Littlefield St., Avon MA 02322. (508) 427-7100. Toll-free fax (800) 872-5628. Website: www.adamsmedia.com. Division of F + W Publications. Jill Alexander, sr. ed. Publishes 230 titles/yr. Receives 5,000 submissions annually. 40 percent of books from first-time authors. Accepts mss through agents or authors. Royalty; variable advance, or outright purchase. Publication within 12-18 mos. Considers simultaneous submissions. Responds to queries in 3 mos. No mss accepted by e-mail. Guidelines on Website; catalog for 9 x 12 SAE/5 stamps.

Nonfiction: Query first by mail; no phone/fax/e-query.

Tips: General publisher that does some inspirational books.

AMBASSADOR BOOKS, INC. 997 MacArthur Blvd., Mahwah NJ 07430. (201) 825-7300. Fax (201) 825-8345 E-mail: info@ambassadorbooks.com, or through Website: www.ambassadorbooks.com. Catholic/Paulist Press. Mr. Chris Driscoll, acq. ed.; submit to: Attn: Submissions. Books of intellectual and spiritual excellence. Publishes 12 titles/yr.; hardcover, trade paperbacks. Receives 1,000 submissions annually. 50 percent of books from first-time authors. Accepts mss through agents or authors. No reprints. Royalty 8-10 percent of net; advance $500-1,000. Publication within 1 yr. Considers simultaneous submissions. Responds in 3-4 mos. Prefers NSRV. Guidelines by mail/e-mail/ Website; free catalog (or on Website).

Nonfiction: Query; no phone/fax/e-query.

Fiction: Query. Juvenile, young adult, adult; picture books & board books.

Photos: Accepts freelance photos for book covers.

Tips: "Our mission for adult books is to celebrate the spiritual dimension of this world by witnessing to the reality of the Way, the Truth, and the Life. For children, it is to foster the knowledge that they are precious to the Lord, while encouraging a friendship with Him that will last a lifetime."

AMBASSADOR-EMERALD, INTL. 427 Wade Hampton Blvd., Greenville SC 29609. (864) 235-2434. Fax (864) 235-2491. E-mail: publisher@emeraldhouse.com. Website: www.emeraldhouse.com. European office: Ambassador Productions, Providence House, Ardenlee, Belfast BT6 8QJ, N. Ireland. Phone 028 90450010. Fax 028 90739659. E-mail: info@ambassador-productions.com. Emerald House Group Inc. Sam Lowry, ed. Dedicated to spreading the gospel of Christ and empowering Christians through the written word. Publishes 35-45 titles/yr.; hardcover, trade paperbacks, mass-market paperbacks, coffee-table books. Receives 300+ submissions annually. 50 to 60 percent of books from first-time authors. Accepts mss through agents or authors. **SUBSIDY PUBLISHES 30 PERCENT**; no print-on-demand. Reprints books. Prefers 30,000+ wds. Royalty 10-18 percent of net; no advance. Average first printing 3,000. Publication within 3.5 mos. Considers simultaneous submissions. Prefers requested ms on CD or by e-mail. Responds in 30-60 days. Prefers KJV. Guidelines by mail/e-mail/Website; free catalog.

Nonfiction: Proposal/3 chapters; phone/fax/e-query OK.

Fiction: Proposal/3chapters; phone/fax/e-query OK. All ages.

Special Needs: Business, finance, biographies, novels, inspirational, devotional, topical, Bible studies.

Also Does: DVDs.

Photos/Artwork: Accepts freelance photos for book covers; open to queries from freelance artists.

Tips: "We're most open to a book which has a clearly defined market and the author's total commitment to the project."

AMERICAN CATHOLIC PRESS. 16565 State St., South Holland IL 60473-2025. (708) 331-5485. Fax (708) 331-5484. E-mail: acp@acpress.org. Website: www.acpress.org or www.leafletmissal.com. Catholic worship resources. Father Michael Gilligan, ed. dir. Publishes 4 titles/yr.; hardcover. Receives 10 submissions annually. Reprints books. Pays $25-100 for outright purchases only. Average first printing 3,000. Publication within 1 yr. No simultaneous submissions. Responds in 2 mos. Prefers NASB. No guidelines; catalog for SASE.

Nonfiction: Query first; no phone/fax/e-query.

Tips: "We publish only materials on the Roman Catholic liturgy. Especially interested in new music for church services. No poetry or fiction."

AMG PUBLISHERS/LIVING INK BOOKS. 6815 Shallowford Rd., Chattanooga TN 37421. Toll-free (800) 266-4977. (423) 894-6060. Toll-free fax (800) 265-6690. (423) 894-9511. E-mail: ricks@amgpublishers.com. Website: www.amgpublishers.com. AMG International. Rick Steele, product development & acquisitions; Dan Penwell, sr. acq. ed; Dr. Warren Baker, sr. ed. To provide biblically oriented books for reference, learning, and personal growth. Imprints: Living Ink Books; God and Country Press. Publishes 30-35 titles/yr.; hardcover, trade paperbacks, and oversized Bible studies. Receives 2,500 submissions annually. 30 percent of books from first-time authors. Accepts mss through agents or authors. Reprints books. Prefers 40,000-60,000 words or 176-224 pgs. Royalty 10-16 percent of net; average advance $2,000. Average first printing 3,500. Publication within 18 mos. Accepts simultaneous submissions. Prefers accepted ms by e-mail. Responds in 1-4 mos. Prefers KJV, NASB, NIV, NKJV, NLT. Guidelines by e-mail/Website; catalog for 9 x 12 SAE/5 stamps.

Nonfiction: Query letter first; e-query preferred. "Looking for historical fiction and nonfiction for our God and Country Press imprint. Need more reference-type works; Bible studies 4-8 weeks in length; and YA fiction."

Fiction: Query letter first; e-query preferred. "Always looking for YA fantasy and historical fiction for adults."

Special Needs: Bible studies and reference—especially reference.

Also Does: Bible software, Bible audio cassettes, CD-ROMs.

Artwork: Open to queries from freelance artists.

Tips: "Most open to a book that is well thought out, clearly written, and finely edited. A professional proposal, following our specific guidelines, has the best chance of acceptance. Spend extra time in developing a good proposal. AMG is always looking for something new and different—with a niche. Write, and rewrite, and rewrite, and rewrite again."

**Note: This publisher serviced by The Writer's Edge and ChristianManuscriptSubmissions.com.

ANGLICANS UNITED/LATIMER PRESS. PO Box 763217, Dallas TX 75376. (972) 293-7443. Fax (972) 293-7559. E-mail: anglicansunited@sbcglobal.net. Website: www.anglicansunited.com; www.latimerpress.com. Episcopal Church USA. Cheryl M. Wetzel, ed. Provides educational materials for biblically orthodox Anglicans and Episcopalians. Publishes 4 titles/yr.; trade paperbacks, mass-market paperbacks. Receives 20 submissions annually. 90 percent of books from first-time authors. Accepts mss through agents or authors. Some subsidy. Reprints books. Prefers up to 225 pgs. Outright purchase for $100-500. Average first printing 1,500-2,000. Publication within 6 mos. Considers simultaneous submissions. Prefers ms by disk or e-mail. Responds in 1 mo. Prefers NIV. Guidelines by mail; catalog for #10 SAE/1 stamp.

Nonfiction: Query letter only first; no phone query; fax/e-query OK. "Looking for Anglican history and practice; adult education."

Ethnic Books: Beginning to translate classical Anglican books into Spanish for Latin American market.

Also Does: Booklets; Videos/DVDs.

Artwork: Open to queries from freelance artists.

Tips: "Most open to (1) a book (60-110 pgs. total), used in Christian education classes for adults and teens; (2) a book (60 pgs.) on baptism, marriage, grief, confirmation, or stewardship."

**Note: This publisher serviced by The Writer's Edge.

ATHENEUM BOOKS FOR YOUNG READERS. 1230 Avenue of the Americas, New York NY 10020. (212) 698-2715. Fax (212) 698-2796. Website: www.simonsayskids.com. Imprint of Simon & Schuster. Submit to The Editor. Publishes books for preschool through high school. Publishes hardcover originals. Prefers mss through agents. Royalty; pays an advance. Considers simultaneous submissions. Guidelines by mail.

Nonfiction: Query only; no phone/fax/e-query. For children/young adult readers only.

Fiction: Query only. For children and teens.

Tips: "Most open to well-written, fast-paced, unique books for middle-grade readers. Subjects include religion."

AVON INSPIRE. HarperCollins, 10 E. 53rd St., New York NY 10022. (212) 207-7000. E-mail: AvonInspire@HarperCollins.com. Website: www.avoninspire.com. Published in partnership with HarperOne. Cynthia DiTiberio, ed. Inspirational women's fiction. Publishes 6-10 titles/yr. Agented submissions only. Royalty and advance negotiable.

Fiction: Historical & contemporary for now; also planning suspense and children's novels.

BAKER ACADEMIC. 6030 E. Fulton Rd, Ada MI 49301. (616) 676-9185. Fax (616) 676-9573. E-mail: submissions@bakeracademic.com. Website: www.bakeracademic.com. Imprint of Baker

Publishing Group. Jim Kinney, ed. dir. Publishes religious academic books and professional books for students and church leaders. Publishes 50 titles/yr.; hardcover, trade paperbacks. 10 percent of books from first-time authors. Accepts mss through agents or authors. Royalty; pays an advance. Publication within 1 yr. Guidelines on Website; catalog for 10 x 13 SAE/3 stamps.

Nonfiction: No unsolicited queries.

BAKER BOOKS. 6030 E. Fulton Rd., Ada MI 49301. (616) 676-9185. Fax (616) 676-9573. Website: www.bakerbooks.com. Imprint of Baker Publishing Group. Submit to Book Editor. Ministry titles for the church. Publishes hardcover, trade paperbacks. No unsolicited proposals. Guidelines by mail; catalog for 10 x 13 SAE/3 stamps. Submit only through an agent, The Writer's Edge, or ChristianManuscriptSubmissions.com.

BAKER'S PLAYS, INC. 45 W. 25th St., New York NY 10010-2035. West coast: 7623 W. Sunset Blvd., Los Angeles CA 90046-2714. (212) 206-8990. E-mail: publications@bakersplays.com. Website: www.bakersplays.com. Samuel French, Inc. Roxane Heinze-Bradshaw, mng. ed. Publishes 2-5 titles/yr. Receives 800 submissions annually. 60 percent of plays from first-time authors. Accepts mss through agents or authors. Reprints plays. Book royalty 10 percent on retail; amateur performance royalty 70 percent; professional performance royalty 80 percent; no advance. Average first printing 1,000. Publication within 6 mos. Considers simultaneous submissions. Accepts requested ms by e-mail. Responds in 6-8 mos. Guidelines by e-mail; separate section in their general catalog, $4.

Plays: E-query. For all ages. "Most open to plays that deal with modern Christian life."

Tips: "We currently publish full-length plays, one-act plays for young audiences, musicals, plays written by high schoolers, and religious plays. We consider plays year round." If your play has been produced, send copies of press clippings. If sending music, you must include a CD.

BALLANTINE PUBLISHING GROUP. 1745 Broadway, 18th Fl., New York NY 10019. (212) 782-9000. Website: www.randomhouse.com/BB. A Division of Random House. Submit to Religion Editor. General publisher that does a few religious books. Mss from agents only. No e-query. Royalty 8-15 percent; variable advances. Nonfiction & fiction. Guidelines on Website; no catalog.

@ B & H PUBLISHING GROUP. 127—9th Ave. N., Nashville TN 37234-0115. (615) 251-2438 Fax (615) 251-3752. E-mail: pat.carter@bhpublishinggroup.com or through Website: www.bhpublishinggroup.com. Book and Bible division of LifeWay Christian Resources. Ricky King, assoc. pub.; Thomas Walters, sr. acq. ed. (nonfiction); Karen Ball, exec. ed. (fiction); Ray Clenden, sr. acq. ed. (academic). Imprints: B & H Books, B & H Academic, Holman Bible Publishers, Holman Reference, Broadman supplies, B & H Español. Publishes books in the conservative, evangelical tradition by and for the larger Christian world. Publishes 90-100 titles/yr.; hardcover, trade paperback. Receives 3,000 submissions annually. 10 percent of books from first-time authors. Requires submissions through agents. Royalty on net; pays an advance. Publication within 18 mos. Considers simultaneous submissions. Responds in 9-12 mos. Prefers HCSB, NIV, NASB. Guidelines by mail/e-mail; free catalog.

Nonfiction: Query first; no phone/fax query.

Fiction: Query first; no phone/fax query. Adult.

Ethnic: Spanish translations.

Also Does: Licensing, Kindle Reader, some audio.

Blog: www.holmantv.com. A series of weekly video episodes for high school and college students.

Tips: "Follow guidelines when submitting. Be informed that the market in general is very crowded with the book you might want to write. Do the research before submitting."

**Note: This publisher serviced by The Writer's Edge and ChristianManuscriptSubmissions.com.

BANTAM BOOKS—See Doubleday Religious.

BARBOUR PUBLISHING INC. 1810 Barbour Dr., PO Box 719, Uhrichsville OH 44683. (740) 922-6045. Fax (740) 922-5948. E-mail: editors@barbourbooks.com. Website: www.barbour books.com. Paul Muckley (pmuckley@barbourbooks.com), sr. ed./nonfiction; Rebecca Germany (rgermany@barbourbooks.com), sr. ed./romance and women's fiction (novels & novellas); Kelly Williams (kwilliams@barbourbooks.com), mng. ed. and youth/children/gift acquisitions. To publish and distribute inspirational products offering exceptional value and biblical encouragement to the masses. Imprints: Barbour Books (fiction and nonfiction) and Heartsong Presents (romance; see separate listing). Publishes 200 titles/yr.; hardcover, trade paperbacks, mass-market paperbacks. Receives 1,500 submissions annually. 40 percent of books from first-time authors. Accepts mss through agents or authors. No subsidy. Prefers 50,000 words (nonfiction) or 80,000-100,000 words (fiction). Royalty 8-12 percent of net; outright purchases $500-5,000; advance $500-5,000. Average first printing 15,000-20,000. Publication within 24 mos. Considers simultaneous submissions & reprints. Responds to queries in 1 mo. Prefers NIV, KJV. Guidelines by mail/Website; catalog for 9 x 12 SAE/2 stamps.

> **Nonfiction:** Proposal/3 chapters; no phone/fax query; e-query OK. E-mail: submissions@ barbourbooks.com.
>
> **Fiction:** Proposal/3 chapters to Rebecca Germany, fiction ed. Novellas 20,000 words. For all ages. "We are interested in a mystery/romance series." E-mail: fictionsubmit@barbourbooks .com. See separate listing for Heartsong Presents & Heartsong Presents—Mysteries.
>
> **Tips:** "We seek solid, evangelical books with the greatest mass appeal. A good title on practical Christian living will go much farther with Barbour than will a commentary on Jude. Do your homework before sending us a manuscript; send material that will work well within our publishing philosophy."
>
> ****Note:** This publisher serviced by The Writer's Edge and ChristianManuscriptSubmissions.com.

BARCLAY PRESS. 211 N. Meridian St., Ste. 101, Newberg OR 97132. (503) 538-9775. Fax (503) 554-8597. E-mail: info@barclaypress.com. Website: www.barclaypress.com. Friends/Quaker. Dan McCracken, gen. mngr. No unsolicited manuscripts.

> ****Note:** This publisher serviced by The Writer's Edge.

BAYLOR UNIVERSITY PRESS. One Bear Pl., 97363, Waco TX 76798-7308. (254) 710-3164. Fax (254) 710-3440. Website: www.baylorpress.com. Baptist. Dr. Carey C. Newman, dir., (254) 710-3522, carey_newman@baylor.edu; Casey Blaine, acq. ed., (254) 710-2846, casey_blaine@ baylor.edu. Imprint: Markham Press Fund. Academic press producing scholarly books on religion and social sciences; church-state studies. Publishes 30 academic titles/yr.; hardcover, trade paperback. Receives 100+ submissions annually. 10 percent of books from first-time authors. Accepts mss through agents or authors. No subsidy publishing. No reprints. Royalty 10 percent on net; no advance. Average first printing 1,000. Publication within 12 mos. Accepts simultaneous submissions. Responds in 2 mos. Guidelines on Website; free catalog.

> **Nonfiction:** Query only first; no phone/fax query; e-query OK. "Looking for academic books; religion and public life."

BEACON HILL PRESS OF KANSAS CITY, PO Box 419527, Kansas City MO 64141. (816) 931-1900. Fax (816) 753-4071. E-mail: jap@bhillkc.com. Website: www.bhillkc.com. Nazarene Publishing House/Church of the Nazarene. Bonnie Perry, pub. dir.; Richard Buckner, ministry line ed.; Judi Perry, consumer ed. A Christ-centered publisher that provides authentically Christian resources that are faithful to God's Word and relevant to life. Imprint: Beacon Hill Books. Publishes 30 titles/ yr.; hardcover, trade paperbacks. Accepts mss through agents or authors. Reprints books. Prefers 30,000-60,000 words or 250 pgs. Royalty 12-14 percent of net; pays an advance; some outright purchases. Average first printing 5,000. Publication within 2 yrs. Considers simultaneous submissions. Responds in 3 mos. or longer. Free guidelines/catalog by mail.

Nonfiction: Proposal/2 chapters; no phone/fax query. "Looking for practical Christian living, felt needs, Christian care, spiritual growth, and ministry resources."

Tips: "Nearly all our titles come through acquisitions, and the number of freelance submissions has declined dramatically. If you wish to submit, follow guidelines above. You are always welcome to submit after sending for guidelines."

**Note: This publisher serviced by The Writer's Edge.

BELIEVE BOOKS. 450 Massachusetts Ave. N.W., Ste. 1223, Washington DC 20001. Phone/fax (202) 787-1532. E-mail: BelieveBooks@gmail.com. Website: www.believebooks.com. Elizabeth Stalcup, ed. Publishes inspirational life stories of people from around the world. E-query.

BETHANY HOUSE PUBLISHERS. 6030 E. Fulton Rd., Ada MI 49301. Website: www.bethanyhouse .com. Baker Publishing Group. To help Christians apply biblical truth in all areas of life—whether through a well-told story, a challenging devotional, or the message of an illustrated children's book. Publishes 90-100 titles/yr.; hardcover, trade paperbacks. 2 percent of books from first-time authors. Accepts mss through agents or authors. Reprints on mass-market paperbacks. Negotiable royalty on net; negotiable advance. Publication within 1 yr. Considers simultaneous submissions. Responds in 3 mos. Guidelines on Website; catalog for 9 x 12 SAE/5 stamps.

Nonfiction: "Seeking well-planned and developed books in the following categories: personal growth, deeper-life spirituality, contemporary issues, women's issues, reference, applied theology, and inspirational."

Fiction: See Website for current acquisitions needs.

Tips: "We do not accept unsolicited queries or proposals via telephone, regular mail, fax, or e-mail."

**Note: This publisher serviced by The Writer's Edge and ChristianManuscriptSubmissions.com.

@ BLUE DOLPHIN PUBLISHING INC. PO Box 8, Nevada City CA 95959. (530) 477-1503. Fax (530) 477-8342. E-mail: Bdolphin@bluedolphinpublishing.com. Website: www.bluedolphin publishing.com. Paul M. Clemens, pub. Imprint: Pelican Pond (fiction & poetry), Papillon Publishing (juvenile), and Symposium Publishing (nonfiction). Books that help people grow in social and spiritual awareness. Publishes 20-24 titles/yr. (includes 10-12 print-on-demand). Receives 4,800 submissions annually. 90 percent of books from first-time authors. Prefers about 60,000 words or 200-300 pgs. Royalty 10-15 percent of net; no advance. Average first printing 300, then on demand. Publication within 10 mos. Considers simultaneous submissions. Requires requested ms on disk. Responds in 3-6 mos. Guidelines by e-mail/Website; catalog for 8.5 x 11 SAE/2 stamps.

Nonfiction: Query or proposal/1 chapter; no phone/e-query. "Looking for books that will increase people's spiritual and social awareness. We will consider all topics."

Fiction: Query/2-pg. synopsis. Pelican Pond Imprint. For teens and adults; no children's board books or picture books.

Also Does: E-books.

Photos/Artwork: Accepts freelance photos for book covers; open to queries from freelance artists.

Tips: "Looking for mature writers whose focus is to help people lead better lives. Our authors are generally professionals who write for others—not just for themselves. We look for topics that would appeal to the general market, are interesting, different, and will aid in the growth and development of humanity. See Website before submitting."

Note: This publisher also publishes books on a range of topics, including cross-cultural spirituality. They also may offer a copublishing arrangement, not necessarily a royalty deal.

BMH BOOKS. PO Box 544, Winona Lake IN 46590. (574) 268-1122. Fax (574) 268-5384. E-mail: tdwhite@bmhbooks.com. Website: www.bmhbooks.com. Blog: www.fgbc-world.blogspot.com. Fellowship of Grace Brethren Churches. Terry White, ed./pub. Trinitarian theology; dispensational eschatology;

emphasis on exegesis. Publishes 15-18 titles/yr.; hardcover, trade paperbacks. Receives 30 submissions annually. 50 percent of books from first-time authors. Accepts mss through agents or authors. Seldom reprints books. Prefers 50,000-75,000 words or 128-256 pgs. Royalty 8-10 percent on retail; rarely pays an advance. Average first printing 2,000. Publication within 1 yr. Prefers not to consider simultaneous submissions. Responds in 3 mos. Prefers KJV or NIV. Requires accepted mss by e-mail. Guidelines by mail/e-mail; free catalog.

Nonfiction: Proposal/2 chapters; no phone/fax query; e-query OK. "Most open to a small-group study book or text for Bible College/Bible Institute."

Tips: "Most open to biblically based, timeless discipleship material."

BOYDS MILLS PRESS. 815 Church St., Honesdale PA 18431. Website: www.boydsmillspress.com. General publisher. Submit to Manuscript Submissions. Publishes a wide range of literary children's titles, for preschool through young adult; very few religious. Publishes 80 titles/yr.; hardcover, trade paperbacks. Receives 15,000 submissions annually. 40 percent of books from first-time authors. Reprints books. Royalty 4-12 percent on retail; advances vary. Considers simultaneous submissions. Guidelines by mail.

Nonfiction: Query/proposal package, outline, 3 sample chapters (expert review/edit of manuscript recommended).

Fiction: Outline/synopsis/first 3 chapters for novels; complete ms for picture books. "We are always interested in multicultural settings."

Tips: "We look for a broad range of books with fresh voices for children and young adults. We publish very few specifically religious books that are not multicultural or otherwise of broad appeal. Please consult our Website for the types of books we publish before submitting your manuscript."

BRANDEN PUBLISHING CO. PO Box 812094, Wellesley MA 02482. (781) 235-3634. Fax (781) 790-1056. E-mail: branden@brandenbooks.com. Website: www.brandenbooks.com. Adolph Caso, ed. Books by or about women, children, military, Italian American or African American themes; religious fiction. Publishes 15 titles/yr.; hardcover, trade paperbacks, coffee-table books. Receives 1,000 submissions annually. 80 percent of books from first-time authors. Accepts mss through agents or authors. Reprints books. Royalty based on profits; no advance. Publication within 10 mos. No simultaneous submissions. Responds within days. Prefers accepted mss by disk or e-mail. Guidelines by mail; no catalog.

Nonfiction: Query only with SASE; no phone/fax queries; e-query OK.

Fiction: Query only with SASE. Ethnic, religious fiction. For adults.

Ethnic Books: African American & Italian.

BRIDGE-LOGOS. 17750 N.W. 115th Ave., Bldg. 200, Ste. 220, Alachua FL 32615. (386) 462-2525. Fax (586) 462-2535. E-mail: editorial@bridgelogos.com or phildebrand@bridge-logos.com. Website: www.bridgelogos.com. Peggy Hildebrand, acq. ed. Publishes classics, books by spirit-filled authors, and inspirational books that appeal to the general evangelical market. Imprint: Unity. Publishes 40 titles/yr.; hardcover, trade paperbacks, mass-market paperbacks. Receives 200+ submissions annually. 30 percent of books from first-time authors. Accepts mss through agents or authors. **SUBSIDY PUBLISHES to 5 PERCENT**; does very little print-on-demand. Reprints books. Prefers 250 pgs. Royalty 10-15 percent on net; rarely pays $500 advance. Average first printing 4,000-5,000. Publication within 3-6 mos. Considers simultaneous submissions. Responds in 6 wks. Prefers accepted mss by e-mail. Guidelines on Website; free catalog.

Nonfiction: Proposal/3-5 chapters; no phone/fax query; e-query OK. "Most open to evangelism, spiritual growth, self-help, and education." Charges a $50 manuscript submission/evaluation fee.

Fiction: Proposal/3-5 chapters; no phone/fax query; e-query OK.

Special Needs: Reference, biography, current issues, controversial issues, church renewal, women's issues, and Bible commentary.

Photos: Accepts freelance photos for book covers.

Tips: "Looking for well-written, timely books that are aimed at the needs of people and that glorify God. Have a great message, a well-written manuscript, and a specific plan and willingness to market your book. Looking for previously published authors with an active ministry who are experts on their subject."

**Note: This publisher serviced by ChristianManuscriptSubmissions.com.

CAMBRIDGE SCHOLARS PUBLISHING. 12 Back Chapman St., Newcastle upon Tyne NE6 2XX, United Kingdom. Fax +44 191 265 2056. E-mail: admin@c-s-p.org. Website: www.c-s-p.org. Dr. Andy Nercessian, ed. Publishes 15 titles/yr. Receives 100 submissions annually. 70 percent of books from first-time authors. No mss through agents. No reprints. No subsidy or print-on-demand. Prefers 100-500 pgs. Royalty 15 percent; no advance. Average first printing 500. Publication within 3 mos. Considers simultaneous submissions. Responds in 3 mos. Prefers accepted ms on disk. Guidelines on Website; free catalog.

Nonfiction: Proposal/1 chapter; e-query OK.

Ethnic Books: African American, Hispanic, and others.

Photos/Artwork: Accepts freelance photos for book covers; open to queries from freelance artists.

Tips: "We will consider very specialized books which others are likely to reject on the grounds of an absence of market. Our titles are mostly of interest to scholars and university academic staff."

CAMBRIDGE UNIVERSITY PRESS. 32 Avenue of the Americas, New York NY 10013-2473. Toll-free (800) 872-7423. (212) 924-3900 or (212) 337-5941. Fax (212) 691-3239. E-mail: newyork@cambridge.org. Website: www.cambridge.org/us. University of Cambridge. Andrew Beck, religion ed. (abeck@cambridge.org). Editors for other topics listed on Website.

Nonfiction: Proposal; no complete mss. Scholarly nonfiction.

CANADIAN INSTITUTE FOR LAW, THEOLOGY & PUBLIC POLICY INC. 89 Douglasview Rise S.E., Calgary AB T2Z 2P5, Canada. (403) 720-8714. Fax (403) 720-4746. E-mail: ciltpp@cs.com. Website: www.ciltpp.com. Will Moore, pres. Integrating Christianity with the study of law and political science. Publishes 2-4 titles/yr.; trade paperbacks. Receives 4-5 submissions annually. 1 percent of books from first-time authors. Accepts mss through agents or authors. Reprints books. Royalty 7 percent on retail; no advance. Average first printing 1,000. Publication within 12-24 mos. No simultaneous submissions. Responds in 6-12 mos. Prefers NIV. Guidelines by mail/e-mail; free catalog.

Nonfiction: Proposal/1 chapter. "Looking for books integrating Christianity with law and political science."

Photos: Accepts freelance photos for book covers.

CANDY CANE PRESS—See Ideals Publications (no freelance for now).

CANTICLE BOOKS. PO Box 2666, Carlsbad CA 92018. (760) 806-3743. Fax (760) 806-3689. E-mail: magnuspress@aol.com. Website: www.magnuspress.com. Imprint of Magnus Press. Warren Angel, ed. dir. To publish Catholic-authored biblical studies that are written for the average person and that minister life to Christ's Church. Publishes 2 titles/yr.; trade paperbacks. Receives 60 submissions annually. 50 percent of books from first-time authors. Accepts mss through agents or authors. Reprints books. Prefers 105-300 pgs. Royalty 6-12 percent on retail; no advance. Average first printing 2,500. Publication within 1 yr. Considers simultaneous submissions. Accepts requested ms on disk. Responds in 1 mo. Guidelines by mail/e-mail; free catalog.

Nonfiction: Query or proposal/2-3 chapters; fax query OK. "Looking for spirituality, thematic biblical studies, unique inspirational/devotional books."

Tips: "Our writers need solid knowledge of the Bible and a mature spirituality that reflects a profound relationship with Jesus Christ. Most open to well-researched, popularly written biblical studies geared to Catholics, or personal experience books that share/emphasize a person's relationship with Christ."

CAREPOINT PUBLISHING. PO Box 870490, Stone Mountain GA 30087. Toll-free (800) 378-9584. (404) 625-9217. E-mail: info@carepointministry.com. Website: www.christiancarepoint.org. Independent Christian publisher. Dr. Scott Philip Stewart, ed. Publishes Christian care books and software to help 21st-century Christians and seekers and those who minister to them. Publishes 12 titles/yr.; trade paperbacks. Receives 100+ submissions annually. 75 percent of books from first-time authors. Accepts mss through agents or authors. Reprints books. Royalty 10-15 percent of net; no advance. Publication within 6 mos. Considers simultaneous submissions, if notified. Accepts requested manuscript on disk or by e-mail. Responds in 4 wks. Guidelines on Website.

Nonfiction: Proposal/2-3 chapters; prefers e-mail query. "Looking for support-group resources."

Photos: Accepts freelance photos for book covers.

Special Needs: Self-help, personal growth, counseling aids, resources for peer and professional Christian caregivers and counselors.

Also Does: Interactive multimedia; book/CD sets.

Tips: "Most open to practical, grace-full support group resources that minister our Lord's healing love, grace, and mercy to the wounded among us. Encourage one another!"

WILLIAM CAREY LIBRARY PUBLISHERS & DISTRIBUTORS. 1605 E. Elizabeth St., Pasadena CA 91104. (626) 720-8210. E-mail through Website: www.missionbooks.org. A ministry of the U.S. Center for World Mission (www.uscwm.org). Naomi Bradley, editorial mngr. (626) 720-8202. Purpose is to publish the latest insights on frontier Christian missions. Publishes 10-15 titles/yr.; trade paperbacks. Reprints books. Variable lengths. Royalty 10 percent on net; no advance. Publication time varies. Guidelines on Website; free catalog.

Nonfiction: Query only; e-query OK. No unsolicited mss. "We are a specialized publisher focusing on books and studies of church growth, missions, world issues, and ethnic/cultural issues."

Special Needs: Anthropology and cross-cultural.

Photos: Accepts freelance photos for book covers.

Tips: "We mostly publish books on missions, evangelization, and unreached people groups. We welcome books that missionaries and mission-minded people would find useful and encouraging. For more information, please click on 'Publishing' on our Website."

CARSON-DELLOSA CHRISTIAN EDUCATION. PO Box 35665, Greensboro NC 27425-5665. (336) 632-0084. Fax (336) 632-0087. E-mail: clayton@carsondellosa.com. Website: www.carsondellosa.com. Carson-Dellosa Publishing, Inc. Carol Layton, ed. dir. Creates high-quality children's products (interactive activities) that teach the Word of God, share his love and goodness, assist in faith development, and glorify his Son, Jesus Christ. Publishes 12 titles/yr.; soft-cover, reproducible, 8.5 x 11, teacher-resource books. Receives 50 submissions annually. 25 percent of books from first-time authors. No reprints. Prefers 64 pgs. Royalty & advance confidential. Publication within 18 mos. Considers simultaneous submissions. Responds in 12 wks. Prefers NIV. Guidelines on Website; free catalog.

Nonfiction: Proposal/2 chapters; hard copy only. "Looking for books that teach the Word of God to children in an engaging and fun way, particularly in a classroom setting."

Fiction: Proposal/2 chapters. "Fiction must be suited for classroom use."

Artwork: Accepts queries from freelance artists.

Also Does: Board games, educational beach balls.

Tips: "Understand the type of books we publish and submit an engaging, well-written proposal. Most open to lesson and activity books that are fun for students and teachers."

**Note: This publisher serviced by ChristianManuscriptSubmissions.com.

CASCADIA PUBLISHING HOUSE LLC. 126 Klingerman Rd., Telford PA 18969. (215) 723-9125. E-mail: editor@cascadiapublishinghouse.com. Website: www.cascadiapublishinghouse.com. Mennonite. Michael A. King, ed. Imprint: DreamSeeker Books. Open to freelance; uses little unsolicited. Some books are subsidized by interested institutions. Guidelines/catalog on Website. Not included in topical listings.

Nonfiction: Query only/vita; e-query OK.

CATHOLIC ANSWERS. 2020 Gillespie Way, El Cajon CA 92020. (619) 387-7200. Fax (619) 387-0042. E-mail through Website: www.catholic.com. Karl Keating, pres.; Mary Jane O'Brien, submissions ed. Publishes 10 titles/yr. Receives 10-15 submissions annually. 1 percent of books from first-time authors. No mss through agents. No subsidy. Reprints books. Prefers 40,000 wds. Royalty on retail; negotiable advance. Average first printing 5,000. Publication within 12 mos. Accepts simultaneous submissions. Responds in 1-3 mos. Prefers RSV—Catholic edition. Guidelines by e-mail; free catalog.

Nonfiction: Query first by mail; no phone/fax/e-query.

Photos: Accepts freelance photos for book covers.

Tips: "Most open to Catholic apologetics and evangelization."

CATHOLIC BOOK PUBLISHING CO. 77 West End Rd., Totowa NJ 07512. (973) 890-2400. Fax (973) 890-2410. E-mail: info@catholicbookpublishing.com. Website: www.catholicbookpublishing .com. Catholic. Anthony Buono, mng. ed. Inspirational books for Catholic Christians. Acquired Resurrection Press and World Catholic Press. Publishes 15-20 titles/yr. Receives 75 submissions annually. 30 percent of books from first-time authors. No mss through agents. Variable royalty or outright purchases; no advance. Average first printing 3,000. Publication within 12-15 mos. No simultaneous submissions. Responds in 2-3 mos. Catalog for 9 x 12 SAE/5 stamps.

Nonfiction: Query letter only; no phone/fax query.

Tips: "We publish mainly liturgical books, Bibles, missals, and prayer books. Most of the books are composed in-house or by direct commission with particular guidelines. We strongly prefer query letters rather than full manuscripts."

CATHOLIC UNIVERSITY OF AMERICA PRESS. 620 Michigan Ave. N.E., Washington DC 20064. (202) 319-5052. Fax (202) 319-4985. E-mail: cua-press@cua.edu. Website: http://cuapress.cua .edu. David J. McGonagle, editor; submit to James Kruggel. Works of original scholarship and works intended for the college/university classroom in various fields, including theology and religious studies. Publishes 10 titles/yr.; hardcover & trade paperback. Receives 230 submissions annually. 25 percent of books from first-time authors. No mss through agents. No reprints. Prefers 200-300 pgs. Royalty 10 percent on net; no advance. Average first printing 750. Publication within 6 mos. Considers simultaneous submissions. Responds as soon as possible. Guidelines by mail/e-mail/ Website; free catalog.

Nonfiction: Query first; no phone/fax/e-query.

Special Needs: Works of original scholarship and works intended for the college and university classroom in theology.

Photos: Accepts freelance photos for book covers.

@ CHALICE PRESS. 1221 Locust St., Ste. 670, St. Louis MO 63103. (314) 231-8500. Fax (314) 231-8524. E-mail: submissions@chalicepress.com. Website: www.chalicepress.com. Christian

Church (Disciples of Christ)/Christian Board of Publication. Lynne Letchworth, ed. (e-mail: lletch worth@chalicepress.com). Books for a thinking, caring church; in Bible, theology, ethics, homiletics, pastoral care, Christian education, Christian living, and spiritual growth. Publishes 35 titles/yr.; hardcover, trade paperbacks, e-books. Receives 550 submissions annually. 15 percent of books from first-time authors. No mss through agents. Prefers 144-240 pgs. for general books, 160-300 pgs. for academic books. Royalty 14 percent of net. Average first printing 2,500-3,000. Publication within 1 yr. Requires requested proposal and ms by e-mail. Responds in 1-3 mos. Guidelines & catalog on Website.

Nonfiction: Query; e-proposal upon publisher's request. "Looking for books on evangelism, leadership, and spiritual growth."

Also Does: Pamphlets.

CHAPTERTWO. Fountain House, Conduit Mews, London SE18 7AP, United Kingdom. Phone ++44 (0)20 8316 5389. Fax ++44(0)20 8854 5963. E-mail: chapter2uk@aol.com. Website: www.chap tertwobooks.org.uk. Plymouth Brethren. Mr. E. Cross, ed. Publishing Plymouth Brethren titles and evangelistic materials to promote New Testament faith and practice. Publishes 20-30 titles/yr.; hardcover, trade paperbacks. No mss through agents. Reprints books. Royalty 0-10 percent on retail (most of their authors donate their work). Average first printing 3,000. Publication within 12 mos. No simultaneous submissions. Prefers KJV, NKJV. No guidelines; free catalog.

Nonfiction: Query first; phone/e-query OK.

Special Needs: Plymouth Brethren commentaries.

Ethnic Books: Hispanic.

Tips: "Writer must be in a Plymouth Brethren assembly and have orthodox Christian doctrine."

CHARISMAKIDS. 600 Rinehart Rd., Lake Mary FL 32746. (407) 333-0600. Fax (407) 333-7100. E-mail: Custsvc@strang.com. Website: www.charismakids.com. Strang Book Group. Submit to The Editor. Books to help children experience God's presence, find his purpose for their lives, and receive the power of the Holy Spirit. Publishes 12 titles/yr. Receives hundreds of submissions annually. 10 percent of books from first-time authors. Prefers mss through agents. No reprints. Prefers 2,400 words or 32 pgs. Royalty on net; pays an advance. Average first printing 10,000. Publication within 1 yr. Considers simultaneous submissions. Responds in 6 mos. Guidelines & catalog on Website.

Nonfiction: Proposal/1 chapter; fax/e-query OK.

Fiction: Proposal/1 chapter. Charismatic children's books; for children 4-8 years. Does not publish 24- to 32-page picture books.

Ethnic Books: African American, Charismatic.

Tips: "Most open to books with a Charismatic worldview for children."

**Note: This publisher serviced by ChristianManuscriptSubmissions.com.

THE CHARLES PRESS, PUBLISHERS. 230 N. 21st St., Ste. 202, Philadelphia PA 19103-1095. (212) 561-2786. Fax (215) 561-0191. E-mail: mailbox@charlespresspub.com. Website: www.charles presspub.com. Lauren Meltzer, pub. (lauren@charlespresspub.com). Responds in 4-16 wks. Guidelines on Website; catalog.

Nonfiction: Proposal (to 10 pgs.); no fax submissions.

CHELSEA HOUSE PUBLISHERS. 132 W. 31st St., Fl. 17, New York NY 10001. Toll-free (800) 322-8755. (212) 896-4211. Toll-free fax (800) 678-3633. E-mail: editorial@factsonfile.com. Website: www.chelseahouse.com. Imprint of Infobase Publishing Group. Submit to Editorial Director. Publishes curriculum-based nonfiction books for middle school and high school students, including on religion. Publishes in hardcover. Reprints books. Considers simultaneous submissions. Guidelines/catalog on Website.

Nonfiction: Query or proposal/2-3 chapters.

Artwork: Open to queries from freelance artists; send photocopies.

CHICKEN SOUP FOR THE SOUL BOOKS. See listing in "Periodicals" section.

CHOSEN BOOKS. Division of Baker Publishing Group, 3985 Bradwater St., Fairfax VA 22031-3702. (703) 764-8250. E-mail: chosenbooks@cox.net. Website: www.chosenbooks.com. Jane Campbell, ed. dir. Charismatic; Spirit-filled-life titles. No unsolicited mss but will respond to e-mails.

CHRISTIAN ED. PUBLISHERS. Box 26639, San Diego CA 92196. (858) 578-4700. Fax (858) 578-2431 (for queries only). E-mail: Editor@cehouse.com. Website: www.christianedwarehouse .com. Blog: www.vbscorner.blogspot.com. Janet Ackelson, asst. ed. An evangelical publisher of Bible club materials for ages 2 through high school, church special-event programs, and online Bible lessons. Publishes 80 curriculum titles/yr. Receives 150 submissions annually. 10 percent of books from first-time authors. No mss through agents. Outright purchases for .03/wd.; no advance. Publication within 1 yr. Accepts requested ms on disk or by e-mail. Responds in 3-5 mos. No simultaneous submissions or reprints. Prefers NIV, KJV. Guidelines by mail/e-mail; catalog for 9 x 12 SAE/4 stamps.

> **Nonfiction:** Query only; phone/fax/e-query OK. Children's Bible studies, curriculum, and take-home papers.
> **Fiction:** For children; on assignment only.
> **Artwork:** Open to freelance illustrators. Send files in Adobe Illustrator.
> **Tips:** "All writing done on assignment. Request our guidelines; then complete a writer application before submitting. Need Bible-teaching ideas for preschool through sixth grade. Also publish Bible stories for preschool and primary take-home papers, 200 words." Using freelance writers mostly for Bible stories rather than for fiction.

CHRISTIAN FAMILY PUBLICATIONS. 312 Point Pleasant Dr., St. Augustine FL 32086. (904) 471-4307. E-mail: christianfamily@mail.com. Website: www.christianfamilybooks.com. Gene Fedele, ed./pub. Imprints: Christian Family Library, Christian Heritage Classics, Great Christian Biographies. Publishes 1-3 titles/yr.; hardcover, trade paperbacks. Receives 30-40 submissions annually. 50 percent of books from first-time authors. No mss through agents. Reprints books. Prefers KJV or NKJV. Accepted mss on disk or by e-mail. Free catalog by mail.

> **Tips:** "Most open to books from a Reformed theological position."

CHRISTIAN FOCUS PUBLICATIONS, LTD. Geanies House, Fearn, Tain, Ross-shire IV20 1TW, Scotland, UK. Phone +44(0) 1862 871011. Fax +44(0) 1862 871699. E-mail: info@christian focus.com. Website: www.christianfocus.com. Willie MacKenzie, adult editorial mngr.; Catherine MacKenzie, children's ed. Focuses on having strong biblical content. Imprints: Mentor, Christian Heritage, Christian Focus, Christian Focus 4 Kids. Publishes 90 titles/yr.; hardcover, trade paperbacks, mass-market paperbacks. Receives 300+ submissions annually. 10 percent of books from first-time authors. Accepts mss through agents or authors. Reprints books. Royalty on net or outright purchase. Publication within 24 mos. Considers simultaneous submissions. Accepts requested ms on disk. Responds typically in 4 mos. Guidelines on Website; free catalog.

> **Nonfiction:** Proposal/2 chapters; fax/e-query OK.
> **Fiction:** Complete ms. For children and teens only. See guidelines for descriptions of children's fiction lines.
> **Photos:** Accepts freelance photos for book covers.
> **Tips:** "We are 'reformed,' though we don't insist all our authors would consider themselves reformed." Most open to issues-based popular books and children's fiction and biography. A prize-winning British publisher with good worldwide coverage.

CHRISTIAN HERITAGE SOCIETY. Box 519, Baldwin Place NY 10505. Phone/fax (914) 962-3287. E-mail: gtkurian@aol.com. Website: www.enyclopediasociety.com. George Kurian, ed. Publishes 6 titles/yr.; hardcover, trade paperbacks. Receives 100 submissions annually. 50 percent of books from first-time authors. Prefers mss through agents. No subsidy. Reprints books. Prefers 120,000 wds. Royalty 10-15 percent on net; no advance. Average first printing 10,000. Publication within 1 yr. Considers simultaneous submissions. Responds in 3 mos. Guidelines by mail; free catalog.

Nonfiction: Query; e-query OK. "Looking for Christian history, reference books, memoirs, devotionals, and evangelism."

CHRISTIAN LIBERTY PRESS. 502 W. Euclid Ave., Arlington Heights IL 60004. (847) 259-4444. Fax (847) 259-2941. E-mail: acquisitions@christianlibertypress.com or larsj@christianlibertypress.com. Website: www.christianlibertypress.com. Publishing arm of Christian Liberty Academy and Christian Liberty Academy School System (CLASS). Lars Johnson, admin. dir. Dedicated to publishing works that are consistent with the Word of God. Curriculum for kindergarten through high school.

Nonfiction: Proposal/2 chapters. A variety of enrichment and support books, including biographies, education resources, and Bible study materials.

Fiction: Proposal/2 chapters. Christian and historical.

@ CHRISTIAN WRITER'S EBOOK NET. PO Box 446, Ft. Duchesne UT 84026. (435) 772-3429. E-mail: editor@writersebook.com. Website: www.writersebook.com. Nondenominational/evangelical Christian. Linda Kay Stewart Whitsitt, ed-in-chief; M. P. Whitsitt, asst. ed.; Terry Gordon Whitsitt, asst. to ed. Gives first-time authors the opportunity to bring their God-given writing talent to the Christian market. Publishes 15 titles/yr. Receives 100 submissions annually. 95 percent of books from first-time authors. Accepts mss through agents or authors. **SUBSIDY PUBLISHES 25 PERCENT**. Reprints books. Prefers 60+ pgs. Royalty 35-50 percent; no advance. E-Books only. Publication within 6 mos. Considers simultaneous submissions. Electronic queries and submissions only; mss need to be in electronic form (MS Word, WordPerfect, ASCII, etc.) to be published; send by e-mail (preferred). No mail submissions accepted without contact by e-mail first. Responds in 1-2 mos. Guidelines on Website.

Nonfiction/Fiction: E-query only. Any topic or genre.

Also Does: Booklets, pamphlets, tracts. E-books.

Tips: "Make sure your work is polished and ready for print. The books we publish are sold in our online store. If you are not sure what an e-book is, check out our Website's FAQ page."

CHURCH GROWTH INSTITUTE. PO Box 7, Elkton MD 21922-0007. (434) 525-0022. Fax (434) 525-0608. E-mail: cgimail@churchgrowth.org. Website: www.churchgrowth.org. Ephesians Four Ministries. Cindy G. Spear, resource development dir. Providing practical tools for leadership, evangelism, and church growth. Publishes 3 titles/yr.; trade paperbacks. Receives 40 submissions annually. 7 percent of books from first-time authors. No mss through agents. Prefers 64-160 pgs. Royalty 6 percent on retail or outright purchase; no advance. Average first printing 100. Publication within 1 yr. Considers simultaneous submissions. Responds in 3 mos. Requires requested ms on disk. Guidelines sent after query/outline is received; catalog for 9 x 12 SAE/4 stamps, or on Website.

Nonfiction: Query; no phone/fax query; e-query OK. "We prefer our writers to be experienced in what they write about, to be experts in the field."

Special Needs: Topics that help churches grow spiritually and numerically; leadership training; attendance and stewardship programs; new or unique ministries (how-to). Self-discovery and evaluation tools, such as our Spiritual Gifts Inventory and Spiritual Growth Survey.

Photos: Accepts freelance photos for book covers.

Tips: "Most open to a practical manual or audio album (CDs/audiotapes and workbooks) for the pastor or other church leaders—something unique with a special niche. Must be practical and different from anything else on the same subject—or must be a topic/slant few others have published. Also very interested in evaluation tools as mentioned above. Please, no devotionals, life testimonies, commentaries, or studies on books of the Bible."

CISTERCIAN PUBLICATIONS INC. The Abbey of Gethsemani, 3642 Monks Rd., Trappist KY 40051. Website: www.cistercianpublications.org. Fr. Mark Scott, OCSO, ed. dir. Works of monastic tradition and studies that foster renewal, spirituality, and ongoing formation of monastics. Publishes 8-14 titles/yr.; hardcover, trade paperbacks, some coffee-table books. Receives 30 submissions annually. 50 percent of books from first-time authors. No mss through agents. Reprints books. Prefers 204-286 pgs. Royalty on net; no advance. Average first printing 1,500. Publication within 2-10 yrs. Requires requested ms on disk. Guidelines on Website; free style sheet/catalog.

Nonfiction: Query only. History, spirituality, and theology.

Photos: Accepts freelance photos for book covers.

Tips: "We publish only on the Christian Monastic Tradition. Most open to a translation of a monastic text, or study of a monastic movement, author, or subject."

CLADACH PUBLISHING. PO Box 336144, Greeley CO 80633. (970) 351-8240. E-mail: staff@ cladach.com. Website: www.cladach.com. Independent Christian publisher. Catherine Lawton, pub. (cathyl@cladach.com); Hannah Lawton, submissions ed. Seeks to influence those inside and outside the body of Christ by giving a voice to talented writers with a clear, articulate, and Christ-honoring vision. Publishes 2-3 titles/yr.; trade paperbacks. Receives 200 submissions annually. 70 percent of books from first-time authors. Accepts proposals through agents or authors. No reprints. Prefers 160-256 pgs. Royalty 7-10 percent on net; no advance. Average first printing 1,500. Publication within 1 yr. Considers simultaneous submissions. Accepted mss by e-mail. Responds in 3-6 mos. Prefers NIV, NRSV. Guidelines on Website; free catalog.

Nonfiction: Query letter only first; e-query OK. "Looking for nonfiction that helps people in their relationship with God."

Fiction: Query letter only first (1-2 pgs.); e-query OK (copied into message). For adults. "Prefer gripping stories depicting inner struggles and real-life issues; well crafted. Would like to see Christian worldview, literary fiction."

Tips: "We want writing that shows God active in our world and that helps readers experience His presence and power in their lives. Check out our Website for current guidelines and published books to see whether your book is a fit for Cladach."

JAMES CLARKE & CO. LTD. PO Box 60, Cambridge CB1 2NT, England. Phone +44 1223 350865. Fax +44 1223 366951. E-mail: publishing@jamesclarke.co.uk. Website: www.jamesclarke.co.uk. Adrian Brink, ed. Publishes scholarly and reference titles in the areas of history & biography, biblical studies and theology. Imprint: The Lutterworth Press (general books, see separate listing). Publishes 25 titles/yr. (5 reprints, 20 new); hardcover & trade paperbacks. Receives 100 submissions annually. 90 percent of books from first-time authors. Accepts mss through agents or authors. Does print-on-demand. Reprints books. **SUBSIDY PUBLISHES 2 PERCENT**. Royalty on retail; pays an advance. Publication within 18 mos. No simultaneous submissions. Responds in 3 mos. Requested ms by mail. Guidelines on Website; free catalog by mail.

Nonfiction: Proposal/2 chapters; e-query OK.

Tips: "For full author guidelines, visit our Website."

+ CLC PUBLICATIONS. PO Box 1449, Fort Washington PA 19034. (215) 542-1242. E-mail: dfessenden@clcpublications.com. Website: www.clcpublications.com. CLC Ministries Intl. David Fessenden, mng. ed. Books that reflect a passion for the topic and a depth of spirituality—a book that grows out of a fervent relationship with Christ. Publishes 12 titles/yr.; hardcover, trade paperbacks, mass-market paperbacks, coffee-table books. Receives 200+ submissions annually. 80 percent of books from first-time authors. Accepts mss through agents or authors. Reprints books. Prefers under 60,000 words or under 300 pgs. Royalty 10-12 percent of net; pays an advance. Average first printing 3,000. Publication within 1 yr. Considers simultaneous submissions. Responds in 2-3 mos. Requires accepted mss on disk or by e-mail. Prefers NKJV. Guidelines by mail/e-mail/Website; catalog for 9 x 12 SAE/2 stamps.

Nonfiction: Query first; proposal/2-3 chapters; e-query OK. Books for the deeper life.
Special Needs: A fresh approach to deepening one's relationship with God.
Ethnic Books: African American.
**Note: This publisher serviced by ChristianManuscriptSubmissions.com.

@ COLLEGE PRESS PUBLISHING CO. INC. 223 W. Third St., Joplin MO 64801. Toll-free (800) 289-3300. (417) 623-6280. Fax (417) 623-8250. E-mail through Website: www.collegepress.com. Christian Church/Church of Christ. Submit to Acquisitions Editor. Christian materials that will help fulfill the Great Commission and promote unity on the basis of biblical truth and intent. Imprint: HeartSpring Publishing (see separate listing). Publishes 15-20 titles/yr.; hardcover, trade paperbacks. Receives 700 submissions annually. 25 percent of books from first-time authors. Accepts mss through agents or authors. Reprints books. Prefers 250-300 pgs. (paperback) or 300-600 pgs. (hardback). Royalty 5-15 percent of net; no advance. Average first printing 3,000. Publication within 6 mos. Considers simultaneous submissions. Requires requested ms on disk; no e-mail submissions. Responds in 2-3 mos. Prefers NIV, NASB, NAS. Guidelines on Website; catalog for 9 x 12 SAE/5 stamps.

> **Nonfiction:** Query only first, then proposal/2-3 chapters; no phone/fax query. "Looking for Bible study, reference, books on divorced leaders, blended families, and leadership." Expanding search for new authors, especially in women's ministry.
> **Ethnic Books:** Reprints their own books in Spanish.
> **Also Does:** E-books.
> **Tips:** "We develop and supply Christian resources for use by individuals, churches, colleges/universities/seminaries, and small groups. We are interested in biblical studies and resources that come from an 'Arminian' view and/or 'amillennial' slant."
> ****Note:** This publisher serviced by ChristianManuscriptSubmissions.com.

@ COMFORT PUBLISHING. 9450 Moss Plantation Ave. S.W., Concord NC 28027. Phone/fax (704) 782-2353. Website: www.comfortpublishing.com. Also has a blog. Comfort Publishing Services, LLC. Pamilla S. Tolen, sr. vp. (ptolen@comfortpublishing.com). To promote Christian literature in a manner that is easy to read and understand, with a message that either teaches a principle or supports the truth of Christian faith. Publishes 10 titles/yr.; hardcover, trade paperbacks. Receives 100 submissions annually. 75 percent of books from first-time authors. Accepts mss through agents or authors. No subsidy; some print-on-demand. Reprints books. Prefers 100,000-150,000 words or 200-300 pgs. Royalty 8-12 percent on retail; some advances $100-2,000. Average first printing 1,000-2,500. Publication within 9-12 mos. Considers simultaneous submissions. Responds in 6 mos. Accepts requested mss by e-mail. Guidelines by mail/e-mail/Website; free catalog.

> **Nonfiction:** Complete ms; fax/e-query OK.
> **Fiction:** Complete ms; fax/e-query OK. For teens & adults. "Looking for mystery/thrillers, mystery romance, and adult/general."
> **Special Needs:** Self-help, spiritual life, tween books, women's issues, money management, inspirational, family life, prophecy.
> **Also Does:** E-books.
> **Photos/Artwork:** Accepts freelance photos for book covers; open to queries from freelance artists.
> **Tips:** "Most open to any well-written book with a message relevant to modern-day Christians."
> ****Note:** This publisher serviced by The Writer's Edge.

CONARI PRESS. 500 Third St., Ste. 230, San Francisco CA 94107. E-mail: info@redwheelweiser.com. Website: www.conari.com or www.redwheelweiser.com. An imprint of Red Wheel/Weiser, LLC. Ms. Pat Bryce, acq. ed. Books on spirituality, personal growth, parenting, and social issues. Publishes 30 titles/yr. Responds in up to 3 mos. Guidelines and catalog on Website. Incomplete topical listings.

CONCILIAR PRESS. PO Box 76, Ben Lomand CA 95005-0076. Toll-free (800) 967-7377. (831) 336-5118. Fax (831) 336-8882. E-mail: Service@conciliarpress.com. Website: www.conciliarpress .com. Antiochian Orthodox Christian Archdiocese of N.A. Father Thomas Zell, ed. Submit to Katherine Hyde (katherinehyde@conciliarmedia.com). Publishes 5-10 titles/yr. Receives 50 submissions annually. 20 percent of books from first-time authors. Accepts mss through agents or authors. **SUBSIDY PUBLISHES 10 PERCENT**. Reprints books. Royalty; no advance. Average first printing 3,000. Prefers e-mail submission. Responds in 3 mos. Prefers NKJV. Guidelines on Website; catalog for 9 x 12 SASE/5 stamps.

Nonfiction: E-query only. Accepts Eastern Orthodox material only.

Photos: Accepts freelance photos for book covers.

Children's Books: Send hard copy to Jane G. Meyer, children's book project mngr., Conciliar Press Ministries, 3112 Calle Rosales, Santa Barbara CA 93105.

Tips: "Please read mission statement posted on Website before submitting."

CONCORDIA ACADEMIC PRESS. 3558 S. Jefferson Ave., St. Louis MO 63118-3968. (314) 268-1098. Fax (314) 268-1329. E-mail: editorial.concordia@cph.org. Website: www.concordiaacademic press.org. Lutheran Church/Missouri Synod. Imprint of Concordia Publishing House. Rev. Paul T. McCain, pub. (paul.mccain@cph.org). Scholarly and professional books in biblical studies, 16th-century studies, historical theology, and theology and culture. Publication within 2 yrs. Responds in 8-12 wks. Guidelines on Website.

Nonfiction: Proposal/sample chapters.

Tips: "Freelance submissions are welcome. Prospective authors should consult the Website for an author prospectus and submission guidelines."

CONCORDIA PUBLISHING HOUSE. 3558 S. Jefferson Ave., St. Louis MO 63118-3968. (314) 268-1187. Fax (314) 268-1329. Website: www.cph.org. Lutheran Church/Missouri Synod. Rev. Paul T. McCain, pub. (paul.mccain@cph.org); Peggy Kuethe: children's resources, children's and family devotions, teaching resources, adult nonfiction, and devotionals; Mark Sell: academic books; Fred Baue: pastoral and congregational resources. Publishes 50 titles/yr.; hardcover, trade paperbacks. Receives 3,000 submissions annually. 10 percent of books from first-time authors. Accepts mss through agents or authors. Royalty 2-12 percent on retail; some outright purchases; some advances $500-1,500. Average first printing 6,000-8,000. Publication within 2 yrs. Considers simultaneous submissions. Responds in 6 mos. Prefers accepted submissions on disk. Prefers NIV. Guidelines on Website; catalog for 9 x 12 SASE/4 stamps.

Nonfiction: Proposal/2 chapters; no phone/fax query. No poetry, personal experience, or biography.

Ethnic Books: Hispanic, Asian American.

Also Does: Pamphlets, booklets.

Tips: "Publishes Christ-centered resources for The Lutheran Church—Missouri Synod. Most open to family, devotional, and teaching resources. Any proposal should be Christ centered, Bible based, and life directed. It must be creative in its presentation of solid scriptural truths. Call for current needs."

**Note: This publisher serviced by The Writer's Edge and ChristianManuscriptSub missions.com.

CONGREGATIONAL LIFE AND LEARNING. Augsburg Fortress Canada, 500 Trillium Dr., Box 9940, Kitchener ON N2G 4Y4, Canada. E-mail: cllsub@augsburgfortress.org. Website: www.afcanada.com. Evangelical Lutheran Church in Canada. Submit using online form. Works to provide congregations with materials and resources for group and individual use that nurture faith, foster learning, and promote spiritual renewal among children, youth, and adults. All material is work-for-hire. Responds in 16 wks. Guidelines at www.afcanada.com/company/submitcongregational.jsp.

Nonfiction: Query first; e-query OK. "Looking for Sunday school materials, Bible study materials, and devotionals."

CONTEMPORARY DRAMA SERVICE. Meriwether Publishing Co., 885 Elkton Dr., Colorado Springs CO 80907. E-mail: merPCDS@aol.com. Website: www.meriwetherpublishing.com. Publishes Christian plays for mainline churches. Also supplemental textbooks on theatrical subjects. Prefers comedy but does publish some serious works. Accepts full-length or one-act plays—comedy or musical. General and Christian. Publishes 30 plays/yr. See the Meriwether Publishing listing for additional details.

@ CONTINUUM INTERNATIONAL PUBLISHING. 80 Maiden Lane, Rm. 704, New York NY 10038-4814. Toll-free (800) 561-7704. (212) 953-5858. Fax (212) 953-5944. E-mail: info@continuum books.com. Website: www.continuumbooks.com. Dr. David Barker, U.S. ed. dir. Imprints: T & T Clark; Burns & Oates. Publishes 60 titles/yr.; hardcover, trade paperbacks. Receives 500 submissions annually. 10 percent of books from first-time authors. Accepts mss through agents or authors. **SUBSIDY PUBLISHES 5 PERCENT**. Does print-on-demand. Reprints books. Royalty to 15 percent; pays an advance. Prefers 60,000-120,000 wds. Publication within 9 mos. No simultaneous submissions. Responds in 1 mo. Guidelines by e-mail/Website; free catalog.

　　Nonfiction: Query, proposal/1 chapter, or complete ms; phone/fax/e-query OK.

　　Photos: Accepts freelance photos for book covers.

　　Contest: Trinity Prize.

DAVID C. COOK. 4050 Lee Vance View, Colorado Springs CO 80918. (719) 536-0100. Fax (719) 536-3269. Website: www.cookministries.com. Dan Rich, sr. vp & pub.; Ingrid Beck, mng. ed. Discipleship is foundational; everything we publish needs to move the reader one step closer to maturity in Christ. Brands: David C. Cook (for teachers or program leaders who want Bible-based discipleship resources; Bible and study resources for serious Bible students; books for Christian families seeking biblical answers to life problems; books to equip kids—birth to age 12—for life); and fiction (inspiring fiction for mature believers). Publishes 85 titles/yr.; hardcover, trade paperbacks. 10 percent of books from first-time authors. Requires mss through agents. Publication within 1-2 yrs. Considers simultaneous submissions. Responds in 3-6 mos. Prefers requested ms by e-mail. Prefers NIV. Guidelines by mail/e-mail/Website.

　　Nonfiction: & Fiction: Accepts submissions only through agents or on request of one of their editors at a writers' conference.

　　**Note: This publisher serviced by The Writer's Edge and ChristianManuscriptSub missions.com.

J. COUNTRYMAN. PO Box 141000, Nashville TN 37214-1000. (615) 902-3134. Fax (615) 902-3200. Website: www.jcountryman.com. Thomas Nelson, Inc. Gift-book imprint. No longer accepting unsolicited manuscripts or proposals.

　　**Note: This publisher serviced by The Writer's Edge.

THE CROSSROAD PUBLISHING CO. 831 Chestnut Ridge Rd., Chestnut Ridge NY 10977-6356. (845) 517-0180. Fax (845) 517-0181. E-mail: info@crossroadpublishing.com. Website: www .cpcbooks.com. Dr. John Jones, ed. dir. Books on religion, spirituality, and personal growth that speak to the diversity of backgrounds and beliefs; hopeful books that inform, enlighten, and heal; particular strengths in Catholic and Anglican titles as well as Christian spirituality and leadership. Imprint: Herder & Herder (see below). Publishes 45 titles/yr.; hardcover, trade paperbacks. Receives 1,200 submissions annually. 10 percent of books from first-time authors. Accepts mss through agents or authors. Does print-on-demand. Reprints books. Prefers 50,000-60,000 words or 160-176 pgs. Royalty 6-14 percent of net; small advance (more for established authors). Average first printing 4,000. Publication within 14 mos. Considers simultaneous submissions. Responds in 6 wks. Accepts requested ms on disk. Guidelines on Website; free catalog.

Nonfiction: Query letter only first; e-query required. Books that explore and celebrate the Christian life.

Tips: "Most authors need some combination of (1) exceptional writing ability, (2) expertise or authority in a field, (3) an existing platform for sales (speaking engagements, etc.). We are independent of all churches yet part of a 200-year tradition of excellent books for enriching Christian life."

Herder & Herder. 200 years of international publishing in the service of theology and church. Monographs, reference works, theological and philosophical discourse. Special focus on younger and emerging theologians as well as the Christian spiritual disciplines.

CROSS TRAINING PUBLISHING. PO Box 1874, Kearney NE 68848. Toll-free (800) 430-8588. Fax (308) 338-2058. E-mail: gordon@crosstrainingpublishing.com. Website: www.crosstraining publishing.com. Gordon Thiessen, pub. Sports books for children and adults.

CROSSWAY BOOKS AND BIBLES. 1300 Crescent St., Wheaton IL 60187. (630) 682-4300. Fax (630) 682-4785. E-mail: editorial@crossway.org. Website: www.crossway.org. A publishing ministry of Good News Publishers. Allan Fisher, VP editorial; submit to Jill Carter, editorial administrator. Publishes books that combine the truth of God's Word with a passion to live it out, featuring unique and compelling Christian content. Publishes 70 titles/yr.; hardcover, trade paperbacks. Receives 1,000 submissions annually. 1 percent of books from first-time authors. Accepts mss through agents or authors. No reprints. Prefers 25,000 words & up. Royalty 10-21 percent of net; advance varies. Average first printing 5,000-10,000. Publication within 18 mos. Considers simultaneous submissions. Responds in 6-8 wks. Prefers ESV. Guidelines by e-mail; free catalog.

    Nonfiction: Currently not accepting unsolicited submissions.

    Also Does: Tracts. See Good News Publishers.

    **Note: This publisher serviced by The Writer's Edge and ChristianManuscriptSubmissions.com.

    **Note: Recipient of five 2006 Silver Angel Awards from Excellence in Media.

CSS PUBLISHING CO. 517 S. Main St., Lima OH 45804. (419) 227-1818. Fax (419) 228-9184. E-mail: editor@csspub.com or through Website: www.csspub.com. Rebecca Allen, mng. ed., (e-mail: ballen@csspub.com). Serves the needs of pastors, worship leaders, and parish program planners in the broad Christian mainline of the American church. Imprints: Fairway Press (subsidy—see separate listing); Academic Renewal Press (reprints textbooks for professors and colleges); B.O.D. (Books On Demand); FaithWalk Books. Publishes 60-70 titles/yr. Receives 1,200-1,500 submissions annually. 50 percent of books from first-time authors. **SUBSIDY PUBLISHES 40 PERCENT** through Fairway Press. Prefers 100-125 pgs. No royalty or advance. Average first printing 1,000. Publication within 6-10 mos. Considers simultaneous submissions. Responds in 3 wks. to 3 mos.; final decision within 12 mos. Requires requested ms on disk and in hard copy. Prefers NRSV. Guidelines by mail/ Website; free catalog.

    Nonfiction: Query or proposal/3 chapters; no e-mail submissions; complete ms for short works. "Looking for pastoral resources for ministry. Our material is practical in nature."

    Fiction: Complete ms. Easy-to-perform dramas and pageants for all age groups. "Our drama interest primarily includes Advent, Christmas, Epiphany, Lent, and Easter. We do not publish long plays."

    Tips: "We're looking for authors who will help with the marketing of their books."

CUSTOM BOOK (formerly Custom Communications Services/Shepherd Press/Custom Book). 77 Main St., Tappan NY 10983. Toll-free (800) 631-1362. (845) 365-0414. Fax (845) 365-0864. E-mail: customusa@aol.com. Website: www.customstudios.com. Norman Shaifer, pres. Publishes 50-75 titles/yr. 50 percent of books from first-time authors. No mss through agents. Royalty on net; some outright purchases for specific assignments. Publication within 6 mos. Responds in 1 mo. Guidelines by mail.

Nonfiction: Query/proposal/chapters. "Histories of individual congregations, denominations, or districts."

Tips: "Find stories of larger congregations (750 or more households) who have played a role in the historic growth and development of the community or region."

DAWN PUBLICATIONS, 12402 Bitney Springs Rd., Nevada City CA 95959. (530) 274-7775. Fax (530) 274-7778. E-mail: submission@dawnpub.com. Website: www.dawnpub.com. Glenn Hovemann, acq. ed. Dedicated to inspiring in children a sense of appreciation for all of life on earth. Publishes 6 titles/yr.; hardcover, trade paperbacks. Receives 3,050 submissions annually. 15 percent of books from first-time authors. Accepts mss through agents or authors. No reprints. Royalty on net; pays an advance. Publication within 1-2 yrs. Considers simultaneous submissions. Responds in 2 mos. Guidelines/catalog on Website.

    Nonfiction: Complete manuscript by mail or e-mail.

    Artwork: Open to queries from freelance artists (send sample c/o Muffy Weaver).

    Tips: "Most open to creative nonfiction. We look for nature awareness and appreciation titles that promote a relationship with the natural world and specific habitats, usually through inspiring treatment and nonfiction."

DEO VOLENTE PUBLISHING. PO Box 119, Humboldt TN 38343. (731) 824-2919. Fax (731) 824-2526. E-mail: books@deovolente.net. Website: www.deovolente.net. Larry Byars, owner. Books that are consistent with reformed theology and promote and assist the Christian walk. Publishes 2-3 titles/yr.; trade paperbacks. Receives 10-20 submissions annually. Accepts mss through agents or authors. Royalty 8-10 percent on retail; no advance. Considers simultaneous submissions. Send accepted mss by disk or e-mail. Guidelines on Website; no catalog.

    Nonfiction: Query first; fax/e-query OK.

    Fiction: Proposal/3 chapters.

DESTINY IMAGE PUBLISHERS. PO Box 310, Shippensburg PA 17257. Toll-free (800) 722-6774, (717) 532-3040. Fax (717) 532-9291. E-mail: rrr@destinyimage.com or through Website: www.destinyimage.com. Ronda Ranalli, ed. mngr. To help people grow deeper in their relationship with God and others. Imprints: Destiny Image Fiction, Destiny Image Dark Matter. Publishes 36 titles/yr. Receives 1,500 submissions annually. 10 percent of books from first-time authors. Accepts mss through agents or authors. **SUBSIDY PUBLISHES 1-2 PERCENT**. Reprints books. Prefers 128-190 pgs. Royalty 10-15 percent on net; no advance. Average first printing 10,000. Publication within 9 mos. Considers simultaneous submissions. Send unsolicited mss via their online Manuscript Submission Form. Responds in up to 6 mos. Guidelines on Website; free catalog.

    Nonfiction: Query or proposal/chapters; no e-query. Charges a $25 fee for unsolicited manuscripts (enclose with submission).

    Fiction: Proposal/1-2 chapters. Adult.

    Tips: "Most open to books on the deeper life or of charismatic interest."

DIMENSIONS FOR LIVING. 201—8th Ave. S., Nashville TN 37203. Fax (615) 749-6512. E-mail: sbriese@umpublishing.org. Website: www.abingdonpress.com. United Methodist Publishing House. Joseph A. Crowe, ed. Submit to Manuscript Submissions (by mail only). Books for the general Christian reader. Publishes 120 titles/yr. Receives 2,000 submissions annually. Less than 1 percent of books from first-time authors. No reprints. Prefers 144 pgs. Royalty 7.5 percent on retail; some outright purchases; no advance. Average first printing 3,000. Publication within 2 yrs. Requires requested ms on disk. Responds in 8 wks. Guidelines on Website; free catalog.

    Nonfiction: Proposal/2 chapters; no phone query. Open to inspiration/devotion, self-help, home/family, special-occasion gift books.

DISCOVERY HOUSE PUBLISHERS. PO Box 3566, Grand Rapids MI 49501. Toll-free (800) 653-8333. (616) 942-9218. Fax (616) 974-2224. E-mail: dhp@dhp.org. Website: www.dhp.org.

RBC Ministries. Carol Holquist, pub. Submit to Manuscript Review Editor. Publishes books that foster Christian growth and godliness. Publishes 12-18 titles/yr.; hardcover, trade paperbacks, mass-market paperbacks. Accepts mss through agents or authors. Reprints books. Royalty 10-14 percent on net; no advance. Publication within 12-18 mos. Considers simultaneous submissions. Requires accepted mss on disk or by e-mail. Responds in 4-6 wks. Guidelines by mail/e-mail/Website; free catalog.

    Nonfiction: Query letter only. If by e-mail, "Attn: Ms Review Editor" in subject line.

    **Note: This publisher serviced by The Writer's Edge and ChristianManuscriptSubmissions.com.

@ DISKUS PUBLISHING. PO Box 43, Albany IN 47320. E-mail: editor@diskuspublishing.com. Submissions to: editor@diskuspublishing.com or submissions@diskuspublishing.com. Website: www.diskuspublishing.com. Marilyn Nesbitt, ed-in-chief; Joyce McLaughlin, inspirational ed. E-book & print publisher. Publishes 50 titles/yr. Royalty 40 percent. Publication within 6-8 mos. Considers simultaneous submissions if noted. Prefers manuscripts by e-mail. Guidelines by mail/Website; catalog online.

    Nonfiction: Complete ms or query by mail or e-mail.

    Fiction: Complete ms by e-mail. Includes religious fiction.

    Tips: This publisher is currently closed to submissions. Check Website under submission guidelines to see when they are going to again open up to submissions.

DOUBLEDAY RELIGIOUS PUBLISHING. 1745 Broadway, New York NY 10019. (212) 782-9000. Fax (212) 782-8338. E-mail: tmurphy@randomhouse.com. Website: www.randomhouse.com. Imprint of Random House Inc. Trace Murphy, ed. dir. Imprints: Image, Galilee, New Jerusalem Bible, Three Leaves Press, Anchor Bible Commentaries, Anchor Bible Reference Library. Publishes 45-50 titles/yr.; hardcover, trade paperbacks. Receives 1,500 submissions annually. 10 percent of books from first-time authors. Requires mss through agents. Reprints books. Royalty 7.5-15 percent on retail; pays an advance. Average first printing varies. Publication within 8 mos. Considers simultaneous submissions. Responds in 4 mos. No disk. No guidelines; catalog for 9 x 12 SASE/3 stamps.

    Nonfiction: Agented submissions only. Proposal/3 chapters; no phone query.

    Fiction: Religious fiction. Agented submissions only.

    Ethnic Books: African American; Hispanic.

    Tips: "Most open to a book that has a big and well-defined audience. Have a clear proposal, lucid thesis, and specified audience."

    **Note: This publisher serviced by ChristianManuscriptSubmissions.com.

DOVE INSPIRATIONAL PRESS. 1000 Burmaster St., Gretna LA 70053. (504) 368-1175. Fax (504) 368-1195. E-mail: editorial@pelicanpub.com. Website: www.pelicanpub.com. Nina Kooij, ed-in-chief. To publish books of quality and permanence that enrich the lives of those who read them. Imprint of Pelican Publishing. Publishes 1 title/yr.; hardcover, trade paperbacks. Receives 250 submissions annually. No books from first-time authors. Accepts mss through agents or authors. Reprints books. Prefers 200+ pgs. Royalty; some advances. Publication within 9-18 mos. No simultaneous submissions. Responds in 1 mo. on queries. Requires accepted ms on disk. Prefers KJV. Guidelines by mail/Website; catalog for 9 x 12 SASE/6 stamps.

    Nonfiction: Proposal/2 chapters; no phone/fax/e-query.

    Fiction: Children's picture books only.

    Photos/Artwork: Accepts freelance photos for book covers; open to queries from freelance artists.

DOVER PUBLICATIONS INC. 31 E. 2nd St., Mineola NY 11501-3852. (516) 294-7000, ext. 173. Fax (516) 873-1401 or (516) 742-6953. E-mail: mwaldrep@doverpublications.com. Website: www.doverpublications.com. Attn: Editorial Dept. Publishes some religious titles, reprints only. Makes outright purchases. Does not return submissions. Guidelines & free catalog on Website.

Nonfiction: Proposal with synopsis/contents/1 chapter; no submissions by e-mail. Religion topics.

EDITORIAL PORTAVOZ. PO Box 2607, Grand Rapids MI 49501-2607. Toll-free (800) 733-2607. (616) 451-4775. Fax (616) 451-9330. E-mail: editor@portavoz.com or portavoz@portavoz.com. Website: www.portavoz.com. Spanish Division of Kregel Publishing. Submit to The Editor. To provide trusted, biblically based resources that challenge and encourage Spanish-speaking individuals in their Christian lives and service. Publishes 40+ titles/yr. 2-5 percent of books from first-time authors. Accepts mss through agents or authors. Does print-on-demand. No reprints. Negotiable royalty on net; negotiable advance. Average first printing 5,000. Publication within 13 mos. Considers simultaneous submissions. Responds in 2-4 mos. Guidelines on Website.

Nonfiction: Send proposal by e-mail or CD-ROM, with 2-3 chapters. "Looking for original Spanish reference works."

Artwork: Purchases artwork outright.

EDITORIAL UNILIT. 1360 N.W. 88th Ave., Miami FL 33172-3093. Toll-free (800) 767-7726. (305) 592-6136. Fax (305) 592-0087. E-mail: info@editorialunilit.com. Website: www.editorialunilit.com. Spanish House. Submit to The Editor. To glorify God by providing the church and Spanish-speaking people with the tools to communicate clearly the gospel of Jesus Christ and help them grow in their relationship with him and his church.

EERDMANS BOOKS FOR YOUNG READERS. 2140 Oak Industrial Dr. N.E., Grand Rapids MI 49505. Toll-free (800) 253-7521. (616) 459-4591. Fax (616) 459-6540. E-mail: youngreaders@eerdmans .com or info@eerdmans.com. Website: www.eerdmans.com/youngreaders. Wm. B. Eerdmans Publishing. Submit to Acquisitions Editor. Produces books for general trade, school, and library markets. Publishes 12-15 titles/yr.; hardcover, trade paperbacks. Receives 5,000 submissions annually. 3 percent of books from first-time authors. Prefers mss through agents. Age-appropriate length. Royalty & advance vary. Average first printing varies. Publication within 36 mos. No simultaneous submissions (mark "Exclusive" on envelope). Responds in 3 mos. Guidelines by mail/e-mail/Website; catalog for 9 x 12 SASE/4 stamps.

Fiction: Proposal/3 chapters for book length; complete ms for picture books. For children and teens. No e-mail or fax submissions.

Artwork: Please do not send illustrations with picture-book manuscripts unless you are a professional illustrator. When submitting artwork, send color copies, not originals. Send illustrations sample to Gayle Brown, art dir.

Tips: "Most open to thoughtful submissions that address needs in children's literature. We are not looking for Christmas stories at this time."

WM. B. EERDMANS PUBLISHING CO. 2140 Oak Industrial Dr. N.E., Grand Rapids MI 49505. Toll-free (800) 253-7521. (616) 459-4591. Fax (616) 459-6540. E-mail: info@eerdmans.com. Website: www.eerdmans.com. Protestant/Academic/Theological. Jon Pott, ed-in-chief. Imprint: Eerdmans Books for Young Readers (see separate listing). Publishes 120-130 titles/yr.; hardcover, trade paperbacks. Receives 3,000-4,000 submissions annually. 10 percent of books from first-time authors. Accepts mss through agents or authors. Reprints books. Royalty; occasional advance. Average first printing 4,000. Publication within 1 yr. Considers simultaneous submissions. Responds to query in 4 wks.; several months for mss. Guidelines by mail/Website (www.eerdmans.com/submit. htm); free catalog.

Nonfiction: Proposal/2-3 chapters; no fax/e-query. "Looking for religious approaches to contemporary issues, spiritual growth, scholarly works."

Fiction: Proposal/chapter; no fax/e-query. For all ages. "We are looking for adult novels with high literary merit."

Tips: "Most open to material with general appeal, but well-researched, cutting-edge material that bridges the gap between evangelical and mainline worlds. Please include e-mail and/or SASE for a response."
**Note: This publisher serviced by The Writer's Edge.

+ **E.F.S. ONLINE PUBLISHING.** 2844 Eighth Ave., Ste. 6E, New York NY 10039. (212) 283-8899. E-mail: efsenterprises@hotmail.com. Website: www.efs-enterprises.com. E.F.S. Enterprises Inc. Zeretha Jenkins, ed. Submit to Rita Baxter. Focuses on extremely well-written fiction and nonfiction that can compete with books published by larger houses; quality work that can stand the test of time. Imprints: E.F.S. Books & E.F.S. Drama Series. Publishes 10-20 titles/yr.; hardcover, trade paperbacks, mass-market paperbacks. Receives 200-250 submissions annually. 90 percent of books from first-time authors. Accepts mss through agents or authors. **SUBSIDY PUBLISHES 10-20 PERCENT** (new/unknown authors). No reprints. Royalty 20-30 percent on net; advance considered for established authors. Average first printing 100-300. Publication within 4-5 mos. No simultaneous submissions. Responds in 1-2 mos. Guidelines on Website; catalog online.
    Nonfiction: Query first (complete ms for subsidy deals); e-query OK.
    Fiction: Query first (complete ms for subsidy deals); e-query OK. "Looking for adult religious fiction; ethnic fiction; contemporary fiction; well-written, clean fiction."
    Special Needs: Very well-written inspirational fiction and nonfiction with a 21st-century flair.
    Ethnic Books: African American and other ethnicities.
    Artwork: Accepts queries from freelance artists.
    Contest: Sponsors three contests: Women's Empowerment Awards Writing Competition, Annual Writing Competition, and Religious Fiction & Nonfiction Writing Competition. See Website for details.
    Tips: "(1) Most open to a well-written book that's plot-driven and supported by a dynamic cast of characters. (2) Proofread your manuscript before submitting. (3) Learn as much as possible about contemporary publishing."

ELDRIDGE PLAYS & MUSICALS. PO Box 14367, Tallahassee FL 32317. (850) 385-2463. Fax (850) 385-2463. E-mail: info@histage.com. Website: www.95church.com. Independent Christian drama publisher. Susan Shore, new plays ed. To provide superior religious drama to enhance preaching and teaching, whatever your Christian denomination. Publishes 15 plays and 2 musicals/yr. Receives 350-400 plays annually. 75 percent of plays from first-time authors. One-act to full-length plays. Outright purchases of $100-1,000 on publication; no advance. Publication within 1 yr. Considers simultaneous submissions. Responds in 2 mos. Requires requested ms on disk or by e-mail. Free guidelines by mail/e-mail/Website; catalog by mail.
    Plays: Complete ms; e-query OK. For children, teens, and adults. Send by e-mail to NewWorks@histage.com or by mail to editor and address above.
    Special Needs: Always looking for high-quality Christmas and Easter plays but open to other holiday and "anytime" Christian plays, too. Can be biblical or contemporary and for performance by all ages, children through adult.
    Tips: "Have play produced at your church and others prior to submission, to work out the bugs. At least try a stage reading."

ELIJAH PRESS. Meadow House Communications Inc., PO Box 317628, Cincinnati OH 45231-7628. (513) 521-7362. Fax (513) 521-7364. Website: www.elijahpress.com. Publishes quality religious/spiritual fiction and nonfiction books and tapes on and related to Christian living, church history, and spiritual reflection. S. R. Davis, ed. Publishes 3-5 titles/yr. Prefers 50,000-100,000 wds. Responds in 1 mo. Guidelines on Website. Incomplete topical listings.
    Nonfiction: One-page query; must have completed ms; no phone/e-query.
    Fiction: Accepts fiction.

EMMAUS ROAD PUBLISHING. 827 N. Fourth St., Steubenville OH 43952. Toll-free (800) 398-5470. (740) 283-2484. Fax (740) 283-4011. E-mail: questions@emmausroad.org. Website: www.emmausroad.org. Catholics United for the Faith. Shannon Minch-Hughes, V.P. Operations. To produce solid Catholic resources. Publishes 8-10 titles/yr.; hardcover, trade paperbacks. Receives 25 submissions annually. 20 percent of books from first-time authors. No mss through agents. No subsidy or print-on-demand. No reprints. Prefers 250 pgs. Royalty on net; no advance. Average first printing 5,000. Publication within 18 mos. Considers simultaneous submissions. Guidelines by e-mail; free catalog.

Nonfiction: Complete ms.
Special Needs: Bible studies.
Ethnic Books: Hispanic.
Also Does: Booklets and pamphlets.

+ **ENCORE PERFORMANCE PUBLISHING**. PO Box 14367, Tallahassee FL 32317. Phone/fax (850) 385-2463. E-mail: info@encoreplay.com. Website: www.encoreplay.com. Eldridge Publishing. Meredith Edwards, mng. dir. Specializes in children's plays and musicals and wholesome family entertainment for schools and churches. Publishes 5-10 titles/yr. Receives 75 submissions annually. Royalty 10 percent on copy sales; 50 percent performance royalty; $100-1,000 for outright purchases; no advance. Print-on-demand. Publication within 6 mos. Considers simultaneous submissions. Responds in 2 mos. Prefers accepted mss by e-mail. Guidelines on Website; catalog.

Nonfiction: Submit synopsis to NewWorks@encore.com. Publishes resource books for all ages on such topics as theatre arts, acting, auditions, improvisation, stage management, etc.
Fiction: Submit synopsis and production history to NewWorks@encore.com. Publishes full-length plays and musicals, skits, and monologue collections, from elementary school through high school. Genres include comedy and drama, multicultural and Christian.
Tips: "We're especially interested in plays and musicals for children, tweens, and teens to help them navigate through the perilous waters of middle school and high school. We're looking for honest but entertaining works."

ETC PUBLICATIONS. 1456 Rodeo Rd., Palm Springs CA 92262. Toll-free (866) 514-9969. (760) 316-9695. Fax (760) 316-9681. Website: www.etcpublications.com. Education Technology Communications. Dr. Richard W. Hostrop, pub.; Lee Ona S. Hostrop, ed. dir. Publishes textbooks for the Christian and general markets at all levels of education. Publishes 6-12 titles/yr.; hardcover, trade paperbacks. Receives 50 submissions annually. 75 percent of books from first-time authors. Accepts mss through agents or authors. No reprints. Prefers 128-256 pgs. Royalty 5-15 percent on net or retail; no advance. Average first printing 1,500-2,500. Publication within 9 mos. No simultaneous submissions. Responds in 10 days. No guidelines (use *Chicago Manual of Style*); catalog for #10 SASE/1 stamp.

Nonfiction: Complete ms; e-query OK. "We are interested only in Christian-oriented, state history textbooks to be used in Christian schools and by homeschoolers."
Photos: Accepts freelance photos for book covers.
Tips: "Open only to state histories that are required at a specific grade level and are Christian oriented, with illustrations."

@ **EVANGELICAL PRESS**. PO Box 825, Webster NY 14580. Toll-free phone/fax (866) 588-6778. E-mail: editor@evangelicalpress.org. Website: www.evangelicalpress.org. Evangelical Press and Services Ltd. Submit to Book Editor. Committed to the dissemination of biblical Christianity throughout the world in numerous languages, and to support local Christians in local churches to live lives that glorify God. Publishes 24 titles/yr.; hardcover, trade paperbacks, mass-market paperbacks. Receives 300+ submissions annually. 80 percent of books from first-time authors. No mss through agents. Does print-on-demand. No reprints. Royalty on net; no advance. Average first printing 3,000. Publication within 12-18 mos. No simultaneous submissions. Accepts requested mss by e-mail. Responds within 3 mos. Prefers NIV/ESV/NKJV. Guidelines by e-mail/Website; free catalog by mail.

Nonfiction: Query, proposal/2 chapters or complete ms; phone/e-query OK.

Also Does: E-books.

Tips: "Understand what our publishing company stands for."

EVERGREEN PRESS. 6140 Rangeline Rd. #A, Theodore AL 36582-5201. (251) 973-0680. Fax (251) 973-0682. E-mail: Brian@evergreenpress.com. Website: www.evergreenpress.com. Genesis Communications. Brian Banashak, pub.; Kathy Banashak, ed-in-chief. Publishes books that empower people for breakthrough living by being practical, biblical, and engaging. Imprints: Evergreen Press, Gazelle Press, Axiom Press (print-on-demand). Publishes 30 titles/yr. Receives 250 submissions annually. 40 percent of books from first-time authors. Accepts mss through agents or authors. **SUBSIDY PUBLISHES 35 PERCENT**. Does print-on-demand. No reprints. Prefers 96-160 pgs. Royalty on net; no advance. Average first printing 4,000. Publication within 6 mos. Considers simultaneous submissions. Requires requested ms on disk or by e-mail. Responds in 4-6 wks. Guidelines on Website; free catalog.

Nonfiction: Complete ms; fax/e-query OK. Submission form on Website.

Fiction: For all ages. Complete ms; phone/fax/e-query OK. Submission form on Website.

Special Needs: Business, finance, personal growth, women's issues, family/parenting, relationships, prayer, humor, and angels.

Also Does: Booklets.

Tips: "Most open to books with a specific market (targeted, not general) that the author is qualified to write for and that is relevant to today's believers and seekers. Author must also be open to editorial direction."

EXTREME DIVA MEDIA, INC. E-mail: query@extremedivamedia.com. Jean Ann Duckworth, ed./pub. Publishes books in 4 areas: reducing stress, increasing joy, simplifying life, and enhancing relationships. Guidelines on Website: www.extremedivamedia.com.

Nonfiction: E-query only. Full manuscripts will be discarded unless requested.

Special Needs: Devotions to Go (30-day devotionals); Self Improvement; Cookbooks/ Entertainment Guides. New series "Girlfriends On . . ." was introduced in 2009. Now accepting submissions. Guidelines on Website.

Tips: "We create books to help women live better lives. Show us how your book contributes to this mission."

FACTS ON FILE INC. 132 W. 31st St., 17th Fl., New York NY 10001. Toll-free (800) 322-8755. (212) 967-8800. Fax (212) 967-9196. E-mail: llikoff@factsonfile.com or editorial@factsonfile .com. Website: www.factsonfile.com. Laurie Likoff, ed. dir. School and library reference and trade books (for middle- to high-school students) tied to curriculum and areas of cross-cultural studies, including religion. Imprint: Checkmark Books. Publishes 3-5 religious titles/yr. Receives 10-20 submissions annually. 2 percent of books from first-time authors. Accepts mss through agents or authors. No reprints. Prefers 224-480 pgs. Royalty 10 percent on retail; outright purchases of $2,000-10,000; advance $5,000-10,000. Some work-for-hire. Average first printing 2,500. Publication within 9-12 mos. Considers simultaneous submissions. Responds in 2 mos. Requires requested ms on disk. Guidelines by mail/Website; free catalog by mail.

Nonfiction: Query or proposal/1 chapter; fax/e-query OK.

Tips: "Most open to reference books tied to curriculum subjects or disciplines."

FAIR HAVENS PUBLICATIONS. PO Box 1238, Gainesville TX 76241-1238. Toll-free (800) 771-4861. (940) 668-6044. Fax (940) 668-6984. E-mail through Website: www.fairhavenspub.com. Submit to Acquisitions Department. Produces quality books, teaching and evangelistic literature, audiotapes and videotapes, CD-ROMs, dramas, and artworks that inspire faith and courage. Publishes 1-2 titles/yr.; hardcover, trade paperbacks. Receives 100 submissions annually. No first-time authors. Accepts mss through agents or authors. **SUBSIDY PUBLISHES 25 PERCENT**; does print-on-demand. Reprints books. Prefers 250-300 pgs. Royalty 10-18 percent on net; no advance (negotiable for published authors). Average first printing 3,000-12,000. Publication within 8 mos. Considers simultaneous submissions. Responds in 12 or more wks. Requires requested ms on disk. Prefers NKJV. Guidelines on Website; no catalog.

Nonfiction: Proposal/3 chapters; no phone/fax/e-query. "We are interested in books based on original research based on compiled data, case studies, etc."

Special Needs: Nonfiction; personal experience; how-to books packed with practical information relating to a felt need.

Also Does: Booklets, audio & videotapes, CD-ROMs, dramas.

Photos/Artwork: Accepts freelance photos for book covers; open to queries from freelance artists.

Tips: "We are flexible and work closely with our authors. We will help authors to self-publish if we do not elect to publish their manuscripts."

FAITH ALIVE CHRISTIAN RESOURCES. 2850 Kalamazoo Ave. S.E., Grand Rapids MI 49560. Toll-free (800) 333-8300. (616) 224-0819 or (616) 224-0728. E-mail: info@faithaliveresources.org. Website: www.faithaliveresources.org. CRC Publications/Christian Reformed Church. Ruth Vanderhart, mng. ed. Guidelines on Website.

Artwork: Open to queries from freelance artists; contact Dean Heetderks, art dir.

+ **FAITH BOOKS & MORE**. 3255 Lawrenceville-Suwanee Rd., Ste. P250, Suwanee GA 30024. (678) 232-6156. Toll-free fax (888) 479-4540. E-mail: publishing@faithbooksandmore.com. Website: www .faithbooksandmore.com. 100% custom publishing. Nicole Smith, mng. ed. Baptist. Imprints: Friends of Faith, Corporate Connoisseur. Publishes 10 titles/yr. Receives 20 submissions annually. 80 percent of books from first-time authors. Accepts mss through agents. **SUBSIDY PUBLISHES 50 PERCENT**; does print-on-demand. Does hardcover, trade paperbacks, and mass-market paperbacks. Reprints books. Any length; no less than 4 pages. Royalty; no advance. Publication within 2 mos. Considers simultaneous submissions. Responds in 3 mos. Prefers NKJV or NIV. Guidelines by e-mail/Website; no catalog.

Nonfiction: Any topic. Complete ms; phone/e-query OK.

Fiction: Any genre, for all ages. Complete ms; phone/e-query OK.

Photos/Artwork: Accepts freelance photos for book covers; considers queries from freelance artists.

FAITH COMMUNICATIONS—See Health Communications.

FAITHWALK PUBLISHING. 517 S. Main St., Lima OH 45804. Toll-free (800) 241-4056. (419) 227-1818. Fax (419) 228-9184. E-mail: submissions@faithwalkpub.com. Website: www.faithwalk pub.com. Imprint of CSS Publishing. Dirk Wierenga, ed. (Send submission c/o Dirk Wierenga, 14140 Payne Forest, Grand Haven MI 49417, or e-query to dirkbw@gmail.com.) Called to publish books that appeal to seekers and believers who might otherwise never purchase a religious book. Publishes 10 titles/yr. Receives 500+ submissions annually. 10 percent of books from first-time authors. Accepts mss through agents or authors. No reprints. Prefers 160-356 pgs. Royalty 6-10 percent on retail; no advance. Average first printing 2,000-5,000. Publication within 12-18 mos. Considers simultaneous submissions (if indicated). Does not respond to submissions unless interested (no SASE needed). Prefers NIV, NRSV. Guidelines by mail/e-mail/Website; catalog.

Nonfiction: Proposal/1-2 chapters; no fax submissions; e-query OK. No children's or gift books.

Fiction: Proposal/1-2 chapters; e-query OK. Adult; adventure, contemporary, and literary.

Photos: Accepts freelance photos for book covers.

FAITHWORDS/HACHETTE BOOK GROUP. 10 Cadillac Dr., Ste. 220, Brentwood TN 37027. (615) 221-0996. Fax (615) 221-0962. Website: www.faithwords.com. Hachette Book Group USA. Anne Horch, ed. Publishes 40 titles/yr.; hardcover, trade paperbacks, mass-market paperbacks. Few books from first-time authors. Requires mss through agents. Prefers 60,000-90,000 wds. Royalty on retail; pays an advance. Publication within 12 mos. Considers simultaneous submissions. Prefers proposals & accepted ms by e-mail.

   Nonfiction: Proposal with table of contents/3 chapters. No phone/fax query; e-query OK.
   Fiction: For teens and adults. Proposal/3 chapters.
   **Note: This publisher serviced by ChristianManuscriptSubmissions.com.

FAMILYLIFE PUBLISHING. PO Box 7111, Little Rock AR 72223. Toll-free (800) 358-6329. E-mail through Website: www.familylife.com. Campus Crusade for Christ. Margie Clark, product development mngr. Our uniqueness is creating/publishing connecting resources: marrying together truth, relationship, and experience. Publishes 10 titles/yr.; hardcover, trade paperbacks. Receives 100 submissions annually. 10 percent of books from first-time authors. Accepts mss through agents or authors. Reprints books. Royalty 2-18 percent of net or outright purchase; pays an advance. Average first printing 10,000. Publication within 12 mos. Considers simultaneous submissions. Requires submissions on disk or by e-mail. Responds in 6 mos. Prefers NASB, ESV, NIV. Guidelines by mail/e-mail/Website; catalog on Website or for 9 x 12 SASE/4 stamps.

   Nonfiction: Proposal/2 chapters; e-query OK. "Looking for books on marriage: intimacy, communication."
   Also Does: Booklets; multipiece activity packs.
   Photos/Artwork: Accepts freelance photos for book covers; open to queries from freelance artists.
   Tips: "Most open to multipiece, interactive products. The query and proposal should be professional. Before you submit to us, be sure to read our writer's guidelines and The Family Manifesto (both on Website). If you don't know who we are or what we do, please send your material elsewhere."
   **Note: This publisher serviced by ChristianManuscriptSubmissions.com.

FATHER'S PRESS. 2424 S.E. 6th St., Lee's Summit MO 64063. Phone/fax (816) 600-6288. E-mail: fatherspress@yahoo.com. Website: www.fatherspress.com. Mike Smitley, owner (mikesmitley2@ yahoo.com). Publishes controversial and risky books that present the biblical truth about issues facing Christians and nonbelievers today. Publishes 6-10 titles/yr.; hardcover, trade paperbacks, mass-market paperbacks, coffee-table books. Receives 800-1,000 submissions annually. 50 percent of books from first-time authors. No mss through agents. No subsidy or print-on-demand. No reprints. Prefers 100 pgs. & up. Royalty 10-15 percent on net; no advance. Average first printing 500. Publication within 6 mos. Considers simultaneous submissions. Accepted mss by disk or e-mail. Responds in 7 days. Prefers KJV. Guidelines by mail/e-mail/Website; no catalog.

   Nonfiction: Query first; proposal/1chapter; phone/e-query OK.
   Fiction: For all ages. Query first; phone/fax/e-query OK.
   Special Needs: Books that deal with issues contributing to the decline of our economy and culture.
   Photos: Accepts freelance photos for book covers.
   Tips: "We prefer books with strong social, economic, and religious relevance. We like writers with a clear marketing strategy with strong sales leads and endorsements."

FREDERICK FELL PUBLISHERS, INC. 2131 Hollywood Blvd., Ste. 305, Hollywood FL 33020. (954) 925-5242. Fax (954) 925-5244. E-mail through Website: www.fellpub.com. Submit to Editorial Dept. General publisher that publishes 2-4 religious titles/yr.; hardcover, trade paperbacks. Receives 4,000 submissions annually. 95 percent of books from first-time authors. Reprints books.

Prefers 60,000 words or 200-300 pgs. Royalty 6-15 percent on retail; advance $500-10,000. Average first printing 7,500. Publication within 1 yr. Considers simultaneous submissions. Responds in 5-13 wks. Requires submissions by e-mail. Guidelines on Website.

Nonfiction: Proposal/2 chapters; no phone/fax/e-query. Looking for self-help and how-to books. Include a clear marketing and promotional strategy.

Fiction: Complete ms; no phone/fax/e-query. For adults; adventure and historical. "Looking for great story lines, with potential movie prospects."

Tips: "Spirituality, optimism, and a positive attitude have international appeal. Steer clear of doom and gloom; less sadness and more gladness benefits all." Also publishes New Age books. SASE required.

FIFTH-ESTATE PUBLISHERS. PO Box 116, Blountsville AL 35031. Toll-free (888) 734-2476. (205) 237-9511. E-mail: admin@fifth-estate.net. Website: www.fifth-estate.net. Joseph Lumpkin, exec. ed. Publishes 10 titles/yr.; hardcover, trade paperbacks, mass-market paperbacks. Receives 100+ submissions annually. 20 percent of books from first-time authors. No mss through agents. No subsidy; does print-on-demand. Reprints books. Prefers 104-732 pgs. Royalty 35-50 percent on net; or outright purchases of $6-30/bk.; no advance. Publication within 3 mos. No simultaneous submissions. Responds in 2 wks. Requires accepted ms on disk or by e-mail. Guidelines on Website; no catalog.

Nonfiction: Query only first; e-query OK. "Looking for spiritual and children's books."

Tips: "When an author tells me their book is different, I usually find it is not. Find what is in demand; write about it; and write it well."

FIRST FRUITS OF ZION, PO Box 649, Marshfield MO 65706-0649. Toll-free (800) 775-4807. (417) 468-2741. Fax (417) 468-2745. E-mail through Website: www.ffoz.org. Hope Egan, ed. A nonprofit ministry devoted to strengthening the love and appreciation of the Body of Messiah for the land, people, and Scripture of Israel. Publishes 2-6 titles/yr.; trade paperbacks. No mss through agents. Royalty; no advance. Publication within 6 mos. Considers simultaneous submissions. Responds in 1 mo. Prefers NASB.

Nonfiction: Query first; no phone/fax/e-query.

Special Needs: Books on Jewish or Hebraic roots only.

Tips: "Be very familiar with our material before submitting to us."

FOCUS ON THE FAMILY BOOK PUBLISHING AND RESOURCE DEVELOPMENT. (street address not required), Colorado Springs CO 80995. (719) 531-3400. Fax (719) 531-3448. E-mail through Website: www.focusonthefamily.com. Exists to support the family; all our products are about topics pertaining to families. Publishes 30-40 titles/yr.; hardcover, trade paperbacks, mass-market paperbacks (rarely). 12 percent of books from first-time authors. Rarely reprints books. Length depends on genre. Royalty or work-for-hire; advance varies. Average first printing varies. Publication within 18 mos. No longer considers unsolicited submissions. Responds in 1-3 mos. Prefers NIV (but accepts 10 others). Guidelines by e-mail/Website; no catalog.

Nonfiction: Query letter only through an agent or writers' conference contact with a Focus editor. "Most open to family advice topics. We look for excellent writing and topics that haven't been done to death—or that have a unique angle."

Fiction: Query letter only through an agent or writer's conference contact with a Focus editor. Stories must incorporate traditional family values or family issues; from 1900 to present day. Also does Mom Lit.

Artwork: Open to queries from freelance artists (but not for specific projects).

**Note: This publisher serviced by The Writer's Edge and ChristianManuscriptSubmissions.com.

FORDHAM UNIVERSITY PRESS. 2546 Belmont Ave., University Box L, Bronx NY 10458. (718) 817-4795. Fax (718) 817-4785. E-mail: tartar@fordham.edu. Website: www.fordhampress.com. Helen

Tartar, ed. dir.; Eric Newman, mng. ed. Publishes for both an academic and general audience; includes religion. Publishes hardcover & trade paperbacks. Reprints books. Guidelines on Website; catalog.

Nonfiction: Query; no e-query.

FORTRESS PRESS. Box 1209, Minneapolis MN 55440-1209. (612) 330-3300. Fax (612) 330-3215. E-mail: booksub@augsburgfortress.org. Website: www.fortresspress.com. Submit to Book Submissions. Publishes religious academic books. Publishes 60 titles/yr.; hardcover, trade paperbacks. Receives 1,000 submissions annually. 10 percent of books from first-time authors. Accepts mss through agents or authors. No reprints. Royalty on net. Considers simultaneous submissions. Responds in 3 mos. Guidelines on Website; free catalog (call 1-800-328-4648).

Nonfiction: Query/sample pages. "Please study guidelines before submitting."
Ethnic Books: African American studies.

FORWARD MOVEMENT. 300 W. 4th St., Cincinnati OH 45202-2666. Toll-free (800) 543-1813. (513) 721-6659. Fax (513) 721-0729. E-mail: rschmidt@forwarddaybyday.com. Website: www.forwardmovement.org. Episcopal. Submit to The Editor. Provides resources to support persons in their lives of prayer and faith. Publishes 2-3 books/yr. and 25 tracts & booklets. Receives 1,000 submissions annually. 50 percent of books from first-time authors. No mss through agents. No reprints. Prefers up to 200 pgs. Onetime honorarium; no advance. Average first printing 5,000. Publication within 9 mos. Considers simultaneous submissions. Prefers requested ms on disk as an RTF file. Responds in 1-2 mos. Prefers NRSV. Guidelines by mail; free catalog.

Nonfiction: Query for book, complete ms if short; no phone/fax/e-query. "Looking for books on prayer and spirituality, devotionals, Christian living, and spiritual life."
Ethnic Books: African American & Hispanic (pamphlets).
Also Does: Booklets, 4-32 pgs.; pamphlets, 4-8 pgs.; tracts.
Tips: "We sell primarily to a mainline Protestant audience. Most open to books that deal with the central doctrines of the Christian faith. Spirituality and Christian living."

FOUNDERS PRESS. PO Box 150931, Cape Coral FL 33915. (239) 772-1400. Fax (239) 772-1140. E-mail through Website: www.founders.org. Founders Ministries/Southern Baptist. Kenneth Puls, ed. Committed to producing and distributing books, pamphlets, and other materials that are consistent with the doctrines of grace and that speak from a historic Southern Baptist perspective. Responds in 4 mos. (or contact them). Guidelines on Website. Incomplete topical listings.

Nonfiction: Proposal plus completed author information sheet (available on the Website).
Also Does: Pamphlets.

FOURSQUARE MEDIA. 1910 W. Sunset Blvd., Ste. 200, Los Angeles CA 90026-0176. (213) 989-4494. E-mail: media@foursquare.org. Website: www.foursquare.org/landing_pages/83,3.html. The Foursquare Church; in partnership with Creation House (Strang Communications). Rick Wulfestieg, dir.; Larry Libby, sr. ed. To capture Foursquare history, vision, and values; for cell study groups, church ministry institutes, and pastoral-led congregational studies. Publishes 4+ titles/yr.

Nonfiction: E-query.
Also Does: Will host writers' conferences in the future to encourage ministry leaders in developing writing and publishing skills.

+ FRESH AIR BOOKS. PO Box 340004, Nashville TN 37203-0004. Website: www.freshairbooks.org. Imprint of Upper Room Books. Submit to Acquisitions Ed. Books that inspire readers to explore Christian faith in a fresh, experimental way. Accepts mss through agents or author. Royalty. Guidelines on Website. Incomplete topical listings.

Nonfiction: Proposal/1chapter by mail; no e-query.
Tips: "Rather than telling readers what to do, our books show the way, mostly through stories of people who live out authentic, compassionate faith in the real world. We believe that faith influences everything we do, and therefore, we consider manuscripts that address

most areas of life. Currently we do not publish fiction or poetry, nor do we publish scholarly or academic works."

FRIENDS UNITED PRESS. 101 Quaker Hill Dr., Richmond IN 47374. (765) 962-7573. Fax (765) 966-1293. E-mail: friendspress@fum.org. Website: www.fum.org/shop. Friends United Meeting (Quaker). Katie Terrell, ed. To gather persons into a fellowship where Jesus Christ is known as Lord and Teacher. Publishes 3 titles/yr. Receives 25 submissions annually. 50 percent of books from first-time authors. No mss through agents. Does print-on-demand. Prefers 150-200 pgs. Royalty 7.5 percent of net; no advance. Publication within 1 yr. Considers simultaneous submissions; e-mail submissions preferred. Responds in 6 mos. Prefers requested ms by e-mail. Guidelines by mail/e-mail/Website; free catalog.

   Nonfiction: Proposal/2 chapters; e-query preferred.

   Ethnic Books: Howard Thurman Books (African American), Underground Railroad.

   Tips: "Primarily open to Quaker authors. Looking for Quaker-related spirituality, or current faith issues/practice addressed from a Christian Quaker experience or practice."

+ **GENTLE PATH PRESS**. PO Box 3172, Carefree AZ 85377. (480) 488-0150. Fax (480) 488-9125. E-mail: info@gentlepath.com. Website: www.gentlepath.com. Greg Ottersbach, pub. Focuses on addiction and recovery from both a secular and spiritual point of view. Imprints: Gentle Path Press, Seasons of Hope. Publishes 2-5 titles/yr.; hardcover, trade paperbacks. Receives 6-12 submissions annually. 75 percent of books from first-time authors. Accepts mss through agents or authors. No subsidy or print-on-demand. No reprints. Prefers 200-350 pgs. Royalty 8-12 percent of net; no advance. Average first printing 2,000-5,000. Publication within 6 mos. Considers simultaneous submissions. Responds in 2-3 mos. Guidelines by e-mail; free catalog.

   Nonfiction: Proposal/3 chapters or complete ms; no phone/fax/e-query.

   Special Needs: "Good material on recovery (personal experience OK). Also spirituality, family issues, women's issues, and grief."

GEORGETOWN UNIVERSITY PRESS. 3240 Prospect St. N.W., Washington DC 20007. (202) 687-5889. Fax (202) 687-6340. E-mail: reb7@georgetown.edu or gupress@georgetown.edu. Website: www.press.georgetown.edu. Georgetown University. Richard Brown, dir. Scholarly books in religion, theology, ethics, and other fields, with an emphasis on cross-disciplinary and cross-cultural studies. Publishes 10 titles/yr. Receives 100 submissions annually. 10 percent of books from first-time authors. Accepts mss through agents or authors. No reprints. Prefers 80,000 wds. Royalty 8-12 percent on net; negotiable advance. Average first printing 2,000-3,000. Publication within 9-10 mos. Considers simultaneous submissions. Requires requested ms on disk. Responds in 6-8 wks. Prefers NRSV. Does print-on-demand. Guidelines on Website; free catalog.

   Nonfiction: Guidelines for submitting a proposal are posted on Website. "Should be thoroughly researched and original."

   Special Needs: Work relations, theology, ethics—with scholarly bent.

   Ethnic Books: Hispanic.

   Also Does: CD-ROMs.

   Photos: Accepts freelance photos for book covers.

GOLLEHON PRESS INC. 6157—28th St. S.E., Grand Rapids MI 49546. (616) 949-3515. Fax (616) 949-8674. E-mail: john@gollehonbooks.com. Website: www.gollehonbooks.com. Becky Anderson, ed. Small press willing to work with first-time authors. Publishes 3-4 titles/yr.; hardcover, trade paperbacks. Receives 50-100 submissions annually. 90 percent of books from first-time authors. Accepts mss through agents or authors. No subsidy publishing. No reprints. Prefers 50,000-80,000 words or 200-250 pgs. Royalty 6-8 percent on retail; advance to $1,000. Average first printing 5,000-10,000. Publication within 8-10 mos. Encourages simultaneous submissions. Responds in 1-2 mos., if interested. Prefers KJV. Guidelines pending; no catalog.

Nonfiction: Query letter only first; if interested will request proposal or full ms. Do not send unsolicited mss. Unable to respond to all queries. No phone/fax query; e-query OK.
Fiction: For teens and adults.
Tips: "Most open to miracles, inspirational, and from the heart. Also more scholarly books, such as the first century church. Will help writers understand publishing, what to expect, and what is expected of them to promote their work. We offer a working relationship that is unusual today.
Note: Gollehon Books also publishes books on gambling, as you will see on their Website. But they are now actively seeking manuscripts on Christian themes as well.

GOOD BOOK PUBLISHING COMPANY. PO Box 837, Kihei HI 96753-0837. Phone/fax (808) 874-4876. E-mail: dickb@dickb.com. Website: www.dickb.com. Christian/Protestant/Bible Fellowship. Ken Burns, pres. Researches and publishes books on the biblical/Christian roots of Alcoholics Anonymous. Publishes 1 title/yr.; publishes trade paperbacks, mass-market paperbacks. Receives 8 submissions annually. 80 percent of books from first-time authors. No mss through agents. Reprints books. Prefers 250 pgs. Royalty 10 percent; no advance. Average first printing 3,000. Publication within 2 mos. Considers simultaneous submissions. Responds in 1 wk. No disk. Prefers KJV. No guidelines; free catalog.
Nonfiction: Proposal; no phone/fax/e-query. Books on the spiritual history and success of AA; 12-step spiritual roots; Bible study.
Also Does: Pamphlets, booklets.

GOOD NEWS PUBLISHERS. 1300 Crescent St., Wheaton IL 60187. (630) 682-4300. Fax (630) 682-4785. E-mail: tracts@gnpcb.org. Website: www.goodnewspublishers.org. Kate Felinski, dir. of Literature Ministries. Tracts only; committed to producing solid, biblically sound gospel tracts, with excellent design, and relevant to today's culture. Publishes 30 tracts/yr. Receives 500 submissions annually. 2 percent of tracts from first-time authors. Prefers 650-800 wds. Pays about $150 or a quantity of tracts. Average first printing 100,000. Publication within 16 mos. Considers simultaneous submissions. Responds in 12 wks. Prefers ESV. Guidelines by mail/Website; free tract catalog.
Tracts: Complete ms.
Also Does: Pamphlets.
Tips: "Most open to seasonal tracts—Easter, Halloween, or Christmas. Be concise, clear, and careful with Christian terms."
**Note: This publisher serviced by ChristianManuscriptSubmissions.com.

GOSPEL LIGHT. 1957 Eastman Ave., Ventura CA 93003. Toll-free (800) 4-GOSPEL. (805) 644-9721, ext. 1223. Website: www.gospellight.com. Anita Griggs, ed. Accepts proposals for Sunday school and Vacation Bible School curriculum and related resources for children from birth through the preteen years; also teacher resources. Guidelines on Website.
Also Does: Sometimes has openings for readers of new curriculum projects. See Website for how to apply.
Tips: "All our curriculum is written and field-tested by experienced teachers; most of our writers are on staff."
**Note: This publisher serviced by ChristianManuscriptSubmissions.com.

GOSPEL PUBLISHING HOUSE. 1445 N. Boonville Ave., Springfield MO 65802. Toll-free (800) 641-4310. (417) 831-8000. E-mail: newproducts@gph.org. Website: www.gospelpublishing.com. Assemblies of God. Julie Horner, ed. The majority of titles specifically address Pentecostal audiences in a variety of ministries in the local church. Publishes 5-10 titles/yr. Receives 250 submissions annually. 5 percent of books from first-time authors. Accepts mss through agents or authors. No reprints. Royalty 5-10 percent of retail; no advance. Average first printing 2,000. Publication within 1 yr. Considers simultaneous submissions. Responds in 4 mos. Requires accepted mss on disk or by e-mail. Guidelines on Website; free catalog.

Nonfiction: Proposal/1 chapter; no phone query, e-query OK. "Looking for Holy Spirit; Pentecostal focus for pastors, local church lay leaders, and individuals; children's ministry programs and resources; small group resources."

Tips: "Most open to a new program or resource for small groups, children's ministry, compassion ministry, or evangelistic outreach, written by someone who is actively leading it at the local church."

GROUP PUBLISHING, INC. 1515 Cascade Ave., Loveland CO 80539-0481. Toll-free (800) 447-1070. (970) 292-4243. Fax (970) 622-4370. E-mail: kloesche@group.com. Website: www.group .com. Nondenominational. Kerri Loesche, contract & copyright administrator. Imprint: Group Books. To equip churches to help children, youth, and adults grow in their relationship with Jesus. Publishes 40 titles/yr.; trade paperbacks. Receives 1,000+ submissions annually. 5 percent of books from first-time authors. Accepts mss through agents or authors. **SOME SUBSIDY**. No reprints. Prefers 128-250 pgs. Outright purchases of $25-3,000 or royalty of 8-10 percent of net; advance $3,000. Average first printing 5,000. Publication within 12-18 mos. Considers simultaneous submissions. Responds in 6 mos. Requires requested ms on disk or by e-mail. Prefers NLT. Guidelines by mail (2 stamps) /e-mail/Website; catalog.

Nonfiction: Query or proposal/2 chapters/intro/cover letter/SASE; no phone/fax/e-query. "Looking for practical ministry tools for youth workers, C. E. directors, and teachers with an emphasis on active learning."

Artists: Open to queries from freelance artists.

Tips: "Most open to a practical resource that will help church leaders change lives; innovative, active/interactive learning. Tell our readers something they don't already know, in a way that they've not seen before."

**Note: This publisher serviced by The Writer's Edge and ChristianManuscriptSubmissions.com.

GRQ, INC. PO Box 1067, Brentwood TN 37024. (615) 776-3275. Fax (615) 507-1709. E-mail: rzaloba@comcast.net. Robert Zaloba, pres. A book packager. Publishes 40-50 titles/yr.; hardcover, trade paperbacks, coffee-table books. Receives 200-300 submissions annually. 70 percent of books from first-time authors. Accepts mss through agents or authors. **SUBSIDY PUBLISHES 5 PERCENT**. Reprints books. Does mostly work-for-hire; rates depend on project; ranges from $1,500-$20,000; pays an advance. Average first printing varies, 10,000-50,000. Publication within 10 mos. Considers simultaneous submissions. Response time varies. Requires accepted ms on disk. No guidelines or catalog.

Nonfiction: Query only first; no phone/fax query; e-query OK.

Tips: "We are a book packager who produces books that speak to the Christian market at large. Our books are found outside of the traditional CBA market. They are uniquely formatted and targeted for an 'average' reader. Most open to practical, unique self-help; unique devotions."

GRUPO NELSON. PO Box 141000, Nashville TN 37214. Toll-free (800) 322-7423. (615) 902-2372/2375. Fax (615) 883-9376. E-mail: storres@thomasnelson.com. Website: www.gruponelson .com. Thomas Nelson has re-formed its Spanish division into Grupo Nelson, with five Spanish-language imprints listed below. Larry Downs, VP/Publisher. Targets the needs and wants of the Hispanic community. Publishes 65-80 titles/yr. Receives 50 submissions annually. 90 percent of books from first-time authors. No mss through agents. Prefers 192 pgs. Royalty on net; advance $500. Average first printing 4,000. Publication within 15 mos. Accepts e-mail submissions. No guidelines; free catalog.

Nonfiction: Query letter only; no phone/fax/e-query.

Ethnic Books: Hispanic imprints.

Also Does: Computer games.

Tips: "Most open to Christian books based on the Bible."

Editorial Diez Puntos: Specializes in parenting & family, personal finance, health & fitness, self-help, and popular culture.

Leader Latino: Business & leadership.

Editorial Caribe: Bibles, Bible reference, and electronic products.

Editorial Betania: Inspirational, popular religious, and children's.

Editorial Catolica: Catholic books and Bibles.

@ GUARDIAN ANGEL PUBLISHING INC. 12430 Teeson Ferry Rd., #186, St. Louis MO 63128. (314) 276-8482. Fax (314) 843-8517. E-mail: publisher@guardianangelpublishing.com. Website: www.guardianangelpublishing.com. Lynda S. Burch, pub. Goal is to inspire children to learn and grow and develop character skills to instill a Christian and healthy attitude of learning, caring, and sharing. Imprints: Wings of Faith, Angel to Angel, Angelic Harmony, Littlest Angels, Academic Wings, Guardian Angel Pets, Guardian Angel Health & Hygiene. Publishes 24-36 titles/yr.; trade paperbacks, coffee-table books. Receives 300-600 submissions annually. 75 percent of books from first-time authors. No subsidy; does print-on-demand. Prefers 100-5,000 words or 32 pgs. Royalty 30-50 percent on download; no advance. Average first printing 50-100. Print books are wholesaled and distributed; e-books are sold through many distribution networks. Publication within 6-12 mos. No simultaneous submissions. Responds in 1 wk.-1 mo. Accepted mss by e-mail. Guidelines on Website; catalog as e-book PDF.

> **Nonfiction:** Complete ms; no phone/fax query; e-query OK. "Looking for all kinds of kids' books."

> **Fiction:** Complete ms; no phone/fax query; e-query OK.

> **Also Does:** E-books.

> **Photos/Artwork:** Accepts freelance photos for book covers; open to queries from freelance artists.

> **Contest:** Sponsors children's writing contest for schools.

> **Tips:** "Most open to books that teach children to read and love books; to learn or grow from books."

GUERNICA EDITIONS. 8075 Marie Brandon, Montreal QC H1E 3P6, Canada. E-mail: guernicaeditions@cs.com. Website: www.guernicaeditions.com. Antonio D'Alfonso, ed. Deals with cultural bridging; interested in the next generation of writers. Publishes 1 religious title/yr.; trade paperbacks, mass-market paperbacks. Receives 100 submissions annually. 5 percent of books from first-time authors. No mss through agents. Reprints books. Prefers 100 pgs. Royalty 8-10 percent of retail; some outright purchases of $200-5,000; advance $200-2,000. Average first printing 1,500. Publication within 10 mos. Responds in 1-6 mos. Requires requested ms on disk; no e-mail. No guidelines (read one of our books to see what we like); catalog online.

> **Nonfiction:** Query only first; no phone/fax/e-query. "Looking for books on world issues."

> **Fiction:** Query only first. "Looking for short and profound literary works."

> **Ethnic Books:** Concentration on other cultures. "We are involved in translations and ethnic issues."

> **Photos:** Accepts freelance photos for book covers.

> **Tips:** "Know what we publish. We're interested in books that bridge time and space, works that fit our editorial literary policies." Responds only if you include International Reply Coupons.

GUIDEPOSTS BOOKS. 16 E. 34th St., 12th Fl., New York NY 10016-4397. (212) 251-8143. Website: www.guidepostsbooks.com. Guideposts Inc. Linda Raglan Cunningham, VP/ed-in-chief; Andrew Attaway, sr. acq. ed. Focuses on inspirational fiction, memoirs, story collections, devotionals, and faith-based true stories. Publishes 20 titles/yr.

Note: This publisher serviced by ChristianManuscriptSubmissions.com.

HANNIBAL BOOKS. PO Box 461592, Garland TX 75046-1592. Toll-free (800) 747-0738. Toll-free fax (888) 252-3022. E-mail: hannibalbooks@earthlink.net. Website: www.hannibalbooks.com. KLMK Communications Inc. Louis Moore, pub. Evangelical Christian publisher specializing in missions, marriage and family, critical issues, and Bible-study curriculum. Publishes 8-10 titles/yr.; trade paperbacks, mass-market paperbacks. Receives 300 submissions annually. 80 percent of books from first-time authors. Accepts mss through agents or authors. Some print-on-demand. Prefers 50,000-60,000 wds. Royalty on net or outright purchase; no advance. Average first printing 2,000-10,000. Publication within 3 mos. No simultaneous submissions. Responds in 3 mos. Prefers NIV. Guidelines/free catalog by mail.

> **Nonfiction:** Book proposal/1-3 chapters; no phone/fax/e-query. "Looking for missionary, marriage restoration, homeschooling, and devotionals."
> **Fiction:** Book proposal/1-3 chapters; no phone/fax/e-query.
> **Tips:** "We are looking for go-get-'em new authors with a passion to be published. Most open to missionary life and Bible studies. Obtain our guidelines and answer each question thoroughly."

HARCOURT RELIGION PUBLISHERS. 6277 Sea Harbor Dr., Orlando FL 32887. Toll-free (800) 922-7696. (407) 345-3800. Fax (407) 345-3798. E-mail: hrpwebmaster@harcourt.com. Website: www.harcourtreligion.com. Catholic. Craig O'Neil, sr. ed. Catholic educational market; high school curriculum. Publishes 50-100 titles/yr. Receives 100-300 submissions annually. Variable royalty or outright purchase; rarely pays advance. Average first printing 1,000-3,000. Publication within 1 yr. Considers simultaneous submissions. Responds in 6 mos. Free catalog.

> **Nonfiction:** Complete ms. "Looking primarily for school and parish textbooks."
> **Photos:** Accepts freelance photos for book covers. Submit to Lynn Molony, production mngr.

HARPERONE. 353 Sacramento St., #500, San Francisco CA 94111-3653. (415) 477-4400. Fax (415) 477-4444. E-mail: hcsanfrancisco@harpercollins.com. Website: www.harpercollins.com. Religious division of HarperCollins. Michael G. Maudlin, ed. dir. Strives to be the preeminent publisher of the most important books across the full spectrum of religion and spiritual literature, adding to the wealth of the world's wisdom by respecting all traditions and favoring none; emphasis on quality Christian spirituality and literary fiction. Publishes 75 titles/yr.; hardcover, trade paperbacks. Receives 10,000 submissions annually. 5 percent of books from first-time authors. Requires mss through agents. No reprints. Prefers 160-256 pgs. Royalty 7.5-15 percent on retail; advance $20,000-100,000. Average first printing 10,000. Publication within 18 mos. Considers simultaneous submissions. Responds in 3 mos. Requires requested ms on disk. No guidelines/catalog.

> **Nonfiction:** Proposal/1 chapter; fax query OK.
> **Fiction:** Complete ms; contemporary adult fiction, literary, fables & parables, spiritual.
> **Tips:** "Agented proposals only."

HARRISON HOUSE PUBLISHERS. Box 35035, Tulsa OK 74153. Toll-free (800) 888-4126. (918) 523-5400. E-mail: customerservice@harrisonhouse.com. Website: www.harrisonhouse.com. Evangelical/charismatic. Julie Lechlider, mng. ed. To challenge Christians to live victoriously, grow spiritually, and know God intimately. Publishes 20 titles/yr.; hardcover, trade paperbacks, mass-market paperbacks. 5 percent of books from first-time authors. No mss through agents. No reprints. Royalty on net or retail; no advance. Average first printing 5,000. Publication within 12-24 mos. Responds in 6 mos. Accepts requested ms by e-mail. No guidelines or catalog. Not currently accepting proposals or manuscripts.

> **Nonfiction:** Query first; then proposal/table of contents/1 chapter; no phone/fax query; e-query OK.
> ****Note:** This publisher serviced by ChristianManuscriptSubmissions.com.

HARVEST DAY BOOKS. 10300 E. Leelanau Ct., Traverse City MI 49684. (231) 929-1999. Fax (231) 929-1993. E-mail: Info@bookmarketingsolutions.com. Website: www.BookMarketingSolutions

.com. Imprint of Book Marketing Solutions LLC. Tom White, pres. (tom@BookMarketingSolutions .com). Publishes works of the Christian faith. Guidelines on Website.

Nonfiction: Submission form on Website.

Poetry: Also accepting submissions for a 5-book poetry series called "Of the Heart." Although not exclusively Christian, they are hoping for an excellent Christian representation. For details, see Website or contact Tom White.

HARVEST HOUSE PUBLISHERS. 990 Owen Loop N., Eugene OR 97402. (541) 343-0123. E-mail: admin@harvesthousepublishers.com. Website: www.harvesthousepublishers.com. Evangelical. Books and products that affirm biblical values and help people grow spiritually strong. Publishes 170 titles/ yr.; hardcover, trade paperbacks, mass-market paperbacks, coffee-table books. No longer accepting unsolicited submissions, proposals, queries, etc. Requires mss through agents. No guidelines/catalog.

Nonfiction: Self-help; Christian living.

Fiction: Interesting women's fiction.

Tips: "Find a good agent."

**Note: This publisher serviced by The Writer's Edge and ChristianManuscriptSubmissions.com.

HAY HOUSE INC. PO Box 5100, Carlsbad CA 92018-5100. (760) 431-7695. Fax (760) 431-6948. E-mail:editorial@hayhouse.com. Website: www.hayhouse.com. Jill Kramer, ed. dir.; Alex Freemon, submissions ed. Books to help heal the planet. Publishes 1 religious title/yr.; hardcover, trade paperbacks. Receives 200 religious submissions annually. 5 percent of books from first-time authors. Accepts mss through agents or authors. Prefers 70,000 words or 250 pgs. Royalty. Average first printing 5,000. Publication within 12-15 mos. Considers simultaneous submissions. Responds in 1-2 mos. Guidelines (www.hayhouse.com/guides.php).

Nonfiction: Proposal/3 chapters; hard copy only. "Looking for self-help/spiritual with a unique ecumenical angle."

Tips: "We are looking for books with a unique slant, ecumenical, but not overly religious. We want an open-minded approach." Includes a broad range of religious titles, including New Age.

HEALTH COMMUNICATIONS INC. 3201 S.W. 15th St., Deerfield Beach FL 33442. Toll-free (800) 441-5569. (954) 360-0909 (no phone calls). Fax (954) 360-0034. E-mail: editorial@hcibooks.com. Website: www.hci-online.com or www.hcibooks.com. Amy Hughes, religion ed.; submit to Editorial Committee. Nonfiction that emphasizes self-improvement, personal motivation, psychological health, and overall wellness; recovery/addiction, self-help/psychology, soul/spirituality, inspiration, women's issues, relationships, and family. Imprint: HCI Teens. Publishes 50 titles/yr.; hard cover, trade paperbacks. 20 percent of books from first-time authors. Accepts mss through agents or authors. Prefers 250 pgs. Royalty 15 percent of net. Publication within 9 mos. Considers simultaneous submissions. Responds in 3 mos. Follow guidelines for submission. Guidelines on Website; catalog for 9 x 12 SASE.

Nonfiction: Query/outline and 2 chapters; no phone/fax/e-query. Needs books for Christian teens.

HEART OF WISDOM PUBLISHERS. 200 Coble Rd., Shelbyville TN 37160-6353. E-mail: info@ heartofwisdom.com. Website: www.heartofwisdom.com. Publishes a variety of academic materials to help Christian families bring up children with a heart's desire for and knowledge of the Lord. Robin Sampson, ed. Query only. Guidelines on Website.

Special Needs: Currently accepting queries for high-quality history, science, and life skills unit studies for grades 4-12. Not accepting any other titles.

Tips: "We market to home educators and Christian schools."

HEARTSONG PRESENTS. Imprint of Barbour Publishing Inc., PO Box 721, 1810 Barbour Dr., Uhrichsville, OH 44683. E-mail: fictionsubmit@barbourbooks.com. Website: www.heartsongpresents .com. JoAnne Simmons, ed. Produces affordable, wholesome entertainment through a book club that also helps to enhance and spread the gospel. Publishes 52 titles/yr.; mass-market paperbacks. Receives

1,000 submissions annually. 10 percent of books from first-time authors. Accepts mss through agents or authors. Prefers 45,000-50,000 wds. Royalty 8 percent of net; advance $2,200. Average first printing 20,000. Publication within 1 yr. Considers simultaneous submissions. Responds in 6-12 mos. Requires electronic submissions; no proposals via regular mail. Prefers KJV for historicals; NIV for contemporary. Guidelines by mail/e-mail; no catalog.

Fiction: Proposal/3 chapters; electronic submissions only (fictionsubmit@barbourbooks .com). Adult. "We publish 2 contemporary and 2 historical romances every 4 weeks. We cover all topics and settings. Specific guidelines available."

Tips: "Romance only, with a strong conservative-Christian theme. Read our books and study our style before submitting."

**Note: This publisher serviced by The Writer's Edge.

HEARTSONG PRESENTS/MYSTERIES. Imprint of Barbour Publishing Inc., PO Box 719, 1810 Barbour Dr., Uhrichsville, OH 44683. (740) 922-6045. Fax (740) 922-5948. E-mail: acquisitions@ barbourbooks.com. Website: www.barbourbooks.com. Editor's blog: www.editcafe.blogspot.com. Susan Downs, ed. Produces affordable, wholesome entertainment through a book club that also helps to enhance and spread the gospel. Publishes 32 titles/yr.; mass-market paperbacks. 25 percent of books from first-time authors. Accepts mss through agents or authors. No subsidy. Prefers 63,000 wds. Royalty or outright purchase; pays an advance. Average first printing 15,000-20,000. Publication within 9-12 mos. Considers simultaneous submissions. Responds in 3-6 mos. Accepts mss by e-mail. Guidelines by mail/e-mail/Website.

Fiction: Proposal/3 chapters; no phone/fax query; e-query OK. Accepts only cozy mysteries with a romance plot thread.

Tips: "Cozy mysteries should feature an amateur sleuth in a setting that has a small-town 'feel.' The inciting crime should occur in the first chapter or two so the majority of the plot focuses on solving the 'whodunit' of the mystery. Study our specific guidelines thoroughly prior to proposal submission."

**Note: This publisher serviced by The Writer's Edge.

HEARTSPRING PUBLISHING. 223 W. Third St. (64801), PO Box 1132, Joplin MO 64802. Toll-free (800) 289-3300. (417) 623-6280. Fax (417) 623-8250. E-mail through Website: www.college press.com. Christian Church/Church of Christ. Submit to Acquisitions Editor. Nonacademic imprint of College Press Publishing Co. Publishes 15-20 titles/yr.; trade paperbacks. Receives 700 submissions annually. 25 percent of books from first-time authors. Accepts mss through agents or authors. Reprints books. Prefers 250-300 pgs. Royalty 5-15 percent of net; no advance. Average first printing 3,000. Publication within 6 mos. Considers simultaneous submissions. Requires requested ms on disk; no e-mail submissions. Responds in 2-3 mos. Prefers NIV, NASB, NAS. Guidelines on Website; catalog for 9 x 12 SAE/5 stamps.

Nonfiction: Query first, then proposal/2-3 chapters; no phone/fax query.

Fiction: Christian fiction.

HENDRICKSON PUBLISHERS. 140 Summit St., PO Box 3473, Peabody MA 01961-3473. (978) 573-2276. Fax (978) 573-8276. E-mail: editorial@hendrickson.com. Website: www.hendrickson .com. Submit to: Editorial Dept./Book Proposals. To provide biblically oriented books for reference, learning, and personal growth, and resources for pastors. Publishes 30 titles/yr.; hardcover, trade paperbacks. Receives 400+ submissions annually. Less than 10 percent of books from first-time authors. Accepts mss through agents or authors. Reprints books. Prefers 150-500 pgs. Royalty; some advances. Average first printing 2,000. Publication within 12-18 mos. No simultaneous submissions. Responds in 4-6 mos. Prefers accepted ms by e-mail. Follow *Chicago Manual of Style.* Prefers NIV. Guidelines by mail/e-mail/Website; catalog for 9 x 12 SAE/$2.38 postage (mark "Media Mail").

Nonfiction: Query first; e-query OK. "Looking for popular reference material." Also publishes academic books through their Academic Book Division. No fiction, devotionals, children's books, or poetry.

Tips: "Best chance: Scholarly/academic or biblical studies. High standards for trade books."

**Note: This publisher serviced by The Writer's Edge and ChristianManuscriptSubmissions.com.

HENSLEY PUBLISHING. 6116 E. 32nd St., Tulsa OK 74135. (918) 664-8520. Fax (918) 664-8562. E-mail: editorial@hensleypublishing.com. Website: www.hensleypublishing.com. Terri Kalfas, dir. of publishing. Goal is to get people studying the Bible instead of just reading books about the Bible; Bible study only. Publishes 5-10 titles/yr.; trade paperbacks. Receives 800 submissions annually. 50 percent of books from first-time authors. No mss through agents. No reprints. Royalty on net; some outright purchases; no advance. Average first printing 2,500. Publication within 12-18 mos. Considers simultaneous submissions. Requires requested ms in MAC format. Responds in 2 mos. Guidelines & catalog on Website.

Nonfiction: Query first, then proposal/first 3 chapters; no phone/fax query. "Looking for Bible studies of varying length for use by small or large groups, or individuals."

**Note: This publisher serviced by The Writer's Edge.

HIDDEN BROOK PRESS. 109 Bayshore Rd., RR #4, Brighton ON K0K 1H0, Canada. (613) 475-2368. E-mail: writers@hiddenbrookpress.com. Website: www.hiddenbrookpress.com. Richard M. Grove, ed./pub. Imprints: Hidden Brook Press, Arc Communications. Does hardcover, trade paperbacks, coffee-table books. Receives 1,000 submissions annually. 98 percent of books from first-time authors. Accepts mss through agents and authors. Does subsidy and print-on-demand, as well as royalty contracts. Reprints books. Royalty on retail or net; no advance. Average first printing 50-5,000. Accepts simultaneous submissions. Guidelines by e-mail.

Nonfiction/Fiction: E-query or e-submissions. All topics; all genres.

HIS WORK CHRISTIAN PUBLISHING. PO Box 5732, Ketchikan AK 99901. Fax (614) 388-0664. Website: www.hisworkpub.com. Angela J. Perez, acq. ed. Books that glorify and honor God. Publishes 4-8 titles/yr.; hardcover, trade paperbacks, electronic. Receives 100+ submissions annually. 95 percent of books from first-time authors. Accepts mss through agents or authors. Reprints books. Royalty 10-20 percent on net. Publication within 2 yrs. Considers simultaneous submissions. Responds in 1-3 mos. Guidelines/current needs/catalog on Website.

Nonfiction: Query with marketing proposal/3 chapters.

Fiction: Religious fiction. Query with marketing proposal/3 chapters.

Tips: "We accept no queries or submissions by e-mail."

HOPE PUBLISHING HOUSE. PO Box 60008, Pasadena CA 91106. (626) 792-6123. Fax (626) 792-2121. E-mail: hopepublishinghouse@gmail.com. Website: www.hope-pub.com. Southern California Ecumenical Council. Faith A. Sand, pub. Produces thinking books that challenge the faith community to be serious about their pilgrimage of faith. Imprint: New Paradigm Books. Publishes 6 titles/yr. Receives 40 submissions annually. 30 percent of books from first-time authors. No mss through agents. Reprints books. Prefers 200 pgs. Royalty 10 percent on net; no advance. Average first printing 3,000. Publication within 6 mos. No simultaneous submissions. Accepts mss by disk or e-mail. Responds in 3 mos. Prefers NRSV. No guidelines; catalog for 7 x 10 SAE/4 stamps.

Nonfiction: Query only first; no phone/fax query; e-query OK.

Tips: "Most open to a well-written manuscript, with correct grammar, that is provocative, original, challenging, and informative."

HOURGLASS BOOKS. 387 Northgate Rd., Lindenhurst IL 60046. E-mail: editor@hourglassbooks .org. Website: www.hourglassbooks.org/submissions.html. Gina Frangello & Molly McQuade, eds.

Publishes anthologies of short stories assembled around a common theme. Accepts simultaneous submissions & reprints. Shared royalties for contributors to the anthologies. Guidelines on Website.

Fiction: Submit by e-mail (copied into message). Literary fiction only. Currently working on Occupational Hazards: Stories from the World of Work. No word limits, or fixed closing dates.

HOWARD BOOKS. 216 Centerview Dr., Ste. 303, Brentwood TN 37027. (615) 873-2080. Website: www.howardpublishing.com. Submit to Manuscript Review Committee. A division of Simon & Schuster Inc. Publishes 65 titles/yr.; hardcover, trade paperbacks. Receives 1,000 submissions annually. 5 percent of books from first-time authors. Prefers 200-250 pgs. Negotiable royalty & advance. Average first printing 10,000. Publication within 16 mos. Considers simultaneous submissions. Accepted ms by e-mail. Responds in 6-8 mos. No disk. Prefers NIV. No guidelines/catalog.

Nonfiction: Accepting queries only, by e-mail; no phone queries.
Fiction: Proposal/3 chapters. Adult.
Tips: "Our authors must first be Christ-centered in their lives and writing, then qualified to write on the subject of choice. Public name recognition is a plus. Authors who are also public speakers usually have a ready-made audience."
**Note: This publisher serviced by The Writer's Edge and ChristianManuscriptSubmissions.com.

IDEALS PUBLICATIONS. 2636 Elm Hill Pike, Ste. 120, Nashville TN 37214. E-mail: pjay@guide posts.org. Website: www.idealsbooks.com. A Guideposts company. Peggy Schaefer, pub. Not currently accepting unsolicited mss.

INKLING BOOKS. 6528 Phinney Ave. N., Seattle WA 98103. (206) 365-1624. E-mail: editor@ inklingbooks.com. Website: www.InklingBooks.com. Michael W. Perry, pub. Publishes 6 titles/yr.; hardcover, trade paperbacks. No mss through agents. Reprints books. Prefers 150-400 pgs. No advance. Print-on-demand. Publication within 2 mos. No guidelines or catalog. Not currently accepting submissions.

INTERNATIONAL AWAKENING PRESS. 139 N. Washington, PO Box 232, Wheaton IL 60187. Phone/fax (630) 653-8616. E-mail: internationalawakening@juno.com. Website: www.international awakening.org. Intl. Awakening Ministries. Richard Owen Roberts, ed./pres. Scholarly books on religious awakenings or revivals. Publishes 4 titles/yr. Receives 12 submissions annually. Reprints books. Royalty negotiated; no advance. Average first printing 3,000. Publication within 6 mos. Responds in 3 mos. Prefers requested ms on disk. Any translation; no paraphrases. No guidelines; free catalog.

Nonfiction: Query only; no phone/fax/e-query. "Looking for scholarly theology, especially Bible commentaries, church history, and revival-related material."
Also Does: Booklets, pamphlets, tracts.
Photos: Accepts freelance photos for book covers.
Tips: "Most open to scholarly books."

@ INTERVARSITY PRESS. Box 1400, Downers Grove IL 60515-1426. Receptionist: (630) 734-4000 or 4036. Fax (630) 734-4200. E-mail: email@ivpress.com. Website: www.ivpress.com. InterVarsity Christian Fellowship. Andrew T. LePeau, ed. dir.; submit to General Book Editor or Academic Editor. IVP books are characterized by a thoughtful, biblical approach to the Christian life that transforms the hearts, souls, and minds of readers in the university, the church, and the world, on topics ranging from spiritual disciplines to apologetics, to current issues, to theology. Imprints: IVP Academic (Gary Deddo, ed.), IVP Connect (Cindy Bunch, ed.), IVP Books (Al Hsu, ed.). Publishes 110-120 titles/yr.; hardcover, trade paperbacks, mass-market paperbacks. Receives 1,300 submissions annually. 15 percent of books from first-time authors. Accepts mss through agents or authors. Reprints books. Prefers 50,000 words or 200 pgs. Negotiable royalty on retail or outright purchase; negotiable advance. Average first printing 5,000. Publication within 12 mos. Considers simultaneous submissions. Responds in 3 mos. Prefers NIV, NRSV. Accepts e-mail submissions after acceptance. Guidelines on Website; catalog for 9 x 12 SAE/5 stamps.

Nonfiction: Query only first, with detailed letter according to submissions guidelines, then proposal with 2 chapters; no phone/fax/e-query.

Ethnic Books: Especially looking for ethnic writers (African American, Hispanic, Asian American).

Also Does: Booklets, 5,000 words; e-books.

Blogs: www.ivpress.com/blogs/behindthebooks; www.ivpress.com/blogs/andyunedited; www.ivpress.com/blogs/addenda-errata.

Tips: "Most open to books written by pastors (though not collections of sermons) or other church staff, by professors, by leaders in Christian organizations. Authors need to bring resources for publicizing and selling their own books, such as a Website, an organization they are part of that will promote their books, speaking engagements, well-known people they know personally who will endorse and promote their book, writing articles for national publication, etc."

**Note: This publisher serviced by The Writer's Edge and ChristianManuscriptSubmissions.com.

INVISIBLE COLLEGE PRESS. PO Box 209, Woodbridge VA 22194-0209. (703) 590-4005. E-mail: submissions@invispress.com. Website: www.invispress.com. Dr. Phillip Reynolds, nonfiction ed.; Paul Mossinger, fiction ed. This publisher majors on the paranormal, science fiction, spiritual, religious, etc. Publishes 12 titles/yr.; trade paperbacks. Receives 150 submissions annually. 75 percent of books from first-time authors. Accepts mss through agents or authors. No reprints. Prefers 70,000 words or more. Royalty 10-25 percent on net; $100 advance. Publication within 4 mos. Considers simultaneous submissions. Responds in 1-3 mos. Guidelines & catalog on Website.

Nonfiction: E-query preferred (copied into message) or query/SASE/proposal package/1 chapter. Reference, religion, spirituality.

Fiction: E-query preferred or query/synopsis & 1 chapter.

JEBAIRE PUBLISHING. PO Box 843, Snellville GA 30078-0843. (770) 823-9017. E-mail: info@ jebairepublishing.com. Website: www.jebairepublishing.com. Shannon Clark, acq. ed. Our mission is "to give gifted writers a voice and hungry souls a full meal." Publishes 2-4 titles/yr.; trade paperbacks. 75 percent of books from first-time authors. No mss through agents. No subsidy, print-on-demand, or reprints. Prefers 125-250 pgs. Royalty 12-15 percent on net; no advance. Average first printing 1,000. Publication within 12 mos. Considers simultaneous submissions. Responds in 4-6 weeks (to proposals). Requires accepted mss on disk or by e-mail. Guidelines by mail/e-mail; no catalog.

Nonfiction: Proposal/2-3 chapters; e-query OK. "Looking for women's devotionals, Christian living, personal growth, and faith."

Photos/Artwork: Accepts freelance photos for book covers; open to queries from freelance artists.

Tips: "We look for writers who have an 'approachable' writing style. We want our readers to feel uplifted and encouraged rather than 'talked down to' or discouraged."

+JESUS FILLED DAY PUBLISHING. PO Box 34, Houston TX 77001. (281) 399-4011. Fax (281) 399-3840. E-mail: team@haveajesusfilledday.com. Website: www.haveajesusfilledday.com. Ann Chapman, VP. Publishes 1 title every 2 yrs.; trade paperback. Receives no submissions. No mss through agents. No reprints.

Nonfiction: Query first; no phone/fax/e-query.

JOSSEY-BASS. A Wiley Imprint, 989 Market St., 5th Fl., San Francisco CA 94103-1741. (415) 782-3145. Fax (415) 433-0499. E-mail: Sfullert@jbp.com. Website: www.jossey-bass.com. John Wiley & Sons Inc. Sheryl Fullerton, exec. ed. Because of a nondenominational focus on Christian spirituality and general corporate ownership, they are able to reach the broadest range of markets and readership. Imprint: Religion and Spirituality. Publishes 30 titles/yr.; hardcover, trade paperbacks. Receives hundreds of submissions annually. Up to 10 percent of books from first-time authors. Accepts mss through agents or authors. No reprints. Prefers 60,000 words or 250 pgs. Royalty negotiable on net; pays an advance. Average first printing 10,000. Publication within 1 yr. Considers simultaneous submissions. Responds in 1 mo. Prefers NRSV, NIV. Guidelines by mail/e-mail; free catalog by mail.

Nonfiction: Proposal/2 chapters; e-query OK. "Looking for fresh, vital resources to deepen faith and Christian identity."

Tips: "Our mission is to provide innovative, thoughtful, and useful resources for people on their faith journeys. Authors with compelling ideas and an established audience (and/or track record) from which to promote and market themselves, as well as clearly relevant credentials and expertise will be enthusiastically received. We are not interested in books that would be considered 'more of the same' or in books that are narrow or marginal in their perspective. We are particularly interested in books that encourage a generous orthodoxy. Create an excellent proposal that clearly presents your idea in a way that is viable for its market and fully describes your platform."

JOURNEYFORTH/BJU PRESS. 1700 Wade Hampton Blvd., Greenville SC 29614. (864) 370-1800, ext. 4350. Fax (864) 298-0268, ext. 4324. E-mail: jb@bju.edu. Website: www.bjupress.com. Bob Jones University Press. Nancy Lohr, youth ed.; Suzette Jordan, adult ed. Our goal is to publish excellent, trustworthy books for children and Christian-living titles for adults. Publishes 15-25 titles/yr.; hardcover, trade paperbacks. Receives 500 submissions annually (100 Christian living/400 youth novels). 10 percent of books from first-time authors. Accepts mss through agents or authors. Reprints youth books only. Royalty. Average first printing varies. Publication within 12-18 mos. Considers simultaneous submissions. No submissions by disk or e-mail. Responds in 8-12 wks. Requires KJV. Guidelines by mail/e-mail; free catalog.

Nonfiction: Proposal/3-5 chapters; e-query OK.

Fiction: Proposal/5 chapters or complete ms. For children & teens. "We prefer overtly Christian or Christian worldview."

Artwork: Open to queries from freelance artists.

Tips: "The precollege, homeschool market welcomes print-rich, well-written novels. No picture books, please, but compelling novels for early readers are always good for us. Biographies on the lives of Christian heroes and statesmen are also a good fit. We focus on conservative biblical books for all ages that will help to develop skill with the written word as well as discernment as a believer; we complement the educational goals of BJU Press, our K-12 textbook division."

**Note: This publisher serviced by The Writer's Edge.

JOURNEY STONE CREATIONS, LLC. 3533 Danbury Rd., Fairfield OH 45014. (513) 860-5616. Fax (513) 860-0176. E-mail: pat@jscbooks.com. Website: www.jscbooks.com. Not currently accepting submissions; check Website for current status.

@ JUBILANT PRESS: AN ELECTRONIC & PRINT PUBLISHER. PO Box 6421, Longmont CO 80501. E-mail: jubilantpress@aol.com or rtthwomen@aol.com. Website: www.jubilantpress.com. Supports Right to the Heart Ministries. Linda Shepherd & Rebekah Montgomery, pubs. Publishes downloadable e-books with instant information to change your life. Publishes 10 e-titles/yr., plus 1 print bk. Acquires print & e-books by invitation only. 0 percent of books from first-time authors. Accepts mss through agents or authors. Reprints books. Prefers 20-100 pgs. Pays for the right to publish, plus a percentage of author's online sales (author must have an active Web page); variable advance. Publication within 6 mos. Prefers NIV. Guidelines provided for specific projects.

Nonfiction: Brief e-mail query only; no phone/fax query.

Special Needs: Women's ministry helps, banquet-planning helps, speaking and writing helps.
Photos: Accepts freelance photos for book covers.
Tips: "Submissions accepted by invitation only. Best to send a brief e-mail with description of your idea. Please see our Web page to best understand our publishing program. Most open to a how-to, informational book with a need-to-know marketability."

JUDSON PRESS. PO Box 851, Valley Forge PA 19482-0851. Toll-free (800) 4-JUDSON. Fax (610) 768-2441. E-mail: jpacquisitions@abc-usa.org. Website: www.judsonpress.com. American Baptist Churches USA/National Ministries. Rebecca Irwin-Diehl, ed. We are theologically moderate, historically Baptist, and in ministry to empower, enrich, and equip the disciples of Jesus and leaders in Christ's church. Publishes 12-15 titles/yr.; hardcover, trade paperbacks. Receives 800 submissions annually. 20 percent of books from first-time authors. Accepts mss through agents or authors. No subsidy; rarely does print-on-demand or reprints. Prefers 100-200 pgs. or 30,000-75,000 wds. Royalty 10-15 percent on net; some work-for-hire agreements or outright purchases; occasional advance $300. Average first printing 3,000. Publication within 18 mos. Considers simultaneous submissions. Requires accepted submissions on disk or by e-mail. Responds in 4-6 mos. Prefers NRSV. Guidelines by e-mail; catalog online.
  Nonfiction: Query or proposal/2 chapters; e-query OK. Practical books for today's church and leaders.
  Ethnic Books: African American & Hispanic.
  Artwork: Open to queries from freelance artists. Attn: Wendy Ronga, creative dir.
  Tips: "Most open to books that are unique, compelling, and practical. Theologically and socially we are a moderate publisher. And we like to see a detailed marketing plan from an author committed to partnering with us."
  **Note: This publisher serviced by The Writer's Edge.

JESSICA KINGSLEY PUBLISHERS. 116 Pentonville Rd., London N1 9JB, United Kingdom. U.S. address: 400 Market St., Ste. 400, Philadelphia PA 19106 (they will forward your proposal). Phone: +44 20 7833 2307. Fax +44 20 7837 2917. E-mail: Post@JKP.com. Website: www.JKP.com. Jessica Kingsley, CEO; submit to: New Book Proposals at JKP. Publishes books that create social change. Imprint: Singing Dragon. Publishes 45+ titles/yr.; hardcover, trade paperbacks. Receives 300+ submissions annually. 60 percent of books from first-time authors. Accepts mss through agents or authors. Print-on-demand for older books. Reprints books. Any length. Royalty 5-10 percent on net; no advance. Average first printing 1,500. Publication within 6 mos. No simultaneous submissions. Responds in up to 6 mos. Requires accepted mss on disk or by e-mail. Prefers NIV. Guidelines by mail/e-mail; free catalog by mail.
  Nonfiction: Proposal/2 chapters; no phone/fax query; e-query OK.
  Special Needs: Practical theology.
  Photos: Accepts freelance photos for book covers.
  Tips: "Most open to books that combine theory with practice; books for practitioners."

KIRK HOUSE PUBLISHERS. PO Box 390759, Minneapolis MN 55439. Toll-free (888) 696-1828. (952) 835-1828. Fax (952) 835-2613. E-mail: publisher@kirkhouse.com. Website: www.kirkhouse .com. Leonard Flachman, pub. Imprints: Lutheran University Press, Quill House Publishers. Publishes 6-8 titles/yr.; hardcover, trade paperbacks, coffee-table books. Receives hundreds of submissions annually. 95 percent of books from first-time authors. No mss through agents. No reprints. Royalty 10-15 percent on net; no advance. Average first printing 500-3,000. Publication within 6 mos. No simultaneous submissions. Requires disk or e-mail submission. Responds in 2-3 wks. Guidelines by e-mail; free catalog by mail.
  Nonfiction: Proposal/1-2 chapters.
  Tips: "Our catalog is eclectic; send a query. Our imprint, Quill House Publishers, accepts adult fiction."

KNB PUBLICATIONS. PO Box 831648, Stone Mountain GA 30083. (404) 294-1457. Fax (404) 294-9732. E-mail: info@knb-publications.com. Website: www.knbpublications.com. Kendra Norman-Bellamy, pub. Guidelines on Website. Incomplete topical listings.

Nonfiction/Fiction: Query by mail or e-mail; no complete mss without permission.

KNIGHT GEORGE PUBLISHING HOUSE, LLC. 24 Leslie Ln., #307, Waterford MI 48328 (check Website for current address before submitting). (586) 481-0466. E-mail: authors@knightgeorge .com. Website: www.knightgeorge.com. Matt Jones, pres. A privately-owned, independent provider of innovative Christian educational materials to Lutherans. New publisher; hardcover, trade paperbacks. 16 percent of books from first-time authors. No mss through agents. No subsidy or print-on-demand. Royalty 2-15 percent of net; no advance. Considers simultaneous submissions. Responds in 3 mos. Accepted mss on disk. Guidelines by mail/e-mail; no catalog.

Nonfiction: Proposal/2 chapters; no phone/fax query; e-query OK.

Fiction: Query only first. Children's stories and classroom reading books. We seek to compete with Golden Books.

Special Needs: Classroom materials: textbooks, workbooks, hands-on learning aids. Innovative teaching methods and newest technology are preferred.

Also Does: Board games, computer games, all hands-on learning methods.

Photos/Artwork: Accepts freelance photos for book covers; open to queries from freelance artists.

Tips: "We prefer books be submitted complete with original artwork. Most open to textbooks (teacher's editions should contain full student's edition within them), workbooks (as applicable), and projects, preferably as a package. Find new and creative ways to teach. We are a publishing house, but will consider any other products (within pricing limits) that educate. Of course, God should be at least implicit, but don't force biblical examples in your work. Write to meet the needs of the market."

KREGEL PUBLICATIONS. PO Box 2607, Grand Rapids MI 49501-2607. (616) 451-4775. Fax (616) 451-9330. E-mail: kregelbooks@kregel.com. Website: www.kregelpublications.com. Blog: www.kregelpublications.blogspot.com. Evangelical/Conservative. Dennis R. Hillman, pub.; Jim Weaver, academic & professional books ed.; submissions policy on Website. To provide tools for ministry and Christian growth from a conservative, evangelical perspective. Imprints: Kregel Kidzone, Kregel Academic and Professional, Kregel Classics. Publishes 75 titles/yr.; hardcover, trade paperbacks. 20 percent of books from first-time authors. Prefers mss through agents. Reprints books. Royalty 8-16 percent of net; some outright purchases; advance $200-2,000. Average first printing 5,000. Publication within 12 mos. Considers simultaneous submissions. Responds in 4 mos. Guidelines by e-mail; catalog for 9 x 12 SAE/3 stamps. No longer reviewing unsolicited queries, proposals, or manuscripts, except through agents, Writer's Edge, or ChristianManuscriptSubmissions.com.

Nonfiction: "Most open to contemporary issues or academic works."

Fiction: For all ages. "Looking for high-quality contemporary fiction with strong Christian themes and characters."

Tips: "We are adding more fiction, but again, we are very selective. Strong story lines with an evident spiritual emphasis are required."

**Note: This publisher serviced by The Writer's Edge and ChristianManuscriptSubmissions.com.

LANGMARC PUBLISHING. PO Box 90488, Austin TX 78709-0488. (512) 394-0989. Fax (512) 394-0829. E-mail: langmarc@booksails.com. Website: www.langmarc.com. Lutheran. Lois Qualben, pub. Focuses on spiritual growth of readers. Publishes 3-5 titles/yr.; hardcover, trade paperbacks. Receives 230 submissions annually. 60 percent of books from first-time authors. Accepts mss through agents or authors. No reprints. Prefers 150-300 pgs. Royalty 10-14 percent on net; no advance. Average first printing varies. Publication usually within 18 mos. Considers simultaneous submissions. Responds in 3 mos. Requires requested ms on disk. Prefers NIV. Guidelines on Website; free catalog.

Nonfiction: Proposal/3 chapters; no phone query. "Most open to inspirational books."

LARSON PUBLICATIONS/PBPF. 4936 NYS Rte. 414, Burdett NY 14818-9729. (607) 546-9342. Fax (607) 546-9344. E-mail: larson@lightlink.com. Website: www.larsonpublications.org. Paul Cash, dir. Books cover philosophy, psychology, religion, and spirituality. Publishes 4-5 titles/yr.; hardcover, trade paperbacks. Receives 1,000 submissions annually. 5 percent of books from first-time authors. Some reprints. Variable royalty; rarely gives an advance. Publication within 1-2 yrs. Considers simultaneous submissions. Requires accepted mss on disk. Responds in 8 wks. Prefers NIV. Guidelines on Website; no catalog.

Nonfiction: Query by mail/outline & SASE; no phone/fax/e-query.

LEGACY PRESS. PO Box 261129, San Diego CA 92196. Toll-free (800) 323-7337. Toll-free fax (800) 331-0297. E-mail: editor@rainbowpublishers.com. Website: www.rainbowpublishers.com. Rainbow Publishers. Submit to Manuscript Submissions. Publishes nondenominational nonfiction and fiction for children in the evangelical Christian market. Publishes 15 titles/yr. Receives 250 submissions annually. 50 percent of books from first-time authors. Reprints books. Prefers 150 pgs. & up. Royalty 8 percent & up on net; advance $500+. Average first printing 5,000. Publication within 2 yrs. Considers simultaneous submissions. Prefers requested ms on disk. Responds in 2-8 wks. Prefers NIV. Guidelines on Website; catalog for 9 x 12 SAE/2 stamps.

Nonfiction: Proposal/3-5 chapters; no e-queries. "Looking for nonfiction for girls and boys ages 2-12."

Fiction: Proposal/3 chapters. For ages 2-12 only. Must include an additional component beyond fiction (e.g., devotional, Bible activities, etc.)

Special Needs: Nonfiction for ages 10-12, particularly Christian twists on current favorites, such as cooking, jewelry making, games, etc.

Artwork: Open to queries from freelance artists.

Tips: "All books must offer solid Bible teaching in a fun, meaningful way that appeals to kids. Research popular nonfiction for kids in the general market, then figure out how to present those fun ideas in ways that teach the Bible. As a smaller publisher, we seek to publish unique niche books that stand out in the market."

LEGACY PUBLISHERS INTERNATIONAL. 1301 S. Clinton St., Denver CO 80247. (303) 283-7480. Fax (303) 283-7536. E-mail: dmiller@hccweb.org. Michele Leonard, acq. ed. To pass the gospel of Jesus Christ on to future generations through the written word. Accepts some freelance. Catalog. Incomplete topical listings.

LIBROS LIGUORI. 1 Liguori Dr., Liguori MO 63057-9999. Toll-free (800) 325-9521. (636) 464-2500. Fax (636) 464-8449. E-mail: manuscript_submission@liguori.org. Website: www.liguori.org. Spanish division of Liguori Publications. To spread the gospel in the Hispanic community by means of low-cost publications. Publishes 5 titles/yr. Receives 6-8 submissions annually. 5 percent of books from first-time authors. Prefers up to 30,000 wds. Royalty 8-10 percent of net or outright purchase of $450 (book and booklet authors get royalties; pamphlet authors get $400 on acceptance); pays an advance. Average first printing 3,500-5,000. Publication within 18 mos. No simultaneous submissions. Requires accepted mss on electronic file. Responds in 4-8 wks. Guidelines on Website; free catalog.

Nonfiction: Four-page summary/1 chapter; fax/e-query OK. "Looking for issues families face today—substance abuse, unwanted pregnancies, etc.; family relations; religion's role in immigrants' experiences, pastoral Catholic faith."

Ethnic Books: Focuses on Spanish-language products.

Also Does: Pamphlets, booklets, tracts, PC software, clip art.

Tips: "Contact us before writing. It's much easier to work together from the beginning of a project. We need books on the Hispanic experience in the U.S. Keep it concise, avoid academic/theological jargon, and stick to the tenets of the Catholic faith. Avoid abstract arguments."

@ LIFE CHANGING MEDIA. 10777 W. Sample Rd., Unit 302, Coral Springs FL 33065-3768. (954) 554-1921. E-mail: submissions@lifechangingmedia.net or through Website: www.lifechangingmedia .net. Life Changing Publications. Paul Gundotra, pres.; Sindhu Roy, chief ed. Mass-market paperbacks. Royalty on retail; no advance. Average first print run varies. Publication within 3 mos. Considers simultaneous submissions (if indicated). Prefers accepted mss by e-mail. Responds in 30-60 days. Guidelines by e-mail/Website; no catalog.

Nonfiction: Query first; e-query OK. "Please include a description of the book project, brief bio including publishing history. Let us know if you have the ability for public speaking."

Also Does: E-books.

Photos: Accepts freelance photos for book covers.

Tips: "Looking for books that entertain, inform, but most of all that are life changing."

LIFE CYCLE BOOKS. PO Box 1008, Niagara Falls NY 14304-1008. Toll-free (800) 214-5849. (416) 690-5860. Toll-free fax (888) 690-8532. (416) 690-8532. E-mail: paulb@lifecyclebooks.com. Website: www.lifecyclebooks.com. Paul Broughton, gen. mngr.; submit to The Editor. Specializes in pro-life material. Publishes 6 titles/yr.; trade paperbacks. Receives 100 submissions annually. No mss through agents. 50 percent of books from first-time authors. Reprints books. Royalty 8-10 percent of net; outright purchase of brochure material, $250+; advance $250-1,000. **SUBSIDY PUBLISHES 10 PERCENT**. Publication within 1 yr. No simultaneous submissions. Responds in 1 mo. Catalog on Website.

Nonfiction: Query or complete ms. "Our emphasis is on pro-life and pro-family titles."

Tips: "We are most involved in publishing leaflets of about 1,500 words, and we welcome submissions of manuscripts of this length."

LIFESONG PUBLISHERS. PO Box 183, Somis CA 93066. (805) 504-3916. Fax (614) 455-5030. E-mail: mailbox@lifesongpublishers.com. Website: www.lifesongpublishers.com. Laurie Donahue, pub. Provides Christian families with tools that will aid in spiritual development of family members. Publishes 1-4 titles/yr.; trade paperbacks. No mss through agents. No reprints. **WOULD CONSIDER SUBSIDY**. Royalty 10 percent on net; small advance. Publication within 12 mos. Considers simultaneous submissions. Responds in 2-4 wks. No guidelines; catalog for 9 x 12 SAE/2 stamps. Not included in nonfiction topical listings.

Nonfiction: Proposal/3 chapters; e-query OK. "Looking for an author with an existing ministry."

LIFT EVERY VOICE. 820 N. LaSalle Blvd., Chicago IL 60610. (312) 329-2140. Fax (312) 329-4157. E-mail: lifteveryvoice@moody.edu. Website: www.lifteveryvoicebooks.com. African American imprint of Moody Publishers. Moody Bible Institute and Institute for Black Family Development. Cynthia Ballenger, acq. ed.; Natalie Harper, asst. coord. To advance the cause of Christ through publishing African American Christians who educate, edify, and disciple Christians. Publishes 15 titles/yr. Receives 50-60 submissions annually. 98 percent of books from first-time authors. Accepts mss through agents or authors. No subsidy. Reprints books. Prefers 50,000 words or 250 pgs. Royalty on retail; pays an advance. Average first printing 5,000. Publication within 12 mos. Considers simultaneous submissions. Responds biannually. Accepts requested ms by e-mail. Prefers KJV. Guidelines by mail; free catalog.

Nonfiction: Proposal/2 chapters; e-query OK.

Fiction: Proposal/2 chapters; e-query OK. For all ages. Send for fiction writer's guidelines.

Special Needs: Children's fiction, especially for boys; nonfiction books for teen girls; also marriage books.

Ethnic Books: African American imprint.

Photos: Accepts freelance photos for book covers.

Tips: "Looking for quality fiction and nonfiction. Good, strong, and focused writing is what LEV is looking for, but mostly writing that is Christ-centered and speaks to the African American community."

**Note: This publisher serviced by ChristianManuscriptSubmissions.com.

@ LIGHTHOUSE PUBLISHING. 251 Overlook Park Ln. Lawrenceville, GA 30043. E-mail: AndyOverett@lighthousechristianpublishing.com. Website: www.lighthousechristianpublishing.com. Nondenominational. Andy Overett, ed.; submit to Chris Wright, sr. ed. To distribute a wide variety of Christian media to vast parts of the globe so people can hear about the gospel for free or very inexpensively (e-books, comics, movies, and online radio). Imprints: Lighthouse Publishing, Lighthouse Music Publishing. Publishes 20-30 titles/yr.; hardcover, trade paperbacks, mass-market paperbacks. Receives 100-150 submissions annually. 60 percent of books from first-time authors. Accepts mss through agents or authors. **SUBSIDY PUBLISHES 15-20 PERCENT**. Does print-on-demand. Reprints books. Any length. Royalty on net; no advance. Average first printing 300-400. Publication within 6 mos. Considers simultaneous submissions. Prefers submissions by e-mail. Responds in 6-8 wks. Prefers NAS. Guidelines on Website; catalog $5.

Nonfiction: Complete ms by e-mail only (info@lighthousechristianpublishing.com). Any topic. "Looking for children's books, Intelligent Design, and science."

Fiction: Complete ms by e-mail only. Any genre, for all ages.

Ethnic Books: Publishes books for almost all foreign-language markets.

Also Does: Comics, animation on CD, music CDs, plans to do Christian computer games in the future. E-books.

Photos/Artwork: Accepts freelance photos for book covers; open to queries from freelance artists.

Tips: "Most open to children's books, comics, and graphic novels; scientific and academic works with a Christian perspective."

LIGHTHOUSE TRAILS PUBLISHING LLC. PO Box 958, Silverton OR 97381. (503) 873-9092. Fax (503) 873-3879. E-mail: editors@lighthousetrails.com. Website: www.lighthousetrails.com. Blog: www.lighthousetrailsresearch.com/blog. David Dombrowski, acq. ed. Books that bring clarity and light to areas of spiritual darkness or deception, and to preserving the integrity of God's Word in all our books. Imprint: Falling Sparrow Series. Publishes 4 titles/yr. Receives 100-150 submissions annually. 35 percent of books from first-time authors. Accepts mss through agents or authors. No subsidy or print-on-demand. Reprints books. Prefers 160-300 pgs. Royalty 12-17 percent of net or 20 percent of retail; advance $1,000. Average first printing 2,500. Publication within 6-9 mos. Considers simultaneous submissions. Requires accepted ms on disk or by e-mail. Responds in 8 wks. Prefers KJV, NAS. Guidelines by e-mail; free catalog by mail.

Nonfiction: Proposal/2 chapters; no phone/fax query; e-query OK.

Fiction: Proposal/2-3 chapters. For all ages. "We are looking for a fiction book or fiction series that would include elements from our books exposing the emerging church and mystical spirituality; bible prophecy/eschatological."

Special Needs: Will look at autobiographies or biographies about people who have courageously endured through overwhelming circumstances (Holocaust survivors, child-abuse survivors, etc.) with a definite emphasis on the Lord's grace and faithfulness.

Artwork: Open to queries from freelance artists.

Tips: "No poetry at this time. Any book we consider will not only challenge the more scholarly reader, but also be able to reach those who may have less experience and comprehension. Our books will include human interest and personal experience scenarios as a means of getting the point across. Read a couple of our books to better understand the style of writing we are looking for. Also check our research Website for an in-depth look at who we are (www.lighthousetrailsresearch.com)."

LIGUORI PUBLICATIONS, 1 Liguori Dr., Liguori MO 63057-9999. Toll-free (800) 325-9521. (636) 464-2500. Fax (636) 464-8449. E-mail: manuscript_submission@liguori.org. Website: www.liguori.org. Catholic/Redemptorists. Submit by e-mail. Spreading the Good News of the gospel by means of low-cost publications. Imprints: Libros Liguori (Spanish language), Liguori Books. Publishes 50 titles/yr.; trade paperbacks. Receives 20-30 submissions annually. 5 percent of books from first-time authors. Reprints books. Prefers up to 30,000 words for books; 40-100 pgs. for booklets; pamphlets 16-18 pgs. Book & booklet authors get royalties; pamphlet authors get flat fee on acceptance; advance varies. No simultaneous submissions. Requires requested ms by e-mail attachment. Responds in 4-8 wks. Requires NRSV. Guidelines on Website; free catalog by mail.

Nonfiction: Send 4-page summary/1 chapter; fax/e-query OK. "Looking for issues families face today—substance abuse, unwanted pregnancies, etc.; family relations; pastoral Catholic faith."

Ethnic Books: Publishes books in Spanish. See separate listing for Libros Liguori.

Also Does: Booklets, pamphlets, tracts; books on Catholic faith.

Tips: "Keep it concise, avoid academic/theological jargon, and stick to the tenets of the Catholic faith. Avoid abstract arguments. Manuscripts accepted by us must have strong, middle-of-the-road, practical spirituality."

LILLENAS PUBLISHING CO., Program Builder Series and Other Drama Resources, PO Box 419527, Kansas City MO 64141-6527. (816) 931-1900. Fax (816) 412-8390. E-mail: drama@lillenas.com. Website: www.lillenasdrama.com. Kimberly R. Messer, product line mngr. Imprint: Lillenas Drama Resources. Publishes 12+ titles/yr.; mass-market paperbacks or electronic versions. Accepts mss through agents or authors. Royalty 10 percent of retail for drama resources; outright purchase of program builder material; no advance. No simultaneous submissions. Responds in 3-4 mos. Guidelines on Website; catalog by mail.

Drama Resources: Query or complete ms; phone/fax/e-query OK. Accepts readings, one-act and full-length plays, program and service features, monologues, and sketch collections. Religion & life issues.

Special Needs: Sketch collections and plays; full-length and one-act plays for adults. Seasonal; children's or youth 5-minute sketches.

Music: For information on submitting musicals, go to: www.lillenas.com.

Tips: "We are focused on providing ministry tools to churches—both large and small. Most open to biblically based sketches and plays that have small- to medium-size casts and are easy to stage; short sketches—4 to 8 minutes."

LION AND LAMB PUBLICATIONS, 8 Three Coins Ct., Fountain Inn SC 29644. (864) 409-0015. E-mail: info@lionandlambpublications.com. Website: www.lionandlambpublications.com. Andriea Chenot, ed.; submit to submissions@lionandlambpublications.com. To win souls, equip saints, and strengthen faith through the power of God's Word and be a part of God's opening doors for new authors. Publishes 25 titles/yr.; hardcover. Receives 300 submissions annually. 80 percent of books from first-time authors. Accepts mss through agents or authors. Does some print-on-demand. No reprints. Royalty 10-15 percent on retail; variable advance. Average first printing 5,000. Publication within 6-12 mos. Considers simultaneous submissions. Responds in 2-4 wks. Accepted mss on disk or by e-mail. Prefers NIV or Good News. Guidelines on Website.

Nonfiction: Proposal/6 chapters; e-query OK. See Website for current needs.

Fiction: Not currently accepting fiction submissions.

Special Needs: Ministry resources primarily for children and youth ministries; Sunday school curriculum; Christian homeschool curriculum.

Also Does: Computer games and other specialty products.

Photos/Artwork: Accepts freelance photos for book covers; open to queries from freelance artists.

Tips: "We are most open to ministry resources and most concerned with books that help win souls, equip saints, and strengthen faith."

LION PUBLISHING, 4050 Lee Vance View, Colorado Springs CO 80918-7102. (719) 536-3271. David C. Cook. Accepts no freelance submissions.

LITTLE LAUREN BOOKS, PO Box 145, Summit Point WV 25446 (Moving to NYC—check Website for new address). Toll-free (888) 769-9931. E-mail: JLouis@LittleLaurenBooks.com. Website: www.littlelauren.com. Jo Louis, ed. Books for teens. Publishes 2-3 titles/yr.; trade paperbacks. Receives 150 submissions annually. 90 percent of books from first-time authors. Prefers mss through agents. No reprints. Does print-on-demand. Prefers 60,000-75,000 wds. Royalty on net; no advance. Average first printing up to 1,000 or POD. Publication within 9-15 mos. Responds in 3 wks. Guidelines on Website; no catalog.

    Nonfiction: Proposal/2-3 chapters; no phone/fax query; e-query preferred.

    Fiction: Proposal/2-3 chapters; no phone/fax query; e-query preferred. For all ages. "Looking for YA fiction from new authors with a fresh style."

    Special Needs: Teen-centered titles.

    Also Does: T-shirts; novelty items.

    Tips: "We are looking for a solid message geared for secular teens or used by Christian teens to give to a friend as a tool for salvation."

    **Note: This publisher serviced by The Writer's Edge.

THE LITURGICAL PRESS, PO Box 7500, St. John's Abbey, Collegeville MN 56321-7500. Toll-free (800) 858-5450, ext. 2218. (320) 363-2213. Toll-free fax (800) 445-5899. (320) 363-3299. E-mail: Sales@litpress.org. Website: www.litpress.org. St. John's Abbey (a Benedictine group). Imprints: Liturgical Press Books, Michael Glazier Books, Pueblo Books, Cistercian Publications. Peter Dwyer, dir.; submit to Hans Christoffersen, ed. dir. (hchristoffe@csbsju.edu). Publishes 75 titles/yr. Prefers 100-300 pgs. Royalty 10 percent of net; some outright purchases; no advance. No simultaneous submissions. Responds in 3 mos. Guidelines by mail/Website; free catalog by mail.

    Nonfiction: Query/proposal. Adult only.

    Tips: "We publish liturgical, scriptural, theological, pastoral, and monastic wisdom resources."

LITURGY TRAINING PUBLICATIONS, Archdiocese of Chicago, 1800 N. Hermitage Ave., Chicago IL 60622-1101. Toll-free (800) 933-1800. (773) 486-8970. Fax (773) 486-7094. E-mail: editorial manager@ltp.org. Website: www.ltp.org. Catholic/Archdiocese of Chicago. Mary Ehle & Mary Fox, eds. Resources for liturgy in Christian life. Imprint: Hillenbrand Books (Kevin Thornton, ed.). Publishes 25 titles/yr.; hardcover, trade paperbacks, coffee-table books. Receives 150 submissions annually. 25 percent of books from first-time authors. Accepts mss through agents or authors. No subsidy or print-on-demand. Reprints books. Variable royalty on net or work-for-hire; pays an advance. Average first printing 2,000-5,000. Publication within 18 mos. Considers simultaneous submissions. Accepts full mss by e-mail. Responds in 3 mos. Prefers RNAB, NRSV Catholic edition. Guidelines by mail/e-mail/Website; free catalog by mail.

    Nonfiction: Proposal/1 chapter; no phone/fax/e-query.

    Ethnic Books: Hispanic.

    Photos/Artwork: Accepts freelance photos for book covers; open to queries from freelance artists.

    Tips: "Our focus is on providing materials to aid in participation in Catholic worship."

LOYOLA PRESS, 3441 N. Ashland Ave., Chicago IL 60657. Toll-free (800) 621-1008. (773) 281-1818. Fax (773) 281-0152. E-mail: editorial@loyolapress.com. Website: www.loyolapress.org. Catholic. Joseph Durepos, acq. ed. (durepos@loyolapress.com). Publishes in the Jesuit and Ignatian spirituality tradition. Publishes 20-30 titles/yr.; hardcover, trade paperbacks. Receives 500 submissions annually. Accepts mss through agents or authors. Prefers 25,000-75,000 words or 150-300 pgs. Standard royalty; reasonable advance. Average first printing 7,500-10,000. Considers simultaneous submissions and first-time authors without agents. Responds in 10-12 wks. Prefers NRSV (Catholic Edition). Guidelines/catalog on Website.

> **Nonfiction:** Query first; proposal/sample chapters; no phone query; e-query OK.
> **Tips:** "Looking for books and authors that help make Catholic faith relevant and offer practical tools for the well-lived spiritual life."

LUTHERAN UNIVERSITY PRESS, PO Box 390759, Minneapolis MN 55439. Toll-free (888) 696-1828. (952) 835-1828. Fax (952) 835-2613. E-mail: publisher@lutheranupress.org. Website: www.lutheranupress.org. Leonard Flachman, pub.; Karen Walhof, ed. Publishes 8-10 titles/yr.; hardcover, trade paperbacks, coffee-table books. Receives dozens of submissions annually. **SUBSIDY PUBLISHES 25 PERCENT**. No print-on-demand or reprints. Royalty 10-15 percent of net; no advance. Average first printing 500-2,000. Publication within 6 mos. No simultaneous submissions. Responds in 3 wks. Guidelines by e-mail; free catalog by mail.

> **Nonfiction:** Proposal/sample chapters in electronic format.
> **Photos:** Accepts freelance photos for book covers.
> **Tips:** "We accept manuscripts only from faculty of Lutheran colleges, universities, seminaries, and Lutheran faculty from other institutions."

LUTHERAN VOICES, Book Submissions, Augsburg Fortress, PO Box 1209, Minneapolis MN 55440-1209. E-mail: lutheranvoices@augsburgfortress.org. Website: www.augsburgfortress.org. Evangelical Lutheran Church in America. Develops quality, accessible books written primarily by ELCA authors that inform, teach, inspire, and renew. Series of books; 96 pgs. ea. Royalty. Responds in 8-12 wks. Guidelines on Website.

> **Nonfiction:** Proposal.
> **Tips:** "We are seeking prophets and preachers, politicians and pastors; educators and scientists; caregivers and counselors; professors and students; scholars and homemakers—people who have a story to tell, topics to illumine, and ideas to explore. It is expected that authors will write out of a foundational understanding of Lutheran theology and practice, though topics may be of interest to a wider Christian audience."

LUTTERWORTH PRESS, PO Box 60, Cambridge CB1 2NT, England. Phone +44 1223 350865. Fax +44 1223 366951. E-mail: publishing@lutterworth.com. Website: www.lutterworth.com. Adrian Brink, ed. Publishes nonfiction, academic, and educational titles in the areas of art, history & biography, literary criticism, religion, biblical studies, and theology. Imprints: Patrick Hardy Books, Acorn Editions. Publishes 25 titles/yr. (5 reprints, 20 new); hardcover & trade paperbacks. Receives 100 submissions annually. 90 percent of books from first-time authors. Accepts mss through agents or authors. **SUBSIDY PUBLISHES 2 PERCENT**. Does print-on-demand. Royalty on retail; pays an advance. Publication within 18 mos. No simultaneous submissions. Responds in 3 mos. Requested ms by mail. Guidelines on Website; free catalog by mail.

> **Nonfiction:** Proposal/2 chapters; e-query OK.
> **Tips:** "For full author guidelines, visit our Website."

MACALESTER PARK PUBLISHING, 24558—546th Ave., Austin MN 55912. Toll-free fax (800) 407-9078. (507) 396-0135. E-mail: Macalesterpark@macalesterpark.com or through Website: www.macalesterpark.com. Focuses on reprinting books. Sue Franklin, owner.

MAGNUS PRESS, PO Box 2666, Carlsbad CA 92018. (760) 806-3743. Fax (760) 806-3689. E-mail: magnuspres@aol.com. Website: www.magnuspress.com. Warren Angel, ed. dir. All books must reflect a strong belief in Christ, solid biblical understanding, and the author's ability to relate to the average person. Imprint: Canticle Books. Publishes 3 titles/yr.; trade paperbacks. Receives 60 submissions annually. 50 percent of books from first-time authors. Accepts mss through agents or authors. Reprints books. Prefers 105-300 pgs. Graduated royalty on retail; no advance. Average first printing 2,500. Publication within 1 yr. Considers simultaneous submissions. Accepts requested ms on disk. Responds in 1 mo. Guidelines by mail/e-mail; free catalog by mail.

> **Nonfiction:** Query or proposal/2-3 chapters; fax query OK. "Looking for spirituality, thematic biblical studies, unique inspirational/devotional books, e.g., *Adventures of an Alaskan Preacher.*"
>
> **Tips:** "Our writers need solid knowledge of the Bible and a mature spirituality that reflects a profound relationship with Jesus Christ. Most open to a popularly written biblical study that addresses a real concern/issue in the church at large today; or a unique inspirational book. Study the market; know what we do and don't publish."
>
> ****Note:** This publisher serviced by The Writer's Edge.

MARCHER LORD PRESS, 8345 Pepperridge Dr., Colorado Springs CO 80920. (719) 266-8874. E-mail: Jeff@marcherlordpress.com. Website: www.marcherlordpress.com. Jeff Gerke, pub. Premier publisher of Christian speculative fiction—it's all they do. Publishes 6-8 titles/yr.; trade paperbacks. Receives 200 submissions annually. 70 percent of books from first-time authors. Accepts mss through agents or authors. No subsidy; does print-on-demand. No reprints. Prefers 90,000 words. Author receives 50 percent after development costs are recouped; pays an advance. Publication within 6 mos. Considers simultaneous submissions. Responds in 6 mos. Guidelines/catalog on Website.

> **Fiction:** Submit only through acquisitions form on Website.
>
> **Special Needs:** Full-length, Christian speculative fiction for an adult and older-teen audience.
>
> **Photos/Artwork:** Accepts freelance photos for book covers; open to queries from freelance artists.
>
> **Tips:** "I'm most open to high fiction craftsmanship and a story that sweeps me away."

+ MASON CREST PUBLISHERS, 370 Reed Rd., Ste. 302, Broomall PA 19008. Toll-free (866) MCP-book, (610) 543-6200. Fax (610) 543-3878. Website: www.masoncrest.com. Publishes correlated materials for grades K-12; includes religious materials.

MASTER BOOKS, PO Box 726, Green Forest AR 72638. (870) 438-5288. Fax (870) 438-5120. E-mail: submissions@newleafpress.net or through Website: www.masterbooks.net. Imprint of New Leaf Press. Amanda Price, ed. Publisher of creation science books; all books are completely evolution free. Publishes 15-20 titles/yr.; hardcover, trade paperbacks. Receives 1,200 submissions annually. 10 percent of books from first-time authors. Accepts mss through agents or authors. No subsidy, print-on-demand, or reprints. Prefers 140-240 pgs. Variable royalty; rarely gives an advance. Average first printing 5,000. Publication within 12 mos. Considers simultaneous submissions. Responds in 3 mos. Guidelines by mail/e-mail/Website; catalog for 9 x 12 SAE/5 stamps.

> **Nonfiction:** Proposal/no chapters; no phone/fax query; e-query OK; submission form on Website. "Looking for biblical creationism, biblical science, creation/evolution debate material."
>
> **Special Needs:** Creation science books and books for the Christian-education/homeschool markets.
>
> **Tips:** "Most open to books for education with lots of hands-on activities."
>
> ****Note:** This publisher serviced by The Writers' Edge.

MCRUFFY PRESS, PO Box 212, Raymore MO 64083. Toll-free (888) 967-1200. Toll-free fax (888) 967-1300. E-mail: brian@mcruffy.com. Website: www.mcruffy.com. Brian Davis, ed. Christian publisher of children's trade books, children's audio, and homeschool materials. Open to freelance. Requires e-query. Incomplete topical listings.

Tips: "Most open to seeing elementary educational materials, any subject area. Not currently accepting picture-book manuscripts."

MERCER UNIVERSITY PRESS, 1400 Coleman Ave., Macon GA 31207-0003. (478) 301-2880. Fax (478) 301-2264. E-mail: jolley_ma@mercer.edu. Website: www.mupress.org. Baptist. Submit to Editor-in-Chief. Publishes 35 titles/yr. Receives 300 submissions annually. 40 percent of books from first-time authors. Accepts some mss through agents. Some reprints. Royalty on net; no advance. Average first printing 800-1,200. Publication within 24 mos. Prefers requested ms in hard copy; no disk or e-mail submissions. Responds in 3-4 mos. Guidelines on Website.

Nonfiction: Proposal/2 chapters; fax/e-query OK. "We are looking for books on history, philosophy, theology, literary studies, and religion, including history of religion, philosophy of religion, Bible studies, and ethics."

Fiction: No religious fiction, only Southern literary. Author information form on Website.

MERIWETHER PUBLISHING LTD./CONTEMPORARY DRAMA SERVICE, 885 Elkton Dr., Colorado Springs CO 80907. (719) 594-4422. Fax (719) 594-9916. E-mail: MerPCDS@aol.com, or editor@meriwether.com. Website: www.meriwetherpublishing.com. Nondenominational. Arthur L. Zapel, exec. ed.; submit to Rhonda Wray, Christian ed. Publishes 30-45 plays & books/yr. Primarily a publisher of plays for Christian and general markets; must be acceptable for use in a wide variety of Christian denominations. Imprint: Contemporary Drama Service. Publishes 3 bks./25 plays/yr. Receives 1,200 submissions annually (mostly plays). 75 percent of submissions from first-time authors. Accepts mss through agents or authors. No reprints. Prefers 225 pgs. Royalty 10 percent of net or retail; no advance. Average first printing of books 1,500-2,500, plays 500. Publication within 6 mos. Considers simultaneous submissions. No e-mail submissions. Responds in up to 2 mos. Any Bible version. Guidelines by mail/e-mail; catalog for 9 x 12 SASE.

Nonfiction: Table of contents/1 chapter; fax/e-query OK. "Looking for creative worship books, i.e., drama; using the arts in worship; how-to books with ideas for Christian education." Submit books to Meriwether.

Fiction: Complete ms for plays. Plays only, for all ages. Always looking for Christmas and Easter plays (1 hr. maximum). Submit plays to Contemporary Drama.

Special Needs: Religious drama—or religious plays—mainstream theology. "We prefer plays that can be staged during a worship service."

Tips: "Our books are on drama or any creative, artistic area that can be a part of worship. Writers should familiarize themselves with our catalog before submitting to ensure that their manuscript fits with the list we've already published." Contemporary Drama Service wants easy-to-stage comedies, skits, one-act plays, large-cast musicals, and full-length comedies for schools (junior high through college) and churches (including chancel dramas for Christmas and Easter). Most open to anything drama-related. "Study our catalog so you'll know what we publish and what would fit our list."

MESSIANIC JEWISH PUBLISHERS, 6120 Day Long Ln., Clarksville MD 21029. (410) 531-6644. Fax (410) 531-9440. E-mail: editor@messianicjewish.net. Website: www.MessianicJewish.net. Lederer/Messianic Jewish Communications. Submit to The Editor. Books that build up the Messianic Jewish community, witness to unbelieving Jewish people, or help Christians understand their Jewish roots. Imprints: Lederer Books. Publishes 6-12 titles/yr.; hardcover, trade paperbacks. Receives 100+ submissions annually. 50 percent of books from first-time authors. No mss through agents. Reprints books. Prefers 50,000-88,000 words. Royalty 7-15 percent on net. Average first printing 5,000. Publication within 12-24 mos. No simultaneous submissions. Responds in 3-6 mos. Requires requested ms on disk. Prefers Complete Jewish Bible. Guidelines on Website; free catalog by mail.

Nonfiction: Read submission guidelines first; then query. Messianic Judaism, Jewish evangelism, or Jewish roots of Christian faith. "Must have Messianic Jewish theme and demonstrate familiarity with Jewish culture and thought."

Fiction: Read submission guidelines first. For adults. Jewish themes only.

Special Needs: Messianic Jewish commentaries.

Ethnic Books: Jewish; Messianic Jewish.

Artwork: Open to queries from freelance artists.

Tips: "Must request guidelines before submitting book proposal; all submissions must meet our requirements. Looking for Messianic Jewish commentaries. Books must address one of the following: Jewish evangelism, Jewish roots of Christianity, or Messianic Judaism."

MILLENNIUM III PUBLISHERS, 174 N. Moore Rd., Simpsonville SC 29680. Willard A. Ramsey, sr. ed. To define the cause of the moral and spiritual decline, and to help restore Christian influence, in our national culture. Publishes 4-5 titles/yr. Receives 100+ submissions annually. 50 percent of books from first-time authors. Accepts mss through agents or authors. Reprints books. Prefers 200-300 pgs. Royalty 10-15 percent on net; some advances. Publication within 10-12 mos. Considers simultaneous submissions. Responds in 6-8 wks. Prefers NKJV. Guidelines by mail.

Nonfiction: Query; no e-query.

Tips: "Most open to nonfiction books applying Christian solutions to contemporary cultural problems."

MISSION CITY PRESS, 202—2nd Ave. S., Franklin TN 37064-2650. (615) 591-1007. Fax (615) 591-1006. E-mail: info@missioncitypress.com. Website: www.missioncitypress.com or www.alifeoffaith.com. Wendy Witherow, ed. coordinator. Provides nondenominational Christian print, gift, and toy products that help young people develop a strong foundation of faith in God. Imprints: A Life of Faith, Faith & Friends. Publishes 5 titles/yr.; hardcover, trade paperbacks. 50 percent of books from first-time authors. Prefers mss through agents. No subsidy publishing or reprints. Prefers 50,000 words/224 pgs.; or 25,000 words/112 pgs. Outright purchases. Publication within 6 months. Free catalog.

Nonfiction: Query only first. All topics indicated are for children and youth only.

Fiction: Proposal/2 chapters. A Life of Faith uses life stories of fictional girls living in the 19th and early 20th centuries to help today's 8- to 14-year-old girls learn to live a lifestyle of faith.

Also Does: Board games, dolls, and accessories.

Artwork: Open to queries from freelance artists.

Contest: Sponsors a contest (see Website).

Tips: "Spend a lot of time on our Website first and only pitch us things that fit our brand."

**Note: This publisher serviced by ChristianManuscriptSubmissions.com.

MONARCH BOOKS, Wilkinson House, Jordan Hill Rd, Oxford OX2 8DR, England. Phone +44 1865 302750. Fax +44 1865 302757. E-mail: info@lionhudson.com. Website: www.lionhudson.com. Lion Hudson PLC. Tony Collins, ed. dir. The largest independent British publisher of books inspired by the Christian faith. Imprints: Monarch, Candle, Lion, Lion Children's. Publishes 160 titles/yr.; hardcover, trade paperbacks, mass-market paperbacks, coffee-table books. Receives 750 submissions annually. 20 percent of books from first-time authors. Accepts mss through agents or authors. No subsidy, print-on-demand, or reprints. Prefers 30,000 words & up. Royalty 12.5-15 percent on net; pays an advance. Average first printing 6,000. Publication within 9 mos. Considers simultaneous submissions. Prefers accepted mss by e-mail. Responds in 4-6 wks. Any Bible version. Guidelines on Website; free catalog (don't send U.S. stamps).

Nonfiction: Proposal/2 chapters; phone/fax/e-query OK.

Fiction: Only Lion Hudson imprint printing any fiction.

Special Needs: Original, saleable books with integrity and Christian core.

Photos/Artwork: Accepts freelance photos for book covers; open to queries from freelance artists.

Tips: "Most open to original, energetic, Spirit-filled books."

MOODY PUBLISHERS, 820 N. LaSalle Blvd., Chicago IL 60610. Fax (312) 329-2144. E-mail: press info@moody.edu. Website: www.moodypublishers.org. Imprints: Northfield Publishing, Lift Every Voice (African American). Moody Bible Institute. Submit to Acquisitions Coordinator. To provide books that evangelize, edify the believer, and educate concerning the Christian life. Publishes 65-70 titles/yr.; hardcover, trade paperbacks, mass-market paperbacks. Receives 3,500 submissions annually. 1 percent of books from first-time authors. Accepts mss through agents or authors. Royalty on net; advance $500-50,000. Average first printing 10,000. Publication within 1 yr. No simultaneous submissions. Requires requested ms on disk. Responds in 2-3 mos. Prefers NASB, NLT, NIV. Guidelines on Website; catalog for 9 x 12 SASE/$2.38 postage (mark "Media Mail").

Nonfiction: Considers agented proposals only; no phone/fax/e-query. "For nonfiction, we review only those proposals that come from professional literary agents." Closed to all other unsolicited mss.

Fiction: Proposal/3-5 chapters; for all ages. "We are looking for stories that glorify God both in content and style. We believe that God gives some of his children the talents to write beautiful works of fiction, and we will seek out those artists and the stories they create. We wish to direct people toward God through beauty and truth." No picture books or romance genre fiction.

Ethnic Books: African American.

Tips: "Most open to books where the writer is a recognized expert and already has a platform to promote the book."

**Note: This publisher serviced by The Writer's Edge and ChristianManuscriptSubmissions.com.

MOPS INTERNATIONAL, 2370 S. Trenton Way, Denver CO 80231-3822. (303) 733-5353. Fax (303) 733-5770. E-mail: jblackmer@MOPS.org. Website: www.MOPS.org. Jean Blackmer, pub. mngr.; Carla Foote, dir. of media. Publishes books dealing with the needs and interests of mothers with young children, who may or may not be Christians. Publishes 4-5 titles/yr. Catalog on Website.

Nonfiction: Query or proposal/3 chapters; by mail, fax, or e-mail.

Tips: "Review existing titles on our Website to avoid duplication."

MOREHOUSE PUBLISHING CO., 4775 Linglestown Rd., Harrisburg PA 17112. (212) 592-1800. E-mail: morehouse@morehousegroup.com. Website: www.churchpublishing.org. Episcopal/Church Publishing Inc. Nancy Fitzgerald, exec. ed. Publishes thought-provoking books that serve the Episcopal Church and bring people of faith closer to God. Imprints: Seabury & Church Publishing. Publishes 60 titles/yr.; hardcover, trade paperbacks. Receives 500 submissions annually. 10 percent of books from first-time authors. Accepts mss through agents or authors. No subsidy or print-on-demand. No reprints. Prefers 100-200 pgs. Royalty 10 percent of net; advance varies. Average first printing varies. Publication within 18 mos. Considers simultaneous submissions. Responds in 3-4 mos. Prefers NRSV. Guidelines on Website; free catalog by mail.

Nonfiction: Proposal/1 chapter by mail; no phone/fax/e-query.

Special Needs: Women's issues, social justice, liturgics—all from an Episcopal/RC/mainline perspective.

Tips: "Please review our Website or catalog before sending proposal. We primarily accept books in our stated categories that are written by Episcopalians and written from an Anglican perspective. Not currently accepting children's book manuscripts."

@ MORE THAN NOVELLAS.COM. E-mail: lizdelayne@hotmail.com. Website: www.MoreThan Novellas.com. Liz DeLayne, ed. To promote and build a library of family-friendly fiction—with values that exemplify the teachings and walk of Christ—for people to read on the Web. Novellas online. No payment. Guidelines on Website.

Nonfiction: Some romantic poetry.

Fiction: Complete ms by e-mail (attached or copied into the message).

Also Does: E-books.

WILLIAM MORROW, 10 E. 53rd St., New York NY 10022. (212) 207-7000. Fax (212) 207-7145. Website: www.harpercollins.com. Imprint of HarperCollins Publishers. General trade imprint; religious titles published by HarperOne. Submit to Acquisitions Editor. Royalty on retail; pays an advance. Agented submissions only.

MOUNTAIN CHURCH BOOKS, 65 Macedonia Rd., Alexander NC 28701. (828) 252-9515. Fax (828) 255-8719. E-mail: pat@abooks.com. Website: www.abooks.com. Imprint of Alexander Books. Submit to Editor. Christian books from a mainly Protestant viewpoint. Publishes hardcover & trade paperbacks. Reprints books. Royalty on net. Guidelines/catalog on Website. Incomplete topical listings.

Nonfiction: Query or proposal/3 sample chapters first; no phone/fax/e-query.

MOUNTAINVIEW PUBLISHING, 1284 Overlook Dr., Sierra Vista AZ 85635-5512. (520) 458-5602. Fax (520) 459-0162. E-mail: leeemory@earthlink.net. Website: www.trebleheartbooks.com. Christian division of Treble Heart Books. Ms. Lee Emory, ed./pub. Online Christian publisher; books never have to go out of print as long as they're being marketed and are selling. Imprints: Treble Heart (see separate listing), Sundowners, Whoodo Mysteries. Publishes 6-9 titles/yr; trade paperbacks. Receives 75 submissions annually. 30 percent of books from first-time authors. Accepts mss through agents or authors. No reprints. No word-length preference. Royalty 35 percent of net on most sales; no advance. Books are published electronically; average first printing 30-500. Publication usually within 1 yr. No simultaneous submissions (a 90-day exclusive is required on all submissions). Responds in 3-4 mos. to submissions, 1-2 wks. to queries. Guidelines on Website.

Nonfiction: Complete ms (by e-mail only) to: 1thbsubmissions2@earthlink.net. Submissions are now open between the 1st and 14th of each month. "Excellent nonfiction, inspirational books are highly desired here."

Fiction: Complete ms (by e-mail only). Genres: Historical romances; contemporary romances; novellas; mainstream and traditional inspirations in most categories; also Christian mysteries, Christian horror, and Christian westerns.

Photos: Accepts high-quality freelance photos for book covers.

Tips: "All inspirational fiction should contain faith elements. Challenge the reader to think, to look at things through different eyes. Avoid point-of-view head-hopping and clichés; avoid heavy-handed preaching. No dark angel stories, hardcore science fiction/fantasy, though will consider futuristic Christian works. Send consecutive chapters, not random. A well-developed marketing plan must accompany all submissions, and no submissions will be accepted for consideration unless guidelines are followed. Actively seeking more nonfiction at this time."

MULTNOMAH BOOKS, 12265 Oracle Blvd., Ste. 200, Colorado Springs CO 80921. (719) 590-4999. Fax (719) 590-8977. E-mail: info@waterbrookmultnomah.com. Website: www.waterbrook multnomah.com. Part of WaterBrook Multnomah, a division of Random House Inc. Ken Petersen, VP/pub.dir. Imprint information listed below. Publishes 75 titles/yr.; hardcover, trade paperbacks. Royalty on net; pays an advance. Multnomah is currently not accepting unsolicited manuscripts, proposals, or queries; no proposals for biographies, poetry, or children's books. Queries will be accepted through literary agents and at writers' conferences at which a Multnomah representative is present. Catalog on Website.

Multnomah Books: Christian living and popular theology books.

Multnomah Fiction: Well-crafted fiction that uses truth to change lives.

NATIONAL BLACK THEATRE INC., 2031-33 National Black Theatre Way, Fifth Ave. (between 125th & 126th Sts.), Harlem NY 10035. (212) 722-3800. E-mail: info@nationalblacktheatre.org. Website: www.nationalblacktheatre.org. Does drama, musicals, and children's plays. Scripts need to reflect an African or African American lifestyle. Especially open to historical or inspirational forms. Also holds workshops and readings.

NATIONAL DRAMA SERVICE, LifeWay Christian Resources, One Lifeway Plaza, Nashville TN 37234. E-mail: terry@lifeway.com. Website: www.lifeway.com. Publishes dramatic material for use in Christian ministry: drama in worship, puppet & clown scripts, Christian comedy, mime/movement scripts, reader's theater, creative worship services, monologues. Open to scripts 2-10 minutes long. E-mail for specific submissions guidelines.

NAVPRESS, Box 35001, Colorado Springs CO 80935. Website: www.navpress.com. To advance the calling of the Navigators by publishing life-transforming products that are biblically rooted, culturally relevant, and that glorify the gospel of Jesus Christ and his Kingdom. This company is restructuring and creating a two-pronged structure, dividing the team into trade publishing and direct publishing groups. Sue Kline leads the trade group, Mike Linder the direct team.
    **Note: This publisher serviced by The Writer's Edge and ChristianManuscriptSubmissions.com.

NAVPRESS TH1NK, 3820 N. 30th St., Colorado Springs CO 80904. Fax (719) 260-7223. E-mail: rebekah.guzman@navpress.com. Website: www.navpress.com. NavPress Publishing. Submit to The Editor. Books for the teen/YA market.

NAZARENE PUBLISHING HOUSE—See Beacon Hill Press of Kansas City.

NEIBAUER PRESS, 20 Industrial Dr., Warminster PA 18974. (215) 322-6200, ext. 255. Fax (215) 322-2495. E-mail: Nathan@Neibauer.com. Website: www.Neibauer.com. Nathan Neibauer, ed. For evangelical/Protestant clergy and church leaders. Publishes 8 titles/yr. Receives 100 submissions annually. 5 percent of books from first-time authors. No mss through agents. Reprints books. Prefers 200 pgs. Royalty on net; some outright purchases; no advance. Average first printing 1,500. Publication within 6 mos. Considers simultaneous submissions. Responds in 4 wks. Prefers e-mail submissions. Prefers NIV. No guidelines/catalog.
    Nonfiction: Query or proposal/2 chapters; fax query OK.
    Also Does: Pamphlets, tracts.
    Photos: Accepts freelance photos for book covers.
    Tips: "Publishes only religious books on stewardship and church enrollment, stewardship and tithing, and church enrollment tracts."

TOMMY NELSON—See Thomas Nelson Publishers.

THOMAS NELSON, FICTION, PO Box 141000, Nashville TN 37214. (615) 889-9000. Website: www.ThomasNelson.com. Thomas Nelson Inc. Ami McConnell, sr. acq. ed.; Amanda Bostic, acq. ed. Fiction from a Christian worldview. Publishes fewer than 70 titles/yr.; hardcover, trade paperbacks, mass-market paperbacks. Requires mss through agents; does not accept unsolicited manuscripts. Prefers 80,000-100,000 words. Royalty on net; pays an advance. Publication within 12 mos. Accepts simultaneous submissions. Responds in about 60 days. No guidelines; free catalog by mail.
    Fiction: Proposal/3 chapters. For teens and adults. All unsolicited manuscripts returned unopened.

THOMAS NELSON PUBLISHERS, PO Box 141000, Nashville TN 37214. (615) 889-9000. Fax (615) 902-2745. Website: www.thomasnelson.com. Does not accept or review any unsolicited queries, proposals, or manuscripts.
    **Note: This publisher serviced by The Writer's Edge and ChristianManuscriptSubmissions.com.

NEW CANAAN PUBLISHING CO. INC., PO Box 752, New Canaan CT 06840. (203) 966-3408. Fax (203) 548-9072. E-mail: info@newcanaanpublishing.com. Website: www.newcanaanpublishing .com. Kathy Mittelstadt, ed. Children's books with strong educational and moral content, for grades 1-9 (ages 5-16); also aggressively building its Christian titles list. Publishes 3-4 titles/yr.; hardcover, trade paperbacks. Receives 120 submissions annually. 50 percent of books from first-time authors. Accepts mss through agents or authors. Reprints books. Prefers 20,000-50,000 words or 120-250 pgs. Royalty 8-10 percent of net; occasional advance. Average first printing 500-5,000. Publication within 1 yr. No simultaneous submissions. Responds in 3-4 mos. Requires requested ms on disk; no e-mail submissions. Guidelines/catalog on Website or for #10 SASE.

Nonfiction: Proposal/2 chapters or complete ms; no e-query. Does not return submissions.
Fiction: Proposal/2 chapters or complete ms; no e-query. For children and teens, 6-14 yrs. "We want children's books with strong educational and moral content; 10,000-20,000 words." Now accepts picture books.
Special Needs: Middle-school-level educational books.
Photos: Accepts freelance photos for book covers.

NEW HOPE PUBLISHERS, Box 12065, Birmingham AL 35202-2065. (205) 991-8100. Fax (205) 991-4015. Website: www.newhopepublishers.com. Division of WMU. Submit to Acquisitions Editor. Publishes Christian nonfiction for women and families and books with a missional focus. Imprints: New Hope Impact (missional-community, social, personal-commitment, church-growth, and leadership issues); New Hope Arise (inspiring women, changing lives); New Hope Grow (Bible-study & teaching resources). Publishes 20-28 titles/yr.; hardcover, trade paperbacks. Receives 350 submissions annually. 25 percent of books from first-time authors. Accepts mss through agents or authors. Reprints books. Royalty on net. Average first printing 5,000-10,000. Publication within 2 yrs. Considers simultaneous submissions. Responds in 3-6 mos. Requires requested ms by e-mail. Guidelines/free catalog by mail.

Nonfiction: Proposal/2 chapters; no phone/fax/e-query. "We look for authors whose messages have a missional emphasis."
Ethnic Books: African American & Hispanic.
Photos: Accepts freelance photos for book covers.
**Note: This publisher serviced by The Writer's Edge and ChristianManuscriptSubmissions.com.

NEW LEAF PUBLISHING GROUP, PO Box 726, Green Forest AR 72638-0726. (870) 438-5288. Fax (870) 438-5120. E-mail: submissions@newleafpress.net. Website: www.nlpg.com. Craig Froman, acq. ed. Endeavors to bring the lost to Christ and understanding to the body of Christ. Imprints: New Leaf Press, Master Books, Attic Books. Publishes 25-30 titles/yr.; hardcover, trade paperbacks, occasionally high-end gift titles. Receives 1,200 submissions annually. 15 percent of books from first-time authors. Accepts mss through agents or authors. No subsidy, print-on-demand, or reprints. No length preference. Variable royalty on net; pays an advance. Average first printing varies. Publication within 8 mos. Considers simultaneous submissions. Responds within 90 days. Requires accepted ms on disk. See Author Proposal form (by e-mail/Website); free catalog by mail.

Nonfiction: Author Proposal form only; no phone query; fax/e-query OK. "Looking for books for the homeschool market, especially grades 1-8."
Special Needs: Stewardship of the earth; ancient man technology, inventions, etc.; educational products for grades K-6.
Tips: "Accepts submissions only with Author Proposal form available by e-mail or on our Website."
**Note: This publisher serviced by The Writer's Edge.

NEW SEEDS BOOKS, 300 Massachusetts Ave., Boston MA 02115. (617) 424-0030. Fax (617) 236-1563. E-mail: editors@shambhala.com. Website: www.newseeds-books.com. Shambhala

Publications Inc. David O'Neal, sr. ed. Imprint devoted to publishing works of the Christian contemplative traditions, cross-traditionally; also new and readable translations of classic texts. Publishes 10 titles/yr.; hardcover & trade paperbacks. Accepts mss through agents or authors. Reprints books. Length open. Royalty 7.5-15 percent on retail; pays an advance. Average first printing 10,000-30,000. Publication within 1 yr. Considers simultaneous submissions. Responds in 3 mos. Prefers accepted ms on disk or by e-mail. Guidelines by e-mail; free catalog by mail.

Nonfiction: Query, proposal/2 chapters, or complete ms; e-query OK.

NEW YORK UNIVERSITY PRESS, 838 Broadway, 3rd Fl., New York NY 10003-4812. (212) 998-2575. Fax (212) 995-3833. E-mail: information@nyupress.org. Website: www.nyupress.org. Jennifer Hammer, religion ed. (jennifer.hammer@nyupress.org). Embraces ideological diversity. Publishes 100 titles/yr.; hardcover, trade paperbacks. Receives 800-1,000 submissions annually. 30 percent of books from first-time authors. Few mss through agents. Royalty on net. Publication within 10-12 mos. Considers simultaneous submissions. Initial response usually within 1 mo. (peer reviewed). Guidelines on Website.

Nonfiction: Query or proposal/1 chapter.

Tips: "As a university press, we primarily publish works with a scholarly foundation written by PhDs affiliated with a university department. Our focus within religious studies is on religion in American history, culture, and politics. We do not publish liturgical studies, pastoral care, spiritual guides, or exegesis. If you are not a university- or seminary-affiliated scholar (or a professional journalist) it is unlikely that your work will be appropriate for our list."

+ **NORDSKOG PUBLISHING**, 4562 Westinghouse St., Ste. E, Ventura CA 93003. (805)642-2070. Fax (805)642-1862. E-mail: jerry@NordskogPublishing.com. Website: www.NordskogPublishing.com. Jerry Nordskog, pub. Driven by a passion to honor God, edify his people, and advance Christ's cause. Imprint: Noble Novels. Publishes 8-12 titles/yr. Receives 25+ submissions annually. 33 percent of books from first-time authors. Prefers mss through agents. Often does print-on-demand. Does hardcover, trade paperbacks, mass-market paperbacks & coffee-table books. Reprints books. Prefers 200-300 pgs. Royalty 10-25 percent; no advance unless well-known author. Average first printing 500-1,000. Publication within 10+ mos. Sometimes considers simultaneous submissions. Accepted ms on disk. Responds in 60-90 days. Guidelines by e-mail; free catalog.

Nonfiction: Proposal with contents & author bio, or complete ms; fax query OK. "We accept anything that is thoroughly biblical, sound theologically, especially if unique and especially if 'meaty.'"

Fiction: Proposal with contents & author bio, or complete ms; fax query OK. Any genre.

Photos/Artwork: Accepts freelance photos for book covers; considers queries from freelance artists.

Tips: "We look for sound theological doctrine and unique topics."

NORTHWESTERN PUBLISHING HOUSE, 1250 N. 113th St., Milwaukee WI 53226-3284. Toll-free (800) 662-6022. Fax (414) 475-7684. E-mail: braunj@nph.wels.net. Website: www.nph.net. Lutheran. Rev. John A. Braun, VP of publishing services. Open to freelance. Responds in 2-3 mos. Guidelines on Website (www.nph.net/cgi-bin/site.pl?aboutUsManuscript). Incomplete topical listings.

Nonfiction: Complete ms/cover letter; or query letter/outline.

OAKTARA PUBLISHERS (formerly Capstone Fiction Group), PO Box 8, Waterford VA 20197. (540) 882-9062. Fax (540) 882-3719. E-mail: inquiries@capstonefiction.com or rtucker@capstonefiction .com. Website: www.capstonefiction.com. Jeff Nesbitt, mng. dir.; Ramona Tucker, ed. dir. To create opportunities for new, talented Christian writers and to promote leading-edge fiction by established Christian authors; inspirational fiction only. Does print-on-demand. Reprints books. Royalty; no advance. Guidelines on Website.

Fiction: Submit by e-mail (attached file) in one Word file. For all ages.

ONE WORLD/BALLANTINE BOOKS, 1745 Broadway, New York NY 10036. (212) 782-9000. Fax (212) 572-4949. Website: www.randomhouse.com. Submit to Senior Editor. Imprint of Ballantine Books. Books are written by and focus on African Americans but from an American perspective. Publishes 24 titles/yr.; hardcover, trade paperbacks, mass-market paperbacks. Receives 850 submissions annually. 50 percent of books from first-time authors. Submissions from agents only. No reprints. Prefers 80,000 words. Royalty 7.5-15 percent on retail; advance $40,000-200,000. Average first printing 10,000. Publication within 18 mos. Considers simultaneous submissions. Responds in 2 mos. No disk or e-mail. No guidelines/catalog. Note: No unsolicited submissions, proposals, manuscripts, or queries at this time.

Nonfiction: Agented submissions only.

Fiction: Agented submissions only. "Contemporary/ethnic novels for African American women."

Ethnic Books: All are ethnic books.

Tips: "You must understand African American culture and avoid timeworn stereotypes."

OREGON CATHOLIC PRESS, PO Box 18030, Portland OR 97218-0030. Toll-free (800) 548-8749. (503) 281-1191. Toll-free fax (800) 462-7329. E-mail: submissions@ocp.org. Website: www.ocp .org. Bari Colombari, sr. ed. To enhance the worship in the Catholic Church in the United States. Imprint: Pastoral Press. Publishes 8 titles/yr. Receives 80 submissions annually. 5 percent of books from first-time authors. No mss through agents. No reprints. Prefers 192 pgs. Royalty 5-12 percent of net; no advance. Average first printing 500. Publication within 12 mos. Considers simultaneous submissions. Prefers requested ms on disk; no e-mail submissions. Responds in 3 mos. Prefers NAB. Guidelines on Website; free catalog by mail.

Nonfiction: Proposal/1 chapter; no phone/fax/e-query. "Looking for liturgical ministries."

Ethnic Books: Hispanic/Spanish language.

Photos: Accepts freelance photos for book covers.

Tips: "Most open to Catholic liturgical works."

OUR SUNDAY VISITOR INC., 200 Noll Plaza, Huntington IN 46750-4303. Toll-free (800) 348-2440. (260) 356-8400. Fax (260) 356-8472. E-mail: booksed@osv.com or oursunvis@osv.com. Website: www.osv.com. Catholic. Submit to Acquisitions Editor. To assist Catholics to be more aware and secure in their faith and capable of relating their faith to others. Publishes 30-40 titles/yr.; hardcover, trade paperbacks. Receives 500+ submissions annually. 10 percent of books from first-time authors. Prefers not to work through agents. Reprints books. Royalty 10-12 percent of net; average advance $1,500. Average first printing 5,000. Publication within 1-2 yrs. No simultaneous submissions. Responds in 3 mos. Requires requested ms on disk. Guidelines on Website; catalog for 9 x 12 SASE.

Nonfiction: Proposal/2 chapters; e-query OK. "Most open to devotional books (not first person), church history, heritage and saints, the parish, prayer, and family."

Also Does: Pamphlets, booklets.

Photos: Occasionally accepts freelance photos for book covers.

Tips: "All books published must relate to the Catholic Church; unique books aimed at our audience. Give as much background information as possible on author qualification, why the topic was chosen, and unique aspects of the project. Follow our guidelines. We are expanding our religious education product line and programs."

PACIFIC PRESS PUBLISHING ASSN., Box 5353, Nampa ID 83653-5353. (208) 465-2500. Fax (208) 465-2531. E-mail: booksubmissions@pacificpress.com. Website: www.pacificpress.com. Seventh-day Adventist. David Jarnes, book ed.; submit to Scott Cady, acq. ed. Books of interest and importance to Seventh-day Adventists and other Christians of all ages. Publishes 35-40 titles/yr.; hardcover, trade paperbacks. Receives 500 submissions annually. 5 percent of books from first-time authors. Accepts mss through agents or authors. No reprints. Prefers 50,000-130,000 words or 160-400 pgs. Royalty

12-15 percent of net; advance $1,500. Average first printing 5,000. Publication within 6 mos. Considers simultaneous submissions. Responds in 1 mo. Requires requested ms on disk or by e-mail. Guidelines at www.pacificpress.com/index/php?pgName=newsSubGuides; no catalog.

Nonfiction: Query only; e-query OK.

Fiction: Query only; almost none accepted; mainly biblical. Children's books: "Must be on a uniquely Seventh-day Adventist topic. No talking animals or fantasy."

Ethnic Books: Hispanic.

Also Does: Booklets.

Tips: "Most open to spirituality, inspirational, and Christian living. Our Website has the most up-to-date information, including samples of recent publications. For more information, see www.adventistbookcenter.com. Do not send full manuscript unless we request it after reviewing your proposal."

P & R PUBLISHING CO., PO Box 817, Phillipsburg NJ 08865. (908) 454-0505. Fax (908) 454-0859. E-mail: editorial@prpbooks.com. Website: www.prpbooks.com. Marvin Padgett, ed. dir.; Melissa Craig, cq. ed. Mission is to publish Reformed material that is consistent with biblical teaching, as summarized in the Westminster Standards. Publishes 40 titles/yr.; hardcover, trade paperbacks. Receives 400 submissions annually. 5 percent of books from first-time authors; electronic submissions only. Accepts mss through agents or authors. Reprints books. Prefers 140-240 pgs. Royalty 10-14 percent of net; pays an advance. Average first printing 4,000. Publication within 10-12 mos. Considers simultaneous submissions. Responds in 2 mos. to proposals. Guidelines by e-mail/ Website (Potential Authors section); catalog by mail.

Nonfiction: Only accepts e-submissions with completion of online author guidelines (hard copy mss not returned).

Fiction: Only accepts e-submissions with completion of online author guidelines (hard copy mss not returned). For children or teens.

Also Does: Booklets.

Tips: "Direct biblical/Reformed content. Clear, engaging, and insightful applications of reformed theology to life. Offer us fully developed proposals and polished sample chapters. All books must be consistent with the Westminster Confession of Faith."

**Note: This publisher serviced by The Writer's Edge and ChristianManuscriptSubmissions.com.

@ PARADISE RESEARCH PUBLICATIONS INC., PO Box 837, Kihei HI 96753-0837. Phone/fax (808) 874-4876. E-mail: dickb@dickb.com. Website: www.dickb.com/index.shtml. Ken Burns, VP. Imprint: Tincture of Time Press. Publishes 5 titles/yr.; trade paperbacks. Receives 8 submissions annually. 80 percent of books from first-time authors. No mss through agents. Reprints books. Prefers 250 pgs. Royalty 10 percent of retail; no advance. Average first printing 5,000. Publication within 2 mos. Considers simultaneous submission. Responds in 1 wk. No disk. Prefers KJV. No guidelines; free catalog.

Nonfiction: Query only; no phone/fax/e-query. Books on the biblical/Christian history of early Alcoholics Anonymous.

Also Does: Pamphlets, booklets, e-books.

Tips: "Most open to the history of early AA Christian Fellowship Program, healing of alcoholism/addiction by power of God."

PARAGON HOUSE, 1925 Oakcrest Ave., Ste. 7, St. Paul MN 55113-2619. (651) 644-3087. Fax (651) 644-0997. E-mail: submissions@paragonhouse.com. Website: www.paragonhouse.com. Rosemary Yokoi, acq. ed. Serious nonfiction and texts with an emphasis on religion, philosophy, and society. Imprints: Omega Books, Vision of. . . . Publishes 12-15 titles/yr.; hardcover, trade paperbacks. Receives 1,200 submissions annually. 20 percent of books from first-time authors. Accepts mss through agents or author. Reprints books. Prefers average 250 pgs. Royalty 7-10 percent of net; advance $1,000. Average first printing 1,500-3,000. Publication within 12-18 mos. Considers few simultaneous submissions. Accepts e-mail submissions (attached file). Responds in 2-3 mos. Guidelines/catalog on Website.

Nonfiction: Query; proposal/2-3 chapters or complete ms; no phone/fax query. "Looking for scholarly overviews of topics in religion and society; textbooks in philosophy; ecumenical subjects; and reference books."

PARSON PLACE PRESS LLC, PO Box 8277, Mobile AL 36689-0277. E-mail: info@parsonplacepress .com. Website: www.parsonplacepress.com. Michael L. White, mng. ed. Devoted to giving both Christian authors and Christian readers a fair deal. Publishes 3-5 titles/yr.; hardcover, trade paperbacks. Receives 50 submissions annually. 75 percent of books from first-time authors. Accepts mss through agents or authors. **SUBSIDY PUBLISHES 10-20 PERCENT**; does print-on-demand. Reprints books. Prefers 104-200 pgs. Royalty 50 percent of net; no advance. Average first printing 4 (because of print-on-demand capabilities). Publication within 3 mos. No simultaneous submissions. Responds in 4-6 wks. Requested mss by e-mail (attached file). Prefers NASB. Guidelines on Website; catalog by e-mail.

Nonfiction: Proposal/2 chapters; e-query OK. Christian topic/content only.

Fiction: Proposal/2 chapters; e-query OK. For all ages.

Special Needs: In nonfiction, discipleship, encouragement, personal growth, pastoral ministry, church growth, development, leadership. In fiction, mystery, suspense, romance, serials.

Contests: Sponsors a poetry contest; guidelines on Website.

Photos/Artwork: Accepts freelance photos for book covers; open to queries from freelance artists.

Tips: "Most open to conservative, biblically based content that ministers to Christians. Write intelligently, clearly, sincerely, and engagingly."

PARSONS PUBLISHING HOUSE, PO Box 488, Stafford VA 22554. (850) 867-3061. Fax (540) 659-9043. E-mail: info@parsonspublishinghouse.com. Website: www.parsonspublishinghouse.com. Nondenominational. Diane Parsons, chief ed. Exists to partner with authors to release their voice into their world. Publishes 5 titles/yr.; hardcover, trade paperbacks. Receives 40 submissions annually. 85 percent of books from first-time authors. Accepts mss through agents or authors. Reprints books. Prefers 120-160 pgs. Royalty 10 percent on net; no advance. Average first printing 300. Publication within 9 mos. Considers simultaneous submissions. Responds in 60 days. Prefers accepted mss by e-mail. Guidelines by e-mail; no catalog.

Nonfiction: Query; e-query OK.

Fiction: Query; proposal/3 chapters; e-query OK. For teens & adults.

Ethnic Books: Hispanic.

Artwork: Open to queries from freelance artists.

Tips: "Most open to Christian living and worship."

PAULINE BOOKS & MEDIA, Daughters of St. Paul, 50 St. Pauls Ave., Jamaica Plain MA 02130-3491. (617) 522-8911. E-mail: editorial@paulinemedia.com. Website: www.pauline.org. Catholic. Sr. Maria Grace Dateno, FSP, and Sr. Sean Mayer, FSP, acq. eds.; Submit to Lauren Koehler, ed. asst. Responds to the hopes and needs of their readers with the Word of God and in the spirit of St. Paul, utilizing all available forms of media so others can find and develop faith in Jesus within the current culture. Imprint: Pauline Kids (see separate listing). Publishes 20 titles/yr.; hardcover, trade paperbacks. Receives 350-400 submissions annually. 10 percent of books from first-time authors. Accepts mss through agents or authors. No subsidy or print-on-demand. Reprints books. Prefers 10,000-60,000 words. Royalty 5-10 percent on net; pays an advance. Average first printing 4,000-10,000. Publication within 12 mos. Considers simultaneous submissions. Responds in 2-3 mos. Prefers requested ms by e-mail. Prefers NRSV. Guidelines by mail/e-mail/Website; free catalog by mail.

Nonfiction: Query; proposal/2 chapters; complete ms; e-query OK.

Special Needs: "Spirituality (prayer/holiness of life/seasonal titles), faith formation (religious instruction/catechesis), family life (marriage/parenting issues), biographies of the saints, prayer books. Of particular interest is our faith and culture line, which includes titles that show how Christ is present and may be more fully embraced and proclaimed within our media culture."

Tips: "Submissions are evaluated on adherence to gospel values, harmony with the Catholic tradition, relevance of topic, and quality of writing."

**Note: This publisher serviced by The Writer's Edge.

PAULINE KIDS, 50 St. Paul's Ave., Boston MA 02130. (617) 522-8911. Fax (617) 524-9805. E-mail: editorial@paulinemedia.com. Website: www.pauline.org. Pauline Books & Media/Catholic. Christina M. Wegendt FSP, children's ed.; Diana Lynch, assoc. children's ed.; submit to Lauren Koehler, ed. asst. Seeks to provide wholesome and entertaining reading that can help children develop strong Christian values. Publishes 20-25 titles/yr.; hardcover, trade paperbacks. Receives 300-450 submissions annually. 10 percent of books from first-time authors. Accepts mss through agents or authors. Reprints books. Royalty 5-10 percent on net; pays an advance. Average first printing 4,000-5,000. Publication within 24 mos. Considers simultaneous submissions. Responds in 2-3 mos. Prefers accepted ms by e-mail. Prefers NRSV. Guidelines by mail/e-mail/Website; free catalog by mail.

Nonfiction/Fiction: Proposal/2 chapters for easy-to-read & middle-grade readers; complete ms for board and picture books; e-query OK.

Special Needs: Easy-to-read and middle-reader chapter fiction.

Photos/Artwork: Accepts freelance photos for book covers; open to queries from freelance artists.

**Note: This publisher serviced by The Writer's Edge.

PAULIST PRESS, 997 Macarthur Blvd., Mahwah NJ 07430. (201) 825-7300. Fax (201) 825-8345. E-mail: info@paulistpress.com. Website: www.paulistpress.com. Catholic. Lawrence Boadt, ed. dir. To bring Catholic values and beliefs into dialogue with the North American culture. Imprints: Newman Press, HiddenSpring, Stimulus. Publishes 80 titles/yr. Receives 1,000 submissions annually. 15 percent of books from first-time authors. Accepts mss through agents or authors. Prefers 150-250 pgs. Royalty 7-10 percent of net; advance $500-1,000. Average first printing 2,000-2,500. Publication within 18-24 mos. Considers simultaneous submissions (prefers 1st option). Requires requested ms on disk. Responds in 2 mos. Prefers NRSV. Guidelines by mail/e-mail/Website; free catalog by mail.

Nonfiction: Proposal/2 chapters or complete ms; e-query OK. "Looking for theology (Catholic and ecumenical Christian), popular spirituality, liturgy, and religious education texts." Children's books for 2-5, 5-8, 8-12, 9-14 years, as per guidelines; complete ms.

Ethnic Books: A few Hispanic.

Also Does: Booklets, pamphlets.

Photos: Accepts freelance photos for book covers.

Tips: "Most open to good spirituality books that have solid input and a clear sense of tradition behind them. Demonstrate grounded convictions. Stay well read. Pay attention to contemporary social needs."

PELICAN PUBLISHING CO. INC., 1000 Burmaster St., Gretna LA 70053. (504) 368-1175. Fax (504) 368-1195. E-mail: editorial@pelicanpub.com. Website: www.pelicanpub.com. Nina Kooij, ed-in-chief. To publish books of quality and permanence that enrich the lives of those who read them. Imprints: Firebird Press, Jackson Square Press, Dove Inspirational Press (see separate listing). Publishes 3 titles/yr.; hardcover, trade paperbacks. Receives 250 submissions annually. No books from first-time authors. Accepts mss through agents or authors. Reprints books. Prefers 200+ pgs. Royalty; some advances. Publication within 9-18 mos. No simultaneous submissions. Responds in 1 mo. on queries. Requires accepted ms on disk. Prefers KJV. Guidelines by mail/Website; catalog for 9 x 12 SAE/6 stamps.

Nonfiction: Proposal/2 chapters; no phone/fax/e-query. Children's picture books to 1,100 words (send complete ms); middle readers about Louisiana (ages 8 & up) at least 25,000 words; cookbooks at least 200 recipes.

Fiction: Complete ms. Children's picture books only. For ages 5-8 only.

Photos/Artwork: Accepts freelance photos for book covers; open to queries from freelance artists.

Tips: "On inspirational titles we need a high-profile author who already has an established speaking circuit so books can be sold at these appearances."

PENGUIN PRAISE, 375 Hudson St., New York NY 10014. (212) 366-2000. Website: www.penguin .com. Joel Fotinos, pub.; Denise Silvestro, exec. ed. Christian publishing imprint of Penguin Group (USA). Will publish books by top-tier Christian authors. Does not usually accept unsolicited mss. Distribution handled by Strang Communications and Noble sales group.

PERIGEE BOOKS, 375 Hudson St., New York NY 10014. (212) 366-2000. Fax (212) 366-2365. Website: www.penguingroup.com. Penguin Group (USA) Inc. John Duff, pub./sr. ed. Publishes 3-5 spirituality titles out of 55-60 titles/yr. Receives 300 submissions annually. 30 percent of books from first-time authors. Strongly prefers mss through agents (but accepts freelance). Prefers 60,000-80,000 words. Royalty 6-7.5 percent; advance $5,000-150,000. Average first printing varies. Publication within 18 mos. Considers simultaneous submissions. Responds in 2 mos. Guidelines available with contract; free catalog.

Nonfiction: Query only; no phone/e-query; fax query OK. "Looking for spiritual, prescriptive, self-help, and women's issues; no memoirs or personal histories."

PFLAUM PUBLISHING GROUP, 2621 Dryden Rd., Ste. 300, Dayton OH 45439. (937) 293-1415. Fax (937) 293-1310. E-mail: kcannizzo@pflaum.com or jeanlarkin@pflaum.com. Website: www .pflaum.com. Peter Li Education Group/Catholic. Karen Cannizzo, ed. dir. or Jean Larkin, ed. dir. Weekly lectionary-based magazines for pre-K through 8; sacramental preparation programs for primary, junior high, and high school; catechetical resources for pre-K through 12, and religious educators. Publishes 20 titles/yr.; trade paperbacks. Receives 25 submissions annually. 10 percent of books from first-time authors. No reprints. Royalty on net or outright purchase; advance depends on author arrangement. Average first printing 2,000. Publication within 9 mos. No simultaneous submissions. Requires accepted ms on disk or by e-mail. Responds as soon as possible. Prefers NRSV. Free guidelines/catalog.

Nonfiction: Proposal with at least 1 chapter; e-query OK. "We like user-friendly resources."

Tips: "We are looking for user-friendly, field-tested resources, particularly related to sacramental preparation and lectionary-based catechesis. We specialize in consumable resources—one book per user—that need to be replaced every year, for example, for Lent and Advent."

THE PILGRIM PRESS, 700 Prospect Ave. E., Cleveland OH 44115-1100. (216) 736-3755. Fax (216) 736-2207. E-mail: sadlerk@ucc.org or stavetet@ucc.org. Website: www.thepilgrimpress.com. United Church of Christ. Timothy G. Staveteig, pub.; Kim Sadler, ed. dir. Church and educational resources. Publishes 55 titles/yr. Receives 500 submissions annually. 60 percent of books from first-time authors. Prefers mss through agents. Reprints books. Royalty 10 percent of net; or work-for-hire, onetime fee; negotiable advance. Average first printing 2,000. Publication within 18 mos. No simultaneous submissions. Responds in 13 wks. Accepts submissions on disk or by e-mail. Guidelines/catalog on Website.

Nonfiction: Query first. Proposal/2 chapters; e-query through Website.

Special Needs: Children's sermons, worship resources, youth materials, and religious materials for ethnic groups.
Ethnic Books: African American, Native American, Asian American, Pacific Islanders, and Hispanic.
Photos: Accepts freelance photos for book covers.
Tips: "Most open to well-written manuscripts that address mainline Protestant Christian needs and that use inclusive language and follow *The Chicago Manual of Style.*"

PLAYERS PRESS INC., PO Box 1132, Studio City CA 91614-0132. (818) 789-4980. E-mail: player spress@att.net. Website: www.ppeps.com. Players Press Inc. Robert W. Gordon, ed. To create is to live life's purpose. Publishes only dramatic works; prides themselves on high-quality titles. Imprints: Phantom Publications, Showcase. Publishes 1-6 religious titles/yr.; hardcover, trade paperbacks, mass-market paperbacks, coffee-table books. Receives 50-80 religious submissions annually. 90 percent of books from first-time authors. Accepts mss through agents or authors. No subsidy publishing. Does print-on-demand with older titles. Rarely reprints books. Variable length. Royalty 10 percent on net; some advances. Average first printing 1,000-10,000. Publication within 12 mos. No simultaneous submissions. No submissions by e-mail. Responds in 1-3 wks. on query; 3-12 mos. on ms. Guidelines by mail; catalog for 9 x 12 SAE/11 stamps or $4.50.
  Nonfiction/Plays: Query only; no phone/fax/e-query. "Always looking for plays and musicals, books on theatre, film, and/or television. For all ages."
  Photos/Artwork: Accepts freelance photos for book covers; open to queries from freelance artists.
  Tips: "Most open to plays; musicals; books on theatre, film, television, and supporting areas: cameras, lighting, costumes, etc."

PONDER PUBLISHING, 15128—27B Ave., Surrey BC V4P 1P2, Canada. Website: www.ponder publishing.ca. Darian Kovacs, pub. Focuses on Canadian writers primarily, writing material for youth and youth workers.

@ POWER PUBLISHING, 13680 N. Duncan Dr., Camby IN 46113. (317) 347-1051. Fax (317) 347-1068. E-mail: info@powerpublishinginc.com. Website: www.powerpublishinginc.com. Janet Schwind, ed.; submit by mail or through Website. Our innovative culture is author-focused, assuming great care and consideration with each manuscript and offering a unique line of publishing programs to meet the needs of nearly every author. Publishes hardcover, trade paperbacks, mass-market paperbacks. Receives 7,200 submissions annually. 50 percent of books from first-time authors. Accepts mss through agents or authors. **SUBSIDY/CO-OP PUBLISHES 10 PERCENT**; print-on-demand up to 10 percent. Reprints books. Prefers 150+ pgs. Royalty on net. Publication within 6 mos. Considers simultaneous submissions. Responds in 2 wks. to initial review; 60-90 days for second review. Prefers accepted mss by e-mail. Prefers NIV. Guidelines by mail/e-mail/Website; no catalog.
  Nonfiction: Proposal/3-6 chapters; complete ms; phone/fax/e-query OK.
  Fiction: Proposal/3-6 chapters; complete ms; phone/fax/e-query OK. For all ages.
  Special Needs: Christian leadership, emergent church, church/pastor resources, and general Christian living.
  Also Does: E-books.
  Photos/Artwork: Accepts freelance photos for book covers; open to queries from freelance artists.
  Tips: "Most open to nonfiction—inspiring and written to appeal to a mass market, as well as spiritual-growth related, or church resources. We require all authors to complete and submit a New Author form with each manuscript submission. Form available by e-mail: info@ powerpublishing.com or on the Website."

PRAEGER PUBLISHERS (formerly listed as Greenwood/Praeger), 130 Cremona Dr., Santa Barbara CA 93117. (805) 968-1911. E-mail: mwilt@abc-clio.com. Website: www.praeger.com or www.abc-clio.com. Imprint of ABC-CLIO. Michael Wilt, sr. acq. ed. Publishes 5-25 titles/yr.; hardcover. Receives 40-60 submissions annually. Accepts mss through agents or authors. No subsidy or reprints. Prefers up to 100,000 words. Variable royalty on net; some advances. Average first printing 1,500. Publication within 8-10 mos. Considers simultaneous submissions. Responds in 1-3 mos. Guidelines by e-mail; catalog on Website.

> **Nonfiction:** Book proposal/1-3 chapters or all chapters available; e-query preferred.
> **Special Needs:** General religious studies; religion & society/culture; religion & contemporary issues.
> **Ethnic Books:** African American studies (general interest); Islamic studies; Jewish studies; Native American studies; Hispanic/Latino studies.
> **Tips:** "Most open to general interest topics; accessible vocabulary and writing style."

PREP PUBLISHING, 1110½ Hay St., Fayetteville NC 28305. (910) 483-2336. Fax (910) 483-2439. E-mail: preppub@aol.com. Website: www.prep-pub.com. PREP Inc. Anne McKinney, mng. ed. (mckinney@prep-pub.com); submit to Frances Sweeney (sweeney@prep-pub.com). Books to enrich people's lives and help them find joy in the human experience. Publishes 10 titles/yr.; hardcover, trade paperbacks. Receives 1,500+ submissions annually. 85 percent of books from first-time authors. Reprints books. Prefers 250 pgs. Royalty 6-10 percent of retail; pays an advance. Average first printing 3,000-5,000. Publication within 18 mos. Considers simultaneous submissions. Responds in 1 mo. Guidelines by mail/Website; catalog for #10 SAE/2 stamps.

> **Nonfiction:** Query only; no phone query. Charges a $350 nonrefundable reading fee.
> **Fiction:** Query only (cover letter and up to 3-page synopsis). All ages. "We are attempting to grow our Judeo-Christian fiction imprint."
> **Tips:** "Rewrite, rewrite, rewrite with your reader clearly in focus."

G. P. PUTNAM'S SONS BOOKS FOR YOUNG READERS, 345 Hudson St., 14th Fl., New York NY 10014. (212) 414-3610. Website: www.penguingroup.com. Submit to Children's Manuscript Editor. Imprint: Penguin Group USA. Publishes 45 titles/yr.; hardcover. Accepts mss through agents or authors. No reprints. Variable royalty on retail; negotiable advance. Considers simultaneous submissions. No disk or e-mail submissions. Responds in 6 mos. Guidelines for SASE.

> **Nonfiction:** Proposal/1-2 chapters. "We publish some religious/inspirational books and books for ages 2-18."
> **Fiction:** For children or teens. Complete ms for picture books; proposal/3 chapters for novels. Primarily picture books or middle-grade novels.

QUIET WATERS PUBLICATIONS, PO Box 34, Bolivar MO 65613-0034. (417) 326-5001. E-mail: QWP@usa.net. Website: www.QuietWatersPub.com. Stephen Trobisch, ed. Books on marriage, family, and missions. Publishes 5-10 titles/yr.; hardcover, trade paperbacks. Prefers mss through agents. No subsidy; does print-on-demand. Reprints books. No length preference. Royalty 8 percent on retail; no advance. Publication within 6 mos. Considers simultaneous submissions. Guidelines on Website; catalog for 9 x 12 SAE/5 stamps.

> **Nonfiction/Fiction:** Query letter first. Fiction for all ages.

+ THE QUILLDRIVER, PO Box 573, Clarksville AR 72830. Phone/fax (479) 497-0321. E-mail: info@thequilldriver.com. Website: www.thequilldriver.com. Donna Lee Schillinger, pub. Inspirational nonfiction directed at young adults (17-25). Imprint: Two-Faced Books. Publishes 3 titles/yr. Receives 12 submissions annually. 85 percent of books from first-time authors. No mss through agents. Would consider reprinting books. Prefers 200 pgs. Royalties; $500 advance. Average first printing 2,000. Publication within 18 mos. Considers simultaneous submissions. Responds in 8 wks. Prefers NIV. Guidelines by e-mail; catalog for #10 SAE/1 stamp.

Nonfiction: Query first; or proposal/2 chapters; e-query OK.

Tips: "Most open to books that are hip—must resonate with young adults."

QUINTESSENTIAL BOOKS, PO Box 8755, Kansas City MO 64114-0755. (816) 561-1555. E-mail: support@quintessentialbooks.com. Website: www.quintessentialbooks.com. Laura C. Joyce, ed. dir. Books that challenge people to think deeply and live passionately in accordance with sound principles. Publishes 5-10 titles/yr.; hardcover, trade paperbacks, mass-market paperbacks. Receives 150 submissions annually. 25 percent of books from first-time authors. Prefers mss through agents. Reprints books. Prefers 60,000-70,000 words or 224 pgs. Royalty on net; negotiable advance. Average first printing varies. Publication within 18 mos. Considers simultaneous submissions. Responds in 3-4 mos. Requires requested ms by e-mail. Prefers NIV or NLT. Guidelines by mail/Website.

Nonfiction: Query only; no phone/fax/e-query. "Nonfiction books must address significant topics in a fresh way, must speak boldly on controversial issues, and must be clear and accurate. Manuscripts on medicine, mental health, and nutrition will only be accepted from credentialed health professionals."

Fiction: Query only; no phone/fax/e-query. For adults. "Fiction must exhibit an understanding of human hearts and relationships, must create a complete and credible world for the reader, and must have multifaceted characters and aesthetic depth."

Photos/Artwork: Accepts freelance photos for book covers; open to queries from freelance artists.

Tips: "We are interested in reaching an intelligent, widely read audience. Avoid submitting simplistic material."

**Note: This publisher serviced by The Writer's Edge.

RAGGED EDGE PRESS, 73 W. Burd St., PO Box 708, Shippenburg PA 17257. (717) 532-2237. Fax (717) 532-6110. E-mail: marketing@whitemane.com or editorial@whitemane.com. Website: www .whitemane.com. White Mane Publishing Co. Inc. Harold E. Collier, acq. ed. Christian, social science, and self-help books that make a difference in people's lives. Publishes 10-15 titles/yr. Receives 50-75 submissions annually. 50 percent of books from first-time authors. **SUBSIDY PUBLISHES 20 PERCENT**. Reprints books. Prefers 200 pgs. Variable royalty on net; no advance. Average first printing 3,000. Publication within 12-18 mos. Considers simultaneous submissions. Responds in 30-90 days. Guidelines by mail/e-mail; catalog online.

Nonfiction: Query only; fax/e-query OK.

Tips: "Most open to a Protestant book in the middle of the spectrum."

RAINBOW PUBLISHERS, PO Box 261129, San Diego CA 92196. Toll-free (800) 323-7337. Toll-free fax (800) 331-0297. E-mail: editor@rainbowpublishers.com. Website: www.rainbowpublishers .com. Submit to The Editor. Publishes Bible-teaching, reproducible books for children's teachers. Publishes 20 titles/yr. Receives 250 submissions annually. 50 percent of books from first-time authors. Reprints books. Prefers 96 pgs. Outright purchases $640 & up. Average first printing 2,500. Publication within 2 yrs. Considers simultaneous submissions. Responds in 3 mos. No disk or e-mail submissions. Prefers NIV. Guidelines by mail/Website; catalog for 9 x 12 SAE/2 stamps.

Nonfiction: Proposal/2-5 chapters; no phone/e-query. "Looking for fun and easy ways to teach Bible concepts to kids, ages 2-12."

Special Needs: Creative puzzles and unique games.

Artwork: Open to queries from freelance artists.

Tips: "Request a catalog or visit your Christian bookstore to see what we have already published. We have over 100 titles and do not like to repeat topics, so a proposal needs to be unique for us but not necessarily unique in the market. Most open to writing that appeals to teachers who work with kids and Bible activities that have been tried and tested on today's kids. No preachy, old-fashioned methods."

@ RANDALL HOUSE DIGITAL, 114 Bush Rd.; PO Box 17306, Nashville TN 37217. Toll-free (800) 877-7030. (615) 361-1221. Fax (615) 367-0535. E-mail through Website: www.randallhouse.com. National Assn. of Free Will Baptists. Alan Clagg, dir. Produces curriculum-on-demand via the Internet and electronic resources to supplement existing printed curriculum. Guidelines by e-mail.

Nonfiction: Query first; e-query OK.

Special Needs: Teacher-training material (personal or group), elective Bible studies for adults, children's curriculum (other than Sunday school), and elective materials for teens.

Also Does: Digital books.

Tips: "We are looking for writers with vision for worldwide ministry who would like to see their works help a greater section of the Body of Christ than served by the conventionally printed products."

RANDALL HOUSE PUBLICATIONS, 114 Bush Rd., Nashville TN 37217. Toll-free (800) 877-7030. (615) 361-1221. Fax (615) 367-0535. E-mail: michelle.orr@randallhouse.com. Website: www .randallhouse.com. Free Will Baptist. Michelle Orr, acq. ed. Publishes Sunday school and Christian education materials to make Christ known, from a conservative perspective. Publishes 5-10 titles/ yr.; hardcover, trade paperbacks, mass-market paperbacks. Receives 100-150 submissions annually. 50 percent of books from first-time authors. Accepts mss through agents or authors. No reprints. Length flexible. Royalty 10-15 percent on net; rarely gives an advance. Average first printing 2,000-5,000. Publication within 12-14 mos. Considers simultaneous submissions. Accepts requested mss by e-mail. Responds in 10-12 wks. Guidelines by mail/e-mail/Website; free catalog.

Nonfiction: Query; e-query OK; proposal/4 chapters. Must fill out book proposal form they provide.

Fiction: For teens & adults. Query first; e-query OK; proposal/6 chapters. Must fill out book proposal form they provide.

Artwork: Open to queries from freelance artists (andrea.young@randallhouse.com).

Tips: "We are expanding our book division with a conservative perspective. We have a very conservative view as a publisher."

**Note: This publisher serviced by ChristianManuscriptSubmissions.com.

RAVENHAWK BOOKS, 7739 E. Broadway Blvd., #95, Tucson AZ 85710. E-mail: ravenhawk6dof@ yahoo.com. Website: www.6dofsolutions.com. Blog: see Website. The 6DOF Group. Hans B. Shepherd or Karl Lasky, eds.; Shelly Geraci, submissions ed. Publishes variable number of titles/yr.; hardcover, trade paperbacks. Receives 20-30 submissions annually. 70 percent of books from first-time authors. Print-on-demand. Reprints books. Royalty 40-50 percent on gross profits; no advance. Average first printing 2,500. Publication in up to 18 mos. Considers simultaneous submissions. Responds in 6 wks. Catalog on Website.

Nonfiction: Query first; e-query OK. "Looking for profitable books from talented writers."

Fiction: Query first. For all ages. Unsolicited full mss returned unopened.

Special Needs: Looking for books from young authors, 16-22 years old.

Photos/Artwork: Accepts freelance photos for book covers; open to queries from freelance artists.

Tips: "Most open to crisp, creative, entertaining writing that also informs and educates. Writing, as any creative art, is a gift from God. Not everyone has the innate talent to do it well. We are author-oriented. We don't play games with the numbers."

REALMS—Fiction for all ages. See Strang Book Group.

REFERENCE SERVICE PRESS, 5000 Windplay Dr., Ste. 4, El Dorado Hills CA 95762. (916) 939-9620. Fax (916) 939-9626. E-mail: info@rspfunding.com. Website: www.rspfunding.com. Stuart Hauser, ed. Books related to financial aid and Christian higher education. Publishes 1 title/yr.; hardcover, trade paperbacks. Receives 3-5 submissions annually. Most books from first-time authors.

No reprints. Royalty 10 percent of net; usually no advance. Publication within 5 mos. May consider simultaneous submissions. No guidelines; free catalog for 2 stamps.

Nonfiction: Proposal/several chapters.

Special Needs: Financial aid directories for Christian college students.

REFORMATION TRUST PUBLISHING, Editorial Dept., 400 Technology Park, Lake Mary FL 32746. Toll-free (800) 435-4343. (407) 333-4244. Fax (407) 333-4233. E-mail: gbailey@ligonier.org. Website: www.ligonier.org/publishing_reformationtrust.php. Imprint of Ligonier Ministries. Greg Bailey, dir. of publications. Exists to publish books true to the historic Christian faith from the best of today's pastors and scholars. Publishes 10-12 titles/yr.; hardcover, trade paperbacks. Receives 100 submissions annually. Open to first-time authors. Accepts mss through agents or authors. No subsidy or reprints. Prefers 40,000-80,000 words. Royalty on net; no advance. Average first printing 5,000. Publication within 10 mos. Considers simultaneous submissions. Responds in 3 mos. Prefers ESV. Guidelines on Website; free catalog.

Nonfiction: Proposal/2 chapters; no complete mss. Accepted ms by disk or e-mail.

Fiction: Proposal/2 chapters. Children's fiction only. "As in all our titles, we want our children's books to touch the deep truths of the Christian faith."

Tips: "We are looking for books that teach the historic Christian faith in layman's language. Our books are not academic, but good scholarship is important. Above all, our books must be based on Scripture. Our theological stance is Reformed/Calvinist."

**Note: This publisher serviced by The Writer's Edge & ChristianManuscriptSubmissions.com.

REGAL BOOKS, 1957 Eastman Ave., Ventura CA 93003. (805) 644-9721. Fax (805) 644-9728. E-mail: editors@gospellight.com. Website: www.regalbooks.com. Gospel Light. Submit to The Editor. To know Christ and to make him known; publishing resources to create meaningful dialogue. Publishes 50 titles/yr.; hardcover, trade paperbacks. Receives 1,000 submissions annually. 20 percent of books from first-time authors. Requires mss through agents. No subsidy, print-on-demand, or reprints. Royalty. Publication within 18 mos. Considers simultaneous submissions. Prefers NIV. No guidelines or catalog.

Nonfiction: All unsolicited mss returned unopened if SASE provided.

Tips: "Most open to books that are well-written, unique in some way. Work through an agent."

**Note: This publisher serviced by The Writer's Edge.

@ RESOURCE PUBLICATIONS INC., 160 E. Virginia St., Ste. 290, San Jose CA 95112-5876. (408) 286-8505. Fax (408) 287-8748. E-mail: info@rpinet.com. Website: www.rpinet.com. William Burns, pub. Publishes 10 titles/yr.; trade paperbacks. Receives 450 submissions annually. 30 percent of books from first-time authors. Prefers 50,000 words. Royalty 8 percent of net; rarely pays advance. Average first printing 3,000. Publication within 1 yr. Responds in 10 wks. Prefers requested ms on disk. Guidelines by e-mail/Website; catalog on Website.

Nonfiction: Proposal/1 chapter; phone/fax/e-query OK.

Fiction: Proposal/2-3 chapters. Adult. Only read-aloud stories for storytellers; fables and parables. "Must be useful in ministerial, counseling, or educational settings."

Also Does: Computer programs; aids to ministry or education; e-books.

Tips: "Know our market. We cater to ministers in Catholic and mainstream Protestant settings. We are not an evangelical house or general interest publisher. Looking for nonfiction ideas that save people time, save money, or help people do their jobs better. Most open to a book that will help a practicing minister understand and deal with a pressing problem he or she faces."

REVELL BOOKS, Fleming H. Revell, Box 6287, Grand Rapids MI 49516. (616) 676-9185. Fax (616) 676-2315. Website: www.revellbooks.com. Imprint of Baker Publishing Group. Publishes inspirational fiction and nonfiction for the broadest Christian market. Guidelines & catalog on Website. No unsolicited mss. Submit through Writer's Edge or ChristianManuscriptSubmissions.com.

REVIEW AND HERALD PUBLISHING ASSN., 55 W. Oak Ridge Dr., Hagerstown MD 21740-7390. (301) 393-3000. Fax (301) 393-4055. E-mail: editorial@rhpa.org. Website: www.rhpa.org. Seventh-day Adventist. Richard Coffen, VP/editorial; Jeannette Johnson, acq. ed. No freelance.

REVIVAL NATION PUBLISHING, PO Box 30001, Sarnia ON N7T 0A7, Canada. Phone/fax (866) 487-1361. E-mail: publishing@revivalnation.com. Website: www.revivalnationpublishing.com. Revival Nation Evangelistic Ministries. Greg Holmes, pres. A not-for-profit publisher; all publishing revenue goes back to building God's Kingdom. Imprint: Revival Nation Kids. Publishes 30-50 titles/yr.; trade paperbacks. Receives 300-400 submissions annually. 95 percent of books from first-time authors. Accepts mss through agents or authors. No subsidy; does print-on-demand. No reprints. Prefers 150-250 pgs. Royalty 20 percent on wholesale; no advance. Average first printing 1,000. Publication within 6 mos. Accepts simultaneous submissions. Responds in 6 wks. Prefers e-mail submissions (attached file in Word). Prefers NIV. Guidelines on Website; no catalog.

> **Nonfiction:** Submit online via Website only. "We look for passion in the writing—something the author would die for."
> **Fiction:** Submit online via Website only. For all ages.
> **Special Needs:** Looking for revival, renewal, holiness, Holy Spirit, prayer, and charismatic.
> **Tips:** Gives preference to Canadian authors but open to all. Only considers unpublished work; does not accept self-published books.

ROSE PUBLISHING, 4733 Torrance Blvd., #259, Torrance CA 90503. Toll-free (800) 532-4278. (310) 353-2100. Fax (310) 353-2116. E-mail: rosepubl@aol.com. Website: www.rose-publishing .com. Nondenominational. Lynnette Pennings, acq./mng. ed. Publishes primarily Bible studies; apologetics; Sunday school wall charts and visual aids. Publishes 30-40 titles/yr. 2 percent of projects from first-time authors. No mss through agents. No reprints. Outright purchases. Publication within 18 mos. Considers simultaneous submissions. Requires accepted mss by disk or e-mail. Responds in 2-3 mos. Catalog for 9 x 12 SAE/4 stamps.

> **Nonfiction:** Query or proposal. No books, mainly booklets/pamphlets, wall charts/posters, or PowerPoints.
> **Special Needs:** Query with sketch of proposed chart or poster (nonreturnable); fax query OK; e-query OK if less than 100 words (copied into message). Open to material that makes difficult Bible topics or theological topics easier; wall charts, study guides and worksheets on sharing your faith and salvation with skeptics. Typical subjects include: cults, books of the Bible, church history, world religions, discipleship, angels, prayer, teens, hot topics.
> **Also Does:** PowerPoint presentations for biblical subjects.
> **Artwork:** Open to queries from freelance artists.
> **Tips:** "Now accepting more freelance submissions. No fiction." Publishes a unique format that makes difficult Bible topics easy to understand.
> ****Note:** This publisher serviced by ChristianManuscriptSubmissions.com.

SAINT CATHERINE OF SIENA PRESS, 4812 N. Park Ave., Indianapolis IN 46205. Toll-free (888) 544-8674, or (888) 232-1492. E-mail: service@saintcatherineofsienapress.com. Website: www .saintcatherineofsienapress.com. Catholic. Jean Zander, ed. dir. Established to promote "excellence in catechesis . . . in faithfulness to Rome." Responds in up to 2 mos. Guidelines/catalog on Website.

> **Nonfiction:** Proposal/2 chapters.

@ SAMARITAN PRESS, PO Box 14451, Knoxville TN 37914. (865) 335-0072. Fax (865) 249-7206. E-mail: ihp@samaritanpress.com. Website: www.samaritanpress.com. R. Michael Henegar, ed.; submit to Kristy Lynn. Believes that every person has a story to tell and readers to enjoy that story. Publishes 15-20 titles/yr.; hardcover, mass-market paperbacks, coffee-table books. Receives 300 submissions annually. 70 percent of books from first-time authors. Accepts mss through agents or authors. **SUBSIDY PUBLISHES 10 PERCENT**; does print-on-demand. Reprints books. Prefers 80+ pgs. Royalty 10-15 percent on retail; no advance. Average first printing 5,000. Publication within 12 mos. No simultaneous submissions. Responds in 3 mos. Wants accepted mss on disk. Prefers NKJV. Guidelines on Website; no catalog.

> **Nonfiction/Fiction:** Query first or complete ms; e-query OK. Fiction for all ages.
> **Special Needs:** All genres of fiction, Christian living, Bible study, and personal experience.
> **Also Does:** E-books.
> **Photos/Artwork:** Accepts freelance photos for book covers; open to queries from freelance artists.
> **Tips:** "All types of fiction are considered, and we enjoy regular people submitting regular stories that can become great lessons of faith and devotion to Jesus Christ."

SCEPTER PUBLISHERS INC., PO Box 211, New York NY 10018. Toll-free (800) 322-8773. (212) 354-0670. Fax (212) 354-0736. E-mail: info@scepterpublishers.org. Website: www.scepterpub lishers.org. Catholic. John Powers, ed. Books on how to struggle to live faith and virtue in one's daily life. Publishes 20 titles/yr. Zero to 2 percent of books from first-time authors. Accepts mss through agents or authors. Reprints books. Prefers 200-250 pgs. Royalty on net; advance $2,000-10,000. Average first printing 2,000. Publication within 24 mos. No simultaneous submissions. Responds after 12 mos. Free catalog.

> **Nonfiction:** Query only first with a 1-2 pg. synopsis; no phone/fax/e-query. Does not return material.
> **Fiction:** Query only first; no phone/fax/e-query.
> **Tips:** "Looking for books that help readers struggle to better live Christian virtues and seriously practice their faith."

SCRIPTURE PRESS—See David C. Cook.

+ SEED FAITH BOOKS LLC, PO Box 230913, Tigard OR 97281. (503) 718-7911. E-mail: helen@ seedfaithbooks.com. Website: www.seedfaithbooks.com. David & Helen Haidle, eds. Christian children & teen books, especially those that have gone out of print. Royalties. Not currently accepting submissions except by request.

> **Tips:** "We plan on selling children's books at Christian school book fairs, as well as by mail order and bookstores, including Amazon."

SHEED & WARD, 4501 Forbes Blvd., Ste. 200, Lanham MD 20706. Toll-free (800) 462-6420. (301) 459-3366. Fax (301) 429-5747. Website: www.sheedandward.com. Imprint of Rowman & Littlefield Publishers Inc. Marcus Boggs, pub. (boggs@rowman.com); submit to Sarah Stanton, ed. (sstanton@rowman.com). Publishes books of contemporary impact and enduring merit in Catholic-Christian thought and action. Publishes 10-20 titles/yr.; hardcover, trade paperbacks. Receives 2,000 submissions annually. 25 percent of books from first-time authors. Prefers 50,000-80,000 words. Royalty 6-12 percent on retail; $2,000 advance. Average first printing 3,000. Publication within 8 mos. Accepts simultaneous submissions. Responds in 2-3 mos. Requires requested ms on disk. Prefers NAB, NRSV (Catholic editions). Guidelines/catalog on Website.

> **Nonfiction:** Proposal/1-2 chapters; e-query OK. "Looking for parish ministry (health care, spirituality, leadership, general trade books for mass audiences, sacraments, small group, or priestless parish facilitating books), Catholic history, Catholic studies."
> **Photos/Artwork:** Considers photos/artwork as part of book package.
> **Tips:** "Looking for general trade titles and academic titles (oriented toward the classroom) in areas of spirituality, parish ministry, leadership, sacraments, prayer, faith formation, church history, and Scripture."

SILOAM—See Strang Book Group.

@ SMYTH & HELWYS PUBLISHING INC., 6316 Peake Rd., Macon GA 31210-3960. Toll-free (800) 747-3016. (478) 757-0564. Fax (478) 757-1305. E-mail: Proposals@helwys.com. Website: www.helwys.com. Submit to Book Editor. Quality resources for the church, the academy, and individual Christians who are nurtured by faith and informed by scholarship. Publishes 25-30 titles/yr. Receives 600 submissions annually. 40 percent of books from first-time authors. Prefers 144 pgs. Royalty 7 percent. Considers simultaneous submissions. Responds in 3 mos. Guidelines by mail/e-mail/Website; free catalog.

> **Nonfiction:** Query only; fax/e-query OK. "Manuscripts requested for topics appropriate for mainline church and seminary/university textbook market."
> **Also Does:** E-books. Copies of print books and original books. Go to: www.nextsunday.com.
> **Tips:** "Most open to books with a strong secondary or special market. Niche titles and short-run options available for specialty subjects."

STANDARD PUBLISHING, 8805 Governor's Hill Dr., Ste. 400, Cincinnati OH 45249. (513) 931-4050. Fax (513) 931-0950. Website: www.standardpub.com. CFM Religion Publishing Group LLC. Provides true-to-the-Bible resources that inspire, educate, and motivate Christians to a growing relationship with Jesus Christ. Prefers mss through agents. Hardcover & trade paperbacks. No reprints. Royalty or outright purchase; pays an advance. No simultaneous submissions. Responds in 3-4 mos. Prefers NIV/KJV. Guidelines by mail/e-mail/Website.

> **Nonfiction:** Query only; e-query OK.
> **Fiction:** Query only; e-query OK. Children's picture or board books; juvenile novels.
> **Special Needs:** Adult and youth ministry resources; children's ministry resources.
> ****Note:** This publisher serviced by The Writer's Edge and ChristianManuscriptSubmissions.com.

ST. ANTHONY MESSENGER PRESS AND FRANCISCAN COMMUNICATIONS, 28 W. Liberty St., Cincinnati OH 45202. Toll-free (800) 488-0488. (513) 241-5615. Fax (513) 241-0399. E-mail: StAnthony@AmericanCatholic.org. Websites: www.AmericanCatholic.org; www.sampbooks.org; www.servantbooks.org. Catholic. Lisa Biedenbach, ed. dir. (lisab@AmericanCatholic.org); Katie Carroll, mng. ed.; Mary Hackett, book ed.; Cynthia Cavnar, acq. ed. (cynthiac@americancatholic.org). Seeks to publish affordable resources for living a Catholic-Christian lifestyle. Imprints: Servant Books, Franciscan Communications, Fischer Productions, Ikonographics (videos). S.A.M.P. publishes 20-35 titles/yr.; Servant publishes 15-18 titles/yr.; trade paperbacks (mostly). Receives 450 submissions annually. 5 percent of books from first-time authors. Accepts mss through agents or authors. Reprints books (seldom). Prefers 25,000-50,000 words or 100-250 pgs. Royalty 10-14 percent on net; advance $1,000-3,000. Average first printing 4,000. Publication within 18 mos. No simultaneous submissions. Requires accepted ms on CD; e-mail OK. Responds in 5-9 wks. Prefers NRSV. Guidelines on Website; catalog for 9 x 12 SAE/4 stamps.

> **Nonfiction:** Query only/500-wd. summary; fax/e-query OK. "Looking for resources for living the Catholic-Christian life at home and in workplace, pastoral resources for parishes and small groups; spiritual self-help from a Catholic perspective; prayer resources; saints and inspirational people; applied Scripture."
> **Special Needs:** Catholic identity, spirituality, resources for new and inactive Catholics, young adult Catholics.
> **Ethnic Books:** Hispanic, African American occasionally.
> **Tips:** "Most open to books with sound Catholic doctrine that include personal experiences or anecdotes applicable to today's culture. Our books are decidedly Catholic."

STARIK PUBLISHING, PO Box 307, Slaton TX 79364. E-mail: submissions@starikpublishing.com. Website: www.starikpublishing.com. Blog: www.starikpublishing.com/wordpress. Stacie Craig, exec. ed. A family-oriented publishing house seeking to improve families through literature. Publishes 1-3 titles/yr.; trade paperbacks. Receives 75 submissions annually. 30 percent of books from first-time authors. No books through agents. No subsidy or reprints. Prefers 100-400 pgs. Royalty; no advance. Average first print run 2,000. Considers simultaneous submissions. Responds in 6-8 wks. Guidelines by mail/e-mail/Website; no catalog.

Nonfiction: Proposal/3 chapters & short author bio; e-query OK. Accepts disk or e-mail submissions.

Fiction: Proposal/3 chapters & short author bio; e-query OK. Teen/young adult & adult Christian fiction.

Artwork: Open to queries from freelance artists.

ST. AUGUSTINE'S PRESS, PO Box 2285, South Bend IN 46680. (574) 291-3500. Fax (574) 291-3700. E-mail: bruce@staugustine.net. Website: www.staugustine.net. A conservative, nondenominational (although mostly Catholic) scholarly publisher of academic titles, mainly in academic philosophy, theology, and cultural history. Bruce Fingerhut, pres. Publishes 20-40 titles/yr.; hardcover, trade paperbacks. Receives 100+ submissions annually. 5 percent of books from first-time authors. Accepts mss through agents or authors. Reprints books. Royalty 6-15 percent of net; advance $1,000. Average first printing 1,000. Publication within 1 yr. Considers simultaneous submissions. Responds in 3 mos. No guidelines; free catalog.

Nonfiction: Query or proposal/chapters. "Most of our titles are philosophy." Cultural history.

Tips: "Most open to books on subjects or by authors similar to what/who we already publish."

ST. BEDE'S PUBLICATIONS, St. Scholastica Priory, PO Box 545, Petersham MA 01366-0545. (978) 724-3213. Fax (978) 724-3216. Catholic/St. Scholastica Priory. Submit to Acquisitions Editor. Publishes 3-4 titles/yr.; hardcover & trade paperbacks. 30-40 percent of books from first-time authors. Accepts mss through agents or authors. Reprints books. Royalty 5-10 percent of net or retail. Publication within 2 yrs. Considers simultaneous submissions. Responds in 2 mos. Prefers NIV. Guidelines on Website; catalog for 9 x 12 SAE/2 stamps.

Nonfiction: Query or outline/sample chapters.

STEEPLE HILL, 233 Broadway, Ste. 1001, New York NY 10279-0001. (212) 553-4200. Fax (212) 277-8969. Website: www.SteepleHill.com. Harlequin Enterprises. Submit to any of the following: Joan Marlow Golan, exec. ed.; Melissa Endlich, sr. ed.; Tina Colombo, sr. ed.; Emily Rodmell, asst. ed.; Sarah McDaniel, ed. asst. (sarah_mcdaniel@harlequin.ca); Elizabeth Mazer, ed. asst. Lines: Love Inspired (mass-market category romances), see listing below; Love Inspired Suspense; Love Inspired Historical, see listing below. Publishes 154 titles/yr.; mass-market paperbacks. Receives 500-1,000 submissions annually. 15 percent of books from first-time authors. Accepts mss through agents or authors. No reprints. Royalty on retail; competitive advance. Publication within 12-24 mos. No simultaneous submissions. Requires accepted ms on disk/hard copy. Responds in 3 mos. Prefers KJV. Guidelines by mail/Website; no catalog.

Fiction: Complete ms for series; no phone/fax/e-query.

STEEPLE HILL LOVE INSPIRED, 233 Broadway, Ste. 1001, New York NY 10279-0001. (212) 553-4200. Fax (212) 277-8969. E-mail: Sarah_McDaniel@harlequin.ca. Website: www.SteepleHill.com. Harlequin Enterprises. Submit to any of the following: Joan Marlow Golan, exec. ed.; Melissa Endlich, sr. ed.; Emily Rodmell, asst. ed.; Sarah McDaniel, ed. asst. Mass-market Christian romance novels. Publishes 72 titles/yr.; mass-market paperbacks. Receives 500-1,000 submissions annually. 15 percent of books from first-time authors. Accepts mss through agents or authors. No reprints. Prefers 55,000-60,000 words. Royalty on retail; competitive advance. Publication within 12-24 mos. Requires ms on disk/hard copy. Responds in 3 mos. Prefers KJV. Guidelines by mail/Website; no catalog.

Fiction: Query letter or 3 chapters and up to 5-page synopsis; no phone/fax/e-query.

Tips: "We want character-driven romance with an author voice that inspires."

**Note: This publisher serviced by ChristianManuscriptSubmissions.com.

STEEPLE HILL LOVE INSPIRED HISTORICAL, 233 Broadway, Ste. 1001, New York NY 10279-0001. (212) 553-4200. Fax (212) 227-8969. Website: www.SteepleHill.com. Harlequin Enterprises. Submit to any of the following: Joan Marlow Golan, exec. ed.; Tina Colombo, sr. ed. in charge of line; Melissa Endlich, sr. ed.; Emily Rodmell, asst. ed.; Sarah McDaniel, ed. asst.; Elizabeth Mazer, ed. asst. Mass-market Christian historical romance novels. Publishes 24 titles/yr.; mass-market paperbacks. Receives 500-1,000 submissions annually. 15 percent of books from first-time authors. Accepts mss through agents or authors. No reprints. Prefers 70,000-75,000 words. Royalty on retail; competitive advance. Publication within 12-36 mos. No simultaneous submissions. Responds in 3 mos. Prefers KJV. Guidelines on Website; no catalog.

> **Fiction:** Proposal/3 chapters. Historical romances featuring Christian characters facing the many challenges of life and love in a variety of historical time periods: biblical fiction, Americana (e.g., westerns, post–Civil War, etc.), European historical eras (e.g., Tudor, Regency, and Victorian England, 18th-century Scotland, etc.), and 20th century (turn-of-the-century through world War II).

STEEPLE HILL LOVE INSPIRED SUSPENSE, 233 Broadway, Ste. 1001, New York NY 10279-0001. (212) 553-4200. Fax (212) 277-8969. E-mail: Sarah_McDaniel@harlequin.ca. Website: www.Steeple Hill.com. Harlequin Enterprises. Submit to any of the following: Joan Marlow Golan, exec. ed.; Tina Colombo, sr. ed. in charge of line; Melissa Endlich, sr. ed.; Emily Rodmell, asst. ed.; Sarah McDaniel, ed. asst.; Elizabeth Mazer, ed. asst. Mass-market inspirational Christian romantic suspense novels. Publishes 48 titles/yr.; mass-market paperbacks. Receives 500-1,000 submissions annually. 15 percent of books from first-time authors. Accepts mss through agents or authors. No reprints. Prefers 55,000-60,000 words. Royalty on retail; competitive advance. Publication within 12-24 mos. No simultaneous submissions. Responds in 3 mos. Prefers KJV. Guidelines on Website; no catalog.

> **Fiction:** Proposal/3 chapters and up to 5-page synopsis; no phone/fax/e-query.
>
> **Special Needs:** "We offer edge-of-the-seat, contemporary romantic suspense tales of intrigue and romance featuring Christian characters facing challenges to their faith and to their lives. Each story should have a compelling mystery or a suspenseful situation threatening the hero and the heroine, combined with an emotional, satisfying, and mature romance. Stories should focus equally on romance and suspense."

STILL WATERS REVIVAL BOOKS, 4710—37A Ave., Edmonton AB T6L 3T5, Canada. (780) 450-3730. Fax (780) 468-1096. E-mail: swrb@swrb.com. Website: www.swrb.com. Covenanter Church. Reg Barrow, pres. Publishes 100 titles/yr. Receives few submissions. Very few books from first-time authors. Reprints books. Prefers 128-160 pgs. Negotiated royalty or outright purchase. Considers simultaneous submissions. Catalog for 9 x 12 SASE/2 stamps.

> **Nonfiction:** Proposal/2 chapters.
>
> **Tips:** "Only open to books defending the Covenanted Reformation, nothing else."

ST. MICHAEL'S ABBEY PRESS, Farnborough, Hampshire, England GU14 7NQ. Phone +44 (0)1252 546105. Fax +44 (0) 1252 372822. E-mail: abbeypress@farnboroughabbey.org or info@farnborough abbey.org. Website: www.farnboroughabbey.org/press/index.php. Open to freelance submissions. Details on Website.

ST. PAULS/ALBA HOUSE. 2187 Victory Blvd., Staten Island NY 10314-6603. (718) 761-0047. Fax (718) 761-0057. E-mail: Edmund_Lane@juno.com. Website: www.stpauls.us. Catholic/Society of St. Paul. Edmund C. Lane, SSP, ed-in-chief; Frank Sadowski, SSP, ed. Imprint: St. Pauls. Publishes 24 titles/yr.; trade paperbacks. Receives 450 submissions annually. 20 percent of books from first-time authors. No mss through agents. Reprints books. Prefers 124 pgs. Royalty 7-10 percent on retail; no advance. Average first printing 3,500. Publication within 9 mos. Prefers requested ms on disk. Responds in 1-2 mos. Free guidelines/catalog by mail.

Nonfiction: Query.
Special Needs: Spirituality in the Roman Catholic tradition; lives of the saints.

STRANG BOOK GROUP, 600 Rinehart Rd., Lake Mary FL 32746. (407) 333-0600. Fax (407) 333-7100. E-mail: creationhouse@strang.com. Website: www.strang.com. Strang Communications. Submit to Acquisitions Assistant. To inspire and equip people to live a Spirit-led life and walk in the divine purpose for which they were called. This house has 8 imprints, which are listed below with descriptions/details. Publishes 150 titles/yr.; hardcover, trade paperbacks, mass-market paperbacks. Receives 1,500 submissions annually. 65 percent of books from first-time authors. Prefers mss through agents. Reprints books. Prefers 55,000 words. Royalty on net or outright purchase; pays an advance. Average first printing 7,500. Publication within 9 mos. Considers simultaneous submissions. Accepts requested ms on disk or on Website. Responds in 6-10 wks. Guidelines by mail/e-mail; free catalog.

> **Nonfiction:** Proposal or complete ms; by mail or e-query OK; no phone query. Book proposal application on Website. "Open to any books that are well written and glorify Jesus Christ."
>
> **Fiction:** Proposal or complete ms; by mail or e-query OK; no phone query. Book proposal application on Website. "For all ages. Fiction must have a biblical worldview and point the reader to Christ."
>
> **Photos:** Accepts freelance photos for book covers.
>
> **Charisma House:** Books on Christian living, mainly from a Charismatic/Pentecostal perspective. Topics: Christian living, work of the Holy Spirit, prophecy, prayer, Scripture, adventures in evangelism and missions, popular theology.
>
> **Siloam:** Books about living in good health—body, mind, and spirit. Topics: alternative medicine; diet and nutrition; and physical, emotional, and psychological wellness. We prefer manuscripts from certified doctors, nutritionists, trainers, and other medical professionals. Proof of credentials may be required.
>
> **FrontLine:** Books on contemporary political and social issues from a Christian perspective.
>
> **Creation House:** Copublishing imprint for a wide variety of Christian books. Author is required to buy a quantity of books from the first press run. This is not self-publishing or print-on-demand.
>
> **Realms:** Christian fiction in the supernatural, speculative genre. Full-length adult novels, 80,000-120,000 words. Will also consider historical or biblical fiction if supernatural element is substantial.
>
> **+ Excel:** Publishes books that are targeted toward success in the workplace and businesses.
>
> **Casa Creacion:** Publishes and translates books into Spanish. (800) 987-8432. E-mail: casacreacion@strang.com. Website: www.casacreacion.com.
>
> **Publicaciones Casa:** Publishes the same as Creation House and is for people who like to copublish in Spanish. Contact info same as Casa Creacion.
>
> ****Note:** This publisher serviced by ChristianManuscriptSubmissions.com.

+ SUMMERSIDE PRESS/LOVE FINDS YOU, 11024 Quebec Cir., Bloomington MN 55438. (612) 321-1015. E-mail: info@summersidepress.com. Website: www.summersidepress.com/index.html. Rachel Meisel, fiction ed. Inspirational romance fiction series. Publishes 12 titles/yr. Prefers 80,000 words or 320 pgs. Guidelines on Website.

> **Fiction:** Send a paragraph overview, plus a 2-3 page synopsis by e-mail (attached file).
>
> **Tips:** "This series features inspirational romance novels set in actual cities and towns across the U.S."

JEREMY P. TARCHER, 375 Hudson St., New York NY 10014. (212) 366-2000. Fax (212) 366-2670. Website: www.penguinputnam.com. Imprint of Penguin Group. Joel Fotinos, VP/pres. Publishes ideas and works about human consciousness that are large enough to include matters of spirit and reli-

gion. Publishes 40-50 titles/yr.; hardcover, trade paperbacks. Receives 2,000 submissions annually. 20 percent of books from first-time authors. Accepts mss through agents or authors. Reprints books. Royalty 5-8 percent of retail; pays an advance. Considers simultaneous submissions. Free catalog.
Nonfiction: Query. Religion.

TAU PUBLISHING, 1422 E. Edgemont Ave., Phoenix AZ 85006. (602) 264-4828. Fax (602) 248-9656. E-mail: phoenixartist@msn.com or through Website: www.tau-publishing.org. Catholic. Jeffrey Campbell, pub. Imprint: Aleph-First. Publishes 3-4 titles/yr. Receives 25 submissions annually. 50 percent of books from first-time authors. Prefers mss through agents. **SOME SUBSIDY.** Reprints books. Prefers 25,000-50,000 words or 100-200 pgs. Royalty on net; no advance. Average first printing 3,000. Publication within 8 mos. Considers simultaneous submissions. Responds in 4-6 mos. Guidelines on Website; no catalog.
Nonfiction: Query; fax/e-query OK. "Looking for Catholic inspirational material; reflections and meditations."
Photos: Accepts freelance photos for book covers.

THIRD WORLD PRESS, PO Box 19730, 7822 S. Dobson Ave., Chicago IL 60619. (773) 651-0700. Fax (773) 651-7286. E-mail: GwenMTWP@aol.com or through Website: www.ThirdWorldPressInc .com. Submit to Asst. to the Publisher. African American publisher. Publishes 20 titles/yr.; hard cover, trade paperbacks. Receives 400-500 submissions annually. 20 percent of books from first-time authors. Accepts mss through agents or authors. Reprints books. Royalty on retail; advance varies. Publication within 18 mos. Considers simultaneous submissions. Responds in 5-6 mos. Guidelines on Website; free catalog.
Nonfiction/Fiction: Query by mail or proposal/5 chapters.
Ethnic Books: African American.
Tips: "Submit complete manuscript for poetry; must be African-American centered." This company is open to submissions in July only. Submissions are not returned.

TORCH LEGACY PUBLICATIONS, PO Box 1733, Joshua TX 76058-1733. (877) TORCHLP or (404) 348-4478. Fax (817) 887-3082. E-mail: info@torchlegacy.com. Website: www.torchlegacy .com. Daniel Whyte III, pres. Dedicated to publishing Bible-based books of all genres by and for African Americans and whosoever will. Publishes 7+ titles/yr. 80 percent of books from first-time authors. Royalty 10 percent of net; no advance. Average first printing 5,000. Publication within 12 mos. No simultaneous submissions. Responds in 2 mos.
Nonfiction: Query first; e-query preferred. "We are especially interested in Christian self-help books for the African American community for all age groups. Outright submissions in all categories are welcome."
Ethnic Books: African American.
Also Does: "We also handle the production and publishing of sermon books by local pastors for local churches, and we transcribe sermons for pastors under our imprint, St. Paul Press."
Tips: "We are looking for books that are Bible-based but at the same time are exciting and life changing. Our mission is to 'turn many from darkness to light' in the Black community in America through presenting a clear, understandable presentation of the gospel of Jesus Christ."

TOUCH PUBLICATIONS, 509 Garden Oaks Blvd., Houston TX 77018. Toll-free (800) 735-5865. (713) 884-8893. Fax (713) 742-5998. E-mail: randall@touchusa.org or from Website: www.touch usa.org. Touch Outreach Ministries. Randall Neighbour, dir. of publishing. To empower pastors, group leaders, and members to transform their lives, churches, and the world through basic Christian communities called cells. Publishes 8 titles/yr. Receives 25 submissions annually. 40 percent of books from first-time authors. Reprints books. Prefers 75-200 pgs. Royalty 10-15 percent of net; no advance. Average first printing 2,000. Guidelines (also by e-mail). Not in topical listings.
Nonfiction: Query only. "Must relate to cell church life."

Photos: Accepts freelance photos for book covers.

Tips: "Our market is extremely focused. We publish books, resources, and discipleship tools for churches, using a cell group strategy."

THE TRACT LEAGUE, 2627 Elmridge Dr., Grand Rapids MI 49534-1329. (616) 453-7695. Fax (616) 453-2460. E-mail: info@tractleague.com. Website: www.tractleague.com. Publishes very few tracts from outside writers, but willing to look at ideas. Submit to General Manager.

TREBLE HEART BOOKS, 1284 Overlook Dr., Sierra Vista AZ 85635. (520) 458-5602. Fax (520) 459-0162. E-mail: leeemory@earthlink.net. Website: www.trebleheartbooks.com. Ms. Lee Emory, ed./pub. Faith-based books without heavy-handed preaching. Online publisher offers four divisions: Romance, Christian, Westerns, Mystery/Suspense. Imprint: Mountain View (Christian division—see separate listing). Receives 100 submissions annually. 20 percent of books from first-time authors. No word/length preference. Reprints few books. Royalty 35 percent of net on most sales. Publication within 12 mos. Books are published electronically in trade-size print. No simultaneous submissions (a 90-day exclusive is required on all submissions, and a viable marketing plan must accompany every submission). Responds in 90 days. Guidelines on Website.

Nonfiction: Submit by e-mail only (with separate marketing plan) to: 1thbsubmissions2@ earthlink.net. Submissions open the 1st-14th of each month. Excellent nonfiction books are highly desired here. Looking for nonfiction.

Fiction: E-mail submissions only. Welcomes most genres for their imprints, but no poetry, alternative life style, porno/erotica, or small children's books. We accept outstanding young adult material.

Photos/Artwork: Accepts high-quality freelance photos for book covers; rarely open to queries from freelance artists.

Tips: "All fiction should be fresh and intriguing. Challenge the reader to think, to look at things through different eyes. Avoid point of view head-hopping and clichés. Send consecutive chapters, not random. A well-developed marketing plan must accompany all submissions. You must follow our guidelines."

THE TRINITY FOUNDATION, PO Box 68, Unicoi TN 37692. (423) 743-0199. Fax (423) 743-2005. E-mail: tjtrinityfound@aol.com. Website: www.trinityfoundation.org. Thomas W. Juodaitis, ed. To promote the logical system of truth found in the Bible. Publishes 5 titles/yr.; hardcover, trade paperbacks. Receives 3 submissions annually. No books from first-time authors. No mss through agents. Reprints books. Prefers 200 pgs. Outright purchases up to $1,500; free books; no advance. Average first printing 2,000. Publication within 9 mos. No simultaneous submissions. Requires requested ms on disk. Responds in 2-3 mos. No guidelines; catalog on Website.

Nonfiction: Query letter only. Open to Calvinist/Clarkian books, Christian philosophy, economics, and politics.

Also Does: Pamphlets, booklets, tracts.

Photos: Accepts freelance photos for book covers.

Tips: "Most open to doctrinal books that conform to the Westminster Confession of Faith; nonfiction, biblical, and well-reasoned books, theologically sound, clearly written, and well organized."

TROITSA BOOKS, 400 Oser Ave., Ste. 1600, Hauppauge NY 11788-3619. (631) 231-7269. Fax (631) 231-8175. E-mail: Novaeditorial@earthlink.net, or through Website: www.novapublishers .com. Religious imprint of Nova Science Publishers Inc. Submit to Editor-in-Chief. Publishes 5-20 titles/yr. Receives 50-100 submissions annually. No mss through agents. Various lengths. Royalty; no advance. Publication within 6-18 mos. Considers simultaneous submissions. Accepts requested ms on disk or by e-mail (prefers e-mail for all submissions and correspondence). Responds in 1 mo. Guidelines on Website; free catalog.

Nonfiction: Proposal/2 chapters by e-mail. Send to above e-mail with a copy to novascil@ aol.com.

Fiction: Proposal/2 chapters by e-mail. For adults.

Photos: Accepts freelance photos for book covers.

TSABA HOUSE, 2252—12th St., Reedley CA 93654. (559) 643-8575. E-mail: info@tsabahouse .com. Website: www.tsabahouse.com. Jodie Nazaroff, VP & sr. ed. Christian publishing company currently publishing fiction, nonfiction, self-help, teaching, and devotionals; no children's books or poetry. Accepts mss through agents or authors. Royalty. Guidelines on Website.

Nonfiction/Fiction: Proposal/cover letter, chapter-by-chapter synopsis, 1 chapter, and word count; no e-query. Accepts during the month of January *only.*

Tips: "Your manuscript must be completed. We offer contracts to authors with a 3 book option only. You must commit to publish one book at least every two years—annually is preferable."

TYNDALE ESPAÑOL, 351 Executive Dr., Carol Stream IL 60188. (630) 784-5272. Fax (630) 344-0943. E-mail: andresschwartz@tyndale.com. Website: www.tyndale.com. Andres Schwartz, dir. Spanish division of Tyndale House Publishers.

@ TYNDALE HOUSE PUBLISHERS, 351 Executive Dr., Carol Stream IL 60188. Toll-free (800) 323-9400. (630) 668-8300. Toll-free fax (800) 684-0247. E-mail through Website: www.tyndale.com. Submit to Manuscript Review Committee. Practical Christian books for home and family. Imprints: Tyndale Español (Spanish imprint); Picket Fence Press (resources for women juggling multiple priorities in and outside the home); Barna Books. Publishes 225-250 titles/yr.; hardcover, trade paperbacks, mass-market paperbacks (reprints). 5 percent of books from first-time authors. Requires mss through agents. Reprints books. Royalty negotiable; outright purchase of some children's books; advance negotiable. Average first printing 5,000-10,000. Publication within 9 mos. Considers simultaneous submissions. Responds in 3-6 mos. Prefers NLT. No unsolicited mss. Guidelines/catalog on Website.

Nonfiction: Query from agents or published authors only; no phone/fax query. No unsolicited mss (they will not be acknowledged or returned).

Fiction: "We accept queries only from agents, Tyndale authors, authors known to us from other publishers, or other people in the publishing industry. Novellas, 25,000-30,000 words; novels 75,000-100,000 words. All must have an evangelical Christian message."

Also Does: E-books.

**Note: This publisher serviced by The Writer's Edge and ChristianManuscriptSubmissions.com.

UMI PUBLISHING, 1551 Regency Court, Calumet City IL 60409. Toll-free (800) 860-8642. (708) 868-7100. Fax (708) 868-6759. E-mail: customerservice@urbanministries.com. Website: www.urban ministries.com. Urban Ministries Inc. Not currently accepting unsolicited manuscripts.

UNITED METHODIST PUBLISHING HOUSE—See Abingdon Press or Dimensions for Living.

UNIVERSITY OF ARKANSAS PRESS, 201 Ozark Ave., Fayetteville AR 72701-1201. Toll-free (800) 626-0090. (479) 575-3246. Fax (479) 575-6044. E-mail: uapress@uark.edu. Website: www.uapress .com. Lawrence J. Malley, ed-in-chief. (lmalley@uark.edu). Academic publisher. Publishes 30 titles/ yr.; hardcover, trade paperbacks. Receives 1,000 submissions annually. 30 percent of books from first-time authors. Accepts mss through agents or authors. Reprints books. Prefers 300 pgs. Royalty on net; no advance. Average first printing 1,000-2,000. Publication within 1 yr. Reluctantly considers simultaneous submissions. Responds in 3 mos. Requires accepted ms on disk. Guidelines on Website; free catalog.

Nonfiction: Query. "All our books are scholarly." Looking for regional books.

Photos: Accepts freelance photos for book covers.

UNIVERSITY PRESS OF AMERICA, 4501 Forbes Blvd., Ste. 200, Lanham MD 20706. (301) 459-3366. Fax (301) 429-5748. E-mail: submitupa@univpress.com. Website: www.univpress.com. Rowman & Littlefield Publishing Group/Academic. Acq. eds.: Brooke Bascietto (e-mail: bbascietto@univpress.com) and Samantha Kirk (skirk@univpress.com). Publishes scholarly works in the social sciences and humanities; established by academics for academics. Imprint: Hamilton Books (biographies & memoirs). Publishes 75 religion titles/yr. Receives 700 submissions annually. 75 percent of books from first-time authors. Accepts mss through agents or authors. **SOME SUBSIDY.** Does digital printing. Reprints books. Prefers 90-300 pgs. Royalty up to 12 percent of net; no advance. Average first printing 200-300. Publication within 4-6 mos. Considers simultaneous submissions. Accepts e-mail submissions. Responds in 2 wks. Accepts requested ms on disk or by e-mail. Guidelines on Website; free catalog.

> **Nonfiction:** Proposal/3 chapters or complete ms; phone/fax/e-query OK. "Looking for scholarly manuscripts."
> **Ethnic Books:** African studies; African American studies.
> **Tips:** "Most open to timely, thoroughly researched, and well-documented books. Moderately controversial topics. We publish academic and scholarly books only. Authors are typically affiliated with a college, university, or seminary."

VBC PUBLISHING, PO Box 9101, Vallejo CA 94591. (707) 315-1219. Fax (707) 648-2169. E-mail: kevin@astroaire.com. Website: www.www.geocities.com/vallejobiblecollege. Vallejo Bible College. Kevin Gordon, pres. To glorify the Lord through Christian literature; to provide the Christian community with material to aid them in their personal studies and to help in their life and ministry. New publisher; plans 1-5 titles/yr.; hardcover, trade paperbacks. Plans to publish 50 percent of books from first-time authors. Accepts mss through agents or authors. Print-on-demand publisher. No reprints. Prefers 100+ pgs. Royalty 8-12 percent on net; no advance. Publication within 8 mos. Considers simultaneous submissions. Responds in 2-6 wks. Accepted mss on disk. Prefers KJV, NKJV, NASB, NIV. Guidelines by mail/Website; no catalog.

> **Nonfiction:** Proposal/2 chapters or complete ms; phone query OK; no fax/e-query.
> **Special Needs:** Biblical theology, Bible study, and Christian living.
> **Artwork:** Open to queries from freelance artists.
> **Tips:** "Most open to doctrinally sound and relevant manuscripts. Have a well-written manuscript and a plan to market your book. Follow guidelines when submitting and trust in the Lord!"

VIRTUAL TALES, E-mail through Website: www.virtualtales.com. P. June Diel, ed. dir; Jake George, acq. ed. Produces eBook and paperback novels and novellas of at least 30,000 words; also open to short story collections. Requires e-mail submissions through Website form. Accepts reprints. Guidelines on Website. Incomplete topical listings.

THE VISION FORUM, 4719 Blanco Rd., San Antonio TX 78212. (210) 340-5250. Fax (210) 340-8577. Website: www.visionforum.com. Douglas W. Phillips, pres. Dedicated to the restoration of the biblical family. Historical fiction.

WALK WORTHY PRESS, (248) 737-1747. Fax (248) 737-1766. E-mail: editor@walkworthypress.net or through Website: www.walkworthypress.net. Denise Stinson, pub. Primarily fiction for the African American Christian. Publishes 10 titles/yr. Receives 200 submissions annually. 95 percent of books from first-time authors. Accepts mss through agents or authors. Reprints books. Prefers 75,000-100,000 words or 300 pgs. Royalty 10-15 percent on retail; variable advance. Average first printing varies. Publication within 9 mos. Considers simultaneous submissions (if informed). No disk or e-mail submissions. Responds in 2-8 wks. Prefers KJV, NKJV, NIV, Amplified. Guidelines on Website; free catalog.

> **Nonfiction:** Proposal/2 chapters by e-mail (see Website). "We do primarily fiction. Our nonfiction is generally from authors who have a high profile."

Fiction: Submission guidelines on Website. Seasoned fiction author may send proposal/3 chapters. For all ages. Contemporary, ethnic, fantasy, juvenile, literary, short-story collection. Big commercial fiction.

Ethnic Books: African American.

Tips: "Present a good package. Read our books first. Do a story synopsis, not book-jacket copy. We like manuscripts that explore little-explored areas of life in Christian books."

+ **WARNER PRESS BOOKS**, 1201 E. 5th St., Anderson IN 46012. Toll-free (800) 741-7721. Fax (765) 640-8005. E-mail: rfogle@warnerpress.org. Website: www.warnerpress.org. Church of God. Karen Rhodes, sr. ed.; submit to Robin Fogle, asst. product ed. Committed to excellence in developing and marketing products and services based on scriptural truths to energize, educate, nurture, inspire, and unite the whole people of God. Hardcover books. Receives 30-50 submissions annually. Rarely accepts mss through agents. **NO SUBSIDY.** No reprints. Prefers 32 pgs. for kid's books; 250-350 pgs. for teen books. Royalty & advance based on the author and type of book. Publication within 12 mos. Considers simultaneous submissions. Responds in 6-8 wks. Prefers KJV/NIV. Guidelines by mail/Website; no catalog.

> **Nonfiction:** Complete ms; fax/e-query OK. Accepts e-mail submissions.
>
> **Fiction:** Complete ms; fax/e-query OK. Accepts e-mail submissions. For children & teens. "We want our books to be biblically sound but with a nondenominational viewpoint/bias."
>
> **Artwork:** Send to Curtis Corzine, Creative Art Director.
>
> **Tips:** "We primarily create books for ages 6-10 (picture books) and 8-12 (fantasy fiction). We are looking for books that are not preachy but do contain a biblical or moral foundation. Well-written, creative books by writers who have done their market research."

WATERBROOK PRESS, 12265 Oracle Blvd., Ste. 200, Colorado Springs CO 80921. (719) 590-4999. Fax (719) 590-8977. E-mail: info@waterbrookmultnomah.com. Website: www.waterbrook multnomah.com. Part of WaterBrook Multnomah, a division of Random House Inc. Ken Petersen, VP/ed. dir. Publishes 75 titles/yr.; hardcover, trade paperbacks. Royalty on net; pays an advance. WaterBrook is currently not accepting unsolicited manuscripts, proposals, or queries; no proposals for biographies or poetry. Queries will be accepted though literary agents and at writers' conferences at which a WaterBrook representative is present. Catalog on Website.

> **Nonfiction/Fiction:** Agented submissions only.

WESLEYAN PUBLISHING HOUSE, PO Box 50434, Indianapolis IN 46250-0434. (317) 774-7900. E-mail: wph@wesleyan.org. Website: www.wesleyan.org/wph. The Wesleyan Church. Attn: Editorial Director. Communicates the life-transforming message of holiness to the world. Publishes 15 titles/yr.; hardcover, trade paperbacks. Receives 150 submissions annually. 20 percent of books from first-time authors. Accepts mss through agents or authors. No reprints. Prefers 25,000-40,000 wds. Royalty and advance. Average first printing 4,000. Publication within 9-12 mos. Will consider simultaneous submissions. Prefers requested ms by e-mail. Responds within 2 mos. Prefers NIV. Guidelines by mail/e-mail/Website; free catalog.

> **Nonfiction:** Proposal/3-5 chapters; no phone/fax/e-query. "Looking for books that help Christians understand the faith and apply it to their lives."
>
> ****Note:** This publisher serviced by ChristianManuscriptSubmissions.com.

WESTBOW PRESS—See Thomas Nelson, Fiction.

WESTMINSTER JOHN KNOX PRESS—See Presbyterian Publishing Corporation.

WHITAKER HOUSE, 1030 Hunt Valley Cir., New Kensington PA 15068. (724) 334-7000. (724) 334-1200. E-mail: publisher@whitakerhouse.com. Website: www.whitakerhouse.com. Whitaker Corp. Tom Cox, sr. ed. To advance God's Kingdom by providing biblically based products that proclaim the power of the gospel and minister to the spiritual needs of people around the world. Publishes 30-40 titles/yr.; hardcover, trade paperbacks, mass-market paperbacks. Receives 500 submissions annually. 25 percent of books from first-time authors. Accepts mss through agents or authors. No subsidy, print-on-demand, or reprints. Prefers 50,000 words. Royalty 6-15 percent on net; some variable advances. Average first printing 5,000. Publication within 10 mos. Will consider simultaneous submissions. Prefers accepted ms by e-mail. Responds in 4 mos. Prefers NIV. Guidelines on Website; no catalog.

Nonfiction/Fiction: Query only first; no phone/fax query; e-query OK.

Special Needs: Charismatic nonfiction.

Ethnic Books: Hispanic translations of current English titles.

Tips: "Looking for quality fiction and previously published authors with a national marketing platform. Most open to high-quality, well-thought-out, compelling pieces of work. Do the research and work required by our guidelines."

@ WHITE ROSE PUBLISHING, PO Box 708, Adams Basin NY 14410. (585) 752-8770. E-mail: rpenders@whiterosepublishing.com or whitequery@whiterosepublishing.com. Website: www.whiterose publishing.com. Rhonda Penders, ed. To give writers a background and forum to perfect their craft; the "garden" is truly a place for new authors to grow and "bloom" along with giving experienced writers a place to gain some flexibility; devoted specifically to inspirational, Christian romances. Publishes about 12 titles/yr; trade paperbacks. Receives 1,000 submissions annually. 40 percent of books from first-time authors. Accepts mss through agents or authors. Does e-publishing for anything under 65,000 words; over that is print & e-publishing. Does print-on-demand. Reprints books. Prefers between 7,500 and 100,000 words. Royalty 35 percent on download; 7 percent on print. No advance. Publication in up to 12 mos. Considers simultaneous submissions reluctantly. Responds to proposals in 60 days; full mss quarterly. Guidelines by e-mail; no catalog.

Fiction: Query only first; romance only. "We are actively seeking both historical and contemporary romances in a variety of subgenres." Accepts short stories as well as full-length manuscripts.

Also Does: E-books.

Tips: "We don't do form rejection slips. We are prompt and believe in communication."

@ WHITE STONE BOOKS, PO Box 2835, Lakeland FL 33806. Toll-free (800) 888-4126. E-mail: info@whitestonebooks.com. Website: www.whitestonebooks.com. Christian books. Amanda Pilgrim, ed. Publishes 25 titles/yr.; hardcover, trade paperbacks, mass-market paperbacks. 30 percent of books from first-time authors. Accepts mss through agents or authors. **SUBSIDY PUBLISHES OCCASIONALLY**. Reprints books. Publication within 18 mos. Considers simultaneous submissions. Guidelines by mail/e-mail; free catalog.

Nonfiction: Proposal/1 chapter.

Fiction: Proposal/1 chapter. For all ages. "We prefer scripts with several connecting layers, with story lines that are compelling and thought provoking."

Special Needs: Adult & teen novels; seasonally appropriate for gift giving, especially for Mother's Day and Christmas.

Also Does: E-books.

Artwork: Open to queries from freelance artists.

Tips: "Most open to books that are seasonally appropriate, but not seasonally specific: Mothers/Mother's Day; Fathers/Father's Day."

**Note: This publisher serviced by The Writers Edge and ChristianManuscriptSubmissions.com.

WILSHIRE BOOK COMPANY, 9731 Variel Ave., Chatsworth CA 91311-4315. (818) 700-1522. Fax (818) 700-1527. E-mail: mpowers@mpowers.com. Website: www.mpowers.com. A general publisher of motivational books. Melvin Powers, pres.; Marcia Powers, ed. Books that help you become who you choose to be tomorrow. Publishes 6 titles/yr. 80 percent of books from first-time authors. Accepts mss through agents or authors. Reprints books. Prefers 30,000 words or 128-160 pgs. Royalty 5 percent on retail; variable advance. Average first printing 5,000. Publication within 6 mos. Considers simultaneous submissions. No disk or e-mail submissions. Responds in 2 mos. Guidelines by e-mail.

Nonfiction: Query or proposal/3 chapters; phone/e-query OK.

Fiction: Allegory for adults that teaches principles of psychological/spiritual growth.

Photos/Artwork: Accepts freelance photos for book covers; open to queries from freelance artists.

Tips: "We are looking for adult allegories such as Illusions, by Richard Bach, The Little Prince, by Antoine de Saint Exupery, and The Greatest Salesman in the World, by Og Mandino. Analyze each one to discover what elements make it a winner. Duplicate those elements in your own style, using a creative, new approach and fresh material. We need 30,000-60,000 words."

WIPF AND STOCK PUBLISHERS, 199 W. 8th Ave., Ste. 3. Eugene OR 97401-2960. (541) 344-1528. Fax (541) 344-1506. E-mail: proposals@wipfandstock.com. Website: www.wipfandstock.com. Submit to Attn: Editorial/Proposals. Specializes in new and reprinted academic books. Imprints: Cascade Books, Pickwick Publications, and Resource Publications. Guidelines/catalog on Website. Incomplete topical listings.

W PUBLISHING GROUP, PO Box 141000, Nashville TN 37214. (615) 889-9000. Fax (615) 902-2112. Website: www.Wpublishinggroup.com. Thomas Nelson Inc. David Moberg, pub.; Greg Daniel, assoc. pub. Publishes 75 titles/yr. Less than 3 percent of books from first-time authors. Requires mss through agents. No reprints. Does not accept unsolicited manuscripts. Prefers 65,000-95,000 wds. Royalty. No guidelines.

Nonfiction: Query letter only first; no unsolicited ms. "Nonfiction dealing with the relationship and/or application of biblical principles to everyday life; 65,000-95,000 words."

**Note: This publisher serviced by The Writer's Edge & ManuscriptSubmissions.com.

WRITE NOW PUBLICATIONS, PO Box 110390, Nashville TN 37222. Toll-free (800) 21-WRITE. E-mail: RegAForder@aol.com. Website: www.writenowpublications.com. Reg A. Forder, exec. ed. To train and develop quality Christian writers; books on writing and speaking for writers and speakers. Royalty division of ACW Press. Publishes 1-2 titles/yr.; trade paperbacks. Receives 6 submissions annually. 0 percent from first-time authors. Accepts mss through agents or authors. Reprints books. Royalty 10 percent of net. Average first printing 2,000. Publication within 12 mos. Considers simultaneous submissions. Requires requested ms on disk. No guidelines/catalog.

Nonfiction: Writing how-to only. Query letter only; e-query OK.

XYZZY PRESS. E-mail: acquisitions@xyzzypress.com. Website: www.xyzzypress.com. Responds in several wks. Guidelines on Website.

Nonfiction/Fiction: Proposal/several chapters by e-mail.

YALE UNIVERSITY PRESS, PO Box 209040, New Haven CT 06518-9040. (203) 432-6807. Fax (203) 436-1064. E-mail: jennifer.banks@yale.edu. Website: www.yalepress.yale.edu. Jennifer Banks, ed. Publishes scholarly and general-interest books, including religion. Publishes 15 religious titles/yr.; hardcover, trade paperbacks. Receives 200 submissions annually. 15 percent of books from first-time authors. Accepts mss through agents or authors. Reprints books. Prefers up to 100,000 words or 400 pgs. Royalty from 0 percent to standard trade royalties; advance $0-100,000. Average first printing 12 mos. Publication within 1 yr. Considers simultaneous submissions. Requires requested ms on disk; no e-mail submissions. Responds in 2 mos. Guidelines/catalog on Website (www.yalebooks.com).

Nonfiction: Query or proposal/sample chapters; fax query OK; no e-query. "Excellent and salable scholarly books."

Contest: Yale Series of Younger Poets competition. Open to poets under 40 who have not had a book of poetry published. Submit manuscripts of 48-64 pages by November 15. Entry fee $15. Send SASE for guidelines (also on Website). Send complete manuscript.

YOUTH SPECIALTIES, 300 S. Pierce St., El Cajon CA 92020. Toll-free (888) 346-4179. (619) 440-2333. Fax (619) 440-8542. E-mail: ideas@youthspecialties.com. Website: www.youthspecialties .com. Zondervan. Books for youth workers and teenagers. Imprint: Invert Books. Publishes 30 titles/yr. Accepts mss through agents or authors. No reprints. Prefers 35,000 words. Royalty on net or outright purchase of $3,000-8,000; pays an advance. Publication within 18 mos. Considers simultaneous submissions. Responds in 4-6 wks. Prefers NIV. Guidelines by e-mail/Website; free catalog.

Nonfiction: Proposal/2 chapters.

Tips: "We prefer books from youth workers who are in the trenches working with students."

ZONDERKIDZ, 5300 Patterson S.E., Grand Rapids MI 49530-0002. (616) 698-6900. Fax (616) 698-3578. E-mail: zpub@zondervan.com. Website: www.zonderkidz.com. Zondervan/ HarperCollins. Children's book line of Zondervan; ages 12 & under. Not currently accepting proposals.

Note: This publisher serviced by ChristianManuscriptSubmissions.com.

ZONDERVAN, 5300 Patterson S.E., Grand Rapids MI 49530-0002. (616) 698-6900. Manuscript submission line: (616) 698-3447. Website: www.zondervan.com. HarperCollins Publishers. Mission is to be the leading Christian communications company meeting the needs of people with resources that glorify Jesus Christ and promote biblical principles. Publishes 120 trade titles/yr.; hardcover, trade paperbacks, mass-market paperbacks. Few books from first-time authors. Accepts mss through agents or authors. No subsidy or reprints. Royalty 12-14 percent of net; variable advance. Publication within 12-18 mos. Considers simultaneous submissions. Requires requested ms by e-mail. Prefers NIV. Guidelines on Website; no catalog.

Nonfiction: Submissions only by e-mail and only certain types of mss. See Website for e-mail address and submission guidelines.

Fiction: No fiction at this time; refer to Website for updates.

Special Needs: Currently accepting unsolicited book proposals in academic, reference, or ministry resources only (see guidelines).

Children's Lines: ZonderKidz and Faithgirlz (not currently accepting new products).

Ethnic Books: Vida Publishers division: Spanish and Portuguese.

Tips: "Almost no unsolicited manuscripts are published. Book proposals should be single-spaced with one-inch margins on all sides."

Note: This publisher serviced by ChristianManuscriptSubmissions.com.

3

Subsidy Publishers

In this section you will find publishers who do 50 percent or more subsidy publishing. For our purposes, I am defining a subsidy publisher as any publisher that requires the author to pay for any part of the publishing costs. They may call themselves by a variety of names, such as book packager, cooperative publisher, self-publisher, or simply someone who helps authors get their books published. Print-on-demand (POD) businesses publish books one at a time and usually print books much faster than typical publishers. Another designation is custom publisher, which refers to a publisher that develops new authors to eventually work with royalty publishers.

To my knowledge the following publishers are legitimate subsidy publishers (as opposed to companies that are simply out to take your money and offer little in return), but I cannot guarantee that. It is important for you to understand that any time you are asked to pay for any part of the production of your book, you are entering into a nontraditional relationship with a publisher. Note that some subsidy publishers also do royalty publishing, so you could approach them as a royalty publisher. You just need to realize that they are likely to offer you a subsidy deal, so if you are interested only in a royalty arrangement, indicate that in your cover letter.

Some subsidy publishers will publish any book, as long as the author is willing to pay for it. Others are as selective about what they publish as a royalty publisher would be. As subsidy publishers become more selective, the professional quality of subsidy books is improving overall. Many will publish only nonfiction—no novels or children's books. These distinctions will be important as you seek the right publisher.

Subsidy publishing can be confusing, and many authors go into agreements with these publishers having little or no knowledge of what to expect. As a result, they come away unhappy or disillusioned; I frequently get complaints from authors who feel they have been cheated or taken advantage of. Each complaint brings with it an expectation that I should drop that publisher from this book. Although I am sensitive to these complaints, I also realize that I am not in a position to pass judgment on which publishers should be dropped. It has been my experience that for every complaint I get about a publisher, I find several other authors who sing the praises of that publisher. For that reason, I feel I can serve the needs of authors better by giving a brief overview of what to expect from a subsidy publisher and what kinds of terms should send up a red flag.

First, unless you know your book has a limited audience or you have your own method of distribution (such as being a speaker who can sell your own books when you speak), I recommend that you try all the appropriate royalty publishers before considering a subsidy house.

If you are unsuccessful with the royalty publishers but still feel strongly about seeing your book published, a subsidy publisher may be able to help you. A subsidy publisher has the contacts, know-how, and resources to make printing your book easier and often less expensive than doing it yourself.

It is always good to get more than one bid to determine whether the terms you are being offered are competitive with those of other such publishers. A legitimate subsidy publisher will be happy to provide you with a list of former clients as references. Don't just ask for that list; follow through and contact more than one of those references. Get a catalog of the publisher's books or a list of those books, and then review a few of them yourself to check the quality of the work, the bindings, etc. See if the books are available through Amazon.com or similar online services. (It's important to understand that the majority of Christian or general bookstores will not carry a self-published book.) Get answers to all your questions before you commit yourself to anything. Also have someone review your contract before you sign it. I do such reviews, as do a number of others listed in the "Editorial Services" section of this book. Be sure that any terms agreed upon are in writing. The listings below include printers who could help you complete the printing process yourself, so you will want to check out those as well.

Keep in mind that the more copies of a book you have printed, the lower the cost per copy. But never let a publisher talk you into publishing more copies than you think is reasonable for your situation. Also, find out up front, and have included in the contract, how much promotion, if any, the publisher is going to do. Some will do as much as a royalty publisher; others do none at all. If the publisher is not doing promotion and you don't have any means of distribution yourself, it may not be a good idea to pursue subsidy publication. You don't want to end up with a garage full of books you can't sell.

Here are some definitions that will help you identify the different types of publishers. Just note that not all publishers may interpret their services as indicated below, so be sure you know what to expect before signing a contract.

Commercial/Mainstream/Traditional Publisher: One who pays all the costs of producing your book (see previous book section).
Vanity Publisher: Prints the books at the author's expense. Will print any book the author is willing to pay for. May offer marketing help, warehousing, editing, or promotion of some sort at the author's expense.
Subsidy Publisher: Shares the cost of printing and binding a book. Often more selective, but the completed books belong to the publisher, not the author. Author may buy books from the publisher and may also collect a royalty for books the publisher sells.
Self-Publishing: Author pays all the costs of publishing the book and is responsible for all the marketing, distribution, promotion, etc. Author may select a service package that defines the cost and services to be rendered. The books belong to the author and he/she keeps all the income from the sale of the books.

Following this section I include the names and addresses of Christian book distributors. I have asked them if they will consider distributing a subsidy-published book, and some have responded positively. You may want to contact some of them to find out their interest before you sign a contract with a subsidy publisher. For more help on self-publishing, go to: www.bookmarket.com/index.html.

+ A plus sign before a listing indicates it is a new listing this year or was not included last year.
@ Indicates the publisher produces e-books.

ACW PRESS, American Christian Writers, PO Box 110390, Nashville TN 37222. Toll-free (800) 21-WRITE. E-mail: Jim@JamesWatkins.com. Website: www.acwpress.com. Reg A. Forder, owner; Jim Watkins, editorial advisor. A self-publishing book packager. Imprint: Write Now Publications (see separate listing). Publishes 40 titles/yr.; hardcover, trade paperbacks, mass-market paperbacks, coffee-table books. Reprints books. **SUBSIDY PUBLISHES 95 PERCENT**; does print-on-demand. Average first printing 2,500. Publication within 4-6 mos. Responds in 48-72 hrs. Request for estimate form available on Website. Not in topical listings; will consider any nonfiction or fiction topic. Guidelines by e-mail/Website.
Nonfiction/Fiction: All types considered.
Tips: "We offer a high quality publishing alternative to help Christian authors get their material into print. High standards, high quality. If authors have a built-in audience, they have the best chance to make self-publishing a success." Has a marketing program available to authors.
**Note: This publisher serviced by The Writer's Edge and ChristianManuscriptSubmissions.com.

AMERICAN BINDING & PUBLISHING CO., PO Box 60049, Corpus Christi TX 78466-0049. Toll-free (800) 863-3708. (361) 658-4221. E-mail: rmagner@grandecom.net. Website: www.american bindingpublishing.com. Rose Magner, pub. Publishes 60 titles/yr. Receives 200 submissions annually. 95 percent of books from first-time authors. No mss through agents. Reprints books. **SUBSIDY PUBLISHES 100 PERCENT;** does print-on-demand. Prefers 200 pgs. Royalty 15 percent on retail; no advance. Publication within 2 wks. Considers simultaneous submissions. Requires requested ms on disk (Microsoft Word format). Responds in 2 wks. Any Bible version. Guidelines by mail/e-mail; free catalog.

Nonfiction: Complete ms; phone/e-query OK. Will consider any topic.
Fiction: Complete ms; phone/e-query OK. For all ages; all genres.
Ethnic Books: African American and Hispanic.
Photos: Accepts freelance photos for book covers.
Tips: "We are print-on-demand; authors are responsible for their own marketing. We will consider any topic—nonfiction or fiction, but most open to fiction."

AMPELOS PRESS, 316 Blanchard Rd., Drexel Hill PA 19026. Phone/fax (610) 626-6833. E-mail: mbagnull@aol.com. Website: www.writehisanswer.com. Marlene Bagnull, LittD, pub./ed. Services (depending on what is needed) include critiquing, editing, proofreading, typesetting, and cover design. Publishes 1-3 titles/yr. **SUBSIDY PUBLISHES 100 PERCENT.** Query only. Not included in topical listings (see "Tips").

Special Needs: Books about missions and meeting the needs of children both at home and abroad.
Tips: "Our vision statement reads: 'Strongly, unashamedly, uncompromisingly Christ-centered. Exalting the name of Jesus Christ. Seeking to teach His ways through holding up the Word of God as the Standard.' (*Ampelos* is the Greek word for 'vine' in John 15:5.) "

ANOMALOS PUBLISHING, 7699 Mount Carmel Dr., Orlando FL 32835. (407) 521-1605. E-mail: info@Anomalos. com. Website: www.anomalos.com. Steve Warner, pub.; Laurie Regan, mng. ed. Self-publisher. Author pays production and publication fees. Publisher distributes, markets, and advertises book. Author receives 80 percent royalty on net. Guidelines/details on Website. Not included in topical listings.

@ BELIEVERSPRESS, (formerly Bethany Press-Custom Solutions), 6820 W. 115th St., Bloomington MN 55438. Toll-free (800) 341-4192. (952) 914-7426. E-mail: info@believerspress.com. Website: www.believerspress.com. A division of Bethany Press International. Sara Rosenberg, ed. Submit by e-mail. A gathering of Christian authors and publishing professionals collaborating to reinvent the way books are published and sold. Offers solutions to fit every budget. Authors pay only for services they need and are in full control. All work done as work-for-hire. Includes: a forum-based publishing community, professional industry blogs, editorial, typesetting, cover design, digital/conventional book production, e-books, distribution, marketing/publicity, author e-store book sales, and author blogs.

BLACK FOREST PRESS/TENNESSEE PUBLISHING HOUSE/SOUTHERN HERITAGE BOOKS, Belle Arden Run Estate, 488 Mountain View Dr., Mosheim TN 37818-3524. Phone/fax (423) 422-4711(call ahead for fax). E-mail: dahkknox@embarqmail.com. Covenant Christian Healing Ministries. Dr. Dahk Knox, pub.; Dr. Jan Knox, CFO. Provides truthful information about an author's book; whether you publish with them or not, you get free help and advice. Imprints: Recht Books, World Truth Publishing House, Abenteure Books, Kinder Books, Sonnerschein Books, Dichter Books, Segen Books. Publishes up to 35 titles/yr.; hardcover, trade paperbacks, coffee-table books. Receives 100 submissions annually. 70 percent of books from first-time authors. Accepts mss through agents. **SUBSIDY PUBLISHES 50 PERCENT;** does print-on-demand. Reprints books (with permission). Prefers 120-325 pgs. Royalty on net (100 percent of sales, minus $1/bk., unless other arrangements made), or outright purchase; no advance. Average first printing 2,000, or 250 POD. Publication within 2 mos. Considers simultaneous submissions. Requires accepted ms by e-mail (attached). Responds in 2 wks. Prefers NIV/NKJV. Guidelines by mail/Website; no catalog.

Nonfiction: Complete ms by e-mail (attached); phone/e-query OK.

Fiction: Complete ms. All genres for all ages.

Special Needs: Historical fiction, nonfiction biographies, religious books of any kind.

Photos/Artwork: Accepts freelance photos for book covers; open to queries from freelance artists.

Tips: "Most open to well-written nonfiction or historical novels. Our imprint, Tennessee Publishing House, provides tax-exemption write-offs with certain religious book offerings."

@ BOOKLOCKER.COM INC., PO Box 2399, Bangor ME 04402-2399. (207) 262-9696. Fax (207) 262-5544. E-mail: angela@booklocker.com. Website: www.booklocker.com. Angela Hoy, pub. We seek unique, eclectic, and different manuscripts. Publishes 300 titles/yr.; hard cover, trade paperbacks, e-books. 70 percent of books from first-time authors. No mss through agents. **SUBSIDY PUBLISHES 100 PERCENT;** does print-on-demand. Reprints books. Prefers 48-740 pgs.; less for children's books. Royalty 35 percent on retail (15 percent on wholesale orders; 35 percent on booklocker.com orders; 50-70 percent for e-books); no advance. Publication within 4-6 wks. Considers simultaneous submissions. Responds in less than a week. Bible version is author's choice. Guidelines on Website; no catalog.

Nonfiction: Complete ms; e-query OK. "We're open to all unique ideas."

Fiction: Complete ms; e-query OK. All genres for all ages.

Ethnic Books: Publishes for all ethnic groups.

Photos/Artwork: Uses stock photos or author-supplied photos/artwork.

Contest: The WritersWeekly.com 24-Hour Short Story Contest is held quarterly.

BOOK PUBLISHERS NETWORK, PO Box 2256, Bothell WA 98041. (425) 483-3040. Fax (425) 483-3098. E-mail: sherynhara@bookpublishersnetwork.com. Website: www.bookpublishersnetwork.com. Sheryn Hara, ed. Publishes 5-8 titles/yr.; hardcover, trade paperbacks. Receives 20 submissions annually. 100 percent of books from first-time authors. Accepts mss through agents. **SUBSIDY PUBLISHES 100 PERCENT.** Reprints books. No preference on length. No royalty/advance. Publication within 3 mos. Considers simultaneous submissions. Responds in 1 mo. Guidelines on Website; no catalog.

Nonfiction: Proposal or complete ms; phone/fax/e-query OK.

Fiction: Proposal or complete ms; phone/fax/e-query OK. For all ages.

Photos: Accepts freelance photos for book covers.

Tips: "We take good care of our authors. We work hand-in-hand with them to produce a quality product."

BOOKS JUST BOOKS.COM, 51 E. 42nd St., Ste. 1202, New York NY 10017. Toll-free (800) 621-2556. Fax (212) 681-8002. E-mail: ron@rjcom.com. Website: www.booksjustbooks.com. R J Communications. Ron Pramschufer, pub. **SUBSIDY PUBLISHES 100 PERCENT.** Guidelines on Website. Not included in topical listings.

@ BOOKSTAND PUBLISHING/EBOOKSTAND.COM, 7790 Eigleberry St., Ste. B, Gilroy CA 95020. Toll-free (866) 793-9365. (408) 852-1832. Fax (408) 413-5443. E-mail: support@bookstandpublishing.com or authorservices@bookstandpublishing.com. Website: www.bookstandpublishing.com. Fast Press Publishing Inc. Kari Baldwin, ed. A POD publisher helping authors get published. Publishes 20+ titles/yr. Receives 20+ submissions annually. 80 percent of books from first-time authors. Accepts mss through agents. **100 PERCENT PRINT-ON-DEMAND.** Reprints books. Royalty 10-30 percent on retail; no advance. Average first printing: 48. Publication within 2 mos. Considers simultaneous submissions. Responds immediately. Guidelines by mail/e-mail/Website; free catalog.

Nonfiction: Complete ms. Christian topics.

Fiction: Complete ms. For all ages. All genres.

Special Needs: Niche books, memoirs, Bible studies.
Photos: Accepts freelance photos for book covers.

BRENTWOOD CHRISTIAN PRESS, 4000 Beallwood Ave., Columbus GA 31904. Toll-free (800) 334-8861. (706) 576-5787. Fax (706) 317-5808. E-mail: Brentwood@aol.com. Website: www .brentwoodbooks.com. Mainline. U. D. Roberts, exec. ed. Publishes 267 titles/yr. Receives 2,000 submissions annually. Reprints books. **SUBSIDY PUBLISHES 95 PERCENT.** Offers InstaBooks and Just in Time publishing (print-on-demand). Average first printing 500. Publication within 1 mo. Considers simultaneous submissions. Responds in 2 days. Guidelines by mail.

> **Nonfiction:** Complete ms. "Collection of sermons on family topics, poetry, relation of Bible to current day."
> **Fiction:** Complete ms. "Stories that show how faith helps overcome small, day-to-day problems."
> **Photos:** Accepts freelance photos for book covers.
> **Tips:** "Keep it short; support facts with reference." This publisher specializes in small print runs of 300-1,000. Can best serve the writer who has a completed manuscript.

BROWN BOOKS PUBLISHING GROUP, 16200 N. Dallas Pkwy., Ste. 170, Dallas TX 75248. (972) 381-0009. Fax (972) 248-4336. E-mail: kgrant@brownbooks.com. Website: www.brownbooks.com. Milli A. Brown, pub.; submit to Kathryn Grant, sr. ed. Publishes books in the areas of self-help, religion/ inspirational, relationships, business, mind/body/spirit, and women's issues. We build relationships with our authors. Imprints: Personal Profiles, The P3 Press. Publishes 10-30 titles/yr.; hardcover, trade paperbacks, coffee-table books. Receives 2,000 submissions annually. 80 percent of books from first-time authors. No mss through agents. **SUBSIDY PUBLISHES 100 PERCENT** through Personal Profiles & P3 imprints. No reprints. Royalty 100 percent of retail; no advance. Authors retain rights to their work. Average first printing 3,000-5,000. Publication in 6 mos. Accepts simultaneous submissions. Responds in 2 wks. Requires mss on disk or by e-mail. Responds in 2 wks. Guidelines on Website.

> **Nonfiction:** Complete ms; phone/e-query OK.
> **Fiction:** Complete ms; phone/e-query OK. For all ages.
> **Tips:** "We accept any type of manuscript."

CHRISTIAN SERVICES NETWORK, 1975 Janich Ranch Ct., El Cajon CA 92019-1150. Toll-free (866) 484-6184. Fax (619) 579-0685. Website: www.csnbooks.com. Michael Wourms, ed. **SELF-PUBLISHING COMPANY.** Details on Website.

CREATION HOUSE, 600 Rinehart Rd., Lake Mary FL 32746-4872. (407) 333-0600. Fax (407) 333-7100. E-mail: creationhouse@strang.com. Website: www.creationhouse.com. Strang Communications Co. Submit to Brenda J. Davis, acq. ed. To inspire and equip people to live a Spirit-led life and to walk in the divine purpose for which they were created. Publishes 125 titles/yr.; hardcover, trade paperbacks, mass-market paperbacks, coffee-table books. Receives 1,500 submissions annually. 80 percent of books from first-time authors. Accepts mss through agents. No subsidy or print-on-demand. Reprints books. Prefers 25,000+ words or 100-200 pgs. Royalty 12-15 percent of net; no advance. Average first printing 6,000. Publication within 5 mos. Considers simultaneous submissions. Responds in 10-12 wks. Open to submissions on disk or by e-mail. Guidelines by mail/e-mail; free catalog.

> **Nonfiction:** Proposal/complete ms; no phone/fax query; e-query OK. "Open to any books that are well written and glorify Jesus Christ."
> **Fiction:** Proposal/complete ms; no phone/fax query; e-query OK. For all ages. "Fiction must have a biblical worldview and point the reader to Christ."
> **Photos:** Accepts freelance photos for book covers.
> **Tips:** "We use the term *copublishing* to describe a hybrid between conventional royalty publishing and self or subsidy publishing, utilizing the best of both worlds. We produce a high quality book for our own inventory, market it, distribute it, and pay the author a royalty

on every copy sold. In return, the author agrees to buy, at a deep discount, a portion of the first print run."

CREDO HOUSE PUBLISHERS, 3148 Plainfield Ave. NE, Ste. 111, Grand Rapids MI 49525-3285. (616) 363-2686. E-mail: connect@credocommunications.net. Website: www.credocommunications .net. A division of Credo Communications LLC. Timothy J. Beals, pres. Works with Christian ministry leaders and organizations to develop life-changing books, Bible-related products and other Christian resources. Estab. 2005. Custom publisher. Publishes 6-12 titles/yr. Publication within 60-90 days. Average first printing 2,500. Guidelines on Website. Not included in topical listings.

Nonfiction/Fiction: Complete online author survey.

+ **CROSSBOOKS**, 1663 Liberty Dr., Ste. 200, Bloomington IN 47403. Toll-free (866)879-0502. E-mail: customerservice@crossbooks.com. Website: www.crossbooks.com. **SUBSIDY OR CO-OP PUBLISHER.** Open to freelance submissions. Not included in topical listings.

CROSSHOUSE PUBLISHING, PO Box 461592, Garland TX 75046. Toll-free (877) 212-0933. Toll-free fax (888) 252-3022. E-mail: crosshousepublishing@earthlink.net. Website: www.cross housepublishing.org. Self-publishing branch of KLMK Communications. Katie Welch, pub. To achieve excellence in Christian self-publishing without sacrificing personal interest and care for customers. Publishes hardcover, trade paperbacks. No mss through agents. **SUBSIDY PUBLISHER.** Royalty 25 percent on net; no advance. Publication within 3 mos. Guidelines by e-mail.

Nonfiction/Fiction: Accepts fiction for all ages.

Photos: Accepts freelance photos for book covers.

Tips: "We provide authors the opportunity to have their books distributed through a wide array of Christian and general bookstores. We aspire to offer the marketplace superior Christian literature that will impact readers' lives."

+ **CROSSLINK PUBLISHING**, PO Box 1232, Rapid City SD 57709. Toll-free (800) 323-0853. Toll-free fax (800) 934-6762. E-mail: publisher@crosslink.org. Website: www.crosslink.org. Christian Church/Church of Christ. Rick Bates, dir. Focused on providing valuable resources to authors as well as bringing vibrant and helpful resources to the Christian community. Estab. 2008. Publishes 6-8 titles/yr.; trade paperbacks. Receives 20 submissions annually. 25 percent of books from first-time authors. Prefers mss through agents. No subsidy; does print-on-demand. No reprints. Prefers 200-300 pgs. Royalty 10 percent of retail; no advance. Average first printing 750. Publication within 3 mos. Considers simultaneous submissions. Responds in 7 days. Requires accepted mss by e-mail. No guidelines/catalog.

Nonfiction: Complete ms; e-query OK.

Special Needs: Devotionals and small-group studies.

Photos/Artwork: Accepts freelance photos for book covers; open to queries from freelance artists.

Tips: "We are particularly interested in providing books that help Christians succeed in their daily walk (inspirational, devotional, small groups, etc.)."

DCTS PUBLISHING, PO Box 40216, Santa Barbara CA 93140. Toll-free (800) 965-8150. Fax (805) 653-6522. E-mail: dennis@dctspub.com. Website: www.dctspub.com. Dennis Stephen Hamilton, ed. Books are designed to enrich the mind, encourage the heart, and empower the spirit. Publishes 5 titles/yr. Receives 25 submissions annually. 35 percent of books from first-time authors. No mss through agents. **SUBSIDY PUBLISHES 70 PERCENT.** No reprints. Prefers 100-300 pgs. Royalty 17 percent of retail; no advance. Average first printing 3,500. Publication within 6-8 mos. No simultaneous submissions. Prefers KJV. Guidelines by mail; free catalog/brochure.

Nonfiction: Query or proposal/2-3 chapters; e-query OK.

@ ROBBIE DEAN PRESS, 2910 E. Eisenhower Parkway, Ann Arbor MI 48108. (734) 973-9511. Fax (734) 973-9475. E-mail: Fairyha@aol.com. Website: www.robbiedeanpress.com. Interested in works that are multiculturally appealing and approach a topic in a unique manner. Dr. Fairy C. Hayes-Scott, owner. Publishes 1 title/yr. Receives 20 submissions annually. 100 percent of books from first-time authors. Accepts mss through agents. **SUBSIDY PUBLISHES 75 PERCENT;** does print-on-demand. Reprints books. Length flexible. Royalty 10-20 percent; no advance. Average first printing 250. Publication within 6 mos. Considers simultaneous submissions. Responds in 2-6 wks. Guidelines by e-mail; free catalog.

Nonfiction: Query first. "We're open to new ideas."
Fiction: "We seldom do fiction." For children only.
Ethnic Books: Multicultural.
Also Does: Booklets; e-books; computer games.
Photos: Accepts freelance photos for book covers.
Tips: "Most open to self-help, reference, senior adult topics, and parenting."

DEEPER REVELATION BOOKS, PO Box 4260, Cleveland TN 37320-4260. (423) 478-2843. Fax (423) 479-2980. Website: www.deeperrevelationbooks.org. Mike Shreve, founder/dir. Publishing in-depth and edifying literature for the body of Christ; producing loving presentations of the gospel to followers of other worldviews. All submissions that match one or both of these descriptions are welcome. (Send $30 with unsolicited submissions.) Responds in 3-6 mos. A partnership publishing house. Authors are partners and associates who fund the printing of their works but own their books. DRB oversees the project to help authors learn the art of publishing, achieve their goals, produce works of excellence, and more easily receive national and international distribution. Does large print runs or print-on-demand. Average print run 2,000-3,000. Publishes 5 titles/yr. All books carry Deeper Revelation Books imprint. Guidelines on Website.

ELDERBERRY PRESS INC., 1393 Old Homestead Rd., 2nd Fl., Oakland OR 97462. (541) 459-6043. Toll-free fax (888) 259-5484. E-mail: editor@elderberrypress.com. Website: www.elderberrypress .com. David W. St. John, exec. ed. Publishes 15 titles/yr. Receives 150-250 submissions annually. 90 percent of books from first-time authors. No mss through agents. **SUBSIDY PUBLISHES 50 PERCENT;** does print-on-demand. Royalty 10-25 percent; no advance. Publication within 3 mos. Considers simultaneous submissions. Accepts disk or e-mail submissions. Responds in 1 mo. Guidelines on Website; free catalog.

Nonfiction: Complete ms; phone/fax/e-query OK. "We consider all topics."
Fiction: Complete ms; phone/fax/e-query OK. All genres for all ages.

ESSENCE PUBLISHING CO. INC., 20 Hanna Ct., Belleville ON K8P 5J2, Canada. Toll-free (800) 238-6376. (613) 962-0234. Fax (613) 962-3055. E-mail: info@essence-publishing.com. Website: www.essence-publishing.com. David Visser, mng. ed.; Sherrill Brunton, acq. mgr.; (sbruton@ essence-publishing. com). Provides affordable, short-run book publishing to the Christian community; dedicated to furthering the work of Christ through the written word. Imprints: Guardian Books, Epic Press. Publishes 100-150+ titles/yr. Receives 250+ submissions annually. 75 percent of books from first-time authors. **SUBSIDY PUBLISHES 90 PERCENT.** Reprints books. Any length. Average first printing 500-1,000. Publication within 3-5 mos. Considers simultaneous submissions. Responds in 3-4 wks. Prefers requested ms on disk or by e-mail. Guidelines by mail/e-mail/Website; catalog online (www.essencebookstore.com).

Nonfiction: Complete ms; phone/fax/e-query OK. Accepts all topics.
Fiction: Complete ms. All genres for all ages. Also picture books.
Also Does: Pamphlets, booklets, tracts.
Photos: Accepts freelance photos for book covers.

FAIRWAY PRESS (subsidy division for CSS Publishing Company), 517 S. Main St., Box 4503, Lima OH 45802-4503. Toll-free (800) 241-4056. (419) 227-1818. Fax (419) 224-4647. E-mail: editor @csspub.com. Website: www.fairwaypress.com. David Runk, ed. (david@csspub.com). Imprint: Express Press. Publishes 100 titles/yr. Receives 200-300 submissions annually. 80 percent of books from first-time authors. Reprints books. **SUBSIDY PUBLISHES 100 PERCENT.** Royalty to 50 percent; no advance. Average first printing 500-1,000. Publication within 6-9 mos. Considers simultaneous submissions. Responds in up to 1 mo. Prefers requested ms on disk; no e-mail submissions. Prefers NRSV. Guidelines on Website; catalog for 9 x 12 SAE.

> **Nonfiction:** Complete ms; phone/fax/e-query OK. All types. "Looking for manuscripts with a Christian theme, and seasonal material."
> **Fiction:** Complete ms. For adults, teens, or children; all types. No longer producing anything in full color or with four-color illustrations.

+ FOREVER BOOKS, 1405–77 University Crescent, Winnipeg MB R3T 3N8, Canada. Toll-free phone/fax (888) 485-2224. E-mail: info@foreverbooks.ca. Website: www.foreverbooks.ca. Beryl Henne, mng. ed.; Gus Henne, acq. ed. Helping others tell their story. Publishes 24+ titles/yr.; hardcover, trade paperbacks, mass-market paperbacks, coffee-table books. Receives 30+ submissions annually. 80 percent of books from first-time authors. Accepts mss through agents. **SUBSIDY PUBLISHES 85 PERCENT;** does print-on-demand. Reprints books. Any length. A contract book publisher; author pays 100 percent. Average first printing 100-1,000. Publication within 4 mos. Considers simultaneous submissions. Responds in 2-3 wks. Accepts mss on disk or by e-mail. Guidelines by mail/e-mail; no catalog.

> **Nonfiction:** Complete ms; e-query OK. All topics.
> **Fiction:** Complete ms; e-query OK. All genres for all ages.
> **Photos/Artwork:** Accepts freelance photos for book covers; open to queries from freelance artists.

FRUITBEARER PUBLISHING, LLC, PO Box 777, Georgetown DE 19947. (302) 856-6649. Fax (302) 856-7742. E-mail: cfa@candyabbott.com. Website: www.fruitbearer.com. Candy Abbott, mng. partner. Offers editing services and advice for self-publishers. Publishes 5-10 titles/yr.; hardcover, picture books. Receives 10-20 submissions annually. 90 percent of books from first-time authors. **SUBSIDY PUBLISHES 100 PERCENT.** No reprints. Average first printing 500-5,000. Publication within 1-6 mos. Responds in 3 mos. Guidelines by mail/e-mail; brochure for #10 SAE/1 stamp.

> **Nonfiction:** Proposal/2 chapters; phone/fax/e-query OK.
> **Fiction:** For all ages.
> **Also Does:** Pamphlets, booklets, tracts.
> **Photos:** Accepts freelance photos for book covers.
> **Tips:** "Accepting limited submissions."

GESHER—See Winer Foundation.

HOLY FIRE PUBLISHING, 717 Old Trolley Rd., Ste. 6, Unit 116, Summerville SC 29485. (843) 628-0319. E-mail: publisher@christianpublish.com. Website: www.christianpublish.com. Venessa Hensel, COO. Important that everything we publish be clean and honoring to Christ and be in line with core Christian beliefs. Publishes 200 titles/yr.; hardcover, trade paperbacks. Receives 3,000 submissions annually. 50 percent of books from first-time authors. Accepts mss through agents. Does only print-on-demand. Reprints books. Prefers 48-750 pgs. Royalty, discounts, and retail price set by author; no advance. Publication within 2 mos. Prefers submissions on disk or by e-mail. Guidelines by mail/e-mail/Website; no catalog.

> **Nonfiction:** Proposal/1 chapter; phone/fax/e-query OK. "Looking for Christian Living or Christian poetry." All topics.
> **Fiction:** Proposal/1 chapter; phone/fax/e-query OK. For all ages. All genres.
> **Artwork:** Open to queries from freelance artists.

IMD PRESS, 7140 Hooker St., Westminster CO 80030-5459. (303) 482-1426. Fax (303) 232-5009. E-mail: JimH@IMDPress.com. Website: www.IMDPress.com. IMD International. Phil Largent, exec. dir.; Jim Hawley, IMD Press project mngr. A nonprofit, self-publishing ministry whose profits support IMD International church planting and Christian leadership development. Publishes 10 titles/yr.; hardcover, mostly trade paperbacks. Receives10-15 submissions annually. 75 percent of books from first-time authors. Accepts mss through agents. **SUBSIDY PUBLISHES 100 PERCENT;** no print-on-demand. Reprints books (with permission). Any length. Royalty or outright purchase; no advance. Average first printing 1,000 (100-5,000+). Publication within 3 mos. Considers simultaneous submissions. Responds in 48 hrs. Prefers NIV. Guidelines/bookstore on Website.

Nonfiction: Complete ms; phone/e-query OK. Generally adult; curriculum for all ages.

Fiction: Complete ms; phone/e-query OK. Generally adult.

Ethnic Books: Translation services for worldwide languages, esp. Indian, Africa, and SE Asia.

Photos/Artwork: Accepts freelance photos for book covers; open to queries from freelance artists.

Also Does: Periodicals

Tips: "We do not buy mss or retain your rights; 15 years editing and 25 years design experience gives you publishing with integrity and excellence. Submit only completed mss. We do not edit."

IMPACT CHRISTIAN BOOKS INC., 332 Leffingwell Ave., Ste. 101, Kirkwood MO 63122. (314) 822-3309. Fax (314) 822-3325. E-mail: info@impactchristianbooks.com. Website: www.impactchristian books.com. William D. Banks, pres. Books of healing, miraculous deliverance, and spiritual warfare, drawing individuals into a deeper walk with God. Publishes 20+ titles/yr. Receives 20-50 submissions annually. 50-70 percent of books from first-time authors. No mss through agents. **SUBSIDY PUBLISHES 50-70 PERCENT.** Reprints books. Average first printing 5,000. Publication within 2 mos. Considers simultaneous submissions. Responds by prior arrangement in 30 days. Requires requested ms on disk. Guidelines by mail; catalog for 9 x 12 SAE/5 stamps. Not in topical listings.

Nonfiction: Query only; phone/fax query OK. Outstanding personal testimonies and Christ-centered books.

INFINITY PUBLISHING, 1094 New Dehaven St., Ste. 100, West Conshohocken PA 19428-2713. Toll-free (877) 289-2665. (610) 941-9999. Fax (610) 941-9959. E-mail: info@infinitypublishing .com. Website: www.infinitypublishing.com. **100 PERCENT PRINT-ON-DEMAND.** Charges $400 up-front fee. First order of books is at 50 percent discount; additional orders 40 percent discount. Royalty 10-30 percent; no advance. 70 percent of books from first-time authors. Prefers mss through agents. Publication within 3 mos. Considers simultaneous submissions. Prefers accepted ms on disk. Guidelines by mail/Website; no catalog.

Nonfiction: Complete ms.

Fiction: Complete ms. All genres; for all ages.

Photos: Accepts freelance photos for book covers.

INSIGHT PUBLISHING GROUP, 8810 S. Yale, Ste. 410, Tulsa OK 74137. (918) 493-1718. Fax (918) 493-2219. E-mail: mail@freshword.com. Website: www.freshword.com. Christian Publisher. John Mason, ed. Owned by a best-selling author who established the company to serve authors. Publishes 50 titles/yr.; hardcover, trade paperbacks, mass-market paperbacks. Receives 50 submissions annually. 50 percent of books from first-time authors. Accepts mss through agents. **60 PERCENT PRINT-ON-DEMAND; 40 PERCENT SUBSIDY.** Reprints books. Prefers 160 pgs. Royalty 15-17 percent on net; no advance. Average first printing 5,000. Publication within 6 mos. Considers simultaneous submissions. Requires disk or e-mail submission. Responds in 2 mos. Guidelines by e-mail/Website. Will consider most fiction and nonfiction topics.

Nonfiction: Complete ms; phone/fax/e-query OK.

Fiction: Complete ms; phone/fax/e-query OK. Nondenominational Christian. For all ages.
Also Does: Booklets.
Tips: "We help people self-publish. To those authors we can offer a variety of services including distribution and small print runs. Most open to books that are unique, authentic, and relevant."

+ INTERMEDIA PUBLISHING GROUP, PO Box 2825, Peoria AZ 85380. (623) 337-8710. Fax (623) 687-9469. E-mail: through online form. Website: www.intermediapub.com. Terry Whalin, ed. Open to freelance submissions. **SUBSIDY PUBLISHER**. Not included in topical listings.

IUNIVERSE (iUniverse), 1663 Liberty Dr., Ste. 300, Bloomington IN 47403. Toll-free (800) 288-4677. Intl. (402) 323-7800. Fax (812) 355-4085. E-mail through Website: www.iuniverse.com. 100 percent self-publishing. Bought out by Author Solutions Inc. (formerly AuthorHouse). Not included in topical listings. Guidelines on Website.

KINDRED BOOKS, 1310 Taylor Ave., Winnipeg MB R3M 3Z6, Canada. Toll-free (800) 545-7322. (204) 669-6575. Fax (204) 654-1865. E-mail: kindred@mbconf.ca. Website: www.kindredproduc tions.com. Mennonite Brethren/Imprint of Kindred Productions. Submit to: Attn. Manager. Publisher for the Mennonite Brethren Church in North America. Publishes 3-4 titles/yr.; hardcover, trade paperbacks. Receives 20 submissions annually. 95 percent of books from first-time authors. No mss through agents. **SUBSIDY PUBLISHES 100 PERCENT;** does print-on-demand. Reprints books. Prefers 60,000 words or 200 pgs. Average first printing 1,000-2,000. Publication within 18 mos. Considers simultaneous submissions. Responds in 4 mos. Accepts requested ms by e-mail. Prefers NIV. Guidelines by mail/e-mail/Website; free catalog.
   Nonfiction: Proposal/2-3 chapters; no phone query, fax/e-query OK. "Looking for Christian living and inspirational books."
   Fiction: Proposal/2-3 chapters. For children & teens.
   Tips: "Most open to Christian living or inspirational books that help everyday people grow in their relationship with Jesus. Books that help meet basic church needs. Material submitted should be in line with the Christian/evangelical faith."

LIFEVEST PUBLISHING, INC., 4901 E. Dry Creek Rd., #170, Centennial CO 80122. Toll-free (877) 843-1007. (303) 221-1007. Website: www.lifevestpublishing.com. Ric Simmons, CEO. Specializes in children's books, educational literature, inspirational works, family/personal histories, and poetry. **SUBSIDY PUBLISHES 100 PERCENT.** Submission form on Website.

LULU.COM. Website: www.lulu.com. Bob Young, pub. **SUBSIDY PUBLISHES 100 PERCENT.** Does print-on-demand. Guidelines/details on Website. Not included in topical listings; will consider any topic.

MARKETING NEW AUTHORS.COM, 2910 E. Eisenhower Pkwy., Ann Arbor MI 48108. Toll-free (800) 431-1579. (734) 975-0028. Fax (734) 973-9475. E-mail: info@marketingnewauthors.com or MarketingNewAuth@aol.com. Website: www.MarketingNewAuthors.com. Imprint of Robbie Dean Press. To primarily serve authors who wish to self-publish. Dr. Fairy C. Hayes-Scott, owner. 100 percent of books from first-time authors. Accepts mss through agents. **SUBSIDY PUBLISHES 100 PERCENT.** Reprints books. Length flexible. Publication within 6 mos. Considers simultaneous submissions. Responds in 2-6 wks. Guidelines by e-mail/Website. Offers 7 different marketing plans; see Website.

MCDOUGAL PUBLISHING, PO Box 3595, Hagerstown MD 21742. (301) 797-6637. Fax (301) 733-2767. E-mail: publishing@mcdougal.org. Website: www.mcdougalpublishing.com. Evangelical. Diane McDougal, pres. Publishes books for the body of Christ. Imprints: McDougal Publishing, Fairmont Books, Parable Publishing, and Serenity Books. Publishes 10-15 titles/yr. Receives 150 submissions annually. 70 percent of books from first-time authors. Accepts mss through agents or authors. **SUBSIDY PUBLISHES 20 PERCENT**. Does print-on-demand (author charged for print setup). Reprints books. Prefers 80-192 pgs. Royalty 10-15 percent of net; no advance. Requires authors to buy minimum of 2,000 copies of their book. Average first printing 3,000-5,000. Publication within 6 mos. Considers simultaneous submissions. Responds in 2 mos. Guidelines by mail/Website; free catalog by mail.

> **Nonfiction:** Proposal/1-2 chapters (preferred); phone/fax/e-query OK. "Looking for titles on all topics relevant to the Christian life."

> **Fiction:** Complete ms. "Now considering adult fiction from authors with an established market; no romance."

> **Tips:** "Know who your audience is, and write to that audience. Also, keep focused on one central theme." Charges a $35 review fee for unsolicited manuscripts.

MILESTONES INTERNATIONAL PUBLISHERS, PO Box 119, Orrstown PA 17244-0119. (717) 477-2230. Fax (717) 477-2261. E-mail: jimrill@milestonesintl.com or milestoneintl@bellsouth.net. Website: www.milestonesintl.com. Jim Rill, pres. Bringing significance to life's journey. Author is asked to buy 3,000 books at $6/ea.

@ **ONE WORLD PRESS**, 1042 Willow Creek Rd., Prescott AZ 86301. Toll-free (800) 250-8171. (928) 445-2081. Fax (928) 717-1779. E-mail: dasya@oneworldpress.com. Website: www.oneworld press.com. Joe Zuccarello, operations mngr. Publishes many titles/yr. Receives 25-50 submissions annually. 50 percent of books from first-time authors. Accepts mss through agents. **SUBSIDY PUBLISHES 100 PERCENT**; does print-on-demand. Reprints books. First printing up to author. Publication within 2 mos. Considers simultaneous submissions. Responds in 2-4 wks. No guidelines or catalog.

> **Nonfiction:** Complete manuscript. All ages. "We publish about anything within decency and reason."

> **Also Does:** Booklets, e-books, pamphlets, tracts.

+ **OUTSKIRTS PRESS, INC.**, 10940 S. Parker Rd. - 515, Parker CO 80134. Toll-free (888) OP-BOOKS. E-mail: info@outskirtspress.com. Website: www.outskirtspress.com. Submit to Book Editor. Open to unsolicited freelance. **CUSTOM/SUBSIDY PUBLISHER**. Not included in topical listings.

@ **PATH PUBLISHING, INC.**, 4302 W. 51st, #121, Amarillo TX 79109-6159. Phone/fax (806) 322-7007 (call first for fax). E-mail: path2@pathpublishing.com. Website: www.pathpublishing.com. John Schmidt, ed. This imprint focuses on self-help and children's books. Has published 21 titles to date (half are Christian); 2-3/yr.; hardcover & trade paperbacks. Receives 150 submissions annually. 90 percent of books from first-time authors. Accepts mss through agents. Reprints books. Prefers 80-120 pgs. **SUBSIDY PUBLISHES 80 PERCENT**. Royalty 10 percent on net for standard contract; 75 percent on subsidy contract; no advance. Considers simultaneous submissions. Responds in days. Guidelines by mail/e-mail/Website; flyer for #10 SASE, no catalog.

> **Nonfiction:** Query letter only first; e-query preferred. "Looking for original, spiritual, creative, and practical."

> **Also Does:** Expanding into e-books, Christian music sales, Website design, and more.

> **Artwork:** Open to queries from freelance artists.

> **Contest:** Periodically sponsors contests.

> **Tips:** "We also do lots of poetry books. Check our Website for 'Tips for Writers' and more."

PATH PUBLISHING IN CHRIST, 4302 W. 51st, #121, Amarillo TX 79109-6159. Phone/fax (806) 322-7007. E-mail: path2@pathpublishing.com. Website: www.pathpublishing.com. Path Publishing, Inc. John Schmidt, ed./pub. Spiritual creations for an aspiring world. Publishing 2-3 titles; hardcover & trade paperbacks. Receives 90 submissions annually. 95 percent of books from first-time authors. Accepts mss through agents. Reprints books. **SUBSIDY PUBLISHES 70 PERCENT;** print-on-demand. Prefers 80-120 pgs. Royalty 10 percent on net for standard contract; 75 percent on subsidy contract; no advance. Average first printing 200. Considers simultaneous submissions. Prefers accepted submissions on disk or by e-mail. Responds in 1 wk. Prefers KJV. Guidelines by mail/e-mail/Website; book fliers for #10 SASE.

> **Nonfiction:** Query letter *only* first; e-query preferred.
> **Fiction:** Does little; maybe a short novella.
> **Special Needs:** Looking for self-help books: original point of view, insightful, and aware of future trends; also devotionals.
> **Also Does:** Christian music, CDs, chapbooks (38-72 pgs.), and CD-ROM books.
> **Photos:** Accepts freelance photos for book covers.
> **Tips:** "We are also a printing broker, literary agent, and writing coach. We are a teaching ministry and will spend more time with a new author than most publishers."

+ PECAN TREE PUBLISHING. Toll-free (877) 207-2442. E-mail: info@pecantreepress.com. Website: www.pecantreepress.com. Submit to Book Editor. Prefers 85,000-120,000 words for fiction; 65,000-85,000 for nonfiction. **SUBSIDY PUBLISHER.** Responds in 8 wks. min. Guidelines on Website.

> **Nonfiction/Fiction:** Query/5 or more chapters; no disk.
> **Tips:** "All material must be legally copyrighted with the Library of Congress (www.loc.gov). Do not call about your manuscript."

@ PLEASANT WORD, 1730 Railroad St., PO Box 428, Enumclaw WA 98022. Toll-free (800) 326-4674. (360) 802-9758. Fax (360) 802-9992. E-mail: acquisitions@pleasantword.com. Website: www.pleasantword.com. Division of The WinePress Group. Submit via Website or call acquisitions dept. In an industry where print-on-demand publishers will print almost anything, Pleasant Word has high standards for both design and content of POD books. Publishes 300 titles/yr.; hardcover, trade paperbacks, coffee-table books. Receives 700+ submissions annually between WinePress and Pleasant Word. 70 percent of books from first-time authors. Accepts mss through agents. **SUBSIDY PUBLISHES 100 PERCENT;** print-on-demand division. Reprints books. Prefers 10,000-150,000 words or 48-740 pgs. Royalties explained on Website; discounts for author purchases. Average first printing 150. Publication within 4-9 mos., depending on editing level. Considers simultaneous submissions. Responds in 48 hrs. Accepted mss on disk. Any Bible version. Guidelines (also by e-mail); free catalog.

> **Nonfiction/Fiction:** Complete ms; e-query OK. Publishes all family-friendly, biblically oriented topics & genres.
> **Also Does:** Audio books, e-books, multimedia, Website design and hosting, blogs, DVD production, CD/book packages, manuals, genuine leather Bibles, full-color children's books, board books, publicity and marketing materials.
> **Photos/Artwork:** Accepts copyright-free photos and artwork.
> **Tips:** "Since 1991, WinePress has been an innovator in the Christian custom printing market. We partner with authors through a wide range of services provided by our in-house departments: including production, design, video, multimedia, Internet, publicity, promotions, warehousing fulfillment, and distribution departments. To ensure the highest quality, everything is coordinated by our unique on-line Co-C.A.P.T.A.I.N. software and friendly staff. We do not accept all manuscripts for publication and advise potential authors to first review our doctrinal standards on our Website."
> ****Note:** This publisher serviced by The Writer's Edge and ChristianManuscriptSubmissions.com.

POEMS BY ME, 4000 Beallwood Ave., Columbus GA 31904. Toll-free (800) 334-8861. E-mail: Brentwood@aol.com. Website: www.PoemsByMe.com. Brentwood Christian Press. Joyce Warren, ed. Poetry that is spiritual, personal, emotional. Receives 80 submissions annually. 75 percent of books from first-time authors. Accepts mss through agents. **SUBSIDY PUBLISHES 100 PERCENT;** does print-on-demand. Reprints books. Need at least 40 poems for a book. Same-week response.

POET'S COVE PRESS, 4000 Beallwood Ave., Columbus GA 31904. Toll-free (800) 334-8861. (706) 576-5787. E-mail: Brentwood@aol.com. Website: www.BrentwoodBooks.com. Subsidiary of Brentwood Publishers Group. U. D. Roberts, exec. dir. Publishes 75 titles/yr. **SUBSIDY OR CUSTOM PUBLISHES 100 PERCENT.** Specializes in self-publishing books of religious or inspirational poetry, in press runs of under 500 copies. Publication in 45 days. Same-day response.

    Tips: "Type one poem per page; include short bio and photo with first submission."

+ PORT HOLE PUBLICATIONS, PO Box 205, Westlake OR 97493. (541) 902-9091. E-mail: info @ellentraylor.com. Website: http://ellentraylor.com. Ellen Traylor, ed./pub. A cooperative publisher requiring a financial investment on the part of their authors.

    Nonfiction/Fiction: Query first.

    Tips: "We are open to publishing family-friendly and/or Christian content books of any length or genre. We are especially open to thought-provoking books on being a Christian in this difficult world, terrific fiction, Christian philosophy, and short-story collections (no poetry or sermons)."

PROVIDENCE HOUSE PUBLISHERS, 238 Seaboard Ln., Franklin TN 37174. Toll-free (800) 321-5692. (615) 771-2020. Fax (615) 771-2002. E-mail: books@providencehouse.com. Website: www .providencehouse.com. Submit to Kelly Bainbridge, acq. ed. Produces books that honor God and reflect the knowledge, commitment, and accomplishments of his people. Publishes 20+ religious titles/yr.; hardcover, trade paperbacks, coffee-table books. Receives 100+ submissions annually. 90 percent of books from first-time authors. No mss through agents. **SUBSIDY PUBLISHES 90 PERCENT;** no print-on-demand. Reprints books. Prefers 96-512 pgs. Author receives 100 percent income from sales. Average first printing 3,000. Publication within 9-10 mos. Considers simultaneous submissions. Responds in up to 6 mos. Prefers accepted ms on disk. Prefers NIV, NKJV. Guidelines by mail; no catalog (see Website).

    Nonfiction: Proposal/2 chapters or complete ms.; phone/fax/e-query OK. Accepts requested ms by e-mail.

    Fiction: Proposal/2 chapters or complete ms. For all ages. "Looking for Christian suspense."

    Special Needs: Biography, church histories, ministry histories, missionary memoirs.

    Artwork: Open to queries from freelance artists.

    Tips: "Most open to biblically based books; history or memoir. Those with a speaking ministry tend to receive more attention. Well-written texts only."

RECOVERY COMMUNICATIONS INC., PO Box 19910, Baltimore MD 21211. (410) 243-8352. Fax (410) 243-8558. E-mail: tdrews3879@aol.com. Website: www.GettingThemSober.com. Toby R. Drews, ed. Publishes 4-6 titles/yr. No mss through agents. **SUBSIDY PUBLISHER.** Prefers 110 pgs. Co-op projects; no royalty or advance. Average first printing 5,000. Publication within 9 mos. Excellent nationwide distribution and marketing in bookstores. Send for their free information packet.

    Nonfiction: Query only.

    Tips: "Although technically we are a subsidy publisher, we are more of a hybrid publisher in that we give the author enough free books to sell in the back of the room to totally recoup all the money they have paid; plus we share 50/50 on net sales at bookstores. Over half of our authors have gotten their money back and made a great profit. We are also aggressive in our pursuit of catalog sales and foreign rights sales. (We recently sold to a German publisher.) We individually coach all our authors, at no cost to them, to help them successfully obtain speaking engagements."

+ **SAGE PRESS**, 40960 California Oaks Rd., Ste. 369, Murrieta CA 92562. Phone/fax (951) 696-5631. E-mail: info@sagepress.com. Website: www.sagepress.us. The Word Works. Sonjia Struthers, ed./pub. To help authors who wish to self-publish get their work before the reading public; to pay them royalties, treat them fairly, teach them about the realities of the book business and how to protect themselves and their intellectual properties, and show them how to succeed. New publisher. Will do hardcover, trade paperbacks, mass-market paperbacks, and coffee-table books. 80 percent of books from first-time authors. Accepts mss through agents. **SUBSIDY PUBLISHES 100 PERCENT;** also does print-on-demand. Reprints books. Prefers a minimum of 50 pgs. Royalty 20-40 percent on net (author retains 100 percent of author-direct sales and all e-book sales); no advance. Average first printing 250. Publication within 1-6 mos. Considers simultaneous submissions. Accepts full mss by e-mail. Guidelines on Website; no catalog yet.

Nonfiction: Query only first; phone/e-query OK.

Fiction: Query only first; phone/e-query OK. For teens/adults.

Tips: "We are subsidy for now, but working toward becoming a traditional royalty publisher as soon as possible."

THE SALT-WORKS, PO Box 37, Roseville CA 95678. (916) 784-0500. Fax (916) 773-7421. E-mail: books@publishersdesign.com. Website: www.publishersdesign.com. Division of Publishers Design Group Inc. Robert Brekke, pub. Seeks to demonstrate through books that God is sovereign, just, and merciful in all he does. Imprints: Salty's Books (children's—see separate listing), PDG, Humpback Books. Publishes 3-5 titles/yr.; hardcover, trade paperbacks, coffee-table books. Receives 100+ submissions annually. 90 percent of Christian books from first-time authors. No mss through agents. **SUBSIDY PUBLISHES 85 PERCENT;** no print-on-demand. Reprints books. Prefers 95,000-150,000 words. Rarely pays royalty of 7-12 percent on net; occasional advance. Average first printing 2,500-10,000. Publication within 4-12 mos. Considers simultaneous submissions. Responds within 45 days. Prefers ESV/NASB/NKJV/NIV (in that order). Guidelines by mail/e-mail/Website; free catalog when available.

Nonfiction: E-query only first; after query & phone meeting, send proposal. Unsolicited mss returned unopened.

Fiction: E-query only first; after query & phone meeting, send proposal. Unsolicited mss returned unopened. For adults and children. "Looking for titles that help believers in exploring and facing common issues surrounding God's sovereignty, His grace and forgiveness, their own sin and idolatry, and the areas where pop culture has influenced the church. Characters are blatantly human."

Special Needs: Looking for titles that communicate a biblical Christian worldview without promoting overly simplistic, idealistic, or theoretical solutions to life's biggest questions; books that honestly show no timidity in addressing our humanness. Looking for manuscripts that demonstrate that society's problems are rooted in the personal and spiritual realms, not in the political, educational, moral, and financial realms.

Also Does: Board games and other specialty products: fitness products, art projects and products, interactive projects for children.

Photos/Artwork: Rarely accepts freelance photos for book covers; open to queries from freelance artists.

Tips: "Most open to books that look at the Christian experience through a realistic biblical and Reformed perspective. Books that address the Christian's real problems as a "heart" problem—not a theological problem; not from a victim mind-set; not a mental or logical one; not from a perspective of merely needing another program, pep talk, or the latest rehash of formulas for victorious living. Books that show the author understands that unless God changes the heart and brings a person to repentance, there are no real and lasting answers."

**Note: This publisher serviced by The Writer's Edge and ChristianManuscriptSubmissions.com.

SALTY'S BOOKS, PO Box 37, Roseville CA 95678. (916) 784-0500. Fax (916) 773-7421. E-mail: books@publishersdesign.com. Website: www.publishersdesign.com. Imprint of The Salt-Works/Division of Publishers Design Group Inc. Robert Brekke, pub. Imprint for children's Christian books. Publishes 2-5 titles/yr.; hardcover, trade paperbacks, coffee-table books. Receives 50+ submissions annually. 90 percent of books from first-time authors. No mss through agents. **SUBSIDY PUBLISHES 75 PERCENT.** Reprints books. Prefers 450-3,500 words for picture books; 8,000-40,000 wds. for early readers. Royalty 7-12 percent on net; no advance. Average first print run for children's books 2,000. Publication within 4-12 mos. Considers simultaneous submissions. Responds within 45 days. Prefers ESV/NASB/NKJV/NIV in that order. Guidelines by mail/e-mail/Website; free catalog when available.

Nonfiction: Query letter only first; after query and phone meeting, send a proposal.

Fiction: Query letter only first; after query and phone meeting, send a proposal. "Looking for titles that help kids in exploring and facing common issues surrounding God's sovereignty."

Special Needs: Looking for manuscripts that offer kids answers from a biblically orthodox Reformed perspective.

Also Does: Board games; books with packaged products; etc.

Artwork: Open to queries from freelance artists.

Tips: "Deal with the difficult issues or subject areas that most Sunday school teachers and youth leaders are either afraid to deal with or are incapable of dealing with. Ask librarians or bookstore owners which books are most popular and why."

**Note: This publisher serviced by The Writer's Edge and ChristianManuscriptSubmissions.com.

SALVATION PUBLISHER AND MARKETING GROUP, PO Box 40860, Santa Barbara CA 93140. (805) 682-0316. Fax (call first). E-mail: opalmaedailey@aol.com. Wisdom Today Ministries. Opal Mae Dailey, ed-in-chief. We encourage, inspire, and educate; author has the choice to be involved as much or little as desired—which gives the opportunity to control income; personal coaching and collective marketing available. Publishes 5-7 titles/yr.; hardcover, trade paperbacks, mass-market paperbacks. 60 percent of books from first-time authors. No mss through agents. **SUBSIDY PUBLISHES 80 PERCENT;** does print-on demand. Reprints books. Prefers 96-224 pgs. Average first printing 1,000. Publication within 3-4 mos. No simultaneous submissions. Accepts requested ms on disk or by e-mail (not attachments). Responds in 1 mo. Prefers KJV. Guidelines (also by e-mail).

Nonfiction: Query only first; phone/fax/e-query OK.

Tips: "Turning taped messages into book form for pastors is a specialty of ours. We do not accept any manuscript that we would be ashamed to put our name on."

@ SELAH PUBLISHING GROUP LLC., 300 Hickory Rd., Bristol TN 37620-6033. Toll-free (877) 616-6451. E-mail: garlen@selahbooks.com. Website: www.selahbooks.com. Garlen Jackson, pub. A publisher that does not water down the author's message. Publishes 45 titles/yr. Receives 20 submissions annually. 75 percent of books from first-time authors. Prefers mss through agents. Reprints books. Prefers 40,000 words or 144 pgs. **SUBSIDY PUBLISHER/BOOK PACKAGER.** Royalty 12-18 percent of net; no advance. Average first printing 2,500. Publication within 6 mos. No simultaneous submissions. Prefers requested ms on disk. Responds in 2 mos. Prefers ASV. Guidelines by e-mail; free catalog.

Nonfiction: Complete ms; no phone/fax/e-query.

Fiction: Complete ms; no phone/fax/e-query. For all ages.

Also Does: E-books.

Photos: Accepts freelance photos for book covers.

Tips: "Most open to time-sensitive, current-events, and controversial books. Writers should spend more time selling who they are in regard to character and integrity."

**Note: This publisher serviced by ChristianManuscriptSubmissions.com.

SELF PUBLISH PRESS, 4000 Beallwood Ave., Columbus GA 31904. Toll-free (800) 334-8861. (706) 576-5787. Fax (706) 317-5808. E-mail: Brentwood@aol.com. Website: www.PublishMyBook .com. Brentwood Publishing Group. U. D. Roberts, exec. ed.; submit to Marie Warren, ed. All books must be family suitable. Receives 100 submissions annually. 98 percent of books from first-time authors. Accepts mss through agents. **SUBSIDY PUBLISHES 98 PERCENT;** does print-on-demand. Offers InstaBooks and Just in Time publishing (print-on-demand). Reprints books. Prefers 64-300 pgs. Publication within 1 mo. Considers simultaneous submissions. Responds in 3 days. Guidelines on Website; no catalog.

> **Nonfiction:** Complete ms/disk; no phone/fax/e-query. All religious—for family or youth.
> **Fiction:** Complete ms/disk; no phone/fax/e-query. For all ages.

SERMON SELECT PRESS, 4000 Beallwood Ave., Columbus GA 31904. Toll-free (800) 334-8861. (706) 576-5787. Fax (706) 317-5808. E-mail: Brentwood@aol.com. Website: www.BrentwoodBooks .com. Subsidiary of Brentwood Publishers Group. U. D. Roberts, exec. dir. **SUBSIDY OR CUSTOM PUBLISHES 100 PERCENT.** Focus is on sermon notes, outlines, illustrations, plus news that pastors would find interesting. Publishes 100 copies. Cost of about $3-4/book. Publication in 45 days. Same-day response.

SOUTHERN BAPTIST PRESS, 4000 Beallwood Ave., Columbus GA 31904. Toll-free (800) 334-8861. (706) 576-5787. E-mail: Brentwood@aol.com. Website: www.SouthernBaptistPress.com. U. D. Roberts, exec. ed. Publishes 25 books/yr. Receives 600 submissions annually. Reprints books. **SUBSIDY OR CUSTOM PUBLISHES 95 PERCENT.** Average first printing 500. Publication within 2 mos. Considers simultaneous submissions. Responds in 1 week. Guidelines by mail.

> **Nonfiction:** Complete ms. "Collections of sermons on family topics; poetry; relation of Bible to current day."
> **Fiction:** Complete ms. "Stories that show how faith helps overcome small, day-to-day problems."
> **Tips:** "Keep it short; support facts with reference."

+ SPARROWCROWNE PRESS, PO Box 172282, Arlington TX 7600392282. E-mail: AngelBeQuick @gmail.com. Sylvia Keck, ed; submit to Careth Villa, acq. ed. Large enough to provide quality printing; small enough to form an old-fashioned business. Publishes 5 titles/yr.; hardcover, coffee-table books. Receives 200 submissions annually. 60 percent of books from first-time authors. No mss through agents. **SUBSIDY PUBLISHES 50 PERCENT;** does print-on-demand. Reprints books. Prefers 25,000-50,000 words or up to 300 pgs. Subsidy contracts vary; no advance. Average first printing 100-1,000. No simultaneous submissions. Responds within 60 days. Requires accepted mss on disk. Prefers KJV, NKJV. Intl. guidelines by mail; no catalog.

> **Nonfiction:** Query first; no phone/fax query; e-query OK. Send SASE; not responsible for unsolicited mss.
> **Tips:** "We do buy certain mss, but they are a rarity. We are mainly self-publish/subsidy and print-on-demand."

STAR BIBLE PUBLICATIONS, 1105 S. Airport Cir., Ste. C, Euless TX 76040. Toll-free (800) 433-7507. (817) 354-6000. Fax (817) 354-6006. E-mail: service@starbible.com. Website: www.star bible.com. Church of Christ. Books that will be in harmony with New Testament principles and useful among general audience markets and among Churches of Christ. Publishes 10-15 titles/yr.; mass-market paperbacks. Receives 20-25 submissions annually. 50 percent of books from first-time authors. No mss through agents. **SUBSIDY PUBLISHES 80 PERCENT.** No reprints. Prefers 110 pgs. Royalty on retail; no advance. Average first printing 1,000-1,500. Publication within 2 mos. No simultaneous submissions. Responds in 1 mo. Accepts mss on disk or by e-mail. Prefers ASV, KJV, NIV. Guidelines by mail/e-mail/Website; catalog on Website.

> **Nonfiction:** Complete ms; phone/fax/e-query OK.
> **Fiction:** Complete ms. For adults.

Photos: Accepts freelance photos for book covers.

Tips: "We are looking for general audience books that focus on the gospel and encourage readers to read the Bible, books that encourage people in their Christian walk, books on doctrine, studies on the Bible or specific books of the Bible, and topical studies."

STRONG TOWER PUBLISHING, PO Box 973, Milesburg PA 16853. E-mail: strongtowerpubs@aol .com. Website: www.strongtowerpublishing.com. Heidi L. Nigro, pub. Specializes in eschatology and books that challenge the reader to think more deeply about their faith and scriptural truths; must be biblically responsible, doctrinally defensible, and consistent with their statement of faith. Publishes 1-2 titles/yr.; trade paperbacks. 50 percent of books from first-time authors. No mss through agents. Reprints books. **PRINT-ON-DEMAND 100 PERCENT.** Royalty 25 percent of net; no advance. Average first printing 50. Publication within 3-4 mos. Guidelines/information/prices on Website.

Nonfiction: Query. Eschatology.

Tips: "We recommend that all first-time authors have their manuscript professionally edited. We will consider putting first-time authors into print, but by invitation only. That invitation comes only after the manuscript has been thoroughly evaluated and we have discussed the pros and cons of our unique on-demand publishing model with the author."

TATE PUBLISHING & ENTERPRISES, LLC., Tate Publishing Bldg., 127 E. Trade Center Ter., Mustang OK 73064-4421. Toll-free (888) 361-9473. Fax (405) 376-4401. E-mail: publish@tatepublishing .com. Website: www.tatepublishing.com. Curtis Winkle, sr. ed.; Dr. Richard Tate, dir. of acquisitions. Owns and operates their own, state-of-the-art printing plant facility; pays to produce audio book. Publishes 120 titles/yr.; hardcover, trade paperbacks, mass-market paperbacks. Receives 60,000-75,000 contacts annually. 60 percent of books from first-time authors. Accepts mss through agents. **SUBSIDY LIKELY** (most authors asked to contribute $3,985.50 toward promotion—refunded if book does well). No print-on-demand. Accepts reprints. Prefers 115,000 words. Royalty 15-40 percent of net; negotiable advance with requirements. Average first printing 5,000. Publication within 4-6 mos. Considers simultaneous submissions. Responds in 3-6 wks. Accepts submissions by disk or e-mail. Any Bible version. Guidelines by mail/e-mail/Website; free catalog.

Nonfiction: Proposal with synopsis & any number of chapters or complete ms; phone/fax/ e-query OK. Any topic. "Looking for books that sell."

Fiction: Proposal with synopsis & any number of chapters or complete ms; phone/fax/e-query OK. For all ages. Any genre.

Ethnic Books: For all ethnic markets.

Contest: For those in author pool.

Artwork: Has 31 full-time artists on staff; open to queries from freelance artists.

Tips: "We invest resources in every work we accept, and accept first-time authors."

**Note: This publisher serviced by The Writer's Edge.

TEACH SERVICES INC., 254 Donovan Rd., Brushton NY 12916. (518) 358-3494. Fax (518) 358-3028. E-mail: publishing@TEACHservices.com. Website: www.teachservices.com. Timothy Hullquist, pres.; submit to Jennifer Aiken, acq. ed. To publish uplifting books for the lowest price. Publishes 48 titles/yr.; hardcover, trade paperbacks, coffee-table books. Receives 100+ submissions annually. 35 percent of books from first-time authors. No mss through agents. **SUBSIDY PUBLISHES 75 PERCENT** (author has to pay for first printing, then publisher keeps it in print); limited print-on-demand. Reprints books. Prefers 40,000 words or 96 pgs. Royalty 10 percent of retail; no advance. Average first printing 2,000. Publication within 6 mos. Considers simultaneous submissions. Responds in 3 wks. Prefers accepted mss by e-mail. Prefers KJV. Guidelines by mail/e-mail/Website; catalog on Website.

Nonfiction: Complete ms; no phone/fax query.

Fiction: Complete ms; allegory and historical. For all ages.

Photos/Artwork: Accepts freelance photos for book covers; open to queries from freelance artists.

TRAFFORD PUBLISHING, 2657 Wilfert Rd., Victoria BC V9B 5Z3, Canada. Toll-free (888) 232-4444. (250) 383-6864. Fax (250) 383-6804. E-mail: info@trafford.com. Website: www.trafford .com. Trafford Holdings Ltd. Your book, your way. Publishes 100-200 titles/yr.; hardcover, trade paperbacks, mass-market paperbacks, coffee-table books. Receives 1,000-2,000 submissions annually. 90 percent of books from first-time authors. No mss through agents. **100 PERCENT PRINT-ON-DEMAND;** no subsidy. Reprints books. Prefers less than 700 pgs. Royalty 60 percent; no advance. Average first printing 40. Publication within 1 mo. Considers simultaneous submissions. Responds immediately. Prefers accepted mss on disk. Guidelines by mail/e-mail/Website; catalog $7.

    Nonfiction: Any appropriate topic.

    Fiction: All genres for all ages.

    Photos: Accepts freelance photos for book covers.

    Tips: "Authors choose the retail price for their books, and their royalty is 60 percent of the gross margin."

VMI PUBLISHERS, 26306 Metolius Meadows Dr., Camp Sherman OR 97730. E-mail: bill@vmi publishers.com, nancie@vmipublishers.com. Website: www.vmipublishers.com. Virtue Ministries Inc. Bill and Nancie Carmichael, pubs. Partnering with new authors. Publishes 8-12 titles/yr.; hardback, trade paperbacks, coffee-table books. Receives dozens of submissions annually. 95 percent of books from first-time authors. Accepts mss through agents. No reprints. Prefers 65,000+ words, or 192-400 pgs. Royalty 12-18 percent of net; no advance. **CUSTOM PUBLISHER;** See Website for details. Average first printing 2,500+. Publication within 6-12 mos. Considers simultaneous submissions. Requires accepted ms on disk or by e-mail. Responds in 2 mos. Guidelines on Website.

    Nonfiction: Query first by e-mail only.

    Fiction: Query first by e-mail only. For all ages. "Anything Christian or inspirational that is well written, especially from new authors."

    Tips: "Go to our Website first, and read how we partner with new authors. Then, if you feel VMI would be a good fit for you, e-mail your proposal."

    **Note: This publisher serviced by ChristianManuscriptSubmissions.com.

@ WINEPRESS PUBLISHING GROUP, PO Box 428, 1730 Railroad St., Enumclaw WA 98022. Toll-free (800) 326-4674. (360) 802-9758. Fax (360) 802-9992. E-mail: acquisitions@winepress group.com. Website: www.winepresspub.com. The WinePress Group. Submit via Website, or call acquisitions department. To ensure the highest quality and service, WP uses custom online software that allows you to track your book project from beginning to end. Imprints: WinePress Publishing, WinePress Kids (children's books), Annotation Press (general market, family friendly), UpWrite Books (writers' resources), Pleasant Word (print-on-demand—see separate listing). Publishes 75 titles/yr.; hardcover, trade paperbacks, mass-market paperbacks, coffee-table books. Receives 700+ submissions annually. 70 percent of books from first-time authors. Accepts mss through agents. **BOOK PACKAGERS 100 PERCENT.** Reprints books. Lengths range from 10,000-150,000 words or 48-1,300 pgs. Author pays production costs, keeps all profit from sales. Average first printing 3,000 (2,500 min.). Publication in 6-9 mos. Considers simultaneous submissions. Responds in 48 hrs. Accepts requested ms on disk. Any Bible version. Guidelines by e-mail; free catalog.

    Nonfiction: Complete ms; e-query OK. Publishes all family-friendly, biblically oriented topics.

    Fiction: Complete ms. Publishes all family-friendly, biblically oriented material and genres. For all ages.

    Also Does: Audio books, eBooks, multimedia, Website design & hosting, blogs, DVD production, CD/book packages, manuals, genuine leather Bibles, full-color children's books, board books, publicity and marketing materials.

Photos/Artwork: Accepts copyright-free photos and artwork.

Tips: "Since 1991, WinePress has been an innovator in the Christian custom printing market. We partner with authors through a wide range of services provided by our in-house departments, including production, design, video, multimedia, Internet, publicity, promotions, warehousing fulfillment, and distribution departments. To ensure the highest quality, everything is coordinated by our unique online Co-C.A.P.T.A.I.N. software and friendly staff. We do not accept all manuscripts for publication and advise potential authors to first review our doctrinal standards on our Website."

**Note: This publisher serviced by The Writer's Edge and ChristianManuscriptSubmissions.com.

WORD ALIVE PRESS, 131 Cordite Rd., Winnipeg MB R3W 1S1, Canada. Toll-free (866) 967-3782. (204) 777-7100. Toll-free fax (800) 352-9272. (204) 669-0947. E-mail: publishing@wordalive .ca. Website: www.wordalivepress.ca. C. Schmidt, publishing consultant. Off-set printing, print-on-demand, editing services, sales, marketing and distribution services, Website development. Guidelines and price list available. Request their Free Guide to Publishing brochure from their Website.

Nonfiction/Fiction: All genres. Fiction for all ages.

XLIBRIS, 1663 Liberty Dr., Ste. 200, Bloomington IN 47403. Toll-Free (888) 795-4274, ext. 278. (610) 915-5214. Fax (610) 915-0294. E-mail: info@xlibris.com or submission@xlibris.com. Website: www.xlibris.com. Division of Random House. Mercedes Bournias, publishing consultant. **SUBSIDY PUBLISHES 100 PERCENT.** Can produce novels to 700 pgs. and picture books to 24 pgs. Basic Package is $499; up to Executive Package at $5,999. Open to any topic.

XULON PRESS INC., 2180 W. State Rd. 434, Ste. 2140, Longwood FL 32779. Toll-free (866) 381-2665. Fax (407) 339-9898. E-mail through Website: www.xulonpress.com. Blog: www.xulonpress .com/blog. Division of Salem Communications. Tom Freiling, VP & gen. mngr. Uses digital and print-on-demand technologies to help Christian authors get published. Imprint: Townhall Press. Publishes 1,500 titles/yr.; hardcover, trade paperbacks. Receives 1,500 submissions annually. 80 percent of books from first-time authors. Accepts mss through agents. Reprints books. **100 PERCENT PRINT-ON-DEMAND.** Royalty 100 percent of net; no advance. Average first printing 1,000. Publication within 30 days. Considers simultaneous submissions. Responds in 1 mo. Not in topical listings; will consider all appropriate Christian topics. Guidelines on Website or by phone; free catalog.

Nonfiction/Fiction: Phone/fax/e-query OK.

Photos: Accepts freelance photos for book covers.

Tips: "We offer on-demand publishing, bookstore distribution, and publicity and promotional services. We also exhibit at the annual International Christian Retail Show (ICRS), BookExpo America (BEA), and Evangelical Christian Publishers Assn. (ECPA). Please refer to the Website for information about how we promote and publicize books."

**Note: This publisher (royalty division) serviced by The Writer's Edge and ChristianManuscriptSubmissions.com.

ZOËLIFEPUBLISHING, 9282 General Dr., Ste. 150, Plymouth MI 78170-4694. Toll-free (877) 841-3400. (734) 254-1043. Fax (734) 254-1063. E-mail: submissions@zoelifepub.com. Website: www.zoelife pub.com. Zoe Life Industries LLC. Sabrina Adams, ed. Imprints: Pen of a Ready Writer, Titus, Business Builders. Publishes 40 titles/yr.; hardcover, trade paperbacks, mass-market paperbacks, coffee-table books. 50+ percent of books from first-time authors. Prefers mss through agents. **SUBSIDY PUBLISHES 50 PERCENT;** no print-on-demand or reprints. Length open. Royalty 5-25 percent; usually no advance. Average first printing 3,000. Publication within 6-12 mos. Responds in 21 days. Open on Bible version. Guidelines by e-mail/Website; free catalog.

Photos: Accepts freelance photos for book covers.

4

Distributors

LISTING OF CHRISTIAN BOOK/MUSIC/GIFT DISTRIBUTORS

ALLIANCE ENTERTAINMENT, LLC, 4250 Coral Ridge Dr., Coral Springs FL 33065-7615. Toll-free (800) 329-7664. (954) 255-4600. Fax (954) 255-4825. E-mail: custsvc@aent.com. Website: www .aent.com. Alliance Entertainment Corp. Music.

AMAZON ADVANTAGE PROGRAM. Go to Amazon.com, scroll down to "Features & Services," and click on "Advantage Program" in left-hand column. This is the site to contact if you want Amazon to distribute your book.

ANCHOR-WHITAKER DISTRIBUTORS, 1030 Hunt Valley Cir., New Kensington PA 15068. Toll-free (800) 444-4484. (724) 334-7000. Toll-free fax (800) 765-1960. (724) 334-1200. E-mail: pur chasing@anchordistributors.com or marketing@anchordistributors.com. Website: www.anchor distributors.com. Christian books, Bibles, music, and gifts. Distributes self-published books on a contract distribution basis. Mail a copy of the book and all pertinent information to John Whitaker.

+ BLACK CHRISTIAN BOOK DISTRIBUTORS, LLC, 8528 Davis Blvd., Ste. 134, N. Richland Hills TX 76180. (817) 240-1256. Fax (817) 887-3089. Website: www.BlackCBD.com.

B. BROUGHTON CO., LTD., 322 Consumers Rd., North York ON M2J 1P8, Canada. Toll-free (800) 268-4449 (Canada only). (416) 690-4777. Fax (416) 690-5357. E-mail: brian@bbroughton.com. Website: www.bbroughton.com. Brian Broughton, owner. Canadian distributor. Distributes books, DVDs, gifts, greeting cards. Does not distribute self-published books.

CAMPUS CRUSADE FOR CHRIST/NEW LIFE RESOURCES, 375 Hwy. 74 S., Ste. A, Peachtree City GA 30269. Toll-free (800) 827-2788. Fax (770) 631-9916. E-mail: pat.pearce@campuscrusade .org. Website: www.campuscrusade.org. Contact: Pat Pearce. Resources for evangelism, discipleship, and spiritual multiplication; books, tracts, Bible studies, and training resources. Does not distribute self-published books.

CBA MAILING LISTS OF CHRISTIAN BOOKSTORES, PO Box 62000, Colorado Springs CO 80962-2000. (719) 265-9895. Fax (719) 272-3510. E-mail: cbender@cbaonline.org. Website: www.cba online.org. Available for rental. Three different lists available, including nonmember stores: 4,700 addresses ($249); member stores: 1,275 addresses ($599); or a combined list of all stores: 5,800 addresses ($699). Prices subject to change. Call toll-free (800) 252-1950 for full details.

CENTRAL SOUTH DISTRIBUTION, 3730 Vulcan Dr., Nashville TN 37211. Toll-free (800) 251-3052. (615) 833-5960. Fax (615) 331-2501. E-mail through Website: www.centralsouthdistribution .com. Contact: Chuck Adams (cadams@csouth.com). Distributes African American gospel music and devotionals.

CHRISTIAN BOOK DISTRIBUTORS, PO Box 7000, Peabody MA 01961-7000. Toll-free (800) 247-4784. (978) 977-5080. Fax (978) 977-5010. E-mail through Website: www.christianbooks .com. Does not distribute self-published books.

CONSORTIUM BOOK SALES & DISTRIBUTION INC., 34—13th Ave. N.E., Ste. 101, Minneapolis MN 55413. (612) 746-2600. Fax (612) 746-2606. E-mail: info@cbsd.com. Website: www.cbsd .com. Distributes a small number of religion titles—more ecumenical in nature than Christian. Does not distribute self-published books.

CORNERSTONE FULFILLMENT SERVICE, LLC, 2915 Chinook Ln., Box 14, Steamboat Springs CO 80487. Phone/fax (970) 870-1518. E-mail: ContactUs@CornerstoneFulfillmentService.com. Website: www.cornerstonefulfillmentservice.com. Sue Leonard, owner. Distributes self-published books, videos, DVDs, CDs. Contact by phone/e-mail.

CROWN DISTRIBUTION. Toll-free (800) 661-9467. (780) 471-1417. Distributes Christian film & video in U.S., Canada, and around the world.

E-FULFILLMENT SERVICE INC., 6893 Sullivan Rd., Grawn MI 49637. Toll-free (866) 922-6783. (231) 276-5057, ext. 100. Fax (231) 276-5074. E-mail: info@efulfillmentservice.com or through Website: www.efulfillmentservice.com. Jordan Lindberg, pres. Services include storage and order fulfillment.

FOUNDATION DISTRIBUTING INC., 9 Cobbledick St., PO Box 98, Orono ON L0B 1M0, Canada. Toll-free (877) 368-3600. (905) 983-1188, ext. 221. Fax (905) 983-1190. E-mail: info@fdi.ca or WebHelp@fdi.ca. Website: www.fdi.ca. Canadian distributor.

GENESIS MARKETING, 850 Wade Hampton Blvd., Bldg. A, Ste. 100, Greenville SC 29609. Toll-free (800) 627-2651. (864) 233-2651. Toll-free fax (800) 849-4363. Website: www.genesislink.com.

+ DOT GIBSON DISTRIBUTION, PO Box 117, Waycross GA 31502. Toll-free (800) 336-8095. (912) 285-2848. Fax (912) 285-0349. E-mail: info@dotgibson.com. Website: www.dotgibson.com. Dot Gibson, owner (dot@dotgibson.com). Distributes cookbooks, children's books, gift books— humorous and inspirational.

GL SERVICES, 1957 Eastman Ave., Ventura CA 93003. Toll-free (888) 610-8011. (805) 677-6815. Fax (805) 644-4729. E-mail through Website: www.glservices.com. A division of Gospel Light. Does not distribute books for individual authors.

INDEPENDENT BOOK PUBLISHERS ASSN. (formerly Publishers Marketing Assn.), 627 Aviation Way, Manhattan Beach CA 90266-7107. (310) 372-2732. Fax (310) 374-3342. E-mail: info@ibpa online.org. Website: www.ibpa-online.org. Trade association of independent publishers. Provides low-cost educational and marketing programs for independent book publishers. Terry Nathan, exec. dir. (terry@ibpa-online.org).

INGRAM BOOK GROUP/DISTRIBUTION, One Ingram Blvd., La Vergne TN 37086-1986. Toll-free (800) 937-8000. (615) 793-5000. Website: www.ingrambookgroup.com. The best way to have your book/product distributed by this company is to go through one of their trading partners. For a list of distributing partners and more information, visit their Website.

KEY MARKETING GROUP, 2448 E. 81st St., Ste. 4802, Jenks OK 74137. Toll-free (877) 727-0697. (918) 298-0232. Fax (918) 299-5912. E-mail through Website: www.keymgc.com. Bryan Norris, owner (bryan@keymgc.com).

LIGHTNING SOURCE INC., 1246 Heil Quaker Blvd., La Vergne TN 37086. (615) 213-5815. Fax (615) 213-4725. E-mail: inquiry@lightningsource.com. Website: www.lightningsource.com.

MALACO CHRISTIAN DISTRIBUTION, 3023 W. Northside Dr., Jackson MS 39213. Toll-free (877) 462-3623. (601) 982-4522. Fax (877) 270-4508. E-mail: malaco@malaco.com or through Website: www.malaco.com. Tony Goodwin, mng. dir. of sales. Music distributor.

MCBETH CORP, Fulfillment and Distribution Headquarters, PO Box 400, Chambersburg PA 17201. Toll-free (800) 876-5112. (717) 263-5600. Fax (717) 263-5909. E-mail: mcbethcorp@supernet .com. Distributes Christian gift products.

NEW DAY CHRISTIAN DISTRIBUTORS, 126 Shivel Dr., Hendersonville TN 37075. Toll-free (800) 251-3633. (615) 822-3633. Toll-free fax (800) 251-3633. E-mail: service@newdaychristian.com. Website: www.newdaychristian.com. Contact: Jeff Stangenberg (jstangenberg@newdaychristian .com). Music (primarily), books, Bibles, gift items. Distributes self-published books. Contact by e-mail.

NOAH'S ARK DISTRIBUTION, 28545 Felix Valdez Ave., Ste. B4, Temecula CA 92590-1859. Toll-free (800) 562-8093. (760) 723-3101. Fax (951) 693-2747. E-mail: slvanyo@msn.com or through Website: www.christianbooksanddvds.com. Contact: Scott Vanyo, mngr.

THE PARABLE GROUP, 3563 Empleo St., San Luis Obispo CA 93401. Toll-free (800) 366-6031, ext. 525. (805) 549-2500. Toll-free fax (800) 543-2136. E-mail: info@parable.com or through Website: www.parable.com. A marketing program for Christian bookstores. Chris Scotti, member services and sales director.

PUBLISHERS GROUP WEST, National Headquarters: 1700 Fourth St., Berkeley CA 94710. (510) 809-3700. Fax (510) 809-3777. E-mail: info@pgw.com. Website: www.pgw.com. Submissions inquiries to: rose.anderson@pgw.com.

QUALITY BOOKS, 1003 W. Pines Rd., Oregon IL 61061. Toll-free (800) 323-4241. (815) 732-4450. Fax (815) 732-4499. E-mail: publisher.relations@quality-books.com. Website: www.quality books.com. Distributes small-press books, audios, DVDs, CD-ROMs, and Blu-ray to public libraries. Distributes self-published books; asks for 1 copy of your book.

RANDOLF PRODUCTIONS INC., 18005 Sky Park Cir., Ste. K, Irvine CA 92614-6514. Toll-free (800) 266-7741. (949) 794-9109. Fax (949) 794-9117. E-mail: sales@go2rpi.com. Website: www. go2rpi.com and www.goccc.com. Distributor of Christian DVDs, books, and music. A subsidiary of Campus Crusade for Christ. Contact: Randy Ray, pres. (randy@go2rpi.com).

SPRING ARBOR DISTRIBUTORS, PO Box 3006, One Ingram Blvd., Mailstop 671, La Vergne TN 37086. Toll-free (800) 395-4340. Toll-free fax (800) 876-0186. (615) 213-5192. E-mail: custserv @springarbor.com or through Website: www.springarbor.com. Contact: Mary Lou Alexander, (800) 395-4340, ext. 33319. E-mail: marylou.alexander@springarbor.com. Books, music, Bibles; no gift items or church supplies.

STL DISTRIBUTION, NORTH AMERICA, 100 Biblica Way, Elizabethton, TN 37643. Toll-free (800) 289-2772. Fax (800) 759-2779. E-mail: david.dykhouse@stl-distribution.com. Website: www .stl-distribution.com. David Dykhouse, VP of marketing. Distributes books, Bibles, CDs, audiobooks, DVDs, gifts, church supplies, marketing materials and services, including the homeschool market, and Catholic products. Distributes self-published books. Submit to the attention of Darren Henry.

TRIUMPH MARKETING, LLC., 2450 Atlanta Hwy., Ste. 1803, Cumming GA 30040. Toll-free (877) 494-0525. (678) 947-5615. Fax (678) 947-1490. Website: www.triumphmarketingllc.com. Stephen McGonigle, pres. (steve@triumphmarketingllc.com); Gary Costello, dir. of sales, marketing, and acquisitions (gary@triumphmarketingllc.com). Submit books/products for consideration.

WORD ALIVE INC., 131 Cordite Rd., Winnipeg MB R3W 1S1, Canada. Toll-free (800) 665-1468. (204) 667-1400. Toll-free fax (800) 352-9272. (204) 669-0947. E-mail: orderdesk@wordalive.ca. Website: www.wordalive.ca. Distributes Christian books. Contact: Caroline Schmidt. Distributes self-published books. Contact by mail.

5

Market Analysis

PUBLISHERS IN ORDER OF MOST BOOKS PUBLISHED PER YEAR

Adams Media 230
Tyndale House 225-250
Barbour Publishing 200
Harvest House 170
Monarch Books 160
Steeple Hill 154
Strang Book Group 150
Zonderkidz 150
Eerdmans, Wm. B. 120-130
Abingdon Press 120
Dimensions for Living 120
Zondervan 120
InterVarsity Press 110-120
New York Univ. Press 100
Still Waters Revival 100
Bethany House 90-120
B & H Publishing 90-100
Christian Focus 90
David C. Cook 85
Boyds Mills Press 80
Christian Ed. Publishers 80
Paulist Press 80
HarperOne 75
Kregel 75
Liturgical Press 75
Multnomah Books 75
Univ. Press/America 75
W Publishing Group 75
Love Inspired 72
Crossway 70
Thomas Nelson, Fiction 70
WaterBrook Press 70
Grupo Nelson 65-80
Moody Publishers 65-70
Howard Books 65
CSS Publishing 60-70
NavPress 60-65
Continuum Intl. 60
Fortress Press 60
Morehouse Publishing 60

Pilgrim Press 55
Heartsong Presents 52
Harcourt Religion 50-100
Custom Commun. 50-75
T & T Clark 50-60
Baker Academic 50
Concordia 50
DiskUs Publishing 50
Liguori Publications 50
Regal Books 50
Love Inspired Suspense 48
Doubleday Religious 45-50
Jessica Kingsley Pub. 45+
Crossroad Publishing 45
G. P. Putnam/Young Readers 45
GRQ 40-50
Jeremy P. Tarcher 40-50
Editorial Portavoz 40+
Bridge-Logos 40
FaithWords 40
Group Publishing 40
P & R Publishing 40
Destiny Image 36
Ambassador-Emerald 35-45
Pacific Press 35-40
Chalice Press 35
Mercer Univ. Press 35
Heartsong Presents/
   Mysteries 32
Revival Nation 30-50
Meriwether Publishing 30-45
Focus on the Family 30-40
Our Sunday Visitor 30-40
Rose Publishing 30-40
Whitaker House 30-40
AMG Publishers 30-35
Baylor Univ. Press 30
Beacon Hill Press 30
Conari Press 30
Contemporary Drama 30 (plays)

Evergreen Press 30
Good News Publishers (tracts)
   30
Hendrickson 30
Jossey-Bass 30
Univ. of AR Press 30
Youth Specialties 30
Ideals Publications 25-30
New Leaf Press 25-30
Smyth & Helwys 25-30
James Clarke 25
Lion and Lamb 25
Liturgy Training 25
Lutterworth Press 25
Meriwether (plays) 25
White Stone Books 25
Guardian Angel Pub. 24-36
Alba House 24
Evangelical Press 24
Love Inspired Historical 24
One World 24
St. Anthony Mess. Press 20-35
St. Augustine's Press 20-40
Chapter Two 20-30
Lighthouse Publishing 20-30
Loyola Press 20-30
New Hope 20-28
Pauline Kids 20-25
Blue Dolphin 20-24
ABC Book Publishing 20
Guideposts Books 20
Harrison House 20
Pauline Books 20
Pflaum Publishing 20
Rainbow Publishers 20
Scepter Publishers 20
Third World Press 20
Eldridge (plays) 17
JourneyForth 15-25
Catholic Book Publishing 15-20

College Press 15-20
Halo Publishing 15-20
HeartSpring Publishing 15-20
Master Books 15-20
Samaritan Press 15-20
BMH Books 15-18
Branden Publishing 15
Cambridge Scholars Pub. 15
Christian Writers Ebook 15
Legacy Press 15
Lift Every Voice 15
Wesleyan Publishing House 15
Yale Univ. Press 15
Discovery House 12-18
Eerdmans/Young Readers 12-15
Judson Press 12-15
Paragon House 12-15
Lillenas 12+
Vintage Romance 12+
CarePoint 12
Carson-Dellosa Christian 12
Charisma Kids 12
CLC Publications 12
Invisible College Press 12
White Rose 12
E.F.S. Online Publishing 10-20
Sheed & Ward 10-20
Wm. Carey Library 10-15
McDougal Publishing 10-15
Ragged Edge 10-15
Reformation Trust 10-12
ACTA Publications 10
Catholic Answers 10
Catholic Univ./America Press 10
Comfort Publishing 10
FaithWalk Publishing 10
FamilyLife Publishing 10
Fifth-Estate Publishers 10
Georgetown University
    Press 10
Jubilant Press 10 (e-books)
New Seeds 10
PREP Publishing 10
Resource Publications 10
Walk Worthy Press 10
Ambassador Books 9
Cistercian Publications 8-14
Emmaus Road 8-10
Hannibal Books 8-10
Lutheran University Press 8-10

Neibauer Press 8
Oregon Catholic Press 8
Touch Publications 8
Torch Legacy 7+
ETC Publications 6-12
Messianic Jewish 6-12
Avon Inspire 6-10
Father's Press 6-10
Mountainview Pub. 6-9
CrossLink Publishing 6-8
Kirk House Publishers 6-8
Christian Heritage 6
Dawn Publications 6
Hope Publishing 6
Inkling Books 6
Life Cycle Books 6
Wilshire Book Co. 6
Praeger Publishers 5-25
Troitsa Books 5-20
Conciliar Press 5-10
Encore Publishing 5-10
Gospel Publishing House 5-10
Hensley Publishing 5-10
Quiet Waters 5-10
Quintessential Books 5-10
Randall House 5-10
Libros Liguori 5
Mission City Press 5
Mt. Olive College Press 5
Paradise Research 5
Parsons Publishing 5
Trinity Foundation 5
His Work 4-8
Larson Publications 4-5
Millennium III 4-5
MOPS Intl. 4-5
Foursquare Media 4+
American Catholic Press 4
Anglicans United 4
Church & Synagogue Library
    Assn. 4
HCI Books 4
Intl. Awakening Press 4
Lighthouse Trails 4
Elijah Press 3-5
Facts On File 3-5
Langmarc Publishing 3-5
Northfield Publishing 3-5
Parson Place Press 3-5
Perigee Books 3-5

Salt-Works Press 3-5
Virginia Pines Press 3-5
Gollehon Press 3-4
New Canaan 3-4
St. Bede's 3-4
Tau Publishing 3-4
Church Growth Institute 3
Friends United Press 3
Magnus Press 3
Pelican Publishing 3
Quill Driver Books 3
First Fruits of Zion 2-6
Baker's Plays 2-5
Gentle Path Press 2-5
Canadian Institute for Law 2-4
Frederick Fell 2-4
Jebaire Publishing 2-4
Cladach Publishing 2-3
Deo Volente 2-3
Forward Movement 2-3
Little Lauren Books 2-3
Canticle Books 2
Players Press 1-6
VBC Publishing 1-5
LifeSong Publishers 1-4
Christian Family 1-3
Starik Publishing 1-3
Fair Havens Publications 1-2
Write Now! 1-2
Aadeon Publishing 1
Dove Inspirational 1
Good Book 1
Guernica Editions 1
Hay House 1
Reference Service 1

SUBSIDY PUBLISHERS
Xulon Press 1,500
Pleasant Word 300
Brentwood 267
Holy Fire 200
Creation House 125
Tate Publishing 120
Trafford Publishing 100-200
Essence Publishing 100-150+
Fairway Press 100
Poet's Cove 75
WinePress 75
American Binding 60
Insight Publishing 50

TEACH Services 48
Selah Publishing 45
Booklocker.com 40-50
ACW Press 40
Zoë Life 40
Black Forest Press 35
Southern Baptist Press 25
Forever Books 24+
Bookstand Publishing 20+
Impact Christian Books 20+
Providence House 20+

Elderberry Press 15
Brown Books 10-30
Star Bible 10-15
IMD Press 10
VMI Publishers 8-12
Credo House 6-12
CrossLink Publishing 6-8
Fruitbearer Publishing 5-10
Book Publishers Network 5-8
Salvation Publisher 5-7
DCTS Publishing 5

Deeper Revelation Books 5
SparrowCrowne Press 5
Recovery Communications 4-6
Kindred Books 3-4
Salt-Works 3-5
Salty's Books 2-5
Path Publishing 2-3
Path Publishing in Christ 2-3
Ampelos Press 1-3
Strong Tower Publishing 1-2
Robbie Dean Press 1

BOOK TOPICS MOST POPULAR WITH PUBLISHERS

The numbers following the topics below indicate how many publishers said they were interested in seeing a book on that topic. To find the list of publishers interested in each topic, go to the Topical Listings for Books (see Contents).

MISCELLANEOUS TALLIES
Art-Freelance 68
Booklets 47
Canadian/Foreign 22
Coffee-table books 28
E-books 39
Minibooks 20
Pamphlets 28
Photographs for covers 97
Print-on-demand 55
Tracts 22

TOPICS BY POPULARITY
1. Christian Living 150
2. Prayer 150
3. Bible/Biblical Studies 149
4. Inspirational 148
5. Family Life 147
6. Religion 145
7. Faith 143
8. Women's Issues 136
9. Devotional Books 133
10. Spirituality 132
11. Theology 125
12. Discipleship 124
13. Fiction: Adult/Religious 123
14. Parenting 121
15. Marriage 120
16. Spiritual Life 119
17. Biography 116
18. Historical 113
19. Church History 111
20. Current/Social Issues 111

21. Personal Growth 109
22. Forgiveness 107
23. Evangelism/Witnessing 105
24. Leadership 103
25. Christian Education 101
26. Church Life 100
27. Self-help 99
28. Worship 99
29. Fiction: Historical 96
30. Bible Commentary 94
31. Fiction: Contemporary 94
32. Ethics 93
33. Apologetics 92
34. Christ 90
35. Health 90
36. Youth Books (nonfiction) 90
37. Ethnic/Cultural 88
38. Healing 88
39. Controversial Issues 87
40. Fiction: Biblical 86
41. Fiction: Juvenile (ages 8-12) 86
42. Relationships 86
43. Men's Books 85
44. Fiction: Teen/Young Adult 84
45. How-To 84
46. Scholarly 84
47. Spiritual Gifts 84
48. Death/Dying 83
49. Personal Renewal 83
50. Reference Books 83
51. Church Renewal 82

52. Fiction: Mystery/Suspense 80
53. Autobiography 78
54. Fiction: Adventure 78
55. Spiritual Warfare 78
56. Christian Business 77
57. Doctrinal 76
58. Holy Spirit 76
59. Humor 76
60. Missionary 76
61. Personal Experience 76
62. Stewardship 76
63. Singles' Issues 75
64. Church Traditions 74
65. Money Management 74
66. Group Study Books 73
67. Dating/Sex 72
68. Philosophy 72
69. Counseling Aids 71
70. Pastors' Helps 71
71. Social Justice Issues 71
72. Encouragement 70
73. Psychology 68
74. Worship Resources 68
75. Children's Picture Books 67
76. Divorce 67
77. Eschatology 67
78. Prophecy 67
79. World Issues 67
80. Fiction: Literary 66
81. Recovery Books 66
82. Fiction: Humor 64
83. Holiday/Seasonal 64
84. Sermons 64

85. Christian Homeschooling 63
86. Miracles 63
87. Politics 63
88. Memoirs 62
89. Exegesis 61
90. Fiction: Fantasy 60
91. Fiction: Romance 60
92. Liturgical Studies 60
93. Fiction: Historical/Romance 59
94. Fiction: Mystery/Romance 59
95. Archaeology 58
96. Christian School Books 58
97. Grief 58
98. Children's Easy Readers 57
99. Church Management 57
100. Holiness 57
101. Homeschooling Resources 56
102. Time Management 56
103. Cookbooks 54
104. Environmental Issues 54
105. Religious Tolerance 54
106. Fiction: Allegory 53
107. Racism 53
108. Fiction: Frontier 52

109. Fiction: Frontier/Romance 52
110. Science 52
111. Charismatic 50
112. Creation Science 50
113. Curriculum 50
114. Economics 50
115. Fiction: Short-Story Collections 50
116. Lifestyle 50
117. Senior Adult Concerns 50
118. Sports/Recreation 50
119. Homiletics 49
120. Fiction: Adult/General 48
121. Fiction: Ethnic 48
122. Poetry 48
123. Sociology 48
124. Cults/Occult 46
125. Drama 46
126. Fiction: Science Fiction 45
127. Travel 44
128. Retirement 43
129. Fiction: Chick Lit 42
130. Fiction: Westerns 42
131. Music-related Books 42
132. Compilations 41
133. Tween Books 41

134. Celebrity Profiles 40
135. Fiction: Novellas 38
136. Popular Culture 38
137. Writing How-To 37
138. Postmodernism 36
139. Youth Programs 36
140. Fiction: Children's Picture Books 34
141. Fiction: Fables/Parables 34
142. Fiction: Speculative 33
143. Exposés 32
144. Program Resources 31
145. Games/Crafts 30
146. Fiction: Plays 29
147. Gift Books 29
148. Lay Counseling 26
149. Hispanic Markets 25
150. Fiction: Cozy Mysteries 24
151. African American Markets 23
152. Novelty Books for Kids 23
153. Christmas Books 19
154. Children's Board Books 15
155. Music/Musicals 11
156. Children's Devotionals 9
157. Praise 5
158. Fiction: Skits 3

BOOK PUBLISHERS WITH THE MOST BOOKS ON THE BEST-SELLER LIST FOR THE PREVIOUS YEAR

This tally is based on actual sales in Christian bookstores reported from August 2008 to May 2009. Numbers behind the names indicate the number of titles each publisher had on that particular best-seller list during that time.

BIBLE STUDIES/ THEOLOGY/MINISTRY

1. Abingdon Press 13
2. Ignatius Press 6
3. Thomas Nelson 6
4. WaterBrook Press 3
5. B & H Publishing 2
6. New Day 2
7. Standard Publishing 2
8. Zondervan 2
9. Barbour 1
10. Harvest House 1
11. InterVarsity 1
12. Regal (Gospel Light) 1

13. Teach All Nations 1
14. Tyndale House 1

CHILDREN'S BOOKS

1. Zondervan 16
2. Thomas Nelson 9
3. Tyndale House 4
4. Barbour 3
5. David C. Cook 2
6. Ideals Books 2
7. Abingdon Press 1
8. Baker Books 1
9. B & H Publishing 1
10. Standard Publishing 1

CHRISTIAN LIVING

1. Thomas Nelson 23
2. Harvest House 14
3. Zondervan 14
4. Moody Press 7
5. B & H Publishing 5
6. Revell (Baker) 5
7. Tyndale House 4
8. WaterBrook 4
9. Charisma 2
10. Gospel Light 2
11. Multnomah 2
12. New Day 2
13. Abingdon 1

14. Augsburg 1
15. Baker Books 1
16. David C. Cook 1
17. FaithWords 1
18. Siloam (Strang) 1
19. Standard 1
20. Wesleyan Publishing 1

FICTION

1. Thomas Nelson 24
2. Bethany House 15
3. Zondervan 9
4. Barbour 7
5. Tyndale House 6
6. Harvest House 4
7. Revell (Baker) 4
8. Center Street (Hachette) 1
9. David C. Cook 1
10. FaithWords 1
11. Multnomah 1
12. Penguin Group USA 1
13. WaterBrook 1
14. Windblown Media 1

INSPIRATIONAL/ GENERAL MEDIA

1. Thomas Nelson 18
2. Zondervan 11
3. Barbour 7
4. Tyndale House 5
5. Charisma 4
6. Harvest House 4
7. Abingdon 3

8. Howard Books 3
9. B & H Publishing 2
10. FaithWords 2
11. Ideals Books 2
12. Simon & Schuster 2
13. David C. Cook 1
14. Crossway 1
15. Kregel 1
16. Penguin Group USA 1
17. Regal 1
18. Revell 1
19. Upper Room 1
20. Whitaker House 1

YOUNG ADULT BOOKS

1. Thomas Nelson 9
2. Harvest House 4
3. Multnomah 4
4. Revell (Baker) 4
5. Bethany House 2
6. NavPress 2
7. Moody Press 2
8. Zondervan 2
9. Barbour 1
10. FaithWords 1

COMBINED BEST-SELLER LISTS

1. Thomas Nelson 89
2. Zondervan 54
3. Harvest House 27
4. Tyndale House 20
5. Barbour 19

6. Abingdon 18
7. Bethany House 17
8. Revell 14
9. B & H Publishing 10
10. Moody Press 9
11. WaterBrook 8
12. Multnomah 7
13. Charisma 6
14. Ignatius 6
15. David C. Cook 5
16. FaithWords 5
17. Ideals 4
18. New Day 4
19. Standard 4
20. Howard Books 3
21. Baker Books 2
22. Gospel Light 2
23. NavPress 2
24. Penguin Group USA 2
25. Regal Books 2
26. Simon & Schuster 2
27. Augsburg 1
28. Center Street (Hachette) 1
29. Crossway Books 1
30. InterVarsity Press 1
31. Kregel 1
32. Siloam (Strang) 1
33. Teach All Nations 1
34. Upper Room Books 1
35. Wesleyan Publishing 1
36. Whitaker House 1
37. Windblown Media 1

TOP 50 BEST SELLERS

This list is based on which publishers had the most books on the list of the Top 50 books each month. It tracks the top 50 sellers regardless of genre (those listed above are in specific genres). It is interesting to note that there were only 27 publishers with books on this list during the last year (7 fewer than last year)—and the field is again dominated by the same top two publishers.

1. Thomas Nelson 36
2. Zondervan 31
3. Harvest House 14
4. Tyndale House 11
5. Barbour 9
6. Abingdon Press 8
7. Moody Press 8
8. B & H Publishing 6
9. Bethany House 6

10. Revell (Baker) 6
11. WaterBrook 5
12. Charisma 3
13. Multnomah 3
14. New Day 3
15. Standard 3
16. FaithWords 2
17. Regal (Gospel Light) 2
18. Center Street (Hachette) 1

19. CLC Publications 1
20. David C. Cook 1
21. Gospel Light 1
22. Howard Books 1
23. Ideals Books 1
24. Siloam (Strang) 1
25. Simon & Schuster 1
26. Upper Room Books 1
27. Windblown Media 1

PART 2

Periodical Publishers

6

Topical Listings of Periodicals

As soon as you have an article or story idea, look up that topic in the following topical listings (see table of contents for a full list of topics). Study the appropriate periodicals in the primary/alphabetical listings (as well as their writers' guidelines and sample copies) and select those that are most likely targets for the piece you are writing.

Note that most ideas can be written for more than one periodical if you slant them to the needs of different audiences, for example, current events for teens, or pastors, or women. Have a target periodical and audience in mind before you start writing. Each topic is divided by age group/audience, so you can pick appropriate markets for your particular slant.

If the magazine prefers or requires a query letter, be sure to write that letter first and then follow any suggestions they make if they give you a go-ahead to write the article.

(R) Takes reprints

(*) Indicates new topic this year

$ Indicates a paying market

($) Indicates a market pays sometimes or pays with books or merchandise

---

AFRICAN AMERICAN MARKETS
Adult/General
African Voices (R)
Chocolate Pages
$ Direction
Light of the World
$ MESSAGE
$ Precepts for Living
Purpose Magazine (R)
3V Magazine
$ Upscale
$ Written

Children
$ JuniorWay
$ Preschool Playhouse
$ Primary Street

Pastors/Leaders
$ African-American Pulpit
$ Torch Legacy Leader

Teen/Young Adult
$ InTeen (R)
$ J.A.M.

Women
Empowering Everyday Women
$ Heart & Soul
Precious Times (R)

APOLOGETICS
Adult/General
$ Arkansas Catholic (R)
$ Aujourd'hui Credo (R)
$ Bible Advocate (R)
Bread of Life (R)
Breakthrough Intercessor (R)
$ Brink Magazine (R)
$ Catholic Insight
CBN.com (R)
$ Celebrate Life (R)
Christian Online
Christian Ranchman
$ Christian Research
$ Christian Standard (R)
$ Christianity Today (R)
Church of England News
$ Columbia (R)
Desert Call (R)
Desert Voice (R)
E-Channels (R)
Evangelical Advocate (R)
$ Focus on the Family
$ Horizons (adult) (R)
($) Impact Magazine (R)
$ In His Presence (R)
$ In Touch
Koinonia
$ Live (R)
$ Lookout
Maine Family Policy (R)
$ Manna (R)
Messianic Perspectives (R)
MovieGuide
$ On Mission
$ Our Sunday Visitor (R)
$ Pathway (R)
Perspectives (R)
Perspectives/Science & Chr. Faith
PrayerWorks (R)
$ Precepts for Living
Priscilla Papers
SCP Journal
$ Seek (R)

$ Social Justice (R)
Sword and Trumpet
Sword of the Lord (R)
$ Way of St. Francis (R)
Wisconsin Christian

Children
$ SHINE brightly (R)

Daily Devotionals
Penned from the Heart (R)

Missions
Lausanne World Pulse (R)

Pastors/Leaders
$ Catholic Servant
$ Christian Century (R)
$ Enrichment Journal (R)
$ Lutheran Partners (R)
$ Outreach (R)
Pulpit Helps (R)
$ SmallGroups.com (R)
Theological Digest (R)

Teen/Young Adult
$ Boundless Webzine (R)
$ Direction Student
$ Horizon Student
$ True Girl
$ Young Salvationist (R)

Women
$ Canticle
Woman of Worth (R)

BIBLE STUDIES
Adult/General
($) AGAIN Magazine (R)
$ Alive Now (R)
$ Annals of St. Anne
$ Arlington Catholic
$ Aujourd'hui Credo (R)
Bread of Life (R)
Breakthrough Intercessor (R)
$ Catholic Peace Voice (R)
$ Catholic Yearbook (R)
CBN.com (R)
Christian Computing (R)
Christian Motorsports
Christian Online
Christian Ranchman
$ Christian Research

$ Christian Standard (R)
Church Herald & Holiness (R)
$ Churchmouse Publications (R)
$ Columbia (R)
Connecting Point (R)
Creation Care (R)
$ Culture Wars (R)
Desert Call (R)
$ DreamSeeker (R)
Eternal Ink (R)
Faithwebbin (R)
$ Foursquare Leader
$ Gem (R)
Gospel Herald
HEARTLIGHT Internet (R)
($) HopeKeepers (R)
$ In His Presence (R)
$ In Touch
$ Lutheran Journal (R)
Maine Family Policy (R)
$ Mature Years (R)
Messianic Perspectives (R)
Methodist History
$ New Wineskins (R)
$ Our Sunday Visitor (R)
Perspectives (R)
$ Positive Thinking (R)
PrayerWorks (R)
$ Precepts for Living
Priscilla Papers
$ Purpose (R)
Quaker Life (R)
Reverent Submissions (R)
$ Seek (R)
$ Social Justice (R)
$ Spiritual Life
Spirituality for Today
$ St. Anthony Messenger
Sword and Trumpet
Sword of the Lord (R)
Trumpeter (R)
Victory Herald (R)
$ War Cry (R)
$ Way of St. Francis (R)
Wisconsin Christian

Children
$ Archaeology
$ Primary Street
$ SHINE brightly (R)

Christian Education/ Library
$ Catechist
Catholic Library
$ Children's Ministry
Congregational Libraries Today
$ Group Magazine
$ Preschool Playhouse (CE)

Missions
MissionsMagazinet
Railroad Evangelist (R)
Women of the Harvest

Pastors/Leaders
$ African-American Pulpit
$ Catholic Servant
$ Let's Worship
Pulpit Helps (R)
Sewanee Theo. Review
Sharing the Practice (R)
$ SmallGroups.com (R)
Theological Digest (R)
$ Word & World

Teen/Young Adult
$ Sharing the Victory (R)
TeensForJC (R)

Women
($) Beyond the Bend (R)
Extreme Woman Magazine
For Every Woman (R)
Jewels of God (R)
Precious Times (R)
Simply Blessed (R)
Virtuous Woman (R)
Woman of Worth (R)
Women's Ministry

BOOK EXCERPTS
Adult/General
($) AGAIN Magazine (R)
$ Alive Now (R)
$ Associated Content (R)
Books & Culture
Bread of Life (R)
$ Catholic Digest (R)
CBN.com (R)
$ Charisma
$ Chicken Soup Books (R)
Christian Observer

$ Christian Renewal (R)
$ Christian Retailing
$ Christianity Today (R)
Church of England News
$ Columbia (R)
$ Converge Point (R)
$ Covenant Companion (R)
Creation Care (R)
$ Culture Wars (R)
E-Channels (R)
Faithwebbin (R)
Good News Journal (R)
Gospel Herald
($) HopeKeepers (R)
$ Indian Life (R)
$ Interim (R)
Island Catholic (R)
$ JC Town Reporter (R)
$ KD Gospel Media
Maine Family Policy (R)
Messianic Perspectives (R)
New Heart (R)
New Identity (R)
$ New Wineskins (R)
$ Power for Living (R)
Priscilla Papers
$ Prism
Quaker Life (R)
Regent Global Bus. Rev. (R)
Single Again Mag. Online (R)
Spirituality for Today
Trumpeter (R)
$ United Church Observer (R)
$ Upscale
Urban Kingdom (R)
Wisconsin Christian
$ Written

Christian Education/ Library
Christian Early Ed. (R)
Christian Library Journal
$ Jour./Adventist Ed. (R)

Missions
Intl. Jour./Frontier Missions(R)

Pastors/Leaders
$ African-American Pulpit
$ Christian Century (R)
Jour./Amer. Soc./Chur.
   Growth (R)

$ Ministry Today
$ Outreach (R)
Rick Warren's Ministry
   Toolbox (R)

Teen/Young Adult
$ Boundless Webzine (R)
$ J.A.M.
TeensForJC (R)

Women
($) Beyond the Bend (R)
Elegance (R)
Extreme Woman Magazine
$ Heart & Soul
Jewels of God (R)
$ Link & Visitor (R)
Share
$ SpiritLed Woman
Unrecognized Woman (R)
Virtuous Woman (R)
Woman of Worth (R)

Writers
$ Freelance Writer's Report (R)
$ Writer

BOOK REVIEWS
Adult/General
$ Abilities
African Voices (R)
($) AGAIN Magazine (R)
$ America
$ Anglican Journal
$ Arkansas Catholic (R)
$ Arlington Catholic
$ Associated Content (R)
$ Atlantic Catholic
$ Aujourd'hui Credo (R)
Blue Ridge Christian News
Books & Culture
Bread of Life (R)
Breakthrough Intercessor (R)
$ Brink Magazine (R)
byFaith
$ Canadian Mennonite (R)
$ Cathedral Age
$ Catholic Insight
$ Catholic Peace Voice (R)
CBN.com (R)
$ Charisma
Charlotte World

Chocolate Pages
Christian Computing (R)
$ Christian Courier/Canada (R)
Christian Family Journal
$ Christian Herald (R)
$ Christian Journal (R)
Christian Media (R)
Christian Observer
Christian Press
Christian Ranchman
$ Christian Renewal (R)
$ Christian Research
$ Christian Retailing
$ Christianity Today (R)
$ ChristianWeek (R)
$ Churchmouse Publications (R)
$ Citizen USA
$ City Light News (R)
Creation Care (R)
$ Cresset
crosshome
$ Culture Wars (R)
Desert Voice (R)
$ DisciplesWorld
Divine Ascent
E-Channels (R)
$ Episcopal Life (R)
Eternal Ink (R)
$ Eureka Street
Evangelical Advocate (R)
$ Faith & Family
$ Faith & Friends (R)
$ Faith Today
Founders Journal
$ Foursquare Leader
Good News Journal (R)
Good News Today
Good News!
Gospel Herald
Halo Magazine
$ Haruah (R)
Heartland Gatekeeper (R)
$ Home Times (R)
($) HopeKeepers (R)
$ Image/WA
$ Imagine
($) Impact Magazine (R)
In Part
$ Indian Life (R)
$ Interim (R)

Island Catholic (R)
$ JC Town Reporter (R)
$ KD Gospel Media
Koinonia
La Nueva Vision
$ Liguorian
Maine Family Policy (R)
($) Mennonite Historian (R)
Methodist History
$ MindFlights (R)
MovieGuide
($) Mutuality (R)
New Christian Voices
New Frontier
$ New Wineskins (R)
$ Our Sunday Visitor (R)
Ozarks Christian News
Penwood Review
Perspectives/Science & Chr. Faith
$ Prairie Messenger (R)
$ Presbyterian Outlook
Priscilla Papers
$ Prism
$ Pure Inspiration (R)
Purpose Magazine (R)
Quaker Life (R)
Radix Magazine
Regent Global Bus. Rev. (R)
Reverent Submissions (R)
$ Search
$ Significant Living (R)
Single Again Mag. Online (R)
$ Social Justice (R)
$ Spiritual Life
Studio (R)
$ Testimony (R)
Time of Singing (R)
Trumpeter (R)
$ Upscale
Urban Kingdom (R)
Victory Herald (R)
$ Way of St. Francis (R)
$ Weavings (R)
Wisconsin Christian
$ World & I (R)
$ Written
Xavier Review

Children
$ New Moon Girls (R)

$ SHINE brightly (R)
$ Sparkle (R)

Christian Education/ Library
Catholic Library
Christian Early Ed. (R)
Christian Librarian (R)
Christian School Ed. (R)
$ Church Libraries (R)
Congregational Libraries Today
$ Group Magazine
Jour. of Christian Ed.
Jour. of Christianity (R)
$ Jour./Adventist Ed. (R)
Jour./Ed. & Christian Belief (R)
Jour./Research on Christian Ed.
$ Momentum
$ Teachers of Vision (R)

Missions
East-West Church & Ministry
    Report
$ Evangelical Missions (R)
$ Glad Tidings (R)
Intl. Jour./Frontier Missions (R)
Missiology
Op. Reveille Interactive Jour. (R)
Women of the Harvest

Music
$ Creator (R)
Hymn

Pastors/Leaders
$ African-American Pulpit
$ Catechumenate
$ Christian Century (R)
CrossCurrents
$ Diocesan Dialogue (R)
$ Emmanuel
$ Enrichment Journal (R)
$ Interpreter
Jour./Amer. Soc./Chur.
    Growth (R)
Jour./Pastoral Care
$ Leadership (R)
$ Let's Worship
$ Lutheran Partners (R)
$ Ministry
Ministry in Motion (R)
$ Ministry Today

Pulpit Helps (R)
$ Reformed Worship (R)
Sharing the Practice (R)
Theological Digest (R)
$ Word & World
$ Worship Leader
$ Your Church (R)

Teen/Young Adult
$ Boundless Webzine (R)
$ Devo'zine (R)
$ Direction Student
G4T Ink (R)
$ Horizon Student
$ J.A.M.
TeensForJC (R)
$ True Girl
$ Young Christian Writers

Women
($) Beyond the Bend (R)
Christian Work at Home
    Moms (R)
$ Dabbling Mum (R)
Empowering Everyday Women
$ Esprit
Extreme Woman Magazine
$ Heart & Soul
Hope for Women
$ Horizons (R)
$ inSpirit (R)
Jewels of God (R)
Live Magazine
$ Pauses . . .
Precious Times (R)
Share
Simply Blessed (R)
Unrecognized Woman (R)
Virtuous Woman (R)
Woman of Worth (R)
Women's Ministry

Writers
$ Advanced Christian Writer (R)
Areopagus
$ Christian Communicator (R)
$ Cross & Quill (R)
Esdras' Scroll (R)
$ Fellowscript (R)
NW Christian Author (R)
$ Spirit-Led Writer (R)
$ Tickled by Thunder

Write Connection
$ Writer
$ Writers' Journal

CANADIAN/FOREIGN MARKETS
Adult/General
$ Abilities
$ Anglican Journal
$ Annals of St. Anne
$ Atlantic Catholic
$ Aujourd'hui Credo (R)
$ Australian Catholics (R)
$ B.C. Catholic (R)
Bread of Life (R)
$ Canada Lutheran (R)
Canadian Lutheran
$ Canadian Mennonite (R)
CanadianChristianity.com
$ Catholic Insight
Catholic Register
Challenge Weekly
$ Christian Courier/Canada (R)
Christian Courier/WI (R)
$ Christian Herald (R)
Christian Outlook
$ Christian Renewal (R)
$ ChristianWeek (R)
Church of England News
$ City Light News (R)
$ Common Ground (R)
Creation
E-Channels (R)
$ Eureka Street
Evangelical Times
$ Faith & Friends (R)
$ Faith Today
Fellowship
Gospel Herald
($) Impact Magazine (R)
$ Indian Life (R)
$ Interim (R)
Island Catholic (R)
LifeSiteNews
Lifetimes Magazine
$ Living Light (R)
($) Mennonite Historian (R)
$ Messenger
$ Messenger/Sacred Heart
$ Messenger/St. Anthony

Mosaic (R)
$ Prairie Messenger (R)
Studio (R)
$ Testimony (R)
$ United Church Observer (R)

Christian Education/Library
$ Christian Educators (R)
Jour. of Christian Ed.
Jour./Ed. & Christian Belief (R)

Daily Devotionals
$ Rejoice!

Missions
$ Glad Tidings (R)
Koinonia
MissionsMagazinet

Music
Church Music

Pastors/Leaders
$ Evangelical Baptist
Technologies for Worship (R)
Theological Digest (R)

Women
Christian Women Today (R)
$ Esprit
Life Tools for Women
$ Link & Visitor (R)
Women Today (R)

Writers
Areopagus
$ Canadian Writer's Jour. (R)
$ Fellowscript (R)
$ Tickled by Thunder
Writers Manual

CELEBRITY PIECES
Adult/General
American Tract (R)
$ Angels on Earth
$ Annals of St. Anne
$ Arlington Catholic
$ Associated Content (R)
$ Australian Catholics (R)
Breakthrough
$ Brink Magazine (R)
$ Catholic Digest (R)
CBN.com (R)

$ Celebrate Life (R)
Christian Family Journal
$ Christian Herald (R)
$ Christian Journal (R)
Christian Motorsports
Christian Online
Christian Ranchman
$ Christianity Today Movies (R)
$ Churchmouse Publications (R)
Church of England News
$ City Light News (R)
$ DisciplesWorld
$ Episcopal Life (R)
$ Focus on the Family
$ Good News in Florida (R)
Good News Journal (R)
$ Good News, Etc. (R)
Gospel Herald
$ Guideposts (R)
Halo Magazine
Heartland Gatekeeper (R)
HEARTLIGHT Internet (R)
$ Home Times (R)
($) HopeKeepers (R)
$ Imagine
($) Impact Magazine (R)
$ In Touch
$ Indian Life (R)
$ JC Town Reporter (R)
$ KD Gospel Media
$ Kindred Spirit (R)
$ Living Light (R)
$ Miracles, Healings
MovieGuide
($) Mutuality (R)
$ New Wineskins (R)
$ Our Sunday Visitor (R)
$ Positive Thinking (R)
$ Power for Living (R)
$ Priority! (R)
$ Prism
$ Pure Inspiration (R)
$ Significant Living (R)
$ St. Anthony Messenger
Tri-State Voice
Trumpeter (R)
Urban Kingdom (R)
$ Vibrant Life (R)
$ War Cry (R)
Wisconsin Christian

Children
$ American Girl (R)
$ Cadet Quest (R)
$ SHINE brightly (R)
$ Sparkle (R)

Music
$ Christian Music Today (R)
Christian Music Weekly (R)

Pastors/Leaders
$ Catholic Servant
$ Ministry Today

Teen/Young Adult
$ Essential Connection (ec)
G4T Ink (R)
$ J.A.M.
$ Listen (R)
$ Sharing the Victory (R)
$ TC Magazine
TeensForJC (R)
$ Young Salvationist (R)

Women
($) Beyond the Bend (R)
$ Canticle
Empowering Everyday Women
Extreme Woman Magazine
$ Heart & Soul
$ Journey
More to Life
Precious Times (R)
Virtuous Woman (R)
Woman of Worth (R)

Writers
$ Cross & Quill (R)
NW Christian Author (R)

CHRISTIAN BUSINESS
Adult/General
$ Angels on Earth
Bread of Life (R)
$ Brink Magazine (R)
$ CBA Retailers
CBN.com (R)
Christian Business
$ Christian Courier/Canada (R)
Christian Family Journal
Christian Motorsports
Christian News NW (R)
Christian Online

Christian Ranchman
$ Christian Retailing
$ ChristianWeek (R)
$ Churchmouse Publications (R)
$ Citizen USA
$ City Light News (R)
Creation Care (R)
Desert Call (R)
Desert Voice (R)
Disciple's Journal (R)
Evangel/OR (R)
$ Faith Today
$ Gem (R)
Good News Journal (R)
Gospel Herald
$ Gospel Today (R)
$ Guideposts (R)
Halo Magazine
Heartland Gatekeeper (R)
HEARTLIGHT Internet (R)
Highway News (R)
$ Home Times (R)
$ In Touch
$ JC Town Reporter (R)
$ KD Gospel Media
Light of the World
$ Living (R)
$ Lookout
$ Manna (R)
Marketplace
MissionWares
New Identity (R)
($) NRB E-Magazine (R)
$ Our Sunday Visitor (R)
($) P.O.W.E.R. Magazine
$ Pathway (R)
$ Power for Living (R)
$ Prism
$ Purpose (R)
Purpose Magazine (R)
Regent Global Bus. Rev. (R)
$ Search
$ Significant Living (R)
Single Again Mag. Online (R)
$ St. Anthony Messenger
$ Together (R)
Trumpeter (R)
Urban Kingdom (R)
$ War Cry (R)
Wisconsin Christian

Christian Education/ Library
Christian School Ed. (R)

Missions
$ Evangelical Missions (R)
Lausanne World Pulse (R)

Music
($) TCP Magazine

Pastors/Leaders
$ African-American Pulpit
$ Catholic Servant
Church Executive
$ Clergy Journal (R)
$ InSite (R)
$ Interpreter
Ministry in Motion (R)
Rick Warren's Ministry
   Toolbox (R)
Technologies for Worship (R)
$ Today's Parish
$ Your Church (R)

Teen/Young Adult
$ Boundless Webzine (R)
$ J.A.M.

Women
($) Beyond the Bend (R)
Christian Women Today (R)
Christian Work at Home
   Moms (R)
$ Dabbling Mum (R)
Elegance (R)
Empowering Everyday Women
$ Heart & Soul
Jewels of God (R)
Precious Times (R)
Simply Blessed (R)
Virtuous Woman (R)
Women Today (R)

Writers
Writing Corner (R)

CHRISTIAN EDUCATION
Adult/General
African Voices (R)
$ America
$ Anglican Journal
$ Animal Trails (R)

$ Annals of St. Anne
$ Arlington Catholic
$ Atlantic Catholic
$ Aujourd'hui Credo (R)
$ B.C. Catholic (R)
Bread of Life (R)
$ Canada Lutheran (R)
$ Canadian Mennonite (R)
$ Catholic Peace Voice (R)
$ Celebrate Life (R)
$ Christian Courier/Canada (R)
$ Christian Examiner
Christian Family Journal
$ Christian Home & School
Christian News NW (R)
Christian Observer
Christian Online
Christian Ranchman
$ Christian Renewal (R)
$ Christian Retailing
$ Christian Standard (R)
$ Christianity Today (R)
$ ChristianWeek (R)
$ Citizen USA
$ City Light News (R)
$ Columbia (R)
$ Company Magazine (R)
Creation Care (R)
$ Cresset
$ Culture Wars (R)
Desert Call (R)
Desert Voice (R)
$ Direction
$ DisciplesWorld
E-Channels (R)
Eternal Ink (R)
Evangelical Advocate (R)
$ Faith & Family
$ Faith Today
Faithwebbin (R)
$ Foursquare Leader
$ Gem (R)
Good News Journal (R)
$ Good News, Etc. (R)
Gospel Herald
$ Gospel Today (R)
Halo Magazine
HEARTLIGHT Internet (R)
Highway News (R)
$ Home Times (R)

$ Homeschooling Today (R)
$ In His Presence (R)
$ JC Town Reporter (R)
$ KD Gospel Media
Koinonia
Light of the World
$ Live (R)
$ Living Church
$ Lookout
Maine Family Policy (R)
$ Manna (R)
$ Messenger/Sacred Heart
Methodist History
Mosaic (R)
MovieGuide
New Identity (R)
$ New Wineskins (R)
Nostalgia (R)
$ Our Sunday Visitor (R)
$ ParentLife
Penned from the Heart (R)
Perspectives (R)
PrayerWorks (R)
$ Precepts for Living
$ Presbyterian Outlook
$ Presbyterians Today (R)
$ Prism
$ Purpose (R)
Reverent Submissions (R)
$ Seek (R)
Single Again Mag. Online (R)
Spirituality for Today
$ St. Anthony Messenger
Sword and Trumpet
Sword of the Lord (R)
$ Testimony (R)
$ Together (R)
Trumpeter (R)
Urban Kingdom (R)
Victory Herald (R)
$ War Cry (R)
$ Way of St. Francis (R)
Wisconsin Christian

Children

$ Guide (R)
$ JuniorWay
$ Kid Zone
$ Primary Street
$ Sparkle (R)

Christian Education/ Library

$ Catechist
$ Children's Ministry
Christian Early Ed. (R)
$ Christian Educators (R)
Christian Librarian (R)
Christian School Ed. (R)
$ Group Magazine
Jour. of Christian Ed.
Jour. of Christianity (R)
$ Jour./Adventist Ed. (R)
Jour./Ed. & Christian
    Belief (R)
Jour./Research on
    Christian Ed.
$ Kids' Ministry Ideas
$ Momentum
$ Preschool Playhouse (CE)
$ Teachers of Vision (R)
$ Today's Catholic Teacher (R)
$ Youth & CE Leadership

Missions

East-West Church & Ministry
    Report
$ Evangelical Missions (R)
$ Glad Tidings (R)

Pastors/Leaders

$ African-American Pulpit
$ Catechumenate
$ Catholic Servant
$ Christian Century (R)
Christian Education Jour. (R)
$ Clergy Journal (R)
CrossCurrents
$ Enrichment Journal (R)
$ Interpreter
$ Lutheran Partners (R)
Ministry in Motion (R)
$ Ministry Today
Pulpit Helps (R)
$ RevWriter Resource
Rick Warren's Ministry
    Toolbox (R)
$ SmallGroups.com (R)
Technologies for Worship (R)
$ Today's Parish
$ Word & World
$ Youthworker

Teen/Young Adult
$ Boundless Webzine (R)
$ Insight (R)
$ J.A.M.
TeensForJC (R)
$ True Girl
$ Young Adult Today

Women
Christian Woman's Page (R)
Crowned with Silver
$ Horizons (R)
$ inSpirit (R)
$ Pauses . . .
Precious Times (R)
Right to the Heart (R)
Share
Woman of Worth (R)

CHRISTIAN LIVING
Adult/General
($) AGAIN Magazine (R)
$ Alive Now (R)
$ America
American Tract (R)
$ Angels on Earth
$ Annals of St. Anne
$ Arkansas Catholic (R)
$ Arlington Catholic
$ Atlantic Catholic
$ Aujourd'hui Credo (R)
$ Australian Catholics (R)
$ B.C. Catholic (R)
$ Bible Advocate (R)
Bread of Life (R)
Breakthrough Intercessor (R)
$ Brink Magazine (R)
$ Canada Lutheran (R)
$ Cathedral Age
$ Catholic Digest (R)
$ Catholic Forester (R)
$ Catholic New York
$ Catholic Yearbook (R)
CBN.com (R)
$ Celebrate Life (R)
Central FL Episcopalian
$ CGA World (R)
$ Charisma
$ Chicken Soup Books (R)
$ Christian Courier/Canada (R)
Christian Courier/WI (R)

$ Christian Examiner
Christian Family Journal
$ Christian Home & School
$ Christian Journal (R)
Christian Observer
Christian Online
Christian Quarterly (R)
Christian Ranchman
$ Christian Research
$ Christian Standard (R)
$ Christianity Today (R)
$ ChristianWeek (R)
Church Herald & Holiness (R)
$ Churchmouse Publications (R)
Church of England News
$ Citizen USA
$ City Light News (R)
$ Columbia (R)
Connecting Point (R)
$ Converge Point (R)
$ Covenant Companion (R)
Creation Care (R)
$ Culture Wars (R)
Desert Call (R)
Desert Voice (R)
$ DisciplesWorld
Divine Ascent
$ DreamSeeker (R)
E-Channels (R)
$ Enfoque a la Familia
Eternal Ink (R)
$ Evangel/IN (R)
Evangel/OR (R)
Evangelical Advocate (R)
$ Faith & Family
$ Faith & Friends (R)
$ Faith Today
Faithwebbin (R)
$ Family Digest (R)
Fit Christian
Florida Baptist Witness
$ Focus on the Family
$ Foursquare Leader
$ Gem (R)
$ Gems of Truth (R)
$ Good News (R)
$ Good News in Florida (R)
Good News Journal (R)
$ Good News, Etc. (R)
Gospel Herald

$ Gospel Today (R)
$ Guideposts (R)
Halo Magazine
$ Haruah (R)
HEARTLIGHT Internet (R)
Highway News (R)
$ Holiness Today
$ Home Times (R)
$ Homeschooling Today (R)
($) HopeKeepers (R)
$ Horizons (adult) (R)
$ Imagine
($) Impact Magazine (R)
$ In His Presence (R)
In Part
$ In Touch
$ Indian Life (R)
Island Catholic (R)
$ JC Town Reporter (R)
$ KD Gospel Media
Keys to Living (R)
Koinonia
La Nueva Vision
Leaves (R)
$ Light & Life
Light of the World
$ Liguorian
$ Live (R)
$ Living (R)
$ Living Church
$ Lookout
$ Lutheran Digest (R)
$ Lutheran Journal (R)
Lutheran Witness
$ Manna (R)
$ Marian Helper
$ Mature Living
$ Mature Years (R)
$ Men of Integrity (R)
Men of the Cross
Men.AG.org (R)
Message of the Open Bible (R)
$ Messenger of the Sacred Heart
Methodist History
$ Miracles, Healings
MissionWares
$ Montgomery's Journey
Mosaic (R)
($) Mutuality (R)
New Heart (R)

New Identity (R)
$ New Wineskins (R)
Nostalgia (R)
$ Our Sunday Visitor (R)
$ Over the Back Fence (R)
$ Ozarks Senior Living (R)
$ ParentLife
Penned from the Heart (R)
Perspectives (R)
$ Positive Thinking (R)
$ Power for Living (R)
PrayerWorks (R)
$ Presbyterians Today (R)
$ Psychology for Living (R)
$ Pure Inspiration (R)
$ Purpose (R)
Quaker Life (R)
Regent Global Bus. Rev. (R)
Reverent Submissions (R)
Saved Magazine
$ Search
$ Seek (R)
Sharing (R)
$ Significant Living (R)
Single Again Mag. Online (R)
$ Spiritual Life
Spirituality for Today
$ Standard (R)
$ St. Anthony Messenger
$ Storyteller (R)
SW Kansas Faith
Sword and Trumpet
Sword of the Lord (R)
$ Testimony (R)
3V Magazine
$ Today's Pentecostal (R)
$ Together (R)
Trumpeter (R)
$ U.S. Catholic
$ United Church Observer (R)
Urban Kingdom (R)
$ Vibrant Life (R)
Victory Herald (R)
$ Victory in Grace (R)
$ Vision (R)
$ Vista (R)
$ War Cry (R)
$ Way of St. Francis (R)
$ Wesleyan Life (R)
Wisconsin Christian

Children
$ Bread for God's Children (R)
$ Cadet Quest (R)
$ Focus/Clubhouse Jr.
$ Guide (R)
$ JuniorWay
$ Kid Zone
$ Partners (R)
$ Passport (R)
$ Pockets (R)
$ Primary Street

Christian Education/ Library
Congregational Libraries Today
$ Group Magazine
$ Momentum
$ Teachers of Vision (R)
$ Youth & CE Leadership

Daily Devotionals
Penned from the Heart (R)

Missions
$ Evangelical Missions (R)
$ Glad Tidings (R)
wec.go
Women of the Harvest

Pastors/Leaders
$ African-American Pulpit
$ Barefoot (R)
$ Catechumenate
$ Catholic Servant
$ Christian Century (R)
$ Foursquare Leader
$ Interpreter
$ Net Results
$ Preaching Well (R)
$ Proclaim (R)
Pulpit Helps (R)
$ Review for Religious
$ RevWriter Resource
Rick Warren's Ministry
   Toolbox (R)
Technologies for Worship (R)
$ Word & World

Teen/Young Adult
$ Boundless Webzine (R)
$ Credo (R)
$ Devo'zine (R)

$ Direction Student
$ Essential Connection (ec)
G4T Ink (R)
$ Horizon Student
$ Insight (R)
$ J.A.M.
$ Real Faith in Life (R)
$ Sharing the Victory (R)
$ TC Magazine
TeensForJC (R)
$ True Girl
$ Young Salvationist (R)

Women
($) Beyond the Bend (R)
$ Canticle
Christian Woman's Page (R)
Christian Work at Home
   Moms (R)
$ Come to the Fire (R)
Crowned with Silver
Elegance (R)
$ Esprit
Extreme Woman Magazine
First Lady
Handmaidens
Hope for Women
$ Horizons (R)
Inspired Women
$ inSpirit (R)
Jewels of God (R)
$ Journey
Just Between Us (R)
$ Link & Visitor (R)
Lutheran Woman's Quar.
$ MomSense (R)
P31 Woman (R)
$ Pauses . . .
Precious Times (R)
Right to the Heart (R)
Share
Simply Blessed (R)
$ SpiritLed Woman
Together with God (R)
Unrecognized Woman (R)
Virtuous Woman (R)
Woman of Worth (R)
Women of the Cross
Women Today (R)
Women's Ministry

CHURCH GROWTH
Adult/General
($) AGAIN Magazine (R)
$ America
$ Annals of St. Anne
$ Atlantic Catholic
$ Bible Advocate (R)
Bread of Life (R)
$ Catholic Peace Voice (R)
$ Christian Examiner
Christian News NW (R)
Christian Online
Christian Quarterly (R)
$ Christian Standard (R)
$ ChristianWeek (R)
$ Churchmouse Publications (R)
Church of England News
$ City Light News (R)
$ Columbia (R)
$ Culture Wars (R)
Desert Call (R)
$ DisciplesWorld
E-Channels (R)
$ EFCA Today
$ Evangel/IN (R)
Evangelical Advocate (R)
$ Faith & Family
$ Faith Today
$ Gem (R)
$ Good News (R)
$ Good News, Etc. (R)
Gospel Herald
Halo Magazine
$ Holiness Today
$ In His Presence (R)
$ In Touch
$ JC Town Reporter (R)
$ KD Gospel Media
Koinonia
$ Liguorian
$ Live (R)
$ Living Church
$ Lookout
Men.AG.org (R)
Message of the Open Bible (R)
$ Messenger of the Sacred Heart
$ Miracles, Healings
Mosaic (R)
New Identity (R)
$ New Wineskins (R)

$ Our Sunday Visitor (R)
Penned from the Heart (R)
$ Presbyterian Outlook
$ Presbyterians Today (R)
$ Purpose (R)
Quaker Life (R)
$ Seek (R)
$ Significant Living (R)
Spirituality for Today
$ St. Anthony Messenger
Sword and Trumpet
Sword of the Lord (R)
$ Testimony (R)
Trumpeter (R)
$ U.S. Catholic
Urban Kingdom (R)
Victory Herald (R)
$ Victory in Grace (R)
$ Way of St. Francis (R)
$ Wesleyan Life (R)
Wisconsin Christian

Christian Education/ Library
$ Children's Ministry
Congregational Libraries Today
$ Group Magazine
$ Youth & CE Leadership

Missions
East-West Church & Ministry
    Report
$ Evangelical Missions (R)
$ Glad Tidings (R)
Lausanne World Pulse (R)
Missiology
$ PIME World (R)

Music
$ Creator (R)
($) TCP Magazine

Pastors/Leaders
$ African-American Pulpit
$ Catechumenate
$ Catholic Servant
$ Christian Century (R)
Christian Education Jour. (R)
Church Executive
$ Clergy Journal (R)
$ Enrichment Journal (R)
$ Foursquare Leader

$ Growth Points (R)
$ Interpreter
Jour./Amer. Soc./Chur.
    Growth (R)
$ Leadership (R)
$ Let's Worship
$ Lutheran Partners (R)
Ministry in Motion (R)
$ Ministry Today
$ Net Results
$ Outreach (R)
Pulpit Helps (R)
Rick Warren's Ministry
    Toolbox (R)
Sharing the Practice (R)
Technologies for Worship (R)
Theological Digest (R)
$ Worship Leader
$ Your Church (R)

Teen/Young Adult
$ Direction Student
$ Horizon Student
$ J.A.M.
TeensForJC (R)

Women
($) Beyond the Bend (R)
Elegance (R)
Hope for Women
$ inSpirit (R)
Share

CHURCH HISTORY
Adult/General
African Voices (R)
$ America
$ Annals of St. Anne
$ Atlantic Catholic
$ Aujourd'hui Credo (R)
Bread of Life (R)
$ Catholic Digest (R)
$ Catholic Insight
$ Catholic Peace Voice (R)
$ Catholic Sentinel
$ Catholic Yearbook (R)
CBN.com (R)
$ Christian History (R)
Christian Online
$ Christian Renewal (R)
$ Christian Standard (R)

Church of England News
$ City Light News (R)
$ Columbia (R)
$ Company Magazine (R)
Creation Care (R)
$ Cresset
Desert Call (R)
Desert Voice (R)
Divine Ascent
E-Channels (R)
Evangelical Advocate (R)
$ Family Digest (R)
Founders Journal
Friends Journal (R)
Gospel Herald
Halo Magazine
$ Holiness Today
$ Horizons (adult) (R)
$ In Touch
Island Catholic (R)
$ JC Town Reporter (R)
Jour. of Church & State
Koinonia
$ Leben (R)
$ Liguorian
$ Lookout
$ Lutheran Journal (R)
($) Mennonite Historian (R)
$ Messiah Journal
Methodist History
Mosaic (R)
MovieGuide
$ New Wineskins (R)
Nostalgia (R)
$ Our Sunday Visitor (R)
$ Pathway (R)
PrayerWorks (R)
$ Presbyterian Outlook
$ Presbyterians Today (R)
Priscilla Papers
$ Purpose (R)
$ Search
$ Social Justice (R)
Spirituality for Today
$ St. Anthony Messenger
Sword and Trumpet
Sword of the Lord (R)
Trumpeter (R)
$ U.S. Catholic
Urban Kingdom (R)

$ Way of St. Francis (R)
$ Wesleyan Life (R)
Wisconsin Christian

Children
$ Archaeology
$ Guide (R)

Christian Education/ Library
$ Catechist
Catholic Library
$ Group Magazine

Daily Devotionals
Penned from the Heart (R)

Missions
$ Evangelical Missions (R)
$ Glad Tidings (R)
Lausanne World Pulse (R)
Missiology
Op. Reveille Interactive Jour. (R)
Railroad Evangelist (R)

Pastors/Leaders
$ African-American Pulpit
$ Catechumenate
$ Christian Century (R)
$ Clergy Journal (R)
CrossCurrents
$ Enrichment Journal (R)
$ Foursquare Leader
$ Leadership (R)
Lutheran Forum
Pulpit Helps (R)
Sharing the Practice (R)
Theological Digest (R)

Teen/Young Adult
$ Boundless Webzine (R)
$ Essential Connection (ec)
$ J.A.M.
$ Living My Faith
$ Real Faith in Life (R)
TeensForJC (R)
$ Young Christian Writers

Women
($) Beyond the Bend (R)
($) History's Women (R)
$ Horizons (R)
$ Link & Visitor (R)
Share

CHURCH LIFE
Adult/General
($) AGAIN Magazine (R)
$ America
$ Annals of St. Anne
$ Arkansas Catholic (R)
$ Atlantic Catholic
$ Aujourd'hui Credo (R)
$ Australian Catholics (R)
Bread of Life (R)
$ Cathedral Age
$ Catholic Digest (R)
$ Catholic Insight
$ Catholic Sentinel
$ Catholic Yearbook (R)
CBN.com (R)
$ Christian Home &
    School
$ Christian Journal (R)
Christian News NW (R)
Christian Online
$ Christian Standard (R)
$ Christianity Today (R)
$ ChristianWeek (R)
$ Churchmouse
    Publications (R)
Church of England News
$ Columbia (R)
$ Company Magazine (R)
$ Covenant Companion (R)
Creation Care (R)
Desert Call (R)
Desert Voice (R)
$ DisciplesWorld
$ DreamSeeker (R)
E-Channels (R)
$ EFCA Today
Encompass
Eternal Ink (R)
$ Evangel/IN (R)
Evangel/OR (R)
Evangelical Advocate (R)
$ Faith & Family
$ Faith Today
$ FGBC World (R)
$ Gem (R)
$ Good News (R)
$ Good News in Florida (R)
$ Good News, Etc. (R)
Gospel Herald

Halo Magazine
$ Holiness Today
$ Home Times (R)
$ Horizons (adult) (R)
$ In His Presence (R)
In Part
$ In Touch
Island Catholic (R)
$ JC Town Reporter (R)
$ KD Gospel Media
Koinonia
Leaves (R)
$ Light & Life
$ Liguorian
$ Live (R)
$ Living Church
$ Lookout
$ Lutheran Journal (R)
Men.AG.org (R)
($) Mennonite
    Historian (R)
$ Messenger/St. Anthony
Mosaic (R)
($) Mutuality (R)
New Identity (R)
$ New Wineskins (R)
Nostalgia (R)
$ Our Sunday Visitor (R)
$ Pathway (R)
Penned from the Heart (R)
$ Presbyterian Outlook
$ Presbyterians Today (R)
Priscilla Papers
$ Purpose (R)
Reverent Submissions (R)
$ Seek (R)
Spirituality for Today
$ Standard (R)
$ St. Anthony Messenger
Sword of the Lord (R)
$ Testimony (R)
$ Today's Pentecostal (R)
Trumpeter (R)
$ U.S. Catholic
Urban Kingdom (R)
Victory Herald (R)
$ War Cry (R)
$ Way of St. Francis (R)
$ Wesleyan Life (R)
Wisconsin Christian

Children
$ Archaeology
$ Bread for God's Children (R)
$ Primary Street

Christian Education/Library
$ Children's Ministry
$ Group Magazine
$ Youth & CE Leadership

Daily Devotionals
Penned from the Heart (R)

Missions
East-West Church & Ministry
    Report
$ Evangelical Missions (R)
$ Glad Tidings (R)

Pastors/Leaders
$ African-American Pulpit
$ Catholic Servant
$ Christian Century (R)
Church Executive
$ Enrichment Journal (R)
$ Foursquare Leader
$ Interpreter
$ Leadership (R)
$ Ministry
$ Ministry & Liturgy (R)
Ministry in Motion (R)
$ Ministry Today
$ Net Results
$ Parish Liturgy (R)
$ Priest
$ RevWriter Resource
Rick Warren's Ministry
    Toolbox (R)
Sharing the Practice (R)
Technologies for Worship (R)
$ Worship Leader
$ Youthworker

Teen/Young Adult
$ Boundless Webzine (R)
$ Direction Student
$ Horizon Student
$ J.A.M.

Women
($) Beyond the Bend (R)
$ Canticle

Christian Woman's Page (R)
$ Esprit
For Every Woman (R)
Handmaiden (R)
Hope for Women
$ Horizons (R)
$ inSpirit (R)
$ Pauses . . .
Share

CHURCH MANAGEMENT
Adult/General
$ America
$ Atlantic Catholic
Bread of Life (R)
Christian Computing (R)
Christian News NW (R)
Christian Online
$ Christian Standard (R)
$ ChristianWeek (R)
$ Churchmouse Publications (R)
Church of England News
$ Covenant Companion (R)
Creation Care (R)
$ Culture Wars (R)
Disciple's Journal (R)
E-Channels (R)
$ EFCA Today
Evangelical Advocate (R)
$ Faith Today
$ Gem (R)
Gospel Herald
$ Gospel Today (R)
Halo Magazine
$ KD Gospel Media
Koinonia
$ Living Church
$ Lookout
Mosaic (R)
$ Our Sunday Visitor (R)
$ Pathway (R)
$ Presbyterian Outlook
Priscilla Papers
$ Purpose (R)
Regent Global Bus. Rev. (R)
$ St. Anthony Messenger
Sword of the Lord (R)
Trumpeter (R)
$ U.S. Catholic
Wisconsin Christian

Christian Education/Library
$ Children's Ministry
$ Group Magazine
$ Youth & CE Leadership

Daily Devotionals
Penned from the Heart (R)

Missions
$ Evangelical Missions (R)

Music
($) TCP Magazine

Pastors/Leaders
$ African-American Pulpit
$ Catholic Servant
Christian Education Jour. (R)
Church Executive
$ Clergy Journal (R)
$ Enrichment Journal (R)
$ Foursquare Leader
$ Growth Points (R)
$ Interpreter
Jour./Amer. Soc./Chur.
    Growth (R)
$ Leadership (R)
$ Lutheran Partners (R)
$ Ministry
Ministry in Motion (R)
$ Ministry Today
$ Net Results
Pulpit Helps (R)
$ RevWriter Resource
Rick Warren's Ministry
    Toolbox (R)
Sharing the Practice (R)
Technologies for Worship (R)
$ Word & World
$ Worship Leader
$ Your Church (R)

Women
Share
Women's Ministry

CHURCH OUTREACH
Adult/General
($) AGAIN Magazine (R)
$ America
$ Annals of St. Anne
$ Atlantic Catholic

Bread of Life (R)
Breakthrough Intercessor (R)
$ Catholic Sentinel
CBN.com (R)
Christian Family Journal
$ Christian Home & School
Christian News NW (R)
Christian Online
$ Christian Research
$ Christian Standard (R)
$ ChristianWeek (R)
$ Churchmouse
    Publications (R)
Church of England News
$ City Light News (R)
$ Columbia (R)
$ Company Magazine (R)
$ Converge Point (R)
$ Covenant Companion (R)
Creation Care (R)
$ Culture Wars (R)
Desert Call (R)
Desert Voice (R)
$ DisciplesWorld
E-Channels (R)
$ EFCA Today
$ Episcopal Life (R)
Eternal Ink (R)
$ Evangel/IN (R)
Evangel/OR (R)
Evangelical Advocate (R)
$ Faith & Friends (R)
$ Faith Today
$ FGBC World (R)
$ Gem (R)
$ Good News (R)
$ Good News in Florida (R)
$ Good News, Etc. (R)
Gospel Herald
Halo Magazine
Heartland Gatekeeper (R)
$ Holiness Today
$ Home Times (R)
($) HopeKeepers (R)
$ In His Presence (R)
In Part
$ In Touch
$ JC Town Reporter (R)
$ KD Gospel Media
Koinonia

$ Light & Life
$ Living Church
$ Lookout
Men.AG.org (R)
Message of the Open
    Bible (R)
$ Miracles, Healings
$ Montana Catholic
Mosaic (R)
Network
New Identity (R)
$ New Wineskins (R)
$ On Mission
$ Our Sunday Visitor (R)
$ Pathway (R)
$ Presbyterian Outlook
$ Presbyterians Today (R)
$ Priority! (R)
Priscilla Papers
$ Prism
$ Purpose (R)
Quaker Life (R)
$ Search
$ Seek (R)
Spirituality for Today
$ Standard (R)
$ St. Anthony Messenger
Sword of the Lord (R)
$ Testimony (R)
Trumpeter (R)
$ U.S. Catholic
Urban Kingdom (R)
Victory Herald (R)
$ Wesleyan Life (R)
Wisconsin Christian

Children
$ Kid Zone
$ Primary Street

Christian Education/Library
$ Children's Ministry
$ Group Magazine
$ Jour./Adventist Ed. (R)
$ Kids' Ministry Ideas
$ Youth & CE Leadership

Missions
East-West Church & Ministry
    Report
$ Evangelical Missions (R)

$ Glad Tidings (R)
Lausanne World Pulse (R)
Missiology
$ PIME World (R)
Railroad Evangelist (R)

Pastors/Leaders
$ African-American Pulpit
$ Catholic Servant
$ Christian Century (R)
Church Executive
$ Clergy Journal (R)
$ Enrichment Journal (R)
$ Foursquare Leader
$ Growth Points (R)
$ Insight Youth (R)
$ Interpreter
Jour./Amer. Soc./Chur.
    Growth (R)
$ Leadership (R)
$ Let's Worship
$ Lutheran Partners (R)
$ Ministry
Ministry in Motion (R)
$ Ministry Today
$ Net Results
$ Outreach (R)
$ RevWriter Resource
Rick Warren's Ministry
    Toolbox (R)
Sharing the Practice (R)
$ SmallGroups.com (R)
Technologies for Worship (R)
$ Today's Parish
$ Word & World
$ Worship Leader
$ Youthworker

Teen/Young Adult
$ Credo (R)
$ Direction Student
$ Horizon Student
$ Insight (R)
TeensForJC (R)
$ True Girl

Women
Christian Woman's Page (R)
Hope for Women
$ inSpirit (R)
Just Between Us (R)
$ Pauses . . .

Share
Women's Ministry

CHURCH TRADITIONS
Adult/General
($) AGAIN Magazine (R)
$ America
$ Annals of St. Anne
$ Arkansas Catholic (R)
$ Atlantic Catholic
$ Aujourd'hui Credo (R)
Bread of Life (R)
$ Brink Magazine (R)
$ Canada Lutheran (R)
$ Catholic Digest (R)
$ Catholic Yearbook (R)
CBN.com (R)
$ Celebrate Life (R)
$ CGA World (R)
$ Christian Examiner
$ Christian History (R)
Christian Online
$ Christian Research
$ Christian Standard (R)
$ Churchmouse
    Publications (R)
Church of England News
$ Columbia (R)
$ Cresset
Desert Call (R)
$ DisciplesWorld
E-Channels (R)
Encompass
Eternal Ink (R)
Evangelical Advocate (R)
$ Faith & Family
$ Faith Today
$ Family Digest (R)
$ FGBC World (R)
$ Gem (R)
Gospel Herald
$ Gospel Today (R)
Halo Magazine
$ Holiness Today
In Part
$ KD Gospel Media
Koinonia
$ Light & Life
$ Liguorian
$ Living Church

$ Lutheran Journal (R)
($) Mennonite Historian (R)
Mosaic (R)
$ New Wineskins (R)
Nostalgia (R)
$ Our Sunday Visitor (R)
Perspectives (R)
$ Presbyterians Today (R)
Priscilla Papers
$ Purpose (R)
$ Search
Spirituality for Today
$ St. Anthony Messenger
$ Testimony (R)
$ Together (R)
Trumpeter (R)
$ U.S. Catholic
Victory Herald (R)
$ Way of St. Francis (R)
Wisconsin Christian

Children
$ Archaeology

Christian Education/ Library
$ Catechist
$ Children's Ministry
$ Group Magazine

Daily Devotionals
Penned from the Heart (R)

Missions
$ Glad Tidings (R)

Pastors/Leaders
$ African-American Pulpit
$ Barefoot (R)
$ Catechumenate
$ Christian Century (R)
$ Clergy Journal (R)
$ Foursquare Leader
$ Interpreter
$ Leadership (R)
Lutheran Forum
$ Ministry Today
$ Parish Liturgy (R)
Pulpit Helps (R)
$ Reformed Worship (R)
Rick Warren's Ministry
    Toolbox (R)

Sharing the Practice (R)
Theological Digest (R)

Teen/Young Adult
$ J.A.M.
TeensForJC (R)
$ True Girl

Women
$ Canticle
Handmaiden (R)
$ Horizons (R)
$ Pauses . . .
Share

CONTROVERSIAL ISSUES
Adult/General
($) AGAIN Magazine (R)
American Tract (R)
$ Animal Trails (R)
$ Associated Content (R)
$ Aujourd'hui Credo (R)
$ Bible Advocate (R)
Biblical Recorder
$ Brink Magazine (R)
CanadianChristianity.com
$ Catholic Insight
$ Catholic Peace Voice (R)
CBN.com (R)
$ Celebrate Life (R)
Challenge Weekly
$ Christian Courier/Canada (R)
$ Christian Examiner
$ Christian Home & School
Christian Media (R)
Christian Online
$ Christian Renewal (R)
$ Christian Response (R)
$ Christian Standard (R)
$ Christianity Today (R)
$ Christianity Today Movies (R)
$ ChristianWeek (R)
$ Churchmouse Publications (R)
Church of England News
$ Citizen USA
$ City Light News (R)
$ Columbia (R)
Creation Care (R)
$ Creative Nonfiction
$ Culture Wars (R)
Desert Christian

Desert Voice (R)
$ DisciplesWorld
$ DreamSeeker (R)
E-Channels (R)
$ EFCA Today
Encompass
$ Enfoque a la Familia
Eternal Ink (R)
$ Eureka Street
Evangelical Advocate (R)
Evangelical Times
$ Faith Today
Faithwebbin (R)
$ Good News (R)
$ Good News in Florida (R)
Good News Today
Good News!
$ Good News, Etc. (R)
Gospel Herald
$ Gospel Today (R)
Halo Magazine
Heartland Gatekeeper (R)
$ Home Times (R)
$ Homeschooling Today (R)
($) Impact Magazine (R)
$ In Touch
$ Indian Life (R)
$ Interim (R)
$ KD Gospel Media
$ Light & Life
$ Live (R)
$ Living Church
$ Lookout
Maine Family Policy (R)
$ Manna (R)
MovieGuide
($) Mutuality (R)
New Identity (R)
$ New Wineskins (R)
$ Now What? (R)
$ Our Sunday Visitor (R)
Perspectives (R)
$ Prairie Messenger (R)
Priscilla Papers
$ Prism
$ Psychology for Living (R)
$ Purpose (R)
$ Search
Single Again Mag. Online (R)
$ Social Justice (R)

$ St. Anthony Messenger
Sword of the Lord (R)
3V Magazine
Tri-State Voice
Trumpeter (R)
$ U.S. Catholic
Urban Kingdom (R)
Victory Herald (R)
$ War Cry (R)
$ Way of St. Francis (R)
Wisconsin Christian
$ World & I (R)
Xavier Review

Children
$ New Moon Girls (R)
Skipping Stones

Christian Education/ Library
Catholic Library
$ Group Magazine
$ Teachers of Vision (R)
$ Today's Catholic Teacher (R)

Missions
East-West Church & Ministry Report
$ Evangelical Missions (R)
Intl. Jour./Frontier Missions (R)
Op. Reveille Interactive
    Jour. (R)

Music
$ Christian Music Today (R)
Hymn

Pastors/Leaders
$ African-American Pulpit
$ Christian Century (R)
Church Executive
$ Clergy Journal (R)
CrossCurrents
$ Enrichment Journal (R)
$ InSite (R)
$ Interpreter
Jour./Pastoral Care
$ Let's Worship
$ Ministry & Liturgy (R)
$ Ministry Today
$ Outreach (R)
Pulpit Helps (R)
$ Word & World
$ Worship Leader

Teen/Young Adult
$ Boundless Webzine (R)
Focus/Dare 2 Dig Deeper
$ J.A.M.
$ Sharing the Victory (R)
$ TC Magazine
TeensForJC (R)
$ True Girl
$ Young Salvationist (R)

Women
($) Beyond the Bend (R)
$ Canticle
$ Esprit
Extreme Woman Magazine
For Every Woman (R)
$ Heart & Soul
Hope for Women
$ inSpirit (R)
Precious Times (R)
Unrecognized Woman (R)

Writers
Areopagus

CRAFTS
Adult/General
$ Associated Content (R)
$ Atlantic Catholic
$ CGA World (R)
Christian Online
$ Churchmouse Publications (R)
$ Faith & Family
Gospel Herald
$ Imagine
$ Indian Life (R)
$ Living (R)
$ Mature Living
$ ParentLife
Sword of the Lord (R)
Urban Kingdom (R)
$ World & I (R)

Children
$ Adventures
$ American Girl (R)
$ Bread for God's Children (R)
$ Cadet Quest (R)
$ Celebrate
$ Focus/Clubhouse
$ Focus/Clubhouse Jr.
$ Junior Companion (R)

$ JuniorWay
$ Kid Zone
$ Passport (R)
$ Pockets (R)
$ Preschool Playhouse (child)
$ SHINE brightly (R)
$ Sparkle (R)
$ Story Mates (R)

*Christian Education/
Library*
$ Catechist
$ Children's Ministry
$ Youth & CE Leadership

Missions
$ Glad Tidings (R)

Pastors/Leaders
$ Interpreter

Teen/Young Adult
$ J.A.M.
TeensForJC (R)
$ True Girl

Women
Christian Woman's Page (R)
Christian Work at Home
    Moms (R)
$ MomSense (R)
P31 Woman (R)
Virtuous Woman (R)
Woman of Worth (R)
Women's Ministry

CREATION SCIENCE
Adult/General
Answers Magazine
$ Bible Advocate (R)
CBN.com (R)
$ Christian Courier/
    Canada (R)
$ Christian Examiner
Christian Observer
$ Christian Renewal (R)
$ Christian Research
$ Citizen USA
$ Creation Illust. (R)
Desert Voice (R)
$ Faith Today
$ Good News in Florida (R)
Gospel Herald

$ Haruah (R)
$ Home Times (R)
$ Homeschooling Today (R)
$ Horizons (adult) (R)
$ Indian Life (R)
$ JC Town Reporter (R)
$ Light & Life
$ Live (R)
$ Living (R)
$ Lookout
$ Pathway (R)
Perspectives/Science &
    Chr. Faith
$ Salvo
$ St. Anthony Messenger
Sword and Trumpet
Sword of the Lord (R)
Trumpeter (R)
$ War Cry (R)
$ Way of St. Francis (R)
Wisconsin Christian

Children
$ Guide (R)
$ Nature Friend (R)
$ Sparkle (R)

*Christian Education/
Library*
$ Jour./Adventist Ed. (R)

Pastors/Leaders
CrossCurrents
Pulpit Helps (R)

Teen/Young Adult
$ Boundless Webzine (R)
$ J.A.M.
$ Real Faith in Life (R)
$ Young Christian Writers
$ Young Salvationist (R)

CULTS/OCCULT
Adult/General
American Tract (R)
$ Annals of St. Anne
CBN.com (R)
$ Christian Examiner
$ Christian Renewal (R)
$ Christian Research
$ Creative Nonfiction
$ Culture Wars (R)

Desert Voice (R)
$ Faith Today
Gospel Herald
Halo Magazine
$ In His Presence (R)
$ In Touch
$ JC Town Reporter (R)
$ Light & Life
$ Lookout
Maine Family Policy (R)
New Heart (R)
$ Now What? (R)
SCP Journal
Sword of the Lord (R)
Trumpeter (R)
Wisconsin Christian

Missions
East-West Church & Ministry
    Report
Intl. Jour./Frontier
    Missions (R)

Pastors/Leaders
$ Ministry Today
$ Word & World

Teen/Young Adult
$ Boundless Webzine (R)
$ Real Faith in Life (R)
$ TC Magazine
TeensForJC (R)
$ Young Salvationist (R)

Women
For Every Woman (R)
$ Journey

CURRENT/SOCIAL ISSUES
Adult/General
American Tract (R)
$ Anglican Journal
$ Apocalypse Chronicles (R)
$ Arlington Catholic
$ Associated Content (R)
$ Aujourd'hui Credo (R)
$ B.C. Catholic (R)
$ Bible Advocate (R)
Biblical Recorder
Breakthrough Intercessor (R)
$ Brink Magazine (R)

Brink Online
CanadianChristianity.com
$ Catholic Insight
$ Catholic New York
$ Catholic Peace Voice (R)
CBN.com (R)
Challenge Weekly
$ Christian Courier/Canada (R)
Christian Courier/WI (R)
$ Christian Examiner
$ Christian Home & School
$ Christian Journal (R)
Christian Observer
Christian Online
Christian Outlook
Christian Ranchman
$ Christian Renewal (R)
$ Christian Research
$ Christian Standard (R)
$ Christianity Today (R)
$ Christianity Today Movies (R)
$ ChristianWeek (R)
Church of England News
$ Citizen USA
$ City Light News (R)
$ Columbia (R)
$ Converge Point (R)
$ Covenant Companion (R)
Creation Care (R)
$ Creative Nonfiction
$ Cresset
$ Culture Wars (R)
Desert Call (R)
Desert Christian
$ Direction
$ Disaster News
$ DisciplesWorld
$ DreamSeeker (R)
E-Channels (R)
Encompass
$ Enfoque a la Familia
$ Eureka Street
Evangel/OR (R)
Evangelical Advocate (R)
Evangelical Times
$ Faith Today
Faithwebbin (R)
$ Focus on the Family
$ Foursquare Leader
Friends Journal (R)

$ Gem (R)
$ Good News (R)
Good News Connection
$ Good News in Florida (R)
Good News Journal (R)
Good News Today
$ Good News, Etc. (R)
Gospel Herald
Halo Magazine
Heartland Gatekeeper (R)
HEARTLIGHT Internet (R)
$ Home Times (R)
$ Homeschooling Today (R)
$ In Touch
$ Indian Life (R)
Island Catholic (R)
$ JC Town Reporter (R)
Jour. of Church & State
$ KD Gospel Media
$ Liberty
LifeSiteNews
$ Light & Life
$ Liguorian
$ Live (R)
$ Living (R)
$ Lookout
Maine Family Policy (R)
$ Manna (R)
$ Marian Helper
$ Men of Integrity (R)
Men.AG.org (R)
$ MESSAGE
$ Messenger/St. Anthony
Messianic Perspectives (R)
$ Montgomery's Journey
More Excellent Way
Mosaic (R)
MovieGuide
($) Mutuality (R)
New Christian Voices
New Heart (R)
New Identity (R)
$ New Wineskins (R)
$ Now What? (R)
$ Our Sunday Visitor (R)
$ Ozarks Senior Living (R)
$ ParentLife
$ Pathway (R)
Perspectives (R)
$ Prairie Messenger (R)

PrayerWorks (R)
$ Priority! (R)
Priscilla Papers
$ Prism
$ Psychology for Living (R)
SCP Journal
$ Seek (R)
Single Again Mag. Online (R)
$ Social Justice (R)
$ Special Living (R)
$ St. Anthony Messenger
$ Storyteller (R)
Sword of the Lord (R)
3V Magazine
$ Together (R)
Tri-State Voice
Trumpeter (R)
$ U.S. Catholic
Urban Kingdom (R)
$ War Cry (R)
$ Way of St. Francis (R)
West Wind Review
Wisconsin Christian
$ World & I (R)
$ Written

Children
$ Bread for God's Children (R)
$ JuniorWay
$ New Moon Girls (R)
$ SHINE brightly (R)
Skipping Stones
$ Sparkle (R)

Christian Education/ Library
Catholic Library
$ Children's Ministry

Daily Devotionals
Penned from the Heart (R)

Missions
East-West Church & Ministry
    Report
$ Glad Tidings (R)
$ New World Outlook
$ One
Op. Reveille Interactive
    Jour. (R)
$ PIME World (R)
Women of the Harvest

Music
$ Christian Music Today (R)

Pastors/Leaders
$ African-American Pulpit
$ Barefoot (R)
$ Catholic Servant
$ Christian Century (R)
$ Enrichment Journal (R)
$ InSite (R)
$ Interpreter
$ Leadership (R)
Lutheran Forum
$ Lutheran Partners (R)
$ Ministry & Liturgy (R)
$ Ministry Today
$ Outreach (R)
Pulpit Helps (R)
$ Word & World

Teen/Young Adult
$ Boundless Webzine (R)
$ Credo (R)
$ Devo'zine (R)
$ Direction Student
Exodus Magazine
Focus/Dare 2 Dig Deeper
$ Horizon Student
$ Insight (R)
$ J.A.M.
$ Listen (R)
$ Risen
$ Sharing the Victory (R)
$ TC Magazine
TeensForJC (R)
$ True Girl
$ Young Adult Today
$ Young Christian Writers
$ Young Salvationist (R)

Women
$ At the Center (R)
($) Beyond the Bend (R)
Christian Work at Home
    Moms (R)
$ Esprit
Extreme Woman Magazine
For Every Woman (R)
$ FullFill
Handmaiden (R)
$ Heart & Soul
Hope for Women

$ Horizons (R)
$ inSpirit (R)
$ Link & Visitor (R)
$ SpiritLed Woman
Unrecognized Woman (R)
Virtuous Woman (R)
Women Today (R)

Writers
Areopagus

DEATH/DYING
Adult/General
($) AGAIN Magazine (R)
$ America
American Tract (R)
$ Arlington Catholic
$ Associated Content (R)
$ Atlantic Catholic
$ Aujourd'hui Credo (R)
$ Bible Advocate (R)
Bread of Life (R)
$ Brink Magazine (R)
CBN.com (R)
$ Celebrate Life (R)
$ Chicken Soup Books (R)
Christian Online
Christian Quarterly (R)
Christian Ranchman
$ Christianity Today (R)
$ ChristianWeek (R)
$ Churchmouse Publications (R)
$ Citizen USA
$ Columbia (R)
$ Converge Point (R)
$ Creative Nonfiction
Desert Call (R)
E-Channels (R)
Evangelical Advocate (R)
$ Faith Today
Faithwebbin (R)
$ Focus on the Family
$ Gem (R)
$ Good News, Etc. (R)
$ Guideposts (R)
Halo Magazine
HEARTLIGHT Internet (R)
$ Homeschooling Today (R)
($) HopeKeepers (R)
$ Horizons (adult) (R)

$ In His Presence (R)
$ In Touch
$ Indian Life (R)
Island Catholic (R)
$ JC Town Reporter (R)
$ KD Gospel Media
$ Light & Life
$ Liguorian
$ Live (R)
$ Lookout
$ Men of Integrity (R)
$ Messenger/Sacred Heart
New Heart (R)
$ New Wineskins (R)
$ Now What? (R)
$ Our Sunday Visitor (R)
$ ParentLife
Perspectives/Science &
     Chr. Faith
$ Positive Thinking (R)
$ Prairie Messenger (R)
PrayerWorks (R)
$ Presbyterian Outlook
$ Presbyterians Today (R)
$ Psychology for Living (R)
$ Seek (R)
Single Again Mag. Online (R)
$ Social Justice (R)
Spirituality for Today
$ Standard (R)
$ St. Anthony Messenger
$ Storyteller (R)
Sword of the Lord (R)
$ Testimony (R)
Trumpeter (R)
$ U.S. Catholic
Urban Kingdom (R)
$ War Cry (R)
$ Way of St. Francis (R)
Wisconsin Christian

Children
$ New Moon Girls (R)
Skipping Stones
$ Sparkle (R)

Daily Devotionals
Penned from the Heart (R)

Missions
$ Glad Tidings (R)

Pastors/Leaders
$ Catholic Servant
$ Christian Century (R)
$ Clergy Journal (R)
$ Enrichment Journal (R)
$ InSite (R)
$ Interpreter
Jour./Pastoral Care
$ Leadership (R)
$ Lutheran Partners (R)
$ RevWriter Resource
Sharing the Practice (R)

Teen/Young Adult
$ Boundless Webzine (R)
$ J.A.M.
TeensForJC (R)
$ True Girl

Women
($) Beyond the Bend (R)
$ Canticle
For Every Woman (R)
Hope for Women
$ inSpirit (R)
$ Pauses . . .
Precious Times (R)
Virtuous Woman (R)
Woman of Worth (R)
Women Today (R)

DEVOTIONALS/ MEDITATIONS
Adult/General
$ Alive Now (R)
$ America
$ Annals of St. Anne
$ Arlington Catholic
$ Aujourd'hui Credo (R)
$ Australian Catholics (R)
Breakthrough Intercessor (R)
$ Catholic Peace Voice (R)
CBN.com (R)
$ Chicken Soup Books (R)
$ Christian Home & School
$ Christian Journal (R)
Christian Online
Christian Quarterly (R)
Christian Ranchman
$ Churchmouse
     Publications (R)

$ Columbia (R)
$ Covenant Companion (R)
Creation Care (R)
crosshome.com
Desert Call (R)
Divine Ascent
Eternal Ink (R)
$ Evangel/IN (R)
Evangelical Advocate (R)
Evangelical Times
$ Faith & Family
$ Faith & Friends (R)
Faithwebbin (R)
$ Family Digest (R)
Founders Journal
$ Foursquare Leader
$ Gem (R)
$ Good News (R)
Good News Journal (R)
Halo Magazine
$ Haruah (R)
HEARTLIGHT Internet (R)
($) HopeKeepers (R)
$ In His Presence (R)
$ In Touch
$ KD Gospel Media
Keys to Living (R)
Koinonia
Leaves (R)
LifeTimes Catholic
$ Liguorian
$ Live (R)
$ Living Church
$ Lutheran Digest (R)
$ Mature Living
$ Messenger/Sacred Heart
$ Messenger/St. Anthony
Mosaic (R)
($) Mutuality (R)
New Christian Voices
New Heart (R)
$ New Wineskins (R)
$ ParentLife
Penned from the Heart (R)
Perspectives (R)
$ Positive Thinking (R)
PrayerWorks (R)
$ Pure Inspiration (R)
Quaker Life (R)
Radix Magazine

Reverent Submissions (R)
$ Sports Spectrum
$ Standard (R)
$ St. Anthony Messenger
Sword of the Lord (R)
$ Today's Pentecostal (R)
Trumpeter (R)
$ U.S. Catholic
Urban Kingdom (R)
Victory Herald (R)
$ Victory in Grace (R)
$ Vision (R)
$ War Cry (R)
$ Way of St. Francis (R)
$ Weavings (R)
$ Wesleyan Life (R)
$ Written

Children
$ Keys for Kids (R)
$ Passport (R)
$ Pockets (R)
$ Sparkle (R)

Christian Education/ Library
Congregational Libraries
    Today
$ Group Magazine

Daily Devotionals
$ Anchor Devotional
ChristianDevotions.us
Daily Dev. for Deaf
$ Devotions
$ Forward Day by Day
Fruit of the Vine
$ Light from the Word
$ My Daily Visitor
Our Daily Journey
Penned from the Heart (R)
$ Quiet Hour
$ Rejoice!
$ Secret Place
$ These Days
$ Upper Room
$ Word in Season

Missions
$ Glad Tidings (R)
$ One
Women of the Harvest

Pastors/Leaders
$ Catholic Servant
$ Emmanuel
$ Ministry Today
$ RevWriter Resource

Teen/Young Adult
$ Devo'zine (R)
G4T Ink (R)
$ J.A.M.
$ Real Faith in Life (R)
$ Take Five Plus
TeensForJC (R)
$ True Girl
$ Young Adult Today

Women
($) Beyond the Bend (R)
$ Canticle
Christian Woman's Page (R)
Christian Work at Home
    Moms (R)
$ Dabbling Mum (R)
Elegance (R)
Extreme Woman Magazine
Handmaidens
$ Horizons (R)
$ InspiredMoms (R)
Jewels of God (R)
$ Journey
$ MD Women of Worship
$ Melody of the Heart
$ Pauses . . .
Precious Times (R)
Simply Blessed (R)
$ SpiritLed Woman
Together with God (R)
Unrecognized Woman (R)
Virtuous Woman (R)
Woman of Worth (R)

Writers
ChristianWriters.com
$ Cross & Quill (R)
$ Fellowscript (R)
$ Shades of Romance (R)
$ Spirit-Led Writer (R)

DISCIPLESHIP
Adult/General
$ Alive Now (R)
$ Arlington Catholic

$ Aujourd'hui Credo (R)
$ Bible Advocate (R)
Breakthrough Intercessor (R)
$ Canada Lutheran (R)
CBN.com (R)
$ Christian Journal (R)
Christian Motorsports
Christian Online
Christian Ranchman
$ Christian Research
$ Christian Standard (R)
$ ChristianWeek (R)
$ Churchmouse
    Publications (R)
Church of England News
$ Columbia (R)
$ Covenant Companion (R)
$ Decision
Desert Call (R)
$ DisciplesWorld
$ EFCA Today
Eternal Ink (R)
$ Evangel/IN (R)
Evangelical Advocate (R)
$ Faith & Family
$ Faith & Friends (R)
$ Faith Today
Faithwebbin (R)
$ Family Digest (R)
$ Gem (R)
$ Good News (R)
Good News Journal (R)
Gospel Herald
Halo Magazine
HEARTLIGHT Internet (R)
Highway News (R)
$ Homeschooling Today (R)
$ Horizons (adult) (R)
$ In His Presence (R)
$ In Touch
$ JC Town Reporter (R)
$ KD Gospel Media
$ Light & Life
$ Liguorian
$ Live (R)
$ Lookout
Maine Family Policy (R)
$ Manna (R)
$ Men of Integrity (R)
Men of the Cross

Men.AG.org (R)
MissionWares
Mosaic (R)
MovieGuide
$ New Wineskins (R)
($) NBR E-Magazine (R)
$ Pathway (R)
Penned from the Heart (R)
Perspectives (R)
Regent Global Bus. Rev. (R)
Reverent Submissions (R)
$ Seek (R)
$ Significant Living (R)
$ Standard (R)
$ St. Anthony Messenger
$ Stewardship (R)
Sword of the Lord (R)
Trumpeter (R)
$ U.S. Catholic
Urban Kingdom (R)
Victory Herald (R)
$ War Cry (R)
$ Way of St. Francis (R)
$ Wesleyan Life (R)
Wisconsin Christian

Children
$ Bread for God's Children (R)
$ Primary Street
$ SHINE brightly (R)
$ Sparkle (R)

Christian Education/ Library
$ Group Magazine
$ Momentum
$ Youth & CE Leadership

Daily Devotionals
Penned from the Heart (R)

Missions
$ Glad Tidings (R)
Lausanne World Pulse (R)
$ PIME World (R)

Pastors/Leaders
$ African-American Pulpit
$ Barefoot (R)
$ Catholic Servant
$ Christian Century (R)
Christian Education Jour. (R)
$ Enrichment Journal (R)

$ Growth Points (R)
$ InSite (R)
$ Interpreter
Jour./Amer. Soc./Chur.
    Growth (R)
$ Leadership (R)
$ Lutheran Partners (R)
Ministry in Motion (R)
$ Net Results
$ Proclaim (R)
Pulpit Helps (R)
$ RevWriter Resource
$ SmallGroups.com (R)
Theological Digest (R)
$ Word & World

Teen/Young Adult
$ Boundless Webzine (R)
$ Credo (R)
$ Devo'zine (R)
$ Direction Student
$ Horizon Student
$ Insight (R)
$ J.A.M.
$ Real Faith in Life (R)
$ TC Magazine
TeensForJC (R)
$ Young Salvationist (R)

Women
($) Beyond the Bend (R)
Christian Woman's Page (R)
Christian Women Today (R)
Elegance (R)
$ Horizons (R)
$ inSpirit (R)
Jewels of God (R)
$ Journey
Just Between Us (R)
$ Link & Visitor (R)
P31 Woman (R)
Precious Times (R)
Virtuous Woman (R)
Woman of Worth (R)
Women of the Cross

DIVORCE
Adult/General
American Tract (R)
$ Angels on Earth
$ Arlington Catholic

$ Associated Content (R)
$ Aujourd'hui Credo (R)
$ Bible Advocate (R)
$ Catholic Digest (R)
CBN.com (R)
$ Christian Examiner
Christian Motorsports
Christian Online
Christian Quarterly (R)
Christian Ranchman
$ ChristianWeek (R)
$ Churchmouse Publications (R)
Church of England News
$ Columbia (R)
$ Culture Wars (R)
Evangelical Advocate (R)
$ Faith Today
Faithwebbin (R)
$ Family Smart E-tips (R)
$ Focus on the Family
$ Gem (R)
$ Good News, Etc. (R)
Gospel Herald
$ Guideposts (R)
Halo Magazine
$ Home Times (R)
$ Homeschooling Today (R)
($) HopeKeepers (R)
$ In His Presence (R)
$ In Touch
Island Catholic (R)
$ JC Town Reporter (R)
$ KD Gospel Media
$ Light & Life
$ Live (R)
$ Living (R)
$ Living Church
$ Lookout
$ Manna (R)
New Heart (R)
$ New Wineskins (R)
$ Now What? (R)
$ Our Sunday Visitor (R)
$ ParentLife
Perspectives (R)
$ Positive Thinking (R)
Priscilla Papers
$ Psychology for Living (R)
$ Seek (R)
Single Again Mag. Online (R)

$ St. Anthony Messenger
$ Storyteller (R)
Trumpeter (R)
Urban Kingdom (R)
$ War Cry (R)
Wisconsin Christian
$ World & I (R)

Missions
$ Glad Tidings (R)

Pastors/Leaders
$ Christian Century (R)
$ Interpreter
$ Lutheran Partners (R)
$ Word & World

Teen/Young Adult
$ Direction Student
$ Horizon Student
$ J.A.M.
$ Young Salvationist (R)

Women
($) Beyond the Bend (R)
For Every Woman (R)
Hope for Women
$ InspiredMoms (R)
$ inSpirit (R)
$ Journey
Precious Times (R)
Unrecognized Woman (R)
Women Today (R)

DOCTRINAL
Adult/General
($) AGAIN Magazine (R)
$ Anglican Journal
$ Atlantic Catholic
$ Aujourd'hui Credo (R)
$ B.C. Catholic (R)
Bread of Life (R)
$ Catholic Insight
CBN.com (R)
Christian Media (R)
Christian Online
$ Christian Research
$ Christian Standard (R)
Creation Care (R)
$ Culture Wars (R)
E-Channels (R)
Evangelical Advocate (R)

Evangelical Times
$ Faith & Family
$ Faith Today
Founders Journal
Gospel Herald
Halo Magazine
$ Homeschooling Today (R)
$ Horizons (adult) (R)
($) Impact Magazine (R)
$ In Touch
$ JC Town Reporter (R)
$ KD Gospel Media
Koinonia
MovieGuide
$ New Wineskins (R)
$ Our Sunday Visitor (R)
$ Pathway (R)
Perspectives (R)
Priscilla Papers
$ Social Justice (R)
$ St. Anthony Messenger
Sword and Trumpet
Sword of the Lord (R)
Trumpeter (R)
$ U.S. Catholic
Urban Kingdom (R)
$ Way of St. Francis (R)
$ Wesleyan Life (R)
Wisconsin Christian

Christian Education/
Library
Catholic Library

Missions
Intl. Jour./Frontier
   Missions (R)
Missiology

Pastors/Leaders
$ Catholic Servant
$ Interpreter
Lutheran Forum
$ Lutheran Partners (R)
Sewanee Theo. Review
Sharing the Practice (R)
Theological Digest (R)
$ Word & World
$ Worship Leader

Teen/Young Adult
$ Direction Student

$ Essential Connection (ec)
$ Horizon Student
$ J.A.M.
$ Real Faith in Life (R)

DVD REVIEWS
Adult/General
$ Christian Journal (R)
$ Churchmouse
   Publications (R)
$ City Light News (R)
Creation Care (R)
$ Eureka Street
Faithwebbin (R)
Gospel Herald
$ Home Times (R)
$ Imagine
Island Catholic (R)
$ JC Town Reporter (R)
$ Our Sunday Visitor (R)
Quaker Life (R)

Missions
East-West Church & Ministry
   Report
$ Glad Tidings (R)

Teen/Young Adult
Exodus Magazine

Women
Christian Work at Home
   Moms (R)
$ Dabbling Mum (R)
For Every Woman (R)

ECONOMICS
Adult/General
$ America
$ Associated Content (R)
$ Aujourd'hui Credo (R)
Brink Online
$ Catholic Peace Voice (R)
$ CBA Retailers
CBN.com (R)
Christian Business
Christian Media (R)
Christian Motorsports
Christian Online
Christian Ranchman
$ Christian Renewal (R)
$ Christian Retailing

$ ChristianWeek (R)
$ Churchmouse Publications (R)
$ City Light News (R)
$ Creative Nonfiction
$ Culture Wars (R)
Evangelical Advocate (R)
$ Faith Today
Faithwebbin (R)
Good News Journal (R)
Gospel Herald
Halo Magazine
$ Home Times (R)
$ Homeschooling Today (R)
$ In Touch
Island Catholic (R)
$ JC Town Reporter (R)
$ Light & Life
$ Live (R)
$ Living (R)
Men.AG.org (R)
MovieGuide
($) NBR E-Magazine (R)
$ Our Sunday Visitor (R)
Perspectives (R)
$ Positive Thinking (R)
Regent Global Bus. Rev. (R)
$ Social Justice (R)
$ St. Anthony Messenger
Trumpeter (R)
Urban Kingdom (R)
Wisconsin Christian
$ World & I (R)

Pastors/Leaders
$ Today's Parish
$ Word & World

Teen/Young Adult
$ Boundless Webzine (R)
$ J.A.M.
TeensForJC (R)

Women
Empowering Everyday Women
Live Magazine
Unrecognized Woman (R)

ENCOURAGEMENT
Adult/General
Ambassador
$ Bible Advocate (R)

Breakthrough Intercessor (R)
$ Bridal Guides (R)
$ Brink Magazine (R)
$ Catholic Digest (R)
$ Catholic Forester (R)
CBN.com (R)
Central FL Episcopalian
Christian Family Journal
$ Christian Home & School
$ Christian Journal (R)
Christian Online
Christian Quarterly (R)
Christian Ranchman
$ Christian Standard (R)
$ Churchmouse
   Publications (R)
$ City Light News (R)
Connections Ldrship/MOPS
$ Converge Point (R)
E-Channels (R)
$ Evangel/IN (R)
Evangelical Advocate (R)
$ Faith & Family
$ Faith & Friends (R)
$ Faith Today
Faithwebbin (R)
$ Family Digest (R)
$ Focus on the Family
$ Gems of Truth (R)
Good News Journal (R)
Gospel Herald
Halo Magazine
$ Home Times (R)
$ Homeschooling Today (R)
($) HopeKeepers (R)
$ Horizons (adult) (R)
$ In His Presence (R)
$ In Touch
$ Indian Life (R)
$ JC Town Reporter (R)
$ KD Gospel Media
Keys to Living (R)
Leaves (R)
$ Lifeglow (R)
$ Light & Life
$ Liguorian
$ Live (R)
$ Lookout
$ Lutheran Digest (R)
$ Manna (R)

$ Mature Living
Men of the Cross
MissionWares
$ Montgomery's Journey
Mosaic (R)
($) Mutuality (R)
New Heart (R)
New Identity (R)
$ New Wineskins (R)
$ Ozarks Senior Living (R)
$ ParentLife
Pegasus Review (R)
Penned from the Heart (R)
PrayerWorks (R)
$ Pure Inspiration (R)
Regent Global Bus. Rev. (R)
Reverent Submissions (R)
$ Seek (R)
$ Significant Living (R)
$ Standard (R)
$ Storyteller (R)
Sword of the Lord (R)
$ Together (R)
Urban Kingdom (R)
Victory Herald (R)
$ Victory in Grace (R)
$ Vision (R)
$ Vista (R)
$ Way of St. Francis (R)
$ Wesleyan Life (R)

Children
$ Bread for God's Children (R)
$ Cadet Quest (R)
$ SHINE brightly (R)
Skipping Stones
$ Sparkle (R)

Christian Education/ Library
$ Teachers of Vision (R)
$ Youth & CE Leadership

Daily Devotionals
Penned from the Heart (R)

Missions
$ Glad Tidings (R)

Pastors/Leaders
Ministry in Motion (R)
Pulpit Helps (R)

Teen/Young Adult
$ Boundless Webzine (R)
$ Direction Student
G4T Ink (R)
$ Horizon Student
$ Insight (R)
$ J.A.M.
$ Young Salvationist (R)

Women
$ Canticle
$ Come to the Fire (R)
Crowned with Silver
Elegance (R)
Empowering Everyday Women
Extreme Woman Magazine
First Lady
For Every Woman (R)
Hope for Women
$ inSpirit (R)
Jewels of God (R)
$ Journey
Just Between Us (R)
P31 Woman (R)
$ Pauses . . .
Precious Times (R)
Simply Blessed (R)
Together with God (R)
Unrecognized Woman (R)
Virtuous Woman (R)
Woman of Worth (R)
Women of the Cross

Writers
$ Christian Communicator (R)
$ Cross & Quill (R)
$ Fellowscript (R)

ENVIRONMENTAL ISSUES
Adult/General
$ America
$ Anglican Journal
$ Animal Trails (R)
$ Associated Content (R)
$ Aujourd'hui Credo (R)
$ Bible Advocate (R)
$ Brink Magazine (R)
$ Cathedral Age
$ Catholic Peace Voice (R)
Christian Online

Christian Outlook
$ ChristianWeek (R)
$ Churchmouse
   Publications (R)
$ Common Ground (R)
$ Covenant Companion (R)
Creation Care (R)
$ Creation Illust. (R)
$ Creative Nonfiction
Desert Call (R)
$ Disaster News
Evangelical Advocate (R)
$ Faith Today
Gospel Herald
Halo Magazine
($) HopeKeepers (R)
$ In Touch
$ JC Town Reporter (R)
$ KD Gospel Media
$ Light & Life
$ Liguorian
$ Living (R)
$ Living Church
$ Lookout
New Identity (R)
$ New Wineskins (R)
$ Our Sunday Visitor (R)
$ ParentLife
Pegasus Review (R)
Perspectives (R)
Perspectives/Science &
   Chr. Faith
$ Prairie Messenger (R)
$ Presbyterian Outlook
$ Prism
Ruminate
$ Search
$ Seek (R)
$ St. Anthony Messenger
Trumpeter (R)
Urban Kingdom (R)
$ War Cry (R)
$ Way of St. Francis (R)
Wisconsin Christian
$ World & I (R)

Children
$ New Moon Girls (R)
$ Pockets (R)
$ SHINE brightly (R)

Skipping Stones
$ Sparkle (R)

Christian Education/ Library
Jour./Research on Christian Ed.

Missions
$ Glad Tidings (R)

Pastors/Leaders
$ Christian Century (R)
$ InSite (R)
$ Interpreter
$ RevWriter Resource
$ Word & World

Teen/Young Adult
$ Boundless Webzine (R)
$ Devo'zine (R)
$ J.A.M.
$ TC Magazine
TeensForJC (R)
$ Young Salvationist (R)

Women
$ Esprit
$ Horizons (R)
$ inSpirit (R)
Share
Unrecognized Woman (R)

ESSAYS
Adult/General
African Voices (R)
$ America
$ Annals of St. Anne
$ Arlington Catholic
$ Associated Content (R)
Books & Culture
Breakthrough Intercessor (R)
$ Cathedral Age
$ Catholic Digest (R)
$ Catholic Peace Voice (R)
$ Chicken Soup Books (R)
$ Christian Courier/Canada (R)
Christian Online
$ Christian Renewal (R)
$ Christianity Today (R)
$ Churchmouse
   Publications (R)
$ Columbia (R)

$ Company Magazine (R)
$ Covenant Companion (R)
Creation Care (R)
$ Creative Nonfiction
$ Culture Wars (R)
$ Direction
$ DisciplesWorld
$ Faith Today
Faithwebbin (R)
$ Gem (R)
Gospel Herald
Halo Magazine
Heartland Gatekeeper (R)
($) HopeKeepers (R)
($) Impact Magazine (R)
$ In Touch
Island Catholic (R)
$ JC Town Reporter (R)
Koinonia
$ Lifeglow (R)
$ Liguorian
$ Lutheran Digest (R)
Maine Family Policy (R)
$ MindFlights (R)
($) Mutuality (R)
New Christian Voices
$ New Wineskins (R)
Nostalgia (R)
$ Our Sunday Visitor (R)
$ Ozarks Senior Living (R)
Penwood Review
$ Precepts for Living
$ Prism
$ Pure Inspiration (R)
Reverent Submissions (R)
$ Rose & Thorn
Ruminate
$ Search
$ Seek (R)
$ Spiritual Life
Spirituality for Today
$ St. Anthony Messenger
$ Storyteller (R)
$ This I Believe
Tiferet (R)
Tri-State Voice
Trumpeter (R)
$ U.S. Catholic
Urban Kingdom (R)
$ War Cry (R)

$ Way of St. Francis (R)
$ World & I (R)
$ Written
Xavier Review

Children
$ Nature Friend (R)
$ New Moon Girls (R)
Skipping Stones

**Christian Education/
Library**
Catholic Library
$ Jour./Adventist Ed. (R)

Missions
$ Evangelical Missions (R)
$ Glad Tidings (R)
$ PFI Global Link Journal (R)
$ PIME World (R)
Railroad Evangelist (R)

Music
$ Creator (R)

Pastors/Leaders
$ African-American Pulpit
$ Catholic Servant
$ Christian Century (R)
CrossCurrents
Jour./Pastoral Care
Lutheran Forum
$ Priest
Theological Digest (R)
$ Torch Legacy Leader
$ Word & World
$ Youthworker

Teen/Young Adult
$ TC Magazine
TeensForJC (R)
$ Young Christian Writers

Women
Christian Woman's Page (R)
$ Dabbling Mum (R)
Extreme Woman Magazine
Handmaidens
$ Horizons (R)
Jewels of God (R)
$ Pauses . . .

WRITERS
$ Advanced Christian
    Writer (R)

$ Christian Communicator (R)
$ Spirit-Led Writer (R)
$ Writer
$ Writer's Digest

ETHICS
Adult/General
($) AGAIN Magazine (R)
$ America
$ Angels on Earth
$ Associated Content (R)
$ Aujourd'hui Credo (R)
$ Brink Magazine (R)
$ Canada Lutheran (R)
$ Cathedral Age
$ Catholic Digest (R)
$ Catholic Insight
$ Catholic Peace Voice (R)
CBN.com (R)
$ Celebrate Life (R)
$ Christian Courier/Canada (R)
$ Christian Examiner
Christian Media (R)
Christian Observer
Christian Online
Christian Ranchman
$ Christian Renewal (R)
$ Christian Research
$ Christian Standard (R)
$ ChristianWeck (R)
$ Churchmouse
    Publications (R)
Church of England News
$ Columbia (R)
Creation Care (R)
$ Creative Nonfiction
$ Cresset
$ Culture Wars (R)
Desert Call (R)
Desert Voice (R)
$ DisciplesWorld
E-Channels (R)
$ Eureka Street
Evangelical Advocate (R)
$ Faith Today
$ Focus on the Family
$ Good News, Etc. (R)
Gospel Herald
Halo Magazine
$ Homeschooling Today (R)

$ Horizons (adult) (R)
$ In His Presence (R)
$ In Touch
$ Interim (R)
Island Catholic (R)
$ JC Town Reporter (R)
Koinonia
$ Light & Life
$ Liguorian
$ Live (R)
$ Living Church
$ Lookout
Maine Family Policy (R)
$ Manna (R)
$ Men of Integrity (R)
Men.AG.org (R)
MissionWares
MovieGuide
New Heart (R)
$ New Wineskins (R)
Nostalgia (R)
($) NBR E-Magazine (R)
$ Our Sunday Visitor (R)
$ Pathway (R)
Perspectives (R)
Perspectives/Science &
    Chr. Faith
$ Positive Thinking (R)
$ Prairie Messenger (R)
$ Presbyterian Outlook
Priscilla Papers
$ Prism
$ Pure Inspiration (R)
Regent Global Bus. Rev. (R)
$ Search
$ Seek (R)
$ Social Justice (R)
$ St. Anthony Messenger
Trumpeter (R)
$ U.S. Catholic
Urban Kingdom (R)
$ War Cry (R)
$ Way of St. Francis (R)
$ World & I (R)

Children
$ Bread for God's
    Children (R)
$ New Moon Girls (R)
Skipping Stones

Christian Education/ Library
Christian Librarian (R)
Jour./Research on Christian Ed.

Daily Devotionals
Penned from the Heart (R)

Missions
$ Glad Tidings (R)

Pastors/Leaders
$ Christian Century (R)
$ Clergy Journal (R)
CrossCurrents
$ Enrichment Journal (R)
$ Interpreter
Jour./Pastoral Care
Lutheran Forum
$ Lutheran Partners (R)
$ Ministry Today
Sewanee Theo. Review
Sharing the Practice (R)
Theological Digest (R)
$ Word & World

Teen/Young Adult
$ Boundless Webzine (R)
$ Devo'zine (R)
$ Direction Student
$ Horizon Student
$ Real Faith in Life (R)
$ Risen
TeensForJC (R)
$ Young Salvationist (R)

Women
$ At the Center (R)
$ Esprit
Handmaiden (R)
Women Today (R)

ETHNIC/CULTURAL PIECES
Adult/General
African Voices (R)
($) AGAIN Magazine (R)
$ America
$ Arlington Catholic
$ Associated Content (R)
$ Aujourd'hui Credo (R)
$ Bible Advocate (R)
Breakthrough Intercessor (R)

$ Brink Magazine (R)
$ Catholic Digest (R)
$ Catholic Peace Voice (R)
$ CBA Retailers
CBN.com (R)
$ Celebrate Life (R)
Chocolate Pages
$ Christian Courier/Canada (R)
$ Christian Home & School
Christian Online
$ ChristianWeek (R)
$ Churchmouse Publications (R)
$ Citizen USA
$ Columbia (R)
$ Commonweal
$ Creative Nonfiction
Desert Call (R)
Desert Voice (R)
E-Channels (R)
$ EFCA Today
Encompass
$ Enfoque a la Familia
$ Episcopal Life (R)
$ Eureka Street
Evangelical Advocate (R)
$ Faith Today
Faithwebbin (R)
$ Foursquare Leader
$ Gem (R)
$ Good News (R)
$ Good News in Florida (R)
Good News!
$ Good News, Etc. (R)
Gospel Herald
$ Gospel Today (R)
Halo Magazine
$ Haruah (R)
$ Homeschooling Today (R)
($) Impact Magazine (R)
$ In Touch
$ Indian Life (R)
$ JC Town Reporter (R)
$ KD Gospel Media
Koinonia
La Nueva Vision
$ Light & Life
$ Live (R)
$ Lookout
$ Manna (R)
$ Men of Integrity (R)

$ MESSAGE
Messianic Perspectives (R)
MovieGuide
($) Mutuality (R)
New Identity (R)
$ New Wineskins (R)
Nostalgia (R)
$ Our Sunday Visitor (R)
$ ParentLife
Penned from the Heart (R)
$ Prairie Messenger (R)
Priscilla Papers
$ Prism
Purpose Magazine (R)
$ Salvo
Saved Magazine
SCP Journal
$ Search
$ Seek (R)
Spirituality for Today
$ St. Anthony Messenger
$ Together (R)
Trumpeter (R)
$ U.S. Catholic
$ Upscale
Urban Kingdom (R)
$ War Cry (R)
$ Way of St. Francis (R)
$ Wesleyan Life (R)
West Wind Review
$ World & I (R)
$ Written
Xavier Review

Children
$ Bread for God's Children (R)
$ Faces
$ New Moon Girls (R)
Skipping Stones
$ Sparkle (R)

Christian Education/ Library
$ Momentum
$ Teachers of Vision (R)

Daily Devotionals
Penned from the Heart (R)

Missions
East-West Church & Ministry
   Report

$ Evangelical Missions (R)
$ Glad Tidings (R)
Intl. Jour./Frontier Missions (R)
Missiology
Op. Reveille Interactive Jour. (R)
$ PIME World (R)
Women of the Harvest

Pastors/Leaders
$ African-American Pulpit
$ Barefoot (R)
$ Christian Century (R)
$ Enrichment Journal (R)
$ Interpreter
Jour./Pastoral Care
$ Lutheran Partners (R)
$ Ministry Today
$ Net Results
Pulpit Helps (R)
$ Torch Legacy Leader
$ Worship Leader

Teen/Young Adult
$ Boundless Webzine (R)
$ Credo (R)
$ Devo'zine (R)
$ Essential Connection (ec)
$ Real Faith in Life (R)
TeensForJC (R)
$ Young Salvationist (R)

Women
$ Esprit
$ Heart & Soul
$ Horizons (R)
$ inSpirit (R)
$ Link & Visitor (R)
Precious Times (R)
$ SpiritLed Woman

EVANGELISM/ WITNESSING
Adult/General
Ambassador
$ America
American Tract (R)
$ Anglican Journal
$ Annals of St. Anne
$ Aujourd'hui Credo (R)
$ Bible Advocate (R)
Breakthrough Intercessor (R)

$ Brink Magazine (R)
$ Canada Lutheran (R)
$ Catholic Telegraph
$ Catholic Yearbook (R)
CBN.com (R)
Central FL Episcopalian
Christian Courier/WI (R)
$ Christian Home & School
Christian Online
Christian Ranchman
$ Christian Research
$ Christian Standard (R)
$ Christianity Today (R)
$ Churchmouse Publications (R)
Church of England News
$ Columbia (R)
$ Converge Point (R)
$ Decision
E-Channels (R)
$ Episcopal Life (R)
$ Evangel/IN (R)
Evangelical Advocate (R)
$ Faith & Family
$ Faith Today
Florida Baptist Witness
$ Gem (R)
$ Good News (R)
Good News Today
$ Good News, Etc. (R)
Gospel Herald
Halo Magazine
Heartbeat/CMA
$ Horizons (adult) (R)
$ In His Presence (R)
$ In Touch
$ JC Town Reporter (R)
$ KD Gospel Media
Koinonia
Leaves (R)
$ Light & Life
$ Live (R)
$ Living Church
$ Lookout
$ Lutheran Journal (R)
Lutheran Witness
$ Manna (R)
$ Men of Integrity (R)
Men.AG.org (R)
Message of the Open Bible (R)
Messianic Perspectives (R)

Mosaic (R)
New Heart (R)
$ New Wineskins (R)
$ On Mission
$ Our Sunday Visitor (R)
$ ParentLife
$ Pathway (R)
Penned from the Heart (R)
$ Power for Living (R)
PrayerWorks (R)
$ Priority! (R)
Regent Global Bus. Rev. (R)
Reverent Submissions (R)
$ Seek (R)
Sharing (R)
Spirituality for Today
$ Standard (R)
$ St. Anthony Messenger
Sword of the Lord (R)
$ Testimony (R)
Trumpeter (R)
Urban Kingdom (R)
Victory Herald (R)
$ War Cry (R)
$ Way of St. Francis (R)
$ Wesleyan Life (R)
Wisconsin Christian

Children
$ Bread for God's Children (R)
$ Focus/Clubhouse Jr.
$ Guide (R)
$ JuniorWay
$ Sparkle (R)

Christian Education/ Library
Catholic Library
$ Group Magazine
$ Kids' Ministry Ideas
$ Youth & CE Leadership

Daily Devotionals
Penned from the Heart (R)

Missions
East-West Church & Ministry
    Report
$ Evangelical Missions (R)
$ Glad Tidings (R)
Intl. Jour./Frontier Missions (R)
Lausanne World Pulse (R)

$ Leaders for Today
Missiology
Op. Reveille Interactive
    Jour. (R)

Music
Christian Music Weekly (R)

Pastors/Leaders
$ Catholic Servant
$ Cook Partners
$ Enrichment Journal (R)
$ Growth Points (R)
$ Interpreter
Jour./Amer. Soc./Chur.
    Growth (R)
$ Leadership (R)
$ Let's Worship
$ Lutheran Partners (R)
Ministry in Motion (R)
$ Ministry Today
$ Outreach (R)
Pulpit Helps (R)
$ RevWriter Resource
Rick Warren's Ministry
    Toolbox (R)
$ SmallGroups.com (R)

Teen/Young Adult
$ Boundless Webzine (R)
$ Credo (R)
$ Devo'zine (R)
$ Essential Connection (ec)
$ Insight (R)
$ J.A.M.
$ Real Faith in Life (R)
$ TC Magazine
TeensForJC (R)
$ True Girl
$ Young Salvationist (R)

Women
$ Canticle
$ Come to the Fire (R)
Extreme Woman Magazine
$ inSpirit (R)
Jewels of God (R)
$ Journey
Just Between Us (R)
$ Link & Visitor (R)
P31 Woman (R)
Precious Times (R)

Share
$ SpiritLed Woman

EXEGESIS
Adult/General
$ Alive Now (R)
$ Aujourd'hui Credo (R)
$ Bible Advocate (R)
$ Catholic Insight
CBN.com (R)
Christian Ranchman
$ Christian Standard (R)
E-Channels (R)
Evangelical Advocate (R)
Halo Magazine
$ In Touch
$ JC Town Reporter (R)
$ Living Church
Messianic Perspectives (R)
$ Our Sunday Visitor (R)
Perspectives (R)
Priscilla Papers
Regent Global Bus. Rev. (R)
Reverent Submissions (R)
$ Social Justice (R)
$ St. Anthony Messenger
Sword and Trumpet
Sword of the Lord (R)
Trumpeter (R)
$ Way of St. Francis (R)
$ Wesleyan Life (R)
Wisconsin Christian

Missions
$ Glad Tidings (R)

Pastors/Leaders
$ Enrichment Journal (R)
Lutheran Forum
Pulpit Helps (R)
Theological Digest (R)

Teen/Young Adult
$ Boundless Webzine (R)
$ Young Adult Today

FAITH
Adult/General
African Voices (R)
$ America
$ Arkansas Catholic (R)

$ Aujourd'hui Credo (R)
Believer's Bay
$ Bible Advocate (R)
Bread of Life (R)
Breakthrough Intercessor (R)
$ Brink Magazine (R)
Brink Online
byFaith
$ Canada Lutheran (R)
$ Canadian Mennonite (R)
$ Catholic Digest (R)
$ Catholic Insight
$ Catholic Peace Voice (R)
$ Catholic Yearbook (R)
CBN.com (R)
$ Christian Courier/Canada (R)
Christian Family Journal
$ Christian Home & School
$ Christianity Today (R)
$ Christian Journal (R)
Christian Online
Christian Quarterly (R)
$ Christian Research
$ Christian Retailing
$ Christian Standard (R)
$ ChristianWeek (R)
Church Herald & Holiness (R)
$ Churchmouse
    Publications (R)
Church of England News
$ City Light News (R)
$ Columbia (R)
$ Converge Point (R)
$ Covenant Companion (R)
Desert Call (R)
Desert Voice (R)
$ Direction
Disciple's Journal (R)
E-Channels (R)
Eternal Ink (R)
Evangelical Advocate (R)
$ Faith & Family
$ Faith & Friends (R)
$ Faith Today
$ Family Digest (R)
$ Focus on the Family
$ Gem (R)
$ Good News in Florida (R)
Good News Journal (R)
Gospel Herald

Halo Magazine
$ Haruah (R)
Highway News (R)
$ Home Times (R)
($) HopeKeepers (R)
$ In His Presence (R)
$ In Touch
$ Indian Life (R)
$ JC Town Reporter (R)
$ KD Gospel Media
Koinonia
La Nueva Vision
LifeTimes Catholic
$ Light & Life
$ Liguorian
$ Live (R)
$ Lookout
$ Lutheran Digest (R)
$ Lutheran Journal (R)
Maine Family Policy (R)
$ Manna (R)
$ Men of Integrity (R)
Men.AG.org (R)
Messianic Perspectives (R)
$ MindFlights (R)
$ Miracles, Healings
Mosaic (R)
New Christian Voices
New Heart (R)
New Identity (R)
$ New Wineskins (R)
$ Our Sunday Visitor (R)
$ ParentLife
Pegasus Review (R)
Penned from the Heart (R)
$ Positive Thinking (R)
$ Prairie Messenger (R)
PrayerWorks (R)
Priscilla Papers
$ Psychology for Living (R)
$ Pure Inspiration (R)
$ Purpose (R)
Reverent Submissions (R)
$ Seek (R)
$ Social Justice (R)
Spirituality for Today
$ Standard (R)
$ St. Anthony Messenger
SW Kansas Faith
Sword and Trumpet

Sword of the Lord (R)
$ Testimony (R)
$ Together (R)
Trumpeter (R)
$ U.S. Catholic
$ United Church
    Observer (R)
Urban Kingdom (R)
$ Victory in Grace (R)
$ Vista (R)
$ Way of St. Francis (R)
$ Weavings (R)
$ Wesleyan Life (R)
$ World & I (R)

Children
$ Bread for God's
    Children (R)
$ Focus/Clubhouse Jr.
$ JuniorWay
$ Kid Zone
$ Our Little Friend (R)
$ Primary Street
$ Primary Treasure (R)
$ SHINE brightly (R)
$ Sparkle (R)

Christian Education/Library
Catholic Library
$ Children's Ministry
Christian Librarian (R)
$ Group Magazine
$ Momentum
$ Youth & CE Leadership

Daily Devotionals
Penned from the Heart (R)

Missions
East-West Church & Ministry
    Report
$ Glad Tidings (R)
Lausanne World Pulse (R)
$ PIME World (R)

Music
Christian Music Weekly (R)

Pastors/Leaders
$ African-American Pulpit
$ Interpreter
$ Ministry Today

Plugged In
$ Proclaim (R)
$ RevWriter Resource
$ SmallGroups.com (R)
$ Worship Leader

Teen/Young Adult

$ Boundless Webzine (R)
$ Credo (R)
$ Devo'zine (R)
$ Direction Student
Exodus Magazine
G4T Ink (R)
$ Horizon Student
$ Insight (R)
$ J.A.M.
$ Risen
$ TC Magazine
TeensForJC (R)
$ True Girl
$ Young Adult Today
$ Young Salvationist (R)

Women

($) Beyond the Bend (R)
$ Canticle
Christian Woman's Page (R)
Christian Work at Home
    Moms (R)
Elegance (R)
$ Esprit
Extreme Woman Magazine
For Every Woman (R)
Hope for Women
$ Horizons (R)
$ inSpirit (R)
Jewels of God (R)
$ Journey
Just Between Us (R)
Life Tools for Women
P31 Woman (R)
$ Pauses . . .
$ SpiritLed Woman
Unrecognized Woman (R)
Virtuous Woman (R)
Woman of Worth (R)
Women of the Cross
Women Today (R)

Writers

Areopagus

FAMILY LIFE
Adult/General

3V Magazine
$ Abilities
African Voices (R)
($) AGAIN Magazine (R)
$ America
$ Angels on Earth
$ Annals of St. Anne
Anointed Pages
$ Arkansas Catholic (R)
$ Arlington Catholic
$ Associated Content (R)
$ Atlantic Catholic
$ Aujourd'hui Credo (R)
$ Australian Catholics (R)
$ B.C. Catholic (R)
Believer's Bay
$ Bible Advocate (R)
Bread of Life (R)
Breakthrough Intercessor (R)
$ Brink Magazine (R)
byFaith
$ Canada Lutheran (R)
$ Catholic Digest (R)
$ Catholic Forester (R)
$ Catholic Insight
CBN.com (R)
$ Chicken Soup Books (R)
$ Christian Courier/Canada (R)
Christian Courier/WI (R)
Christian Family Journal
$ Christian Home & School
$ Christian Journal (R)
Christian Online
Christian Quarterly (R)
Christian Ranchman
$ Christian Renewal (R)
$ ChristianWeek (R)
Church Herald & Holiness (R)
$ Churchmouse
    Publications (R)
$ City Light News (R)
$ Columbia (R)
Connecting Point (R)
$ Converge Point (R)
$ Covenant Companion (R)
Creation Care (R)
$ Creative Nonfiction
$ Culture Wars (R)

Desert Call (R)
Desert Voice (R)
Disciple's Journal (R)
E-Channels (R)
Eternal Ink (R)
Evangelical Advocate (R)
$ Faith & Family
$ Faith & Friends (R)
$ Faith Today
Faithwebbin (R)
$ Family Digest (R)
$ Family Smart E-tips (R)
$ Focus on the Family
$ Foursquare Leader
$ Gem (R)
$ Good News in Florida (R)
Good News Journal (R)
$ Good News, Etc. (R)
Gospel Herald
$ Guideposts (R)
Halo Magazine
HEARTLIGHT Internet (R)
Highway News (R)
$ Home Times (R)
$ Homeschooling Today (R)
$ Horizons (adult) (R)
$ In His Presence (R)
$ In Touch
$ Indian Life (R)
$ JC Town Reporter (R)
$ KD Gospel Media
Keys to Living (R)
Koinonia
LifeSiteNews
LifeTimes Catholic
$ Liguorian
$ Live (R)
$ Living (R)
$ Living Church
$ Living Light (R)
$ Lookout
$ Lutheran Digest (R)
Maine Family Policy (R)
$ Manna (R)
$ Mature Years (R)
$ Men of Integrity (R)
Men of the Cross
Men.AG.org (R)
($) Mennonite Historian (R)
$ Messenger/St. Anthony

$ Montgomery's Journey
($) Mutuality (R)
New Christian Voices
New Identity (R)
$ New Wineskins (R)
Nostalgia (R)
$ Our Sunday Visitor (R)
$ Over the Back Fence (R)
$ ParentLife
$ Pathway (R)
Pegasus Review (R)
Penned from the Heart (R)
$ Positive Thinking (R)
$ Power for Living (R)
$ Prairie Messenger (R)
PrayerWorks (R)
Priscilla Papers
$ Psychology for Living (R)
$ Purpose (R)
Quaker Life (R)
Reverent Submissions (R)
$ Search
$ Seek (R)
$ Significant Living (R)
Single Again Mag. Online (R)
$ Social Justice (R)
$ Special Living (R)
Spirituality for Today
$ St. Anthony Messenger
$ Storyteller (R)
SW Kansas Faith
Sword and Trumpet
Sword of the Lord (R)
$ Testimony (R)
$ Today's Pentecostal (R)
$ Together (R)
Trumpeter (R)
$ U.S. Catholic
$ United Church Observer (R)
Urban Kingdom (R)
$ Vibrant Life (R)
$ Victory in Grace (R)
$ Vision (R)
$ Vista (R)
$ War Cry (R)
$ Way of St. Francis (R)
$ Wesleyan Life (R)
West Wind Review
Wisconsin Christian
$ World & I (R)

Children
$ Bread for God's
    Children (R)
$ Focus/Clubhouse
$ Focus/Clubhouse Jr.
$ Guide (R)
$ JuniorWay
$ Kid Zone
$ New Moon Girls (R)
$ Pockets (R)
$ Sparkle (R)

Christian Education/ Library
$ Children's Ministry
$ Group Magazine
$ Youth & CE Leadership

Daily Devotionals
Penned from the Heart (R)

Missions
$ Glad Tidings (R)
Women of the Harvest

Pastors/Leaders
$ African-American Pulpit
$ Catholic Servant
$ Enrichment Journal (R)
$ InSite (R)
$ Interpreter
Jour./Pastoral Care
Ministry in Motion (R)
$ Ministry Today
$ Preaching Well (R)
$ RevWriter Resource
$ Today's Parish
$ Word & World

Teen/Young Adult
$ Credo (R)
$ Direction Student
Exodus Magazine
$ Horizon Student
$ Insight (R)
$ J.A.M.
$ Real Faith in Life (R)
$ TC Magazine
TeensForJC (R)
$ Young Adult Today
$ Young Christian Writers
$ Young Salvationist (R)

Women
$ Canticle
Christian Woman's Page (R)
Christian Work at Home
    Moms (R)
$ Come to the Fire (R)
Crowned with Silver
$ Dabbling Mum (R)
Elegance (R)
$ Esprit
Extreme Woman Magazine
For Every Woman (R)
$ Girlfriend 2 Girlfriend
Handmaiden (R)
Hope for Women
$ Horizons (R)
$ InspiredMoms (R)
$ inSpirit (R)
Jewels of God (R)
$ Journey
Just Between Us (R)
Life Tools for Women
$ Link & Visitor (R)
Live Magazine
Lutheran Woman's Quar.
$ MomSense (R)
P31 Woman (R)
$ Pauses . . .
Precious Times (R)
Share
Simply Blessed (R)
$ SpiritLed Woman
Together with God (R)
Unrecognized Woman (R)
Virtuous Woman (R)
Woman of Worth (R)
Women of the Cross
Women Today (R)

FEATURE ARTICLES
Adult/General
$ Angels on Earth
Breakthrough Intercessor (R)
$ Bridal Guides (R)
$ Brink Magazine (R)
$ Capper's
$ Catholic Digest (R)
Christian Family Journal
Christian Quarterly (R)
$ Churchmouse Publications (R)

$ City Light News (R)
$ Columbia (R)
$ Covenant Companion (R)
Creation Care (R)
Desert Christian
Eternal Ink (R)
Evangelical Advocate (R)
$ Faith & Family
$ Faith Today
$ FGBC World (R)
$ Good News in Florida (R)
Good News Journal (R)
$ Good News, Etc. (R)
Gospel Herald
Halo Magazine
Heartland Gatekeeper (R)
$ Home Times (R)
$ Homeschooling Today (R)
$ In His Presence (R)
$ JC Town Reporter (R)
Jour. of Church & State
$ Light & Life
$ Lookout
$ Manna (R)
$ Marian Helper
Messianic Perspectives (R)
$ Montana Catholic
$ Montgomery's Journey
More Excellent Way
New Identity (R)
Nostalgia (R)
$ Our Sunday Visitor (R)
$ Over the Back Fence (R)
$ ParentLife
$ Prairie Messenger (R)
Regent Global Bus. Rev. (R)
$ Relevant
$ Significant Living (R)
Trumpeter (R)
$ Vibrant Life (R)

Children
$ Archaeology

Christian Education/ Library
Christian Early Ed. (R)
$ Momentum

Missions
$ Glad Tidings (R)
MissionsMagizinet

Pastors/Leaders
Church Executive
$ InSite (R)
$ Outreach (R)
Preaching
$ RevWriter Resource

Teen/Young Adult
$ Devo'zine (R)
$ Direction Student
$ Horizon Student
$ Young Christian (R)

Women
Christian Women Today (R)
Elegance (R)
Extreme Woman Magazine
Just Between Us (R)
$ Pauses . . .
Unrecognized Woman (R)
Virtuous Woman (R)
Woman of Worth (R)

Writers
$ Writer

FILLERS: ANECDOTES
Adult/General
$ Alive Now (R)
$ Angels on Earth
$ Animal Trails (R)
Breakthrough Intercessor (R)
$ Bridal Guides (R)
$ Catholic Digest (R)
$ Catholic Yearbook (R)
$ Chicken Soup Books (R)
$ Christian Journal (R)
Christian Motorsports
Christian Quarterly (R)
Christian Ranchman
$ Christian Response (R)
Church Herald & Holiness (R)
$ Churchmouse Publications (R)
$ City Light News (R)
Desert Call (R)
Disciple's Journal (R)
E-Channels (R)
Eternal Ink (R)
$ Faith & Family
$ Family Digest (R)
$ Foursquare Leader

$ Gem (R)
Good News Journal (R)
Halo Magazine
HEARTLIGHT Internet (R)
Highway News (R)
$ Home Times (R)
($) Impact Magazine (R)
$ In His Presence (R)
$ JC Town Reporter (R)
$ Living (R)
$ Lutheran Digest (R)
$ Lutheran Journal (R)
$ Manna (R)
MovieGuide
New Heart (R)
$ Purpose (R)
Reverent Submissions (R)
$ Significant Living (R)
Single Again Mag. Online (R)
Spirituality for Today
$ St. Anthony Messenger
$ Today's Pentecostal (R)
Urban Kingdom (R)
Victory Herald (R)
$ Vista (R)
$ War Cry (R)

Children
Skipping Stones

Christian Education/ Library
Christian Librarian (R)

Missions
Railroad Evangelist (R)

Music
$ Creator (R)

Pastors/Leaders
$ Barefoot (R)
$ Enrichment Journal (R)
$ Leadership (R)
$ Preaching Well (R)
$ PreachingToday.com
Pulpit Helps (R)
Sharing the Practice (R)
$ Sunday Sermons (R)

Teen/Young Adult
$ Young Christian (R)
$ Young Salvationist (R)

Women
($) Beyond the Bend (R)
Christian Woman's Page (R)
Just Between Us (R)
Right to the Heart (R)
Virtuous Woman (R)

Writers
$ Canadian Writer's Jour. (R)
$ Cross & Quill (R)
$ Fellowscript (R)
$ New Writer's Mag.
NW Christian Author (R)
$ Tickled by Thunder
Write Connection
$ Writers' Journal

FILLERS: CARTOONS
Adult/General
African Voices (R)
American Tract (R)
$ Angels on Earth
$ Animal Trails (R)
$ Bridal Guides (R)
$ Catholic Digest (R)
$ Chicken Soup Books (R)
Christian Computing (R)
$ Christian Herald (R)
$ Christian Journal (R)
Christian Motorsports
Christian Quarterly (R)
Christian Ranchman
$ Churchmouse Publications (R)
$ Citizen USA
$ City Light News (R)
Connecting Point (R)
$ Culture Wars (R)
Disciple's Journal (R)
E-Channels (R)
$ Eureka Street
$ Evangel/IN (R)
Evangel/OR (R)
$ Faith & Family
$ Faith & Friends (R)
$ Foursquare Leader
$ Gem (R)
Good News Journal (R)
$ Gospel Today (R)
Halo Magazine
HEARTLIGHT Internet (R)

Highway News (R)
$ Home Times (R)
($) Impact Magazine (R)
$ In His Presence (R)
$ Interchange
$ Interim (R)
$ JC Town Reporter (R)
Light of the World
$ Liguorian
$ Lutheran Digest (R)
$ Mature Years (R)
MovieGuide
New Heart (R)
Pegasus Review (R)
$ Power for Living (R)
$ Presbyterians Today (R)
$ Significant Living (R)
$ Special Living (R)
$ St. Anthony Messenger
$ Storyteller (R)
Trumpeter (R)
$ United Church Observer (R)
Urban Kingdom (R)

Children
$ American Girl (R)
$ Passport (R)
$ SHINE brightly (R)
Skipping Stones

Christian Education/ Library
$ Children's Ministry
Christian Librarian (R)
$ Group Magazine
$ Jour./Adventist Ed. (R)
$ Teachers of Vision (R)
$ Today's Catholic Teacher (R)
$ Youth & CE Leadership

Missions
$ Glad Tidings (R)
Mission Frontiers
Railroad Evangelist (R)

Music
Christian Music Weekly (R)
$ Creator (R)
Tradition

Pastors/Leaders
$ Barefoot (R)
$ Catholic Servant

$ Christian Century (R)
$ Diocesan Dialogue (R)
$ Enrichment Journal (R)
$ Leadership (R)
$ Lutheran Partners (R)
$ Priest
Pulpit Helps (R)
Sharing the Practice (R)
$ SmallGroups.com (R)
$ Your Church (R)

Teen/Young Adult
G4T Ink (R)
$ Listen (R)
TeensForJC (R)
$ Young Christian (R)
$ Young Salvationist (R)

Women
Simply Blessed (R)

Writers
$ Canadian Writer's Jour. (R)
$ Cross & Quill (R)
$ New Writer's Mag.
$ Writer
$ Writers' Journal

FILLERS: FACTS
Adult/General
$ Animal Trails (R)
Bread of Life (R)
$ Bridal Guides (R)
$ Catholic Digest (R)
$ Catholic Yearbook (R)
$ Chicken Soup Books (R)
$ Christian Herald (R)
Christian Motorsports
Christian Ranchman
$ Christian Response (R)
$ Churchmouse Publications (R)
$ City Light News (R)
Desert Call (R)
Disciple's Journal (R)
$ Gem (R)
Good News Journal (R)
Halo Magazine
Highway News (R)
$ Home Times (R)
$ Interchange

$ JC Town Reporter (R)
$ Lutheran Digest (R)
$ Lutheran Journal (R)
Message of the Open Bible (R)
MovieGuide
PrayerWorks (R)
$ Significant Living (R)
Single Again Mag. Online (R)
$ St. Anthony Messenger
Sword and Trumpet
Sword of the Lord (R)
$ Today's Pentecostal (R)
Urban Kingdom (R)
$ Vista (R)
$ Written

Children
$ Kid Zone
$ Nature Friend (R)

Christian Education/ Library
$ Teachers of Vision (R)
$ Today's Catholic Teacher (R)

Pastors/Leaders
$ Enrichment Journal (R)
$ Interpreter

Teen/Young Adult
$ Real Faith in Life (R)
TeensForJC (R)
$ True Girl
$ Young Christian (R)
$ Young Salvationist (R)

Women
($) Beyond the Bend (R)
Christian Woman's Page (R)
Simply Blessed (R)
Unrecognized Woman (R)
Virtuous Woman (R)
Woman of Worth (R)

Writers
Areopagus
$ New Writer's Mag.
Write Connection
$ Writers' Journal

FILLERS: GAMES
Adult/General
$ Catholic Yearbook (R)

$ CGA World (R)
$ Christian Herald (R)
Christian Motorsports
Christian Ranchman
$ Churchmouse
    Publications (R)
$ Citizen USA
Connecting Point (R)
Disciple's Journal (R)
$ Faith & Friends (R)
$ Family Smart E-tips (R)
$ Gem (R)
Good News Journal (R)
Halo Magazine
HEARTLIGHT Internet (R)
$ JC Town Reporter (R)
$ Lutheran Journal (R)
MovieGuide
Victory Herald (R)

Children
$ American Girl (R)
$ Guide (R)
$ Pockets (R)
$ SHINE brightly (R)
$ Sparkle (R)

Christian Education/ Library
Catholic Library
$ Group Magazine

Missions
$ Glad Tidings (R)

Pastors/Leaders
$ Barefoot (R)

Teen/Young Adult
$ Listen (R)
TeensForJC (R)
$ Young Salvationist (R)

FILLERS: IDEAS
Adult/General
$ Animal Trails (R)
$ Bridal Guides (R)
$ CGA World (R)
$ Christian Home & School
Christian Motorsports
Christian Quarterly (R)
Christian Ranchman

$ Churchmouse
    Publications (R)
Disciple's Journal (R)
Evangel/OR (R)
$ Family Smart E-tips (R)
$ Gem (R)
Good News Journal (R)
Halo Magazine
HEARTLIGHT Internet (R)
Highway News (R)
$ Home Times (R)
$ JC Town Reporter (R)
$ KD Gospel Media
$ Manna (R)
MovieGuide
New Identity (R)
Reverent Submissions (R)
$ Seek (R)
Single Again Mag. Online (R)
Urban Kingdom (R)

Christian Education/ Library
$ Children's Ministry
Christian Librarian (R)
Congregational Libraries Today
$ Group Magazine
$ Preschool Playhouse (CE)
$ Youth & CE Leadership

Missions
$ Evangelical Missions (R)
Mission Connection

Music
$ Creator (R)

Pastors/Leaders
$ Barefoot (R)
$ Interpreter
$ Lutheran Partners (R)
$ Preaching Well (R)
$ RevWriter Resource
$ SmallGroups.com (R)

Teen/Young Adult
$ Real Faith in Life (R)
$ Young Christian (R)

Women
($) Beyond the Bend (R)
Christian Woman's Page (R)
Empowering Everyday Women
Just Between Us (R)

P31 Woman (R)
Right to the Heart (R)
Virtuous Woman (R)

Writers
Areopagus
$ Canadian Writer's Jour. (R)
$ Tickled by Thunder
Write Connection
$ Writers' Journal

FILLERS: JOKES
Adult/General
$ Catholic Digest (R)
$ Christian Journal (R)
Christian Motorsports
Christian Ranchman
$ Churchmouse Publications (R)
$ City Light News (R)
Desert Voice (R)
Disciple's Journal (R)
Eternal Ink (R)
$ Faith & Friends (R)
$ Gem (R)
Good News Journal (R)
Halo Magazine
HEARTLIGHT Internet (R)
$ Home Times (R)
($) Impact Magazine (R)
$ In His Presence (R)
$ Interchange
$ JC Town Reporter (R)
Light of the World
$ Liguorian
$ Lutheran Digest (R)
$ Mature Years (R)
$ Miracles, Healings
MovieGuide
New Heart (R)
PrayerWorks (R)
Reverent Submissions (R)
$ Significant Living (R)
Single Again Mag. Online (R)
$ St. Anthony Messenger

Music
$ Creator (R)

Pastors/Leaders
$ Preaching Well (R)
Pulpit Helps (R)
Sharing the Practice (R)

Teen/Young Adult
G4T Ink (R)
TeensForJC (R)

Women
Virtuous Woman (R)

Writers
Write Connection
$ Writers' Journal

FILLERS: KID QUOTES
Adult/General
$ Animal Trails (R)
$ Bridal Guides (R)
$ Chicken Soup Books (R)
$ Christian Journal (R)
Desert Voice (R)
Eternal Ink (R)
Halo Magazine
Highway News (R)
$ Home Times (R)
$ Indian Life (R)
$ JC Town Reporter (R)
$ KD Gospel Media
MovieGuide
Reverent Submissions (R)
Single Again Mag. Online (R)
$ Upscale
Victory Herald (R)

Christian Education/ Library
$ Children's Ministry
Christian Early Ed. (R)

Missions
$ Glad Tidings (R)

FILLERS: NEWSBREAKS
Adult/General
$ Anglican Journal
$ Arkansas Catholic (R)
$ B.C. Catholic (R)
$ Canada Lutheran (R)
$ Catholic Telegraph
$ Christian Journal (R)
Christian Motorsports
Christian Ranchman
$ Christian Renewal (R)
$ Churchmouse Publications (R)
$ City Light News (R)

Disciple's Journal (R)
Evangel/OR (R)
Friends Journal (R)
$ Gem (R)
Good News Journal (R)
Halo Magazine
HEARTLIGHT Internet (R)
Highway News (R)
$ Home Times (R)
$ JC Town Reporter (R)
$ KD Gospel Media
MovieGuide
New Identity (R)
($) NRB E-Magazine (R)
Sword and Trumpet
Sword of the Lord (R)
Urban Kingdom (R)
$ Vista (R)

Christian Education/ Library
Christian Librarian (R)

Missions
Op. Reveille Interactive
    Jour. (R)

Pastors/Leaders
$ Preaching Well (R)

Teen/Young Adult
$ Real Faith in Life (R)

Women
Hope for Women

Writers
Areopagus
$ New Writer's Mag.
$ Writers' Journal

FILLERS: PARTY IDEAS
Adult/General
$ Animal Trails (R)
$ Bridal Guides (R)
Christian Ranchman
$ Churchmouse Publications (R)
Disciple's Journal (R)
Good News Journal (R)
Halo Magazine
Highway News (R)
$ JC Town Reporter (R)
$ KD Gospel Media

$ Manna (R)
MovieGuide
Urban Kingdom (R)
Victory Herald (R)

Children
$ Sparkle (R)

Christian Education/
Library
$ Youth & CE Leadership

Music
$ Creator (R)

Pastors/Leaders
$ Barefoot (R)

Teen/Young Adult
TeensForJC (R)
$ Young Christian (R)

Women
Hope for Women
P31 Woman (R)
Right to the Heart (R)
Virtuous Woman (R)

FILLERS: PRAYERS
Adult/General
$ Alive Now (R)
$ Angels on Earth
$ Animal Trails (R)
Breakthrough Intercessor (R)
$ Bridal Guides (R)
$ Catholic Yearbook (R)
$ CGA World (R)
$ Christian Herald (R)
$ Christian Journal (R)
Christian Motorsports
Christian Online
Christian Ranchman
$ Churchmouse
    Publications (R)
Desert Call (R)
Disciple's Journal (R)
E-Channels (R)
Eternal Ink (R)
$ Family Digest (R)
$ Gem (R)
Good News Journal (R)
Halo Magazine
HEARTLIGHT Internet (R)

Highway News (R)
$ Home Times (R)
$ JC Town Reporter (R)
LifeTimes Catholic
$ Mature Years (R)
MovieGuide
PrayerWorks (R)
Reverent Submissions (R)
Single Again Mag. Online (R)
Spirituality for Today
Urban Kingdom (R)
Victory Herald (R)
$ Vista (R)

Children
$ SHINE brightly (R)
$ Sparkle (R)

Daily Devotionals
$ Word in Season

Missions
$ Glad Tidings (R)

Teen/Young Adult
G4T Ink (R)
TeensForJC (R)
$ True Girl
$ Young Christian (R)
$ Young Salvationist (R)

Women
Just Between Us (R)
Right to the Heart (R)
Simply Blessed (R)
Unrecognized Woman (R)
Virtuous Woman (R)

Writers
$ Cross & Quill (R)
Write Connection
$ Writers' Journal

FILLERS: PROSE
Adult/General
$ Animal Trails (R)
$ Bible Advocate (R)
Bread of Life (R)
$ Bridal Guides (R)
Christian Motorsports
Christian Online
Christian Ranchman
$ Churchmouse Publications (R)

$ Decision
Desert Call (R)
Disciple's Journal (R)
Eternal Ink (R)
Evangel/OR (R)
$ Faith & Family
$ Gem (R)
Good News Journal (R)
Halo Magazine
HEARTLIGHT Internet (R)
Highway News (R)
$ JC Town Reporter (R)
MovieGuide
Pegasus Review (R)
$ Purpose (R)
Reverent Submissions (R)
Single Again Mag. Online (R)
Sword and Trumpet
Sword of the Lord (R)
$ Today's Pentecostal (R)
Urban Kingdom (R)
Victory Herald (R)

Children
$ Partners (R)

Pastors/Leaders
$ Preaching Well (R)

Teen/Young Adult
$ Listen (R)
$ Real Faith in Life (R)
TeensForJC (R)
$ Young Christian (R)

Women
$ Melody of the Heart

Writers
Areopagus
$ Freelance Writer's Report (R)
Write Connection
$ Writer
$ Writers' Journal

FILLERS: QUIZZES
Adult/General
$ Animal Trails (R)
$ Bridal Guides (R)
$ Catholic Yearbook (R)
Christian Motorsports
Christian Online

Christian Ranchman
Church Herald & Holiness (R)
$ Churchmouse Publications (R)
Disciple's Journal (R)
$ Faith & Friends (R)
$ Gem (R)
Good News Journal (R)
Halo Magazine
($) Impact Magazine (R)
$ JC Town Reporter (R)
Light of the World
$ Lutheran Journal (R)
MovieGuide
Urban Kingdom (R)
Children
$ Cadet Quest (R)
$ Focus/Clubhouse
$ Guide (R)
$ Nature Friend (R)
$ Partners (R)
$ SHINE brightly (R)
Skipping Stones
$ Sparkle (R)
$ Story Mates (R)

Teen/Young Adult
G4T Ink (R)
$ Listen (R)
$ Real Faith in Life (R)
TeensForJC (R)
$ True Girl
$ Young Christian (R)
$ Young Salvationist (R)

Women
$ Melody of the Heart
Virtuous Woman (R)

Writers
$ Writers' Journal

FILLERS: QUOTES
Adult/General
$ Alive Now (R)
$ Animal Trails (R)
Bread of Life (R)
$ Bridal Guides (R)
$ Catholic Digest (R)
$ Catholic Yearbook (R)
$ Chicken Soup Books (R)
$ Christian Herald (R)

$ Christian Journal (R)
Christian Motorsports
Christian Quarterly (R)
Christian Ranchman
$ Christian Response (R)
$ Churchmouse
   Publications (R)
$ Culture Wars (R)
Desert Call (R)
Desert Voice (R)
Disciple's Journal (R)
$ Faith & Friends (R)
$ Family Smart E-tips (R)
$ Gem (R)
Good News Journal (R)
Halo Magazine
HEARTLIGHT Internet (R)
$ Home Times (R)
$ Indian Life (R)
$ JC Town Reporter (R)
$ Lutheran Journal (R)
Message of the Open Bible (R)
MovieGuide
New Identity (R)
Pegasus Review (R)
PrayerWorks (R)
Reverent Submissions (R)
$ Seek (R)
Spirituality for Today
$ St. Anthony Messenger
$ Storyteller (R)
Urban Kingdom (R)
$ Vista (R)
$ Written

Children
$ Partners (R)
Skipping Stones

Missions
Railroad Evangelist (R)

Pastors/Leaders
Pulpit Helps (R)

Teen/Young Adult
$ True Girl
$ Young Christian (R)

Women
($) Beyond the Bend (R)
Just Between Us (R)

Right to the Heart (R)
Unrecognized Woman (R)

Writers
$ Canadian Writer's Jour. (R)
$ Fellowscript (R)
Write Connection
$ Writers' Journal

FILLERS: SERMON ILLUSTRATIONS
Adult/General
$ Churchmouse
   Publications (R)
Halo Magazine
$ JC Town Reporter (R)
Urban Kingdom (R)

Pastors/Leaders
$ Preaching Well (R)
$ PreachingToday.com
Pulpit Helps (R)
$ RevWriter Resource
$ Sunday Sermons (R)

Women
($) Beyond the Bend (R)

FILLERS: SHORT HUMOR
Adult/General
$ Angels on Earth
$ Animal Trails (R)
$ Bridal Guides (R)
$ Chicken Soup Books (R)
$ Christian Journal (R)
Christian Motorsports
Christian Online
Christian Quarterly (R)
Christian Ranchman
$ Churchmouse Publications (R)
$ Citizen USA
$ City Light News (R)
Disciple's Journal (R)
Eternal Ink (R)
$ Family Digest (R)
Friends Journal (R)
$ Gem (R)
Good News Journal (R)
Halo Magazine
HEARTLIGHT Internet (R)
Highway News (R)
$ Home Times (R)

($) Impact Magazine (R)
$ In His Presence (R)
$ Indian Life (R)
$ JC Town Reporter (R)
$ Leben (R)
$ Living (R)
$ Lutheran Digest (R)
$ Manna (R)
$ Mature Living
Message of the Open Bible (R)
MovieGuide
New Heart (R)
PrayerWorks (R)
$ Presbyterians Today (R)
Reverent Submissions (R)
$ Rose & Thorn
$ Seek (R)
$ Significant Living (R)
Single Again Mag. Online (R)
Urban Kingdom (R)
Victory Herald (R)

Children
$ SHINE brightly (R)
$ Sparkle (R)

Christian Education/ Library
Christian Librarian (R)

Missions
$ Glad Tidings (R)

Music
Christian Music Weekly (R)
$ Creator (R)

Pastors/Leaders
$ Barefoot (R)
$ Catholic Servant
$ Enrichment Journal (R)
$ Interpreter
$ Leadership (R)
$ Preaching Well (R)
Pulpit Helps (R)
Sharing the Practice (R)

Teen/Young Adult
G4T Ink (R)
$ Real Faith in Life (R)
TeensForJC (R)
$ Young Christian (R)
$ Young Salvationist (R)

Women
($) Beyond the Bend (R)
Christian Woman's Page (R)
Just Between Us (R)
$ Melody of the Heart
Unrecognized Woman (R)
Woman of Worth (R)

Writers
Areopagus
$ Christian Communicator (R)
$ Fellowscript (R)
$ New Writer's Mag.
$ Tickled by Thunder
Write Connection
$ Writers' Journal

FILLERS: TIPS
Adult/General
$ Animal Trails (R)
$ Bridal Guides (R)
Christian Ranchman
$ Churchmouse Publications (R)
Halo Magazine
Highway News (R)
$ Home Times (R)
$ JC Town Reporter (R)
$ KD Gospel Media
$ Manna (R)
MovieGuide
New Identity (R)
Reverent Submissions (R)
Single Again Mag. Online (R)
$ Special Living (R)
$ Storyteller (R)
Urban Kingdom (R)
Victory Herald (R)
$ Written

Children
$ Cadet Quest (R)

Christian Education/ Library
$ Youth & CE Leadership

Missions
Mission Connection

Pastors/Leaders
$ Barefoot (R)
$ Enrichment Journal (R)
$ Your Church (R)

Teen/Young Adult
TeensForJC (R)
$ Young Christian (R)

Women
($) Beyond the Bend (R)
Christian Woman's Page (R)
Hope for Women
$ MomSense (R)
Simply Blessed (R)
Unrecognized Woman (R)
Virtuous Woman (R)
Woman of Worth (R)
Women's Ministry

Writers
$ Fellowscript (R)
$ Freelance Writer's
   Report (R)
NW Christian Author (R)
Write Connection
$ Writers' Journal

FILLERS: WORD PUZZLES
Adult/General
$ Animal Trails (R)
$ Bridal Guides (R)
$ Catholic Yearbook (R)
$ CGA World (R)
$ Christian Herald (R)
$ Christian Journal (R)
Christian Quarterly (R)
Christian Ranchman
$ Churchmouse
   Publications (R)
$ Citizen USA
Connecting Point (R)
Desert Voice (R)
Disciple's Journal (R)
$ Evangel/IN (R)
$ Faith & Friends (R)
Friends Journal (R)
$ Gem (R)
Good News Journal (R)
$ Gospel Today (R)
Halo Magazine
HEARTLIGHT Internet (R)
$ Horizons (adult) (R)
($) Impact Magazine (R)
$ JC Town Reporter (R)

Light of the World
$ Mature Years (R)
MovieGuide
$ Power for Living (R)
$ Significant Living (R)
$ Standard (R)

Children
$ Adventures
$ American Girl (R)
$ Cadet Quest (R)
$ Faces
$ Focus/Clubhouse
$ Guide (R)
$ Kid Zone
$ Nature Friend (R)
$ Our Little Friend (R)
$ Partners (R)
$ Passport (R)
$ Pockets (R)
$ SHINE brightly (R)
Skipping Stones
$ Story Mates (R)

Christian Education/ Library
$ Youth & CE Leadership

Missions
$ Glad Tidings (R)
Teen/Young Adult
G4T Ink (R)
$ Real Faith in Life (R)
TeensForJC (R)
$ True Girl
$ Young Christian (R)
$ Young Salvationist (R)

Women
$ Melody of the Heart

Writers
$ Writers' Journal

FOOD/RECIPES
Adult/General
$ Animal Trails (R)
$ Associated Content (R)
$ Bridal Guides (R)
CBN.com (R)
Christian Online
Christian Quarterly (R)

$ Columbia (R)
$ Faith & Family
Good News Journal (R)
Gospel Herald
($) HopeKeepers (R)
($) Impact Magazine (R)
$ In His Presence (R)
$ Indian Life (R)
$ KD Gospel Media
$ Mature Living
New Identity (R)
$ ParentLife
$ Significant Living (R)
$ St. Anthony Messenger
Urban Kingdom (R)
$ World & I (R)
$ Written

Children
$ Adventures
$ American Girl (R)
$ Celebrate
$ Faces
$ Focus/Clubhouse
$ Focus/Clubhouse Jr.
$ Pockets (R)
$ SHINE brightly (R)
$ Sparkle (R)

Missions
$ Glad Tidings (R)
Women of the Harvest

Teen/Young Adult
$ Boundless Webzine (R)
$ J.A.M.
TeensForJC (R)

Women
($) Beyond the Bend (R)
Christian Women Today (R)
Christian Work at Home
   Moms (R)
Crowned with Silver
$ Dabbling Mum (R)
Elegance (R)
Empowering Everyday Women
First Lady
For Every Woman (R)
$ Girlfriend 2 Girlfriend
Hope for Women
$ Melody of the Heart

Precious Times (R)
Unrecognized Woman (R)
Virtuous Woman (R)
Woman of Worth (R)
Women Today (R)

GRANDPARENTING
Adult/General
$ CGA World (R)
Christian Family Journal
$ Christian Home & School
$ Churchmouse
   Publications (R)
$ Columbia (R)
$ Family Digest (R)
$ Focus on the Family
Good News Journal (R)
Gospel Herald
Halo Magazine
$ Home Times (R)
$ In His Presence (R)
$ In Touch
$ Indian Life (R)
Island Catholic (R)
$ JC Town Reporter (R)
$ KD Gospel Media
$ Liguorian
$ Live (R)
$ Lutheran Digest (R)
$ Mature Living
Nostalgia (R)
$ Our Sunday Visitor (R)
$ ParentLife
PrayerWorks (R)
$ Purpose (R)
$ Seek (R)
$ Significant Living (R)
$ Today's Pentecostal (R)
$ Vista (R)
Wisconsin Christian

Missions
$ Glad Tidings (R)

Women
Christian Work at Home
   Moms (R)
Crowned with Silver
Elegance (R)
$ Pauses . . .
Virtuous Woman (R)

HEALING
Adult/General
$ America
$ Angels on Earth
Anointed Pages
$ Associated Content (R)
Breakthrough Intercessor (R)
$ Canada Lutheran (R)
CBN.com (R)
$ Celebrate Life (R)
$ Christian Home & School
Christian Motorsports
Christian Online
Christian Quarterly (R)
Christian Ranchman
$ ChristianWeek (R)
$ Churchmouse Publications (R)
Connecting Point (R)
E-Channels (R)
Evangelical Advocate (R)
$ Faith Today
$ Foursquare Leader
$ Gem (R)
$ Good News (R)
Gospel Herald
$ Guideposts (R)
Halo Magazine
$ Home Times (R)
($) HopeKeepers (R)
Island Catholic (R)
$ JC Town Reporter (R)
$ KD Gospel Media
$ Light & Life
$ Live (R)
$ Miracles, Healings
New Heart (R)
New Identity (R)
$ Now What? (R)
$ Our Sunday Visitor (R)
Perspectives (R)
$ Positive Thinking (R)
Prayer Closet
$ Pure Inspiration (R)
$ Seek (R)
Sharing (R)
Single Again Mag. Online (R)
$ Sound Body (R)
$ Spiritual Life
$ St. Anthony Messenger
$ Testimony (R)

Trumpeter (R)
$ United Church Observer (R)
Urban Kingdom (R)
$ Way of St. Francis (R)
$ World & I (R)

Children
$ Bread for God's Children (R)
Skipping Stones

Daily Devotionals
Penned from the Heart (R)

Missions
$ Glad Tidings (R)

Music
($) TCP Magazine

Pastors/Leaders
$ Word & World

Teen/Young Adult
$ Boundless Webzine (R)
$ J.A.M.

Women
$ Canticle
Christian Woman's Page (R)
Extreme Woman Magazine
Hope for Women
$ Pauses . . .
Precious Times (R)
Share
$ SpiritLed Woman
Unrecognized Woman (R)
Virtuous Woman (R)
Woman of Worth (R)

Writers
Areopagus

HEALTH
Adult/General
$ Abilities
$ Angels on Earth
$ Anglican Journal
Anointed Pages
$ Apocalypse Chronicles (R)
$ Associated Content (R)
$ Aujourd'hui Credo (R)
$ B.C. Catholic (R)
$ Bible Advocate (R)
$ Brink Magazine (R)

$ Canada Lutheran (R)
$ Catholic Forester (R)
CBN.com (R)
$ Celebrate Life (R)
$ CGA World (R)
$ Christian Courier/Canada (R)
Christian Courier/WI (R)
Christian Health Care
$ Christian Home & School
Christian Online
Christian Quarterly (R)
Christian Ranchman
$ ChristianWeek (R)
$ Churchmouse Publications (R)
$ Common Ground (R)
$ Creative Nonfiction
Disciple's Journal (R)
E-Channels (R)
Evangelical Advocate (R)
$ Faith Today
Faithwebbin (R)
Fit Christian
Good News Journal (R)
Gospel Herald
$ Gospel Today (R)
$ Guideposts (R)
Halo Magazine
$ Home Times (R)
($) HopeKeepers (R)
$ In His Presence (R)
Island Catholic (R)
$ JC Town Reporter (R)
$ KD Gospel Media
$ Lifeglow (R)
$ Light & Life
$ Live (R)
$ Lookout
$ Mature Years (R)
$ MESSAGE
Message of the Open Bible (R)
New Heart (R)
New Identity (R)
$ Our Sunday Visitor (R)
$ Ozarks Senior Living (R)
($) P.O.W.E.R. Magazine
$ ParentLife
Penned from the Heart (R)
Perspectives/Science &
   Chr Faith
$ Positive Thinking (R)

$ Pure Inspiration (R)
Purpose Magazine (R)
Single Again Mag. Online (R)
$ Sound Body (R)
$ Special Living (R)
$ St. Anthony Messenger
$ Testimony (R)
$ Today's Pentecostal (R)
Trumpeter (R)
$ Upscale
Urban Kingdom (R)
$ Vibrant Life (R)
$ Vista (R)
$ War Cry (R)
Wisconsin Christian
$ World & I (R)
$ Written

Children
$ American Girl (R)
$ Bread for God's Children (R)
$ Guide (R)
$ New Moon Girls (R)
Skipping Stones
$ Sparkle (R)

Daily Devotionals
Penned from the Heart (R)

Missions
$ Glad Tidings (R)

Pastors/Leaders
$ Christian Century (R)
$ InSite (R)
$ Interpreter
$ Word & World

Teen/Young Adult
$ Boundless Webzine (R)
$ Devo'zine (R)
G4T Ink (R)
$ J.A.M.
$ Listen (R)
TeensForJC (R)
$ True Girl

Women
$ At the Center (R)
Christian Woman's Page (R)
Christian Women Today (R)
$ Dabbling Mum (R)
Elegance (R)

Empowering Everyday Women
$ Esprit
Extreme Woman Magazine
$ Heart & Soul
$ Horizons (R)
$ InspiredMoms (R)
$ inSpirit (R)
$ Journey
Life Tools for Women
Live Magazine
Lutheran Woman's Quar.
$ Pauses . . .
Precious Times (R)
Share
Simply Blessed (R)
$ SpiritLed Woman
Unrecognized Woman (R)
Virtuous Woman (R)
Woman of Worth (R)
Women Today (R)

HISPANIC MARKETS
Adult/General
$ El Herald Cristiano
$ Enfoque a la Familia
La Nueva Vision

HISTORICAL
($) AGAIN Magazine (R)
$ Angels on Earth
$ Arlington Catholic
$ Associated Content (R)
$ Capper's
$ Catholic Peace Voice (R)
CBN.com (R)
$ Celebrate Life (R)
$ Christian Courier/
   Canada (R)
$ Christian History (R)
Christian Motorsports
Christian Observer
Christian Online
$ Christian Renewal (R)
$ Citizen USA
$ Columbia (R)
$ Company Magazine (R)
Creation Care (R)
E-Channels (R)
$ Eureka Street
Evangelical Advocate (R)

Evangelical Times
$ Faith Today
$ Family Digest (R)
$ FGBC World (R)
Gospel Herald
Halo Magazine
$ Haruah (R)
$ Home Times (R)
$ In His Presence (R)
$ In Touch
$ Indian Life (R)
Island Catholic (R)
$ JC Town Reporter (R)
$ KD Gospel Media
$ Leben (R)
$ Lifeglow (R)
$ Light & Life
$ Lutheran Digest (R)
($) Mennonite Historian (R)
$ Messiah Journal
Messianic Times
Methodist History
New Identity (R)
$ New Wineskins (R)
Nostalgia (R)
$ Our Sunday Visitor (R)
$ Over the Back Fence (R)
Perspectives (R)
Perspectives/Science &
   Chr. Faith
$ Power for Living (R)
PrayerWorks (R)
$ Presbyterian Outlook
Priscilla Papers
Sharing (R)
$ Social Justice (R)
$ St. Anthony Messenger
$ Storyteller (R)
Sword of the Lord (R)
Trumpeter (R)
$ U.S. Catholic
$ Upscale
Urban Kingdom (R)
$ Way of St. Francis (R)
$ Wesleyan Life (R)
Wisconsin Christian
$ World & I (R)

Children
$ Archaeology

$ Bread for God's Children (R)
$ Faces
$ Focus/Clubhouse Jr.
$ Guide (R)
$ New Moon Girls (R)
$ Sparkle (R)

Christian Education/ Library
Catholic Library

Missions
East-West Church & Ministry
   Report
$ Glad Tidings (R)
$ One
Women of the Harvest

Music
$ Creator (R)
Hymn

Pastors/Leaders
$ Leadership (R)
Lutheran Forum
$ Ministry Today
$ Priest
Pulpit Helps (R)
Sewanee Theo. Review
Theological Digest (R)
$ Today's Parish
$ Word & World

Teen/Young Adult
$ Boundless Webzine (R)
$ J.A.M.
$ Real Faith in Life (R)
TeensForJC (R)
$ Young Adult Today
$ Young Christian Writers

Women
($) History's Women (R)
$ SpiritLed Woman

Writers
Areopagus
$ Tickled by Thunder

HOLIDAY/SEASONAL
Adult/General
$ Alive Now (R)
American Tract (R)

$ Angels on Earth
$ Animal Trails (R)
$ Annals of St. Anne
$ Arlington Catholic
Bread of Life (R)
$ Brink Magazine (R)
$ Canada Lutheran (R)
$ Capper's
$ Cathedral Age
$ Catholic Digest (R)
$ Catholic New York
CBN.com (R)
$ CGA World (R)
$ Chicken Soup Books (R)
$ Christian Courier/Canada (R)
Christian Courier/WI (R)
Christian Family Journal
$ Christian Home & School
$ Christian Journal (R)
Christian Online
$ Christian Renewal (R)
$ Christian Retailing
$ ChristianWeek (R)
$ Churchmouse Publications (R)
$ City Light News (R)
$ Columbia (R)
Connecting Point (R)
$ Converge Point (R)
$ Covenant Companion (R)
Desert Call (R)
E-Channels (R)
Eternal Ink (R)
Evangelical Advocate (R)
$ Faith & Family
$ Faith Today
Faithwebbin (R)
$ Family Digest (R)
$ Family Smart E-tips (R)
$ Focus on the Family
$ Foursquare Leader
$ Gem (R)
$ Gems of Truth (R)
$ Good News in Florida (R)
Good News Journal (R)
$ Good News, Etc. (R)
Gospel Herald
$ Guideposts (R)
Halo Magazine
HEARTLIGHT Internet (R)
$ Home Times (R)

($) HopeKeepers (R)
$ Horizons (adult) (R)
$ In His Presence (R)
$ In Touch
$ JC Town Reporter (R)
$ KD Gospel Media
$ Lifeglow (R)
$ Light & Life
$ Liguorian
$ Live (R)
$ Living (R)
$ Living Church
$ Living Light (R)
$ Lookout
$ Manna (R)
$ Mature Living
$ Mature Years (R)
Messianic Perspectives (R)
$ Miraculous Medal
$ Montana Catholic
$ Montgomery's Journey
$ On Mission
$ Our Sunday Visitor (R)
$ Over the Back Fence (R)
$ ParentLife
Penned from the Heart (R)
$ Positive Thinking (R)
$ Power for Living (R)
$ Prairie Messenger (R)
PrayerWorks (R)
$ Psychology for Living (R)
$ Pure Inspiration (R)
$ Purpose (R)
Reverent Submissions (R)
$ Seek (R)
Sharing (R)
$ Special Living (R)
$ St. Anthony Messenger
Sword of the Lord (R)
$ Today's Christian (R)
$ Together (R)
Trumpeter (R)
$ U.S. Catholic
$ United Church Observer (R)
Urban Kingdom (R)
$ Vibrant Life (R)
Victory Herald (R)
$ Victory in Grace (R)
$ Vision (R)
$ Vista (R)

$ War Cry (R)
$ Way of St. Francis (R)
$ Wesleyan Life (R)
$ World & I (R)

Children
$ Archaeology
$ Focus/Clubhouse
$ Focus/Clubhouse Jr.
$ Guide (R)
$ Junior Companion (R)
$ JuniorWay
$ Nature Friend (R)
$ Pockets (R)
$ Primary Street
$ SHINE brightly (R)
Skipping Stones
$ Sparkle (R)

Christian Education/ Library
$ Group Magazine
$ Today's Catholic Teacher (R)
$ Youth & CE Leadership

Daily Devotionals
Penned from the Heart (R)
$ These Days

Missions
$ Glad Tidings (R)
Railroad Evangelist (R)
Women of the Harvest

Music
$ Creator (R)

Pastors/Leaders
$ Catholic Servant
$ Interpreter
$ Preaching Well (R)
Pulpit Helps (R)
$ Sunday Sermons (R)

Teen/Young Adult
$ Boundless Webzine (R)
$ Credo (R)
$ Essential Connection (ec)
$ J.A.M.
$ Real Faith in Life (R)
TeensForJC (R)
$ True Girl
$ Young Christian (R)

$ Young Christian Writers
$ Young Salvationist (R)

Women
($) Beyond the Bend (R)
$ Canticle
Christian Women Today (R)
Elegance (R)
$ Esprit
For Every Woman (R)
Handmaiden (R)
($) History's Women (R)
Hope for Women
$ InspiredMoms (R)
$ inSpirit (R)
$ Journey
Just Between Us (R)
Lutheran Woman's Quar.
P31 Woman (R)
$ Pauses . . .
Precious Times (R)
Together with God (R)
Unrecognized Woman (R)
Virtuous Woman (R)

Writers
Areopagus
$ Cross & Quill (R)

HOLY SPIRIT
Adult/General
Bread of Life (R)
Breakthrough Intercessor (R)
$ Christian Home & School
$ Christian Journal (R)
Christian Quarterly (R)
Christian Ranchman
$ Churchmouse
   Publications (R)
$ Columbia (R)
$ EFCA Today
Eternal Ink (R)
Faithwebbin (R)
Gospel Herald
Halo Magazine
$ Home Times (R)
$ In Touch
$ JC Town Reporter (R)
$ KD Gospel Media
$ Light & Life
$ Live (R)

Maine Family Policy (R)
$ Our Sunday Visitor (R)
PrayerWorks (R)
$ Pure Inspiration (R)
Reverent Submissions (R)
Saved Magazine
$ Seek (R)
Spirituality for Today
Urban Kingdom (R)
Victory Herald (R)
$ Vista (R)
$ Way of St. Francis (R)
Wisconsin Christian

Children
$ Bread for God's
   Children (R)

Missions
$ Glad Tidings (R)

Music
($) TCP Magazine

Pastors/Leaders
$ Enrichment Journal (R)
$ Lutheran Partners (R)
$ Ministry Today

Teen/Young Adult
$ Boundless Webzine (R)

Women
$ Come to the Fire (R)
Elegance (R)
For Every Woman (R)
Jewels of God (R)
Just Between Us (R)
$ Pauses . . .
Unrecognized Woman (R)
Woman of Worth (R)

HOMESCHOOLING
Adult/General
$ Animal Trails (R)
Christian Family Journal
$ Columbia (R)
Desert Voice (R)
Faithwebbin (R)
$ Good News in Florida (R)
$ Good News, Etc. (R)
Gospel Herald
$ Home Times (R)

$ In His Presence (R)
$ In Touch
$ JC Town Reporter (R)
$ KD Gospel Media
$ Our Sunday Visitor (R)
$ ParentLife
Wisconsin Christian

Children
$ Archaeology
$ Bread for God's Children (R)
$ New Moon Girls (R)
Skipping Stones

Christian Education/ Library
Jour./Ed. & Christian Belief (R)

Missions
$ Glad Tidings (R)
Women of the Harvest

Teen/Young Adult
$ Boundless Webzine (R)
$ Insight (R)
$ J.A.M.
$ True Girl
$ Young Christian (R)

Women
$ Canticle
Christian Woman's Page (R)
Christian Work at Home
    Moms (R)
Crowned with Silver
For Every Woman (R)
Hope for Women
$ InspiredMoms (R)
$ inSpirit (R)
Jewels of God (R)
$ Journey
Unrecognized Woman (R)
Virtuous Woman (R)
Woman of Worth (R)

HOMILETICS
Adult/General
CBN.com (R)
Christian Ranchman
$ Columbia (R)
E-Channels (R)
Evangelical Advocate (R)
Gospel Herald

Halo Magazine
$ In Touch
$ New Wineskins (R)
Perspectives (R)
Priscilla Papers
$ Social Justice (R)
$ St. Anthony Messenger
$ Stewardship (R)
$ Testimony (R)
Trumpeter (R)
$ Wesleyan Life (R)

Missions
$ Glad Tidings (R)

Pastors/Leaders
$ African-American Pulpit
$ Christian Century (R)
$ Clergy Journal (R)
$ Enrichment Journal (R)
$ Lutheran Partners (R)
$ Ministry & Liturgy (R)
Preaching
$ Preaching Well (R)
$ Priest
$ Proclaim (R)
Sewanee Theo. Review

Women
$ SpiritLed Woman
Unrecognized Woman (R)

HOW-TO
Adult/General
$ Animal Trails (R)
$ Associated Content (R)
$ Bridal Guides (R)
$ Brink Magazine (R)
$ CBA Retailers
CBN.com (R)
$ Celebrate Life (R)
$ CGA World (R)
Christian Motorsports
Christian Observer
Christian Online
$ Christian Retailing
$ Churchmouse
    Publications (R)
Connecting Point (R)
$ Direction
E-Channels (R)

$ Faith & Family
$ Faith Today
$ Family Digest (R)
$ Family Smart E-tips (R)
$ Focus on the Family
Good News Journal (R)
$ Good News, Etc. (R)
Gospel Herald
Halo Magazine
$ Home Times (R)
($) HopeKeepers (R)
$ Imagine
$ In Touch
$ JC Town Reporter (R)
$ Live (R)
$ Living (R)
$ Living Church
$ MESSAGE
($) Mutuality (R)
$ On Mission
$ ParentLife
$ Positive Thinking (R)
PrayerWorks (R)
$ Presbyterians Today (R)
Regent Global Bus. Rev. (R)
$ Significant Living (R)
$ St. Anthony Messenger
$ Testimony (R)
Trumpeter (R)
$ U.S. Catholic
Urban Kingdom (R)
$ Vibrant Life (R)
Victory Herald (R)
$ Vista (R)
$ World & I (R)
$ Written

Children
$ Archaeology
$ Cadet Quest (R)
$ Sparkle (R)

Christian Education/ Library
$ Catechist
Catholic Library
$ Christian Educators (R)
Christian Librarian (R)
$ Church Libraries (R)
Congregational Libraries Today
$ Group Magazine

$ Jour./Adventist Ed. (R)
$ Kids' Ministry Ideas
$ Preschool Playhouse (CE)
$ Teachers of Vision (R)
$ Today's Catholic Teacher (R)
$ Youth & CE Leadership

Missions
$ Glad Tidings (R)
$ PFI Global Link Journal (R)

Pastors/Leaders
$ African-American Pulpit
$ Insight Youth (R)
$ Lead Magazine (R)
$ Lutheran Partners (R)
$ Ministry
$ Ministry & Liturgy (R)
$ Ministry Today
$ Net Results
$ Newsletter Newsletter
$ Outreach (R)
$ RevWriter Resource
$ Worship Leader
$ Your Church (R)

Teen/Young Adult
$ Listen (R)
$ Real Faith in Life (R)
TeensForJC (R)
$ True Girl

Women
($) Beyond the Bend (R)
Christian Woman's Page (R)
Christian Women Today (R)
Christian Work at Home
    Moms (R)
$ Dabbling Mum (R)
Elegance (R)
Extreme Woman Magazine
Hope for Women
Jewels of God (R)
Just Between Us (R)
$ Melody of the Heart
Precious Times (R)
Unrecognized Woman (R)
Virtuous Woman (R)
Woman of Worth (R)

Writers
$ Advanced Christian Writer (R)
Author-Me

$ Cross & Quill (R)
Esdras' Scroll (R)
$ Fellowscript (R)
$ Freelance Writer's
    Report (R)
$ Poets & Writers
$ Spirit-Led Writer (R)
$ Writer's Digest

HOW-TO ACTIVITIES (JUV.)
Adult/General
$ Animal Trails (R)
$ Associated Content (R)
$ Christian Home & School
Christian Online
$ Churchmouse
    Publications (R)
E-Channels (R)
$ Faith & Family
$ Family Smart E-tips (R)
$ Homeschooling Today (R)
$ JC Town Reporter (R)
Keys to Living (R)
$ On Mission
$ ParentLife
$ St. Anthony Messenger
$ World & I (R)

Children
$ Adventures
$ American Girl (R)
$ Archaeology
$ Bread for God's
    Children (R)
$ Cadet Quest (R)
$ Celebrate
$ Faces
$ Focus/Clubhouse
$ Focus/Clubhouse Jr.
$ Guide (R)
$ Junior Companion (R)
$ JuniorWay
$ Kid Zone
$ Nature Friend (R)
$ Pockets (R)
$ Preschool Playhouse
$ Seeds
$ SHINE brightly (R)
$ Sparkle (R)

Christian Education/Library
$ Children's Ministry
Christian Early Ed. (R)
$ Group Magazine
$ Kids' Ministry Ideas
$ Preschool Playhouse (CE)

Missions
$ Glad Tidings (R)

Pastors/Leaders
$ Interpreter

Teen/Young Adult
$ Listen (R)
$ True Girl
$ Young Christian (R)

Women
Christian Work at Home Moms
    (R)
Elegance (R)

HUMOR
Adult/General
$ Abilities
American Tract (R)
$ Angels on Earth
$ Associated Content (R)
$ Brink Magazine (R)
$ Catholic Digest (R)
$ Catholic Forester (R)
$ Catholic Peace Voice (R)
CBN.com (R)
$ CGA World (R)
$ Chicken Soup Books (R)
Christian Computing (R)
$ Christian Courier/Canada (R)
$ Christian Home & School
$ Christian Journal (R)
Christian Online
Christian Quarterly (R)
Christian Ranchman
$ Christianity Today (R)
$ Churchmouse Publications (R)
$ City Light News (R)
Connecting Point (R)
Creation Care (R)
$ Creative Nonfiction
Desert Voice (R)
Disciple's Journal (R)

E-Channels (R)
Eternal Ink (R)
$ Faith & Family
$ Faith Today
$ Family Smart E-tips (R)
$ Focus on the Family
$ Gem (R)
$ Good News in Florida (R)
Good News Journal (R)
$ Good News, Etc. (R)
Gospel Herald
Halo Magazine
$ Haruah (R)
Highway News (R)
$ Home Times (R)
$ Homeschooling Today (R)
($) HopeKeepers (R)
$ Horizons (adult) (R)
$ In His Presence (R)
$ In Touch
$ Indian Life (R)
Island Catholic (R)
$ JC Town Reporter (R)
$ KD Gospel Media
$ Lifeglow (R)
$ Liguorian
$ Living (R)
$ Living Church
$ Living Light (R)
$ Lookout
$ Manna (R)
$ Mature Living
Men.AG.org (R)
$ Miracles, Healings
More Excellent Way
New Christian Voices
New Heart (R)
$ New Wineskins (R)
Nostalgia (R)
$ Our Sunday Visitor (R)
$ Over the Back Fence (R)
$ Ozarks Senior Living (R)
Pegasus Review (R)
Penned from the Heart (R)
$ Positive Thinking (R)
PrayerWorks (R)
$ Psychology for Living (R)
Reverent Submissions (R)
$ Rose & Thorn
Ruminate

$ Seek (R)
$ Significant Living (R)
$ St. Anthony Messenger
$ Storyteller (R)
$ Testimony (R)
$ Together (R)
Trumpeter (R)
$ U.S. Catholic
Urban Kingdom (R)
Victory Herald (R)
$ Victory in Grace (R)
$ Vista (R)
$ War Cry (R)
$ Way of St. Francis (R)
$ Weavings (R)
$ Wildwood Reader (R)
$ World & I (R)
Xavier Review

Children
$ Cadet Quest (R)
$ Faces
$ Focus/Clubhouse Jr.
$ SHINE brightly (R)
$ Sparkle (R)

Christian Education/ Library
$ Children's Ministry

Daily Devotionals
Penned from the Heart (R)

Missions
$ Glad Tidings (R)
Women of the Harvest

Music
Christian Music Weekly (R)
$ Creator (R)

Pastors/Leaders
$ Catholic Servant
$ Enrichment Journal (R)
$ Leadership (R)
$ Lutheran Partners (R)
Ministry in Motion (R)
$ Preaching Well (R)
$ Priest
$ Today's Parish

Teen/Young Adult
$ Boundless Webzine (R)

$ Direction Student
$ Essential Connection (ec)
G4T Ink (R)
$ Horizon Student
$ Real Faith in Life (R)
$ TC Magazine
TeensForJC (R)
$ Young Christian Writers
$ Young Salvationist (R)

Women
($) Beyond the Bend (R)
Crowned with Silver
Elegance (R)
$ Esprit
Extreme Woman Magazine
Hope for Women
$ Horizons (R)
Jewels of God (R)
$ Journey
Lutheran Woman's Quar.
$ MD Women of Worship
$ Melody of the Heart
$ MomSense (R)
Simply Blessed (R)
$ SpiritLed Woman
Unrecognized Woman (R)

Writers
Areopagus
$ Christian Communicator (R)
$ New Writer's Mag.

INNER LIFE
Adult/General
$ Bible Advocate (R)
$ Catholic Digest (R)
CBN.com (R)
$ Christian Journal (R)
Christian Ranchman
$ ChristianWeek (R)
$ Churchmouse
   Publications (R)
Divine Ascent
E-Channels (R)
$ Faith & Family
$ Faith Today
$ Focus on the Family
Gospel Herald
Halo Magazine
$ In Touch

Island Catholic (R)
$ JC Town Reporter (R)
LifeTimes Catholic
$ Light & Life
$ Live (R)
$ Living (R)
$ Mature Years (R)
$ Men of Integrity (R)
$ MindFlights (R)
Mosaic (R)
$ New Wineskins (R)
$ Our Sunday Visitor (R)
($) P.O.W.E.R. Magazine
Penned from the Heart (R)
$ Positive Thinking (R)
$ Presbyterians Today (R)
$ Pure Inspiration (R)
Regent Global Bus. Rev.(R)
Reverent Submissions (R)
$ Seek (R)
Spirituality for Today
$ Testimony (R)
$ Together (R)
Urban Kingdom (R)
Victory Herald (R)
$ Way of St. Francis (R)
$ Weavings (R)
$ Wildwood Reader (R)
$ World & I (R)

Missions
$ Glad Tidings (R)

Pastors/Leaders
$ Interpreter
Jour./Pastoral Care
$ Lutheran Partners (R)

Teen/Young Adult
$ Boundless Webzine (R)
Exodus Magazine
$ TC Magazine
TeensForJC (R)
$ Young Salvationist (R)

Women
$ Canticle
Christian Woman's Page (R)
$ Come to the Fire (R)
Crowned with Silver
Empowering Everyday Women
$ FullFill

$ Journey
Just Between Us (R)
$ Pauses . . .
Unrecognized Woman (R)
Women Today (R)

INSPIRATIONAL
Adult/General
African Voices (R)
$ Alive Now (R)
$ Angels on Earth
$ Animal Trails (R)
$ Annals of St. Anne
$ Arlington Catholic
$ Associated Content (R)
$ Aujourd'hui Credo (R)
Bread of Life (R)
Breakthrough Intercessor (R)
$ Bridal Guides (R)
$ Brink Magazine (R)
$ Canada Lutheran (R)
$ Canadian Mennonite (R)
$ Capper's
$ Catholic Forester (R)
$ Catholic Peace Voice (R)
CBN.com (R)
$ Celebrate Life (R)
$ CGA World (R)
$ Chicken Soup Books (R)
Christian Family Journal
$ Christian Home & School
$ Christian Journal (R)
Christian Motorsports
Christian Online
Christian Quarterly (R)
Christian Ranchman
$ Churchmouse
    Publications (R)
$ Columbia (R)
Connecting Point (R)
$ Covenant Companion (R)
$ Decision
$ Direction
$ DisciplesWorld
Divine Ascent
$ DreamSeeker (R)
E-Channels (R)
Eternal Ink (R)
$ Evangel/IN (R)
Evangelical Advocate (R)

$ Faith & Family
$ Faith Today
Faithwebbin (R)
$ Family Digest (R)
$ Focus on the Family
$ Foursquare Leader
$ Gem (R)
$ Good News (R)
$ Good News in Florida (R)
Good News Journal (R)
Gospel Herald
$ Gospel Today (R)
$ Guideposts (R)
Halo Magazine
HEARTLIGHT Internet (R)
Highway News (R)
$ Home Times (R)
($) HopeKeepers (R)
$ In His Presence (R)
$ In Touch
$ Indian Life (R)
$ JC Town Reporter (R)
$ KD Gospel Media
Keys to Living (R)
Koinonia
Leaves (R)
$ Lifeglow (R)
$ Liguorian
$ Live (R)
$ Living (R)
$ Living Church
$ Lookout
$ Lutheran Digest (R)
$ Marian Helper
$ Mature Living
($) Mennonite Historian (R)
$ MESSAGE
Message of the Open Bible (R)
$ Messenger/Sacred Heart
Messianic Perspectives (R)
$ MindFlights (R)
$ Miracles, Healings
Mosaic (R)
($) Mutuality (R)
New Heart (R)
New Identity (R)
Nostalgia (R)
$ ParentLife
Pegasus Review (R)
Penned from the Heart (R)

$ Positive Thinking (R)
$ Power for Living (R)
$ Prairie Messenger (R)
PrayerWorks (R)
$ Precepts for Living
$ Presbyterians Today (R)
$ Priority! (R)
$ Psychology for Living (R)
$ Pure Inspiration (R)
$ Purpose (R)
Quaker Life (R)
Reverent Submissions (R)
$ Seek (R)
$ Significant Living (R)
Single Again Mag. Online (R)
Spirituality for Today
$ Standard (R)
$ St. Anthony Messenger
$ Stewardship (R)
$ Storyteller (R)
SW Kansas Faith
Sword and Trumpet
Sword of the Lord (R)
$ Testimony (R)
$ Today's Christian (R)
$ Together (R)
Trumpeter (R)
$ U.S. Catholic
$ United Church
   Observer (R)
$ Upscale
Urban Kingdom (R)
Victory Herald (R)
$ Victory in Grace (R)
$ Vista (R)
$ War Cry (R)
$ Way of St. Francis (R)
$ Wesleyan Life (R)
$ Wildwood Reader (R)
$ World & I (R)

Children
$ Archaeology
$ Bread for God's Children (R)
$ Cadet Quest (R)
$ Partners (R)
$ Passport (R)
$ Primary Street
$ SHINE brightly (R)
$ Sparkle (R)

Christian Education/ Library
Catholic Library
$ Children's Ministry
Congregational Libraries Today
$ Jour./Adventist Ed. (R)
$ Youth & CE Leadership

Daily Devotionals
Penned from the Heart (R)
$ Rejoice!

Missions
$ Glad Tidings (R)
Women of the Harvest

Music
$ Creator (R)
($) TCP Magazine

Pastors/Leaders
$ African-American Pulpit
$ Catholic Servant
$ Interpreter
$ Let's Worship
$ Ministry Today
$ Preaching Well (R)
$ Priest
Technologies for Worship (R)

Teen/Young Adult
$ Boundless Webzine (R)
$ Devo'zine (R)
$ Direction Student
Exodus Magazine
G4T Ink (R)
$ Horizon Student
$ Insight (R)
$ J.A.M.
TeensForJC (R)
$ True Girl
$ Young Christian (R)
$ Young Salvationist (R)

Women
($) Beyond the Bend (R)
Christian Women Today (R)
$ Come to the Fire (R)
Elegance (R)
Empowering Everyday Women
$ Esprit
Extreme Woman Magazine
For Every Woman (R)

$ FullFill
Handmaiden (R)
Hope for Women
$ Horizons (R)
$ InspiredMoms (R)
$ inSpirit (R)
Jewels of God (R)
$ Journey
$ Link & Visitor (R)
Lutheran Woman's Quar.
$ MomSense (R)
P31 Woman (R)
$ Pauses . . .
Precious Times (R)
Right to the Heart (R)
Share
Simply Blessed (R)
$ SpiritLed Woman
Unrecognized Woman (R)
Virtuous Woman (R)
Woman of Worth (R)

Writers
Areopagus
NW Christian Author (R)
$ Writer's Digest

INTERVIEWS/PROFILES
Adult/General
$ Abilities
($) AGAIN Magazine (R)
American Tract (R)
$ Anglican Journal
Anointed Pages
$ Arkansas Catholic (R)
$ Arlington Catholic
$ Associated Content (R)
$ Australian Catholics (R)
Baptist Standard
Biblical Recorder
Books & Culture
Breakthrough Intercessor (R)
$ Brink Magazine (R)
$ Canadian Mennonite (R)
CanadianChristianity.com
$ Cathedral Age
$ Catholic New York
$ Catholic Peace Voice (R)
CBN.com (R)
$ Celebrate Life (R)

Challenge Weekly
$ Charisma
Charlotte World
Christian Business
Christian Chronicle
Christian Courier/WI (R)
$ Christian Herald (R)
Christian Motorsports
Christian Observer
Christian Online
Christian Ranchman
$ Christianity Today (R)
$ Christianity Today Movies (R)
$ ChristianWeek (R)
$ Churchmouse Publications (R)
Church of England News
$ City Light News (R)
$ Columbia (R)
Creation Care (R)
$ Culture Wars (R)
Desert Call (R)
Desert Christian
$ DisciplesWorld
Divine Ascent
E-Channels (R)
Encompass
$ Episcopal Life (R)
Eternal Ink (R)
Evangel/OR (R)
$ Faith Today
Faithwebbin (R)
$ FGBC World (R)
$ Focus on the Family
$ Gem (R)
$ Good News (R)
Good News Connection
$ Good News in Florida (R)
Good News Journal (R)
Good News Today
$ Good News, Etc. (R)
Gospel Herald
$ Gospel Today (R)
$ Guideposts (R)
Halo Magazine
Heartland Gatekeeper (R)
HEARTLIGHT Internet (R)
$ Home Times (R)
($) HopeKeepers (R)
$ In His Presence (R)
$ In Touch

$ Indian Life (R)
$ Interim (R)
$ JC Town Reporter (R)
$ KD Gospel Media
$ Kindred Spirit (R)
$ Lifeglow (R)
LifeSiteNews
$ Light & Life
$ Liguorian
$ Living Church
$ Lookout
$ Manna (R)
$ MESSAGE
Messianic Perspectives (R)
$ MindFlights (R)
More Excellent Way
($) Mutuality (R)
New Heart (R)
New Identity (R)
$ On Mission
$ Our Sunday Visitor (R)
$ Ozarks Senior Living (R)
$ ParentLife
$ Positive Thinking (R)
$ Power for Living (R)
PrayerWorks (R)
$ Presbyterian Outlook
$ Priority! (R)
$ Prism
$ Pure Inspiration (R)
Regent Global Bus. Rev. (R)
$ Search
$ St. Anthony Messenger
$ Stewardship (R)
$ Testimony (R)
$ Today's Christian (R)
Tri-State Voice
Trumpeter (R)
$ United Church Observer (R)
$ Upscale
Urban Kingdom (R)
$ Vibrant Life (R)
$ War Cry (R)
$ Way of St. Francis (R)
$ Weavings (R)
Wisconsin Christian
$ World & I (R)

Children
$ American Girl (R)

$ Cadet Quest (R)
$ Faces
$ New Moon Girls (R)
$ Pockets (R)
$ Primary Street
$ SHINE brightly (R)
Skipping Stones
$ Sparkle (R)

Christian Education/ Library
$ Children's Ministry
$ Church Libraries (R)
$ Youth & CE Leadership

Missions
East-West Church & Ministry
    Report
$ Evangelical Missions (R)
$ Glad Tidings (R)
$ Leaders for Today
Op. Reveille Interactive
    Jour. (R)
$ PFI Global Link Journal (R)

Music
$ Christian Music Today (R)

Pastors/Leaders
$ African-American Pulpit
$ Catholic Servant
$ Christian Century (R)
$ Enrichment Journal (R)
$ InSite (R)
Ministry in Motion (R)
$ Ministry Today
$ Outreach (R)
$ Priest

Teen/Young Adult
$ Boundless Webzine (R)
$ Credo (R)
$ Direction Student
$ Essential Connection (ec)
Exodus Magazine
$ Horizon Student
$ J.A.M.
$ Listen (R)
$ Risen
$ Spirit
$ TC Magazine
TeensForJC (R)
$ True Girl

$ Young Salvationist (R)
$ YouthWalk

Women
Christian Work at Home Moms
  (R)
Elegance (R)
Empowering Everyday Women
$ Esprit
Extreme Woman Magazine
$ Horizons (R)
$ Journey
Just Between Us (R)
$ Link & Visitor (R)
More to Life
$ Pauses . . .
Precious Times (R)
Unrecognized Woman (R)
Virtuous Woman (R)
Woman of Worth (R)

Writers
$ Advanced Christian Writer (R)
Areopagus
$ Christian Communicator (R)
$ Cross & Quill (R)
$ Fellowscript (R)
$ New Writer's Mag.
$ Poets & Writers
Write Connection
$ Writer
$ Writer's Digest
Writers Manual
$ Writers' Journal

LEADERSHIP
Adult/General
African Voices (R)
$ Angels on Earth
CBN.com (R)
Christian Business
$ Christian Courier/
  Canada (R)
$ Christian Home & School
Christian Motorsports
$ Christian Retailing
$ Christian Standard (R)
$ ChristianWeek (R)
$ Churchmouse Publications (R)
$ Columbia (R)
Connections Ldrship/MOPS

$ Culture Wars (R)
Desert Voice (R)
Disciple's Journal (R)
E-Channels (R)
$ EFCA Today
Encompass
Evangelical Advocate (R)
$ Faith Today
$ Foursquare Leader
$ Gem (R)
$ Good News (R)
Good News Journal (R)
$ Good News, Etc. (R)
Gospel Herald
Halo Magazine
HEARTLIGHT Internet (R)
($) HopeKeepers (R)
$ In Touch
$ JC Town Reporter (R)
$ KD Gospel Media
$ Light & Life
$ Living Church
$ Lookout
Maine Family Policy (R)
$ Manna (R)
$ Men of Integrity (R)
Men of the Cross
Men.AG.org (R)
MissionWares
Mosaic (R)
($) Mutuality (R)
$ New Wineskins (R)
($) NBR E-Magazine (R)
$ Our Sunday Visitor (R)
$ Presbyterian Outlook
Priscilla Papers
Quaker Life (R)
Regent Global Bus. Rev. (R)
Reverent Submissions (R)
$ St. Anthony Messenger
$ Stewardship (R)
$ Testimony (R)
Trumpeter (R)
$ United Church Observer (R)
Urban Kingdom (R)
Victory Herald (R)
$ Vista (R)
$ Way of St. Francis (R)
Wisconsin Christian
$ World & I (R)

Children
$ Bread for God's Children (R)

Christian Education/ Library
Catholic Library
$ Children's Ministry
Christian Early Ed. (R)
Christian Librarian (R)
Christian School Ed. (R)
$ Group Magazine
Jour./Research on Christian Ed.
$ Momentum
$ Teachers of Vision (R)
$ Today's Catholic Teacher (R)
$ Youth & CE Leadership

Missions
East-West Church & Ministry
  Report
$ Glad Tidings (R)
$ Leaders for Today
Mission Connection

Pastors/Leaders
$ African-American Pulpit
$ Catholic Servant
$ Christian Century (R)
Christian Education Jour. (R)
$ Clergy Journal (R)
$ Enrichment Journal (R)
$ Growth Points (R)
$ InSite (R)
$ Interpreter
Jour./Amer. Soc. for Church
  Growth (R)
$ Lead Magazine (R)
$ Leadership (R)
$ Lutheran Partners (R)
$ Ministry
Ministry in Motion (R)
$ Ministry Today
$ Net Results
$ Outreach (R)
Plugged In
Pulpit Helps (R)
$ RevWriter Resource
Rick Warren's Ministry
  Toolbox (R)
$ SmallGroups.com (R)
Theological Digest (R)

$ Word & World
$ Worship Leader
$ Your Church (R)

Teen/Young Adult
$ Boundless Webzine (R)
$ Direction Student
$ Horizon Student
TeensForJC (R)
$ Young Christian Writers

Women
($) Beyond the Bend (R)
Elegance (R)
$ Esprit
For Every Woman (R)
$ Horizons (R)
Just Between Us (R)
Precious Times (R)
Right to the Heart (R)
Share
$ SpiritLed Woman
Unrecognized Woman (R)
Women of the Cross
Women Today (R)

LIFESTYLE ARTICLES
Adult/General
Anointed Pages
$ Bible Advocate (R)
Breakthrough
$ Brink Magazine (R)
Brink Online
byFaith
$ Catholic Insight
CBN.com (R)
Christian Family Journal
$ Christian Journal (R)
Christian Ranchman
$ ChristianWeek (R)
$ Churchmouse
   Publications (R)
$ City Light News (R)
Connections Ldrship/MOPS
Creation Care (R)
$ FGBC World (R)
Fit Christian
$ Focus on the Family
$ Good News in Florida (R)
Good News Journal (R)
$ Good News, Etc. (R)

Gospel Herald
Halo Magazine
$ Home Times (R)
$ In His Presence (R)
$ In Touch
Island Catholic (R)
$ JC Town Reporter (R)
$ KD Gospel Media
$ Light & Life
$ Liguorian
$ Live (R)
$ Lookout
$ Manna (R)
$ Mature Living
Men.AG.org (R)
$ Montgomery's Journey
New Identity (R)
Nostalgia (R)
$ Our Sunday Visitor (R)
Ozarks Christian News
$ ParentLife
$ Priority! (R)
$ Pure Inspiration (R)
Saved Magazine
$ Seek (R)
3V Magazine
Urban Kingdom (R)
$ Vibrant Life (R)
$ Way of St. Francis (R)

Children
$ Bread for God's
   Children (R)

Missions
$ Glad Tidings (R)
wec.go

Teen/Young Adult
$ Boundless Webzine (R)
$ Direction Student
Exodus Magazine
$ Horizon Student
$ Insight (R)
$ TC Magazine

Women
($) Beyond the Bend (R)
Christian Woman's Page (R)
Crowned with Silver
Elegance (R)
Empowering Everyday Women

For Every Woman (R)
$ FullFill
Hope for Women
Jewels of God (R)
Live Magazine
Unrecognized Woman (R)
Women Today (R)

LITURGICAL
Adult/General
($) AGAIN Magazine (R)
$ Alive Now (R)
$ Arlington Catholic
$ Aujourd'hui Credo (R)
$ Cathedral Age
$ Catholic Yearbook (R)
$ Columbia (R)
$ Culture Wars (R)
Divine Ascent
E-Channels (R)
$ Episcopal Life (R)
Gospel Herald
Halo Magazine
Island Catholic (R)
$ Living Church
$ Lutheran Journal (R)
$ Messenger/Sacred Heart
$ New Wineskins (R)
$ Our Sunday Visitor (R)
Perspectives (R)
$ Prairie Messenger (R)
$ Social Justice (R)
$ St. Anthony Messenger
$ Testimony (R)
Urban Kingdom (R)
$ Way of St. Francis (R)

Christian Education/
Library
$ Mommentum

Missions
East-West Church & Ministry
   Report
$ Glad Tidings (R)

Pastors/Leaders
$ African-American Pulpit
$ Barefoot (R)
$ Catholic Servant
$ Christian Century (R)

$ Clergy Journal (R)
CrossCurrents
$ Diocesan Dialogue (R)
Lutheran Forum
$ Lutheran Partners (R)
$ Ministry & Liturgy (R)
$ Parish Liturgy (R)
$ Preaching Well (R)
$ Reformed Worship (R)
Rick Warren's Ministry
    Toolbox (R)
Sewanee Theo. Review
$ Today's Parish
$ Word & World

Women
$ Horizons (R)

MARRIAGE
Adult/General
$ Angels on Earth
Anointed Pages
$ Arlington Catholic
$ Associated Content (R)
$ Atlantic Catholic
Breakthrough Intercessor (R)
$ Bridal Guides (R)
$ Brink Magazine (R)
$ Canada Lutheran (R)
$ Catholic Digest (R)
CBN.com (R)
$ Celebrate Life (R)
$ Christian Courier/Canada (R)
$ Christian Examiner
Christian Family Journal
$ Christian Home & School
$ Christian Journal (R)
Christian Motorsports
Christian Online
Christian Quarterly (R)
Christian Ranchman
$ Christian Research
$ Christian Standard (R)
$ ChristianWeek (R)
Church Herald & Holiness (R)
$ Churchmouse
    Publications (R)
$ Columbia (R)
$ Converge Point (R)
$ Culture Wars (R)

$ Decision
Desert Voice (R)
Disciple's Journal (R)
E-Channels (R)
$ Evangel/IN (R)
Evangelical Advocate (R)
$ Faith & Family
$ Faith Today
Faithwebbin (R)
$ Family Digest (R)
$ Family Smart E-tips (R)
$ Focus on the Family
$ Foursquare Leader
$ Gem (R)
$ Good News in Florida (R)
Good News Journal (R)
$ Good News, Etc. (R)
Gospel Herald
$ Guideposts (R)
Halo Magazine
HEARTLIGHT Internet (R)
$ Home Times (R)
$ Homeschooling Today (R)
($) HopeKeepers (R)
$ In His Presence (R)
$ In Touch
$ Indian Life (R)
Island Catholic (R)
$ JC Town Reporter (R)
$ KD Gospel Media
$ Lifeglow (R)
$ Light & Life
$ Liguorian
$ Live (R)
$ Living (R)
$ Living Church
$ Living Light (R)
$ Lookout
Maine Family Policy (R)
$ Manna (R)
$ Mature Living
$ Men of Integrity (R)
Men of the Cross
Men.AG.org (R)
$ Montgomery's Journey
More Excellent Way
Mosaic (R)
($) Mutuality (R)
New Christian Voices
New Identity (R)

$ New Wineskins (R)
$ Now What? (R)
$ Our Sunday Visitor (R)
$ ParentLife
Pegasus Review (R)
Penned from the Heart (R)
Perspectives (R)
$ Positive Thinking (R)
$ Prairie Messenger (R)
PrayerWorks (R)
Priscilla Papers
$ Psychology for Living (R)
$ Pure Inspiration (R)
$ Purpose (R)
$ Seek (R)
$ Significant Living (R)
Single Again Mag. Online (R)
Spirituality for Today
$ St. Anthony Messenger
$ Testimony (R)
3V Magazine
$ Together (R)
Trumpeter (R)
$ U.S. Catholic
Urban Kingdom (R)
$ Vibrant Life (R)
$ Vista (R)
$ War Cry (R)
$ Way of St. Francis (R)
$ Wesleyan Life (R)
$ Wildwood Reader (R)
Wisconsin Christian
$ World & I (R)

Daily Devotionals
Penned from the Heart (R)

Missions
$ Glad Tidings (R)

Pastors/Leaders
$ African-American Pulpit
$ Catholic Servant
$ Christian Century (R)
$ Interpreter
Jour./Pastoral Care
$ Lutheran Partners (R)
$ Ministry & Liturgy (R)
$ Ministry Today
$ Preaching Well (R)
$ SmallGroups.com (R)

Theological Digest (R)
$ Today's Parish
$ Word & World

Teen/Young Adult
$ Boundless Webzine (R)
TeensForJC (R)
$ Young Adult Today

Women
Christian Woman's Page (R)
Christian Work at Home
    Moms (R)
$ Come to the Fire (R)
Crowned with Silver
$ Dabbling Mum (R)
Elegance (R)
Empowering Everyday Women
Extreme Woman Magazine
First Lady
For Every Woman (R)
$ Girlfriend 2 Girlfriend
$ Heart & Soul
Hope for Women
$ Horizons (R)
$ inSpirit (R)
Jewels of God (R)
$ Journey
Lutheran Woman's Quar.
$ MomSense (R)
P31 Woman (R)
$ Pauses . . .
Precious Times (R)
Simply Blessed (R)
$ SpiritLed Woman
Unrecognized Woman (R)
Virtuous Woman (R)
Woman of Worth (R)
Women of the Cross
Women Today (R)

MEN'S ISSUES
Adult/General
$ Annals of St. Anne
$ Arlington Catholic
$ Associated Content (R)
$ Brink Magazine (R)
CBN.com (R)
$ Chicken Soup Books (R)
$ Christian Examiner
$ Christian Journal (R)

Christian News NW (R)
Christian Online
Christian Quarterly (R)
Christian Ranchman
$ ChristianWeek (R)
$ Churchmouse Publications (R)
$ Columbia (R)
$ Converge Point (R)
$ Creative Nonfiction
Desert Voice (R)
Disciple's Journal (R)
E-Channels (R)
$ EFCA Today
$ Evangel/IN (R)
$ Faith Today
Faithwebbin (R)
$ Family Digest (R)
$ Family Smart E-tips (R)
$ Focus on the Family
$ Foursquare Leader
$ Gem (R)
$ Good News in Florida (R)
Good News Journal (R)
$ Good News, Etc. (R)
Gospel Herald
Halo Magazine
HEARTLIGHT Internet (R)
Highway News (R)
$ Home Times (R)
$ Homeschooling Today (R)
($) HopeKeepers (R)
$ In His Presence (R)
$ In Touch
$ Indian Life (R)
$ JC Town Reporter (R)
$ KD Gospel Media
$ Light & Life
$ Live (R)
$ Living (R)
$ Lookout
$ Manna (R)
$ Men of Integrity (R)
Men of the Cross
Men.AG.org (R)
MissionWares
$ Montgomery's Journey
Mosaic (R)
($) Mutuality (R)
New Identity (R)
$ Our Sunday Visitor (R)

Penned from the Heart (R)
Perspectives (R)
$ Positive Thinking (R)
PrayerWorks (R)
$ Presbyterian Outlook
Priscilla Papers
$ Psychology for Living (R)
$ Purpose (R)
Regent Global Bus. Rev. (R)
$ Significant Living (R)
Single Again Mag. Online (R)
$ St. Anthony Messenger
$ Testimony (R)
3V Magazine
$ Together (R)
Trumpeter (R)
$ U.S. Catholic
$ United Church Observer (R)
Urban Kingdom (R)
$ Vibrant Life (R)
$ Wesleyan Life (R)
West Wind Review
Wisconsin Christian
$ World & I (R)
$ Written

Pastors/Leaders
$ African-American Pulpit
$ Interpreter
$ Lutheran Partners (R)
$ SmallGroups.com (R)
$ Word & World

Teen/Young Adult
$ Boundless Webzine (R)
TeensForJC (R)

Women
Hope for Women
Unrecognized Woman (R)

MIRACLES
Adult/General
($) AGAIN Magazine (R)
$ Angels on Earth
$ Anglican Journal
$ Animal Trails (R)
$ Aujourd'hui Credo (R)
$ B.C. Catholic (R)
Breakthrough
    Intercessor (R)

$ Catholic Yearbook (R)
CBN.com (R)
$ CGA World (R)
$ Chicken Soup Books (R)
$ Christian Home & School
Christian Motorsports
Christian Online
Christian Quarterly (R)
Christian Ranchman
$ Christian Standard (R)
$ Christianity Today (R)
$ ChristianWeek (R)
$ Churchmouse Publications (R)
$ Columbia (R)
Connecting Point (R)
$ Culture Wars (R)
$ Decision
Disciple's Journal (R)
Divine Ascent
E-Channels (R)
$ Episcopal Life (R)
Evangelical Advocate (R)
$ Faith Today
$ Gem (R)
$ Good News (R)
Gospel Herald
$ Guideposts (R)
Halo Magazine
$ Home Times (R)
($) HopeKeepers (R)
$ Horizons (adult) (R)
$ In His Presence (R)
$ In Touch
$ JC Town Reporter (R)
$ KD Gospel Media
$ Lifeglow (R)
$ Light & Life
$ Live (R)
$ Living Church
$ Lookout
$ Lutheran Journal (R)
$ Men of Integrity (R)
$ Miracles, Healings
Mosaic (R)
New Heart (R)
$ New Wineskins (R)
$ Our Sunday Visitor (R)
Pegasus Review (R)
Penned from the Heart (R)
Perspectives (R)

$ Positive Thinking (R)
$ Power for Living (R)
PrayerWorks (R)
$ Presbyterian Outlook
$ Priority! (R)
Priscilla Papers
$ Pure Inspiration (R)
$ Seek (R)
$ Significant Living (R)
Spirituality for Today
$ St. Anthony Messenger
$ Storyteller (R)
Sword and Trumpet
Sword of the Lord (R)
$ Testimony (R)
Trumpeter (R)
Urban Kingdom (R)
Wisconsin Christian

Children
$ Bread for God's Children (R)
$ Guide (R)
$ Sparkle (R)

Christian Education/ Library
Catholic Library
$ Children's Ministry
$ Youth & CE Leadership

Daily Devotionals
Penned from the Heart (R)

Missions
$ Evangelical Missions (R)
Intl. Jour./Frontier Missions (R)
$ Leaders for Today
Missiology
Mission Frontiers
$ New World Outlook
$ One
Op. Reveille Interactive Jour. (R)
$ PFI Global Link Journal (R)
$ PIME World (R)
Railroad Evangelist (R)
Women of the Harvest

Pastors/Leaders
$ African-American Pulpit
$ Clergy Journal (R)
$ Interpreter
Jour./Amer. Soc. for Church
    Growth (R)

$ Lutheran Partners (R)
$ Ministry Today
Pulpit Helps (R)
Rick Warren's Ministry
    Toolbox (R)
$ Word & World

Teen/Young Adult
$ Boundless Webzine (R)
$ Credo (R)
$ Devo'zine (R)
G4T Ink (R)
$ Insight (R)
$ Real Faith in Life (R)
$ Young Salvationist (R)

Women
$ Come to the Fire (R)
Elegance (R)
$ Esprit
Hope for Women
$ Horizons (R)
$ Journey
$ Link & Visitor (R)
$ SpiritLed Woman
Unrecognized Woman (R)

MISSIONS
Adult/General
Breakthrough Intercessor (R)
$ Brink Magazine (R)
$ Christian Home & School
Christian Ranchman
Church Herald & Holiness (R)
$ Churchmouse
    Publications (R)
$ City Light News (R)
$ Columbia (R)
$ EFCA Today
$ Good News in Florida (R)
$ Good News, Etc. (R)
Gospel Herald
Halo Magazine
$ In Touch
$ KD Gospel Media
$ Live (R)
Messianic Perspectives (R)
New Identity (R)
$ On Mission
$ Our Sunday Visitor (R)
$ ParentLife

PrayerWorks (R)
Quaker Life (R)
Spirituality for Today
Victory Herald (R)
$ Way of St. Francis (R)

Children
$ Bread for God's Children (R)

Christian Education/ Library
Christian Librarian (R)

Missions
East-West Church & Ministry
     Report
$ Glad Tidings (R)
Intl. Jour./Frontier
     Missions (R)
Lausanne World Pulse (R)
Mission Connection
MissionsMagizinet
wec.go

Pastors/Leaders
Church Executive
$ Enrichment Journal (R)
Ministry in Motion (R)

Teen/Young Adult
$ Direction Student
Exodus Magazine
$ Horizon Student
$ Young Christian Writers

Women
Jewels of God (R)

MONEY MANAGEMENT
Adult/General
$ Anglican Journal
$ Associated Content (R)
$ Bridal Guides (R)
$ Brink Magazine (R)
Brink Online
byFaith
$ Catholic Forester (R)
$ CBA Retailers
CBN.com (R)
$ Christian Journal (R)
Christian Motorsports
Christian Online
Christian Quarterly (R)

Christian Ranchman
$ ChristianWeek (R)
$ Churchmouse
     Publications (R)
Connecting Point (R)
$ Creative Nonfiction
Disciple's Journal (R)
E-Channels (R)
Evangelical Advocate (R)
$ Faith & Family
$ Faith Today
Faithwebbin (R)
$ Family Smart E-tips (R)
$ Focus on the Family
$ Gem (R)
Gospel Herald
Halo Magazine
HEARTLIGHT Internet (R)
Highway News (R)
$ Home Times (R)
$ Homeschooling Today (R)
$ In His Presence (R)
$ In Touch
$ JC Town Reporter (R)
$ KD Gospel Media
$ Lifeglow (R)
$ Live (R)
$ Lookout
$ Manna (R)
$ Mature Years (R)
Men.AG.org (R)
($) NBR E-Magazine (R)
$ Our Sunday Visitor (R)
($) P.O.W.E.R. Magazine
$ ParentLife
Penned from the Heart (R)
$ Significant Living (R)
Single Again Mag. Online (R)
$ St. Anthony Messenger
$ Testimony (R)
$ Together (R)
Trumpeter (R)
Urban Kingdom (R)
$ War Cry (R)
Wisconsin Christian
$ World & I (R)

Children
$ Bread for God's Children (R)
$ SHINE brightly (R)

Daily Devotionals
Penned from the Heart (R)

Missions
$ Glad Tidings (R)

Pastors/Leaders
$ African-American Pulpit
$ Clergy Journal (R)
$ Enrichment Journal (R)
$ Interpreter
$ Lutheran Partners (R)
Ministry in Motion (R)
Rick Warren's Ministry
     Toolbox (R)
$ SmallGroups.com (R)
$ Today's Parish
$ Your Church (R)

Teen/Young Adult
$ Boundless Webzine (R)
$ Direction Student
$ Horizon Student
$ Real Faith in Life (R)

Women
Christian Women Today (R)
Christian Work at Home
     Moms (R)
Elegance (R)
Empowering Everyday Women
$ Heart & Soul
Hope for Women
$ Horizons (R)
$ InspiredMoms (R)
$ Journey
Life Tools for Women
More to Life
Precious Times (R)
Simply Blessed (R)
Unrecognized Woman (R)
Virtuous Woman (R)
Woman of Worth (R)
Women Today (R)

MOVIE REVIEWS
Adult/General
$ Abilities
$ Associated Content (R)
$ Atlantic Catholic
Breakthrough Intercessor (R)
byFaith

CBN.com (R)
Charlotte World
Christian Family Journal
$ Christian Herald (R)
$ Christian Journal (R)
$ Christianity Today
    Movies (R)
$ Churchmouse
    Publications (R)
$ City Light News (R)
Creation Care (R)
$ Cresset
$ Eureka Street
$ Faith & Friends (R)
$ Good News in Florida (R)
Good News Today
Gospel Herald
Heartland Gatekeeper (R)
$ Home Times (R)
$ Interim (R)
Island Catholic (R)
$ JC Town Reporter (R)
$ KD Gospel Media
MovieGuide
New Christian Voices
$ Our Sunday Visitor (R)
Perspectives (R)
$ Prairie Messenger (R)
Urban Kingdom (R)

Children
$ Sparkle (R)

Missions
$ Glad Tidings (R)

Music
Hymn

Teen/Young Adult
Exodus Magazine
$ Risen
$ TC Magazine

Women
Christian Work at Home
    Moms (R)
Empowering Everyday Women
Extreme Woman Magazine
Hope for Women
Jewels of God (R)
Virtuous Woman (R)
Woman of Worth (R)

MUSIC REVIEWS
Adult/General
$ Arlington Catholic
$ Associated Content (R)
$ Atlantic Catholic
$ Aujourd'hui Credo (R)
$ Canadian Mennonite (R)
$ Catholic Peace Voice (R)
CBN.com (R)
$ Charisma
Charlotte World
Christian Family Journal
$ Christian Herald (R)
$ Christian Journal (R)
Christian Media (R)
$ Christian Renewal (R)
$ Christian Retailing
$ Churchmouse
    Publications (R)
$ City Light News (R)
$ Cresset
Desert Voice (R)
E-Channels (R)
$ Eureka Street
$ Faith & Family
$ Faith Today
Faithwebbin (R)
$ Foursquare Leader
$ Good News in
    Florida (R)
Gospel Herald
Halo Magazine
$ Haruah (R)
Heartland Gatekeeper (R)
HEARTLIGHT Internet (R)
$ Interim (R)
$ JC Town Reporter (R)
$ KD Gospel Media
MovieGuide
New Christian Voices
$ Our Sunday Visitor (R)
$ Prairie Messenger (R)
$ Presbyterians Today (R)
$ Prism
$ Pure Inspiration (R)
$ Rose & Thorn
$ Testimony (R)
Trumpeter (R)
Urban Kingdom (R)
$ World & I (R)

Children
$ Sparkle (R)

Christian Education/ Library
Catholic Library
$ Church Libraries (R)

Missions
$ Glad Tidings (R)
Women of the Harvest

Music
$ Christian Music Today (R)
Christian Music Weekly (R)
$ Creator (R)
Tradition

Pastors/Leaders
$ Barefoot (R)
$ Christian Century (R)
$ Interpreter
$ Ministry Today
$ Parish Liturgy (R)
$ Reformed Worship (R)
Technologies for Worship (R)
$ Worship Leader

Teen/Young Adult
$ Credo (R)
$ Devo'zine (R)
Exodus Magazine
$ Risen
$ Sharing the Victory (R)
$ TC Magazine
TeensForJC (R)
$ True Girl

Women
Christian Work at Home
    Moms (R)
Empowering Everyday Women
Extreme Woman Magazine
Hope for Women
Jewels of God (R)
Precious Times (R)
Virtuous Woman (R)

NATURE
Adult/General
$ Animal Trails (R)
$ Associated Content (R)
$ Aujourd'hui Credo (R)

$ Brink Magazine (R)
CBN.com (R)
$ Christian Courier/
   Canada (R)
$ Christian Renewal (R)
$ Churchmouse
   Publications (R)
Creation
Creation Care (R)
$ Creation Illust. (R)
$ Creative Nonfiction
$ Gem (R)
Gospel Herald
Halo Magazine
$ In Touch
$ JC Town Reporter (R)
$ KD Gospel Media
Keys to Living (R)
$ Lifeglow (R)
$ Lutheran Digest (R)
New Identity (R)
$ Our Sunday Visitor (R)
$ Over the Back Fence (R)
Pegasus Review (R)
Penned from the Heart (R)
PrayerWorks (R)
Ruminate
$ Salvo
$ Search
$ Seek (R)
$ St. Anthony Messenger
$ Storyteller (R)
$ Testimony (R)
Trumpeter (R)
Urban Kingdom (R)
$ Way of St. Francis (R)
$ Wildwood Reader (R)
Wisconsin Christian
$ World & I (R)

Children
$ Archaeology
$ Bread for God's Children (R)
$ Cadet Quest (R)
$ Focus/Clubhouse Jr.
$ Guide (R)
$ Nature Friend (R)
$ Partners (R)
$ SHINE brightly (R)
Skipping Stones

$ Sparkle (R)

Missions
$ Glad Tidings (R)

Pastors/Leaders
$ Word & World

Teen/Young Adult
$ Boundless Webzine (R)
$ Devo'zine (R)
$ Young Christian Writers

Women
Jewels of God (R)
Virtuous Woman (R)
Woman of Worth (R)

NEWS FEATURES
Adult/General
Ambassador
$ Arkansas Catholic (R)
$ Associated Content (R)
$ Atlantic Catholic
Baptist Standard
Biblical Recorder
Blue Ridge Christian News
$ Canadian Mennonite (R)
CanadianChristianity.com
$ Cathedral Age
$ Catholic Insight
$ Catholic New York
$ Catholic Peace Voice (R)
$ Catholic Sentinel
CBN.com (R)
Challenge Weekly
$ Charisma
Charlotte World
Christian Chronicle
Christian Courier/WI (R)
$ Christian Examiner
Christian News NW (R)
Christian Press
Christian Ranchman
$ Christian Renewal (R)
$ Christian Research
$ Christian Response (R)
$ Christian Retailing
$ Christianity Today Movies (R)
$ ChristianWeek (R)
Church of England News
$ City Light News (R)

$ Commonweal
$ Compass Direct
Creation Care (R)
Desert Christian
Desert Voice (R)
$ Disaster News
Encompass
$ Eureka Street
Evangel/OR (R)
$ Faith Today
Florida Baptist Witness
Founders Journal
Good News Connection
Good News Journal (R)
Good News Today
Good News!
$ Good News, Etc. (R)
Gospel Herald
Heartland Gatekeeper (R)
$ Home Times (R)
($) HopeKeepers (R)
($) Impact Magazine (R)
$ Indian Life (R)
$ Interchange
Island Catholic (R)
$ JC Town Reporter (R)
$ KD Gospel Media
La Nueva Vision
$ Liberty
LifeSiteNews
Louisiana Baptist
Maine Family Policy (R)
$ Manna (R)
Messianic Perspectives (R)
$ Miracles, Healings
$ Montana Catholic
More Excellent Way
MovieGuide
Network
$ Our Sunday Visitor (R)
Ozarks Christian News
$ Priority! (R)
$ Search
$ St. Anthony Messenger
Sword and Trumpet
$ Testimony (R)
Tri-State Voice
Trumpeter (R)
$ Upscale
Urban Kingdom (R)

$ War Cry (R)
$ World & I (R)

Children
$ Partners (R)
$ Pockets (R)

Missions
East-West Church & Ministry
    Report
$ Glad Tidings (R)
Op. Reveille Interactive Jour. (R)

Music
$ Christian Music Today (R)

Pastors/Leaders
$ Christian Century (R)
Church Executive
$ Ministry Today
Pulpit Helps (R)
Rick Warren's Ministry
    Toolbox (R)

Teen/Young Adult
$ Listen (R)

Women
Empowering Everyday Women
Hope for Women

Writers
$ Poets & Writers

NEWSPAPERS/TABLOIDS
Ambassador
$ Anglican Journal
$ Arkansas Catholic (R)
$ Arlington Catholic
$ Atlantic Catholic
$ B.C. Catholic (R)
Baptist Standard
Biblical Recorder
Blue Ridge Christian News
CanadianChristianity.com
$ Catholic New York
Catholic Register
$ Catholic Sentinel
$ Catholic Servant
$ Catholic Telegraph
Challenge Weekly
Charlotte World
Christian Chronicle

$ Christian Courier/Canada (R)
Christian Courier/WI (R)
$ Christian Examiner
$ Christian Herald (R)
$ Christian Journal (R)
Christian Media (R)
Christian News NW (R)
Christian Observer
Christian Press
Christian Ranchman
$ Christian Renewal (R)
$ ChristianWeek (R)
Church of England News
$ Citizen USA
$ City Light News (R)
$ Common Ground (R)
Desert Christian
Desert Voice (R)
Disciple's Journal (R)
$ Episcopal Life (R)
Evangelical Times
Florida Baptist Witness
Good News Connection
Good News Journal (R)
Good News Today
Good News!
$ Good News, Etc. (R)
Heartland Gatekeeper (R)
$ Home Times (R)
$ In His Presence (R)
$ Indian Life (R)
$ Interchange
$ Interim (R)
Island Catholic (R)
$ JC Town Reporter (R)
La Nueva Vision
$ Layman
LifeSiteNews
Light of the World
$ Living (R)
$ Living Light (R)
Living Stones
Louisiana Baptist
$ Manna (R)
Messianic Times
$ Montana Catholic
Mosaic (R)
Network
New Frontier
$ Our Sunday Visitor (R)

Ozarks Christian News
$ Ozarks Senior Living (R)
$ Prairie Messenger (R)
PrayerWorks (R)
Pulpit Helps (R)
Senior Connection
SW Kansas Faith
Sword of the Lord (R)
$ Together (R)
Tri-State Voice
Wisconsin Christian

NOSTALGIA
Adult/General
$ Associated Content (R)
$ Catholic Forester (R)
$ Churchmouse Publications (R)
Good News Journal (R)
$ Good News, Etc. (R)
Gospel Herald
Halo Magazine
$ Home Times (R)
$ In Touch
$ Lutheran Digest (R)
$ Mature Living
Nostalgia (R)
$ Over the Back Fence (R)
PrayerWorks (R)
$ Seek (R)
$ Storyteller (R)
$ Testimony (R)
Urban Kingdom (R)

Children
$ Faces

Missions
$ Glad Tidings (R)

Pastors/Leaders
$ Priest

Women
Crowned with Silver
$ Journey

ONLINE PUBLICATIONS
Adult/General
$ America
$ Anglican Journal
Answers Magazine
$ Apocalypse Chronicles (R)

$ Associated Content (R)
Behind the Hammer
Believer's Bay
Books & Culture
Breakthrough
$ Brink Magazine (R)
CanadianChristianity.com
$ Cathedral Age
$ Catholic Digest (R)
CBN.com (R)
Challenge Weekly
$ Charisma
Chocolate Pages
Christian Chronicle
Christian Computing (R)
$ Christian Examiner
$ Christian Journal (R)
Christian Media (R)
Christian Online
Christian Outlook
$ Christian Standard (R)
$ Christianity Today (R)
$ Christianity Today Movies (R)
$ Columbia (R)
$ Company Magazine (R)
$ Compass Direct
crosshome.com
$ Decision
$ Disaster News
Disciple's Journal (R)
Divine Ascent
$ Drama Ministry (R)
$ DreamSeeker (R)
Eternal Ink (R)
$ Eureka Street
Faithwebbin (R)
$ Family Smart E-tips (R)
$ Foursquare Leader
Good News Connection
$ Good News in Florida (R)
Good News!
Gospel Herald
Halo Magazine
$ Haruah (R)
HEARTLIGHT Internet (R)
($) Impact Magazine (R)
$ Interim (R)
$ JC Town Reporter (R)
$ KD Gospel Media
Koinonia

$ Layman
$ Leben (R)
LifeSiteNews
LifeTimes Catholic
$ Lookout
Maine Family Policy (R)
$ Manna (R)
$ Marian Helper
Men of the Cross
Men.AG.org (R)
$ Messenger/St. Anthony
$ MindFlights (R)
MissionWares
More Excellent Way
$ New Wineskins (R)
$ Now What? (R)
($) NBR E-Magazine (R)
$ On Mission
Perspectives (R)
PrayerWorks (R)
$ Priority! (R)
Regent Global Bus. Rev. (R)
$ Relevant
$ Rose & Thorn
Single Again Mag. Online (R)
$ Sound Body (R)
$ St. Anthony Messenger
$ Testimony (R)
$ Today's Christian (R)
$ Today's Pentecostal (R)
Touched By the Hand
Trumpeter (R)
$ U.S. Catholic
Urban Kingdom (R)
Victory Herald (R)
$ World & I (R)

Children

$ American Girl (R)
$ Archaeology
$ Focus/Clubhouse
$ Focus/Clubhouse Jr.
Girls Connection
$ Keys for Kids (R)
$ Kids' Ark (R)

Daily Devotionals

$ Forward Day by Day

Missions

Mission Frontiers

Op. Reveille Interactive Jour. (R)
Women of the Harvest

Music

$ Christian Music Today (R)
$ Creator (R)

Pastors/Leaders

$ Barefoot (R)
$ Cook Partners
$ InSite (R)
$ Interpreter
$ Leadership (R)
$ Living Church
$ Lutheran Partners (R)
Ministry in Motion (R)
$ Net Results
$ Newsletter Newsletter
Preaching
$ PreachingToday.com
Pulpit Helps (R)
$ Reformed Worship (R)
$ RevWriter Resource
Rick Warren's Ministry
    Toolbox (R)
$ SmallGroups.com (R)
Technologies for Worship (R)
$ Youthworker

Teen/Young Adult

$ Boundless Webzine (R)
Connected
StudentLife
TeensForJC (R)
$ Young Salvationist (R)

Women

$ At the Center (R)
Breathe Again
Christian Ladies Connect
Christian Woman's Page (R)
Christian Women Today (R)
Christian Work at Home
    Moms (R)
$ Come to the Fire (R)
$ Dabbling Mum (R)
Elegance (R)
Empowering Everyday Women
For Every Woman (R)
$ FullFill
$ Girlfriend 2 Girlfriend
Handmaidens

($) History's Women (R)
Hope for Women
Inspired Women
$ InspiredMoms (R)
Jewels of God (R)
Life Tools for Women
Live Magazine
$ Melody of the Heart
Right to the Heart (R)
Virtuous Woman (R)
Women of the Cross
Women Today (R)
Women's Ministry

Writers
Author-Me
ChristianWriters.com
Esdras' Scroll (R)
$ Freelance Writer's Report (R)
$ Shades of Romance (R)
$ Spirit-Led Writer (R)
WriteToInspire.com
Writing Corner (R)

OPINION PIECES
Adult/General
$ Annals of St. Anne
$ Arkansas Catholic (R)
$ Arlington Catholic
$ Associated Content (R)
$ B.C. Catholic (R)
$ Brink Magazine (R)
$ Catholic New York
$ Catholic Peace Voice (R)
CBN.com (R)
$ Christian Courier/Canada (R)
$ Christian Examiner
Christian News NW (R)
$ Christian Renewal (R)
$ Christian Research
$ Christianity Today (R)
$ Christianity Today Movies (R)
$ ChristianWeek (R)
$ Churchmouse Publications (R)
Church of England News
$ Citizen USA
$ Culture Wars (R)
$ DisciplesWorld
$ Episcopal Life (R)
$ Eureka Street

$ Faith Today
Faithwebbin (R)
$ Good News in Florida (R)
$ Good News, Etc. (R)
Gospel Herald
Halo Magazine
$ Home Times (R)
($) HopeKeepers (R)
$ In Touch
$ Indian Life (R)
$ Interim (R)
Island Catholic (R)
$ JC Town Reporter (R)
$ Living Church
$ Lookout
Maine Family Policy (R)
Mosaic (R)
MovieGuide
($) NBR E-Magazine (R)
$ Our Sunday Visitor (R)
Perspectives (R)
$ Prairie Messenger (R)
$ Presbyterian Outlook
Regent Global Bus. Rev. (R)
$ Salvo
$ Social Justice (R)
$ St. Anthony Messenger
$ Testimony (R)
Trumpeter (R)
$ U.S. Catholic
$ United Church Observer (R)
Urban Kingdom (R)
$ World & I (R)
$ Written

Children
$ New Moon Girls (R)
Skipping Stones

Christian Education/Library
Catholic Library
$ Group Magazine
Jour. of Christianity/Foreign
   Lang. (R)
$ Teachers of Vision (R)

Missions
$ Evangelical Missions (R)
$ Glad Tidings (R)
Op. Reveille Interactive
   Jour. (R)

Music
$ Christian Music Today (R)

Pastors/Leaders
$ Catholic Servant
$ Ministry Today
$ Priest
$ Word & World
$ Worship Leader

Teen/Young Adult
TeensForJC (R)

Women
($) Beyond the Bend (R)
Crowned with Silver
$ Esprit
Hope for Women
Unrecognized Woman (R)

Writers
$ Advanced Christian Writer (R)
Areopagus
$ New Writer's Mag.

PARENTING
Adult/General
American Tract (R)
$ Angels on Earth
$ Annals of St. Anne
$ Arkansas Catholic (R)
$ Arlington Catholic
$ Associated Content (R)
$ Atlantic Catholic
$ Canada Lutheran (R)
$ Catholic Digest (R)
$ Catholic Yearbook (R)
CBN.com (R)
$ Celebrate Life (R)
$ Chicken Soup Books (R)
$ Christian Courier/Canada (R)
Christian Family Journal
$ Christian Home & School
Christian Motorsports
Christian Observer
Christian Quarterly (R)
Christian Ranchman
$ Christian Renewal (R)
$ Christian Research
$ ChristianWeek (R)
$ Churchmouse Publications (R)
$ Columbia (R)

$ Converge Point (R)
Creation Care (R)
$ Culture Wars (R)
Disciple's Journal (R)
Evangelical Advocate (R)
$ Faith & Family
$ Faith Today
Faithwebbin (R)
$ Family Digest (R)
$ Family Smart E-tips (R)
$ Focus on the Family
$ Foursquare Leader
$ Gem (R)
$ Good News in Florida (R)
Good News Journal (R)
$ Good News, Etc. (R)
Gospel Herald
Halo Magazine
HEARTLIGHT Internet (R)
Highway News (R)
$ Home Times (R)
$ Homeschooling Today (R)
($) HopeKeepers (R)
$ In His Presence (R)
$ In Touch
$ Indian Life (R)
$ JC Town Reporter (R)
$ KD Gospel Media
Koinonia
$ Light & Life
$ Liguorian
$ Live (R)
$ Living (R)
$ Living Light (R)
$ Lookout
$ Lutheran Journal (R)
$ Manna (R)
$ Men of Integrity (R)
Men.AG.org (R)
$ Montgomery's Journey
Mosaic (R)
MovieGuide
($) Mutuality (R)
New Christian Voices
$ New Wineskins (R)
$ Our Sunday Visitor (R)
$ ParentLife
Pegasus Review (R)
Penned from the Heart (R)
$ Positive Thinking (R)

$ Power for Living (R)
$ Prairie Messenger (R)
$ Psychology for Living (R)
$ Purpose (R)
$ Seek (R)
Single Again Mag. Online (R)
$ Special Living (R)
Spirituality for Today
$ St. Anthony Messenger
SW Kansas Faith
$ Testimony (R)
$ Today's Pentecostal (R)
$ Together (R)
Trumpeter (R)
$ U.S. Catholic
Urban Kingdom (R)
$ Vibrant Life (R)
Victory Herald (R)
$ Vista (R)
$ War Cry (R)
$ Wesleyan Life (R)
Wisconsin Christian
$ World & I (R)

Christian Education/ Library
$ Children's Ministry

Daily Devotionals
Penned from the Heart (R)

Missions
$ Glad Tidings (R)

Pastors/Leaders
$ Catholic Servant
$ Interpreter
Plugged In

Women
$ Canticle
Christian Woman's Page (R)
Christian Work at Home
   Moms (R)
$ Come to the Fire (R)
$ Dabbling Mum (R)
Elegance (R)
$ Esprit
Extreme Woman Magazine
For Every Woman (R)
$ Girlfriend 2 Girlfriend
Handmaiden (R)

$ Heart & Soul
Hope for Women
$ InspiredMoms (R)
$ inSpirit (R)
Jewels of God (R)
$ Journey
Just Between Us (R)
$ Link & Visitor (R)
Lutheran Woman's Quar.
$ MomSense (R)
P31 Woman (R)
$ Pauses . . .
Precious Times (R)
Simply Blessed (R)
$ SpiritLed Woman
Unrecognized Woman (R)
Virtuous Woman (R)
Woman of Worth (R)
Women Today (R)

PEACE ISSUES
Adult/General
$ Associated Content (R)
$ Aujourd'hui Credo (R)
$ Bible Advocate (R)
Breakthrough Intercessor (R)
$ Cathedral Age
CBN.com (R)
$ ChristianWeek (R)
$ Churchmouse Publications (R)
$ Columbia (R)
$ Eureka Street
Evangel/OR (R)
Gospel Herald
Halo Magazine
$ In Touch
Island Catholic (R)
$ JC Town Reporter (R)
$ Liguorian
$ Living (R)
$ Lookout
($) Mennonite Historian (R)
Messianic Perspectives (R)
Mosaic (R)
$ Our Sunday Visitor (R)
Penned from the Heart (R)
Perspectives (R)
$ Pure Inspiration (R)
$ Purpose (R)
Quaker Life (R)

$ Seek (R)
Spirituality for Today
$ Testimony (R)
$ Together (R)
$ U.S. Catholic
Urban Kingdom (R)
$ Way of St. Francis (R)

Children
$ New Moon Girls (R)
$ Pockets (R)
Skipping Stones

Christian Education/ Library
Catholic Library

Missions
$ Glad Tidings (R)

Pastors/Leaders
$ African-American Pulpit
$ Christian Century (R)
$ Clergy Journal (R)
$ Interpreter
$ Lutheran Partners (R)

Teen/Young Adult
$ True Girl

Women
$ Esprit
Extreme Woman Magazine
$ Horizons (R)
$ Pauses . . .
Unrecognized Woman (R)
Women Today (R)

PERSONAL EXPERIENCE
Adult/General
African Voices (R)
($) AGAIN Magazine (R)
$ Alive Now (R)
$ Angels on Earth
$ Annals of St. Anne
$ Associated Content (R)
$ Australian Catholics (R)
$ B.C. Catholic (R)
Behind the Hammer
$ Bible Advocate (R)
Breakthrough
Breakthrough Intercessor (R)
$ Bridal Guides (R)

$ Brink Magazine (R)
$ Catholic Digest (R)
$ Catholic New York
$ Catholic Peace Voice (R)
$ Catholic Yearbook (R)
CBN.com (R)
$ Celebrate Life (R)
$ CGA World (R)
$ Chicken Soup Books (R)
$ Christian Courier/Canada (R)
$ Christian Journal (R)
Christian Motorsports
Christian Observer
Christian Online
Christian Quarterly (R)
$ Christianity Today (R)
$ ChristianWeek (R)
$ Churchmouse Publications (R)
$ Columbia (R)
$ Commonweal
$ Converge Point (R)
$ Creative Nonfiction
$ Decision
$ DisciplesWorld
E-Channels (R)
$ Evangel/IN (R)
Evangelical Advocate (R)
$ Faith Today
Faithwebbin (R)
$ Family Digest (R)
$ Focus on the Family
$ Gem (R)
$ Good News, Etc. (R)
Gospel Herald
$ Guideposts (R)
Halo Magazine
Highway News (R)
$ Home Times (R)
($) HopeKeepers (R)
$ Horizons (adult) (R)
$ In His Presence (R)
$ In Touch
Island Catholic (R)
$ JC Town Reporter (R)
$ KD Gospel Media
Keys to Living (R)
Leaves (R)
$ Lifeglow (R)
$ Light & Life
$ Liguorian

$ Live (R)
$ Living (R)
$ Living Church
$ Lookout
$ Lutheran Journal (R)
$ Marian Helper
$ Mature Living
$ MESSAGE
$ MindFlights (R)
More Excellent Way
($) Mutuality (R)
New Heart (R)
New Identity (R)
$ New Wineskins (R)
Nostalgia (R)
$ Now What? (R)
$ On Mission
$ Ozarks Senior Living (R)
$ ParentLife
Penned from the Heart (R)
$ Positive Thinking (R)
$ Power for Living (R)
PrayerWorks (R)
$ Psychology for Living (R)
$ Pure Inspiration (R)
Quaker Life (R)
Reverent Submissions (R)
Ruminate
$ Seek (R)
Sharing (R)
$ Spiritual Life
$ St. Anthony Messenger
$ Storyteller (R)
$ Testimony (R)
$ Together (R)
Trumpeter (R)
$ Upscale
Urban Kingdom (R)
Victory Herald (R)
$ Victory in Grace (R)
$ Vision (R)
$ War Cry (R)
$ Way of St. Francis (R)
$ Wesleyan Life (R)
$ World & I (R)

Children
$ Bread for God's Children (R)
$ Faces
$ Guide (R)

$ New Moon Girls (R)
$ Partners (R)
Skipping Stones
$ Sparkle (R)

Christian Education/ Library
$ Children's Ministry
$ Group Magazine
$ Jour./Adventist Ed. (R)
$ Teachers of Vision (R)

Daily Devotionals
Penned from the Heart (R)
$ Rejoice!

Missions
$ Evangelical Missions (R)
$ Glad Tidings (R)
$ PIME World (R)
Railroad Evangelist (R)
Women of the Harvest

Pastors/Leaders
$ Catholic Servant
Jour./Pastoral Care
$ Lead Magazine (R)
$ Lutheran Partners (R)
$ Priest
$ Today's Parish
$ Worship Leader
$ Youthworker

Teen/Young Adult
$ Boundless Webzine (R)
$ Devo'zine (R)
$ Direction Student
Exodus Magazine
$ Horizon Student
$ Insight (R)
$ Real Faith in Life (R)
$ Spirit
$ TC Magazine
TeensForJC (R)
$ True Girl
$ Young Salvationist (R)

Women
Christian Woman's Page (R)
Christian Work at Home
    Moms (R)
$ Come to the Fire (R)
Elegance (R)

Empowering Everyday Women
$ Esprit
Extreme Woman Magazine
Handmaiden (R)
Hope for Women
Inspired Women
Jewels of God (R)
$ Journey
Just Between Us (R)
$ Melody of the Heart
$ MomSense (R)
$ Pauses . . .
Precious Times (R)
Simply Blessed (R)
$ SpiritLed Woman
Unrecognized Woman (R)
Virtuous Woman (R)
Woman of Worth (R)
Women Today (R)

Writers
Areopagus
$ New Writer's Mag.
NW Christian Author (R)

PERSONAL GROWTH
Adult/General
$ Alive Now (R)
$ Annals of St. Anne
$ Associated Content (R)
$ Bible Advocate (R)
Breakthrough Intercessor (R)
$ Catholic Digest (R)
$ Catholic Forester (R)
$ Catholic Peace Voice (R)
CBN.com (R)
$ Christian Courier/Canada (R)
$ Christian Journal (R)
Christian Online
Christian Quarterly (R)
Christian Ranchman
$ Churchmouse Publications (R)
$ Columbia (R)
$ Common Ground (R)
Connections Ldrship/MOPS
$ Decision
Divine Ascent
E-Channels (R)
$ Evangel/IN (R)
Evangelical Advocate (R)

$ Faith & Family
$ Faith & Friends (R)
$ Faith Today
Faithwebbin (R)
$ Family Digest (R)
$ Focus on the Family
$ Gem (R)
$ Good News in Florida (R)
Good News Journal (R)
$ Good News, Etc. (R)
Gospel Herald
Halo Magazine
$ Home Times (R)
($) HopeKeepers (R)
$ Horizons (adult) (R)
$ In His Presence (R)
$ In Touch
$ Indian Life (R)
Island Catholic (R)
$ JC Town Reporter (R)
$ KD Gospel Media
Keys to Living (R)
Leaves (R)
$ Light & Life
$ Liguorian
$ Live (R)
$ Living (R)
$ Living Church
$ Lookout
$ Lutheran Digest (R)
$ Manna (R)
$ Mature Living
$ Mature Years (R)
$ Men of Integrity (R)
$ MindFlights (R)
$ Montgomery's Journey
More Excellent Way
Mosaic (R)
($) Mutuality (R)
New Heart (R)
New Identity (R)
$ New Wineskins (R)
$ ParentLife
Penned from the Heart (R)
$ Positive Thinking (R)
$ Prairie Messenger (R)
PrayerWorks (R)
$ Psychology for Living (R)
$ Pure Inspiration (R)
$ Purpose (R)

Regent Global Bus. Rev. (R)
Reverent Submissions (R)
$ Seek (R)
Single Again Mag. Online (R)
$ St. Anthony Messenger
$ Stewardship (R)
$ Testimony (R)
$ Together (R)
Trumpeter (R)
Urban Kingdom (R)
Victory Herald (R)
$ Victory in Grace (R)
$ War Cry (R)
$ Way of St. Francis (R)
$ Wildwood Reader (R)
$ World & I (R)

Children
$ Bread for God's Children (R)
$ Guide (R)
Skipping Stones
$ Sparkle (R)

Christian Education/ Library
$ Children's Ministry
$ Youth & CE Leadership

Daily Devotionals
Penned from the Heart (R)

Missions
$ Glad Tidings (R)
Women of the Harvest

Pastors/Leaders
$ Ministry Today

Teen/Young Adult
$ Boundless Webzine (R)
$ Direction Student
Exodus Magazine
$ Horizon Student
$ Insight (R)
TeensForJC (R)
$ True Girl
$ Young Adult Today
$ Young Salvationist (R)

Women
Christian Woman's Page (R)
$ Come to the Fire (R)
$ Dabbling Mum (R)
Elegance (R)

Empowering Everyday
    Women
$ Esprit
Extreme Woman Magazine
$ FullFill
Hope for Women
$ Horizons (R)
$ inSpirit (R)
Jewels of God (R)
$ Journey
Just Between Us (R)
$ MomSense (R)
P31 Woman (R)
$ Pauses . . .
Precious Times (R)
Simply Blessed (R)
$ SpiritLed Woman
Unrecognized Woman (R)
Virtuous Woman (R)
Women Today (R)

Writers
Areopagus

PHOTO ESSAYS
Adult/General
$ Associated Content (R)
$ Cathedral Age
Christian Motorsports
Creation Care (R)
Desert Voice (R)
$ Faith & Family
$ Good News in Florida (R)
$ Good News, Etc. (R)
$ Imagine
Island Catholic (R)
$ KD Gospel Media
Nostalgia (R)
$ Our Sunday Visitor (R)
$ Ozarks Senior Living (R)
$ Priority! (R)
$ Prism
$ Salvo
$ St. Anthony Messenger
Urban Kingdom (R)
$ Wildwood Reader (R)
$ World & I (R)

Children
$ Faces
Skipping Stones

Christian Education/ Library
$ Jour./Adventist Ed. (R)

Missions
$ Glad Tidings (R)

Pastors/Leaders
Church Executive
$ Outreach (R)
$ Priest
$ Youthworker

Teen/Young Adult
$ Credo (R)
TeensForJC (R)

Women
Christian Woman's Page (R)
$ Horizons (R)

PHOTOGRAPHS
Note: "Reprint" indicators (R)
have been deleted from this section and "B" for black & white
glossy prints or "C" for color
transparencies has been inserted.
Many publishers will also accept/
prefer digital photos. An asterisk
(*) before a listing indicates they
buy photos with articles only.

Adult/General
African Voices—B
American Tract
Ancient Paths—B
Anglican Journal—B/C
*Animal Trails—B/C
*Annals of St. Anne—B/C
*Arkansas Catholic—C
Arlington Catholic—B
Associated Content—C
Bible Advocate—C
*Breakthrough Intercessor—C
*Bridal Guides—B/C
Canada Lutheran—B
*Catholic Digest—B/C
Catholic Forester—B/C
*Catholic Insight
Catholic New York—B
Catholic Peace Voice—B/C
Catholic Sentinel—B/C
Catholic Telegraph—B

Catholic Yearbook—C
CBA Retailers—C
*Celebrate Life—C
*Charisma—C
*Christian Courier/Canada—B
*Christian Examiner—C
Christian Family Journal—C
Christian Herald—C
*Christian History—B/C
Christian Home & School—C
*Christianity Today—C
*Christian Motorsports—B
*Christian Online
Christian Retailing—C
*Christian Standard—B/C
ChristianWeek—B/C
*Churchmouse Publications
*Church of England News
*Citizen USA—C
City Light News—B/C
*Commonweal—B/C
Connecting Point—B
Converge Point—C
Covenant Companion—B/C
Culture Wars—B/C
Decision
*Desert Voice
*DisciplesWorld
Divine Ascent—B
Episcopal Life—B
Eureka Street—B/C
*Evangel/IN—B
*Evangel/OR—B/C
Evangelical Advocate—C
Faith & Family—C
*Faith & Friends—C
*Faith Today—C
FGBC World—C
Focus on the Family—B/C
*Foursquare Leader
*Good News in Florida—C
Good News Journal
Gospel Herald—C
Gospel Today
*Guideposts—B/C
Halo Magazine
Highway News—B
Holy House Ministries—B
*Home Times—B/C
Homeschooling Today—B/C

*HopeKeepers—B/C
*Horizons (adult)
Imagine—C
*Impact Magazine—C
*In His Presence
*In Touch
Indian Life—B/C
Interchange—B
*Interim—B/C
Island Catholic—B/C
KD Gospel Media—B/C
*Layman—B
Leaves—B/C
*Leben—C
Liberty—B/C
*Lifeglow—B/C
Light & Life—B/C
*Liguorian—C
*Live—B/C
Living—B/C
Living Church—B/C
*Living Light—B/C
*Lookout—B/C
*Lutheran Journal—C
*Manna—C
Marian Helper—B/C
*Mature Living
*Mature Years—C
Messianic Perspectives—B
Miracles, Healings—B
Montana Catholic
Montgomery's Journey
*Mosaic—B/C
Mutuality—B/C
*New Heart—C
*New Identity—C
New Wineskins—B/C
Nostalgia—B/C
On Mission—B/C
Our Sunday Visitor—B/C
Over the Back Fence—C
P.O.W.E.R. Magazine
*Pathway
*Perspectives—B
Power for Living—B
Presbyterian Outlook—B/C
*Presbyterians Today—B/C
*Prism—B/C
*Psychology for Living—C
*Purpose—B

Quaker Life—B/C
Salvo—C
*Seek—C
*Special Living—B/C
Spiritual Life—B
Sports Spectrum—C
Standard—B
*St. Anthony Messenger—B/C
*Storyteller—B
*Testimony—B/C
Tiferet—B/C
Today's Pentecostal—B/C
*Together—B/C
*United Church Observer—B/C
Upscale
Urban Kingdom—C
*Vibrant Life—C
Vision—B/C
*War Cry—B/C
Way of St. Francis—B/C
West Wind Review—B
*World & I—B/C

Children
American Girl—C
Cadet Quest—C
Celebrate—C
*Focus/Clubhouse—C
*Focus/Clubhouse Jr.—C
Nature Friend—B/C
*Pockets—C
SHINE brightly—C
Skipping Stones

Christian Education/ Library
*Christian Early Ed.—C
Christian Librarian—B
*Church Libraries—B/C
Jour./Adventist Ed.—B
*Teachers of Vision—C
*Today's Catholic Teacher—C
*Youth & CE Leadership—C

Daily Devotionals
Our Daily Journey—C
Secret Place—B
Upper Room

Missions
Evangelical Missions
*Glad Tidings—C

Intl. Jour./Frontier Missions (R)
*New World Outlook—C
*One—C
Op. Reveille Interactive Jour.—
   B/C
PFI Global Link Journal
*PIME World—B/C

Music
Christian Music Weekly—B
*Creator—B/C

Pastors/Leaders
Catechumenate—C
Catholic Servant
Christian Century—B/C
*Church Executive—C
*InSite—C
*Leadership—B
*Lutheran Partners—B
Ministry—B
Priest
*Pulpit Helps
Today's Parish—B/C
*Worship Leader—C
*Your Church—C
*Youthworker

Teen/Young Adult
Credo—B/C
*Direction Student—B/C
Essential Connection
   (ec)—B/C
Exodus Magazine
Listen—B/C
*Real Faith in Life—B
*Sharing the Victory—C
*Spirit
Take Five Plus—B/C
Young Adult Today—B
*Young Christian—B/C

Women
At the Center—C
Beyond the Bend—B/C
*Canticle
*Esprit—B
Handmaidens
*Link & Visitor—B
*Precious Times—C
Right to the Heart
*Unrecognized Woman

Woman of Worth—B/C

Writers
Best New Writing—C
*Cross & Quill—B
Esdras' Scroll—B/C
*New Writer's Mag.
*Poets & Writers
Tickled by Thunder
Write Connection—B
*Writer's Digest—B

POETRY
Adult/General
African Voices (R)
$ Alive Now (R)
$ America
$ Ancient Paths (R)
Angel Face (R)
$ Associated Content (R)
$ Aujourd'hui Credo (R)
$ Bible Advocate (R)
Bread of Life (R)
Breakthrough Intercessor (R)
$ Bridal Guides (R)
$ Capper's
$ Catholic Forester (R)
$ Catholic Peace Voice (R)
$ Catholic Yearbook (R)
$ Christian Courier/Canada (R)
$ Christian Journal (R)
Christian Motorsports
$ Christian Research
$ Churchmouse
   Publications (R)
$ Commonweal
Connecting Point (R)
Creation Care (R)
$ Creation Illust. (R)
$ Cresset
crosshome.com
$ Culture Wars (R)
Desert Call (R)
$ DisciplesWorld
E-Channels (R)
Eternal Ink (R)
$ Eureka Street
$ Evangel/IN (R)
Evangel/OR (R)
Friends Journal (R)

$ Gem (R)
Good News Journal (R)
Haiku Hippodrome
Halo Magazine
$ Haruah (R)
Highway News (R)
$ Home Times (R)
$ Image/WA
($) Impact Magazine (R)
$ In His Presence (R)
$ Indian Life (R)
Island Catholic (R)
$ JC Town Reporter (R)
$ KD Gospel Media
Keys to Living (R)
Leaves (R)
$ Liberty
LifeTimes Catholic
$ Light & Life
Light of the World
$ Live (R)
$ Lutheran Digest (R)
$ Lutheran Journal (R)
$ Mature Living
$ Mature Years (R)
Men of the Cross
$ MindFlights (R)
$ Miraculous Medal
New Heart (R)
New Identity (R)
$ New Wineskins (R)
($) P.O.W.E.R. Magazine
Pegasus Review (R)
Penned from the Heart (R)
Penwood Review
Perspectives (R)
$ Poetry Scout
$ Prairie Messenger (R)
Priscilla Papers
$ Pure Inspiration (R)
$ Purpose (R)
Quaker Life (R)
Radix Magazine
Relief Journal
Reverent Submissions (R)
$ Rose & Thorn
Ruminate
Sharing (R)
Silver Wings (R)
Single Again Mag. Online (R)

$ Standard (R)
$ St. Anthony Messenger
$ Storyteller (R)
Studio (R)
Sword and Trumpet
Sword of the Lord (R)
$ Testimony (R)
Tiferet (R)
Time of Singing (R)
$ U.S. Catholic
Urban Kingdom (R)
Victory Herald (R)
$ Vision (R)
$ Way of St. Francis (R)
$ Weavings (R)
West Wind Review
$ World & I (R)
Xavier Review

Children
$ American Girl (R)
$ Faces
$ Focus/Clubhouse Jr.
$ Partners (R)
$ Pockets (R)
$ SHINE brightly (R)
Skipping Stones
$ Story Mates (R)

Christian Education/ Library
$ Teachers of Vision (R)
$ Today's Catholic Teacher (R)

Daily Devotionals
ChristianDevotions.us
Penned from the Heart (R)
$ Secret Place
$ These Days

Missions
$ Glad Tidings (R)
Railroad Evangelist (R)

Pastors/Leaders
$ Catechumenate
$ Christian Century (R)
CrossCurrents
$ Emmanuel
Jour./Pastoral Care
Lutheran Forum
$ Lutheran Partners (R)
$ Preaching Well (R)

$ Review for Religious
Sharing the Practice (R)

Teen/Young Adult
$ Credo (R)
$ Devo'zine (R)
$ Essential Connection (ec)
Exodus Magazine
G4T Ink (R)
$ Insight (R)
$ Take Five Plus
TeensForJC (R)
$ Young Christian (R)
$ Young Christian Writers
$ Young Salvationist (R)

Women
Christian Woman's Page (R)
$ Esprit
Handmaiden (R)
Handmaidens
$ Link & Visitor (R)
$ Melody of the Heart
$ MomSense (R)
Unrecognized Woman (R)
Virtuous Woman (R)
Woman of Worth (R)

Writers
Areopagus
$ Best New Writing
$ Canadian Writer's Jour. (R)
$ Christian Communicator (R)
ChristianWriters.com
$ Cross & Quill (R)
Esdras' Scroll (R)
$ New Writer's Mag.
NW Christian Author (R)
$ Tickled by Thunder
Write Connection
$ Writer's Digest
$ Writers' Journal

POLITICS
Adult/General
African Voices (R)
$ Anglican Journal
$ Arlington Catholic
$ Associated Content (R)
$ Bible Advocate (R)
$ Brink Magazine (R)

Brink Online
$ Cathedral Age
$ Catholic Insight
$ Catholic Peace Voice (R)
CBN.com (R)
Christian Business
$ Christian Courier/Canada (R)
Christian Courier/WI (R)
$ Christian Examiner
$ Christianity Today (R)
Christian Media (R)
$ Christian Renewal (R)
$ ChristianWeek (R)
$ Churchmouse
   Publications (R)
Church of England News
$ Commonweal
Creation Care (R)
$ Creative Nonfiction
$ Cresset
Desert Voice (R)
$ DisciplesWorld
$ Faith Today
$ Good News in Florida (R)
$ Good News, Etc. (R)
Gospel Herald
Halo Magazine
$ Home Times (R)
$ In Touch
Island Catholic (R)
$ JC Town Reporter (R)
Jour. of Church & State
$ KD Gospel Media
$ Light & Life
Maine Family Policy (R)
MovieGuide
Network
New Christian Voices
$ New Wineskins (R)
$ Our Sunday Visitor (R)
Perspectives (R)
$ Presbyterian Outlook
$ Social Justice (R)
$ St. Anthony Messenger
$ Testimony (R)
Tri-State Voice
Trumpeter (R)
Urban Kingdom (R)
Wisconsin Christian
$ World & I (R)

Children
$ New Moon Girls (R)

Missions
East-West Church & Ministry
    Report
$ One

Pastors/Leaders
$ Christian Century (R)
$ Interpreter
$ Lutheran Partners (R)
$ Word & World

Teen/Young Adult
$ Boundless Webzine (R)
$ InTeen (R)

Women
Empowering Everyday Women
$ Esprit
$ inSpirit (R)

PRAISE*
Adult/General
Bread of Life (R)
Breakthrough Intercessor (R)
Christian Quarterly (R)
$ Churchmouse
    Publications (R)
Good News Journal (R)
Gospel Herald
Halo Magazine
$ Imagine
$ In Touch
$ JC Town Reporter (R)
$ KD Gospel Media
$ Live (R)

Children
$ Bread for God's
    Children (R)

Pastors/Leaders
$ SmallGroups.com (R)

Women
Extreme Woman Magazine
Jewels of God (R)

PRAYER
Adult/General
African Voices (R)
($) AGAIN Magazine (R)

$ Alive Now (R)
$ Angels on Earth
$ Annals of St. Anne
Believer's Bay
$ Bible Advocate (R)
Breakthrough Intercessor (R)
$ Brink Magazine (R)
$ Canada Lutheran (R)
$ Cathedral Age
$ Catholic Digest (R)
$ Catholic Peace Voice (R)
$ Catholic Yearbook (R)
CBN.com (R)
$ Celebrate Life (R)
$ CGA World (R)
$ Christian Home & School
$ Christianity Today (R)
$ Christian Journal (R)
Christian Online
Christian Quarterly (R)
Christian Ranchman
$ Christian Research
$ Christian Standard (R)
$ ChristianWeek (R)
$ Churchmouse
    Publications (R)
$ Columbia (R)
Connecting Point (R)
$ Converge Point (R)
$ Covenant Companion (R)
$ Culture Wars (R)
$ Decision
Desert Call (R)
Desert Voice (R)
Divine Ascent
$ Episcopal Life (R)
$ Evangel/IN (R)
Evangelical Advocate (R)
$ Faith & Family
$ Faith Today
Faithwebbin (R)
$ Family Digest (R)
$ Foursquare Leader
$ Gem (R)
$ Good News (R)
$ Good News in Florida (R)
Good News Journal (R)
$ Good News, Etc. (R)
Gospel Herald
Halo Magazine

HEARTLIGHT Internet (R)
Holy House Ministries (R)
$ Home Times (R)
($) HopeKeepers (R)
$ Horizons (adult) (R)
$ In His Presence (R)
$ In Touch
Island Catholic (R)
$ JC Town Reporter (R)
$ KD Gospel Media
Leaves (R)
$ Lifeglow (R)
$ Light & Life
$ Liguorian
$ Live (R)
$ Living Church
$ Lookout
$ Lutheran Digest (R)
$ Lutheran Journal (R)
Maine Family Policy (R)
$ Manna (R)
$ Marian Helper
$ Mature Years (R)
$ Men of Integrity (R)
Men.AG.org (R)
Message of the Open Bible (R)
$ Montgomery's Journey
Mosaic (R)
$ New Wineskins (R)
$ Our Sunday Visitor (R)
$ ParentLife
Pegasus Review (R)
Penned from the Heart (R)
Perspectives (R)
$ Positive Thinking (R)
Prayer Closet
PrayerWorks (R)
$ Presbyterian Outlook
$ Presbyterians Today (R)
$ Priority! (R)
$ Pure Inspiration (R)
Reverent Submissions (R)
$ Seek (R)
$ Spiritual Life
$ Standard (R)
$ St. Anthony Messenger
Sword of the Lord (R)
$ Testimony (R)
$ Today's Pentecostal (R)
Trumpeter (R)

$ U.S. Catholic
Urban Kingdom (R)
Victory Herald (R)
$ War Cry (R)
$ Way of St. Francis (R)
$ Wesleyan Life (R)
Wisconsin Christian

Children
$ Bread for God's Children (R)
$ Guide (R)
$ Primary Street
$ Sparkle (R)

Christian Education/ Library
Catholic Library
$ Children's Ministry
$ Group Magazine
$ Teachers of Vision (R)
$ Youth & CE Leadership

Daily Devotionals
Penned from the Heart (R)

Missions
$ Glad Tidings (R)
Intl. Jour./Frontier
    Missions (R)
$ PFI Global Link Journal (R)
Railroad Evangelist (R)

Music
$ Creator (R)

Pastors/Leaders
$ Catholic Servant
$ Clergy Journal (R)
$ Diocesan Dialogue (R)
$ Emmanuel
$ Interpreter
$ Leadership (R)
$ Lutheran Partners (R)
$ Ministry & Liturgy (R)
$ Ministry Today
$ Proclaim (R)
$ Reformed Worship (R)
$ Review for Religious
Rick Warren's Ministry
    Toolbox (R)
Sewanee Theo. Review
$ SmallGroups.com (R)
Theological Digest (R)

$ Today's Parish
$ Word & World
$ Worship Leader

Teen/Young Adult
$ Boundless Webzine (R)
$ Devo'zine (R)
$ Direction Student
$ Horizon Student
$ Insight (R)
$ InTeen (R)
$ J.A.M.
$ Real Faith in Life (R)
TeensForJC (R)
$ True Girl
$ Young Salvationist (R)

Women
($) Beyond the Bend (R)
$ Canticle
Christian Woman's Page (R)
$ Come to the Fire (R)
Crowned with Silver
Elegance (R)
Extreme Woman Magazine
For Every Woman (R)
Hope for Women
$ Horizons (R)
$ InspiredMoms (R)
$ inSpirit (R)
$ Journey
Just Between Us (R)
Lutheran Woman's Quar.
P31 Woman (R)
Precious Times (R)
Right to the Heart (R)
$ SpiritLed Woman
Unrecognized Woman (R)
Virtuous Woman (R)
Woman of Worth (R)
Women Today (R)

Writers
Areopagus

PROPHECY
Adult/General
$ Apocalypse Chronicles (R)
Believer's Bay
$ Bible Advocate (R)
CBN.com (R)

Christian Media (R)
Christian Online
Christian Quarterly (R)
$ Christian Research
$ Churchmouse
    Publications (R)
Evangelical Advocate (R)
Faithwebbin (R)
$ Foursquare Leader
Gospel Herald
Halo Magazine
$ In His Presence (R)
$ In Touch
$ JC Town Reporter (R)
$ KD Gospel Media
$ Light & Life
$ Live (R)
Midnight Call
$ Our Sunday Visitor (R)
Single Again Mag. Online (R)
$ St. Anthony Messenger
Sword of the Lord (R)
$ Testimony (R)
Trumpeter (R)
Urban Kingdom (R)

Pastors/Leaders
$ Ministry Today
Rick Warren's Ministry
    Toolbox (R)
$ Word & World

Teen/Young Adult
$ InTeen (R)
$ Real Faith in Life (R)
TeensForJC (R)
$ Young Salvationist (R)

Women
Jewels of God (R)
$ SpiritLed Woman
Unrecognized Woman (R)

PSYCHOLOGY
Adult/General
$ Associated Content (R)
$ Aujourd'hui Credo (R)
$ Catholic Peace Voice (R)
CBN.com (R)
$ Christian Courier/Canada (R)
Christian Online

$ Churchmouse Publications (R)
$ Creative Nonfiction
Evangelical Advocate (R)
$ Gem (R)
Gospel Herald
Halo Magazine
$ In Touch
Island Catholic (R)
$ JC Town Reporter (R)
$ KD Gospel Media
$ Light & Life
More Excellent Way
$ Our Sunday Visitor (R)
Perspectives/Science & Chr. Faith
$ Psychology for Living (R)
$ Search
$ Spiritual Life
$ St. Anthony Messenger
$ Testimony (R)
Trumpeter (R)
Urban Kingdom (R)
$ Vibrant Life (R)
$ World & I (R)

Children
$ New Moon Girls (R)

Missions
$ Glad Tidings (R)

Pastors/Leaders
Jour./Pastoral Care
$ Word & World

Women
($) Beyond the Bend (R)

PUPPET PLAYS
$ Children's Ministry
Christian Early Ed. (R)
$ Churchmouse Publications (R)
$ Imagine
$ JC Town Reporter (R)

RACISM
Adult/General
$ Aujourd'hui Credo (R)
$ Brink Magazine (R)
$ Catholic Peace Voice (R)
CBN.com (R)
$ Christianity Today (R)
$ ChristianWeek (R)

$ Churchmouse
    Publications (R)
$ Citizen USA
$ Columbia (R)
$ Creative Nonfiction
$ Eureka Street
$ Faith Today
Faithwebbin (R)
Gospel Herald
Halo Magazine
$ In Touch
Island Catholic (R)
$ JC Town Reporter (R)
$ KD Gospel Media
$ Light & Life
$ Live (R)
$ Lookout
$ Manna (R)
$ Men of Integrity (R)
($) Mutuality (R)
$ New Wineskins (R)
$ Our Sunday Visitor (R)
Perspectives (R)
Priscilla Papers
$ Prism
$ St. Anthony Messenger
$ Testimony (R)
$ Together (R)
Trumpeter (R)
$ U.S. Catholic
$ Upscale
Urban Kingdom (R)
$ Way of St. Francis (R)
$ World & I (R)

Children
$ Guide (R)
$ New Moon Girls (R)
$ Our Little Friend (R)
$ Primary Treasure (R)
Skipping Stones
$ Sparkle (R)

Missions
East-West Church & Ministry
    Report

Pastors/Leaders
$ Clergy Journal (R)
CrossCurrents
Jour./Pastoral Care

$ Ministry Today

Teen/Young Adult
$ Boundless Webzine (R)
$ Direction Student
$ Horizon Student
TeensForJC (R)
$ True Girl
$ Young Salvationist (R)

Women
$ Horizons (R)
$ SpiritLed Woman

RECOVERY
Adult/General
CBN.com (R)
$ Christian Journal (R)
$ Churchmouse
    Publications (R)
$ Creative Nonfiction
$ Disaster News
Evangelical Advocate (R)
$ Focus on the Family
$ Good News in Florida (R)
Gospel Herald
Halo Magazine
$ Home Times (R)
($) HopeKeepers (R)
$ In Touch
$ JC Town Reporter (R)
$ KD Gospel Media
$ Light & Life
$ Live (R)
$ Lookout
$ Manna (R)
$ Men of Integrity (R)
Men.AG.org (R)
$ Miracles, Healings
$ Now What? (R)
$ Our Sunday Visitor (R)
$ Priority! (R)
$ Prism
Reverent Submissions (R)
Ruminate
$ Seek (R)
Urban Kingdom (R)
$ Way of St. Francis (R)
$ Wildwood Reader (R)
Wisconsin Christian
$ Written

Missions
$ Glad Tidings (R)

Pastors/Leaders
Jour./Pastoral Care
$ Ministry Today

Teen/Young Adult
$ Boundless Webzine (R)

Women
($) Beyond the Bend (R)
Extreme Woman Magazine
$ inSpirit (R)
Right to the Heart (R)
Women Today (R)

RELATIONSHIPS
Adult/General
$ Angels on Earth
$ Annals of St. Anne
Anointed Pages
$ Associated Content (R)
$ Aujourd'hui Credo (R)
$ Bridal Guides (R)
$ Brink Magazine (R)
$ Canada Lutheran (R)
$ Canadian Mennonite (R)
$ Catholic Digest (R)
$ Catholic Forester (R)
CBN.com (R)
$ Celebrate Life (R)
$ Chicken Soup Books (R)
Christian Family Journal
$ Christian Home & School
$ Christian Journal (R)
Christian Online
Christian Quarterly (R)
Christian Ranchman
$ ChristianWeek (R)
$ Churchmouse
    Publications (R)
$ Converge Point (R)
$ Creative Nonfiction
Desert Call (R)
E-Channels (R)
Eternal Ink (R)
$ Evangel/IN (R)
Evangelical Advocate (R)
$ Faith Today
Faithwebbin (R)

$ Family Digest (R)
$ Family Smart E-tips (R)
$ Focus on the Family
$ Foursquare Leader
$ Gem (R)
$ Gems of Truth (R)
$ Good News in Florida (R)
Good News Journal (R)
Gospel Herald
$ Gospel Today (R)
$ Guideposts (R)
Halo Magazine
HEARTLIGHT Internet (R)
Highway News (R)
$ Home Times (R)
$ Homeschooling Today (R)
($) HopeKeepers (R)
$ Horizons (adult) (R)
$ In His Presence (R)
$ In Touch
Island Catholic (R)
$ JC Town Reporter (R)
$ KD Gospel Media
Keys to Living (R)
$ Lifeglow (R)
$ Light & Life
$ Liguorian
$ Live (R)
$ Living (R)
$ Lookout
$ Manna (R)
$ Mature Years (R)
$ Men of Integrity (R)
Men of the Cross
Men.AG.org (R)
$ Montgomery's Journey
More Excellent Way
($) Mutuality (R)
New Heart (R)
New Identity (R)
$ New Wineskins (R)
$ Our Sunday Visitor (R)
Ozarks Christian News
($) P.O.W.E.R. Magazine
$ ParentLife
Pegasus Review (R)
Penned from the Heart (R)
Perspectives (R)
$ Positive Thinking (R)
PrayerWorks (R)

Priscilla Papers
$ Pure Inspiration (R)
Reverent Submissions (R)
$ Search
$ Seek (R)
Single Again Mag. Online (R)
$ Special Living (R)
Spirituality for Today
$ St. Anthony Messenger
$ Storyteller (R)
$ Testimony (R)
3V Magazine
$ Today's Pentecostal (R)
$ Together (R)
Trumpeter (R)
$ Upscale
Urban Kingdom (R)
$ Vibrant Life (R)
$ Vision (R)
$ Vista (R)
$ War Cry (R)
$ Way of St. Francis (R)
$ Wesleyan Life (R)
$ Wildwood Reader (R)
$ World & I (R)

Children
$ Bread for God's Children (R)
$ Cadet Quest (R)
$ Guide (R)
$ New Moon Girls (R)
$ Passport (R)
$ SHINE brightly (R)
Skipping Stones
$ Sparkle (R)

Christian Education/ Library
$ Group Magazine
$ Teachers of Vision (R)
$ Youth & CE Leadership

Missions
$ Glad Tidings (R)

Pastors/Leaders
$ Leadership (R)
$ SmallGroups.com (R)
$ Word & World

Teen/Young Adult
$ Boundless Webzine (R)
$ Credo (R)

$ Direction Student
G4T Ink (R)
$ Horizon Student
$ Insight (R)
$ Listen (R)
$ Real Faith in Life (R)
$ TC Magazine
TeensForJC (R)
$ True Girl
$ Young Salvationist (R)

Women
$ At the Center (R)
($) Beyond the Bend (R)
$ Canticle
Christian Woman's Page (R)
$ Come to the Fire (R)
Crowned with Silver
$ Dabbling Mum (R)
Elegance (R)
Empowering Everyday Women
Extreme Woman Magazine
First Lady
For Every Woman (R)
$ Girlfriend 2 Girlfriend
$ Heart & Soul
Hope for Women
$ InspiredMoms (R)
$ inSpirit (R)
Jewels of God (R)
$ Journey
Just Between Us (R)
Life Tools for Women
$ Link & Visitor (R)
Live Magazine
Lutheran Woman's Quar.
$ MomSense (R)
P31 Woman (R)
$ Pauses . . .
Precious Times (R)
Simply Blessed (R)
$ SpiritLed Woman
Unrecognized Woman (R)
Virtuous Woman (R)
Woman of Worth (R)
Women Today (R)

RELIGIOUS FREEDOM
Adult/General
$ Arlington Catholic

$ Aujourd'hui Credo (R)
$ Brink Magazine (R)
$ Catholic Peace Voice (R)
CBN.com (R)
Christian Courier/WI (R)
$ Christian Examiner
$ Christian Home & School
$ Christianity Today (R)
Christian Observer
Christian Online
Christian Ranchman
$ Christian Response (R)
$ ChristianWeek (R)
$ Churchmouse Publications (R)
Church of England News
$ Columbia (R)
$ Commonweal
$ Compass Direct
Connecting Point (R)
Desert Voice (R)
E-Channels (R)
$ Episcopal Life (R)
$ Eureka Street
Evangelical Advocate (R)
$ Faith Today
$ Gem (R)
$ Good News in Florida (R)
Good News Today
Gospel Herald
Halo Magazine
$ Home Times (R)
$ In His Presence (R)
$ In Touch
$ Interim (R)
Island Catholic (R)
$ JC Town Reporter (R)
Jour. of Church & State
$ KD Gospel Media
$ Liberty
$ Lifeglow (R)
$ Light & Life
$ Live (R)
$ Lookout
Maine Family Policy (R)
$ Manna (R)
Message of the Open Bible (R)
Messianic Perspectives (R)
$ New Wineskins (R)
$ Our Sunday Visitor (R)
$ Pathway (R)

Pegasus Review (R)
Perspectives (R)
$ Prairie Messenger (R)
$ Presbyterian Outlook
$ Prism
$ Pure Inspiration (R)
$ Salvo
$ Search
$ Seek (R)
Spirituality for Today
$ Spiritual Life
$ St. Anthony Messenger
$ Testimony (R)
Trumpeter (R)
Urban Kingdom (R)
Victory Herald (R)
$ Way of St. Francis (R)
Wisconsin Christian
$ World & I (R)

Children
$ Guide (R)
$ New Moon Girls (R)
Skipping Stones

Christian Education/ Library
$ Teachers of Vision (R)

Missions
East-West Church & Ministry
    Report
$ Evangelical Missions (R)
$ Glad Tidings (R)
Lausanne World Pulse (R)
Op. Reveille Interactive Jour. (R)
wec.go

Pastors/Leaders
$ Catholic Servant
$ Christian Century (R)
CrossCurrents
$ Word & World

Teen/Young Adult
$ Boundless Webzine (R)
$ Direction Student
$ Horizon Student
$ InTeen (R)
TeensForJC (R)

Women
$ SpiritLed Woman

RELIGIOUS TOLERANCE
Adult/General
$ Aujourd'hui Credo (R)
$ Brink Magazine (R)
$ Catholic Peace Voice (R)
CBN.com (R)
$ Christian Examiner
$ Christian Home & School
$ Christianity Today (R)
Christian Online
$ ChristianWeek (R)
$ Churchmouse
    Publications (R)
Church of England News
$ Columbia (R)
$ Compass Direct
E-Channels (R)
$ Eureka Street
Evangelical Advocate (R)
$ Faith Today
$ Good News, Etc. (R)
Gospel Herald
Halo Magazine
$ In Touch
$ Interim (R)
Island Catholic (R)
$ JC Town Reporter (R)
Jour. of Church & State
$ KD Gospel Media
$ Light & Life
$ Live (R)
$ Lookout
Maine Family Policy (R)
$ Manna (R)
Messianic Perspectives (R)
More Excellent Way
$ New Wineskins (R)
$ Our Sunday Visitor (R)
Perspectives (R)
$ Prairie Messenger (R)
$ Pure Inspiration (R)
$ Search
$ Seek (R)
Spirituality for Today
$ St. Anthony Messenger
$ Testimony (R)
Trumpeter (R)
Urban Kingdom (R)
$ Way of St. Francis (R)
$ World & I (R)

Children
$ New Moon Girls (R)
$ Primary Treasure (R)
Skipping Stones

Missions
East-West Church & Ministry
    Report
$ Glad Tidings (R)
Op. Reveille Interactive Jour. (R)

Pastors/Leaders
$ Christian Century (R)
Church Executive
$ Clergy Journal (R)
CrossCurrents

Teen/Young Adult
$ Boundless Webzine (R)
$ Direction Student
$ Horizon Student
TeensForJC (R)

Women
$ Esprit
Hope for Women

REVIVAL
Adult/General
$ Bible Advocate (R)
Breakthrough Intercessor (R)
CBN.com (R)
$ Christian Home & School
Christian Quarterly (R)
Christian Ranchman
$ Churchmouse Publications (R)
$ Columbia (R)
$ Converge Point (R)
Evangelical Advocate (R)
$ Good News, Etc. (R)
Gospel Herald
Halo Magazine
$ Home Times (R)
$ In His Presence (R)
$ In Touch
$ KD Gospel Media
$ Light & Life
$ Live (R)
$ Lookout
$ Manna (R)
Reverent Submissions (R)
Urban Kingdom (R)

Missions
East-West Church & Ministry
    Report

Pastors/Leaders
Jour./Amer. Soc./Chur. Growth
    (R)
$ Ministry Today

Teen/Young Adult
$ Boundless Webzine (R)
$ Insight (R)

Women
$ Come to the Fire (R)
Hope for Women

SALVATION
TESTIMONIES
Adult/General
American Tract (R)
Believer's Bay
Breakthrough Intercessor (R)
CBN.com (R)
$ Christian Home & School
$ Christian Journal (R)
Christian Motorsports
Christian Online
Christian Quarterly (R)
Christian Ranchman
$ Christian Research
$ Churchmouse
    Publications (R)
$ Columbia (R)
Connecting Point (R)
$ Converge Point (R)
$ Decision
E-Channels (R)
$ Evangel/IN (R)
Evangelical Advocate (R)
$ Faith Today
$ FGBC World (R)
$ Gem (R)
$ Good News, Etc. (R)
Gospel Herald
$ Guideposts (R)
Halo Magazine
Heartbeat/CMA
Highway News (R)
$ Home Times (R)
$ In His Presence (R)

$ In Touch
$ JC Town Reporter (R)
$ KD Gospel Media
Leaves (R)
$ Lifeglow (R)
$ Light & Life
$ Live (R)
$ Men of Integrity (R)
$ MESSAGE
Messianic Perspectives (R)
New Heart (R)
New Identity (R)
$ Now What? (R)
$ On Mission
$ Pathway (R)
$ Power for Living (R)
PrayerWorks (R)
$ Priority! (R)
Reverent Submissions (R)
$ Seek (R)
$ St. Anthony Messenger
Sword of the Lord (R)
$ Testimony (R)
$ Together (R)
Trumpeter (R)
Urban Kingdom (R)
$ War Cry (R)
$ Wesleyan Life (R)
Wisconsin Christian

Children
$ Guide (R)
$ Sparkle (R)

Christian Education/ Library
Catholic Library
$ Group Magazine

Missions
Railroad Evangelist (R)

Teen/Young Adult
$ Boundless Webzine (R)
$ Direction Student
Exodus Magazine
$ Horizon Student
$ InTeen (R)
TeensForJC (R)

Women
($) History's Women (R)
Hope for Women

$ Journey
$ MD Women of Worship
Precious Times (R)
$ SpiritLed Woman
Unrecognized Woman (R)
Women Today (R)

Writers
Areopagus

SCIENCE
Adult/General
$ Animal Trails (R)
Answers Magazine
$ Associated Content (R)
$ Aujourd'hui Credo (R)
CBN.com (R)
$ Christian Courier/Canada (R)
$ Churchmouse Publications (R)
Creation
Creation Care (R)
$ Creation Illust. (R)
$ Creative Nonfiction
$ Eureka Street
$ Faith Today
Gospel Herald
$ Home Times (R)
$ In Touch
Island Catholic (R)
$ Light & Life
$ Our Sunday Visitor (R)
Perspectives (R)
Perspectives/Science & Chr. Faith
$ Salvo
$ Search
$ St. Anthony Messenger
$ Testimony (R)
Trumpeter (R)
Urban Kingdom (R)
$ World & I (R)

Children
$ Archaeology
$ Cadet Quest (R)
$ Nature Friend (R)
$ New Moon Girls (R)
Skipping Stones
$ Sparkle (R)

Missions
Intl. Jour./Frontier Missions (R)

Pastors/Leaders
$ Lutheran Partners (R)
$ Word & World

Teen/Young Adult
$ InTeen (R)
TeensForJC (R)
$ Young Christian Writers

SELF-HELP
Adult/General
$ Associated Content (R)
$ Catholic Digest (R)
CBN.com (R)
$ CGA World (R)
$ Churchmouse
    Publications (R)
Disciple's Journal (R)
$ Family Smart E-tips (R)
Gospel Herald
Halo Magazine
$ Home Times (R)
($) HopeKeepers (R)
$ In Touch
$ JC Town Reporter (R)
$ KD Gospel Media
$ Lifeglow (R)
$ Light & Life
$ Liguorian
$ Lookout
$ Manna (R)
Men of the Cross
$ Pure Inspiration (R)
Reverent Submissions (R)
$ Seek (R)
$ Significant Living (R)
Single Again Mag. Online (R)
$ Special Living (R)
$ St. Anthony Messenger
$ Testimony (R)
Trumpeter (R)
Urban Kingdom (R)
$ Vibrant Life (R)
$ World & I (R)

Children
Skipping Stones

Missions
$ Glad Tidings (R)
Women of the Harvest

Pastors/Leaders
$ Interpreter

Teen/Young Adult
$ Listen (R)
TeensForJC (R)

Women
Christian Woman's Page (R)
Elegance (R)
Extreme Woman Magazine
For Every Woman (R)
$ FullFill
Jewels of God (R)
$ Journey
Women of the Cross

SENIOR ADULT ISSUES
Adult/General
$ Angels on Earth
$ Anglican Journal
$ Annals of St. Anne
$ Arkansas Catholic (R)
$ Associated Content (R)
$ B.C. Catholic (R)
byFaith
$ Canada Lutheran (R)
$ Catholic Forester (R)
CBN.com (R)
$ CGA World (R)
Christian Quarterly (R)
Christian Ranchman
$ Christian Standard (R)
$ ChristianWeek (R)
$ Churchmouse Publications (R)
$ City Light News (R)
$ Columbia (R)
$ Converge Point (R)
Desert Voice (R)
$ Evangel/IN (R)
Evangelical Advocate (R)
$ Family Digest (R)
$ Family Smart E-tips (R)
$ Focus on the Family
$ Gem (R)
$ Good News in Florida (R)
Good News Journal (R)
Gospel Herald
Halo Magazine
$ Home Times (R)
$ Homeschooling Today (R)
($) HopeKeepers (R)

$ In His Presence (R)
$ In Touch
Island Catholic (R)
$ JC Town Reporter (R)
$ Lifeglow (R)
$ Light & Life
$ Liguorian
$ Live (R)
$ Mature Living
$ Mature Years (R)
$ Montgomery's Journey
$ Our Sunday Visitor (R)
$ Ozarks Senior Living (R)
Penned from the Heart (R)
$ Power for Living (R)
PrayerWorks (R)
Reverent Submissions (R)
$ Seek (R)
Senior Connection
$ Significant Living (R)
Single Again Mag. Online (R)
$ St. Anthony Messenger
$ Testimony (R)
Trumpeter (R)
$ U.S. Catholic
$ War Cry (R)
$ Way of St. Francis (R)
$ Wesleyan Life (R)

Christian Education/ Library
$ Youth & CE Leadership

Daily Devotionals
Penned from the Heart (R)

Missions
$ Glad Tidings (R)

Pastors/Leaders
$ Diocesan Dialogue (R)
$ Interpreter
$ Word & World

Women
For Every Woman (R)
$ inSpirit (R)
Simply Blessed (R)
Unrecognized Woman (R)

SERMONS
Adult/General
$ Arlington Catholic

Breakthrough Intercessor (R)
$ Catholic Yearbook (R)
$ Churchmouse Publications (R)
Evangelical Advocate (R)
Gospel Herald
$ In His Presence (R)
$ KD Gospel Media
$ Lutheran Journal (R)
Pegasus Review (R)
$ St. Anthony Messenger
$ Stewardship (R)
Sword of the Lord (R)
$ Testimony (R)
Trumpeter (R)
Urban Kingdom (R)
Victory Herald (R)
$ Weavings (R)
Wisconsin Christian

Pastors/Leaders
$ African-American Pulpit
$ Clergy Journal (R)
$ Ministry Today
Preaching
$ Preaching Well (R)
$ Proclaim (R)
Pulpit Helps (R)
Sharing the Practice (R)
$ Sunday Sermons (R)
$ Today's Parish
$ Torch Legacy Leader

SHORT STORY: ADULT/GENERAL
$ Best New Writing
CBN.com (R)
Desert Call (R)
Desert Voice (R)
$ DisciplesWorld
$ Esprit
Faithwebbin (R)
$ Glad Tidings (R)
Halo Magazine
Handmaidens
$ Haruah (R)
$ Imagine
$ In His Presence (R)
$ Liguorian
Maine Family Policy (R)
$ Ministry & Liturgy (R)
$ Miraculous Medal

$ New Writer's Mag.
$ Over the Back Fence (R)
Perspectives (R)
PrayerWorks (R)
$ Preaching Well (R)
$ Purpose (R)
Ruminate
$ Seek (R)
$ Significant Living (R)
Tiferet (R)
Unrecognized Woman (R)
Urban Kingdom (R)
$ Wildwood Reader (R)

SHORT STORY: ADULT/RELIGIOUS

African Voices (R)
$ Alive Now (R)
$ Ancient Paths (R)
$ Angels on Earth
$ Anglican Journal
$ Annals of St. Anne
Areopagus
$ Associated Content (R)
$ Aujourd'hui Credo (R)
$ Bridal Guides (R)
$ Canadian Writer's Jour. (R)
$ Catholic Forester (R)
$ Catholic Yearbook (R)
CBN.com (R)
$ CGA World (R)
$ Christian Century (R)
$ Christian Courier/Canada (R)
$ Christian Educators (R)
$ Christian Home & School
$ Christian Journal (R)
Christian Online
Christian Ranchman
$ Christian Renewal (R)
$ Christian Research
Christian Woman's Page (R)
$ Churchmouse
    Publications (R)
$ City Light News (R)
$ Come to the Fire (R)
Connecting Point (R)
$ Covenant Companion (R)
CrossCurrents
Desert Voice (R)
$ DisciplesWorld

Esdras' Scroll (R)
$ Esprit
$ Eureka Street
$ Evangel/IN (R)
$ Faith & Family
Faithwebbin (R)
$ Foursquare Leader
$ Gem (R)
$ Gems of Truth (R)
$ Glad Tidings (R)
Handmaidens
$ Haruah (R)
HEARTLIGHT Internet (R)
$ Home Times (R)
$ Horizons (R)
$ Horizons (adult) (R)
$ Image/WA
$ Imagine
($) Impact Magazine (R)
$ In His Presence (R)
$ Indian Life (R)
$ inSpirit (R)
Intl. Jour./Frontier
    Missions (R)
Island Catholic (R)
$ JC Town Reporter (R)
Jewels of God (R)
Koinonia
$ Liguorian
$ Live (R)
$ Lutheran Journal (R)
Lutheran Woman's Quar.
$ Melody of the Heart
$ Messenger/Sacred Heart
$ Messenger/St. Anthony
$ MindFlights (R)
$ Miraculous Medal
$ New Wineskins (R)
$ On Mission
($) P.O.W.E.R. Magazine
Perspectives (R)
PrayerWorks (R)
Precious Times (R)
$ Presbyterian Outlook
$ Proclaim (R)
$ Purpose (R)
Railroad Evangelist (R)
Relief Journal
Reverent Submissions (R)
Ruminate

Seeds of Hope
$ Seek (R)
$ Shades of Romance (R)
$ Sharing the Victory (R)
$ Significant Living (R)
Simply Blessed (R)
Spirituality for Today
$ Standard (R)
$ St. Anthony Messenger
Studio (R)
$ Testimony (R)
Tiferet (R)
$ U.S. Catholic
Unrecognized Woman (R)
Urban Kingdom (R)
$ Vision (R)
$ Vista (R)
$ Way of St. Francis (R)
$ Wesleyan Life (R)
West Wind Review
$ Written

SHORT STORY: ADVENTURE
Adult

$ Angels on Earth
$ Animal Trails (R)
$ Annals of St. Anne
$ Associated Content (R)
$ Best New Writing
$ Capper's
CBN.com (R)
Desert Voice (R)
Esdras' Scroll (R)
$ Gem (R)
$ Glad Tidings (R)
Halo Magazine
$ Haruah (R)
HEARTLIGHT Internet (R)
$ In His Presence (R)
$ Indian Life (R)
$ JC Town Reporter (R)
$ Liguorian
PrayerWorks (R)
$ Rose & Thorn
$ Standard (R)
$ Storyteller (R)
Studio (R)
Unrecognized Woman (R)
Urban Kingdom (R)

$ Vision (R)
$ Weavings (R)

Children
$ American Girl (R)
$ Animal Trails (R)
$ Archaeology
$ Bread for God's Children (R)
$ Cadet Quest (R)
Connecting Point (R)
Eternal Ink (R)
$ Focus/Clubhouse Jr.
$ Junior Companion (R)
$ Kid Zone
$ Kids' Ark (R)
$ New Moon Girls (R)
$ Partners (R)
$ SHINE brightly (R)
Skipping Stones
$ Sparkle (R)
Sword of the Lord (R)
$ Young Christian (R)

Teen/Young Adult
$ Animal Trails (R)
$ Archaeology
$ Bread for God's Children (R)
$ Cadet Quest (R)
$ Credo (R)
$ Direction Student
$ Horizon Student
$ InTeen (R)
$ Partners (R)
$ SHINE brightly (R)
$ Storyteller (R)
Sword of the Lord (R)
TeensForJC (R)
$ Young Adult Today
$ Young Christian (R)
$ Young Christian Writers
$ Young Salvationist (R)

SHORT STORY: ALLEGORY
Adult
$ Alive Now (R)
$ Associated Content (R)
CBN.com (R)
$ Christian Journal (R)
Christian Woman's Page (R)
$ City Light News (R)

$ Covenant Companion (R)
Esdras' Scroll (R)
$ Gem (R)
$ Glad Tidings (R)
Halo Magazine
HEARTLIGHT Internet (R)
$ Home Times (R)
$ Imagine
$ In His Presence (R)
$ Indian Life (R)
$ JC Town Reporter (R)
$ Liguorian
Maine Family Policy (R)
Men of the Cross
$ New Wineskins (R)
PrayerWorks (R)
Railroad Evangelist (R)
Reverent Submissions (R)
Studio (R)
$ Vision (R)
$ Way of St. Francis (R)
Women of the Cross

Children
$ Animal Trails (R)
$ Nature Friend (R)
Sword of the Lord (R)
$ Young Christian (R)

Teen/Young Adult
$ Animal Trails (R)
$ Direction Student
$ Home Times (R)
$ Horizon Student
Sword of the Lord (R)
$ Young Christian Writers
$ Young Salvationist (R)

SHORT STORY: BIBLICAL
Adult
$ Alive Now (R)
$ Anglican Journal
$ Annals of St. Anne
$ Aujourd'hui Credo (R)
Bread of Life (R)
$ Catholic Yearbook (R)
CBN.com (R)
$ CGA World (R)
$ Christian Journal (R)
Christian Online

Christian Ranchman
Christian Woman's Page (R)
Congregational Libraries
   Today
Connecting Point (R)
Crowned with Silver
Desert Call (R)
Desert Voice (R)
Esdras' Scroll (R)
$ Evangel/IN (R)
Faithwebbin (R)
$ Gem (R)
$ Glad Tidings (R)
Halo Magazine
$ Haruah (R)
HEARTLIGHT Internet (R)
$ Horizons (R)
$ In His Presence (R)
$ JC Town Reporter (R)
Jewels of God (R)
$ Kindred Spirit (R)
$ Lutheran Journal (R)
Lutheran Woman's Quar.
Maine Family Policy (R)
$ New Wineskins (R)
PrayerWorks (R)
$ Purpose (R)
Railroad Evangelist (R)
Reverent Submissions (R)
$ Seek (R)
Spirituality for Today
Studio (R)
Urban Kingdom (R)
Victory Herald (R)
$ Vista (R)
$ Way of St. Francis (R)
$ Wesleyan Life (R)

Children
$ Adventures
$ Animal Trails (R)
$ Bread for God's Children (R)
Christian Ranchman
Eternal Ink (R)
Faithwebbin (R)
$ Focus/Clubhouse
$ Nature Friend (R)
$ Pockets (R)
$ Sparkle (R)
Sword of the Lord (R)

Victory Herald (R)
$ Young Christian (R)

Teen/Young Adult
$ Anglican Journal
$ Animal Trails (R)
$ Bread for God's Children (R)
Christian Ranchman
Crowned with Silver
$ Direction Student
$ Essential Connection (ec)
Faithwebbin (R)
$ Home Times (R)
$ Horizon Student
$ InTeen (R)
Spirituality for Today
Sword of the Lord (R)
TeensForJC (R)
Victory Herald (R)
$ Young Adult Today

SHORT STORY: CONTEMPORARY
Adult
African Voices (R)
$ Alive Now (R)
$ Ancient Paths (R)
$ Angels on Earth
$ Annals of St. Anne
$ Associated Content (R)
$ Aujourd'hui Credo (R)
$ Canada Lutheran (R)
CBN.com (R)
$ Christian Century (R)
$ Christian Courier/Canada (R)
$ Christian Home & School
$ Christian Renewal (R)
Christian Woman's Page (R)
$ Churchmouse Publications (R)
Connecting Point (R)
$ Covenant Companion (R)
$ DisciplesWorld
Esdras' Scroll (R)
$ Esprit
$ Eureka Street
$ Evangel/IN (R)
Faithwebbin (R)
$ Gem (R)
$ Glad Tidings (R)
Halo Magazine
$ Haruah (R)

HEARTLIGHT Internet (R)
$ Horizons (adult) (R)
$ In His Presence (R)
$ Indian Life (R)
$ JC Town Reporter (R)
$ Liguorian
$ Mature Living
$ New Wineskins (R)
$ New Writer's Mag.
Perspectives (R)
PrayerWorks (R)
Precious Times (R)
Railroad Evangelist (R)
Relief Journal
Reverent Submissions (R)
Ruminate
$ Seek (R)
$ Shades of Romance (R)
Simply Blessed (R)
Spirituality for Today
$ Standard (R)
$ Storyteller (R)
Studio (R)
Tiferet (R)
$ U.S. Catholic
Urban Kingdom (R)
$ Vision (R)
West Wind Review
$ Wildwood Reader (R)
$ Written
Xavier Review

Children
$ Adventures
$ American Girl (R)
$ Animal Trails (R)
$ Bread for God's
    Children (R)
$ Cadet Quest (R)
Faithwebbin (R)
$ Focus/Clubhouse
$ Focus/Clubhouse Jr.
$ Kids' Ark (R)
$ New Moon Girls (R)
$ Partners (R)
$ Pockets (R)
$ SHINE brightly (R)
$ Sparkle (R)
$ Story Mates (R)
$ Young Christian (R)

Teen/Young Adult
$ Animal Trails (R)
$ Cadet Quest (R)
$ Direction Student
$ Essential Connection (ec)
Faithwebbin (R)
$ Home Times (R)
$ Horizon Student
$ Living My Faith
$ Partners (R)
$ Real Faith in Life (R)
$ Spirit
$ Storyteller (R)
TeensForJC (R)
$ Young Christian Writers
$ Young Salvationist (R)

SHORT STORY: ETHNIC
Adult
African Voices (R)
$ Associated Content (R)
$ CGA World (R)
$ DisciplesWorld
Esdras' Scroll (R)
$ Eureka Street
Faithwebbin (R)
$ Gem (R)
$ Glad Tidings (R)
Halo Magazine
$ Haruah (R)
$ Indian Life (R)
$ JC Town Reporter (R)
PrayerWorks (R)
Relief Journal
$ Seek (R)
Spirituality for Today
Studio (R)
$ U.S. Catholic
Unrecognized Woman (R)
Urban Kingdom (R)
Xavier Review

Children
$ American Girl (R)
$ Animal Trails (R)
Faithwebbin (R)
$ Focus/Clubhouse
$ Kids' Ark (R)
$ New Moon Girls (R)
Skipping Stones

$ Sparkle (R)
$ Young Christian (R)

Teen/Young Adult
$ Animal Trails (R)
Faithwebbin (R)
$ SHINE brightly (R)
TeensForJC (R)
$ Young Christian (R)

SHORT STORY: FANTASY
Adult
$ Associated Content (R)
Connecting Point (R)
$ Eureka Street
Faithwebbin (R)
$ Gem (R)
$ Glad Tidings (R)
Halo Magazine
($) Impact Magazine (R)
$ In His Presence (R)
$ JC Town Reporter (R)
$ MindFlights (R)
$ Rose & Thorn
$ Storyteller (R)
Studio (R)
$ Tickled by Thunder
$ Written

Children
Faithwebbin (R)
$ Focus/Clubhouse
$ New Moon Girls (R)
$ SHINE brightly (R)
$ Sparkle (R)
Sword of the Lord (R)

Teen/Young Adult
$ Credo (R)
Faithwebbin (R)
$ InTeen (R)
$ SHINE brightly (R)
$ Storyteller (R)
Sword of the Lord (R)
TeensForJC (R)
$ Young Adult Today
$ Young Christian Writers

SHORT STORY:
FRONTIER
Adult
$ Associated Content (R)

$ Capper's
Connecting Point (R)
Desert Voice (R)
$ Gem (R)
$ Glad Tidings (R)
Halo Magazine
$ Haruah (R)
$ In His Presence (R)
$ Indian Life (R)
$ JC Town Reporter (R)
PrayerWorks (R)
$ Storyteller (R)
Studio (R)

Children
$ Animal Trails (R)
Eternal Ink (R)
$ Kids' Ark (R)
$ New Moon Girls (R)
$ SHINE brightly (R)
Sword of the Lord (R)
$ Young Christian (R)

Teen/Young Adult
$ Credo (R)
$ Home Times (R)
$ Storyteller (R)
Sword of the Lord (R)

SHORT STORY:
FRONTIER/ROMANCE
$ Associated Content (R)
$ Capper's
Connecting Point (R)
$ Gem (R)
Halo Magazine
$ Haruah (R)
$ JC Town Reporter (R)
$ Shades of Romance (R)
Studio (R)
Unrecognized Woman (R)
Urban Kingdom (R)

SHORT STORY:
HISTORICAL
Adult
$ Alive Now (R)
$ Ancient Paths (R)
$ Associated Content (R)
$ Aujourd'hui Credo (R)
$ Capper's

CBN.com (R)
$ Christian Renewal (R)
$ City Light News (R)
Connecting Point (R)
Desert Voice (R)
Faithwebbin (R)
$ Gem (R)
$ Glad Tidings (R)
Halo Magazine
$ Haruah (R)
HEARTLIGHT Internet (R)
$ Home Times (R)
$ Imagine
$ In His Presence (R)
$ Indian Life (R)
$ JC Town Reporter (R)
Lutheran Woman's Quar.
$ New Writer's Mag.
$ Purpose (R)
Railroad Evangelist (R)
$ Rose & Thorn
$ Seek (R)
Spirituality for Today
$ Storyteller (R)
Studio (R)
Urban Kingdom (R)

Children
$ American Girl (R)
$ Animal Trails (R)
$ Archaeology
$ Bread for God's Children (R)
Christian Ranchman
Faithwebbin (R)
$ Focus/Clubhouse
$ Focus/Clubhouse Jr.
$ Home Times (R)
$ Kids' Ark (R)
$ Nature Friend (R)
$ New Moon Girls (R)
$ Partners (R)
$ SHINE brightly (R)
$ Sparkle (R)
Sword of the Lord (R)
$ Young Christian (R)

Teen/Young Adult
$ Animal Trails (R)
$ Archaeology
$ Bread for God's Children (R)
Christian Ranchman

$ Credo (R)
Faithwebbin (R)
$ Home Times (R)
$ InTeen (R)
$ Partners (R)
$ SHINE brightly (R)
Spirituality for Today
$ Storyteller (R)
Sword of the Lord (R)
$ Young Adult Today
$ Young Christian Writers

SHORT STORY: HISTORICAL/ROMANCE
African Voices (R)
Areopagus
$ Associated Content (R)
$ Capper's
CBN.com (R)
Connecting Point (R)
Faithwebbin (R)
$ Gem (R)
Halo Magazine
$ Haruah (R)
$ JC Town Reporter (R)
$ Liguorian
$ Shades of Romance (R)
Studio (R)
Unrecognized Woman (R)
Urban Kingdom (R)
$ Written

SHORT STORY: HUMOROUS
Adult
African Voices (R)
$ Ancient Paths (R)
$ Associated Content (R)
$ Canada Lutheran (R)
$ Catholic Forester (R)
CBN.com (R)
$ CGA World (R)
$ Christian Courier/Canada (R)
$ Christian Journal (R)
$ City Light News (R)
Congregational Libraries Today
Connecting Point (R)
$ Covenant Companion (R)
$ Esprit
$ Eureka Street

$ Gem (R)
$ Glad Tidings (R)
Halo Magazine
$ Haruah (R)
HEARTLIGHT Internet (R)
$ Home Times (R)
$ Horizons (adult) (R)
$ Imagine
$ In His Presence (R)
$ JC Town Reporter (R)
Jewels of God (R)
$ Liguorian
$ Mature Living
$ Mature Years (R)
Men of the Cross
$ Miraculous Medal
$ New Writer's Mag.
$ Over the Back Fence (R)
Pegasus Review (R)
PrayerWorks (R)
$ Presbyterian Outlook
Reverent Submissions (R)
$ Seek (R)
$ Significant Living (R)
Spirituality for Today
$ Storyteller (R)
Studio (R)
$ U.S. Catholic
Unrecognized Woman (R)
Urban Kingdom (R)
$ Vista (R)
West Wind Review

Children
$ Cadet Quest (R)
Christian Ranchman
Congregational Libraries Today
Eternal Ink (R)
$ Focus/Clubhouse
$ Home Times (R)
$ New Moon Girls (R)
$ SHINE brightly (R)
Skipping Stones
$ Sparkle (R)
$ Story Mates (R)
Sword of the Lord (R)
$ Young Christian (R)

Teen/Young Adult
$ Animal Trails (R)
$ Cadet Quest (R)

Christian Ranchman
$ Credo (R)
$ Direction Student
$ Essential Connection (ec)
$ Home Times (R)
$ Horizon Student
$ InTeen (R)
Pegasus Review (R)
$ Storyteller (R)
Sword of the Lord (R)
TeensForJC (R)
$ Young Adult Today
$ Young Christian Writers
$ Young Salvationist (R)

SHORT STORY: JUVENILE
$ Adventures
$ American Girl (R)
Areopagus
$ Associated Content (R)
$ Beginner's Friend (R)
$ Cadet Quest (R)
$ Catholic Forester (R)
CBN.com (R)
$ Christian Renewal (R)
Church Herald & Holiness (R)
Congregational Libraries Today
Desert Voice (R)
Esdras' Scroll (R)
$ Faces
$ Faith & Family
$ Focus/Clubhouse
$ Focus/Clubhouse Jr.
Halo Magazine
$ In His Presence (R)
Jewels of God (R)
$ Junior Companion (R)
$ Keys for Kids (R)
$ Kid Zone
$ Kids' Ark (R)
$ Nature Friend (R)
$ New Moon Girls (R)
$ Partners (R)
$ Pockets (R)
$ Primary Pal (R)
$ Seek (R)
$ SHINE brightly (R)
Skipping Stones
$ Sparkle (R)
$ Story Mates (R)

TeensForJC (R)
$ United Church Observer (R)
$ Young Christian Writers

SHORT STORY: LITERARY
Adult
African Voices (R)
$ Ancient Paths (R)
$ Associated Content (R)
$ Christian Courier/
   Canada (R)
$ Covenant Companion (R)
Esdras' Scroll (R)
$ Eureka Street
Faithwebbin (R)
$ Gem (R)
$ Glad Tidings (R)
Halo Magazine
Handmaidens
$ Haruah (R)
$ Horizons (adult) (R)
$ Imagine
$ JC Town Reporter (R)
$ New Wineskins (R)
Pegasus Review (R)
Perspectives (R)
Relief Journal
Reverent Submissions (R)
$ Rose & Thorn
Ruminate
$ Seek (R)
$ Standard (R)
$ Storyteller (R)
Studio (R)
$ Tickled by Thunder
Tiferet (R)
$ U.S. Catholic
Urban Kingdom (R)
West Wind Review
$ Wildwood Reader (R)
$ Written
Xavier Review

Children
$ New Moon Girls (R)
Skipping Stones

Teen/Young Adult
Faithwebbin (R)
$ Home Times (R)

Pegasus Review (R)
Spirituality for Today
$ Storyteller (R)

SHORT STORY: MYSTERY/ROMANCE
$ Associated Content (R)
$ Capper's
Connecting Point (R)
$ Direction Student
Faithwebbin (R)
$ Gem (R)
Halo Magazine
$ Haruah (R)
$ Horizon Student
$ JC Town Reporter (R)
$ Shades of Romance (R)
Studio (R)
TeensForJC (R)
Unrecognized Woman (R)
Urban Kingdom (R)

SHORT STORY: MYSTERY/SUSPENSE
Adult
$ Associated Content (R)
$ Best New Writing
$ Capper's
CBN.com (R)
Connecting Point (R)
Desert Voice (R)
Esdras' Scroll (R)
Faithwebbin (R)
$ Gem (R)
$ Glad Tidings (R)
Halo Magazine
$ Haruah (R)
HEARTLIGHT Internet (R)
$ JC Town Reporter (R)
Relief Journal
$ Storyteller (R)
Studio (R)
$ Tickled by Thunder
Unrecognized Woman (R)

Children
$ American Girl (R)
$ Animal Trails (R)
Faithwebbin (R)
$ Kids' Ark (R)

$ New Moon Girls (R)
$ SHINE brightly (R)
$ Sparkle (R)
Sword of the Lord (R)
$ Young Christian (R)

Teen/Young Adult
$ Animal Trails (R)
$ Credo (R)
$ Direction Student
Faithwebbin (R)
$ Horizon Student
$ InTeen (R)
$ SHINE brightly (R)
$ Storyteller (R)
Sword of the Lord (R)
TeensForJC (R)
$ Young Adult Today
$ Young Christian Writers

SHORT STORY: PARABLES
Adult
$ Annals of St. Anne
$ Associated Content (R)
$ Catholic Yearbook (R)
$ Christian Courier/Canada (R)
$ Christian Journal (R)
$ Covenant Companion (R)
Esdras' Scroll (R)
$ Esprit
$ Gem (R)
$ Glad Tidings (R)
HEARTLIGHT Internet (R)
$ Imagine
($) Impact Magazine (R)
$ In His Presence (R)
$ JC Town Reporter (R)
Jewels of God (R)
$ Liguorian
$ Lutheran Journal (R)
$ Ministry & Liturgy (R)
$ New Wineskins (R)
Perspectives (R)
$ Preaching Well (R)
Railroad Evangelist (R)
Reverent Submissions (R)
$ Seek (R)
Studio (R)
$ Testimony (R)

Urban Kingdom (R)
$ Way of St. Francis (R)

Children
$ Animal Trails (R)
$ Archaeology
Eternal Ink (R)
$ Faces
$ Focus/Clubhouse Jr.
$ Sparkle (R)
$ Young Christian (R)

Teen/Young Adult
$ Animal Trails (R)
$ Archaeology
$ Home Times (R)
$ InTeen (R)
$ SHINE brightly (R)
TeensForJC (R)
$ Testimony (R)
$ Young Adult Today
$ Young Christian Writers
$ Young Salvationist (R)

SHORT STORY: PLAYS
Areopagus
$ Drama Ministry (R)
Esdras' Scroll (R)
$ Faces
$ Focus/Clubhouse Jr.
$ Imagine
$ J.A.M.
$ New Wineskins (R)
$ SHINE brightly (R)
Studio (R)
TeensForJC (R)
Unrecognized Woman (R)
Urban Kingdom (R)

SHORT STORY: ROMANCE
Adult
$ Associated Content (R)
$ Bridal Guides (R)
$ Capper's
CBN.com (R)
Connecting Point (R)
Faithwebbin (R)
$ Gem (R)
Halo Magazine
$ Haruah (R)
$ JC Town Reporter (R)

Precious Times (R)
$ Rose & Thorn
$ Shades of Romance (R)
$ Storyteller (R)
Studio (R)
Unrecognized Woman (R)
Urban Kingdom (R)
$ Wildwood Reader (R)
$ Written

Teen/Young Adult
$ Animal Trails (R)
$ Direction Student
$ Horizon Student
TeensForJC (R)

SHORT STORY: SCIENCE FICTION
Adult
African Voices (R)
$ Associated Content (R)
Connecting Point (R)
$ Eureka Street
Faithwebbin (R)
$ Gem (R)
$ Glad Tidings (R)
Halo Magazine
$ JC Town Reporter (R)
$ MindFlights (R)
$ Rose & Thorn
$ Storyteller (R)
Studio (R)
$ Tickled by Thunder
$ Written

Children
Faithwebbin (R)
$ Kids' Ark (R)
$ New Moon Girls (R)
$ SHINE brightly (R)
$ Sparkle (R)
Sword of the Lord (R)

Teen/Young Adult
$ Credo (R)
$ Direction Student
Faithwebbin (R)
$ Home Times (R)
$ Horizon Student
$ InTeen (R)
$ J.A.M.

$ SHINE brightly (R)
$ Storyteller (R)
Sword of the Lord (R)
$ Young Adult Today

SHORT STORY: SENIOR ADULT FICTION
Adult
Desert Voice (R)
$ Glad Tidings (R)
Halo Magazine
$ Imagine
$ In His Presence (R)
$ Liguorian
$ Live (R)
$ Mature Living
$ Mature Years (R)
PrayerWorks (R)
Reverent Submissions (R)
$ Seek (R)
$ St. Anthony Messenger
Unrecognized Woman (R)
$ Vista (R)

SHORT STORY: SKITS
Adult
Desert Voice (R)
$ Drama Ministry (R)
Esdras' Scroll (R)
$ Imagine

Children
$ Drama Ministry (R)
$ Focus/Clubhouse Jr.
$ SHINE brightly (R)
Sword of the Lord (R)

Teen/Young Adult
Crowned with Silver
$ Drama Ministry (R)
$ J.A.M.
$ SHINE brightly (R)
Sword of the Lord (R)
TeensForJC (R)

SHORT STORY: SPECULATIVE
Adult
$ Associated Content (R)
$ Eureka Street
Faithwebbin (R)

Halo Magazine
$ JC Town Reporter (R)
Relief Journal
Reverent Submissions (R)
Studio (R)
$ Tickled by Thunder
Urban Kingdom (R)
$ Written

Children
$ New Moon Girls (R)

Teen/Young Adult
Faithwebbin (R)
$ Home Times (R)
TeensForJC (R)
$ Young Salvationist (R)

SHORT STORY: TEEN/ YOUNG ADULT
$ Anglican Journal
$ Animal Trails (R)
$ Bread for God's Children (R)
$ Canada Lutheran (R)
$ Catholic Forester (R)
CBN.com (R)
$ Credo (R)
Crowned with Silver
Desert Voice (R)
$ Direction Student
Esdras' Scroll (R)
$ Essential Connection (ec)
Halo Magazine
$ Horizon Student
$ In His Presence (R)
$ InTeen (R)
$ J.A.M.
$ JC Town Reporter (R)
Jewels of God (R)
$ Living My Faith
$ New Moon Girls (R)
Pegasus Review (R)
Precious Times (R)
$ Real Faith in Life (R)
$ Seek (R)
$ Sharing the Victory (R)
Skipping Stones
$ Spirit
$ Storyteller (R)
TeensForJC (R)
$ Testimony (R)

Tiferet (R)
Unrecognized Woman (R)
Urban Kingdom (R)
Victory Herald (R)
West Wind Review
$ Written
$ Young Adult Today
$ Young Christian (R)
$ Young Christian Writers
$ Young Salvationist (R)
$ Youth Compass (R)

SHORT STORY: WESTERNS
Adult
$ Associated Content (R)
$ Bridal Guides (R)
$ Capper's
$ JC Town Reporter (R)
$ Storyteller (R)
Studio (R)
$ Tickled by Thunder

Children
$ Animal Trails (R)
Christian Ranchman
$ Kids' Ark (R)
$ Sparkle (R)
Sword of the Lord (R)
$ Young Christian (R)

Teen/Young Adult
$ Animal Trails (R)
Christian Ranchman
$ Credo (R)
$ Storyteller (R)
Sword of the Lord (R)

SINGLES' ISSUES
Adult/General
African Voices (R)
$ Annals of St. Anne
Anointed Pages
$ Associated Content (R)
$ Bible Advocate (R)
$ Brink Magazine (R)
CBN.com (R)
$ Christian Examiner
Christian Family Journal
Christian Online
Christian Ranchman

$ ChristianWeek (R)
$ Churchmouse Publications (R)
$ Columbia (R)
$ Converge Point (R)
Desert Voice (R)
Disciple's Journal (R)
E-Channels (R)
$ Evangel/IN (R)
Evangelical Advocate (R)
$ Faith Today
Faithwebbin (R)
$ Family Smart E-tips (R)
$ Focus on the Family
$ Foursquare Leader
$ Gem (R)
$ Good News in Florida (R)
Good News Journal (R)
Gospel Herald
Halo Magazine
HEARTLIGHT Internet (R)
$ Home Times (R)
$ Homeschooling Today (R)
($) HopeKeepers (R)
$ In His Presence (R)
$ In Touch
$ JC Town Reporter (R)
$ KD Gospel Media
$ Light & Life
$ Live (R)
$ Lookout
Men.AG.org (R)
$ Montgomery's Journey
($) Mutuality (R)
New Identity (R)
$ Our Sunday Visitor (R)
$ ParentLife
Penned from the Heart (R)
$ Power for Living (R)
Priscilla Papers
$ Psychology for Living (R)
$ Seek (R)
Single Again Mag. Online (R)
$ St. Anthony Messenger
$ Testimony (R)
$ Together (R)
Trumpeter (R)
$ U.S. Catholic
Urban Kingdom (R)
$ Vibrant Life (R)
$ War Cry (R)

$ Wesleyan Life (R)
$ Wildwood Reader (R)
Wisconsin Christian
$ World & I (R)

Christian Education/ Library
$ Youth & CE Leadership

Daily Devotionals
Penned from the Heart (R)

Missions
$ Glad Tidings (R)
Women of the Harvest

Pastors/Leaders
$ Interpreter
$ Ministry Today
$ Word & World

Teen/Young Adult
$ Boundless Webzine (R)
$ InTeen (R)
$ TC Magazine
TeensForJC (R)
$ Young Salvationist (R)

Women
$ Canticle
Christian Woman's Page (R)
Christian Women Today (R)
Elegance (R)
Hope for Women
$ inSpirit (R)
Simply Blessed (R)
$ SpiritLed Woman
Unrecognized Woman (R)
Women of the Cross
Women Today (R)

SMALL-GROUP HELPS
Adult/General
$ Christian Standard (R)
$ Churchmouse
    Publications (R)
$ Good News in Florida (R)
Gospel Herald
$ In Touch
$ KD Gospel Media
Reverent Submissions (R)
$ Seek (R)
Urban Kingdom (R)

Missions
$ Glad Tidings (R)

Pastors/Leaders
Ministry in Motion (R)
$ Ministry Today
Pulpit Helps (R)
$ RevWriter Resource
$ SmallGroups.com (R)

Teen/Young Adult
$ Boundless Webzine (R)

Women
For Every Woman (R)

SOCIAL JUSTICE
Adult/General
$ Arkansas Catholic (R)
$ Arlington Catholic
$ Associated Content (R)
$ Aujourd'hui Credo (R)
$ Brink Magazine (R)
Brink Online
$ Catholic Peace Voice (R)
CBN.com (R)
$ Christian Courier/Canada (R)
Christian Online
$ Christian Response (R)
$ Christian Standard (R)
$ Christianity Today (R)
$ ChristianWeek (R)
$ Churchmouse Publications (R)
$ Citizen USA
$ Columbia (R)
$ Commonweal
$ Company Magazine (R)
$ Covenant Companion (R)
Creation Care (R)
$ Creative Nonfiction
$ Cresset
$ Culture Wars (R)
Desert Call (R)
Desert Voice (R)
$ Disaster News
E-Channels (R)
$ Eureka Street
Evangel/OR (R)
Evangelical Advocate (R)
$ Faith & Family
$ Faith Today

$ Foursquare Leader
$ Gem (R)
$ Good News in Florida (R)
Gospel Herald
Halo Magazine
$ In Touch
$ Indian Life (R)
Island Catholic (R)
$ JC Town Reporter (R)
$ KD Gospel Media
$ Light & Life
$ Liguorian
$ Lookout
$ Men of Integrity (R)
More Excellent Way
Mosaic (R)
($) Mutuality (R)
New Identity (R)
$ New Wineskins (R)
$ Our Sunday Visitor (R)
Penned from the Heart (R)
Perspectives (R)
$ Prairie Messenger (R)
$ Precepts for Living
Priscilla Papers
$ Prism
$ Salvo
$ Search
$ Seek (R)
$ Social Justice (R)
$ Spiritual Life
Spirituality for Today
$ St. Anthony Messenger
$ Testimony (R)
$ Together (R)
Trumpeter (R)
$ U.S. Catholic
$ United Church Observer (R)
Urban Kingdom (R)
$ Way of St. Francis (R)
$ World & I (R)

Children
$ Pockets (R)
Skipping Stones

Christian Education/ Library
Catholic Library
$ Jour./Adventist Ed. (R)
$ Momentum

Missions

East-West Church & Ministry
   Report
$ Glad Tidings (R)
Lausanne World Pulse (R)
Missiology

Pastors/Leaders

$ African-American Pulpit
$ Barefoot (R)
$ Christian Century (R)
$ Clergy Journal (R)
$ Interpreter
Jour./Pastoral Care
Sharing the Practice (R)
Theological Digest (R)
$ Torch Legacy Leader

Teen/Young Adult

$ Boundless Webzine (R)
$ Devo'zine (R)
$ Spirit
$ TC Magazine
TeensForJC (R)
$ True Girl
$ Young Salvationist (R)

Women

$ Esprit
$ Horizons (R)
$ inSpirit (R)

SOCIOLOGY

Adult/General

$ Anglican Journal
$ Associated Content (R)
$ Catholic Peace Voice (R)
$ Christian Courier/Canada (R)
Christian Online
$ Churchmouse
   Publications (R)
$ Creative Nonfiction
$ Culture Wars (R)
Evangelical Advocate (R)
$ Faith Today
$ Gem (R)
Gospel Herald
Halo Magazine
$ In Touch
Island Catholic (R)
$ JC Town Reporter (R)
Jour. of Church & State

$ KD Gospel Media
$ Light & Life
More Excellent Way
$ Our Sunday Visitor (R)
Perspectives (R)
Perspectives/Science & Chr. Faith
Priscilla Papers
$ Salvo
$ Search
$ Social Justice (R)
$ St. Anthony Messenger
$ Testimony (R)
Trumpeter (R)
Urban Kingdom (R)
$ World & I (R)

Missions

East-West Church & Ministry
   Report

Pastors/Leaders

Jour./Amer. Soc./Chur. Growth
   (R)
$ Torch Legacy Leader
$ Word & World

Teen/Young Adult

$ Boundless Webzine (R)
$ InTeen (R)
TeensForJC (R)

Women

($) Beyond the Bend (R)
Women of the Cross

SPIRITUAL GIFTS

Adult/General

African Voices (R)
Bread of Life (R)
$ Brink Magazine (R)
CBN.com (R)
$ Christian Home & School
Christian Motorsports
Christian Online
Christian Quarterly (R)
Christian Ranchman
$ Christian Standard (R)
$ Christianity Today (R)
$ ChristianWeek (R)
$ Churchmouse
   Publications (R)
$ Columbia (R)

$ Covenant Companion (R)
E-Channels (R)
Evangelical Advocate (R)
$ Faith & Family
$ Faith & Friends (R)
$ Faith Today
Faithwebbin (R)
Gospel Herald
Halo Magazine
$ Home Times (R)
($) HopeKeepers (R)
$ In Touch
Island Catholic (R)
$ JC Town Reporter (R)
$ KD Gospel Media
$ Light & Life
$ Live (R)
$ Mature Years (R)
$ Men of Integrity (R)
$ Miracles, Healings
Mosaic (R)
($) Mutuality (R)
$ New Wineskins (R)
Penned from the Heart (R)
$ Positive Thinking (R)
PrayerWorks (R)
Priscilla Papers
Regent Global Bus. Rev. (R)
Reverent Submissions (R)
$ Seek (R)
Spirituality for Today
$ St. Anthony Messenger
$ Stewardship (R)
Sword and Trumpet
$ Testimony (R)
$ Together (R)
Trumpeter (R)
Urban Kingdom (R)
Victory Herald (R)
$ Vista (R)
$ Way of St. Francis (R)
Wisconsin Christian

Children

$ Bread for God's Children (R)
$ Our Little Friend (R)
$ Primary Treasure (R)
$ Sparkle (R)

Daily Devotionals

Penned from the Heart (R)

Missions
Lausanne World Pulse (R)

Pastors/Leaders
$ Interpreter
$ Ministry Today
$ RevWriter Resource
$ Worship Leader

Teen/Young Adult
$ Direction Student
$ Horizon Student
$ TC Magazine
TeensForJC (R)

Women
($) Beyond the Bend (R)
Christian Woman's Page (R)
Elegance (R)
Extreme Woman Magazine
For Every Woman (R)
Hope for Women
$ inSpirit (R)
Jewels of God (R)
$ Journey
Just Between Us (R)
P31 Woman (R)
Precious Times (R)
$ SpiritLed Woman
Unrecognized Woman (R)
Virtuous Woman (R)
Woman of Worth (R)
Women Today (R)

SPIRITUALITY
Adult/General
African Voices (R)
($) AGAIN Magazine (R)
$ Alive Now (R)
American Tract (R)
$ Angels on Earth
$ Annals of St. Anne
Anointed Pages
$ Arkansas Catholic (R)
$ Arlington Catholic
$ Associated Content (R)
$ Atlantic Catholic
$ Aujourd'hui Credo (R)
Bread of Life (R)
Breakthrough Intercessor (R)
$ Brink Magazine (R)
$ Catholic Digest (R)

$ Catholic Peace Voice (R)
CBN.com (R)
$ CGA World (R)
$ Christian Courier/Canada (R)
$ Christian Journal (R)
Christian Online
$ Christianity Today (R)
$ ChristianWeek (R)
$ Churchmouse Publications (R)
Church of England News
$ Common Ground (R)
$ Covenant Companion (R)
$ Culture Wars (R)
Desert Call (R)
Divine Ascent
E-Channels (R)
$ Episcopal Life (R)
$ Eureka Street
Evangelical Advocate (R)
$ Faith & Family
$ Faith & Friends (R)
$ Faith Today
Faithwebbin (R)
$ Family Digest (R)
$ Gem (R)
$ Good News (R)
$ Good News in Florida (R)
Gospel Herald
$ Guideposts (R)
Halo Magazine
HEARTLIGHT Internet (R)
$ Horizons (adult) (R)
$ In Touch
$ Indian Life (R)
Island Catholic (R)
$ JC Town Reporter (R)
$ KD Gospel Media
Koinonia
Leaves (R)
$ Lifeglow (R)
LifeTimes Catholic
$ Light & Life
$ Live (R)
$ Living Church
$ Lookout
Maine Family Policy (R)
$ Mature Years (R)
$ Men of Integrity (R)
$ Messenger/Sacred Heart
$ Messenger/St. Anthony

Messianic Perspectives (R)
New Heart (R)
$ New Wineskins (R)
$ Our Sunday Visitor (R)
Pegasus Review (R)
Penned from the Heart (R)
Penwood Review
$ Positive Thinking (R)
$ Prairie Messenger (R)
$ Presbyterian Outlook
$ Presbyterians Today (R)
Priscilla Papers
$ Pure Inspiration (R)
Quaker Life (R)
$ Seek (R)
Single Again Mag. Online (R)
$ Spiritual Life
Spirituality for Today
$ St. Anthony Messenger
$ Stewardship (R)
Sword and Trumpet
$ Testimony (R)
$ Together (R)
Trumpeter (R)
$ U.S. Catholic
Urban Kingdom (R)
Victory Herald (R)
$ Vista (R)
$ War Cry (R)
$ Way of St. Francis (R)
$ Weavings (R)
Wisconsin Christian
$ World & I (R)

Children
$ Bread for God's Children (R)
$ New Moon Girls (R)
Skipping Stones

Christian Education/ Library
Catholic Library
$ Children's Ministry
Jour./Ed. & Christian Belief (R)
Jour./Research on Christian Ed.
$ Momentum

Daily Devotionals
Penned from the Heart (R)

Missions
$ Evangelical Missions (R)

$ Glad Tidings (R)
Missiology

Pastors/Leaders
$ Christian Century (R)
$ Diocesan Dialogue (R)
$ Emmanuel
$ Interpreter
Jour./Pastoral Care
$ Leadership (R)
$ Lutheran Partners (R)
$ Ministry & Liturgy (R)
$ Ministry Today
$ Proclaim (R)
$ Review for Religious
$ RevWriter Resource
Rick Warren's Ministry
   Toolbox (R)
Sharing the Practice (R)
Theological Digest (R)
$ Today's Parish
$ Word & World
$ Worship Leader

Teen/Young Adult
$ Boundless Webzine (R)
$ Direction Student
$ Horizon Student
$ InTeen (R)
$ TC Magazine
TeensForJC (R)
$ True Girl
$ Young Adult Today

Women
($) Beyond the Bend (R)
$ Canticle
Christian Woman's Page (R)
Elegance (R)
Extreme Woman Magazine
Handmaiden (R)
$ Heart & Soul
Hope for Women
$ Horizons (R)
$ inSpirit (R)
$ Journey
Lutheran Woman's Quar.
$ Pauses . . .
Precious Times (R)
$ SpiritLed Woman
Unrecognized Woman (R)

Women of the Cross
Women Today (R)

Writers
Areopagus

SPIRITUAL LIFE
Adult/General
$ Arkansas Catholic (R)
$ Associated Content (R)
$ Atlantic Catholic
$ Aujourd'hui Credo (R)
$ Bible Advocate (R)
Bread of Life (R)
Breakthrough Intercessor (R)
$ Brink Magazine (R)
$ Cathedral Age
$ Catholic Digest (R)
$ Catholic Peace Voice (R)
$ Catholic Yearbook (R)
CBN.com (R)
$ Christian Examiner
$ Christian Home & School
$ Christian Journal (R)
Christian Online
Christian Quarterly (R)
Christian Ranchman
$ Christian Research
$ ChristianWeek (R)
$ Churchmouse
   Publications (R)
$ Columbia (R)
Connections Ldrship/MOPS
$ Covenant Companion (R)
Divine Ascent
E-Channels (R)
$ Enfoque a la Familia
Eternal Ink (R)
Evangelical Advocate (R)
$ Faith & Family
$ Faith & Friends (R)
$ Faith Today
Faithwebbin (R)
$ Family Digest (R)
$ Focus on the Family
$ Good News in Florida (R)
Gospel Herald
Halo Magazine
$ Home Times (R)
$ Homeschooling Today (R)

$ Horizons (adult) (R)
$ In His Presence (R)
In Part
$ In Touch
Island Catholic (R)
$ JC Town Reporter (R)
$ KD Gospel Media
Koinonia
$ Light & Life
$ Liguorian
$ Live (R)
$ Lookout
$ Lutheran Journal (R)
Lutheran Witness
$ Mature Living
$ Men of Integrity (R)
Messianic Perspectives (R)
Mosaic (R)
New Heart (R)
New Identity (R)
$ New Wineskins (R)
$ Our Sunday Visitor (R)
($) P.O.W.E.R. Magazine
$ ParentLife
Penned from the Heart (R)
Perspectives (R)
PrayerWorks (R)
$ Presbyterians Today (R)
Priscilla Papers
$ Pure Inspiration (R)
Regent Global Bus. Rev. (R)
Reverent Submissions (R)
Ruminate
$ Search
$ Seek (R)
$ Significant Living (R)
Single Again Mag. Online (R)
Spirituality for Today
$ Standard (R)
$ St. Anthony Messenger
$ Stewardship (R)
Sword and Trumpet
$ Testimony (R)
$ Together (R)
$ U.S. Catholic
Urban Kingdom (R)
Victory Herald (R)
$ Way of St. Francis (R)
$ Weavings (R)
$ Wildwood Reader (R)

Children
$ Bread for God's Children (R)
$ Sparkle (R)

Christian Education/Library
$ Momentum
$ Teachers of Vision (R)
$ Youth & CE Leadership

Daily Devotionals
Penned from the Heart (R)

Missions
$ Glad Tidings (R)
wec.go

Pastors/Leaders
$ African-American Pulpit
$ Barefoot (R)
Christian Education Jour. (R)
$ Interpreter
Jour./Pastoral Care
$ Leadership (R)
$ Ministry
$ Ministry & Liturgy (R)
Ministry in Motion (R)
$ Ministry Today
$ Review for Religious
$ RevWriter Resource
$ SmallGroups.com (R)

Teen/Young Adult
$ Boundless Webzine (R)
$ Direction Student
G4T Ink (R)
$ Horizon Student
$ TC Magazine
$ True Girl
$ Young Salvationist (R)

Women
$ Canticle
Christian Woman's Page (R)
Christian Work at Home
    Moms (R)
Elegance (R)
Extreme Woman Magazine
First Lady
$ FullFill
Hope for Women
$ Horizons (R)
$ inSpirit (R)

Jewels of God (R)
$ Journey
Just Between Us (R)
More to Life
P31 Woman (R)
$ Pauses . . .
Precious Times (R)
Right to the Heart (R)
Simply Blessed (R)
Unrecognized Woman (R)
Women Today (R)

SPIRITUAL RENEWAL
Adult/General
$ Arkansas Catholic (R)
$ Associated Content (R)
$ Bible Advocate (R)
Bread of Life (R)
Breakthrough Intercessor (R)
$ Brink Magazine (R)
CBN.com (R)
Christian Family Journal
$ Christian Home & School
Christian Online
Christian Quarterly (R)
Christian Ranchman
$ ChristianWeek (R)
$ Churchmouse Publications (R)
$ Columbia (R)
$ Converge Point (R)
Eternal Ink (R)
$ Evangel/IN (R)
Evangelical Advocate (R)
Faithwebbin (R)
$ Good News, Etc. (R)
Gospel Herald
Halo Magazine
$ Home Times (R)
$ In His Presence (R)
$ In Touch
Island Catholic (R)
$ JC Town Reporter (R)
$ KD Gospel Media
Koinonia
$ Light & Life
$ Liguorian
$ Live (R)
$ Lookout
$ Manna (R)
$ Men of Integrity (R)

Messianic Perspectives (R)
Mosaic (R)
New Identity (R)
$ New Wineskins (R)
$ ParentLife
PrayerWorks (R)
$ Pure Inspiration (R)
Reverent Submissions (R)
$ Seek (R)
Spirituality for Today
$ Standard (R)
Sword and Trumpet
$ Testimony (R)
$ Today's Pentecostal (R)
Urban Kingdom (R)
Victory Herald (R)
$ Way of St. Francis (R)
$ Wildwood Reader (R)
Wisconsin Christian

Children
$ Bread for God's Children (R)
$ Sparkle (R)

Pastors/Leaders
$ African-American Pulpit
$ Christian Century (R)
Christian Education Jour. (R)
$ Interpreter
$ Leadership (R)
$ Lutheran Partners (R)
$ Ministry & Liturgy (R)
Ministry in Motion (R)
$ Ministry Today
Theological Digest (R)

Teen/Young Adult
$ Boundless Webzine (R)
$ Direction Student
$ Horizon Student
$ TC Magazine
$ True Girl
$ Young Salvationist (R)

Women
$ Canticle
Christian Woman's Page (R)
$ Come to the Fire (R)
Extreme Woman Magazine
Hope for Women
$ Horizons (R)
$ inSpirit (R)

Jewels of God (R)
$ Journey
Just Between Us (R)
$ Pauses . . .
Precious Times (R)
Right to the Heart (R)
Unrecognized Woman (R)
Virtuous Woman (R)
Women Today (R)

SPIRITUAL WARFARE
Adult/General
 ($) AGAIN Magazine (R)
$ Angels on Earth
$ Associated Content (R)
Believer's Bay
$ Bible Advocate (R)
Bread of Life (R)
Breakthrough Intercessor (R)
$ Brink Magazine (R)
CBN.com (R)
$ Celebrate Life (R)
$ CGA World (R)
$ Christian Home & School
Christian Online
Christian Quarterly (R)
Christian Ranchman
$ Christian Research
$ Christianity Today (R)
$ ChristianWeek (R)
$ Churchmouse
   Publications (R)
$ Columbia (R)
E-Channels (R)
Evangelical Advocate (R)
$ Faith & Friends (R)
$ Faith Today
Faithwebbin (R)
$ Gem (R)
$ Good News (R)
$ Good News, Etc. (R)
Gospel Herald
Halo Magazine
HEARTLIGHT Internet (R)
$ In His Presence (R)
$ JC Town Reporter (R)
$ KD Gospel Media
Koinonia
Leaves (R)
$ Light & Life

$ Live (R)
$ Lookout
Maine Family Policy (R)
$ Manna (R)
$ Men of Integrity (R)
Messianic Perspectives (R)
Mosaic (R)
New Heart (R)
$ New Wineskins (R)
Penned from the Heart (R)
Prayer Closet
PrayerWorks (R)
Reverent Submissions (R)
$ Seek (R)
$ St. Anthony Messenger
Sword and Trumpet
Sword of the Lord (R)
$ Testimony (R)
Trumpeter (R)
Urban Kingdom (R)
Victory Herald (R)
Wisconsin Christian

Children
$ Bread for God's Children (R)

Daily Devotionals
Penned from the Heart (R)

Missions
Railroad Evangelist (R)

Music
($) TCP Magazine

Pastors/Leaders
$ Growth Points (R)
$ Let's Worship
$ Ministry Today
Rick Warren's Ministry
   Toolbox (R)
$ SmallGroups.com (R)

Teen/Young Adult
TeensForJC (R)
$ Young Salvationist (R)

Women
$ At the Center (R)
Elegance (R)
Extreme Woman Magazine
Handmaiden (R)
Hope for Women

$ inSpirit (R)
Jewels of God (R)
$ Journey
Just Between Us (R)
Precious Times (R)
Simply Blessed (R)
Unrecognized Woman (R)
Women Today (R)

SPORTS/RECREATION
Adult/General
$ Abilities
$ Angels on Earth
$ Arlington Catholic
$ Associated Content (R)
CBN.com (R)
Christian Courier/WI (R)
$ Christian Renewal (R)
$ Churchmouse Publications (R)
$ Citizen USA
$ City Light News (R)
Connecting Point (R)
Creation Care (R)
$ Eureka Street
$ Faith Today
$ Family Smart E-tips (R)
$ Gem (R)
$ Good News, Etc. (R)
Gospel Herald
$ Gospel Today (R)
$ Guideposts (R)
Heartbeat/CMA
Heartland Gatekeeper (R)
$ Home Times (R)
$ In His Presence (R)
$ In Touch
$ JC Town Reporter (R)
$ KD Gospel Media
$ Lifeglow (R)
$ Living Light (R)
$ Lookout
$ Miracles, Healings
$ Our Sunday Visitor (R)
$ Over the Back Fence (R)
Reverent Submissions (R)
$ Sports Spectrum
$ St. Anthony Messenger
$ Storyteller (R)
$ Testimony (R)
Urban Kingdom (R)

$ Vibrant Life (R)
Wisconsin Christian
$ World & I (R)

Children
$ American Girl (R)
$ Cadet Quest (R)
$ SHINE brightly (R)
$ Sparkle (R)

Christian Education/ Library
$ Teachers of Vision (R)

Missions
$ Glad Tidings (R)

Pastors/Leaders
$ Insight Youth (R)

Teen/Young Adult
$ Boundless Webzine (R)
$ Credo (R)
$ Direction Student
G4T Ink (R)
$ InTeen (R)
$ Listen (R)
$ Real Faith in Life (R)
$ Sharing the Victory (R)
$ TC Magazine
TeensForJC (R)
$ Young Salvationist (R)

Women
Hope for Women

STEWARDSHIP
Adult/General
$ Angels on Earth
$ Bible Advocate (R)
$ Catholic Yearbook (R)
CBN.com (R)
$ Celebrate Life (R)
$ Christian Courier/Canada (R)
Christian News NW (R)
Christian Online
Christian Ranchman
$ Christian Standard (R)
$ ChristianWeek (R)
$ Churchmouse Publications (R)
$ Columbia (R)
Creation Care (R)
E-Channels (R)

$ Evangel/IN (R)
Evangelical Advocate (R)
$ Faith Today
$ Family Digest (R)
$ Focus on the Family
$ Gem (R)
$ Good News in Florida (R)
Gospel Herald
Halo Magazine
Highway News (R)
$ Home Times (R)
$ In His Presence (R)
$ In Touch
$ JC Town Reporter (R)
$ KD Gospel Media
$ Lifeglow (R)
$ Light & Life
$ Liguorian
$ Live (R)
$ Living Church
$ Lookout
$ Lutheran Journal (R)
$ Manna (R)
New Identity (R)
($) NBR E-Magazine (R)
$ Our Sunday Visitor (R)
Penned from the Heart (R)
Perspectives (R)
$ Positive Thinking (R)
$ Power for Living (R)
$ Presbyterian Outlook
$ Prism
$ Purpose (R)
Quaker Life (R)
Regent Global Bus. Rev. (R)
$ Seek (R)
$ St. Anthony Messenger
$ Stewardship (R)
$ Testimony (R)
Trumpeter (R)
$ U.S. Catholic
$ United Church Observer (R)
Urban Kingdom (R)
$ Way of St. Francis (R)
$ Wesleyan Life (R)
Wisconsin Christian
$ Written

Children
$ Bread for God's Children (R)

$ Guide (R)
$ SHINE brightly (R)
$ Sparkle (R)

Christian Education/ Library
$ Momentum

Daily Devotionals
Penned from the Heart (R)

Missions
East-West Church & Ministry
    Report
$ Glad Tidings (R)

Pastors/Leaders
$ Clergy Journal (R)
$ InSite (R)
$ Interpreter
$ Let's Worship
Ministry in Motion (R)
$ Ministry Today
$ Net Results
$ Preaching Well (R)
$ RevWriter Resource
Sharing the Practice (R)
$ Your Church (R)

Teen/Young Adult
$ Boundless Webzine (R)
$ Direction Student
$ Horizon Student
$ TC Magazine
TeensForJC (R)
$ Young Salvationist (R)

Women
Crowned with Silver
$ Esprit
Hope for Women
$ Horizons (R)
$ Journey
P31 Woman (R)
Precious Times (R)
Woman of Worth (R)

TAKE-HOME PAPERS
Adult/General
$ Evangel/IN (R)
$ Gem (R)
$ Gems of Truth (R)
$ Horizons (adult) (R)

$ Live (R)
$ Power for Living (R)
$ Purpose (R)
$ Seek (R)
$ Standard (R)
$ Vision (R)
$ Vista (R)

Children
$ Adventures
$ Beginner's Friend (R)
$ Celebrate
$ Faith Detectives
$ God's Explorers
$ Good News (R)
$ Good News (child)
$ Guide (R)
$ Junior Companion (R)
$ JuniorWay
$ Kid Zone
$ Our Little Friend (R)
$ Partners (R)
$ Passport (R)
$ Preschool Playhouse (child)
$ Primary Pal (R)
$ Primary Street
$ Primary Treasure (R)
$ Promise
$ Seeds
$ Story Mates (R)
$ Venture

Teen/Young Adult
$ Insight (R)
$ Living My Faith
$ Spirit
$ Visions
$ Youth Compass (R)

TEACHER HELPS
Adult/General
$ Animal Trails (R)
$ Churchmouse Publications (R)
$ EFCA Today
$ Precepts for Living
$ Seek (R)

Christian Education/ Library
Christian Early Ed. (R)
Christian School Ed. (R)

Pastors/Leaders
Christian Education Jour. (R)
Ministry in Motion (R)
$ Ministry Today
Pulpit Helps (R)

Teen/Young Adult
$ Young Christian (R)

THEOLOGICAL
Adult/General
($) AGAIN Magazine (R)
$ Alive Now (R)
$ America
$ Anglican Journal
$ Annals of St. Anne
$ Arkansas Catholic (R)
$ Arlington Catholic
$ Atlantic Catholic
$ Aujourd'hui Credo (R)
$ B.C. Catholic (R)
$ Bible Advocate (R)
Bread of Life (R)
Breakthrough Intercessor (R)
$ Brink Magazine (R)
byFaith
$ Cathedral Age
$ Catholic Peace Voice (R)
$ Catholic Yearbook (R)
CBN.com (R)
$ Christian Courier/Canada (R)
Christian Online
Christian Ranchman
$ Christian Renewal (R)
$ Christian Research
$ Christian Standard (R)
$ Christianity Today (R)
$ Churchmouse Publications (R)
Church of England News
Creation Care (R)
$ Cresset
$ Culture Wars (R)
Divine Ascent
E-Channels (R)
$ Episcopal Life (R)
$ Eureka Street
Evangelical Advocate (R)
Evangelical Times
$ Faith Today
Founders Journal

$ Good News (R)
Gospel Herald
Halo Magazine
$ Horizons (adult) (R)
$ In His Presence (R)
$ In Touch
Koinonia
$ Light & Life
$ Living Church
$ Lookout
$ Lutheran Journal (R)
$ Messenger/Sacred Heart
Messianic Perspectives (R)
MovieGuide
$ New Wineskins (R)
$ Our Sunday Visitor (R)
Perspectives (R)
Perspectives/Science & Chr. Faith
$ Prairie Messenger (R)
PrayerWorks (R)
$ Presbyterian Outlook
Priscilla Papers
Purpose Magazine (R)
Quaker Life (R)
$ Search
$ Social Justice (R)
$ Spiritual Life
$ St. Anthony Messenger
$ Testimony (R)
Trumpeter (R)
$ U.S. Catholic
$ United Church Observer (R)
Urban Kingdom (R)
$ Way of St. Francis (R)

Christian Education/ Library
Jour. of Christianity (R)

Daily Devotionals
Penned from the Heart (R)

Missions
East-West Church & Ministry
   Report
$ Glad Tidings (R)
Lausanne World Pulse (R)
Missiology

Pastors/Leaders
$ African-American Pulpit
$ Catechumenate

$ Christian Century (R)
$ Clergy Journal (R)
CrossCurrents
$ Diocesan Dialogue (R)
$ Growth Points (R)
Jour./Amer. Soc./Chur.
   Growth (R)
Jour./Pastoral Care
Lutheran Forum
$ Lutheran Partners (R)
$ Ministry & Liturgy (R)
$ Preaching Well (R)
$ Proclaim (R)
$ Reformed Worship (R)
$ RevWriter Resource
Rick Warren's Ministry
   Toolbox (R)
Sewanee Theo. Review
Sharing the Practice (R)
$ SmallGroups.com (R)
$ Today's Parish
$ Word & World
$ Worship Leader

Teen/Young Adult
$ Boundless Webzine (R)
$ InTeen (R)
TeensForJC (R)
$ Young Salvationist (R)

Women
$ Canticle
$ Esprit
$ Horizons (R)

THINK PIECES
Adult/General
$ Alive Now (R)
$ Annals of St. Anne
$ Associated Content (R)
Baptist Standard
$ Bible Advocate (R)
$ Brink Magazine (R)
$ Catholic Forester (R)
$ Catholic Peace Voice (R)
$ CGA World (R)
$ Christian Courier/
   Canada (R)
$ Christianity Today (R)
Christian Online
$ ChristianWeek (R)

$ Churchmouse
   Publications (R)
$ City Light News (R)
Desert Call (R)
$ Episcopal Life (R)
$ Eureka Street
Evangelical Advocate (R)
$ Faith Today
$ Gem (R)
Good News Journal (R)
Gospel Herald
Halo Magazine
$ Haruah (R)
HEARTLIGHT Internet (R)
$ In Touch
Island Catholic (R)
$ JC Town Reporter (R)
$ KD Gospel Media
$ Lifeglow (R)
$ Light & Life
$ Lookout
$ Manna (R)
Men of the Cross
$ MindFlights (R)
New Identity (R)
$ New Wineskins (R)
$ Our Sunday Visitor (R)
Pegasus Review (R)
Penned from the Heart (R)
Penwood Review
$ Positive Thinking (R)
PrayerWorks (R)
$ Presbyterian Outlook
Purpose Magazine (R)
Reverent Submissions (R)
$ Search
$ Seek (R)
$ St. Anthony Messenger
$ Stewardship (R)
$ Testimony (R)
Trumpeter (R)
$ U.S. Catholic
Urban Kingdom (R)
$ World & I (R)

Children
Skipping Stones

Christian Education/ Library
$ Children's Ministry

Missions
$ Glad Tidings (R)
Lausanne World Pulse (R)

Pastors/Leaders
$ Catholic Servant
$ Enrichment Journal (R)
$ Ministry Today
Rick Warren's Ministry
   Toolbox (R)
$ Word & World

Teen/Young Adult
$ Boundless Webzine (R)
$ Real Faith in Life (R)
$ TC Magazine
TeensForJC (R)
$ Young Salvationist (R)

Women
Crowned with Silver
Elegance (R)
Jewels of God (R)
$ MomSense (R)
Unrecognized Woman (R)
Women of the Cross

Writers
Areopagus

TIME MANAGEMENT
Adult/General
$ Associated Content (R)
$ Bridal Guides (R)
$ Brink Magazine (R)
$ Catholic Forester (R)
$ CBA Retailers
CBN.com (R)
Christian Business
Christian Online
$ ChristianWeek (R)
$ Churchmouse
   Publications (R)
Disciple's Journal (R)
Evangelical Advocate (R)
Faithwebbin (R)
$ Focus on the Family
$ Gem (R)
Good News Journal (R)
Gospel Herald
Halo Magazine
$ Home Times (R)

$ Homeschooling Today (R)
($) HopeKeepers (R)
$ In Touch
$ JC Town Reporter (R)
$ KD Gospel Media
$ Lifeglow (R)
$ Light & Life
$ Live (R)
$ Living Light (R)
$ Lookout
Men of the Cross
MissionWares
($) NBR E-Magazine (R)
$ ParentLife
Penned from the Heart (R)
$ Positive Thinking (R)
Regent Global Bus. Rev. (R)
$ St. Anthony Messenger
$ Stewardship (R)
$ Testimony (R)
$ Together (R)
Trumpeter (R)
Urban Kingdom (R)
$ Victory in Grace (R)
$ World & I (R)

Christian Education/ Library
Catholic Library
Christian Librarian (R)
Christian School Ed. (R)
$ Youth & CE Leadership

Daily Devotionals
Penned from the Heart (R)

Pastors/Leaders
$ Enrichment Journal (R)
$ Interpreter
Ministry in Motion (R)
Rick Warren's Ministry
   Toolbox (R)
$ Your Church (R)

Teen/Young Adult
$ Boundless Webzine (R)
$ Direction Student
$ Horizon Student
TeensForJC (R)
$ True Girl

Women
Christian Woman's Page (R)

Christian Work at Home
   Moms (R)
Elegance (R)
$ Girlfriend 2 Girlfriend
Hope for Women
$ InspiredMoms (R)
$ inSpirit (R)
$ Journey
Just Between Us (R)
Life Tools for Women
P31 Woman (R)
Precious Times (R)
Unrecognized Woman (R)
Virtuous Woman (R)
Woman of Worth (R)
Women Today (R)

Writers
$ Advanced Christian Writer (R)
$ Christian Communicator (R)
$ Fellowscript (R)
Write Connection
$ Writer
$ Writers' Journal

TRAVEL
Adult/General
$ Abilities
$ Angels on Earth
$ Arlington Catholic
$ Associated Content (R)
$ Bridal Guides (R)
$ Brink Magazine (R)
$ Capper's
CBN.com (R)
Christian Family Journal
$ Churchmouse
   Publications (R)
$ City Light News (R)
$ Common Ground (R)
Creation Care (R)
$ Creative Nonfiction
Desert Voice (R)
$ DisciplesWorld
Evangelical Advocate (R)
$ Family Digest (R)
$ Gem (R)
Gospel Herald
Halo Magazine
($) HopeKeepers (R)

$ In His Presence (R)
$ In Touch
Island Catholic (R)
$ JC Town Reporter (R)
$ KD Gospel Media
$ Lifeglow (R)
$ Mature Living
$ Mature Years (R)
MovieGuide
New Identity (R)
$ Over the Back Fence (R)
$ Ozarks Senior Living (R)
$ ParentLife
$ Seek (R)
Single Again Mag. Online (R)
$ Special Living (R)
$ Testimony (R)
$ Upscale
Urban Kingdom (R)
$ Way of St. Francis (R)
Wisconsin Christian
$ World & I (R)

Children
$ Archaeology
$ Faces
$ SHINE brightly (R)
Skipping Stones
$ Sparkle (R)

Missions
$ Glad Tidings (R)
$ PIME World (R)

Teen/Young Adult
$ Boundless Webzine (R)
TeensForJC (R)

Women
Hope for Women
$ InspiredMoms (R)
Live Magazine
Precious Times (R)
Unrecognized Woman (R)

TRUE STORIES
Adult/General
African Voices (R)
$ Angels on Earth
Baptist Standard
Behind the Hammer
Biblical Recorder

Breakthrough Intercessor (R)
$ Bridal Guides (R)
$ Brink Magazine (R)
byFaith
$ Catholic Digest (R)
CBN.com (R)
$ Celebrate Life (R)
Challenge Weekly
Charlotte World
Christian Observer
Christian Online
Christian Quarterly (R)
Christian Ranchman
$ Churchmouse Publications (R)
$ City Light News (R)
$ Columbia (R)
$ Creative Nonfiction
$ Culture Wars (R)
$ Disaster News
E-Channels (R)
$ Enfoque a la Familia
Eternal Ink (R)
Evangelical Advocate (R)
Evangelical Times
$ Faith & Family
$ Family Digest (R)
$ Focus on the Family
$ Foursquare Leader
$ Gem (R)
$ Gems of Truth (R)
$ Good News in Florida (R)
Good News Today
$ Good News, Etc. (R)
Gospel Herald
$ Guideposts (R)
Halo Magazine
$ Haruah (R)
Heartland Gatekeeper (R)
HEARTLIGHT Internet (R)
Highway News (R)
$ Home Times (R)
($) HopeKeepers (R)
$ Horizons (adult) (R)
$ In His Presence (R)
$ In Touch
$ Indian Life (R)
$ JC Town Reporter (R)
$ KD Gospel Media
$ Lifeglow (R)
$ Light & Life

$ Live (R)
$ Lutheran Digest (R)
$ Mature Living
Men of the Cross
Message of the Open Bible (R)
Messianic Perspectives (R)
MissionWares
New Heart (R)
New Identity (R)
$ New Wineskins (R)
Nostalgia (R)
$ Now What? (R)
$ On Mission
$ ParentLife
Penned from the Heart (R)
$ Power for Living (R)
PrayerWorks (R)
$ Priority! (R)
$ Pure Inspiration (R)
Reverent Submissions (R)
$ Search
$ Seek (R)
$ St. Anthony Messenger
$ Storyteller (R)
$ Testimony (R)
$ Today's Pentecostal (R)
Tri-State Voice
Trumpeter (R)
Urban Kingdom (R)
Victory Herald (R)
$ Victory in Grace (R)
$ Vision (R)
$ Vista (R)
$ War Cry (R)
$ Way of St. Francis (R)
$ Written

Children
$ Bread for God's Children (R)
$ Cadet Quest (R)
$ Focus/Clubhouse Jr.
$ Guide (R)
$ Nature Friend (R)
$ New Moon Girls (R)
$ Our Little Friend (R)
$ Partners (R)
$ Pockets (R)
$ Primary Treasure (R)
$ SHINE brightly (R)
Skipping Stones

$ Sparkle (R)
$ Story Mates (R)

Christian Education/ Library
$ Children's Ministry
Christian Early Ed. (R)

Missions
$ Glad Tidings (R)
$ Leaders for Today

Pastors/Leaders
$ Leadership (R)
$ Preaching Well (R)
Sharing the Practice (R)

Teen/Young Adult
$ Boundless Webzine (R)
$ Credo (R)
$ Direction Student
$ Essential Connection (ec)
$ Horizon Student
$ Insight (R)
$ Listen (R)
$ Real Faith in Life (R)
$ Sharing the Victory (R)
$ Spirit
$ TC Magazine
TeensForJC (R)
$ True Girl
$ Young Christian (R)
$ Young Christian Writers
$ Young Salvationist (R)
$ YouthWalk

Women
$ Canticle
Elegance (R)
Empowering Everyday Women
Extreme Woman Magazine
For Every Woman (R)
($) History's Women (R)
Hope for Women
$ Journey
$ MomSense (R)
$ Pauses . . .
Precious Times (R)
Simply Blessed (R)
Unrecognized Woman (R)
Women Today (R)

Writers
Areopagus

VIDEO REVIEWS
Adult/General
$ Arlington Catholic
$ Atlantic Catholic
$ Canadian Mennonite (R)
$ Catholic Peace Voice (R)
CBN.com (R)
Charlotte World
Christian Family Journal
$ Christianity Today
    Movies (R)
$ Christian Renewal (R)
$ Churchmouse
    Publications (R)
$ Citizen USA
Creation Care (R)
Desert Call (R)
Desert Voice (R)
E-Channels (R)
Eternal Ink (R)
$ Eureka Street
$ Faith & Family
$ Foursquare Leader
Gospel Herald
Halo Magazine
Heartland Gatekeeper (R)
$ Home Times (R)
$ Imagine
$ Interim (R)
$ JC Town Reporter (R)
$ KD Gospel Media
MovieGuide
New Christian Voices
$ Our Sunday Visitor (R)
$ Presbyterians Today (R)
$ Pure Inspiration (R)
Quaker Life (R)
$ Rose & Thorn
Single Again Mag. Online (R)
$ Testimony (R)
Trumpeter (R)
Urban Kingdom (R)

Children
$ Sparkle (R)

Christian Education/ Library
$ Church Libraries (R)
Congregational Libraries Today
Jour. of Christianity (R)

Missions
East-West Church & Ministry
    Report
$ Glad Tidings (R)

Music
$ Christian Music Today (R)

Pastors/Leaders
$ Christian Century (R)
$ Interpreter
$ Ministry Today
Technologies for Worship (R)
$ Worship Leader

Teen/Young Adult
$ Credo (R)
$ Devo'zine (R)
Exodus Magazine
TeensForJC (R)
$ True Girl

Women
Christian Woman's Page (R)
$ Dabbling Mum (R)
Empowering Everyday Women
Extreme Woman Magazine
Hope for Women
Jewels of God (R)
Precious Times (R)
Virtuous Woman (R)
Woman of Worth (R)

WEBSITE REVIEWS
Adult/General
$ Atlantic Catholic
Brink Online
$ Catholic Peace Voice (R)
CBN.com (R)
Charlotte World
$ Christianity Today (R)
$ Churchmouse
    Publications (R)
$ Citizen USA
Eternal Ink (R)
Gospel Herald
Heartland Gatekeeper (R)
($) HopeKeepers (R)
$ JC Town Reporter (R)
$ MindFlights (R)
New Christian Voices
New Identity (R)

$ New Wineskins (R)
($) NBR E-Magazine (R)
$ On Mission
$ Our Sunday Visitor (R)
Single Again Mag. Online (R)
$ Upscale
Urban Kingdom (R)
$ World & I (R)

Missions
East-West Church & Ministry
    Report
Op. Reveille Interactive
    Jour. (R)

Pastors/Leaders
$ Interpreter
Ministry in Motion (R)

Teen/Young Adult
TeensForJC (R)
$ True Girl

Women
Empowering Everyday Women
Hope for Women

Writers
NW Christian Author (R)
$ Writers' Journal

WOMEN'S ISSUES
Adult/General
$ Abilities
$ Alive Now (R)
$ Anglican Journal
$ Annals of St. Anne
$ Arlington Catholic
$ Associated Content (R)
$ Brink Magazine (R)
$ Catholic Forester (R)
$ Catholic Peace Voice (R)
$ CBA Retailers
CBN.com (R)
$ Celebrate Life (R)
$ CGA World (R)
$ Chicken Soup Books (R)
$ Christian Courier/Canada (R)
$ Christian Examiner
Christian Family Journal
$ Christian Journal (R)
Christian News NW (R)

Christian Online
Christian Quarterly (R)
Christian Ranchman
$ ChristianWeek (R)
$ Churchmouse Publications (R)
Church of England News
$ Citizen USA
$ Columbia (R)
$ Converge Point (R)
$ Creative Nonfiction
Desert Voice (R)
Disciple's Journal (R)
$ EFCA Today
$ Episcopal Life (R)
$ Evangel/IN (R)
Evangelical Advocate (R)
$ Faith & Family
$ Faith Today
$ Family Smart E-tips (R)
$ Foursquare Leader
$ Gem (R)
$ Good News in Florida (R)
Good News Journal (R)
Gospel Herald
$ Gospel Today (R)
Halo Magazine
HEARTLIGHT Internet (R)
Holy House Ministries (R)
$ Homeschooling Today (R)
($) HopeKeepers (R)
$ In His Presence (R)
$ In Touch
$ Indian Life (R)
Island Catholic (R)
$ JC Town Reporter (R)
$ KD Gospel Media
$ Light & Life
$ Liguorian
$ Live (R)
$ Lookout
$ Manna (R)
$ Montgomery's Journey
More Excellent Way
Mosaic (R)
($) Mutuality (R)
New Identity (R)
$ New Wineskins (R)
$ Our Sunday Visitor (R)
$ ParentLife
Penned from the Heart (R)

Perspectives (R)
$ Prairie Messenger (R)
PrayerWorks (R)
$ Presbyterian Outlook
Priscilla Papers
$ Psychology for Living (R)
$ Purpose (R)
Purpose Magazine (R)
Reverent Submissions (R)
$ Seek (R)
$ St. Anthony Messenger
$ Storyteller (R)
$ Testimony (R)
$ Together (R)
Trumpeter (R)
$ U.S. Catholic
$ United Church Observer (R)
Urban Kingdom (R)
$ Vibrant Life (R)
$ War Cry (R)
$ Wesleyan Life (R)
West Wind Review
$ World & I (R)
$ Written

Children
$ New Moon Girls (R)
Skipping Stones

Christian Education/Library
$ Teachers of Vision (R)

Daily Devotionals
Penned from the Heart (R)

Missions
$ Glad Tidings (R)
Women of the Harvest

Pastors/Leaders
$ African-American Pulpit
$ Interpreter
$ SmallGroups.com (R)
$ Word & World

Teen/Young Adult
$ Boundless Webzine (R)
TeensForJC (R)
$ True Girl

Women
$ At the Center (R)

($) Beyond the Bend (R)
Breathe Again
$ Canticle
Christian Ladies Connect
Christian Woman's Page (R)
Christian Women Today (R)
Christian Work at Home
   Moms (R)
$ Come to the Fire (R)
Crowned with Silver
$ Dabbling Mum (R)
Elegance (R)
Empowering Everyday
   Women
$ Esprit
Extreme Woman Magazine
First Lady
For Every Woman (R)
$ FullFill
$ Girlfriend 2 Girlfriend
Handmaiden (R)
Handmaidens
$ Heart & Soul
Hope for Women
$ Horizons (R)
Inspired Women
$ inSpirit (R)
Jewels of God (R)
$ Journey
Just Between Us (R)
Life Tools for Women
$ Link & Visitor (R)
Lutheran Woman's Quar.
$ Melody of the Heart
$ MomSense (R)
More to Life
P31 Woman (R)
$ Pauses . . .
Precious Times (R)
Right to the Heart (R)
Share
Simply Blessed (R)
$ SpiritLed Woman
Together with God (R)
Unrecognized Woman (R)
Virtuous Woman (R)
Woman of Worth (R)
Women of the Cross
Women Today (R)
Women's Ministry

WORKPLACE ISSUES
Adult/General
$ Associated Content (R)
$ Bible Advocate (R)
byFaith
CBN.com (R)
Christian Business
$ Christian Examiner
Christian Online
Christian Ranchman
$ Christian Retailing
$ ChristianWeek (R)
$ Churchmouse
    Publications (R)
$ Converge Point (R)
Desert Voice (R)
E-Channels (R)
$ Eureka Street
$ Evangel/IN (R)
Evangelical Advocate (R)
$ Faith & Friends (R)
$ Faith Today
$ Good News in Florida (R)
Good News Journal (R)
Good News Today
$ Good News, Etc. (R)
Gospel Herald
$ Gospel Today (R)
Halo Magazine
Highway News (R)
($) HopeKeepers (R)
$ In His Presence (R)
$ In Touch
Island Catholic (R)
$ JC Town Reporter (R)
$ KD Gospel Media
$ Light & Life
$ Live (R)
$ Lookout
$ Manna (R)
$ Men of Integrity (R)
$ Montana Catholic
$ Montgomery's Journey
More Excellent Way
New Christian Voices
New Heart (R)
$ Now What? (R)
$ Our Sunday Visitor (R)
$ ParentLife
Penned from the Heart (R)

Perspectives (R)
$ Positive Thinking (R)
$ Purpose (R)
Purpose Magazine (R)
Regent Global Bus. Rev. (R)
Reverent Submissions (R)
$ Seek (R)
$ Testimony (R)
$ Together (R)
$ U.S. Catholic
Urban Kingdom (R)
$ World & I (R)

Christian Education/ Library
Catholic Library
Christian Librarian (R)
$ Group Magazine
$ Teachers of Vision (R)
$ Today's Catholic Teacher (R)

Missions
$ Glad Tidings (R)

Pastors/Leaders
Church Executive
$ Interpreter
$ Your Church (R)

Teen/Young Adult
$ Boundless Webzine (R)

Women
Elegance (R)
Empowering Everyday Women
$ FullFill
Hope for Women
Inspired Women
$ InspiredMoms (R)
$ Journey
Life Tools for Women
Live Magazine
More to Life
Unrecognized Woman (R)
Women Today (R)

Writers
$ Advanced Christian Writer (R)

WORLD ISSUES
Adult/General
 ($) AGAIN Magazine (R)
American Tract (R)

$ Annals of St. Anne
$ Arlington Catholic
$ Associated Content (R)
$ Aujourd'hui Credo (R)
Baptist Standard
$ Bible Advocate (R)
Biblical Recorder
Breakthrough Intercessor (R)
$ Brink Magazine (R)
CanadianChristianity.com
$ Catholic Peace Voice (R)
Catholic Register
CBN.com (R)
$ CGA World (R)
Challenge Weekly
Charlotte World
Christian Chronicle
$ Christian Examiner
Christian Observer
Christian Online
$ Christian Renewal (R)
$ ChristianWeek (R)
$ Churchmouse
    Publications (R)
$ Columbia (R)
$ Compass Direct
$ Creative Nonfiction
$ Culture Wars (R)
Desert Christian
Desert Voice (R)
$ Eureka Street
$ Evangel/IN (R)
Evangelical Advocate (R)
Evangelical Times
$ Faith Today
Friends Journal (R)
$ Gem (R)
Good News Connection
Good News Today
$ Good News, Etc. (R)
Gospel Herald
Halo Magazine
Heartland Gatekeeper (R)
HEARTLIGHT Internet (R)
$ Home Times (R)
$ In Touch
$ Indian Life (R)
$ JC Town Reporter (R)
Jerusalem Connection
$ Liberty

LifeSiteNews
$ Light & Life
$ Living Church
$ Lookout
Maine Family Policy (R)
Messianic Perspectives (R)
MovieGuide
($) Mutuality (R)
New Identity (R)
$ New Wineskins (R)
$ Our Sunday Visitor (R)
Penned from the Heart (R)
Perspectives (R)
$ Presbyterian Outlook
$ Prism
$ Purpose (R)
Purpose Magazine (R)
$ Salvo
$ Seek (R)
$ Social Justice (R)
$ St. Anthony Messenger
$ Testimony (R)
Tri-State Voice
Trumpeter (R)
$ United Church Observer (R)
Urban Kingdom (R)
$ War Cry (R)
$ Way of St. Francis (R)
West Wind Review
$ World & I (R)

Children
$ New Moon Girls (R)
Skipping Stones

Christian Education/ Library
Catholic Library

Missions
East-West Church & Ministry
    Report
$ Glad Tidings (R)
Intl. Jour./Frontier Missions (R)
Lausanne World Pulse (R)
$ Leaders for Today
Missiology
Mission Frontiers
$ New World Outlook
$ One
Op. Reveille Interactive Jour. (R)

$ PFI Global Link Journal (R)
$ PIME World (R)

Pastors/Leaders
$ Christian Century (R)
$ Ministry Today
$ Word & World

Teen/Young Adult
$ Boundless Webzine (R)
$ TC Magazine
TeensForJC (R)
$ True Girl

Women
$ Canticle
$ Esprit
Hope for Women
$ Horizons (R)
$ SpiritLed Woman

Writers
Areopagus

WORSHIP
Adult/General
($) AGAIN Magazine (R)
$ Angels on Earth
$ Annals of St. Anne
$ Arlington Catholic
$ Aujourd'hui Credo (R)
Bread of Life (R)
Breakthrough Intercessor (R)
$ Brink Magazine (R)
$ Catholic Yearbook (R)
CBN.com (R)
$ CGA World (R)
$ Christian Examiner
$ Christianity Today (R)
Christian Online
Christian Ranchman
$ Christian Standard (R)
$ ChristianWeek (R)
$ Churchmouse
    Publications (R)
$ Columbia (R)
$ Converge Point (R)
Creation Care (R)
$ Culture Wars (R)
E-Channels (R)
Eternal Ink (R)
$ Evangel/IN (R)

Evangelical Advocate (R)
$ Faith Today
$ Foursquare Leader
Gospel Herald
Halo Magazine
($) HopeKeepers (R)
$ Imagine
$ In His Presence (R)
$ In Touch
$ Lifeglow (R)
$ Light & Life
$ Liguorian
$ Live (R)
$ Living Church
$ Lookout
$ Lutheran Journal (R)
$ Manna (R)
Mosaic (R)
New Identity (R)
$ New Wineskins (R)
Penned from the Heart (R)
Perspectives (R)
$ Power for Living (R)
PrayerWorks (R)
$ Presbyterian Outlook
$ Presbyterians Today (R)
Priscilla Papers
Purpose Magazine (R)
Quaker Life (R)
Reverent Submissions (R)
$ Seek (R)
$ Spiritual Life
$ St. Anthony Messenger
$ Stewardship (R)
Sword and Trumpet
Sword of the Lord (R)
$ Testimony (R)
Time of Singing (R)
Trumpeter (R)
$ United Church Observer (R)
Urban Kingdom (R)
$ Vista (R)
$ War Cry (R)
$ Way of St. Francis (R)
$ Wesleyan Life (R)
$ World & I (R)

Children
$ Bread for God's
    Children (R)

$ Keys for Kids (R)
$ Promise
$ Sparkle (R)

Christian Education/ Library
$ Group Magazine
$ Youth & CEs Leadership

Daily Devotionals
Penned from the Heart (R)

Missions
$ Glad Tidings (R)
Lausanne World Pulse (R)

Music
Church Music
$ Creator (R)

Pastors/Leaders
$ African-American Pulpit
$ Barefoot (R)
$ Clergy Journal (R)
$ Enrichment Journal (R)
$ Growth Points (R)
$ Interpreter
Jour./Amer. Soc./Chur.
   Growth (R)
$ Leadership (R)
$ Let's Worship
$ Lutheran Partners (R)
$ Ministry & Liturgy (R)
$ Ministry Today
$ Parish Liturgy (R)
Preaching
Pulpit Helps (R)
$ Reformed Worship (R)
$ RevWriter Resource
Rick Warren's Ministry
   Toolbox (R)
Sharing the Practice (R)
Theological Digest (R)
$ Today's Parish
$ Word & World
$ Worship Leader
$ Your Church (R)

Teen/Young Adult
$ Boundless Webzine (R)
$ Direction Student
$ Horizon Student

$ Insight (R)
$ TC Magazine
TeensForJC (R)
$ True Girl

Women
Christian Woman's Page (R)
Elegance (R)
Extreme Woman Magazine
For Every Woman (R)
Hope for Women
$ Horizons (R)
Jewels of God (R)
$ Journey
Virtuous Woman (R)
Women Today (R)

WRITING HOW-TO
Adult/General
$ Associated Content (R)
$ CBA Retailers
CBN.com (R)
Christian Observer
Christian Online
$ Churchmouse
   Publications (R)
Good News Journal (R)
$ Haruah (R)
$ Home Times (R)
($) HopeKeepers (R)
Pegasus Review (R)
Penwood Review
Reverent Submissions (R)
Single Again Mag. Online (R)
$ St. Anthony Messenger
Urban Kingdom (R)
$ World & I (R)

Children
Skipping Stones

Christian Education/ Library
$ Group Magazine
$ Teachers of Vision (R)

Pastors/Leaders
$ Newsletter Newsletter

Teen/Young Adult
$ Boundless Webzine (R)
TeensForJC (R)

Women
$ Dabbling Mum (R)
Elegance (R)
Extreme Woman Magazine
Hope for Women
Precious Times (R)
Right to the Heart (R)

Writers
$ Advanced Christian Writer (R)
Areopagus
Author-Me
$ Best New Writing
$ Canadian Writers Journal
$ Christian Communicator (R)
$ Cross & Quill (R)
$ Fellowscript (R)
$ Freelance Writer's Report (R)
$ New Writer's Mag.
NW Christian Author (R)
$ Poets & Writers
$ Shades of Romance (R)
$ Spirit-Led Writer (R)
$ Tickled by Thunder
Write Connection
$ Writer
$ Writer's Digest
Writers Manual
$ Writers' Journal
WriteToInspire.com
Writing Corner (R)

YOUNG-WRITER MARKETS
Note: These publications have indicated they will accept submissions from children or teens (C or T).

Adult/General
African Voices
$ Ancient Paths (T)
$ Animal Trails
Anointed Pages
$ Aujourd'hui Credo (C or T)
Breakthrough Intercessor
   (C or T)
$ Bridal Guides (C or T)
$ Catholic Peace Voice (T)
$ Catholic Yearbook (C or T)
CBN.com (T)

$ Celebrate Life (C or T)
$ Christian Herald (T)
$ Christian Home & School
    (C or T)
$ Christian Journal (C or T)
Christian Online (C or T)
$ ChristianWeek (T)
Church Herald & Holiness
    (C or T)
$ Citizen USA (T)
$ City Light News (T)
$ Creative Nonfiction (T)
Desert Voice (T)
$ Drama Ministry (T)
$ DreamSeeker (C or T)
E-Channels (T)
Eternal Ink (C or T)
Gospel Herald (C or T)
$ Gospel Today
Haiku Hippodrome (C or T)
Halo Magazine
$ Haruah (T)
Holy House Ministries (C or T)
$ Home Times (T)
($) HopeKeepers (T)
$ In His Presence (C or T)
$ Indian Life (C or T)
$ Interchange (C or T)
Island Catholic (C or T)
$ KD Gospel Media (T)
$ Leben (T)
LifeTimes Catholic (T)
$ Light & Life (C or T)
$ Lutheran Journal (C or T)
$ Manna (C or T)
Men of the Cross (T)
$ MindFlights (T)
$ Miracles, Healings (C or T)
MissionWares (T)
$ Montgomery's Journey (T)
Mosaic
$ New Wineskins (C or T)
Pegasus Review (T)
Penned from the Heart (C or T)
$ Priority! (C or T)
$ Pure Inspiration (C or T)
Purpose Magazine (C or T)
Quaker Life (C or T)
Reverent Submissions (C or T)
Silver Wings (C or T)

$ Storyteller (C or T)
Urban Kingdom (T)
Victory Herald (C or T)
$ Vista (C or T)
$ Way of St. Francis (C or T)
Wisconsin Christian (C or T)

Children
$ American Girl
$ Archaeology (C or T)
$ Focus/Clubhouse (C)
$ Kids' Ark (C or T)
$ New Moon Girls (C or T)
$ Pockets (C)

Christian Education/ Library
Catholic Library
$ Children's Ministry (C or T)

Daily Devotionals
Penned from the Heart
    (C or T)

Missions
$ Glad Tidings (T)
Koinonia
$ PIME World (T)

Pastors/Leaders
$ Insight Youth (T)
$ Let's Worship
$ Reformed Worship (C or T)

Teen/Young Adult
$ Boundless Webzine (T)
$ Credo (T)
$ Direction Student (T)
$ Essential Connection (ec) (T)
G4T Ink (T)
$ Horizon Student (T)
$ Insight (T)
$ Listen (T)
$ Take Five Plus (T)
$ TC Magazine (T)
TeensForJC (T)
$ True Girl (T)
$ Young Christian (T)
$ Young Christian Writers (T)

Women
$ Dabbling Mum (T)
Elegance (T)

Extreme Woman
    Magazine (T)
($) History's Women (T)
Jewels of God (T)
Precious Times (T)
Together with God (T)
Unrecognized Woman (T)
Women of the Cross (T)
Women Today (T)

Writers
$ Canadian Writer's Jour. (T)
Esdras' Scroll (C or T)
$ Fellowscript (T)
NW Christian Author (T)
$ Spirit-Led Writer (T)
$ Tickled by Thunder (C or T)
Write Connection (T)
$ Writers' Journal (T)

YOUTH ISSUES
Adult/General
American Tract (R)
$ Annals of St. Anne
Anointed Pages
$ Arlington Catholic
$ Associated Content (R)
$ Atlantic Catholic
$ Aujourd'hui Credo (R)
$ Catholic Forester (R)
$ Catholic Peace Voice (R)
CBN.com (R)
$ Chicken Soup Books (R)
$ Christian Examiner
Christian Family Journal
$ Christian Home & School
Christian Motorsports
Christian News NW (R)
Christian Online
Christian Ranchman
$ Christian Renewal (R)
$ ChristianWeek (R)
$ Churchmouse Publications (R)
$ Citizen USA
$ Columbia (R)
$ Converge Point (R)
$ Culture Wars (R)
Desert Voice (R)
E-Channels (R)
$ EFCA Today

$ Eureka Street
Evangelical Advocate (R)
$ Faith & Family
$ Faith Today
$ Family Smart E-tips (R)
$ Good News in Florida (R)
Gospel Herald
Halo Magazine
$ Home Times (R)
$ Homeschooling Today (R)
$ In His Presence (R)
$ In Touch
$ Indian Life (R)
Island Catholic (R)
$ JC Town Reporter (R)
$ KD Gospel Media
Koinonia
LifeTimes Catholic
$ Living Church
$ Lookout
$ Manna (R)
Message of the Open Bible (R)
Mosaic (R)
$ Our Sunday Visitor (R)
Pegasus Review (R)
Penned from the Heart (R)
$ Presbyterian Outlook
Quaker Life (R)
$ Seek (R)
Single Again Mag. Online (R)
Spirituality for Today
$ St. Anthony Messenger
Sword of the Lord (R)

$ Testimony (R)
Trumpeter (R)
$ U.S. Catholic
Urban Kingdom (R)
$ Way of St. Francis (R)
$ Wesleyan Life (R)
$ World & I (R)

Children
$ American Girl (R)
$ Bread for God's Children (R)
$ Cadet Quest (R)
$ Keys for Kids (R)
$ New Moon Girls (R)
$ SHINE brightly (R)
Skipping Stones
$ Sparkle (R)

Christian Education/ Library
Catholic Library
$ Group Magazine
$ Jour./Adventist Ed. (R)
$ Teachers of Vision (R)
$ Youth & CE Leadership

Missions
East-West Church & Ministry
     Report

Pastors/Leaders
$ Barefoot (R)
$ Catholic Servant
$ Insight Youth (R)
$ InSite (R)

$ Interpreter
$ Lutheran Partners (R)
Plugged In
$ Word & World
$ Youthworker

Teen/Young Adult
$ Boundless Webzine (R)
Connected
$ Credo (R)
$ Direction Student
Exodus Magazine
Focus/Dare 2 Dig Deeper
G4T Ink (R)
$ Horizon Student
$ Insight (R)
$ Listen (R)
$ Risen
$ Sharing the Victory (R)
$ Spirit
StudentLife
$ TC Magazine
$ True Girl
$ Visions
$ Young Salvationist (R)
$ YouthWalk

Women
$ At the Center (R)
$ Esprit
Extreme Woman Magazine
P31 Woman (R)
Together with God (R)
Unrecognized Woman (R)

7

Periodicals and E-zines

Following are the listings of periodicals. They are arranged alphabetically by type of periodical. (See table of contents for a list of types.) Nonpaying markets are indicated within those listings, e.g., **NO PAYMENT**. Paying markets are indicated with a $ in front of the listing.

A plus sign (+) before an entry indicates that it is a new listing. It is important that freelance writers request writers' guidelines and a recent sample copy or visit a periodical's Website before submitting to any of these publications.

An @ sign in front of a listing indicates that it's an online publication. This year just over 30 percent of the entries are online publications.

If you do not find the publication you are looking for, look in the General Index in the back of the book. See the introduction of that index for the codes used to identify the current status of each unlisted publication.

For a detailed explanation of how to understand and get the most out of these listings, as well as solid marketing tips, see "How to Use This Book" at the front of the book. Unfamiliar terms are explained in the Glossary.

+ A plus sign indicates a new listing.

$ A dollar sign indicates a paying market.

($) A dollar sign in parentheses indicates the market sometimes pays or pays in books, subscriptions, advertisements, or other merchandise.

@ Indicates an online publication.

ADULT/GENERAL MARKETS

$ **ABILITIES MAGAZINE**, 401—340 College St., Toronto ON M5T 3A9, Canada. (416) 923-1885. Fax (416) 923-9829. E-mail: ray@abilities.ca. Website: www.abilities.ca. Canadian Abilities Foundation; general. Raymond Cohen, ed-in-chief. Canada's foremost cross-disabilities lifestyle magazine. Open to freelance. Query; e-query preferred. Pays $50-250 Cdn. for 1st rts. Articles 750-2,000 wds. No simultaneous submissions. Requires disk. Kill fee 50 percent. Guidelines/theme list on Website. (Ads)

> **Tips:** "Ensure your query is strongly Canadian and includes strategies, news, or ideas on living with a disability. We don't publish material with an overtly religious tone. Articles must be disability-related with a positive tone and practical advice."

AFRICAN VOICES, 270 W. 96th St., New York NY 10025. (212) 865-2982. Fax (212) 316-3335. E-mail: africanvoices@aol.com or general@africanvoices.com. Website: www.africanvoices.com. African Voices Communications Inc. Layding Kaliba, mng. ed.; Kim Horne, fiction ed.; Debbie Officer, book review ed. Publishes original fiction, nonfiction, and poetry by artists of color. Quarterly mag.; 48 pgs.; circ. 20,000. Subscription $12. 75 percent unsolicited freelance; 25 percent assigned. Query/clips; e-query OK. **PAYS IN COPIES** for 1st rts. Articles 500-2,500 words (25/yr.); fiction 500-2,000 words (20/yr.); book reviews 500-1,200 words. Responds in 16 wks. Seasonal 4 mos. ahead. Accepts simultaneous submissions & reprints (tell when/where appeared). Requires accepted submissions by e-mail (copied into message). Uses some sidebars. Guidelines on Website; copy $5/9 x 12 SAE/$2.38 postage (mark "Media Mail"). (Ads)

Poetry: Layding Kaliba, poetry ed. Accepts 75-80/yr. Avant-garde, free verse, light verse, haiku, traditional; to 3 pgs. Submit max. 3 poems.

Fillers: Accepts 10/yr. Cartoons.

($) AGAIN MAGAZINE, 10090-A Hwy 9, PO Box 76, Ben Lomond CA 95005. Toll-free (800) 967-7377. (831) 336-5118. Fax (831) 336-8882. E-mail: mgillis@conciliarmedia.com. Website: www.conciliarpress.com. Antiochian Orthodox Archdiocese of North America/Conciliar Press. Fr. Michael Gillis, ed. Historic Eastern Orthodox Christianity applied to our modern times. Quarterly mag.; 32 pgs.; circ. 5,000. Subscription $16. 1 percent unsolicited freelance; 99 percent assigned. Query; e-query OK. **USUALLY PAYS IN COPIES**. Articles 1,500-2,500 words (4/yr.); book reviews 800-1,000 words. Responds in 6-8 wks. Seasonal 4-6 mos. ahead. Serials 2 parts. Accepts reprints (tell when/where appeared). Prefers requested ms on disk or by e-mail (copied into message). Uses some sidebars. Prefers NKJV. Guidelines on Website; copy for 9 x 12 SAE/4 stamps. (No ads)

  Tips: "We are Orthodox in orientation, and interested in thoughtful, intelligent articles dealing with church history, Protestant/Orthodox dialog, relations between Protestants and Orthodox in foreign countries, also in modern ethical dilemmas—no fluff."

$ ALIVE NOW, PO Box 340004, Nashville TN 37203-0004. (615) 340-7218. Fax (615) 340-7267. E-mail: alivenow@upperroom.org. Website: www.alivenow.org. The Upper Room. JoAnn Evans Miller, ed. Short, theme-based writings in attractive graphic setting for reflection and meditation. Bimonthly mag.; 48 pgs.; circ. 40,000. Subscription $17.95. 30 percent unsolicited freelance; 70 percent assigned. Complete ms/cover letter; e-query OK. Pays $35-120 on acceptance for all rts. Articles 200-400 words (25/yr.); fiction 200-400 words. Responds 13 wks. before issue date. Seasonal 6-8 mos. ahead. Accepts simultaneous submissions & reprints (tell when/where appeared). Accepts e-mail submissions (copied into message). Uses some sidebars. Prefers NRSV. Guidelines/theme list by mail/Website; copy for 6 x 9 SAE/4 stamps.

  Poetry: Avant-garde, free verse, traditional; 10-45 lines; $25-100. Submit max. 5 poems. On issue's theme.

  Fillers: Anecdotes, prayers, quotes; no payment.

  Tips: "We can only accept submissions that fit with our themes. Write for our theme list and make your submission relevant to the topic. Avoid the obvious and heavy-handed preachiness."

  **Note: This periodical was #46 on the 2009 Top 50 Christian Publishers list (#46 in 2008).

THE AMBASSADOR, 712 Onstott Rd. #112, Yuba City CA 95993. (530) 933-1385. Fax (360) 937-1385. E-mail: editor@Ambassadornewspaper.com. Seth Halpern, ed./pub. To encourage the local Christian community. Monthly newspaper; circ. 6,000. Subscription $30. Open to unsolicited freelance. Query. Incomplete topical listings. (Ads)

$ @ AMERICA, 106 W. 56th St., New York NY 10019-3893. (212) 581-4640. Fax (212) 399-3596. E-mail: articles@americamagazine.org. Website: www.americamagazine.org. Catholic. Submit to Editor-in-Chief. For thinking Catholics and those who want to know what Catholics are thinking. Weekly mag. & online version; 32+ pgs.; circ. 46,000. Subscription $48. 100 percent unsolicited freelance. Complete ms/cover letter; fax/e-query OK. Pays $150-300 on acceptance. Articles 1,500-2,000 wds. Responds in 6 wks. Seasonal 3 mos. ahead. Does not use sidebars. Guidelines by mail/Website; copy for 9 x 12 SAE. (Ads) Incomplete topical listings.

  Poetry: Buys avant-garde, free verse, light verse, traditional; 20-35 lines; $2-3/line.

AMERICAN TRACT SOCIETY, Box 462008, Garland TX 75046-2008. (972) 276-9408. Fax (972) 272-9642. E-mail: PBatzing@ATSTracts.org. Website: www.ATStracts.org. Peter Batzing, tract ed. Majority of tracts written to win unbelievers. New tract releases bimonthly; 40 new titles produced annually. 5 percent unsolicited freelance; 2 percent assigned. Complete ms/cover letter; e-query OK.

PAYS IN COPIES on publication for exclusive tract rts. Tracts 600-1,200 wds. Responds in 6-8 wks. Seasonal 1 yr. ahead. Accepts simultaneous submissions & reprints (tell when/where appeared). Accepts requested ms on disk or by e-mail (attached or copied into message). Prefers NIV, KJV. Guidelines by mail/e-mail; free samples for #10 SAE/1 stamp. (No ads)

Special Needs: Youth issues, African American, cartoonists, critical issues.

Tips: "Read our current tracts; submit polished writing; relate to people's needs and experiences. Follow guidelines—almost no one does."

$ ANCIENT PATHS, PO Box 7505, Fairfax Station VA 22039. E-mail: ssburris@cox.net. Website: www.editorskylar.com. Christian/nondenominational. Skylar Hamilton Burris, ed. For a literate Christian audience or non-Christians open to and moved by traditional-themed poetry and fiction. Biennial literary mag; 80+ pgs.; circ. 175. Subscription $12. 100 percent unsolicited freelance. Features 2 select poets (15-20 pgs. of poetry ea.) & 2 select writers (6,000-9,000 words ea.). Each will be paid $50 & 1 copy; artists $10 & 1 copy. To be considered, submit query/3 pgs. of prose or 3 best poems. Indicate how much writing/poetry you have to submit. Stories should be 1,000-9,000 words, poems 8 lines min. (no maximum). Not copyrighted. No articles or devotions. Responds in 4 wks. No seasonal. Accepts simultaneous submissions & reprints (if less than half of full submission; tell when/where appeared). Pays on publication for onetime or reprint rts & electronic excerpt rts. No kill fee. Does not use sidebars. Prefers KJV. Also accepts submissions from teens (but must compete with adults). Guidelines by mail/Website; copy $10 (make check to Skylar Burris). (Ads—1/2 pg. $30)

Poetry: Buys 30-50/issue. Free verse, traditional; 8 lines min.; pays $50 & 1 copy total to 2 featured poets (15-20 pgs. ea.). Submit query & 3 best poems.

Tips: "Order a sample copy and review it before querying to see if you think we are a good match. Read the great Christian writers—O'Connor, Lewis, Hopkins, Done, Tennyson, Greene, Chesterton. Stir your reader's emotions; make your reader think and feel without being too obvious. Don't be overly didactic. Follow guidelines carefully." Query period for Issue 16 closes June 1, 2010 and reopens for Issue 17 March 1, 2012.

ANGEL FACE, PO Box 102, Huffman TX 77336. E-mail: MaryAnka_50@msn.com. Website: www .maryanka.com. MaryAnka Press/Catholic. Mary Agnes Dalrymple, pub. Religious or general poetry based on the rosary, birth, rebirth, joy, light, sorrow, epiphany, hope, Jesus, Mary, the seasons of nature and the cycles of life, the search for God in everyday life, etc. (but open to all denominations). Annual literary mag.; 50 pgs.; circ. 100. Subscription $14. 10 percent unsolicited freelance. Complete ms/cover letter (by mail only); no phone/fax/e-query. **PAYS 1 COPY** for onetime rts. Poetry only. Responds in 1-6 mos. Accepts simultaneous submissions & reprints (tell when/where appeared). No submissions by e-mail or on disk. Guidelines by mail/Website; copy $7 (checks payable to Mary Dalrymple).

Poetry: Accepts 35/yr. Free-verse, 60-65 lines. Submit max. 5 poems (typed).

Tips: "I am open to all viewpoints and have published poems by non-Christians as well as Catholic and protestant writers. Send your best work even if you are not sure it fits the rosary pattern. Info on the rosary and sample poems from past issues can be found on my Website."

$ ANGELS ON EARTH, 16 E. 34th St., New York NY 10016. (212) 251-8100. Fax (212) 684-1311. E-mail: submissions@angelsonearth.com. Website: www.angelsonearth.com. Guideposts. Colleen Hughes, ed-in-chief; Meg Belviso, depts. ed. for features and fillers. Presents true stories about God's angels and humans who have played angelic roles on earth. Bimonthly mag.; 75 pgs.; circ. 550,000. Subscription $19.95. 90 percent unsolicited freelance. Complete ms/cover letter; no phone/fax/e-query. Pays $25-400 on publication for all rts. Articles 100-2,000 words (100/yr.); all stories must be true. Responds in 13 wks. Seasonal 6 mos. ahead. E-mail submissions from Website. Guidelines on Website (www.angelsonearth.com/writers_Guidelines.asp); copy for 7 x 10 SAE/4 stamps.

Fillers: Buys many. Anecdotal shorts of similar nature (angelic); 50-250 words; $50-100.
Columns/Departments: Buys 50/yr. Messages (brief, mysterious happenings), $25. Earning Their Wings (good deeds), 150 words, $50. Only Human? (human or angel?/mystery), 350 words; $100. Complete ms.
Tips: "We are not limited to stories about heavenly angels. We also accept stories about human beings doing heavenly duties."

$ ANGLICAN JOURNAL, 80 Hayden St., Toronto ON M4Y 2J6, Canada. (416) 924-9199, ext. 307. Fax (416) 921-4452. E-mail: editor@national.anglican.ca. Website: www.anglicanjournal.com. Anglican Church of Canada. Josie De Lucia, ed. asst. (jdelucia@national.anglican.ca). National newspaper of the Anglican Church of Canada; informs Canadian Anglicans about the church at home and overseas. Newspaper (10x/yr.) & online; 12-16 pgs.; circ. 200,000. Subscription $10 Cdn., $17 U.S. & foreign. 10 percent unsolicited freelance. Query only; fax/e-query OK. Pays $50-250 or .23/ word Cdn., on acceptance for 1st & electronic rts. Articles to 1,000 words (12-15/yr.); fiction for early teens, teens, and adults. Responds in 2 wks. Seasonal 2 mos. ahead. No reprints. Guidelines by e-mail/Website. (Ads)
Tips: "Select subject matter that would be of interest to a national audience."

$ ANIMAL TRAILS, 2660 Peterborough St., Oak Hills VA 20171. E-mail: animaltrails@yahoo.com. Website: www.shoutlife.com/animaltrails. Tellstar Publishing. Shannon Bridget Murphy, ed. Keeping animal memories alive through writing. Quarterly mag. 85 percent unsolicited freelance. Complete ms/cover letter; e-query OK. Pays .02-.05/word on acceptance for 1st, onetime, reprint, or simultaneous rts. Articles to 2,000 words; fiction to 2,000 words. Responds in 2-8 wks. Seasonal 3 mos. ahead. Accepts simultaneous submissions & reprints (tell when/where appeared). Accepts disk or e-mail submissions (attached or copied into message.). No kill fee. Regularly uses sidebars. Prefers KJV. Guidelines by e-mail. (No ads)
Poetry: Buys variable number. Avant-garde, free verse, haiku, light verse, traditional; any length. Pays variable rates. Submit any number.
Fillers: Buys most types, to 1,000 wds.
Tips: "Most open to articles, stories, poetry, and fillers that explain the value of animals and their relationship with God. The value of animals is the mission of *Animal Trails*. Include a Scripture reference."

$ THE ANNALS OF SAINT ANNE, 9795 St. Anne Blvd., St. Anne de Beaupre QC G0A 3C0, Canada. (418) 827-4538. Fax (418) 827-4530. E-mail: mag@revuesteannedebeaupre.ca (for subscriptions only). Catholic/Redemptorist Fathers. Fr. Guy Desrochers, C.Ss.R., ed; Fr. Bernard Mercier, C.Ss.R., interim mng. ed. Promotes Catholic family values. Bimonthly mag.; 32 pgs.; circ. 25,000. Subscription $20 U.S. 80 percent unsolicited freelance. Complete ms/cover letter; no phone/fax/ e-query. Pays $60 for 650 words; $90 for 900 words; $40 for fiction (700 words) on acceptance for 1st N.A. serial rts. only. Responds in 4-5 wks. Seasonal 6 mos. ahead. No simultaneous submissions or reprints. No disk or e-mail submission. Does not use sidebars. Prefers NRSV. Guidelines by mail; copy for #10 or 9 x 12 SAE. (No ads)
Tips: "Writing must be uplifting and inspirational, clearly written, not filled with long quotations. We tend to stay away from extreme controversy and focus on the family, good family values, devotion, and Christianity. Most open to Christian education, Christian living, Christian growth, church life and testimonies. Write a well-researched, current story with 'across the board' appeal." Rights must be clearly stated. Typed manuscripts only.

ANOINTED PAGES MAGAZINE, 3900 W. Brown Deer Rd, Ste. A-149, Milwaukee WI 53209. (414) 517-8876 or (414) 759-4959. E-mail: info@anointedpages.com. Website: www.anointedpages.com. Interdenominational. Marvin Ivy, pub. (marvinivy@anointedpages.com); Jodine Ivy, editorial administrator (jodineive@anointedpages.com). To profile religious and community leaders and the lives that they are changing within their ministry and community, and to meet the needs of people with articles on the holistic lifestyle. Bimonthly mag. Subscription $19.99. Estab. 2007. Open to unsolicited freelance. Query. Articles. Also accepts submissions from teens.

ANSWERS MAGAZINE & ANSWERSMAGAZINE.COM, PO Box 510, Hebron KY 41048. (859) 727-2222. Fax (859) 727-4888. E-mail: nationaleditor@answersmagazine.com. Website: www .answersmagazine.com. Answers in Genesis. Mike Matthews, exec. ed-in-chief. Bible-affirming, creation based. Quarterly mag. Articles to 300-600 wds. Responds in 30 days. Details on Website.

$ @ THE APOCALYPSE CHRONICLES, Box 448, Jacksonville OR 97530. Phone/fax (541) 899-8888. E-mail: James@ChristianMediaNetwork.com. Website: www.Christianmedia.tv. Christian Media. James Lloyd, ed./pub. Deals with the apocalypse exclusively. Quarterly & online newsletter; circ. 2,000-3,000. Query; prefers phone query. Payment negotiable for reprint rts. Articles. Responds in 3 wks. Requires KJV. No guidelines; copy for #10 SAE/2 stamps.
> **Tips:** "It's helpful if you understand your own prophetic position and are aware of its name, i.e., Futurist, Historicist, etc."

$ ARKANSAS CATHOLIC, PO Box 7417, Little Rock AR 72217. (501) 664-0125. Fax (501) 664-6572. E-mail: mhargett@dolr.org. Website: www.arkansas-catholic.org. Catholic Diocese of Little Rock. Malea Hargett, ed.; Tara Little, assoc. ed. Statewide newspaper for the local diocese. Weekly tabloid; 16 pgs.; circ. 7,700. Subscription $18. 1 percent unsolicited freelance; 10 percent assigned. Query/clips; e-query OK. Pays $3/inch on publication for 1st rts. Articles 1,000 wds. Accepts simultaneous submissions & reprints. Accepts requested ms on disk or by e-mail. Uses some sidebars. Prefers Catholic Bible. Guidelines by mail/e-mail; copy for 9 x 12 SAE/2 stamps. (Ads)
> **Columns/Departments:** Tara Little, ed. Buys 2/yr. Seeds of Faith (education). Complete ms. Pays $20.
> **Tips:** "All stories and columns must have an Arkansas and Catholic connection."

$ ARLINGTON CATHOLIC HERALD, 200 N. Glebe Rd., Ste. 600, Arlington VA 22203. (703) 841-2590. Fax (703) 524-2782. E-mail: editorial@catholicherald.com. Website: www.catholicherald .com. Catholic Diocese of Arlington. Michael F. Flach, ed. Regional, for the local diocese. Weekly newspaper; 28 pgs.; circ. 53,000. Subscription $14. 10 percent unsolicited freelance. Query; phone/fax/e-query OK. Pays $50-150 on publication for onetime rts. Articles 500-1,500 wds. Responds in 2 wks. Seasonal 3 mos. ahead. Accepts simultaneous submissions. Prefers accepted ms on disk. Regular sidebars. Guidelines by mail/Website; copy for 11 x 17 SAE. (Ads)
> **Columns/Departments:** Sports; School News; Local Entertainment; 500 wds.
> **Tips:** "All submissions must be Catholic related. Avoid controversial issues within the church."

$ @ ASSOCIATED CONTENT, 88 Steele St., Ste. 400, Denver CO 80206-5715. (720) 255-9185. E-mail: miguel@associatedcontent.com. Website: www.associatedcontent.com. *Associated Content.* Miguel Chacon, submissions mngr. Weekly e-zine; 1000+ pgs. Free online. 100 percent unsolicited freelance. Query online. Pays $3-20 on acceptance for nonexclusive, electronic rts. Articles 400-5,000 words (1,000+/yr.); fiction 400-5,000 words (1,000+/yr.). Responds in 2 wks. Seasonal 1 mo. ahead. Accepts simultaneous submissions & reprints (tell when/where appeared). Accepts submissions online only. Guidelines on Website; copy online.
> **Poetry:** Avant-garde, free verse, haiku, light verse, traditional.
> **Tips:** "Look over Website and see what the other writers are doing. Sign up, fill out a profile, and submit your work."
> ****Note:** This periodical was #6 on the 2008 Top 50 Christian Publishers list (#6 in 2007, #7 in 2006).

$ ATLANTIC CATHOLIC, 88 College St., Antigonish NS B2G 2L7, Canada. (902) 863-4370. Fax (902) 863-1943. E-mail: editor@thecasket.ca or atlanticcatholic@thecasket.ca. Website: www.thecasket

.ca. The Casket Printing and Publishing Co. Ken Sims, pub.; Brian Lazzuri, mng. ed. Reports religious news that will inform, educate, and inspire Catholics. Biweekly tabloid; circ. 2,000. Subscription $28. Open to unsolicited freelance. Pays $25/story. Articles to 800 wds. Accepts e-mail submissions of mss up to 800 wds. (Ads)

> **Tips:** "Most open to book and movie reviews, less than 700 words; also celebrity profiles, less than 700 words."

$ AUJOURD'HUI CREDO, 1332 Victoria, Longueuil QC J4V 1L8, Canada. (450) 466-7733. Fax (450) 466-2664. E-mail: davidfines@egliseunie.org. Website: www.united-church.ca. United Church of Canada. David Fines, dir. The only French Reformed magazine in North America. Monthly mag.; 28 pgs.; circ. 250. Subscription $25 Cdn. 20 percent unsolicited freelance. Complete ms; fax/e-query OK. Pays $100 on publication for nonexclusive rts. Not copyrighted. Articles 1,500 words (10/yr.); fiction 800 words (6/yr.); reviews 100 words. Responds in 4 wks. Seasonal 2 mos. ahead. Accepts simultaneous submissions & reprints (tell when/where appeared). Requires e-mail submissions (attached or copied into message). No kill fee. Uses some sidebars. Also accepts submissions from children/teens. Prefers TOB. Guidelines/theme list by e-mail; free copy. (Ads)

> **Poetry:** Accepts free verse.
> **Tips:** "Most likely to break in by being inclusive and intelligent. Looking for theological reflection or social topics. Contact director. Must write in French."

$ AUSTRALIAN CATHOLICS, PO Box 553, Richmond Victoria 3121, Australia. Tel. (61) (3) 9421 9666. Fax (61) (3) 9421 9600. E-mail: auscaths@jespub.jesuit.org.au or through Website: www .australiancatholics.com.au. Jesuit Communications. Michael McVeigh, ed. Stories of faith and living for a contemporary Catholic audience. Mag. published 5x/yr.; 36 pgs.; circ. 200,000. Open to unsolicited freelance. Query or complete ms; e-query OK. Payment by negotiation on publication for 1st rts. Articles 800-1,200 wds. Seasonal 4 mos. ahead. Accepts reprints (tell when/where appeared). Uses some sidebars.

> **Tips:** "We generally prefer articles on people, either as interviews or reflections on personal experiences. We generally don't consider an overseas submission, unless it can be made relevant for an Australian audience."

THE BAPTIST STANDARD, PO Box 660267, Dallas TX 75266-0267. (214) 630-4571. Fax (214) 638-8535. E-mail: marvknox@baptiststandard.com or through Website: www.baptiststandard.com /postnuke/index.php. Marv Knox, ed. The Texas Baptist news journal. Biweekly newspaper. Subscription $20.50. Incomplete topical listings.

$ B.C. CATHOLIC, 150 Robson St., Vancouver BC V6B 2A7, Canada. (604) 683-0281. Fax (604) 683-8117. E-mail: bcc@rcav.bc.ca. Website: http://bcc.rcav.org. Roman Catholic Archdiocese of Vancouver. Paul Schratz, ed. News, education, and inspiration for Canadian Catholics. Weekly (48x) newspaper; 20 pgs.; circ. 20,000. Subscription $32. 20 percent unsolicited freelance. Query; phone query OK. Pays .15/wd. on publication for 1st rts. Photos $30. Articles 300-3,000 wds. Responds in 6 wks. Seasonal 4 wks. ahead. Accepts simultaneous submissions & reprints (.05/wd.). Prefers e-mail submission (copied into message). Guidelines on Website; free copy. (Ads)

> **Tips:** "Items of relevance to Catholics in British Columbia are preferred."

@ BEHIND THE HAMMER, 1018 Main St., Akron PA 17501. (717) 859-2210. Fax (717) 859-4910. E-mail: communications@mds.mennonite.net. Website: www.mds.mennonite.net. Mennonite Disaster Services. Scott Sundberg, ed. Quarterly & online mag. Subscription free. Open to freelance. Complete ms/cover letter. **NO PAYMENT**. Articles. Guidelines on Website; free copy. Not in topical listings.

> **Tips:** "By sharing our stories we hope to encourage and motivate one another to continue expressing the love of God through MDS activity."

@ BELIEVER'S BAY, 1202 S. Pennsylvania St., Marion IN 46953. E-mail: publisher@BelieversBay .com. Website: www.BelieversBay.com. Tim Russ, pub. To share the love of God with common sense. Monthly online mag. Mostly freelance. Complete ms by e-mail only (attached); e-query OK. **NO PAYMENT** for 1st & electronic rts. (permanently archives pieces). Articles 500-1,000 wds. Guidelines/monthly topical themes listed at www.believersbay.com/submission_guidelines.htm.

> **Columns/Departments:** Columns 300-500 wds.
> **Special Needs:** Living in Responsible Grace.
> **Tips:** "Only accepts e-mail submissions: submission@believersbay.com."

$ BIBLE ADVOCATE, Box 33677, Denver CO 80233. (303) 452-7973. Fax (303) 452-0657. E-mail: bibleadvocate@cog7.org. Website: www.cog7.org/BA. Church of God (Seventh-day). Calvin Burrell, ed.; Sherri Langton, assoc. ed. Adult readers; 50 percent not members of the denomination. Monthly (8x) mag.; 32 pgs.; circ. 13,500. Subscription free. 25-35 percent unsolicited freelance. Complete ms/cover letter; no phone/fax/e-query. Pays $25-55 on publication for 1st, onetime, reprint, electronic, simultaneous rts. Articles 600-1,200 words (10-20/yr.). Responds in 4-8 wks. Seasonal 9 mos. ahead (no Christmas or Easter pieces). Accepts simultaneous submissions & reprints (tell when/where appeared). Accepts requested ms by e-mail (copied into message—preferred—or attached). Regularly uses sidebars. Prefers NIV, NKJV. Guidelines/theme list by mail/Website; copy for 9 x 12 SAE/3 stamps. (No ads)

> **Poetry:** Buys 6-10/yr. Free verse, traditional; 5-20 lines; $20. Submit max. 5 poems.
> **Fillers:** Buys 5/yr. Prose; 100-400 words; $20.
> **Special Needs:** Articles centering on upcoming themes (see Website).
> **Tips:** "If you write well, all areas are open to freelance, especially personal experiences that tie in with the monthly themes. Articles that run 650-700 words are more likely to get in. Also, fresh writing with keen insight is most readily accepted. Writers may submit sidebars that fit our theme for each issue."

BIBLICAL RECORDER, PO Box 18808, Raleigh NC 27619-8808. (919) 847-2127. Fax (919) 847-6939. E-mail: editor@biblicalrecorder.org. Website: www.biblicalrecorder.org. Baptist. Steve DeVane, mng. ed. Newspaper. Subscription $15. Incomplete topical listings.

+ BLUE RIDGE CHRISTIAN NEWS, 29 Crystal St., #101, Spruce Pine NC 28777. (828) 766-7048. Fax (828) 765-9128. E-mail: info@blueridgechristiannews.com. Website: www.blueridgechristiannews .com. Nondenominational. Steve Parker, ed./pub. Semimonthly newspaper; circ. 11,000. Subscription $24. Open to unsolicited freelance. Query first. Articles. Incomplete topical listings. (Ads)

> **Tips:** "We are committed to bringing health, unity, and spiritual maturity to the Body of Christ while releasing the power of the Holy spirit into every segment of society: home, church, education, business, media, arts, and government."
> ** 2009 Award of Merit—Most Imroved Publication.

@ BOOKS & CULTURE, 465 Gundersen Dr., Carol Stream IL 60188. (630) 260-6200. Fax (630) 260-0114. E-mail: booksandculture@christianitytoday.com or jwilson@christianitytoday.com. Website: www.booksandculture.com. Christianity Today Intl. John Wilson, ed. To edify, sharpen, and nurture the evangelical intellectual community by engaging the world in all its complexity from a distinctly Christian perspective. Bimonthly & online newsletter.; circ. 12,000. Subscription $19.95. Open to freelance. Query. Articles & reviews. Incomplete topical listings. (Ads)

THE BREAD OF LIFE, 35—5100 S. Service Rd., PO Box 127, Burlington ON L7R 3X5, Canada. (905) 634-5433. E-mail: info@thebreadoflife.ca. Website: www.thebreadoflife.ca. Catholic. Fr. Peter Coughlin, ed. Catholic Charismatic; to encourage spiritual growth in areas of renewal in the Catholic Church today. Bimonthly mag.; 48 pgs.; circ. 2,500. Subscription $35 Cdn.; $40 elsewhere. 5 percent unsolicited freelance. Complete ms/cover letter; fax query OK. **NO PAYMENT**. Articles 750 words;

book reviews 250 words. Responds in 4-6 wks. Seasonal 6 mos. ahead. Accepts reprints (tell when/ where appeared). No disk. Does not use sidebars. Prefers NAB, NJB. Guidelines; copy for 9 x 12 SAE/$2.38 postage (mark "Media Mail"). (Some ads)

Poetry: Accepts little.

Fillers: Accepts 10-12/yr. Facts, prose, quotes; to 250 wds.

Tips: "Most open to testimonies; contact managing editor. We do appreciate poetry submissions and 750 word testimonies of the power of Jesus/Holy spirit active in your life. It is best if a writer includes a 2-3 line biography and photo for publication."

THE BREAKTHROUGH INTERCESSOR, PO Box 121, Lincoln VA 20160-0121. (540) 338-5522. Fax (540) 338-1934. E-mail: editor@intercessors.org. Website: www.intercessors.org. Nondenominational. Cherise Ryan, mng. ed. Preparing and equipping people who pray; encouraging in prayer and faith. Quarterly mag.; 36 pgs.; circ. 5,000. Subscription $18. 100 percent unsolicited freelance. Complete ms; fax/e-query OK. Accepts full mss by e-mail. **PAYS 5 COPIES** for 1st, reprint rts. Articles 1,000 words (50/yr.); book reviews 300-600 words; music/video reviews 300 words. Responds in 3 weeks. Seasonal 6 mos. ahead. Accepts simultaneous submissions. Accepts requested ms by e-mail (copied into message). Uses some sidebars. Also accepts submissions from children/ teens. Any Bible version. Guidelines by mail/e-mail/Website; copy for 6 x 9 SAE/3 stamps. (No ads)

Poetry: Accepts 4/yr. Any type, 4-32 lines. Submit any number (as long as they're about prayer).

Fillers: Accepts 8/yr. Anecdotes, prayers; to 300 wds.

Special Needs: Moving personal stories in how prayer has changed your life.

Contest: Pays $25 for article with most reader impact, plus one free subscription.

Tips: "Break in by submitting true articles/stories about prayer and its miraculous results, and articles that teach about an aspect of prayer using scripture to support each point." Manuscripts acknowledged but not returned.

BREAKTHROUGH MAGAZINE, (517) 882-3595. E-mail: editor@breakthroughonlinemag.com. Website: www.breakthroughonlinemag.com. Baraka Miller, ed. "Every struggle endures a break-through, every breakthrough endures a struggle." Showcases those who have made their break-through in life and who are impacting their communities; sharing the joy of life, family, success, and above all Christ, the one who gives us strength to "Breakthrough." Webzine.

BRETHREN IN CHRIST, [formerly Seek (BIC)], 431 Grantham Rd., PO Box A, Grantham PA 17027. (717) 697-2634. Fax (717) 697-7714. E-mail: biccomm@bic-church.org. Website: www .BIC-church.org/seek. Denominational/Brethren in Christ Church. Rebekah Basinger, ed. Highlights the spiritual journeys and writings of our members. Quarterly magazine. Subscription free to mem-bers. Open to unsolicited freelance. Query preferred. **NO PAYMENT**. Articles & reviews. Not in topical listings.

$ BRIDAL GUIDES, 2660 Peterborough St., Oak Hill VA 20171. E-mail: bridalguides@yahoo.com. Tellstar Publishing. Shannon Bridget Murphy, ed. Theme-based wedding/reception ideas and plan-ning for Christian wedding planners. Quarterly mag. 85 percent unsolicited freelance. Complete ms/ cover letter; e-query OK. Pays .02-.05/word on acceptance for 1st, onetime, reprint, simultaneous rts. Articles to 2,000 words; fiction to 2,000 words. Responds in 2-8 wks. Seasonal 3 mos. ahead. Accepts simultaneous submissions & reprints (tell when/where appeared). Accepts disk or e-mail submissions (attached or copied into message.). No kill fee. Regularly uses sidebars. Also accepts submissions from children/teens. Prefers KJV. Guidelines by e-mail. (No ads)

Poetry: Buys variable number. Avant-garde, free verse, haiku, light verse, traditional; any length. Pays variable rates. Submit any number.

Fillers: Buys most types, to 1,000 words; .02-.05/wd.

Special Needs: "Most open to wedding and planning articles that show readers how to successfully complete plans for their events. Illustrations and art either with or without manuscript packages. Romance fiction related to weddings, travel, and home."

+ @ **THE BRINK ONLINE**, 114 Bush Rd., Nashville TN 37217. Toll-free (800) 877-7030. (615) 361-1221. Fax (615) 367-0535. E-mail: thebrink@randallhouse.com. Website: www.randallhouse .com. Randall House. Jacob Riggs, ed. Webzine for twentysomethings, including articles focusing on but not limited to: faith, media, dating, culture, politics, religion, technology, social justice, and finance. Updated weekly. Articles 500-1,500 wds. Accepts reprints. Requires e-query.

$ @ **THE BRINK MAGAZINE**, 114 Bush Rd., Nashville TN 37217. Toll-free (800) 877-7030. (615) 361-1221. Fax (615) 367-0535. E-mail: thebrink@randallhouse.com. Website: www.thebrinkonline .com. Randall House. Jacob Riggs, ed. Devotional magazine for young adults; focusing on Bible studies, life situations, discernment of culture, and relevant feature articles. Quarterly & online mag.; 64 pgs.; circ. 10,000. Estab. 2008. 30 percent unsolicited freelance; 70 percent assigned. Query, query/ clips; prefers e-query. Accepts full mss by e-mail. Pays $50-150 on acceptance for all rts. Articles 500-1,500 words (10-15/yr.). Responds in 1-2 wks. Seasonal 6 mos. ahead. Accepts simultaneous submissions & reprints (tell when/where appeared). Requires accepted articles by e-mail (attached file). No kill fee. Regularly uses sidebars. No guidelines or copy; theme list available. (No ads)
   Fillers: Buys 4/yr. Ideas, newsbreaks, quizzes; 50-100 wds. No payment.
   Columns/Departments: Buys 4/yr.; query. What____Says About____ (hot cultural topic, movie, song, event, or TV show is used to draw out a certain theme). Pays $50-100.
   Tips: "A writer can best get in by writing for the online version by pitching the editor an idea. After familiarity has been built, the editor could contact the writer for printed pieces."

BYFAITH (byFaith), 1700 N. Brown Rd., Ste. 105, Lawrenceville GA 30043. (678) 825-1005. Fax (678) 825-1001. E-mail: editor@byfaithonline.com. Website: www.byfaithonline.com. Presbyterian Church in America (PCA). Dick Doster, ed. (ddoster@byfaithonline.com). Provides news of the PCA; connects members, guests, and staff members to the denomination. Bimonthly mag.; 54 pgs. Subscription $19.95. Open to unsolicited freelance. Complete ms by e-mail ("Editorial Submission" in subject line). **NO MENTION OF PAYMENT**. Articles 500-3,000 wds. Guidelines on Website. Incomplete topical listings.
   Tips: "We publish in 5 areas: stories that provoke thinking and creativity; very practical theology; articles that help readers understand the arts and culture; sensible, down-to-earth information; and PCA news."
   ** 2008, 2006 EPA Award of Excellence—Denominational; 2007 EPA Award of Merit—Denominational.

$ **CANADA LUTHERAN**, 302—393 Portage Ave., Winnipeg MB R3B 3H6, Canada. Toll-free (888) 786-6707, ext. 172. (204) 984-9172. Fax (204) 984-9185. E-mail: editor@elcic.ca, or canaluth@ elcic.ca. Website: www.elcic.ca/clweb. Evangelical Lutheran Church in Canada. Trina Gallop, ed. dir. (tgallop@elcic.ca); Lucia Carruthers, ed. Denominational. Monthly (8x) mag.; 42 pgs.; circ. 14,000. Subscription $22. 60 Cdn.; $42 U.S. 40 percent unsolicited freelance; 60 percent assigned. Query or complete ms/cover letter; fax/e-query OK. Pays $40-110 (.10/wd.) Cdn. on publication for onetime rts. Articles 700-1,200 words (15/yr.); fiction 850-1,200 words (4/yr.). Responds in 5 wks. Seasonal 10 mos. ahead. Accepts simultaneous submissions & reprints. Prefers e-mail submission (copied into message). Uses some sidebars. Prefers NRSV. Guidelines by mail/e-mail. (Ads)
   Tips: "Canadians/Lutherans receive priority here; others considered but rarely used. Want material that is clear, concise, and fresh. Articles that talk about real life experiences of faith receive our best reader response."

@ **CANADIANCHRISTIANITY.COM**, #200-20316—56 Ave., Langley BC V3A 3Y7, Canada. Toll-free (888) 899-3777. E-mail: editor@canadianchristianity.com. Website: www.CanadianChristianity

.com. A ministry of the Christian Info Society. David Dawes, mng. ed. Online newspaper. Incomplete topical listings.

THE CANADIAN LUTHERAN, 3074 Portage Ave., Winnipeg MB R3K 0Y2, Canada. Toll-free (800) 588-4226. (204) 895-3433. Fax (204) 897-4319. E-mail: communications@lutheranchurch.ca. Website: www.lutheranchurch.ca. Lutheran Church—Canada. Ian Adnams, ed. Monthly (10x) mag. Subscription $20. Open to unsolicited freelance. Not in topical listings. (Ads)

$ CANADIAN MENNONITE, 490 Dutton Dr., Unit C5, Waterloo ON N2L 6H7, Canada. Toll-free (800) 378-2524. (519) 884-3810. Fax (519) 884-3331. E-mail: submit@canadianmennonite.org. Website: www.canadianmennonite.org. Canadian Mennonite Publishing Service. Ross W. Muir, mng. ed. Seeks to promote covenantal relationships within the Mennonite Church Canada constituency (guided by Hebrews 10:23-25). Biweekly mag.; 32-40 pgs.; circ. 16,500. Subscription $32.50 Cdn.; $52.50 U.S. Open to unsolicited freelance. Query; phone/e-query OK. Pays .10/wd.; .05/wd. for reprints; for 1st rts. Articles 400-800 words; reviews 500 words (pays .10/wd.). Responds in 2-4 wks. Accepts reprints (tell when/where appeared). Prefers e-mail submissions (attached file). Some kill fees 50 percent. Uses some sidebars. Guidelines and past issues on Website. Incomplete topical listings. (Ads)
> **Tips:** "We provide channels for sharing accurate and fair information, faith profiles, inspirational and educational materials, news, and analysis of issues facing the church. We use very little from outside the Mennonite Church."

$ CAPPER'S, 1503 S.W. 42nd St., Topeka KS 66609. (785) 274-4300. Fax (785) 274-4305. E-mail: cappers@cappers.com. Website: www.cappers.com. Ogden Publications. K. C. Compton, ed-in-chief. Timely news-oriented features with positive messages. Monthly mag.; 40-56 pgs.; circ. 150,000. Subscription $18. 95. 40 percent unsolicited freelance. Complete ms/cover letter by mail only. Pays about $2.50/printed inch for nonfiction on publication, pays $100-400 for fiction on acceptance for onetime rts. Articles to 1,000 words (50/yr.); fiction to 2,000 words, serials to 25,000 words (20/yr.). Responds in 2-6 mos. Seasonal 6 mos. ahead. No simultaneous submissions or reprints. Prefers requested ms by e-mail. Uses some sidebars. Guidelines by mail/Website; copy $4/9 x 12 SASE/4 stamps. (Ads)
> **Poetry:** Attn: Poetry Editor. Buys 50/yr. Free verse, light verse, traditional; 4-16 lines. Pays $10-15 on acceptance. Submit max. 5 poems.
> **Columns/Departments:** Buys 12/yr. Garden Path (gardens/gardening), 500-1,000 wds. Payment varies. This column most open.
> **Tips:** "Our publication is all original material either written by our readers/freelancers or occasionally by our staff. Every department, every article is open. Break in by reading at least 6 months of issues to know our special audience. Most open to nonfiction features and garden stories." Submissions are not acknowledged or status reports given.

$ @ CATHEDRAL AGE, 3101 Wisconsin Ave. N.W., Washington DC 20016. (202) 537-5681. Fax (202) 364-6600. E-mail: Cathedral_Age@cathedral.org. Website: www.cathedralage.org. Protestant Episcopal Cathedral Foundation. Craig W. Stapert, pub. mngr. News from Washington National Cathedral and stories of interest to friends and supporters of WNC. Quarterly & online mag.; 36 pgs.; circ. 30,000. Subscription $15. 50 percent assigned freelance. Query; e-query OK. Pays to $750 on publication for all rts. Articles 1,200-1,500 words (10/yr.); book reviews 600 words, ($250). Responds in 6 wks. Seasonal 6 mos. ahead. Requires requested ms on disk or by e-mail (attached file). Kill fee 50 percent. Uses some sidebars. Prefers NRSV. No guidelines; copy $5/9 x 12 SAE/5 stamps. (No ads)
> **Special Needs:** Art, architecture, music.
> **Tips:** "We assign all articles, so query with clips first. Always write from the viewpoint of an individual first, then move into a more general discussion of the topic. Human-interest angle important."

$ @ CATHOLIC DIGEST, PO Box 6015, 1 Montauk Ave., Ste. 200, New London CT 06320-1789. (860)ˉ437-3012. Fax (860) 536-5600. E-mail: cdsubmissions@bayard-us.com. Website: www .CatholicDigest.com. Catholic/Bayard Publications. Dan Connors, ed-in-chief (dconnors@catholic digest.com); Julie Rattey, mng. ed.; submit to Kathryn Oates, asst. ed. Readers have a stake in being Catholic and a wide range of interests: religion, family, health, human relationships, good works, nostalgia, and more. Monthly & online mag.; 128 pgs.; circ. 400,000. Subscription $19.95. 15 percent unsolicited freelance; 20 percent assigned. Complete ms (for original material)/cover letter, tear sheets for reprints; no e-query. Pays $200-300 ($100 for reprints) on acceptance for 1st rts. Online-only articles receive $100, plus half of any traceable revenue. Articles 1,000-2,000 words; feature articles 1,200-1,700 words (60/yr.). Responds in 6-8 wks. Seasonal 5 mos. ahead. Accepts reprints (tell when/where appeared). Accepts requested ms on disk or by e-mail (copied into message). Regularly uses sidebars. Prefers NAB. Guidelines on Website; copy for 7 x 10 SAE/2 stamps. (Ads)

> **Fillers:** Fillers Editor. Buys 200/yr. Anecdotes, cartoons, facts, jokes, quotes; 1 line to 300 words; $2/published line on publication. Submit to cdfillers@bayard-inc.com.
> **Columns/Departments:** Buys 75/yr. Open Door (personal stories of conversion to Catholicism); 200-500 words; $2/published line. See guidelines for full list.
> **Special Needs:** Family and career concerns of Baby Boomers who have a stake in being Catholic.
> **Contest:** See Website for current contest, or send an SASE.
> **Tips:** "We favor the anecdotal approach. Stories must be strongly focused on a definitive topic that is illustrated for the reader with a well-developed series of true-life, interconnected vignettes."
> ** This periodical was #29 on the 2009 Top 50 Christian Publishers list (#31 in 2008, #37 in 2007, #31 in 2006, #48 in 2005).

$ CATHOLIC FORESTER, Box 3012, Naperville IL 60566-7012. Toll-free (800) 552-0145. (630) 983-3381. Toll-free fax (800) 811-2140. (630) 983-3384. E-mail: magazine@catholicforester.com. Website: www.catholicforester.com. Catholic Order of Foresters. Mary Anne File, ed. For mixed audience, primarily parents and grandparents between the ages of 30 and 80+. Quarterly mag.; 40 pgs.; circ. 100,000. Free/membership. 20 percent unsolicited freelance. Complete ms/cover letter; no phone/fax/e-query. Pays .50/wd. on acceptance for 1st rts. Articles 1,000-1,500 words (12-16/yr.); fiction for all ages 500-1,500 words (12-16/yr.). Responds in 3 mos. Seasonal 6 mos. ahead. Accepts simultaneous submissions & reprints (tell when/where appeared). Accepts requested ms by e-mail. Uses some sidebars. Prefers Catholic Bible. Guidelines on Website; copy for 9 x 12 SAE/4 stamps. (No ads)

> **Poetry:** Buys 3/yr. Light verse, traditional; to 15 lines. Pay.50/wd. Submit max. 5 poems.
> **Tips:** "Looking for informational, inspirational articles on finances and health. Writing should be energetic with good style and rhythm. Most open to general interest and fiction."
> ** This periodical was #36 on the 2009 Top 50 Christian Publishers list (#23 in 2008, #26 in 2007, #19 in 2006, #36 in 2005).

$ CATHOLIC INSIGHT, PO Box 625, Adelaide Sta., 31 Adelaide St. E., Toronto ON M5C 2J8, Canada. (416) 204-9601. Fax (416) 204-1027. E-mail: reach@catholicinsight.com. Website: www.catholic insight.com. Life Ethics Information Center. Fr. Alphonse de Valk, ed./pub. News, analysis, and commentary on social, ethical, political, and moral issues from a Catholic perspective. Monthly (11x) mag.; 44 pgs.; circ. 3,700. Subscription $35 Cdn., $55 U.S. 2 percent unsolicited freelance; 98 percent assigned. Query preferred; phone/fax/e-query OK. Pays $200 for 1,500 words ($250 for 2,000 words) on publication for 1st rts. Articles 750-1,500 words (20-30/yr.); book reviews 750 words ($85). Responds in 6-8 wks. Seasonal 2 mos. ahead. Accepts requested ms on disk. Uses some sidebars. Prefers RSV (Catholic). Guidelines by mail/e-mail; copy $4 Cdn./9 x 12 SAE/$2 Cdn. postage or IRC. (Ads)

Tips: "We are interested in intelligent, well-researched, well-presented commentary on a political, religious, social, or cultural matter from the viewpoint of the Catholic Church."

$ CATHOLIC NEW YORK, 1011—1st Ave., Rm. 1721, New York NY 10022. (212) 688-2399. Fax (212) 688-2642. E-mail: cny@cny.org. Website: www.cny.org. Catholic. John Woods, ed-in-chief. To inform New York Catholics. Biweekly newspaper; 40 pgs.; circ. 135,000. Subscription $24. 2 percent unsolicited freelance. Query or complete ms/cover letter. Pays $15-100 on publication for onetime rts. Articles 500-800 wds. Responds in 5 wks. Copy $3.

Tips: "Most open to columns about specific seasons of the Catholic Church, such as Advent, Christmas, Lent, and Easter."

$ CATHOLIC PEACE VOICE, 532 W. 8th, Erie PA 16502-1343. (814) 453-4955, ext. 235. Fax (814) 452-4784. E-mail: info@paxchristiusa.org. Website: www.paxchristiusa.org. Dave Robinson, exec. dir. (Dave@paxchristiusa.org). For members of Pax Christi USA, the national Catholic Peace Movement. Bimonthly newsmag.; 16-20 pgs.; circ. 23,000. Subscription $20, free to members. 15-20 percent unsolicited freelance; 25-30 percent assigned. Complete ms; phone/fax/e-query OK. Pays $50-75 on publication for all & electronic rts. Articles 500-1,500 words (10-15/yr.); reviews 750 words, $50. Responds in 1-2 wks. Accepts simultaneous submissions & reprints (tell when/where appeared). Accepted ms on disk or by e-mail (attached or copied into message). Uses some sidebars. Also accepts submissions from teens. Guidelines by mail/e-mail; copy for 9 x 12 SAE/2 stamps. (Ads)

Poetry: Accepts 1-5/yr. Avant-garde, free verse, haiku, light verse, traditional. Submit max. 2 poems. No payment.

Tips: "Most open to features and news, as well as reviews and resources. E-mailing us and pitching a story is the best way to break into our publication. Emphasis is on nonviolence. No sexist language."

THE CATHOLIC REGISTER, 1155 Yonge St., Ste. 401, Toronto ON M4T 1W2, Canada. (416) 934-3410. Fax (416) 934-3409. E-mail: editor@catholicregister.org, or news@catholicregister.org or through Website: www.catholicregister.org. Joe Sinasac, ed./pub.; Mickey Conlon, mng. ed. To provide reliable information about the world from a Catholic perspective. Weekly (47x) tabloid; circ. 33,000. Subscription $42.70. Open to unsolicited freelance. Not in topical listings. (Ads)

$ CATHOLIC SENTINEL, 5536 N.E. Hassalo St., Portland OR 97213. (503) 281-1191. Fax (503) 460-5496. E-mail: sentinel@ocp.org. Website: www.sentinel.org. Oregon Catholic Press. Bob Pfohman, ed. Weekly tabloid; 20 pgs.; circ. 16,000. Subscription $32. 2 percent unsolicited freelance; 0 percent assigned. Query/clips. Payment negotiable on publication for onetime rts. Articles 600-1,500 wds. Responds in 4 wks. Seasonal 2 mos. ahead. Accepts requested ms on disk or by e-mail (copied into message). Uses some sidebars. Prefers NAS. Incomplete topical listings. Guidelines on Website; copy for 9 x 12 SAE/3 stamps. (Ads)

Tips: "We're most open to local church news and feature articles."

$ CATHOLIC TELEGRAPH, 100 E. 8th St., Cincinnati OH 45202. (513) 421-3131. Fax (513) 381-2242. E-mail: cteditorial@catholiccincinnati.org. Website: www.thecatholictelegraph.com. Tricia Hempel, ed. Diocese newspaper for Cincinnati area (all articles must have a Cincinnati or Ohio connection). Weekly newspaper; 24-28 pgs.; circ. 100,000. Subscription $24. Limited unsolicited freelance; mostly assigned. Send résumé and writing samples for assignment. Pays varying rates on publication for all rts. Articles. Responds in 2-3 wks. Kill fee. No guidelines; copy $2/#10 SASE.

Fillers: Newsbreaks (local).

Special Needs: Personality features for "Everyday Evangelists" section. These are feature stories that offer a slice of life of a person who is making a difference as a Roman Catholic Christian in their community. Prefer to have a tie within the Archdiocese of Cincinnati; must be an Ohioan. Complete ms; 800 words; pays $40 (extra for photos of individual interviewed).

Tips: "Most likely to accept an article about a person, event, or ministry with an Ohio connection—Cincinnati-Dayton area."

$ THE CATHOLIC YEARBOOK, 7010—6th St. N., Oakdale MN 55128. (651) 702-0086. Fax (651) 702-0074. E-mail: catholic2@msn.com. Apostolic Publishing Co. Inc. Roger Jensen, ed. Family magazine of articles and prayers, promoting the sharing of Christian fellowship among Catholics. Annual mag.; 68-72 pgs.; circ. 400,000. 60 percent unsolicited freelance; 40 percent assigned. Complete ms/cover letter. Pays $5-50 on publication for 1st rts. Articles 750-1,500 words (20/yr.). Response time varies. No simultaneous submissions; accepts reprints. Accepts articles on disk or by e-mail (attached file). No kill fee. Uses some sidebars. Prefers NIV. Also accepts submissions from children/teens. Guidelines by mail. (Ads)

> **Poetry:** Buys 10/yr. Light verse, traditional; 15-50 words, up to 150 words. Pays $8-30. Submit max. 3 poems.
> **Fillers:** Buys 5-10/yr. Anecdotes, facts, games, prayers, quizzes, quotes, and word puzzles; 50-300 wds. Pays $5-30.

$ @ CBA RETAILERS + RESOURCES, 9240 Explorer Dr., Colorado Springs CO 80920. Toll-free (800) 252-1950. (719) 272-3555. Fax (719) 272-3510. E-mail: publications@cbaonline.org. Website: www.cbaonline.org. Christian Booksellers Assn. Submit queries to Kathleen Samuelson, publications dir. (samuelson@cbaonline.org). To provide Christian retail store owners and managers with professional retail skills, product information, and industry news. Monthly trade journal (also in digital edition); 48-100 pgs.; circ. 5,000. Subscription $59.95 (for nonmembers). 10 percent unsolicited freelance; 80 percent assigned. Query/clips; fax/e-query OK. Pays .30/wd. on publication for all rts. Articles 800-2,000 words (30/yr. assigned); book/music/video reviews, 150 words, $35. Responds in 8 wks. Seasonal 4-5 mos. ahead. Prefers requested ms mailed in MS Word file. Regularly uses sidebars. Accepts any modern Bible version. (Ads/Dunn & Dunn/856-582-0690)

> **Special Needs:** Trends in retail, consumer buying habits, market profiles. By assignment only.
> **Tips:** "Looking for writers who have been owners/managers/buyers/sales staff in Christian retail stores. Most of our articles are by assignment and focus on producing and selling Christian products or conducting retail business. We also assign reviews of books, music, videos, giftware, kids products, and software to our regular reviewers."

@ CBN.COM (CHRISTIAN BROADCASTING NETWORK), 977 Centerville Turnpike, Virginia Beach VA 23463. (757) 226-3557. Fax (757) 226-3575. E-mail: chris.carpenter@cbn.org or through Website: www.CBN.com. Christian Broadcasting Network. Chris Carpenter, dir. of internal programming; Belinda Elliott, books ed. Online mag.; 1.6 million users/mo. Free online. Open to unsolicited freelance. E-mail submissions (attached as a Word document). Query/clips; e-query OK. **NO PAYMENT.** Devotions 500-700 words; Spiritual Life Teaching, 700-1,500 words; Living Features (Family, Entertainment, Health, Finance), 700-1,500 words; Movie/TV/Music Reviews, 500-1,000 words; Hard News, 300-700 words; News Features, 700-1,500 words; News Interviews, 1,000-2,000 words; fiction. Accepts reprints (tell when/where appeared). Also accepts submissions from teens. Prefers NLT/NASB/NKJV. Guidelines by e-mail; copy online. (No ads)

> **Special Needs:** Adoption stories/references, world religions from Judeo/Christian perspective.
> **Tips:** "In lieu of payment, we link to author's Website and provide a link for people to purchase the author's materials in our Web store."

$ CELEBRATE LIFE, PO Box 1350, Stafford VA 22555. (540) 659-4171. Fax (540) 659-2586. E-mail: CLMag@all.org. Website: www.clmagazine.org. American Life League. Stephanie Hopping, ed. Covers all right-to-life matters according to Catholic teaching. Bimonthly mag.; 48 pgs.; circ. 70,000. Subscription $12.95. 50 percent unsolicited freelance; 50 percent assigned. E-query preferred. Pays on publication according to quality of article for 1st or reprint rts.; or work-for-hire assignments. Articles 400-1,600 wds. Seasonal 4 mos. ahead. Accepts few reprints. Prefers e-mail submissions or disk. No kill fee. Also accepts submissions from children/teens. Prefers Jerusalem Bible (Catholic). Guidelines/theme list on Website. (No ads)

> **Special Needs:** Personal experience about abortion, post-abortion stress/healing, adoption, activism/young people's involvement, death/dying, euthanasia, eugenics, special needs children, personhood, chastity, large families, stem-cell science, and other right-to-life topics.
>
> **Tips:** "We are no-exceptions pro-life in keeping with the Catholic Church. Looking for interviews with pro-life leaders and nonfiction stories about people who live according to pro-life ethics despite diversity. Photos are preferred for personal stories. No fiction or poetry. Break in by submitting work."
>
> ** This periodical was #43 on the 2007 Top 50 Christian Publishers list.

+ **CELEBRATIONS**, PO Box 53, Cordele GA 31010. (229) 938-1760. E-mail: nancybgibbs@aol .com. Website: www.nancybgibbs.com. Southern Baptist. Nancy B. Gibbs, ed. We are a good news Christian newspaper reaching teens to senior adults with stories and articles with a positive attitude toward today's world. Monthly newspaper; 12 pgs.; circ. 900. Subscription free. Estab. 2008. 25 percent unsolicited freelance. Complete ms/cover letter; e-query OK. Accepts full mss by e-mail. **NO PAYMENT** for one-time, reprint, or nonexclusive rts. Not copyrighted. Articles 200-400 wds. (25/yr.). Responds in 4 wks. Seasonal 4 mos. ahead. Accepts simultaneous submissions & reprints. Prefers e-mail submissions (copied into message). Uses some sidebars. Prefers KJV. Copy for $1/9 x 12 SAE/$2.50 postage. (Ads)

> **Poetry:** Accepts 12/yr. Light verse, traditional; 10-20 lines. Submit max. 1 poem.
>
> **Fillers:** Anecdotes, ideas, prayers, prose, quotes, sermon illustrations, short humor; 50-100 wds.
>
> **Columns/Departments:** Accepts 25/yr. Pet Page (nothing about dying pets), 300 wds.; Dinner Page (stories to tell around dinner table), 400 wds.; Sports Page (sports interest), 400 wds.; Family Matters (fun ideas to share with family), 200 wds.; and Happiness Corner (travel ideas, ideas to share with others), 350 wds.
>
> **Tips:** "Columns and fillers most open to freelancers."

CENTRAL FLORIDA EPISCOPALIAN, 1017 E. Robinson St., Orlando FL 32801. Toll-free (800) 299-3567. (407) 423-3567. Fax (407) 872-0006. E-mail: joethoma@aol.com. Website: www.cfdiocese .org. Episcopal Diocese of Central Florida. Joe Thoma, ed. To spread the Good Word of Jesus Christ to the people of Central Florida, the U.S., and the world. Monthly mag.; circ. 24,000. Subscription $10. Open to unsolicited freelance. Articles. Incomplete topical listings. (Ads)

$ **CGA WORLD**, PO Box 249, Olyphant PA 18447. Toll-free (800) 836-5699. (570) 586-1091. Fax (570) 586-7721. E-mail: cgaemail@aol.com. Website: www.catholicgoldenage.org. Catholic Golden Age. Barbara Pegula, mng. ed. For Catholics 50+. Quarterly newsletter. Subscription/membership $12. Uses little freelance. Query. Pays .10/wd. on publication for 1st, onetime, or reprint rts. Articles 600-1,000 words; fiction 600-1,000 words. Responds in 6 wks. Seasonal 6 mos. ahead. Accepts reprints (tell when/where appeared). Accepts requested ms on disk. Guidelines by mail; copy for 9 x 12 SAE/3 stamps. (Ads)

@ **CHALLENGE WEEKLY**, PO Box 68-800, Newton, Auckland, New Zealand 1032. Tel. (64-9) 378 4052, or +64 027 271 2849. Fax (64-9) 376 3855. E-mail: editor@challengeweekly.co.nz or through Website: www.challengeweekly.co.nz. Challenge Publishing Society. Garth George, ed. New Zealand's Christian Newspaper. Proclaiming the good news that Jesus is the Christ. Weekly online newspaper. Subscription $68. Incomplete topical listings.

$ @ **CHARISMA**, 600 Rinehart Rd., Lake Mary FL 32746. (407) 333-0600. Fax (407) 333-7100. E-mail: charisma@strang.com. Website: www.charismamag.com. Strang Communications. J. Lee

Grady, exec. ed.; Jimmy Stewart, mng. ed.; submit to Adrienne S. Gaines, assoc. ed. Primarily for the Pentecostal and Charismatic Christian community. Monthly & online mag.; 100+ pgs.; circ. 250,000. Subscription $19.97. 80 percent assigned freelance. Query only; no phone query, e-query OK. Pays up to $1,000 (for assigned) on publication for all rts. Articles 2,000-3,000 words (40/yr.); book/music reviews, 200 words, $20-35. Responds in 8-12 wks. Seasonal 5 mos. ahead. Kill fee $50. Prefers accepted ms by e-mail. Regularly uses sidebars. Guidelines on Website; free copy. (Ads)

   Tips: "Most open to news section, reviews, or features. Query (published clips help a lot)."
   ** #1 Best-selling magazine in Christian retail stores.

THE CHARLOTTE WORLD, 4701 Beech Crest Pl., Charlotte NC 28269. (704) 661-9137. Fax (704) 295-7919. E-mail: warren.smith@thecharlotteworld.com. Website: www.thecharlotteworld.com. World Newspaper Publishing. Warren Smith, ed. To report unreported, under-reported, or badly reported news, from a Christian perspective. Online newspaper; circ. 20,000. Subscription $36. Open to unsolicited freelance. Query preferred. Articles; reviews. Incomplete topical listings. (Ads)

   ** 2007 EPA Award of Merit—Newspaper; 2006 EPA Award of Excellence—Newspaper.

$ CHICKEN SOUP FOR THE SOUL BOOK SERIES, PO Box 700, Cos Cob CT 06807. Fax (203) 861-7194. E-mail: webmaster@chickensoupforthesoul.com. Website: www.chickensoup.com. Barbara LoMonaco, ed. (blomonaco@chickensoupforthesoul.com). Inspirational anthologies to open your heart and rekindle your spirit; audience is open to all ages, races, etc. Quarterly trade paperback books; 385 pgs.; circ. 60 million. $14.95/book. 98 percent unsolicited freelance. Make submissions via Website. Pays $200 (plus 10 free copies of the book, worth more than $110) on publication for reprint, simultaneous, & electronic rts. Articles 1,200 words max. Seasonal anytime. Accepts simultaneous submissions & reprints (tell when/where appeared). Prefers e-mail submissions: Go to www. chickensoupforthesoul.com and click on "Submit Your Story" on the left tool bar. No kill fee. Guidelines/themes on Website; free sample. (No ads)

   Fillers: Anecdotes, cartoons, facts, kid quotes, quotes, short humor; 10-200 wds. Pays.
   Special Needs: See Website for a list of upcoming titles.
   Contest: See Website for list of current contests.
   Tips: "Visit our Website and be familiar with our book series. Send in stories via mail or e-mail, complete with contact information. Submit story typed, double-spaced, max. 1,200 words, in a Word document."

@ CHOCOLATE PAGES ONLINE MAGAZINE, 33011 Tall Oaks St., Farmington Hills MI 48336-4551. (248) 249-2300. Fax (248) 471-2422. E-mail: pamperry@ministrymarketingsolutions .com. Website: www.ministrymarketingsolutions.com or www.chocolatepagesnetwork.com. Ministry Marketing Solutions. Pam Perry, pub. About current books targeting the African American Christian market; goes to bookstores, book clubs, black media, Christian media, church reading groups, and writer's clubs. Books for review accepted via mail and press kits via e-mail.

@ CHRISTIAN BUSINESS DAILY.COM, c/o Selling Among Wolves LLC, 379 Interstate Blvd., Sarasota FL 34240. (941) 377-9384. Fax (941) 371-6211. E-mail: articles@christianbusinessdaily.com or through Website: www.christianbusinessdaily.com. Jeremy Harrison, online dir. Business news from a Christian worldview. E-zine. Open to freelance. Query. **NO PAYMENT**. Articles. Incomplete topical listings. (Ads)

@ THE CHRISTIAN CHRONICLE, PO Box 11000, Oklahoma City OK 73013. (405) 425-5070. Fax (405) 425-5076. E-mail: bailey.mcbride@oc.edu, or through Website: www.christianchronicle .org. Churches of Christ. Bobbie Ross Jr, ed.; Tamie Ross, online ed. An international newspaper for members of the Church of Christ. Monthly newspaper & online. Subscription $20 (onetime fee). Incomplete topical listings.

$ CHRISTIAN CITIZEN USA, PO Box 49365, Dayton OH 45377-0365. Toll-Free (877) 428-6397. (937) 233-6227. Fax (937) 233-6231. E-mail: editor@ccn-usa.net. Website: www.citizenusa.us. Christian Media Group Inc. Pendra Lee Snyder, pub. Only Judeo-Christian newspaper in Ohio; news features, current events presented from Judeo-Christian worldview. Monthly newspaper; circ. 30,000. Subscription $52. 10 percent unsolicited freelance; 75 percent assigned. Query/clips; phone/fax/e-query OK. Accepts full mss by e-mail. Pay up to $25 on publication for all (if assigned) or 1st rts. Articles 600-800 words; book reviews, 500-600 words; music reviews, 200-300 words; video reviews, 500 words (pays $20-25). Responds in 4 wks. Seasonal 2-3 mos. ahead. Prefers e-mail submissions (copied into message). No kill fee. Uses some sidebars. Also accepts submissions from teens. Prefers KJV. (Ads) Guidelines by e-mail/Website.

> **Fillers:** Buys 4/yr. Cartoons, games, short humor, word puzzles. Pays $20-25.
>
> **Columns/Departments:** Buys 4/yr. News features, under 800 words, $20-50 or no payment. E-query.
>
> **Tips:** "Most open to current news features, or current events/political."

@ CHRISTIAN COMPUTING MAGAZINE, PO Box 319, Belton MO 64012. Toll-free phone/fax (800) 456-1868. (816) 331-8142. E-mail: steve@ccmag.com or through Website: www.ccmag.com. Steve Hewitt, ed-in-chief. For Christian/church computer users. Monthly (11x) & online mag.; 2 pgs.; circ. 30,000. Subscription $14.95, or free digital version. 40 percent unsolicited freelance. Query/clips; fax/e-query OK. **NO PAYMENT** for all rts. Articles 1,000-1,800 words (12/yr.). Responds in 4 wks. Seasonal 2 mos. ahead. Accepts reprints. Requires requested ms on disk. Regularly uses sidebars. Guidelines by mail; copy for 9 x 12 SAE.

> **Fillers:** Accepts 6 cartoons/yr.
>
> **Columns/Departments:** Accepts 12/yr. Telecommunications (computer), 1,500-1,800 words.
>
> **Special Needs:** Articles on Internet, DTP, computing.

$ CHRISTIAN COURIER (Canada), 5 Joanna Dr., St. Catherines ON L2N 1V1, Canada. (U.S. address: Box 110, Lewiston NY 14092-0110). Toll-free (800) 969-4838. (905) 682-8311. Toll-free fax (800) 969-4838. (905) 682-8313. E-mail: editor@christiancourier.ca. Website: www.christian courier.ca. Reformed Faith Witness. Bert Witvoet, interim ed. (bert.witvoet@sympatico.ca). To present Canadian and international news, both religious and general, from a Reformed Christian perspective. Biweekly tabloid; 24-28 pgs.; circ. 4,000. Subscription $40 Cdn.; $32, U.S. 20 percent unsolicited freelance; 80 percent assigned. Complete ms/cover letter; fax/e-query OK. Pays $75-120 U.S., up to. 10/wd. for assigned ($50-100 for unsolicited); 30 days after publication for onetime, reprint, or simultaneous rts. Not copyrighted. Articles 700-1,200 words (40/yr.); fiction to 1,200-2,500 words (6/yr.); book reviews 800-1,200 words. Responds in 1-3 wks. Seasonal 3 mos. ahead. Accepts simultaneous submissions & reprints (tell when/where appeared). Prefers accepted ms by e-mail (attached file). No kill fee. Uses some sidebars. Prefers NIV. Guidelines/deadlines on Website; no copy. (Ads)

> **Poetry:** Buys 12/yr. Avant-garde, free verse, light verse, traditional; 10-30 lines; $20-30. Submit max. 5 poems.
>
> **Tips:** "Suggest an aspect of the theme which you believe you could cover well, have insight into, could treat humorously, etc. Show that you think clearly, write clearly, and have something to say that we should want to read. Have a strong biblical worldview and avoid moralism and sentimentality." Responds only if material is accepted.

CHRISTIAN COURIER (WI), 1933 W. Wisconsin Ave., Milwaukee WI 53233. (414) 345-3545. Fax (414) 918-4503. E-mail: editor@ChristianCourierNewspaper.com. Website: www.christiancourier newspaper.com. ProBuColls Assn. Dr. Dennis Hill, ed. To propagate the gospel of Jesus Christ and cover those events which demonstrate Christian unity. Monthly newspaper; circ. 10,000. 10 percent freelance. Query; e-query OK. **PAYS IN COPIES**, for onetime rts. Not copyrighted. Articles 300-1,500 words (6/yr.). Responds in 4-8 wks. Seasonal 2 mos. ahead. Accepts reprints. Guidelines by mail; free copy. (Ads)

> **Special Needs:** Human interest, special ministries; see editorial calendar for details.
>
> **Tips:** "We are looking for bloggers who can objectively cover nondenominational Christian events in Wisconsin, the U.S. and globally."

$ @ **CHRISTIAN EXAMINER**, PO Box 2606, El Cajon CA 92021. (619) 668-5100. Fax (619) 668-1115. E-mail: info@christianexaminer.com. Website: www.christianexaminer.com. Keener Communications. Lori Arnold, ed. To report on current events from an evangelical Christian perspective, particularly traditional family values and church trends. Monthly & online newspaper; 24-36 pgs.; circ. 180,000. Subscription $19.95. 5 percent assigned. Query/clips. Pays .10/wd., on publication for 1st & electronic rts. Articles 600-900 wds. Responds in 4-5 wks. Seasonal 3 mos. ahead. No simultaneous submissions or reprints. Prefers e-mail submissions (copied into message). No kill fee. Uses some sidebars. Guidelines by e-mail; copy $1.50/9 x 12 SAE. (Ads)

> **Tips:** "We prefer news stories."
>
> ** 2007, 2006, 2005 EPA Award of Merit—Newspaper. Member of Fellowship of Christian Newspapers (FCN).

@ **CHRISTIAN FAMILY JOURNAL**, 312 Point Pleasant Dr., St. Augustine FL 32086. (904) 471-4307. E-mail: laurie@christianfamilypublications.com. Website: www.christianfamilypublications .com. Providing positive, Christian information to families across the Southeast (more than one publication). Laurie Stroud, pub. Monthly & online mags.; 24-36 pgs; circ. 10,000-30,000/market. Subscription free or available for $25. Open to unsolicited freelance. Query; e-query OK. **NO PAYMENT**. Articles 500 words (150/yr.); reviews 300-500 words; rarely uses fiction. Responds in a few wks. Seasonal 3 mos. ahead. No simultaneous submissions or reprints. Prefers e-mail submission (attached file in Word doc.). Uses some sidebars. Guidelines by e-mail; copy for 9 x 12 SAE/$3 postage. (Ads)

> **Columns/Departments:** Accepts 10-15/mo. Query.

CHRISTIAN HEALTH CARE NEWSLETTER, PO Box 3618, Peoria IL 61612-3618. Toll-free (888) 268-4377. Fax (309) 689-0764. E-mail: infopac@smchcn.org. Website: www.samaritanministries.org. Samaritan Ministries Intl. Ray King, ed. Health issues. Monthly newsletter; circ. 12,000. Subscription $12. Open to unsolicited freelance. Articles & reviews. Incomplete topical listings. (Ads)

$ **THE CHRISTIAN HERALD**, PO Box 68526, Brampton ON L6R 0J8, Canada. (905) 874-1731. Fax (905) 874-1781. E-mail: info@christianherald.ca. Website: www.christianherald.ca. Covenant Communications. Fazal Karim Jr., ed-in-chief. A Canadian-Christian tabloid with a focus on Christian arts and entertainment. Monthly tabloid; 24 pgs.; circ. 30,000. Subscription free, or $25 if mailed (Canadian residents add 5 percent sales tax). 5 percent unsolicited freelance; 95 percent assigned. Query; fax/e-query OK. Pays $20-100 or.10/wd. on publication for 1st rts. Articles 500-1,500 words; product reviews 150-200 words. Responds in 4 wks. Seasonal 3 mos. ahead. Accepts simultaneous submissions & reprints (tell when/where appeared). Prefers e-mail submissions (attached file). No kill fee. Uses some sidebars. Also accepts submissions from teens. Prefers ESV, KJV, NLT. Guidelines by mail/e-mail; copy for 9 x 12 SAE/$2 Canadian postage. (Ads)

> **Fillers:** Accepts 10/yr. Cartoons, facts, games, jokes, prayers, quotes, and word puzzles; 20-100 wds. No payment.
>
> **Columns/Departments:** Interviews (Christian newsmakers/personalities), 900 words, $20-50.
>
> **Tips:** "Most open to articles/columns with specific reference to Canadians, with Canadian quotes, relevance, etc."

$ **CHRISTIAN HISTORY**, 465 Gundersen Dr., Carol Stream IL 60188. (630) 480-2004. Fax (630) 260-0114. E-mail: CHeditor@christianhistory.net. Website: www.christianhistory.net. Christianity

Today Intl. Submit to Assistant Editor. To teach Christian history to educated readers in an engaging manner. Quarterly mag. & newsletter; 52 pgs.; circ. 50,000. Subscription $12. 5 percent unsolicited freelance; 95 percent assigned. Query only. Pays .10-.25/wd. on publication for 1st rts. Articles 500-3,000 words (1/yr.). Responds in 2 mos. Accepts reprints (tell when/where appeared). Prefers accepted ms by e-mail (attached or copied into message). Kill fee 50 percent. Regularly uses sidebars. Prefers NIV. Guidelines/theme list by mail/e-mail; copy for 9 x 12 SASE. (Ads)

> **Tips:** "Let us know your particular areas of specialization and any books or articles you have published in the area of Christian history. Theme-related articles are usually assigned. Most open to non-themed departments: Story Behind; People Worth Knowing; Turning Point. Please familiarize yourself with our magazine before querying."
>
> ** 2009, 2008, 2005 EPA Award of Merit—General.

$ CHRISTIAN HOME & SCHOOL, 3350 East Paris Ave. S.E., Grand Rapids MI 49512. Toll-free (800) 635-8288. (616) 957-1070, ext. 239. Fax (616) 957-5022. E-mail: mleon@CSIonline.org. Website: www.CSIonline.org. Christian Schools Intl. Amy Bross, ed. For parents of children of all ages; offering a biblical perspective on all areas of parenting. Biannual mag.; 36 pgs.; circ. 67,000. Subscription $13.95. 95 percent unsolicited; 5 percent assigned. Complete ms or query, prefers e-query. Pays $50-250 on publication for 1st rts. Articles 1,000-2,000 words (30/yr.); Christmas fiction 1,000-2,000 words (5/yr.); book reviews $25 (assigned). Responds in 4 wks. Seasonal 7 mos. ahead. Accepts simultaneous query. Prefers mss by e-mail (attached or copied into message). Regularly uses sidebars. Accepts submissions from children/teens. Prefers NIV. Guidelines/theme list by mail/Website; copy for 7 x 10 SAE/4 stamps. (Ads)

> **Note:** Check Website for changes at this publication.
>
> **Fillers:** Parenting ideas; 100-250 words; $25-40.
>
> **Tips:** "Writers can break in by having articles written about parenting (at all stages of life), geared from a Christian perspective and current with the times."
>
> ** 2007 EPA Award of Merit—Organizational. This periodical was #41 on the 2009 Top 50 Christian Publishers list (#36 in 2008, #44 in 2007, #32 in 2006, #44 in 2005).

$ @ CHRISTIANITY TODAY, 465 Gundersen Dr., Carol Stream IL 60188-2498. (630) 260-6200. Fax (630) 260-8428. E-mail: cteditor@christianitytoday.com. Website: www.christianitytoday.com/ctmag. Christianity Today Inc. Mark Galli, ed. For evangelical Christian thought leaders who seek to integrate their faith commitment with responsible action. Monthly & online mag.; 65-120 pgs.; circ. 155,000. Subscription $24.95. Not currently accepting freelance submissions; if you have written for them in the past, contact the editor you worked with or e-mail them to find out how to contact that editor. Pays .25-.35/wd. on publication for 1st rts. Articles 1,000-4,000 words (60/yr.); book reviews 800-1,000 words (pays per-page rate). Responds in 13 wks. Seasonal 8 mos. ahead. Accepts reprints (tell when/where appeared—payment 25 percent of regular rate). Kill fee 50 percent. Does not use sidebars. Prefers NIV. Guidelines on Website; copy for 9 x 12 SAE/3 stamps. (Ads)

> **Tips:** "Read the magazine." Does not return unsolicited manuscripts.
>
> ** #8 Best-selling Magazine in Christian retail stores. 2008, 2006, 2005 EPA Award of Excellence—General. 2009 Award of Merit—General. 2006, 2005 EPA Award of Merit—Online (for ChristianityToday Online).

$ @ CHRISTIANITY TODAY MOVIES, 465 Gundersen Dr., Carol Stream IL 60188. (630) 260-6200. Fax (630) 260-8428. E-mail: CTmovies@christianitytoday.com. Website: www.ChristianityTodayMovies.com. Christianity Today Intl. Mark Moring, ed. To inform and equip Christian moviegoers to make discerning choices about films, through timely coverage, insightful reviews and interviews, educated opinion, and relevant news, all from a Christian worldview. Weekly e-zine. Subscription free. 10 percent unsolicited freelance; 90 percent assigned. Query; fax/e-query OK. Accepts full mss by e-mail. Pays $75-125 on acceptance for 1st rts. Articles 500-2,000 words (150/yr.) & movie reviews 700-

1,000 words ($110). Responds in 2 wks. No seasonal. Sometimes accepts simultaneous submissions and reprints (tell when/where appeared). Prefers e-mail submissions (attached file). Some kill fees 50 percent. Uses some sidebars. Prefers NIV. No guidelines; copy online. (Ads)

Tips: "Study our Website; know what we're doing. Always looking for commentaries and/or news pieces on trends in the industry, especially as they relate to a Christian audience."

** 2009, 2007 EPA Award of Merit—Online. This periodical was #37 on the 2009 Top 50 Christian Publishers list (#35 in 2008).

\$ @ **THE CHRISTIAN JOURNAL**, 1032 W. Main, Medford OR 97501. (541) 773-4004. Fax (541) 773-9917. E-mail: info@thechristianjournal.org. Website: www.TheChristianJournal.org. Lifting the Cross Ministries. Chad McComas, ed. Dedicated to sharing encouragement with the body of Christ in Southern Oregon and Northern California. Monthly & online newspaper; 16-24 pgs.; circ. 15,000. Subscription $20; most copies distributed free. 50 percent unsolicited freelance; 50 percent assigned. Complete ms; phone/fax query OK. Pays .01/wd. on publication for onetime rts. Articles & fiction to 500 words; reviews to 500 words; children's stories 500 words. Prefers articles by e-mail to info@ thechristianjournal.org (attached file). Also accepts submissions from children/teens. Guidelines/ theme list by e-mail/Website; copy online. (Ads)

Poetry: Accepts 12-20/yr. Free verse, haiku, light verse, traditional; 4-12 lines. Submit max. 2 poems.

Fillers: Accepts 50/yr. Anecdotes, cartoons, jokes, kid quotes, newsbreaks, prayers, quotes, short humor, or word puzzles; 100-300 wds.

Columns/Departments: Accepts 6/yr. Youth; Seniors; Children's stories; all to 500 words.

Tips: "Send articles on themes; each issue has a theme. Theme articles get first choice."

@ **CHRISTIAN MEDIA**, Box 448, Jacksonville OR 97530. (541) 899-8888. E-mail: James@ ChristianMediaNetwork.com. Website: www.ChristianMediaDaily.com or www.ChristianMediaNetwork .com. James Lloyd, ed./pub. Updates on world conditions, politics, economics, in the light of prophecy. Quarterly & online tabloid; 24 pgs.; circ. 25,000. Query; prefers phone query. **NO PAYMENT** for negotiable rts. Articles; book & music reviews, 3 paragraphs. Accepts simultaneous submissions & reprints. Prefers requested ms on disk. Requires KJV. Copy for 9 x 12 SAE/2 stamps.

Special Needs: Particularly interested in stories that expose dirty practices in the industry— royalty rip-offs, misleading ads, financial misconduct, etc. No flowery pieces on celebrities; wants well-documented articles on abuse in the media.

CHRISTIAN MOTORSPORTS ILLUSTRATED, 1066 W. Taft, Ste. 166, Sapulpa, OK 47066. (607) 742-3407. E-mail: articles@christianmotorsports.com or through Website: www.christianmotorsports .com. CPO Publishing. Roland Osborne, pub.; Tammy Maxey, ed. Covers the entire world of motorsports, from NASCAR to dirt, snowmobile, drag boat, NHRA, go-karts, Moto-X, car shows, bike rallies, lawnmower races, etc., with a unique Christian spin. Quarterly mag.; 64 pgs.; circ. 74,000. Subscription $20. 50 percent unsolicited freelance. Complete ms; e-query OK. **PAYS IN COPIES**. Articles 650-1,200 words (30/yr.). Seasonal 4 mos. ahead. Requires requested ms by e-mail or through Website. Regularly uses sidebars. Guidelines on Website. (Ads)

Fillers: Accepts 100/yr. Anecdotes, cartoons, facts, games, ideas, jokes, newsbreaks, prayers, prose, quizzes, quotes, short humor.

Columns/Departments: Accepts 10/yr.

Tips: "Christians involved in motorsports, tech-tips, bike ministries, etc. CMI is chrome, smoke, and big engines—with Jesus in the middle! If it relates to motorsports, try us. Relevant photos to accompany article required. Browse Website and read one of our mags to get a flavor for the publication."

CHRISTIAN NEWS NORTHWEST, PO Box 974, Newberg OR 97132. Phone/fax (503) 537-9220. E-mail: cnnw@cnnw.com. Website: www.cnnw.com. John Fortmeyer, ed./pub. News of ministry in the evangelical Christian community in western and central Oregon and southwest Washington; distributed primarily through evangelical churches. Monthly newspaper; 28-40 pgs.; circ. 29,000. Subscription $20. 10 percent unsolicited freelance; 5 percent assigned. Query; phone/fax/e-query OK. **NO PAYMENT**. Not copyrighted. Articles 300-400 words (100/yr.). Responds in 4 wks. Seasonal 3 mos. ahead. Accepts reprints (tell when/where appeared). Accepts e-mail submissions. Regularly uses sidebars. Guidelines by mail/e-mail; copy $1.50. (Ads)

> **Tips:** "Most open to ministry-oriented features. Our space is always tight, but stories on lesser-known, Northwest-based ministries are encouraged. Keep it very concise. Since we focus on the Pacific Northwest, it would probably be difficult for anyone outside the region to break into our publication."
> ** 2006 EPA Award of Merit—Newspaper.

THE CHRISTIAN OBSERVER, 9400 Fairview Ave., Ste. 200, Manassas VA 22110. (703) 335-2844. Fax (703) 368-4817. E-mail: editor@christianobserver.org, or christianobserver@comcast.net. Website: www.ChristianObserver.org. Christian Observer Foundation; Presbyterian Reformed. Dr. Edwin P. Elliott, mng. ed. To encourage and edify God's people and families; print version of Presbyterians-Week. Monthly newspaper; 32 pgs.; circ. 2,000. Subscription $27. 10 percent unsolicited freelance; 90 percent assigned. Query; phone/e-query OK. **NO PAYMENT**. Accepts e-mail submissions. (Ads)

@ CHRISTIAN ONLINE MAGAZINE. E-mail: submissions@christianmagazine.org. Website: www.ChristianMagazine.org. Darlene Osborne, pub. Strictly founded on the Word of God, this magazine endeavors to bring you the best Christian information on the net. Monthly e-zine. Subscription free. 10 percent unsolicited freelance; 90 percent assigned. E-query. Articles 500-700 wds. Responds in 1 wk. Seasonal 2 mos. ahead. Prefers accepted ms by e-mail (attached file). **NO PAYMENT**. Regularly uses sidebars. Also accepts submissions from children/teens. Prefers KJV. Guidelines on Website. (Ads)

> **Fillers:** Accepts 50/yr. Prayers, prose, quizzes, short humor; 500 wds.
> **Columns/Departments:** Variety Column, 700-1,000 wds. Query.
> **Tips:** "Most open to solid Christian articles founded on the Word of God."

@ THE CHRISTIAN OUTLOOK, 492 Hob Moor Rd., Yardley, Birmingham B25 8UB, United Kingdom. Phone +44 870 383 0197. Fax +44 870 199 2302. E-mail through Website: www.thechristianoutlook.net. Nondenominational. Issues on life and living from a Christian perspective. Online newspaper. Free online. Open to unsolicited freelance. Submit through Website. Incomplete topical listings.

> **Tips:** "We also maintain forums for online interaction among Christians, and between Christians and non-Christians."

CHRISTIAN PRESS NEWSPAPER (formerly *The Chronicle*—Kansas Edition), 504 N. Main St., Newton KS 67114. (316) 283-8300. Fax (316) 283-6090. E-mail: editor@christianpress.com. Website: www.christianpress.com. Russ Jones, pub. Monthly Newspaper; circ. 80,000. Articles/reviews. See Website for details.

> **Tips:** "We inform the public of issues that affect our decision making, encourage and build up the body of Christ, and are a tool to bring others to a life-changing decision for Christ and give back to our community."

+ CHRISTIAN QUARTERLY, PO Box 311, Palo Cedro CA 97073. Phone/fax (530) 247-7500. E-mail: ChristQtly@aol.com. Nondenominational. Cathy Jansen, pub. Uplifting and encouraging articles. Quarterly tabloid; 28 pgs; circ. 15,000. Subscription free. 100 percent unsolicited freelance. Phone or e-query. Accepts full mss by e-mail. **NO PAYMENT**. Not copyrighted. Articles to 1,200 wds. Responds immediately. Accepts reprints (tell when/where appeared). Accepts e-mail (attached or copied into message). Never uses sidebars. Also accepts submissions from children/teens. Guidelines by e-mail; copy for 10 x 13 SAE/$2 postage. (Ads)

Poetry: Accepts 6-10/yr. Free verse, traditional.

Fillers: Accepts anecdotes, cartoons, ideas, quotes, short humor, and word puzzles.

Columns/Departments: Uses many. Marriage & Family; Health; Financial; (testimonies).

Special Needs: "Articles helping people grow in their Christian walk."

THE CHRISTIAN RANCHMAN/COWBOYS FOR CHRIST, 311 FM 718, Newark TX 76071, or PO Box 7557, Fort Worth TX 76111. (817) 236-0023. Fax (817) 236-0024. E-mail: cwb4christ@ cowboysforchrist.net. Website: www.CowboysforChrist.net. Interdenominational. Ted Pressley, ed. Monthly tabloid; 20 pgs.; circ. 43,800. No subscription. 85 percent unsolicited freelance. Complete ms/cover letter. **NO PAYMENT** for all rts. Articles 350-1,000 words; book/video reviews (length open). Does not use sidebars. No guidelines; sample copy.

Poetry: Accepts 40/yr. Free verse. Submit max. 3 poems.

Fillers: Accepts all types.

Tips: "We're most open to true-life Christian stories, Christian testimonies, and Christian or livestock news. Contact us with your ideas first."

$ CHRISTIAN RENEWAL, Box 770, Lewiston NY 14092-0770, or PO Box 777, Jordan Sta., ON L0R 1S0, Canada. (905) 562-5059. Fax (905) 562-1368. E-mail: JVANDYK@aol.com. Website: www.crmag .com. Reformed (Conservative). John Van Dyk, ed. Church-related and world news for members of the Reformed community of churches in North America. Biweekly newspaper; 40-48 pgs.; circ. 3,500. Subscription $41 U.S./$43 Cdn. (christianrenewal@hotmail.com). 5 percent unsolicited freelance; 20 percent assigned. Query/clips; e-query OK. Pays $25-100 for onetime rts. Articles 500-3,000 words; fiction 2,000 words (6/yr.); book reviews 50-200 words. Seasonal 3 mos. ahead. Accepts simultaneous submissions & reprints. Prefers e-mail submission (copied into message). Uses some sidebars. Prefers NIV, ESV. No guidelines; copy $2. (Ads: christianrenewal@hotmail.com)

$ CHRISTIAN RESEARCH JOURNAL, PO Box 8500, Charlotte NC 28271-8500. (704) 887-8200. Fax (704) 887-8299. E-mail: submissions@equip.org. Website: www.equip.org. Christian Research Institute. Elliot Miller, ed-in-chief; Melanie Cogdill, ed. Probing today's religious movements, promoting doctrinal discernment and critical thinking, and providing reasons for Christian faith and ethics. Quarterly mag.; 64 pgs.; circ. 30,000. Subscription $30. 75 percent freelance. Query or complete ms/cover letter; fax query OK; e-query & submissions OK. Pays .16/wd. on publication for 1st rts. Articles to 4,200 words (25/yr.); book reviews 1,100-2,500 words. Responds in 4 mos. Accepts simultaneous submissions. Kill fee to 50 percent. Guidelines by mail/e-mail (guidelines@ equip.org); copy $6. (Ads)

Columns/Departments: Effective Evangelism, 1,700 words; Viewpoint, 875 words; News Watch, to 2,500 words.

Special Needs: Viewpoint on Christian faith and ethics, 1,700 words; news pieces, 800-1,200 words.

Tips: "Be familiar with the Journal in order to know what we are looking for. We accept freelance articles in all sections (features and departments). E-mail for writer's guidelines."

$ THE CHRISTIAN RESPONSE, PO Box 125, Staples MN 56479-0125. (218) 894-1165. E-mail: happyc@arvig.net. Website: www.brainerd.net/~hapco2. HAPCO Industries. Hap Corbett, ed./pub. Exposes anti-Christian bias in America and encourages readers to write letters against such bias. Bimonthly newsletter; 6 pgs. Subscription $13. 10 percent unsolicited freelance. Complete ms/ cover letter; e-query OK. Accepts full mss by e-mail after acceptance. Pays $5-20 on acceptance for onetime rts. Articles 50-700 words (4-6/yr.). Responds in 2 wks. Seasonal 6 mos. ahead. Accepts simultaneous submissions & reprints. Does not use sidebars. Guidelines; copy for $2 or 5 stamps. (Ads—classified only)

Fillers: Buys 2-3/yr. Anecdotes, facts, quotes; up to 150 words; $5-10.

Special Needs: Articles on anti-Christian bias; tips on writing effective letters to the editor; pieces on outstanding accomplishments of Christians in the secular media.

Tips: "The best way to break in is to uncover an instance of a Christian being denied civil rights by any public unit or government agency because of being a Christian, and writing a concise 500-700 word article about it."

$ @ **CHRISTIAN RETAILING**, 600 Rinehart Rd., Lake Mary FL 32746. (407) 333-0600. Fax (407) 333-7133. E-mail: Christian.Retailing@strang.com. Website: www.christianretailing.com. Strang Communications. Andy Butcher, ed. (andy.butcher@strang.com). For Christian product industry manufacturers, distributors, retailers. Trade journal published 14x/yr.; circ. 9,500 (print), 14,000 (digital). Subscription $75. 10 percent assigned. Query/clips; no phone/fax/e-query. Pays .25/wd. on publication for articles; book reviews (no payment). No simultaneous submissions. Accepts requested mss by e-mail (attached file). Kill fee. Uses some sidebars. Prefers NIV. Guidelines available from mng. ed. as needed. (Ads)

Tips: Also publishes 2 supplements: The Church Bookstore (7x/yr.) and Inspirational Gift Trends (4x/yr.).

$ @ **CHRISTIAN STANDARD**, 8805 Governor's Hill Dr., Ste. 400, Cincinnati OH 45249. (513) 931-4050. Fax (513) 931-0950. E-mail: christianstandard@standardpub.com. Website: www.christian standard.com. Standard Publishing/Christian Churches/Churches of Christ. Mark A. Taylor, ed. Devoted to the restoration of New Testament Christianity, its doctrines, its ordinances, and its fruits. Weekly & online mag.; 16 pgs.; circ. 30,000. Subscription $45. 40 percent unsolicited freelance; 60 percent assigned. Complete ms; no phone/fax/e-query. Pays $20-200 on publication for onetime, reprint, & electronic rts. Articles 800-1,600 words (200/yr.). Responds in 9 wks. Seasonal 8-12 mos. ahead. Accepts reprints (tell when/where appeared). Guidelines/copy on Website. (Ads)

Tips: "We would like to hear ministers and elders tell about the efforts made in their churches. Has the church grown? developed spiritually? overcome adversity? succeeded in missions?"

+ @ **CHRISTIAN VOICE MAGAZINE**, PO Box 147, Kennedy AL 35574. (205) 662-4826. Fax (205) 596-4375. E-mail: news@christianvoicemagazine.com or editor@christianvoicemagazine .com. Website: www.christianvoicemagazine.com. Distributed by Wilds & Assocs. John Lanier, exec. ed. Christian music news & information. Monthly print and digital mag. Estab. 2006. Subscription $20 print; $10 digital download. Open to unsolicited freelance. Complete ms/copy ready. Music-related news articles. Guidelines on Website. Not included in topical listings.

$ **CHRISTIANWEEK**, Box 725, Winnipeg MB R3C 2K3, Canada. Toll-free (800) 263-6695. (204) 982-2060. Fax (204) 947-5632. E-mail: admin@christianweek.org. Website: www.christianweek .org. Fellowship for Print Witness. Doug Koop, edit. dir.; Jerrod Peters, mng. ed. Canada's leading Christian news source; telling the stories of God and His people in Canada. Biweekly tabloid newspaper; 8-24 pgs.; circ. 2,000. Subscription $44.95 (Cdn.), $65.95 (U.S.). Query; phone/fax/e-query OK. Accepts full mss by e-mail. Pays .10/wd. on publication for onetime & electronic rts. Not copyrighted. Articles 400-1,500 words (200/yr.); book reviews 400 words (pays free book). Responds in 1-2 wks. Seasonal 4 mos. ahead. Accepts simultaneous submissions & reprints (tell when/where appeared). Prefers accepted ms by e-mail (attached). Sometimes pays kill fee. Uses some sidebars. Prefers NRSV. Guidelines on Website; copy for 9 x 12 SASE. (Ads)

Tips: "Most open to general news, profiles, and features. Writers are encouraged to query first with ideas about people or news events in their own community (Canadian angles, please) or denomination that would be of interest to readers in other denominations or in other areas of the country."

CHURCH HERALD AND HOLINESS BANNER, 7407 Metcalf, Overland Park KS 66212. Fax (913) 722-0351. E-mail: HBeditor@juno.com. Website: www.heraldandbanner.com. Church of God

(Holiness)/Herald and Banner Press. Mark D. Avery, gen mngr. Offers the conservative holiness movement a positive outlook on their church, doctrine, future ministry, and movement. Monthly mag.; 24 pgs.; circ. 1,100. Subscription $12.50. 5 percent unsolicited freelance; 5 percent assigned. Query; e-query OK. Accepts full mss by e-mail. **NO PAYMENT** for onetime, reprint, or simultaneous rts. Not copyrighted. Articles 600-1,200 words (3-5/yr.). Responds in 9 wks. Seasonal 6 mos. ahead. Accepts simultaneous submissions & reprints (tell when/where appeared). Accepts requested ms on disk or by e-mail (attached file). Uses some sidebars. Prefers KJV. Also accepts submissions from children/teens. No guidelines; copy for 9 x 12 SAE/2 stamps. (No ads)

Fillers: Anecdotes, quizzes; 150-400 words.

Tips: "Most open to short inspirational/devotional articles. Must be concise, well written, and get one main point across; 200-600 wds. Be well acquainted with the Wesleyan/Holiness doctrine and tradition. Articles which are well written and express this conviction are very likely to be used."

$ CHURCHMOUSE PUBLICATIONS LLC, PO Box 9, Hudson NH 03051. E-mail: submissions@ churchmousepublications.com. Website: www.churchmousepublications.com. Estab. 2008. Clarice G. James, ed. Web-based Christian publishing syndicate serving the Christian community. 80 percent unsolicited freelance; 10 percent assigned. Send complete ms through Website. Markets to periodicals, newspapers, churches, faith-based organizations. Payment split 50/50 between syndicate and author; for 1st, onetime, reprint, or simultaneous rts. Articles & fiction to 1,200 words; reviews 330-600 words. Seasonal 2 mos. ahead. Accepts simultaneous submissions & reprints (tell when/ where appeared). No kill fee. Regularly uses sidebars. Prefers NIV, NAS, NKJV. Guidelines/theme list on Website. (Ads)

Poetry: Open to free verse, haiku, light verse, traditional, 8-24 lines. Submit max. 5 poems.

Fillers: Open to all types except kid quotes; 20-35 or 50-60 wds.

Columns/Departments: Open to columns; 500-750 wds. Sermon illustrations 100-700 wds. "We are open to new columnists in a variety of topics. Need columns from seniors, Christian business leaders, and youth ministries. Send a few samples through Website."

Special Needs: Holiday, special occasion material, children's material, church administration material, Christian business.

Tips: "Go to our Website; open an account as a producer; review our guidelines, list of features, current features, etc. Upload a feature or two. We will respond within a few weeks. Our needs are varied and wide-open now. If you are excellent at what you do (whether it's writing a column, devotional, or how-to feature or creating a comic or puzzle) we're much more interested in accepting your work than rejecting it. See complete guidelines for wide range of material we accept."

CHURCH OF ENGLAND NEWSPAPER, Religious Intelligence Ltd., 14 Great College St., London SW1P 3RX, England. Phone +44 20 7878 1001. Fax +44 20 7878 1031. E-mail: colin.blakely@churchnews paper.com. Website: www. churchnewspaper.com. Religious Intelligence LTD. Colin Blakely, ed. Weekly newspaper; circ. 25,000. Subscription 60 pounds (UK); 85 pounds (U.S.). Query: phone/e-query OK. Accepts e-mail submissions (attached file). Uses some sidebars. Guidelines by e-mail. (Ads)

Tips: "Most open to news reports and general features."

$ CITY LIGHT NEWS, 459 Astoria Cres. S.E., Calgary AB T2J 0Y6, Canada. (403) 640-2011. Fax (403) 640-2000. E-mail: info@calgarychristian.com. Website: www.calgarychristian.com. CLN Productions. Peter McManus, ed./pub. A Christian newspaper serving the church audience in Central and Southern Alberta and Southeastern BC. Monthly tabloid; 20-36 pgs.; circ. 11,000+. Subscription $24.95 Cdn. 10 percent unsolicited freelance; 60 percent assigned. Query/clips; phone/fax/e-query OK. Pays .10-.15/wd. Cdn. on publication for 1st rts. Articles 550 words; fiction 300 words; reviews 300 words (.10/wd.). Responds in 2 wks. Seasonal 1 mo. ahead. Accepts simultaneous submissions

& reprints (tell when/where appeared). Prefers e-mail submissions (attached file). Some kill fees 100 percent. Uses some sidebars. Also accepts submissions from teens. Prefers NIV. Guidelines by e-mail/Website; copy for 10 x 13 SAE/$3 postage. (Ads)

Fillers: Buys 24/yr. Anecdotes, cartoons, facts, jokes, newsbreaks, quotes, short humor; 100-150 wds. Pays .10/wd.

Columns/Departments: Query. Opinion column. Pays .10-.15/wd.

Special Needs: Current blogs.

Tips: "Most open to uplifting, personal stories of real-life situations; upcoming events."

$ @ **COLUMBIA**, PO Box 1670 (06507-0981), 1 Columbus Plaza, New Haven CT 06510-3326. (203) 752-4398 or (203) 752-4303. Fax (203) 752-4109. E-mail: columbia@kofc.org or through Website: www.kofc.org. Knights of Columbus. Tim S. Hickey, ed. Geared to a general Catholic family audience. Monthly & online mag.; 32 pgs.; circ. 1.6 million. Subscription $6; foreign $8. 25 percent unsolicited freelance; 75 percent assigned. Query; fax/e-query OK. Pays $250-600 on acceptance for 1st & electronic rts. Articles 500-1,500 words (12/yr.). Responds in 2 wks. Seasonal 3 mos. ahead. Occasional reprint (tell when/where appeared). Prefers e-mail submission (copied into message). Kill fee. Regularly uses sidebars. Guidelines by mail/e-mail; free copy. (No ads)

Special Needs: Essays on spirituality, personal conversion. Catholic preferred. Query first.

Tips: "We welcome contributions from freelancers in all subject areas. An interesting or different approach to a topic will get the writer at least a second look from an editor. Most open to feature writers who can handle church issues, social issues from an orthodox Roman Catholic perspective. Must be aggressive, fact-centered writers for these features."

** This periodical was #45 on the 2007 Top 50 Christian Publishers list (#45 in 2006, #49 in 2005).

$ **COMMON GROUND**, #204—4381 Fraser St., Vancouver BC V6V 4G4, Canada. (604) 733-2215. Fax (604) 733-4415. E-mail: editor@commonground.ca. Website: www.commonground.ca. Common Ground Publishing. Joseph Roberts, sr. ed. Covers health, environment, spirit, creativity, and wellness. Monthly tabloid; circ. 70,000. Subscription $60 Cdn.; U.S. $50. 10 percent unsolicited freelance. Query by e-mail. Pays .10/wd. (Cdn.) on publication (although most articles are donated) for onetime or reprint rts. Articles 600-1,500 words (to 2,500 words), (12/yr.). Responds in 6-13 wks. (returns material only if clearly specified). Seasonal 3 mos. ahead. Accepts simultaneous submissions & reprints. Requires requested ms by e-mail. Guidelines on Website; copy $5. Incomplete topical listings. (Ads)

Tips: "Donated articles are given priority over paid articles. Once an article has been published, we will contact you with the final word count, after which you may submit an invoice."

$ **COMMONWEAL**, 475 Riverside Dr., Rm. 405, New York NY 10115-0499. (212) 662-4200. Fax (212) 662-4183. E-mail: editors@commonwealmagazine.org. Website: www.commonwealmagazine.org. Commonweal Foundation/Catholic. Paul Baumann, ed. A review of public affairs, religion, literature, and the arts, for an intellectually engaged readership. Biweekly jour.; 32 pgs.; circ. 19,000. Subscription $55. 20 percent unsolicited freelance. Query/clips; phone query OK. Pays $75-100 on publication for all rts. Articles 750-1,000 or 2,000-3,000 words (30/yr.). Responds in 3-4 wks. Seasonal 2 mos. ahead. Prefers requested ms by e-mail. Kill fee 2 percent. Uses some sidebars. Guidelines on Website; free copy. (Ads)

Poetry: Rosemary Deen, poetry ed. Buys 30/yr. Free verse, traditional; to 75 lines; .75/line. Submit max. 5 poems. Submit October-May, by mail only.

Columns/Departments: Upfronts (brief, newsy facts and information behind the headlines), 750-1,000 words; The Last Word (commentary based on insight from personal experience or reflection), 700 words.

Tips: "Most open to meaningful articles on social, political, religious, and cultural topics; or columns."

$ @ COMPANY MAGAZINE: THE WORLD OF JESUITS AND THEIR FRIENDS, PO Box 60790, Chicago IL 60660. (773) 761-9432. Fax (773) 761-9443. E-mail: editor@companymagazine.org. Website: www.companymagazine.org. Martin McHugh, ed.; Megan Austin, asst. ed. For people interested in or involved with Jesuit ministries. Quarterly & online mag.; 32 pgs.; circ. 120,000. Free subscription. 40 percent unsolicited freelance; 60 percent assigned. Complete ms/cover letter; e-query OK. Pays $250-450 on publication for onetime rts. Articles 1,500 wds. Responds in 6 wks. Seasonal 3 mos. ahead. Accepts simultaneous submissions & reprints (tell when/where appeared). Prefers e-mail submission (attached file). Prefers NRSV, NAB, NJB. Guidelines by mail/e-mail; copy for 9 x 12 SAE/4 stamps. (No ads)

> **Columns/Departments:** Books with a Jesuit connection; Minims and Maxims (short items of interest to Jesuit world), 100-150 words/photo; Letters to the Editor; Obituaries. No payment (usually).
> **Tips:** "We welcome manuscripts as well as outlines of story ideas and indication of willingness to accept freelance assignments (please include résumé and writing samples with the latter two). Articles must be Jesuit-related, and writers usually have some prior association with and/or knowledge of the Jesuits. Looking for feature articles (Jesuit-related), historical, essays, or ministry-related articles."

$ @ COMPASS DIRECT NEWS, PO Box 27250, Santa Ana CA 92799. (949) 862-0304. Fax (949) 752-6536. E-mail: info@compassdirect.org. Website: www.compassdirect.org. Compass Direct. Jeff M. Sellers, mng. ed. To raise awareness of and encourage prayer for Christians worldwide who are persecuted for their faith. Online news source; circ. 785. E-mail subscription $25; for reprint rights $40. Uses little unsolicited freelance. Pays $125-175. Articles 800-1,200 words; no reviews. Query only. Guidelines by e-mail. (No ads)

> **Tips:** "An international journalist could submit an article query on a current/specific instance of Christian persecution in a country with religious liberty restrictions. Be on the scene where persecution of Christians is taking place, and report it thoroughly and professionally."

CONNECTING POINT, PO Box 685, Cocoa FL 32923. (321) 632-0130. Fax (321) 632-5540. E-mail: lhoward@specialgatherings.com or info@specialgatherings.com. Linda G. Howard, ed. For and by the mentally challenged (mentally retarded) community; primarily deals with spiritual and self-advocacy issues. Monthly mag.; 12 pgs.; circ. 1,000. Free. 75 percent unsolicited freelance. Complete ms; phone/fax/e-query OK. **NO PAYMENT** for 1st rts. Articles (24/yr.) & fiction (12/yr.), 250-300 wds. Responds in 3-6 wks. Seasonal 3 mos. ahead. Accepts simultaneous submissions & reprints. Guidelines by mail/e-mail; copy for 9 x 12 SAE/$2.38 postage (mark "Media Mail").

> **Poetry:** Accepts 4/yr. Any type; 4-30 lines. Submit max. 10 poems.
> **Fillers:** Accepts 12/yr. Cartoons, games, word puzzles; 50-250 words.
> **Columns/Departments:** Accepts 24/yr. Devotion Page, 250 words; Bible Study, 250 wds. Query.
> **Special Needs:** Self-advocacy, integration/normalization, justice system.
> **Tips:** "All manuscripts need to be in primary vocabulary."

CONNECTIONS LEADERSHIP/MOPS, 2370 S. Tenton Way, Denver CO 80231. (303) 733-5353. Fax (303) 733-5770. E-mail: Connections@MOPS.org. Website: www.MOPS.org. MOPS Intl. Carla Foote, ed. To provide leadership training and encouragement for leaders of chartered MOPS (Mothers of Preschoolers) groups. Quarterly; circ. 25,000. Subscription $10. Open to unsolicited freelance. Query. Articles. Incomplete topical listings.

$ THE COVENANT COMPANION, 5101 N. Francisco Ave., Chicago IL 60625. (773) 907-3328. Fax (773) 784-4366. E-mail: communication@covchurch.org. Website: www.covchurch.org. Evangelical Covenant Church. Jane Swanson-Nystrom, ed.; Cathy Norman Peterson, features ed. Informs, stimulates thought, and encourages dialog on issues that affect the denomination. Monthly mag.; 40 pgs.;

circ. 12,000. Subscription $19.95. 10-15 percent unsolicited freelance; 75 percent assigned. Query or complete ms/cover letter; fax/e-query OK. Pays $35-100 after publication (within 3 wks.) for one-time or simultaneous rts. Articles 600-1,800 words (40/yr.). Prefers e-mail submission. Responds in 4 wks. Seasonal 4 mos. ahead. Accepts simultaneous submissions & reprints (tell when/where appeared). Some kill fees. Regularly uses sidebars. Prefers NRSV. Guidelines by mail/e-mail; copy for 9 x 12 SAE/5 stamps or $2.50. (Ads)

CREATION, PO Box 4545, Eight Mile Plains QLD 4113, Australia. Phone 07 3840 9888. Fax 07 3840 9889. E-mail: mail@creation.info. Website: www.creation.com. Creation Ministries Intl. Carl Wieland, managing dir. A family, nature, science magazine focusing on creation/evolution issues. Quarterly mag.; 56 pgs.; circ. 55,000. Subscription $28. 30 percent unsolicited freelance. Query; phone/fax/e-query OK. **NO PAYMENT** for all rts. Articles to 1,500 words (20/yr.). Responds in 2-3 wks. Prefers requested ms on disk or by e-mail (attached file). Regularly uses sidebars. Guidelines by mail/e-mail; copy $7.50. (No ads)

   Tips: "Get to know the basic content/style of the magazine and emulate. Send us a copy of your article, or contact us by phone."

CREATION CARE, 275 Edgewood Dr., Americus GA 31709. (678) 541-0747 (office) or (404) 414-7906 (direct). E-mail: een@creationcare.org. Website: www.creationcare.org/magazine. Evangelical Environmental Network. Rusty Prichard, PhD, ed. (submit to: rusty@creativecare.org). For Christians who care about stewardship of natural resources, environmental responsibility, sustainability, and simplicity. Quarterly mag.; 40 pgs.; circ. 6,000. Subscription fee $30 (free to supporters). 40 percent unsolicited freelance. Query; e-query OK. **NO PAYMENT**. Articles 750-2,100 words (20/yr.); book reviews 250 words. Responds in 6-8 wks. Seasonal 4 mos. ahead. No simultaneous submissions. Accepts reprints (tell when/where appeared). Prefers accepted ms by e-mail. Regularly uses sidebars. Prefers NRSV, NIV. Guidelines by e-mail. (Ads)

   Tips: "Feature articles and reviews are often done by freelancers, also interviews/profiles, news features, essays. Writing is especially sought that conveys the concrete, real-life connections between care of creation, social justice, Christian ministry, personal discipleship, parenting, and community. Articles should focus on or appeal to evangelicals and other Christians with a vibrant, orthodox faith and a high view of Scripture."

$ CREATION ILLUSTRATED, PO Box 7955, Auburn CA 95604. (530) 269-1424. Fax (530) 269-1428. E-mail: ci@creationillustrated.com. Website: www.creationillustrated.com. Tom Ish, ed./pub. An uplifting, Bible-based Christian nature magazine that glorifies God; for ages 9-99. Quarterly mag.; 68 pgs.; circ. 20,000. Subscription $19.95. 60 percent unsolicited freelance; 40 percent assigned. Query or query/clips; fax/e-query OK. Pays $75-125 within 30 days of publication for 1st rts. (holds rts. for 6 mos.). Articles 1,000-2,000 words (20/yr.). Responds in 2 mos. Seasonal 6 mos. ahead. Accepts simultaneous submissions & reprints (tell when/where appeared). Prefers e-mail submission (copied into message). Kill fee 25 percent. Uses some sidebars. Prefers NKJV. Guidelines/theme list by mail/Website; copy $3/9 x 12 SAE/$2.38 postage (mark "Media Mail"). (Some ads)

   Poetry: Short, usually 4-8 verses. Needs to have both nature and spiritual thoughts. Pays about $15.

   Columns/Departments: Creation Up Close Feature, 1,500-2,000 words, $100; Re-Creation and Restoration Through Outdoor Adventure, 1,500-2,000 words, $100; Creatures Near and Dear to Us, 1,500-2,000 words, $100; Children's Story, 500-1,000 words, $50-75; My Walk with God, 1,000-1,500 words, $75; Gardens from Eden Around the World, 1,000-1,500 words, $75; Creation Day (a repeating series). 1,500-2,000 words, $100.

   Tips: "Most open to an experience with nature/creation that brought you closer to God and will inspire the reader to do the same. Include spiritual lessons and supporting Scriptures—at least 3 or 4 of each."

$ CREATIVE NONFICTION, 5501 Walnut St., Ste. 202, Pittsburgh PA 15232. (412) 688-0304. Fax (412) 688-0262. E-mail: information@creativenonfiction.org. Website: www.creativenonfiction.org. Lee Gutkind, ed. Publishes compelling nonfiction stories with a strong narrative and research element. Triannual jour.; 150 pgs.; circ. 5,000. Subscription $29.95 for 4 issues. 80 percent unsolicited freelance; 20 percent assigned. Complete ms/cover letter; no phone/fax/e-query. Pays $10/published page on publication for all rts. Articles to 5,000 words (30/yr.). Responds in 5 mos. Accepts simultaneous submissions; no reprints. No disk or e-mail submissions. No kill fee. Does not use sidebars. Also accepts submissions from teens. Guidelines by e-mail/Website; copy $10/$3 postage. (Ads)

Contests: Sometimes sponsor contests; see Website for details.

$ THE CRESSET: A REVIEW OF ARTS, LITERATURE & PUBLIC AFFAIRS, Huegli Hall, Valparaiso University, Valparaiso IN 46383. (219) 464-6809. E-mail: cresset@valpo.edu. Website: www.valpo.edu/cresset. Valparaiso University/Lutheran. James Paul Old, ed. (tom.kennedy@valpo.edu). For college-educated, professors, pastors, laypeople; serious review essays on religious-cultural affairs. Mag. published 5x/yr.; 60 pgs.; circ. 4,500. Subscription $20. 10 percent unsolicited freelance; 90 percent assigned. Query; e-query OK. Pays $100-500 on publication for all rts. Articles 2,000-4,500 words (2/yr.); book/music reviews, 1,000 words ($150). Responds in 15 wks. No simultaneous submissions or reprints. Prefers requested ms by e-mail (attached or copied into message). Regularly uses sidebars. Prefers NRSV. Guidelines on Website; copy $4. (No ads)

Poetry: John Ruff, poetry ed. Buys 20/yr. Avant-garde, free verse, light verse, traditional; to 40 lines; $15-25. Submit max. 4 poems.

Columns/Departments: Buys 20/yr. Books; Music; Science & Technology; World Views; all 1,000 words, $100-250. Query.

@ CROSSHOME.COM: YOUR CHRISTIAN HOME ON THE NET! E-mail: webmaster@crosshome.com. Website: www.crosshome.com. Online mag. Open to unsolicited freelance. Complete ms by e-mail; e-query OK. **NO PAYMENT** for onetime rts. Articles 300-1,000 words; devotionals 300-1,000 words (prefers 350-650 words); book reviews 300-800 words. Responds in 1-3 wks. (if accepted). Requires accepted ms by e-mail (attached file in Word). Prefers KJV, NKJV, NIV, NASB. Guidelines on Website (www.crosshome.com/guidelines.shtml); copy online. (Ads)

Poetry: Accepts free verse, traditional; 30-500 wds.

Columns/Departments: Open to submissions for regular columns or ideas for new ones. (See guidelines.)

Special Needs: See Website/guidelines for list of channels where your writing might fit.

Tips: "We do archive all writing, but any submissions can be deleted by request of the author by e-mail."

$ CULTURE WARS, 206 Marquette Ave., South Bend IN 46617-1111. (574) 289-9786. Fax (574) 289-1461. E-mail: jones@culturewars.com or letters@culturewars.com or fidelitypress@sbcglobal.net. Website: www.culturewars.com. Ultramontagne Associates Inc. Dr. E. Michael Jones, ed. Issues relating to Catholic families and issues affecting America that affect all people. Monthly (11x) mag.; 48 pgs.; circ. 3,500. Subscription $39. 20 percent unsolicited freelance. Complete ms/cover letter; fax/e-query OK. Pays $100 & up on publication for all rts. Articles (25/yr.); book reviews $50. Responds in 12-24 wks. Query about reprints. Prefers requested ms on disk. Uses some sidebars. Developing guidelines; copy for 9 x 12 SAE/5 stamps.

Poetry: Buys 15/yr. Free verse, light verse, traditional; 10-50 lines; $25. Submit max. 2 poems.

Fillers: Buys 15/yr. Cartoons, quotes; 25 words & up; payment varies.

Columns/Departments: Buys 25/yr. Commentary, 2,500 words; Feature, 5,000 words; $100-250.

Tips: "All fairly open except cartoons. Single-spaced preferred; photocopies must be legible."

$ @ DECISION/DECISION ONLINE, 1 Billy Graham Pkwy., Charlotte NC 28201-0001. (704) 401-2432. Fax (704) 401-3009. E-mail: submissions@bgea.org. Website: www.decisionmag.org. Billy Graham Evangelistic Assn. Bob Paulson, ed. Evangelism/Christian nurture; all articles must have connection to BGEA. Monthly (11x) & online mag.; 44 pgs.; circ. 400,000. Subscription $15. 5 percent unsolicited freelance; written mostly in-house. Query preferred; no phone/fax/e-query. Pays $200-500 on publication for 1st rts. Articles 400-1,000 words (8/yr.). Response time varies. Seasonal 3-5 mos. ahead. Accepts ms by e-mail (attached file). Uses some sidebars. Prefers NIV. Guidelines by mail/e-mail/Website; copy for 10 x 13 SAE/3 stamps. (No ads)

> **Columns/Departments:** Buys 11/yr. Finding Jesus (people who have become Christians through Billy Graham ministries), 500-600 words; $200. Complete ms.
> **Special Needs:** Personal experience articles telling how a Billy Graham ministry helped you live out your faith.
> **Tips:** "Nearly all of our articles have some connection with a ministry of the Billy Graham Evangelistic Assn.—through the author's participation in the ministry or through the author's being touched by the ministry."
> ** 2009, 2005 EPA Award of Merit—Organizational.

DESERT CALL: CONTEMPLATIVE CHRISTIANITY AND VITAL CULTURE, Box 219, Crestone CO 81131. (719) 256-4778. Fax (719) 256-4719. E-mail: nada@spirituallifeinstitute.org. Website: www.spirituallifeinstitute.org. Spiritual Life Institute/Catholic. Suzie Ryan, ed. Practical spirituality and contemplative prayer; interfaith/interreligious dialog, the arts and culture, fiction. Quarterly mag.; 32 pgs.; circ. 2,000. Subscription $20. 15 percent unsolicited freelance; 10 percent assigned. Complete ms/cover letter; no phone/fax/e-query. **PAYS 3 COPIES** for 1st rts. Articles 1,000-2,500 words (4/yr.); some fiction. Responds in 15 wks. Seasonal 8 mos. ahead. Accepts reprints (tell when/where appeared). No disk or e-mail submissions. Uses some sidebars. No guidelines; copy $2.50/10 x 13 SAE. (No ads)

> **Poetry:** Accepts 3/yr. Free verse, haiku, traditional; to 25 lines.
> **Fillers:** Accepts 3/yr. Anecdotes, facts, prayers, prose, quotes; 50-250 words.

DESERT CHRISTIAN NEWS, PO Box 4196, Palm Desert CA 92261. (760) 772-2027. E-mail: smiller@desertchristiannews.org. Website: www.desertchristiannews.org. Susan Miller, ed. To encourage communication and unity among Christians in the Coachella Valley by sharing inspiring local news stories, feature articles, and information. Monthly newspaper; weekly TV/radio programs. Subscription $35. Open to freelance. Articles 500-750 wds. Query preferred. Articles; reviews. Guidelines on Website. (Ads) Incomplete topical listings.

THE DESERT VOICE, PO Box 567, Imperial CA 92251. (760) 337-9200. Fax (760) 355-0197. E-mail: editor@desertvoice.info. Website: www.desertvoice.info. Witness Publishing Inc. Alex Arroyave, ed. To reach the lost and to provide family-friendly news not found elsewhere by bias or neglect or simply because they don't feel it's important. Monthly newspaper; 20 pgs.; circ. 5,200. No subscriptions. Open to freelance. Complete ms/cover letter. **NO PAYMENT**. Articles & fiction 500-800 words; reviews 300 words. Seasonal 2 mos. ahead. Accepts simultaneous submissions & reprints (tell when/where appeared). Prefers e-mail submissions (attached file). Uses some sidebars. Occasionally accepts submissions from teens. No guidelines or copy. (Ads)

> **Fillers:** Jokes, kid quotes, quotes, word puzzles.
> **Special Needs:** News.

$ DIRECTION, PO Box 436987, Chicago IL 60643. (708) 868-7100, ext. 236. Fax (708) 868-6759. E-mail: ecarey@urbanministries.com. Website: www.urbanministries.com. Urban Ministries Inc. Submit to Evangeline Carey, developmental ed. An adult-level Sunday school quarterly publication consisting of student book and teacher's guide. Quarterly mag; 64 pgs.; $19.45 (student) and $29.45 (teacher). 100 percent assigned. Query or query/clips; phone/fax/e-query OK. Accepts full manuscripts by e-mail. Pays to $200 ($300 for lessons) on acceptance, for all rts. Articles 1,500-3,500 wds. Responds in 4 wks. Seasonal 12 mos. ahead. No simultaneous submissions or reprints. Requires accepted ms on disk or by e-mail (attached or copied into message). Kill fee 50 percent. Does not use sidebars. Prefers KJV. Guidelines by e-mail; copy for SASE. (No ads)

> **Tips:** "Send query with a writing sample, or attend our annual conference on the first weekend in November each year."

$ @ DISASTER NEWS NETWORK, 8815 Centre Park Dr., #240, Columbia MD 21045. (443) 393-3330. Fax (443) 445-6935. E-mail: info@villagelife.org. Website: www.disasternews.net. Village Life Co. Submit to Editor. Online; an interactive daily news site on the World Wide Web. Query by e-mail only. Pays $100-150 after publication for all rts. Articles 1,000 words (varies). Requires accepted ms by e-mail. Guidelines on Website. (Ads)

> **Tips:** "Most open to 'people stories' related to faith-based disaster response and/or mitigation. Also, faith-based response to incidents of public violence, and volunteer stories. Authors are expected to have an e-mail submission address. Check our Website." Authors must be DNN pre-approved contractor writers. This publication is moving so check Website for new address.

@ DISCIPLE'S JOURNAL, 10 Fiorenza Dr., Wilmington MA 01887-4421. Toll-free (800) 696-2344. (978) 657-7373. Fax (978) 657-5411. E-mail: kadorothy@yahoo.com. Website: www.disciples directory.com. Kenneth A. Dorothy, ed. To strengthen, edify, inform, and unite the body of Christ. Monthly & online newspaper; 24-32 pgs.; circ. 8,000. Subscription $14.95. 5 percent unsolicited freelance. Query; fax/e-query OK. **NO PAYMENT** for onetime rts. Articles 400 words (24/yr.); book/music/video reviews 200 words. Responds in 2 wks. Seasonal 2 mos. ahead. Accepts simultaneous submissions & reprints (tell when/where appeared). Prefers requested ms on disk or by e-mail (attached file). Uses some sidebars. Prefers NIV. Guidelines/theme list by mail/e-mail; copy for 9 x 12 SAE/$2.38 postage (mark "Media Mail"). (Ads)

> **Fillers:** Accepts 12/yr. All types; 100-400 wds.
>
> **Columns/Departments:** Financial; Singles; Men; Women; Business; Parenting; all 400 words.
>
> **Tips:** "Most open to men's, women's, or singles' issues; missions; or homeschooling. Send sample of articles for review."

$ DISCIPLESWORLD, 6325 Guilford Ave., Ste. 213, Indianapolis IN 46220-1992. (317) 375-8846. Fax (317) 375-8849. E-mail: editor@disciplesworld.com or through Website: www.disciplesworld .com. Christian Church (Disciples of Christ). Sherri Wood Emmons, mng. ed. The journal of news, opinion, and mission for this denomination in North America. Monthly (10x) mag.; 48 pgs.; circ. 14,000. Subscription $31. 30 percent unsolicited freelance; 70 percent assigned. Complete ms/cover letter or query with/without clips; e-query OK. Pays .16/wd. on publication for 1st rts. Articles 1,200-1,800 words (40/yr.); fiction 700-1,500 words (8-10/yr.); reviews 600 words (no payment). Responds in 1 mo. Seasonal 3 mos. ahead. Accepts simultaneous submissions; no reprints. Requires submissions by disk or e-mail (attached file). No kill fee. Uses some sidebars. Prefers NRSV. Guidelines/theme list on Website; copy for #10 SASE. (Ads)

> **Poetry:** Buys 6-10/yr. Free verse, light verse; 12-30 lines. Pays $10-50. Submit max. 3 poems.
>
> **Columns/Departments:** Buys 12-15/yr. Speak Out (opinion on an issue), 700 words; Disciples Go (travel to places relevant to Disciples), 700 words, plus photos; $100. Quotable Quotes, 200 words (no pay).
>
> **Tips:** "Our readers are mostly college-educated, active in their churches, proud of their Disciples heritage, and all over the board politically and theologically. We like things with a Disciples connection."
>
> ** This periodical was #33 on the 2009 Top 50 Christian Publishers list (#48 in 2008, #40 in 2007, #46 in 2006, #45 in 2005).

@ DIVINE ASCENT: A Journal of Orthodox Faith, PO Box 439, 21770 Ponderosa Way, Manton CA 96059. (530) 474-5964. Fax (530) 474-3564. E-mail: office@monasteryofstjohn.org. Website: www.monasteryofstjohn.org. Monastery of St. John of Shanghai & San Francisco/Orthodox Church in America. Archimandrite Memetios, abbot & ed-in-chief. Focuses on contemporary Orthodox spirituality as seen in the lives and writings of saints, and holy men and women of our own time. Semiannual & online jour.; 150 pgs. Subscription $25/2 yrs. 20 percent unsolicited freelance; 65 percent assigned. Query. **NO PAYMENT** for all rts. Articles (6/yr.); book reviews 500 wds. Responds in 4-8 wks. No reprints. Prefers disk or e-mail submissions (attached file). Does not use sidebars. Prefers RSV, KJV, NKJV. Guidelines by e-mail. (Ads, from Orthodox Christian businesses)

   Tips: "Nothing Protestant."

$ @ DRAMA MINISTRY, PO Box 40387, Nashville TN 37204. Toll-free (866) 859-7622. Fax (615) 463-9139 E-mail: service@dramaministry.com or through Website: www.dramaministry.com. Belden Street Music Company. Regi Stone, pub. Mag. published 8x/yr. & online; page count varies. Subscription $99.95. 75 percent unsolicited freelance; 25 percent assigned. Complete ms/cover letter for scripts; query for articles; e-query OK. Accepts full scripts by e-mail. Pays $100 for scripts on publication for onetime & online rts. Articles 500-700 words (80/yr.); scripts 2-10 minutes (80/ yr.). Responds in 6-8 wks. Seasonal 6 mos. ahead. Accepts simultaneous submissions & reprints (tell when/where appeared). Requires submissions by e-mail (attached file or copied into message). No kill fee or sidebars. Also accepts submissions from teens. Any Bible version. Guidelines on Website. (No ads)

   Tips: "If your script is well written and you have a true understanding of what works within the church drama ministry, then you will break into our publication easily. Please adhere to and read writers' guidelines thoroughly (see Website). We do not respond unless we choose to publish your script. All scripts written by freelancers."

$ @ DREAMSEEKER MAGAZINE, 126 Klingerman Rd., Telford PA 18969. (215) 723-9125. E-mail: DSM@CascadiaPublishingHouse.com or editor@CascadiaPublishingHouse.com. Website: www. CascadiaPublishingHouse.com. Cascadia Publishing House. Submit to The Editor. For readers committed to exploring from the heart, with passion, depth, and flair, their own visions and issues of the day. Quarterly print & online mag.; 52 pgs.; circ. 1,000 (including online). Subscription $14.95. 10 percent unsolicited freelance; 90 percent assigned. Query; e-query OK. Accepts full mss by e-mail. Pays $5 or .01/wd. on publication for 1st or onetime rts. Articles 750-1,500 words (10/yr.). Responds in 8 wks. No seasonal. No simultaneous submissions; rarely buys reprints (tell when/where appeared). Prefers submissions on disk or by e-mail (attached file). No kill fee or sidebars. Also accepts submissions from children/teens. Guidelines on Website; copy online. Incomplete topical listings.

@ E-CHANNELS, 3819 Bloor St. W., Toronto ON M9P 1K7, Canada. Phone/fax (519) 651-2232. E-mail: cbbrown@rogers.com. Website: http://renewalfellowship.presbyterian.ca. The Renewal Fellowship/Presbyterian (P.C.C.). Calvin Brown, ed. For Presbyterians seeking spiritual renewal and biblical orthodoxy. Online mag.; 20 pgs.; circ. 2,000. Subscription $12. 10 percent unsolicited freelance; 90 percent assigned. Query; e-query OK. **PAYS IN COPIES** for onetime rts. Articles 1,000-1,500 words (15/yr.); book reviews 300 words. Responds in 4 wks. Seasonal 4-6 mos. ahead. Accepts reprints (tell when/where appeared). Prefers mss by e-mail (attached file/RTF). Regularly uses sidebars. Also accepts submissions from teens. No guidelines; copy for #10 SAE/3 stamps. (Ads)

   Poetry: Accepts 3/yr. Free verse, haiku, light verse, traditional; 3 lines & up. Submit max. 6 poems.

   Fillers: Accepts 4/yr. Anecdotes, cartoons, prayers.; 6-100 words.

$ EFCA TODAY, 418 Fourth St. N.E., PO Box 315, Charlottesville VA 22902. (434) 961-2500. Fax (434) 961-2507. E-mail: Today@EFCA.org, or DianeMc@journeygroup.com. Website: www.efca today.org. Evangelical Free Church of America/Journey Communications Group. Diane McDougall, ed. Denominational. Quarterly mag.; 32 pgs.; circ. 44,000. Subscription $10. 5 percent unsolicited freelance; 95 percent assigned. Query (preferred) or complete ms/cover letter; fax/e-query OK. Pays .23/wd. on acceptance for 1st and subsidiary rts. (free use on EFCA Website or church bulletins). Articles 300-500 words (4/yr.). Responds in 6 wks. Seasonal 6 mos. ahead. Prefers e-mail (attached file) or hard copy. Kill fee 50 percent. Regularly uses sidebars. Guidelines by mail/e-mail/Website; copy $1/10 x 13 SAE/$2.38 postage (mark "Media Mail"). (Ads)

Columns/Departments: Cover-Theme Section (variety of topics applicable to church leadership), 500-1,000 words; pays $46-250.

Special Needs: Stories of EFCA churches in action.

Tips: "Read samples—really can't beat it—and make sure the articles are about EFCA vision and/or activities, geared to leaders, not pew-sitters. We are not a general-interest publication. 'Inspirational' pieces are not applicable."

** 2008, 2007, 2006 EPA Award of Merit—Denominational. 2009, 2005 EPA Award of Excellence—Denominational. This periodical was #39 on the 2009 Top 50 Christian Publishers list (#41 in 2007, #50 in 2006).

$ EL HERALDO CRISTIANO (THE CHRISTIAN HERALD), PO Box 2955, 639 Cleveland St., Ste. 245, Clearwater FL 33755. (813) 200-7055. E-mail: info@elheraldocristiano.org. Website: www .elheraldocristiano.org. Pentecostal/published in Spanish. Joseph Diaz, ed./pub. Embracing the family for Christ. Estab. 2007; 36 pgs. Distributed in Tampa Bay area but nationwide eventually. Pays. Call or e-mail. Incomplete topical listings.

ENCOMPASS, 2296 Henderson Mills Rd. N.E., Ste. 406, Atlanta GA 30345-2739. Toll-free (800) 914-2000. (770) 414-1515. Fax (770) 414-1518. E-mail: rlundy@americananglican.org. Website: www.americananglican.org. The American Anglican Council. Robert Lundy, ed. To provide news and information regarding the Episcopal Church and worldwide Anglican Communion; to provide inspirational articles for the spread of Christ's kingdom; to offer encouragement and challenge to the larger church. Monthly newsletter; 4-6 pgs.; circ. 45,000. Subscription free. Open to freelance. Query preferred; phone/e-query OK. **NO PAYMENT**. Articles 200-2,000 wds. Responds in 2 wks. Accepts articles by e-mail (attached file). Uses some sidebars. No guidelines; copy for 9 x 12 SAE/2 stamps.

Tips: "Most open to features or aspects of important people in the Anglican scene in America; commentary on current events in the Anglican community from the orthodox point of view."

$ ENFOQUE A LA FAMILIA, 8675 Explorer Dr., Colorado Springs CO 80920. Toll-free (800) 434-2345. (719) 548-4660. Fax (719) 531-3383. E-mail: ardilama@fotf.org. Website: www.enfoque .org. Focus on the Family. Marta Ardila, ed. To provide family-friendly material to our domestic Spanish constituents and inform the Hispanic community of culturally relevant issues that affect their families. Bimonthly mag.; circ. 30,000. Subscription free. Open to freelance. Complete ms/cover letter. Articles; no reviews. Incomplete topical listings. (No ads)

$ @ EPISCOPAL LIFE AND EPISCOPAL LIFE ONLINE, 815—2nd Ave., New York NY 10017. Toll-free (800) 334-7626. (212) 716-6000. Fax (212) 949-8059. E-mail: mdavies@episcopalchurch .org or elife@aflwebprinting.com. Website: www.episcopal-life.org. Episcopal Church. Solange De Santis, newspaper ed.; Matthew Davies, online ed. Denominational. Monthly newspaper; 28 pgs.; circ. 200,000. Subscription $27.00. 10 percent assigned. Query/clips or complete ms/cover letter; phone query on breaking news only; e-query OK. Pays $50-300 on publication for 1st, onetime, or simultaneous rts. Articles 800 words (24/yr.); assigned book reviews 200-300 words ($50). Responds in 1-4 wks. Seasonal 3 mos. ahead. Accepts simultaneous submissions & reprints. Accepts e-mail submission. Kill fee 50 percent. No guidelines; free copy. (Ads)

Columns/Departments: Commentary on political/religious topics; 300-600 words; $35-75. Query.

Tips: "All articles must have Episcopal Church slant or specifics. We need topical/issues, not devotional stuff. Most open to feature stories about Episcopalians—clergy, lay, churches, involvement in local efforts, movements, ministries."
** This periodical was #50 on the 2009 Top 50 Christian Publishers list (#50 in 2008).

@ **ESDRAS SCROLL**, PO Box 63, McDonaugh GA 30253. (678) 826-0648. Fax (928) 563-3225. E-mail: submissions@voicesofchrist.org. Website: www.voicesofchrist.org. Voices of Christ Literary Ministries. Theresa H. Johnson, ed. We prefer poetry, and creative writing that is relevant to time/seasons in which we live. Seasonal e-zine/literary mag.; circ. 5,000. Subscription free. 100 percent unsolicited freelance. Call or query; e-query OK. Accepts full mss by e-mail. **NO PAYMENT** for onetime, reprint, electronic rts. Articles & fiction 500-1,500 words; book reviews 250 words. Responds in 6 wks. Seasonal 2 mos. ahead. Accepts simultaneous submissions & reprints (tell when/where appeared). Prefers e-mail submissions (attached). Uses some sidebars. Also accepts submissions from children/teens. Prefers KJV. Guidelines on Website; copy online. (Ads)
   Poetry: Accepts up to 100/yr. Any type; 3-30 lines. Submit max. 3-5 poems. "Poetry is our main focus, specifically poetry that addresses social issues."
   Fillers: Accepts up to 20/yr. Cartoons, sermon illustrations, short humor; 250 words.
   Tips: "Submit creative work that is relevant to the times/seasons in which we live. In particular, writings that address social, government, educational, or even religious issues from a spiritual perspective. We readily review and accept poetry that addresses current social issues of concern to the church and society that uphold Christian principles. In addition, we actively seek poetry that deals with end-time ministry." Fiction for children and teens, 12 years and up.

@ **ETERNAL INK**, 4706 Fantasy Ln., Alton IL 62002. E-mail: eternallyours8@yahoo.com. Nondenominational. E-mail publication; open to any serious effort or submission. Mary-Ellen Grisham, ed; Carl Phillips, features ed. (CarlPhil10@aol.com); Pat Earl, devotions ed. Biweekly e-zine; 1 pg.; circ. 450. Subscription free. 25 percent unsolicited freelance; 75 percent assigned. Complete ms/cover letter by e-mail only. **NO PAYMENT** for onetime rts. Not copyrighted. Articles/devotions 300-500 words (26/yr.); reviews 300-500 words. Responds in 6 wks. Seasonal 2 mos. ahead. Accepts simultaneous submissions & reprints. Accepts e-mail submissions (copied into message). No kill fee or sidebars. Prefers NIV. Occasionally accepts submissions from children/teens. Guidelines/copy by e-mail/Website. (No ads)
   Poetry: Elizabeth Pearson, poetry ed. (roybet@sbcglobal.net). Accepts 24-30/yr. Free verse, traditional, inspirational; to 30 lines. Submit max. 3 poems.
   Fillers: Ivie Bozeman, fillers ed. (ivie@rose.net). Accepts 24-30/yr. Anecdotes, jokes, kid quotes, prayers, prose, short humor; 150-250 words.
   Columns/Departments: Accepts many/yr. See information on Website. Query.
   Contest: Annual Prose/Poetry Contest in November-December, with 1st, 2nd, and 3rd-place winners in each category. Book awards for first-place winners. See Website.
   Tips: "Please contact Mary-Ellen Grisham by e-mail with questions."

$ @ **EUREKA STREET: An Online Magazine of Public Affairs, the Arts, and Theology**, PO Box 553, Richmond VIC 3121, Australia. Tel. +61 3 9421 9666 or 1300 72 88 46. Fax +61 3 9421 9600. E-mail: eureka@eurekastreet.com.au. Website: www.eurekastreet.com.au. Jesuit Communications. Michael Mullins, ed.; submit to Tim Kroenert, asst. ed. An online magazine of public affairs, the arts, and theology. Daily e-zine; circ. 30,000. Subscription free. 35 percent unsolicited freelance; 35 percent assigned. Query; phone/e-query OK (complete ms for fiction). Accepts full mss by e-mail (submissions@eurekastreet.com.au). Pays $200 on publication for onetime rts. Articles 600-800 words; fiction 700-1,000 words; reviews 400 words (pays $100). Responds in 1 wk. Seasonal 1 mo. ahead. No simultaneous submissions or reprints. Requires submissions by e-mail (attached). Uses some sidebars. Guidelines on Website (www.eurekastreet.com.au/ab_write.html).

Poetry: Philip Harvey (poetry@eurekastreet.com.au). Buys 50/yr. Avant-garde, free verse, haiku, light verse, traditional. Pays $50 for a set of 4 poems. Submit max. 3 poems.
Contest: Eureka Street/Reader's Feast Award for social justice/human rights writing; and Margaret Dooley Award for Young Writers. Website: www.crimeandjusticefestival.com/eureka.
**This periodical was #12 on the 2009 Top 50 Christian Publishers list.

$ EVANGEL (IN), Box 535002, Indianapolis IN 46253-5002. (317) 244-3660. E-mail: evangeleditor @fmcna.org. Free Methodist/Light and Life Communications. Julie Innes, ed. For young to middle-aged adults; encourages spiritual growth. Weekly take-home paper (published quarterly); 8 pgs.; circ. 11,000. Subscription $9. 100 percent unsolicited freelance. Complete ms/cover letter; no e-query. Pays .04/wd. ($10 min.) on publication for onetime rts. Articles 1,200 words (100/yr.); fiction 1,200 words (100/yr.). Responds in 6-8 wks. Seasonal 12-15 mos. ahead. Accepts some simultaneous submissions & reprints (tell when/where appeared). Accepts requested mss by e-mail. Some sidebars. Prefers NIV. Guidelines by mail/e-mail; copy for #10 SAE/1 stamp. (No ads)
   Poetry: Buys 40+/yr. Free verse, light verse, traditional; 3-16 lines; $10. Submit max. 5 poems. Rhyming poetry not usually taken seriously.
   Fillers: Buys 20/yr. Cartoons, crypto-word puzzles; to 100 words; $10.
   Tips: "Bring fresh insight to a topic. Submit material appropriate for the market and audience. Although we will cover a specific issue of concern to men or to women, we prefer that the problem be addressed universally. Don't ramble; stick to one thesis. A returned manuscript isn't always because of poor writing. Can also use short devotional material, 600 words or less."

@ EVANGEL (OR), 199 S.E. 193rd Ave., Portland OR 97233. (971) 506-3947. Fax (503) 669-6877. E-mail: director@onwordcommunications.com. Website: www.pnmc.org. Pacific Northwest Mennonite Conference. Susan M. Palmer, ed. Official publication of the Pacific Northwest Mennonite Conference, featuring news and features about the churches, organizations, and people of the Mennonite Church USA in WA, OR, ID, AK, and W. MT. Quarterly & online mag.; 8 pgs.; circ. 25,000. Subscription free. 5 percent unsolicited freelance; 50 percent assigned. Query; fax/e-query OK. Accepts full mss by e-mail. **PAYS IN COPIES** for onetime rts. Not copyrighted. Articles 500-1,000 words (4/yr.). Responds in 2-4 wks. Seasonal 4 mos. ahead. No simultaneous submissions; accepts reprints (tell when/where appeared). Accepts requested mss on disk or by e-mail (attached file). Uses some sidebars. Guidelines by mail/e-mail; copy for 9 x 12 SAE/1.05 postage. (No ads)
   Fillers: Accepts 2-4/yr. Newsbreaks, prose, 50-150 wds.
   Special Needs: Features on local congregational activities.
   Tips: "Become familiar with the views, beliefs of Mennonite Church USA. Visiting www .mennoniteusa.org is a good place to start. Please address issues from a Mennonite perspective. Check our Website."

THE EVANGELICAL ADVOCATE, Box 30, 1426 Lancaster Pike, Circleville OH 43113. (740) 474-8856. Fax (740) 477-7766. E-mail: directordoc@cccuhq.org or info@cccuhq.org. Website: www .cccuhq.org. Churches of Christ in Christian Union. Ralph Hux, dir. of communications. Provides news, information, and features that emphasize current events and worldview, appealing to the needs of our constituency, emphasizing fundamental evangelical holiness. Bimonthly mag.; 32-36 pgs.; circ. 4,000. Subscription $12. 15 percent unsolicited freelance; 15 percent assigned. Query (preferred) or complete ms/cover letter; fax/e-query OK. **NO PAYMENT**. Articles 500-1,000 words (15-20/yr.). Seasonal 2-3 mos. ahead. Accepts simultaneous submissions & reprints (tell when/where appeared). Prefers e-mail submissions (attached file). Regularly uses sidebars. Prefers KJV, NIV, NRSV. Theme list/guidelines by e-mail; copy for 9 x 12 SAE. (No ads)
   Poetry: Accepts 6-12/yr. Traditional.
   Tips: "Best way to break in is to submit material for review by e-mail."

EVANGELICAL TIMES, Faverdale North Industrial Estate, Darlington DL3 0PH, United Kingdom. Tel. +44 1325 380232. E-mail: theeditors@evangelicaltimes.org. Website: www.evangelical-times. org. Edgar Andrews & Roger Fay, eds. For churches who hold a biblical, Christ-centered theology & the doctrines of grace; circulated worldwide. Monthly tabloid newspaper; 32 pgs.; circ. 40,000. Subscription $18 (surface), $28 (airmail). Incomplete topical listings.

> **Tips:** "Our paper offers UK and world news, Christian comment, and a wide variety of articles (biblical, devotional, practical, topical, doctrinal, and historical), with a strong missionary dimension."

$ FAITH & FAMILY: The Magazine of Catholic Living, 432 Washington Ave., North Haven CT 06473. (203) 230-3809. Fax (203) 230-3838. E-mail: editor@faithandfamilymag.com. Website: www.faithandfamilymag.com. Catholic/Circle Media Inc. Tom & April Hoopes, eds.; submit to Robyn Lee, asst. ed. Features writing for Catholics and/or Christian families of all ages. Bimonthly mag.; 100 pgs.; circ. 32,000. Subscription $17.95. 10 percent unsolicited freelance; 90 percent assigned. Query/clips; e-query preferred; no phone query. Pays .33/wd. on publication for 1st rts. Articles 700-3,000 words (35/yr.); brief reviews. Responds in 6-8 wks. Seasonal 6-9 mos. ahead. No reprints. Prefers e-mail submission (attached file). Kill fee. Regularly uses sidebars. Accepts illustrations from children. Prefers NAB. Guidelines by mail/Website; copy $4.50/10 x 13 SAE. (Ads)

> **Fillers:** Buys 10/yr. Anecdotes, cartoons, prose (brief).

> **Columns/Departments:** Buys 75/yr. The Home Front (news); The Insider; Flair; The Season; Life Lessons; Faith & Folklore; Celebrations; Entertainment; The Where & How Guide; Spiritual Directions; and Back Porch; 600-1,200 wds. Query.

> **Tips:** "Most open to well-written feature articles employing good quotations, anecdotes, and transitions about an interesting aspect of family life; departments; news items. To break in, submit ideas for The Home Front." Wants only Catholic theme-related material.

> ** This periodical was #22 on the 2008 Top 50 Christian Publishers list (#33 in 2007, #21 in 2005).

$ FAITH & FRIENDS, 2 Overlea Blvd., Toronto ON M4H 1P4, Canada. (416) 422-6226. Fax (416) 422-6120. E-mail: faithandfriends@can.salvationarmy.org. Website: www.faithandfriends.ca. The Salvation Army. Colonel Jim Champ, asst. ed-in-chief; Geoffrey Moulton, ed.; Ken Ramstead, mng. ed. Monthly mag.; 32 pgs.; circ. 50,000. Subscription $16.50 Cdn. 90 percent assigned. Query/clips; e-query OK. Pays up to $200 Cdn. on publication for onetime rts. Articles 500-1,000 wds. Responds in 2 wks. Seasonal 6 mos. ahead. Accepts simultaneous submissions & reprints (tell when/where appeared). Prefers accepted ms by e-mail (attached file). Uses some sidebars. Prefers TNIV. Guidelines by mail/Website; free copy. (No ads)

> **Fillers:** Buys 10/yr. Cartoons, games, jokes, quizzes, quotes, word puzzles; 50 words; $25.

> **Columns/Departments:** God in My Life (how Christians in the workplace find faith relevant), 600 words; Words to Live By (simple Bible studies/discussions of faith), 600 words; Faith Builders (movie & TV reviews from a spiritual and faith perspective), 750-1,000 words; Between the Lines (book reviews), 500 words; Someone Cares.

$ FAITH TODAY: To Connect, Equip, and Inform Evangelical Christians in Canada, M.I.P. Box 3745, Markham ON L3R 0Y4, Canada. (905) 479-5885. Fax (905) 479-4742. E-mail: editor@faithtoday.ca. Website: www.faithtoday.ca. Evangelical Fellowship of Canada. Gail Reid, mng. ed.; Bill Fledderus, sr. ed.; Karen Stiller, assoc. ed. A general-interest publication for Christians in Canada; almost exclusively about Canadians, including Canadians abroad. Bimonthly mag.; 56 pgs.; circ. 18,000. U.S. subscription $30.15 Cdn. 20 percent unsolicited freelance; 80 percent assigned. Query only; fax/e-query preferred. Pays $80-500 (.20-.25 Cdn./wd.) on publication for 1st & electronic rts.; reprints. 15/wd. Features 800-1,700 words; cover stories 2,000 words; essays 650-1,200 words; profiles 900 words; reviews 300 words (75-100/yr.) Responds in 6 wks. Prefers e-mail submission.

Kill fee 30-50 percent. Regularly uses sidebars. Any Bible version. Guidelines at www.evangelical fellowship.ca/FTwriters; copy for 9 x 12 SAE/$2.05 in Canadian funds. (Ads)

Tips: "Most open to short, colorful items, statistics, stories, profiles for Kingdom Matters department. Content (not author) must be Canadian." Unsolicited manuscripts will not be returned.

** This periodical was #42 on the 2006 Top 50 Christian Publishers list (#37 in 2005).

@ **FAITHWEBBIN ONLINE MAGAZINE**, PO Box 8732, Columbia SC 29202. Fax (775) 908-9660. E-mail: editor@faithwebbin.net. Website: www.faithwebbin.net. Tywebbin Creations. Mrs. Tyora Moody, ed. For Christian families. Monthly online mag. 100 percent unsolicited freelance. Complete ms by e-mail only; e-query OK. **NO PAYMENT**. Articles 800-1,000 words (15-20/yr.). Responds in 1-2 wks. Seasonal 2 mos. ahead. Accepts reprints (tell when/where appeared). Requires e-mail submission (attached file). Regularly uses sidebars. Any Bible version. Guidelines/theme list on Website. (No ads)

Columns/Departments: Accepts 12/yr. Seek (original Bible study lessons and devotions), 1,000-1,200 words; Grow (Christian living: family, finance, marriage, etc.), 800-1,000 words. Needs more health and finance articles.

Special Needs: Book reviews and author interviews.

Tips: "The two areas exclusively open to freelancers are Seek and Grow. Articles are normally accepted if they meet the length requirement and are not similar to what is already included on the site. Looking for fresh articles; love testimonial type devotions or articles that encourage and motivate the reader. Devotions are accepted frequently."

$ **THE FAMILY DIGEST**, PO Box 40137, Fort Wayne IN 46804. Catholic. Corine B. Erlandson, manuscript ed. Dedicated to the joy and fulfillment of Catholic family life and its relationship to the Catholic parish. Quarterly booklet; 48 pgs.; circ. 150,000. Distributed through parishes. 95 percent unsolicited freelance. Complete ms/cover letter; no phone/fax/e-query. Pays $50-60, 4-9 wks. after acceptance, for 1st N.A. rts. Articles 700-1,200 words (40/yr.). Responds in 4-9 wks. Seasonal 7 mos. ahead. Occasionally buys reprints (tell when/where appeared). Prefers hard copy by mail. Uses some sidebars. Prefers NAB. Guidelines by mail; copy for 6 x 9 SAE/2 stamps. (Ads)

Fillers: Buys 12/yr. Anecdotes drawn from experience, prayers, short humor; 25-100 words; pays $25.

Tips: "Prospective freelance writers should be familiar with the types of articles we accept and publish. We are looking for upbeat articles which affirm the simple ways in which the Catholic faith is expressed in daily life. Articles on family life, parish life, seasonal articles, how-to pieces, inspirational, prayer, spiritual life, and church traditions will be gladly reviewed for possible acceptance and publication."

$ @ **FAMILY SMART E-TIPS**, PO Box 3667, Escondido CA 92033. (858) 513-7150. Fax (951) 461-3526. E-mail: plewis@smartfamilies.com or info@smartfamilies.com. Website: www.smartfamilies .com. Smart Families Inc. Paul Lewis, ed./pub. Christian parenting, with strong crossover to general families. E-newsletter. 20 percent unsolicited freelance. Complete ms preferred; fax/e-query OK. Pays $50-250 on publication for 1st rts. Articles 200-1,000 wds. Responds in 1-3 wks. Seasonal 4 mos. ahead. Accepts simultaneous submissions & reprints. Prefers e-mail submission (attached file). Uses some sidebars. Prefers NIV. No guidelines or copy. (No ads)

Fillers: Games, ideas, quotes.

Tips: "We are not a typical 'magazine' and have tight length requirements. Because of crossover audience, we do not regularly print Scripture references or use traditional God-word language."

FELLOWSHIP MAGAZINE, PO Box 412, 1109 Garner Ave., Fenwick ON L0S 1C0, Canada. Toll-free (800) 678-2607. (905) 892-1441. E-mail: minister@pelhamcentre.org. Website: www.fellowship magazine.org. Fellowship Publications/United Church of Canada. Diane Walker, sr. ed. (pmiller17@

cogeco.ca). To provide a positive voice for orthodoxy and uphold the historic Christian faith within the denomination; general lay audience. Quarterly mag.; circ. 9,000. Subscription free for donation. Open to unsolicited freelance. **NO PAYMENT**. Not in topical listings. (Ads)

$ FGBC WORLD, PO Box 576, Winona Lake IN 46590. (574) 268-1122. Fax (574) 268-5384. E-mail: lcgates@bmhbooks.com. Website: www.fgbcworld.com. Brethren Missionary Herald Co. Liz Cutler Gates, edit. dir. Connecting people and churches of the Fellowship of Grace Brethren Churches. Bimonthly tabloid; 8 pgs.; circ. 16,000. Subscription free. Open to unsolicited freelance; 10 percent assigned. Query/clips; fax/e-query OK. Accepts full mss by e-mail. Pays to $100 on publication. Seasonal 4-5 months ahead. No simultaneous submissions; accepts reprints (tell when/where appeared). Prefers accepted articles on disk or by e-mail (attached file). Uses some sidebars. Theme list; no guidelines; copy on Website. (Ads)

   Tips: "Articles must have a Grace Brethren tie."

+ THE FIT CHRISTIAN, PO Box 5732, Ketchikan AK 99901. (206) 274-8474. Fax (614) 388-0664. E-mail: editor@hisworkpub.com or hiswork@hisworkpub.com. Website: www.fitchristian.com. His Work Christian Publishing. Angela J. Perez, ed. A Christian health and fitness magazine. Bimonthly mag. Subscription free. Open to unsolicited freelance. Articles. Incomplete topical listings. (Ads)

FLORIDA BAPTIST WITNESS, 1230 Hendricks Ave., Jacksonville FL 32207. (904) 596-3165. Fax (904) 346-0696. E-mail: jhannigan@floridabaptistwitness.com. Website: www.floridabaptistwitness .com. Florida Baptist Witness Inc./Southern Baptist. Joni B. Hannigan, mng. ed. Publishes good news about God's work that edifies, exhorts, and empowers Florida Baptists to exalt God and extend his Kingdom. Biweekly newspaper; circ. 33,000. Subscription $17.95. Open to unsolicited freelance. Query, query/clips; e-query OK; no calls. Articles. Incomplete topical listings. (Ads)

   Tips: "Submit queries on ideas for specific articles, interviews, Q & A's of particular personalities, conferences, topics related to Southern Baptist or evangelical interest. This is a denominational publication. No columns or fiction; follow AP style."

$ FOCUS ON THE FAMILY MAGAZINE, Colorado Springs CO 80995 (no street address required). (719) 531-3400. Fax (719) 531-3499. Website: www.family.org. Focus on the Family. Sheila Seifert, mng. ed.; Linda Arnold, ed. asst. To help families use Christian principles to strengthen marriages, improve child rearing, purposefully embrace midlife, hold a biblical worldview, and deal with the problems of everyday life. Monthly mag.; 32 pgs.; circ. 800,000. Free subscription. 5 percent unsolicited freelance; 80 percent assigned; 15 percent staff written. Query; no phone/fax/e-query. No full mss by e-mail. Pays .30-.35 cents/wd. on acceptance for 1st & electronic rts. Articles 375-1,100 wds. Responds in 6 wks. Seasonal 7 mos. ahead. Accepts simultaneous submissions; no reprints. Accepts purchased or assigned articles by e-mail (attached file in text or Word). Uses some sidebars. Prefers NIV. Guidelines by mail/e-mail; copy for 9 x 12 SAE/2 stamps. (No ads)

   Tips: "This magazine is 90 percent generated from within our ministry. It's very hard to break in. We look for unique angles and personal stories on common family-life topics. Writing must be concise, compelling, and accurate."
   ** 2005 EPA Award of Merit—Most Improved Publication.

THE FOUNDERS JOURNAL, PO Box 150931, Cape Coral FL 33915. (239) 772-1400. Fax (239) 772-1140. E-mail from Website: www.founders.org. Founders Ministries/Southern Baptist. Thomas K. Ascol, ed. Consistent with the doctrines of grace that speak from a historic Southern Baptist perspective. Quarterly jour. Subscription $20. Complete ms/cover letter & completed author-information form from Website. Articles & book reviews. Responds in 4 mos., or you may contact them. Guidelines on Website. Incomplete topical listings.

FRIENDS JOURNAL: Quaker Thought and Life Today, 1216 Arch St., #2A, Philadelphia PA 19107-2835. (215) 563-8629. Fax (215) 568-1377. E-mail: info@friendsjournal.org. Website: www

.friendsjournal.org. Quaker. Robert Dockhorn, sr. ed. Reflects Quaker life with commentary on social issues, spiritual reflection, Quaker history, and world affairs. Monthly mag.; circ. 8,000. Subscription $39. 70 percent freelance. Complete ms by e-mail preferred; e-query OK. **NO PAYMENT**. Articles to 2,500 words; news items 50-200 words; reports of Quaker events 450 words. Responds in 3-16 wks. Accepts simultaneous submissions or reprints, if notified. Also accepts disk. Guidelines on Website; free copy. Incomplete topical listings.

Poetry: To 25 lines.

Fillers: Games, short humor, newsbreaks, and word puzzles.

$ **THE GEM**, 700 E. Melrose Ave., Box 926, Findlay OH 45839-0926. (419) 424-1961. Fax (419) 424-3433. E-mail: communications@cggc.org or through Website: www.cggc.org. Churches of God, General Conference. Rachel L. Foreman, ed. To encourage and motivate people in their Christian walk. Monthly (13x) take-home paper for adults; 8 pgs.; circ. 6,000. Subscription $14. 80 percent unsolicited freelance; 20 percent assigned. Complete ms/cover letter; phone/fax/e-query OK. Pays $15 after publication for onetime rts. Articles 300-1,200 words (125/yr.); fiction 1,200 words (125/yr.). Responds in 12 wks. Seasonal 3 mos. ahead. Accepts simultaneous submissions & reprints (tell when/where appeared). Accepts requested ms on disk or by e-mail. Uses some sidebars. Prefers NIV. Guidelines on Website; copy for #10 SAE/2 stamps. (No ads)

Poetry: Buys 100/yr. Any type, 3-40 lines; $5-15. Submit max. 3 poems.

Fillers: Buys 100/yr. All types except party ideas; 25-100 words; $5-10.

Special Needs: Missions and true stories. Be sure that fiction has a clearly religious/Christian theme.

Tips: "Most open to real-life experiences where you have clearly been led by God. Make the story interesting and Christian."

** This periodical was #9 on the 2009 Top 50 Christian Publishers list (#7 in 2008, #9 in 2007, #37 in 2006, #24 in 2005).

$ **GEMS OF TRUTH**, PO Box 4060, Overland Park KS 66204. (913) 432-0331. Fax (913) 722-0351. E-mail: sseditor1@juno.com. Website: www.heraldandbanner.com. Church of God (Holiness)/Herald & Banner Press. Arlene McGehee, Sunday school ed. Denominational. Weekly adult take-home paper; 8 pgs.; circ. 14,000. Subscription $2.45. Complete ms/cover letter; phone/fax/e-query OK (prefers mail or e-mail). Pays .005/wd. on publication for 1st rts. Fiction 1,000-2,000 wds. Seasonal 6-8 mos. ahead. Accepts simultaneous submissions & reprints (tell when/where appeared). Prefers KJV. Guidelines/theme list/copy by mail. Not in topical listings. (No ads)

$ **GOOD NEWS**, PO Box 150, Wilmore KY 40390. (859) 858-4661. Fax (859) 858-4972. E-mail: steve@goodnewsmag.org or info@goodnewsmag.org. Website: www.goodnewsmag.org. United Methodist/Forum for Scriptural Christianity Inc. Steve Beard, ed. Focus is evangelical renewal within the denomination. Bimonthly mag.; 44 pgs.; circ. 100,000. Subscription $20. 20 percent unsolicited freelance. Query first; no phone/fax/e-query. Pays $100-150 on publication for onetime rts. Articles 1,500-1,850 words (25/yr.). Responds in 24 wks. Seasonal 4-6 mos. ahead. Accepts simultaneous submissions & reprints (tell when/where appeared). Accepts requested ms on disk. Kill fee. Regularly uses sidebars. Prefers NIV. Guidelines by mail/Website; copy $2.75/9 x 12 SAE. (Ads)

Tips: "Most open to features."

@ **GOOD NEWS!** 440 W. Nyack Rd., West Nyack NY 10994. (845) 620-7438, ext. 20438. Fax (845) 620-7723. E-mail: warren_maye@use.salvationarmy.org. Website: www.SAgoodnews.org. The Salvation Army. Warren Maye, ed. Monthly & online newspaper; 16 pgs.; circ. 30,000. 5 percent unsolicited freelance; 20 percent assigned.

@ **GOOD NEWS CONNECTION**, 105 Harris Ave., Portland ME 04103. Toll-free (800) 357-0203. (207) 797-4915. E-mail: Info@goodnewsconnection.com. Website: www.goodnewsconnection.com. Jim Duran, pub. Enriching thousands of families in Maine and New Hampshire through churches, bookstores, numerous retail outlets, and the Web. Bimonthly & online newspaper; circ. 6,000. Subscription $16.95. Query preferred. Articles; no reviews. Incomplete topical listings.

$ **GOOD NEWS, ETC.**, PO Box 2660, Vista CA 92085. (760) 724-3075. E-mail: goodnewseditor@ cox.net. Website: www.goodnewsetc.com. Good News Publishers Inc. of California. Rick Monroe, ed. Feature stories and local news of interest to Christians in San Diego County. Monthly tabloid; 24-32 pgs.; circ. 38,000. Subscription $30. 5 percent unsolicited freelance; 5 percent assigned. Query; e-query OK. Pays $40-150 on publication for all, 1st, onetime, or reprint rts. Articles 500-900 words (15/yr.). Responds in 2 wks. Seasonal 2 mos. ahead. Accepts simultaneous submissions & reprints (tell when/where appeared). Prefers accepted ms on disk. Regularly uses sidebars. Prefers NIV. No guidelines; copy for 9 x 12 SAE/4 stamps. (Ads)
> **Tips:** "Most open to local (San Diego), personality-type articles. A San Diego connection is needed."
> ** 2005 EPA Award of Merit—Newspaper.

$ @ **GOOD NEWS IN FLORIDA**, PO Box 935148, Margate FL 33093. (954) 564-5378. Fax (866) 587-2911. E-mail: editor@goodnewsfl.org. Website: www.goodnewsfl.org. Blackstone Media Group. Grif Blackstone, ed. To report truth, provoke thought, and honor Jesus Christ. Monthly & online newspaper; 24-56 pgs.; circ. 80,000. Subscription $19.95. Open to freelance. Query/published clips; e-query OK. Accepts full mss by e-mail. Pays .10/wd. for all, 1st, onetime rts. Articles 500-800 wds. Responds in 1 wk. Seasonal 2 mos. ahead. Accepts simultaneous submissions & reprints. Prefers e-mail submissions (attached file). Uses some sidebars. Prefers NLT. Guidelines on Website. (Ads)
> ** 2008, 2007 EPA Award of Merit—Newspaper.

GOOD NEWS JOURNAL, 9701 Copper Creek Dr., Austin TX 78729-3543. (512) 249-6535. Fax (512) 249-0018. E-mail: goodnews98@aol.com. Website: www.thegoodsnewsjournal.net. Evelyn W. Davison, pub. Christian paper for national circulation by subscription, and Central Texas by free distribution. Monthly newspaper; 24 pgs.; circ. 60,000. Subscription $29.95. 40 percent unsolicited freelance; 60 percent assigned. Query; fax/e-query OK. **NO PAYMENT** for onetime rts. Articles 200-600 wds. Accepts reprints. Prefers accepted ms by e-mail. Guidelines by mail/e-mail/Website; copy for 9 x 12 SAE/2 stamps. (Ads)
> **Poetry:** Accepts 4-6/yr. Traditional.
> **Fillers:** Accepts many. All types; 10-50 wds.
> **Tips:** "Most open to short help articles; hope articles; and humor articles."

THE GOOD NEWS TODAY, PO Box 2558, Providence RI 02906. Phone/fax (401) 619-0418. E-mail: larry@goodnewsinri.org or larry@thegoodnewstoday.org. Website: www.thegoodnewstoday .org. Good News Outreach. Lawrence L. Lepore, mng. ed. To evangelize the lost and unite the body of Christ in Rhode Island and S.E. Massachusetts. Monthly newspaper; circ. 16,000. Subscription $20. Open to unsolicited freelance. Complete ms. Articles; book & movie reviews. Starting a new Boston edition. Incomplete topical listings. (Ads)

+ @ **THE GOSPEL HERALD**, 1507—4769 Hazel St., Burnaby BC V5H 1S7, Canada. (604) 715-6288. Fax (604) 608-9152. E-mail: edward@gospelherald.com. Website: www.gospelherald.net. Interdenominational. Edward Shih, pub. The only global Chinese Christian daily news source in English. Daily online journal. All rts. Prefers e-mail submissions (attached or copied into message). Accepts submissions from children/teens. No guidelines; copy online. (Ads)

$ **GOSPEL TODAY MAGAZINE**, 115 Scarlett Oak Way, PO Box 800, Fairburn GA 30213-3448. (770) 719-4825. Fax (770) 716-2660. E-mail: gteditorial@aol.com or Gospeltodaymag@aol.com. Website: www.gospeltoday.com. Horizon Concepts Inc. Teresa Hairston, pub. Ministry/Christian life-style directed toward urban marketplace. Bimonthly (8x) mag.; 64-80 pgs.; circ. 200,000. (drhair-stongt@aol.com). Subscription $14.97. 5 percent unsolicited freelance; 90 percent assigned. Query;

e-query OK. Pays $75-250 on publication for all rts. Articles 1,000-3,500 words (4/yr.). Responds in 2 wks. Seasonal 3 mos. ahead. Accepts simultaneous submissions & reprints (tell when/where appeared). Prefers accepted ms by e-mail (attached file). Kill fee 15 percent. Uses some sidebars. Prefers NKJV. Guidelines on Website; copy $3.50. (Ads)

Fillers: Accepts 2-3/yr. Cartoons, word puzzles. No payment.

Columns/Departments: Precious Memories (historic overview of renowned personality), 1,500-2,000 words; From the Pulpit (issue-oriented observation from clergy), 2,500-3,000 words; Life & Style (travel, health, beauty, fashion tip, etc.), 1,500-2,500 words; Broken Chains (deliverance testimony), 1,200 words. Query. Pays $50-75.

Tips: "Looking for great stories of great people doing great things to inspire others."

+ GREATER PHOENIX CHRISTIAN CHRONICLE, 7070 E. 3rd Ave., Scottsdale AZ 85251. (480) 481-2960. E-mail: gpcceditor@gpchristianchronicle.com. Website: www.gpchristianchronicle.com. David Singer, pub. Monthly newspaper; circ. 25,000. Subscription $20. Open to unsolicited freelance. Query. Articles/reviews. Incomplete topical listings. (Ads)

Tips: "We exist to inform our readers from a biblical perspective, raising the standard for family values, sourcing and networking within the Phoenix community."

$ GUIDEPOSTS, 16 E. 34th St., 21st Fl., New York NY 10016-4397. (212) 251-8100. E-mail: sub missions@guideposts.com. Website: www.guideposts.com. Interfaith. Submit to articles editor. Per sonal faith stories showing how faith in God helps each person cope with life in some particular way. Monthly mag.; 86 pgs.; circ. 2.5 million. Subscription $13.94. 40 percent unsolicited freelance; 20 percent assigned. Complete ms/cover letter by e-mail (attached or copy into message). Pays $100-500 on publication for all rts. Articles 750-1,500 words (40-60/yr.), shorter pieces 250-750 words ($100-250). Responds only to mss accepted for publication in 2 mos. Seasonal 6 mos. ahead. Accepts simultaneous submissions & reprints. Kill fee 20 percent. Uses some sidebars. Free guidelines on Website: www.guideposts.com/tellusyourstory; copy. (Ads)

Columns/Departments: Mysterious Ways (divine intervention), 250 words; What Prayer Can Do, 250 words; Angels Among Us, 400 words; Divine Touch (tangible evidence of God's help), 400 words.

Contest: Writers Workshop Contest held on even years with a late June deadline. Winners attend a week-long seminar in New York (all expenses paid) on how to write for Guideposts.

Tips: "Be able to tell a good story, with drama, suspense, description, and dialog. The point of the story should be some practical spiritual help that subjects learned through their experience. Use unique spiritual insights, strong and unusual dramatic details." First person only.

@ HAIKU HIPPODROME, PO Box 2340, Clovis CA 93613-2340. (559) 347-0194. E-mail: clovis wings@aol.com. Poetry on Wings. Jackson Wilcox, ed. Bimonthly mag. & e-zine; 8 pgs.; circ. 100. Subscription by donation. 100 percent unsolicited freelance. Complete ms/cover letter; phone query OK. No full mss by e-mail. **PAYS 1 COPY & SUBSCRIPTION** on publication for 1st rts. Haiku 3 lines. Responds in 4 wks. Seasonal 3+ mos. ahead. No simultaneous submissions or reprints. Also accepts submissions from children/teens. Prefers KJV. Guidelines by mail; copy for #10 SAE/1 stamp. (No ads)

Poetry: Accepts 225/yr. Haiku; 3 lines. Submit max. 3 poems.

Contest: Every issue includes a Hippodrome Tanka: 3 lines (5-7-5) which are given. The contestant then provides 2 lines of 7 syllables each. Prize for best 2 is publication in next issue.

Tips: "We accept a broad range of what many call English Haiku: (3 lines—often 5-7-5 syllables). However we encourage the style of the early haiku poets—seizing the actuality of the moment in nature and expressing it in the purity of a word or phrase." Prefers no more than 2 haiku on a page.

@ HALO MAGAZINE, 148 Banks Dr., Winchester VA 22602. (540) 877-3568. Fax (540) 877-3535. E-mail: halomag@aol.com. Website: www.halomag.com. Marian Newman Braxton, pres./ed.

Designed to minister to the unsaved and encourage the Christian; reaches a wide audience, including churches, hospitals, and prison ministries across many states. Quarterly & online mag.; 40-54 pgs. Subscription $20. Open to unsolicited freelance. Fax or e-query; complete ms for fiction. Accepts full mss by e-mail. **NO PAYMENT**. Articles & fiction 600-1,500 wds. Submit seasonal 3-4 mos. ahead. Accepts simultaneous submissions & reprints. Prefers submissions by disk/e-mail (attached or copied into message). Uses some sidebars. Accepts submissions from children/teens. Prefers KJV. No guidelines; sample copy for 9 x 12 SAE/$2 postage. (Ads)

> **Poetry:** Accepts original poems; any type or length.
> **Fillers:** Any type or length.
> **Contest:** Sponsors some contests: Presidents' Day (your favorite president; why); Thanksgiving (what you're thankful for), etc.
> **Tips:** "Contact us via e-mail and sign up to write for regular columns such as marriage, death, dealing with illness, teen corner, caregiver's corner, women's corner, divorce, etc."

$ @ HARUAH: Breath of Heaven, 9618 Misty Brook Grove, Memphis TN 38016. (901) 213-3878. E-mail: editor@haruah.com. Website: www.haruah.com. Double-Edge Publishing. Steve Forstner, ed. A magazine dedicated to the art of writing; wanting to inspire and encourage our readers to think in new ways. Monthly e-zine & literary mag.; circ. 9,000. Subscription free online. 75 percent unsolicited freelance; 25 percent assigned. Complete ms/cover letter; no phone/fax query; e-query OK. No full mss by e-mail; use online submission form on Website. Pays $5 for onetime & electronic rts. No length limitations on articles (20+/yr.) or fiction (60+/yr.); reviews 500 wds. Responds in 4-6 wks. Seasonal several mos. ahead. No simultaneous submissions; some reprints (tell when/where appeared). Submit through their online submissions system. Does not use sidebars. Also accepts submissions from teens (students). Any Bible version. Guidelines/copy on Website. (No ads)

> **Poetry:** Rochita Loenen-Ruiz, poetry ed. Accepts 24+/yr. Free verse, light verse, traditional, literary; any number of lines. Pays $2. Submit max. 3 poems.
> **Tips:** "Your story doesn't have to mention God, but we would prefer it to point to Him in one way or another. We have a family atmosphere and love to help emerging writers. But be aware that we keep our expectations for our publication high and do not settle just to fill space. If you are thinking of submitting and aren't sure if your submission fits our guidelines, always feel free to e-mail a query. We have wonderful forums to mingle with the staff. Take advantage of those and get to know us."

HEARTBEAT/CMA, PO Box 9, Hatfield AR 71945. (870) 389-6196. Fax (870) 389-6199. E-mail: heartbeat@cmausa.org or through Website: www.cmausa.org. Christian Motorcyclists Assn. Jennifer Hayes, ed. To encourage members and give them a tool when they are witnessing in the general world. Monthly; circ. 18,000. Subscription $20. Open to freelance. Complete ms/cover letter. Articles; no reviews. Incomplete topical listings. (Ads)

THE HEARTLAND GATEKEEPER, PO Box 34038, Omaha NE 68134. (402) 926-2633. Fax (402) 391-8744. E-mail: publisher@heartlandgatekeeper.org or through Website: www.heartlandgate keeper.org. Faith Missions Intl./nondenominational. Irene Jensen, ed./pub. To promote unity in the body of Christ, to encourage spiritual growth, to testify to the goodness of God through reporting from a Christian perspective, to reach those who have yet to know Jesus; for Omaha/Council Bluffs region. Monthly newspaper; circ. 10,000. Subscription $24. Open to freelance. Prefers query; e-query OK; use online submission form. **NO PAYMENT** for onetime or reprint rts. Articles 150-300 words, 300-700 words, or feature articles 500-1,000 words. Accepts reprints (tell when/where appeared). E-mail submissions only. Guidelines on Website. Incomplete topical listings. (Ads)

@ HEARTLIGHT INTERNET MAGAZINE, PO Box 7044, Abilene TX 79608. E-mail: phil@heart light.org. Website: www.heartlight.org. Westover Hills Church of Christ. Phil Ware, ed. Offers positive Christian resources for living in today's world. Weekly online mag.; 20+ pgs.; circ. 70,000+.

Subscription free. 20 percent unsolicited freelance. E-query. **NO PAYMENT** for electronic rts. Articles 300-450 words (25-35/yr.); fiction 500-700 words (12-15/yr.). Responds in 3 wks. Seasonal 2 mos. ahead. Accepts simultaneous submissions & reprints (tell when/where appeared). Prefers e-mail submission. Regularly uses sidebars. Prefers NIV. Copy on Website.

Fillers: Accepts 12/yr. Anecdotes, cartoons, games, ideas, jokes, newsbreaks, prayers, prose, quotes, short humor, word puzzles; to 350 wds.

Tips: "Most open to feature articles, Just for Men or Just for Women, or Heartlight for Children."

HIGHWAY NEWS AND GOOD NEWS, PO Box 117, Marietta PA 17547-0117. For UPS or FedEx: 1525 River Rd., Marietta PA 17547. (717) 426-9977. Fax (717) 426-9980. E-mail: tfcio@transport forchrist.org. Website: www.transportforchrist.org. Transport for Christ. Inge Koenig, ed. For truck drivers and their families; evangelistic, with articles for Christian growth. Monthly mag.; 16 pgs.; circ. 35,000. Subscription $30 or donation. 60 percent unsolicited freelance. Complete ms/cover letter; fax query OK; e-query preferred. **PAYS IN COPIES** for rights offered. Articles 600 or 1,500 wds. Seasonal 4 mos. ahead. Accepts simultaneous submissions & reprints (tell when/where appeared). Prefers requested ms by e-mail (attached or copied into message). Uses some sidebars. Prefers NIV. Guidelines/theme list by mail; free copy for 9 x 12 SAE. (No ads)

Poetry: Accepts 2/yr.; any type; 3-20 lines. Submit max. 5 poems.

Fillers: Accepts 12/yr. Anecdotes, cartoons, facts, ideas, prayers, prose, short humor, tips; to 100 wds.

Tips: "Looking for items affecting the trucking industry. Need pieces (any length) on health, marriage, and fatherhood. Most open to features and true stories about truckers. Send pictures."

$ + **HOLINESS TODAY**, 17001 Prairie Star Pkwy, Lenexa KS 66220. (913) 577-0500. E-mail: HolinessToday@Nazarene.org. Website: www.holinesstoday.org. Church of the Nazarene. Carmen Ringhiser, ed. Bimonthly mag.; circ. 50,000. Subscription $12. Accepts unsolicited freelance. Query first. Pays. Articles. Guidelines by e-mail. Incomplete topical listings. (No ads)

Tips: "Keeps readers connected with the Nazarene experience and provides tools for everyday faith."

HOLY HOUSE MINISTRIES NEWSLETTER, 9641 Tujunga Canyon Blvd., Tujunga CA 91042. (818) 249-3477. Fax (818) 249-3432. E-mail: HolyHouse9@aol.com. Website: http://holyhouseministries .tripod.com. Rev. Kimberlie Zakarian, pres. Ministers to the unity of families by writing to individual members. Bimonthly newsletter; 6 pgs. Subscription free. 20 percent unsolicited freelance; 80 percent assigned. Query; e-query OK. Prefers accepted ms by e-mail. **PAYS 5 COPIES** for onetime rts. Articles 300 words (50/yr.). Responds in 2 wks. Seasonal 3 mos. ahead. Accepts reprints (tell when/ where appeared). Uses some sidebars. Also accepts submissions from children/teens. No guidelines; copy for $1.25. Incomplete topical listings.

Tips: "Most open to women's issues and prayer tips."

$ **HOMECOMING**, PO Box 562, Alexandria IN 46001. Toll-free (800) 520-4664. (765) 724-8405. Contact by e-mail from their Website: www.gaithernet.com/home.php. Click on "Magazine." Bill & Gloria Gaither, pubs.; Joy MacKenzie, ed-at-large; Roberta Croteau, ed-in-chief. Open to submissions to several columns.

$ **HOMESCHOOLING TODAY**, PO Box 244, Abingdon VA 24212. (276) 628-7730. Fax (208) 692-5505. E-mail: editor@homeschooltoday.com. Website: www.homeschoolingtoday.com. Nehemiah Four LLC. Jim Bob Howard, ed-in-chief. Practical articles, encouragement, news, and lessons for homeschoolers. Bimonthly mag.; 72 pgs.; circ. 12,000. Subscription $21.99. 40 percent unsolicited freelance; 60 percent assigned. Complete ms by e-mail (attached file) or disk; fax/e-query OK. Pays .08/published wd. on publication for 1st rts. Feature articles 2,000-2,200 words; articles 700-1,100 words (30/yr.); book reviews 500 words. Responds in 5-9 wks. Seasonal 1 yr. ahead. Accepts simultaneous submissions; occasional reprints. Requires requested ms by e-mail (attached file). Kill fee 25 percent. Uses some sidebars, 200-400 wds. KJV, NKJV, ESV, or 1599 Geneva. Guidelines/theme list on Website; free copy. (Ads)

> **Columns/Departments:** Buys 20-24/yr. Abacus (teaching math), 700-950 words; Living Literature (unit study with Living Books), 1,100-1,350 words; Thinking (biblical worldview), 850-1,000 words; Hearth and Homeschool (encouraging words for moms), 1,200-1,5,00 words. Pays .08/wd. (See guidelines for additional departments.) Monthly e-newsletter: Homeschooling Helper (1 article, 1,000 words max.; .06/wd.). Semimonthly e-newsletter: Father-Led Home Education (1 article, 850 words max; display banner advertising in lieu of payment). Query.

$ HOME TIMES FAMILY NEWSPAPER, PO Box 22547, West Palm Beach FL 33416-2547. Toll-free (888) 439-3509. Fax (561) 249-4932. E-mail: hometimes@aol.com. Website: www.hometimes.org. Neighbor News Inc. Dennis Lombard, ed./pub. Conservative, pro-Christian community newspaper. Monthly tabloid; 24 pgs.; circ. 4,000. Subscription $24. 15 percent unsolicited freelance; 25 percent assigned. Complete ms only/cover letter; no phone/fax/e-query. Pays $5-25 on acceptance for one-time rts. Articles 100-1,000 words (15/yr.); fiction 300-1,500 words (3/yr.). Responds in 2-3 wks. Seasonal 2 mos. ahead. Accepts simultaneous submissions & reprints (tell when/where appeared). Accepts requested ms by e-mail. No kill fee. Regularly uses sidebars. Also accepts submissions from teens. Any Bible version. Guidelines by mail; 3 issues $3. (Ads)

> **Poetry:** Buys a few/yr. Free verse, traditional; 2-16 lines; $5. Submit max. 3 poems.
> **Fillers:** Uses a few/yr. Anecdotes, cartoons, facts, ideas, jokes, kid quotes, newsbreaks, prayers, quotes, short humor, tips; to 100 words; pays 3-6 copies, if requested.
> **Columns/Departments:** Buys 30/yr. See guidelines for departments, to 600 words; $5-15.
> **Special Needs:** Good short stories (creative nonfiction or fiction). More faith, miracles, personal experiences, and people stories.
> **Tips:** "Most open to personal stories or home/family pieces. Very open to new writers, but study guidelines and sample first; we are different. Published by Christians, but not 'religious.' Looking for more positive articles and stories. Now seeking stringers in multiple viable markets to write local people features with photos. Journalism experience is preferred. E-mail query for more info with your name, brief background, and your address to hometimes2@ aol.com. We strongly suggest you read *Home Times*. Also consider our manual for writers, *101 Reasons Why I Reject Your Manuscript* ($19)."

($) @ HOPEKEEPERS MAGAZINE, PO Box 502928, San Diego CA 92150. Toll-free (888) 751-7378. (858) 486-4685. Toll-free fax (800) 933-1078. E-mail: rest@restministries.org. Website: www.hopekeepersmagazine.com. Rest Ministries Inc. Lisa Copen, ed. For people who live with chronic illness or pain; offers encouragement, support, and hope dealing with everyday issues. Quarterly mag.; 64 pgs.; digital only. Subscription $17.97. 60 percent unsolicited freelance; 40 percent assigned. Query; fax/e-query OK. **PAYS IN COPIES.** Writers receive passwords to give to friends for digital access. Sometimes pay is determined for articles with extensive research; on publication. Articles 375-1,500 words; book reviews 300 words. Responds in 6-8 wks. Seasonal 6 mos. ahead. Accepts simultaneous submissions & reprints. Prefers e-mail submissions (attached or copied into message). Regularly uses sidebars. Also accepts submissions from teens. Guidelines by mail/e-mail/ Website; free copy (call or see Website). (Ads)

> **Fillers:** Accepts 25/yr. Facts, newsbreaks, tips; 40-90 wds.
> **Columns/Departments:** Accepts 4/yr. Refreshments (devotional-style/journal writing), 350 wds.
> **Tips:** "Topics should be 'attention grabbers' about specific emotions (Is it okay to be mad at God?) or experiences (parenting with a chronic illness), or helpful (5 things

you should know about illness on the job). Most open to upbeat topical articles that give reader motivation to change/reflect; should be balanced with personal experience, others' experiences, facts, and Scripture. Devotionals or 'my illness story' not accepted. Please read guidelines; 90 percent of submissions ignore guidelines. Content also accepted for online publications. Fiction is considered but not used frequently."

$ HORIZONS, 1300 N. Meacham Rd., Schaumburg IL 60173-4888. (847) 843-1600. Fax (847) 843-3757. E-mail: takehomepapers@garbc.org. Website: www.RegularBaptistPress.org. General Assn. of Regular Baptist Churches/Regular Baptist Press. Joan E. Alexander, ed. For adults associated with fundamental Baptist churches. Weekly take-home paper that supports the adult curriculum by assisting adults in being grounded and growing Christians; 4 pgs. weekly. Open to freelance. Complete ms/cover letter including personal testimony; no phone/fax/e-query. Pays .05/wd. and up, on acceptance (usually) for 1st rts. Articles 800-1,000 words (if over 600 words, use subheads); fiction 1,000-1,200 words. Responds in 8-12 wks. Seasonal 1 yr. ahead. No simultaneous submissions; some reprints. Some sidebars. Prefers KJV. Guidelines/theme list on Website. Incomplete topical listings. (No ads)

Fillers: Buys 10-15/yr. Word puzzles.

Tips: "We are especially happy to meet competent writers who are using RBP materials in church, or are well acquainted with churches in which our materials are used. We recommend that prospective contributors purchase and study a full quarter of issues before submitting. We look for personal experience stories (both first person and as-told-to), articles with a story element to them, and well-written fiction that helps readers know more of God's character and ways. Check Website quarterly for updates concerning needs, themes, etc.; we're planning one year in advance. Also buy a copy of *Blueprint for Spiritual Maturity* on Website. It articulates our educational philosophy and identifies a broad list of areas where we want to help people grow spiritually. We look for articles that address those areas."

$ IMAGE, 3307 Third Ave. W., Seattle WA 98119. (206) 281-2988. Fax (206) 281-2335. E-mail: image@imagejournal.org. Website: www.imagejournal.org. Gregory Wolfe, pub./ed.; Mary Kenagy, mng. ed. Publishes the best literary fiction, poetry, nonfiction, and visual arts that engages the Judeo-Christian tradition. Quarterly jour.; 128 pgs.; circ. 5,200. Subscription $39.95. 50 percent unsolicited freelance; 50 percent assigned. Queries preferred; phone/fax/e-query OK. Pays $10/pg. ($200 max.) on acceptance for 1st rts. Articles/essays 4,000-6,000 words (10/yr.); fiction 4,000-6,000 words (8/yr.); book reviews 2,000 words. Responds in 1-2 mos. No seasonal. Accepts simultaneous submissions; no reprints. No kill fees. Does not use sidebars. Any Bible version. Guidelines by mail/Website; copy $16 (postpaid). (Ads)

Poetry: Buys 24/yr. Good poetry. Pays $2/line (up to $150). Submit max. 5 poems.

Tips: "Read the journal to understand what we publish. We're always thrilled to see high quality literary work in the unsolicited freelance pile, but we really can't typify what we're looking for other than good writing that's honest about faith and the life of faith. No genre fiction."

$ IMAGINE: Arts Ministry Magazine for IMAGO DEI, 1015 Minnesota Ave., Kansas City KS 66101. Phone/fax (913) 233-0266. E-mail: lori@imagodeiarts.org. Website: www.imagodeiarts.org. IMAGO DEI: Friends of Christianity and the Arts. Calista Baker, submissions ed.; Kathleen Laverick, nonfiction ed.; Lori L. Triplett, fiction ed. For Christians interested in a broad view of the arts. Semiannual mag.; 48 pgs.; circ. 1,000. Estab. 2008. 100 percent unsolicited freelance. Complete ms/cover letter; no phone/fax/e-query. No full mss by e-mail. Pays $15-25 on publication for onetime rts. Articles/fiction/reviews 1,000-2,500 wds. Responds in 12 wks. Accepts simultaneous submissions; no reprints. Prefers disk. No kill fee. Does not use sidebars. Accepts submissions from children/teens. Any Bible version. Guidelines on Website; copy $9.95/9 x 12 SAE/$2 postage. (Ads)

Poetry: Marie Asner, poetry ed. Buys 25-50/yr. Avant-garde, free verse, light verse, traditional; to 40 lines. Pays $15-25. Submit max. 3 poems.

Special Needs: Any type of art: songs, visual art, choreography, drama.
Tips: "Entire magazine is freelance written; open to any art form."

($) @ IMPACT MAGAZINE, 301 Geylang Rd., #03-04 Geylang Centre, Singapore 389344. Tel. 65 6748 1244. Fax 65 748 3744. E-mail: editor@impact.com.sg. Website: www.impact.com.sg. Impact Christian Comm. Ltd. Andrew Goh, ed.; Loy Chin Fen, copy ed. To help young working adults apply Christian principles to contemporary issues. Bimonthly & online mag.; 56 pgs.; circ. 6,000. Subscription $20. 10 percent unsolicited freelance. Query or complete ms/cover letter; phone/fax/e-query OK. Accepts full ms by e-mail. Ranges from no payment up to $40/pg. for all rts. Articles 1,200-1,500 words (12/yr.) & fiction (6/yr.); 1,000-2,000 words. Seasonal 2 mos. ahead. Accepts reprints. Prefers e-mail submission (attached file). Uses some sidebars. Prefers NIV. Guidelines by mail/e-mail; copy for $4/$3 postage (surface mail). (Ads)
   Poetry: Accepts 2-3 poems/yr. Free verse, 20-40 lines. Submit max. 3 poems.
   Fillers: Accepts 6/yr. Anecdotes, cartoons, jokes, quizzes, short humor, and word puzzles.
   Columns/Departments: Closing Thoughts (current social issues), 600-800 words; Testimony (personal experience), 1,500-2,000 words; Parenting (Asian context), 1,000-1,500 words; Faith Seeks Understanding (answers to tough questions of faith/Scripture), 80-1,000 words.
   Tips: "We're most open to fillers and testimonies."

$ INDIAN LIFE, PO Box 3765, Redwood Post Office, Winnipeg MB R2W 3R6, Canada. U.S. address: PO Box 32, Pembina ND 58271. (204) 661-9333. Fax (204) 661-3982. E-mail: ilm@indianlife.org. Website: www.indianlife.org. Indian Life Ministries/nondenominational. Jim Uttley, ed. An evangelistic publication for English-speaking aboriginal people in North America. Bimonthly tabloid newspaper; 16 pgs.; circ. 16,000. Subscription $15. 5 percent unsolicited freelance; 5 percent assigned. Query (query or complete ms for fiction); phone/fax/e-query OK. Pays .15/wd (to $200) on publication for 1st rts. Articles 150-2,500 words (20/yr.); fiction 500-2,000 words (8/yr.); reviews, 250 words ($40). Responds in 6 wks. Seasonal 4 mos. ahead. Accepts simultaneous submissions & reprints (tell when/where appeared). Accepts requested ms by e-mail (copied into message preferred). Some kill fees 50 percent. Uses some sidebars. Accepts submissions from children/teens. Prefers New Life Version, NIV. Guidelines by mail/ e-mail/Website; copy for 9 x 12 SAE/$2 postage (check or money order). (Ads)
   Poetry: Buys 4 poems/yr.; free verse, light verse, traditional, 10-100 words; pays $40. Submit max. 5 poems.
   Fillers: Kid quotes, quotes, short humor, 50-200 words; $10-25.
   Special Needs: Celebrity pieces must be aboriginal only. Looking for legends.
   Tips: "Most open to testimonies from Native Americans/Canadians—either first person or third person—news features, or historical fiction with strong and accurate portrayal of Native American life from the Indian perspective. A writer should have understanding of some Native American history and culture. We suggest reading some Native American authors. Native authors preferred, but some others are published. Aim at a 10th-grade reading level; short paragraphs; avoid multisyllable words and long sentences."
   **This periodical was #30 on the 2009 Top 50 Christian Publishers list.

$ IN HIS PRESENCE, PO Box 14451, Knoxville TN 37914. (865) 335-0072. Fax (865) 524-5277. E-mail: ihp@samaritanpress.com. Website: www.samaritanpress.com. Samaritan Press. R. Michael Henegar, pres. Offers ongoing serial-form stories and new articles and interviews to interest Christian communities. Monthly tabloid; 36+ pgs; circ. 25,000. Subscription $25. 80 percent unsolicited freelance; 20 percent assigned. Query; e-query OK. Pay negotiable on publication. Articles 600-1,200 words; fiction 2,000+ words. Responds in 4-6 wks. Seasonal 3 mos. ahead. Accepts simultaneous submissions & reprints (tell when/where appeared). Wants accepted mss by e-mail. Sometimes pays kill fee. Also accepts submissions from children/teens. Prefers NKJV. Guidelines (also by e-mail/ Website); copy for 9 x 12 SAE/$2 postage. (Ads)

Poetry: Buys 10-15/yr. Light verse, traditional; 12-36 lines. Pay negotiable. Submit max. 2 poems.

Fillers: Buys 12-15/yr. Anecdotes, cartoons, jokes, short humor; 60-600 wds. Pay negotiable.

Tips: "All sections and departments are open to new writers and freelancers. Just let us see your work and have confidence in yourself and your ability. "

+ **IN PART**, 431 Grantham Rd., Box A, Grantham PA 17027. (717) 697-2634. E-mail: inpart@ bic-church.org or through Website: www.inpart.org. Brethren in Christ Church. Kristine N. Frey, ed. Quarterly mag.; circ. 24,000. Subscription free. Open to unsolicited freelance. Query first. Articles/ reviews. Guidelines/theme list on Website. Incomplete topical listings. (No ads)

Tips: "We communicate the life, teachings, and mission of the Brethren in Christ Church."

$ **INTERCHANGE**, 412 Sycamore St., Cincinnati OH 45202-4179. (513) 421-0311. Fax (513) 421-0315. E-mail: rthompson@diosohio.org or through Website: www.episcopal-dso.org. Episcopal Diocese of Southern Ohio. Richelle Thompson, dir. of communications. Regional paper for the Episcopal and Anglican Church in southern Ohio. Monthly (11x) newspaper; 16 pgs.; circ. 12,000. Free. 20 percent unsolicited freelance. Query or complete ms/cover letter. Pays $50-150 on acceptance for all rts. Articles 500-2,000 words (8-10/yr.). Responds in 4 wks. Accepts simultaneous submissions. Prefers requested ms on disk/CD. Regularly uses sidebars. Also accepts submissions from children/teens. Copy for 9 x 12 SASE.

Fillers: Cartoons, facts, jokes.

Tips: "Most open to features, especially with a local angle."

$ @ **THE INTERIM**, 104 Bond St., Third Floor, Toronto ON M5B 1X9, Canada. (416) 204-1687. Fax (416) 204-1027. E-mail: interim@lifesite.net or lsn@lifesitenews.com. Website: www.lifesite .net. The Interim Publishing Co. Paul Tuns, ed. Abortion, euthanasia, pornography, feminism, and religion from a pro-life perspective; Catholic and evangelical Protestant audience. Monthly & online newspaper; 24 pgs.; circ. 20,000. Subscription $35 Cdn. or U.S. 60 percent unsolicited freelance. Query; phone/e-query OK. Pays $50-150 Cdn. on publication. Articles 400-750 words; book, music, video reviews, 500 words ($50-75 Cdn.). Responds in 2 wks. Seasonal 2 mos. ahead. Accepts simultaneous submissions & reprints (tell when/where appeared). Prefers e-mail submission (copied into message). Kill fee. Uses some sidebars. Prefers RSV & others. No guidelines; catalog by mail. (Ads)

Fillers: Cartoons.

Tips: "We are most open to news on life, family, and moral issues; informative commentary."

$ **IN TOUCH**, 3836 DeKalb Technology Pkwy., Atlanta GA 30340. (770) 451-1001. E-mail: writers@ intouch.org. Website: www.intouch.org. In Touch Ministries. Tonya Stoneman, ed. Publishing arm of Dr. Charles Stanley's international ministry. Monthly mag.; 48 pgs.; circ. 1 million. Subscription free. 25 percent unsolicited freelance; 25 percent assigned. Query, e-query OK. No full mss by e-mail. Pays varying rates on acceptance for 1st, electronic, nonexclusive rts. Articles 800-2,000 words (60/ yr.). Responds in 6-8 wks. Seasonal 6 mos. ahead. No simultaneous submissions or reprints. Prefers e-mail submissions (attached or copied into message). Kill fee 50 percent. Uses some sidebars. Prefers NASB. Guidelines by e-mail/Website; copy for 6 x 9 SAE. (No ads)

Columns/Departments: Strong in Spirit (exegetical), 1,200 words; Family Room (family topics), 800-1,200 words; By Faith (profiles), 800-1,200 words; Solving Problems (life issues), 800-1,200 words. Payment varies.

** 2007 EPA Award of Merit—Devotional.

ISLAND CATHOLIC NEWS, PO Box 5424 LCD9, Victoria BC V8R 6S4, Canada. (250) 727-9429. Fax (250) 727-3647. E-mail: Icn@telus.net (editorial); icn@islandnet.com (administration). Website:

www.islandnet.com/~icn. Island Catholic News Society. Patrick Jamieson, mng. ed. Submit to Louise Beinhauer (250-727-3247). Dissenting but concerned Catholics critical of the institution of the Catholic church. Monthly tabloid; 12-16 pgs.; circ. 2,000. Subscription $35 Cdn./U.S. 90 percent unsolicited freelance; 10 percent assigned. Query; phone/fax/e-query OK. Accepts full mss by e-mail. **PAYS IN COPIES OR AD SPACE** on publication for 1st, onetime or reprint rts. Articles 250/350/500 words (2-4/yr.); fiction 1,500 words (1-2/yr.); reviews 250-750 words. Responds in 4 wks. Seasonal 2 mos. ahead. Accepts simultaneous submissions & reprints (tell when/where appeared). Accepts e-mail submissions. Regularly uses sidebars. Prefers Jerusalem Bible. Also accepts submissions from children/teens. Guidelines by mail; copy for #10 SAE/3 stamps. (Ads)

> **Poetry:** Accepts 10-20/yr. Avant-garde, free verse, haiku; 5-20 lines. Submit max. 4 poems.
> **Fillers:** Prayers, prose, quotes.
> **Tips:** "Call to chat."

$ + @ **THE JC REPORTER**, 3190 Lancaster Dr. N.E., Salem OR 97305. (503) 316-1220. Fax (503) 585-7228. E-mail: cindy@thejctown.com. Website: www.thejctown.com. The JC Media Group. Cindy Smith, pres./pub. Combined with radio & Web, we spread the Word and encourage, equip, and unite the local body of Christ. Monthly & online newspaper; 24-32 pgs; circ. 20,000. Subscription $20. Estab. 2007. 70 percent unsolicited freelance; 30 percent assigned. Query/clips; fax/e-query OK. Accepts full mss by e-mail (attached file). Pays $25-75 for onetime rts. Not copyrighted. Articles to 700 words (100/yr.); fiction to 700 words (100/yr.); reviews 200 words, pays $10. Responds in 4-6 wks. Seasonal 2 mos. ahead. Accepts simultaneous submissions & reprints (tell when/where appeared). No kill fee. Uses some sidebars. Guidelines by e-mail; copy for 10 x 13 SAE/$2 postage. (Ads)

> **Poetry:** Accepts 24/yr. Any type. No payment. Submit any number.
> **Fillers:** Accepts many/yr. All types; 300-500 wds.
> **Columns/Departments:** Buys many/yr. Query or complete ms, $20-50.

THE JERUSALEM CONNECTION, PO Box 20295, Washington DC 20041. (703) 707-0014. Fax (703) 707-9514. E-mail: jmh@tjci.org. Website: www.tjci.org. The Jerusalem Connection Intl. James M. Hutchens, ed. To inform, educate, and activate support for Israel and Jewish people; advocates for Christian Zionism. Bimonthly mag.; circ. 3,500. Subscription $30. Open to unsolicited freelance. Query. Articles. Incomplete topical listings. (Ads)

JOURNAL OF CHURCH AND STATE, Oxford University Press, 2001 Evans Rd., Cary NC 27513. Toll-free (800) 852-7323. (919) 677-0977. Fax (919) 677-1714. E-mail: Carolyn.wilson@oxfordjournals .org. Website: www.oxfordjournals.org. Submit to The Editor. Provides a forum for the critical examination of the interaction of religion and government worldwide. Quarterly jour.; 225 pgs.; circ. 1,700. Subscription $25 (indiv.); $39 (institution). 75 percent unsolicited freelance; 25 percent assigned. Complete ms (3 copies)/cover letter (also by e-mail); phone/fax query OK; no e-query. **NO PAYMENT** for all rights. Articles 25-30 pgs./footnotes (24/yr.). Responds in 9-18 wks. Prefers requested ms on disk; e-mail submission OK. Does not use sidebars. Prefers KJV. Guidelines by mail/e-mail/Website; copy $8/$3.16 postage (mark "Media Mail"). (Ads)

> **Special Needs:** Church-state issues, philosophy, religion.
> **Tips:** "Open to feature articles only. Send three copies of essay and cover letter. Follow writers' guidelines."

$ + @ **KD GOSPEL MEDIA MAGAZINE**, PO Box 1211, Hartford CT 06143-1211. (860) 833-2360. Fax (860) 461-7928. E-mail: deanne@kdgmmag.com. Website: www.kdgmmag.com. To bring the God perspective into the homes of our readers in a motivating and encouraging way. Deanne Williams, chief ed. Quarterly & online mag.; 84 pgs. Subscription $14.50. Estab. 2009. 20 percent unsolicited freelance; 80 percent assigned. Query/clips; e-query OK. Accepts full mss by e-mail. Pays $100-200 on publication for all rts. Articles 1,050 words; reviews 500 words. Responds in 3-6 wks. Seasonal 4 mos. ahead. Accepts simultaneous submissions. Accepts articles on disk or by e-mail (attached file).

No kill fee. Uses some sidebars. Also accepts submissions from teens. Guidelines by e-mail/Website; theme list online; no copy. (Ads)

Poetry: Buys 6/yr. Any type of religious poetry; 15-20 lines. Pays $50. Submit max. 2 poems.

Fillers: Buys 12/yr. Ideas, kid quotes, newsbreaks, party ideas, tips; 200-300 wds. Pays $25.

Columns/Departments: Buys 12/yr., 500-1,000 words, $100-200. Complete ms.

Special Needs: Beauty, fashion, missions, sports, men's/women's/youth issues, holiday/seasonal, movie reviews, time management, food/recipes, and politics.

Contest: Sponsors a poetry contest once a year from January 1 to August 30. Winner published in October issue.

Tips: "Creativity is a huge plus. Sending photos with queries helps a lot. Be clear in what you are offering because you never know when we will be looking to fill a position. Be sure to check your facts and reference others' work. All articles should be positive, educational, and/or faith based."

KEYS TO LIVING, 105 Steffens Rd., Danville PA 17821. (570) 437-2891. E-mail: owcam@verizon .net. Website: www.keystoliving.homestead.com. Connie Mertz, ed./pub. Educates, encourages, and challenges readers through devotional and inspirational writings; also nature articles, focusing primarily on wildlife in eastern U.S. Quarterly newsletter; 12 pgs. Subscription $10. 20 percent unsolicited freelance (needs freelance). Complete ms/cover letter; prefers e-mail submissions; no phone query. **PAYS 2 COPIES** for onetime or reprint rts. Articles 350-500 wds. Responds in 4 wks. Accepts reprints. No disk; e-mail submission OK (copied into message). Prefers NIV. Guidelines/theme list on Website (owcam@verizon.net); copy for 7 x 10 SAE/2 stamps. (No ads)

Poetry: Accepts if geared to family, nature, personal living, or current theme. Traditional with an obvious message.

Special Needs: More freelance submissions on themes only.

Tips: "We are a Christ-centered family publication. Seldom is freelance material used unless it pertains to a current theme. No holiday material accepted. Stay within word count."

@ $ KINDRED SPIRIT, 3909 Swiss Ave., Dallas TX 75204. (214) 841-3556. Fax (972) 222-1544. E-mail: sglahn@dts.edu. Website: www.dts.edu/ks. Dallas Theological Seminary. Sandra Glahn, ed-in-chief. Publication of Dallas Theological Seminary. Tri-annual mag. & online; 16-20 pgs.; circ. 30,000. Subscription free. 75 percent unsolicited freelance. Query/clips; fax/e-query OK. Pays $300 flat fee on publication for 1st & electronic rts. Articles 1,100 words; biblical fiction. Responds in 6 wks. Seasonal 8 mos. ahead. No simultaneous submissions; accepts reprints. Requires accepted mss by e-mail (attached or copied into message). Regularly uses sidebars. Prefers NIV. Guidelines on Website; copy by mail. (No ads)

Special Needs: Profiles/interviews of DTS grads and faculty are open to anyone.

Tips: "Any news or profiles or expositions of Scripture with a link to DTS will receive top consideration; all topics other than interviews need to come from DTS graduates."

** 2009 Award of Merit—Online.

@ KOINONIA, 8107 Holmes Rd., Kansas City MO 64131. (816) 361-7242. Fax (816) 361-2144. E-mail: koinoniaemail@gmail.com. Website: www.holycatholicanglican.org. Holy Catholic Church/ Anglican Rite. Holly Michael, ed. Seeks a variety of articles pertaining to the orthodox Christian faith. Quarterly online newsletter; 12-16 pgs. Subscription $10. Complete ms/cover letter; e-query OK. **PAYS IN COPIES & SUBSCRIPTION** for one-time rts. Articles/short stories to 2,000 wds. Guidelines by e-mail; copy online. (Ads)

Tips: "All sections open."

+ LA NUEVA VISION, 13 Warwick St., Auburn MA 01501. (401) 528-7762. Newspaper in Spanish for multidenominational Christians. Edwin Cancel, pub.; Rev. Israel Mercedes, ed. Monthly newspaper. Open to unsolicited freelance. Query first. Articles/reviews. Incomplete topical listings. (Ads)

$ @ THE LAYMAN, 136 Tremont Park Dr. N.E., PO Box 2210, Lenoir NC 28645. (828) 758-8716. Fax (828) 758-0920. E-mail: laymanletters@layman.org. Website: www.layman.org. Presbyterian Lay Committee. Carman Fowler, pres. & exec. dir.; Parker T. Williamson, ed. emeritus; Paula R. Kincaid, ed. of *The Layman* & *The Layman Online*. For evangelical Christians interested in the Presbyterian and reformed denominations. Bimonthly & online newspaper; 24 pgs.; circ. 100,000. No subscriptions. 10 percent unsolicited freelance. Query. Pays negotiable rates on publication for 1st rts. Articles 800-1,200 words (12/yr.). Responds in 2 wks. Seasonal 2 mos. ahead. Prefers requested ms on disk. Regularly uses sidebars. Copy for 9 x 12 SAE/3 stamps. (No ads)

LEAVES, PO Box 87, Dearborn MI 48121-0087. (313) 561-2330. Fax (313) 561-9486. E-mail: leaves-mag@juno.com. Website: www.rc.net/detroit/mariannhill/leaves.htm. Catholic/Mariannhill Fathers of Michigan. Jacquelyn M. Lindsey, ed. For all Catholics; promotes devotion to God and his saints and publishes readers' spiritual experiences, petitions, and thanksgivings. Bimonthly mag.; 24 pgs.; circ. 50,000. Subscription free. 50 percent unsolicited freelance. Complete ms/cover letter; phone/fax/e-query OK. **NO PAYMENT** for 1st or reprint rts. Not copyrighted. Articles 500 words (6-12/yr.). Responds in 4 wks. Seasonal 4 mos. ahead. Accepts reprints. Accepts e-mail submissions (copied into message). Does not use sidebars. Prefers NAB, RSV (Catholic edition). No guidelines or copy. (No ads)
  Poetry: Accepts 6-12/yr. Traditional; 8-20 lines. Submit max. 4 poems.
  Special Needs: Testimonies of conversion or reversion to Catholicism.
  Tips: "Besides being interestingly and attractively written, an article should be confidently and reverently grounded in traditional Catholic doctrine and spirituality. The purpose of our magazine is to edify our readers."

$ @ LEBEN, 2150 River Plaza Dr., Ste. 150, Sacramento CA 95833. (916) 473-8866, ext. 4. E-mail: editor @Leben.us. Website: www.Leben.us. City Seminary Press. Wayne Johnson, ed. Focuses on Protestant Christian history and biography. Quarterly & online mag.; 24 pgs.; circ. 5,000. Subscription $9.95. 20 percent unsolicited freelance; 80 percent assigned. Complete ms; e-query OK. Accepts full mss by e-mail. Pays $175 or .05/wd. (copies & subscription) on acceptance for 1st & electronic rts. Articles 500-3,000 words (4/yr.). Responds in 2 wks. Accepts simultaneous submissions & reprints (tell when/ where appeared). Prefers e-mail submissions (attached file). Uses some sidebars. Also accepts submissions from teens. Prefers KJV. Guidelines on Website; copy for 9 x 12 SASE/$2 postage. (Ads)
  Fillers: Buys 4-6/yr. Short humor. Pays $5-10.
  Special Needs: Reprints from old publications; historical, humor, etc.
  Tips: "We feature stories that are biographical, historically accurate, and interesting—about Protestant martyrs, patriots, missionaries, etc., with a 'Reformed' slant."

$ LIBERTY, Dept. of Public Affairs and Religious Liberty, 12501 Old Columbia Pike, Silver Springs MD 20904-1608. (301) 680-6690. Fax (301) 680-6695. E-mail: steeli@nad.adventist.org. Website: www.libertymagazine.org. Seventh-day Adventist. Lincoln Steed, ed. (lincoln.steed@nad.adventist .org). Deals with religious-liberty issues for government officials, civic leaders, and laymen. Bimonthly mag.; 32 pgs.; circ. 200,000. Subscription $6.95. 95 percent unsolicited freelance. Query/clips; phone/fax/e-query OK. Pays $100-500 on acceptance for 1st rts. Articles & essays 1,000-2,500 wds. Responds in 5-13 wks. Requires requested ms on disk or by e-mail. Guidelines/copy by mail.

$ LIFEGLOW, Box 6097, Lincoln NE 68506-0097. (402) 448-0981. Fax (402) 488-7582. E-mail: info@christianrecord.org. Website: www. christianrecord.org. Christian Record Services for the Blind. Bert Williams, ed. For sight-impaired adults; interdenominational Christian audience. Published as large-print magazine.

LIFESITE NEWS.COM, Canadian address: 104 Bond St. E., Third Fl., Toronto ON M5B 1X9, Canada. U.S. address: LPO Box 1008, Niagara Falls NY 14304-1008. Toll-free (866) 787-9947. E-mail: editor

@lifesitenews.com or lsn@lifesitenews.com. Website: www.lifesitenews.com. An originally written online daily news service covering life, faith, family, and freedom. John-Henry Westen, ed. 20 million page views/yr. Free subscription at www.lifesite.net/ldn/subscribe. Incomplete topical listings.

Tips: "Highly regarded as a leader in the field of pro-life and pro-family news."

@ **LIFETIMES CATHOLIC E-ZINE**. (877) 585-3816. E-mail: bjubar@parishwebmaster.com (see guidelines for e-mail address for each department). Website: www.ParishWebmaster.com/writers .htm. Catholic. Brandon Jubar, ed. Designed to spread the Good News and minister to people online. Weekly online publication. Open to submissions. Query first. **NO PAYMENT**. Articles 300-600 words (300/yr.). Also accepts submissions from teens. Guidelines on Website.

Columns: Weekly Reflection; Catholic Life; Faith & Spirituality; Family; Self-Improvement; Teen Issues; Teen 2 Teen.

+ **LIFETIMES MAGAZINE**, Providence House, Ardenlee St., Belfast BT6 8QJ, Northern Ireland. Toll-free (800) 209-8570. E-mail: tlowry@emeraldhouse.com. Website: www.emeraldhouse.com. Ambassador Intl. Gillian Graham, ed. An upbeat, heartwarming look at Christian life. Monthly mag. Subscription 65 pounds/yr.

$ **LIGHT & LIFE**, Box 535002, Indianapolis IN 46253-5002. (317) 244-3660. Fax (317) 244-1247. E-mail: LLMAuthors@fmcna.org. Website: www.freemethodistchurch.org/Magazine. Free Methodist Church of North America. Doug Newton, ed.; Cynthia Schnereger, mng. ed.; submit to Margie Newton, ms manager. Interactive magazine for maturing Christians; contemporary-issues oriented, thought-provoking; emphasizes spiritual growth, discipline, holiness as a lifestyle. Bimonthly mag.; 32 pgs. (plus pullouts); circ. 13,000. Subscription $16. 95 percent unsolicited freelance. Query first; e-query OK. Pays .15/wd. on acceptance for 1st rts. Articles 800-1,700 words (24/yr.). Responds in 8-12 wks. Seasonal 12 mos. ahead. No simultaneous submissions. Prefers e-mail submission (attached file) after acceptance. No kill fee. Uses some sidebars. Prefers NIV. Also accepts submissions from children/teens. Guidelines on Website; copy $4. (Ads)

Tips: "Best to write a query letter. We are emphasizing contemporary issues articles, well researched. Ask the question 'What topics are not receiving adequate coverage in the church and Christian periodicals?' Seeking unique angles on everyday topics."

LIGHT OF THE WORLD NEWSPAPER, 177-34 Troutville Rd., Jamaica NY 11434. (718) 938-7966. E-mail: Christislight@aol.com. Julius Ogunnaya, ed. Primarily targets African Christians and non-Christians. Monthly newspaper; 28 pgs.; circ. 20,000. Open to unsolicited freelance. E-query. **NO PAYMENT**. Articles 2 pgs. max. Guidelines by e-mail. Incomplete topical listings. (Ads)

Poetry: Accepts poetry.

Fillers: Cartoons, jokes, quizzes, and word puzzles.

Contest: Youth Annual Essay Competition.

$ **LIGUORIAN**, One Liguori Dr., Liguori MO 63057-9999. Toll-free (800) 464-2555. (636) 464-2500. Toll-free fax (800) 325-9526. (636) 464-8449. E-mail: manuscript_submissions@liguori .org. Website: www.liguorian.org. Catholic/Liguori Publications. Rick Potts, C.Ss.R., ed-in-chief; Cheryl Plass, mng. ed. To help Catholics of all ages better understand the gospel and church teachings and to show how these teachings apply to life and the problems confronting them as members of families, the church, and society. Monthly (10x) mag.; 40 pgs.; circ. 120,000. Subscription $20. 30-40 percent unsolicited freelance; 60 percent assigned. Query, query/clips, or complete ms; phone/fax/e-query OK. Pays .12-.15/wd. on acceptance for 1st rts. Articles 1,200-2,200 words (30-50/yr.); fiction 1,800-2,000 words (10/yr.); book reviews 250 words. No simultaneous submissions or reprints. Responds in 8-12 wks. Seasonal 6-8 mos. ahead. Prefers requested ms by e-mail (attached file). Sometimes pays kill fee. Uses some sidebars. Prefers NRSV. Guidelines by mail/e-mail/Website; copy for 9 x 12 SAE/3 stamps. (Ads)

Fillers: Buys 10/yr. Cartoons, jokes.

Tips: "Most open to 1,000-word meditations; 1,800-word fiction; or 1,500-word personal testimonies. Send complete manuscript for fiction. Polish your own manuscript."

** This periodical was #16 on the 2009 Top 50 Christian Publishers list (#13 in 2008, #16 in 2007, #22 in 2006, #6 in 2005).

$ LIVE, 1445 N. Boonville Ave., Springfield MO 65802-1894. (417) 862-2781. Fax (417) 862-6059. E-mail: rl-live@gph.org. Website: www.gospelpublishing.com. Assemblies of God/Gospel Publishing House. Richard Bennett, adult ed. Inspiration and encouragement for adults. Weekly take-home paper; 8 pgs.; circ. 46,000. Subscription $14.80. 100 percent unsolicited freelance. Complete ms/cover letter; no phone/fax query; e-query OK. Pays .10/wd. (.07/wd. for reprints) on acceptance for onetime or reprint rts. Articles 400-1,100 words (80-90/yr.); fiction 400-1,100 words (20/yr.). Responds in 4-6 wks. Seasonal 18 mos. ahead. Accepts simultaneous submissions & reprints (tell when/where appeared). Accepts e-mail submissions (attached file). No kill fees. Few sidebars. Prefers NIV, KJV. Guidelines by mail/e-mail; copy for #10 SAE/1 stamp. (No ads)

Poetry: Buys 12-18/yr. Free verse, light verse, traditional; 8-25 lines; $60 ($35 for reprints) when scheduled. Submit max. 3 poems.

Tips: "We are often in need of good shorter stories (400-600 words), especially true stories or based on true stories. Often need holiday stories that are not 'how-to' stories, particularly for patriotic or nonreligious holidays. All areas open to freelance—human interest, inspirational, and difficulties overcome with God's help. Fiction must be especially good with biblical application. Follow our guidelines. Most open to well-written personal experience with biblical application. Send no more than two articles in the same envelope and send an SASE."

** This periodical was #3 on the 2009 Top 50 Christian Publishers list (#5 in 2008, #1 in 2007, #8 in 2006, #19 in 2005).

$ LIVING FOR THE WHOLE FAMILY (formerly Living), 1251 Virginia Ave., Harrisonburg VA 22802. (540) 433-5351. Fax (540) 434-0247. E-mail: mediaforliving@gmail.com. Website: www.livingforthewholefamily.com. Media for Living. Melodie M. Davis, ed. A positive, practical, and uplifting publication for the whole family; mass distribution. Quarterly tabloid; 28-36 pgs.; circ. 50,000. Subscription free. 95 percent unsolicited freelance. Query or complete ms/cover letter; e-query OK. Pays $50 after publication for onetime rts. Articles 1,000-1,200 words (40-50/yr.). Responds in 13-18 wks. Seasonal 4 mos. ahead. Accepts simultaneous submissions & reprints (tell when/where appeared). Accepts requested ms by e-mail (copied into message; include e-mail address in message). Uses some sidebars. Prefers NIV. Guidelines by mail/e-mail; copy for 9 x 12 SAE/4 stamps. (Ads)

Fillers: Buys 4-8/yr. Anecdotes, short humor; 100-200 words; $20-25.

Tips: "We are directed toward the general public, many of whom have no Christian interests, and we're trying to publish high-quality writing on family issues/concerns from a Christian perspective. That means religious language must be low key. Too much of what we receive is directed toward a Christian reader. We get far more than we can use, so something really has to stand out. Please carefully consider before sending. Need more articles of interest to men. Our articles need to have a family slant or fit the descriptor 'encouragement for families.'" When submitting by e-mail, put title of magazine and title of your piece in subject line. Also include your e-mail address in body of message.

$ LIVING LIGHT NEWS, #200, 5306—89th St., Edmonton AB T6E 5P9, Canada. (780) 468-6397. Fax (780) 468-6872. E-mail: shine@livinglightnews.com. Website: www.livinglightnews.com. Living Light Ministries. Jeff Caporale, ed. To motivate and encourage Christians; witnessing tool to the lost. Bimonthly tabloid; 36 pgs.; circ. 75,000. Subscription $24.95 U.S. 40 percent unsolicited freelance; 60 percent assigned. Query; e-query OK. Pays $20-125 (.05-.10/wd. Cdn. or.10/wd. U.S.) on publication for all, 1st, onetime, simultaneous, or reprint rts. Articles 350-700 words (75/yr.). Responds in 4 wks. Seasonal 3-4 mos. ahead. Accepts simultaneous submissions & reprints (tell when/where appeared). Guidelines by e-mail/Website; copy for 9 x 12 SAE/$2.50 Cdn. postage or IRCs (no U.S. postage). (Ads)

Columns/Departments: Buys 20/yr., 450-600 words, $10-30 Cdn. Parenting; relationships. Query.

Special Needs: Celebrity interviews/testimonials of well-known personalities. Fun or informative articles (250-700 words) for Christian-education supplement.

Tips: "Most open to a timely article about someone who is well known in North America, in sports or entertainment, and has a strong Christian walk."

** This periodical was #34 on the 2007 Top 50 Christian Publishers list (#38 in 2006, #34 in 2005).

LIVING STONES NEWS, 2031 E. First St., Duluth MN 55812. (218) 728-4945. E-mail: corinne@ livingstonesnews.com, editor@livingstonesnews.com or through Website: www.livingstonesnews .com. Corinne E. Scott, pub. To glorify God, to reach out to the unsaved, and to bring hope, encouragement, peace, and the unconditional love of Jesus Christ to our readers. Monthly newspaper; circ. 15,000. Subscription free to churches & businesses; $18 for individuals. Open to freelance. Query preferred. Articles. (Ads) Not included in topical listings.

$ @ THE LOOKOUT, 8805 Governor's Hill Dr., Ste. 400, Cincinnati OH 45249. (513) 931-4050. Fax (513) 931-0950. E-mail: lookout@standardpub.com. Website: www.lookoutmag.com. Standard Publishing. Shawn McMullen, ed. For adults who are interested in learning more about applying the gospel to their lives. Weekly & online mag.; 16 pgs.; circ. 62,000. Subscription $45. 30 percent unsolicited freelance; 70 percent assigned. Query for theme articles; e-query OK. Pays $175-225 on publication. Articles 500-1,600 words (200/yr.). Responds in 10 wks. Seasonal 9 mos. ahead. Accepts simultaneous submissions; no reprints. No disks or e-mail submissions. Kill fee 50 percent. Regularly uses sidebars. Prefers NIV. Guidelines/theme list by mail/e-mail/Website: www.lookout mag.com/write/default.asp); copy for #10 SAE/$1. (Ads)

Columns/Departments: Buys 24/yr. Outlook (personal opinion); Salt & Light (innovative ways to reach out into the community); Faith Around the World; all 800 wds. Pays $125. Query.

Tips: "Most open to feature articles according to our theme list. Get a copy of our theme list and query about a theme-related article at least six months in advance. Request sample copies of our magazine to familiarize yourself with our publishing needs (also available online)."

** This periodical was #10 on the 2009 Top 50 Christian Publishers list (#17 in 2008, #10 in 2007, #30 in 2006, #4 in 2005).

@ LOUISIANA BAPTIST MESSAGE, PO Box 311, Alexandria LA 71309. (318) 442-7728. Fax (318) 445-8328. E-mail: editor@baptistmessage.com. Website: www.baptistmessage.com. Louisiana Southern Baptists. Kelly Boggs, ed. To report the news of what God is doing through Southern Baptists in Louisiana. Weekly & online newspaper; circ. 30,000. Subscription $14. Open to unsolicited freelance. Complete ms. Articles & reviews. Incomplete topical listings. (Ads)

$ THE LUTHERAN DIGEST, Box 4250, Hopkins MN 55343. (952) 933-2820. Fax (952) 933-5708. E-mail: tldi@lutherandigest.com. Website: www.lutherandigest.com. The Lutheran Digest, Inc. Nick Skapyak, ed. Blend of general and light theological material used to win nonbelievers to the Lutheran faith. Quarterly literary mag.; 64 pgs.; circ. 60,000. Subscription $16. 100 percent unsolicited freelance. Query or complete ms/cover letter; phone/fax/e-query OK. Pays $35-100+ ($25-50 for reprints) on acceptance for onetime & reprint rts. Articles to 1,000 words or no more than 7,000 characters—3,000 preferred (25-30/yr.). Accepts full mss by e-mail. Responds in 4-9 wks. Seasonal 6-9 mos. ahead. Accepts simultaneous submissions & reprints (tell when/where appeared). Accepts e-mail submissions (attached). No kill fee. Uses some sidebars. Rarely accepts submissions from children/teens. Guidelines by mail/Website; copy $3.50/6 x 9 SAE. (Ads)

Poetry: Accepts 20+/yr. Light verse, traditional; short/varies; no payment. Submit max. 3 poems/mo.

Fillers: Anecdotes, facts, short humor, tips; length varies; no payment.

Tips: "We want our readers to feel uplifted after reading our magazine. Therefore, short, hopeful pieces are encouraged. We need well-written short articles that would be of interest to middle-aged and senior Christians—and also acceptable to Lutheran Church pastors. We prefer real-life stories over theoretical essays. Personal tributes and testimony articles are discouraged. Please read sample articles and follow our writers' guidelines prior to submission—a little research goes a long way. Too much inappropriate and irrelevant material received."

**This periodical was #24 on the 2009 Top 50 Christian Publishers list.

$ THE LUTHERAN JOURNAL, PO Box 28158, Oakdale MN 55128. (651) 702-0086. Fax (651) 702-0074. E-mail: christianad2@msn.com. Vance Lichty, pub.; Roger S. Jensen, ed. Family magazine for, by, and about Lutherans, and about God at work in the Lutheran world. Annual mag.; 48 pgs.; circ. 200,000. Subscription $6. 60 percent unsolicited freelance; 40 percent assigned. Complete ms/cover letter; fax query OK. Pays .01-.04/wd. on publication for all or 1st rts. Articles 750-1,500 words (25-30/yr.); fiction 1,000-1,500 wds. Response time varies. Seasonal 4-5 mos. ahead. Accepts reprints. Uses some sidebars. Prefers NIV, NAS, KJV. Accepts requested ms on disk. Also accepts submissions from children/teens. Guidelines by mail; copy for 9 x 12 SAE/2 stamps. (Ads)

Poetry: Buys 4-6/yr. Light verse, traditional; 50-150 words; $10-30. Submit max. 3 poems.

Fillers: Buys 5-10/yr. Anecdotes, facts, games, prayers, quizzes, quotes; 50-300 words; $5-30.

Columns/Departments: Buys 40/yr. Apron Strings (short recipes); About Books (reviews), 50-150 words; $5-25.

Tips: "Most open to Lutheran lifestyles or Lutherans in action." Does not return rejected manuscripts.

THE LUTHERAN WITNESS, 1333 S. Kirkwood Rd., St. Louis MO 63122-7295. (314) 996-1202. Fax (314) 996-1126. E-mail: david.strand@lcms.org. Website: www.lcms.org/pages/witness.asp. The Lutheran Church Missouri Synod. David L. Strand, ed. Official periodical of the denomination, for lay members of its congregations; to encourage responsible Christian action in church and society. Monthly mag.; circ. 200,000. Subscription $18. Open to unsolicited freelance. Complete ms. Articles. Incomplete topical listings. (Ads)

MAINE FAMILY POLICY COUNCIL RECORD, (formerly The Christian Civic League of Maine Record), 70 Sewall St., Augusta ME 04330. (207) 622-7634. Fax (207) 621-0035. E-mail: email@mainefamilypolicycouncil.com. Website: www.mainefamilypolicycouncil.com. Michael Hein, administrator. Christian political publication and commentary. Publishes occasionally. Subscription free. Some freelance. Query; phone/fax/e-query OK. **NO PAYMENT** for onetime rts. Articles 800-1,200 words (10-12/yr.). Responds in 4-8 wks. Accepts simultaneous query & reprints. Guidelines by e-mail/Website; free copy. (No ads)

Tips: "Most open to news articles and reporting."

$ @ THE MANNA, PO Box 130, Princess Anne MD 21853. Phone/fax (410) 543-9652. E-mail: manna@mylifeline.net. Website: www.wolc.org. Maranatha Inc. Randy Walter, ed. A free monthly tabloid featuring evangelical articles and distributed in the marketplace in Delaware, Maryland, and Virginia. Monthly & online tabloid; 32-40 pgs; circ. 42,000. Subscription free. 10-15 percent unsolicited freelance; 15 percent assigned. Query/clips; e-query OK. No full mss by e-mail. Pays $30-50 on publication for 1st, onetime, or reprint rts. Articles 1,000-1,200 wds. Responds in 1-2 wks. Seasonal 3-4 mos. ahead. No simultaneous submissions. Accepts reprints (tell when/where appeared). Accepted articles on disk or by e-mail (copied into message). Uses some sidebars. Also accepts submissions from children/teens. No guidelines; copy for 9 x 12 SAE/2 stamps. (Ads)

Fillers: Anecdotes, ideas, party ideas, short humor, and tips. No payment.

Columns/Departments: Accepts up to 12/yr. Finances (business or personal); Counseling (Q & A); Personal Integrity (scriptural); all 800 wds. No payment.

Special Needs: Themes: marital fidelity, conquering fear, hypocrites, heaven, showing compassion, and What Is Your Hope? Most open to these theme pieces.

Tips: "E-mail your query."

** 2009 Award of Excellence—Newspaper.

$ @ **MARIAN HELPER**, Marian Helpers Center, Eden Hill, Stockbridge MA 01263. (413) 298-3691. Fax (413) 298-3583. E-mail: came@marian.org. Website: www.marian.org. Catholic/Marians of the Immaculate Conception. Dave Came, exec. ed.; Felix Carroll, review ed. Quarterly & online mag.; circ. 500,000. Rarely uses unsolicited; 25 percent assigned freelance. Query/clips or complete ms/cover letter. Pays $250 for 1,000-1,200 words (2-page feature) for 1st rts. Articles 500-900 wds. Responds in 6 wks. Seasonal 6 mos. ahead. Kill fee 30 percent. Guidelines/copy for #10 SAE. (No ads)

Tips: "Write about God's mercy touching people's everyday lives or about devotion to the Blessed Virgin Mary in a practical, inspirational, or fresh way."

MARKETPLACE, 12900 Preston Rd., Ste. 1215, Dallas TX 75230-1328. Toll-free (800) 775-7657. (972) 385-7657. Fax (972) 385-7307. E-mail: artstricklin@mchapusa.com. Website: www.mchapusa.com. Marketplace Ministries. Art Stricklin, VP/Public Relations. Focus is on working in the corporate workplace. Triannual literary mag.; 12-18 pgs.; circ. 16,000. Subscription free. 10 percent assigned. Query; e-query OK. Accepts full mss by e-mail. **NO PAYMENT** for all rts. Articles. Prefers e-mail submission. No copy. Incomplete topical listings. (No ads)

Tips: "We are attempting to cut back on freelance and use only assigned stories."

$ **MATURE LIVING**, One Lifeway Plaza, MSN 175, Nashville TN 37234-0175. (615) 251-5677. E-mail: matureliving@lifeway.com. Website: www.lifeway.com. LifeWay Christian Resources/Southern Baptist. Rene Holt, content ed. Christian leisure reading for senior adults (55+) characterized by human interest and Christian warmth. Monthly mag.; 60 pgs.; circ. 318,000. Subscription $22.50. 90 percent unsolicited freelance; 10 percent assigned. Complete ms/cover letter; no phone/fax/e-query. Accepts full mss by e-mail (attached or copied into message). Pays $85-115 for feature articles ($105-115 for fiction) on acceptance for all rts. Articles 400-1,200 words (85/yr.); senior adult fiction 900-1,200 words (12/yr.). Responds in 6-8 wks. Seasonal 6-8 mos. ahead. No simultaneous submissions or reprints. No kill fee. Uses some sidebars. Prefers KJV, HCSB. Guidelines by mail/e-mail (rene.holt@lifeway.com); copy for 9 x 12 SAE/4 stamps. (Ads)

Poetry: Buys 24-30/yr. Light verse, traditional; 12-16 lines; $35. Submit max. 3 poems.

Fillers: Accepts 144/yr. Grandchildren stories, 50-100 words; $15.

Columns/Departments: Buys 300+/yr. Cracker Barrel, 4-line verse, $15; Grandparent's Brag Board, 50-100 words, $15; Over the Garden Fence (gardening), 300-350 words; Communing with God (devotional), 125-200 words; Fun 'n Games (wordsearch/crossword puzzles), 300-350 words; Crafts; Recipes; $15-50. Complete ms. See guidelines for full list.

Tips: "Almost all areas open to freelancers except medical and financial matters. Study the magazine for its style. Write for our readers' pleasure and inspiration. Fiction for senior adults needs to underscore a biblical truth."

** This periodical was #22 on the 2009 Top 50 Christian Publishers list (#44 in 2008, #13 in 2007, #10 in 2006).

$ **MATURE YEARS**, Box 801, Nashville TN 37202. (615) 749-6292. Fax (615) 749-6512. E-mail: matureyears@umpublishing.org. United Methodist. Marvin W. Cropsey, ed. To help persons in and nearing retirement years understand and appropriate the resources of the Christian faith in dealing with specific problems and opportunities related to aging. Quarterly mag.; 112 pgs.; circ. 55,000. Subscription $21. 60 percent unsolicited freelance; 40 percent assigned. Complete ms/cover letter; fax/e-query OK. Pays .07/wd. on acceptance for onetime rts. Articles 900-2,000 words (60/yr.); fiction 1,200-2,000 words (4/yr.). Responds in 9 wks. Seasonal 14 mos. ahead. Accepts reprints. Prefers accepted ms by e-mail (copied into message). Regularly uses sidebars. Prefers NRSV, NIV. Guidelines by mail/e-mail; copy $5. (No ads)

> **Poetry:** Buys 24/yr. Free verse, haiku, light verse, traditional; 4-16 lines; .50-1.00/line. Submit max. 6 poems.
>
> **Fillers:** Buys 20/yr. Anecdotes (to 300 words), cartoons, jokes, prayers, word puzzles (religious only); to 30 words; $5-25.
>
> **Columns/Departments:** Buys 20/yr. Health Hints, 900-1,200 words; Modern Revelations (inspirational), 900-1,100 words; Fragments of Life (true-life inspirational), 250-600 words; Going Places (travel), 1,000-1,500 words; Money Matters, 1,200-1,800 words.
>
> **Special Needs:** Articles on crafts and pets. Fiction on older adult situations. All areas open except Bible studies.
>
> ** This periodical was #30 on the 2007 Top 50 Christian Publishers list (#35 in 2006, #31 in 2005).

@ **MEN.AG.ORG**, 1445 N. Boonville Ave., Springfield MO 65802. (417) 862-2781. Fax (417) 832-0574. E-mail: men@ag.org. Website: www.men.ag.org. Assemblies of God. Darian Amsler, field & commun. coord. Targeting men, ages 25-60; Christian/Pentecostal distinctive. Weekly e-zine. 10 percent unsolicited freelance; 90 percent assigned. Prefers e-query. **NO PAYMENT** for 1st rts. Articles 600-1,000 wds. Responds in 1 wk. Seasonal 5 mos. ahead. Accepts simultaneous submissions & reprints (tell when/where appeared). Prefers e-mail submissions (attached file). Prefers NIV. Guidelines by e-mail/Website; copy online. (Ads)

> **Tips:** "In being familiar with Website, submit articles (by e-mail) relevant to the faith, life, and culture. "

($) **MENNONITE HISTORIAN**, 600 Shaftesbury Blvd., Winnipeg MB R3P 0M4, Canada. (204) 888-6781. E-mail: aredekopp@mennonitechurch.ca. Or, 1310 Taylor Ave., Winnipeg MB R3M 3Z6, Canada. (204) 669-6575. E-mail: dheidebrecht@mbconf.ca. Website: www.mennonitechurch.ca/programs. Mennonite Heritage Centre of Mennonite Church Canada, and the Centre for Mennonite Brethren Studies of the Canadian Conference of Mennonite Brethren churches. Alf Redekopp (MHC), and Doug Heidebrecht (CMBS), co-eds; Conrad Stoesz (CMBS/MHC), assoc. ed. Gathers and shares historical material related to Mennonites; focus on North America but also beyond. Quarterly newsletter; 8-12 pgs.; circ. 600. Subscription $13. 40 percent unsolicited freelance; 20 percent assigned. Complete ms/cover letter; phone/e-query OK. **NO PAYMENT EXCEPT BY SPECIAL ARRANGEMENT** for 1st rts. Articles 250-1,000 wds. Accepts simultaneous submissions & reprints (tell when/where appeared). Prefers e-mail submission (attached file). Does not use sidebars.

> **Tips:** "Must be Mennonite related (i.e., related to the life and history of the denomination, its people, organizations, and activities). Most open to lead articles. Write us with your ideas. Also genealogical articles."

$ **MEN OF INTEGRITY**, 465 Gundersen Dr., Carol Stream IL 60188. (630) 260-6200. Fax (630) 260-0451. E-mail: mail@menofintegrity.net. Website: www.MenofIntegrity.net. Christianity Today Intl. Harry Genet, mng. ed. Uses narrative to apply biblical truth to specific gritty issues men face. Bimonthly pocket-size mag.; 64 pgs.; circ. 70,000. Subscription $19.95. 10 percent unsolicited freelance. Complete ms. Pays $50 on acceptance for onetime & electronic rts. Articles 225 words (15/yr.). Responds in 6 wks. Accepts simultaneous submissions & reprints (tell when/where appeared). Accepts requested ms on disk or e-mail (attached file or copied into message). Does not use sidebars. Prefers NLT. Guidelines/theme list by mail/e-mail; copy $4/#10 SAE. (Ads)

> ** 2006 EPA Award of Merit—Devotional

@ MEN OF THE CROSS, 920 Sweetgum Creek, Plano TX 75023. (972) 517-8553. E-mail: info@ menofthecross.com. Website: www.menofthecross.com. Greg Paskal, content mngr. (greg@greg paskal.com). Encouraging men in their walk with the Lord; strong emphasis on discipleship and relationship. Online community. 50 percent unsolicited freelance. Query by e-mail. **NO PAYMENT**. Not copyrighted. Articles 500-1,500 words (10/yr.). Responds in 2-4 wks. Seasonal 3 mos. ahead. Accepts simultaneous submissions; no reprints. Prefers e-mail submissions (attached or copied into message). Uses some sidebars. Prefers NIV, NKJV, NASB. Also accepts submissions from teens. Guidelines by e-mail; copy online. (No ads)

   Poetry: Accepts 1/yr. Avant-garde, free verse; 50-250 lines. Submit max. 1 poem.

   Special Needs: Christian living in the workplace.

   Tips: "Appropriate topic could be a real, first-hand account of how God worked in the author's life. We are looking for humble honesty in hopes it will minister to those in similar circumstances. View online forums for specific topics."

$ MESSAGE, Review and Herald Pub. Assn., 55 W. Oak Ridge Dr., Hagerstown MD 21740. (301) 393-4100. Fax (301) 393-4103. E-mail: message@RHPA.org. Website: www.messagemagazine.org. Review & Herald/Seventh-day Adventist. Washington Johnson II, ed. (wjohnson@rhpa.org). Pat Harris, asst. ed. (pharris@rhpa.org). For African Americans and all people seeking practical Christian guidance on current events and a better lifestyle. Bimonthly mag.; 32 pgs.; circ. 125,000. Subscription $14.95. 10-20 percent freelance written. Query or complete ms/cover letter; fax/e-query OK. Pays $50-250 on acceptance for 1st rts. Articles 700-1,200 words; fiction for children (ages 5-8), 500 words. Responds in 6-10 wks. Seasonal 6 mos. ahead. Prefers requested ms by e-mail. Regularly uses sidebars. Prefers KJV. Guidelines on Website; copy for 9 x 12 SAE/2 stamps. (Ads)

   Columns/Departments: Buys for each issue. Healthspan (health issues), 700 words; MESSAGE Jr. (biblical stories or stories with clear-cut moral for ages 5-8), 500 words; $50-300.

   Tips: "As with any publication, writers should have a working knowledge of *Message*. They should have some knowledge of our style and our readers."

MESSAGE OF THE OPEN BIBLE, 2020 Bell Ave., Des Moines IA 50315-1096. (515) 288-6761. Fax (515) 288-2510. E-mail: message@openbible.org. Website: www.openbible.org. Open Bible Standard Churches. Andrea Johnson, ed. To inspire, inform, and educate the Open Bible family. Bimonthly mag.; 16 pgs.; circ. 3,000. Subscription $9.95. 3 percent unsolicited freelance; 3 percent assigned. Query or complete ms/cover letter; e-query OK. **PAYS 5 COPIES**. Not copyrighted. Articles 750 words (2/yr.). Responds in 4 wks. Seasonal 4 mos. ahead. Accepts simultaneous submissions & reprints (tell when/where appeared). Accepts requested ms on disk or by e-mail. Regularly uses sidebars. Prefers NIV. Guidelines/theme list by mail/e-mail; copy for 9 x 12 SAE/2 stamps. (No ads)

   Fillers: Accepts 6/yr. Facts, quotes, short humor; 50 wds.

   Tips: "A writer can best break in by giving us material for an upcoming theme or something inspiring, specifically as it would relate to an Open Bible layperson."

$ THE MESSENGER, 440 Main St., Steinbach MB R5G 1Z5, Canada. (204) 326-6401. Fax (204) 326-1613. E-mail: messenger@emconf.ca or through Website: www.emconf.ca/Messenger. Evangelical Mennonite Conference. Terry M. Smith, ed.; Rebecca Buhler, asst. ed. Serves Evangelical Mennonite Conference members and general readers. Mag. published 22x/yr.; 16-24 pgs. Subscription $12. Uses little freelance, but open. Query preferred; phone/fax/e-query OK. Accepts full mss by e-mail. Pays $50-120 on publication for 1st rts. only. Articles. Not included in topical listings.

$ @ THE MESSENGER OF SAINT ANTHONY, Via Orto Botanico 11, 35123 Padova, Italy (U.S. address: Anthonian Assn., 101 Saint Anthony Dr., Mt. Saint Francis IN 47146). (812) 923-6356 or 049 8229924. Fax (812) 923-3200 or 049 8225651. E-mail: m.conte@santantonio.org (editor);

messenger@santantonio.org (ed. sec.); or info@santantonio.org. Website: www.saintanthonyof padua.net. Catholic/Provincia Padovana F.M.C. Fr. Mario Conte OFM, ed.; Corrado Roeper, ed. sec. For middle-aged and older Catholics in English-speaking world; articles that address current issues. Monthly & online mag.; 50 pgs.; circ. 45,000. Subscription $25 U.S. 10 percent unsolicited freelance; 90 percent assigned. Query (complete ms for fiction); phone/fax/e-query OK. Pays $40/pg. (600 words/pg.) for onetime rts. Articles 600-2,400 words (40/yr.); fiction 900-1,200 words (11/yr.). Responds in 8-10 wks. Seasonal 3 mos. ahead. Prefers e-mail submission (attached file or copied into message). Regularly uses sidebars. Prefers NEB (Oxford Study Edition). Guidelines by mail/e-mail; free copy. (No ads)

> **Columns/Departments:** Buys 50-60/yr. Documentary (issues), 600-2,000 words; Spirituality, 600-2,000 words; Church Life, 600-2,000 words; Saint Anthony (devotional), 600-1,400 words; Living Today (family life), 600-1,400 words; $55-200. Complete ms.
> **Special Needs:** Short story of a moral or religious nature; St. Anthony.
> **Tips:** "Most open to short stories; Saint Anthony, and devotional articles on parishes named after Saint Anthony, local feasts/shrines in Saint Anthony's honour. All writers should bring a uniquely Catholic perspective to their articles."

$ MESSENGER OF THE SACRED HEART, 661 Greenwood Ave., Toronto ON M4J 4B3, Canada. (416) 466-1195. Catholic/Apostleship of Prayer. Rev. F. J. Power, S.J., ed. Help for daily living on a spiritual level. Monthly mag.; 32 pgs.; circ. 11,000. Subscription $14. 20 percent freelance. Complete ms; no phone query. Pays .10/wd. on acceptance for 1st rts. Articles 700-1,500 words (30/yr.); fiction 700-1,500 words (12/yr.). Responds in 5 wks. Seasonal 5 mos. ahead. No disk. Does not use sidebars. Guidelines by mail; no copy. (No ads)

> **Tips:** "Most open to inspirational stories and articles."

$ MESSIAH JOURNAL (formerly *Messiah* magazine), PO Box 649, Marshfield MO 65706-0649. (417) 468-2741. Fax (417) 468-2745. E-mail: amber@ffoz.org or through Website: www.ffoz.org. First Fruits of Zion. Boaz Michael, ed. Dedicated to the study, exploration, and celebration of our righteous and sinless, Torah-observant King—Yeshua of Nazareth. Quarterly mag.; 34 pgs.; circ. 10,000. Subscription for donation. Open to freelance. Query; fax query OK. Pays on acceptance for all rts. Articles (15-20/yr.). Responds in 3 wks. Seasonal 6 mos. ahead. Accepts simultaneous submissions; no reprints. Requires e-mail submissions (attached file). Does not use sidebars. Prefers NASB. Copy for $4/9 x 12 SAE/5 stamps. Incomplete topical listings. (No ads)

> **Tips:** "F.F.O.Z. is a nonprofit ministry devoted to strengthening the love and appreciation of the Body of the Messiah for the land, people, and Scriptures of Israel. Since our focus is unique, please be very familiar with our magazine before submitting your query. Our Torah Testimony column is always open, as are some of the others. Looking for something on Hebrew roots."

MESSIANIC PERSPECTIVES, 611 Broadway, San Antonio TX 78215. (210) 226-0421, ext. 130. Fax (210) 226-2140. E-mail: rachelz@cjfm.org. Website: www.cjfm.org. CJF Ministries. Rachel Zanardi, ed. To provide for our constituency ministry-related news along with Bible teaching from a messianic perspective. Bimonthly newspaper; 20 pgs.; circ. 30,000. Subscription $10. Open to unsolicited freelance. Query; e-query OK. Accepts full mss by e-mail. Articles & reviews. Responds in 4 wks. Seasonal 4 mos. ahead. Accepts simultaneous submissions & reprints (tell when/where appeared). Prefers e-mail submissions (attached file). Regularly uses sidebars. Prefers NKJV. No guidelines or copy. (No ads)

THE MESSIANIC TIMES, 14080 Palm Dr., Ste. D #432, Desert Hot Springs CA 92240. Toll-free (866) 612-7770. (905) 685-4072. Fax (905) 685-7371. E-mail: mteditor@bellsouth.net or through Website: www.messianictimes.com. Times of the Messiah Ministries. Paul Liberman, pub. To unify the Messianic Jewish community around the world, to serve as an evangelistic tool to the Jewish community, and to educate Christians about the Jewish roots of their faith. Bimonthly newspaper; circ. 35,000. Subscription $19.99. Accepts freelance. Query preferred. Articles & reviews. Not in topical listings. (Ads)

METHODIST HISTORY, PO Box 127, Madison NJ 07940. (973) 408-3189. Fax (973) 408-3909. E-mail: RWilliams@gcah.org. Website: www.gcah.org. United Methodist. Robert J. Williams, ed. History of the United Methodism and Methodist/Wesleyan churches. Quarterly jour.; 64 pgs.; circ. 800. Subscription $20. 100 percent unsolicited freelance. Query; phone/fax/e-query OK. **PAYS 3 COPIES** for all rts. Historical articles to 5,000 words (15/yr.); book reviews 500 words. Responds in 8 wks. Requires requested ms on disk. Does not use sidebars. Guidelines by mail/Website; no copy. (Ads)

  Special Needs: United Methodist church history.

MIDNIGHT CALL MAGAZINE, PO Box 280008, Columbia SC 29228. Toll-free (800) 845-2420. (803) 755-0733. Fax (803) 755-6002. E-mail: info@midnightcall.com. Website: www.midnightcall .com. Arno Froese, ed. The world's only international voice of prophecy regarding end-time events. Subscription $22.50.

$ @ **MINDFLIGHTS**, 9618 Misty Brook Cove, Cordova TN 38016. E-mail: editor@mindflights .com. Website: http://mindflights.com/index.html. Double-Edged Publishing Inc. Submit to Editorial Staff. Publishes speculative (sci-fi/fantasy) short fiction and poetry with a Christian or Christian-friendly slant. Monthly online & quarterly print mag. Estab. 2008. 100 percent unsolicited freelance. Complete ms/cover letter submitted via online form (no e-mail submissions). Pays .005/wd. with a min. of $5 & max. of $25 on acceptance for 1st, reprint, and electronic rts. Articles under 2,000 words (1/yr.); fiction under 5,000 words (80/yr.). Responds in 3-4 wks. Seasonal 3 mos. ahead. No simultaneous submissions; reprints rarely (tell when/where appeared). No kill fee or sidebars. Also accepts submissions from teens. Guidelines on Website; copy of print edition. (Ads)

  Poetry: Buys 60-80/yr. Any type. Pays .005/wd. (min. $5 & max. $25). Submit max. 3 poems.
  Special Needs: Book and music reviews must be sci-fi/fantasy related.
  Contest: Planning a poetry contest. All contests announced on Website.
  Tips: "We like work that is original, interesting, and successfully melds the speculative and the spiritual without being preachy." Updates are posted online 2-3 times a week.

$ + **MIRACLES, HEALINGS, & THE UNEXPLAINED**, 13527 N.E. Rose Pkwy, Portland OR 97230. (503) 793-3026. Fax (503) 206-4792. E-mail: solidgoldpub@comcast.net. Website: www.miracles magazine.com. Sue Wade, ed. Showing through the overwhelming evidence of miracles that Jesus is healing and revealing himself to people every day. Annual mag., 80-100 pgs. Estab. 2007. 99 percent freelance. Complete ms by mail/cover letter or through Website. Pays $10-25 on publication for onetime rts. Not copyrighted. Articles 100-2,000 wds. Responds in 3-4 wks. Seasonal 6 mos. ahead. Accepts simultaneous submissions; no reprints. Uses some sidebars. Also accepts submissions from children/teens. Any Bible version. Guidelines/copy on Website. (Ads)

  Fillers: Accepts 20/yr. Anecdotes, cartoons, facts, ideas, jokes, kid quotes, short humor; 50-60 words; pays $10.
  Contest: Sometimes holds a contest for the most unique miracle story.
  Tips: "Keep stories active, yet brief. Use description such as time of day, atmosphere, people around, what it smelled like, witnesses (if any), what you look like, colors you remember, etc. Express your feelings and the importance to you. Include a picture of yourself or those in the story. The stories must be true and can be verified if necessary. Stories are meant to increase faith and hope in those who read them."

$ **THE MIRACULOUS MEDAL**, 475 E. Chelten Ave., Philadelphia PA 19144-5785. Toll-free (800) 523-3674. (215) 848-1010. Fax (215) 848-1014. E-mail through Website: www.cammonline.org.

Catholic. Rev. James O. Kiernan, C.M., ed. Fiction and poetry for Catholic adults, mostly women. Quarterly mag.; 36 pgs.; circ. 200,000. Subscription free to members. 40 percent unsolicited freelance. Query by mail only. Pays .03/wd. and up on acceptance for 1st rts. Religious fiction 1,000-2,000 words; some 1,000-1,500 words (6/yr.). Responds in 13 wks. Seasonal anytime. Accepts simultaneous submissions. Guidelines by mail/e-mail; copy for 6 x 9 SAE/2 stamps. (No ads) Incomplete topical listings.

Poetry: Buys 6/yr. Free verse, traditional; to 20 lines; $1 & up/line. Send any number. "Must have religious theme, preferably about the Blessed Virgin Mary."

Tips: "Most open to good short stories, 1,500-2,500 words, or poetry, with light religious theme."

@ MISSIONWARES.COM, 920 Sweetgum Creek, Plano TX 75023. (972) 517-8553. E-mail: info@missionwares.com. Website: www.missionwares.com. Greg Paskal, owner. Website targeted toward Christian technologists. E-zine. 50 percent unsolicited freelance. Complete ms; e-query OK. Accepts full mss by e-mail. **NO PAYMENT** for onetime rts. Not copyrighted. Articles 1,500-5,000 words (3-5/yr.). Responds in 3-4 wks. No seasonal. No simultaneous submissions or reprints. Accepts e-mail submissions (attached file in Word or PDF). Does not use sidebars. Also accepts submissions from teens. Prefers NIV, NKJV, NLT. Guidelines by e-mail; copy online. (No ads)

Special Needs: Technical White Papers. Best practices in technology as outlined by biblical precedence.

Tips: "We are looking for out-of-the-box thinking when it comes to the usage of current and new technologies."

$ THE MONTANA CATHOLIC, PO Box 1729, Helena MT 59624. (406) 442-5820. Fax (406) 442-5191. E-mail: rstmartin@diocesehelena.org. Website: www.diocesehelena.org. Catholic Diocese of Helena. Renee St. Martin Wizeman, ed. Publishes news and features from a Catholic perspective, particularly as they pertain to the church in western Montana. Monthly tabloid; 20 pgs.; circ. 9,000. Subscription $12.16. 5 percent freelance. Query or complete ms; e-query OK. Pays .05-.10/wd. on acceptance for 1st, onetime, simultaneous rts. Articles 400-1,200 words (5/yr.). Responds in 5 wks. Accepts simultaneous submissions. Kill fee 25 percent. Guidelines on Website. Incomplete topical listings. (Ads)

Tips: "Most open to seasonal pieces or articles with a tie to western Montana. Must have a Catholic angle."

$ MONTGOMERY'S JOURNEY, 555 Farmington Rd., Montgomery AL 36109-4609. (334) 213-7940. Fax (334) 213-7990. E-mail: deanne@montgomerysjourney.com. Website: www.montgomerys journey.com. Keep Sharing LLC. DeAnne Watson, ed. For protestant Christians and Christian families. Monthly mag.; 60-72 pgs.; circ. 18,000. Open to freelance. Complete ms by e-mail. Pays $25 on publication for onetime or reprint rts. Articles 900-1,500 wds. Seasonal 3 mos. ahead. Accepts requested ms on disk or by e-mail (attached file). No kill fee. Regularly uses sidebars. Also accepts submissions from teens. Guidelines by e-mail; no copy. (Ads)

Tips: "Most open to feature articles, instructional in nature, with subheaders and sidebars."

@ THE MORE EXCELLENT WAY (formerly Society for the Prevention of Cruelty to Humans), PO Box 3032, Clackamas OR 97015. E-mail: spch.email@yahoo.com. Website: www.preventcruelty tohumans.com. Stan Baldwin, ed/pub. To encourage personal acts of decency and kindness; to challenge and change the prevailing culture of cruelty. Mostly e-zine. Subscription free. Open to unsolicited freelance. Complete ms/cover letter; no phone/fax query; e-query preferred. Submit by e-mail. **PAYS COPIES & SUBSCRIPTION** for onetime rts. Not copyrighted. Articles 350-800 words (18/yr.) Responds in 1 wk. Accepts reprints (tell when/where appeared). Does not use sidebars. Accepts submissions from teens. Guidelines by e-mail; copy on Website. (No ads)

Columns/Departments: Accepts 24/yr. Friends of the Dolphins (profile/experience of service, compassion, kindness); Mom Factor (teaching children in the home, character building). Complete ms.

Tips: "Write to touch the heart. Nonfiction with a fictional story style. Everything must encourage others to love their neighbors. Minimize the religious talk."

MOSAIC, 4315 Village Centre Ct., Mississauga ON L4Z 1S2, Canada. (905) 848-2600. Fax (905) 848-2603. E-mail: mosaic@fmc-canada.org. Website: www.fmc-canada.org. Free Methodist Church in Canada. Lisa Howden, mng. ed. (howdenl@fmc-canada.org). Reflecting the diversity of ministry expression within the Free Methodist family. Bimonthly tabloid; 8 pgs.; circ. 4,000. Open to unsolicited freelance. Query; phone/e-query OK. **NO PAYMENT**. Articles 800-1,200 wds. Responds in 2 wks. Seasonal 4 mos. ahead. Accepts reprints (tell when/where appeared). Accepts e-mail submissions (attached file). Guidelines/theme list by e-mail/Website; no sample copy. (Ads)

    Tips: "Most open to inspirational pieces."

MOVIEGUIDE, 1151 Avenida Acaso, Camarillo CA 93012. Toll-free (800) 577-6684. (770) 825-0084. Fax (805) 383-4089. E-mail through Website: www.movieguide.org. Good News Communications/Christian Film & Television Commission. Dr. Theodore Baehr, pub. Family guide to media entertainment from a biblical perspective. Monthly mag.; 48 pgs.; circ. 2,500. Subscription $40. 40 percent unsolicited freelance. Query/clips. **PAYS IN COPIES** for all rts. Articles 1,000 words (100/yr.); book/music/video/movie reviews, 750-1,000 words. Responds in 6 wks. Seasonal 6 mos. ahead. Accepts requested ms on disk. Regularly uses sidebars. Guidelines/theme list; copy for SAE/4 stamps. (Ads)

    Fillers: Accepts 1,000/yr.; all types; 20-150 wds.

    Columns/Departments: Movieguide; Travelguide; Videoguide; CDguide, etc.; 1,200 wds.

    Contest: Scriptwriting contest for movies with positive Christian content. Go to www .kairosprize.com.

    Tips: "Most open to articles on movies and entertainment, especially trends, media literacy, historical, and hot topics."

($) MUTUALITY, 122 W. Franklin Ave., Ste. 218, Minneapolis MN 55404-2451. (612) 872-6898. Fax (612) 872-6891. E-mail: mgreulich@cbeinternational.org or cbe@cbeinternational.org. Website: www.cbeinternational.org. Christians for Biblical Equality. Megan Greulich, ed. Seeks to provide inspiration, encouragement, and information about equality within the Christian church around the world. Quarterly mag.; 32 pgs.; circ. 2,000. Subscription $40/free to members. 80 percent assigned freelance. Query/clips; fax/e-query OK. **PAYS A GIFT CERTIFICATE TO THEIR BOOKSTORE** on publication for 1st or electronic rts. Articles 1,000-2,000 words (12/yr.); book reviews 500-800 words. Responds in 6 wks. Accepts reprints (tell when/where appeared). Accepts requested ms on disk or by e-mail (attached file). Regularly uses sidebars. Prefers NRSV, TNIV. Guidelines by mail/ Website; copy for 9 x 12 SAE/3 stamps. (Ads)

    ** 2009 Award of Merit—Most Improved Publication.

+ @ NASHVILLE CHRISTIAN TIMES, 455 Sam Ridley Blvd., Ste. 263, Smyrna TN 37167. E-mail: editor@nashvillechristiantimes.com. Website: www.nashvillechristiantimes.com. Nashville Christian Writers Assn. Carol Harper, exec. ed. An online resource for Nashville's Christian Community. E-zine. Welcomes submissions for *The Christian View* department.

NETWORK, PO Box 131165, Birmingham AL 35213-6165. (205) 328-7112. E-mail: dolores@net worknewspaper.org. Website: www.networknewspaper.org. Interdenominational. Dolores Milazzo-Hicks, ed./pub. To encourage and nurture dialog, understanding, and unity in Christian communities. Monthly tabloid; 12-16 pgs.; circ. 10,000. Subscription $17.50. 50 percent unsolicited freelance. Phone/fax/e-query OK. **NO PAYMENT**. Not copyrighted. Articles to 500 wds. Accepts simultaneous submissions. Articles and news.

    Tips: "Most open to feature stories that express the unity of the body of Christ and articles that encourage and uplift our readers. We also cover state, local, national, and international news."

+ @ **NEW CHRISTIAN VOICES.COM**. E-mail: editor@newchristianvoices.com. Website: www
.NewChristianVoices.com. Nondenominational. Joanne Brokaw, ed. Humor/lifestyle Website. Open
to unsolicited freelance. Pays on acceptance for all rts. (but will negotiate on rts.); pay based on
experience and quality of work. Articles 300-600 words; devotionals 150-250 words (buys all rts. to
devotionals). Responds in 1-4 wks. Guidelines on Website. Incomplete topical listings.
  Special Needs: Looking for bloggers. Put "Blog Query" in subject line of e-mail.
  Tips: "We're looking for good writers who can write funny (amusing to hilarious) essays,
  commentaries, editorials, and columnlike material for our channels. We're interested in
  creating relationships with writers who will write for us regularly. "

NEW FRONTIER, 180 E. Ocean Blvd., 4th Fl., Long Beach CA 90802. (562) 491-8331. Fax (562)
491-8791. E-mail: New.frontier@usw.salvationarmy.org. Website: www.salvationarmy.usawest
.org/newfrontier. Salvation Army Western Territory. Robert L. Docter, ed. To share the Good News
of the gospel and the work of The Salvation Army in the western territory with salvationists and
friends. Biweekly newspaper; circ. 25,500. Subscription $15. Open to freelance. Prefers query. **NO
PAYMENT**. Articles & reviews; no fiction. Not in topical listings. (Ads)

A NEW HEART, PO Box 4004, San Clemente CA 92674-4004. (949) 496-7655. Fax (949) 496-8465.
E-mail: HCFUSA@gmail.com. Website: www.HCFUSA.com. Aubrey Beauchamp, ed. For Christian healthcare givers; information regarding medical/Christian issues. Quarterly mag.; 16 pgs.; circ. 5,000.
Subscription $25. 20 percent unsolicited freelance; 10 percent assigned. Complete ms/cover letter;
phone/fax/e-query OK. **PAYS 2 COPIES** for onetime rts. Not copyrighted. Articles 600-1,800 words
(20-25/yr.). Responds in 2-3 wks. Accepts simultaneous submissions & reprints. Accepts e-mail sub-
mission. Does not use sidebars. Guidelines by mail/fax; copy for 9 x 12 SAE/3 stamps. (Ads)
  Poetry: Accepts 1-2/yr. Submit max. 1-3 poems.
  Fillers: Accepts 3-4/yr. Anecdotes, cartoons, facts, jokes, short humor; 100-120 wds.
  Columns/Departments: Accepts 20-25/yr. Chaplain's Corner, 200-250 words; Physician's
  Corner, 200-250 words.
  Tips: "Most open to real-life situations which may benefit and encourage healthcare givers
  and patients. True stories with medical and evangelical emphasis."

+ @ **NEW IDENTITY MAGAZINE**, PO Box 375, Torrrance CA 90508. (310) 947-8707. E-mail:
inquiry@newidentitymagazine.com. Website: www.newidentitymagazine.com. Cailin Henson, ed-in-
chief. To help new Christians with their new identity in Christ. Quarterly & online mag.; 48-52 pgs.
Subscription free online. 50 percent unsolicited freelance; 50 percent assigned. Query; e-query OK.
Accepts full mss by e-mail. **NO PAYMENT** for 1st rts. Articles 500-4,000 wds. Responds in 1-4 wks.
No simultaneous submissions; accepts reprints (tell when/where appeared). Accepts e-mail sub-
missions (attached or copied into message). Uses some sidebars. Prefers NIV, *The Message*, AMP.
Guidelines/copy on Website. (Ads)
  Poetry: Accepts 4-8/yr. Any type or length. Submit max. 4 poems.
  Fillers: Ideas, newsbreaks, quotes, tips, events, ordinary Christians doing extraordinary things.
  Columns/Departments: See guidelines.
  Tips: "Share your perspective, your story, or how you're living out your passions and using
  your gifts."

$ @ **NEW WINESKINS**, PO Box 41028, Nashville TN 37204-1028. (615) 292-2940. Fax (615) 292-
2931. E-mail: info@wineskins.org. Website: www.wineskins.org. The ZOE Group Inc. Greg Taylor,
mng. ed. Combines biblical and cultural scholarly focus with popular-level articles and art for a
powerful journal/magazine hybrid. Bimonthly e-zine; 15-20 articles/mo. 50 percent unsolicited freelance; 50 percent assigned. Query; e-query preferred. Pays $50 for online articles by year end, for
onetime and electronic rts. Articles 800-2,500 words (100/yr.); fiction 1,000-2,500 words (10/yr.);
book reviews 800-1,200 words ($50). Responds in 1-2 mos. Seasonal 6 mos. ahead. Accepts simul-

taneous submissions & reprints (tell when/where appeared). Prefers e-mail submissions (attached or copied into message). No kill fee. Sometimes uses sidebars. Also accepts submissions from children/teens. Prefers NIV or NRSV. Guidelines by e-mail/Website; copy on Website. (Ads)

Poetry: Buys 4-5/yr. Avant-garde, free verse, light verse; 100-2,000 wds. Pays $50. Submit max. 1 poem.

Tips: "Best way to break in is by reviewing books, specifically ones we request. Also by writing well-shaped and well-researched pieces that are more than just opinions."

**This periodical was #38 on the 2009 Top 50 Christian Publishers list.

NOSTALGIA, PO Box 203, Spokane WA 99210-0203. (509) 299-4041. E-mail: editor@Nostalgia Magazine.net. Website: www.nostalgiamagazine.net. King's Publishing Group, Inc. Mark Carter, ed. We provide a forum for baby boomers and before to share photos and stories of yesterday that enrich life today; we use exclusively dated images/photos. Bimonthly mag.; 48 pgs. Subscription $22.95. 90 percent unsolicited freelance; 10 percent assigned. Complete ms/cover letter; e-query OK. **PAYS COPIES** on publication for 1st, onetime, reprint, simultaneous, or electronic rts. Articles 400-1,500 words (150/yr.). Responds in up to 1 yr. Seasonal 4 mos. ahead. Accepts simultaneous submissions & reprints (tell when/where appeared). Prefers e-mail submissions (attached or copied into message). No kill fee. Regularly uses sidebars. Guidelines by mail/e-mail; query for themes/topics; copy $5/9 x 12 SAE. (Ads)

Special Needs: Photos and family memories from 1940s, 1950s, and 1960s.

Tips: "Looking for personal family memories with interesting photos: traveling, camping, working together. Specific episodes are better than generalities (400-2,000 words, 1 photo/400 words). Dig out a great fun photo showing people engaged in life, write a caption, submit. No genealogies. Send us a first-person account showing everyday life from the years 1950-1968, with great photos."

$ @ **NOW WHAT?** Box 33677, Denver CO 80233. (303) 452-7973. Fax (303) 452-0657. E-mail: nowwhat@cog7.org. Website: http://nowwhat.cog7.org. Church of God (Seventh-day). Sherri Langton, assoc. ed. Articles on salvation, Jesus, social issues, life problems, that are seeker sensitive. Monthly online mag.; available only online. 100 percent unsolicited freelance. Complete ms/cover letter; no query. Pays $25-55 on publication for first, onetime, electronic, simultaneous, or reprint rts. Articles 1,000-1,500 words (20/yr.). Responds in 4-8 wks. Accepts simultaneous submissions & reprints (tell when/where appeared). Accepts requested ms by e-mail. Regularly uses sidebars. Prefers NIV. Guidelines by mail/Website; copy of online article for #10 SAE/1 stamp. (No ads)

Special Needs: "Personal experiences must show a person's struggle that either brought him/her to Christ or deepened faith in God. The entire Now What? site is built around a personal experience each month."

Tips: "The whole e-zine is open to freelance. Think how you can explain your faith, or how you overcame a problem, to a non-Christian. It's a real plus for writers submitting a personal experience to also submit an objective article related to their story. Or they can contact Sherri Langton for upcoming personal experiences that need related articles."

($) @ **NRB E-MAGAZINE**, 9510 Technology Dr., Manassas VA 20110-4167. (703) 330-7000. Fax (703) 330-7100. E-mail: vfraedrich@nrb.org or info@nrb.org. Website: www.nrb.org. National Religious Broadcasters. Laurel MacLeod, sr. ed. Topics relate to Christian radio, television, satellite, church media, Internet, and all forms of communication; promoting access and excellence in Christian communications. Monthly (9x) & online mag.; 52 pgs.; circ. 9,300. Subscription $24; Canadians add $6 U.S.; foreign add $24 U.S. 70 percent unsolicited freelance. Complete ms/cover letter; fax/e-query OK. **PAYS 6 COPIES** ($100-200 for assigned) on publication for 1st or reprint rts. Articles 1,000-2,000 words (30/yr.). Responds in 6 wks. Seasonal 6 mos. ahead. Accepts simultaneous submissions & reprints (tell when/where appeared). Prefers accepted ms by e-mail. Regularly uses sidebars. Prefers NAS. Guidelines/theme list by mail/e-mail; free copy. (Ads)

Columns/Departments: Valerie Fraedrich, asst. ed. Accepts 9/yr. Trade Talk (summary paragraphs of news items/events in Christian broadcasting), 50 words; Opinion (social issues), 750 words. Columns coordinated in-house, 500 wds.
Special Needs: Electronic media; education. All articles must relate in some way to broadcasting: radio, TV, programs on radio/TV, or Internet.
Tips: "Most open to feature articles relevant to Christian communicators. Become acquainted with broadcasters in your area and note their struggles, concerns, and victories. Find out what they would like to know, research the topic, then write about it." Contact assistant editor for guidelines, reprint permission, classified ads, additional copies, etc.

$ @ **ON MISSION**, 4200 North Point Pkwy., Alpharetta GA 30022-4176. (770) 410-6382. Fax (770) 410-6105. E-mail: onmission@namb.net. Website: www.onmission.com. North American Mission Board, Southern Baptist. Carol Pipes, ed. Helping readers share Christ in the real world. Quarterly & online mag.; 32 pgs.; circ. 200,000. Subscription free. One to 5 percent unsolicited freelance; 50-60 percent assigned. Query (complete ms for fiction); no phone/fax query; e-query OK. Accepts full mss by e-mail. Pays .25/wd. on acceptance for 1st rts. Articles 500-1,000 words (20/yr.). Responds in 8 wks. Seasonal 8 mos. ahead. No simultaneous submissions or reprints. Accepts e-mail submissions (attached or copied into message). Kill fee. Regularly uses sidebars. Prefers HCSB. Guidelines by mail/e-mail/Website; copy for 9 x 12 SAE/$2.07 postage. (Ads)
   Columns/Departments: Buys 4-8/yr. The Pulse (outreach/missions ideas); 500 wds. Query.
   Special Needs: Needs articles on these topics: sharing your faith, interviews/profiles of missionaries, starting churches, volunteering in missions, sending missionaries.
   Tips: "We are primarily a Southern Baptist publication reaching out to Southern Baptist pastors and laypeople, equipping them to share Christ, start churches, volunteer in missions, and impact the culture. Write a solid, 750-word how-to article geared to 20- to 40-year-old men and women who want fresh ideas and insight into sharing Christ in the real world in which they live, work, and play. Send a résumé, along with your best writing samples. We are an on-assignment magazine, but occasionally a well-written manuscript gets published."
   ** 2007, 2006 EPA Award of Merit—Missionary; 2005 EPA Award of Merit—Most Improved Publication.

+ @ **OREGON FAITH REPORT.COM**. (503) 644-1300. E-mail: oregon@oregonreport.com. Website: www.oregonfaithreport.com. A daily Web magazine that features the latest local religion news that is missed by the local newspaper. Jason Williams, pub. Online. Open to unsolicited free-lance. **NO PAYMENT**. Articles. Complete mss by e-mail.
   Tips: "We're looking for guest opinion pieces on news related to topics and insightful commentary on the issues facing Oregonians. This is an opportunity for Oregon writers to get their articles circulated and build a support base of readers."

$ **OUR SUNDAY VISITOR**, 200 Noll Plaza, Huntington IN 46750. Toll-free (800) 348-2440. (260) 356-8400. Fax (260) 359-9117. E-mail: oursunvis@osv.com. Website: www.osv.com. Catholic. John Norton, ed.; Sarah Hayes, article ed. Vital news analysis, perspective, spirituality for today's Catholic. Weekly newspaper; 24 pgs.; circ. 68,000. 10 percent unsolicited freelance; 90 percent assigned. Query or complete ms; fax/e-query OK. Pays $100-800 within 4 wks. of acceptance for 1st & electronic rts. Articles 500-3,500 words (25/yr.). Responds in 4-6 wks. Seasonal 2 mos. ahead. No simultaneous submissions; rarely accepts reprints (tell when/where appeared). Kill fee. Regularly uses sidebars. Prefers RSV. Guidelines by mail/e-mail/Website; copy for $2/10 x 13 SASE/$1postage. (Ads)
   Columns/Departments: Faith; Family; Trends; Profile; Heritage; Media; Q & A. See guidelines for details.
   Tips: "Our mission is to examine the news, culture, and trends of the day from a faithful and

sound Catholic perspective—to see the world through the eyes of faith. Especially interested in writers able to do news analysis (with a minimum of 3 sources), or news features."
** This periodical was #11 on the 2009 Top 50 Christian Publishers list (#48 in 2006, #14 in 2005).

$ OVER THE BACK FENCE, PO Box 756, Chillicothe OH 45601. Toll-free (800) 718-5727. Fax (330) 220-3083. E-mail: SarahW@longpointmedia.com Website: www.backfencemagazine.com. Long Point Media. Sarah Williamson, ed. Positive news about southern Ohio. Bimonthly mag.; 74 pgs.; circ. 15,000. Subscription $13.95. 60 percent unsolicited freelance. Query/clips; fax/e-query OK. Pays .15-.20/wd. (.10/wd. for fiction) on publication for onetime rts. Articles 750-1,000 words (9-12/yr.); fiction 300-850 words (8/yr.). Responds in 12 wks. Seasonal 1 yr. ahead. Accepts simultaneous submissions & reprints (tell when/where appeared). Requires requested ms on disk or by e-mail (copied into message). Regularly uses sidebars. Guidelines by mail/Website; copy $4/9 x 12 SAE or on Website. (Ads)
   Columns/Departments: Buys 8/yr. Memory Lane (interesting history that never made the headlines), 800-1,000 words; Heartstrings (touching essays), 800 words; Shorts (humorous essays), 800 words. Complete ms. Pays $80-120.
   Special Needs: Think upbeat and positive. Articles on nature, history, travel, nostalgia, and family.
   Tips: "We need material for our columns most often—Humorous Shorts, Memory Lane, and Heartstrings. It is best for writers to send things with appeal for Midwest readers and be generally positive. We do not publish articles that criticize or create a negative feeling about a geographical area or people."

THE OZARKS CHRISTIAN NEWS, 149 Grand Ave., Branson MO 65616. Phone/fax (417) 336-3636. E-mail: lila@ozarkschristiannews.com. Website: www.OzarksChristianNews.com. John Sacoulas, ed. Celebrating the common ground in the body of Christ. Monthly newspaper; circ. 20,000. Subscription $28. Open to unsolicited freelance. Complete ms. Articles & reviews. Incomplete topical listings. (Ads)

$ OZARKS SENIOR LIVING NEWSPAPER, 2010 S. Steward, Springfield MO 65804. (417) 862-0852. Fax (417) 862-9079. E-mail: seniorliving@sbcglobal.net. Website: www.slnewspaper.net. Metropolitan Radio Group Inc. Joyce Yonker O'Neal, mng. ed. Positive, upbeat paper for people 55+; includes religious articles. Monthly newspaper; 40 pgs.; circ. 40,000. 25-50 percent unsolicited freelance. Query or complete ms/cover letter; no phone/fax/e-query. Pays $20-35 for assigned; $5-35 for unsolicited; 30 days after publication for 1st, reprint, electronic rts. Articles 600 words (65/yr.). Responds in 2-5 wks. Seasonal 4 mos. ahead. Guidelines by mail; copy for 9 x 12 SAE/5 stamps.

$ PARENTLIFE, One Lifeway Plaza, Nashville TN 37234-0172. (615) 251-2196. Fax (615) 277-8142. E-mail: parentlife@lifeway.com. Website: www.lifeway.com/parentlife. Blog: www.lifeway.com/parentlifeblog. LifeWay Christian Resources. Jodi Skulley, ed. (jodi.skulley@lifeway.com). A child-centered magazine for parents of children 12 and under. Monthly mag.; 52 pgs.; circ. 72,000. Subscription $29.65. 5 percent unsolicited freelance; 95 percent assigned. Query; e-query OK. Accepts full mss by e-mail. Pays $150-500 on acceptance for nonexclusive rts. Articles 500-1,500 words (60/yr.) Responds in 6 mos. Seasonal 1 yr. ahead. Accepts simultaneous submissions; no reprints. Prefers e-mail submissions (attached file). No kill fee. Regularly uses sidebars. Prefers HCSB. Guidelines/theme list by mail/e-mail/Website; copy for 10 x 13 SASE. (Ads)
   Columns/Departments: Buys 60/yr. A Healthy Life (parent health issues), to 500 words; On the Way (expectant-parent topics), to 500 words; The Funny Life (funny family stories), 100 words; Single Parent Life, to 500 words; Working Life, to 500 words. Pays $20-150. Query.
   Tips: "Most open to feature articles, articles on single parents, working parents, expectant parents. Fill out the online application: www.lifeway.com/people, and then submit article ideas to editor after application is completed."
   **This periodical was #13 on the 2009 Top 50 Christian Publishers list.

$ + @ THE PATHWAY, 400 E. High St., Jefferson City MO 65101. (573) 636-0400. E-mail: dhinkle @mobaptist.org. Website: www.mbcpathway.com. Missouri Baptist Convention. Don Hinkle, ed. For Missouri Southern Baptists. Biweekly & online tabloid; 20 pgs; circ. 15,000. Subscription $10. 1 percent unsolicited freelance; 20 percent assigned. Query; phone/fax/e-query OK. Pays $50-200 for all rts. Articles 700-800 words (30/yr.). Responds in 2 wks. Seasonal 2 mos. ahead. Accepts simultaneous submissions & reprints (tell when/where appeared). Accepts disk or e-mail submissions (attached or copied into message). No kill fee. Uses some sidebars. Prefers NIV/KJV/NAS.

THE PEGASUS REVIEW, PO Box 88, Henderson MD 21640-0088. (410) 482-6736. E-mail: editor @pegasus review.com. Art Bounds, ed. Theme-oriented poetry, short fiction, and essays; not necessarily religious; in calligraphy format. Quarterly mag.; 12-14 pgs.; circ. 150. Subscription $12. 100 percent unsolicited freelance. Query or complete ms/cover letter (include background); e-query OK. No complete mss by e-mail. **PAYS 2 COPIES** for onetime rts. Fiction 2.5 pgs. is ideal, single-spaced (6-10/yr.); also one-page essays. Responds in 4 wks. Accepts simultaneous submissions & reprints (tell when/where appeared). No disk or e-mail submissions. Does not use sidebars. Also accepts submissions from teens. Prefers KJV. Guidelines/theme list by e-mail; copy $2.50. (No ads)

> **Poetry:** Accepts 40-50/yr. Free verse, haiku, traditional; 5-25 lines (shorter the better; pay attention to line length). Theme oriented. Submit max. 3 poems.
>
> **Fillers:** Accepts 20/yr. Cartoons, prose, quotes; 100-150 wds.
>
> **Special Needs:** 2010 themes: January—The Home; April—Humor; July—Youth & Age; October—On Writing.
>
> **Tips:** "Write and circulate your work. Get involved with a local writers' group or form one of your own. Persevere."

THE PENTECOSTAL MESSENGER, PO Box 850, Joplin MO 64802. Toll-free (800) 444-4674. (417) 624-7050. Toll-free fax (800) 982-5687. (417) 624-7102. E-mail: johnm@pcg.org. Website: www.messengerpublishing.com. Pentecostal Church of God. John Mallinak, ed. Denominational publication; ministry resource. Monthly (11x) mag.; circ. 5,000. Subscription $12. Accepts freelance. Prefers query. Complete ms. Articles. Copy $1.50. Not in topical listings. (Ads)

> ** 2009 Award of Excellence—Most Improved Publication.

THE PENWOOD REVIEW, PO Box 862, Los Alamitos CA 90720-0862. E-mail: submissions@penwood review.com. Website: www.penwoodreview.com. Lori Cameron, ed. Poetry, plus thought-provoking essays on poetry, literature, and the role of spirituality and religion in the literary arts. Biannual jour.; 40+ pgs.; circ. 80-100. Subscription $12. 100 percent unsolicited freelance. Complete ms; no e-query. **NO PAYMENT** ($2 off subscription & 1 free copy), for onetime and electronic rts. Articles 1 pg. (single-spaced). Responds in 9-12 wks. Accepts requested ms by e-mail (copied into message). Guidelines by mail/e-mail/Website; copy $6.

> **Poetry:** Accepts 120-160/yr. Any type, including formalist; to 2 pgs. Submit max. 5 poems.
>
> **Special Needs:** Faith and the literary arts; religion and literature. Needs essays (up to 2 pgs., single-spaced).
>
> **Tips:** "We publish poetry almost exclusively and are looking for well-crafted, disciplined poetry, not doggerel or greeting-card-style poetry. Poets should study poetry, read it extensively, and send us their best, most original work. Visit our Website or buy a copy for an idea of what we publish."

@ PERSPECTIVES: A Journal of Reformed Thought, 4500—60th Ave. S.E., Grand Rapids MI 49512. (616) 392-8555, ext. 131. Fax (616) 392-7717. E-mail: perspectives@rca.org. Website: www.perspectivesjournal.org. Reformed Church Press. Dr. Scott Hoezee, Dr. James Bratt, and Steve Mathonnet-VanderWell, eds. To express the Reformed faith theologically; to engage issues that Reformed Christians meet in personal, ecclesiastical, and societal life; and thus to contribute to the mission of the church of Jesus Christ. Monthly (10x) & online mag.; 24 pgs.; circ. 3,000. Subscription $30. 75 percent unsolicited freelance; 25 percent assigned. Complete ms/cover letter or query; fax/e-query OK. **PAYS 6 COPIES** for 1st rts. Articles (10/yr.) and fiction (3/yr.), 2,500-3,000 words; reviews 1,000 words. Responds in 20 wks. Seasonal 10 mos. ahead. Accepts reprints (tell when/where appeared). Prefers requested ms by e-mail (attached file). Uses some sidebars. Prefers NRSV. Guidelines on Website; no copy. (Ads)

    Poetry: Accepts 2-3/yr. Traditional. Submit max. 3 poems. Hard copy only to above address.

    Columns/Departments: Accepts 12/yr. As We See It (editorial/opinion), 750-1,000 words; Inside Out (biblical exegesis), 750 words. Complete ms.

    Tips: "Most open to feature-length articles. Must be theologically informed, whatever the topic. Avoid party-line thinking and culture-war approaches. I would say that a reading of past issues and a desire to join in a contemporary conversation on the Christian faith would help you break in here. Also the 'As We See It' column is a good place to start."

PERSPECTIVES ON SCIENCE & CHRISTIAN FAITH, PO Box 668, Ipswich MA 01938. (978) 356-5656. Fax (978) 356-4375. E-mail: asa@asa3.org. Website: www.asa3.org. American Scientific Affiliation. Submit to Arie Leegwater, ed. (Calvin College, 1726 Knollcrest Cir. S.E., Grand Rapids MI 49546; leeg@calvin.edu). Quarterly journal; 72 pgs.; circ. 2,000+. Subscription $40/yr. 75 percent unsolicited freelance; 25 percent assigned. E-query. Accepts full mss by e-mail. **NO PAYMENT**. Articles 6,000 wds. (20/yr.). Responds in 2 wks. Seasonal 4 mos. ahead. No simultaneous submissions or reprints. Accepts submissions by disk or e-mail (attached file). Regularly uses sidebars. Guidelines on Website.

    Special Needs: Science and faith; bioethics.

    Tips: "Freelancer must have credentials to write about their subject, i.e., advanced degree in science or theology. Article must be well researched and will be peer-reviewed."

$ POETRY SCOUT CENTRE MINISTRY, 6512 Arbor Lane, #614, Fort Worth TX 76132. E-mail: director@poetryscout-centreministry.com. Website: www.poetryscout-centreministry.com. Poetry Scout—Centre Ministry. Thomas L. Means, dir. Seeking Christian inspirational poetry writers to cost-share in a partnership book publishing contract. Poetry only. (Ads only as Website links)

    Poetry: Accepts 10 pages per poet per publishing contract; ten pages of theme-oriented poetry, quotes, and elaborating thoughts. Free verse or traditional (theme oriented); up to 32 lines/poem. Payment is based on contractual agreement with affiliated publisher, and within a partnership cost-share plan. Prescreen required of a 10-line inspirational poem reflecting the Trinity of God. Mail complete ms; send e-mail; or submit through Website.

$ POINT (formerly BGC World), 2002 S. Arlington Heights Rd., Arlington Heights IL 60005-4102. Toll-free (800) 323-4215, ext. 3217. (847) 228-0200, ext. 3217. Fax (847) 228-5376. E-mail: bputman@baptistgeneral.org. Website: www.convergeww.org. Converge Worldwide/Baptist General Conference. Bob Putman, ed. Almost exclusively by, for, and about the people and ministries of the Converge Worldwide (Baptist General Conference). Bimonthly mag.; 16 pgs.; circ. 46,000. Subscription free. 5 percent unsolicited freelance; 95 percent assigned. Query/clips; e-query preferred. Pays $60-280 on publication for 1st, reprint, electronic rts. Articles 300-1,400 words (20-30/yr.). Responds in 5-9 wks. Seasonal 6 mos. ahead. Accepts simultaneous submissions & reprints (tell when/where appeared). Prefers accepted mss by e-mail (attached file). Kill fee 50 percent. Uses some sidebars. Prefers NIV. Guidelines/theme list by mail/e-mail; free copy for #10 SAE. (Ads)

    Columns/Departments: Buys 30/yr. Converge Connection (short news blurbs of happenings in Converge churches), 75-250 words; New Life (first-person or "as-told-to" story of Converge church member transformation or church transformation), 750-1,400 words; Outreach Ideas (from Converge churches), 250-400 words.

Tips: "To break in, report on interesting happenings/ministry in Converge (BGC) churches close to you for our Converge connection or Outreach Ideas columns."
** 2007 EPA Award of Excellence—Denominational. This periodical was #47 on the 2008 Top 50 Christian Publishers list (#50 in 2007).

$ POSITIVE THINKING: Finding Joy & Fulfillment Every Day, 66 E. Main St., Pauling NY 12564. (212) 251-8100. Fax (845) 855-1036. E-mail: awong@guideposts.org. Website: www.guideposts .org. Guideposts. Amy Wong, ed. Spiritually oriented, based on positive thinking and faith. Bimonthly mag.; 36 pgs.; circ. 400,000. Subscription $15. 30 percent unsolicited freelance. Query preferred; phone/fax/e-query OK. Pays $75/pg. on publication for onetime rts. Articles 500-2,300 words (8/ yr.). Responds in 3-4 wks. Seasonal 6 mos. ahead. Accepts reprints. Accepts submissions by e-mail. Does not use sidebars. Guidelines by mail; copy for #10 SAE/1 stamp.
    Special Needs: Contemporary heroes; overcoming (addiction, etc.) through faith. (1) Life-changing experiences that bring about faith in Jesus Christ. (2) Ways to improve prayer and spiritual life. (3) How positive thinking and faith provide answers to life's problems.
    Tips: "Most open to true stories of finding faith through difficult circumstances. Avoid preachiness. How-tos (if applicable), stories (nonfiction only) that touch the heart and soul. Have a deep, living knowledge of Christianity. Our audience is 65-70 percent female; average age is 55."

$ POWER FOR LIVING, MS #104—Manuscript Submission, 4050 Lee Vance View, Colorado Springs CO 80918. Toll-free (800) 708-5550. (719) 536-0100. Fax (719) 535-2928. Website: www.cook ministries.org. Cook Communications/Scripture Press Publications. Don Alban Jr., ed. To expressly demonstrate the relevance of specific biblical teachings to everyday life via captivating profiles of exceptional Christians. Weekly take-home paper; 8 pgs.; circ. 250,000. Subscription $12. 15 percent unsolicited freelance; 85 percent assigned. Complete ms; no phone/fax/e-query. Pays up to .15/ word (reprints up to .10/word) on acceptance for onetime rts. Profiles 700-1,500 words (20/yr.). Responds in 10 wks. Seasonal 1 yr. ahead. Accepts simultaneous submissions & reprints (tell when/ where appeared). Accepts requested ms on disk. Kill fee. Requires KJV. Guidelines on Website; copy for #10 SAE/1 stamp (Use address above, but change to MS #205—Sample Request). (No ads)
    Special Needs: "Third-person profiles of truly out-of-the-ordinary Christians who express their faith uniquely. We use very little of anything else."
    Tips: "Most open to vignettes, 450-1,500 words, of prominent Christians with solid testimonies or profiles from church history. Focus on the unusual. Signed releases required."

($) @ P.O.W.E.R. MAGAZINE, 3030 E. 35th St., Indianapolis IN 46218. Toll-free (888) 415-2224. E-mail: info@powermagazine.org. Website: www.powermagazine.org. Kimberly Stewart, ed. Compelling people to come to Christ. Online mag. Subscription $6. Open to unsolicited freelance. Pays sometimes. Articles. Guidelines by e-mail or through Website. Incomplete topical listings. (Ads)

$ PRAIRIE MESSENGER: Catholic Journal, PO Box 190, Muenster SK S0K 2Y0, Canada. (306) 682-1772. Fax (306) 682-5285. E-mail: pm.canadian@stpeterspress.ca. Website: www.prairie messenger.ca. Catholic/Benedictine Monks of St. Peter's Abbey. Peter Novecosky, OSB, ed.; Maureen Weber, assoc. ed. For Catholics in Saskatchewan and Manitoba, and Christians in other faith communities. Weekly tabloid (46x); 20 pgs.; circ. 6,900. Subscription $32 Cdn. 10 percent unsolicited freelance; 90 percent assigned. Complete ms/cover letter; phone/fax/e-query OK. Pays $55 ($2.75/ column inch for news items) on publication for 1st, onetime, simultaneous, reprint rts. Not copyrighted. Articles 800-900 (15/yr.). Responds in 9 wks. Seasonal 3 mos. ahead. Accepts simultaneous submissions & reprints. Regularly uses sidebars. Guidelines by e-mail/Website; copy for 9 x 12 SAE/$1 Cdn./$1.39 U.S. postage. (Ads)
    Poetry: Accepts 35/yr. Avant-garde, free verse, haiku, light verse; 3-30 lines. Pays $20 Cdn.
    Columns/Departments: Accepts 5/yr. Pays $55 Cdn.

Special Needs: Ecumenism; social justice; native concerns.

Tips: "Comment/feature section is most open; send good reflection column of about 800 words; topic of concern or interest to Prairie readership. It's difficult to break into our publication. Piety not welcome."

THE PRAYER CLOSET, PO Box 278, Hickory, MS 39332. (601) 646-2295. E-mail: prayer@prayer closetministries.org. Website: www.prayerclosetministries.org. Dr. Kevin Meador, ed. Challenges and equips believers in the areas of prayer, fasting, spiritual warfare, journaling, and healing. Monthly newsletter; circ. 3,000. Free subscription online. **PAYS IN COPIES**. Prefers NKJV. Guidelines by mail.

Tips: "We are looking for sound, biblically based articles concerning the indicated topics (see topical listings)."

@ **PRAYERWORKS**, PO Box 301363, Portland OR 97294. (503) 761-2072. E-mail: VannM1@ aol.com. Website: www.prayerworksnw.org. The Master's Work. V. Ann Mandeville, ed. For prayer warriors in retirement centers; focuses on prayer. Weekly newspaper and online (soon); 4 pgs.; circ. 1,500. Subscription free. 100 percent unsolicited freelance. Complete ms. **PAYS IN COPIES/ SUBSCRIPTION** for onetime rts. Not copyrighted. Articles (30-40/yr.) & fiction (30/yr.); 350-500 wds. Responds in 3 wks. Seasonal 2 mos. ahead. Accepts simultaneous submissions & reprints. Does not use sidebars. Guidelines by mail; copy for #10 SAE/1 stamp. (No ads)

Poetry: Accepts 20-30/yr. Free verse, haiku, light verse, traditional. Submit max. 10 poems.

Fillers: Accepts up to 50/yr. Facts, jokes, prayers, quotes, short humor; to 50 wds.

Tips: "Write tight and well. Half our audience is over 70, but 30 percent is young families. Subject matter isn't important as long as it is scriptural and designed to help people pray. Have a strong, catchy takeaway."

$ **PRECEPTS FOR LIVING**, Annual Sunday School Commentary, PO Box 436987, Chicago IL 60643. E-mail: ecarey@urbanministries.com. Website: www.urbanministries.com. Urban Ministries Inc. Dr. Vincent Bacote, ed; submit to Evangeline Carey, developmental ed. *Precepts for Living* is a verse-by-verse Sunday School commentary geared toward an African American adult audience. Word studies are presented in the original Greek and Hebrew languages to further illuminate understanding of the text. KJV Scriptures. 500 pgs. Strict adherence to guidelines. Query/writing samples & clips; e-query OK. Lessons are assigned. Pays $200 per Bible Study lesson and $300 for More Light on the Text, a verse-by-verse commentary which includes Greek and Hebrew word studies, 120 days after acceptance, for all rts. Requires accepted ms by e-mail (attached).

Tips: "Must be able to write adult Christian curriculum. Send résumé, including educational experience. Should be astute in biblical education and how to correctly exegete Scripture."

$ **THE PRESBYTERIAN OUTLOOK**, Box 85623, Richmond VA 23285-5623. Toll-free (800) 446-6008. (804) 359-8442. Fax (804) 353-6369. E-mail: editor@pres-outlook.org. Website: www.pres outlook.org. Presbyterian Church (USA) /Independent. Jack Haberer, ed.; Randy Harris, book review ed. For ministers, members, and staff of the denomination. Weekly (43x) mag.; 16-40 pgs.; circ. 10,000. Subscription $44.95. 5 percent unsolicited freelance; 95 percent assigned. Query; phone/ fax/e-query OK. Payment varies for all rts. Not copyrighted. Articles/fiction to 1,000 words; book reviews 1 pg. Responds in 1-2 wks. Seasonal 2 mos. ahead. Accepts e-mail submissions. Uses some sidebars. Prefers NRSV. Guidelines by mail/e-mail; free copy. (Ads)

Tips: "Correspond (mail or e-mail) with editor regarding current needs; most open to features. Most material is commissioned; anything submitted should be of interest to Presbyterian church leaders."

$ **PRESBYTERIANS TODAY**, 100 Witherspoon St., Louisville KY 40202-1396. Toll-free (800) 227-2872. (502) 569-5000. Toll-free fax (800) 541-5113. (502) 569-8632. E-mail: today@pcusa.org.

Website: www.pcusa.org/today. Presbyterian Church (USA). Eva Stimson, ed.; John Sniffen, assoc. ed. Denominational; not as conservative or evangelical as some. Monthly (10x) mag.; 48 pgs.; circ. 58,000. Subscription $19.95. 25 percent freelance. Query or complete ms/cover letter; phone/fax/e-query OK. Pays $75-300 on acceptance for 1st rts. Articles 800-2,000 words (prefers 1,000-1,500), (20/yr.). Also uses short features 250-600 wds. Responds in 2-5 wks. Seasonal 3 mos. ahead. Few reprints. Accepts requested ms on disk or by e-mail. Kill fee 50 percent. Prefers NRSV. Guidelines on Website: www.pcusa.org/today/guidelines/guidelines.htm; free copy. (Ads)

Fillers: Cartoons, $25; and short humor to 150 words, no payment.

Tips: "Most open to feature articles about Presbyterians—individuals, churches with special outreach, creative programs, or mission work. Do not often use inspirational or testimony-type articles."

** This periodical was #40 on the 2006 Top 50 Christian Publishers list (#32 in 2005).

$ @ **PRIORITY!** 440 W. Nyack Rd., West Nyack NY 10994. (845) 620-7450. Fax (845) 620-7723. E-mail: linda_johnson@use.salvationarmy.org. Website: www.prioritypeople.org. The Salvation Army. Linda D. Johnson, ed.; Robert Mitchell, assoc. ed. Quarterly & online mag.; 48-56 pgs.; circ. 28,000. Subscription $8.95. 50 percent assigned. Query/clips; e-query OK. Pays $200-800 on acceptance for 1st rts. Articles 400-1,700 words (8-10/yr.). All articles assigned. Responds in 2 wks. Occasionally buys reprints (tell when/where appeared). Prefers accepted ms by e-mail (in Word or copied into message). Kill fee 50 percent. Regularly uses sidebars. Prefers NIV. Occasionally buys submissions from children/teens. Guidelines/theme list by e-mail; copy $1/9 x 12 SAE. (Ads)

Columns/Departments: Buys 5-10/yr. Prayer Power (stories about answered prayer, or harnessing prayer power); Who's News (calling attention to specific accomplishments or missions); Q & A (answers to current questions); My Take (unpublished writer's view); all 400-700 words; $200-400. Query.

Special Needs: All articles must have a connection to The Salvation Army. Can be from any part of the U.S. Looking especially for freelancers with Salvation Army connections; Christmas recollections (by August 1); people/program features.

Tips: "Most open to features on people. Every article, whether about people or programs, tells a story and must feature the Salvation Army. Stories focus on evangelism, holiness, prayer. The more a writer knows about The Salvation Army, the better."

PRISCILLA PAPERS, 122 W. Franklin Ave., Ste. 218, Minneapolis MN 55404-2451. Send submissions to editor at: 130 Essex St., Gordon-Conwell Theological Seminary, S. Hamilton MA 01982. (612) 872-6898. Fax (612) 872-6891. E-mail: debbeattymel@aol.com. Website: www.cbeinternational.org. Christians for Biblical Equality. William David Spencer, ed.; Deb Beatty Mel, assoc. ed. Addresses biblical interpretation and its relationship to women and men sharing authority and ministering together equally not according to gender, ethnicity, or class but according to God's gifting. Quarterly jour.; 32 pgs.; circ. 2,000. Subscription $40 (includes subscription to Mutuality). 85 percent unsolicited freelance; 15 percent assigned. Query preferred; fax/e-query OK. **PAYS 3 COPIES, PLUS A GIFT CERTIFICATE AT CBE'S MINISTRY** for 1st & electronic rts. Articles 600-5,000 words (1/yr.); no fiction; book reviews 600 words (free book). Slow and careful response. No reprints. Seasonal 12 mos. ahead. Prefers proposed ms on disk or by e-mail (attached file) with hard copy. No kill fee. Uses some sidebars. Guidelines on Website; copy for 9 x 12 SAE/$2.07 postage. (Ads)

Poetry: Accepts 1/yr. Avant-garde, free verse, traditional (on biblical gender equality themes); pays a free book.

Tips: "P.P. is the academic voice of CBE. Our target is the informed lay reader. All sections are open to freelancers. Any well-written, single-theme article (no potpourri) presenting a solid exegetical and hermeneutical approach to biblical equality from a high view of Scripture will be considered for publication." Seeks original cover art work. Use *Chicago Manual of Style*.

$ PRISM: America's Alternative Evangelical Voice, 6 E. Lancaster Ave., Wynnewood PA 19096-3495. (484) 384-2990. Fax (610) 649-8090. E-mail: kristyn@esa-online.org. Website: www.esa online.org/prism. Evangelicals for Social Action. Kristyn Komarnicki, ed. For Christians who are interested in the social and political dimensions of the gospel. Bimonthly mag.; 40 pgs.; circ. 2,500. Subscription $35. 50 percent unsolicited freelance. Complete ms/cover letter; e-query OK. Accepts full mss by e-mail. Pays $75-450 on publication for 1st & electronic rts. Articles 1,500-3,000 words (10-12/yr.); no fiction; book reviews, 500 words ($75). Responds within 12 wks. Seasonal 9 mos. ahead. No reprints. Regularly uses sidebars. Prefers NRSV. Guidelines by e-mail; copy $3. (Ads)

> **Tips:** "Open to features on social justice issues (profiles of cutting-edge and/or particularly effective holistic ministries) and on living out the Christian faith within contemporary culture. Understand progressive evangelicals and E.S.A. Read Tony Campolo, Ron Sider, and Richard Foster. Most open to features. We don't assign work to writers we haven't published before, so send a full manuscript."
>
> ** 2008 Award of Merit—Organizational.

$ PSYCHOLOGY FOR LIVING, 250 W. Colorado Blvd., Ste. 200, Arcadia CA 91007. (626) 821-8400. Fax (626) 821-8409. E-mail: editor@ncfliving.org. Website: www. ncfliving.org. Narramore Christian Foundation. Robert & Melanie Whitcomb, eds. Addresses issues of everyday life from a Christian and psychological viewpoint. Quarterly mag.; 8 pgs. (one issue 24 pgs.); circ. 7,000. Subscription for $20 donation. Open to freelance. Complete ms/cover letter; fax OK, e-query preferred. Pays $75-200, plus a subscription, on publication for 1st, onetime, or reprint rts. Articles 1,000-1,700 wds. Responds in 2-4 wks. Seasonal 4 mos. ahead. Accepts reprints (tell when/where appeared). Prefers accepted ms by e-mail (attached file). Uses some sidebars. Prefers NIV. Guidelines by mail/e-mail; free copy. (No ads)

> **Tips:** "Tell a story or illustration that shows how a psychological/emotional problem was dealt with in a biblical and psychologically sound manner. Not preachy."

$ PURE INSPIRATION, 7 Waterloo Rd., Stanhope NJ 07874. (973) 347-6900. Fax (973) 347-6909. E-mail: marnold@lightstreampublishing.com. Website: www.pureinspirationmag.com. Lightstream Publishing LLC. Robert Becker, ed.; Marie Arnold, mng. ed. Inspires people to live positive, healthier lives—spiritually and emotionally—emphasizing our similarities, not our differences; readership is 75 percent women. Quarterly mag.; 100 pgs.; circ. 25,000. Subscription $19.97. 50 percent unsolicited freelance; 25 percent assigned. Query, query/clips, or complete ms/cover letter; fax/e-query OK. Pays $100-125/pg. on publication for 1st rts. Articles 1,500-2,000 words (25-30/yr.). Responds in 2-3 wks. Seasonal 6 mos. ahead. No simultaneous submissions; reprints negotiable (tell when/where appeared). Prefers e-mail submissions (attached file). Some kill fees. Some sidebars. Also accepts submissions from children/teens. Guidelines on Website; copy for 9 x 12 SAE/$2 postage. (Ads)

> **Poetry:** Only inspirational poems.
>
> **Columns/Departments:** Buys 10-12/yr. Share Your Story (true personal stories of inspiration), 1,000-1,500 words, $100.
>
> **Tips:** "Most open to any topic which is helpful to our readers, such as those that will help to improve their lives spiritually and inspire them."

$ PURPOSE, 616 Walnut Ave., Scottdale PA 15683-1999. (724) 887-8500. Fax (724) 887-3111. E-mail: Horsch@mpn.net. Website: www.mpn.net. Mennonite Publishing Network/Agency of Mennonite Church USA & Canada. James E. Horsch, ed. Denominational, for older youth & adults. Monthly take-home paper; 32 pgs.; circ. 8,900. Subscription $22.65; $23.78 Cdn. 80 percent unsolicited freelance; 20 percent assigned. Complete ms (only) /cover letter; e-mail submissions preferred. Pays $10-42 or .06-.07/wd. on acceptance (or when editor chooses) for onetime rts. Articles & fiction, 300-600 words (95/yr.). Responds in 6 mos. Seasonal 1 yr. ahead. Accepts simultaneous submissions & reprints (tell when/where appeared). Regularly uses sidebars. Guidelines by mail/e-mail; copy $2/6 x 9 SAE/2 stamps. (No ads)

Poetry: Buys 120/yr. Free verse, haiku, traditional; 3-12 lines; up to $2/line ($7.50-20). Submit max. 5 poems.

Fillers: Buys 25/yr. Anecdotes, prose; up to 300 words; up to.06/wd.

Tips: "Read our guidelines. All areas are open. Articles must carry a strong story line. First person is preferred. Don't exceed maximum word length, send no more than 3 works at a time." ** This periodical was #25 on the 2009 Top 50 Christian Publishers list (#19 in 2008, #38 in 2007, #43 in 2006, #50 in 2005).

PURPOSE MAGAZINE, 2720 Airport Dr., Columbus OH 43219. (614) 418-1785. Fax (614) 253-2283. E-mail: purposeforlife@gmail.com. Website: www.purposemagazine.com. Ellavation Enterprises Inc. Ella Coleman, pub./ed-in-chief. Christian magazine for a predominately African American audience; personal and family empowerment to inspire, motivate, and educate readers to live their God-given purpose. Bimonthly mag.; 32-40 pgs.; circ. 5,000. Subscription $25. 25 percent unsolicited freelance; 75 percent assigned. Query/clips; e-query OK. **PAYS A SUBSCRIPTION & PROMOTION**. Articles. Accepts reprints (tell when/where appeared). Prefers e-mail submissions (attached file in Word). Regularly uses sidebars. Also accepts submissions from children/teens. Prefers NKJV. Guidelines on Website; copy for 9 x 12 SASE. (Ads)

   Poetry: Accepts very few; 30-40 lines. Submit max. 20 poems.

   Fillers: Most types; 200-500 wds.

   Columns/Departments: Financial wisdom. Complete ms.

   Contests: Occasionally sponsors a contest.

QUAKER LIFE, 101 Quaker Hill Dr., Richmond IN 47374. (765) 962-7573. Fax (765) 962-1293. E-mail: quakerlife@fum.org. Website: www.fum.org. Friends United Meeting. Katie Terrell, ed. For Christian Quakers, focusing on news around the world, peace and justice, simplicity, and inspiration. Bimonthly mag.; 44 pgs.; circ. 4,000. Subscription $24. 50 percent unsolicited freelance; 50 percent assigned. Query; fax/e-query OK. Accepts full ms by e-mail. **PAYS 3 COPIES** on publication for 1st rts. Articles to 1,500 words (40/yr.); book reviews 300 words; music/video reviews, 200 words. Responds in 4 wks. Seasonal 4 mos. ahead. Accepts some reprints (tell when/where appeared). Accepts e-mail submissions (attached in Word or copied into message). No kill fee. Uses some sidebars. Prefers RSV. Also accepts submissions from children/teens. Guidelines/theme list by e-mail/ Website; copy for 9 x 12 SAE. (Ads)

   Poetry: Accepts 2/yr.

   Columns/Departments: Peace Notes (peace and justice news and ideas); Inspirations (1st person personal experience); Scripture for Living (applying biblical teachings); Perspectives (opinion); each 750 wds. Query or complete ms.

   Special Needs: Leadership, church growth, personal experience.

   Tips: "All articles must fit within the theme (list on Website). Write on current issues or a personal spiritual experience from a Christian perspective. Be more practical than academic. For general readers who are Christian Quakers."

RADIX MAGAZINE, PO Box 4307, Berkeley CA 94704. (510) 548-5329. E-mail: RadixMag@aol .com. Website: www.RadixMagazine.com. Sharon Gallagher, ed.; Luci Shaw, poetry ed. Features in-depth articles for thoughtful Christians who are interested in engaging the culture. Quarterly mag.; 32 pgs. Subscription $15. 10 percent unsolicited freelance; 90 percent assigned. E-queries only. **PAYS IN COPIES** for 1st rts. Meditations, 300-500 words (2/yr.); book reviews 700 words. Responds in 6 wks. to e-mail only. Seasonal 6 mos. ahead. No simultaneous submissions or reprints. Accepted submissions by e-mail only (attached file). Uses some sidebars. Prefers NRSV. Guidelines by e-mail; copy $5. (Ads)

   Poetry: Accepts 12/yr. Avant-garde, free verse, haiku, traditional; 4-30 lines. Submit max. 1 poem.

Tips: "Most open to poetry, book reviews, meditations. Familiarity with the magazine is key."

@ REGENT GLOBAL BUSINESS REVIEW, 1000 Regent University Dr., Virginia Beach VA 23464. (757) 226-4074. E-mail: rgbr@regent.edu. Website: www.regent.edu/rgbr. Regent University— School of Global Leadership & Entrepreneurship. Julianne R. Cenac, exec. ed. (Jcenac@regent.edu). For Christian leaders and managers who take their faith seriously and who give genuine thought to how to live out that faith in the workplace and everywhere else. Bimonthly e-zine; 30 pgs.; circ. 10,000. Free online. 25 percent unsolicited freelance; 75 percent assigned. Query/clips by e-mail only. **NO PAYMENT** for electronic rts. Feature articles 1,200-2,500 words; case studies 2,500-4,000 words (not including any data appendices); Tool Kit/Executive Summaries 250-500 words. Responds in 2 wks. Seasonal 6 mos. ahead. No simultaneous submissions; accepts reprints. Requires accepted mss by e-mail (attached file). Regularly uses sidebars. Prefers NIV. Guidelines on Website.

> **Columns/Departments:** Tool Kit (tips and resources) 250-500 words; Research Translations, 1,000-1,500 words.

> **Tips:** "If you are interested in contributing to the exploration and advancement of global business, we are interested in hearing from you. We seek articles from contributors who are recognized experts in their field or who have requisite experience and credentials to be qualified to speak authoritatively on the subject matter."

$ @ RELEVANT & RELEVANTMAGAZINE.COM, 1220 Alden Rd., Orlando FL 32803-2546. Toll-free (877) 538-4417. (407) 660-1411. Fax (407) 401-9100. E-mail: corene@relevantmediagroup .com. Website: www.RelevantMagazine.com. Relevant Media Group. Roxanne Wieman, ed. dir. (roxanne @relevantmediagroup.com). Targets culture-savvy twentysomethings who are looking for purpose, depth, and spiritual truth. Bimonthly & online mag.; 100 pgs. Subscription $12. 80 percent freelance. Send a one-paragraph query/clips; prefers e-mail; no phone/fax query. Pays $100-400 within 45 days of publication for 1st rts. & all electronic rts. for 6 mos.; nonexclusive rts. thereafter. Features 600-1,000 words; reviews 400-600 words. Prefers submissions as Word attachments. Guidelines on Website (www.relevantmagazine.com/editorial); copy $2.98.

RELIEF JOURNAL, 60 W. Terra Cotta Ave, Ste. B, #156, Crystal Lake IL 60014-3548. E-mail: editor@ reliefjournal.com. Website: www.reliefjournal. com. CC Publishing, NFP. Kimberly Culbertson, ed-in-chief; Lisa Ohlen Harris, nonfiction ed.; Chris Fisher, fiction ed. Edgy Christian Journal. Quarterly literary mag.; 175 pgs.; circ. 300. Subscription $48. 90 percent unsolicited freelance; 10 percent assigned. Use online submissions system only; no mail or e-mail submissions. Complete ms. **PAYS IN COPIES** for 1st rts. Creative nonfiction (20/yr.) & fiction (24/yr.) to 8,000 wds. Responds in 16 wks. Accepts simultaneous submissions & reprints (only when solicited). Prefers NKJV. Guidelines on Website. Incomplete topical listings. (Ads)

> **Poetry:** Brad Fruhauff, poetry ed. Accepts 80-100/yr. Poetry that is well-written and makes sense; to 1,000 wds. Submit max. 5 poems.

$ + RENEWED & READY: Adventist Living for Today, 16617 Kendle Rd., Williamsport MD 21795. (301) 223-6738. E-mail: editor@RenewedandReady.com. Website: www.RenewedandReady .com. Seventh-day Adventist. Ginger Church, ed. To inspire Adventists, over 50, to have a zest for life. Monthly mag.; 62 pgs. Subscription $17.99. Articles 500-1,500 words (see guidelines). Guidelines & copy by mail. Incomplete topical listings. (Ads)

REVERENT SUBMISSIONS JOURNAL, #2835, 1420 N.W. Gilman Blvd., Ste. 2, Issaquah WA 98027. (425) 255-8825. E-mail: reverentsubmissions@comcast.net. Bev Fowler, pub. A theme-based journal for Christians of all faiths, seeking to provide experience, exposure, and credibility for Christian writers while encouraging others in their daily life and spiritual walk. Quarterly newsletter; 12 pgs.; circ. 125. Subscription $12. 100 percent unsolicited freelance. Query; e-query OK. Accepts full mss by e-mail. **PAYS 2 COPIES** for 1st, onetime, reprint rts. Not copyrighted. Articles & fiction to 800 words (up to 48/yr. for ea.); book reviews to 600 words. Responds in 12 wks. Seasonal 3 mos. ahead. Accepts simultaneous submissions and reprints (tell when/where appeared). Prefers e-mail submissions (attached file). Does not use sidebars. Also accepts submissions from children/teens. Prefers NIV. Guidelines/theme list by mail/e-mail; copy for 9 x 12 SAE/2 stamps. (No ads)

Poetry: Accepts 12-15/yr. Free verse, haiku, light verse, traditional; up to 400 wds. Format conducive to column format.

Fillers: Buys as needed. Anecdotes, ideas, jokes, kid quotes, prayer, prose, quotes, short humor, tips; up to 100 wds.

Tips: "Christian-focused articles/fiction/poetry on the theme of each issue, with bio, contact information, and correct word count. Order upcoming theme list. Manuscripts will not be returned."

$ @ THE ROSE & THORN: A Literary E-zine. E-mail: BAQuinn@aol.com. Website: www.therose andthornezine.com. General. B. A. Quinn, ed. Showcases short fiction, poetry, essays, and anything of a literary nature; no children's or juvenile stories. Quarterly online literary mag. Complete ms. Pays $5 and will provide a link to your Website. Onetime nonexclusive rts. Articles/fiction to 2,000 words. Requires submissions by e-mail (copied into message). Guidelines on Website.

Poetry: Now accepting poetry. Submit max. 3 poems; prefers shorter poems. E-mail to poetryeditor@hotmail.com. Pays $5.

Special Needs: Fiction, vignettes, and flash fiction; creative essays, perspective, humor.

Tips: "We have eclectic tastes, so go ahead and give us a shot." This publication is not always open to submissions, so check submissions page on their Website to see when they are open.

RUMINATE: Faith in Literature and Art, 140 N. Roosevelt Ave., Fort Collins CO 80521. (970) 449-2726. E-mail: editor@ruminatemagazine.com. Website: www.ruminatemagazine.com. Brianna Van Dyke, ed.; submit to submissions@ruminatemagazine.com. An intimate and hip publication of faith, literature and art; publishes work with both subtle and overt associations with the Christian faith as well as work that has no direct association. Quarterly mag.; 70 pgs.; circ. 1,500. Subscription $28. 100 percent unsolicited freelance. Complete ms/cover letter by e-mail only. **PAYS 3 COPIES OR SUBSCRIPTION** for 1st rts. Articles to 5,000 words (4-8/yr.); fiction to 5,000 words (8-12/ yr.). Responds in 16 wks. Accepts simultaneous submissions; no reprints. Requires disk or e-mail submissions (attached file). Does not use sidebars. Guidelines/theme list on Website; order copy on Website/$9. (Ads)

Poetry: Lacee Perrin, poetry ed. (poetry@ruminatemagazine.com). Accepts 50/yr. Avant-garde, free verse, traditional; to 40 lines. Submit max. 4 poems.

Contest: Annual poetry contest deadline is May 15. Annual fiction contest deadline is November 15. Entry fee: $15. Prizes: $300 1st prize; $150 to runner-up. Details on Website.

Tips: "We are looking for writers and artists who are interested in the process of creating quality work that reveals the nature of Christ."

$ SALVO MAGAZINE, PO Box 410788, Chicago IL 60641. (773) 481-1090. Fax (773) 481-1095. E-mail: editor@salvomag.com. Website: www.salvomag.com. Fellowship of St. James. Bobby Maddex, ed. Geared toward young adults, 25-45, who want to free themselves from the false world-views emanating from Hollywood, the media, and the Academy. Quarterly mag.; 96 pgs.; circ. 2,800. Subscription $25.99. 25 percent unsolicited freelance; 75 percent assigned. Query/clips; no phone/ fax query, e-query OK. Accepts full mss by e-mail. Pays .20/wd. on publication for 1st rts. Articles 600-2,500 words (16/yr.). Responds in 4 wks. No seasonal. No simultaneous submissions or reprints. Prefers e-mail submissions (attached file). Kill fee $100. Regularly uses sidebars. No Bible references. Guidelines/theme list on Website; copy $6.99. (Ads)

Columns/Departments: Buys 12/yr. Dispatches (features) 2,000 words; The Trenches (tales of academic bias) 1,200 words; Random Flak (minifeatures) 1,200 words; .20/wd.

Tips: "We are most open for features on science, sex, and society—anything that deconstructs false ideology and worldviews, using reason and logic alone."

SAVED MAGAZINE, PO Box 22-2302, Hollywood FL 33022-3100. Toll-free (877) 34SAVED. (954) 921-4700. Fax (954) 921-4724. E-mail: editorial@savedmagazine.com. Website: www.savedmaga zine.com. Christian. Teri Tavernier, pub. (teri@savedmagazine.com). Targets diverse Christian population by infusing area businesses, neighborhoods, and ministries across economic and ethnic lines. Bimonthly mag. Subscription $15. Open to unsolicited freelance. No mention of payment. Articles. Editorial schedule on Website. Incomplete topical listings. (Ads)

SCP JOURNAL, PO Box 4308, Berkeley CA 94704. (510) 540-0300. Fax (510) 540-1107. E-mail: scp@scp-inc.org. Website: www.scp-inc.org. Spiritual counterfeits Project Inc. Tal Brooke, ed. Deals with topics from apologetics to New Age, new religions, cults, occult, and cultural trends. Quarterly jour.; circ. 15,000. Subscription $25. Open to queries only. Articles. Incomplete topical listings. Guidelines on Website. (No ads)

$ SEARCH MAGAZINE (formerly Science & Spirit Magazine), 1319 Eighteenth St. N.W., Washington DC 20036-1802. (202) 296-6267. E-mail: editors@searchmagazine.org. Website: www.searchmaga zine.org. Science & Spirit Resources Inc./Heldref Publications. Peter Manseau, ed. For intellectually curious, educated readers who have an interest in how technology, faith, ethics, and the arts connect in both global affairs and their everyday lives. Bimonthly mag; 66 pgs.; circ. 7,500. Subscription $30. 20 percent freelance. Query by e-mail only. Pays .20-.75/wd. for assigned,.20-.50/wd. for unsolicited for articles on acceptance for all rts. Makes work-for-hire assignments. No reprints. Articles 1,200-2,500 words (40/yr.) Responds in 1 mo. Seasonal 6 mos. ahead. Guidelines on Website; copy on Website.
   Columns/Departments: Interlude (social/science environmental topic), 1,200-1,600 words; Critical Mass (news briefs covering all areas of science—physics, gender, space, psychology, etc.); pays $200-300. See Website for samples of departments.
   Tips: "Common mistakes include shallow reporting, lack of in-depth writing, lack of diversity in religious perspectives. We're looking for well-researched articles that include interviews with scientists, theologians, and everyday people. The best articles include citations for recent research and current books. Thoughtful leads, transitions, and conclusions based on the writer's research and insight are a must."

SEEDS OF HOPE: Hope for the Healing of Hunger and Poverty, 602 James Ave., Waco TX 76706-1476. (254) 755-7745. Fax (254) 753-1909. E-mail: Seedseditor@clearwire.net. Website: www.seedspublishers.org. Seeds of Hope Publishers. Katie Cook, ed. Committed to the healing of hunger and poverty in our world. Quarterly worship packet; 20 pgs. of camera-ready resources. Subscription $120. Individual packet $50. Back issues less expensive. Also quarterly newsletter, Hunger News & Hope, published through denominational offices of national churches. E-query OK. **NO PAYMENT**.

$ SEEK, 8805 Governor's Hill Dr., Ste. 400, Cincinnati OH 45249. E-mail: seek@standardpub.com. Website: www.Standardpub.com. Standard Publishing. Margaret K. Williams, ed. Light, inspirational, take-home reading for young and middle-aged adults. Weekly take-home paper; 8 pgs.; circ. 29,000. Subscriptions $16.99 (sold only in sets of 5). 75 percent unsolicited freelance; 25 percent assigned. Complete ms; no phone/fax/e-query. Pays .07/wd. on acceptance for 1st rts., .05/wd. for reprints (tell when/where appeared). Articles 500-1,200 words (150-200/yr.); fiction 500-1,200 words. Responds in 18 wks. Seasonal 1 yr. ahead. Prefers submissions by e-mail (attached file). Uses some sidebars. Guidelines/theme list by mail/Website; copy for 6 x 9 SAE/2 stamps. (No ads)
   Fillers: Buys 50/yr. Ideas, short humor; $15.
   Tips: "We now work with a theme list. Only articles tied to these themes will be considered for publication. Check Website for theme list and revised guidelines."

** This periodical was #19 on the 2009 Top 50 Christian Publishers list (#11 in 2008, #7 in 2007, #26 in 2006, #27 in 2005).

SENIOR CONNECTION, PO Box 38, Dundee IL 60118. (847) 428-0205. E-mail: churchpb@flash .net. Website: www.seniorconnectionnewspaper.com. Churchill Publications/Catholic. Peter Rubino, ed. For Catholics ages 50 and up with ties to the Chicago area. Monthly newspaper; circ. 190,000. Subscription $18.95. Open to unsolicited freelance. Articles. Incomplete topical listings.

SHARING: A Journal of Christian Healing, 6807 Forest Haven, San Antonio TX 78240. (210) 681-5146. Fax (210) 681-5146. E-mail: Marjorie.George@dwtx.org. Website: www.orderofstluke .org. Order of St. Luke the Physician. Marjorie George, ed. For Christians interested in spiritual and physical healing. Monthly (10x) jour.; 16 pgs.; circ. 9,000. Subscription $20. 100 percent unsolicited freelance. Complete ms/cover letter. **NO PAYMENT** for onetime or reprint rts. Articles 750-900 words (50/yr.). Responds in 3 wks. Seasonal 2 mos. ahead. Accepts simultaneous submissions & reprints (tell when/where appeared). Prefers ms by e-mail. Some sidebars. Prefers RSV. Guidelines by mail; copy for 8 x 10 SAE/2 stamps.
>   **Poetry:** Accepts 10-12/yr. Free verse, traditional; 6-14 lines.
>   **Tips:** "We're looking for crisp, clear, well-written articles on the theology of healing and personal witness of healing. We are totally open; best to send manuscript. We do not return manuscripts or poems, nor do we reply to inquiries regarding manuscript status."

$ SIGNIFICANT LIVING/TODAY'S CHRISTIAN: Maximizing Life After 50, 2800 Vision Ct., Aurora IL 60506. (630) 801-3838. Fax (630) 801-3839. E-mail: pshort@TLN.com. Website: www .significantliving.org. Peg Short, ed-in-chief. Dedicated to serving adults in the second half of life (boomers to seniors), empowering them to live with Christlike vitality, and inspiring them to serve others, so that our nation may be strengthened and God may be honored. Bimonthly mag.; 40 pgs.; circ. 25,000. Subscription by membership only $19.95. Estab. 2007. 5-10 percent unsolicited freelance; 90-95 percent assigned. Query; e-query OK. Accepts full mss by e-mail. Pays .20-.30/wd. on acceptance for all rts. Articles & fiction 1,000-1,200 wds. Responds in up to 2-3 wks. Seasonal 6 mos. ahead. Accepts simultaneous submissions & reprints (tell when/where appeared). Prefers e-mail submissions (attached file). Kill fee $25. Uses some sidebars. Guidelines by e-mail/Website; free copy. (Ads)
>   **Fillers:** For boomers & seniors. Anecdotes, cartoons, facts, jokes, short humor, word puzzles.
>   **Tips:** "Most open to features—role-model stories that reflect issues for boomers and seniors. Open to celebrity and athlete stories, and features that are issue-oriented to boomers and seniors. Human interest and role-model stories of middle and senior adult issues."
>   ** This periodical was #14 on the 2009 Top 50 Christian Publishers list.

SILVER WINGS, PO Box 2340, Clovis CA 93613-2340. (559) 347-0194. E-mail: cloviswings@aol .com. Poetry on Wings/Evangelical. Jackson Wilcox, ed. Christian understanding and uplift through poetry. Bimonthly mag.; 16 pgs.; circ. 300. Subscription free with donation. 100 percent unsolicited freelance. Query or complete ms; phone query OK. **PAYS ONE COPY & SUBSCRIPTION** for poetry only for 1st rts.; book reviews 200 wds. Not copyrighted. Poetry only. Responds in 3 wks. Seasonal 3-12 mos. ahead. No disk or e-mail submissions. Does not use sidebars. Prefers KJV. Also accepts submissions from children/teens. Guidelines by mail; copy for 6 x 9 SASE/2 stamps. (No ads)
>   **Poetry:** Accepts 175/yr. Free verse, haiku, light verse, traditional; 3-20 lines. Submit max. 3 poems. No payment. "Any poetry that conforms to Christian conduct, teaching, and morality. No profanity or mention of alcoholic beverages."
>   **Contest:** Annual poetry contest on a theme (December 31 deadline); send SASE for details. Winners published in March. $325 in prizes. $3 entry fee.
>   **Tips:** "We like poems with clear Christian message, observation, or description. Poetry should be easy to read and understand. Short poems get best attention. We are open to topics

and material making a point that agrees with Christian teaching. We will even consider views that vary within the Christian community. Encourages submissions from teens."

@ SINGLE AGAIN.COM WEBZINE & MAGAZINE, 7405 Greenback Ln., #129, Citrus Heights CA 95610-5603. (916) 773-1111. Fax (916) 773-2999. E-mail: publisher@singleagain.com. Website: www.singleagain.com. Messenger Publishing Group. Rev. Paul Scholl, pub. Caters to people trying to put their lives back together after divorce, separation, or death of a significant other. Quarterly & online newsletter; 8-10 pgs. Subscription $12. Open to freelance. Complete ms/cover letter by mail or e-mail (preferred). **NO PAYMENT** for simultaneous rts. Articles 500 words & up (50-75/ yr.). Responds in 6 wks. Accepts simultaneous submissions & reprints (tell when/where appeared). Accepts requested mss by e-mail (attached file in Word only). Does not use sidebars. Guidelines on Website. Incomplete topical listings. (Ads)

> **Poetry:** Accepts 6-12/yr. Any type to 24 lines. Submit max. 6 poems.
> **Fillers:** Accepts 15-12/yr. Anecdotes, facts, ideas, jokes, kid quotes, prayers, prose, short humor, tips.
> **Tips:** "Write from your heart first. Don't worry about your article being perfect. We will help you with any final editing."

$ SOCIAL JUSTICE REVIEW, 3835 Westminster Pl., St. Louis MO 63108-3472. (314) 371-1653. Fax (314) 371-0889. E-mail: centbur@sbcglobal.net. Website: www.socialjusticereview.org. Central Bureau of the Catholic Central Verein. Rev. Edward Krause, C.S.C., ed. For those interested in the social teaching of the Catholic Church. Bimonthly mag.; 32 pgs.; circ. 5,000. Subscription $20. 90 percent unsolicited freelance. Query or complete ms/cover letter; no phone/fax/e-query. Pays .02/ wd. on publication for onetime rts. Not copyrighted. Articles 1,500-3,000 words (80/yr.); book reviews 500 words (no payment). Responds in 1 wk. Seasonal 3 mos. ahead. Accepts reprints (tell when/where appeared). Prefers submissions on disk. No kill fee. Does not use sidebars. No guide- lines; copy for 9 x 12 SAE/3 stamps. (No ads)

> **Columns/Departments:** Virtue; Economic Justice (Catholic views); variable length. Query or complete ms. Pays .02/wd.
> **Tips:** "Articles and reviews open to freelancers. Fidelity to papal teaching and clarity and simplicity of style; thoughtful and thought-provoking writing."

$ @ SOUND BODY, Box 448, Jacksonville OR 97530. Phone/fax (541) 899-8888. E-mail: Susan@ ChristianMediaNetwork.com. Websites: www.SoundBody.tv. Christian Media. James Lloyd, ed./pub. A health newsletter with an alternative slant. Quarterly & online newsletter. Query; prefers phone query. Payment negotiable for reprint rts. Articles. Responds in 3 wks. Requires KJV. No guidelines; copy for #10 SAE/2 stamps.

SOUTHWEST KANSAS FAITH AND FAMILY, PO Box 1454, Dodge City KS 67801. (620) 225- 4677. Fax (620) 225-4625. E-mail: info@swkfaithandfamily.org. Website: www.swkfaithandfamily .org. Independent. Stan Wilson, pub. Dedicated to sharing the Word of God and news and informa- tion that honors Christian beliefs, family traditions, and values that are the cornerstone of our nation. Monthly newspaper; circ. 5,000. Subscription $18. Accepts freelance. Prefers e-query; complete ms OK. Articles; no reviews. Guidelines on Website. Incomplete topical listings. (Ads)

$ SPECIAL LIVING, PO Box 1000, Bloomington IL 61702. (309) 661-9277. E-mail: gareeb@aol .com. Website: www.specialiving.com. Betty Garee, pub./ed. For and about physically disabled adults, mobility impaired individuals. Quarterly mag.; 88 pgs.; circ. 12,000. Subscription $12. 90 percent unsolicited freelance; 5 percent assigned. Query; phone/fax/e-query OK. Pays .10/wd. on publication for 1st rts. Articles 300-800 words (50/yr.). Responds in 3 wks. Seasonal 6 mos. ahead. Accepts simultaneous submissions & reprints (tell when/where appeared). Prefers requested ms on disk. No kill fee. Uses some sidebars. No guidelines; copy $2. (Ads)

Fillers: Buys 20/yr. Cartoons, tips.

Tips: "Query with a specific idea. Have good photos to accompany your article. Most open to mobility impaired concerns and successes."

SPIRITUALITY FOR TODAY, PO Box 7466, Greenwich CT 06836. (203) 316-9394. Fax (203) 316-9396. E-mail: Clemons10@aol.com. Website: www.spirituality.org. Clemons Productions Inc. Dorothy Riera, asst. ed. Adults' spiritual renewal with articles that challenge reflection. Monthly mag.; 13-15 pgs.; circ. 495,000. Subscription free. Open to freelance. E-query OK. **NO PAYMENT**. Articles & short stories 1,000 wds. Guidelines by e-mail. (Ads)

    Fillers: Accepts anecdotes, prayers, quotes.

    Tips: "Most open to human interest pertaining to the church (2 pages); and human values. Just submit an e-mail with article attached. We always respond to our e-mails." Spanish page included.

$ SPIRITUAL LIFE, 2131 Lincoln Rd. N.E., Washington DC 20002-1199. Toll-free (888) 616-1713. (202) 832-5505. Fax (202) 832-8967. E-mail: edodonnell@aol.com. Website: www.Spiritual-Life.org. Catholic. Edward O'Donnell, O.C.D., ed. Essays on Christian spirituality with a pastoral application to everyday life. Quarterly jour.; 64 pgs.; circ. 12,000. Subscription $22. 80 percent unsolicited freelance. Complete ms/cover letter; phone/fax/e-query OK. Pays $50-250 ($50/pg.) on acceptance for 1st rts. Articles/essays 3,000-5,000 words (20/yr.); book reviews 1,500 words ($15). Responds in 9 wks. Seasonal 9 mos. ahead. Accepts simultaneous submissions. Requires requested ms on disk. Does not use sidebars. Prefers NAB. Guidelines by mail; copy for 7 x 10 SAE/5 stamps.

    Tips: "No stories of personal healing, conversion, miracles, etc."

$ SPORTS SPECTRUM, PO Box 2037, Indian Trail NC 28079. Toll-free (866) 821-2971. (704) 821-2971. Fax (704) 821-2669. E-mail: editor@sportsspectrum.com or info@sportsspectrum .com. Website: www.sportsspectrum.com. Sports Spectrum Publishing. Brett Honeycutt, mng. ed. (bhoneycutt@sportsspectrum.com). Designed to feature sports people and issues as a way of introducing the gospel to non-Christian sports fans and of encouraging Christian sports fans. Quarterly mag.; 68 pgs.; circ. 20,000. Subscription $27.52. 80 percent assigned. Query/clips; e-query OK. Pays .21/wd. on acceptance for all rts. Not copyrighted. Articles 1,200-1,500 words (40/yr.). Responds in 3-4 wks. Requires accepted ms by e-mail (attached file). Kill fee 30-50 percent. Regularly uses sidebars. Prefers NIV. Guidelines by mail/e-mail/Website; no sample copy. (Ads)

    Tips: "The best thing a writer can do is to be aware of the special niche *Sports Spectrum* has developed in sports ministry. Then find athletes who fit that niche and who haven't been covered in the magazine."

    ** 2007, 2006, 2005 EPA Award of Merit—General.

$ STANDARD, 2923 Troost Ave., Kansas City MO 64109. (816) 931-1900. Fax (816) 412-8306. E-mail: DCBrush@wordaction.com. Website: www.wordaction.com. Nazarene. Duane C. Brush, ed. Examples of Christianity in everyday life for adults, college-age through retirement. Weekly take-home paper; 8 pgs.; circ. 100,000. 100 percent unsolicited freelance. Complete ms. Pays .035/wd. (.02/wd. for reprints) on acceptance for onetime rts. Articles (20/yr.) or fiction (200/yr.) 700-1,500 wds. Responds in 12 wks. Seasonal 15 mos. ahead. Accepts simultaneous submissions & reprints (tell when/where appeared). No disk; accepts e-mail submissions (attached). Does not use sidebars. Prefers NIV. Guidelines by e-mail; copy for #10 SAE/2 stamps. (No ads)

    Poetry: Buys 30/yr. Free verse, haiku, traditional; to 30 lines; .25/line. Submit max. 5 poems.

    Fillers: Buys 50/yr. Word puzzles; $20.

    Tips: "Fiction or true-experience stories must demonstrate Christianity in action. Show us, don't tell us. Action in stories must conform to Wesleyan-Arminian theology and practices." Themes follow the Christian year, not celebrating national holidays.

    ** This periodical was #26 on the 2009 Top 50 Christian Publishers list (#29 in 2008, #24 in 2007, #27 in 2006).

$ @ ST. ANTHONY MESSENGER, 28 W. Liberty St., Cincinnati OH 45202-6498. (513) 241-5615. Fax (513) 241-0399. E-mail: StAnthony@AmericanCatholic.org. Website: www.AmericanCatholic .org. Fr. Pat McCloskey, O.F.M., ed. For Catholic adults & families. Monthly & online mag.; 64 pgs.; circ. 305,000. Subscription $28. 55 percent unsolicited freelance. Query/clips (complete ms for fiction); e-query OK. Pays .20/wd. on acceptance for 1st, reprint (right to reprint), and electronic rts. Articles 1,500-3,000 words, prefers 1,500-2,500 (35-50/yr.); fiction 1,500-2,500 words (12/ yr.); book reviews 500 words, $50. Responds in 3-9 wks. Seasonal 6 mos. ahead. Kill fee. Uses some sidebars. Prefers NAB. Guidelines on Website; copy for 9 x 12 SAE/4 stamps. (Ads)

> **Poetry:** Christopher Heffron, poetry ed. Buys 20/yr. Free verse, haiku, traditional; 3-25 lines; $2/line ($20 min.) Submit max. 2 poems.
>
> **Fillers:** Cartoons.
>
> **Tips:** "Many submissions suggest that the writer has not read our guidelines or sample articles. Most open to articles, fiction, profiles, interviews of Catholic personalities, personal experiences, and prayer. Writing must be professional; use Catholic terminology and vocabulary. Writing must be faithful to Catholic belief and teaching, life, and experience. Our online writers' guidelines indicate the seven categories of articles. Texts of articles reflecting each category are linked to the online writers' guidelines for nonfiction articles."
>
> ** This periodical was #28 on the 2009 Top 50 Christian Publishers list (#25 in 2008, #22 in 2007, #33 in 2006, #40 in 2005).

$ STEWARDSHIP, PO Box 1561, New Canaan CT 06840. Toll-free (888) 320-5576. (203) 966-6470. Fax (203) 966-4654. E-mail: guy@parishpublishing.org, or info@parishpublishing.org. Website: www.parishpublishing.org. Parish Publishing, LLC. Guy Brossy, principal. Inspires parish-ioners to give to their church—abilities, time, and monies. Monthly newsletter; 4 pgs.; circ. 1 million. 50 percent unsolicited freelance; 50 percent assigned. Fax/e-query with cover letter. Pays $50 on acceptance for all & reprint rts. Articles 150, 200, or 300 words (50/yr.) Responds in 2 wks. Seasonal 3 mos. ahead. Accepts simultaneous submissions & reprints. Accepts e-mail submissions (attached or copied into message). Regularly uses sidebars. Free guidelines/copy by mail. (No ads)

> **Tips:** "Write articles that zero in on stewardship—general, time, talent, or treasure—as it relates to the local church."

$ THE STORYTELLER, 2441 Washington Rd., Maynard AR 72444. (870) 647-2137. E-mail: story tellermag1@yahoo.com. Website: www.thestorytellermagazine.com. Fossil Creek Publishing. Regina Cook Williams, ed./pub.; Ruthan Riney, review ed. Family audience. Quarterly jour.; 72 pgs.; circ. 600. Subscription $20. 100 percent unsolicited freelance. Complete ms/cover letter; phone/e-query OK. Pays .0025/wd. on publication for 1st rts. Articles 2,500 words (60/yr.); fiction 2,500 words (100-125/yr.). Responds in 1 wk. Seasonal 3 mos. ahead. Accepts simultaneous submissions & reprints (tell when/where appeared). Responds in 1-2 wks. No disk or e-mail submissions; does not use sidebars. Also accepts submissions from children/teens (not children's stories). Guidelines by mail/Website; copy $6/9 x 12 SAE/5 stamps. (Ads)

> **Poetry:** Jamie Johnson, poetry ed. Accepts 100/yr. Free verse, haiku, light verse, traditional; 5-40 lines. Submit max. 3 poems. Pays $1/poem.
>
> **Fillers:** Accepts 10-20/yr. Cartoons, quotes, tips; 25-50 wds. Writing-related only.
>
> **Special Needs:** Original artwork. Funny or serious stories about growing up as a pastor's child or being a pastor's wife. Also westerns and mysteries.
>
> **Contest:** Offers 1 or 2 paying contests per year, along with People's Choice Awards, and Pushcart Prize nominations.See Website for announcements of all forthcoming contests for the year.
>
> **Tips:** "We look for stories that are written well, flow well, have believable dialogue, and good endings. So many writers write a good story but fizzle at the ending. All sections of the magazine are open except how-to articles. Study the craft of writing. Learn all you can before

you send anything out. Pay attention to detail, make sure manuscripts are as free of mistakes as possible. Follow the guidelines—they aren't hard."
** This periodical was #42 on the 2007 Top 50 Christian Publishers list.

STUDIO: A Journal of Christians Writing, 727 Peel St., Albury NSW 2640, Australia. Phone/fax +61 2 6021 1135. E-mail: studio00@bigpond.net.au. Submit to Studio Editor. Quarterly jour.; 36 pgs.; circ. 300. Subscription $60 AUS. 90 percent unsolicited freelance; 10 percent assigned. Query. **PAYS IN COPIES** for onetime rts. Articles 3,000 words (15/yr.); fiction 3,000 words (50/yr.); book reviews 300 words. Responds in 3 wks. Accepts simultaneous submissions & reprints (tell when/where appeared). No disks; e-mail submissions OK. Does not use sidebars. Guidelines by mail (send IRC); copy for $10 AUS. (Ads)
Poetry: Accepts 200/yr. Any type; 4-100 lines. Submit max. 3 poems.
Contest: See copy of journal for details.
Tips: "We accept all types of fiction and literary article themes."

THE SWORD AND TRUMPET, PO Box 575, Harrisonburg VA 22803-0575. Phone/fax (540) 867-9419. E-mail: swandtrump@verizon.net. Website: www.swordandtrumpet.org. Mennonite. Paul Emerson, ed. Primarily for conservative Bible believers. Monthly mag.; 37 pgs.; circ. 3,300. Subscription $15. **NO PAYMENT**. Articles. Prefers KJV. (No ads)

SWORD OF THE LORD NEWSPAPER, PO Box 1099, Murfreesboro TN 37133-1099. Toll-free (800) 247-9673. (615) 893-6700. Fax (615) 895-7447. E-mail: guyking@swordofthelord.com or through Website: www.swordofthelord.com. Independent Baptists and other fundamentalists. Dr. Shelton Smith, pres./ed.; submit to Guy King. Revival and soul-winning. Biweekly newspaper; 24 pgs.; circ. 70,000. Subscription $15. Open to freelance. Query; phone/fax/e-query OK. **NO PAYMENT**. Articles 500-1,000 words; fiction for 4-7 & 8-12 yrs. and teenagers. Responds in 13 wks. Seasonal 3 mos. ahead. Accepts simultaneous submissions & reprints (tell when/where appeared). Accepts disk or e-mail submissions (attached file). No kill fee. Does not use sidebars. Requires KJV. Guidelines by mail/e-mail; no copy. (Ads)
Poetry: Accepts variable number. Free verse, light verse, traditional; any length.
Fillers: Accepts variable number. Facts, newsbreaks, prose.
Columns/Departments: Accepts variable number. Kid's Korner (children's stories); Teen Talk (teen issues); both 500-700 wds.
Tips: "Most open to Bible study, soul-winning material, Christian growth, and youth character building that does not stress graphic portrayals of 'what's really going on out there.' Only works from a fundamentalist viewpoint and using the KJV are considered." Does not reprint articles from Mennonite, Lutheran, or Catholic publications.

$ @ **TESTIMONY**, 2450 Milltower Ct., Mississauga ON L5N 5Z6, Canada. (905) 542-7400. Fax (905) 542-7313. E-mail: testimony@paoc.org. Website: www.testimonymag.com. The Pentecostal Assemblies of Canada. Steve Kennedy, ed. To encourage a Christian response to a wide range of issues and topics, including those that are peculiar to Pentecostals. Monthly & online mag.; 24 pgs.; circ. 14,000. Subscription $24 U.S./$19.05 Cdn. (includes GST). 10 percent unsolicited freelance; 90 percent assigned. Query; fax/e-query OK. Pays $20-75 on publication for 1st rts. (no pay for reprint rts.). Articles 700-900 wds. Responds in 6-8 wks. Seasonal 4 mos. ahead. Accepts reprints (tell when/where appeared). Prefers e-mail submission (copied into message). Regularly uses sidebars. Prefers NIV. Guidelines/theme list by mail/e-mail/Website; copy $2/9 x 12 SAE. (Ads)
Tips: "View theme list on our Website and query us about a potential article regarding one of our themes. Our readership is 98 percent Canadian. We prefer Canadian writers or at least writers who understand that Canadians are not Americans in long underwear. We also give preference to members of this denomination, since this is related to issues concerning our fellowship."

$ THIS I BELIEVE ESSAYS, 2424 Frankfort Ave., Louisville KY 40206-3515. (502) 259-9889. E-mail through Website: www.npr.org/thisibelieve/guide.html. National Public Radio (NPR). Write and submit your own story of personal belief; those accepted will be recorded and read on the air. Guidelines & contract included on the Website. Complete ms. submitted through Website. Pays $200, 30 days after your essay is recorded. Personal essay 350-500 wds. Details on Website.

3V MAGAZINE, PO Box 143, McKeesport PA 15132. Toll-free (877) 279-5212. E-mail through Website: www.3VMagazine.com. National Christian Men's publication. Jamar Subert, pub. A comprehensive resource directly related to the daily spiritual walk of Christian men and offers key insight concerning today's issues. Bimonthly mag. Subscription $10. Open to unsolicited freelance. Submit up to 100-word query through Website. No mention of payment. Articles. Incomplete topical listings.

TIFERET: A Journal of Spiritual Literature, 211 Dryden Rd., Bernardsville NJ 07924-1108. (908) 432-2149. E-mail: editors@tireretjournal.com. Website: www.tiferetjournal.com. Donna Baier Stein, pub./Ed-in-chief. Publishes writings from authors of many faiths. Quarterly literary mag.; 176 pgs. Open to unsolicited freelance. Only accepts electronic submissions via Website. **NO PAYMENT** for 1st rts. Articles; fiction. Responds in 4 mos. Accepts simultaneous submissions & rarely reprints. Guidelines on Website.

    Poetry: Renee Ashley, poetry ed. Submit max. 6 poems.

    Special Needs: Accepts artwork, black & white for interior; color for cover.

TIME OF SINGING: A Magazine of Christian Poetry, PO Box 149, Conneaut Lake PA 16316. E-mail: timesing@zoominternet.net. Website: www.timeofsinging.com. Lora Zill, ed. We try to appeal to all poets and lovers of poetry. Quarterly booklet; 44 pgs.; circ. 250. Subscription $17. 95 percent unsolicited freelance; 5 percent assigned. Complete ms; e-query OK. **PAYS IN COPIES** for 1st, one-time, or reprint rts. Poetry only (some book reviews by assignment). Responds in 12 wks. Seasonal 6 mos. ahead. Accepts simultaneous submissions & reprints (tell when/where appeared). Accepts e-mail submission (attached file). Guidelines by mail/e-mail/Website; copy $4 ea. or 2/$6.

    Poetry: Accepts 150-200/yr. Free verse, haiku, light verse, traditional; 3-60 lines. Submit max. 5 poems. Always need form poems (sonnets, villanelles, triolets, etc.) with Christian themes. Fresh rhyme. "Cover letter not needed; your work speaks for itself."

    Contest: Sponsors 1-2 annual poetry contests on specific themes or forms ($2 entry fee/ poem) with cash prizes (send SASE for rules).

    Tips: "Study poetry, read widely—both Christian and non-Christian. Work at the craft. Be open to suggestions and critique. If I have taken time to comment on your work, it is close to publication. If you don't agree, submit elsewhere. I appreciate poets who take chances, who write outside the box. Time of Singing is a literary poetry magazine, so I'm not looking for greeting card verse or sermons that rhyme."

$ @ TODAYSCHRISTIAN.COM, 465 Gundersen Dr., Carol Stream IL 60188-2498. (630) 260-6200. Fax (630) 260-0114. E-mail: tceditor@christianitytoday.com. Website: www.todays-christian .com. Dawn Zemke, ed. Uses both reprints and original material. Online mag. Complete ms/cover letter; e-query OK. Pays .05-.10/wd. on acceptance for 1st electronic rts. Articles 500-1,500 wds. Responds in 6-8 wks. Seasonal 9 mos. ahead. Accepts reprints. Accepts e-mail submissions (copied into message). Prefers NIV. Guidelines/theme list by mail/e-mail/Website; copy online

    Tips: "Looking for profiles, inspirational stories, and seasonal."

$ TODAY'S PENTECOSTAL EVANGEL, 1445 N. Boonville, Springfield MO 65802-1894. (417) 862-2781. Fax (417) 862-0416. E-mail: tpe@ag.org. Website: www.tpe.ag.org. Assemblies of God. Ken Horn, ed.; submit to Scott Harrup, sr. assoc. ed. Assemblies of God. Weekly & online mag.; 32 pgs.; circ. 175,000. Subscription $28.99. 5 percent unsolicited freelance; 95 percent assigned.

Complete ms/cover letter; no phone/fax/e-query. Accepts full mss by e-mail. Pays .06/wd. (.04/wd. for reprints) on acceptance for 1st & electronic rts. Articles 500-1,200 words (10-15/yr.); testimonies 200-300 words. Responds in 6-8 wks. Seasonal 6-8 mos. ahead. No simultaneous submissions; accepts reprints (tell when/where appeared). Kill fee 100 percent. Prefers e-mail submissions (attached file). Uses some sidebars. Prefers NIV, KJV. Guidelines by mail/e-mail/Website; copy for 9 x 12 SAE/$1.39 postage. (Ads)

> **Fillers:** Anecdotes, facts, personal experience, testimonies; 250-500 wds. Practical, how-to pieces on family life, devotions, evangelism, seasonal, current issues, Christian living; 250 words; pays about $25.
>
> **Special Needs:** "TPE offers a free e-mail/online devotional, Daily Boost. Contributors are not paid, but a number of these writers have been published in the magazine."
>
> **Tips:** "True, first-person inspirational material is the best bet for a first-time contributor. We reserve any controversial subjects for writers we're familiar with. Positive family-life articles work well near Father's Day, Mother's Day, and holidays."

$ TOGETHER, 1251 Virginia Ave., Harrisonburg VA 22802. (540) 433-5351. Fax (540) 434-0247. E-mail: Tgether@aol.com. Website: www.churchoutreach.com. Media for Living. Melodie Davis, ed. An outreach magazine distributed by churches to attract the general public to Christian faith and life. Quarterly tabloid; 8 pgs.; circ. 25,000. Free. 90 percent unsolicited freelance. Complete ms/cover letter or query; e-query OK. Pays $35-60 after publication for 1st & electronic rts. Articles 500-1,200 words (16/yr.). Responds in 9-17 wks. Seasonal 6 mos. ahead. Accepts simultaneous submissions & reprints. Accepts requested ms on disk or by e-mail (copied into message). Uses some sidebars. Prefers NIV. Guidelines/theme list by mail/e-mail/Website; copy on Website. (No ads)

> **Tips:** "Deal with contemporary themes with fresh style. We need a variety of salvation testimonies from all racial/ethnic groups, with excellent photos available (don't submit photos until requested)." When submitting by e-mail, put title of magazine and title of your piece in subject line. Also include your e-mail address in body of message.

@ TOUCHED BY THE HAND OF GOD. Website: www.touchedbythehandofgod.com. Barrett Batson, ed. People share stories of how God has opened doors, hearts, or minds for them in remarkable ways and at just the right time. Website. Free online. Open to unsolicited freelance. Complete ms. Use submission form on Website. NO PAYMENT for onetime or reprint rts. Personal stories to 600 wds. Guidelines on Website.

TRI-STATE VOICE, 38 Sioux Ave., Oakland NJ 07436-2133. (201) 644-7062. E-mail: tristatevoice@aol.com. Website: www.tristatevoice.com. Tom Campisi, ed. To be a voice to the Christian community in Greater NYC. Monthly newspaper; circ. 15,000. Subscription $24. Open to freelance. Query preferred. Articles; no reviews. Incomplete topical listings. (Ads)

@ THE TRUMPETER, 20969 Certosa Ter., Boca Raton FL 33433. (305) 274-4880. Fax (302) 370-1485. E-mail: info@thetrumpeter.com. Website: www. thetrumpeter.com. Swanko Communications. Martiele Swanko, ed-in-chief. Unites all South Florida Christian denominations, ethnic groups, and cultures. Online mag.; 80+ pgs.; circ. 20,000. Subscription $19.95. 90 percent unsolicited freelance. Query; fax/e-query OK. NO PAYMENT for onetime rts. Features & sports, 900-1,000 words; articles 500-1,200 words; book/music/video reviews, 100 words. Responds in 4 wks. Accepts reprints (tell when/where appeared). Requires requested ms on disk or by e-mail. Regularly uses sidebars. Prefers KJV. Guidelines/theme list by mail/ e-mail/Website. (Ads)

> **Fillers:** Cartoons.
>
> **Columns/Departments:** Accepts 100/yr. Around Town (local talk), 100-125 words; Arts & Entertainment, 400 words; Legal, 450 words; Political/Viewpoint, 100-125 words.
>
> **Tips:** "Call us for a special feature assignment. Be a good writer. Know how to effectively write a paragraph by the rules and use active verbs instead of passive verbs."

+ **TRUTH TREASURES/COVENANT TREASURES**, 1302 E. 30th, Apt. A, Texarkana AR 71854. E-mail: tonya@truth-treasures.com. Website: www.truth-treasures.com. Blog: www.truth-treasures .com/blog. Covenant Treasures Ministries, Inc. Tonya Taylor, ed.; submit to Submission for *Covenant Treasures*. Devotionals, testimonials, and humor. Open to unsolicited freelance.

$ **THE UNITED CHURCH OBSERVER**, 478 Huron St., Toronto ON M5R 2R3, Canada. (416) 960-8500. Fax (416) 960-8477. E-mail through Website: www.ucobserver.org. United Church of Canada. David Wilson, ed./pub. To voice hope for individual Christians, for the United Church, for God's world. Monthly (11x) mag.; circ. 70,000. Subscription $23 Cdn.; $30 U.S. 20 percent freelance written; uses a limited amount of material from non-United Church freelancers. Pays variable rates for 1st rts. (sometimes all rts.). Articles to 1,200 wds. Accepts reprints (tell when/where appeared). (Ads)

$ **UPSCALE MAGAZINE: Exposure to the World's Finest**, 600 Bronner Brothers Way S.W., Atlanta GA 30310. (404) 758-7467. Fax (404) 755-9892. E-mail: features@upscalemag.com (department editors listed on Website). Website: www.upscalemagazine.com. Upscale Communications Inc. Joyce E. Davis, sr. ed. To inspire, inform, and entertain African Americans. Monthly mag.; circ. 250,000. Subscription $20. 75-80 percent unsolicited freelance. Query; fax/e-query OK. Pays $100 & up on publication for 1st rts. Articles (135/yr.); novel excerpts. Seasonal 6 mos. ahead. Accepts simultaneous submissions. Responds in 5-9 wks. Kill fee 25 percent. Guidelines/copy on Website.

    Columns/Departments: Buys 6-10/yr. News & Business (factual, current); Lifestyle (travel, home, wellness, etc.); Beauty & Fashion (tips, trends, upscale fashion, hair); Arts & Entertainment. Query. Payment varies. These columns most open to freelance.

    Tips: "We are open to queries for exciting and informative nonfiction." Uses inspirational and religious articles.

@ **URBAN KINGDOM MAGAZINE.COM**, PO Box 77622, Washington DC 20013-8622. Toll-free (800) 346-5589. E-mail: info@urbankingdommagazine.com. Website: www.urbankingdommagazine .com. Urban Kingdom Media Group LLC. Vashti Dominique, pub. & ed-in-chief. Characterizes the contemporary lifestyle of Christian young men and young women; a media source of realism and truth, encouragement, and entertainment. Webzine; circ. 3,000. Open to freelance. Query/2 clips by e-mail to: writers@urbankingdommagazine.com; phone/e-query OK. **NO PAYMENT**. Articles to 1,000 words; fiction length varies; book reviews 500 words. Responds in 3 wks. Seasonal 3 mos. ahead. Accepts simultaneous submissions & reprints (tell when/where appeared). Requires e-mail submissions (attached file). Uses some sidebars. Also accepts submissions from teens. Guidelines/ theme list by e-mail/Website; copy online. (Ads)

    Poetry: Uses regularly. All types; any length.

    Fillers: Uses regularly. Anecdotes, cartoons, facts, ideas, newsbreaks, party ideas, prayers, prose, quizzes, quotes, sermon illustrations, short humor, tips; 200-300 words or 350-500 wds.

    Columns: Has a number of columns in these areas: music, urban mode, arts & entertainment, health, beauty & grooming, community, news & political commentary/current events, sports, business/finance/technology, lifestyle, testimony, book review.

    Special Needs: Music; style; arts & entertainment; community; business, finance & technology; health, beauty & grooming; home & living; travel. "We would like to give a more balanced focus to men's issues and interest in fashion, sports, etc."

    Tips: "Writer must be a good writer and spiritually active. We appeal to a very contemporary, nontraditional Christian market. Most open to music, arts & entertainment, book review, fashion, boy's lounge."

$ @ **U.S. CATHOLIC**, 205 W. Monroe St., Chicago IL 60606. (312) 236-7782. Fax (312) 236-8207. E-mail: editors@claretians.org. Website: www.uscatholic.org. The Claretians. Meinrad Schrer-Emunds, exec. ed. (emundsm@claretians.org); Rev. John Molyneau C.M.F., ed/pub. Devoted to starting and continuing a dialog with Catholics of diverse lifestyles and opinions about the way they live their faith. Monthly & online mag.; 52 pgs.; circ. 40,000. Subscription $22. 95 percent unso-licited freelance. Complete ms/cover letter; phone/fax/e-query OK. Pays $200-500 (fiction $300-400) on acceptance for all rts. Articles 2,500-3,200 words; fiction to 2,500 words. Responds in 5 wks. Seasonal 6 mos. ahead. Accepts requested ms on disk or by e-mail. Regularly uses sidebars. Guidelines on Website; copy for 10 x 13 SASE. (Ads: Tom Toussaint, 312-236-7782, ext. 854)

> **Poetry:** Submit poetry (and fiction) to literaryeditor@uscatholic.org. All types except light verse, to 50 lines; $75.
>
> **Columns/Departments:** (See guidelines first.) Sounding Board, 1,100-1,300 words, $250; Practicing Catholic, 750 words, $150.
>
> **Tips:** "Most open to features and essays. All manuscripts (except for fiction or poetry) should have an explicit religious dimension that enables readers to see the interaction between their faith and the issue at hand. Fiction should be well written, creative, with solid character development."
>
> ** This periodical was #31 on the 2009 Top 50 Christian Publishers list (#20 in 2008, #23 in 2007, #23 in 2006, #22 in 2005).

$ VIBRANT LIFE, 55 W. Oak Ridge Dr., Hagerstown MD 21740-7390. (301) 393-4019. Fax (301) 393-4055. E-mail: vibrantlife@rhpa.org. Website: www.vibrantlife.com. Seventh-day Adventist/Review & Herald. Charles Mills, ed. Total health publication (physical, mental, and spiritual); plus articles on family and marriage improvement; ages 30-50. Bimonthly mag.; 32 pgs.; circ. 30,000. Subscription $20. 50 percent unsolicited freelance; 30 percent assigned. Query/clips; fax/e-query OK. Pays $100-300 on acceptance for 1st, onetime, reprint, or electronic rts. Articles 450-650 words; feature articles to 1,000 words (50-60/yr.). Responds in 5 wks. Seasonal 9 mos. ahead. Accepts simultaneous submissions & reprints (tell when/where appeared). Accepts e-mail submissions (attached file). Kill fee 50 percent. Regularly uses sidebars. Prefers NIV. Guidelines/themes on Website; copy $1/9 x 12 SAE. (Ads)

> **Tips:** "Articles need to be very helpful, practical, and well documented. Don't be preachy. Sidebars are a real plus." Not accepting submissions until end of year; see Website.
>
> ** This periodical was #40 on the 2009 Top 50 Christian Publishers list (#26 in 2007, #7 in 2005).

@ VICTORY HERALD, Box 190, Tipton OK 73570. Phone/fax (580) 667-4178. E-mail:dsmith@pldi .net. Website: www.victoryherald.com. To promote and encourage writers to submit works of inspi-rational content and purpose that will reach out and touch the hearts of readers. Donna Smith, ed. Monthly e-zine. 70 percent unsolicited freelance; 30 percent assigned. Complete ms; e-query OK. Accepts full mss by e-mail. NO PAYMENT for onetime rts. Articles 500-750 words; fiction 750-1,200 words. Responds in 2 wks. Seasonal 2 mos. ahead. Accepts simultaneous submissions & reprints (tell when/where appeared). Prefers submissions by e-mail (attached file or copied into message). Uses some sidebars. Also accepts submissions from children/teens. Guidelines/copy on Website. (No ads)

> **Poetry:** Accepts 24-36/yr. Free verse, haiku, traditional; 40-45 lines max. Submit max. 3 poems.
>
> **Fillers:** Accepts 24-36/yr. Anecdotes, games, kid quotes, party ideas, prayers, prose, short humor, tips; 50-150 wds.
>
> **Columns/Departments:** Complete ms; no payment.
>
> **Tips:** "More open to inspirational works; any writing that encourages and inspires one to live for Christ."

$ @ VICTORY IN GRACE, 60 Quentin Rd., Lake Zurich IL 60047. (847) 438-4494. Fax (847) 438-4232. E-mail: cameron@victoryingrace.org, or julie@victoryingrace.org. Website: www.victory ingrace.org. Teaching and print ministry of Dr. James Scudder. Cameron Edwards, mng. ed. Serves to help and inspire viewers and listeners of Victory in Grace with Dr. James Scudder. Online mag. 5 percent unsolicited freelance; 95 percent assigned/in-house. E-query only. Pays .15/wd. on publication for 1st rts. Not copyrighted. Articles 1,200-1,500 words (20/yr.). Responds in 4-6 wks. Seasonal 6 mos. ahead. Accepts simultaneous submissions & reprints (tell when/where appeared). Prefers e-mail submissions (attached file). Sometimes pays kill fee. Regularly uses sidebars. Prefers KJV. Guidelines by mail/e-mail; copy online.

Special Needs: True stories of how someone's life has changed through the ministry of Victory in Grace.

Tips: "Most open to a strong story about how God helps His people to cope with or overcome obstacles."

$ THE VISION, 8855 Dunn Rd., Hazelwood MO 63042-2299. (314) 837-7300. Fax (314) 837-1803. E-mail: WAP@upci.org. Website: www.upci.org/wap. United Pentecostal Church. Richard M. Davis, ed.; submit to Karen Myers, administrative aide. Denominational. Weekly take-home paper; 4 pgs.; circ. 6,000. Subscription $2.49/quarter. 95 percent unsolicited freelance. Complete ms/cover letter; no e-query. Pays $8-25 on publication for 1st rts. Articles 500-1,600 words (to 120/yr.); fiction 1,200-1,600 words (to 120/yr.); devotionals 350-400 words. Seasonal 9 months ahead. Accepts simultaneous submissions & reprints. Guidelines by mail/e-mail/Website; free copy/#10 SASE. (No ads)

Poetry: Buys 30/yr.; traditional; $3-12.

Tips: "Most open to fiction short stories, real-life experiences, and short poems. Whether fiction or nonfiction, we are looking for stories depicting everyday life situations and how Christian principles are used to solve problems, resolve issues, or enhance one's spiritual growth. Be sure manuscript has a pertinent, spiritual application. Best way to break into our publication is to send a well-written article that meets our specifications."

$ VISTA, PO Box 50434, Indianapolis IN 46250-0434. (317) 774-7900. E-mail: submissions@wesleyan.org. Website: www.wesleyan.org/wph. Wesleyan Publishing House. Jim Watkins, ed. Weekly take-home paper; 8 pgs. 62 percent unsolicited freelance; 38 percent assigned. Accepts full mss by e-mail. Pays $5-35 on publication for onetime and reprint rts. Articles 500-550 words; fiction 500-550 words; humor 250 words. Seasonal 9 mos. ahead. No simultaneous submissions. Prefers e-mail submission (attached). No kill fee. Regularly uses sidebars. Also accepts submissions from children/teens. Prefers NIV. Guidelines by mail/e-mail; copy $2.50. (No ads)

Fillers: Buys many/yr. Anecdotes, facts, newsbreaks, prayers, quotes; 30-75 wds.

Special Needs: Book excerpts from WPH products.

Tips: "Great market for beginning writers. Any subject related to Christian growth."

+ THE VOICE OF GRACE & TRUTH, PO Box 43, Brandamore PA 19316. (610) 942-3053. E-mail: joycetilney@comcast.com or mail@thevoiceofgraceandtruth.com. Website: www.thevoiceofgraceand truth.com. A paper with purpose! Joyce Tilney, ed. Bimonthly newspaper; 16 pgs.; circ. 15,000. Subscription free. Open to unsolicited freelance. Query first. Articles. Incomplete topical listings. (Ads)

Tips: "We offer teaching, news, and testimonies to inspire, educate, and challenge the Body of Christ, and to share Jesus with the world."

$ WAR CRY, 615 Slaters Ln., Alexandria VA 22314. (703) 684-5500. Fax (703) 684-5539. E-mail: War_cry@USN.salvationarmy.org. Website: www.salvationarmypublications.org. The Salvation Army. Maj. Ed Forster, ed-in-chief; Jeff McDonald, mng. ed. Pluralistic readership reaching all socioeconomic strata and including distribution in institutions. Biweekly mag.; 24 pgs.; circ. 250,000. Subscription $10. 5 percent unsolicited freelance. Complete ms/brief cover letter; no phone/fax query; e-query OK. Accepts full mss by e-mail. Pays .15/wd. on acceptance for 1st, onetime rts. Articles 500-1,000 words; no fiction or poetry. Responds in 4-6 wks. Seasonal 1 yr. ahead. Accepts simultaneous submissions and reprints (tell when/where appeared). Prefers accepted ms by e-mail (attached or copied into message). No kill fee. Uses some sidebars. Prefers NIV. Guidelines by mail/e-mail; copy for 9 x 12 SASE. (No ads)

Fillers: Buys 10/yr. Anecdotes (inspirational), 200-500 words; .15/wd.

** This periodical was #45 on the 2009 Top 50 Christian Publishers list (#40 in 2008, #17 in 2006, #33 in 2005).

$ THE WAY OF ST. FRANCIS, 1112—26th St., Sacramento CA 95816-5610. (916) 443-5717. Fax (916) 443-2019. E-mail: ofmcaway@att.net. Website: www.sbfranciscans.org. Franciscan Friars of California/Catholic. Sharon E. Melberg, mng. ed. For those interested in the message of St. Francis of Assisi as lived out by contemporary people. Bimonthly mag.; 49 pgs.; circ. 5,000. Subscription $15; $17 foreign. 60 percent unsolicited freelance; 40 percent assigned. Complete ms/cover letter; phone/ fax/e-query OK. Accepts full mss by e-mail. Pays $50 (or up to 10 copies & 2 subscriptions) on publication for 1st rts. Articles 900-1,800 words (25/yr.); fiction 500-2,000 words (12/yr.); reviews 250 words. Responds in 2 wks. Seasonal 6 mos. ahead. No simultaneous submissions; reprints accepted (tell when/where appeared). Prefers requested ms on disk or by e-mail (attached file). No kill fee. Uses some sidebars. Prefers NAB. Also accepts submissions from children/teens. Guidelines/theme list by mail/e-mail/Website; copy for 6 x 9 SAE/$2.77 postage (mark "Media Mail"). (No ads)

Poetry: Accepts 4-6 poems/yr.; any type; 4-50 lines; pays $50.

Tips: "Write a piece that explores an aspect of Franciscan spirituality that is fresh and provocative. All fiction must have a Franciscan tie-in."

**This periodical was #35 on the 2009 Top 50 Christian Publishers list.

$ WEAVINGS, 1908 Grand Ave., PO Box 340004, Nashville TN 37203-0004. (615) 340-7200. E-mail: weavings@upperroom.org. Website: www.upperroom.org. The UpperRoom. Submit to The Editor. For clergy, lay leaders, and all thoughtful seekers who want to deepen their understanding of, and response to, how God's life and human lives are being woven together. Quarterly mag. Subscription $28. Open to freelance. Complete ms. Pays .12/wd. & up on acceptance. Articles 1,250-2,000 words; sermons & meditations 500-2,000 words; stories (short vignettes or longer narratives) to 2,000 words; book reviews 750 words. Responds within 13 wks. Accepts reprints. Accepts requested ms on disk or by e-mail. Guidelines/theme list on Website; copy for 7.5 x 10.5 SAE/5 stamps. Incomplete topical listings.

Poetry: Pays $75 & up.

Tips: Note that this publication is transitioning as they go to press and will likely be changing format, as well as other aspects of this listing. Check their Website for current information.

$ WESLEYAN LIFE, Box 50434, Indianapolis IN 46250-0434. (317) 774-7909. Fax (317) 774-7913. E-mail: communications@wesleyan.org. Website: www.wesleyan.org. The Wesleyan Church Corp. Dr. Ronald D. Kelly, gen. ed.; Jerry Brecheisen, mng. ed. Denominational. Quarterly mag.; 40 pgs.; circ. 50,000. Subscription controlled. 10 percent freelance. E-mail submissions only. Pays $50-80 for unsolicited on publication for 1st or simultaneous rts. Articles 400-500 words (50/yr.). Responds in 2 wks. Seasonal 6 mos. ahead. Accepts simultaneous submissions & reprints (tell when/ where appeared). Guidelines by mail/e-mail/Website; copy $2. (Ads—limited)

Tips: "Most open to 400-500 word articles. Must be submitted electronically. No poetry."

WEST WIND REVIEW, 1250 Siskiyou Blvd., Ashland OR 97520. (541) 552-6518 or (541) 552-6641. E-mail: cwright@sou.edu, or WestWind@sou.edu. Website: www.westwindreview.blogspot .com. Southern Oregon University. Student editor changes each year; Craig Wright, advisor. Strives to bring well-written, insightful stories and poems to the public. Annual anthology; 100-200 pgs.; circ. 250-500. 100 percent unsolicited freelance. Complete ms/cover letter & bio; no phone/e-query. **PAYS 1 COPY OF ANTHOLOGY** for 1st rts. Not copyrighted. Fiction (8-15/yr.). Accepts mss from May 15 through December 1. Responds in 5-10 wks. No simultaneous submissions or reprints. Does not use sidebars. No e-mail submissions. Guidelines on Website; copy $3. (No ads)

Poetry: Any type; any length. Submit max. 5 poems. Pays one copy of the anthology.

Special Needs: Poetry or short stories that reflect moving, human interest—in a tasteful manner. Fiction should be thoughtful, literary, and contemporary.

Tips: "We accept all submissions for consideration, and observe no borders in order to encourage original creativity. We accept all forms of poetry, prose, short story, and black & white photos. No erotica, sci-fi/fantasy, or racial bias."

$ THE WILDWOOD READER, PO Box 55-0898, Jacksonville FL 32255. (904) 705-6806. E-mail: publisher@wildwoodreader.com. Website: www.wildwoodreader.com. Timson Edwards Co. Alex Gonzalez, pub. Focus is on adult, literary short fiction that is uplifting and motivational for living life in wellness and spirit. Biweekly jour.; 16 pgs.; circ. 100. Subscription $12. 100 percent unsolicited freelance. Query in writing. Pays $10-75, 60 days after publication for onetime rts. Fiction 800-2,400 words (18/yr.). Responds in 6 wks. Seasonal 4 mos. ahead. Accepts simultaneous submissions & reprints (tell when/where appeared). Requires CD by mail. Guidelines by mail; no copy. (Ads)

Contest: Sponsors regular contests with winners being published. Readers pick the best of the year for an annual award.

Tips: "Most open to good, solid, ready-to-print short stories that follow the indications above. I prefer new and emerging writers; we are not a high end publication yet, but working our way there. Your work must be edited and ready to publish."

WISCONSIN CHRISTIAN NEWS, PO Box 756, 1007 W. Arlington St., Marshfield WI 54449. (715) 486-8066. E-mail: christiannews@charter.net. Website: www.wisconsinchristiannews.com. Rob E. Pue, ed. Regional Christian newspaper for all of Wisconsin; nondenominational/evangelical. Monthly newspaper; 48 pgs.; circ. 10,000. Subscription $25. Open to freelance. **NO PAYMENT**. Articles 500-1,500 wds. Responds in 1 wk. Seasonal 2 mos. ahead. Accepts e-mail submissions (copied into message). Uses some sidebars. Also accepts submissions from children/teens. No guidelines; copy $2. (Ads)

$ THE WITTENBURG DOOR, 5620 Columbia Ave., Dallas TX 75214, or PO Box 1444, Waco TX 76703-1444. (214) 827-2625. Fax (254) 827-7938. E-mail (submissions): dooreditor@earthlink .net. Website: www.wittenburgdoor.com. Trinity Foundation. Robert Darden, sr. ed. Currently on a publishing hiatus.

WORD & WAY, 3236 Emerald Ln., Ste. 400, Jefferson City MO 65109-3700. (573) 635-5939, ext. 206. Fax (573) 635-1774. E-mail: wordandway@wordandway.org. Website: www.wordandway.org. Baptist. Bill Webb, ed. (bwebb@wordandway.org/ext. 206). Biweekly. Subscription $17.50. To glorify God.

$ @ THE WORLD & I ONLINE: The Magazine for Lifelong Learners, 3600 New York Ave. N.E., Washington DC 20002-1947. (202) 635-4054. Fax (202) 832-5780. E-mail: editors@world andi. com. Website: www.worldandi.com. New World Communications. Charles Kim, pub. Scholarly and encyclopedic. Monthly online journal. Subscription rates on Website. 10-20 percent unsolicited freelance. Considers draft articles on speculation, or queries on specific topics (offer evidence of research/qualification on topic). E-query only. Pays $100 following publication for all electronic rts. Articles 1,200-2,000 words (550-600/yr.). Requests free use of original photos to illustrate, if available (don't submit unless requested). Responds in 6-10 wks. Query for seasonal 5 mos. ahead. No reprints. Prefers requested ms by e-mail (unformatted Word). Uses some sidebars. Guidelines on Website.

Special Needs: Areas of interest include Arts, Life, Travel (first person); Profiles [(A) individuals who make a difference in community; (b) successful first generation immigrants for ESL section, (c) exceptional writers, literary figures.] Culture (peoples/societies worldwide, American regional and ethnic heritage), Civil War. Other sections include Science, Analysis, Commentary on Current Affairs (specialist contributors only), and Book Reviews.

Tips: "Life, Culture, Profiles areas most open to freelancers. Offer a great/original idea (with established background as a writer). Tone of essay should be objective. Avoid advocacy

and undue partisanship. Audience is educated, nonspecialist, nonsectarian. We especially appreciate scholarly contributions."
** This periodical was #32 on the 2009 Top 50 Christian Publishers list (#34 in 2008, #32 in 2007, #41 in 2006).

+ **WRECKED FOR THE ORDINARY**, 2421 Ellington Cir., Nashville TN 37211. (615) 512-5488. E-mail: editor@wreckedfortheordinary.com. Website: www.wrecked.org. Jeff Goins, ed. Seeks to awake and challenge a generation of young adults to follow an unsafe Christ in a world numbed by pop Christianity. **NO PAYMENT**. Articles 600-800 words (longer pieces divided into 2-part series).

$ **WRITTEN**, PO Box 250504, Atlanta GA 30325. (404) 753-8315. E-mail: editor@written mag.com. Website: www.writtenmag.com. Zipporah Publications, LLC. Michelle Gipson, pub. Celebrates the word and the reader; nationally syndicated insert to African American newspapers across the country. Bimonthly tabloid; 12-16 pgs; circ. 130,000. Subscription $8. 20 percent unsolicited freelance; 80 percent assigned. Query/clips; e-query OK. Pays $10-75 or.10/wd. on publication for onetime rts. Articles 500-750 words (6-8/yr.); reviews 250 words ($75). Responds in 3 wks. Seasonal 3 mos. ahead. Accepts simultaneous submissions; no reprints. Requires e-mail submissions (attached file in Word). No kill fee. Regularly uses sidebars. Also accepts submissions from teens. Guidelines by mail/Website; copy for 9 x 12 SAE/$1 postage. (Ads—media kit available on Website)
   Fillers: Accepts 1-3/yr. Facts, quotes, tips.
   Contest: Next New Writer Contest.
   Tips: "Our column for freelancers is "First Person Singular." We look for heartfelt stories from writers who have something to share with readers. We look for moving stories that 'bleed on the page.'"

XAVIER REVIEW, 1 Drexel Dr., Box 110C, New Orleans LA 70125. (504) 520-7549 or (504) 520-7303. Fax (504) 520-7944. Website: www.xula.edu. Xavier University of Louisiana. Nicole Pepinster Greene, ed. (ngreene@xula.edu). Publishes nondogmatic, thought-provoking, and sometimes humorous and even irreverent work on religious subject matters. Semiannual literary jour; 75 pgs.; circ. 300. Subscription $10 (individuals), $15(institutions). 90 percent unsolicited freelance; 10 percent assigned. Complete ms/cover letter; e-query OK. **PAYS IN COPIES** for 1st rts. Articles 250-5,000 words (3/yr.); fiction 250-5,000 words (6/yr.); book reviews 250-750 words. Responds in 4 wks. Accepts simultaneous submissions; no reprints. Prefers accepted mss by e-mail (attached). No kill fee. Does not use sidebars. Guidelines on Website; copy for $2/7 x 10 SAE/3 stamps. (No ads)
   Poetry: Accepts 20/yr. Avant-garde, free verse, traditional; 5-60 lines. Submit max. 5 poems.

CHILDREN'S MARKETS

$ **ADVENTURES**, 2923 Troost Ave., Kansas City MO 64109-1538. (816) 931-1900. Fax (816) 412-8306. E-mail through Website: www.wordaction.com. Donna Fillmore, ed. For 6- to 8-yr.-olds (1st & 2nd graders); emphasis on principles, character building. Weekly take-home paper; 4 pgs.; circ. 40,000. Subscription $11.96 ($2.99/child/quarter). 25 percent unsolicited freelance. Query; e-query OK. Pays $15 on acceptance for multiple-use rts. Articles 200 wds. Responds in 4-6 wks. Accepts simultaneous submissions; no reprints. Accepts requested ms by e-mail (attached file). Prefers NIV. Guidelines/theme list by mail/e-mail; copy for #10 SAE/1 stamp. (No ads)
   Special Needs: Recipes and crafts; activities.
   Tips: "Looking for creative activities that 1st and 2nd graders can do on their own at home; crafts, recipes, simple science projects that can be connected to the theme."

$ @ **AMERICAN GIRL**, PO Box 620497, Middleton WI 53562-0497. Toll-free (800) 360-1861. (608) 836-4848. Fax (608) 831-7089. E-mail: im_agmag_editor@pleasantco.com. Website: www .americangirl.com. Pleasant Company Publications. Kristi Thom, ed.; Barbara E. Stretchberry, mng.

ed. General market; for girls ages 8-12 to recognize and celebrate girls' achievements yesterday and today, inspire their creativity, and nurture their hopes and dreams. Bimonthly & online mag.; 50 pgs.; circ. 700,000. Subscription $22.95. 5 percent unsolicited freelance; 10 percent assigned. Query (complete ms for fiction); no e-query. Pays $1/wd. ($300 minimum) on acceptance for 1st or all rts. Articles 150-1,000 words (10/yr.); fiction to 2,300 words (6/yr.; $500 min.). Responds in 13 wks. Seasonal 6 mos. ahead. Accepts simultaneous submissions & reprints. Kill fee 50 percent. Uses some sidebars. Guidelines on Website; copy $3.95 (check/9 x 12 SAE/$2.38 postage (mark "Media Mail"). (No ads)

Poetry: All poetry is by children.

Fillers: Cartoons, puzzles, word games; $50.

Columns/Departments: Buys 10/yr. Girls Express (short profiles on girls), to 150 words (query); Giggle Gang (visual puzzles, mazes, word games, math puzzles, seasonal games/ puzzles), send complete ms. Pays $50-200.

Contest: Contests vary from issue to issue.

Tips: "Girls Express offers the most opportunities for freelancers. We're looking for short profiles of girls who are doing great and interesting things. Key: a girl must be the 'star' and the story written from her point of view. Be sure to include the ages of the girls you are pitching to us. Write for 8- to 12-year-olds—not teenagers."

$ @ ARCHAEOLOGY. E-mail: shannondustytrails@yahoo.com. Shannon Bridget Murphy, ed./pub. Biblical archaeology for children and teens. Quarterly mag. Open to unsolicited freelance. Complete ms/cover letter; e-query OK. Pays .02-.05/wd. on acceptance for 1st, onetime rts. Articles 500-2,000 words; fiction 500-2,000 words. Responds in 2-4 wks. Seasonal 6-8 mos. ahead. Accepts simultaneous submissions & reprints (tell when/where appeared). No kill fee. Regularly uses sidebars. Also accepts submissions from children/teens. Prefers KJV. Guidelines by e-mail.

Poetry: Open to any type of poetry from children and teens.

Fillers: Anecdotes, cartoons, facts, games, ideas, kid quotes, newsbreaks, party ideas, prayers, prose, quizzes, quotes, sermon illustrations, short humor, tips, and word puzzles.

$ BEGINNER'S FRIEND, PO Box 4060, Overland Park KS 66204. (913) 432-0331. Fax (913) 722-0351. E-mail: sseditor1@juno.com. Website: www.heraldandbanner.com. Church of God (Holiness) /Herald and Banner Press. Arlene McGehee, Sunday school ed. Denominational; for young children. Weekly take-home paper; 4 pgs.; circ. 2,700. Subscription $1.50. Complete ms/cover letter; phone/ fax/e-query OK (prefers mail or e-mail). Pays .005/wd. on publication for 1st rts. Fiction 500-800 wds. Seasonal 6-8 mos. ahead. Accepts simultaneous submissions & reprints (tell when/where appeared). Prefers KJV. Guidelines/theme list; copy. Not in topical listings.

$ BREAD FOR GOD'S CHILDREN, Box 1017, Arcadia FL 34265-1017. (863) 494-6214. Fax (863) 993-0154. E-mail: Bread@breadministries.org. Website: www.breadministries.org. Bread Ministries Inc. Judith M. Gibbs, ed. A family magazine for serious Christians who are concerned about their children or grandchildren. Bimonthly mag.; 32 pgs.; circ. 5,000. Subscription free. 20-25 percent unsolicited freelance. Complete ms; no e-query. Pays $10-30 ($40-50 for fiction) on publication for 1st rts. Not copyrighted. Articles 500-800 words (6/yr.); fiction & true stories 500-900 words for 4-10 yrs., 900-1,500 words for teens 13 and up (6/yr.). Responds in 8-12 wks. (may hold longer). Uses some simultaneous submissions & reprints (tell when/where appeared). Some sidebars. Prefers KJV. Guidelines by mail/e-mail; 3 copies for 9 x 12 SAE/5 stamps; 1 copy 3 stamps. (No ads)

Columns/Departments: Buys 5-8/yr. Let's Chat (discussion issues facing children), 500-800 words; Teen Page (teen issues), 600-900 words; and Idea Page (object lessons or crafts for children), 300-800 words; $10-30.

Tips: "Most open to fiction and articles. Our child and youth fiction can always use a well-written piece about living out godly principles. We need good stories for the younger children—ages 4-10 years. Most open to fiction or real-life stories of overcoming through faith in Jesus Christ. No tag endings or adult solutions coming from children. Create realistic characters and situations. No 'sudden inspiration' solutions. Open to any areas of family life related from a godly perspective."

$ **CADET QUEST**, PO Box 7259, Grand Rapids MI 49510. (616) 241-5616. Fax (616) 241-5558. E-mail: submissions@CalvinistCadets.org. Website: www.CalvinistCadets.org. Calvinist Cadet Corps. G. Richard Broene, ed. To show boys ages 9-14 how God is at work in their lives and in the world around them. Mag. published 7x/yr.; 24 pgs.; circ. 8,000. Subscription $14.35. 35 percent unsolicited freelance. Complete ms/cover letter. Pays .04-.06/wd. on acceptance for 1st, onetime, or reprint rts. Articles 800-1,500 words (12/yr.); fiction 1,000-1,300 words (14/yr.). Responds in 4-6 wks. Accepts simultaneous submissions & reprints (tell when/where appeared). Accepts ms by e-mail (copied into message). Uses some sidebars. Prefers NIV. Guidelines/theme list by mail/Website; copy for 9 x 12 SAE/3 stamps. (Ads—limited)
   Fillers: Buys several/yr. Quizzes, tips, puzzles; 20-200 words; $5 & up.
   Tips: "Most open to fiction or fillers tied to themes; request new theme list in January of each year (best to submit between February and April each year). Also looking for simple projects/ crafts, and puzzles (word, logic)."

$ **CELEBRATE**, 2923 Troost Ave., Kansas City MO 64109. (816) 931-1900. Fax (816) 753-4071. E-mail through Website: www.wordaction.com. Word-Action Publishing Co./Church of the Nazarene. Melissa Hammer, sr. ed. Weekly activity/story paper connects Sunday school learning to life for preschoolers (3 & 4), kindergartners (5 & 6), and their families. Weekly take-home paper; 4 pgs.; circ. 40,000. Subscription $10. 50 percent unsolicited freelance. Query or complete ms/cover letter; e-query OK. Pays $15 or.25/line on acceptance for multiple-use rts. Articles 200 wds. Responds in 4-6 wks. No seasonal. Accepts simultaneous submissions; no reprints. Accepts e-mail submissions (attached file). Prefers NIV. Guidelines by e-mail; theme list/copy for #10 SAE/1 stamp. (No ads)
   Special Needs: Activities, recipes, poems, piggyback songs, and crafts for 3- to 6-year-olds.
   Tips: "Activities should be something a preschooler or kindergartener can do mostly on their own at home. Supplies should be things commonly found around the house or easily obtained at craft stores."

$ **FACES**, 30 Grove St., Ste. C, Peterborough NH 03458. Toll-free (800) 821-0115. (603) 924-7209. Fax (603) 924-7380. E-mail: facesmag@yahoo.com. Website: www.cobblestonepub.com. Cobblestone Publishing/general. Elizabeth Crooker Carpentiere, ed. Introduces young readers (ages 9-14) to different world cultures, religion, geography, government, and art. Monthly mag.; 52 pgs.; circ. 15,000. Subscription $29.95. 90-100 percent freelance. Query only; e-query OK. Pays .20-.25/ wd. on publication for all rts. Articles 300-800 words (45-50/yr.); fiction to 800 words (retold folktales, legends, plays; related to theme). Responds in 4 wks. to 4 mos. Accepts simultaneous submissions. Prefers disk or hard copy. Kill fee 50 percent. Guidelines/themes by mail/Website; copy $4.95/9 x 12 SAE/$2.07 postage; also online.
   Poetry: Any type to 100 wds.
   Fillers: Activities, 100-600 words; .20-.25/wd.

$ **FAITH DETECTIVES**, 1300 N. Meacham Rd., Schaumburg IL 60173-4888. (847) 843-1600. Fax (847) 843-3757. E-mail: takehomepapers@garbc.org. Website: www.RegularBaptistPress .org. General Assn. of Regular Baptist Churches/Regular Baptist Press. Joan E. Alexander, ed. New Publication for juniors (grades 5 & 6). Guidelines still under development.

$ @ **FOCUS ON THE FAMILY CLUBHOUSE**, 8605 Explorer Dr., Colorado Springs CO 80920. (719) 531-3400. Website: www.clubhousemagazine.com. Focus on the Family. Jesse Florea, ed.; Joanna Lutz, asst. ed.; submit to Jamie Dangers, ed. asst. For children 8-12 years who desire to know more about God and the Bible. Monthly & online mag.; 24 pgs.; circ. 90,000. Subscription $18. 15 percent unsolicited freelance; 25 percent assigned. Complete ms/cover letter; no phone/fax/e-query. Pays .15-.25/wd. for articles, up to $300 for fiction on acceptance for nonexclusive license. Articles to 800 words (5/yr.); fiction 500-1,800 words (30/yr.). Responds in 8 wks. Seasonal 6 mos. ahead. Accepts simultaneous submissions; no reprints. No disk or e-mail submissions. Kill fee. Uses some sidebars. Prefers NIV. Also accepts submissions from children once a year. Guidelines by mail; copy (call 800-232-6459). (No ads)

Fillers: Buys 6-8/yr. Quizzes, word puzzles, recipes; 200-800 words; .15-.25/wd.

Tips: "Most open to fiction, personality stories, quizzes, and how-to pieces with a theme. Avoid stories dealing with boy-girl relationships, poetry, and contemporary, middle-class family settings (current authors meet this need). We look for fiction in exciting settings with ethnic characters. Creatively retold Bible stories and historical fiction are easy ways to break in. Send manuscripts with list of credentials. Read past issues."

** 2009, 2008, 2007, 2006, 2005, 2004 EPA Award of Merit—Youth.

$ @ **FOCUS ON THE FAMILY CLUBHOUSE JR.**, 8605 Explorer Dr., Colorado Springs CO 80920. (719) 531-3400. Fax (719) 531-3499. E-mail: joanna.lutz@fotf.org. Website: www.clubhousemag azine.com. Focus on the Family. Suzanne Hadley, ed.; Joanna Lutz, asst. ed.; submit to Jamie Dangers, ed. asst. For 4- to 8-year-olds growing up in a Christian family. Monthly & online mag.; 24 pgs.; circ. 65,000. Subscription $18. 25 percent unsolicited freelance; 50 percent assigned. Complete ms/ cover letter; no phone/fax/e-query. Pays $25-200 ($50-100 for fiction) on acceptance for nonexclusive rts. Articles 100-500 words (1-2/yr.); fiction 250-1,000 words (10/yr.); Bible stories 250-800 words; one-page rebus stories to 200 words. Responds in 8 wks. Seasonal 6-9 mos. ahead. Kill fee 25 percent. Uses some sidebars. Guidelines by mail; copy (call 800-232-6459). (No ads)

Poetry: Buys 4-8/yr. Traditional; 10-25 lines (to 250 words); $50-100.

Fillers: Buys 4-8/yr. Recipes/crafts; 100-500 words; $50-100.

Special Needs: Bible stories, rebus, fiction, and crafts.

Tips: "Most open to short, nonpreachy fiction, beginning reader stories, and read-to-me. Be knowledgeable of our style and try it out on kids first. Looking for stories set in exotic places; nonwhite, middle-class characters; historical pieces; humorous quizzes; and craft and recipe features are most readily accepted."

** 2007 EPA Award of Merit—Youth.

@ **GIRLS CONNECTION**, 1445 N. Boonville Ave., Springfield MO 65802-1894. Website: http://mgc .ag.org/connection. Missionettes Girls Clubs/Assemblies of God. A program for winning girls to Jesus Christ through love and acceptance. Webzine.

$ **GOD'S EXPLORERS**, 1300 N. Meacham Rd., Schaumburg IL 60173-4888. (847) 843-1600. Fax (847) 843-3757. E-mail: takehomepapers@garbc.org. Website: www.RegularBaptistPress .org. General Assn. of Regular Baptist Churches/Regular Baptist Press. Joan E. Alexander, ed. New Publication for primaries (grades 1 & 2). Guidelines still under development.

$ **GOOD NEWS**, 2621 Dryden Rd., Moraine OH 45439. (937) 293-1415. Fax (937) 293-1310. E-mail: service@pflaum.com. Website: www.pflaum.com. Catholic. Joan Mitchell CSJ, ed. For children in grades 2 and 3. Weekly (32x) take-home paper. Not in topical listings.

$ **GUIDE**, 55 W. Oak Ridge Dr., Hagerstown MD 21740. (301) 393-4037. Fax (301) 393-4055. E-mail: Guide@rhpa.org. Website: www.guidemagazine.org. Seventh-day Adventist/Review and Herald Publishing. Randy Fishell, ed.; Rachel Whitaker, assoc. ed. A Christian journal for 10- to 14-yr.-olds, presenting true stories relevant to their needs. Weekly mag.; 32 pgs.; circ. 27,000. Subscription $49.95/yr. 90 percent unsolicited freelance; 10 percent assigned. Complete ms/cover letter; fax/e-query OK. Pays .06-.12/wd. ($25-140) on acceptance for 1st, reprint rts. True stories 750-1,500 words (300/yr.). Responds in 5 wks. Seasonal 8 mos. ahead. Accepts reprints (tell when/

where appeared; pays 50 percent of standard rate). Prefers requested ms by e-mail (attached file). Uses some sidebars. Prefers NIV. Guidelines on Website; copy for 6 x 9 SAE/2 stamps. (No ads)

Fillers: Buys 50/yr. Games, quizzes, word puzzles on a spiritual theme; 20-50 words; $25-40. Accepting very few games, only the most unusual concepts.

Special Needs: "Most open to true action/adventure, Christian humor, and true stories showing God at work in a 10- to 14-year-old's life. Stories must have energy and a high level of intrinsic interest to kids. Put it together with dialog and a spiritual slant, and you're on the 'write' track for our readers. School life."

Tips: "We use only true stories, including school situations, humorous circumstances, adventure, short historical and biographical stories, and almost any situation relevant to 10- to 14-year-olds. Stories must have a spiritual point or implication. We publish multipart true stories regularly; 3-12 chapters, 1,200 words each. We can no longer accept nature or historical stories without documentation."

** This periodical was #23 on the 2009 Top 50 Christian Publishers list (#24 in 2008, #27 in 2007, #44 in 2006, #25 in 2005).

$ JUNIOR COMPANION, PO Box 4060, Overland Park KS 66204. (913) 432-0331. Fax (913) 722-0351. E-mail: sseditor1@juno.com. Website: www.heraldandbanner.com. Church of God (holiness) /Herald and Banner Press. Arlene McGehee, Sunday school ed. Denominational; for 4th-6th graders. Weekly take-home paper; 4 pgs.; circ. 3,500. Subscription $1.50. Complete ms/cover letter; phone/fax/e-query OK (prefers mail or e-mail). Pays .005/wd. on publication for 1st rts. Fiction 500-1,200 wds. Seasonal 6-8 mos. ahead. Accepts simultaneous submissions & reprints (tell when/where appeared). Prefers KJV. Guidelines/theme list/copy by mail. Not in topical listings.

$ JUNIORWAY, PO Box 436987, Chicago IL 60643. Fax (708) 868-6759. Website: www.urbanministries.com. Urban Ministries Inc. K. Steward, ed. (ksteward@urbanministries.com). Sunday school magazine with accompanying teacher's guide and activity booklet for 4th-6th graders. Open to freelance queries; 100 percent assigned. Query and/or e-query with writing sample and/or clips; no phone queries. Pays $150 for curriculum, 120 days after acceptance for all rts. Articles 1,200 words (4/yr.), pays $80. Responds in 4 wks. No simultaneous submissions. Requires requested material by e-mail (attached file). Guidelines by e-mail. (No ads) Incomplete topical listings.

Poetry: Buys 8/yr.; 200-400 words; pays $40.

Tips: "*Juniorway* principally serves an African American audience; editorial content addresses broad Christian issues. Looking for those with educational or Sunday school teaching experience who can actually explain scriptures in an insightful and engaging way and apply those scriptures to the lives of children 9-11 years old."

$ @ KEYS FOR KIDS, PO Box 1001, Grand Rapids MI 49501-1001. (616) 647-4971. Fax (616) 647-4950. E-mail: Hazel@cbhministries.org, or geri@cbhministries.org. Website: www.cbhministries.org. CBH Ministries. Hazel Marett, ed.; Geri Walcott, ed. A daily devotional booklet for children (8-14) or for family devotions. Bimonthly booklet & online version; 80 pgs.; circ. 70,000. Subscription free. 100 percent unsolicited freelance. Complete ms; e-query OK. Accepts full mss by e-mail. Pays $25 on acceptance for 1st, reprint, or simultaneous rts. Devotionals (includes short fiction story) 375-425 words (60-70/yr.). Responds in 4-8 wks. Seasonal 4-5 mos. ahead. Accepts simultaneous submissions & reprints. Prefers NKJV. Guidelines by mail/e-mail; copy for $1.39 postage. (No ads)

Tips: "We want children's devotions. If you are rejected, go back to the sample and study it some more. We use only devotionals, but they include a short fiction story. Any appropriate topic is fine."

$ @ THE KIDS' ARK CHILDRENS CHRISTIAN MAGAZINE, PO Box 3160, Victoria TX 77903. Toll-free (800) 455-1770. (361) 485-1770. E-mail: editor@thekidsark.com. Website: http://thekids

ark.com. Interdenominational. Joy Mygrants, sr. ed. To give kids 6-10 a biblical foundation on which to base their choices in life. Quarterly mag. (soon to be online); 32 pgs.; circ. 8,000. 100 percent unsolicited freelance. Complete ms; e-query OK. Accepts full ms by e-mail. Pays $100 max. on publication for 1st, reprint ($25), electronic, worldwide rts. Fiction 600 words (12/yr.); no articles. Responds in 3-4 wks. No reprints. Prefers accepted submissions by e-mail (attached file). Kill fee 15 percent. Uses some sidebars. Also accepts submissions from children/teens. Prefers NIV. Guidelines/ theme list on Website; copy for $1 postage. (Ads-limited)

> **Tips:** "Open to fiction only. Think outside the box! Must catch children's attention and hold it; be biblically based and related to theme. We want to teach God's principles in an exciting format. Every issue contains the Ten Commandments and the plan of salvation."

$ KID ZONE, 2923 Troost Ave., Kansas City MO 64109. (816) 931-1900. Fax (816) 412-8306. E-mail: vlfolsom@wordaction.com or lslohberger@wordaction.com. Website: www.wordaction.com. Nazarene/Word Action Publishing. Virginia Folsom, ed.; submit to Laura Lohberger, asst. ed. For 8- to 10-yr.-olds, emphasizing Christian values and holy living; follows theme of Sunday school curriculum. Weekly take-home paper; 4 pgs.; circ. 30,000. 80 percent unsolicited freelance; 20 percent assigned. Query; phone/fax/e-query OK. Accepts full mss by e-mail. Pays $25. Articles & fiction 450 wds. Guidelines/theme list by mail/e-mail; copy for #10 SAE/1 stamp.

> **Fillers:** Puzzles & trivia; 250 words; $15.

> **Tips:** "Request our theme list and samples. Send a sample of your material that you think would be appropriate for our publication. Break in by writing exciting, relevant, realistic stories and trivia pieces about info pertinent to kids."

$ NATURE FRIEND: Helping Children Explore the Wonders of God's Creation, 4253 Woodcock Ln., Dayton VA 22821. (540) 867-0764. Fax (540) 867-9516. E-mail: editor@nature friendmagazine.com. Website: www.naturefriendmagazine.com. Dogwood Ridge Outdoors. Kevin Shank, ed. For ages 6-16. Monthly mag.; 24 pgs.; circ. 13,000. Subscription $34. 50-80 percent freelance written. Complete ms/cover letter; no phone/fax/e-query. Pays .05/wd. on publication for 1st rts. Articles 250-900 words (50/yr.); or fiction 500-750 words (40/yr.). Responds in 12-13 wks. Seasonal 4 mos. ahead. Accepts simultaneous submissions & reprints. Submit accepted articles on disk (Word format) or by e-mail. Uses some sidebars. KJV only. Guidelines $5 (www.nature friendmagazine.com/index.pl?linkid=12;class=gen); copy $5/9 x 12 SAE/$2 postage. (No ads)

> **Fillers:** Buys 12/yr. Quizzes, word puzzles; 100-500 words; $10-15.

> **Columns/Departments:** "Month" Nature Trails (seasonal, nature activity for each month); 100-450 wds. Write up as something you do each year, such as mushroom hunting, wildflower walk, snowshoeing, Christmas bird count, viewing a specific meteor shower, etc.

> **Tips:** "We want to bring joy and knowledge to children by opening the world of God's creation to them. We endeavor to create a sense of awe about nature's Creator and a respect for His creation. I'd like to see more submissions of hands-on things to do with a nature theme (not collecting rocks or leaves—real stuff). The best way to learn about the content we use is to be a current, active subscriber."

$ NEW MOON: The Magazine for Girls and Their Dreams, 2 W. First St., #101, Duluth MN 55802. Toll-free (800) 381-4743. (218) 728-5507. Fax (218) 728-0314. E-mail: Newmoon@new moongirlmedia.com. Website: www.newmoon.org. New Moon Publishing. Submit to Editorial Dept. A feminist publication for girls 8-14 years of age; we value diversity and take girls seriously. Bimonthly & online mag.; 49 pgs.; circ. 30,000. Subscription $29.95. 40 percent unsolicited freelance; 50 percent assigned. Query or complete ms/cover letter; e-query OK. Accepts full mss by e-mail. Pays .06/wd. on publication for all rts. Articles 600-1,200 words (12/yr.); fiction 1,200-1,500 words (6/yr.); book reviews 300 words. Responds in 24 wks. No seasonal/holiday. Accepts simultaneous submissions & reprints (tell when/where appeared). Prefers accepted articles by e-mail (copied into message). No kill fee. Regularly uses sidebars. Also accepts submissions from girls and teens. Guidelines/theme list on Website; copy $7/9 x 12 SAE. (No ads)

Poetry: Buys 12/yr. Poetry from girls 8-14 only. Pays $10. Submit any number/any length.

Columns/Departments: Buys 18/yr. Herstory (women from history), 600 words; Women's Work (women in careers), 600 words; Body Language (health & puberty issues for girls), 600 words; pays .06/wd.

Tips: "We accept work from girls and women only. Girls can submit to any department. Adults must limit their submissions to fiction and the columns listed above."

$ OUR LITTLE FRIEND, Box 5353, Nampa ID 83653-5353. (208) 465-2580. Fax (208) 465-2531. E-mail: ailsox@pacificpress.com. Website: www.pacificpress.com. Seventh-day Adventist. Aileen Andres Sox, ed. To help children understand their infinite value to their Creator and Redeemer; learn how to respond to God; show love to their family and friends; serve others in their world; find fulfillment participating in the Seventh-day Adventist Church. Weekly take-home paper for 1- to 6-yr.-olds; 8 pgs. Subscription $25.96. 25 percent unsolicited freelance (or reprints); 50 percent assigned. Complete ms by e-mail. Pays $25-40 on acceptance for onetime or reprint rts. True stories 450-550 words (52/yr.); no articles. Responds in 26 wks. Seasonal 7 mos. ahead. Accepts simultaneous submissions & reprints; no serials. Prefers e-mail submissions (attached file). Guidelines by mail/Website; copy for 9 x 12 SAE/2 stamps. (No ads)

$ PARTNERS, Christian Light Publications Inc., Box 1212, Harrisonburg VA 22803-1212. (540) 434-0768. Fax (540) 433-8896. E-mail: partners@clp.org. Website: www.clp.org. Mennonite. Etta G. Martin, ed. Helping 9- to 14-yr.-olds to build strong Christian character. Weekly take-home paper; 4 pgs.; circ. 6,707. Subscription $10.90. 99 percent unsolicited freelance; 1 percent assigned. Complete ms; e-query OK. Pays .04-.06/wd. on acceptance for 1st, multiuse, or reprint rts. Articles 200-800 words (100/yr.); fiction & true stories 400-1,600 words (200/yr.); serial stories up to 1,600 words/installment; short-short stories to 400 words. Responds in 6 wks. Seasonal 6 mos. ahead. Accepts reprints only 5 yrs. or more after last publication (tell when/where appeared); serials 2 parts. Prefers e-mail submissions (attached or copied into message). No kill fee. Requires KJV. Guidelines/theme list by mail/e-mail; copy for 9 x 12 SAE/3 stamps. (No ads)

Poetry: Buys 250/yr. Traditional, story poems; 4-24 lines; .65-.75/line.

Fillers: Buys 275/yr. Prose, quizzes, quotes, word puzzles (Bible-related); 200-800 words; .03-.05/wd.

Columns/Departments: Character Corner; Cultures & Customs; Historical Highlights; Maker's Masterpiece; Missionary Mail; Torches of Truth; or Nature Nook; all 200-800 wds.

Tips: "Most open to character-building articles and stories that teach a spiritual lesson. New approaches to old themes, or new theme relevant to age level. Please ask for our guidelines before submitting manuscripts. Write in a lively way (showing, not telling) and on a child's level of understanding (ages 9-14). We do not require that you be Mennonite, but we do send a questionnaire for you to fill out if you desire to write for us."

** This periodical was #2 on the 2009 Top 50 Christian Publishers list (#3 in 2008, #14 in 2007, #15 in 2006, #15 in 2005).

$ PASSPORT, 2923 Troost Ave., Kansas City MO 64109. (816) 931-1900. Fax (816) 412-8306. E-mail: rrpettit@wordaction.com or lslohberger@wordaction.com. Website: www.wordaction.com. Word Action/Nazarene Publishing House. Ryan Pettit, ed.; submit to Laura Lohberger, asst. ed. For preteens, 10- to 12-year-olds; supports the Sunday school lesson and provides an exciting way to learn about God and life. Weekly take-home paper; 4 pgs.; circ. 18,000. 30 percent unsolicited freelance. Pays $25. Articles 500 words; no fiction. Accepts reprints. Guidelines/theme list by mail/e-mail; copy for #10 SAE/1 stamp.

Fillers: Cartoons & word puzzles; $15.

Tips: "Most open to creative, true-to-life stories, or creative puzzles and cartoons."

$ POCKETS, PO Box 340004, Nashville TN 37203-0004. (615) 340-7333. Fax (615) 340-7267. E-mail: pockets@upperroom.org. Website: www.pockets.org. United Methodist/The Upper Room. Submit to Lynn W. Gilliam, ed. Devotional magazine for children (6-11 yrs.). Monthly (11x) mag.; 48 pgs.; circ. 67,000. Subscription $21.95. 75 percent unsolicited freelance. Complete ms/brief cover letter; no phone/fax/e-query. Pays .14/wd. on acceptance for onetime rts. Articles 400-800 words (10/yr.) & fiction 600-1,400 words (40/yr.). Responds in 8 wks. Seasonal 1 yr. ahead. Accepts simultaneous submissions & reprints (tell when/where appeared). No mss by e-mail. Uses some sidebars. Prefers NRSV. Also accepts submissions from children through age 12. Guidelines/theme list by mail/e-mail/Website; copy for 9 x 12 SAE/4 stamps. (No ads)

> **Poetry:** Buys 25/yr. Free verse, haiku, light verse, traditional; to 25 lines; $25-48. Submit max. 7 poems.
>
> **Fillers:** Buys 50/yr. Games, word puzzles; $25-50.
>
> **Columns/Departments:** Buys 20/yr. Complete ms. Kids Cook; Pocketsful of Love (ways to show love in your family), 200-300 words; Peacemakers at Work (children involved in environmental, community, and peace/justice issues; include action photos and name of photographer), to 600 words; Pocketsful of Prayer, 400-600 words; Someone You'd Like to Know (preferably a child whose lifestyle demonstrates a strong faith perspective), 600 words. Pays .14/wd.
>
> **Special Needs:** Two-page stories for ages 5-7, 600 words max. Need role model stories, retold Biblical stories, Someone You'd Like to Know, and Peacemakers at Work.
>
> **Contest:** Fiction-writing contest; submit between 3/1 & 8/15 every year. Prize $1,000 and publication in Pockets. 1,000-1,600 wds. Must be unpublished and not historical fiction. Previous winners not eligible. Send to Pockets Fiction Contest at above address, and include an SASE for return of manuscript and response. Write "Fiction Contest" on envelope and on title/first page of manuscript.
>
> **Tips:** "Well-written fiction that fits our themes is always needed. Make stories relevant to the lives of today's children and show faith as a natural part of everyday life. All areas open to freelance. Nonfiction probably easiest to sell for columns (we get fewer submissions for those). Read, read, read, and study. Be attentive to guidelines, themes, and study past issues."
>
> ** This periodical was #6 on the 2009 Top 50 Christian Publishers list (#8 in 2008, #11 in 2007, #12 in 2006, #10 in 2005).

$ PRESCHOOL PLAYHOUSE, PO Box 436987, Chicago IL 60643. (708) 868-7100. E-mail: jgrier@urbanministries.com. Website: www.urbanministries.com. Urban Ministries Inc. Janet Grier, ed. Quarterly Sunday school curriculum including student magazine, teacher's guide, and teaching resources for 2- to 5-year-olds. Open to freelance; 100 percent assigned. Query/clips and/or writing sample; no phone query. Pays $150 for curriculum 120 days after acceptance for all rts. Assignments only. No simultaneous submissions or reprints. Requires accepted ms by e-mail only (attached file). No kill fee. Requires NIV. Include sample of age-appropriate curriculum writing/Bible explanation for children with request for guidelines. Guidelines for #10 SASE. (No ads)

> **Tips:** "Preschool Playhouse principally serves an urban, African American audience; editorial content addresses broad Christian issues. Looking for writers with educational or Sunday school teaching experience who can accurately explain Scripture in an insightful and engaging way and apply those Scriptures to the lives of children 2-5 years old."

$ PRIMARY PAL, PO Box 4060, Overland Park KS 66204. (913) 432-0331. Fax (913) 722-0351. E-mail: sseditor1@juno.com. Website: www.heraldandbanner.com. Church of God (holiness)/Herald and Banner Press. Arlene McGehee, Sunday school ed. Denominational; for 1st-3rd graders. Weekly take-home paper; 4 pgs.; circ. 2,900. Subscription $1.50. Complete ms/cover letter; phone/fax/e-query OK (prefers mail or e-mail). Pays .005/wd. on publication for 1st rts. Fiction 500-1,000 wds. Seasonal 6-8 mos. ahead. Accepts simultaneous submissions & reprints (tell when/where appeared). Prefers KJV. Guidelines/theme list/copy by mail. Not in topical listings.

$ PRIMARY STREET, PO Box 436987, Chicago IL 60643. (708) 868-7100. E-mail: jgrier@urban ministries.com. Website: www.urbanministries.com. Urban Ministries Inc. Janet Grier, ed. Quarterly Sunday school curriculum including student magazine, teacher's guide, and teaching resources for 6- to 8-year-olds. Open to freelance queries; 100 percent assigned. Pays $150 for curriculum 120 days after acceptance for all rts. Assignments only. No simultaneous submissions or reprints. Requires accepted ms by e-mail only (attached file). No kill fee. Will accept sidebars on assigned educational topics; pay varies. Requires NIV. Include sample of age-appropriate curriculum writing/ Bible explanation for children with request for guidelines. Guidelines for #10 SASE. (No ads)

> **Tips:** "Primary Street principally serves an urban, African American audience; editorial content addresses broad Christian issues. Looking for writers with educational or Sunday school teaching experience who can accurately explain scripture in an insightful and engaging way and apply those scriptures to the lives of children 6 to 8 years old."

$ PRIMARY TREASURE, Box 5353, Nampa ID 83653-5353. (208) 465-2500. Fax (208) 465-2531. E-mail: ailsox@pacificpress.com. Website: www.pacificpress.com. Seventh-day Adventist. Aileen Andres Sox, ed. To help children understand their infinite value to their Creator and Redeemer; learn how to respond to God; show love to their family and friends; serve others in their world; find fulfillment participating in the Seventh-day Adventist Church. Weekly take-home paper for 6- to 9-yr.-olds (1st-4th grades); 16 pgs. 50 percent freelance (assigned), 25 percent reprints or unsolicited. Complete ms by e-mail preferred. Pays $25-50 on acceptance for onetime or reprint rts. True stories 900-1,000 words (52/yr.); articles used rarely (query). Responds in 13 wks. Seasonal 7 mos. ahead. For simultaneous submissions & reprints see guidelines; serials to 10 parts (query). E-mail submission preferred (attached file). Guidelines by mail/Website; copy for 9 x 12 SAE/2 stamps. (No ads)

> **Tips:** "We need true adventure stories with a spiritual slant; positive, lively stories about children facing modern problems and making good choices. We always need strong stories about boys and stories featuring dads. We need a spiritual element that frequently is missing from submissions."

$ PROMISE, 2621 Dryden Rd., Moraine OH 45439. Toll-free (800) 543-4383. (937) 293-1415. Fax (937) 293-1310. E-mail: service@pflaum.com. Website: www.pflaum.com. Catholic. Joan Mitchell CSJ, ed. For kindergarten and grade 1; encourages them to participate in parish worship. Weekly (32x) take-home paper. Not in topical listings.

$ SEEDS, 2621 Dryden Rd., Moraine OH 45439. (937) 293-1415. Fax (937) 293-1310. E-mail: service@pflaum.com. Website: www.pflaum.com. Catholic. Joan Mitchell CSJ, ed. Prepares children to learn about God; for preschoolers. Weekly (32x) take-home paper; 4 pgs. Not in topical listings.

$ SHINE BRIGHTLY, Box 7259, Grand Rapids MI 49510. (616) 241-5616, ext. 3034. Fax (616) 241-5558. E-mail: servicecenter@gemsgc.org. Website: www.gemsgc.org. GEMS Girls Clubs. Sara Hilton, ed. (734-478-1596; sara@gemsgc.org). To show girls ages 9-14 that God is at work in their lives and in the world around them. Monthly (9x) mag.; 24 pgs.; circ. 13,000. Subscription $13.25. 80 percent unsolicited freelance; 20 percent assigned. Complete ms; no e-query. Pays .03-.05/wd. on publication for 1st or reprint rts. Articles 100-400 words (35/yr.); fiction 400-900 words (30/ yr.). Responds in 4-6 wks. Seasonal 10 mos. ahead. Accepts simultaneous submissions & reprints. Accepts requested ms on disk. Regularly uses sidebars. Prefers NIV. Guidelines/theme list on Website; copy $1/9 x 12 SAE/3 stamps. (No ads)

> **Fillers:** Buys 10/yr. Cartoons, games, party ideas, prayers, quizzes, short humor, word puzzles; 50-200 words; $5-10.
>
> **Special Needs:** Craft ideas that can be used to help others. Articles on how words can help build others up or tear people down.
>
> **Tips:** "Be realistic—we get a lot of fluffy stories with Pollyanna endings. We are looking for real-life-type stories that girls relate to. We mostly publish short stories but are open to short

reflective articles. Know what girls face today and how they cope in their daily lives. We need angles from home life and friendships, peer pressure, and the normal growing-up challenges girls deal with."

SKIPPING STONES: A Multicultural Magazine, PO Box 3939, Eugene OR 97403. (541) 342-4956. E-mail: editor@skippingstones.org. Website: www.skippingstones.org. Interfaith/multicultural. Arun N. Toké, exec. ed. A multicultural awareness and nature appreciation magazine for young people 7-17, worldwide. Bimonthly (5x) mag.; 36 pgs.; circ. 2,500. Subscription $25. 85 percent unsolicited freelance; 15 percent assigned. Query or complete ms/cover letter; no phone query; e-query/submissions OK. **PAYS IN COPIES** (40 percent discount on extra issues) for 1st, electronic, and nonexclusive reprint rts. Articles (15-25/yr.) 750-1,000 words; fiction for teens, 750-1,000 words. Responds in 9-13 wks. Seasonal 2-4 mos. ahead. Accepts simultaneous submissions. Accepts ms on disk or by e-mail. Regularly uses sidebars. Guidelines/theme list by mail/e-mail/Website; copy $6/4 stamps. (No ads)

> **Poetry:** Only from kids under 18. Accepts 100/yr. Any type; 3-30 lines. Submit max. 4-5 poems.
> **Fillers:** Accepts 10-20/yr. Anecdotes, cartoons, games, quizzes, short humor, word puzzles; to 250 wds.
> **Columns/Departments:** Accepts 10/yr. Noteworthy News (multicultural/nature/international/social, appropriate for youth), 200 wds.
> **Special Needs:** Stories and articles on your community and country, peace, nonviolent communication, compassion, kindness, spirituality, tolerance, and giving.
> **Contest:** Annual Book Awards for published books and authors (deadline February 1); Annual Youth Honor Awards for students 7-17 (deadline June 25). Send SASE for guidelines.
> **Tips:** "Most of the magazine is open to freelance. We're seeking submissions by minority, multicultural, international, and/or youth writers. Do not be judgmental or preachy; be open or receptive to diverse opinions."

$ SPARKLE, PO Box 7259, Grand Rapids MI 49510. (616) 241-5616. Fax (616) 241-5558. E-mail: amy@gemsgc.org, or servicecenter@gemsgc.org. Website: www.gemsgc.org. GEMS Girls' Clubs (nondenominational). Sara Hilton, ed. (734-478-1596/sara@gemsgc.org). To prepare girls, grades 1-3, to live out their faith and become world changers; to help girls make a difference in the world. Published 6x/yr. (October-March). Subscription $10.25. 80 percent unsolicited freelance; 20 percent assigned. Complete ms; no e-query. Pays .03/wd. on publication for 1st, reprint, or simultaneous rts. Articles 200-400 words (10/yr.); fiction 200-400 words (6/yr.). Responds in 6 wks. Seasonal 10 mos. ahead. Accepts simultaneous submissions & reprints. Accepts requested ms on disk. Regularly uses sidebars. Prefers NIV. Guidelines/theme list by mail/e-mail/Website; copy $1/9 x 12 SAE/3 stamps. (No ads)

> **Fillers:** Buys 10/yr. Games, party ideas, prayers, quizzes, short humor; 50-200 words; $5-15.
> **Tips:** "Send in pieces that teach girls how to be world-changers for Christ, or that fit our annual theme. We also are always looking for games, crafts, and recipes. Keep the writing simple. Keep activities short. Engage a third-grader, while being easy enough for a first-grader to understand."

$ STORY MATES, Box 1212, Harrisonburg VA 22803-1212. (540) 434-0750. Fax (540) 433-8896. E-mail: StoryMates@clp.org. Website: www.clp.org. Mennonite/Christian Light Publications Inc. Crystal Shank, ed. For 4- to 8-yr.-olds. Weekly take-home paper; 4 pgs.; circ. 6,500. Subscription $11.45. 90 percent unsolicited freelance. Complete ms. Pays up to.05/wd. on acceptance for 1st rts. (.06/wd. for 1st rts., plus reprint rts.). Realistic or true stories, 800-900 words (50-75/yr.); picture stories 120-150 words. Responds in 6 wks. Seasonal 6 mos. ahead. Accepts simultaneous submissions & reprints (tell when/where appeared). No disk. Requires KJV. Guidelines/theme list by mail/ e-mail; copy for 9 x 12 SAE/3 stamps. Will send questionnaire to fill out. (No ads)

Poetry: Buys 25/yr. Traditional, any length. Few story poems. Pays up to.65/line.
Fillers: Quizzes, word puzzles, craft ideas. "Need fillers that correlate with theme list; Bible related." Pays about $10.
Special Needs: True or true-to-life stories the children can relate to.
Tips: "Carefully read our guidelines and understand our conservative Mennonite applications of Bible principles." Very conservative.
** This periodical was #49 on the 2007 Top 50 Christian Publishers list.

$ TRUTH TRAVELERS, 1300 N. Meacham Rd., Schaumburg IL 60173-4888. (847) 843-1600. Fax (847) 843-3757. E-mail: takehomepapers@garbc.org. Website: www.RegularBaptistPress .org. General Assn. of Regular Baptist Churches/Regular Baptist Press. Joan E. Alexander, ed. New Publication for middlers (grades 3 & 4). Subscription $3.29. Guidelines by mail.

$ VENTURE, 2621 Dryden Rd., Moraine OH 45439. (937) 293-1415. Fax (937) 293-1310. E-mail: service@pflaum.com. Website: www.pflaum.com. Catholic. Joan Mitchell CSJ, ed. For grades 4-6. Weekly (32x) take-home paper. Not in topical listings.

+ THE VIRTUOUS GIRL, A Magazine by Girls for Girls. Website: www.thevirtuousgirl.org. Quarterly magazine.

CHRISTIAN EDUCATION/LIBRARY MARKETS

$ CATECHIST, 2621 Dryden Rd., 3rd Fl., Dayton OH 45439. (937) 847-5900. Fax (314) 638-6812. E-mail: kdotterweich@peterli.com. Website: www.catechist.com. Catholic; Peter Li Education Group . Kass Dotterweich, ed. For Catholic school teachers and parish volunteer catechists. Mag. published 7x/yr.; 52 pgs.; circ. 52,000. Subscription $26.95. 30 percent unsolicited freelance; 70 percent assigned. Query (preferred) or complete ms. Pays $25-150 (variable rates) on publication. Articles 1,200 wds. Responds in 9-18 wks. Guidelines by mail/Website; copy $3.
   Tips: "Most open to 'From the Field' column: Classroom ideas to 600 wds."

CATHOLIC LIBRARY WORLD, 100 North St., Ste. 224, Pittsfield MA 01201-5178. (413) 443-2252. Fax (413) 442-2252. E-mail: cla@cathla.org. Website: www.cathla.org. Catholic Library Assn. Sr. Mary E. Gallagher SSJ, gen. ed. For libraries at all levels—preschool to postsecondary to academic; parish, public, and private. Quarterly jour.; 80 pgs.; circ. 1,000. Subscription $60/$85 foreign. 90 percent unsolicited freelance; 10 percent assigned. Query or complete ms; phone/fax/e-query OK. **PAYS 1 COPY** for all rts. Articles (12-16/yr.); book/video reviews, 300-500 wds. Responds in 4-6 wks. No simultaneous submissions or reprints. Accepts requested ms on disk. Uses some sidebars. No guidelines; copy for 9 x 12 SAE. (Ads)
   Special Needs: Topics of interest to academic libraries, high school and children's libraries, parish and community libraries, archives, and library education. Reviewers cover areas such as theology, spirituality, pastoral, professional, juvenile books and material, and media.
   Tips: "Review section considers taking on new reviewers who are experts in field of librarianship, theology, and professional studies. No payment except a free copy of the book or materials reviewed. Query us by mail or e-mail."

$ CHILDREN'S MINISTRY MAGAZINE, 1515 Cascade Ave., Loveland CO 80539. Toll-free (800) 447-1070. Fax (970) 292-4373. E-mail: jhooks@cmmag.com or info@group.com. Website: www .childrensministry.com. Group Publishing/nondenominational. Christine Yount Jones, exec. ed.; submit to Jennifer Hooks, mng. ed. (jhooks@cmmag.com). The leading resource for adults who work with children (ages 0-12) in the church. Bimonthly mag.; 140 pgs.; circ. 60,000. Subscription $29.95. 40 percent unsolicited freelance; 60 percent assigned. Complete ms/cover letter; e-query OK. Pays $25-400 on acceptance for all & electronic rts. Articles 50-1,800 words (250-300/yr.). Responds in 8-10 wks. Seasonal 6-9 mos. ahead. No simultaneous submissions or reprints. Accepts requested ms by e-mail (attached or copied into message). Regularly uses sidebars. Also accepts submissions from children/teens. Sometimes pays kill fee. Prefers NLT. Guidelines by mail/e-mail/Website; copy $2/9 x 12 SAE/$2.38 postage (mark Media Mail). (Ads)

Fillers: Buys 25-50/yr. Cartoons, kid quotes; 25-50 words; $25-60.

Columns/Departments: Submit to Carmen Kamrath (ckamrath@cmmag.com). Buys 200+/yr. Age-level insights (age-appropriate ideas); Family Ministry (family ideas); Reaching Out (outreach ideas); 150-250 wds. Teacher Telegram (ideas for teachers); For Parents Only (parenting ideas); 150-300 words; $40-150. Complete ms.

Special Needs: Seasonal ideas, outreach ideas, volunteer management, and family ministry. Always looking for new ideas, crafts, games, and activities.

Tips: "All areas open to freelancers. Start small—ideas, activities, and personal essays. Or go big—wow us with a profoundly inspiring article that fits the magazine's makeup. We're looking for stand-out ideas and the very latest in this important ministry area. If you're in the trenches, we want to hear from you. We seek features from experts in practice or in theory. No poetry or fiction."

** This periodical was #5 on the 2009 Top 50 Christian Publishers list (#4 in 2008, #8 in 2007, #5 in 2006, #1 in 2005).

CHRISTIAN EARLY EDUCATION, PO Box 65130, Colorado Springs CO 80921. Toll-free (888) 892-4258. (719) 528-6906. Fax (719) 531-0631. E-mail: earlyeducation@acsi.org. Website: www .acsi.org. Assn. of Christian Schools Intl. D'Arcy Maher, sr. ed. Equips individuals serving children ages 0-5 from a biblical perspective. Quarterly mag.; 40 pgs.; circ. 7,000. Subscription $14. 10 percent unsolicited freelance; 90 percent assigned. Query; phone/fax/e-query OK. Accepts full mss by e-mail. **PAYS IN COPIES** for 1st, reprint rts. Articles 400-1,800 words (12-15/yr.); book reviews 100 words. Responds in 4 wks. Seasonal 10 mos. ahead. Accepts reprints (tell when/where appeared). Requires e-mail submissions (attached file). Uses some sidebars. Prefers NIV. Guidelines/theme list by e-mail; free copy. (Ads)

Fillers: Accepts 4/yr; kid quotes, 10-30 wds.

Columns/Departments: Accepts up to 10/yr. Staff Training (training for teachers of young children, to use in staff meeting), 400 words; Parents' Place (material suitable for parents of young children), 400 words. Complete ms.

Tips: "Most open to these columns: Unique Perspectives, Footprints in Development, Professional Edge, Resource Review, Heart 2 Heart, and Field Trip."

$ CHRISTIAN EDUCATORS JOURNAL, 73 Highland Ave., St. Catherines ON L2R 4H9, Canada. Phone/fax (905) 684-3991. E-mail: bert.witvoet@sympatico.ca. Website: www.CEJonline.com. Christian Educators Journal Assn. Bert Witvoet, mng. ed. For educators in Christian day schools at the elementary, secondary, and college levels. Quarterly jour.; 36 pgs.; circ. 4,200. Subscription $7.50 (c/o James Rauwerda, 2045 Boston St. S.E., Grand Rapids MI 49506, 616-243-2112). 50 percent unsolicited freelance; 50 percent assigned. Query; phone/e-query OK. Pays $30 on publication for onetime rts. Articles 750-1,500 words (20/yr.); fiction 750-1,500 words. Responds in 5 wks. Seasonal 4 mos. ahead. Accepts simultaneous submissions & reprints. Guidelines/theme list; copy $1.50 or 9 x 12 SAE/4 stamps. (Limited ads)

Poetry: Buys 6/yr. On teaching day school; 4-30 lines; $10. Submit max. 5 poems.

Tips: "No articles on Sunday school, only Christian day school. Most open to theme topics and features."

THE CHRISTIAN LIBRARIAN, Ryan Library, PLNU, 3600 Lomaland Dr., San Diego CA 92106. (619) 849-2208. Fax (619) 849-7024. E-mail: apowell@pointloma.edu. Website: www.acl.org. Assn. of Christian Librarians. Anne-Elizabeth Powell, ed-in-chief. Geared toward academic librarians of the Christian faith. Triannual jour.; 40 pgs.; circ. 800. Subscription $30. 50 percent unsolicited freelance; 50 percent assigned. E-mail; fax/e-query OK. **NO PAYMENT** for onetime rts. Not copyrighted. Articles

1,000-3,500 words; research articles to 5,000 words (6/yr.); reviews 150-300 words. Responds in 5 wks. Accepts simultaneous submissions & reprints (tell when/where appeared). Prefers accepted ms by e-mail (attached file). Uses some sidebars. Guidelines by mail/e-mail/Website; copy $5. (No ads)

Fillers: Anecdotes, ideas, short humor; 25-300 words.

Special Needs: Articles dealing with the intersection of faith and professional duties in libraries. Interviews with library leaders, profiles of Christian academic libraries, international librarianship. Deals with all topics as they can be applied to librarianship. Articles on Christian librarianship for peer review.

Tips: "Reviews are a good way to gain publication. Write a tight, well-researched article about a current 'hot topic' in librarianship as it is defined in a Christian setting, or ethics of librarianship. Articles on 'how we did it right' are good entry publications."

+ CHRISTIAN LIBRARY JOURNAL, 2107 Highway 101, #153, Florence OR 97439. E-mail: nlhesch@christianlibraryj.org. Website: www.christianlibraryj.org. Christian Library Services. Nancy L. Hesch, pub. Provides reviews from a Christian viewpoint of both Christian and non-Christian books for Christian schools, homeschools, and family libraries. Book reviews & some articles comparing books; to be posted on blog.

Tips: "If interested in doing reviews, send us your name, mailing address, phone number, and e-mail. We will respond with guidelines, and books will be sent from publisher."

CHRISTIAN SCHOOL EDUCATION, PO Box 65130, Colorado Springs CO 80962-5130. (719) 528-6906. Fax (719) 531-0631. E-mail: cse@acsi.org. Website: www.acsi.org. Association of Christian Schools Intl. Steven C. Babbitt, ed. To provide accurate information as well as provoke thought and reflection about the ministry of Christian school education worldwide. Quarterly mag.; 56 pgs.; circ. 70,000. Subscription $16. 2 percent unsolicited freelance; 98 percent assigned. Query preferred; phone query OK. **NO PAYMENT**. Asks for photocopy permission for member schools. Articles 650-2,600 words; book reviews 600 words. Responds in 12 wks. No seasonal material. Accepts simultaneous submissions & reprints (tell when/where appeared). Requires submissions by disk or e-mail (attached file). Regularly uses sidebars. Prefers NIV, NKJV. Guidelines by mail/e-mail. (Ads)

Tips: "Most articles for publication are solicited, therefore freelancers 'breaking into publication' is highly unlikely. Most open to Christian business and leadership."

$ CHURCH LIBRARIES, 9118 W. Elmwood Dr., #1G, Niles IL 60714-5820. (847) 296-3964. Fax (847) 296-0754. E-mail: linjohnson@ECLAlibraries.org. Website: www.ECLAlibraries.org. Evangelical Church Library Assn. Lin Johnson, mng. ed. To assist church librarians in setting up, maintaining, and promoting church libraries and media centers. Quarterly mag.; 32-36 pgs.; circ. 400. Subscription $35. 25 percent unsolicited freelance. Complete ms or queries by e-mail only. Pays .05/wd. on acceptance for 1st or reprint rts. Articles 500-1,000 words (24-30/yr.); book/music/DVD reviews by assignment, 75-150 words, free product. Responds in 4-6 wks. Seasonal 6 mos. ahead. Accepts reprints (tell when/where appeared). Requires e-mail submission. Regularly uses sidebars. Prefers NIV. Guidelines by mail/e-mail/Website); copy for 9 x 12 SAE/4 stamps. (Ads)

Tips: "Talk to church librarians or get involved in library or reading programs. Most open to articles and promotional ideas; profiles of church libraries. Book reviews assigned; need for reviewers fluctuates; if interested e-mail for availability."

CONGREGATIONAL LIBRARIES TODAY, 2920 S.W. Dolph Ct., Portland OR 97219-4055. (503) 244-6919. Fax (503) 977-3734. E-mail: csla@worldaccessnet.com. Website: www.cslainfo.org. Church and Synagogue Library Assn. Judith Janzen, exec. dir. To help librarians run congregational libraries. Quarterly; 32 pgs.; circ. 3,000. Subscription $40 U.S.; $50 Cdn. (USD), $60 foreign (USD). Query; no e-query. **NO PAYMENT**. Requires accepted ms on disk. Articles. Book & video reviews 1-2 paragraphs. Guidelines/copies by mail. (Ads)

Fillers: Ideas.

$ GROUP MAGAZINE, Box 481, Loveland CO 80539. (970) 669-3836. Fax (970) 292-4373. E-mail: rlawrence@group.com or sfirestone@group.com or info@group.com. Website: www.group .com or www.youthministry.com. Rick Lawrence, ed.; Scott Firestone, assoc. ed. For leaders of Christian youth groups; to supply ideas, practical help, inspiration, and training for youth leaders. Bimonthly mag.; 85 pgs.; circ. 25,000. Subscription $29.95. 50 percent unsolicited freelance; 50 percent assigned. Query; fax/e-query OK. Pays $150-350 on acceptance for all rts. Articles 175-2,000 words (100/yr.). Responds in 6-9 wks. Seasonal 5 mos. ahead. No simultaneous submissions or reprints. Accepts e-mail submissions (copied into message). No kill fee. Uses some sidebars. Any Bible version. Guidelines on Website; copy $2/9 x 12 SAE/3 stamps. (Ads)

> **Fillers:** Buys 5-10/yr. Cartoons, games, ideas; $40.
> **Columns/Departments:** Buys 30-40/yr. Try This One (youth group activities), to 300 words; Hands-on-Help (tips for leaders), to 175 words; Strange But True (profiles remarkable youth ministry experience), 500 words. Pays $50. Complete ms.
> **Special Needs:** Articles geared toward working with teens; programming ideas; youth-ministry issues.
> **Tips:** "We're always looking for effective youth-ministry ideas, especially those tested by youth leaders in the field. Most open to Hands-On-Help column (use real-life examples, personal experiences, practical tips, Scripture, and self-quizzes or checklists). We buy the idea, not the verbatim submission."
> ** This periodical was #36 on the 2007 Top 50 Christian Publishers list.

$ THE JOURNAL OF ADVENTIST EDUCATION, 12501 Old Columbia Pike, Silver Spring MD 20904-6600. (301) 680-5069. Fax (301) 622-9627. E-mail: rumbleb@gc.adventist.org. Website: http://jae.education.org. General Conference of Seventh-day Adventists. Beverly J. Robinson-Rumble, ed. For Seventh-day teachers teaching in the church's school system, kindergarten to university, and educational administrators. Bimonthly (5x) jour.; 48 pgs.; circ. 10,800. Selected articles are translated into French, Spanish, and Portuguese for a twice-yearly International Edition. Subscription $18.25 (add $3 outside U.S.). Percentage of freelance varies. Query or complete ms; phone/fax/e-query OK. Pays $25-300 on publication for 1st North American and translation rts. and permission to post on Website. Articles 1,000-2,000 words (2-20/yr.). Responds in 6-17 wks. Seasonal 6 mos. ahead. Accepts reprints (tell when/where appeared). Accepts requested ms on disk. Regularly uses sidebars. Guidelines on Website; copy for 10 x 12 SAE/5 stamps.

> **Fillers:** Cartoons only, no payment.
> **Special Needs:** "All articles in the context of parochial schools (not Sunday school tips); professional enrichment and teaching tips for Christian teachers. Need feature articles and articles on the integration of faith and learning."

JOURNAL OF CHRISTIAN EDUCATION, PO Box 602, Epping NSW 1710, Australia. Phone/fax 61 2 9868 6644. E-mail: business@acfe.org.au, submit to editor@acfe.org.au. Website: www.jce .org.au. Australian Christian Forum on Education Inc. Dr. Grant Maple & Dr. Ian Lambert, eds. To consider the implications of the Christian faith for the entire field of education. Triannual jour.; 80 pgs.; circ. 400. Subscription $55 AUS, $55 U.S. for individuals; $70 AUS, $70 U.S. for institutions. 40 percent unsolicited freelance; 60 percent assigned. Complete ms/cover letter; phone/fax/e-query OK. **NO PAYMENT** for onetime rts. Articles 3,000-6,000 words (6/yr.); book reviews 400-600 words. Responds in 4 wks. Seasonal 6 mos. ahead. Accepts requested ms on disk or by e-mail (attached file). Does not use sidebars. Guidelines by e-mail/Website; free copy. (No ads)

> **Tips:** "Send for a sample copy, study guidelines, and submit manuscript. Most open to articles or book reviews. Open to any educational issue from a Christian perspective."

JOURNAL OF CHRISTIANITY AND FOREIGN LANGUAGES, Dept. of Germanic and Asian Languages, Calvin College, 3201 Burton St. S.E., Grand Rapids MI 49546. (616) 957-8609. Fax (616)

526-8583. E-mail: dsmith@calvin.edu. Website: www.nacfla.net. North American Christian Foreign Language Assn. Dr. David Smith, ed. Scholarly articles dealing with the relationship between Christian belief and the teaching of foreign languages and literatures; mainly for college faculty. Annual jour.; 100 pgs.; circ. 100. Subscription $16 (indiv.), $27 (library). Open to freelance. Complete ms/cover letter; phone/fax/e-query OK. **PAYS IN COPIES/OFFPRINTS**. Articles 2,000-4,000 words (6/yr.); book/video reviews, 750 words. Responds in 12-16 wks. Rarely accepts reprints (tell when/where appeared). Requires requested ms on disk or by e-mail (attached file). Does not use sidebars. Guidelines by mail/ Website); no copy. (Ads)

> **Columns/Departments:** Accepts 1-3/yr. Forum (position papers, pedagogical suggestions), 1,000-1,500 words.
>
> **Tips:** "Most open to Forum column; guidelines at www.spu.edu/orgs/nacfla. Also see Website for abstracts and samples. Book reviews and opinion pieces must be related to Christianity and education in foreign languages and literature."

JOURNAL OF EDUCATION & CHRISTIAN BELIEF, Dept. of Germanic Languages, Calvin College, 3201 Burton St. S.E., Grand Rapids MI 49546. (616) 526-8609. Fax (616) 526-7502. E-mail: jecb@stapleford-centre.org. Website: www.jecb.org. Association of Christian Teachers; The Stapleford Centre; The Kuyers Institute for Christian Teaching and Learning. Editors: Dr. David Smith (use above address) & Dr. John Shortt, 1 Kiteleys Green, Leighton Buzzard, Beds LU7 3LD, United Kingdom. Phone +44 1525 379709. Semiannual jour.; 80 pgs.; circ. 400. Subscription $45. 80 percent unsolicited freelance; 20 percent assigned. Complete ms/cover letter; e-query OK. **NO PAYMENT** for 1st rts. Articles 5,000 words (12/yr.). Responds in 4-8 wks. Accepts reprints (tell when/where appeared). Prefers requested ms by e-mail (attached file). Does not use sidebars. Guidelines by e-mail; no copy. (No ads)

> **Tips:** "Most open to reviews of books related to education and Christian belief; should be expert reviews addressed to an academic audience. Must address Christian education in competent, scholarly manner."

JOURNAL OF RESEARCH ON CHRISTIAN EDUCATION, Andrews University, Information Services Bldg., Ste. 101, Berrien Springs MI 49104. (269) 471-6080. Fax (269) 471-6224. E-mail: jrce@andrews.edu. Website: www.andrews.edu/jrce. Andrews University. Larry D. Burton, ed.; Janet Mallory, book rev. ed. Research related to Christian schooling (all levels) within the Protestant tradition. Triennial jour.; 100+ pgs.; circ. 400. Subscription $60. 100 percent unsolicited freelance. Complete ms/cover letter; phone/fax/e-query OK. **NO PAYMENT**. Articles 13-26 double-spaced pgs. (12-18/yr.); book reviews, 2-5 pgs. Responds in 1 wk.; decision within 6 mos. (goes through review board). No simultaneous submissions. Requires e-mail submissions. Does not use sidebars. Guidelines by mail/e-mail. (No ads)

> **Tips:** "This is a research journal. All manuscripts should conform to standards of scholarly inquiry. Manuscripts are submitted to a panel of 3 experts for their review. Publication decision is based on recommendation of reviewers. Authors should submit manuscripts written in scholarly style and focused on Christian schooling. Submit an electronic copy along with a 100-word abstract and 30-word bio-sketch indicating institutional affiliation."

$ KIDS' MINISTRY IDEAS, 55 W. Oak Ridge Dr., Hagerstown MD 21740. (301) 393-3178. Fax (301) 393-3209. E-mail: KidsMin@rhpa.org. Website: www.kidsministryideas.org. Seventh-day Adventist. Candy DeVore, ed. For adults leading children (birth-8th grade) to Christ. Quarterly mag.; 32 pgs.; circ. 2,500. Complete ms/cover letter; e-query OK. Pays $20-100 within 5-6 wks. of acceptance. Accepts full ms by e-mail. Guidelines on Website.

$ MOMENTUM, 1077—30th St. N.W., Ste. 100, Washington DC 20007-3852. Toll-free (800) 711-6232. (202) 337-6232. Fax (202) 333-6706. E-mail: momentum@ncea.org, or through Website: www.ncea.org/news/momentum/WritingforMomentum.asp. National Catholic Educational Assn. Brian

Gray, ed. Features outstanding programs, issues, and research in Catholic education. Quarterly jour.; 96 pgs.; circ. 23,000. Subscription $20 (free to members). 50 percent unsolicited freelance; 30 percent assigned. Query or complete ms; phone/e-query OK. Pays $50-100 on publication for 1st rts. Articles 500-1,500 words (25-30/yr.); research articles 3,500-5,000 words; book reviews 300 words ($50). No simultaneous submissions. Accepts full mss by e-mail (attached—preferred—or copied into message). Pays some kill fees. Regularly uses sidebars. Prefers NAB (Catholic). Guidelines/theme list by e-mail/Website; copy $5/9 x 12 SAE/$2.38 postage (mark "Media Mail"). (Ads)

> **Columns/Departments:** From the Field (success ideas that can be used by other Catholic schools); DRE Directions (guidance for directors of religious education programs); both 700 words.
>
> **Tips:** "All sections are open, but first visit our Website to understand the organization and then call or e-mail to discuss ideas. Much higher rate of acceptance when we've had a conversation first."

$ PRESCHOOL PLAYHOUSE, PO Box 436987, Chicago IL 60643. E-mail: rsailes@urbanministries .com. Website: www.urbanministries.com. Urban Ministries Inc. Dr. R. Sailes, dir. of children's curriculum. Quarterly Sunday school curriculum for 2- to 5-year-olds with accompanying teacher's guide and curriculum resource materials. Open to freelance; 100 percent assigned. Query/clips and/ or writing sample; no phone query. Pays $150 for curriculum 120 days after acceptance for all rts. Articles accepted only on assignment. No simultaneous submissions or reprints. Requires accepted ms by e-mail only (attached file). No kill fee. Will accept sidebars on assigned educational topics; pay varies. Requires NIV. Guidelines for #10 SASE. (No ads)

> **Tips:** "Preschool Playhouse principally serves an African American audience; editorial content addresses broad Christian issues. Looking for those with educational or Sunday school teaching experience who can accurately explain Scripture in an insightful and engaging way and apply those Scriptures to the lives of preschool children."

$ @ TEACHERS OF VISION MAGAZINE, 227 N. Magnolia Ave., Ste. 2, Anaheim CA 92801. (714) 761-1476. Fax (714) 761-1679. E-mail: judy@ccai.org. Website: www.ceai.org. Christian Educators Assn., Intl. Judy Turpen, contributing ed.; F. L. Turpen, editorial dir.; Denise Trippett, mng. ed. To encourage, equip, and empower Christian educators serving in public and private schools. Quarterly & online mag.; circ. 10,000. Subscription $20. 50 percent unsolicited freelance; 50 percent assigned. Query; prefers e-query (judy@ceai.org). Pays $20-40 ($30 for reprints) on publication for 1st or reprint rts. Articles 600-2,500 words (15-20/yr.); minifeatures 400-750 words, $25; very few book reviews 50 words, pays copies. Responds in 4-12 wks. Seasonal 4 mos. ahead. Accepts simultaneous submissions & reprints (tell when/where appeared). Accepts requested ms on disk or by e-mail (attached or copied into message). Regularly uses sidebars. Any Bible version. Guidelines/theme list on Website: www.ceai.org/fbenefits/teachers_of_vision/tov_index_ed.htm; copy for 9 x 12 SAE/4 stamps. (Ads)

> **Poetry:** Accepts 2-3/yr. Free verse, haiku, light verse, traditional; 4-16 lines. Submit max. 3 poems.
>
> **Fillers:** Educational only.
>
> **Special Needs:** Legal and other issues in public education. Interviews, classroom resource reviews, living out your faith in your work.
>
> **Tips:** "Know public education; write from a positive perspective as our readers are involved in public education by calling and choice. Most open to tips for teachers for living out their faith in the classroom in legally appropriate ways. No preachy articles."

$ TODAY'S CATHOLIC TEACHER, 2621 Dryden Rd., Dayton OH 45439. Toll-free (800) 523-4625, ext. 1139. (937) 293-1415. Fax (937) 293-1310. E-mail: mnoschang@peterli.com. Website: www .catholicteacher.com. Catholic; Peter Li Education Group. Mary C. Noschang, ed-in-chief; submit to

Betsy Shepard (bshepard@peterli.com). Directed to personal and professional concerns of teachers and administrators in K-12 Catholic schools. Monthly mag. (6x during school yr.); 60 pgs.; circ. 45,000. Subscription $14.95. 30 percent unsolicited freelance; 30 percent assigned. Query; phone/fax/e-query OK. Pays $150-250 on publication for 1st rts. Articles 600-800, 1,000-1,200, or 1,500-2,500 words (40-50/yr.). Responds in 18 wks. Seasonal 3 mos. ahead. Accepts simultaneous submissions & reprints (tell when/where appeared). Prefers requested ms by e-mail (attached file). Regularly uses sidebars. Guidelines/theme list on Website; copy $3/9 x 12 SAE. (Ads)

Special Needs: Activity pages teachers can copy and pass out to students to work on. Try to provide classroom-ready material teachers can use to supplement curriculum.

Tips: "Looking for material teachers in grades 3-9 can use to supplement curriculum material. Most open to articles related to school curriculum and other areas, or lesson plans."

** This periodical was #35 on the 2007 Top 50 Christian Publishers list.

$ YOUTH AND CHRISTIAN EDUCATION LEADERSHIP, 1080 Montgomery Ave., Cleveland TN 37311. Toll-free (800) 553-8506. (423) 478-7597. Fax (423) 478-7616. E-mail: jonathanm@renovatuscommunity.com. Website: www.pathwaypress.org. Church of God/Pathway Press. Jonathan Martin, ed. To inform, equip, and inspire Christian education teachers and leaders. Quarterly mag.; 32 pgs.; circ. 10,000. Subscription $8. 10 percent unsolicited freelance; 90 percent assigned. Complete ms/cover letter; phone/e-query OK. Accepts full mss by e-mail (attached). Pays $25-50 on publication for 1st or onetime rts. Articles 500-1,000 words (20/yr.). Responds in 2 wks. Seasonal 4 mos. ahead. Accepts simultaneous submissions; no reprints. Accepts requested ms on disk or by e-mail (attached file). No kill fee. Uses some sidebars. Prefers NIV. Guidelines on Website; copy $1.25/9 x 12 SAE. (No ads)

Fillers: Buys 4/yr. Cartoons, ideas, party ideas, tips, word puzzles; 250-300 wds. Pays $35.

Special Needs: Most open to how-to articles relating to Christian education. Local church ministry stories; articles on youth ministry, children's ministry, Christian education, and Sunday school.

DAILY DEVOTIONAL MARKETS

Due to the nature of the daily devotional market, the following market listings give a limited amount of information. Because most of these markets assign all material, they do not wish to be listed in the usual way.

If you are interested in writing daily devotionals, send to the following markets for guidelines and sample copies, write up sample devotionals to fit each one's particular format, and send to the editor with a request for an assignment. *Do not* submit any other type of material to these markets unless indicated.

$ ANCHOR DEVOTIONAL, PO Box 79997, Riverside CA 92513-1997. Toll-free (800) 65HAVEN. Fax (951) 710-1115. E-mail: ministry@haventoday.org. Website: www.haventoday.org/anchor.php. Haven Ministries. Kathy Doane, ed. Monthly devotional mag. Devotions 185 wds. Send sample devotional and request an assignment. Assigns one month of devotions on a theme (author picks theme). Query first for theme. Accepts simultaneous submissions; no reprints. Payment discussed at appropriate time.

+ CHRISTIANDEVOTIONS.US, PO Box 6494, Kingsport TN 37663. (423) 384-4821. Fax (423) 239-7103. E-mail: cindy@christiandevotions.us. Website: www.christiandevotions.us. Cindy Sproles & Eddie Jones, eds. Prefers completed devotions; 300-400 wds. **NO PAYMENT**. Accepts poetry. Accepts reprints & e-mail submissions.

DAILY DEVOTIONS FOR THE DEAF, 21199 Greenview Rd., Council Bluffs IA 51503-4190. (712) 322-5493. Fax (712) 322-7792. E-mail: JoKrueger@deafmissions.com. Website: www.deafmissions

.com. Jo Krueger, ed. Quarterly. Circ. 26,000. Prefers to see completed devotionals; 225-250 wds. **NO PAYMENT**. E-mail submissions OK.

$ DEVOTIONS, 8805 Governor's Hill Dr., Ste. 400, Cincinnati OH 45249-3319. (513) 931-4050. Fax (513) 931-0904. E-mail: gwilde1@cfl.rr.com. Website: www.standardpub.com. Gary Allen, ed. Assigned by work-for-hire contract to previously published writers only. Query by e-mail only. Pays $20/devotion. Send list of credits rather than a sample.

$ FORWARD DAY BY DAY, 300 W. Fourth St., Cincinnati OH 45202-2666. Toll-free (800) 543-1813. (513) 721-6659. Fax (513) 721-0729. E-mail: rschmidt@forwarddaybyday.com. Website: www.forwardmovement.org. Richard H. Schmidt, ed./dir. Also online version. Send a couple of samples and request an assignment. Likes author to complete an entire month's worth of devotions; 215 wds. Subscription $13. No e-mail submissions. Pays $300 for a month of devotions. Accepts reprints. (No ads)

FRUIT OF THE VINE, Barclay Press, 211 N. Meridian St., #101, Newberg OR 97132. (503) 538-9775. Fax (503) 554-8597. E-mail: info@barclaypress.com. E-mail submissions accepted at phampton @barclaypress.com. Website: www.barclaypress.com. Editorial team: Paula Hampton & Judy Woolsey. Send samples and request assignment. Accepts e-mail submissions & reprints. Subscription $18. Prefers 250-290 wds. **PAYS FREE SUBSCRIPTION & 6 COPIES**. Guidelines by mail.

+ FUSION, 114 Bush Rd., Nashville TN 37217. (615) 361-1221. Fax (615) 367-0535. E-mail: jonathan.yandell@randallhouse.com or through Website: www.randallhouse.com. Randall House. Jonathan Yandell, ed. For adults 35-55, combines truth and faith in daily life. Encourages application of Scripture through devotions and experience; instructional and inspirational articles. Quarterly mag.; circ. 20,000. Subscription $20. Open to freelance. Query with samples by e-mail.

$ LIGHT FROM THE WORD, PO Box 50434, Indianapolis IN 46250-0434. (317) 774-7900. E-mail: submissions@wesleyan.org. Website: www.wesleyan.org/wph. Wesleyan. Attn: Editorial Director. Devotions 220-230 wds. Pays $100 for 7 devotions. Electronic submissions only. Send a couple of sample devotions to fit their format and request an assignment. No reprints.

MUSTARDSEED MINISTRIES DEVOTIONAL, PO Box 501, Bluffton IN 46714. E-mail: devotionals @mustardseedministries.org. Website: www.mustardseedministries.org. MustardSeed Ministries. Wayne Steffen, ed. (Wayne@mustardseedministries.org). Devotional mag. 100 percent unsolicited freelance. Complete ms; e-mail submissions preferred. **PAYS A UNIQUE, ATTRACTIVE PLAQUE**. Devotions 225-275 wds. Guidelines on Website.

   Special Needs: Also looking for articles for their newsletter. Guidelines on Website.
   Tips: "We do not return any submissions and prefer that they are e-mailed to us. We are looking for submissions that are biblically based. Sincerity is as important as your writing skills. Most of us have a story to tell about how Christ touched our life in some situation that others in this world would benefit from; please send this to us."

$ MY DAILY VISITOR, 200 Noll Plaza, Huntington IN 46750. (260) 356-8400. Fax (260) 356-8472. E-mail: mdvisitor@osv.com. Website: www.osv.com. Catholic. Submit to The Editor. Scripture meditations based on the day's Catholic Mass readings. Bimonthly devotional booklet. Open to freelance from Catholic writers only. Pays $500 for a month's devotions (28-31 days) plus 5 copies on acceptance for onetime rts. Not copyrighted. Devotions 125-135 words ea. (assigns a full month at a time). Guidelines on Website.

OUR DAILY JOURNEY, 3000 Kraft Ave. S.E., Grand Rapids MI 49512. (616) 974-2663. Fax (616) 957-5741. E-mail: tfelten@rbc.org. Website: www.rbc.org. RBC Ministries. Tom Felten, ed. Devotionals for today's young adult; features meditations on God's leading through life and community participation. Monthly devotional; 64 pgs. Subscription $5 or for donation. Open to unsolicited freelance. Complete ms (as a Word attachment). **PAYS 10 COPIES**. Articles/devotions 325-350 wds. Guidelines on Website. (No ads)

Special Needs: Art and photographs. See guidelines.

Tips: "Submit one article at a time, once a month."

PENNED FROM THE HEART, 304 Stow Neck Rd., Salem NJ 08079-3431. (856) 339-9422. E-mail: ed4penned@gmail.com. Website: www.gloriaclover.com. Son-Rise Publications (toll-free 800-358-0777). Jana Carman, ed. Annual daily devotional book; about 240 pgs.; 5,000 copies/yr. 100 percent unsolicited freelance. Complete ms/cover letter; phone/e-query OK. **PAYS ONE COPY OF THE BOOK + A DISCOUNT TO RESELL BOOKS**. Onetime rts. Devotions up to 250 words (365/yr.). Responds in 9-13 wks. Considers simultaneous submissions; accepts reprints (tell when/ where appeared). Prefers mss by e-mail (attached). Also accepts submissions from children/teens. Guidelines/examples on Website: www.gloriaclover.com/guidelines.html. (No ads)

Poetry: To 24 lines. Pays one copy.

Tips: "Devotions must be biblically based, and something with an unexpected 'punch' is preferred. Build faith, encourage, and glorify God. No New Age material. Follow guidelines, specifically 250 words or less."

$ THE QUIET HOUR, 4050 Lee Vance View, Colorado Springs CO 80919. (719) 536-0100. Fax (407) 359-2850. E-mail: gwilde1@cfl.rr.com. Website: www.davidccook.com/index.cfm. David C. Cook. Gary Wilde, ed. Subscription $3.49/quarter. 100 percent freelance (makes 13 assignments/ yr.). Pays $15-35/devotional on acceptance. Currently using only previously published writers. Send list of credits only, rather than a sample. Accepts e-mailed sample devotional. Responds in 3 mos.

$ REJOICE! 600 Shaftesbury Blvd., Winnipeg MB R3P 0M4, Canada. (204) 488-0610. Fax (204) 831-5675. E-mail: ByronRB@mph.org. Website: www.mpn.net/rejoice. Faith & Life Resources/ Mennonite Publishing Network. Byron Rempel-Burkholder, ed. Daily devotional magazine grounded in Anabaptist theology. Quarterly mag.; 112 pgs.; circ. 12,000. Subscription $29.60. 5 percent unsolicited freelance; 95 percent assigned. Pays $100-125 for 7-day assigned meditations, 250-300 words each, on publication for 1st rts. Also accepts testimonies 500-600 words (8/yr.) Prefers that you send a couple of sample devotions and inquire about assignment procedures; fax/e-query OK. Accepts assigned mss by e-mail (attached). Responds in 4 wks. Seasonal 8 mos. ahead. No simultaneous submissions or reprints. Some kill fees 50 percent. Does not use sidebars. Prefers NRSV. Guidelines by e-mail.

Poetry: Buys 8/yr. Free verse, light verse; 60 characters. Pays $25. Submit max. 3 poems.

Tips: "Don't apply for assignment unless you are familiar with the publication and Anabaptist theology."

$ THE SECRET PLACE, Box 851, Valley Forge PA 19482-0851. (610) 768-2434. Fax (610) 768-2441. E-mail: thesecretplace@abc-usa.org. Website: www.judsonpress.com. Kathleen Hayes, sr. ed. Prefers to see completed devotionals, 200 words (use unfamiliar Scripture passages). 64 pgs. Circ. 150,000. 100 percent freelance. Pays $20 for 1st rts. Accepts poetry. Prefers e-mail submissions. No reprints. Guidelines by mail.

$ THESE DAYS, 100 Witherspoon St., Louisville KY 40202-1396. (502) 569-5102. Fax (502) 569-5113. E-mail: vpatton@presbypub.com. Website: www.ppcpub.com. Presbyterian Publishing Corp. Vince Patton, ed. Quarterly booklet; circ. 200,000. Subscription $7.95. Query/samples. 95 percent unsolicited freelance. Pays $14.25/devotion on acceptance for 1st and nonexclusive reprint rts. (makes work-for-hire assignments); 200 words (including key verse and short prayer). Pays $15 for short, contemporary poetry (15 lines, 33-character/line maximum) on church holidays and seasons of the year—overtly religious. Query for their two feature segments (short articles): "These Moments" and "These Times." Guidelines by mail; copy for 6 x 9 SAE/3 stamps.

Poetry: Accepts poetry.

Photos: Buys digital photos for the cover.

$ THE UPPER ROOM, PO Box 340004, Nashville TN 37203-0004. (615) 340-7252. Fax (615) 340-7267. E-mail: TheUpperRoomMagazine@upperroom.org. Website: www.upperroom.org. Mary Lou Redding, ed. dir. 95 percent unsolicited freelance. Pays $25/devotional on publication. 72 pgs. Wants freelance submissions and does not make assignments. Phone/fax/e-query OK. Send devotionals up to 250 wds. Buys explicitly religious art, in various media, for use on covers only (transparencies/slides requested); buys onetime, worldwide publishing rts. Accepts e-mail submissions (copied into message). Guidelines by mail/Website; copy for 5 x 7 SAE/2 stamps. (No ads)

   Tips: "We do not return submissions. Accepted submissions will be notified in 6-9 wks. Follow guidelines. Need meditations from men." Always include postal address with e-mail submissions.

$ + WORD AGLOW, 8855 Dunn Rd., Hazelwood MO 63042. (314) 837-7300. Fax (314) 837-1803. E-mail: WAP@upci.org. Website: www.upci.org/wap. United Pentecostal Church. Submit to The Editor. Devotionals 350-400 wds. Pays on publication. Submit by mail or e-mail. Requires KJV.

@ THE WORD AMONG US, 9639 Doctor Perry Rd., #126, Ijamsville MD 21754. Toll-free (800) 775-9673. (301) 831-1262. Fax (301) 831-1188. E-mail: lrz@wau.org. Website: www.wau.org. Catholic. Leo Zanchettin, ed. Daily meditations based on the Mass readings, inspirational essays, and stories of the saints and other heroes of the faith. Print & online mag.; circ. 500,000. Subscription $34.95 (print & online); $9.95 (online only).

$ THE WORD IN SEASON, PO Box 1209, Minneapolis MN 55440-1209. Fax (612) 330-3215. E-mail: rochelle@rightnowcoach.com. Website: www.augsburgfortress.org. Augsburg Fortress. Rev. Rochelle Y. Melander, ed./mngr. 96 pgs. Devotions to 200 wds. Pays $20/devotion; $75 for prayers. Accepts e-mail submissions (copied into message) after reading guidelines. Guidelines at www.augsburgfortress.org, type "The Word in Season" in search box.

   Tips: "We prefer that you write for guidelines. We will send instructions for preparing sample devotions. We accept new writers based on the sample devotions we request and make assignments after acceptance."

MISSIONS MARKETS

ACTION MAGAZINE: Men for Missions Intl., PO Box A, Greenwood IN 46142. (317) 881-6752. Fax (317) 865-1076. E-mail: keller@omsinternational.org. Website: www.mfmi.org. Kent Eller, dir. Informs the public of ministry opportunities, as well as reporting on the various OMS mission teams. Quarterly mag. Open to unsolicited freelance. Complete ms. Articles.

EAST-WEST CHURCH & MINISTRY REPORT, Southern Wesleyan University, Box 1020, Central SC 29630. (864) 644-5221. Fax (864) 644-5902. E-mail: melliott@swu.edu. Website: www.east westreport.org. Dr. Mark R. Elliott, ed. Encourages Western Christian ministry in Central and Eastern Europe and the former Soviet Union that is effective, culturally sensitive, and cooperative. Quarterly literary magazine; 16 pgs.; circ. 430. Print subscription $49.45; e-mail subscription $22.95. 25 percent unsolicited freelance; 75 percent assigned. Query; phone/fax/e-query OK. **PAYS IN COPIES** for all rts. Articles 1,400-2,000 words (4/yr.); book reviews, 400 words. Responds in 4 wks. Prefers requested ms on disk or by e-mail. Regularly uses sidebars. Any Bible version. Guidelines on Website; copy $11.95. (No ads)

   Tips: "All submissions must relate to Central and Eastern Europe or the former Soviet Union."

$ EVANGELICAL MISSIONS QUARTERLY, PO Box 794, Wheaton IL 60187. (630) 752-7158. Fax (630) 752-7155. E-mail: emis@wheaton.edu. Website: www.emisdirect.com. Evangelism and Missions Information Service (EMIS). A. Scott Moreau, ed.; Laurie Fortunak, mng. ed.; Dave Broucek, book review ed. For missionaries and others interested in missions trends, strategies, issues, problems, and resources. Quarterly jour.; 136 pgs.; circ. 7,000. Subscription $24.95. 67 percent unsolicited; 33 percent assigned. Query; phone/fax/e-query OK. Pays $100 on publication for all & electronic rts. Articles 3,000-3,500 words (30/yr.); book reviews 400 words (query/pays $25). Responds in 2 wks. Accepts few reprints (tell when/where appeared). Prefers requested ms on disk or by e-mail (copied into message). Uses some sidebars. Kill fee negotiable. Prefers NIV. Guidelines on Website; free copy. (Ads)

    Columns/Departments: Buys 8/yr. In the Workshop (tips to increase missionary effectiveness), 800-2,000 words; Perspectives (opinion), 800 words. Pays $50-100.

    Tips: "We consider all submissions. It is best to check our Website for examples and guidelines. Present an article idea and why you are qualified to write it. All articles must target evangelical, cross-cultural missionaries. 'In the Workshop' is most open to freelancers. Most authors have a credible connection to and experience in missions."

$ GLAD TIDINGS, 50 Wynford Dr., Toronto ON M3C 1J7, Canada. Toll-free (800) 619-7301. (416) 441-1111. Fax (416) 441-2825. E-mail: cwood@presbyterian.ca. Website: www.presbyterian.ca/wms. Women's Missionary Society/Presbyterian Church in Canada. Colleen Wood, ed. Challenges concerned Christians to reflect on their faith through articles and reports related to mission and social justice issues, locally, nationally, and internationally. Bimonthly mag.; 48 pgs.; circ. 4,000. Subscription $14 Cdn. 20 percent unsolicited freelance; 80 percent assigned. Query; e-query OK. Accepts full mss by e-mail. Pays $15-50 on publication for onetime or reprint rts. Articles 800-1,600 words (2-4/yr.); fiction 400-1,200 words (6/yr.); reviews 200 words (no payment). Responds in 3 wks. Seasonal 3-4 mos. ahead. Accepts simultaneous submissions & reprints (tell when/where appeared). Prefers e-mail submissions (attached or copied into message). No kill fee. Uses some sidebars. Also accepts submissions from teens. Prefers NRSV. Guidelines by e-mail; no copy. (Limited ads)

    Poetry: Buys 6/yr. Avant-garde, free verse, haiku, light verse, traditional; 5-100 wds. Pays $10-20. Submit max. 5 poems.

    Fillers: Buys 4-6/yr. cartoons, games, kid quotes, prayers, short humor, word puzzles; $10-20.

    Tips: "Writers can best break in with submissions of poetry, puzzles, or fiction. It is best to query as we often use themes."

INTERNATIONAL JOURNAL OF FRONTIER MISSIOLOGY, 1605 E. Elizabeth St., Pasadena CA 91104. (626) 398-2119. Fax (626) 398-2101. E-mail: ijfm@wciu.edu. Website: www.ijfm.org. William Carey Intl. University. Rory Clark, ed. Dedicated to frontiers in missions. Quarterly jour.; 48 pgs.; circ. 500. Subscription $18. 75 percent unsolicited freelance. Complete ms/cover letter; phone/fax/e-query OK. **NO PAYMENT** for onetime rts. Articles 2,000-8,500 words. Seasonal 3 mos. ahead. Accepts simultaneous submissions & reprints. Accepts e-mail submissions. Does not use sidebars. Guidelines/theme list by e-mail/Website; no copy. (Ads)

    Special Needs: Contextualization, church in missions, training for missions, mission trends and paradigms, de-westernization of the gospel and missions from the Western world, biblical worldview development, mission theology, Animism, Islam, Buddhism, Hinduism, nonliterate peoples, tent making, mission member care, reaching nomadic peoples, mission history, new religious movements and missions, science and missions, etc.

    Tips: "Writers on specific issues we cover are always welcome. Although the circulation is small, the print run is 2,000 and used for promotional purposes. Highly recommended for mission schools, libraries, and mission executives."

@ LAUSANNE WORLD PULSE, PO Box 794, Wheaton IL 60189. (630) 752-7158. Fax (630) 752-7155. E-mail: info@lausanneworldpulse.com. Website: www.lausanneworldpulse.com. Lausanne Committee for World Evangelism/Wheaton College. Laurie Fortunak, editorial coord. News and information on evangelism and missions from around the world. Monthly e-zine; 40 pgs.; circ. 8,000. Subscription free online. 20 percent unsolicited freelance; 80 percent assigned. Query or complete ms/cover letter; e-query OK. Accepts full mss by e-mail. **NO PAYMENT** for 1st, reprint, electronic, nonexclusive rts. Articles 600-1,500 wds. Responds in 2-3 wks. Seasonal 6 mos. ahead. Accepts simultaneous submissions; might accept reprints (tell when/where appeared). Prefers accepted mss by e-mail (attached file). Uses some sidebars. Guidelines/theme list on Website. (No ads)

$ LEADERS FOR TODAY, Box 13, Atlanta GA 30370. (770) 449-8869. Fax (770) 449-8457. E-mail: ingridalbuquerque@yahoo.com. Website: www.haggai-institute.com. Haggai Institute. Ingrid Albuquerque, ed. Primarily for donors to ministry; focus is alumni success stories. Quarterly mag.; 16 pgs.; circ. 7,500. Subscription free. 100 percent assigned to date. Query; fax query OK. Pays .10-.25/wd. on acceptance for all rts. Articles 1,000-2,000 wds. Responds in 2-3 wks. Requires requested ms on disk or by e-mail (attached file). Kill fee 100 percent. Regularly uses sidebars. Prefers NIV. Guidelines/theme list by mail; copy for 9 x 12 SAE/4 stamps. (No ads)

   Tips: "If traveling to a developing country, check well in advance regarding the possibility of doing an alumni story. All articles are preassigned; query first."
   ** 2005 EPA Award of Merit—Missionary.

MISSIOLOGY: An International Review, Covenant Theological Seminary, 12330 Conway Rd., St. Louis MO 63141. (314) 434-4044, ext. 4207. Fax (314) 392-4212. E-mail: missiology@cov enantseminary.edu. Website: www.asmweb.org. American Society of Missiology/Asbury Theological Seminary. J. Nelson Jennings, ed. A scholarly journal for those who study and practice missions worldwide. Quarterly jour.; 128-136 pgs.; circ. 1,500. Subscription $26. 60 percent unsolicited freelance; 40 percent assigned. Complete ms/cover letter. **PAYS 20 COPIES** for 1st rts. Articles 3,000-5,000 words (20/yr.); book reviews 400 words. Responds in 8 wks. No seasonal. No simultaneous submissions or reprints. Prefers requested ms by e-mail (attached file) or on disk. Uses some sidebars. Any Bible version. Guidelines on Website; copy for 6 x 9 SAE/$3.16 postage ($6 foreign). (Ads)

@ MISSION CONNECTION, 17001 Prairie Star Pkwy., Lenexa KS 66220. (816) 333-7000, ext. 2350. Fax (816) 822-8296. E-mail: missionconnection@nazarene.org. Website: www.nazarene missions.org. Nazarene Missions Intl. Gail L. Sawrie, ed. A meeting place for equipping NMI leaders through interaction and resource exchange. Monthly e-zine. Subscription free. Open to unsolicited freelance. Complete ms. **NO PAYMENT**. Not copyrighted. Articles to 400 wds. Guidelines on Website. Incomplete topical listings. (No ads)

@ MISSION FRONTIERS, 1605 Elizabeth St., Pasadena CA 91104. (626) 797-1111. Fax (626) 398-2263. E-mail: mission.frontiers@uscwm.org. Website: www.missionfrontiers.org. U.S. Center for World Mission. Dr. Ralph Winter, ed.; Rick Wood, mng. ed. To stimulate a movement to establish indigenous churches where still needed around the world. Bimonthly & online mag.; 24 pgs.; circ. 100,000. Subscription free for donation. No unsolicited freelance; 100 percent assigned. Query. **NO PAYMENT**. Articles & reviews. Rarely responds. Accepts requested ms on disk or by e-mail (copied into message). Regularly uses sidebars. No guidelines; free copy. Incomplete topical listings. (Ads— MFAds@uscwm.org)

   Fillers: Cartoons.
   Tips: "Be a published missionary or former missionary. Be on the cutting edge of a strategic breakthrough or methods of reaching an unreached ethnic group." Looking for true-life, short sidebars of Muslims accepting Jesus or impact of prayer in missions.

MISSIONS MAGIZINET, PO Box 17, Uppsala, S-751 03, Sweden. Phone +4618 489-8000, or +4618 489 8182. E-mail: info@livetsord.se. Website: www.livetsord.se. Livets Ord/Word of Life Church. Rune Borgso, ed. To provide Bible teaching and to inform of our missions work through reports and feature stories. Published 7x/yr.; circ. 64,000. Open to unsolicited freelance. Query. Articles. Incomplete topical listings. (Ads)

$ NEW WORLD OUTLOOK, 475 Riverside Dr., Rm. 1476, New York NY 10115-0122. (212) 870-3765. Fax (212) 870-3940. E-mail: nwo@gbgm-umc.org. Website: http://gbgm-umc.org/nwo. United Methodist. Christie R. House, ed. Denominational missions. Bimonthly mag.; 48 pgs.; circ. 24,000. Subscription $15. 20 percent unsolicited freelance. Query; fax/e-query OK. Pays $50-300 on publication for all & electronic rts. Articles 500-2,000 words (24/yr.); book reviews 200-500 words (assigned). No guaranteed response time. Seasonal 4 mos. ahead. Kill fee 50 percent or $100. Prefers e-mail submission (WordPerfect 6.1 or 8.1 in attached file). Regularly uses sidebars. Prefers NRSV. Guidelines by mail; copy $3. (Ads)

> **Tips:** "Ask for a list of United Methodist mission workers and projects in your area. Investigate them, propose a story, and consult with the editors before writing. Most open to articles and/or color photos of U.S. or foreign mission sites visited as a stringer, after consultation with the editor."

$ ONE, 1011 First Ave., New York NY 10022-4195. Toll-free (800) 442-6392. (212) 826-1480. Fax (212) 826-8979. E-mail: cnewa@cnewa.org, or through Website: www.cnewa.org. Catholic Near East Welfare Assn. Michael La Civita, exec. ed. Interest in cultural, religious, and human rights development in Middle East, N.E. Africa, India, or Eastern Europe. Bimonthly mag.; 40 pgs.; circ. 100,000. Subscription $20. 50 percent unsolicited freelance; 50 percent assigned. Query/clips; fax query OK. Pays .20/edited wd. ($200) on publication for all rts. Articles 1,200-1,800 words (15/yr.). Responds in 9 wks. Accepts requested ms on disk. Kill fee $200. Prefers NASB. Guidelines by mail/e-mail; copy for 8 x 11 SAE/2 stamps.

> **Tips:** "We strive to educate our readers about the culture, faith, history, issues, and people who form the Eastern Christian churches. Anything on people in Palestine/Israel, Eastern Europe, or India. Material should not be academic. Include detailed photographs with story or article."

@ OPERATION REVEILLE INTERACTIVE JOURNAL, PO Box 3488, Monument CO 80132-3488. (719) 572-5908. Fax (775) 248-8147. E-mail: bside@oprev.org. Website: www.oprev.org. Mission to Unreached Peoples. Bruce T. Sidebotham, dir. Provides information to equip U.S. military Christians for cross-cultural ministry. Quarterly & online newsletter; 8 pgs.; circ. 1,500. Subscription free. 40 percent unsolicited freelance; 60 percent assigned. Query; phone/e-query OK. **PAYS IN COPIES** for onetime rts. Not copyrighted. Articles 250-1,000 words (4/yr.). Responds in 4 wks. Seasonal 4 mos. ahead. Accepts simultaneous submissions & reprints (tell when/where appeared). Accepts requested ms on disk. Regularly uses sidebars. Prefers NIV. No guidelines; copy .50/9 x 12 SAE/4 stamps. (No ads)

> **Fillers:** Accepts 4/yr. Newsbreaks to 150 words.
>
> **Columns/Departments:** Accepts 4/yr. Agency Profile (describes a mission agency's history and work), 200-300 words; Area Profile (describes spiritual landscape of a military theater of operations), 300-750 words; Resource Review (describes a cross-cultural ministry tool), 100-200 words. Query.
>
> **Special Needs:** Ministry in Afghanistan and Iraq. World news and analysis; cross-cultural communication; area profiles and people profiles on military theaters of operation.
>
> **Tips:** "We need insights for military personnel on understanding and relating the gospel to Muslims."

$ PFI GLOBAL LINK JOURNAL, Box 17434, Washington DC 20041. (703) 481-0000. Fax (703) 481-0003. E-mail: communications@pfi.org. Website: www.pfi.org. Prison Fellowship Intl. Seldom uses freelance articles, but would consider articles with a direct connection to a Prison Fellowship organization outside of the United States.

$ PIME WORLD, 17330 Quincy St., Detroit MI 48221-2765. (313) 342-4066. Fax (313) 342-6816. E-mail: pimeworld@pimeusa.org. Website: www.pimeusa.org. Pontifical Inst. for Foreign Missions/Catholic. Rick Schulte, ed. For those interested in and supportive of foreign missions. Published 5x/

yr., plus newsletter supplement; 24 pgs.; circ. 16,000. Subscription $15. 10 percent unsolicited free-lance. Complete ms; e-query OK. Pays $15-25 on publication for onetime rts. Photos $10. Articles 500-1,000 wds. Responds in 2 wks. Seasonal 4 mos. ahead. Accepts reprints (tell when/where appeared). Prefers e-mail submission (attached file). Uses some sidebars. Prefers NAB. Also accepts submissions from teens. Guidelines/theme list by mail; copy for 6 x 9 SAE/2 stamps. (No ads)

Tips: "Features are open to freelancers. Needs missionary profiles; articles on PIME missionaries; interfaith dialog/experiences; and missions in Africa, especially Ivory Coast, Guinea Bissau, and Cameroon. Also issues like hunger, human rights, women's rights, peace, and justice as they are dealt with in developing countries by missionaries and locals alike."

THE RAILROAD EVANGELIST, PO Box 5026, Vancouver WA 98668-5026. (360) 699-7208. E-mail: rrjoe@comcast.net, or REA@comcast.net. Website: www.railroadevangelist.com. Railroad Evangelistic Assn. Joe Spooner, ed. For railroad and transportation employees and their families. Tri-annual mag.; 16 pgs.; circ. 2,500. Subscription $8. 100 percent unsolicited freelance. Complete ms/no cover letter; phone query OK. **NO PAYMENT**. Articles 100-700 words (10-15/yr.); railroad-related fiction only, for children 5-12 yrs. Seasonal 4 mos. ahead. Accepts simultaneous submissions & reprints. Accepts e-mail submissions. Does not use sidebars. Guidelines by mail/e-mail; copy for 9 x 12 SAE/2 stamps. (No ads)

Poetry: Accepts 4-8/yr. Traditional, any length. Send any number.

Fillers: Accepts many. Anecdotes, cartoons, quotes; to 100 wds.

Tips: "We need 400- to 700-word railroad-related salvation testimonies, or railroad-related human-interest stories, or model railroads. Since we publish only three times a year, we are focusing on railroad-related articles only. Just write and tell us or send us what you have. We'll let you know if we can use it or not."

+ **WEC.GO**, PO Box 1707, Fort Washington PA 19034. (215) 646-2322. Fax (215) 646-6202. E-mail: wec.go@wec-usa.org. Website: www.wec-usa.org/wec.go. Worldwide Evangelism for Christ International. Kay Negly, ed. Quarterly mag.; circ. 9,500. Subscription free. Open to unsolicited free-lance. Query first. **NO PAYMENT**. Articles. Incomplete topical listings.

Tips: "Our purpose is to inform the Christian public about WEC International, and missions in general—through life stories that challenge our readers spiritually and stir their hearts for His Great Commission."

@ **WOMEN OF THE HARVEST**, PO Box 151297, Lakewood CO 80215-9297. Toll-free (877) 789-7778. (303) 985-2148. Fax (303) 989-4239. E-mail: editor@womenoftheharvest.com. Website: www.womenoftheharvest.com. Women of the Harvest Ministries Intl. Inc. Cindy Blomquist, ed. To support and encourage women serving in cross-cultural missions. Bimonthly e-zine; 35 pgs.; circ. 8,000. Free online. 90 percent unsolicited freelance; 10 percent assigned. Complete ms; e-query OK. Accepts full ms by e-mail. **NO PAYMENT** for onetime & electronic rts. Articles 300-1,200 wds. Responds in 2 wks. Seasonal 3 mos. ahead. No simultaneous submissions or reprints. Prefers requested ms by e-mail (copied into message or attached file). Uses some sidebars. Guidelines/theme list/copy on Website. (No ads)

Tips: "This is a magazine designed especially for women serving cross-culturally. We need articles, humor, and anecdotes related to this topic. Best way to break in is by having a cross-cultural missions experience or to be heading to the mission field."

** 2008 EPA Award of Excellence—Online; 2006 EPA Award of Merit—Online.

MUSIC MARKETS

$ @ **CHRISTIAN MUSIC TODAY**, 465 Gundersen Dr., Carol Stream IL 60188. (630) 620-6200. Fax (630) 260-8428. E-mail: music@christianitytoday.com. Website: www.ChristianMusicToday .com. Christianity Today Intl. Tod Hertz & Mark Moring, eds. To inspire and inform readers about today's Christian music, artists, and industry trends through timely coverage, relevant news, insightful reviews and interviews, and educated opinion, all from a Christian worldview. Weekly e-zine. 5 percent unsolicited freelance; 95 percent assigned. Query; fax/e-query OK. Accepts full mss by e-mail. Pays $50-200 on acceptance for 1st rts. Articles 400-2,000 words (200/yr.); music reviews, 300-700 words, payment varies. Responds in 2 wks. Occasionally accepts simultaneous submissions & reprints (tell when/where appeared). Prefers e-mail submissions (attached file). Sometimes pays kill fee 50 percent. Uses some sidebars. Prefers NIV. No guidelines; copy online. (Ads)

    Columns/Departments: Buys 6-8/yr. Glimpses of God (spiritual leanings in secular music), 1,000 wds. Pays $75-100. Query.

    Special Needs: Reviews of music videos.

    Tips: "Most open to news/trends, interviews, and commentaries."

    ** This periodical was #42 on the 2009 Top 50 Christian Publishers List (#27 in 2008).

CHRISTIAN MUSIC WEEKLY, 7057 Bluffwood Ct., Brownsburg IN 46112-8650. (317) 892-5031. Fax (317) 892-5034. Canadian address: 775 Pam Cres, Newmarket ON L3Y 5B7, Canada. E-mail through Website: www.ChristianMusicWeekly.com. Joyful Sounds. Rob Green, ed. Trade paper for Worship, Inspirational, Adult Contemporary, and Southern Gospel Music radio formats. Weekly trade paper; 12 pgs.; circ. 300-1,200. Subscription $49 (paper) or free (PDF via e-mail). 25 percent unsolicited freelance; 75 percent assigned. Query by e-mail only. **PAYS IN COPIES** (will publish photo of writer and tiny bio). Articles 600-2,000 words; music reviews, 100-300 words. Responds in 2 wks. Seasonal 2 mos. ahead. Accepts reprints. Requires requested ms on disk (DOS-ASCII), prefers e-mail submission. Guidelines by e-mail; copy for 9 x 12 SAE/2 stamps. (Ads)

    Fillers: Cartoons, short humor (particularly radio or music related).

    Columns/Departments: Insider (artist interview); Programming 101 (radio technique); retail, inspirational, especially for musicians and radio people; 600-2,000 words.

    Special Needs: Songwriting and performance.

    Tips: "Most open to artist interviews. Must be familiar with appropriate music formats."

+ **CHRISTIAN VOICE MAGAZINE**, PO Box 147, Kennedy AL 35574. (205) 662-4826. Fax (205) 596-4375. E-mail: news@christianvoicemagazine.com or editor@christianvoicemagazine.com. Website: www.christianvoicemagazine.com. Distributed by Wilds & Assocs. John Lanier, exec. ed. Christian music news & information. Monthly print and digital mag. Estab. 2006. Subscription $20 print; $10 digital download. Open to unsolicited freelance. Complete ms/copy ready. Music-related news articles. Guidelines on Website. Not included in topical listings.

CHURCH MUSIC QUARTERLY, 19 The Close, Salisbury, Wiltshire, SP1 2EB, United Kingdom. Phone +44 1722 424848. Fax +44 1722 424849. E-mail: cmq@rscm.com. Website: www.rscm.com. Royal School of Church Music. Submit to: Julian Elloway, ed., Highmead, Field Rd., Stroud, Glos. GL5 2JA, UK; phone/fax 01453 840388; cmqreviews@rscm.com. Advice and inspiration for church musicians around the world. Quarterly mag.; 60 pgs; circ. 12,000. Subscription free with RSCM membership. 5 percent unsolicited freelance; 95 percent assigned. Query/clips; phone/fax/e-query OK. Accepts full mss by e-mail. Pays on publication. Articles. Incomplete topical listings. (Ads)

$ @ **CREATOR MAGAZINE**, PO Box 3538, Pismo Beach CA 93448. Toll-free (800) 777-6713. (707) 837-9071. E-mail: creator@creatormagazine.com. Website: www.creatormagazine.com. Rod Ellis, ed. For interdenominational music ministry; promoting quality, diverse music programs in the church. Bimonthly & online mag.; 48-56 pgs.; circ. 6,000. Subscription $32.95. 35 percent unsolicited freelance. Query or complete ms/cover letter; fax/e-query OK. Pays $30-75 for assigned, $30–$60 for unsolicited, on publication for 1st, onetime, reprint rts. Articles 1,000–10,000 words (20/yr.); book reviews ($20). Responds in 4-12 wks. Seasonal 4 mos. ahead. Accepts simultaneous submissions & reprints (tell when/where appeared). Prefers requested ms on disk. Regularly uses sidebars. Prefers NRSV. Guidelines/theme list/copy for 9 x 12 SAE/5 stamps. (Ads)

Fillers: Buys 20/yr. Anecdotes, cartoons, ideas, jokes, party ideas, short humor; 10-75 words; $5-25.

Special Needs: Articles on worship; staff relationships.

THE HYMN: A Journal of Congregational Song, School of Theology, Boston University, 745 Commonwealth Ave., Boston MA 02215-1401. Toll-free (800) THEHYMN. Fax (617) 353-7322. E-mail: hymneditor@amural.com. Website: www.bu.edu/sth/hymn or www.hymnsociety.org. Hymn Society in the U.S. & Canada. Nancy E. Hall, ed. For church musicians, hymnologists, scholars; articles related to the congregational song. Quarterly jour.; 60 pgs.; circ. 3,000. Subscription $75. 85 percent unsolicited freelance; 15 percent assigned. Query; phone/e-query OK. **NO PAYMENT** for all rts. Articles any length (12/yr.); book & music reviews any length. Responds in 6 wks. Seasonal 4 mos. ahead. Prefers requested ms on disk or by e-mail. Regularly uses sidebars. Any Bible version. Guidelines on Website; free copy. (Ads)

> **Special Needs:** Articles on history of hymns or practical ways to teach or use hymns. Controversial issues related to hymns and songs. Contact editor.
>
> **Contest:** Hymn text & tune contests for special occasions or themes.
>
> **Tips:** "Focus all articles on congregational song. No devotional material."

I AM MAGAZINE, 13055 Riverdale Dr. N.W., Ste. 500-222, Coon Rapids MN 55448. (651) 248-9671, or (763) 221-7119. E-mail: jerrvals2003@yahoo.com. Website: www.myspace.com/iam magazine. Jerrvals Records. Jerry Griffis, pub.; Val Griffis, ed. To reach gospel music listeners in the urban communities through genres such as gospel, traditional, contemporary, rap, and gospel hip-hop, as well as giving independent and national gospel artists and record companies an opportunity to gain exposure. Quarterly mag. Subscription $12. Open to unsolicited freelance. Query or complete ms. Articles. Guidelines on Website. Not in topical listings. (Ads)

($) + TCP MAGAZINE, 181—104 Wind Chime Ct., Raleigh NC 27615. (919) 676-0263. E-mail: info@theconnectionplace.com. Website: www.tcpmagazine.com. The Connection Place Inc. Peggy Tatum, ed. To connect music, ministries, and Christian businesses. Quarterly mag.; 36 pgs; circ. 20,000. Subscription $15. 100 percent assigned. Query/clips; e-query OK. **PAYS IN COPIES & ADVERTISEMENT**. Articles 550 words; short story to 300 words.

> **Special Needs:** Trends in religion.

TRADITION MAGAZINE, PO Box 492, Anita IA 50020. Phone/fax (712) 762-4363. E-mail: bobever hart@yahoo.com. National Traditional Country Music Assn. Inc. Bob Everhart, pres./ed. Bimonthly mag.; 56 pgs.; circ. 3,500. Subscription $25. 30 percent unsolicited freelance; 70 percent assigned. Query. **PAYS IN COPIES** for onetime rts. Articles 1,000-2,000 words (4/yr.). Responds in 6-8 wks. Uses some sidebars. Prefers KJV. Guidelines; copy for 9 x 12 SAE/2 stamps. (Ads)

> **Fillers:** Cartoons.
>
> **Columns/Departments:** Accepts 4-6/yr. Query.
>
> **Tips:** "Most articles need to deal with traditional or old-time music."
>
> Note: Also see "Resources: Songwriting" in the resources section for this book (on CD).

PASTOR/LEADERSHIP MARKETS

$ THE AFRICAN-AMERICAN PULPIT, PO Box 381587, Germantown TN 38183. Toll-free (800) 509-8227. Phone/fax (412) 364-1688. E-mail: mcgoeyeditor@comcast.net, Info@theafrican americanpulpit.com or through Website: www.TheAfricanAmericanPulpit.com. Hope for Life Intl. Inc. Martha Simmons, pub.; Eugene L. Gibson Jr. & Maria Mallory White, co-eds. The only journal focused exclusively on the art of black preaching. Quarterly jour.; 96 pgs.; circ. 4,000. Subscription $40 ($59 to libraries). 50 percent unsolicited freelance; 50 percent assigned. Complete ms/cover letter by e-mail only. Pays $50 (flat fee) on publication for all rts. Articles 1,500 words, sermons

2,500 words. Responds in 13-26 wks. Seasonal 6-9 mos. ahead. Requires requested ms on disk or by e-mail. Does not use sidebars. Any Bible version. Guidelines by mail/e-mail/Website; copy. (Ads)

Special Needs: Any type of sermon by African American preachers and related articles or essays.

Contest: Sponsors contest occasionally; advertised in the magazine.

Tips: "The entire journal is open to freelancers. We strongly encourage freelancers to submit to us (as many pieces as you can), and freelancers can call anytime with questions. We are always looking for how-to articles, sermon helps, homiletic-method essays, seminarian pieces, and practical pieces."

$ BAREFOOT, 2923 Troost Ave., Kansas City MO 64109-1593. Toll-free (866) 355-9933. (816) 931-1900. Fax (816) 412-8306. E-mail: bfeditor@barefootministries.com or through Website: www.barefootministries.com. Bo Cassell, ed. Dedicated to resourcing and equipping youth workers. 10 percent unsolicited freelance; 90 percent assigned. E-query preferred; fax query OK. Pays $50-100 on publication for all rts. Articles for youth workers 1,000-2,000 words (20-25/yr.); reviews 500 words ($25). Responds in 8 wks. Seasonal 6 mos. ahead. Accepts reprints (tell when/where appeared). Accepts e-mail submissions (attached or copied into message). Some kill fees. Does not use sidebars. Prefers NIV. Guidelines by e-mail; copy online. (No ads)

Fillers: Buys 20-40/yr. Anecdotes, cartoons, games, ideas, party ideas, short humor, and tips, 100-200 words; $20-40.

Special Needs: Youth worker and youth issues.

Tips: "We are most open to freelancers in the areas of product, music, and entertainment reviews. Where youth ministry articles and curricular pieces are concerned, we usually assign those to established youth ministry professionals."

$ CATECHUMENATE: A Journal of Christian Initiation, 1800 N. Hermitage Ave., Chicago IL 60622-1101. Toll-free (800) 933-1800. (773) 486-8970. E-mail: editors@ltp.org. Website: www .LTP.org. Catholic. Mary Fox, ed. For clergy and laity who work with those who are planning to become Catholic. Bimonthly mag.; 48 pgs.; circ. 5,600. Subscription $20. 60 percent unsolicited freelance; 40 percent assigned. Query; phone/fax/e-query OK. Accepts full ms by e-mail. Pays $100-300 on publication for all rts. Articles 2,000-3,000 words (10/yr.); book reviews 800 words. Responds in 2 wks. Seasonal 6 mos. ahead. No simultaneous submissions or reprints. Requires requested ms by e-mail (attached). No kill fee. Uses some sidebars. Guidelines by e-mail; copy for 6 x 9 SAE/4 stamps. (No ads)

Poetry: Buys 6/yr. Any type; 5-20 lines; $75. Submit max. 5 poems. Onetime rts.

Columns/Departments: Buys 26/yr. Sunday Word (Scripture reflection on Sunday readings, aimed at catechumen); 450 words; $200-250. Query for assignment.

Special Needs: Christian initiation; reconciliation.

Tips: "Writers should have worked at parishes or dioceses or taught in universities about Christian initiation."

$ THE CATHOLIC SERVANT, PO Box 24142, Minneapolis MN 55424. (612) 729-7321. Cell (612) 275-0431. Fax (612) 724-8695. E-mail: JohnSondag@sainthelena.us. Website: www.CatholicServant .org. Catholic. John Sondag, ed./pub. For Catholic evangelization, catechesis, and apologetics. Monthly tabloid; 12 pgs.; circ. 41,000 during school yr.; 33,000 summer. Query/clips; fax query OK. Pays $60 on publication. Articles 750-1,000 words (12/yr.). Responds in 4 wks. Seasonal 3 mos. ahead. Requested mss by e-mail only. Uses some sidebars. (Ads)

Fillers: Cartoons & short humor.

Columns/Departments: Opinion column, 500-750 words.

Tips: "We buy features or columns only." Be sure to indicate "Ms for Catholic Servant" in subject line of e-mail.

$ THE CHRISTIAN CENTURY, 104 S. Michigan Ave., Ste. 700, Chicago IL 60603. (312) 263-7510. Fax (312) 263-7540. E-mail: submissions@christiancentury.org. Website: www.christiancentury.org. Christian Century Foundation. Submit to: Attention Manuscripts. For ministers, educators, and church leaders interested in events and theological issues of concern to the ecumenical church. Biweekly mag.; 48 pgs.; circ. 30,000. Subscription $49. 20 percent unsolicited freelance; 80 percent assigned. Query (complete ms for fiction); phone/fax query OK. Pays $125 on publication for all or onetime rts. Articles 1,500-3,000 words (150/yr.); fiction 1,000-3,000 words (3/yr.); book reviews 800-1,500 words; music or video reviews 1,000 words; pays $0-75. Responds in 1-9 wks. Seasonal 4 mos. ahead. No simultaneous submissions. Accepts reprints (tell when/where appeared). No kill fee. Regularly uses sidebars. Prefers NRSV. Guidelines/theme list by mail/e-mail/Website; copy $5. (Ads)

> **Poetry:** Poetry Editor (poetry@christiancentury.org). Buys 50/yr. Any type (religious but not sentimental); to 20 lines; $50. Submit max. 10 poems.
>
> **Special Needs:** Film, popular-culture commentary; news topics and analysis.
>
> **Tips:** "Keep in mind our audience of sophisticated readers, eager for analysis and critical perspective that goes beyond the obvious. We are open to all topics if written with appropriate style for our readers."

CHRISTIAN EDUCATION JOURNAL, 13800 Biola Ave., LaMirada CA 90639. (562) 903-6000, ext. 5528. Fax (562) 906-4502. E-mail: editor.cej@biola.edu. Website: www.biola.edu/cej. Talbot School of Theology, Biola University. Kevin E. Lawson, ed. Academic journal on the practice of Christian education; for students, professors, and thoughtful ministry leaders in Christian education. Semiannual jour.; 200-250 pgs.; circ. 750. Subscription $28. Open to freelance. Query; e-query OK. Accepts full mss by e-mail. **NO PAYMENT** for 1st rts. Articles 3,000-6,000 words (20/yr.); book reviews 2-5 pgs. Responds in 4-6 wks. No seasonal. Might accept simultaneous submissions & reprints (tell when/where appeared). Requires e-mail submissions (attached file in Word format). Does not use sidebars. Any Bible version. Guidelines on Website; no copy. (Ads)

> **Tips:** "Focus on foundations and/or research with implications for the conception and practice of Christian education." Book reviews must be preassigned and approved by the editor; guidelines on Website.

+ CHURCH EXECUTIVE, 4742 N. 24th St., Ste. 340, Phoenix AZ 85016. (602) 265-7600. Fax (602) 265-4300. E-mail: ron@churchexecutive.com. Website: www.churchexecutive.com. Power Trade Media. Ronald E. Keener, ed. Business magazine for larger churches and megachurches, read by pastors, executive pastors, and business administrators. Monthly mag.; 52 pgs; circ. 20,000. Subscription $39. 5 percent unsolicited freelance; 95 percent assigned. Query; phone/e-query OK. Accepts full mss by e-mail. **NO PAYMENT**. Articles 1,200 wds. Responds in 2 wks. Seasonal 3 mos. ahead. Accepts simultaneous submissions; no reprints. Accepts e-mail submissions (attached file). Regularly uses sidebars. Prefers NIV. Guidelines/theme list by e-mail; copy for 9 x 12 SAE/$2 postage. (Ads)

> **Columns/Departments:** Accepts 5/yr. Query.
>
> **Special Needs:** Church construction; economic impact on giving.
>
> **Tips:** "Relate your piece to our editorial calendar and product categories."

$ THE CLERGY JOURNAL, 6160 Carmen Ave. E., Inver Grove Heights MN 55076-4422. (651) 451-9945. Fax (651) 457-4617. E-mail: sfirle@logosstaff.com. Website: www.logosproductions .com. Logos Productions Inc. Sharon Firle, mng. ed. Directed mainly to clergy—a practical guide to church leadership and personal growth. Monthly (9x) mag.; 56 pgs.; circ. 6,000. Subscription $46.95. 5 percent unsolicited freelance; 95 percent assigned. Complete ms/cover letter; fax/e-query OK. Pays $75-150 on publication for 1st rts. Articles 1,000-1,500 words (25/yr.). Responds in 4 wks. Seasonal 8 mos. ahead. Accepts simultaneous submissions & reprints (tell when/where appeared). Prefers requested ms by e-mail (attached file). No kill fee. Uses some sidebars. Prefers NRSV. Guidelines/ theme list by mail/e-mail/Website; copy for 9 x 12 SAE/4 stamps. (Ads—struran@logosstaff.com)

Columns/Departments: Ministry Issues; Preaching & Worship; Personal Issues; $75-150.
Special Needs: Church technology issues.
Tips: "Our greatest need is sermon writers who can write on assigned texts. Instructions sent on request. Our readers are mainline Protestant. We are interested in meeting the personal and professional needs of clergy in areas like worship planning, church and personal finances, and self-care—spiritual, physical, and emotional."

$ @ **COOK PARTNERS**, (formerly Cook International), 4050 Lee Vance View, Colorado Springs CO 80918. (719) 536-0100. Fax (719) 536-3266. E-mail: kim.pettit@cookinternational.org. Website: www.cookinternational.org. Cook International. Kim Pettit, mng. ed. Seeks to encourage self-sufficient, effective indigenous Christian publishing worldwide to spread the life-giving message of the gospel. Bimonthly online publication; circ. 2,000. Subscription free. Open to unsolicited freelance. Query or complete ms. Articles & reviews 400-1,500 wds. Responds in 1-4 wks. Most writers donate their work, but will negotiate for payment if asked. Wants all rts. Incomplete topical listings. (No ads)

CROSS CURRENTS, 475 Riverside Dr., Ste. 1945, New York NY 10015. (212) 870-2544. Fax (212) 870-2539. E-mail: editors@crosscurrents.org. Website: www.crosscurrents.org. Association for Religion and Intellectual Life. Charles P. Henderson, exec. dir. (cph@crosscurrents.org); submit to Managing Editor. For thoughtful activists for social justice and church reform. Quarterly mag.; 144 pgs.; circ. 5,000. Subscription $42. 25 percent unsolicited freelance; 75 percent assigned. Mostly written by academics. Complete ms/cover letter; e-query OK. **PAYS IN COPIES** for all rts. Articles 3,000-5,000 words; fiction 3,000 words; book reviews 1,000 words. Responds in 4-8 wks. Seasonal 6 mos. ahead. No simultaneous submissions or reprints. Prefers requested ms on disk or by e-mail (attached file). Does not use sidebars. Guidelines on Website; no copy. (Ads)
   Poetry: Accepts 12/yr. Any type or length; no payment. Submit max. 5 poems.
   Tips: "Looking for focused, well-researched articles; creative fiction and poetry. Send two double-spaced copies; SASE; use Chicago Manual of Style and nonsexist language."

$ **DIOCESAN DIALOGUE**, 16565 S. State St., South Holland IL 60473. (708) 331-5485. Fax (708) 331-5484. E-mail: acp@acpress.org. Website: www.americancatholicpress.org. American Catholic Press. Father Michael Gilligan, editorial dir. Targets Latin-Rite dioceses in the U.S. that sponsor a Mass broadcast on TV or radio. Annual newsletter; 8 pgs.; circ. 750. Free. 20 percent unsolicited freelance. Complete ms/cover letter; no phone/fax/e-query. Articles 200-1,000 wds. Pays variable rates on publication for all rts. Responds in 10 wks. Accepts simultaneous submissions & reprints. Uses some sidebars. Prefers NAB (Confraternity). No guidelines; copy $3/9 x 12 SAE/2 stamps. (No ads)
   Fillers: Cartoons, 2/yr.
   Tips: "Writers should be familiar with TV production of the Mass and/or the needs of senior citizens, especially shut-ins."

$ **EMMANUEL**, 5384 Wilson Mills Rd., Cleveland OH 44143. (440) 449-2103. Fax (440) 449-3862. E-mail: emmanuel@blessedsacrament.com. Website: www.blessedsacrament.com. Catholic. Rev. Paul Bernier SSS, ed. (pbernier@blessedsacrament.com); Patrick Riley, book review ed. Eucharistic spirituality for priests and others in church ministry. Bimonthly mag.; 96 pgs.; circ. 3,000. Subscription $31; $36 foreign. 30 percent unsolicited freelance. Query or complete ms/cover letter; e-query OK. Pays $75-150 for articles, $50 for meditations, on publication for all rts. Articles 2,000-2,750 words; meditations 1,000-1,250 words; book reviews 500-750 words. Responds in 2 wks. Seasonal 4 mos. ahead. Accepts manuscripts on disk or as e-mail attachments. Guidelines/theme list by mail/e-mail. (Ads)
   Poetry: Buys 15/yr. Free verse, light verse, traditional; 8 lines & up; $35. Submit max. 3 poems.
   Tips: "Most open to articles, meditations, poetry oriented toward Eucharistic spirituality, prayer, and ministry."

$ ENRICHMENT: A Journal for Pentecostal Ministry, 1445 N. Boonville Ave., Springfield MO 65802. (417) 862-2781, ext. 4095. Fax (417) 862-0416. E-mail: enrichmentjournal@ag.org. Website: www.enrichmentjournal.ag.org. Assemblies of God. Gary R. Allen, exec. ed.; Rick Knoth, mng. ed. (rknoth@ag.org). Enriching and encouraging Pentecostal ministers to equip and empower Spirit-filled believers for effective ministry. Quarterly jour.; 144-160 pgs.; circ. 33,000. Subscription $24; foreign add $30. 15 percent unsolicited freelance. Complete ms/cover letter. Pays up to .15/wd. ($75-350) on acceptance for 1st rts. Articles 1,000-2,800 words (25/yr.); book reviews, 250 words ($25). Responds in 8-12 wks. Seasonal 1 yr. ahead. Accepts simultaneous submissions & reprints (tell when/where appeared). Requires requested ms on disk or by e-mail (copied into message or attached). Kill fee up to 50 percent. Regularly uses sidebars. Prefers NIV. Guidelines/theme list on Website; copy for $7/10 x 13 SAE. (Ads)

> **Fillers:** Buys over 100/yr. Anecdotes, cartoon, facts, short humor, tips; $25-40, or .10-.20/wd.
> **Columns/Departments:** Buys 40/yr. For Women in Ministry (leadership ideas), Associate Ministers (related issues), Managing Your Ministry (how-to), Financial Concepts (church stewardship issues), Family Life (minister's family), When Pews Are Few (ministry in smaller congregation), Worship in the Church, Leader's Edge, Preaching That Connects, Ministry & Medical Ethics, History Is His Story; all 1,200-2,500 words; $75-275. Query or complete ms.
> **Tips:** "Most open to EShorts: short (150-250 word) think pieces covering a wide range of topics related to ministry and church life, such as culture, worship, generational issues, church/community, trends, evangelism, surveys, time management, and humor."
> ** 2009 Award of Merit—Christian Ministries. 2008, 2007 EPA Award of Excellence— Christian Ministry. This periodical was #15 on the 2009 Top 50 Christian Publishers list (#43 in 2008, #47 in 2006).

$ THE EVANGELICAL BAPTIST, PO Box 457, Guelph, ON N1H 6K9, Canada. (519) 821-4830, ext. 229. Fax (519) 821-9829. E-mail: eb@fellowship.ca. Website: www.fellowship.ca. Fellowship of Evangelical Baptist Churches in Canada. Jennifer Bugg, mng. ed. To enhance the life & ministry of pastors and leaders in local churches. Quarterly mag. Subscription $12. Query preferred. Pays .05/wd. on publication for onetime rts. Articles 800-2,400 words; book reviews 200-500 words. Guidelines on Website.

$ + @ FOURSQUARE LEADER (formerly *Advance*), 1910 W. Sunset Blvd., Ste. 400, PO Box 26902, Los Angeles CA 90026-0176. Toll-free (888) 635-4234. (213) 989-4230. Fax (213) 989-4590. E-mail: comm@foursquare.org, or through Website: www.foursquarechurch.org. International Church of the Foursquare Gospel. Marcia Graham, ed. For credentialed Foursquare leaders. 5x/yr & online mag. with bonus missions issue & online version; 20 pgs.; circ. 10,000. Subscription free. Estab. 2009. 100 percent assigned. Query/clips. No full mss by e-mail. Payment negotiated. Pays on publication for all rts. Articles 800-2,000 words; book/music/video reviews 150 words. Responds in 4 wks. Seasonal 4 mos. ahead. No simultaneous submissions or reprints. Requires e-mail submissions (attached file). Kill fee negotiable. Uses some sidebars. Prefers NKJV. Guidelines by mail/e-mail/Website; free copy on request. (No ads)

> **Tips:** "Query only via e-mail on relevant real-life topics related to Foursquare ministry."

$ GROWTH POINTS, PO Box 892589, Temecula CA 92589-2589. Phone/fax (951) 506-3086. E-mail: cgnet@earthlink.net. Website: www.churchgrowthnetwork.com. Dr. Gary L. McIntosh, ed. For pastors and church leaders interested in church growth. Monthly newsletter; 2 pgs.; circ. 8,000. Subscription $16. 10 percent unsolicited freelance; 90 percent assigned. Query; fax/e-query OK. Pays $25 for onetime rts. Not copyrighted. Articles 1,000-2,000 words (2/yr.). Responds in 4 wks. Accepts simultaneous submissions & reprints. Accepts requested ms on disk. Does not use sidebars. Guidelines by mail; copy for #10 SAE/1 stamp. (No ads)

> **Tips:** "Write articles that are short (1,200 words), crisp, clear, with very practical ideas that

church leaders can put to use immediately. All articles must have a pro-church-growth slant, be very practical, have how-to material, and be very tightly written with bullets, etc."

$ **INSIGHT YOUTH RESOURCE**, (formerly *Cornerstone Youth Resource*), 55 W. Oak Ridge Dr., Hagerstown MD 21740. E-mail: iyr_editor@yahoo.com. Seventh-day Adventist. Patricia Humphrey, ed. For Christian youth leaders; a practical resource filled with ideas for creative youth ministry and programming. Quarterly mag.; 48 pgs.; circ. 2,200. 5 percent unsolicited freelance; 95 percent assigned. Query/clips; fax query OK; best to e-mail, as editor lives in Texas. Pays $25-350 on acceptance for nonexclusive full rts. Articles 700-900 words (16/yr.). Responds in 8-12 wks. Seasonal 12 mos. ahead. Accepts reprints (tell when/where appeared). Accepts e-mail submissions (attached file in Microsoft Word). No kill fee. Regularly uses sidebars. Prefers KJV, NKJV, NIV. Also accepts submissions from teens. Guidelines by mail/e-mail; copy for 9 x 12 SAE/$2.38 postage (mark "Media Mail"). (Ads)

> **Columns/Departments:** Outreach Ideas (service activity ideas for teens), 800-1,000 words; Super Social Suggestions (social activities and games for teen groups), 800-1,000 words; Program Ideas (creative youth programming ideas), variable lengths.
>
> **Special Needs:** Articles dealing with understanding and teaching youth. Innovative concepts in youth ministry.
>
> **Tips:** "Areas most open to freelancers are the Super Social and Outreach Ideas. We are always looking for creative activity ideas that teen leaders can do with youth, ages 14-18. The activities should be fun to do and well written with clear, easy-to-follow instructions. Ideas that are tested and have worked well with your own youth group are preferred."

$ **INSITE**, PO Box 62189, Colorado Springs CO 80962-2189. (719) 260-9400. Fax (719) 260-6398. E-mail: editor@ccca.org, or info@ccca.org. Website: www.ccca.org. Christian Camp and Conference Assn. Alison Phillips, ed. To inform and inspire professionals serving in the Christian camp and conference community. Bimonthly mag.; 40 pgs.; circ. 9,000. Subscription $29.95. 15 percent unsolicited freelance; 85 percent assigned. Query; e-query OK. Pays .20/wd. on publication for 1st and electronic rts. Cover articles 1,500-2,000 words (12/yr.); features 1,200-1,500 words (30/yr.); sidebars 250-500 words (15-20/yr.) Responds in 4 wks. Seasonal 6 mos. ahead. Accepts simultaneous submissions & reprints (tell when/where appeared). Prefers e-mail submission (attached file). Kill fee. Regularly uses sidebars. Prefers NIV. Guidelines on Website; copy $4.95/10 x 13 SAE/$1.73 postage. (Ads)

> **Special Needs:** Outdoor setting; purpose & objectives; administration & organization; personnel development; camper/guest needs; programming; health & safety; food service; site/facilities maintenance; business/operations; marketing & PR; relevant spiritual issues; fund-raising.
>
> **Tips:** "Most open to profiles and how-to pieces; get guidelines, then query first. Don't send general camping-related articles. We print stories specifically related to Christian camp and conference facilities; innovative programs or policies; how a Christian camp or conference experience affected a present-day leader. Review several issues so you know what we're looking for."
>
> ** 2008, 2006, 2005, 2004 EPA Award of Merit—Christian Ministries; 2007 EPA Award of Excellence—Christian Ministries; 2006 EPA Award of Merit—Most Improved Publication.

$ @ **INTERPRETER and INTERPRETER ONLINE**, PO Box 320, Nashville TN 37202-0320. (615) 742-5407. Fax (615) 742-5460. E-mail: knoble@umcom.org, or through Website: www .InterpreterMagazine.org. United Methodist Church. Joey Butler, mng. ed.; Kathy Noble, ed. For lay leaders and pastors of the United Methodist Church; focus on ministry ideas & resources, spiritual-growth issues, with a practical slant. Bimonthly & online mag.; 44+ pgs.; circ. 225,000. Subscription $12. Some assigned freelance; very little unsolicited material. Query/clips. Pays on acceptance for all rts. Articles 500-1,000 words (6 print/yr.; some Web exclusive). Seasonal 6 mos. ahead. No simultaneous submissions or reprints. Use submission form on Website or submit via e-mail. No kill fee. Uses some sidebars. Prefers NRSV. Guidelines on Website; copy for 9 x 12 SAE/4 stamps. (Ads)

> **Columns/Departments:** Lighter Fare (limited/occasional humor), Leadership Link (leadership theory & practice), IdeaMart (resources to support local church ministry), The World is My Parish (stories of United Methodists around the world); all 200-250 words; payment varies.
>
> **Tips:** "All articles must have a specific and prominent United Methodist connection. Very difficult for unsolicited freelancers to break in, as we have an excellent pool and depend on them for referrals. No stories about organizations, ministries, missions with an official United Methodist equivalent. All writers must have an understanding of United Methodist organization."
>
> ** This periodical was #19 on the 2005 Top 50 Christian Publishers list. Received awards from the Associated Church Press in 2008 and United Methodist Assn. of Communicators in 2007.

THE JOURNAL OF PASTORAL CARE & COUNSELING, 1549 Clairmont Rd., Ste. 103, Decatur GA 30033-4635. (404) 320-0195. Fax (404) 320-0849. E-mail: MngEd@jpcp.org. Website: www .jpcp.org. Dr. Terry R. Bard, mng. ed. For chaplains/pastors/professionals involved with pastoral care and counseling in other than a church setting. Quarterly jour.; 116 pgs.; circ. 10,000. Subscription $35. 95 percent unsolicited freelance; 5 percent assigned. Query; phone/fax/e-query OK. **PAYS 10 COPIES** for 1st rts. Articles 5,000 words or 20 pgs. (30/yr.); book reviews 5 pgs. Responds in 8 wks. Accepts requested ms electronically (instructions on Website). Does not use sidebars. Guidelines on Website; no copy. (Ads)

> **Poetry:** Accepts 16/yr. Free verse; 5-16 lines. Submit max. 3 poems.
>
> **Special Needs:** "We publish brief (500-600 words) 'Personal Reflections,' but they need to deal with clinical experiences that have led the writer to reflect on the religious and/or theological meaning generated."
>
> **Tips:** "Most open to poems and personal reflections. Readers are highly trained clinically, holding professional degrees in religion/theology. Writers need to be professionals on topics covered."

JOURNAL OF THE AMERICAN SOCIETY FOR CHURCH GROWTH, c/o Dr. Gary L. McIntosh, ed., Talbot School of Theology, 13800 Biola Ave., LaMirada CA 90639. (562) 944-0351. Fax (562) 906-4502. E-mail: gary.mcintosh@biola.edu. Website: www.ascg.org. American Society for Church Growth. Dr. Gary L. McIntosh, ed. Targets professors, pastors, denominational executives, and seminary students interested in church growth and evangelism. Biannual jour. (winter & summer); 150 pgs.; circ. 400. Subscription $24. 66 percent unsolicited freelance; 33 percent assigned. Complete ms/cover letter; phone/fax/e-query OK. **PAYS IN COPIES** for onetime rts. Not copyrighted. Articles 15 pgs. or 4,000-5,000 words (10/yr.); book reviews 750-2,000 words. Responds in 8-12 wks. Accepts simultaneous submissions & reprints (tell when/where appeared). Prefers requested ms on disk or by e-mail. Does not use sidebars. Any Bible version. Guidelines by mail (also in journal)/ theme list; copy $10. (Ads)

> **Tips:** "Provide well-researched and tightly written articles related to some aspect of church growth. Articles should be academic in nature, rather than popular in style. We're open to new writers at this time."

$ @ **LEADERSHIP**, 465 Gundersen Dr., Carol Stream IL 60188. (630) 260-6200. Fax (630) 260-0451. E-mail: LJEditor@LeadershipJournal.net. Website: www.leadershipjournal.net. Christianity Today Intl. Marshall Shelley, ed-in-chief. Practical help for pastors/church leaders, covering the spectrum of subjects from personal needs to professional skills. Quarterly & online jour.; 104 pgs.; circ. 48,000. Subscription $24.95. 20 percent unsolicited freelance; 80 percent assigned. Query or complete ms/cover letter; fax/e-query OK. Accepts full mss by e-mail. Pays .15-20/wd. on acceptance for 1st & electronic rts. Articles 500-3,000 words (10/yr.).; book reviews 100 words (pays $25-50). Responds in 6 wks. Seasonal 6 mos. ahead. Accepts reprints (tell when/where appeared). Accepts requested ms by e-mail (copied into message or attached Word doc). Kill fee 30 percent. Regularly uses sidebars. Prefers NLT. Guidelines on Website; copy for 9 x 12 SAE/$2 postage. (Ads)

> **Fillers:** Buys 80/yr. Cartoons, short humor; to 150 words; $25-50.
>
> **Columns/Departments:** Skye Jethani, mng. ed. Buys 12/yr. Tool Kit (practical stories or resources for preaching, worship, outreach, pastoral care, spiritual formation, & administration); 100-700 wds. Complete ms. Pays $50-250.
>
> **Tips:** "Leadership is a practical journal for pastors. Tell real-life stories of church life—defining moments—dramatic events. What was learned the hard way—by experience. We look for articles that provide practical help for problems church leaders face, not essays expounding on a topic, editorials arguing a position, or homilies explaining biblical principles. We want 'how-to' articles based on first-person accounts of real-life experiences in ministry in the local church."
>
> ** 2008 Award of Merit—General; 2009 & 2006 Award of Excellence—Christian Ministries; 2007 EPA Award of Merit—Christian Ministries. This periodical was #21 on the 2009 Top 50 Christian Publishers list (#18 in 2008, #15 in 2007, #14 in 2006, #8 in 2005).

$ LEAD MAGAZINE, 55 W. Oak Ridge Dr., Hagerstown MD 21740. (301) 393-4095. Fax (301) 393-4055. E-mail: fcrumbly@rhpa.org, or sabbathscholleadership@rhpa.org. Website: www.mylead magazine.org. Seventh-day Adventist/Review & Herald. Faith Crumbly, ed. Nurtures, educates, and supports adult Bible study and program leaders by providing training in leadership & interpersonal skills, plus programs. Monthly mag.; 32 pgs.; circ. 8,100. Subscription $34.95 (add $6 for addresses outside U.S., Canada, & Bermuda). 10 percent unsolicited freelance; 90 percent assigned. Complete ms. Pays $25-100 on acceptance for 1st rts. Articles 600-1,200 words (120-150/yr.). Responds in 1-2 wks. Seasonal 6-8 mos. ahead. Accepts reprints (tell when/where appeared). Prefers accepted ms by e-mail (attached file). Uses some sidebars. Guidelines/theme list on Website; copy for $2.36 in postage. (For ads, contact Genia Blumenberg at gblumenberg@rhpa.org.)

> **Columns/Departments:** Buys 5/yr. Tool Kit (interpersonal skills, organization, mentoring, training), 600-800 wds. Query. Pays $70-100.

$ LET'S WORSHIP, One Lifeway Plaza, MSN 175, Nashville TN 37234-0170. (615) 251-3775. Fax (615) 251-2795. E-mail: craig.adams@lifeway.com. Website: www.lifeway. com. Southern Baptist/LifeWay Christian Resources. Craig Adams, ed-in-chief. Resources for pastors and worship leaders; countering the norm with contagious ideas. Quarterly mag.; 96 pgs.; circ. 5,500. Subscription $14.95. 10 percent unsolicited freelance; 90 percent assigned. Complete ms by e-mail only. Pays .105/wd. on acceptance for all, 1st, or onetime rts. Articles 1,500 words (50/yr.); book reviews 300 words ($50). Responds in 10 wks. Seasonal 10 mos. ahead. Accepts simultaneous submissions. Requires ms by e-mail (attached file or copied into message). Regularly uses sidebars. Prefers HCSB. No guidelines/copy. (No ads)

> **Columns/Departments:** Wednesday Words (4-week Bible study with listening sheets); Bible study, 625 words; church choir; instrumental music; worship media; student worship; children's worship; listening sheet, 200 words; drama (original scripts), 900 words.
>
> **Special Needs:** New worship songs, staff communication tools and tips, fresh hymn arrangements, children's worship ideas, media techniques and tools, drama scripts, puppet scripts, singing techniques & exercises, etc.
>
> **Tips:** "This periodical exists to bring the entire church staff to the same page with regards to worship culture in the church community."

$ @ THE LIVING CHURCH, PO Box 514036, Milwaukee WI 53203-3436. Toll-free (800) 211-2771. (414) 276-5420. Fax (414) 276-7483. E-mail: tlc@livingchurch.org. Website: www.livingchurch .org. Episcopal/The Living Church Foundation Inc. John Schuessler, mng. ed. Independent news coverage of the Episcopal Church for clergy and lay leaders. Weekly & online mag.; 24+ pgs.; circ. 9,000. Subscription $42.50. Open to freelance. Query; phone/fax/e-query OK. Pays $25-100 (for solicited articles; nothing for unsolicited) for onetime rts. Articles 1,000 words (10/yr.). Responds in 2-4 wks. Seasonal 2 mos. ahead. Prefers requested ms by e-mail (attached or copied into message). Uses some sidebars. Guidelines by mail/e-mail; free copy. (Ads)

> **Columns/Departments:** Accepts 5/yr. Benediction (devotional/inspirational), 200 wds. Complete ms. No payment.
>
> **Tips:** "Most open to features, as long as they have something to do with the Episcopal Church."

LUTHERAN FORUM, PO Box 327, Delhi NY 13753-0327. (607) 746-7511. E-mail: dkralpb@aol .com. Website: www.lutheranforum.org. American Lutheran Publicity Bureau. Sarah Hinlicky Wilson, ed. (editor@lutheranforum.org). For church leadership—clerical and laity. Quarterly mag.; 64 pgs.; circ. 3,200. Subscription $26.95. 20 percent unsolicited freelance; 80 percent assigned. E-query only. **PAYS 2 COPIES** for onetime rts. Articles 2,000-3,000 words (48/yr.) Responds in 26-32 wks. No simultaneous submissions or reprints. Accepts full mss by e-mail only (attached file). Does not use sidebars. Prefers ESV. Guidelines/theme list on Website; copy for 9 x 12 SAE/$8. (Ads)

> **Poetry:** Accepts 2-8/yr. Avant-garde, free verse, traditional. Submit max. 5 poems.
>
> **Special Needs:** Hymns written by Lutheran composers only. Submit to Sally Messner, messner@lutheranforum.org.
>
> **Tips:** "Review the departments on our Website and read back issues. 95 percent of material is by Lutheran writers. Clarity of expression and sophistication of theological analysis are essential. No devotions or personal essays."

$ @ LUTHERAN PARTNERS, 8765 W. Higgins Rd., Chicago IL 60631-4101. Toll-free (800) 638-3522, ext. 2884. (773) 380-2884. Fax (773) 380-2829. E-mail: Lutheran_partners@ecunet .org. Website: www.elca.org/lutheranpartners. Evangelical Lutheran Church in America. Submit to William A. Decker, ed.; David von Schlichten, book review ed. (drdlphn@yahoo.com); Geoffrey L. Scott, video review ed. (revgeoff@welcome2clc.org). To encourage and challenge rostered leaders in the ELCA, including pastors and lay ministers. Bimonthly & online mag.; 40 pgs.; circ. 20,000. Subscription $13 (free to leaders), $19.50 outside North America. 10-15 percent unsolicited freelance; 85-90 percent assigned. Query; phone/fax/e-query OK. Pays $125-170 on publication for onetime rts. Articles 750-1,500 words (12-15/yr.). Responds in 16 wks. Seasonal 6-12 mos. ahead. Accepts simultaneous submissions & reprints (tell when/where appeared). Kill fee (rare). Prefers requested ms on disk or by e-mail (attached file). Regularly uses sidebars. Prefers NRSV. Guidelines/ theme list by mail/e-mail/Website; copy $2/9 x 12 SAE/5 stamps. (Ads)

> **Poetry:** Buys 6/yr. Free verse, traditional; $50-75. Keep concise. Submit max. 6 poems.
>
> **Fillers:** Buys 4-5/yr. Cartoons; ideas for parish ministry; to 500 words; $25.
>
> **Special Needs:** Book reviews. Query the editor. Uses books predominately from mainline denominational and some evangelical publishers. Payment is copy of book. Youth and family issues, rural and urban ministry issues, men's issues. More articles from women and ethnic authors (especially if ordained or are in official lay-ministry leadership roles).
>
> **Tips:** "Query me with ideas which show you know our audience, can feel their heartbeats, and walk in their shoes. First, we are a leadership publication. Our audience includes pastors and lay church staff. Your articles must answer concerns that leadership has. Secondly, understand Lutheran Church theology and ELCA congregational life. Pertinent topics include preaching, Christian education, youth and family issues, Lutheran identity, worship, Scripture and theology, and social issues."

** This periodical was #44 on the 2009 Top 50 Christian Publishers list (#28 in 2008, #48 in 2007).

$ MINISTRY & LITURGY, 160 E. Virginia St., #290, San Jose CA 95112. Toll-free (888) 273-7782. (408) 286-8505. Fax (408) 287-8748. E-mail: editor@rpinet.com. Website: www.rpinet.com/ml. Resource Publications Inc. Donna M. Cole, ed. dir. To help liturgists and ministers make the imaginative connection between liturgy and life. Monthly (10x) mag.; 50 pgs.; circ. 20,000. Subscription $50. 5 percent unsolicited freelance; 5 percent assigned. Query only; fax/e-query OK. Pays $50-200 on publication for 1st rts. Articles & fiction 1,500 words (30/yr.). Responds in 4 wks. Seasonal 6 mos. ahead. Accepts reprints (tell when/where appeared). Requires requested ms on disk. Regularly uses sidebars. Guidelines/theme list by mail; copy $4/11 x 14 SAE/2 stamps. (Ads)

Special Needs: The practice of ministry: music ministry, youth ministry, pastoral ministry, and liturgical ministry.

Contest: Visual Arts Awards.

Tips: "Writers need to be able to help our reader do his or her job better. Be familiar enough with contemporary issues in ministry to provide perceivable value to the reader. Provide new insight or valuable insight into issues of concern to members of a ministry team. Credibility (training and experience in ministry) is important."

@ MINISTRY IN MOTION E-ZINE, 7357 Brandtvista Ave., Huber Heights OH 45424-3330. (932) 233-6594. E-mail: hanover@dbmim.net. Website: www.ministryinmotion.net. Nondenominational. Thomas Hanover, ed. We seek to equip lay and clergy leaders for ministry in the 21st century through the resources of publications, coaching, consulting, and other Website tools. Bimonthly e-zine; circulation 1,000+. Subscription free online. 25 percent unsolicited freelance; 75 percent assigned. Query; e-query OK. Accepts full mss by e-mail. **NO PAYMENT** for onetime & electronic rts. Articles 1,000-1,200 words (10-12/yr.); book reviews 750 words. Responds in 2 wks. Seasonal 3 mos. ahead. Accepts simultaneous submissions & reprints (tell when/where appeared). Prefers submissions by e-mail (attached file). Regularly uses sidebars. Prefers NIV or NRSV. Guidelines on Website; copy by e-mail/Website. (Ads)

Fillers: Short humor.

Columns/Departments: Accepts 4-6/yr. Ministry Employment (how to find employment in ministry field); Women's Ministries (how to lead effective women's ministries); 700-1,000 wds. Query.

Tips: "Share leadership tips and insights. The more practical and how-to, the better. No theology or heavily scholastic articles; we are for the everyday church worker. Avoid church culture terms and lingo related to your own denomination. If no experience, send us some samples. We'll work with you."

$ MINISTRY MAGAZINE: International Journal for Pastors, 12501 Old Columbia Pike, Silver Spring MD 20904. (301) 680-6510. Fax (301) 680-6502. E-mail: MinistryMagazine@gc.adventist .org. Website: www.ministrymagazine.org. Seventh-day Adventist. Nikolaus Satelmajer, ed.; Willie E. Hucks II, assoc. ed. For pastors. Monthly jour.; 32 pgs.; circ. 19,000. Subscription $30.50. 90 percent unsolicited freelance. Query; fax/e-query OK. Pays $50-300 on acceptance for all rts. Articles 1,000-1,500 words; book reviews 100-150 words ($25). Responds within 13 wks. Prefers requested ms by e-mail. Uses some sidebars. Guidelines/theme list by mail/Website; copy for 9 x 12 SAE/5 stamps. (Ads)

$ @ MINISTRY TODAY, 600 Rinehart Rd., Lake Mary FL 32746. (407) 333-0600. Fax (407) 333-7133. E-mail: ministrytoday@strang.com. Website: www.ministrytodaymag.com. Strang Communications. Submit to The Editor. Helps for pastors and church leaders, primarily in Pentecostal/charismatic churches. Bimonthly & online mag.; 112 pgs.; circ. 30,000. Subscription $24.95. 60-80 percent freelance. Query; fax/e-query preferred. Pays $50 or $500-800 on publication for all rts.

Articles 1,800-2,500 words (25/yr.); book/music/video reviews, 300 words, $25. Responds in 4 wks. Prefers accepted ms by e-mail. Kill fee. Regularly uses sidebars. Prefers NIV. Guidelines by mail; copy $6/9 x 12 SAE. For free subscription to online version go to: www.digital.ministrytoday.com/ signup. (Ads)

> **Tips:** "Most open to columns. Write for guidelines and study the magazine. Please correspond with editor before sending an article proposal."

$ @ NET RESULTS, 300 W. Blvd. N., Columbia MO 65203. (806) 726-8094, ext. 198. Fax (806) 762-8873. E-mail: submissions@netresults.org, or netresults@netresults.org. Website: www.net results.org. Net Results Inc. Bill Tenny-Brittian, sr. ed. (billtb@netresults.org). Offers Christian church leaders practical, ministry-vitalization ideas & methods. Digital mag.; 32 pgs.; circ. 12,000. Subscription $49.95 for digital. 20 percent unsolicited freelance; 80 percent assigned. Query; fax/e-query OK. Accepts full ms through e-mail. Now pays a small amount on publication for onetime rts. Articles 1,000-2,000 words (20/yr.). Response time varies. Seasonal 6 mos. ahead. No simultaneous submissions or reprints. Requires accepted ms by e-mail (attached file). No kill fee. Regularly uses sidebars. Prefers TNIV. Copy for 9 x 12 SAE. (Limited ads)

> **Tips:** "We prefer practical, how-to articles on ideas that have worked in a local church setting."

$ @ THE NEWSLETTER NEWSLETTER, PO Box 36269, Canton OH 44735. Toll-free (800) 992-2144. E-mail: jburns@comresources.com or through Website: www.newsletternewsletter.com. Communication Resources. John Burns, ed. To help church secretaries and church newsletter editors prepare their newsletter. Monthly & online newsletter; 14 pgs. Subscription $49.95. 100 percent assigned. Complete ms; e-query OK. Pays $50-150 on acceptance for all rts. Articles 800-1,000 words (12/yr.). Responds in 4 wks. Seasonal 4 mos. ahead. Accepts simultaneous submissions. Requires requested ms by e-mail. Kill fee. Guidelines by mail/e-mail.

> **Tips:** "Most open to how-to articles on various aspects of newsletter production—writing, graphics, layout and design, postal, printing, etc."

$ OUTREACH MAGAZINE, 2230 Oak Ridge Way, Vista CA 92081-8341. (760) 940-0600. Fax (760) 597-2314. E-mail: llowry@outreach.com. Website: www.outreachmagazine.com. Lindy Lowry, ed. Tells the ideas, insights, and stories of today's outreach-focused churches and is designed to inspire, challenge, and equip churches to connect with their communities and show the love of God to people both locally and globally. Bimonthly mag.; 130 pgs.; circ. 35,000. Subscription $29.95. 20 percent unsolicited freelance; 80 percent assigned. Query/clips; e-query OK. Pays $400 for articles; $700-1,000 for feature articles; on publication for 1st rts. Articles 1,200-2,500 wds. Responds in 6-8 wks. Seasonal 6 mos. ahead. No simultaneous submissions; rarely accepts reprints (tell when/ where appeared). Prefers submissions by e-mail (attached file). Sometimes pays kill fee. Regularly uses sidebars. Guidelines on Website; free copy. (Ads)

> **Columns/Departments:** Accepts fewer than 10/yr. Pulse (tight & bright stories about churches finding unique ways to outreach), 50-250 words; From the Frontline (profile of one church & the unique way it's reaching its community), 800 words; SoulFires (as-told-to pieces from interview with someone doing outreach), 950 words; .30/wd. or flat fee. Query.
> **Special Needs:** Interviews with non-Christians.
> **Tips:** "Most open to interviews/profiles (Soulfires, Frames, The Outreach Interview); church stories (Pulse, Idea Bank, From the Front Line); outreach ideas from churches (Idea Bank, Connections, Big Idea).

$ PARISH LITURGY, 16565 S. State St., South Holland IL 60473. (708) 331-5485. Fax (708) 331-5484. E-mail: acp@acpress.org. Website: www.americancatholicpress.org. American Catholic Press. Father Michael Gilligan, ed. dir. A planning tool for Sunday and holy day liturgy. Quarterly mag.; 40 pgs.; circ. 1,200. Subscription $24. 5 percent unsolicited freelance. Query; no phone/e-query. Pays variable rates for all rts. Articles 400 wds. Responds in 4 wks. Seasonal 4 mos. ahead. Accepts simultaneous submissions & reprints (tell when/where appeared). Uses some sidebars. Prefers NAB. No guidelines; copy available. (No ads)

Tips: "We only use articles on the liturgy—period. Send us well-informed articles on the liturgy."

PLUGGED IN, Colorado Springs CO 80920 (no street address needed). Toll-free (800) 232-6459. (719) 531-3400. Fax (719) 548-5823. E-mail: waliszrs@fotf.org, or pluggedin@family.org. Website: www.pluggedinonline.com. Focus on the Family. Steven Isaac, ed.; Bob Smithhouser, sr. ed. To assist parents and youth leaders in better understanding popular youth culture and equip them to impart principles of discernment to young people. Monthly newsletter; circ. 43,000. Subscription $24. Open to queries only. Articles. Incomplete topical listings. (No ads)

PREACHING, PREACHING ON-LINE, & PREACHING NOW, 750 Old Hickory Blvd., Ste. 150-1, Brentwood TN 37027. (615) 386-3011. Fax (615) 312-4277. E-mail: editor@preaching.com. Website: www.preaching.com. Salem Communications. Dr. Michael Duduit, ed. Bimonthly; circ. 9,000. Subscription $24.95/2 yrs. 50 percent unsolicited freelance; 50 percent assigned. Query; fax/e-query OK. **PAYS A SUBSCRIPTION** for onetime & electronic rts. Responds in 4-8 wks. Seasonal 10-12 mos. ahead. Reprints from books only. Prefers requested ms by e-mail (attached file). Uses some sidebars. Guidelines on Website; copy online. (ads). *Preaching Online* is a professional resource for pastors that supplements Preaching Magazine. Includes all content from magazine, plus additional articles and sermons. Feature articles, 2,000-2,500, $50. Sermons 1,500-2,000 words; $35. Preaching Now is a weekly e-mail/e-zine; circ. 19,000. No freelance submissions; accepts books for review. Guidelines on Website; copy $8. (Ads)

$ PREACHINGTODAY.COM, 465 Gundersen Dr., Carol Stream IL 60188-2498. Toll-free (877) 247-4787. (630) 260-6200. Fax (630) 260-0451. E-mail: blarson@christianitytoday.com. Website: www.preachingtoday.com. Christianity Today Intl. Brian Larson, ed. Open to fresh sermon illustrations from various sources for preachers (no recycled illustrations from other illustration sources). E-mail submissions only; use online submission form. Articles 250-500 wds. Responds in 1 mo. Guidelines on Website. Sermon illustrations only.

$ PREACHING WELL, PO Box 3102, Margate NJ 08402. Toll-free (800) 827-9401. (609) 822-9401. Fax (609) 822-1638. E-mail: techsupport@voicings.com. Website: www.voicings.com. Voicings Publications. James Colaianni Jr., pub. Sermon illustration resource for professional clergy. Monthly newsletter, 8 pgs. Subscription $47. 5 percent unsolicited freelance. Complete ms; e-query OK. Pays .10/wd. on publication for any rts. Illustrations/anecdotes 50-250 wds. Responds in 6 wks. Seasonal 4 mos. ahead. Accepts reprints. Prefers requested ms on disk or by e-mail. Guidelines/topical index by mail/e-mail; copy for 9 x 12 SAE. (Ads)

Poetry: Light verse, traditional; 50-250 lines; .10/wd. Submit max. 3 poems.

Fillers: Various; sermon illustrations; 50-250 words; .10/wd.

Tips: "All sections open."

$ THE PRIEST, 200 Noll Plaza, Huntington IN 46750-4304. Toll-free: (800) 348-2440. (260) 356-8400. Fax (260) 359-9117. E-mail: tpriest@osv.com. Website: www.osv.com. Catholic/Our Sunday Visitor Inc. Msgr. Owen F. Campion, ed.; submit to Murray Hubley, assoc. ed. For Catholic priests, deacons, and seminarians; to help in all aspects of ministry. Monthly jour.; 48 pgs.; circ. 6,500. Subscription $39.95. 40 percent unsolicited freelance. Query (preferred) or complete ms/cover letter; phone/fax/e-query OK. Pays $50-250 on acceptance for 1st rts. Not copyrighted. Articles to 1,500 words (96/yr.); some 2-parts. Responds in 5-13 wks. Seasonal 3 mos. ahead. Uses some sidebars. Prefers disk or e-mail submissions (attached file). Prefers NAB. Guidelines on Website; free copy. (Ads)

Fillers: Murray Hubley, fillers ed. Cartoons; $35.

Columns/Departments: Buys 36/yr. Viewpoint, to 1,000 words; $75.
Tips: "Write to the point, with interest. Most open to nuts-and-bolts issues for priests, or features. Keep the audience in mind; need articles or topics important to priests and parish life. Include Social Security number."

$ @ PROCLAIM, PO Box 1561, New Canaan CT 06840. Toll-free (888) 320-5576. Fax (203) 966-4654. E-mail: meg@parishpublishing.org, or info@parishpublishing.org. Website: www.parishpub lishing.org. Parish Publishing LLC. Meg Brossy, ed. The leading inspirational preaching resource for church leaders. Weekly newsletter; 4 pgs. Subscription $69.95. Also available digitally at www .proclaimsermons.com for $59.95, which includes archives of sermons. 20 percent unsolicited freelance; 80 percent assigned. Query/clips. Pays to $100 on publication or acceptance for reprint rts. Articles or fiction. Responds in 2 wks. Seasonal 3 mos. ahead. Prefers accepted mss by e-mail (attached file). (No ads)
    Tips: "*Proclaim* follows the Catholic Lectionary and the Revised Common Lectionary (RCL). Writers are usually priests and ministers, or in seminary."

@ PULPIT HELPS, 6815 Shallowford Rd., Chattanooga TN 37421. Toll-free (800) 251-7206. (423) 894-6060. Fax (423) 894-1055. E-mail: publisher@pulpithelps.com. Website: www.pulpithelps .com. AMG International. Justin Lonas, pub. Primarily reaches Bible-believing Christian pastors and functions as their primary source for information for sermon preparation and news from the Christian world. Monthly & online; 40 pgs; circ. 12,000. Subscription $25. 10 percent unsolicited freelance; 70 percent assigned. Complete ms/cover letter; e-query OK. Accepts full mss by e-mail. **NO PAYMENT.** Articles 800-1,000 words (50-75/yr.); book reviews 250 words. Responds in 2-4 wks. Seasonal 2-3 mos. ahead. Accepts simultaneous submissions & reprints (tell when/where appeared). Requires e-mail submission (attached file). Uses some sidebars. Prefers NASB (others accepted). Guidelines by mail/e-mail; copy for 9 x 12 SAE/2 stamps. (Ads)
    Fillers: Accepts 50-100/yr. Anecdotes, cartoons, jokes, quotes, sermon illustrations, short humor, word puzzles; 25-150 words.
    Columns/Departments: Ted Kyle, mng. ed. (editor@pulpithelps.com) Accepts 2-4/yr. Missions Spotlight (innovative approaches to reaching the lost for Christ around the world); 800-1,200 words.
    Tips: "Most open to Sermon Starters—sermon outlines designed to give a busy pastor a leg up; any good missions-focused pieces; any good essays reflecting thoughtful Christian scholarship."

$ @ REFORMED WORSHIP, 2850 Kalamazoo S.E., Grand Rapids MI 49560-0001. Toll-free (800) 777-7270. (616) 224-0763. Toll-free fax (888) 642-8606. (616) 224-0803. E-mail: info@reformed worship.org. Website: www.reformedworship.org. Faith Alive Christian Resources. Rev. Joyce Borger, ed. To provide worship leaders and committees with practical assistance in planning, structuring, and conducting congregational worship in the Reformed tradition. Quarterly & online mag.; 48 pgs.; circ. 4,600. Subscription $25.95. 30 percent unsolicited freelance; 70 percent assigned. Query; e-query OK. Accepts full mss by e-mail. Pays .05/wd. on publication for 1st & electronic rts. Articles 1,400 words; book reviews 200 words. Responds in 4 wks. Seasonal 6 mos. ahead. Rarely accepts reprints (tell when/where appeared). Prefers e-mail submission (attached file). Uses some sidebars. Also accepts submissions from children/teens. Prefers TNIV. Guidelines on Website; copy for 9 x 12 SAE/$2.38 postage (mark "Media Mail"). (No ads)
    Columns/Departments: Songs for the Season (music and background notes, usually 3 songs), 2,000 words; Worship Technology (intersection of worship and technology), 900 words. Query.
    Tips: "Most open to liturgies for worship, prayers. Practical themes or ideas for worship that have been tried. You need to understand and focus on the Reformed tradition of worship."
    ** 2004 EPA Award of Merit—General.

$ REVIEW FOR RELIGIOUS, 3601 Lindell Blvd., St. Louis MO 63108-3393. (314) 633-4610. Fax (314) 633-4611. E-mail: review@slu.edu. Website: www.reviewforreligious.org. Catholic/Jesuits of Missouri Province. Rev. David L. Fleming, S.J., ed. A forum for shared reflection on the lives and experience of all who find that the church's rich heritages of spirituality support their personal and apostolic Christian lives. Quarterly mag.; 112 pgs.; circ. 4,000. Subscription $30. 100 percent unsolicited freelance. Complete ms/cover letter; no phone/fax/e-query. Accepts full ms by e-mail. Pays $6/printed pg. on publication for 1st rts. Articles 1,500-5,000 words (50/yr.). Responds in 9 wks. Seasonal 8 mos. ahead. Accepts requested ms on disk. Does not use sidebars. Prefers RSV, NAB. Guidelines on Website; copy for 10 x 13 SAE/5 stamps. (No ads)

> **Poetry:** Buys 10/yr. Light verse, traditional; 3-12 lines; $6. Submit max. 4 poems.
> **Tips:** "Read the journal. Do not submit an article without reading at least one issue. Submit an article based on our guidelines."

$ @ THE REVWRITER RESOURCE, PO Box 81, Perkasie PA 18944. Phone/fax (215) 453-8128. E-mail: editor@revwriter.com. Website: www.revwriter.com. Nondenominational/RevWriter Resources LLC. Rev. Susan M. Lang, ed. An electronic newsletter for busy lay and clergy congregational leaders. Monthly e-zine.; circ. 650. Subscription free. 90 percent unsolicited freelance; 10 percent assigned. Query; e-query preferred. Pays $20 on publication for 1st electronic rts. & one-year archival rts.; $10 for devotions. Articles 1,500 words; questions or exercises for group use, 250-500 words. No simultaneous submissions or reprints. Also accepts submissions from teens. Guidelines by e-mail/Website; copy online. (Ads)

> **Fillers:** Buys 10/yr. Ministry ideas; Ministry Resources List to accompany article; 250-400 wds. These are usually written by the feature-article writer. Also Practical Wisdom section.
> **Tips:** "I'm always looking for articles for the Practical Wisdom section, which focuses on program or ministry ideas that worked for you. This is an easy area to break into. They are short pieces, usually 250-400 wds. Articles should be practical how-tos for busy church leaders—materials they can use in their ministry settings. Be sure to read archived issues for previous formats and ministry resources already covered. Looking for a new approach to stewardship. Most open to devotion writing in Lent and Advent, and the monthly articles and discussion questions. Send me an e-query detailing the article you'd like to write and include your expertise in this area. The material must be practical and applicable to life as a busy congregational leader. They want information they can use."

SEWANEE THEOLOGICAL REVIEW, School of Theology, Box 46-W, Sewanee TN 37383-0001. (931) 598-1475. E-mail: STR@sewanee.edu. Website: www.sewanee.edu/theology/str/strhome .html. Anglican/Episcopal. Submit to Managing Editor. For Anglican/Episcopal clergy and interested laity. Quarterly jour.; 120 pgs. Subscription $24. Open to freelance. Complete ms/cover letter; no e-query. **NO PAYMENT** for all rts. Articles (24/yr.). Responds in 9-26 wks. Seasonal 24 mos. ahead. No simultaneous submissions or reprints. Prefers requested ms on disk or by e-mail (attached file). Prefers NRSV. No guidelines; copy $8. Incomplete topical listings. (Ads)

> **Special Needs:** Anglican and Episcopal theology, religion, history, doctrine, ethics, homiletics, liturgies, hermeneutics, biography, prayer, practice.

SHARING THE PRACTICE, c/o Central Woodward Christian Church, 3955 W. Big Beaver Rd., Troy MI 48084-2610. (248) 644-0512. Website: www.apclergy.org. Academy of Parish Clergy/Ecumenical/ Interfaith. Rev. Dr. Robert Cornwall, ed-in-chief (drbobcornwall@msn.com); Dr. Forrest V. Fitzhugh, book rev. ed. (s.spade@att.net). Growth toward excellence through sharing the practice of parish ministry. Quarterly international jour.; 40 pgs.; circ. 250 (includes 80 seminary libraries & publishers). Subscription $30/yr. (send to APC, 2249 Florinda St., Sarasota FL 34231-1414). 100 percent unsolicited freelance. Complete ms/cover letter; e-query OK; query/clips for fiction. **NO PAYMENT** for 1st, reprint, simultaneous, or electronic rts. Articles 500-2,500 words (25/yr.); reviews 500-

1,000 words. Responds in 2 wks. Seasonal 6 mos. ahead. Accepts simultaneous submissions & reprints (tell when/where appeared). Prefers e-mail submissions (copied into message). Uses some sidebars. Prefers NRSV. Guidelines/theme list by mail/e-mail; free copy. (No ads)

Poetry: Accepts 12/yr. Any type; 25-35 lines. Submit max. 2 poems.

Fillers: Accepts 6/yr. Anecdotes, cartoons, jokes, short humor; 50-100 wds.

Columns/Departments: Academy News; President's.

Contest: Book of the Year Award ($100+), Top Ten Books of the Year list, Parish Pastor of the Year Award ($200+). Inquire by e-mail to DIELPADRE@aol.com.

Tips: "We desire articles and poetry by practicing clergy of all kinds who wish to share their practice of ministry. Join the Academy."

$ @ SMALL GROUPS.COM, 465 Gundersen Dr., Carol Steam IL 60188. (630) 260-6200. Fax (630) 260-0451. E-mail: smallgroups@christianitytoday.com. Website: www.smallgroups.com. Christianity Today Intl. Sam O'Neal, mng. ed. Serves small group leaders and churches and provides training and curriculum that is easy to use. Weekly e-zine; circ. 50,000. Subscription $99. 10 percent unsolicited freelance; 50 percent assigned. Complete ms/cover letter; e-query OK. Accepts full mss by e-mail. Pays $50-100 for articles, $350-750 for curriculum, on acceptance for electronic & nonexclusive rts. Articles 750-1,500 words (50/yr.). Responds in 2 wks. Seasonal 2 mos. ahead. Accepts simultaneous submissions & reprints (tell when/where appeared). Prefers requested ms by e-mail (attached file). Some kill fees 50 percent. Does not use sidebars. Accepts reprints. Prefers NIV. Guidelines/copy by e-mail. (Ads)

Fillers: Small group cartoons.

Special Needs: Video Bible studies.

Tips: "It's best to submit articles that you have used to train and support small groups and leaders in your own church."

$ SUNDAY SERMONS, PO Box 3102, Margate NJ 08402. Toll-free (800) 827-9401. (609) 822-9401. Fax (609) 822-1638. E-mail: techsupport@voicings.com. Website: www.voicings.com. Voicings Publications. James Colaianni Jr., pub. Full-text sermon resource serving professional clergy since 1970. Bimonthly booklet; 60 pgs. Subscription $62 or $89. 5 percent unsolicited freelance. Complete ms; e-query OK. Pays .10/wd. on publication for any rts. Complete sermon manuscripts 1,200-1,500 words; illustrations/anecdotes 50-250 words. Responds in 6 wks. Seasonal 4 mos. ahead. Accepts reprints. Prefers requested ms on disk or by e-mail. Guidelines/topical index by mail/e-mail; copy for 9 x 12 SAE. Incomplete topical listings.

Fillers: Various; sermon illustrations; 50-250 words; .10/wd.

Tips: "Submit complete sermon, 1,200-1,500 wds. Read sample sermons on our Website."

@ TECHNOLOGIES FOR WORSHIP, 3891 Holborn Rd., Queensville ON L0G 1R0, Canada. (905) 473-9822. Fax (905) 473-9928. E-mail: krc@tfwm.com. Website: www.tfwm.com. ITC Inc. Kevin Rogers Cobus, ed. Bimonthly & online mag.; 92+ pgs.; circ. 35,000. Subscription $14.95. 100 percent unsolicited freelance. Query; phone/fax/e-query OK. **NO PAYMENT** for onetime rts. Articles 700-1,200 wds. Responds in 2 wks. Seasonal 2 mos. ahead. Accepts simultaneous submissions & reprints (tell when/where appeared). Prefers accepted ms by e-mail (attached or copied into message). Uses some sidebars. Guidelines/theme list by mail/Website; copy by mail. (Ads)

Special Needs: Website streaming resources for churches and ministries; technologies: audio, video, music, computers, broadcast, lighting, & drama; 750-2,500 words.

Tips: "Call/fax/e-mail the editor to discuss idea for article or column. The publication is open to technical, educational articles that can benefit the church, providing hints, tips, guidelines, examples, studies, tutorials, etc. on new technology and new uses for it in the church."

THEOLOGICAL DIGEST & OUTLOOK, 415 Linwell Rd., St. Catherines ON L2M 2P3, Canada. (905) 935-5369. Fax (905) 935-7134. E-mail: p-d@niagara.com or paul@firstgrantham.org.

Website: www.ITCanada.com/~theology. United Church of Canada. Rev. Paul Miller, ed. For clergy & informed laity; evangelical/orthodox slant within denomination. Semiannual mag.; 36 pgs.; circ. 400. Subscription $15 Cdn., $19 U.S. 100 percent unsolicited freelance. Complete ms; phone/fax/e-query OK. **NO PAYMENT**. Articles 1,500-5,000 words (6-8/yr.). Responds in 2 wks. Accepts reprints (tell when/where appeared). Prefers disk or e-mail submissions. Does not use sidebars. Any Bible version. No guidelines. (No ads)

> **Tips:** "Just submit."

$ TODAY'S PARISH, 1 Montauk Ave., Ste. 200, New London CT 06320. Toll-free (800) 321-0411, ext. 188 (editor). (860) 536-2611. Fax (860) 536-5674. E-mail: NWagner@twentythirdpublications .com. Websites: www.todaysparish.com or www.twentythirdpublications.com. Catholic/Twenty-Third Publications. Nick Wagner, ed. Practical ideas & issues relating to parish life, management, & ministry. Mag. published 7x/yr.; 40 pgs.; circ. 14,800. Subscription $24.95. Very little unsolicited freelance. Query or complete ms. Pays $75-100 on publication for 1st rts. Articles 800-1,800 words (15/yr.). Responds 13 wks. Seasonal 6 mos. ahead. Guidelines by mail; copy for 9 x 12 SASE.

$ @ TORCH LEGACY LEADER, PO Box 1733, Joshua TX 76058. Toll-free (877) TORCHLP. (404) 348-4478. Fax (817) 887-3089. E-mail: info@torchlegacy.com. Website: www.torchlegacy.com. Torch Ministries Intl. Daniel Whyte III, pres./ed. A biblically based journal for black church leaders & community leaders. Online jour. 60 percent unsolicited freelance; 40 percent assigned. Complete ms/cover letter; e-query OK. Pays $50 (flat fee) on publication for 1st rts. Best Black Sermon of the quarter receives $100 on publication. Articles 1,500 wds. Responds in 12 wks. Seasonal 6 mos. ahead. Requires requested ms on disk. Uses some sidebars. Prefers KJV. Guidelines by mail/e-mail/Website. Incomplete topical listings.

> **Special Needs:** Sermons; articles; essays on the spiritual, social, & moral crisis facing the black community in America, with biblically based solutions.
> **Tips:** "We are looking for sound, biblically based material that can be used by God to help lift up black America to where it needs to be in every area of life."

@ RICK WARREN'S MINISTRY TOOLBOX, 1 Saddleback Pkwy., Lake Forest CA 92630-2244. Toll-free (877) 727-8677. (949) 609-8703. E-mail: info@pastors.com. Website: www.pastors.com (archive: www.pastors.com/Legacy/RWMT/MTAchive.asp). Tobin Perry, ed. dir. To mentor pastors worldwide. Weekly e-zine; circ. 177,000. Free e-mail newsletter. 10 percent unsolicited freelance; 90 percent assigned. Query; e-query OK. **NO PAYMENT** for onetime, reprint, simultaneous, & electronic rts. Will link readers to your site or book on Amazon in exchange for article. Articles 800-1,000 words (250/yr.). Responds in 6-8 wks. Seasonal 4 mos. ahead. Accepts simultaneous submissions & reprints (tell when/where appeared). Prefers accepted ms by e-mail (attached file). Uses some sidebars. Guidelines/copy by e-mail. (No ads)

> **Special Needs:** Issues facing pastors and other ministry leaders. Time management, conflict resolution, facilitating change, communication & preaching, stewardship, worship, lay ministry, temptation, spiritual vitality, family matters, finances, creative ideas for ministry, vision, power, authority, encouragement, ministry & missions mobilization, small group leadership, facilitating spiritual growth, missions (specifically battling spiritual lostness, egocentric leadership, poverty, disease, & illiteracy locally & globally). Uses a lot of church leadership & pastoral book excerpts & articles adapted from books. The key is that the submission relates to church leaders, specifically pastors.
> **Tips:** "We're very open to freelance contributions. Although we are unable to pay, this is a worldwide ministry to pastors."

$ WORD & WORLD: Theology for Christian Ministry, 2481 Como Ave., St. Paul MN 55108. (651) 641-3210. Fax (651) 641-3354. Website: www.luthersem.edu/word&world. E.L.C.A./Luther Theological Seminary. Frederick J. Gaiser, ed. (fgaiser@luthersem.edu); Mark Thronveit, book rev.

ed. (mthrontv@luthersem.edu). Addresses ecclesiastical and general issues from a theological perspective & addresses pastors & church leaders with the best fruits of theological research. Quarterly jour.; 104 pgs.; circ. 2,500. Subscription $24. 10 percent unsolicited freelance. Complete ms/cover letter; phone query OK. Pays $50 on publication for all rts. Articles 3,500 wds. Responds in 2-8 wks. Guidelines/theme list on Website; copy $7.

> **Tips:** "Most open to general articles. We look for serious theology addressed clearly and interestingly to people in the practice of ministry. Creativity and usefulness in ministry are highly valued."

$ @ WORSHIP LEADER, 32234 Paseo Adelanto, Ste. A, San Juan Capistrano CA 92675-3622. Toll-free (888) 881-5861. (949) 240-9339. Fax (949) 240-0038. E-mail: editor@wlmag.com. Website: www.worshipleader.com. The Worship Leader Partnership. Julie Reid, exec. ed. A resource for current trends, theological insights, & planning programs for all those involved in church worship. Bimonthly (8x) & digital mag.; 64-72 pgs.; circ. 50,000. Subscription $19.95. 20 percent unsolicited freelance; 80 percent assigned. Query/clips or complete ms by fax/e-mail OK. Pays $200-800 for assigned, $200-500 for unsolicited, on publication for all or 1st rts. Articles 1,200-2,000 words (15-30/yr.); reviews 300 words. Responds in 6-13 wks. Seasonal 6 mos. ahead. Accepts e-mail submissions (attached file—MS Word). Kill fee 50 percent. Uses some sidebars. Prefers NIV. Guidelines/theme list on Website; copy $5. (Ads)

> **Tips:** "Read our magazine. Become familiar with our themes. Submit a detailed and well-thought-out idea that fits our vision."

$ YOUR CHURCH, 465 Gundersen Dr., Carol Stream IL 60188. (630) 260-6200. Fax (630) 260-0114. E-mail: YCEditor@yourchurch.net. Website: www.yourchurch.net. Christianity Today Intl. Submit to Matt Branaugh, ed. Gives pastors and church leaders practical information to help them in managing the business side of the church. Bimonthly trade journal; 52+ pgs.; circ. 75,000. Subscription free to church administrators. 10 percent unsolicited freelance; 90 percent assigned. Query/clips; phone/fax/e-query OK. Accepts full mss by e-mail. Pays .20/wd. on acceptance for 1st & electronic rts. Articles 1,000-2,000 words (10/yr.). Responds in 4 wks. Seasonal 6 mos. ahead. Accepts simultaneous submissions & reprints (tell when/where appeared). Prefers e-mail submission (attached file). Accepts full manuscripts by e-mail. Kill fee 50 percent. Regularly uses sidebars. Prefers NIV. Guidelines/theme list by e-mail; copy for 9 x 12 SASE. (Ads: 630-260-6202)

> **Fillers:** Buys 18/yr. Cartoons, $125.
>
> **Columns/Departments:** Query. Church Makeover (recent remodeling project), 500-700 wds, plus several high-resolution photos, before/after project; Ask the Experts (Q & A), 100-300 words; $50-200.
>
> **Special Needs:** Church management articles; audio/visual equipment; books/curriculum resources; music equipment; church products; furnishings; office equipment; computers/software; transportation (bus, van); video projectors; church architecture/construction.
>
> **Tips:** "Write and ask to be considered for an assignment; tell of your background, experience, strengths, and writing history. All areas are open to freelancers—articles on every topic we cover. Writers who can research a topic, interview experts, and present clear, concise writing should persistently and consistently ask for assignments. It might take several months to get an assignment."
>
> ** This periodical was #27 on the 2009 Top 50 Christian Publishers list (#16 in 2008, #12 in 2007, #13 in 2006, #16 in 2005).

$ @ YOUTHWORKER JOURNAL, c/o Salem Publishing, 150 Old Hickory Blvd., Ste. 150-1, Brentwood TN 37027. (615) 386-3011. Fax (615) 386-3380. E-mail: proposals@youthworker .com. Website: www.Youthworker. com. Salem Communications. Steve & Lois Rabey, eds. For youth workers/church & parachurch. Bimonthly & online jour.; 72 pgs.; circ. 15,000. Subscription

$39.95. 100 percent unsolicited freelance. Query or complete ms (only if already written); e-query preferred. Pays $50-300 on publication for 1st/perpetual rts. Articles 250-3,000 words (30/yr.); length may vary. Responds in 26 wks. Seasonal 6 mos. ahead. No reprints. Kill fee $50. Guidelines/theme list on Website: www.youthworker.com/editorial_guidelines.php; copy $5/10 x 13 SAE. (Ads)

> **Columns/Departments:** Buys 10/yr. International Youth Ministry, Technology in Youth Ministry.
>
> **Tips:** "Read Youthworker; imbibe its tone (professional, though not academic; conversational, though not chatty). Query me with specific, focused ideas that conform to our editorial style. It helps if the writer is a youth minister, but it's not required. Check Website for additional info, upcoming themes, etc. WorldView column on mission activities and trips is about only one open to outsiders."

TEEN/YOUNG ADULT MARKETS

$ @ BOUNDLESS WEBZINE, Focus on the Family, Colorado Springs CO 80995 (no street address needed). (719) 531-5181. Fax (719) 531-3349. E-mail: editor@boundless.org. Website: www.boundless.org. Focus on the Family. Ted Slater, ed. For Christian singles up to their mid-30s. Weekly e-zine; 200,000 visitors/mo.; 130 page views/mo. on blog. Free online. 5 percent unsolicited freelance; 95 percent assigned. Query/clips; e-query OK. Accepts full ms by e-mail. Pays .30/wd. on acceptance for nonexclusive rts. Articles 1,200-1,800 words (140/yr.). Responds in 4 wks. Seasonal 4 mos. ahead. Accepts simultaneous submissions & reprints (tell when/where appeared). Requires e-mail submission (attached—preferred—or copied into message). No kill fee. Does not use sidebars. Also accepts submissions from teens. Prefers ESV, NIV. Guidelines by mail/Website; copy online. (No ads)

> **Tips:** "See author guidelines on our Website. Most open to conversational, winsome, descriptive, and biblical."
>
> ** This periodical was #18 on the 2009 Top 50 Christian Publishers list (#12 in 2008, #25 in 2007, #24 in 2006, #23 in 2005).

@ CONNECTED, Box 6097, Lincoln NE 68506-0097. (402) 488-0981. Fax (402) 488-7582. E-mail: editor@christianrecord.org. Website: http://connected.christianrecord.org. Christian Record Services for the Blind. Bert Williams, ed. For visually impaired adults; for interdenominational Christian audience. E-zine. Not included in topical listings.

$ CREDO MAGAZINE, PO Box 419527, Kansas City MO 64141. (816) 931-1900. Fax (816) 412-8312. E-mail: credomag@barefootministries.com. Website: www.credomagazine.com. Barefoot Ministries/Nazarene Publishing House. Stefanie Hendrickson, ed. A cutting-edge devotional magazine that also challenges teens in their spiritual walk with relevant articles dealing with the issues they are facing. Monthly mag.; 48 pgs.; circ. 15,000. Subscription $23.40. 20-30 percent unsolicited freelance; 70-80 percent assigned. Query. Pays $30-60 for articles; $60 for fiction; on acceptance for all rts. Articles 500-800 words (20-30/yr.); fiction 700-800 words (10-15/yr.); reviews 500 words ($25). Responds in 4-6 wks. Seasonal 4-6 mos. ahead. No simultaneous submissions; accepts reprints (tell when/where appeared). Requires e-mail submission (attached or copied into message). Kill fee. Uses some sidebars. Prefers NIV. Encourages submissions from teens. Guidelines/theme list by mail/e-mail/Website); copy for 6 x 9 SAE/$1 postage (additional copies $1.95 ea.). (No ads)

> **Poetry:** Accepts 10-15/yr. Any type. Will be used in the magazine or on the Web. No payment. Submit any number.
>
> **Columns/Departments:** Buys 30-40/yr. Real Deal (life issues/relationships), 700-850 words; Kung Pao (features student's creative work—poetry, lyrics, short stories, essays, art, photos. etc.), 100-500 words; Unreal (fiction piece—looking for 4-6 part series with each part able to stand on its own), 800 words; Tune-Up (interviews/profiles/news on Christian

artists and bands), 800-850 words; Life Zone (articles about youth God is using in cool ways), 800 words; $40-60.

Special Needs: All topics must be geared to teens.

Tips: "We are most open to freelancers in the areas of Kung Pao (teens only), Tune-Up, Life Zone, and Unreal (fiction). Also to music and entertainment reviews."

** This periodical was #47 on the 2009 Top 50 Christian Publishers list (#42 in 2008, #18 in 2007, #9 in 2006).

$ @ DEVO'ZINE, PO Box 340004, Nashville TN 37203-0004. (615) 340-7247. Fax (615) 340-1783. E-mail: devozine@upperroom.org, or smiller@upperroom.org. Websites: www.devozine.org and www.devozine.info. Upper Room Ministries. Sandy Miller, ed. Devotional; to help teens (12-18) develop and maintain their connection with God and other Christians. Bimonthly online mag.; 80 pgs.; circ. 90,000. Subscription $21.95. 85 percent unsolicited freelance; 15 percent assigned. Query; phone/fax/e-query OK. Pays $25 for meditations, $100 for feature articles (assigned) on acceptance for these onetime rts.: newspaper, periodical, electronic, and software-driven rts., and the right to use in future anthologies. Meditations 150-250 words (350/yr.); articles 650-700 words; book/music/video reviews 650-700 words, $100. Responds in 16 wks. Seasonal 6-8 mos. ahead. Accepts occasional reprints (tell when/where appeared). Accepts requested ms by e-mail or online submission. Regular sidebars. Prefers NRSV, NIV, CEV. Guidelines/theme list on Website; copy/7 x 10 SASE. (No ads)

    Poetry: Buys 25-30/yr. Free verse, light verse, haiku, traditional; to 150 words or 10-20 lines; $25. Submit max. 1 poem/theme, 9 themes/issue.

    Tips: "E-mail with ideas for weekend features related to specific themes."

    ** This periodical was #1 on the 2009 Top 50 Christian Publishers list (#2 in 2008, #3 in 2007, #1 in 2006, #2 in 2005).

$ DIRECTION STUDENT MAGAZINE (formerly Clear Direction), PO Box 17306, Nashville TN 37217. (615) 361-1221. Fax (615) 367-0535. E-mail: clearmag@randallhouse.com. Website: www.randallhouse.com. Randall House. Jonathan Yandell, ed.; submit to Derek Lewis, ed. asst. Bringing junior high students to a closer relationship with Christ through devotionals, relevant articles, and pertinent topics. Quarterly mag.; 52 pgs.; circ. 5,300. Open to freelance. Complete ms/cover letter; query for fiction. Accepts full mss by e-mail. Pays $35-150 for nonfiction; $35-125 for fiction; on publication for 1st rts. Articles 600-1,500 words (35/yr.); book reviews 600-800 words ($35). Responds in 6 wks. Seasonal 9 mos. ahead. Accepts simultaneous submissions; no reprints. Prefers e-mail submissions (attached file). No kill fee. Regularly uses sidebars. Also accepts submissions from teens. Prefers KJV. Guidelines by e-mail/Website; copy for 9 x 12 SAE. (No ads)

    Columns/Departments: Buys 10/yr. Changing Lanes (describe how God is changing you), 600-800 words; Between the Lines (review of book selected by Randall House), 600-800 words; $35-50.

    Tips: "We are open to freelancers by way of articles and submissions to 'Changing Lanes' (600-800 words) and for feature articles (1,200-1,500 words). All articles should be about an aspect of the Christian life or contain a spiritual element, as the purpose of this magazine is to bring junior high students closer to Christ. We are happy to accept personal testimonies or knowledgeable articles on current hot topics and how they compare to biblical standards."

$ ESSENTIAL CONNECTION (EC), One Lifeway Plaza, Nashville TN 37234-0174. (615) 251-2008. Fax (615) 277-8271. E-mail: ec@lifeway.com. Website: www.lifeway.com. LifeWay Christian Resources of the Southern Baptist Convention. Mandy Crow, ed. Christian leisure reading and devotional guide for 7th-12th graders. Monthly mag.; 60 pgs.; circ. 120,000. Subscription $24.95. 10 percent unsolicited freelance; 90 percent assigned. Query; e-query OK. Pays $80-120 on acceptance for all rts. Articles 800-1,200 words (12/yr.); fiction 1,200 words (12/yr.). Responds in 10 wks. Seasonal 9 mos. ahead. No simultaneous submissions or reprints. Prefers e-mail submission (attached file or copied into message). No kill fee. Uses some sidebars. Prefers NIV. Guidelines by mail/e-mail; free copy. (No ads)

Poetry: Accepts 36/yr. All types. From teens only.

Special Needs: Always in search of Christian humor; sports profiles. Most open to fiction (send complete ms).

Tips: "We generally prefer writers to complete the writer process at www.lifeway.com/people."

EXODUS MAGAZINE, 1108 SW Tennessee Ave., Lawton OK 73501. E-mail: submissions@exodus mag.com. Website: www.exodusmag.com. Rochelle Moyd, pub. For an urban youth/young adult audience, ages 15-25, moderately to highly computer literate, and most likely a minority. Mag. Open to unsolicited freelance. Submit by mail or e-mail. NO PAYMENT for onetime rts. Articles 1,000-2,000 wds. Guidelines on Website.

Columns/Departments: Accepts many/yr., all 1,000-2,000 wds. Da Message (how to grow as Christians); Da Movement (profiles of youth groups or organizations); Story-2-Tell (testimonies); Young & Successful (young entrepreneurs); Shout! (submissions from youth); On the Grind (up and coming gospel artists); Hot or Not (ratings of new albums); Fashion & Faith (glorifying God through clothing).

$ FOCUS ON THE FAMILY DARE 2 DIG DEEPER SERIES, Youth Culture Dept., Colorado Springs CO 80995 (no street address needed). (719) 531-3400. Fax (719) 531-3448. Website: www.family .org. Submit to Acquisitions Editor. A series of small booklets that deal with hard topics that teens (ages 12-18) are struggling with. Query editor with your ideas to be sure they haven't already covered the topic.

G4T INK, 419 Mason St., Ste. 108, Vacaville CA 95688. (707) 446-4463. E-mail: info@generation s4truth.org. Website: www.generations4truth.org. Generations 4 Truth. Diana Ventura, dir. Ministry written for and by teens, college students, and adults who address teen issues. Quarterly mag.; 30-40 pgs; circ. 2,500. Estab. 2007. 70 percent unsolicited freelance; 30 percent assigned. Query/clips; e-query OK. **NO PAYMENT** for nonexclusive rts. Not copyrighted. Articles 200-400 wds. Responds in 4-6 wks. Accepts simultaneous submissions & reprints (tell when/where appeared). Accepts e-mail submissions (attached file in word.doc). Uses some sidebars. Prefers NIV. Accepts submissions from teens. Guidelines on Website; copy for 9 x 12 SAE.

Poetry: Accepts 4-8/yr.

Fillers: Accepts cartoons, jokes, prayers, quizzes, short humor, and word puzzles.

Tips: "Submit short articles that encourage teens. Issues pertinent to today's teens. Also, filler content such as poetry and cartoons."

$ HORIZON STUDENT MAGAZINE (formerly Clear Horizon), PO Box 17306, Nashville TN 37217. (615) 361-1221. Fax (615) 367-0535. E-mail: clearmag@randallhouse.com. Website: www.randall house.com. Randall House. Jonathan Yandell, ed.; submit to Derek Lewis, ed. asst. Bringing high school students to a closer relationship with Christ through devotionals, relevant articles, and pertinent topics. Quarterly mag.; 56 pgs. Open to freelance. Query or complete ms/cover letter; query for fiction; e-query OK. Accepts full mss by e-mail. Pays $35-150 for articles, $50-125 for fiction, on publication for 1st rts. Articles 600-1,500 words (35/yr.); book reviews 600-800 words ($35). Responds in 6 wks. Seasonal 9 mos. ahead. Accepts simultaneous submissions; no reprints. Prefers e-mail submissions (attached file). No kill fee. Regularly uses sidebars. Also accepts submissions from teens. Prefers KJV. Guidelines by e-mail/Website; copy for 9 x 12 SAE. (No ads)

Columns/Departments: Buys 10/yr. Changing Lanes (describe how God is changing you), 600-800 words; Between the Lines (review of book selected by Randall House), 600-800 words; $35-50.

Tips: "We are open to freelancers by way of articles and submissions to 'Changing Lanes' (600-800 words) All articles should be about an aspect of the Christian life or contain a spiritual element, as the purpose of this magazine is to bring high school students closer to Christ. We are happy to accept personal testimonies or knowledgeable articles on current hot topics and how they compare to biblical standards."

$ INSIGHT, 55 W. Oak Ridge Dr., Hagerstown MD 21740-7301. (301) 393-4038. Fax (301) 393-4055. E-mail: insight@rhpa.org. Website: www.insightmagazine.org. Review and Herald Publishing Assn./Seventh-day Adventist. Dwain Esmond, ed. A magazine of positive Christian living for Seventh-day Adventist high school students, ages 13-19. Weekly take-home mag.; 16 pgs.; circ. 20,000. Subscription $49.95. 80 percent unsolicited freelance. Complete ms/cover letter; fax/e-query OK. Pays $50-85, on publication for 1st rts. Not copyrighted. Articles 1,200-1,700 words (120/yr.). Seasonal 6 mos. ahead. Accepts reprints (tell when/where appeared). Prefers e-mail submission (attached file). Kill fee. Regularly uses sidebars. Prefers NIV. Also accepts submissions from teens. Guidelines on Website; copy $2/#10 SASE. (No ads)
   Poetry: Buys to 36/yr. All types; to 1 pg.; $10. By high school and college students only.
   Columns/Departments: Buys 50/yr. On the Edge (drama in real life), 800-1,500 words, $50-100; It Happened to Me (personal experience in first person), 600-900 words, $50-75; Big Deal (big topics, such as prayer, premarital sex, knowing God's will, etc.) with sidebar, 1,200-1,700 words, $75 + $25 for sidebar; So I Said (first-person opinion), 300-500 words, $25-125. Complete ms.
   Contest: Sponsors a nonfiction and poetry contest; includes a category for students under 21. Prizes to $250. June deadline (varies). Send SASE for rules.
   Tips: "We look for teen-written or stories written from a teen perspective that are first-person accounts of experiencing God in everyday life. Also need stories by male authors, particularly some humor. Also profiles of Seventh-day Adventist teenagers who are making a notable difference."
   ** This periodical was #43 on the 2009 Top 50 Christian Publishers list (#28 in 2006, #28 in 2005).

$ INTEEN, PO Box 436987, Chicago IL 60643. (708) 868-7100, ext. 362. Fax (708) 868-6759. Website: www.urbanministries.com. Urban Ministries Inc. Submit to Editor. Teen curriculum for ages 15-17 (student and teacher manuals). Quarterly booklet; 32 pgs.; circ. 20,000. Subscription $11.25. 1 percent unsolicited freelance; 99 percent assigned. Query/clips; phone query OK; no e-query. Pays $75-150 on acceptance for all rts. Articles & fiction 1,200 wds. Responds in 4 wks. Seasonal 9 mos. ahead. Accepts some reprints (tell when/where appeared). Accepts requested ms on disk or by e-mail (copied into message). Prefers NIV. Free guidelines/theme list/copy for 10 x 13 SAE. (No ads)
   Poetry: Buys 4/yr. Free verse; variable length; $25-60.
   Tips: "Write in with sample writings and be willing and ready to complete an assignment. We prefer to make assignments. Most open to Bible study guides applicable and interesting for teens. Writers who can accurately explain Scriptures to teens are always welcome."

$ J.A.M.: JESUS AND ME, PO Box 436987, Chicago IL 60643. (708) 868-7100, ext. 373. Fax (708) 868-6759. E-mail: tlee@urbanministries.com. Website: www.urbanministries.com. Urban Ministries Inc. Timothy Lee, ed. Quarterly Sunday school magazine for 12- to 14-year-olds. Open to freelance. Query/clips; fax/e-query OK. Pays up to $150 for curriculum. 120 days after acceptance for all rts. Lessons up to 900 words, which includes a story approx. 250 words. Responds in 4 wks. Seasonal 6 mos. ahead. No simultaneous submissions or reprints. Requires accepted ms by e-mail (attached file). Prefers NIV. Guidelines/copy for #10 SASE. (No ads)
   Tips: "J.A.M. principally serves an African American audience; editorial content addresses

broad Christian issues. Looking for those with educational or Sunday school teaching experience who can accurately explain scripture in an insightful and engaging way and apply those scriptures to the lives of 12-14 year olds."

$ LISTEN MAGAZINE, 55 W. Oak Ridge Dr., Hagerstown MD 21740. (301) 393-4019. E-mail: editor @listenmagazine.org. Website: www.listenmagazine.org. The Health Connection. Celeste Perrino-Walker, ed. Positive lifestyle magazine for teens/young adults; emphasizes values in a general tone. Monthly mag. (September-May); 32 pgs.; circ. 20,000/exposure 100,000. Subscription $26.95. 50 percent unsolicited freelance; 50 percent assigned. Query or complete ms; e-query OK. Pays .06-.10/ wd. ($50-150) on acceptance for 1st or reprint rts. Articles 800 words (30-50/yr.); true stories 800 words (15/yr.). Responds in 2 wks. to 3 mos. Seasonal 1 yr. ahead. Accepts simultaneous submissions & reprints (tell when/where appeared). Accepts requested ms on CD or by e-mail (attached file). Uses some sidebars. Guidelines/theme list on Website; copy $2/9 x 12 SASE/2 stamps. (No ads)

Fillers: Uses 500-word quizzes based on topic in our theme list.

Special Needs: Antidrug, tobacco, alcohol; positive role models. For true stories, needs stories dealing with everyday problems: peer pressure, decision making, friendship, family conflict, self-discipline, divorce, abuse, anorexia/bulimia, and making positive choices.

Tips: "Need good true stories and celebrity features. We've stopped using fiction. While it isn't always possible, we like to feature stories about individuals who overcome the temptation to experiment with drugs and alcohol, and/or who find a creative way to deal with a bad situation. We have a narrow focus. By offering us cutting edge articles on our subjects, you'll have a greater chance of breaking in."

** This periodical was #39 on the 2008 Top 50 Christian Publishers list (#29 in 2007, #20 in 2006, #13 in 2005).

$ LIVING MY FAITH, 1300 N. Meacham Rd., Schaumburg IL 60173-4888. (847) 843-1600. Fax (847) 843-3757. E-mail: livingmyfaith@garbc.org or realfaith@garbc.org. Website: www.rbpstudent ministries.org. Regular Baptist Press. Submit to Editor. For junior high youth (12-14); conservative/ fundamental. Weekly devotional booklet; 12 pgs. Complete ms; no e-query. Articles. Pays .05/wd. and up, on acceptance. True & fiction stories to 1,000 wds. Responds in 4-8 wks. Requires KJV. Guidelines on Website.

Tips: "Check Website quarterly for updates concerning needs, themes, etc. This is written chiefly by assignment."

$ MERLYN'S PEN: Fiction, Essays, and Poems by America's Teens, 11 S. Angell St., Ste. 301, Providence RI 02906. Toll-free (800) 247-2027. (401) 751-3766. Fax (401) 274-1541. E-mail: merlyn@merlynspen.org. Website: www.merlynspen.com. General. R. James Stahl, ed. Magazine; circ. 5,000. Subscription $29.95. Query; no e-query. Pays $20-200 on publication for all rts. Articles 500-5,000 words; fiction to 8,500 words. Responds in 10-12 wks.

Poetry: Free verse, metric verse; $20-50.

$ REAL FAITH IN LIFE, 1300 N. Meacham Rd., Schaumburg IL 60173-4888. (847) 843-1600. Fax (847) 843-3757. E-mail: realfaith@garbc.org. Website: www.rbpstudentministries.org. Regular Baptist Press. For senior high youth (14-17); conservative/fundamental. Quarterly devotional book; 112 pgs. Complete ms; no e-query. Pays .05/wd. and up, on acceptance for first (preferred) or onetime rts. Articles 700-1,200 wds. Responds in 4-8 wks. Using mostly assignment writers who are using the RBP student ministries materials or are familiar with churches who do. Some reprints. Guidelines on Website; copy.

Tips: "Check Website quarterly for updates concerning needs, themes, etc. Written chiefly by assignment."

$ @ RISEN MAGAZINE: The Art & Soul of Pop Culture, 5677 Oberlin Dr., Ste. 202, San Diego CA 92121. (858) 481-5650. Fax (858) 481-5660. E-mail: matthew@risenmagazine.com or chris@

risenmagazine.com. Website: www.risenmagazine.com (online version of the magazine). Risen Media LLC. Submit to Managing Editor. Audience is 18- to 35-year-old seekers and new believers; original photos and one-on-one interviews cut to the heart of today's cultural icons. Bimonthly mag.; 34 pgs.; circ. 45,000+. Subscription $19.95. Open to freelance. Query; phone/e-query OK. Pays $150-700. Articles. (Ads)

$ @ **SHARING THE VICTORY**, 8701 Leeds Rd., Kansas City MO 64129-1680. Toll-free (800) 289-0909. (816) 921-0909. Fax (816) 921-8755. E-mail: stv@fca.org. Website: www.SharingTheVictory .com (online version of the magazine). Fellowship of Christian Athletes (Protestant and Catholic). Jill Ewert, ed. Equipping and encouraging athletes and coaches to take their faith seriously, in and out of competition. Monthly (9x—double issues in Jan., Jun. & Aug.) mag.; 40 pgs.; circ. 80,000. Subscription $19.95. 10 percent unsolicited freelance; 40 percent assigned. Query only/clips; e-query OK. Pays $150-400 on publication for 1st rts. Articles 1,000 words (5-20/yr.). Responds in 13 wks. Seasonal 6 mos. ahead. Accepts reprints, pays 50 percent (tell when/where appeared). Accepts requested ms on disk or by e-mail (attached or copied into message). Kill fee .05 percent. Uses some sidebars. Prefers HCSB. Guidelines on Website; copy $1/9 x 12 SASE/3 stamps. (Ads)

    Special Needs: Articles on FCA camp experiences. All articles must have an athletic angle. Need stories featuring Christian female professional athletes with an FCA connection.

    Tips: "FCA angle important; pro and college athletes and coaches giving solid Christian testimony; we run stories according to athletic season. Need articles on Christian pro athletes—all sports. It is suggested that the writer actually look at the magazine for general style and presentation."

$ **SPIRIT**, 1884 Randolph Ave., St. Paul MN 55105-1700. (651) 690-7010. Fax (651) 690-7039. E-mail: jmcsj9@aol.com. Catholic/Good Ground Press. Joan Mitchell, CSJ, ed. Religious education for Catholic high schoolers. Weekly newsletter; circ. 20,000. 50 percent freelance written. Complete ms/cover letter or query; fax/e-query OK. Pays $250-300 on publication for all rts. Articles 1,000-1,200 words (4/yr.); fiction 1,000-1,200 words (10/yr.; $125-300). Responds in 5 wks. Seasonal 6 mos. ahead. Accepts simultaneous submissions. Free guidelines/copy by mail.

    Tips: "No born-again pieces. Articles about teens must be written from their point of view."

@ **STUDENTLIFE BIBLE STUDY** (formerly Clarity Publishers), PO Box 36040, Birmingham AL 35236. Toll-free (800) 718-2267. Fax (205) 403-3969. E-mail: slpublishing@studentlife.net. Website: www.studentlife.net. Andy Blanks, exec. ed. Bible study curriculum intended to take jr. high and sr. high school students through the Bible in 6 years. Ty Gullick, exec. ed. for new Bible study curriculum for adult learners. Weekly online. Subscriptions on a sliding scale. Open to freelance. Complete ms/cover letter. (No ads)

+ **SUSIE, Magazine for Teen Girls**, (615) 216-6147. E-mail: susieshell@comcast.net. Susie Shellenberger, owner. A publication appealing and relevant for today's girl. Estab. 2009. Monthly mag. Open to unsolicited freelance. E-mail complete manuscripts labeled "Free Freelance." **NO PAYMENT FOR THE FIRST YEAR.** Nonfiction & fiction. Not included in topical listings.

$ **TAKE FIVE PLUS YOUTH DEVOTIONAL GUIDE**, 1445 N. Boonville Ave., Springfield MO 65802-1894. (417) 862-2781, ext. 4208. Fax (417) 862-6059. E-mail: rl-take5plus@gph.org. Assemblies of God. Glen Ellard, ed. Devotional for teens. By assignment only. Query. Accepts e-mail submissions. Pays $25/devotion. Devotions may range from 210 to 235 words (max.). Guidelines on request.

    Poetry: Accepts poetry from teens; no more than 25 lines.

    Tips: "The sample devotions need to be based on a Scripture reference available by query. You will not be paid for the sample devotions." Also accepts digital photos.

$ **TC MAGAZINE**, 915 E. Market, Ste. 10750, Searcy AR 72149. (501) 279-4660. Fax (501) 279-4931. E-mail: editor@tcmagazine.org. Website: www.tcmagazine.org. Institute for Church & Family. Laura

Kaiser, ed. To help teenagers (13-19) discover style in faith and love. Quarterly mag.; 52 pgs.; circ. 8,000. Subscription $12.95. 10 percent unsolicited freelances; 40 percent assigned. Complete ms; fax or e-query OK. Accepts full mss by e-mail. Pays variable rates on publication for all rts. Articles 500-1,200 words (10/yr.); no fiction. Responds only if chosen for publication. Seasonal 6 mos. ahead. No simultaneous submissions or reprints. No kill fee. Uses some sidebars. Also accepts submissions from teens. Guidelines on Website; copy $3.95/9 x 12 SAE. (Ads—e-mail to request rate book & media kit)

> **Columns/Departments:** Buys 5/yr. Complete ms. College (college prep for high schoolers), 800-1,000 words; Humor (funny article in first person), 800 words.
>
> **Tips:** "We really look for teen writers. First-person articles about personal experience are desired. No fiction at this time."

@ TEENS FOR JC, 2855 Lawrenceville-Suwanee Rd., Ste. 760-355, Suwanee GA 30024. Phone/fax (770) 831-8622. E-mail: uvaldes@aol.com. Website: www.plgkmedia.com. PLGK Communications Inc. Quentin Plair, pres./CEO. Salutes the fun and exhilaration of being a Christian teen. Monthly e-zine. 90 percent unsolicited freelance; 10 percent assigned. Complete ms/cover letter; no phone/fax/e-query. Accepts requested ms on disk or by e-mail (attached file). **NO PAYMENT** for onetime rts. Not copyrighted. Articles 100-5,000 words (15/yr.) & fiction 100-5,000 words (12/yr.); reviews 200 words. Responds in 12 weeks. Seasonal 4 mos. ahead. Accepts simultaneous submissions & reprints (tell when/where appeared). No kill fee. Uses some sidebars. Also accepts submissions from teens. Guidelines by mail/Website. (Ads)

> **Poetry:** Accepts many; any type; 1-200 lines.
>
> **Fillers:** Accepts many; cartoons, facts, games, jokes, party ideas, prayers, prose, quizzes, short humor, tips, word puzzles; 10-750 words.
>
> **Columns/Departments:** Accepts 36/yr. School tips (teen tips for scholarly excellence); Scoop (current info); Music (music reviews/stories); Speak Out (opinion articles by teens); all 100-500 words.
>
> **Tips:** "Provide information teens need to lay a foundation for a successful life. Looking for great stories."

$ TG! MAGAZINE, 703 Michigan Ave., Ste. 2, LaPorte IN 46350. (219) 324-2780. E-mail: editor@ tgmagazine.net. Website: www.tgmagazine.net. Catholic. Brandi Lee, ed-in-chief. For Catholic teenage girls; covers faith, life, and fashion. Bimonthly mag.; 32 pgs.; circ. 3,500. Subscription $18.95. Open to freelance. E-query preferred; no phone/fax query. Accepts full mss by e-mail. Pays .15-.20/ wd. for 1st & electronic rts. Articles 800-1,200 words; no fiction; reviews 50-100 words ($25). Responds in 4-6 wks. Seasonal 12 mos. ahead. No simultaneous submissions or reprints. Some kill fees. Regularly uses sidebars. Also accepts submissions from teens (no pay). Prefers NAB or NRSV (Catholic editions only). Guidelines by mail/e-mail; copy $4.99/7 x 10 SAE. (Ads)

> **Fillers:** Buys unlimited number. Facts, prayers, quizzes, quotes, word puzzles.
>
> **Columns/Departments:** Social Justice; Health/Hygiene/Beauty; Teen Issues; Life Plan; Entertainment; Make-It-Your-Own; True Girl Saint. Pays by the word.
>
> **Tips:** "Our feature articles are most open to freelancers. Reading back issues is imperative to understanding our mission, style, tone, and audience. A firm grasp of our readers' needs for educational, spiritual, and entertainment resources will help guide submissions."

$ VISIONS, 2621 Dryden Rd., Moraine OH 45439. (937) 293-1415. Fax (937) 293-1310. E-mail: service@pflaum.com. Website: www.pflaum.com. Catholic. Joan Mitchell CSJ, ed. For grades 7 & 8. Weekly (32x) take-home paper. Not in topical listings.

$ YOUNG ADULT TODAY, PO Box 436987, Chicago IL 60643. (708) 868-7100, ext. 362. Fax (708) 868-6759. Website: www.urbanministries.com. Urban Ministries Inc. C. Submit to Editor. Magazine for 18- to 24-year-olds. Open to freelance. Query/clips; fax/e-query OK. Pays $75-150, 120 days after acceptance for all rts. Articles 200-400 wds. Responds in 4 wks. Seasonal 6 mos. ahead. Accepts simultaneous submissions. Accepts requested ms on disk. Prefers NIV. Free guidelines/theme list/ copy for #10 SASE. (No ads)

Poetry: Buys 4/yr. Free verse; variable length; $25-60.

Tips: "Send query with a writing sample, or attend our annual conference on the first weekend in November each year. Manuscripts are evaluated at the conference."

$ YOUNG CHRISTIAN, 2660 Petersborough St., Oak Hill VA 20171. E-mail: youngchristianmagazine @yahoo.com. Website: www.shoutlife. com/youngchristian. Shannon Bridget Murphy, ed. Christian writing with the Lord's message for children and teens. Quarterly mag. 85 percent unsolicited freelance. Complete ms/cover letter; e-query OK. Pays .02-.05/wd. on acceptance for 1st or onetime rts. Articles 500-2,000 words; fiction 500-2,000 words. Responds in 2-8 wks. Seasonal 3-6 mos. ahead. Accepts simultaneous submissions & reprints (tell when/where appeared). Accepts disk; prefers e-mail submissions (attached or copied into message). No kill fee. Regularly uses sidebars. Prefers KJV. Guidelines by e-mail. (No ads)

Poetry: Buys variable number. Avant-garde, free verse, haiku, light verse, traditional; any length; variable rates. Submit any number.

Fillers: Buys anecdotes, cartoons, facts, ideas, kid quotes, party ideas, prayers, prose, quizzes, quotes, short humor, tips, and word puzzles; to 1,000 wds.

Tips: "Most open to nonfiction, fiction, poetry, and fillers written by children and teens. Include a Scripture reference. Young Christian will provide information to teachers and educational employees on request. Accepts books, CDs, or tapes to be reviewed, but no written reviews."

$ + YOUNG CHRISTIAN WRITERS MAGAZINE, PO Box 34116, Knoxville TN 37930. (865) 223-3627. E-mail: editor@youngchristianwriters.com. Website: www.YoungChristianWriters.com. Pete Zanoni, dir.; Alicia Zanoni (age 15), ed. Publishes stories, essays, poems, comics, and book reviews written from a Christian worldview by students ages 12-18. Quarterly mag.; 20 pgs. Subscription $14. 90 percent unsolicited freelance; 10 percent assigned. Complete ms by mail or e-mail. Accepts full mss by e-mail. Pays $15-20 on publication for all rts. (will negotiate, if asked). Articles/short stories/ essays to 3,000 wds. Responds in 6 wks. Seasonal 2 mos. ahead. No simultaneous submissions or reprints. Prefers e-mail submissions (attached file). Prefers KJV, NAS, NIV. Guidelines/themes on Website; copy $3.50/9 x 12 SASE/$1.17 postage. (No ads)

Poetry: Buys 16/yr.; free verse, haiku, light verse, traditional; to 300 words; pays $10-15. Submit max. 2 poems.

Special Needs: Looking for creative, well-written work—fiction, essays (current issues, nature, history, true stories, biography, nature, creation science), book reviews of high quality literature, variety of poetry. Accurate, well-organized current news articles from a biblical worldview and analysis.

Tips: "Our vision is to inspire teens to honor God with their creative writing. If interested in being a book reviewer, send us a sample book review you have written. (We'll contact you with a book to review if we're interested.)"

$ @ YOUNG SALVATIONIST, PO Box 269, Alexandria VA 22313-0269. (703) 684-5500. Fax (703) 684-5539. E-mail: ys@usn.salvationarmy.org. Website: http://publications.salvationarmyusa.org. The Salvation Army. Amy Reardon, ed. For teens and young adults in the Salvation Army. Monthly (10x) & online mag.; 24 pgs.; circ. 48,000. Subscription $4.50. 80 percent unsolicited freelance; 20 percent assigned. Complete ms preferred; e-query OK. Pays .15/wd. (.10/wd. for reprints) on acceptance for 1st, onetime, or reprint rts. Articles (60/yr.) & fiction (10/yr.), 600-1,200 words; short evangelistic pieces, 350-600 words. Responds in 9 wks. Seasonal 6 mos. ahead. Accepts reprints (tell when/where appeared). Accepts requested ms on disk or by e-mail. Uses some sidebars. Prefers NIV. Guidelines/theme list by mail/Website; copy for 9 x 12 SASE/3 stamps. (No ads)

** This periodical was #4 on the 2009 Top 50 Christian Publishers list (# 9 in 2008, #5 in 2007, #3 in 2006, #12 in 2005).

$ YOUTH COMPASS, PO Box 4060, Overland Park KS 66204. (913) 432-0331. Fax (913) 722-0351. E-mail: sseditor1@juno.com. Church of God (holiness)/Herald and Banner Press. Arlene McGehee, Sunday school ed. Denominational; for teens. Weekly take-home paper; 4 pgs.; circ. 4,800. Subscription $1.50. Complete ms/cover letter; phone/fax/e-query OK (prefers mail or e-mail). Pays .005/wd. on publication for 1st rts. Fiction 800-1,500 wds. Seasonal 6-8 mos. ahead. Accepts simultaneous submissions & reprints (tell when/where appeared). Prefers KJV. Guidelines/theme list/copy by mail. Not in topical listings.

$ YOUTHWALK, 4201 N. Peachtree Rd., Atlanta GA 30341. (770) 451-9300. Fax (770) 454-9313. E-mail: yw@ywspace.org. Website: www.ywspace.org. Walk Thru the Bible Ministries. Laurin Makohon, ed. (laurin@ywspace.org). To help students navigate their Bibles, connect with God, and their own faith. Monthly devotional mag.; circ. 30,000. Subscription $18. 5 percent unsolicited freelance; 25 percent assigned. Complete ms. Pays $50-250. Articles 600-1,500 words; no reviews. Requires NIV. (No ads)

> **Tips:** "We accept freelance for feature articles only; no devotionals. Submit a complete manuscript of a real-life teen story."
> ** 2009, 2008, 2007 EPA Award of Excellence—Devotional; 2006 EPA Award of Merit—Devotional.

WOMEN'S MARKETS

$ @ AT THE CENTER, PO Box 309, Fleetwood PA 19522. Toll-free phone/fax (800) 588-7744. E-mail: sonya@rightideas.us. Website: www.atcmag.com. Right Ideas Inc. Jerry Thacker, ed.; submit to Sonya Valentino, asst. ed. Designed to help staff, volunteers, and board members of Crisis Pregnancy Centers/Pregnancy Care Centers with relevant information and encouragement. Quarterly online mag. Subscription free. 20 percent unsolicited freelance; 80 percent assigned. Query/clips; e-query preferred. Accepts full mss by e-mail. Pays $150 on publication for 1st, reprint, or simultaneous rts. Articles 1,000 wds. Responds in 4 wks. Seasonal 6 mos. ahead. Accepts simultaneous submissions & reprints (tell when/where appeared). Accepts e-mail submissions (attached file). No kill fee. Uses some sidebars. Accepts submissions from teens. Prefers ESV. Guidelines/idea list by e-mail; copy online. (Ads)

> **Special Needs:** Stories of Christian leaders who were almost aborted.
> **Tips:** "Looking for practical articles of help and encouragement for those involved in the work of CPC/PCC ministry—center directors, staff, and volunteers. If someone has been involved in crisis pregnancy work, their insight into many areas of the ministry can be helpful to staff and board. Need good techniques for counseling abortion-minded clients."

($) @ BEYOND THE BEND, 22 Williams St., Batavia NY 14020. (585) 343-2810. Fax (585) 343-3245. E-mail: submissions@beyondthebend.com. Website: www.beyondthebend.com. PC Publications. Patti Chadwick, ed. (Patti@beyondthebend.com). For women in midlife. Monthly e-zine. Subscription free online. 50 percent unsolicited freelance; 50 percent assigned. Complete ms/cover letter or query; e-query OK. **PAYS IN FREE BOOKS** for onetime and reprint rts. Articles 500-1,000 words (25/yr.); reviews 500 words. Responds in 1 wk. Seasonal 6 mos. ahead. Accepts simultaneous submissions & reprints (tell when/where appeared). Prefers e-mail submissions (attached or copied into message). Uses some sidebars. Guidelines on Website; copy online. (Ads)

> **Fillers:** Accepts 20/yr. Anecdotes, facts, ideas, quotes, sermon illustrations, short humor, and tips; 25-50 wds.
> **Tips:** "Make sure articles pertain to issues of women in midlife."

@ BREATHE AGAIN MAGAZINE, 222 W. 21st St., Ste. F126, Norfolk VA 23517. (757) 404-1582. Fax (757) 626-1669. E-mail: info@breatheagain.org. Website: www.breatheagainmagazine.com. Nicole Cleveland, ed./pub. (editor@breatheagain.org). Stirring stories about overcoming adversity and living triumphant, successful lives encourage and motivate women not only to endure but to overcome life's most challenging moments. Bimonthly digital mag. Open to stories of overcoming.

$ CANTICLE, 325 Scarlet Blvd., Oldsmar FL 34677. Toll-free (800) 558-5452. (734) 429-2952. E-mail: editor@canticlemagazine.com. Website: www.canticlemagazine.com. Women of Grace/Catholic. Susan Brinkman, OCDS, ed. Dedicated solely to the woman's vocation within the church. Bimonthly jour.; 32 pgs.; circ. 4,000. Subscription $29.95. 75 percent unsolicited freelance; 25 percent assigned. Query or complete ms; e-query OK. Pays $50-150 on publication for 1st rts. Articles 600 or 1,200 wds. Responds in 4-6 wks. Seasonal 4 mos. ahead. Requires e-mail submissions in attached file after acceptance. No kill fee. Regularly uses sidebars. Prefers NAB or RSV (Catholic version). Guidelines/theme list on Website; copy online. (Ads)
> **Columns/Departments:** Buys 6/yr. Send complete ms. Solitary Genius (singles, widows; religious perspective), 600 words; pays $50-75. List of columns in guidelines; 500-750 words; $75 for assigned, less for unsolicited.
> **Tips:** "Read guidelines and theme list."

+ @ CHRISTIAN LADIES CONNECT, E-mail: submissions@christianladies.net. Website: www.christianladies.net. Demetria Brown Zinga, pub. Online mag. Open to unsolicited freelance. Query by e-mail only. **NO PAYMENT** for onetime or reprint rts. Articles 500-1,500 wds. Responds in 4-6 wks. Seasonal 3-6 mos. ahead. Uses some sidebars. Guidelines & editorial calendar on Website. Incomplete topical listings.

@ CHRISTIAN WOMAN'S PAGE. E-mail: editor@christianwomanspage.org. Website: www.christianwomanspage.org. Nondenominational. Janel Messenger, ed./pub. Strives to provide women with the whys and hows to live Christianity lovingly and practically in day-to-day life. Monthly e-zine & weekly blog. Carries 12-16 articles/issue; 90,000 unique visitors/yr. 98 percent unsolicited freelance; 2 percent assigned. Complete ms/cover letter by e-mail only. **NO PAYMENT** for 1st, onetime, reprint, simultaneous, nonexclusive rts. Articles 1,200-1,700 words; devotions no less than 700 words; larger articles can be broken into parts; reviews 500-700 words; fiction 1,800 words. Responds in 3-5 wks. Seasonal 2 mos. ahead. Accepts simultaneous submissions & reprints (tell when/where appeared). Requires e-mail submissions (copied into message). Does not use sidebars. Prefers NIV. Guidelines/needs list/copy on Website. (No ads)
> **Poetry:** Accepts 3-5/yr. Light verse, traditional. Submit max. 3 poems.
> **Fillers:** Accepts several/yr. Anecdotes, facts, ideas, short humor, and tips.
> **Columns/Departments:** No columns, but open to them.
> **Tips:** "We are an excellent new writer's market. We will use almost every well-written article submitted if it fits with our mission—encouraging women to live with passion and love for Jesus Christ."

@ CHRISTIAN WOMEN TODAY, Box 300, Sta. A, Vancouver BC V6C 2X3, Canada. (604) 514-2000. Fax (604) 514-2124. E-mail: editor@christianwomentoday.com. Website: www.christianwomentoday.com. French Website: www.chretiennes.com. Campus Crusade for Christ, Canada. Karen Schenk, pub.; Stacy Wiebe, ed. For Christian women, 20-60 yrs. Monthly online mag.; 2 million hits/mo. 30 percent unsolicited freelance. Query first; e-query preferred. **NO PAYMENT**. Lifestyle articles 200-500 words; features 500-1,000 words; life stories 500 words. Seasonal 4 mos. ahead. Accepts simultaneous submissions & reprints (tell when/where appeared). Prefers e-mail submission (attached file). Guidelines/theme list on Website: www.christianwomentoday.com/volunteer/submissions.html. (Ads)
> **Tips:** "The writer needs to have a global perspective, have a heart to build women in their faith, and help develop them to win others to Christ. Text should be written for online viewing with subheads and bullets in the body of the article."

+ @ **CHRISTIAN WORK AT HOME MOMS**, PO Box 974, Bellevue NE 68005. Toll-free (888) 44-CWAHM. E-mail: jill@cwahm.com. Website: www.cwahm.com. Christian Work at Home Inc. Jill Hart, pres. Primary audience is moms looking for information and advice about working from home. Weekly online mag.; 2,000 pgs. sitewide; circ. 15,000-20,000 unique visitors/mo. Subscription free online. 50 percent unsolicited freelance; 50 percent assigned. Query or complete ms; e-query OK. Accepts full mss by e-mail. **NO PAYMENT** for nonexclusive rts. Articles 600 words & up (50-75/yr.); reviews 300 words. Responds in 2 wks. Seasonal 2 mos. ahead. Accepts reprints. Requires accepted mss by e-mail (copied into message). Uses some sidebars. Guidelines/theme list/copy on Website. (Ads)

  Special Needs: More how-to on home schooling with a home business.

  Tips: "We are always looking for great devotions, recipes, and craft ideas. We also look for how-to articles related to running a home business, and profiles of successful work-at-home moms."

CHURCHWOMAN, 475 Riverside Dr., Ste. 1626A, New York NY 10115. Toll-free (800) 298-5551. (212) 870-2347. Fax (212) 870-2338. E-mail: cwu@churchwomen.org. Website: www.church women.org. Church Women United. Julie Drews, ed. Shares stories of women acting on their faith and engaging in the work for peace and justice around the world. Quarterly mag.; 28 pgs.; circ. 3,000. Subscription $10. 1 percent unsolicited freelance. Query. **PAYS IN COPIES**. Articles to 3 pgs. Prefers accepted ms by e-mail (copied into message). Guidelines by mail; copy $1.

$ @ **COME TO THE FIRE COMMUNITY ONLINE MAGAZINE**, PO Box 480052, Kansas City MO 64148. (816) 777-2003. E-mail: pam@cometothefire.org. Website: www.cometothefire.org. Pam Enderby, mng. ed. To encourage women to live holy lives by applying Scripture to their daily lives. Weekly online e-zine. Subscription free. 90 percent unsolicited freelance. Complete ms/no cover letter. Accepts full mss by e-mail. Pays $15-50 on publication for onetime, simultaneous, or reprint rts. Articles 500-1,200 words (30/yr.). Responds in 4-6 wks. Seasonal 6 mos. ahead. Accepts simultaneous submissions & reprints (tell when/where appeared). Uses some sidebars. Prefers e-mail submissions (attached file). Prefers NIV. Guidelines/theme list by e-mail/Website; copy online. (No ads)

  Special Needs: Looking for keys to building healthy relationships between mothers/daughters and mothers/sons with a spiritual emphasis; caring for elderly parents; and loving your husband God's way.

  Tips: "We look for articles that draw women into a deeper spiritual life—articles on surrender, prayer, parenting—yet written with personal illustrations."

@ **CROWNED WITH SILVER**, PO Box 10, Masonville CO 80541. E-mail: crownedwithsilver@yahoo. com. Website: www.crownedwithsilver.com. Submit to The Editor. Return to biblical femininity; Christian homemaking encouragement regarding home schooling, etiquette, marriage, womanhood, and nostalgic wisdom from the past. Quarterly online mag. Subscription $14. Articles & fiction.

  Tips: "Send your article via e-mail and follow the topics indicated. Write 500 words—no longer—not shorter."

$ @ **THE DABBLING MUM**, 508 W. Main St., Beresford SD 57004. (605) 763-2549. E-mail: dm@ thedabblingmum.com. Website: www.thedabblingmum.com. Alyice Edrich, ed. Balance your life while you glean from successful entrepreneurs, parents, writers, cooks, and Christians—just like you. Biweekly e-zine; circ. 30,000-40,000. Subscription free online. 90 percent unsolicited freelance; 10 percent assigned. Complete ms submitted online; e-query OK. Accepts full mss by e-mail. Pays $10-40 (reprints $5-10) on acceptance for 1st & reprint rts, and nonexclusive indefinite archival rts. Articles 500-1,500 words (48-96/yr.); book & video reviews 500 words (no payment). Responds in 4-12 wks. Seasonal 1 mo. ahead. No simultaneous submissions; accepts reprints (tell when/where appeared). Accepts e-mail submissions (copied into message). No kill fee or sidebars. Also accepts submissions from teens. Prefers KJV or NAS. Guidelines/editorial calendar/copy on Website. (Ads)

  Special Needs: Simple living articles; small-business articles.

Columns/Departments: Query; pays $10-25. "We have a 'current needs' section and editorial calendar online that is updated frequently with columnists wanted, article needs, word count, and payment."
Tips: "Write something that is not readily available on the Internet. Add a personal twist to your how-to piece, and talk to readers in a conversational tone. Also write a business article—it's the most difficult area to fill. If we like what we see we'll consider more of your work outside that area."
** This periodical was #49 on the 2008 Top 50 Christian Publishers list (#39 in 2007).

@ **ELEGANCE**, PO Box 2084, Waldorf MD 20604. (301) 870-9009. E-mail: greatness@youare royalty.org. Website: www.YouAreRoyalty.org. Royalty Inc. Brenda Douglas, pub. For women and teen girls. Quarterly e-zine. Subscription free online. 90 percent unsolicited freelance. Query; e-query OK. Accepts full mss by e-mail. **NO PAYMENT**. Articles. Seasonal 2 mos. ahead. Accepts simultaneous submissions & reprints (tell when/where appeared). Accepts articles by e-mail (attached in Word). Uses some sidebars. Guidelines by e-mail; copy online.
   Fillers: Cartoons, facts, ideas, jokes, quotes, short humor, tips, and word puzzles.
   Columns/Departments: Seeking His Face (spiritual growth); In His Image (character development); Focus on the Family (family life); Health & Fitness (diet & exercise); Majestic Teens (teen interests); Women in Leadership; Appreciation for Diversity; all 1,000-1,500 words.
   Tips: "All sections open to freelancers."

+ @ **EMPOWERING EVERYDAY WOMEN**. Toll-free (877) 419-6560, ext. 4. E-mail: submissions @eewmagazine.com or articles@eewmagazine.com. Website: www.eewmagazine.com. Dianna Hobbs, ed-in-chief (dhobbs@eewmagazine.com). For African American Christian Women. Online mag. Open to unsolicited freelance. Complete ms or query by e-mail only. **NO PAYMENT** for onetime electronic rights & right to archive. Articles 800-1,500 wds. Responds in up to 12 wks. Guidelines on Website. Incomplete topical listings. (Ads)
   Tips: "The EEW woman is a forward-thinking woman. She is looking for new information to help enhance her spiritually, emotionally, physically, and financially. When she logs onto our site she expects to carry away practical tools that can be applied to her daily life."

$ **ESPRIT**, Evangelical Lutheran Women, 302-393 Portage Ave., Winnipeg MB R3B 3H6, Canada. (204) 984-9160. Fax (204) 984-9162. E-mail: esprit@elcic.ca. Website: www.elw.ca. Catherine Pate, ed. For Christian women. Quarterly mag.; 36 pgs.; circ. 4,000. Subscription $25 Cdn., $27 U.S. 65 percent unsolicited freelance; 35 percent assigned. Complete ms/cover letter; phone/e-query OK. Pays $18-54 Cdn. on publication for 1st or onetime rts. Articles & fiction 350-1,300 wds. Responds in 2-4 wks. Seasonal 4 mos. ahead. Accepts simultaneous submissions. Prefers accepted mss by e-mail (attached). Uses some sidebars. Requires NRSV. Guidelines by mail/Website; copy for #10 SAE/$6.25 Cdn. postage or $8 U.S. (Limited ads)
   Poetry: Light verse, traditional; 8-100 lines; $18. Submit max. 3 poems.
   Columns/Departments: Buys 4/yr. Family Matters, 1,300 words.
   Tips: "Most open to social justice, world issues, and women's issues (justice, violence). We are currently focusing on topical, well-researched articles with a particular eye on world events. Any submissions should emphasize this research-based approach."
   ** This periodical was #32 on the 2008 Top 50 Christian Publishers list (#20 in 2007, #34 in 2006, #30 in 2005).

+ @ **EXTREME WOMAN MAGAZINE**, PO Box 1562, Clemmons NC 27012. (336) 301-3016. Fax (336) 712-1355. E-mail: eic@extremewomanmagazine.com. Website: www.extremewoman magazine.com. Rochelle L. Valasek, ed-in-chief. Spotlights women (20-100 yrs.) who live extremely for God. Monthly & online mag. (also a quarterly PDF mag.); 32 pgs. Subscription free for now. 100 percent unsolicited freelance. Complete ms/cover letter; fax/e-query OK. **NO PAYMENT** for onetime rts. Articles 500-1,000 words (60/yr.); reviews up to 300 words. Responds in 2-4 wks. Seasonal 6 mos. ahead. Accepts simultaneous submissions; no reprints (negotiable). Prefers e-mail submissions (attached file). Uses some sidebars. Also accepts submissions from teens. Prefers KJV. Guidelines/theme list by mail/e-mail; copy by mail. (Ads)

> **Poetry:** Accepts 12/yr. Free verse, light verse, traditional; 5-20 lines. Submit max. 3 poems.
> **Fillers:** Accepts 12/yr. Anecdotes, cartoons, facts, jokes, quotes, short humor, and tips, 24+ wds.
> **Tips:** "As we revamp the magazine, we will look at all freelance to fit in. Best way to break in is to check out our online magazine."

FIRST LADY, PO Box 1233, Mableton GA 30126. E-mail: FLMezine@gmail.com. Website: www.firstladymagazine.com or www.FLMezine.com. Tracey L. Smith, pub. To educate, encourage, and inspire women about many aspects of life from a Christian viewpoint. Monthly mag.; circ. 30,000. Subscription $10. Articles.

@ **FOR EVERY WOMAN** (formerly WT Online), 1445 N. Boonville Ave., Springfield MO 65802-1894. (417) 862-2781, ext. 4066. Fax (417) 862-0503. E-mail: dhampton@ag.org. Website: www.women.ag.org. Assemblies of God Women's Ministries Dept. D. Hampton, admin. coord. Inspirational online magazine for women. Ongoing Webzine. 20 percent unsolicited freelance. Complete ms; e-query OK. Accepts full mss by e-mail. **NO PAYMENT** for onetime rts. Articles 500-800 words (20/yr.). Responds within 1 yr. Seasonal 4-6 mos. ahead. Accepts reprints (tell when/where appeared). Accepts e-mail submissions (attached file). Uses some sidebars. Prefers NIV. Guidelines/theme list by e-mail/Website; copy by e-mail. (Ads)

> **Columns/Departments:** Buys 30/yr. The Single Woman (never married, widowed, divorced), 400 words; Family Matters (single or married moms); I Still Do! (marriage), 400 words. See site for column information.
> **Special Needs:** Prayer focus.
> **Tips:** "Always need articles that encourage and have biblical support text."
> ** 2008, 2005 EPA Award of Merit—General.

$ @ **FULLFILL**, 2370 S. Trenton Way, Denver CO 80231-3822. E-mail: write@fullfill.org. Website: www.fullfill.org. MOPS Intl. Submit to FullFill Editor. Encourages women in all seasons of life to realize, utilize, and maximize their influence. Quarterly mag. & online community. Open to unsolicited freelance. Complete ms preferred; considers queries. Pays varying amounts on publication. Articles 1,000-1,500 wds. Requires e-mail submissions (attached or copied into message—write@fullfill.org). Guidelines/themes on Website (click on "About Us," then "Write"). Incomplete topical listings.

> **Columns/Departments:** Coaching Corner (coaching on personal growth, life management, professional growth), 650 wds.

$ @ **GIRLFRIEND 2 GIRLFRIEND** (formerly Simple Joy). E-mail: submission@g2gzine.com. Website: www.simplejoy.org. Jean Ann Duckworth, pub.; submit to The Editor (editor@g2gzine.com). For women (target age 30-55) interested in a simpler way of life; general. Monthly online mag. Open to freelance. Complete mss; e-query OK. Pays $10 honorarium on publication for articles to 1,000 words (72-120/yr.); within 60 days of publication; for onetime rts. Seasonal 4 mos. ahead. Prefers e-mail (attached file in Word format). Guidelines on Website. Incomplete topical listings.

> **Special Needs:** Focuses on 4 specific areas: reducing stress, enhancing joy, simplifying life, and building/strengthening relationships.
> **Tips:** "Read the current issue to better understand our mission and market. We like working with first-time authors."

THE HANDMAIDEN, PO Box 76, Ben Lomond CA 95005. Toll-free (800) 967-7377. (831) 336-5118. Fax (831) 336-8882. E-mail: czell@conciliarpress.com. Website: www.conciliarpress.com/

magazines/the-handmaiden. Antiochian Orthodox Archdiocese of North America. Carla Zell, ed. For women serving God within the Eastern Orthodox tradition. Quarterly jour.; 64 pgs.; circ. 3,000. Subscription $16.50. 5 percent unsolicited freelance; 95 percent assigned. Query; e-query OK. **PAYS IN COPIES/SUBSCRIPTION**. Articles 1,000-2,000 words (8/yr.). Responds in 6-8 wks. Seasonal 6 mos. ahead. Accepts reprints (tell when/where appeared). Prefers hard copy or e-mail submissions (copied into message). Uses some sidebars. Prefers NKJV. Guidelines/theme list by mail/e-mail; copy for 7 x 10 SASE/4 stamps. (No ads)

> **Poetry:** Katherine Grace Bond, poetry ed. (PO Box 1711, Duvall WA 98019; 425-788-8275; handmaiden@KatherineGraceBond.com). Accepts 4-8/yr. Free verse, light verse, traditional. Submit max. 3 poems.

> **Columns/Departments:** Heroines of the Faith (lives of women saints within Orthodox tradition), 1,000-2,000 words.

> **Tips:** "Most open to theme features, sidebars, and poetry."

@ HANDMAIDENS. E-mail: iona@handmaidens.org. Website: www.handmaidens.org. Iona Hoeppner, ed. For women of all (or no) denominations; consider the sensitivities of those whose theology may differ from your own. E-zine. Open to unsolicited freelance. Complete ms. **NO PAYMENT** for onetime rts. Articles; fiction. Requires e-mail submissions (copied into message). Guidelines on Website.

> **Poetry:** Accepts poetry.

> **Tips:** "We welcome your art, photos, poetry, essays, articles, short stories, devotional material, links, almost anything of interest to Christian women."

$ HEART & SOUL, 2514 Maryland Ave., Baltimore MD 21218. Toll-free (800) 834-8813, ext. 105. (410) 576-9199. Fax (410) 662-4596. E-mail: editor@heartandsoul.com. Website: www.heartand soul.com. General. Submit to Editorial Dept. The African American woman's ultimate guide to total well-being (body, mind, and spirit). Bimonthly mag.; 88-96 pgs.; circ. 300,000. Subscription $18. Open to unsolicited freelance. Query preferred. Pays on acceptance. Articles 800-1,500 wds. Guidelines on Website. (Ads) Incomplete topical listings.

($) @ HISTORY'S WOMEN, 22 Williams St., Batavia NY 14020. (585) 343-2810. Fax (585) 343-3245. E-mail: submissions@historyswomen.com. Website: www.historyswomen.com. PC Publications. Patti Chadwick, ed. Online magazine highlighting the extraordinary achievements of women throughout history. Monthly e-zine; 20 pgs.; circ. 21,000. Subscription free online. 20 percent unsolicited freelance. E-query/e-submissions only. **PAYS IN COPIES & FREE E-BOOKS** (occasionally pays $10, if budget permits) for 1st, onetime, reprint, or electronic rts. Articles 400-1,200 words (20/yr.). Responds in 1-2 wks. Seasonal 3 mos. ahead. Accepts simultaneous submissions & reprints (tell when/where appeared). Prefers e-mail submission (copied into message). Does not use sidebars. Also accepts submissions from teens. Guidelines on Website; copy on site archive. (Ads)

> **Columns/Departments:** Buys 10-20/yr. Women to Admire, in these columns: Women of Faith; First Women (pioneers in their field); Social Reformers; Amazing Moms; Women Who Ruled (women rulers); Early America; all 500-1,000 words, $10. Query or complete ms.

HOPE FOR WOMEN MAGAZINE, PO Box 3241, Muncie IN 47307. Toll-free fax (800) 936-2214. E-mail: Editor@hopeforwomenmag.com. Website: www.hopeforwomenmag.com. Virtuous Publications Inc. Submit to Editor. Quarterly mag.; 72 pgs.; circ. 10,000. Subscription $14.95. 95 percent unsolicited freelance; 5 percent assigned. Query/clips; e-query OK. Accepts full mss by e-mail. **NO PAYMENT** for 1st rts. Articles 500-2,000 words; reviews 300 words. Responds in 4-6 wks. Seasonal 2-3 mos. ahead. No simultaneous submissions or reprints. Accepts e-mail submissions (attached file). Guidelines/theme list by mail/e-mail; copy for #10 SASE. (Ads)

> **Fillers:** Newsbreaks, party ideas, tips; .10/wd.

> **Columns/Departments:** Relationships (nurturing and maintaining positive relationships), 800-1,200 words; Light (tough issues usually kept quiet in the church), 800-1,000 words;

Journey (helps for a woman's life journey), 500-800 words; .10-. 15/wd. Query. Additional columns listed on Website.

Tips: "Each issue features at least one interview with a woman of faith—often a celebrity— who has come through a difficult time and grown stronger in her faith because of it."

$ HORIZONS, 100 Witherspoon St., Louisville KY 40202-1396. (502) 569-5897. Fax (502) 569-8085. E-mail: yhileman@ctr.pcusa.org, or sharon.gillies@pcusa.org. Website: www.pcusa.org/horizons. Presbyterian Church (USA)/Presbyterian Women. Yvonne Hileman, asst. ed. Justice issues and spiritual life for Presbyterian women. Bimonthly mag. & annual Bible study; 40 pgs.; circ. 25,000. Subscription $18. 10 percent unsolicited freelance; 90 percent assigned. Complete ms preferred; fax/e-query OK. Pays $50/600 words on publication for all rts. Articles 600-1,800 words (10/yr.) & fiction 800-1,200 words (5/yr.); book reviews 100 words ($25). Responds in 3 mos. Seasonal 6 mos. ahead. Accepts simultaneous submissions & reprints (tell when/where appeared). Accepts requested ms on disk or by e-mail (attached file or copied into message). Kill fee. Regularly uses sidebars. Prefers NRSV. Guidelines/theme list by mail/e-mail/Website; copy $4/9 x 12 SAE. (No ads)

Poetry: Buys 5/yr. All types; $50-100. Submit max. 5 poems.

Fillers: Cartoons, church-related graphics; $50.

Tips: "Most open to devotionals, mission stories, justice and peace issues. Writer should be familiar with constituency of Presbyterian women and life in the Presbyterian Church (USA)."

** This periodical was #6 on the 2006 Top 50 Christian Publishers list (#11 in 2005).

$ @ INSPIREDMOMS.COM, PO Box 293477, Lewisville TX 75077. (972) 979-7438. E-mail: wendy@inspiredmoms.com. Website: www.inspiredmoms.com. Wind Spirit Press. Wendy Hamilton, site ed. Bimonthly e-zine & resource Website for moms. Open to unsolicited freelance on themes. Complete ms/bio by e-mail only (indicate theme/edition for submission in e-mail subject line). Pays $25/published article. Articles to 1,000-1,200 words (48/yr.). Accepts reprints not published within previous 6 months. Responds in 2-3 wks. Guidelines/theme list on Website or by e-mail.

Tips: "We need writers skilled at conversational writing and approaching tough topics relevant to moms."

@ INSPIRED WOMEN MAGAZINE, E-mail: publisher@inspiredwomenmagazine.com. Website: www.inspiredwomenmagazine.com. Christian. Adriana Zamot, pub. Offers the women of the world information about the issues that affect us every day. Monthly online mag. Open to unsolicited freelance. Query first; e-query preferred. **NO PAYMENT** for onetime rts. Articles. Guidelines/copy online. Incomplete topical listings.

$ INSPIRIT MAGAZINE, 5101 N. Francisco Ave., Chicago IL 60625. (773) 907-3332. Fax (773) 784-4366. E-mail: wmc@covchurch.org. Website: www.covchurch.com/women/inspirit-magazine. Dept. of Women Ministries. Ruth Hill, ed-in-chief (ruth.hill@covchurch.org). To inform and inspire women across the Evangelical Covenant denomination. Quarterly mag.; 50 pgs.; circ. 2,500. Subscription $12. 40 percent unsolicited freelance; 60 percent assigned. Complete ms/cover letter; phone/fax/e-query OK. Must include e-mail contact address. Pays $25-35 on publication. Articles about 750 words (4/yr.); fiction 750-800 words (4/yr.). Seasonal 2.5 mos. ahead. Accepts simultaneous submissions & reprints (tell when/where appeared). Prefers e-mail submissions (attached file). Uses some sidebars. Prefers TNIV or NIV. Guidelines/theme list on Website; copy for 6 x 9 SAE/$2.50. (Ads)

Tips: "Follow themes printed in issues and guidelines posted on our Website."

+ @ JEWELS OF GOD.COM, E-mail: info@jewelsofgod.com. Website: http://jewelsofgod.com. Covenant Treasures Ministries Inc. Tonja Taylor, ed. Weekly e-zine for women. Estab. 2008. 90 percent unsolicited freelance; 10 percent assigned. Query or complete ms/cover letter; e-query OK.

Accepts full mss by e-mail. **NO PAYMENT** for onetime rts. Not copyrighted. Articles to 1,000 words (100/yr.); fiction to 3,000 words (100/yr.); reviews 100 words. Responds in 2 wks. Seasonal 3 mos. ahead. Accepts simultaneous submissions & reprints (tell when/where appeared). Prefers e-mail submissions (attached file). Uses some sidebars. Accepts submission from teens (with parental OK by e-mail). Prefers NIV, AMP, Message. Guidelines by e-mail; copy online. (Ads)

Poetry: Accepts 60/yr. Avant-garde, free verse; to 30 lines. Submit max. 5 poems.

Fillers: Accepts 36/yr. Anecdotes, facts, games, ideas, kid quotes, prayers, quizzes, and word puzzles, 10-100 words.

Tips: "All areas open to freelancers."

$ JOURNEY: A Woman's Guide to Intimacy with God, One Lifeway Plaza, Nashville TN 37234-0175. (615) 251-5659. E-mail: journey@lifeway.com. Website: www.lifeway.com. LifeWay Christian Resources. Articles to: Manuscript Submissions at address above. Devotional submissions to: Susan Nelson, Walk Through the Bible, 4201 N. Peachtree Rd., Atlanta GA 30341. Pamela Nixon, lead ed.; Tammy Drolsum, ed. Devotional magazine for women 30-50 years old. Monthly mag.; 44 pgs.; circ. 215,000. Subscription $24.95. 15 percent unsolicited freelance; 85 percent staff or assigned. Subscription $22.05. Query/clips or complete ms/cover letter; no phone/fax/e-query or e-submissions. Pays $50-100 on acceptance for all rts. Articles 350-1,000 words (10-12/yr.). Responds in 8 wks. Seasonal 6-7 mos. ahead. Regularly uses sidebars. Prefers HCSB. Accepts requested ms on disk. Guidelines by mail; copy for 6 x 9 SASE/2 stamps.

Special Needs: Strong feature articles, 750-1,000 words (including sidebars) on topics of interest to women 30-50 years old ranging from practical applications of faith to spiritual growth, as well as profiles of Christian women in leadership positions.

Tips: "Most open to feature articles that are well written with a thorough understanding of our magazine and target audience. Strong sample devotionals written in Journey style may be considered for assignment of a devotional."

JUST BETWEEN US, 777 S. Barker Rd., Brookfield WI 53045. Toll-free (800) 260-3342. (262) 786-6478. Fax (262) 796-5752. E-mail: jbu@elmbrook.org. Website: www.justbetweenus.org. Elmbrook Church Inc. Shelly Esser, ed. Ideas, encouragement, and resources for wives of evangelical ministers and women in leadership. Quarterly mag.; 40 pgs.; circ. 8,000. Subscription $19.95. 85 percent unsolicited freelance; 15 percent assigned. Query; phone/fax/e-query OK. **NO PAYMENT** for onetime rts. Articles 250-500 words or 1,200-1,500 words (50/yr.). Responds in 8 wks. Accepts simultaneous submissions & reprints. Regularly uses sidebars. Prefers NIV. Guidelines by mail/e-mail/Website; copy $4/9 x 12 SAE. (Ads)

Fillers: Accepts 15/yr. Anecdotes, ideas, prayers, quotes, short humor; 50-250 wds.

Tips: "Most open to feature articles addressing the unique needs of women in leadership (Bible-study leaders, women's ministry directors, pastors' wives, missionary wives, etc.); or "Ideas to Inspire" column with short ministry tips for readers. Some of these needs would include relationship with God, staff, leadership skills, ministry how-tos, balancing ministry and family, and marriage. The best way to break in is to contact the editor with a query."

@ LIFE TOOLS FOR WOMEN: Online Women's Lifestyle Magazine, 40 MacEwan Park Rise, N.W., Calgary AB T3K 3Z9, Canada. (403) 295-1932. Fax (403) 291-2515. E-mail: editor@life toolsforwomen.com. Website: www.lifetoolsforwomen.com. Judy Rushfeldt, ed. Equipping women to reach their potential. Monthly online mag. Monthly page views: 45,000. Articles 500-1,200 wds. **NO PAYMENT**. Provides a byline and up to 50-word bio, including e-mail & Website link. Prefers e-query & e-submission (attached file). Guidelines on Website.

$ THE LINK & VISITOR, 100-304 The East Mall, Etobicoke ON M9B 6E2, Canada. (416) 651-8967. Fax (416) 622-2308. E-mail: rjames@baptistwomen.com. Website: www.baptistwomen.com. Baptist Women of Ontario and Quebec. Renee James, ed. A positive, practical Baptist magazine for Canadian women who want to reach others for Christ. Bimonthly mag.; 24 pgs.; circ. 4,000. Subscription $17 Cdn., $17 U.S. 50 percent freelance. Complete ms; e-query OK. Pays .06-.10/wd. Cdn., on publication for onetime or simultaneous rts.; some work-for-hire. Articles 600-1,000 words (30-35/yr.). Responds in 16 wks. Seasonal 4 mos. ahead. Accepts simultaneous submissions & reprints (tell when/where appeared). Requires e-mail submission (copied into message). No kill fee. Uses some sidebars. Prefers NIV (inclusive language), NRSV, NLT. Guidelines/theme list on Website; copy for 9 x 12 SASE/2 Cdn. stamps. (Ads—limited/Canadian)

Poetry: Buys 6/yr. Free verse; 12-32 lines; pays $10-20. Submit max. 3 poems.

Tips: "Feature writers who know our magazine and our readers will know what topics and types of stories we are looking for. Canadian writers only, please."

@ **LIVE MAGAZINE**, (formerly L.I.V.E.). E-mail: info@liv-magazine.com. Website: www.livein victory.org. Suber Media Group. Cheryl A. Pullins, ed-in-chief. A Christian publication for the affluent Christian woman; dedicated to excellence, enlightenment, and empowerment. Online mag. Free subscription. Open to freelance. Send query by e-mail. E-mail for guidelines. (Ads—advertising@ liv-magazine.com)

Tips: "Our mission is to promote the application of the principles of the Word of God by using the magazine as a tool to empower people to live in victory in every area of their lives! The magazine is a ministry. Through articles and imagery LIVE Magazine showcases, shares, and encourages people around the globe with the message of victory!"

LUTHERAN WOMAN'S QUARTERLY, PO Box 411993, St. Louis MO 63141-1993. Toll-free (800) 252-5965. Fax (314) 268-1532. E-mail: editor@lwml.org. Website: www.lwml.org. Lutheran Women's Missionary League. Nancy Graf Peters, ed-in-chief. For women of the Lutheran Church— Missouri Synod. Quarterly mag.; 44 pgs.; circ. 200,000. Subscription $5.50. 25 percent unsolicited freelance; 75 percent assigned. Complete ms/cover letter. **NO PAYMENT**. Not copyrighted. Articles 750-1,200 words (4/yr.); fiction 750-1,200 words (4/yr.). Responds in 2 wks. Seasonal 5 mos. ahead. Regularly uses sidebars. Prefers NIV. Guidelines/theme list by mail/e-mail; no copy.

Tips: "Most open to articles. Must reflect the Missouri Synod teachings. Most of our writers are from the denomination. We set themes two years ahead. Contact us for themes and guidelines."

$ @ **MARYLAND WOMEN OF WORSHIP**, 3117 Ferndale Ave., Baltimore MD 21207. E-mail: mdwomenofworship@yahoo.com. Website: www.marylandwomenofworship.com. Wilhelmina Street, ed. Online mag. & quarterly devotional guide. Open to unsolicited freelance. Complete ms by mail or e-mail. Pays $12. Articles 300 wds. Guidelines, themes, deadlines, & devotional format on Website.

Special Needs: Study lessons (see Website).

$ @ **MELODY OF THE HEART: Reconciling Hearts; Offering Hope**, 8409 S. Elder Ave., Broken Arrow, OK 74011-8286. (918) 451-4017. E-mail inquiries: Please use Online Contact Form (No mail submissions). Website: http://www.epistleworks.com/HeartMelody. Epistleworks Creations. JoAnn Reno Wray, ed./pub. Christian publication for women 30-65+ yrs.; heart-stirring, tight writing to bring practicality and joy to life. Bimonthly online publication; over 100,000 hits monthly. Open to freelance. Query with online form for most submissions (including short fiction). Pays on publication for reprint or 1st electronic rights: $40 for columnists (1st rights only. Currently filled; open to queries. Columnists commit to one year/6 columns.); $20-25 for articles and short fiction. Published material includes short bio (150 words plus current photo in "JPG" format). Any rights purchased include one month exclusive publication in our online magazine, then may sell elsewhere. Pays by check or PayPal. After initial publication, articles archived for 6 months. Articles 750-900 words; short fiction under 1000 words. Response only if work accepted due to high volume of submissions. Writers should check the online guidelines often to note any changes in editorial needs. Guidelines PDF available for download. Not currently accepting submissions.

$ MOMSENSE (MomSense), 2370 S. Trenton Way, Denver CO 80231. (303) 733-5353. Fax (303) 733-5770. E-mail: MomSense@mops.org. Website: www.MomSense.org, or www.MOPS.org. MOPS Intl. Inc. (Mothers of Preschoolers). Mary Darr, ed. Nurtures mothers of preschoolers from a Christian perspective with articles that both inform and inspire on issues relating to womanhood and motherhood. Bimonthly mag.; 32 pgs.; circ. 120,000. Subscription $23.95. 20 percent unsolicited freelance; 30 percent assigned. Complete ms/cover letter & bio; e-query OK. Accepts full mss by e-mail. Pays .15/wd. on publication for 1st & reprint rts. Articles 600 words (15-20/yr.). Responds in 10-12 wks. Seasonal 6 mos. ahead. Accepts simultaneous submissions & reprints (tell when/where appeared). Prefers requested ms by e-mail (attached file or copied into message). Some kill fees 10 percent. Uses some sidebars. Prefers NIV. Guidelines/theme list by mail/e-mail/or at www.MOPS.org/write; copy for 9 x 12 SASE/$1.39 postage. (Ads)

> **Poetry:** Buys 6/yr. Any type to 400 wds. Pays .15/wd. Submit max. 6 poems.
> **Fillers:** Accepts 10/yr. Tips. No payment.
> **Special Needs:** "We always need practical articles to the woman as a woman, and to the woman as a mom."
> **Contest:** Sponsors several contests per year for writing and photography. Check Website for details on current contests.
> **Tips:** "Most open to theme-specific features. Writers are more seriously considered if they are a mother with some connection to MOPS (but not required). Looking for original content ideas that appeal to Christian and non-Christian readers."
> ** This periodical was #34 on the 2009 Top 50 Christian Publishers list (#14 in 2008, #21 in 2007).

MORE TO LIFE (MTL), 415 Second St., Indian Rocks Beach FL 33785. (727) 596-7625. Fax (727) 593-3523. E-mail: info@munce.com. Website: www.MTLMagazine.com. The Munce Group. Andrea Stock, ed. Lifestyle magazine for women who are discovering their spiritual core and true purpose. 8x/yr. mag.; 36-72 pgs.; circ. 250,000-2 million. Incomplete topical listings. (Ads)

> **Tips:** "This magazine will draw attention to the quality, variety, and relevance of Christian products for everyday living and guide the readers back to Christian retail stores."

+ THE MOTHER'S HEART MAGAZINE, PO Box 231, Oxford MI 48370. E-mail: Editor@TMHMag.com. Website: www.The-Mothers-Heart.com. Kym Wright, ed. Serves and encourages mothers in the many facets of staying at home and raising a family. Bimonthly online mag.; 80-100 pgs; circ. 20,000. Subscription by donation. 30% unsolicited freelance; 50% assigned. Query or complete ms; e-query OK. Pays $10-75 on publication for 1st, reprint, electronic rts. Articles 1,500-2,000 words (45/yr.); book & video reviews 150-200 wds. Responds in 3-6 wks. Seasonal 4-6 mos. ahead. No simultaneous submissions; possibly reprints (tell when/where appeared). Requires e-mail submissions, attached (.doc or.docx files only) or copied into message. No kill fee. Regularly uses sidebars. Prefers NIV. Also accepts submissions from teens. Guidelines by e-mail/Website; download copy from Website. (Ads)

> **Fillers:** Buys up to 20/yr. Anecdotes, facts, ideas, kid quotes, short humor, and tips; 100-250 wds. Pays $10-20.
> **Columns/Departments:** Query, then send complete ms/15 article ideas for column topic. Pays $50-75.
> **Special Needs:** Adoption stories. Large families: how you do it, organization, travel. Money management in our economic times. Raising special-needs children. "Coming Home" stories about mothers who choose to stay home with their children. Homocentric pieces. Homeschool unit studies.
> **Tips:** "Editor will work with author to develop article idea. To break in, read back issues, then query with your idea. Inspirational, encouragement, upbeat pieces will be considered over others. Sound biblical concepts, articles based on and including scripture. Write from

an outline. Begin with a scenario, story, or hook to spark reader's interest." Open to almost any topic.

+ @ OREGON WOMENS REPORT.COM. (503) 644-1300. E-mail: Oregon@oregonreport.com. Website: www.OregonWomensReport.com. Online women's magazine that features intelligent ideas, thoughtful opinions, and real-life experiences of local women. Jason Williams, pub. Webzine. Open to freelance. Complete ms by e-mail. Articles. **NO PAYMENT**.

Tips: "Our open-comment webzine allows people to discuss articles and build an online community around our writers. We are seeking volunteer article submissions on topical issues, insightful commentary, and true-to-life testimonies."

$ PAUSES: An Oasis for Today's Catholic Woman, N1261Briarwood Ln., Merrill WI 54452. (715) 536-2450. E-mail: sallie.2@netzero.com. Catholic. Sallie Bachar, ed. To inspire, encourage, and enable Catholic women to reach the fullness of their potential through the Catholic Church. Quarterly newsletter; 8 pgs. Subscription $10. 100 percent unsolicited freelance. Complete ms/ cover letter; e-query OK. Pays $10 on publication for onetime rts. Articles 300-500 words (50/yr.); reviews 200 words. Responds in 4 wks. Seasonal 3 mos. ahead. Accepts simultaneous submissions; no reprints. Accepts submissions by e-mail (attached). Does not use sidebars. Guidelines by mail/e-mail; copy for 6 x 9 SASE/2 stamps. (Ads)

PRECIOUS TIMES, 3857 Birch St., Ste. 215, Newport Beach CA 92660. Toll-free (800) 299-0696. (714) 564-3949. E-mail: precioustimesmag@gmail.com or bookrevieweditor@precioustimesmag .com. Website: www.precioustimesmag.com. Independent. Marilyn White, pub/ed-in-chief. To help black women (ages 20-60) grow in their relationship with God, self, and others; biblical, but not preachy. Quarterly mag.; 76 pgs.; circ. 350,000. Subscription $18. 90 percent unsolicited freelance; 10 percent assigned. Complete ms; e-query OK. **PAYS 5 COPIES** for 1st rts. Personal testimonies, 1,800-2,000 words; everyday-life information, 1,200-2,400 words; health/fitness/beauty, 1,200 words; celebrity/personality interviews, 1,800-2,400 words; book reviews, 250-300 words; music reviews, 200-500 words; fiction, 2,400-3,200 words. (20 articles/yr.; 4 fiction). Responds in 12 wks. Seasonal 10 mos. ahead. Accepts simultaneous submissions & reprints (tell when/where appeared). Requires e-mail submissions (attached or copied into message in Word only). Uses some sidebars. Prefers NIV. Also accepts submissions from teens. Guidelines by mail/e-mail/Website; copy $5/9 x 12 SAE. (Ads)

Columns/Departments: Business, Health, Beauty, Finance; 600 words.

Tips: "Provide practical theology for contemporary issues. All articles should have a personal perspective, be relevant, and use real life anecdotes. We prefer a black woman's perspective on life issues."

P31 WOMAN, 616-G Matthews-Mint Hill Rd., Matthews NC 28105. (704) 849-2270. Fax (704) 849-7267. E-mail: editor@proverbs31.org. Website: www.proverbs31.org. Proverbs 31 Ministries. Glynnis Whitwer, ed.; submit to Janet Burke, asst. ed. (janet@proverbs31.org). Seeks to offer a godly woman's perspective on life. Monthly mag.; 16 pgs.; circ. 10,000. Subscription for donation. 50 percent unsolicited freelance; 50 percent assigned. Complete ms; e-query OK. **PAYS IN COPIES** for onetime rts. Not copyrighted. Articles 200-1,000 words (40/yr.). Responds in 4-6 wks. Seasonal 3 mos. ahead. Accepts simultaneous submissions & reprints (tell when/where appeared). Prefers accepted ms by e-mail (attached file or copied into message). Uses some sidebars. Prefers NIV. Guidelines/theme list by mail/Website; copy on Website. (No ads)

Fillers: Accepts 12/yr. Ideas, party ideas, prose; to 100 words.

Tips: "Looking for articles that encourage women and offer practical advice as well."

@ RIGHT TO THE HEART OF WOMEN E-ZINE, 2217 Lake Park Dr., Longmont CO 80503. (303) 772-2035. Fax (303) 678-0260. E-mail: rmontgomery@rebekahmontgomery.com. Website: www .righttotheheartofwomen.com. Rebekah Montgomery, ed. Encouragement and helps for women in ministry. Weekly online e-zine; 5 pgs.; circ. 18,000. Subscription free. 10 percent unsolicited freelance; 90 percent assigned. Query; e-query OK. **NO PAYMENT** for nonexclusive rts. Articles 100-800 words (20/yr.). Responds in 2 wks. Seasonal 2 mos. ahead. Accepts simultaneous submissions & reprints (tell when/where appeared). Requires accepted mss by e-mail (copied into message). Does not use sidebars. No guidelines; copy on Website. (Ads)

Columns/Departments: Accepts 10/yr. Women Bible Teachers; Profiles of Women in Ministry; Women's Ministry Tips; Author's and Speaker's Tips; 100 wds. Query.
Special Needs: Book reviews must be in first person, by the author. Looking for women's ministry event ideas. Topics related to women and women's ministries.
Tips: "For free subscription, subscribe at Website above; also view e-zine. We want to hear from those involved in women's ministry or leadership. Also accepts manuscripts from AWSAs (see www.awsawomen.com). Query with your ideas."

SHARE, 10 W. 71st St., New York NY 10023-4201. (212) 877-3041. Fax (212) 724-5923. E-mail: CDofANatl@aol.com. Website: www.catholicdaughters.org. Catholic Daughters of the Americas. Peggy O'Brien, exec. dir.; submit to Peggy Eastman, ed. For Catholic women. Quarterly mag.; circ. 85,000. Free with membership. Most articles come from membership, but is open. **NO PAYMENT**. Buys color photos & covers. Guidelines/copy by mail. (Ads)

Tips: "We use very little freelance material unless it is written by Catholic Daughters."

SIMPLY BLESSED CHRISTIAN WOMEN'S MAGAZINE, PO Box 291205, Columbia SC 29229. (803) 968-5196. Fax (803) 234-4071. E-mail: jjpublisher@yahoo.com. Website: www.simplyblessedmag .com. J and J Publishing Co. Stephanie McKenny, ed./pub. (editor@simplyblessedmag.com). For all women 25-55, focusing on encouraging and empowering them to perform in their roles at a greater capacity along with sharing information that will assist them in their day-to-day lifestyles. Bimonthly mag.; 40+ pgs. Subscription $18. Estab. 2007. 60 percent unsolicited freelance; 40 percent assigned. Query/clips; e-query OK. Accepts full mss by e-mail. **NO PAYMENT**. Not copyrighted. Articles 800-1,000 words (3/yr.); fiction 800-1,000 words (3/yr.); reviews 500 words. Responds in 2 wks. Seasonal 3 mos. ahead. Accepts reprints (tell when/where appeared). Accepts e-mail submissions (attached file). Uses some sidebars. Prefers KJV or AMP. Guidelines by mail/e-mail; copy for $2/9 x 12 SAE. (Ads)

Fillers: Accepts 6/yr. Cartoons, facts, prayers, tips; 200-300 words.
Columns/Departments: Accepts 6-10/yr. Seasoned Sisters (women 50+); Pastor's Wives Corner (encouragement for pastor's wives); Health Awareness; Single & Satisfied; all 500-800 wds. Query.
Tips: "Most open to health, marriage, singles, wealth, and business."

$ SPIRITLED WOMAN, 600 Rinehart Rd., Lake Mary FL 32746. (407) 333-0600. Fax (407) 333-7100. E-mail: spiritledwoman@strang.com. Website: www.spiritledwoman.com. Strang Communications. Brenda J. Davis, ed. To call women, ages 20-60, into intimate fellowship with God so He can empower them to fulfill His purpose for their lives. Bimonthly mag.; 100 pgs.; circ. 100,000. Subscription $17.95. 1 percent unsolicited freelance; 99 percent assigned. Query (limit to 500 words); e-query OK. Pays to $300 ($50 for humor, $75 for testimonies) on publication for 1st and all electronic rts. Articles 1,200-2,000 wds. Responds in 18-26 wks. No simultaneous submissions. Guidelines by mail/e-mail; copy. (Ads)

Columns/Departments: Testimonies; Final Fun (funny stories or embarrassing moments, to 200 words); cartoons; $25-50.
Tips: "Most of our articles are commissioned. Mainly we want high-impact feature articles that depict a practical and spiritual application of Scriptural teachings. Need brief testimonies of 350 words or less (open to all); profiles of women in ministry. Articles need to deal with the heart issues that hold a woman back. Also humorous anecdotes and book excerpts."
** 2007 EPA Award of Merit—Most Improved Publication.

TOGETHER WITH GOD, PO Box 5002, Antioch TN 37011. Toll-free (877) 767-7662. (615) 731-6812. Fax (615) 731-0771. E-mail: twg@wnac.org. Website: www.wnac.org. Women Nationally Active for Christ of National Assn. of Free Will Baptists. Sarah Fletcher, ed. A women's magazine with emphasis on fulfilling the Great Commission. Bimonthly mag.; 32 pgs.; circ. 7,500. Subscription $12. Estab. 2007. 25 percent unsolicited freelance; 75 percent assigned. Complete ms/cover letter. Accepts full ms by e-mail. **PAYS IN COPIES** for 1st rts. Articles 750-1,200 words (10/yr.). Responds in 8 wks. Seasonal 12 mos. ahead. No simultaneous submissions; accepts reprints (tell when/where appeared). Prefers e-mail submissions (attached file). Regularly uses sidebars. Also accepts submissions from teens. Prefers KJV. Guidelines/theme list by e-mail; copy for 10 x 13 SAE/$1. (No ads)

> **Columns/Departments:** What Works (practical tips/lists about women's health, homes, fitness, fashion, or finances; My Mentor (women 13-40 write about older women's influence in life); 500-700 words.
> **Special Needs:** Christian life, family issues, creative outreach.
> **Contest:** Annual Creative Arts Contest. March 1 deadline. Categories include Programs, Articles, Poetry, Plays/Skits, Devotionals, Art/Photography. Open to our subscribers, Women Active for Christ, or any woman active in the Free Will Baptist Church.
> **Tips:** "Most open to articles. Bulk of material comes from Women Active for Christ or Free Will Baptist writers."

+ @ THE UNRECOGNIZED WOMAN ONLINE MAGAZINE & E-ZINE, 412 Cornwallis Ct., Ashland VA 23005. (804) 496-6449. E-mail: cookashland@aol.com. Website: www.theunrecognizedwoman.com. Outstretched Hands. Joan Cook, ed-in-chief. A Christian, inspirational magazine for all women. Bimonthly e-zine; 45 pgs; circ. 5,000. Subscription free. Estab. 2007. 30 percent unsolicited freelance; 70 percent assigned. Query/e-query OK. Accepts full mss by e-mail. **NO PAYMENT** for one-time & electronic rts. Articles 500 words (4/yr.); fiction (4/yr.); book reviews 75 words. Responds in 8 wks. Seasonal 2 mos. ahead. No simultaneous submissions. Accepts reprints (tell when/where appeared). Requires e-mail submissions (attached file). Accepts submissions from teens. Guidelines/theme list/copy on Website. (Ads)

> **Poetry:** Accepts 20/yr. Any type; 3-20 lines. Submit max. 3 poems.
> **Fillers:** Accepts facts, prayers, quotes, short humor, and tips, 50-100 wds.
> **Columns/Departments:** Accepts 30/yr. Complete ms.
> **Contest:** Essay contest for teen girls to write about a woman who has—and how she has—impacted her life; and what she inspired the girl to do to impact the lives of others.
> **Tips:** "All areas are open to freelancers. Besides checking topical listings here, you can refer to our article submission topics on the Website."

@ A VIRTUOUS WOMAN, 594 Ivy Hill, Harlan KY 40831. (606) 573-6506. E-mail: submissions@avirtuouswoman.org. Website: www.avirtuouswoman.org. Independent Seventh-day Adventist ministry. Melissa Ringstaff, dir./ed. Strives to provide practical articles for women ages 20-60 years; based on Proverbs 31. Monthly e-zine; circ. 20,000+ online. 80 percent unsolicited freelance; 20 percent assigned. Complete ms/cover letter; e-query OK. Accepts full mss by e-mail. **NO PAYMENT** for first, reprint, electronic, anthology rts. Articles 500-2,000 words (150+/yr.); reviews 500-1,000 words. Responds in 6-8 wks. Seasonal 6 mos. ahead. No simultaneous submissions; accepts reprints (tell when/where appeared). Accepts e-mail submissions (attached file in DOC or TXT or copied into message). Uses some sidebars. Prefers KJV, NIV, NLT. Guidelines/theme list on Website; copy for 9 x 12 SASE/$2.02 postage & $3.50. (Ads)

> **Poetry:** Accepts 5/yr. Free verse, traditional. Submit max. 2 poems.
> **Fillers:** Accepts 12/yr. Anecdotes, facts, ideas, jokes, party ideas, prayers, quizzes, and tips; to 200 wds.
> **Tips:** "Write practical articles that appeal to the average woman—articles that women can identify with. Do not preach. Read our writer's helps for ideas."

A WOMAN OF WORTH, 594 Ivy Hill, Harlan KY 40831. (606) 573-6506. E-mail: submissions@ avirtuouswoman.org. Website: www.avirtuouswoman.org. A Virtuous Woman. Melissa Ringstaff, dir./ ed. Strives to provide practical articles for women ages 20-60 years; based on Proverbs 31. Quarterly jour. & cookbook; 40-48 pgs.; circ. 20,000. Subscription $24.95. 90 percent unsolicited freelance. Complete ms/cover letter; e-query OK. Accepts full mss by e-mail. **PAYS 1 COPY** for first, reprint, electronic, & anthology rts. Articles 500-2,000 words (100/yr.); fiction 500-2,000 (1-2/yr.); reviews 500 words. Responds in 6-8 wks. Seasonal 6 mos. ahead. No simultaneous submissions; accepts reprints (tell when/where appeared). Accepts submissions on disk or by e-mail (copied into message or attached in DOC or TXT). Regularly uses sidebars. Prefers KJV, NIV, NLT. Guidelines/theme list on Website; copy for 9 x 12 SAE/$6.75.

Poetry: Accepts 4-6/yr. Free verse, traditional; 20-30 lines. Submit max. 2 poems.

Fillers: Accepts 5-10/yr. Facts, short humor, and tips; 100-500 wds.

Columns/Departments: Accepts 100+/yr. Has a number of columns open to freelancers. See Website for list and length.

Contests: Occasionally runs contests for readers.

Tips: "Articles should be practical, giving reader useful ideas to apply to her own life. We like inspiring articles that offer encouragement and hope."

@ WOMEN OF THE CROSS, 920 Sweetgum Creek, Plano TX 75023. (972) 517-8553. Greg Paskal, content mngr. (greg@gregpaskal.com). Encouraging women in their walk with the Lord; strong emphasis on discipleship and relationship. Online community. 50 percent unsolicited freelance. Complete ms by e-mail; e-query OK. **NO PAYMENT**. Articles 500-1,500 words (10/yr.). Responds in 2-4 wks. Seasonal 3 mos. ahead. Accepts simultaneous submissions; no reprints. Prefers e-mail submissions (attached or copied into message). Uses some sidebars. Prefers NIV, NKJV, NASB. Also accepts submissions from teens. Guidelines by e-mail. (No ads)

Poetry: Accepts 2/yr. Avant-garde, free verse, haiku, or light verse; 50-250 lines. Submit max. 1 poem.

Columns/Departments: Accepts 10/yr. Features (Christian living, encouragement); Article (to other women); all 500-1,500 words.

Special Needs: Personal stories of growing in the Lord; faith-stretching stories about international adoption.

Tips: "Appropriate topics could be first-hand accounts of how God worked in the author's life through a personal or family experience. View online forum for specific topics."

@ WOMEN'S MINISTRY MAGAZINE, 4319 S. National Ave., #303, Springfield MO 65810-2607. (417) 888-2067. Fax (866) 360-2611. E-mail: publisher@womensministry.net. Website: www .womensministry.net, or www.jenniferrothschild.com. Jennifer and Philip Rothschild, pubs. Where more than 25,000 women's ministry leaders find news, events, and tips for women's ministry in the local church. Online newsletter. Subscription free. Open to freelance. Use online submission form. Guidelines on Website.

Special Needs: Punchy, practical tips and ideas related to leading effective women's ministry.

@ WOMEN TODAY MAGAZINE, Box 300, Sta. A, Vancouver BC V6C 2X3, Canada. Toll-free (800) 563-1106, ext. 252. (604) 514-2000 (no phone calls). Fax (604) 514-2002. E-mail: editor@ womentodaymagazine.com. Website: www.womentodaymagazine.com. Campus Crusade for Christ, Canada. Karen Schenk, pub.; Claire Colvin, sr. ed. For the professional, preseeking woman, 20-60 years; provides quality information that leads into a discussion of spiritual things and a presentation of the gospel. Monthly e-zine; 1.5 million hits/mo.; 100,000 unique visitors/mo. 60 percent unsolicited freelance; up to 10 percent assigned. Must use online submission system on Website; e-query OK. Accepts full ms by e-mail. **NO PAYMENT** for onetime or reprint rts. Articles 300-1,000 words (12-24/yr.). Responds in 8-12 wks. to accepted material only. Seasonal 4 mos. ahead. Accepts simultaneous submissions & reprints. Requires use of online submission form. Does not use sidebars. Also accepts submissions from teens. Guidelines/theme list on Website. (Ads)

Columns/Departments: Columns tend toward how-to; 600-1,000 wds. Beauty & Fashion; Health & Fitness; Food & Cooking; Advice.

Tips: "Write on a topic from the theme list 4-5 months in advance. Beauty/fashion, relationships, and self-esteem are big draws on our site, and we can always use more great content. To break in, make your article approachable to an unchurched audience, avoid Christian jargon, and speak the truth plainly."

WRITERS' MARKETS

$ ADVANCED CHRISTIAN WRITER, 9118 W. Elmwood Dr., #1G, Niles IL 60714-5820. (847) 296-3964. Fax (847) 296-0754. E-mail: ljohnson@wordprocommunications.com. Website: www .ACWriters.com. American Christian Writers/Reg Forder, Box 110390, Nashville TN 37222. Toll-free (800) 21-WRITE. E-mail: ACWriters@aol.com (for samples, advertising, and subscriptions). Lin Johnson, mng. ed. A professional newsletter for published writers. Bimonthly newsletter; 8 pgs.; circ. 500. Subscription $19.95. 50 percent unsolicited freelance. Query, correspondence, & mss by e-mail only. Pays $20 on publication for 1st or reprint rts. Articles 500-1,200 words (18/yr.). Responds in 4-6 wks. Seasonal 6 mos. ahead. Accepts reprints (tell when/where appeared). Uses some sidebars. Requires e-mail submission. Prefers NIV. Guidelines by mail/e-mail; copy for #10 SAE/1 stamp. (Ads)

Special Needs: Behind the scenes look at a publishing house (how it started, how editorial operates, current needs, submission procedures); how-to; opinion pieces; time management; workplace issues.

Tips: "We accept articles only from professional, well-published writers and from editors. We need manuscripts about all aspects of building a freelance career and how to increase sales and professionalism; on the advanced level; looking for depth beyond the basics."

AREOPAGUS MAGAZINE. E-mail editor@areopagus.org.uk. Website: www.areopagus.org.uk. Areopagus Publications. Julian Barritt, ed. For amateur Christian writers, producing both general and Christian writing. Quarterly mag.; 32 pgs.; circ. 100. Subscription $17 U.S. 0 percent unsolicited freelance. Complete ms/cover letter (if subscriber); e-query OK. **NO PAYMENT.** Articles 1,800 words (6/ yr.); fiction 1,800 words (5/yr.); book reviews 300 words. Responds in 1 mo. Seasonal 4 mos. ahead. Accepts e-mail submissions (attached or copied into message). Does not use sidebars. Any Bible version. Guidelines by mail; copy on Website.

Poetry: Accepts 40/yr.; any type; to 60 lines. Submit max. 3 poems.

Fillers: Accepts 10/yr. Facts, ideas, newsbreaks, prose, short humor, to 200 wds.

Contest: Sponsors a quarterly, subscribers-only, writing competition (fiction, nonfiction, or poetry).

Tips: "Items are selected by merit from subscribers only. If not accepted, a recommendation for resubmission is given if there is potential."

AUTHOR-ME.COM, PO Box 451, Dundee IL 60118. E-mail: cookcomm@gte.net. Website: www .Author-Me.com. Independent. Bruce L. Cook, pub.; Adam W. Smith, ed. dir. (awsmith@patriot.net); Winona Rasheed, mng. ed. (mzcoffeecake2001@yahoo.com). Endeavors to encourage and nurture new writers in their craft. Accepts freelance. Complete ms. **NO PAYMENT.** No submissions from writers under age 14. Edit manuscripts before submitting. Requires e-mail submissions from Website form. Guidelines on Website.

Poetry: Submit max. 4 poems.

$ BEST NEW WRITING, PO Box 11, Titusville NJ 08560. E-mail: editor@hopepubs.com. Website: www.bestnewwriting.com. Christopher Klim, exec. ed.; Robert Gover, ed. In 2006, *Writers' Notes Magazine* was transformed in this annual anthology, which carries the results of the Eric Hoffer

Award for Books and Prose. Submit books via mail; no queries. The prose category is for creative fiction and nonfiction less than 10,000 wds. Annual award for books features 14 categories. Pays $500 for winning prose; $1,500 for winning book. Guidelines at www.HofferAward.com.

$ CANADIAN WRITER'S JOURNAL, White Mountain Publications, Box 1178, New Liskeard ON P0J 1P0, Canada. Canada-wide toll-free (800) 258-5451. (705) 647-5424. Fax (705) 647-8366. E-mail: cwj@cwj.ca. Website: www.cwj.ca. Deborah Ranchuk, ed./pub. How-to articles for writers. Bimonthly mag.; 64 pgs.; circ. 350. Subscription $35. 75 percent unsolicited freelance; 15 percent assigned. Complete ms/cover letter or query; phone/fax/e-query OK. Pays $7.50 Cdn./published pg. (about 450 words) on publication (2-9 mos. after acceptance) for onetime rts. Articles 400-2,000 words (200/ yr.); fiction to 1,200 words (see contest below); book/music/video reviews 250-500 words ($7.50). Responds in 9 wks. Seasonal 3 mos. ahead. Accepts simultaneous submissions & reprints (tell when/ where appeared). Prefers e-mail submission (copied into message only). Some sidebars. Prefers KJV. Also accepts submissions from teens. Guidelines by mail/e-mail/Website; copy $9. (Ads)

   Poetry: Buys 40-60/yr. All types; to 40 lines; $2-5. Submit max. 10 poems.
   Fillers: Buys 15-20/yr. Anecdotes, cartoons, ideas, quotes; 20-200 words; $3-5.
   Contest: Sponsors semiannual short fiction contest (March 31 and September 30 deadlines); to 1,200 wds. Entry fee $5. Prizes $100, $50, $25. All fiction needs are filled by this contest. E-mail: cwc-calendar@cwj.ca.
   Tips: "Send clear, complete, concise how-to-write articles with a sense of humor and usefulness. Read the guidelines and follow them, please."
   ** This periodical was #20 on the 2009 Top 50 Christian Publishers list (#30 in 2008, #19 in 2007).

$ CHRISTIAN COMMUNICATOR, 9118 W. Elmwood Dr., #1G, Niles, IL 60714-5820. (847) 296-3964. Fax (847) 296-0754. E-mail: ljohnson@wordprocommunications.com. Website: www .ACWriters.com. American Christian Writers/Reg Forder, Box 110390, Nashville TN 37222. Toll-free (800) 21-WRITE. Fax (615) 834-0450. E-mail: ACWriters@aol.com (for samples, advertising or subscriptions). Lin Johnson, mng. ed.; Mona Hodgson, poetry ed. For Christian writers/speakers who want to improve their writing craft and speaking ability, stay informed about writing markets, and be encouraged in their ministries. Monthly (11x) mag.; 20 pgs.; circ. 3,000. Subscription $29.95. 70 percent unsolicited freelance. Complete ms/queries by e-mail only. Pays $5-10 on publication for 1st or reprint rts. Articles 650-1,000 words (90-100/yr.). Responds in 4-6 wks. Seasonal 6 mos. ahead. Accepts reprints (tell when/where appeared). Requires e-mail submission. Guidelines by e-mail; copy for 9 x 12 SAE/3 stamps to Nashville address. (Ads)

   Poetry: Buys 22/yr. Free verse, haiku, light verse, traditional; to 20 lines. Poems on writing or speaking; $5. Send to Mona Hodgson: mona@monahodgson.com.
   Columns/Departments: Buys 35/yr. A Funny Thing Happened on the Way to Becoming a Communicator (humor), 75-300 words; Interviews (published authors or editors), 650- 1,000 words; Speaker's Corner (techniques for speakers), 650-1,000 words.
   Tips: "I need anecdotes for the "Funny Thing Happened" column and articles on speaking, research, creativity."

CHRISTIANWRITERS.COM. Website: www.christianwriters.com. A free online writers' resource community to provide a supportive, family atmosphere where writers may easily access the tools and resources to create, market, and publish their work. Accepts articles, short fiction, poetry, and devotionals. Submit through Website. Guidelines on Website.

$ CROSS & QUILL, 1624 Jefferson Davis Rd., Clinton SC 29325-6401. (864) 697-6035. E-mail: CQarticles@aol.com or cwfi@cwfi-online.org. Website: www.cwfi-online.org. Christian Writers Fellowship Intl. Sandy Brooks, ed./pub. For Christian writers, editors, agents, conference directors. Bimonthly newsletter; 16 pgs.; circ. 1,000+. Subscription $25; CWFI membership $45. 75 percent unsolicited freelance; 25 percent assigned. Complete ms; query for electronic submissions. Pays $5-50 on publication for 1st or reprint rts. Articles 200-800 words (50/yr.); book reviews 100 words ($5). Responds in 2 mos. Seasonal 6 mos. ahead. Accepts reprints (tell when/where appeared). Uses some sidebars. Accepts e-mail submission (copied into message) to CQArticles@cwfi-online .org. Guidelines by mail/e-mail/Website); copy $2/9 x 12 SASE/3 stamps. (No ads)

Poetry: Accepts 12/yr. Any type; to 12 lines. Submit max. 3 poems. Must pertain to writing/ publishing.

Fillers: Accepts 12/yr. Anecdotes, cartoons, prayers; 25-100 wds. Pays in copies.

Columns/Departments: Accepts 36/yr. Writing Rainbows! (devotional), 500-600 words; Writers Helping Writers (how-to), 200-800 words; Editor's Roundtable (interview with editor), 200-800 words; Tots, Teens & In-Betweens (juvenile market), 200-800 words; BusinessWise (business side of writing), 200-800 words; Connecting Points (how-to on critique group), 200-800 words.

Special Needs: Good "meaty" informational articles on children's writing; fiction market; studying the markets; program ideas for groups; etc.

Tips: "Most open to informational articles that explain how to improve writing skills, how to keep records, how to organize and run a writers' group. Keep in mind our audience is primarily writers and others associated with Christian publishing. Stick to informational, nuts and bolts type articles, and follow our guidelines."

$ FELLOWSCRIPT, PO Box 26016, 650 Portland St., Dartmouth NS B2W 6P3, Canada. E-mail: submissions@inscribe.org. Website: www.inscribe.org. InScribe Christian Writers' Fellowship. Joanna Mallory, acq. ed. To provide encouragement, instruction, news, and helpful information for the membership of InScribe Christian Writers' Fellowship. Quarterly newsletter; 28-44 pgs.; circ. 150-200. Subscription $40 (includes membership). 45 percent unsolicited freelance; 55 percent assigned. Complete ms; e-query OK. Pays $5 or .025/wd. Cdn. on publication for 1st or onetime rts. or.015/wd. for reprint rts. Articles 600-1,200 words (70/yr.); book reviews (writing related), 300-500 words ($5). Responds in 4-6 wks. Seasonal 3-4 mos. ahead. Accepts simultaneous submissions & reprints (tell when/where appeared). Requires mss by e-mail (attached or copied into message). No kill fee. Uses some sidebars. Also accepts submissions from teens. Prefers NIV or NKJV. Guidelines on Website; copy for $3.50 in U.S. or Cdn. stamps or IRCs. (Ads if writing related)

Fillers: Accepts 4-8/yr. Anecdotes, quotes, short humor, tips (all writing-related); 300-600 wds. Pays $5.

Special Needs: Articles of practical help to writers, from beginners to advanced.

Contest: Fall contest in conjunction with InScribe's fall conference every year in September (August deadline). Categories include fiction, poetry, children's stories, essays, and nonfiction. Details on Website, or write and ask to be put on mailing list.

Tips: "The best submissions for us are practical articles on an aspect of writing, written in conversational style and with a good take-away."

$ FICTION FIX NEWSLETTER: The Nuts and Bolts of Crafting Better Fiction. E-mail: adminis tration@coffeehouseforwriters.com. Website: www.coffeehouseforwriters.com/news.html. Carol Lindsay, ed. For writers and aspiring writers of short stories and novels. Monthly newsletter; circ. 5,000. To subscribe, send blank e-mail to FictionFix-subscribe@topica.com. E-query only. Responds in 2-3 wks. Pays to $20 ($30-50 for assigned) within 10 days of publication for 1st electronic rts. How-to articles 300-1,500 wds. Prefers submission by e-mail (copied into message only/see guide-lines for specifics). Guidelines on Website.

Columns/Departments: This Writer's Opinion (reviews of writing books), 300-500 words; The Writing Life (personal writing stories). No payment.

Tips: "Articles must be received by the 10th of the previous month. Articles received after the 10th will be considered for a later publication."

$ FREELANCE WRITER'S REPORT, 45 Main St., PO Box A, North Stratford NH 03590-0167. (603) 922-8383. E-mail: editor@writers-editors.com. Website: www.writers-editors.com. General/CNW Publishing Inc. Dana K. Cassell, ed. Covers marketing and running a freelance writing business. Monthly newsletter; 8 pgs. 25 percent freelance. Complete ms via e-mail (attached or copied into message). Pays .10/wd. on publication for onetime rts. Articles to 900 words (50/yr.). Responds within 1 wk. Seasonal 2 mos. ahead. Accepts simultaneous submissions & reprints (tell when/where appeared). Does not use sidebars. Guidelines on Website; copy for 6 x 9 SASE/2 stamps (for back copy); $4 for current copy.

Fillers: Prose fillers to 400 wds.

Contest: Open to all writers. Deadline March 15, 2009. Nonfiction, fiction, children's, poetry. Prizes; $100, $75, $50. Details on Website.

Tips: "No articles on the basics of freelancing; our readers are established freelancers. Looking for marketing and business building for freelance writers/editors/book authors."

$ NEW WRITER'S MAGAZINE, PO Box 5976, Sarasota FL 34277-5976. (941) 953-7903. E-mail: newriters@aol.com. General/Sarasota Bay Publishing. George S. Haborak, ed. Bimonthly mag.; circ. 5,000. 95 percent freelance. Query or complete ms by mail. Pays $10-50 ($20-40 for fiction) on publication for 1st rts. Articles 700-1,000 words (50/yr.); fiction 700-800 words (2-6/yr.). Responds in 5 wks. Guidelines by mail; copy $3.

Poetry: Buys 10-20/yr. Free verse, light verse; 8-20 lines. Pays $5 min. Submit max. 3 poems.

Fillers: Buys 25-45/yr. Writing-related cartoons; buys 20-30/yr.; pays $10 max. Anecdotes, facts, newsbreaks, short humor; 20-100 words; buys 5-15/yr. Pays $5 max.

Tips: "We like interview articles with successful writers."

NORTHWEST CHRISTIAN AUTHOR, NCWA, PO Box 428, Enumclaw WA 98022. Toll-free (800) 731-6292. E-mail: acquisitions@nwchristianwriters.org. Website: www.nwchristianwriters.org. Northwest Christian Writers Assn. Mike Owens, acq. ed. To encourage Christian authors to share the gospel through the written word and to promote excellence in writing. Bimonthly newsletter; 12 pgs.; circ. 200. Subscription $12; or $25 including membership. 40 percent unsolicited freelance; 60 percent assigned. Complete ms/cover letter; e-query OK. **PAYS 3 COPIES** for onetime or reprint rts. Not copyrighted. Articles 300-1,000 words (20/yr.); book reviews 100 words. Responds in 2 wks. Accepts simultaneous submissions & reprints (tell when/where appeared). Prefers e-mail submission (attached file). Uses some sidebars. Also accepts submissions from teens. Guidelines on Website; no copy. (No ads)

Poetry: Accepts 3/yr. Free verse, light verse. Submit max. 3 poems.

Fillers: Anecdotes, tips; 50-250 wds.

Profiles: Every issue includes a profile (800-1,000 words) of a NWCW member and short sample of their work.

Special Needs: How-tos on nonfiction and fiction writing. Focus on genre techniques. Interviews with Christian authors.

Tips: "Most open to articles on writing techniques, particularly for specific genres. Stay within word count. E-queries should have 'NW Christian Author' in subject line. Include 1-3 sentence author bio with article."

$ POETS & WRITERS MAGAZINE, 90 Broad St., Ste. 2100, New York NY 10004-2272. (212) 226-3586. Fax (212) 226-3963. E-mail: editor@pw.org. Website: www.pw.org. General. Submit to The Editors. Professional trade journal for poetry, fiction, and nonfiction writers. Subscription $19.95. Bimonthly mag.; circ. 60,000. Query/clips by mail; e-query OK. Pays $150-500 on acceptance for 1st & nonexclusive rts. Articles 500-3,000 words (35/yr.). Responds in 4-6 wks. Seasonal 4 mos. ahead. Some kill fees 25 percent. Guidelines on Website; copy $4.95. (Ads)

Tips: "Most open to News & Trends, The Literary Life, and The Practical Writer (columns)."

$ @ SHADES OF ROMANCE MAGAZINE, 7127 Minnesota Ave., St. Louis MO 63111. E-mail: sor mag@yahoo.com. Website: www.sormag.com. Blog: www.sormag.blogspot.com. LaShaunda Hoffman, ed. A guide for readers and writers of multicultural romance and fiction. E-zine. E-query only. Pays $20 for articles, $25 for fiction within 30 days of publication (through PayPal) for electronic rts. Articles 500-800 words (6/yr.); short stories 500-1,500 words (6/yr.); devotions 200-500 words. Responds in 2-4 wks. Seasonal 2 mos. ahead. Accepts simultaneous submissions & reprints (tell when/where appeared; pays $10). Accepts e-mail submissions (attached file). Does not use sidebars. Guidelines/themes by e-mail/Website; copy online. (Ads)

$ @ SPIRIT-LED WRITER. E-mail: query@spiritledwriter.com. Website: www.SpiritLedWriter.com. Lisa A. Crayton, pub./ed. Internet magazine for Christian beginning, intermediate, and advanced writers. Monthly e-zine. Query by e-mail (put "Query: [subject]" in subject line). Pays $20 on publication for onetime, reprint, and electronic rts. Articles 800-1,200 words (70+/yr.); reviews to 500 words. Responds in 6-8 wks. Accepts reprints. Submit accepted mss by e-mail (no attachments). Regularly uses sidebars. Also accepts submissions from teens. Guidelines by e-mail/Website; copy online. (Ads)

> **Columns/Departments:** Buys several/yr. Musing Dept. (writing-related personal reflections), 700-900 words; God's Glory Dept. (writing success stories), 500-700 words; Business (articles on the business of writing), to 1,200 words; Children's Column (how-to on writing for youth), to 1,200 words; $10-20.
>
> **Special Needs:** Writing-related devotionals; conference coverage (700-900 words); and book reviews of writing books, 250-500 words ($5-10, depending on whether they supply the book). Also articles on writing for youth or on advanced writing topics.
>
> **Tips:** "Easiest to break in with a success story (God's glory), musing article, or devotional. We seek how-to and feature articles with a writing theme. We are not a general, Christian-living publication. We reject many manuscripts because they are general, not writing-related. Make it relevant to writing and writers."

$ TICKLED BY THUNDER, 14076—86A Ave., Surrey BC V3W 0V9, Canada. (604) 591-6095. E-mail: info@tickledbythunder.com. Website: www.tickledbythunder.com. Larry Lindner, ed. For writers wanting to better themselves. Quarterly chapbook (3-4x); 24 pgs.; circ. 1,000. Subscription $10 Cdn. or U.S. 90 percent unsolicited freelance; 10 percent assigned. Complete ms/cover letter; e-query OK from subscribers only (use online form). Pays $2-5 (in Cdn. or U.S. stamps) on publication for onetime rts. Articles 1,500 words (5/yr.); fiction 2,000 words (20/yr.); book/music/video reviews 1,000 words. Responds in 16 wks. Seasonal 6 mos. ahead. Accepts simultaneous submissions. Prefers requested ms on disk, no e-mail submission. Uses some sidebars. Also accepts submissions from children/teens. Guidelines by mail/e-mail/Website; copy $2.50/6 x 9 SAE. (Ads)

> **Poetry:** Accepts 20-40/yr. Any type; to 40 lines. Submit max. 5-7 poems. "Try sending seasonal poetry well in advance."
>
> **Contest:** For fiction (February 15 annual deadline) and poetry (February 15, May 15, August 15, and October 15 annual deadlines). Article contests for subscribers only (February 15, May 15, August 15, and October 15 deadlines). Send SASE for guidelines.
>
> **Tips:** "Write a 300-word article describing how you feel about your successes/failures as a writer. Be specific, and focus—don't be at all general or vague; tell what works for you. Be original; say something classic in a new way. Use imagery. For fiction, surprise me. Write to put me on the edge of my seat—hold my attention—then wrap it up with something unexpected. Need book reviews of writing books."

THE WRITE CONNECTION, 3706 N.E. Shady Lane Dr., Gladstone MO 64119. Phone/fax (816) 459-8016. E-mail: HACWN@earthlink.net. Website: www.hacwn.org. Heart of America Christian Writers' Network. Jeanette Littleton, exec. ed.; Pat Mitchell, ed. Monthly newsletter; 4 pgs.; circ. 150. Subscription free with HACWN membership $25. 50 percent unsolicited freelance; 50 percent assigned. Complete ms/ cover letter; e-query OK. **NO PAYMENT** for 1st or reprint rts. Articles 400 words (12/yr.); book reviews 200 words. Responds in 8 wks. Accepts simultaneous submissions; no reprints. Accepts requested mss by e-mail. Uses some sidebars. Also accepts submissions from teens. (Ads)

Poetry: Accepts 5/yr. Free verse, light verse, traditional; to 12 lines. Submit max. 3 poems.

Fillers: Accepts 25/yr. Anecdotes, facts, ideas, jokes, prayers, prose, quotes, short humor, tips—solely dealing with writing.

$ THE WRITER, 21027 Crossroads Cir., Waukesha WI 53186. (262) 796-8776. Fax (262) 798-6468. E-mail: queries@writermag.com. Website: www.writermag.com. General. Ron Kovach, sr. ed. (rkovach@writermag.com); Sarah Lange, assoc. ed. (slange@writermag.com). How-to for writers; lists religious markets on Website. Monthly mag.; 60-68 pgs.; circ. 30,000. Subscription $32.95. 80 percent unsolicited freelance. Query; no phone/fax query (prefers hard copy or e-query). Pays $300-500 for feature articles; book reviews ($40-80, varies); on acceptance for 1st rts. Features 600-3,500 words (60/yr.). Responds in 4-6 wks. Uses some sidebars. Guidelines by mail/Website. (Ads)

Fillers: Prose; writer-related cartoons $50. Send cartoons to slange@writermag.com.

Columns/Departments: Buys 24+/yr. Freelance Success (shorter pieces on the business of writing); Off the Cuff (personal essays about writing; avoid writer's block stories). All 600-1,600 wds. Pays $100-300 for columns; $25-75 for Take Note. Query 4 months ahead. See guidelines for full list of columns.

Special Needs: How-to on the craft of writing only.

Contests: Occasionally sponsors a contest.

Tips: "Get familiar first with our general mission, approach, tone, and the types of articles we do and don't do. Then, if you feel you have an article that is fresh and well suited to our mission, send us a query. Personal essays must provide takeaway advice and benefits for writers; we shun the 'navel-gazing' type of essay. Include plenty of how-to, advice, and tips on techniques. Be specific. Query for features six months ahead. All topics indicated must relate to writing."

** This periodical was #17 on the 2009 Top 50 Christian Publishers list (#45 in 2008).

$ THE WRITER'S CHRONICLE: The Magazine for Serious Writers, The Association of Writers & Writing Programs, George Mason University, MSN 1E3, 4400 University Dr., Fairfax VA 22030-4444. (703) 993-4301. Fax (703) 993-4302. E-mail: chronicle@awpwriter.org. Website: www.awpwriter .org. D. W. Fenza, ed-in-chief. Mag. published 6x during academic yr. Subscription $20. Pays $11/100 words on publication for 1st rts. Articles to 7,000 words max. No kill fee. Guidelines on Website.

Special Needs: Author interviews, essays, trends, and literary controversies. No poetry or fiction.

$ WRITER'S DIGEST, 4700 E. Galbraith Rd., Cincinnati OH 45236. (513) 531-2690, ext. 1739. Fax (513) 891-7153. E-mail: wdsubmissions@fwpubs.com. Website: www.writersdigest.com. General/F & W Publications. Submit to Acquisitions Editor. To inform, instruct, or inspire the freelancer and author. Monthly (8x) mag.; 88 pgs.; circ. 140,000. Subscription $14.96. 20 percent unsolicited; 60 percent assigned. Strongly prefers e-query (responds in 8-12 wks.). Pays. 30-.50/wd. on acceptance for 1st & electronic (sometimes) rts. Articles 800-1,500 words (75/yr.). Responds to mail query in 2 mos. Seasonal 8 mos. ahead. Requires requested ms by e-mail (copied into message). Kill fee 25 percent. Regularly uses sidebars. Guidelines/editorial calendar on Website; copy $5.25 (attn: Lyn Menke). (Ads)

Contests: Sponsors annual contest for articles, short stories, poetry, and scripts. Also The National Self-Publishing Book Awards. Send SASE for rules.

Tips: "We're looking for fiction technique pieces by published authors."

** This periodical was #49 on the 2009 Top 50 Christian Publishers list (#38 in 2008).

$ WRITERS' JOURNAL, PO Box 394, Perham MN 56573-0394. (218) 346-7921. Fax (218) 346-7924. E-mail: editor@writersjournal.com. Website: www.writersjournal.com. Val-Tech Media/General. Leon Ogroske, ed. Advice, tools, and markets for writers, communicators, and poets. Bimonthly mag.; 68 pgs.; circ. 20,000. Subscription $19.97. 90 percent unsolicited freelance; 10 percent assigned. Complete ms/cover letter; phone/fax/e-query OK. Usually pays $30, plus subscription, on publication for onetime rts. Articles 1,200-2,200 words (30-40/yr.); fiction 2,000 words (contest entries only). Responds in 6-28 wks. Accepts simultaneous submissions; no reprints. Accepts requested ms by e-mail (copied into message). No kill fee. Uses some sidebars. Also accepts submissions from teens. Guidelines on Website; copy $5/SASE/$2.07 postage. (Ads)

> **Poetry:** Esther M. Leiper, poetry ed. Buys 25/yr. All types; to 10 lines; $5/poem. Submit max. 4 poems.
> **Fillers:** Buys 20/yr. Any type, 10-200 wds. Pays $1-10.
> **Contest:** Runs several contests each year. Prizes up to $500. Categories are short story, horror/ghost, romance, travel writing, and fiction; 3 poetry; 2 photo. Guidelines on Website.
> **Tips:** "Be concise; no wordiness. Avoid personal essays. Write to the reader. We are looking for a well-written article on freelance income; articles on how to write better and how to sell what authors write. Also looking for articles on obscure income markets for writers. General story construction and grammar tips."

WRITERS MANUAL, Ste. 402, 7231—120th St., Delta BC V4C 6P5, Canada. E-mail: editor@writers manual.com. Website: www.writersmanual.com (click on "Get Interviewed!"). Krista Barrett, ed-in-chief. Looking for author and/or freelance interviews. Onetime rts.

+ @ THE WRITER'S NOTEBOOK, 106 Fletcher Dr., Logansport LA 71049. (318) 609-4751. E-mail: marcies04@bellsouth.net. Website: http://writersnotebook.homestead.com. Marcella Simmons, pub. For poets and writers. Bimonthly online mag. E-mail submissions only. How-to & features, 250-1,500 wds.; personal experience 250-1,000 wds. Open to freelance. **NO PAYMENT.** Accepts reprints. Guidelines on Website; copy online. Not in topical listings.

> **Fillers:** 50-250 wds. (My first Sales, etc.).
> **Tips:** "Deadline for submissions is the 25th of each month."

WRITETOINSPIRE.COM, E-mail: editor@writetoinspire.com. Website: www.writetoinspire.com. Online publication. Provides good how-to information for Christian writers. **NO PAYMENT** for 1st or onetime rts. Articles 500-700 words, written in an online style. Send submissions in body of e-mail (no attachments). Guidelines on Website.

WRITING CORNER, E-mail: submission-wc@writingcorner.com or through Website: www.writing corner.com. Online publication. Open to unsolicited freelance. Query or complete ms by e-mail (no attachments). **NO PAYMENT** for nonexclusive rts. Articles 600-900 words; fiction 600-900 words. Responds in 2 wks. Accepts reprints. Guidelines at: www.writingcorner.com/admin/subguidelines .htm.

8

Market Analysis for Periodicals

PERIODICALS IN ORDER BY CIRCULATION

ADULT/GENERAL
Guideposts 2,500,000
Columbia 1,600,000
In Touch 1,000,000
Stewardship 1,000,000
Focus on the Family 800,000
Angels on Earth 550,000
Marion Helpers 500,000
Spirituality for Today 495,000
Catholic Digest 400,000
Catholic Yearbook 400,000
Decision 400,000
Positive Thinking 400,000
Mature Living 318,000
St. Anthony Messenger 305,000
Charisma 250,000
Power for Living 250,000
Upscale Magazine 250,000
War Cry 250,000
Anglican Journal 215,000
Australian Catholics 200,000
Gospel Today 200,000
Liberty 200,000
Lutheran Journal 200,000
Lutheran Witness 200,000
Miraculous Medal 200,000
On Mission 200,000
Today's Pentecostal Evangel
   175,000
Christianity Today 155,000
Cappers 150,000
Family Digest 150,000
Written 130,000
MESSAGE 125,000
Company 120,000
Liguorian 120,000
Catholic Forester 100,000
CGA World 100,000
Good News (KY) 100,000
Standard 100,000

Christian Motorsports 74,000
ParentLife 72,000
HEARTLIGHT Internet 70,000+
Celebrate Life 70,000
Common Ground 70,000
Men of Integrity 70,000
United Church Observer 70,000
Christian Home & School 67,000
Lookout 62,000
Lutheran Digest 60,000
Presbyterians Today 58,000
Creation 55,000
Mature Years 55,000
Arlington Catholic 53,000
Discovery Years 52,600
Christian History 50,000
Chronicle—IN Edition 50,000
Faith & Friends 50,000
Holiness Today 50,000
Leaves 50,000
Wesleyan Life 50,000
America 46,000
Point 46,000
Live 46,000
Encompass 45,000
LarkNews.com 45,000
Messenger of St. Anthony 45,000
EFCA Today 44,000
The Manna 42,000
Alive Now 40,000
Senior Living 40,000
U.S. Catholic 40,000
Highway News 35,000
Lifeglow 34,000
Florida Baptist Witness 33,000
Faith & Family 32,000
Cathedral Age 30,000
Christian Computing 30,000
Christian Research 30,000
Christian Standard 30,000

Eureka Street 30,000
Homeschooling Today 30,000
Kindred Spirit 30,000
Louisiana Baptist Message
   30,000
Messianic Perspectives 30,000
Vibrant Life 30,000
World & I 30,000
Christian News NW 29,000
Seek 29,000
Priority! 28,000
Annals of St. Anne 25,000
Arizona Family News 25,000
Evangel (OR) 25,000
In His Presence 25,000
LifeLine Journal 25,000
Pure Inspiration 25,000
Significant Living 25,000
Central FL Episcopalian 24,000
In Part 24,000
Catholic Peace Voice 23,000
Majellan 23,000
African Voices 20,000
Creation Illustrated 20,000
Interim 20,000
Ozarks Christian 20,000
Trumpeter 20,000
Commonweal 19,000
Faith Today 18,000
Heartbeat 18,000
Montgomery's Journey 18,000
Canadian Mennonite 16,500
Marketplace 16,000
Over the Back Fence 15,000
The Pathway 15,000
SCP Journal 15,000
Tri-State Voice 15,000
Victory in Grace 15,000
Canada Lutheran 14,000
DisciplesWorld 14,000

Gems of Truth 14,000
Testimony 14,000
Bible Advocate 13,500
Light & Life 13,000
Books & Culture 12,000
Christian Health Care 12,000
Covenant Companion 12,000
Special Living 12,000
Spiritual Life 12,000
Evangel 11,000
Messenger/Sacred Heart 11,000
Sports Spectrum 11,000
Christian Family 10,000-30,000
The Brink 10,000+
Messiah Magazine 10,000
Presbyterian Outlook 10,000
Regent Global Bus. Rev.
    10,000
Vision 10,000
Christian Retailing 9,500
NRB E-Magazine 9,300
Fellowship 9,000
Haruah 9,000
Living Church 9,000
Montana Catholic 9,000
Sharing 9,000
Purpose 8,900
Disciple's Journal 8,000
Friends Journal 8,000
Arkansas Catholic 7,700
Science & Spirit 7,500
Psychology for Living 7,000
Creation Care 6,000
Gem 6,000
Impact 6,000
Vision 6,000
Image 5,200
AGAIN 5,000
Ambassador 5,000
Breakthrough Intercessor 5,000
CBA Retailers 5,000
Creative Nonfiction 5,000
Cross Currents 5,000
Leben 5,000
New Heart 5,000
Pentecostal Messenger 5,000
Prism 5,000
Purpose Magazine 5,000
Review for Religious 5,000
Social Justice Review 5,000

Way of St. Francis 5,000
Maine Family Record 4,600
Cresset 4,500
Evangelical Advocate 4,000
Home Times 4,000
Mensajero Ala Blanca 4,000
Quaker Life 4,000
Wireless Age 4,000
Catholic Insight 3,700
Culture Wars 3,500
Evangel 3,500
JerUSAlem Connection 3,500
Sword and Trumpet 3,300
Message of the Open Bible 3,000
Perspectives 3,000
Prayer Closet 3,000
Urban Kingdom 3,000
Salvo 2,800
Bread of Life 2,500
MovieGuide 2,500
Railroad Evangelist 2,500
Apocalypse Chronicles 2,000-
    3,000
Perspectives/Science & Chr. Faith
    2,000+
Atlantic Catholic 2,000
Channels 2,000
Desert Call 2,000
Mutuality 2,000
Priscilla Papers 2,000
Jour./Church & State 1,700
Mennonite Historian 1,600
Ruminate 1,500
Church Herald/Holiness Banner
    1,100
Connecting Point 1,000
DreamSeeker 1,000
Imagine 1,000
Methodist History 800
Compass Direct 785
Storyteller 600
Eternal Ink 450
Gold Country Families 450
Relief 300
Silver Wings 300
Studio 300
Xavier Review 300
West Wind Review 250-500
Aujourd'hui Credo 250
Time of Singing 250

Ancient Paths 175
Pegasus Review 150
Reverent Submissions 125
Angel Face 100
Haiku Hippodrome 100
Wildwood Reader 100
Penwood Review 80-100

CHILDREN
American Girl 700,000
Focus/Clubhouse 90,000
Keys for Kids 70,000
Pockets 67,000
Focus/Clubhouse Jr. 65,000
Our Little Friend 45,000-50,000
Adventures 40,000
Celebrate 40,000
Primary Treasure 35,000
Kid Zone 30,000
New Moon 30,000
Guide 27,000
Primary Street 20,000
Passport 18,000
Faces 15,000
Nature Friend 13,000
SHINE brightly 13,000
Bread for God's Children
    10,000
Cadet Quest 8,000
Kids' Ark 8,000
Partners 6,519
Story Mates 6,500
Junior Companion 3,500
Primary Pal (KS) 2,900
Beginner's Friend 2,700
Skipping Stones 2,500

**CHRISTIAN EDUCATION/
LIBRARY**
Christian School Education
    70,000
Children's Ministry 60,000
Catechist 52,000
Today's Catholic Teacher 45,000
Group 25,000
Momentum 23,000
Jour./Adventist Education 10,800
Teachers of Vision 10,000
Youth & CE Leadership 10,000
Christian Early Education 7,000

Christian Educators Journal 4,200

Church & Synagogue Libraries 3,000

Kids' Ministry Ideas 2,500

Catholic Library World 1,000

Christian Librarian 800

Church Libraries 400

Jour./Christian Education 400

Jour./Education & Christian Belief 400

Jour./Research on Christian Education 400

Jour./Christianity & Foreign Lang. 100

DAILY DEVOTIONALS

These Days 200,000

Secret Place 150,000

Our Journey 80,000

Daily Devotions for the Deaf 26,000

Rejoice! 12,000

Penned from the Heart 5,000

MISSIONS

One 100,000

Mission Frontiers 75,000

MissionsMagazinet 64,000

New World Outlook 24,000

Montgomery's Journey 18,000

PIME World 16,000

Mission Connection 14,400

wec.go 9,500

Women of the Harvest 8,000

Leaders for Today 7,500

Evangelical Missions 7,000

Glad Tidings 4,500

Railroad Evangelist 2,500

Missiology 1,500

Op. Reveille Interactive Jour. 1,500

Intl. Jour./Frontier Missions500

East-West Church & Ministry Report 250

MUSIC

CCM Magazine 70,000

Senior Musician 32,000

TCP Magazine 20,000

I AM Magazine 15,000

Church Music 12,000

Creator 6,000

Tradition 3,500

Hymn 3,000

Christian Radio 500

Christian Music 300-1,200

NEWSPAPERS

Layman 450,000

Episcopal Life 280,000

Anglican Journal 200,000

Alpha News 195,000

Christian Examiner 180,000

Catholic New York 135,000

Catholic Telegraph 100,000

Living 90,000

Christian Press 80,000

Good News in South Florida 80,000

Living Light News 75,000

Common Ground 70,000

Sword of the Lord 70,000

Our Sunday Visitor 68,000

Good News Journal 60,000

Arlington Catholic Herald 53,000

Chronicle/Kansas 50,000

Living 50,000

Christian Ranchman 43,800

Evangelical Times 40,000

Senior Living 40,000

Good News, Etc. 38,000

Messianic Times 35,000

Minnesota Christian Chronicle 35,000

Catholic Register 33,000

Christian Herald 30,000

Christian News NW 30,000

Citizen USA 30,000

Good News! 30,000

Interim 30,000

New Frontier 25,500

Christian Media 25,000

Greater Phoenix Christian Chronicle 25,000

Together 25,000

Life Gate 23,000

B.C. Catholic 20,000

Charlotte World 20,000

JC Reporter 20,000

Light of the World 20,000

HeartBeat/CMA 18,000

Catholic Sentinel 16,000

Good News Today 16,000

Indian Life 16,000

Christian Journal 15,000

Christian Quarterly 15,000

Christian Voice 15,000

Living Stones News 15,000

Voice of Grace & Truth 15,000

Interchange 12,000

City Light News 11,000+

Blue Ridge Christian News 11,000

Christian Courier (WI) 10,000

Heartland Gatekeeper 10,000

Network 10,000

Spiritual Voice News 10,000

Wisconsin Christian News 10,000

Star of Zion 9,200

Catholic New Times 8,500

Choice Newspaper 8,000

Disciple's Journal 8,000

Arkansas Catholic 7,700

Prairie Messenger 6,900

Home Times 6,000

Desert Voice 5,200

SW KS Faith & Family 5,000

Christian Courier (Canada) 4,000

Christian Renewal 3,500

Atlantic Catholic 2,000

Christian Observer 2,000

ChristianWeek 2,000

Island Catholic News 2,000

PrayerWorks 1,500

B.C. Christian News 1,000

Hunted News 1,000

Anglican 300

PASTORS/LEADERS

Interpreter 225,000

Alpha News 195,000

Rick Warren's Ministry 177,000

Your Church 75,000

Church Life Inspiration 65,000

Plugged In 50,000

SmallGroups.com 50,000

Worship Leader 50,000

Leadership 48,000

Plugged In 43,000
Catholic Servant 41,000
OUTreach 35,000
Technologies/Worship 35,000
Enrichment 33,000
Christian Century 30,000
Ministry Today 30,000
Torch Legacy Leader 22,000
Church Executive 20,000
Lutheran Partners 20,000
Ministry & Liturgy 20,000
Ministry 19,000
Preaching Now 19,000
This Rock 15,870
Youthworker 15,000
Today's Parish 14,800
Net Results 12,000
Pulpit Helps 12,000
Foursquare Leader 10,000
Jour./Pastoral Care 10,000
Preaching 9,000
InSite 8,750
Sabbath School Leadership 8,100
Growth Points 8,000
Priest 6,500
Clergy Journal 6,000
Catechumenate 5,600
Let's Worship 5,500
Cross Currents 5,000
Reformed Worship 4,600
African-American Pulpit 4,000
Review for Religious 4,000
Lutheran Forum 3,200
Emmanuel 3,000
Single Adult Min. Jour. 3,000
Environment & Art 2,500
Word & World 2,500
Cornerstone Youth Resource
    2,200
Church Worship 1,500
Parish Liturgy 1,200
Ministry in Motion 1,000+

Christian Ed. Jour. 750
Diocesan Dialogue 750
RevWriter Resource 650
Jour./Amer. Soc./Chur. Growth
    400
Theological Digest 400
Sharing the Practice 250

TEEN/YOUNG ADULT
Essential Connection 120,000
Devo'zine 90,000
Sharing the Victory 80,000
Young Salvationist 48,000
Risen Magazine 45,000+
YouthWalk 30,000
Young & Alive 25,000
Insight 20,000
InTeen 20,000
Listen 20,000
Spirit 20,000
Credo 15,000
Student Leadership 8,500
TC Magazine 8,000
Direction Student 5,300
Youth Compass 4,800
True Girl 3,500
G4T Ink 2,500

WOMEN
Precious Times 350,000
Heart & Soul 300,000
More to Life 250,000-2,000,000
Journey 215,000
Today's Christian Woman
    210,000
Lutheran Woman's Quarterly
    200,000
Melody of the Heart 130,000
MomSense 120,000
SpiritLed Woman 100,000
Share 95,000
Life Tools for Women 45,000

Dabbling Mum 30,000-40,000
First Lady 30,000
Connections Leadership/MOPS
    25,000
Horizons 25,000
Women's Ministry 25,000
History's Women 21,000
A Virtuous Woman 20,000+
A Woman of Worth 20,000
Right to the Heart 18,000
Hope for Women 10,000
P31 Woman 10,000
Just Between Us 8,000
Together with God 7,500
CoLaborer 7,300
Unrecognized Woman 5,000
Esprit 4,000
Link & Visitor 4,000
Women Alive 4,000
ChurchWoman 3,000
Handmaiden 3,000
inSpirit 2,500

WRITERS
Writer's Digest 140,000
Poets & Writers 60,000
The Writer 30,000
Writers' Journal 20,000
Fiction Fix 5,000
New Writer's 5,000
Poetic Voices 5,000
Christian Communicator 3,000
Beginnings 1,500
Cross & Quill 1,000+
Tickled by Thunder 1,000
Advanced Christian Writer 500
Canadian Writer's Journal 385
NW Christian Author 200
FellowScript 150-200
Write Connection 150
Areopagus (UK) 100
The Write Touch 40

PERIODICAL TOPICS IN ORDER OF POPULARITY

Note: Following is a list of topics in order by popularity. To find the list of publishers interested in each of these topics, go to the topical listings for periodicals and find the topic you are interested in. The numbers indicate how many periodical editors said they were interested in seeing something of that type or on that topic. An asterisk (*) indicates a new topic this year.

MISCELLANEOUS TALLIES

African American Markets 20
Canadian/Foreign 69
Newspapers/Tabloids 79
Online Publications 164
Photographs 216
Take-home Papers 38
Young Writer Markets 112

TOPICS BY POPULARITY
1. Christian Living 268
2. Family Life 225
3. Book Reviews 211
4. Current/Social Issues 208
5. Inspirational 204
6. Interviews/Profiles 190
7. Faith 185
8. Prayer 180
9. Personal Experience 176
10. Relationships 169
11. Holiday/Seasonal 167
12. Poetry 163
13. Marriage 161
14. Christian Education 159
15. Spirituality 157
16. Women's Issues 156
17. Devotionals/Meditations 147
18. Controversial Issues 146
19. Evangelism/Witnessing 146
20. True Stories 145
21. Church Outreach 144
22. Humor 144
23. Church Life 142
24. Spiritual Life 142
25. Discipleship 135
26. Ethnic/Cultural Pieces 135
27. Parenting 135
28. Personal Growth 133
29. Leadership 127
30. Encouragement 126
31. Worship 126
32. Health 121

33. Miracles 119
34. Ethics 118
35. Youth Issues 117
36. Church Growth 116
37. How-to 114
38. World Issues 111
39. Essays 110
40. Theological 110
41. Death/Dying 107
42. Church History 105
43. Social Justice 104
44. Short Story: Adult/Religious 103
45. Historical 100
46. News Features 100
47. Fillers: Cartoons 96
48. Stewardship 96
49. Church Traditions 95
50. Money Management 94
51. Bible Studies 93
52. Christian Business 92
53. Men's Issues 92
54. Religious Freedom 91
55. Spiritual Renewal 91
56. Short Story: Contemporary 90
57. Singles' Issues 90
58. Celebrity Pieces 89
59. Spiritual Gifts 89
60. Opinion Pieces 83
61. Spiritual Warfare 83
62. Time Management 83
63. Workplace Issues 83
64. Divorce 79
65. Environmental Issues 79
66. Music Reviews 79
67. Salvation Testimonies 79
68. Fillers: Anecdotes 78
69. Think Pieces 78
70. Fillers: Short Humor 77
71. Short Story: Biblical 76
72. Short Story: Humorous 76
73. Homeschooling 75

74. Feature Articles 74
75. Healing 74
76. Lifestyle Articles 74
77. Book Excerpts 73
78. Senior Adult Issues 71
79. Church Management 70
80. Political 69
81. Apologetics 68
82. Inner Life 65
83. Video Reviews 65
84. Religious Tolerance 64
85. Short Story: Historical 63
86. Doctrinal 62
87. Short Story: Adventure 62
88. Sports/Recreation 61
89. Racism 60
90. Travel 59
91. Nature 58
92. Fillers: Ideas 57
93. Fillers: Facts 56
94. Fillers: Quotes 56
95. Fillers: Word Puzzles 55
96. Economics 54
97. Food/Recipes 54
98. Peace Issues 53
99. Fillers: Prayers 52
100. Writing How-to 51
101. How-to Activities (juv.) 48
102. Crafts 47
103. Holy Spirit 47
104. Self-help 47
105. Creation Science 46
106. Liturgical 46
107. Missions 46
108. Movie Reviews 46
109. Short Story: Parables 46
110. Recovery 44
111. Fillers: Prose 42
112. Fillers: Tips 42
113. Short Story: Literary 42
114. Sociology 42
115. Science 41

116. Short Story: Teen/Young Adult 41
117. Fillers: Jokes 40
118. Short Story: Mystery/Suspense 40
119. Fillers: Quizzes 39
120. Short Story: Allegory 39
121. Prophecy 38
122. Fillers: Newsbreaks 37
123. Grandparenting 37
124. Short Story: Juvenile 37
125. Cults/Occult 36
126. Short Story: Ethnic 36
127. Psychology 35
128. Exegesis 34
129. Photo Essays 34
130. Website Reviews 34
131. Homiletics 32
132. Short Story: Science Fiction 32
133. Fillers: Games 31
134. Short Story: Fantasy 31
135. Revival 30
135. Sermons 30
136. Short Story: Adult/General 30
137. Short Story: Frontier 25
138. Fillers: Party Ideas 24
139. Nostalgia 23
140. Short Story: Romance 23
141. DVD Reviews 20
142. Fillers: Kid Quotes 20
143. Short Story: Skits 20
144. Short Story: Westerns 18
145. Praise 17
146. Short Story: Historical/Romance 17
147. Small Group Helps 17
148. Short Story: Speculative 16
149. Short Story: Mystery/Romance 15
150. Short Story: Senior Adult Fiction 15
151. Short Story: Plays 13
152. Teacher Helps 13
153. Short Story: Frontier/Romance 11
154. Fillers: Sermon Illustrations 10
155. Puppet Plays 5
156. Hispanic Publications 2

SUMMARY OF INFORMATION ON CHRISTIAN PERIODICAL PUBLISHERS FOUND IN THE ALPHABETICAL LISTINGS

Note: Following is some general information based on typical averages of the information supplied by the periodical publishers in this guide. This information will be valuable in determining what numbers or percentages are typical in the various categories.

Wants Query or Complete Manuscript
Not all periodicals indicate a preference, but 45-50 percent prefer or accept a complete manuscript, 35-38 percent want or will accept a query, 3-5 percent require a query, and 12-15 percent will accept either.

Accepts Phone/Fax/E-mail Query
Every year fewer periodical publishers are accepting phone or fax queries, and at this point almost none do. The majority now prefer e-mail queries—either directly or through an online form available on their Website. It is suggested that you reserve phone queries for timely projects or assignments that require immediate answers to questions. If you call, be sure you have your question or idea well thought out and can present it succinctly and articulately. It is always important to use the form of communication they indicate in their listing.

Submissions on Disk
This question has almost become obsolete, as the majority of publishers that don't want a hard copy now want an e-mail submission. Individual listings will indicate which ones still want or accept a disk. There are still a few.

Submissions by E-mail
This area continues to show some significant changes in editors' perceptions of e-mail submissions. When asked if they would accept submissions by e-mail, now more than half say yes. Of those, 40 percent wanted the article copied into the message, 42 percent wanted them sent as an attached file, and the last 18 percent would accept them either way. Generally speaking, those who prefer the article copied into the message fear viruses, while those who prefer an attached copy don't like losing the coding when you copy it into the message.

Pays on Acceptance or Publication
Of the publishers that indicated, 40 percent pay on acceptance, while 60 percent pay on publication.

Percentage of Freelance

Many of the publishers responded to the question about how much freelance material they use. Based on the figures we have, for the average publisher, 35 percent of the material purchased is unsolicited freelance, and 65 percent is assigned.

Circulation

In dividing the list of periodicals into three groups, according to size of circulation, the list comes out as follows: Publications with a circulation of 100,000 or more (up to 3,000,000) make up 15 percent of periodicals; publications with a circulation between 50,000 and 100,000, 10 percent; the remaining 75 percent have a circulation of 50,000 or less. If we break that last group into three more groups by circulation, we come out with circulations of 33,000-50,000 making up 10 percent; 18 percent with circulations of 17,000-32,000; and the remaining 72 percent with less than 17,000. That means that 52 percent of all the periodicals that reported their circulation are at a circulation of 17,000 or less. Not all publications update their circulation every year, but for those that did this year, 73 percent reported a decline in circulation, while 27 percent showed an increase.

Response Time

The average response time is just over eight weeks, one week longer than reported three or four years ago. Those who are writing and submitting regularly will have no problem confirming that most publishers are taking longer to respond to submissions—both for queries and complete manuscripts.

Reprints

Just over 49 percent of the periodicals included in the market guide accept reprints. Most Christian publishers now want a tear sheet of the original publication, or at least a cover letter telling when and where it appeared originally. Be sure to check the individual listings to see if a publisher wants to know when and where a piece has appeared previously. Most are also paying less for reprints than for original material.

Preferred Bible Version

The most preferred Bible version is the New International Version, the preference of more than half the publishers. Other preferred versions are the King James Version, the New Revised Standard Version, the New American Bible, New American Standard, Revised Standard Version, and New King James. The NIV seems a good choice for those who didn't indicate a preference, although the more conservative groups seem to favor the KJV.

PART 3
Specialty Markets

9

Greeting Card/Gift/Specialty Markets

This listing contains both Christian/religious card publishers and secular publishers that have religious lines or produce some religious or inspirational cards. Keep in mind that the secular companies may produce other lines of cards that are not consistent with your beliefs, and that for a secular company, inspirational cards usually do not include religious imagery. All of these are paying markets. A support group for greeting card writers can be found at http://groups.yahoo.com/group/GreetingCardWriters.

+ Indicates new listing

Note: See the end of this listing for specialty product topical lists.

GREETING CARD PUBLISHERS

AFRICAN AMERICAN EXPRESSIONS, 10266 Rockingham Dr., Sacramento CA 95827-2515. Toll-free (800) 684-1555. (916) 424-5000. Fax (916) 424-5053. E-mail: gperkins@black-gifts.com or info@black-gifts.com. Website: www.black-gifts.com. Greg Perkins, pres. Christian card publisher and specialty products. Open to freelance; buys 5-10 ideas/yr. Prefers outright submissions. Pays $35 on acceptance. No royalty. Responds in 2 wks. Uses rhymed, unrhymed, traditional, and light verse. Produces invitations and conventional, humorous, informal, inspirational, juvenile, novelty, and religious cards. Needs anniversary, birthday, Christmas, friendship, get well, graduation, keep in touch, love, miss you, Mother's Day, new baby, relatives (all occasions), sympathy, valentines, wedding, and pastor appreciation. Holiday/seasonal 9 mos. ahead. Open to ideas for new card lines, calendars/journals, novelty/gift items, magnets, and stationery. No guidelines; free catalog.

ALEGRIA COLLECTION, PO Box 835008, Miami FL 33283-5008. (305) 253-4646. Fax (305) 253-4604. E-mail: ventas@alegriacollection.com. Website: www.alegriacollection.com. Spanish greeting cards.

AMERICAN GREETINGS, One American Rd., Cleveland OH 44144-2398. (216) 252-7300. Fax (216) 252-6778. Website: www.americangreetings.com. Kathleen McKay, ed. No unsolicited material.

ARTFUL GREETINGS, PO Box 52428, Durham NC 27717. Toll-free (800) 638-2733. (919) 484-0100. Fax (919) 484-3099. E-mail: myw@artfulgreetings.com. Website: www.artfulgreetings.com. Black art greeting cards and gifts.

BLUE MOUNTAIN ARTS INC., PO Box 4549, Boulder CO 80306. (303) 449-0536. Fax (303) 447-0939. E-mail: editorial@sps.com. Website: www.sps.com. Submit to Editorial Department. General card publisher that does a few inspirational cards. Open to freelance; buys 50-100 ideas/yr. Prefers outright submissions. Pays $300 for all rts. for use on a greeting card, or $50 for onetime use in a book, on publication. No royalties. Responds in 12-16 wks. Uses unrhymed or traditional poetry; short or long, but no one-liners. Produces inspirational and sensitivity. Needs anniversary, birthday, Christmas, congratulations, Easter, Father's Day, friendship, get well, graduation, keep in touch, love, miss you, Mother's Day, new baby, please write, relatives, sympathy, thank you, valentines, wedding, reaching for dreams. Holiday/seasonal 3 mos. ahead. Open to ideas for new card lines. Send any number of ideas (1 per pg.). Open to ideas for gift books. Guidelines; no catalog.

Contest: Sponsors a poetry card contest online. Details on Website.

Tips: "We are interested in reviewing poetry and writings for greeting cards, and expanding our field of freelance poetry writers."

C4YOURSELF GREETING CARDS, 1406 Sycamore St., Cincinnati OH 45202. (513) 608-1878. E-mail through Website: www.c4yourself.biz. Angela Morrow, creator. Christmas cards & cards for all occasions. Also does desk calendars. E-mail with card ideas.

CREATIVE CHRISTIAN GIFTS, PO Box 915441, Longwood FL 32791-5441. Toll-free (866) 325-1857. (407) 610-9535. E-mail: sales@creativechristiangifts.com. Website: www.creativechristiangifts .com. Greeting cards & note cards.

CURRENT INC., PO Box 2559, Colorado Springs CO 80901. (719) 594-4100. Fax (719) 534-6259. No freelance.

DAYSPRING CARDS INC., Box 1010, 21154 Hwy 16 East, Siloam Springs AR 72761. Fax (479) 524-9477. E-mail: info@dayspring.com (type "write" in message or subject line). Website: www .dayspring.com. Christian/religious card publisher. Please read guidelines before submitting. Prefers outright submission. Pays $60/idea on acceptance for all rts. No royalty. Responds in 4-8 wks. Uses unrhymed, traditional, light verse, conversational, contemporary; various lengths. Looking for inspirational cards for all occasions, including anniversary, birthday, relative birthday, congratulations, encouragement, friendship, get well, new baby, sympathy, thank you, wedding. Also needs seasonal cards for friends and family members for Christmas, Valentine's Day, Easter, Mother's Day, Father's Day, Thanksgiving, graduation, and Clergy Appreciation Day. Include Scripture verse with each submission. Send 10 ideas or less. Guidelines by phone or e-mail; no catalog.

Tips: Prefers submissions on 8.5 x 11 inch sheets, not 3x5 cards (one idea per sheet).

DESIGN DESIGN INC., 19 La Grave S.E., Grand Rapids MI 49503. (616) 771-2448. Fax (616) 774-4020. Website: www.designdesign.us. Rebecca Cooper, ed. (rebecca.cooper@designdesign.us). A general card publisher that does a few inspirational and religious cards. Open to freelance submissions. Prefers outright submissions (but not of artwork). Rights purchased depend on product. Uses rhymed, unrhymed, traditional, and light verse. Produces anniversary, birthday, Christmas, congratulations, Easter, Father's Day, friendship, get well, graduation, Halloween, love, miss you, Mother's Day, new baby, relative (all occasions), St. Patrick's Day, sympathy, Thanksgiving, thank you, valentines, and wedding. Open to new card lines. Open to ideas for gift/novelty items, greeting books, magnets, and stationery. Guidelines on Website; no catalog.

DICKSON'S LIFE PUBLISHING, 709 B Ave. East, Seymour IN 47274. (812) 522-1308. Fax (812) 522-1319. E-mail: rtocquigny@aol.com. Website: www.dicksonsgifts.com. Rick Tocquigny, pres. Christian/religious card publisher. Open to freelance; buys 25-50 ideas/yr. Prefers outright submissions. Pays $50 on acceptance for nonexclusive rts. Royalties 2-3 percent. Responds in 4 wks. Uses rhymed, unrhymed, traditional, light verse; under 75 words Produces all types of cards. Needs anniversary, birthday, Christmas, congratulations, Easter, Father's Day, friendship, get well, graduation, keep in touch, love, miss you, Mother's Day, new baby, please write, relative (all occasions), St. Patrick's Day, sympathy, Thanksgiving, thank you, valentines, wedding, adult baptism, mission trip blessings, confirmation, and first communion. Holiday/seasonal 18 mos. ahead. Open to ideas for new card lines; submit max. 3 ideas. Open to ideas for activity/coloring books, bookmarks, calendars/journals, gift/novelty items, magnets, mugs, plaques, stationery, T-shirts/apparel, and toys. No guidelines/catalog.

HEAVENLY DESIGNS, 118 Burnell Pl. S.E., Leesburg VA 20175. Toll-free (866) 707-0113. Phone/fax (703) 737-0113. E-mails: cindyjames@birthverse.com, or bjames@birthverse.com. Website: www.birthverse.com. Bob & Cindy James, owners. Inspirational greeting cards.

HERMITAGE ART CO. INC., 5151 N. Ravenswood Ave., Chicago IL 60640. Toll-free (800) 621-7992. (773) 561-3773. Fax (773) 561-4422. E-mail: Office@hermitageart.com. Website: www.her mitageart.com. Color bulletins, bookmarks, specialty items.

INSPIRATIONART & SCRIPTURE INC., PO Box 5550, Cedar Rapids IA 52406-5550. Toll-free (800) 728-5550. (319) 365-4350. Fax (319) 861-2103. E-mail: Customerservice@inspirationart .com. Website: www.inspirationart.com. Publishes Christian posters only. Charles Edwards, creative dir. Open to freelance. Buys 20-30 ideas/yr. Prefers e-mail contact. Pays $150-250, 30 days after publication, for right to publish as a poster; or royalties 5 percent of net. Responds in 4 wks. Seasonal 6 mos. ahead. Open to new ideas for posters. Submit up to 3 ideas. Artist's guidelines on Website.

+ JESUS FILLED DAY PUBLISHING CO., PO Box 34, Houston TX 77001. (281) 399-4011. Fax (281) 399-3840. E-mail: team@haveajesusfilledday.com. Website: www.haveajesusfilledday.com. Ann Chapman, VP. Produces cards and specialty items.

NORTHERN CARDS, Creative Department, 5035 Timberlea Blvd., Unit #9, Mississauga ON L4W 2W9, Canada. Toll-free (877) 627-7444. (905) 625-4944. Fax (905) 625-5995. E-mail: artists@northern cards.com. Website: www.northerncards.com/docs/artists.shtml. Open to writers and artists. Greeting cards.

NOVO CARD PUBLISHERS INC., 7570 N. Croname Rd., Niles IL 60714-3904. Toll-free (800) 624-2426. (847) 588-3220. Fax (847) 588-3508. E-mail: art@novocard.net. Website: www.novocard .net. Submit to Art Production. General card publisher that does a few inspirational & religious cards. Open to freelance; buys 10 ideas/yr. Prefers outright submissions. Pays $2/line on acceptance for all rts. No royalties. Responds in 5 wks. Uses traditional & light verse; 5-20 lines (nothing too brief). Produces baby announcements, conventional, humorous, inspirational, invitations, juvenile, religious, studio. Needs anniversary, birthday, Christmas, congratulations, Easter, Father's Day, friendship, get well, miss you, Mother's Day, new baby, relatives (all occasions), sympathy, Thanksgiving, thank-you, valentines, wedding. Seasonal 6-8 mos. ahead. Open to ideas for new card lines. Submit enough ideas to show style. Guidelines/needs list; no catalog.
  Tips: "We don't want anything too brief or too lengthy. We like verse that holds everyone's hearts, especially the male gender."

OATMEAL STUDIOS, PO Box 138CW, Rochester VT 05767. (802) 767-3171. E-mail: Dawn@oat mealstudios.com. Website: www.oatmealstudios.com. Dawn Abraham, editor. Always needs birthday ideas. No holiday copy needed. E-mail for guidelines for submitting online, or submit ideas on 3 x 5 index cards with your name and address on each one.

PLESH CREATIVE GROUP INC., 38 A Park St., Medfield MA 02052. (508) 359-6400. Fax (508) 359-6448. E-mail: pleshcreative@gmail.com. Website: www.PleshCreative.com. Submit to: Suzanne Comeau. General card publisher with a religious line. Open to freelance. Prefers outright submissions. Buys all rts. Pays $30-50 on acceptance. No royalties. Responds in several wks. Uses rhymed, unrhymed, traditional, and light verse; 8-10 lines or shorter. Produces conventional, humorous, inspirational, juvenile, religious.

P. S. GREETINGS/FANTUS PAPER PRODUCTS, 5730 N. Tripp Ave., Chicago IL 60646-6723. Toll-free (800) 621-8823. (773) 267-6150. Fax (773) 267-6055. E-mail: artdirector@psgreetings .com. Website: www.psgreetings.com. General card publisher with a religious line. Submit to Design Director; Re: Freelance Writer. Open to freelance. Holiday/seasonal 6 mos. ahead. Responds in 1 mo. Pays flat fee on publication; no royalty. Rhymed, unrhymed, traditional, light verse. Produces announcements, conventional, humorous, informal, inspirational, invitations, juvenile, novelty, religious, sensitivity, softline, studio. Not open to ideas for new card lines or specialty products. Guidelines/copy for #10 SASE (also on Website).

RED FARM STUDIO, 1135 Roosevelt Ave., Pawtucket RI 02861-0347. Toll-free (877) REDFARM. (401) 728-9300. Toll-free fax (888) 860-3276. E-mail: redfarm@quadrigaart.com. Website: www .redfarmstudio.com. Thomas Scott, pres.; Steven Scott, VP; submit to Production Coordinator. General card publisher with a religious line. 100 percent freelance; buys 100 ideas/yr. Outright submission. Pays variable rates (about $4/line) within 1 mo. of acceptance for exclusive rts. No royalties. Responds in 2 mos. Uses traditional and light verse; 1-4 lines. Produces announcements, invitations, religious. Needs anniversary, birthday, Christmas, friendship, get well, new baby, sympathy, wedding. Holiday 6 mos. ahead. Not open to ideas for new card lines. Submit any number of ideas. Guidelines/needs list for SASE.

BOB SIEMON DESIGNS INC., 3501 W. Segerstrom Ave., Santa Ana CA 92704-6497. (714) 549-0678. Fax (714) 979-2627. Website: www.bobsiemon.com. No freelance.

SOLE SOURCE GREETINGS, Attn: Art Submissions or Attn: Copy Submissions, 1 Idea Way, Caldwell ID 83605-6902. Toll-free (800) 346-5860 or (800) 285-1657. Toll-free fax (800) 455-0642. E-mail through Website: www.solesourcegreetings.com. Send artwork via e-mail as a JPG or PDF file (see Website for size details). Check Website for samples of greetings. Open to: thinking of you, birthday, thank-you, sympathy, new baby, congratulations, anniversary, wedding, etc. Also business-specific cards. Pays up to $500 for artwork; pays $25/message. Royalties 5 percent on retail sales; 2.5 percent on wholesale catalog sales.

WARNER PRESS INC., 1201 E. 5th St., PO Box 2499, Anderson IN 46018-9988. (765) 644-7721. Fax (765) 640-8005. E-mail: rfogle@warnerpress.org. Website: www.warnerpress.org. Karen Rhodes, product mktg. ed.; Robin Fogle, ed. asst. Producer of church resources (greeting cards, bulletins, coloring books, puzzle books). 30 percent freelance; buys 30-50 ideas/yr. Query for guidelines. Pays $30-35 on acceptance (for bulletins); material for bulletins cannot be sold elsewhere for bulletin use but may be sold in any other medium. No royalties. Responds in 6-8 wks. Uses rhymed, unrhymed, traditional verse, and devotionals for bulletins; 16-24 lines. Accepts 10 ideas/submission. Guidelines for bulletins; no catalog.
    Also Does: Also open to ideas for coloring books, church-resource items.

WORLD LIBRARY PUBLICATIONS, 3708 River Rd., Ste. 400, Franklin Park IL 60131. Toll-free (800) 621-5197, ext. 2800. (847) 233-2800. Fax (847) 233-2762. E-mail: odegardj@jspaluch .com. Website: www.wlpmusic.com. A division of J. S. Paluch Co. Jennifer Odegard, marketing dir. A music, liturgy, and art publisher with some greeting cards in their line. Open to freelance. Query. Pays on publication; pays some negotiable royalties. Traditional verse. Produces inspirational & religious cards; anniversary, birthday, Christmas, Easter, St. Patrick's Day, sympathy. Holiday/seasonal 10-12 mos. ahead. Not open to ideas for new card lines. Open to ideas for various specialty items; all religious themed. Also does books/CDs. Send any number of ideas. Guidelines; catalog for 9 x 12 SASE.

ADDITIONAL CARD PUBLISHERS
Note: Following is a list of card publishers who did not respond to our questionnaire. You may want to contact them on your own to see if they are open to freelance submissions.

BERG CHRISTIAN ENTERPRISES, 4525 S.E. 63rd Ave., Portland OR 97206. (503) 777-4101.

BLACK FAMILY GREETING CARDS, 20 Cortlandt Ave., New Rochelle NY 10801. Bill Harte, pres.

BLACKSMITH CARDS & PRINTS, 37535 Festival Dr., Palm Desert CA 92211. Bob Smith, pres.

CD GREETING CARDS, PO Box 5084, Brentwood TN 37024-5084.

CRT CUSTOM PRODUCTS, INC., 7532 Hickory Hills Ct., Whites Creek TN 37189.

DESIGNS FOR BETTER LIVING, 1716 N. Vista St., Los Angeles CA 90046.

KRISTIN ELLIOTT INC., 6030 N. Orchard Rd., Tucson AZ 85704-5310.

GOOD NEWS IN SIGHT, 2610 Mirror Lake Dr., Fayetteville NC 28303-5212.

GRACE PUBLICATIONS, PO Box 9432, Wyoming MI 49509-0432.

GREENLEAF, INC., 951 S. Pine St., #250, Spartanburg SC 29302-3370. Greenleaf Foundation, Inc.

HIGHER HORIZONS, PO Box 78399, Los Angeles CA 90016-0399.

LUCY & ME GALLERY, 13232 Riviera Pl. N.E., Seattle WA 98125-4645. Diane Roger, card ed.

ALFRED MAINZER INC., 3527—35th St, Astoria NY 11106-1608. Toll-free (800) 22-cards. (718) 392-4200. Fax (718) 392-2681.

MORE THAN A CARD, 5010 Baltimore Ave., Bethesda MD 20816.

OAKSPRINGS IMPRESSIONS, PO Box 572, Woodacre CA 94973-0572. (415) 488-9194. Fax (415) 488-0194.

FREDERICK SINGER & SONS INC., 520 S. Fulton Ave, Mount Vernon NY 10550-5011.

RANDALL WILCOX PUBLISHING, 826 Orange Ave., #544, Coronado CA 92118.

CAROL WILSON FINE ARTS, PO Box 17394, Portland OR 97217. Gary Spector, ed.

GAME MARKETS

Note: Some of the following markets for games, gift items, and videos have not indicated their interest in receiving freelance submissions. Contact these markets on your own for information on submission procedures before sending them anything.

BIBLE GAMES CO., 14389 Cassell Rd., PO Box 237, Fredericktown OH 43019. Toll-free (800) 824-2637. (740) 694-8042. Fax (740) 694-8072. E-mail: info@biblegamescompany.com. Website: www.biblegamescompany.com. JoAnn Vozar, operations mngr. Produces Bible games. 10 percent freelance. Buys 1-2 ideas/yr. Query. Pays on publication for all rts (negotiable). Royalties 8 percent. Responds in 6-8 wks. Open to new ideas. One game per submission. Guidelines & catalog online.

   Tips: "Send developed and tested game play, target market, and audience. Must be totally nonsectarian and fully biblical—no fictionalized scenarios." Board games, CD-ROMs, computer games, and video games.

GOODE GAMES INTERNATIONAL, Original Family Fun Games, PO Box 1099, Nicholasville KY 40356. (859) 881-4513. E-mail: info@goodegames.com. Website: www.goodegames.com. Contact: Mike Goode.

TALICOR, 901 Lincoln Pkwy., Plainwell MI 49080. (269) 685-2345. Fax (269) 685-6789. E-mail: webmaster@Talicor.com. Website: www.Talicor.com. Nicole Hancock, pres. Produces board games and puzzles. 100 percent freelance; buys 10 ideas/yr. Outright submissions. Pays variable rates on publication for all rts. Royalty 4-6 percent. Responds in 4 wks. Seasonal 6 mos. ahead. Open to new ideas for board games, novelty items, puzzles, or toys. Submit 1-4 ideas. No guidelines; catalog for 9 x 12 SAE/$2.38 postage (mark "Media Mail").

WISDOM TREE, PO Box 8682, Tucson AZ 85738-8682. Fax (520) 825-5702. E-mail: Thuff80691@ aol.com. Website: www.wisdomtreegames.com. Brenda Huff, owner. Produces Bible-based computer games and does sales and marketing of Bible-based and family-friendly educational games. Responds in 1-6 wks. Seasonal 8 mos. ahead. Open to review of beta versions of computer games, computer software, or video games. Also networks with Christian Game Developers Group to put projects together. Catalog on request.

Special Needs: "Storybook/puzzle game engine."

GIFT/SPECIALTY-ITEM MARKETS

ANCHOR WALLACE PUBLISHERS, 1000 Hwy 4 S., PO Box 7000, Sleepy Eye MN 56085-0007. Toll-free (800) 533-3570. Toll-free fax (800) 582-2352. E-mail: contactus@anchorwallace.com. Website: www.anchorwallace.com. Worship bulletins, foil & 4-color elegant certificates.

ARTBEATS, 129 Glover Ave., Norwalk CT 06850-1311. (203) 847-2000. Fax (203) 846-2105. E-mail: Richard@nygs.com or mail@nygs.com. Website: www.NYGS.com. New York Graphic Society. Richard Fleischmann, pub. Produces prints and posters. Open to freelancers; purchases 100 ideas/yr. Outright submissions. Pays on publication. Royalties 10 percent. Responds in 3 wks. Does conventional, inspirational, juvenile, religious, and sensitivity prints and posters. Open to new ideas. Guidelines on Website; no catalog.

ASHLEIGH MANOR, PO Box 3851, Frederick MD 21705-3851. Toll-free (800) 327-4212. Fax (301) 631-0108. E-mail: TLawton@ashleighmanor.com. Website: www.ashleighmanor.com. Produces specialty products: religious frames & giftware, bookmarks, gift/novelty items. Free catalog.

BE ONE SPORTSWEAR, 3208 Merrywood Dr., Sacramento CA 95825. (916) 483-7630. E-mail: Blane@beone.com. Website: www.BeOne.com. Christian clothing.

CARPENTREE INC., Carpentree Design, 2724 N. Sheridan, Tulsa OK 74115. Toll-free (800) 736-2787. (918) 582-3600. Fax (918) 587-4329. E-mail through Website: www.carpentree.com. Submit to Design Dept. Produces framed art and verse. Buys several ideas/yr. Prefers outright submission. Rights purchased are negotiable. Pays on publication; negotiable royalty. Responds in 12-15 wks. Uses rhymed, unrhymed, and traditional verse for framed art; 4-16 lines. Open to ideas for new specialty items. Submit max 3-10 ideas. Open to ideas for framed art, tabletop items, and gift/novelty items. Guidelines; catalog $5/10 x 13 SAE.

CHRISTIAN ART GIFTS INC., 1025 N. Lombard Rd., PO Box 1443, Lombard IL 60148. Toll-free (800) 521-7807. (630) 599-0240. Fax (630) 599-0245. Website: www.christianartgifts.com. Friendship cards, greeting books, bookmarks, mugs.

+ CROSS GIFT DIVISION/DICKSONS INC., 513 Warrenville Rd., Warren NJ 07059. Jewelry ideas. E-mail: amonteschio@dicksongifts.com. Website: www.dicksongifts.com/contact_us.aspx. Attn: Alda Monteschio. Guidelines on Website.

DESTINY IMAGE GIFTS, PO Box 310, Shippensburg PA 17257. Toll-free (800) 722-6774. (717) 532-3040. Fax (717) 532-9291. E-mail: rrr@destinyimage.com, or through Website: www.destinyimage.com. Ronda Ranalli, ed. mngr. No unsolicited e-mail submissions; use online submission form. Gift products. Guidelines on Website.

DEXSA: The Giving Company, PO Box 109, Hudson WI 54016. Toll-free (800) 933-3972. (715) 386-8701. Toll-free fax (888) 559-1603. E-mail through Website: www.dexsa.com. John Larson, owner. Gifts.

EAGLES WINGS, 2101 Old Hickory Tree Rd., St. Cloud FL 34772. (407) 892-6358. Fax (407) 892-6759. E-mail: info@eagleswings.com. Website: www.eagleswings.com. Apparel.

GREENACRE WORKSHOP. Toll-free (877) 733-3276. Toll-free fax (888) 860-3276. (401) 728-0350. E-mail: redfarm@quadrigaart.com. Website: www.greenacreworkshop.com. Coloring/activity books; paintables.

HERITAGE PUZZLE INC., PO Box 328, Pfafftown NC 27040-0328. Toll-free (888) 348-3717. Toll-free fax (866) 727-8209. E-mail: heritagepuzzle@triad.rr.com. Website: www.heritagepuzzle.com. Religious jigsaw puzzles.

JODY HOUGHTON DESIGNS INC., 5434 River Rd. N. #135, Keizer OR 97303-4429. Toll-free (800) 733-8253. (503) 656-7748. E-mail: jody@jodyhoughton.com. Website: www.jodyhoughton .com.

KNOW HIM CHRISTIAN GEAR, 6200 S. Troy Cir., Ste. 140, Englewood CO 80111-6474. Toll-free (888) 256-6944. (303) 662-9512. Fax (303) 662-9942. E-mail: Doug.Mckenna@knowhim.com or through Website: www.KnowHim.com. Doug McKenna, pres. Christian apparel.

JAMES LAWRENCE COMPANY, 1501 Livingstone Rd., PO Box 188, Hudson WI 54016. Toll-free (800) 546-3699. (715) 386-3082. Fax (715) 386-3699. E-mail: brian@jameslawrencecompany .com. Website: www.jameslawrencecompany.com. Brian Johnson, gen. mngr. Producer of specialty products. Open to freelance. Buys variable number/yr. Prefers e-mail contact. Prefers exclusive rts. Pays $50-100/verse on acceptance. Negotiable royalties. Responds in 3-4 wks. Inspirational verse no shorter than 4 lines and no longer than 5 stanzas of 4 lines ea. Holiday 6-9 mos. ahead. Open to new ideas for gift/novelty items, magnets, mugs, plaques. Send any number of ideas. No guidelines or catalog. View Website before submitting.

LIVING EPISTLES, 2232 S. Main St., #444, Ann Arbor MI 48103. Toll-free (800) 294-8637. Fax (205) 759-9889. E-mail: LivingEpistlesService@livingepistles.com, or through Website: www.living epistles.com. Apparel.

LORENZ CORP., 501 E. Third St., Dayton OH 45401. Toll-free (800) 444-1144, ext. 1. (937) 228-6118. Fax (937) 223-2042. E-mail: info@lorenz.com. Website: www.lorenz.com. Gift products, stationery, bookmarks, buttons, postcards, posters, and more. Guidelines on Website.

MCBETH CORP, PO Box 400, Chambersburg PA 17201. Toll-free (800) 876-5112. (717) 263-5600. Fax (717) 263-5909. E-mail: mcbethcorp@supernet.com. Website: www.wholesalecentral .com/mcbethcorp. Gifts, jewelry, calendars, Christmas items, activity books, greeting cards, and more.

NOT OF THIS WORLD CLOTHING CO., 169 Radio Rd. #8, Corona CA 92879. (951) 354-9528. Fax (951) 354-9529. E-mail: info@notw.com, or info@c28.com. Website: www.notw.com. Shirts, wallets, belts, belt buckles.

RED LETTER 9, 2910 Kerry Forest Pkwy, #D4, Tallahassee FL 32309. Toll-free (866) 804-4833. Toll-free fax (866) 804-4832. E-mail: info@redletter9.com. Website: www.redletter9.com. Apparel and gift items.

SERENDIPITY PUZZLE CO., INC. W228 N821 Westmound Dr., Waukesha WI 53186. (262) 549-8930. Fax (262) 549-8910. E-mail: diane.bucher@serendipitypuzzles.com. Website: www.serendipity puzzles.com. A division of The Marek Group, Diane Bucher-Gilboy, dir. of sales. Produces specialty products. Open to freelance. Purchases 50+ ideas/yr. Prefers outright submissions through e-mail. Payment & royalty (decided case-by-case) on acceptance. Responds in 2 wks. Seasonal 2 mos. ahead. Open to new ideas for specialty items. Submit 2 or more ideas at a time. Manufactures custom orders. Free catalog.

> **Tips:** "The Marek Group is a nationally recognized, high quality commercial printing and manufacturing company, specializing in catalogs, publications, direct mail, variable data, Web-to-print applications, and the manufacturing of puzzles and board games."

SONTEEZ CHRISTIAN T-SHIRTS, PO Box 44106, Phoenix AZ 85064. Toll-free (800) 874-4485. Website: www.sonteez.com. T-shirts.

VIDA ENTERTAINMENT, 201 East City Hall Ave., Norfolk VA 23451. Toll-free (877) YES-VIDA. (757) 626-3102. E-mail: sales@vidaentertainment.com. Website: www.vidaentertainment.com. Books, DVDs, comics, & toys.

SOFTWARE DEVELOPERS

AMG SOFTWARE, 6815 Shallowford Rd. (37421), PO Box 22000, Chattanooga TN 37422. Toll-free (800) 266-4977. (423) 894-6060, ext. 277. Toll-free fax (800) 265-6690. (423) 894-9511. Ricks@amgpublishers.org. Website: www.amgpublishers.org. AMG International. Contact: Rick Steele, Dir. of Electronic Media.

BAKER SOFTWARE, Box 6287, Grand Rapids MI 49516-6287. (616) 676-9185. Fax (616) 676-9573. Website: www.BakerBooks.com. Baker Publishing Group.

B & H SOFTWARE, 127 Ninth Ave. N., Nashville TN 37234. (615) 251-3638. Website: www .BHpublishinggroup.com.

BIBLESOFT, 22014—7th Ave. S., Seattle WA 98198-6235. (206) 824-0547. Fax (206) 824-1828. Website: www.biblesoft.com. Makers of PC Study Bible.

ELLIS ENTERPRISES INC., 5100 N. Brookline, #465, Oklahoma City OK 73112. (405) 948-1766. Fax (405) 917-2250. E-mail: mail@ellisenterprises.com. Website: www.ellisenterprises.com or www.BibleLibrary.com. Contact: Dr. John Ellis. Produces the Micro Bible, Ultra Bible, Mega Bible, and Maxima Bible. Check out additional products on their Website.

LOGOS BIBLE SOFTWARE, 1313 Commercial St., Bellingham WA 98225-4307. (360) 527-1700. Fax (360) 527-1707. E-mail: suggest@logos.com. Website: www.logos.com. Contact: Dan Pritchett (Dan@logos.com). Publishes the Logos Bible Software Series X Scholar's Library, Leader's Library, Bible Study Library, and more. Over 8,000 titles from more than 100 publishers now compatible with the system.

NAVPRESS SOFTWARE, 16002 Pool Canyon Rd., Austin TX 78734. Website: www.navpress.com.

OLIVE TREE BIBLE SOFTWARE, PO Box 48271, Spokane WA 99228-1271. (509) 465-0302. Fax (509) 467-4976. E-mail: drew@olivetree.com, or support@olivetree.com. Website: www.OliveTree .com. Drew Hunter, pres. Bible software.

ZONDERVAN DIGITAL MEDIA, (formerly Zondervan New Media), 5300 Patterson St. S.E., Grand Rapids MI 49530. Toll-free (800) 226-1122. (616) 698-6900. Fax (616) 698-3483. Website: www .zondervan.com. Contact: Jody DeNeef. Software.

VIDEO/CD/DVD MARKETS

+ ALL THAT PRODUCTIONS INC., PO Box 1594, Humble TX 77347-1594. (218) 878-2062. E-mail: thelma@itsathelma.com. Website: www.ItsAThelma.com. Deborah Elum, dir. Produces videos and movies of comedy series "It's a Thelma." Not open to freelance.

ALPHA OMEGA PUBLICATIONS, 804 N. 2nd Ave. E., Rock Rapids IA 51246. Toll-free (800) 622-3070. Website: www.AOP.com. Videos & DVDs.

AMG PUBLISHERS/CD/CD-ROMS, 6815 Shallowford Rd. (37421), PO Box 22000, Chattanooga TN 37422. Toll-free (800) 266-4977. (423) 894-6060, ext. 277. Toll-free fax (800) 265-6690. (423) 894-9511. E-mail: ricks@amgpublishers.org. Website: www.amgpublishers.org. AMG International. Contact: Rick Steele, dir. of prod. dev./acq. Bible CD-ROMs.

CANDLELIGHT MEDIA GROUP, 3323 State Hwy. 276, Emory TX 75440. Toll-free (800) 747-2696. E-mail: info@candlelightmedia.com. Website: www.candlelightmedia.com. Videos, DVDs.

CLOUD TEN PICTURES, PO Box 1440, Niagara Falls NY 14302. (905) 684-5561. Fax (905) 684-7946. Website: www.cloudtenpictures.com. Film production and acquisition, video distribution, and marketing. Cloud Ten Pictures (maker of the Left Behind movies) is committed to making quality, Christian-themed films. For all inquiries, contact C.E.O.: Andre van Heerden; andrev@cloudten pictures.com.

DALLAS CHRISTIAN VIDEO. Toll-free (877) 516-2900. Fax (972) 644-5926. E-mail: DCV6681@ aol.com. Website: www.dallaschristianvideo.com. Contact: Bob Hill. Videos.

RUSS DOUGHTEN FILMS INC., 5907 Meredith Dr., Des Moines IA 50322. Toll-free (800) 247-3456. (515) 278-4737. Fax (515) 278-4738. E-mail: cneufeld@rdfilms.com. Website: www.rdfilms .com. Russell S. Doughton Jr., pres. Submit to Production Dept. Produces and distributes feature-length Christian movies. Open to ideas. Guidelines; free catalog.

GOSPEL COMMUNICATIONS, PO Box 455, Muskegon MI 49443-0455. Toll-free (800) 253-0413. (231) 773-3361. Fax (231) 777-1847. E-mail: info@gospelcommunications.org. Website: www .GospelCommunications.org. Contact: Marilyn Bush. Videos, DVDs, books, Bibles, and music.

TOMMY NELSON VIDEOS, PO Box 141000, Nashville TN 37214. Website: www.tommynelson.com. Contact: Bill Reeves, entertainment dir. Video producer.

PROPHECY PUBLICATIONS, PO Box 7000, Oklahoma City OK 73153. Toll-free (800) 475-1111. Fax (405) 636-1054. E-mail: Krissie@prophecyinthenews.com. Website: www.prophecyinthenews .com. Contact: J. R. Church. Religious education videos; fiction videos.

TYNDALE FAMILY VIDEO, 351 Executive Dr., Carol Stream IL 60188. (630) 668-8300. Website: www.tyndale.com. Videos.

VISION VIDEO/GATEWAY FILMS, PO Box 540, Worcester PA 19490-0540. Toll-free (800) 523-0226. (610) 584-3500. Fax (610) 584-6643. E-mail: info@VisionVideo.com. Website: www .VisionVideo.com. Contact: Karen Rutt.

WACKY WORLD STUDIOS, 148 E. Douglas Rd., Oldsmar FL 34677-2939. (813) 818-8277. Fax (813) 818-8396. E-mail: info@wackyworld.tv, or through Website: www.wackyworld.tv. Full service custom art and design studio. Videos, DVDs.

ZONDERVAN AUDIO AND VIDEO (formerly Zondervan New Media), 5300 Patterson St. S.E., Grand Rapids MI 49530. Toll-free (800) 226-1122. (616) 698-6900. Fax (616) 698-3483. Website: www.zondervan.com. Contact: T. J. Rathbun. Audio & video.

SPECIALTY-PRODUCTS TOPICAL LISTINGS
Note: Most of the following publishers are greeting card/specialty market publishers, but some will be found in the book-publisher listings.

An A in parentheses (A) before a listing indicates an agent is required.
An asterisk (*) after a category indicates the category is new this year.

Activity/Coloring Books
(A) Cook, David C.
Dickson's Life Pub.
Greenacre Workshop
Knight George Pub.
McBeth Corp.

Rainbow Publishers
Serendipity Puzzle
Warner Press
World Library Pub.

Audiotapes
(A) Tyndale House

(A) W Publishing
AMG Publishers
AMG Software
Bible Games
Eldridge Plays
Fair Havens

McRuffy Press
Zondervan Audio/Video

Banners
Serendipity Puzzle
World Library Pub.

Board Games/Games
(A) Cook, David C.
(A) Tyndale House
Bethel Publishing
Bible Games
Carson-Dellosa
Goode Games
Knight George Pub.
Master Books
Mission City Press
Morris, William
Rainbow Publishers
Review and Herald
Salt Works
Serendipity Puzzle
Standard Publishing
Talicor
WinePress

Bookmarks
Ashleigh Manor
Blue Mountain Arts
Christian Art Gifts
Dickson's Life Pub.
Hermitage Art
Lorenz
Serendipity Puzzle
Warner Press
World Library Pub.

Bulletins
Hermitage Art

Calendars/Daily Journals
(A) Tyndale House
Abingdon Press
African American Expressions
American Tract
Barbour
Blue Mountain Arts
C4Yourself
Dickson's Life Pub.
Group Publishing
McBeth Corp.
Neibauer Press
Serendipity Puzzle

Women of the Promise
World Library Pub.

CD-ROMs
(A) Cook, David C.
AMG Publishers
AMG Video/CD
Bible Games
Fair Havens
Georgetown Univ. Press
Group Publishing
Our Sunday Visitor
World Library Pub.

Charts
Rose Publishing
Serendipity Puzzle

Comic books
(A) Nelson, Thomas
Kaleidoscope Press
Lighthouse Publishing
Serendipity Puzzle
Vida Entertainment
ZonderKidz

Computer games
(A) Cook, David C.
Bible Games
Dean Press, Robbie
Grupo Nelson
Knight George Pub.
Lion and Lamb
WinePress
Wisdom Tree

Computer Software
(A) Regal
AMG Publishers
AMG Software
B & H Software
Baker Software
BibleSoft
Ellis Enterprises
Libros Liguori
Logos Bible Software
NavPress Software
Olive Tree Bible Software
Resource Public.
Wisdom Tree
World Library Pub.
Zondervan Digital

DVDs
Anglicans United
Candlelight Media
Gospel Communications
Vida Entertainment
Wacky World
WinePress
World Library Pub.

Gift/Novelty Items
(A) Cook, David C.
Abingdon Press
African American Expressions
Artful Greetings
Ashleigh Manor
Blue Mountain Arts
Carpentree
Carson-Dellosa
Christian Art Gifts
Design Design
Destiny Image
Dexsa
Dickson's Life Pub.
Hermitage Art
Houghton Designs, Jody
Lawrence Co., James
Lion and Lamb
Lorenz
McBeth Corp.
Mission City Press
Red Letter 9
Salt Works
Serendipity Puzzle
Talicor

Gift Books
(A) Ballantine
 (A) Cook, David C.
(A) Countryman, J.
(A) HarperOne
(A) Regal
ACTA Publications
Adams Media
Ambassador Books
American Binding
B & H Publishing
Baker Books
Barbour
Black Forest/Tennessee
Blue Mountain Arts
Booklocker.com

Book Publishers
Brown Books
Christian Writer's Ebook
Contemporary Drama
Creation House
DCTS Publishing
Dean Press, Robbie
Dimensions for Living
Editorial Portavoz
Eerdmans Pub., Wm. B.
Elderberry Press
Essence
Evergreen Press
Fairway Press
Faith Communications
Gollehon Press
GRQ
Guardian Angel
Hay House
Hidden Brook Press
Holy Fire Publishing
Howard Books
IMD Press
Kaleidoscope Press
Lift Every Voice
Lighthouse Publishing
Mission City Press
Monarch Books
New Leaf
New Seeds
One World
Our Sunday Visitor
Pleasant Word
Providence Pub.
Ravenhawk Books
Review and Herald
Rose Publishing
Salt Works
Serendipity Puzzle
Tate Publishing
Trafford Publishing
Vida Entertainment
VMI Publishers
White Stone Books
WinePress
Word Alive
World Library Pub.

Greeting Books
Blue Mountain Arts

Christian Art Gifts
Design Design
Houghton Designs, Jody
Serendipity Puzzle

Jewelry*
Cross Gift Division

Magnets
African American Expressions
Blue Mountain Arts
Design Design
Dickson's Life Pub.
Houghton Designs, Jody
Lawrence Co., James
World Library Pub.

Mugs
Christian Art Gifts
Dickson's Life Pub.
Lawrence Co., James

Note Cards
Creative Christian Gifts

Plaques
Dickson's Life Pub.
Houghton Designs, Jody
Lawrence Co., James

Postcards
Abingdon Press
Houghton Designs, Jody
Lorenz
Serendipity Puzzle
Warner Press
World Library Pub.

Posters
ArtBeats
InspirationArt
Life Cycle Books
Lorenz
Serendipity Puzzle
World Library Pub.

Puzzles
Bible Games
Heritage Puzzle
Rainbow Publishers
Serendipity Puzzle
Talicor

Stationery
African American Expressions
Design Design

Dickson's Life Pub.
Lorenz
Serendipity Puzzle

Sunday Bulletins
Anchor Wallace
Serendipity Puzzle
Warner Press
World Library Pub.

T-shirts/Apparel
Be One Christian
Dickson's Life Pub.
Eagles Wings
Know Him
Living Epistles
Not of This World
Red Letter 9
SonTeez
World Library Pub.

Toys
Dickson's Life Pub.
Mission City Press
Standard Publishing
Talicor
Vida Entertainment

Videos/Video Games
(A) Cook, David C.
(A) Regal
(A) Tyndale House
(A) W Publishing
Abingdon Press
Alpha Omega
AMG Video/CD
Anglicans United
Bible Games
Candlelight Media
Cloud Ten
Dallas Christian Video
Destiny Image
Doughten Films, Russ
Editorial Unilit
Fair Havens
Focus on the Family
Gospel Communications
Group Publishing
Howard Books
Master Books
Nelson Videos, Tommy
Pauline Books

Prophecy Publications   Vision Video   Wisdom Tree
Tyndale Family Video   Wacky World   Zondervan Audio/Video

PART 4

Helps for Writers

10

Christian Writers' Conferences and Workshops

Visit the following Websites for information on these and other conferences available across the country: www.freelancewriting.com/conferences, or www.screenwriter.com/insider/WritersCalendar. html. Link to these conference Websites at www.stuartmarket.com. Because many of the conferences had not yet set 2010 dates, you will need to check their Websites for exact dates.

+ Indicates a new listing

ALABAMA

SOUTHERN CHRISTIAN WRITERS CONFERENCE. Tuscaloosa/First Baptist Church; June 2010. Contact: Joanne Sloan, SCWC, PO Box 1106, Northport AL 35473. (205) 333-8603. Fax (205) 339-4528. E-mail: SCWCworkshop@bellsouth.net. Website: http://web.mac.com/wmdsloan/iweb/SCWC. Editors/agents in attendance. Attendance: 200+.

ARIZONA

AMERICAN CHRISTIAN WRITERS PHOENIX CONFERENCE. Grace Inn; October 22-23, 2010. Contact: Reg A. Forder, Box 110390, Nashville TN 37222. Toll-free (800) 21-WRITE. E-mail: ACWriters@aol.com. Website: www.ACWriters.com. Attendance: 40-80.

CATHOLIC SCREENWRITERS WORKSHOP. Tucson; March 21-24, 2010. Contact: Fr. Tom Santa, CSsR, 7101 W. Picture Rocks Rd., Tucson AZ 85743-9645. Toll-free (866) 737-5751. (520) 744-3400. Fax (520) 744-8021. E-mail: office@desertrenewal.org. Website: www.desertrenewal.org. See Website for additional writers' events.

ARKANSAS

ANNUAL ARKANSAS WRITERS CONFERENCE. Little Rock; June 4-5, 2010 (always 1st Friday & Saturday of June). Website: www.geocities.com/penwomen. Attendance: 150-175. Sponsors 30 contests; one entry fee covers all contests.

+ **SILOAM SPRINGS WRITERS WORKSHOP**. Siloam Springs; September (probably 3rd Saturday). Contact: Margaret Weathers, 716 W. University St., Siloam Springs AR 72761. (479) 524-6598. Sponsors a contest. No editors/agents in attendance. No scholarships. Attendance: 30.

CALIFORNIA

ACT ONE: WRITING PROGRAM. Hollywood; summer of 2010. Contact: Vicki Peterson, 2690 N. Beachwood Dr., Hollywood CA 90068. (323) 464-0815. Fax (323) 468-0315. E-mail: info@ actoneprogram.com. Website: www.ActOneProgram.com. These are intensive training sessions for screenwriters, taught by professionals working in Hollywood. Offers track for television writers. No editors/agents in attendance. Limited to 30 students (by application).

ANTELOPE VALLEY CHRISTIAN WRITERS' CONFERENCE. Lancaster (near Los Angeles); May 14-15, 2010. Presented by High Desert Christian Writer's Guild and Quartz Hill School of Theology. Free critiques; writing contest. Contact: Steve Hutson, dir., 5022 Avenue N, Ste. 102-128, Palmdale CA 93551. (661) 722-4896. Toll-free fax (866) 501-4280. E-mail: info@avwriters.com. Website:www .avwriters.com.

BIOLA MEDIA CONFERENCE. La Mirada; April or May 2010 (date varies). Contact: Craig Detweiler, Biola University, 13800 Biola Ave., La Mirada CA 90639. Toll-free (866) 334-2266. Website: www .biolamedia.com.

CASTRO VALLEY CHRISTIAN WRITERS SEMINAR. Castro Valley; February 2010. Contact: Pastor Jon Drury, 19300 Redwood Rd., Castro Valley CA 94546-3465. (510) 886-6300. Fax (510) 581-5022. E-mail: jdrury@redwoodchapel.org. Website: www.christianwriter.org. No editors/agents in attendance. Offers full or partial scholarships. Attendance: 200.

MOUNT HERMON CHRISTIAN SONGWRITERS CONFERENCE. Near Santa Cruz. August 31-September 3, 2010. Call (888) MH-CAMPS or visit Website: www.mounthermon.org/song writers.

MOUNT HERMON CHRISTIAN WRITERS CONFERENCE. Mount Hermon (near Santa Cruz); March 26-30, 2010; also Head-Start Clinic (mentoring) March 24-25, 2010; April 15-19, 2011. Also offers a Career Track for professional writers (details on Website); and a teen track. Contact: Rachel A. Williams, Box 413, Mount Hermon CA 95041-0413. (831) 335-4466. Fax (831) 335-9213. E-mail: rachel.williams@mounthermon.org. Website: www.mounthermon.org/adult/professionals/ writers-conference (no brochure; all details on Website December 1). Many editors and agents in attendance. Offers partial scholarships. Cash awards. Attendance: 450.

MOUNT HERMON HEAD START MENTORING CLINIC. Mount Hermon, CA. This mentoring session is held the two days prior to the regular spring conference; March 24-25, 2010. See the listing for Mount Hermon Christian Writers' Conference for details.

ORANGE COUNTY CHRISTIAN WRITERS FELLOWSHIP SPRING WRITERS DAY. Mariners Church/Irvine; April 2010. Contact: John DeSimone, dir.; Peg Matthew Rose, ed., PO Box 5056, Fullerton CA 92838. (714) 538-7070. Fax (949) 458-1807. E-mail: editor@occwf.org. Website: www.occwf.org. Editors and possibly agents in attendance. Offers full and partial scholarships. See Website for list of faculty and conference date. Attendance: 100-150+.

SAN DIEGO CHRISTIAN WRITERS GUILD FALL CONFERENCE. San Diego; September 2010. Contact: Jennie Gillespie, PO Box 270403, San Diego CA 92198. (760) 294-3269. E-mail: info@ sandiegocwg.org. Website: www.sandiegocwg.org. Editors/agents in attendance. Attendance: 180.

SANTA BARBARA CHRISTIAN WRITERS CONFERENCE. Westmont College; October 2010. Contact: Opal Mae Dailey, PO Box 40860, Santa Barbara CA 93140. Phone/fax (805) 682-0316 (call first for fax). E-mail: opalmaedailey@aol.com. Website: www.cwgsb.com. Attendance: 50.

SOCIETY OF CHILDREN'S BOOK WRITERS & ILLUSTRATORS CONFERENCE IN CHILDREN'S LITERATURE. New York City, early February 2010; Los Angeles, early August 2010. Society of Children's Book Writers & Illustrators. Contact: Lin Oliver, 8271 Beverly Blvd., Los Angeles CA 90048. (323) 782-1010. Fax (323) 782-1892. E-mail: scbwi@scbwi.org. Website: www.scbwi.org. Includes a track for professionals. Editors/agents in attendance. Attendance: 900.

WRITERS SYMPOSIUM BY THE SEA. San Diego/Point Loma Nazarene University; February 24-26 & March 24-26, 2010. Contact: Dean Nelson, Professor, Journalism Dept., PLNU, 3900 Lomaland Dr., San Diego CA 92106. (619) 849-2592. Fax (619) 849-2566. E-mail: deannelson@pointloma.edu. Website: www.pointloma.edu/writers. No editors/agents in attendance. No scholarships. Attendance: 500.

COLORADO

AD LIB CHRISTIAN ARTS RETREAT. Franciscan Retreat Center; Colorado Springs; September 2010. Contact: Prof. Richard Terrell, 6905 Forest Lake Blvd., Lincoln NE 68516. (402) 486-4198. Cell (402) 440-8851. E-mail: richard.terrell@doane.edu, or kiwi@neb.rr.com. Website: www.adlib christianarts.org. Gather for Sabbath, fellowship, display/discuss art/writing projects, and work on what we love to do. Guest artists are the editors of Ruminate, CO-based arts journal. No working editors/agents. Attendance: limited to 20.

COLORADO CHRISTIAN WRITERS CONFERENCE. Estes Park; May 12-15, 2010 at the YMCA of the Rockies. Director: Marlene Bagnull, LittD, 316 Blanchard Rd., Drexel Hill, PA 19026-3507. Phone/fax (610) 626-6833. E-mail: mbagnull@aol.com. Website: www.writehisanswer.com/Colorado. Conferees choose 6 hour-long workshops from 42 offered or a Fiction or Nonfiction Clinic (by application) plus one 6.5 hour continuing session from 7 offered. One-on-one appointments, paid critiques, editors' panels, and general sessions. Teens Write Saturday afternoon, plus teens are welcome to attend the entire conference at 60 percent off. Contest awards (registered conferees only), includes 50 percent off 2011 conference. Faculty of 60 authors, editors, and agents. Attendance: 260.

GLEN EYRIE FICTION WRITER'S CONFERENCE. Colorado Springs; January 2010. Contact: Craig Dunham, 3820 N. 30th, Colorado Springs CO 80904. Toll-free (800) 944-4536. (719) 634-0808. Fax (719) 272-7448. Website: www.gleneyriegroup.org. Some editors/agents in attendance. Attendance: 100. Check Website for conferences and dates.

JERRY B. JENKINS CHRISTIAN WRITERS GUILD WRITING FOR THE SOUL CONFERENCE. Grand Hyatt, Denver; February 18-21, 2010; February 9-12, 2011. Sponsored by the Jerry B. Jenkins Christian Writers Guild. Host: Jerry B. Jenkins. Speakers for 2010 include Max Lucado, Phil Vischer, and Philip Yancey. Appointments with publishers' reps & agents. More than 30 editors & agents in attendance. Payment plans available. Special meal rates offered for nonparticipating spouses or parents of teens. General sessions with national keynote speakers and in-depth workshops on 6 tracks. Contact: Admissions Manager, 5525 N. Union Blvd., Ste. 200, Colorado Springs CO 80918. Toll-free (866) 495-5177. Fax (719) 495-5181. E-mail: ContactUs@christianwritersguild.com. Website: www.christianwritersguild.com. Offers partial scholarships. Attendance: 400.

CONNECTICUT

WESLEYAN WRITERS CONFERENCE. Wesleyan University/Middletown; June 2010 (tentative, see Website). Contact: Anne Greene, Director, Wesleyan Writers Conference, 294 High St., Rm. 207, Middletown CT 06459. (860) 685-3604. Fax (860) 685-2441. E-mail: agreene@wesleyan.edu. Website: www.wesleyan.edu/writers. Includes an advanced track. Editors/agents in attendance. Offers fellowship and scholarship awards. Attendance: 100.

DELAWARE

DELAWARE CHRISTIAN WRITERS CONFERENCE. Word of Life Christian Center, Newark; April 2010. E-mail: johnriddle@sprintmail.com. Website: www.DelawareChristianWritersConference .com. Director: John Riddle, 6 Basset Pl., Bear DE 19701. (302) 834-4910. Editors, agents, advanced track, young writers program, writing contests, editorial appointments, & evaluations.

FLORIDA

AMERICAN CHRISTIAN WRITERS ORLANDO CONFERENCE. November 20, 2010. Contact: Reg A. Forder, Box 110390, Nashville TN 37222. Toll-free (800) 21-WRITE. E-mail: ACWriters@aol.com. Website: www.ACWriters.com. Attendance: 40-80.

CHRISTIANS IN THEATRE ARTS (CITA) ANNUAL NETWORKING CONFERENCE. Orlando FL; June 2010. Contact: Bryanne Barker, PO Box 26471, Greenville SC 29616. (864) 679-1898. E-mail: admin@cita.org. Website: www.cita.org. Offers workshops and advanced tracks. Sponsors a play contest & sketch contest (rules on Website). Attendance: 200.

FLORIDA CHRISTIAN WRITERS CONFERENCE. Lake Yale Conference Center; Leesburg FL; March 4-7, 2010. Contact: Billie Wilson, 2344 Armour Ct., Titusville FL 32780. (321) 269-5831. Fax (321) 747-0246. E-mail: billiewilson@cfl.rr.com. Website: www.flwriters.org. Offers advanced track (15 hours of class time—by application only) & teen track. Speakers: Cec Murphey & Jerry Jenkins. Editors and agents in attendance. Offers full & partial scholarships. Offers awards in 11 categories. Awards open to registrants; mss submitted to conference for review are considered for an award. Attendance: 350.

INTERNATIONAL CHRISTIAN RETAIL SHOW. (Held in a different location each year.) St. Louis MO; June 27-July 1, 2010. Contact: Scott Graham, Box 62000, Colorado Springs CO 80962-2000. Toll-free (800) 252-1950. (719) 265-9895. Fax (719) 272-3510. E-mail: info@cbaonline.org. Website: www.christianretailshow.com. Entrance badges available through book publishers or Christian bookstores. Attendance: 8,000.

GEORGIA

AMERICAN CHRISTIAN WRITERS ATLANTA CONFERENCE. Airport Clarion Inn; May 21-22, 2010. Contact: Reg Forder, Box 110390, Nashville TN 37222. Toll-free (800) 21-WRITE. E-mail: ACWriters@aol.com. Website: www.ACWriters.com. Attendance: 40-80.

CATCH THE WAVE WRITERS CONFERENCE. Woodstock; September 2010. See Website for conference details: www.christianauthorsguild.org. Sponsors a short story contest & an article contest. Editors/agents in attendance. No scholarships. Attendance: 60.

EAST METRO ATLANTA CHRISTIAN WRITERS CONFERENCE. Covington; July 2010. Contact: Colleen Jackson, PO Box 2896, Covington GA 30015. (404) 444-7514. E-mail: cjac401992@aol.com. Website: www.emacw.org. Check Website for location and details.

GEORGIA CHRISTIAN WRITERS' SPRING FESTIVAL. Atlanta area; May 1, 2010 (first Saturday in May each year). Contact: Lloyd Blackwell, 3049 Scott Rd. N.E., Marietta GA 30066. (770) 421-1203. E-mail: lloydblackwell@worldnet.att.net.

SOUTHEASTERN WRITERS ASSN. ANNUAL WORKSHOP. St. Simons Island; June 21-26, 2010. Contact: Sheila Hudson, registrar, 161 Woodstone Dr., Athens GA 30605. E-mail: sheilahudson@charter.net. Website: www.southeasternwriters.com. Attendance: limited to 100. Sponsors contests on the Website. Agents/editors in attendance. Evaluations with 3-day registrations.

ILLINOIS

KARITOS CHRISTIAN ARTS CONFERENCE. Bolingbrook; August 2010. Contact: Bob Hay, 1122 Brentwood Ln., Wheaton, IL 60189. (847) 925-8018. E-mail: bob@karitos.com. Website: www.karitos.com. Features workshops in all areas of the arts, including writing. Also general sessions and evening celebrations. Attendance: 300-400.

WRITE-TO-PUBLISH CONFERENCE. Wheaton (Chicago area); June 9-12, 2010. Contact: Lin Johnson, 9118 W. Elmwood Dr., #1G, Niles IL 60714-5820. (847) 296-3964. Fax (847) 296-0754. E-mail: lin@WriteToPublish.com. Website: www.WriteToPublish.com. Offers freelance career track (prerequisite: 1 published book). Majority of faculty are editors; also has agents. No scholarships. Attendance: 250.

INDIANA

AMERICAN CHRISTIAN WRITERS FORT WAYNE CONFERENCE. Clarion Downtown; April 16-17, 2010. Contact: Reg A. Forder, Box 110390, Nashville TN 37222. Toll-free (800) 21-WRITE. E-mail: ACWriters@aol.com. Website: www.ACWriters.com. Attendance: 40-80.

AMERICAN CHRISTIAN WRITERS INDIANAPOLIS CONFERENCE. July 24, 2010. Contact: Reg A. Forder, Box 110390, Nashville TN 37222. Toll-free (800) 21-WRITE. E-mail: ACWriters@aol.com. Website: www.ACWriters.com. Attendance: 40-80.

BETHEL COLLEGE CHRISTIAN WRITERS' WORKSHOP. Bethel College/Mishawaka; spring 2011. Contact: English Dept. Chair, 1001 W. McKinley Ave., Mishawaka IN 46544. (574) 257-3427. Website: www.BethelCollege.edu/writersworkshop. Editors sometimes in attendance; no agents. Sometimes offers full or partial scholarships. Attendance: 130.

EARLHAM SCHOOL OF RELIGION: THE MINISTRY OF WRITING COLLOQUIUM. Richmond; late October 2010 & 2011. Contact: Susan Yanos, Earlham School of Religion, 228 College Ave., Richmond IN 47374-4095. Toll-free (800) 432-1377. (765) 983-1420. Fax (765) 983-1688. E-mail: yanossu@earlham.edu. Website: www.esr.earlham.edu. Editors in attendance. No scholarships. Attendance: 100-200.

MIDWEST WRITERS WORKSHOP. Muncie/Ball State University Alumni Center; July 29-31, 2010 (always the last Thursday, Friday, and Saturday of July). Contact: Dept. of Journalism, Ball State University, Muncie IN 47306-0484. Director: Jama Kehoe Bigger. (765) 282-1055. E-mail: midwest writers@yahoo.com. Website: www.midwestwriters.org. Sponsors a contest. Editors/agents in attendance. Offers full scholarships. Attendance: 150.

IOWA

+ AMERICAN CHRISTIAN WRITERS DES MOINES CONFERENCE. Holiday Inn; August 14, 2010. Contact: Reg A. Forder, Box 110390, Nashville TN 37222. Toll-free (800) 21-WRITE. E-mail: ACWriters@aol.com. Website: www.ACWriters.com. Attendance: 40-80.

CEDAR FALLS CHRISTIAN WRITERS' WORKSHOP. Riverview Conference Center/Cedar Falls; June 9-12, 2010. June 8-11, 2011. Contact: Jean Vaux, 1703 Sunnyside Dr., Cedar Falls IA 50613-4644. (319) 277-7444. Fax (318) 277-1721. E-mail: vauxcom@cfu.net. Website: www.shellybeach online.com. No editor/agents in attendance. Offers full & partial scholarships. Attendance: 35.

CHRISTIAN WRITERS SEMINAR. Arnolds Park; September 2010. Contact: Denise Triggs, PO Box 281, Okoboji IA 51355. (712) 332-7191. E-mail: waterfalls42@hotmail.com. Website: www.water fallsretreats.com. No editors/agents in attendance. No scholarships. Attendance: 20.

IOWA SUMMER WRITING FESTIVAL. University of Iowa/Iowa City; June & July 2010. This is a general writer's conference that comes highly recommended for good, solid instruction. Contact: Amy Margolis, Iowa Summer Writing Festival, C215 Seashore Hall, University of Iowa, Iowa City IA 52242-5000. (319) 335-4160. Fax (319) 335-4743. E-mail: iswfestival@uiowa.edu. Website: www .uiowa.edu/~iswfest. For two months, June and July, you can sign up for either one-week workshops or weekend workshops on a wide variety of topics. Write for a catalog of offerings (available in February).

QUAD-CITIES CHRISTIAN WRITERS' CONFERENCE. Eldridge; April 9-10, 2010. Contact: Twila Belk, 4350 Tanglewood Rd., Bettendorf IA 52722. (563) 332-1622. e-mail: twilabelk@mchsi.com. Website: www.qccwc.com. Speakers include: Cynthia Ruchti, Jim Pence. No editors or agents in attendance. Offers full scholarships. Attendance 100+.

KANSAS

CALLED TO WRITE. Girard/Pittsburg; April 9-10, 2010. Contact: Deborah Vogts, 17300 Ness Rd., Erie KS 66733. E-mail: debvogts@gmail.com. Website: www.christianwritersfellowship.blogspot .com. Speaker: Cec Murphey. Attendance: 50-60.

KENTUCKY

KENTUCKY CHRISTIAN WRITERS' CONFERENCE. Elizabethtown; June 11-12, 2010. E-mail: registrar@kychristianwriters.com. Website: www.kychristianwriters.com. Speaker: Virginia Smith. Editors in attendance. Workshops and appointments with editors. Attendance: 100.

MARYLAND

SANDY COVE CHRISTIAN COMMUNICATORS' EXPERIENCE. Sandy Cove/North East; September-October 2010 (unconfirmed). This conference changing format; see Website. Contact: Sharon Norris Elliott, Writers' Conference Director, Sandy Cove Ministries, 60 Sandy Cove Rd., North East MD 21901. Toll-free (800) 234-2683. E-mail: info@sandycove.org. Website: www.sandy cove.org/writers.

MASSACHUSETTS

CAPE COD ANNUAL SUMMER WRITERS' CONFERENCE. Craigville Conference Center; third week in August, 2010. Contact: Anne-Elizabeth Tom, exec. dir., PO Box 408, Osterville MA 02655-0408. (508) 420-0200. Fax (508) 420-0212. E-mail: writers@capecodwriterscenter.org. Website: www.capecodwriterscenter.org. Classes capped at 18; smaller for advanced. Editors, publishers, and agents in attendance. Seven and a half hour workshops are $185; two and a half hour $60; 5 one-hour combined manuscript evaluation/mentoring $150. Deadline for registration is July 15. No registration fee for CCWC members; for nonmembers $35. Attendance: 200.

MICHIGAN

AMERICAN CHRISTIAN WRITERS GRAND RAPIDS CONFERENCE. Howard Johnson; June 11-12, 2010. Contact: Reg Forder, Box 110390, Nashville TN 37222. Toll-free (800) 21-WRITE. E-mail: ACWriters@aol.com. Website: www.ACWriters.com. Attendance: 40-80.

FESTIVAL OF FAITH & WRITING. Calvin College, Grand Rapids; April 15-17, 2010 (held every other year). Contact: Shelly LeMahieu Dunn, Calvin College, 1795 Knollcrest Cir. S.E., Grand Rapids MI 49546. (616) 526-6770. Fax (616) 526-8508. E-mail: ffw@calvin.edu. Website: www.calvin.edu/ festival. Editors/agents in attendance; no scholarships.

MARANATHA CHRISTIAN WRITERS SEMINAR. Maranatha Bible & Missionary Conference/ Muskegon; September 2010. Contact: Verna Kokmeyer, 4759 Lake Harbor Rd., Muskegon MI 49441-5299. (231) 798-2161. Fax (231) 798-2152. E-mail: info@writewithpurpose.org. Website: www .WriteWithPurpose.com. Speakers include: Dennis Hensley, Holly Miller, Sally Stuart, Bill Crowder, and Anne Fenske. Editors/agents in attendance. Offers partial scholarships. Attendance: 100.

ORIGINAL & ADVANCED SPEAK UP WITH CONFIDENCE SEMINARS. Cornerstone University, Grand Rapids MI, June 23-26, 2010. For details & to register, go to: www.carolkent.org, click on "Speak Up Seminars." Contact: Carol Kent, 3141 Winged Foot Dr., Lakeland FL 33803-5437. Toll-free in U.S. (888) 870-7719; outside U.S. (810) 982-0898. Fax (810) 987-4163. E-mail: Speakupinc@ aol.com. Website: www.SpeakUpSpeakerServices.com. Speaking seminars. Offers advanced training and opportunities to be coached in small groups. Also offers a workshop on writing for speakers who write for publication. Upcoming conferences listed on Website. Attendance: 100.

MINNESOTA

AMERICAN CHRISTIAN WRITERS MINNEAPOLIS CONFERENCE. Country Inn (St. Paul); August 6-7, 2010. Contact: Reg Forder, Box 110390, Nashville TN 37222. Toll-free (800) 21-WRITE. Website: www.ACWriters.com. Attendance: 40-80.

MINNESOTA CHRISTIAN WRITERS GUIDE SPRING & FALL SEMINARS. Minneapolis/St. Paul; spring seminar, March or April 2010; fall seminar, October or November 2010. Contact: Mrs. Pat Van der Merwe, 19820 Olde Sturbridge Rd., Corcoran MN 55340. (763) 478-6145. E-mail: pdvdm@comcast.net. Website: www.mnchristianwriters.org. No editors/agents in attendance; no scholarships. Attendance: 50.

THE WRITING ACADEMY SEMINAR. Mount Olivet Retreat Center outside Minneapolis; July 30-August 3, 2010. Sponsors year-round correspondence writing program and annual seminar. Contact: Nancy Remmert, 312 St. Louis Ave., St. Louis MO 63135-2756. (314) 522-3718. E-mail: info@wams.org, or nremm10335@aol.com. Website: www.wams.org. Attendance: 30. Sponsors a writing contest open to members (rules are posted on Website).

WRITING SEMINARS/NORTH HENNEPIN COMMUNITY COLLEGE. Minneapolis; new classes every Monday and Thursday, year round. Instructor: Louise B. Wyly. Topics include Fiction Writing, Novel Writing, Mystery Novels, Writing for Children and Teens, The Artist's Way; Memoirs, and other beginning and advanced courses. Offers a Creative Writing Certificate and an Advanced Creative Writing Certificate. Contact: Louise Wyly, 6315 55th Ave. N., Minneapolis MN 55428-358, or call (763) 533-6207. E-mail: Lsnowbunny@aol.com. Website: www.nhcc.edu/cect.

MISSOURI

+ AMERICAN CHRISTIAN WRITERS SPRINGFIELD. Lamplighter North; August 21, 2010. Contact: Reg A. Forder, Box 110390, Nashville TN 37222. Toll-free (800) 21-WRITE. E-mail: ACWriters@aol.com. Website: www.ACWriters.com. Attendance: 40-80.

HEART OF AMERICA CHRISTIAN WRITERS NETWORK CONFERENCES. Kansas City, November 11-13, 2010, check Website for dates of additional events. Contact: Jeanette Littleton, 3706 N.E. Shady Lane Dr., Gladstone MO 64119. Phone/fax (816) 459-8016. E-mail: HACWN@earthlink.net. Website: www.HACWN.org. Offers classes for new and advanced writers. Editors/agents in attendance. Contest details on brochure. Attendance: 125.

WRITER'S BREAKTHROUGH WORKSHOP. Kansas City; May 2010. Contact: Dr. Grace LaJoy Henderson, PO Box 181, Raymore MO 64083. E-mail: poetry@gracelajoy.com. Website: www.writers breakthrough.com. Churches, groups, community organizations, libraries, etc., can request a mini Writer's Breakthrough Workshop to be held at their facility at anytime during the year. Attendance: 100.

NEW HAMPSHIRE

WRITERS WORKSHOPS BY MARY EMMA ALLEN. Taught on request by writer's groups, conferences, schools, and libraries. Topics include: Workshops for Young Writers (for schools and home-parenting groups); Writing Your Family Stories; Blogging for Fun, Profit, & Promotion; Scrapbooking Your Stories. Contact: Mary Emma Allen (instructor), 55 Binks Hill Rd., Plymouth NH 03264. (603) 536-2641. E-mail: me.allen@juno.com. Blogs: http://maryemmallen.blogspot.com and http://bookbagblog.blogspot.com.

NEW MEXICO

CLASS CHRISTIAN WRITERS' CONFERENCE (formerly Glorieta Christian Writers' Conference). Ghost Ranch/Abiquiu; October 13-17, 2010 (tentative). Editors and agents in attendance. Contact:

Linda Gilden, dir., PO Box 52103, Albuquerque NM 87181-2103. E-mail: kaeporter@gmail.com. Website: www.classeminars.org. Editors/agents in attendance. Partial scholarships. Attendance: 400.

THE GLEN WORKSHOP. St. John's College/Santa Fe; first full week in August 2010. Includes fiction, poetry, nonfiction, memoir, on-site landscape painting, figure drawing, collage and mixed media, and several master classes. Contact: Julie Mullins, 3307 Third Ave. W., Seattle WA 98119. (206) 281-2988 (*Image Journal*). Fax (206) 281-2979. (*Image Journal*). E-mail: image@imagejournal.org. Website: www.imagejournal.org/page/events/the-glen-workshop. Two Image editors; no agents in attendance. Offers partial scholarships. Attendance: 200.

SOUTHWEST WRITERS MINIWORKSHOPS. Albuquerque; various times during the year (check Website for dates). Contact: Conference Chair, 3721 Morris St. N.E., Ste. A, Albuquerque NM 87111-3611. (505) 265-9485. E-mail: swwriters@juno.com. Website: www.southwestwriters .com. General conference. Sponsors the Southwest Writers Contests annually and quarterly (see Website). Agents/editors in attendance. Attendance: 50.

NEW YORK

53rd INTERNATIONAL CONFERENCE ON HUMOR, HOPE AND HEALING. Saratoga Springs; May or June 2010. General. Contact: The HUMOR Project Inc., 480 Broadway, Ste. 210, Saratoga Springs NY 12866. (518) 587-8770. E-mail: info@humorproject.com. Website: www.humor project.com.

NORTH CAROLINA

+ AMERICAN CHRISTIAN WRITERS CHARLOTTE CONFERENCE. Marriott Executive Park; May 14-15, 2010. Contact: Reg A. Forder, Box 110390, Nashville TN 37222. Toll-free (800) 21-WRITE. E-mail: ACWriters@aol.com. Website: www.acwriters.com. Attendance: 40-80.

BLUE RIDGE MOUNTAIN CHRISTIAN WRITERS CONFERENCE. LifeWay Ridgecrest Conference Center; May 16-20, 2010. Contact: Alton Gansky, 9983 Rose Dr., Oak Hills CA 92344-0220. (760) 949-8075. E-mail: alton@altongansky.com. Website: www.brmcwc.com, or www.Lifeway.com/ christianwriters. Editors and agents in attendance. Sponsors a contest. Full & partial scholarships. Attendance: 350-400.

SHE SPEAKS CONFERENCE. Concord; July 30-August 1, 2010; July 22-24, 2011. Contact: LeAnn Rice, Proverbs 31 Ministries, 616-G Matthews-Mint Hill Rd., Matthews NC 28105. (704) 849-2270. Fax (704) 849-7267. E-mail: office@Proverbs31.org. Website: www.SheSpeaksConference. com. 2010 speakers: Lysa TerKeurst, Renee Swope. Editors/agents in attendance; no scholarships. Attendance: 450.

OHIO

AMERICAN CHRISTIAN WRITERS' COLUMBUS CONFERENCE. Clarion Hotel; June 5, 2010. Hosted by Columbus Christian Writers Assn./Pat Zell, (937) 593-9207. Contact: Reg Forder, Box 110390, Nashville TN 37222. Toll-free (800) 21-WRITE. E-mail: ACWriters@aol.com. Website: www .ACWriters.com. Attendance: 40-80.

NORTHWEST OHIO CHRISTIAN WRITERS ONE-DAY SEMINAR. Toledo; October 9, 2010. Contact: Kathy Douglas, 5702 Angola Rd, Lot 139, Toledo OH 43615. (419) 867-0805. E-mail: mlka@toast.net. Speaker 2010: Dr. Dennis Hensley. No editors/agents in attendance; no scholarships. Attendance: 50.

NORTHWEST OHIO CHRISTIAN WRITERS SPRING 2-DAY RETREAT. Lial Retreat Center/ Whitehouse; April 30-May 1, 2010. Contact: Kathy Douglas, 5702 Angola Rd., Lot 139, Toledo OH 43615. (419) 867-0805. E-mail: mlka@toast.net. Website: www.nwocw.org. Advance registration required. Attendance: about 12.

PEN TO PAPER LITERARY SYMPOSIUM. Dayton; October 1-2, 2010; September 30-October 1, 2011. Contact: Valerie L. Coleman, Pen of the Writer, 893 S. Main St., PMB 175, Dayton OH 45322. (937) 307-0760. Fax (515) 474-3643. E-mail: info@penofthewriter.com. Website: www.penofthe writer.com/pentopaper. Editors/agents in attendance. For Power Awards contest details, go to: www.pen ofthewriter.com/awards.

WRITE ON! WORKSHOP. Dayton; March 27, 2010; March 26, 2011. Contact: Valerie L. Coleman, Pen of the Writer, PMB 175—893 S. Main St., Dayton OH 45322. (937) 307-0760. Fax (515) 474-3643. E-mail: info@penofthewriter.com. Website: www.penofthewriter.com/WriteOn. Speakers: Valerie L. Coleman & Wendy Beckman. Editors in attendance. Full and partial scholarships. Attendance: 50.

OKLAHOMA

AMERICAN CHRISTIAN WRITERS' OKLAHOMA CITY CONFERENCE. La Quinta Airport; March 19-20, 2010. Contact: Reg Forder, Box 110390, Nashville TN 37222. Toll-free (800) 21-WRITE. E-mail: ACWriters@aol.com. Website: www.ACWriters.com. Attendance: 40-80.

OREGON

HEART TALK. A workshop for people beginning to speak or write for publication. Portland/ Western Seminary; March 9-10, 2010 original seminar; March 11-12, 2010 advanced seminar (on speaking). Contact: Women's Center for Ministry, Western Seminary, 5511 S.E. Hawthorne Blvd., Portland OR 97215-3367. (503) 517-1931. Fax (503) 517-1889. E-mail: wcm@westernseminary .edu. Website: www.westernseminary.edu/women. Beverly Hislop, exec. dir. of Women's Center for Ministry. Conference alternates between writing one year and speaking the next. Workshops and editors/publicists available for consultation. Check Website for details. Offers partial scholarships based on need. Attendance: 125.

OREGON CHRISTIAN WRITERS COACHING CONFERENCE. Portland/Salem area; August 2-5, 2010. Website: www.OregonChristianWriters.org. Includes about 7 hours of training under a specific coach/topic. Offers advanced track. E-mail: scregistration@OregonChristianWriters.org. Speaker: Bill Myers. Editors/agents in attendance. Attendance: 250.

ORIGINAL & ADVANCED SPEAK UP WITH CONFIDENCE SEMINARS. Western Seminary, Portland OR, March 9-12, 2010. For details & to register, go to: www.carolkent.org, click on "Speak Up Seminars." Contact: Carol Kent, 3141 Winged Foot Dr., Lakeland FL 33803-5437. Toll-free in U.S. (888) 870-7719; outside U.S. (810) 982-0898. Fax (810) 987-4163. E-mail: Speakupinc@aol.com. Website: www.SpeakUpSpeakerServices.com. Speaking seminars. Offers advanced training and opportunities to be coached in small groups. Also offers a workshop on writing for speakers who write for publication. Upcoming conferences listed on Website. Attendance: 100.

PENNSYLVANIA

GREATER PHILADELPHIA CHRISTIAN WRITERS' CONFERENCE. Philadelphia Biblical University, Langhorne; August 5-7, 2010 (tentative). Founder and director: Marlene Bagnull, LittD, 316 Blanchard Rd., Drexel Hill, PA 19026-3507. Phone/fax (610) 626-6833. E-mail: mbagnull@aol.com. Website: www.writehisanswer.com/Philadelphia. Conferees choose 6 hour-long workshops from 42 offered or a Fiction or Nonfiction Clinic (by application) plus one 6.5-hour continuing session from 7 offered.

One-on-one appointments, paid critiques, editors panels, and general sessions. Contest (registered conferees only) for 50 percent off 2011 conference. Especially encourages African American writers. Faculty of 50-60 authors, editors, and agents. Attendance: 250.

HIGHLIGHTS FOUNDATION FOUNDERS WORKSHOPS. Honesdale; February-December 2010. Contact: Kent Brown, Highlights Foundation, 814 Court St., Honesdale PA 18431. (570) 253-1192. Fax (570) 253-0179. E-mail: contact@highlightsfoundation.org. Website: www.HighlightsFoundation .org. Editors and agents in attendance. For children's writers. Targeted workshops that allow you to select a topic that fits your writing needs—from sports to nature, magazine to books, fiction to nonfiction, and picture books to young adult novels. Offers a track for advanced writers. General conference. Modest grants may be available.

HIGHLIGHTS FOUNDATION WRITERS WORKSHOP AT CHAUTAUQUA. Chautauqua NY; July 17-24, 2010. Contact: Kent Brown, Highlights Foundation, 814 Court St., Honesdale PA 18431. (570) 253-1192. Fax (570) 253-0179. E-mail: contact@highlightsfoundation.org. Website: www.highlights foundation.org. For children's writers and illustrators. Week-long conference. Choose workshops for your level, genre, and interests. Editors/agents in attendance. General conference. Offers full and partial scholarships (applications received through January 2010). Attendance 100.

MERCER COUNTY ANNUAL ONE-DAY WRITERS' WORKSHOP (sponsored by St. David's Writers' Conference); Stoneboro; April 24, 2010. Contact: Gloria Clover, 26 Everbreeze Dr., Hadley PA 16130. (724) 253-2635. E-mail: gloworm@certainty.net. Websites: www.gloriaclover.com; www.stdavids writers.com. Occasionally has editors, but rarely agents in attendance. Sponsors a contest. No scholarships. Attendance: 120.

MONTROSE CHRISTIAN WRITERS CONFERENCE. Montrose; July 25-30, 2010. Contact: Montrose Bible Conference, 5 Locust St., Montrose PA 18801-1112. Toll-free (800) 598-5030. (570) 278-1001. Fax (570) 278-3061. E-mail: mbc@montrosebible.org. Website: www.montrose bible.org. Tracks for advanced writers and teens. Editors/agents in attendance. Provides a few partial scholarships. Attendance: 100.

ST. DAVIDS CHRISTIAN WRITERS' CONFERENCE. Grove City College, Grove City; June 2010. Lora Zill, director. Contact: Audrey Stallsmith, registrar, 87 Pines Rd. E., Hadley PA 16130-1019. (724) 253-2738. E-mail: registrar@stdavidswriters.com. Website: www.stdavidswriters.com. Offers writer's retreat & track for advanced writers. Contest in 10 categories for attendees only. See Website for information on their Writers' Colony. Editors in attendance. Full and partial scholarships. Attendance: 60-70.

SUSQUEHANNA VALLEY WRITERS WORKSHOP. Best Western Country Cupboard Inn, Lewisburg; October 2010. Contact: Marsha Hubler. (570) 837-0002. E-mail: ckwriter@evenlink.com. Website: www.marshahubler.com. Editors/agents in attendance.

SOUTH CAROLINA

+ **UPSTATE SOUTH CAROLINA ACW FALL WORKSHOP**. Anderson; October 2010. Contact: Elva Martin, 104 Oak Knoll Ter., Anderson SC 29625-2507. Phone/fax (864) 226-7024. E-mail: elvamartin ministries@charter.net. Offers track for advanced writers and possibly a teen track. Sponsors a contest. Editors/agents in attendance. Offers partial & full scholarships.

TENNESSEE

+ **AMERICAN CHRISTIAN WRITERS' DIRECTORS FORUM**. Nashville; January 12-14, 2010. Contact: Reg A. Forder, Box 110390, Nashville TN 37222. Toll-free (800) 21-WRITE. E-mail: ACWriters@ aol.com. Website: www.ACWriters.com. Attendance: 40-80.

AMERICAN CHRISTIAN WRITERS' MEMPHIS CONFERENCE. First Baptist Church; May 1, 2010. Contact: Reg A. Forder, Box 110390, Nashville TN 37222. Toll-free (800) 21-WRITE. E-mail: ACWriters@aol.com. Website: www.ACWriters.com. Attendance: 40-80.

AMERICAN CHRISTIAN WRITERS' NASHVILLE MENTORING RETREAT. Opryland Guest House; April 9-10, 2010. Contact: Reg Forder, Box 110390, Nashville TN 37222. Toll-free (800) 21-WRITE. E-mail: ACWriters@aol.com. Website: www.ACWriters.com. Attendance: 40-80.

+ **SOUTHEASTERN CHRISTIAN WRITERS CONFERENCE**. Cleveland; October 22-23, 2010. Contact: Homer Rhea, PO Box 6102, Cleveland TN 37320. (423) 339-2576. Fax (423) 478-7334. E-mail: homer8238@gmail.com. Website: www.homerrhea.com. Speaker: Cecil Murphey. Attendance: 50+.

TEXAS

AMERICAN CHRISTIAN WRITERS' DALLAS CONFERENCE. Holiday Inn Select; March 12-13, 2010. Contact: Reg Forder, Box 110390, Nashville TN 37222. Toll-free (800) 21-WRITE. E-mail: ACWriters@aol.com. Website: www.ACWriters.com. Attendance: 40-80.

AUSTIN CHRISTIAN WRITERS' WORKSHOP. February 2010 (check Website). Contact: Lin Harris, 129 Fox Hollow Cove, Cedar Creek TX 78612-4844. (512) 601-2216. Fax (240) 208-3201. E-mail: linharris@austin.rr.com. Attendance: 100.

EAST TEXAS CHRISTIAN WRITERS CONFERENCE. Marshall; April 9-10, 2010; April 8-9, 2011 (2nd weekend of April annually). Contact: Dr. Jerry Hopkins, East Texas Baptist University, 1209 N. Grove St., Marshall TX 75670. (903) 923-2083. Fax (903) 923-2077. E-mail: Jhopkins@etbu.edu. Website: www.etbu.edu/news/CWC/default.htm. Offers an advanced & teen track; contest. Editors/agents in attendance. Partial scholarships for students only. Attendance: 200.

INSPIRATIONAL WRITERS ALIVE! AMARILLO SEMINAR. April 10, 2010 (always first Saturday after Easter). Contact: Jerry McClenagan, 6808 Cloud Crest, Amarillo TX 79124. (806) 355-7117. E-mail: jerrydalemc@sbcglobal.net. Sponsors an annual contest. Attendance: 50.

NORTH TEXAS CHRISTIAN WRITERS' CONFERENCE. Keller; September 17-18, 2010; September 16-17, 2011 (second Friday & Saturday after Labor Day). Contact: NTCW Conference, PO Box 820802, Fort Worth TX 76182. (817) 715-2597. E-mail: info@ntchristianwriters.com. Website: www.ntchristianwriters.com. Offers track for advanced writers. No editors or agents in attendance. Offers partial scholarships. Sponsors a contest for conference registrants only. Attendance: 250.

TEXAS CHRISTIAN WRITERS CONFERENCE. Houston; August 7, 2010. Contact: Martha Rogers, 6038 Greenmont, Houston TX 77092-2332. (713) 686-7209. E-mail: marthalrogers@sbcglobal.net. Editors/agents in attendance. Sponsors a contest: Inspirational Writers Alive! Open Competition; May 15 deadline. Attendance: 70. If you want to start another group in Texas, contact Martha Rogers.

YWAM HANDS-ON SCHOOL OF WRITING AND WRITERS-TRAINING WORKSHOPS. Lindale; September-December 2010. Contact: Carol Scott, 15186 CR 440, Lindale TX 75771. (903) 882-9663. Fax (903) 882-1161. E-mail: contactus@ywamwoodcrest.com, or through Website: www.ywamwoodcrest.com. List of workshops on Website or for SASE. Attendance: 10-20.

UTAH

UTAH CHRISTIAN WRITERS' CONFERENCE. Bluffdale; fall 2010 (tentative). Contact: Julie Scott, PO Box 3, Bountiful UT 84011-0003. (801) 294-5485. E-mail: julie.scott@mac.com. Website: www.utahchristianwriters.com. Editors in attendance; no agents. Offers partial scholarships. ACW Chapter.

VIRGINIA

NATIONAL CHRISTIAN WRITERS CONFERENCE. Norfolk; March 2010. Contact: Antonio L. Crawford, PO Box 1458, National City CA 91951-1458. (619) 791-5810. E-mail: ncwcsd@yahoo .com. Website: www.nationalchristianwritersconference.com.

RICHMOND CHRISTIANS WHO WRITE CONFERENCE. Richmond; September 17-18, 2010. Contact: Rev. Thomas C. Lacy, 12114 Walnut Hill Dr., Rockville VA 23146-1854. (804) 749-4050. Fax (804) 749-4939. Or codirector Rebekah Robb, 9600 January Way, Richmond VA 23238. (804) 527-0913. E-mail: tcrobb@integrity.com. E-mail: RichmondCWW@aol.com. Blog: http://rcww.blog spot.com.

WASHINGTON

AMERICAN CHRISTIAN WRITERS SPOKANE CONFERENCE. Mirabeau Park Hotel; September 24-25, 2010. Contact: Reg Forder, Box 110390, Nashville TN 37222. Toll-free (800) 21-WRITE. E-mail: ACWriters@aol.com. Website: www.ACWriters.com. Attendance: 40-80.

NORTHWEST CHRISTIAN WRITERS RENEWAL. Bothell; May 7-8, 2010. Contact: Judy Bodmer, 11108 NE 141 Pl., Kirkland WA 98034. (425) 488-2900. E-mail: jbodmer@msn.com. Website: www .nwchristianwriters.org. Speaker: Brandilyn Collins. Editors/agents in attendance. Offers full scholarships. Attendance: 175.

WISCONSIN

+ AWAKENING THE SOUL OF THE WRITER. La Crosse; March 2010. Contact: Theresa Washburn, Franciscan Spirituality Center, FSPA, 912 Market St., La Crosse WI 54601. E-mail: twashburn@fspa .org. Website: www.franciscanspiritualitycenter.org.

GREEN LAKE CHRISTIAN WRITER'S CONFERENCE. Green Lake; August 22-27, 2010; August 21-26, 2011. Contact: Jan White, Green Lake Conference Center, W2511 State Rd. 23, Green Lake WI 54941-9599. (920) 294-3323 for reservations. E-mail for information: janwhite@glcc.org. Website: www.glcc.org. For new or well-published writers in Christian or secular markets. Editors in attendance. Offers partial scholarships. Sponsors a contest for conference attendees only. Attendance: 40-80.

CANADA/FOREIGN

AMERICAN CHRISTIAN WRITERS CARIBBEAN CRUISE. November 28-December 5, 2010. Contact: Reg A. Forder, Box 110390, Nashville TN 37222. Toll-free (800) 21-WRITE. E-mail: ACWriters@aol.com. Website: www.ACWriters.com. Attendance: 15-30.

ASSOCIATION OF CHRISTIAN WRITERS (UK) MEMBERS CONFERENCE. Hoddesdon, Herts UK. E-mail through Website for dates & locations: www.christianwriters.org.uk. Membership (900) open. Sponsors an occasional writers' weekend for members only. Editors in attendance; no agents. No scholarships.

COMIX35 CHRISTIAN COMICS TRAINING SEMINAR. Various international locations & dates. Contact: Nate Butler, PO Box 4458, Albuquerque NM 87196-4458. E-mail: comix35@comix35.org. Website: www.comix35.org. Speakers: Nate Butler & others. Sometimes has editors/agents in attendance. Sponsors a contest (details on Website). Attendance: 15-20.

INSCRIBE CHRISTIAN WRITERS' FELLOWSHIP FALL CONFERENCE. Edmonton AB, Canada; September 2010. Contact: Marcia Laycock, Box 637, Blackfalds AB T0M 0J0, Canada. (430) 885-9828. Fax (403) 885-4777. E-mail: query@inscribe.org. Website: www.inscribe.org (click on "Events").

Some editors in attendance; no agents. Sponsors a fall contest open to nonmembers; details on Website. Attendance: 70+.

ISRAEL TOUR FOR CHRISTIAN WRITERS. Leaves from Chicago; February 8-17, 2010. American Christian Writers. Contact: Reg A. Forder, Box 110390, Nashville TN 37222. Toll-free (800) 21-WRITE. E-mail: ACWriters@aol.com. Website: www.ACWriters.com. Attendance: 15-30.

LITTWORLD CONFERENCE. Next conference won't be held until 2012. Contact: John D. Maust, director, 351 S. Main Pl., Ste. 230, Carol Stream IL 60188-2455. (630) 260-9063. Fax (630) 260-9265. E-mail: MaiLittWorld@sbcglobal.net. Website: www.littworld.org.

WRITE! CANADA. Guelph, Ontario; June 17-19, 2010. Contact: Shannon Liebold, The Word Guild, PO Box 28087, Waterloo ON N2L 6J8, Canada. (519) 886-4196. E-mail: writecanada@rogers.com. Website: www.thewordguild.com. Hosted by The Word Guild, an association of Canadian writers and editors who are Christian. Offers an advanced track. Editors/agents in attendance. Contests for attendees. Offers full & partial scholarships. Attendance: 250. Also sponsors one-day conferences in various Canadian cities.

CONFERENCES THAT CHANGE LOCATIONS

ACT ONE: SCREENWRITING WEEKENDS. Two-day workshops; see Website for dates and locations. Contact: Conference Coordinator, 2690 Beachwood Dr., Lower Fl., Hollywood CA 90068. (323) 464-0815. Fax (323) 468-0315. E-mail: info@ActOneProgram.com. Website: www.ActOneprogram.com. Open to anyone who is interested in learning more about the craft of screenwriting. Speakers vary: Sheryl Anderson, Thom Parham, Dean Batali, Chris & Kathy Riley. No editors/agents in attendance. Attendance: 75.

AMERICAN CHRISTIAN FICTION WRITERS CONFERENCE. Rotates cities; Indianapolis, September (3rd weekend) 2010. Contact: Robin Miller, conf. dir., PO Box 101066, Palm Bay FL 32910-1066. E-mail: cd@acfw.com. Website: www.ACFW.com. Offers varied skill level tracks for published and unpublished writers. Editors/agents in attendance. Sponsors 2 contests (details on Website). Offers scholarships each year to ACFW members only.

AMERICAN CHRISTIAN WRITERS CONFERENCES. Various dates and locations (see individual states where held). Also sponsors an annual Caribbean cruise in November/December. Contact: Reg A. Forder, Box 110390, Nashville TN 37222. Toll-free (800) 21-WRITE. E-mail: ACWriters@aol.com. Website: www.ACWriters.com. Attendance 30-40.

AUTHORIZEME. Various locations and dates. Contact: Sharon Norris Elliott, PO Box 1519, Inglewood CA 90308-1519. (310) 508-9860. Fax (323) 567-8557. E-mail: AuthorizeMe@sbc global.net. Website: www.AuthorizeMe.net. AuthorizeMe is a 12-hour, hands-on seminar that teaches you how to get your book idea out of your head, down onto paper, and into a professional book proposal. Seminars offered nationwide. For a list of scheduled seminars, or to sponsor a seminar in your area, check Website. Offers full & partial scholarships. Attendance: 5-50.

CATHOLIC MEDIA CONVENTION. Anaheim, CA; May 2010. Contact: Thomas Conway, exec. dir., 205 W. Monroe St., Chicago IL 60606-5013. (312) 380-6789. Fax (312) 361-0256. E-mail: cath journ@catholicpress.org. Website: www.catholicmediaconvention.org. For media professionals. Editors/agents in attendance. Partial scholarships. Annual book awards. Attendance: 550.

CHILDREN'S AUTHORS' BOOTCAMPS. Held in several locations each year; various dates. General. Contact: Bootcamp c/o Linda Arms White, PO Box 231, Allenspark CO 80510. Phone/fax (303) 747-1014. E-mail: CABootcamp@msn.com. Website: www.WeMakeWriters.com. Upcoming dates and details on Website.

CHRISTIAN LEADERS AND SPEAKERS SEMINARS (The CLASSeminar). PO Box 36551, Albuquerque NM 87176. (702) 882-0638. Website: www.classeminars.org. Sponsors several seminars across the country each year. Check Website for CLASSeminar dates and locations. For those who want to improve their communication skills for either the spoken or written word, for professional or personal reasons. Speakers: Florence Littauer and others. Attendance: 75-100.

CRUISIN' FOR CHRIST. Caribbean cruise; September 2010. Contact: Kendra Norman-Bellamy (blessed_to_write@yahoo.com), PO Box 831648, Stone Mountain GA 30083. E-mail: Cruisin_For_ Christ@yahoo.com. Website: ww.cruisinforchrist.org. Writing workshops onboard.

EVANGELICAL PRESS ASSOCIATION CONVENTION. Irvine TX, May 5-7, 2010; May 4-6, 2011. Contact: Doug Trouten, dir., PO Box 28129, Minneapolis MN 55428. (763) 535-4793. Fax (763) 535-4794. E-mail: director@epassoc.org. Website: www.epassoc.org. Attendance: 300-400. Annual convention for editors of evangelical periodicals; freelance communicators welcome.

THE EXPERTIZING WORKSHOP. Held in Boston, New York, and San Francisco; every 6 mos. (October, April). Contact: Alyza Harris, Expertizing.com, PO Box 590239, Newton MA 02459. (617) 630-0945. E-mail: alyza@PublishingGame.com. Website: www.Expertizing.com, or www.Expertizing .com/forum.htm. Learn how to get more media attention for your book and business. Speaker: Fern Reiss. Attendance: Limited to 6.

FAITHWRITERS CONFERENCE. Date & location on Website. Contact: Scott Lindsay. Website: www .faithwriters.com/conference.php.

INTERNATIONAL CHRISTIAN RETAIL SHOW. (Held in a different location each year); July 2010. Contact: CBA, Box 62000, Colorado Springs CO 80962-2000. Toll-free (800) 252-1950. (719) 265-9895. E-mail: info@cbaonline.org. Website: www.cbaonline.org. Entrance badges available through book publishers or Christian bookstores. Attendance: 8,000.

MUSE ONLINE WRITERS CONFERENCE. Contact: Lea Schizas. E-mail: museitupeditor@yahoo .ca. Website: www.freewebs.com/themuseonlinewritersconference. This is a free online conference. Check Website for upcoming conferences.

NEW ENGLAND CHRISTIAN WRITERS CONFERENCE. This conference is currently on hold. Contact: Lauren Yarger, exec. dir./producer, Masterworks Productions, Inc., 2 Long Lott Rd., West Granby CT 06090. (860) 658-7733. E-mail: masterworkproductions@yahoo.com. Website: www .masterworkproductions.org.

THE PUBLISHING GAME WORKSHOP. Various cities throughout the year (check Website for dates and locations). Workshops held every 3 mos. (September, December, March, and June). Contact: Alyza Harris, Peanut Butter and Jelly Press, PO Box 590239, Newton MA 02459. Phone/fax (617) 630-0945. E-mail: info@PublishingGame.com, or Alyza@publishinggame.com. Website: www.PublishingGame .com (dates, locations, and registration forms on Website). Speaker: Fern Reiss. Editors and agents in attendance. Attendance: limited to 18.

"WRITE HIS ANSWER" SEMINARS & RETREATS. Various locations around U.S.; dates throughout the year; a choice of focus on periodicals or books (includes self-publishing or mastering the craft). Contact: Marlene Bagnull, LittD, 316 Blanchard Rd., Drexel Hill PA 19026-3507. Phone/fax (610) 626-6833. E-mail: mbagnull@aol.com. Website: www.writehisanswer.com/Writing_Seminars .htm. Attendance: 20-60. One- and two-day seminars by the author of Write His Answer: A Bible Study for Christian Writers.

WRITER'S NUDGE WORKSHOPS. Various locations & dates. Contact: Mary Busha, 1370-B Deerfield Rd., Lebanon OH 45036. (513) 228-1205. E-mail: marybusha@writersnudge.com. Website: www .writersnudge.com.

11

Area Christian Writers' Clubs, Fellowship Groups, and Critique Groups

We highly recommend finding and joining a group in your area.

+ A plus sign indicates a new listing.

ALABAMA

CHRISTIAN FREELANCERS. Tuscaloosa. Contact: Joanne Sloan, 4195 Waldort Dr., Northport AL 35473. (205) 333-8603. E-mail: cjosloan@bellsouth.net. Membership (25) open.

ARIZONA

+ **CHRISTIAN WRITERS OF THE WEST** (ACFW Chapter). Mesa. Contact: Pamela Tracy, Mesa AZ. (623) 910-0524. E-mail: pamwrtr@aol.com. Blog: http://christianwritersofthewest.blogspot.com. Membership (21) open to members of national ACFW.

EAST VALLEY CHRISTIAN WRITERS. Mesa. Contact: Brenda Jackson, Mesa AZ. (480) 827-1545. E-mail: BrendaAtTheRanch@yahoo.com. Membership (5) open.

FOUNTAIN HILLS CHRISTIAN WRITERS GROUP. Contact: Jewell Johnson, 14223 N. Westminster Pl., Fountain Hills AZ 85268. (480) 836-8968. E-mail: tykeJ@juno.com. Membership (10-16) open. ACW Chapter.

ARKANSAS

LITTLE ROCK ACW CHAPTER. Contact: Mary Larmoyeux. E-mail: mlarmoyeux@familylife.com. Membership (20) open. Sponsors a contest open to nonmembers if they have attended before.

SILOAM SPRINGS WRITERS. Contact: Margaret Weathers, 716 W. University St., Siloam Springs AR 72761. (479) 524-6598. E-mail: Rosie1st2000@yahoo.com. Membership (28) open. Periodically sponsors a contest open to nonmembers, and a seminar in September.

CALIFORNIA

+ **AMADOR FICTION WRITERS CRITIQUE GROUP**. Meetings in Jackson & Ione. Contact: Kathy Boyd Fellure, 520 Sutter Ln., Ione CA 95640-9771. (209) 274-0205. E-mail: kathyfellure2@juno.com. Membership (10) ; waiting list for writers; open to readers.

BAY AREA WRITERS CRITIQUE GROUP. Fremont. Contact: Carol Hall, PO Box 853, Union City CA 94587. (510) 206-2358. E-mail: Info@CarolLeeHall.com. Membership (10) open to experienced writers only.

CASTRO VALLEY CHRISTIAN WRITERS GROUP. Contact: Pastor Jon Drury, 19300 Redwood Rd., Castro Valley CA 94546-3465. (510) 886-6300. E-mail: jdrury@redwoodchapel.org. Website: www.christianwriter.org. Membership (10-14) open. Sponsoring a Christian Writers Seminar, February 2010.

+ CHAIRS: THE CHRISTIAN AUTHORS, ILLUSTRATORS, & READERS SOCIETY. Montclair. Contact: Nancy I. Sanders, 6361 Prescott Ct., Chino CA 91710-7105. (909) 590-0226. E-mail: jeff andnancys@gmail.com. Website: www.chairs7.wordpress.com. Membership (15-20) open.

CHRISTIAN WRITERS GUILD OF SANTA BARBARA. Contact: Opal Mae Dailey, (805) 682-0316 or (805) 252-9822. E-mail:opalmaedailey@aol.com or cwgsb@sbcglobal.net. Meets monthly. Membership open.

DIABLO VALLEY CHRISTIAN WRITERS GROUP. Danville. Contact: Cynthia Herrmann, 65 S. "C" St., Tracy CA 95376. (209) 607-5118. E-mail: cherrmn@pacbell.net. Membership (12-18) open.

HIGH DESERT CHRISTIAN WRITERS. Quartz Hill. Contact: Don Patterson, 6223 Almond Valley Way, Quartz Hill CA 93536. (661) 722-5695. E-mail: don@theology.edu. Website: www.theology .edu/writers. Membership (30) open. Presents the Sable Quill-Pacesetter Award each year to the writer in the group who has shown the most progress or professional achievement. Cosponsors the Antelope Valley Christian Writers Conference, May 2010.

+ INSPIRE CHRISTIAN WRITERS. Meetings in Sacramento and Roseville. Contact: Elizabeth Thompson, 9359 Silverbend Ln., Elk Grove CA 95624-3985. (916) 670-1937. E-mail: elizabeth mthompson@comcast.net. Group e-mail: inspiregroup@comcast.net. Blog site: www.inspirewriters .com. Membership (18) open. Sponsoring a speaker and a meal May 15, 2010. Check Website for details.

NOVEL IDEA CHRISTIAN WRITERS SWARM. Norwalk/Cerritos. Contact: Derrell B. Thomas, 11239 1/2 Ferina St., Norwalk CA 90650-5507. (562) 292-9997. E-mail: derrell.writer@gmail.com. Membership (15) open.

ORANGE COUNTY CHRISTIAN WRITERS FELLOWSHIP. Various groups meeting throughout the county. Contact: Peggy Matthews Rose (editor@occwf.org) or write OCCWF, PO Box 5056, Fullerton CA 92838. Membership (190) open. Annual membership includes a bimonthly newsletter, information on local critique groups, advance notice of writing opportunities through an e-mail list, and reduced fees for annual Spring Writer's Day (usually on a Saturday in April; see Website for details). Conference includes keynote speakers, workshops, and consultations. See Website for details: www .occwf.org.

PEGGY LESLIE'S CRITIQUE GROUP/SAN DIEGO CHRISTIAN WRITERS GUILD. El Cajon. Contact: Peggy Leslie, 329 Quail Run, El Cajon CA 92019. (619) 447-6258. E-mail: gnpleslie@cox .net. Website: www.sandiegocwg.org. Membership (6) open.

SACRAMENTO CHRISTIAN WRITERS. Citrus Heights. Contact: Beth Miller Self, 2012 Rushing River Ct., Elverta CA 95626-9756. (916) 992-8709. E-mail: cwbself@msn.com. Website: www.sc writers.org. Membership (25) open. Sponsors a contest for members. Sponsors a seminar every 5 years in Sacramento; the next one, May 15, 2010, will be their 30th anniversary as a group.

SAN DIEGO COUNTY CHRISTIAN WRITERS' GUILD. Contact: Jennie & Bob Gillespie, PO Box 270403, San Diego CA 92198. (760) 294-3269. E-mail: info@sandiegocwg.org. Website: www.san diegocwg.org. Membership (200) open. To join their Internet newsgroup, e-mail your name and address to: info@sandiegocwg.com. Sponsors 10 critique groups, fall seminar (September 2010), and spring fellowship brunch.

SANTA CLARA VALLEY CHRISTIAN WRITER'S GROUP. Cupertino. Contact: Richard M. Hinz, 550 S. 4th St., Apt. E, San Jose CA 95112, (408) 297-3336, Rickhinz@yahoo.com. Membership (14) open.

S.C.U.M. San Leandro. Contact: John B. Olson, 1261 Estrudillo Ave., San Leandro CA 94577. (510) 357-4441. E-mail: johno@litany.com. Membership (12) open.

SOUTH VALLEY CHRISTIAN WRITERS/ACW CHAPTER. Group connects by e-mail only. Contact: Mary E. Kirk, 2727 N. 11th Ave., apt. 321, Hanford CA 93230-3362. (559) 582-8442. E-mail: mkirk@cnetech.com.

TEMECULA CHRISTIAN WRITERS CRITIQUE GROUP. Contact: Rebecca Farnbach, 41403 Bitter Creek Ct., Temecula CA 92591-1545. (951) 699-5148. Fax (951) 699-4208. E-mail: sunbrook@hotmail.com. Membership (12) open. Part of San Diego Christian Writers Guild.

+ VISION WRITERS/ACW CHAPTER. Los Angeles. Contact: Bertha Sanders, 2127 W. 73rd St., Los Angeles CA 90047-2111. (323) 971-4319. E-mail: bwsander1@ca.rr.com. Membership (6) open.

WORDSMITHS (PROFESSIONAL CHRISTIAN WRITERS). Montclair. Contact: Nancy I. Sanders, 6361 Prescott Ct., Chino CA 91710-7105. (909) 590-0226. E-mail: jeffandnancys@gmail.com. Website: www.wordsmiths8.wordpress.com. Membership (8) not open (contact for membership information).

THE WRITE BUNCH. Stockton. Contact: Shirley Cook, 3123 Sheridan Way, Stockton CA 95219-3724. (209) 477-8375. E-mail: shirleymcp@sbcglobal.net. Membership (8) not currently open.

COLORADO

+ ACFW COLORADO GROUP & 3 CHAPTERS. Website: www.acfwcolorado.com. Sponsors ongoing blog, annual retreat, 2 miniconferences/yr., plus the following 3 chapters: **HIS Writers**, North Denver; www.acfwcolorado.com/denver.html. **W!W!W!**, Colorado Springs; www.acfwcolorado.com/cosprings.html. **Mile High Scribes**, South Denver, contact: Jan Parrish; jan_parish@comcast.net.

WORDS FOR THE JOURNEY CHRISTIAN WRITERS GUILD/ROCKY MOUNTAIN REGION. Parker. Contact: Michele Cushatt, 1907 Ross Ln., Highlands Ranch CO 80126. (720) 271-2367. E-mail: michele@MicheleCushatt.com. Website: www.wordsforthejourney.org and www.wftj.blogspot.com. Membership (100+) open. See separate listing for Southeast Texas region.

DELAWARE

DELMARVA CHRISTIAN WRITERS' FELLOWSHIP. Georgetown. Contact: Candy Abbott, PO Box 777, Georgetown DE 19947-0777. (302) 856-6649. Fax (302) 856-7742. E-mail: cfa@candyabbot.com. Website: www.delmarvawriters.com. Membership (20+) open.

FLORIDA

ADVENTURES IN CHRISTIAN WRITING. Orlando (First Presbyterian Church). Contact: Joanna Adicks Wallace, 1107 E. Amelia St., Orlando FL 32803-5327. Phone/fax (407) 841-2157. E-mail: hughjohj@yahoo.com. Membership (20) open.

BRANDON CHRISTIAN WRITERS/ACW CHAPTER. Contact: Ruth C. Ellinger, (813) 685-7387. E-mail: Writer@Ruthellinger.com. Membership (30) open.

FIRST COAST CHRISTIAN WRITERS/ACW CHAPTER. Jacksonville. Contact: Lorraine Haataia, PhD., PO Box 600956, Jacksonville FL 32260-0956. E-mail: president@FirstCoastChristianWriters.org. Website: www.FirstCoastChristianWriters.org. Blog: http://FirstCoastChristianWriters.blogspot.com. Membership (10+) open.

HOBE SOUND WRITERS GROUP/ACW CHAPTER. Hobe Sound. Contact: Faith Tofte, 9342 Bethel Way, Hobe Sound FL 33455. (772) 545-4023. E-mail: faithtofte@bellsouth.net. Membership (5) open.

MID-FLORIDA CHRISTIAN WRITERS. Oakland. Contact: Joy Shelton, 1040 Glensprings Ave., Winter Garden FL 34787. (407) 654-9076. E-mail: JoyShelton4@aol.com. Membership (10) open.

PALM BEACH CHRISTIAN WRITERS ASSN. West Palm Beach. Contact: Natalie Ferrone, 964 Imperial Lake Rd., West Palm Beach FL 33413. (561) 574-0201. E-mail: nataliekim71@msn.com. Membership (10) open. ACW Chapter.

SUNCOAST CHRISTIAN WRITERS. Seminole. Contact: Elaine Creasman, 13014—106th Ave. N., Largo FL 33774-5602. Phone/fax (727) 595-8963. E-mail: emcreasman@aol.com. Membership (10-15) open.

WORD WEAVERS. Longwood. Contact: Larry J. Leech II, 911 Alameda Dr., Longwood FL 32750. (407) 925-6411. E-mail: lleech@cfl.rr.com. Website: www.WordWeaversonline.com. Membership (90+) open. Sponsors a contest for members. Planning a conference for February 2010 in Lake Yale.

GEORGIA

EAST METRO ATLANTA CHRISTIAN WRITERS/ACW CHAPTER. Covington. Contact: Colleen Jackson, PO Box 2896, Covington GA 30015. (404) 444-7514. E-mail: cjac401992@aol.com. Website: www.emacw.org. Membership (40) open. Sponsoring a seminar; date and location to be decided. Check Website for monthly meeting and seminar dates and location.

GEORGIA WRITERS ASSN./CHRISTIAN WRITERS POD. Woodstock/Marietta. Contact: Lloyd Blackwell, 3049 Scott Rd. N.E., Marietta GA 30066. (770) 421-1203. E-mail: lloydblackwell@world net.att.net. Membership (73) open. Meets twice monthly. Sponsors a contest, an annual cooperative published book, and a seminar in May.

NORTHEAST GEORGIA WRITERS. Gainesville. Contact: Elouise Whitten, 660 Crestview Ter., Gainesville GA 30501-3110. (770) 532-3007. E-mail: elouisewhitten@netzero.net. Membership (38) open. Sponsors contest open to members. Sponsors a conference in even years at Brenau University in Gainesville.

IDAHO

ACW SANDPOINT. Contact: Anita Aurit, 403 Louis Ln., Sandpoint ID 83864. (208) 610-0626. E-mail: AnitaAurit@gmail.com. Website: www.heroes.com/ACW.htm. Membership (10) open.

IDAHOPE WRITERS (IDAhope). Boise. Contact: Angela Meuser, c/o Rediscover Bookshop, 7079 Overland Rd., Boise ID 83709. (208) 327-7679. E-mail: ameuser@cableone.net. Membership (20) open.

+ WE IS WRITERS/ACW. Moscow. Contact: Susan Thomas, 540 N. Grant, Moscow ID 83843. (208) 882-9038. E-mail: susanethomas@juno.com. Blog: www.weiswriters@blogspot.com. Membership (7) open.

INDIANA

+ MORGAN COUNTY CHRISTIAN WRITERS/ACW CHAPTER. Mooresville. Contact: Barbara Manning or Margaret Walker, Life Pointe Community Church, 825 N. Indiana St., Mooresville IN 46158. (317) 831-0659. E-mail: morgancountywriters@yahoo.com. Website: www.ourchurch.com/member/m/morgancounty. Membership (20) open.

IOWA

IOWA SCRIBES. Marion. Contact: Kimn Swenson Gollnick, 550 Edinburgh Ave., Marion IA 52302-5614. (319) 373-2302. E-mail: kimn-gollnick@uiowa.edu. Facebook: www.facebook.com/group.php?gid=57127652115. Website: www.KIMN.net/scribes.htm. Membership (6-10) open.

CEDAR RAPIDS CHRISTIAN WRITER'S GROUP. Contact: Susan Fletcher, 513 Knollwood Dr. S.E., Cedar Rapids IA 52403. (319) 365-9844. E-mail: skmcfate@msn.com. Membership (4) open but by invitation only.

FELLOWSHIP OF CHRISTIAN WRITERS/ORANGE CITY IA. Contact: Judith Vander Wege, 304 Frankfort Ave. S.E., Orange City IA 51041-1708. Phone/fax (712) 707-9313 (call first for fax). E-mail: judithvanderwege@orangecitycomm.net. Website: http://Spokesman-Ink.org. Membership (2) open. For critique, teaching, motivation, and fellowship. Sponsors a fall poetry contest open to nonmembers.

KANSAS

CHRISTIAN WRITERS FELLOWSHIP. Girard. Contact: Deborah Vogts, 17300 Ness Rd., Erie KS 66733. (620) 244-5619. E-mail: debvogts@gmail.com. Website: www.ChristianWritersFellowship .blogspot.com. Membership (35) open. Sponsors a contest open to nonmembers and a seminar April 9-10, 2010 (see listing in conference section).

CREATIVE WRITERS FELLOWSHIP. Newton, North Newton, Hesston, Moundridge, Halstead. Contact: Esther Groves, sec., 405 W. Bluestem, Apt. H4, North Newton KS 67117-8069. (316) 283-7224. Membership (21) open.

KENTUCKY

LOUISVILLE CHRISTIAN WRITERS/ACW CHAPTER. Crystal Murray, pres. Contact: Lana Jackson, 7804 Foxlair Way, Louisville KY 40220-3283. (502) 968-3602. E-mail: info@lcwriters.com or LanaHJackson@insightbb.com. Website: www.LCWriters.com. Meeting details on Website. Membership (22) open.

LOUISIANA

SOUTHERN CHRISTIAN WRITERS GUILD. Mandeville. Contact: Grace Booth or Marlaine Peachey, 806 Harmony Ln., Mandeville LA 70471. (985) 626-4282. Fax (985) 624-3108. E-mail: peachlane@bellsouth.net. Website under construction. Has monthly speakers. Membership (30) open.

MAINE

+ MAINE FELLOWSHIP OF CHRISTIAN WRITERS. China. Contact: Vicki Schad, 180 S. Stanley Hill Rd., Vassalboro ME 04989. (207) 923-3956. E-mail: jvschad@gmail.com. Membership (15) open. Sponsors an August seminar in Belfast ME.

MARYLAND

ANNAPOLIS FELLOWSHIP OF CHRISTIAN WRITERS. Annapolis. Contact: Jeri Sweany, 3107 Ervin Ct., Annapolis MD 21403-4620. (410) 267-0924. Membership (15) open.

BALTIMORE AREA CHRISTIAN WRITERS/ACW CHAPTER. Owings Mills. Contact: Theresa V. Wilson, MEd, PO Box 47182, Windsor Mill MD 21244-3571. (443) 622-4907. E-mail: writerseminar @aol.com. Website: www.writersinthemarketplace.org. Membership (36) open.

MCC WRITERS' GROUP. Joppa. Contact: Virginia Colclasure or Dawn Sexton, c/o Mountain Christian Church, 1824 Mountain Rd., Joppa MD 21085. (410) 877-1824 (church). E-mail: Vcolclasure@ zoominternet.net or mccwriters@zoominternet.net. Devotional blog: http://portionsofgrace.blog spot.com. Sponsors a one-day seminar in September. Membership (15) open.

THIRD SATURDAY CHRISTIAN WRITERS GROUP. Howard County. Contact: Claire K. DeBakey. (443) 413-6790. E-mail: c.debakey@att.net. Membership (12+) open.

MASSACHUSETTS

CENTRAL MASSACHUSETTS CHRISTIAN WRITERS FELLOWSHIP. Sturbridge. Contact: Barbara Shaffer, 168 Warren Rd., Brimfield MA 01010-9615. (413) 245-9620. E-mail: historyfind2@aol.com. Membership (10) open.

MICHIGAN

AMERICAN CHRISTIAN WRITERS DETROIT. Contact: Pamela Perry, 33011 Tall Oaks St., Farmington MI 48336-4551. (248) 426-2300. Fax (248) 471-2422. E-mail: PamPerry@ministry marketingsolutions.com. Website: www.ministrymarketingsolutions.com. Membership (219) open. Sponsors a fall seminar in Detroit.

THE CALLED AND READY WRITERS. Detroit. Contact: Wanda Burnside, PO Box 211018, Detroit MI 48221. (313) 792-2801. Fax (313) 861-7578. E-mail: wtvision@hotmail.com. Website: www .thecalledandreadywriters.org. Poetry critique available. Membership (70) open (more than 25 published book authors).

MINNESOTA

MINNESOTA CHRISTIAN WRITERS GUILD. Minneapolis/St. Paul. Contact: Mary Fran Heitzman, pres., 10417 Colorado Rd., Bloomington MN 55438. (952) 831-7790. Fax: (952) 253-0712. E-mail: maryfheitzman@comcast.net. Website: www.mnchristianwriters.org. Membership (110) open. Sponsors a spring contest for members only and annual spring (March) and fall (October) seminars in Minneapolis/St. Paul area. Monthly meetings (Sept.-May); monthly newsletter. Sponsors critique circles throughout Minnesota.

MISSISSIPPI

BYHALIA CHRISTIAN WRITERS/ACW CHAPTER. Contact: Marylane Wade Koch, 2573 Church St., Byhalia MS 38611-9576. (901) 351-0870. E-mail: bcwriters@gmail.com. Has an online yahoo group. Membership (50) open. Works with ACW on an annual seminar in Memphis area; April 30-May 1, 2010.

MISSOURI

CHRISTIAN WRITERS WORKSHOP OF ST. LOUIS/ACW CHAPTER. Brentwood area. Contact: Ruth Houser, 3148 Arnold-Tenbrook Rd., Arnold MO 63010-4732. (636) 464-1187. E-mail: HouserRA@juno.com. Membership (10-12) open.

HEART OF AMERICA CHRISTIAN WRITERS' NETWORK. Kansas City metro area. Contact: Mark and Jeanette Littleton, 3706 N.E. Shady Lane Dr., Gladstone MO 64119. Phone/fax (816) 459-8016. E-mail: HACWN@earthlink.net. Website: www.HACWN.org. Membership (150) open. Sponsors monthly meetings, weekly critique groups, professional writers' fellowships, a contest (open to non-members), a newsletter, marketing e-mails, and a conference in November.

OZARKS CHAPTER OF AMERICAN CHRISTIAN WRITERS. Springfield. Meets monthly, Sept. to May. Contact: Jeanetta Chrystie, pres., OCACW, 5042 E. Cherry Hills Blvd., Springfield MO 65809-3301. (417) 832-8409. E-mail: DrChrystie@mchsi.com. Susan Willingham, newsletter ed.; OzarksACW@ yahoo.com. Guidelines on Website: www.ClearGlassView.org/OzarksACW/index.htm. Sponsor an annual contest (open to nonmembers) ; genre, dates, and guidelines on Website. See Website for other events. Membership (38) open. Newsletter-only subscriptions available.

NEBRASKA

CENTRAL NEBRASKA FELLOWSHIP OF CHRISTIAN WRITERS, ARTISTS, AND MUSICIANS (C-WAM). Kearney. Contact: Carolyn R. Scheidies, 415 E. 15th, Kearney NE 68847-6959. (308) 234-3849. E-mail: crscheidies@mail2faith.com (put C-WAM in subject line). Membership (10) open; more on Internet Loop.

MY THOUGHTS EXACTLY WRITERS GROUP. Fremont. Contact: Cheryl A. Paden, PO Box 1073, Fremont NE 68025. (402) 727-6508. Membership (6-8) open. Sponsoring a writers' retreat in January 2010.

WORDSOWERS CHRISTIAN WRITER'S GROUP/ACW CHAPTER. Omaha area. Contact: Kelly Haack, 16268 Orchard Cir., Omaha NE 68135-1336. (402) 593-7936. E-mail: haackkj@cox.net. Website: www.wordsowers.com. Membership (20) open.

NEW JERSEY

NORTH JERSEY CHRISTIAN WRITER'S GROUP. Ringwood. Contact: Louise Bergmann DuMont, PO Box 36, Ringwood NJ 07456. (973) 962-9267. E-mail: LouiseDumont@gmail.com. Writers blog: www.njcwg.blogspot.com. Membership (30) open. E-mail for information.

NEW MEXICO

SOUTHWEST WRITERS. Albuquerque. Contact: Rob Spiegel, pres., 3721 Morris St. N.E., Ste. A, Albuquerque NM 87111-3611. (505) 265-9485. E-mail: swwriters@juno.com. Website: www.south westwriters.com. Membership (700) open. Sponsors an annual and a monthly contest (open to nonmembers), a series of miniconferences in Albuquerque (see Website for dates), workshops and classes. Semimonthly e-lert notices are open to nonmembers. General.

NEW YORK

NEW YORK CHRISTIAN WRITERS GROUP. Manhattan. Contact: Marilyn Driscoll, 350—1st Ave., New York, NY 10010 (Manhattan). (212) 529-6087. E-mail: madrisc@rcn.com. Membership (8) open.

THE SCRIBBLERS/ACW CHAPTER. Riverhead. Contact: Bill Batcher, pres., c/o First Congregational Church, 103 First St., Riverhead NY 11901. E-mail: bbatcher@optonline.net. Membership (12) open. Meets monthly and sponsors annual writing retreat.

SOUTHERN TIER CHRISTIAN WRITERS' FELLOWSHIP. Johnson City. Contact: Jean Jenkins, 3 Snow Ave., Binghamton NY 13905-3810. (607) 797-5852. E-mail: jdjenkins2@verizon.net. Membership (8) open.

NORTH CAROLINA

COVENANT WRITERS. Lincolnton. Contact: Robert Redding, 3392 Hwy. 274, Cherryville NC 28021-9634. (704) 445-4962. E-mail: minwriter@yahoo.com. Membership (10) open.

SEVEN SERIOUS SCRIBES. Cary. Contact: Katherine W. Parrish, 103 Chimney Rise Dr., Cary NC 27511-7214. (919) 467-1924. E-mail: servantsong@aol.com. Critique group. Membership (7) not currently open, but encourages others to start similar groups in the area.

OHIO

COLUMBUS CHRISTIAN WRITERS ASSN. Contact: Barbara Taylor Sanders, (614) 306-3637. E-mail: BTSanders@columbus.rr.com. Website: www.cwacolumbus.com. Meets third Saturday of each month. Membership (25) open.

CREATIVE FORCE ACW NORTHGATE. Sunbury. Contact: Lark Lamontagne, 450 Township Rd. 208, Marengo OH 43334-9501. (740) 625-6535. Fax (740) 625-6572. E-mail: lark@L3VS.com. Membership (20) not currently open.

DAYTON CHRISTIAN SCRIBES. Kettering. Contact: Lois Pecce, PO Box 41613, Dayton OH 45441-0613. (937) 433-6470. E-mail: epecce@compuserve.com. Membership (30) open.

CENTEX CHAPTER—AMERICAN CHRISTIAN FICTION WRITERS (ACFW). Englewood. Contact: Tina Toles, PO Box 251, Englewood OH 45322. (937) 836-6600. E-mail: daytonwriters@ureach.com. Website: www.daytonwriters.com. Membership (25) open. Sponsoring a conference in June 2010.

FAITH WRITERS. Milford. Contact: Sharon Siepel or Vicki Clarke, 5910 Price Rd., Milford OH 45150. (513) 831-3770. E-mail: ssiepel@faithchurch.net. Website: www.faithchurch.net. Meets January-October, 4th Wednesday of the month. Membership (25) open.

MIDDLETOWN AREA CHRISTIAN WRITERS, Franklin. Contact: Donna J. Shepherd, Healing Word Assembly of God, 5303 S. Dixie Hwy, Franklin OH 45005. (513) 423-1627. E-mail: donnashepherd@cinci.rr.com. Website: www.middletownwriters.blogspot.com. Membership (15) open.

+ MOVING AHEAD ACW CHAPTER. Marion. Contact: Diana Barnum, 3288 Darby Glen Blvd., Hilliard OH 43026. (614) 529-9459. E-mail: diana@ohiohelp.net. Membership open to inmates of the Marion Correctional Institution (MCI); adult male inmates in a reentry program for prisoners getting ready to reenter society. May expand group to include those in the community.

NORTHWEST OHIO CHRISTIAN WRITERS/ACW CHAPTER. Bowling Green. Contact: Katherine Douglas, pres., 5702 Angola Rd., Lot 139, Toledo OH 43615. (419) 867-0805. E-mail: mlka@toast.net. Website: www.nwocw.org. Meets the 4th Fridays of January, March, May, July, and October. Membership (45-50) open. Sponsors a spring writers' retreat and a fall writers' seminar in September/October.

OKLAHOMA

FELLOWSHIP OF CHRISTIAN WRITERS (FCW). Tulsa. Contact: Lavon Lewis, PO Box 471031, Tulsa, OK 74147. (918) 256-2138. E-mail: fcw@fellowhipofchristianwriters.org. Website: http://fellowshipofchristianwriters.org. Founded as Tulsa Christian Writers, FCW has helped to encourage, equip, launch, and inspire hundreds of writers for over 30 years. Membership (50+) open; includes a monthly, full-color 8-10 page newsletter, eligibility to members-only contests, book and CD discounts. FCW also conducts a free e-mail group with over 800 members, at Yahoo Groups—http://groups.yahoo.com/group/FCW—or send an email to above e-mail address. Local membership $35/yr. At-large membership $25/yr.

SONRISE CHRISTIAN WRITERS. Oklahoma City. Contact: Marlys Norris, 6209 N.W. 82nd St., Oklahoma City OK 73132. E-mail: marlysj@sbcglobal.net. Starting a new group; membership open.

WORDWRIGHTS, OKLAHOMA CITY CHRISTIAN WRITERS. Contact: Milton Smith, 6457 Sterling Dr., Oklahoma City OK 73132-6804. (405) 721-5026. E-mail: HisWordMatters@yahoo.com. Website: www.shadetreecreations.com. Membership (20+) open. Occasional contests for members only. Hosts an annual writers' conference with American Christian Writers, February, in Oklahoma City; send an SASE for information.

OREGON

+ CHRISTIAN CRITIQUERS. Gresham (near 182nd & Powell). Contact: Susan Thogerson Maas, 27526 S.E. Carl St., Gresham OR 97080-8215. (503) 663-7834. E-mail: susan.maas@verizon.net. Membership (5) possibly open.

OREGON CHRISTIAN WRITERS. Contact: Mary Hake, pres. E-mail: president@oregonchristian writers.org. Website: www.oregonchristianwriters.org. Meets for 3 all-day Saturday conferences annually: February, in Salem; May, in Eugene; and October, in Portland. Newsletter published one month before each one-day conference. Annual 4-day Coaching Conference late July/early August, in Portland/Salem metro area. Membership (400) open.

PORTLAND CHRISTIAN WRITERS GROUP. Contact: Stan Baldwin, (503) 659-2974. Serious group; must write regularly. Currently full, but waiting list available.

ROYAL PEN-DANTS. Salem/Portland area. Primarily for those writing for children. Contact: Carole Farmen. (503) 362-2148. E-mail: cfarmen@msn.com. Membership (6) open only to committed, producing writers.

SALEM I CHRISTIAN WRITERS GROUP. Contact: Sam Hall, 6840 Macleay Rd. S.E., Salem OR 97301. (503) 363-7586. Membership (9) not currently open.

WRITER'S DOZEN CRITIQUE GROUP. Springfield. Contact: Denise Nash, 42892 Leaburg Dr., Leaburg OR 97489-9619. (541) 896-3816. E-mail: dcarlson@efn.org. Membership (12) not currently open.

PENNSYLVANIA

ARTISTS' JUNCTION WRITERS' GATHERING. Lancaster. Contact: Deb Munson or Jan Brenneman, PO Box 282, Lancaster PA 17608. (717) 295-2533. E-mail: aji@artistsjunction.org. Website: www.artistsjunction.org. Membership open.

THE FIRST WORD. Sewickley (near Pittsburgh). Contact: Shirley S. Stevens, 712 Ridge Ave., Pittsburgh PA 15202-2223. (412) 761-2618. E-mail: poetcat@comcast.net. Membership (10) open. Affiliated with the St. Davids Christian Writers' Conference.

GREATER PHILADELPHIA CHRISTIAN WRITERS' FELLOWSHIP. Newton Square. Contact: Marlene Bagnull, 316 Blanchard Rd., Drexel Hill, PA 19026. Phone/fax (610) 626-6833. E-mail: Mbagnull@aol.com. Website: www.writehisanswer.com. Membership (25) open. Meets one Thursday morning a month, September-June. Sponsors annual writers' conference (August 2010) and contest (open to registered conferees only).

INDIANA CHRISTIAN WRITERS FELLOWSHIP. Indiana. Contact: Jan Woodard, 270 Sunset Dr., Indiana PA 15701. (724) 465-5886. E-mail: jjwoodward@verizon.net. This group is currently inactive, but Jan Woodard can put you in contact with other writers in the area.

INDIAN VALLEY CHRISTIAN WRITERS FELLOWSHIP/ACW CHAPTER. Telford (Bucks County). Contact: Cheryl Wallace, 952 Route 113, Sellersville PA 18960-2962. (215) 453-0415. E-mail: wallace writer@verizon.net. Membership (24) open.

INSPIRATIONAL WRITERS' FELLOWSHIP. Brookville. Contact: Jan R. Sady, 2026 Langville Rd., Mayport PA 16240-5610. (814) 856-2560. E-mail: janfran@windstream.net. Membership (15) open. Sometimes sponsors a contest. No conference in 2010.

JOHNSTOWN CHRISTIAN WRITERS' GUILD. Johnstown. Contact: Betty Rosian, 108 Deerfield Ln., Johnstown PA 15905-5703. (814) 255-4351. E-mail: wordsforall@atlanticbb.net. Membership (12) open.

LANCASTER CHRISTIAN WRITERS/ACW CHAPTER. Lititz. Contact: Jeanette Windle, 121 E. Woods Dr., Lititz PA 17543. (717) 626-8752. E-mail: jeanette@jeanettewindle.com. Website: www.lancasterchristianwriters.org. Membership (100+) open. Sponsors a one-day spring conference, March 20, 2010.

+ **LEHIGH VALLEY CHRISTIAN WRITERS FELLOWSHIP**. Allentown. Contact: Beth Morgan, 1541 Cherry Ln., Macungie PA 18062. (610) 391-1090. E-mail: bethmorgan@rcn.com. Membership open. Sponsors a seminar in March.

SOUTH CAROLINA

COLUMBIA CHRISTIAN WRITERS. Contact: Kim Andrysczyk, 201 Sutton Way, Irmo SC 29063. (803) 781-3510. E-mail: kimbocraig@juno.com. Meets monthly. Membership (6) open.

GREENVILLE CHRISTIAN WRITERS GROUP. Contact: Nancy Parker, 3 Ben St., Greenville SC 29601. (864) 313-3116. E-mail: Nancy@jjparker.com. Membership (24) open.

UPSTATE SOUTH CAROLINA ACW CHAPTER. Anderson. Contact: Elva Martin, 104 Oak Knoll Ter., Anderson SC 29625-2507. Phone/fax (864) 226-7024. E-mail: elvamartinministries@charter.net. Membership (36) open. Sponsors a conference in October and a contest for conference attendees.

WRITING 4 HIM. Spartanburg. Contact: Linda Gilden, PO Box 2928, Spartanburg SC 29304. E-mail: RoseWriter@aol.com. Membership (25) open.

TENNESSEE

+ **NASHVILLE CHRISTIAN WRITERS ASSN./ACW CHAPTER**. Nashville & Greater Middle TN area. Contact: D. Lynn Jacobs, pres., 455 Sam Ridley Blvd., Ste. 263, Smyrna TN 37167, email@dlynn jacobs.com; or Carol Harper, VP, crharper@gmail.com. Website: www.nashvillechristianwriters .com. Membership open (cost is $20 annually). Supports the *Nashville Christian Times* (see listing in periodical section).

TEXAS

+ **ACFW WRITERS ON THE STORM**. The Woodlands. Contact: Linda P. Kozar, 7 S. Chandler Creek Cir., The Woodlands TX 77381. (281) 362-1791. Prefers cell (832) 797-7522. E-mail: zarcom1@aol .com. Blog: http://acfwwritersonthestorm.blogspot.com. Visitors welcome (e-mail contact person).

CENTEX CHAPTER—AMERICAN CHRISTIAN FICTION WRITERS (ACFW). Englewood. Contact: Tina Toles, PO Box 251, Englewood OH 45322. (937) 836-6600. E-mail: daytonwriters@ ureach.com. Website: www.daytonwriters.com. Membership (25) open. Sponsoring a conference in June 2010.

CHRISTIAN WRITERS GROUP OF GREATER SAN ANTONIO. Universal City/San Antonio area. Contact: Brenda Blanchard, 2827 Olive Ave., Schertz TX 78154-3719. (210) 945-4163. E-mail: brendablanchard1@aol.com. Has quarterly guest speakers. Membership (25) open.

+ **CROSS REFERENCE WRITERS**. Brazos Valley. E-mail: CrossRefWriters@yahoo.com. Website: http://sites.google.com/site/crossreferencewriters. Membership open.

DALLAS CHRISTIAN WRITERS GUILD. Plano. Contact: Jan Winebrenner, 2709 Winding Hollow, Plano TX 75093. E-mail: janwrite@earthlink.net. Website: www.dallaschristianwriters.com. Membership (30) open.

DALLAS-FORT WORTH READY WRITERS/ACFW BRANCH. Colleyville. Contact: Lena Nelson Dooley. E-mail: safe-ldwrites@flash.net. Blog: www.dfwreadywriters.blogspot.com. Meeting info on Website. Membership open.

DENTON CHRISTIAN WRITERS GUILD. Denton. Contact: Sonjia Bradshaw, 3821 Willowick Dr., Denton TX 76210. E-mail: sonjia.bradshaw@dentonchristianwriters.com. Website: www.denton christianwriters.com. Membership (4) open.

INSPIRATIONAL WRITERS ALIVE! Groups meet in Houston, Pasadena, Jacksonville, Amarillo, Humble, Tyler, and Port Neches. Contact: Martha Rogers, 6038 Greenmont, Houston TX 77092-2332. (713) 686-7209. E-mail: marthalrogers@sbcglogal.net. Membership (130 statewide) open. Sponsors summer seminar, August 2010; monthly newsletter; and annual contest (January 1-May 15) open to nonmembers.

INSPIRATIONAL WRITERS ALIVE!/AMARILLO CHAPTER. Contact: Jerry McClenahan, pres., 6808 Cloud Crest, Amarillo TX 79124. (806) 674-3504. E-mail: jerrydalemc@sbcglobal.net. Membership (35) open. Sponsors a contest open to members, and a seminar the Saturday after Easter.

INSPIRATIONAL WRITERS ALIVE!/EAST TEXAS CHAPTER. Jacksonville. Contact: Maxine Holder, director & founding member, 4785 FM 1248 S., Rusk TX 75785-5254. (903) 795-3986. E-mail: mholder787@aol.com. Membership (14) open. Sponsors a contest through First Baptist Chapter/Houston.

+ INSPIRATIONAL WRITERS ALIVE!/TYLER CHAPTER. Tyler. Contact: Judith Robinson, (903) 894-3586 or (903) 714-9720. Membership (15) open.

NORTH TEXAS CHRISTIAN WRITERS/ACW CHAPTERS. Meetings held in Argyle, Arlington, Dallas, Fort Worth, Keller, Lewisville. Contact: NTCW, PO Box 820802, Fort Worth TX 76182-0802. (817) 715-2597. E-mail: info@ntchristianwriters.com. Website: www.ntchristianwriters .com. Membership (100+) open. Sponsors an annual seminar after Labor Day, September 2010.

ROCKWALL CHRISTIAN WRITERS' GROUP. Lake Pointe Church/Rockwall. Contact: Leslie Wilson, 535 Cullins Rd., Rockwall TX 75032-6017. (972) 772-3442. Cell (214) 505-5336. E-mail: LesliePWilson@aol.com. Website: http://rcwg.blogspot.com. Membership (20) open.

WORDS FOR THE JOURNEY CHRISTIAN WRITERS GUILD/SOUTHEAST TEXAS REGION. Contact: Sharen Watson, 2635 Imperial Grove Ln., Conroe TX 77385. (281) 292-5634 or (303) 906-1573. E-mail: IRite4Him@aol.com. Website: www.wordsforthejourney.org. Membership (100+) open. See separate listing for Rocky Mountain CO Region.

UTAH

UTAH CHRISTIAN WRITERS FELLOWSHIP/ACW CHAPTER. Salt Lake City area. Contact: Julie Scott, PO Box 3, Bountiful UT 84011-0003. (801) 294-5485. E-mail: ucwf@markjulie.com. Website: www.utahchristianwriters.com. Sponsoring a writers' conference in fall 2010 in Bluffdale UT. Membership (20) open.

VERMONT

+ AMERICAN CHRISTIAN WRITERS OF NEW ENGLAND. Jericho. Contact: Laurel Decher, 1375 North Ave., Burlington VT 05408. (802) 660-4080. E-mail: ldecher@gmail.com. Website: http:// hime.myfairpoint.net/ldecher/vermontwriters.html. Membership (4-6) open.

VIRGINIA

CAPITAL CHRISTIAN WRITERS. Fairfax. Leader: Betsy Dill, PO Box 873, Centreville VA 20122-0873. Phone/fax (703) 803-9447. E-mail: ccwriters@gmail.com. Website: www.ccwriters.org. Sponsors Saturday workshops 1-2 times a year. Membership (45) open.

+ JOYWRITERS/ACW CHAPTER. Galax. Contact: Vie Herlocker, PO Box 342, Fancy Gap VA 24328-0342. (276) 237-1972. E-mail: info@joywriters.org. Website: www.joywriters.org. Membership (20) open.

NEW COVENANT WRITER'S GROUP. Newport News. Contact: Mary Tatem, 451 Summer Dr., Newport News VA 23606-2515. (757) 930-1700. E-mail: rwtatem@juno.com. Membership (8) open.

PENINSULA CHRISTIAN WRITERS/ACW CHAPTER. Yorktown. Contact: Yvonne Ortega, PO Box 955, Yorktown VA 23692. E-mail: yvonne@yvonneortega.com. Membership (5) open. Sponsors annual writers workshop, likely in the spring.

RICHMOND CHRISTIANS WHO WRITE/ACW CHAPTER. Contact: Rev. Thomas C. Lacy, 12114 Walnut Hill Dr., Rockville VA 23146-1854. (804) 749-4050; or Rebekah Robb, 9600 January Way, Richmond VA 23238, (804) 527-0913, tcrobb@integrity.com. E-mail: RichmondCWW@aol.com. Blog: http://rcww.blogspot.com. Sponsoring a conference September 17-18, 2010. Membership (50+) open.

TIDEWATER CHRISTIAN WRITERS FORUM/ACW CHAPTER. Norfolk. Contact: Peter D. Mallett, 1270 Pall Mall St., #A, Norfolk VA 23513. (757) 889-9917. E-mail: F18Pete@aol.com. Website: http://groups.yahoo.com/group/TidewaterChristianWF. Membership (21) open. ACW Chapter (www.acwriters.com).

WASHINGTON

NORTHWEST CHRISTIAN WRITERS ASSN. Bothell. Contact: President, PO Box 428, Enumclaw WA 98022-0428. Toll-free (800) 731-6292. Fax (360) 802-9992. E-mail: president@nwchristian writers.org. Website: www.nwchristianwriters.org. Speakers clearinghouse available on Website. Click on "Speakers Connection." Membership (200+) open. Meets monthly; bimonthly newsletter. Sponsors a contest and Northwest Christian Writers Renewal in May (see separate listing).

SPOKANE CHRISTIAN WRITERS. Spokane. Contact: Ruth McHaney Danner, PO Box 18425, Spokane WA 99228-0425. (509) 328-3359. E-mail: ruth@ruthdanner.com. Membership (20) open.

WALLA WALLA CHRISTIAN WRITERS. Walla Walla. Contact: Helen Heavirland, PO Box 146, College Place WA 99324-0146. Phone/fax (541) 938-3838. E-mail: hlh@bmi.net. Membership open.

WALLA WALLA VALLEY CHRISTIAN SCRIBES. College Place. Contact: Helen Heavirland, PO Box 146, College Place WA 99324-0146. Phone/fax (541) 938-3838. E-mail: hlh@bmi.net. Membership (8) open.

WRITERS IN THE ROUGH. Arlington. Contact: Rick Bell, 9111—96th St. N.E., Arlington WA 98223-8865. (360) 653-7420. E-mail: bellvista@verizon.net. Membership (10) open.

WISCONSIN

LIGHTHOUSE CHRISTIAN WRITERS. Klondike. Contact: Lois Wiederhoeft, 901 Aubin St., Lot 115, Peshtigo WI 54157. (715) 582-1024. E-mail: 2loisann@myway.com. Or, Mary Jansen, PO Box 187, Mountain WI 54149. (715) 276-1706. Website: www.lighthousechristianwriters.com. Membership (8) open.

THE LIVING WORD/ACW CHAPTER. Superior. Contact: Amy Trees, pres., 1421 E. 5th St., Superior WI 54880. (715) 398-7244. E-mail: TheLivingWordSuperior@yahoogroups.com. Website: http://LivingWordWriters.bravehost.com. Membership (30) open.

PENS OF PRAISE CHRISTIAN WRITERS. Manitowoc. Contact: Cofounders Becky McLafferty, 9225 Carstens Lake Rd., Manitowoc WI 54220. (920) 758-9196; or Sue Kinney, 4516 Laurie Ln., Two Rivers WI 54241. (920) 793-2922. E-mail: mclafferty@lakefield.net, or cal-suek@charter.net. Membership (12-14) open. Meets monthly.

ROCK RIVER STORY WEAVERS CRITIQUE GROUP. Johnson Creek. Contact: James B. Robar, N2963 Buena Vista Rd., Fort Atkinson WI 53538. (920) 568-1677. Fax (920) 397-7334. E-mail: jim@jamesbrobar.com. Membership (6) closed. You may join waiting list.

WORD AND PEN CHRISTIAN WRITERS CLUB/ACW CHAPTER. Menasha. Contact: Chris Stratton, 107 E. McArthur St., Appleton WI 54911-2109. (920) 739-0752. E-mail: wordandpen@mychristian site.com. Website: www.mychristiansite.com/ministries/wordandpen. Membership (17) open.

CANADIAN/FOREIGN

ASSOCIATION OF CHRISTIAN WRITERS. Mainly London. Contact: Lin Ball or Rev. Simon Baynes, 23 Moorend Ln., Thame, Oxon, OX9 3BQ, United Kingdom. Phone 01844-213 673. E-mail: admin@ christianwriters.org.uk. Website: www.christianwriters.org.uk. Membership (750) open. Sponsors a contest open to nonmembers; a biennial conference; and writers' days in March, June, and October in London.

FRASER VALLEY CHRISTIAN WRITERS GROUP. Abbotsford BC. Contact: Helmut Fandrich, 2461 Sunnyside Pl., Abbotsford BC V2T 4C4, Canada. Phone/fax (604) 850-0666. E-mail: helmut10@ coneharvesters.com. Membership (20) open.

INSCRIBE CHRISTIAN WRITERS' FELLOWSHIP. Edmonton (various locations across Canada). Contact: Eunice Matchett, 4304—45 St., Drayton Valley AB T7A 1G7, Canada. (780) 542-7950. E-mail: scrappi@telusplanet.net. Website: www.inscribe.org. Membership (250) open. Sponsors a newsletter and 2 contests, details on Website (one open to nonmembers). Also sponsors annual conference in September.

+ MANITOBA CHRISTIAN WRITERS ASSN. Winnipeg MB. Contact: Irene LoScerbo, 78 River Elm Dr., West St. Paul MB R2V 4G1, Canada. (204) 334-7780. E-mail: solonoi@mts.net. Membership (25) open.

NEW ZEALAND CHRISTIAN WRITERS GUILD. Contact: Janet Fleming, Box 115, Kaeo 0448, New Zealand. E-mail: MJflamingos@xtra.co.nz. Website: www.freewebs.com/nzchristianwritersguild. Membership (120) open. Workshops, biannual weekend retreat, local groups, home study courses, contest for members, and bimonthly magazine.

SWAN VALLEY CHRISTIAN WRITERS GUILD. Swan River, MB. Contact: Addy Oberlin, Box 132, Swan River MB R0L 1Z0, Canada. Phone/fax (204) 734-4269. E-mail: waltadio@mts.net. Membership (10) open. Sponsors a contest open to nonmembers.

THE WORD GUILD. Meets in various cities. Contact: Jeanette Duncan, PO Box 28087, Waterloo ON N2L 6J8, Canada. (519) 886-4196. E-mail: questions@thewordguild.com. Website: www.the wordguild.com. Membership (320) open. Sponsors contests open to nonmembers (see contest listings). Sponsoring an annual conference in Guelph ON, June 17-19, 2010.

NATIONAL/INTERNATIONAL GROUPS (NO STATE LOCATION)

AMERICAN CHRISTIAN FICTION WRITERS. Cynthia Ruchti, pres.; PO Box 101066, Palm Bay FL 32910. Phone/fax (321) 984-4018. E-mail: Publicity Officer, Angela Breidenbach, pr@acfw .com. Website: www.ACFW.com. E-mail loop, online courses, critique groups, and e-newsletter for members. Send membership inquiries to membership@acfw.com. Membership (1,800) open. Sponsors contests for published and unpublished members. Sponsors annual seminar in September.

AMERICAN CHRISTIAN WRITERS SEMINARS. Sponsors conferences in various locations around the country (see individual states for dates and places). Call or write to be placed on mailing list for any conference. Events are Friday and Saturday unless otherwise noted. Brochures usually mailed three months prior to event. Contact: Reg Forder, Box 110390, Nashville TN 37222. Toll-free (800) 21-WRITE. Website: www.ACWriters.com.

CHRISTIAN WRITERS FELLOWSHIP INTL. (CWFI). Contact: Sandy Brooks, 1624 Jefferson Davis Rd., Clinton SC 29325-6401. (864) 697-6035. E-mail: cwfi@cwfi-online.org. Website: www.cwfi online.org. To contact Sandy Brooks personally: sandybrooks@cwfi-online.org. No meetings, but offers market consultations, critique service, writers books, and conference workshop tapes. Connects writers living in the same area and helps start writers' groups. Membership (1,000+) open.

CHRISTIAN WRITERS' GROUP INTL. (CWGI). Website: http://christianwritersgroup.org. An international organization of born-again Christians who write. Purpose: to assist Christians as they fulfill their calling to write by offering resources, information, education, support, networking, and interaction with Christian writers, editors, and publishers. Includes critique and prayer subgroups for members only. Periodically offers CWGI members scholarships to writing conferences. Editors and publishers are welcome. To join, send a blank e-mail to CWG-subscribe@yahoogroups.com or sign up at http://groups.yahoo.com/group/CWGI. Executive director: Brandy Brow. Membership (700+) open.

FAITH, HOPE & LOVE is the inspirational chapter of Romance Writers of America. Charges yearly dues (see Website), but you must also be a member of RWA to join (see their Website for annual dues). Chapter offers these services: online list service for members, a Web page, 20-pg. bimonthly newsletter, annual contest, monthly online guest chats with multipublished authors and industry professionals, connects critique partners by mail or e-mail, and latest romance-market information. To join, contact RWA National Office, 16000 Stuebner Airline Rd., Ste. 140, Spring TX 77379. (832) 717-5200. Fax (832) 717-5201. E-mail: info@rwanational.org. Website: www.rwanational.org. Or go to FHL Website: www.faithhopelove-rwa.org. Inspirational Readers Choice Contest by subgenre categories for published works; deadline April 1; cash prizes. Send SASE for guidelines. Membership (150+) open.

JERRY B. JENKINS CHRISTIAN WRITERS GUILD. Contact: Kerma Murray, 5525 N. Union Blvd., Ste. 200, Colorado Springs, CO 80918. Toll-free (866) 495-5177. Fax (719) 495-5187. E-mail: ContactUs@ChristianWritersGuild.com. Website: www.ChristianWritersGuild.com. This international organization of 1,800 members offers annual memberships, mentor-guided correspondence courses for adults (two-year Apprentice; advanced one-year Journeyman; and Craftsman) and youth (Pages: ages 9-12, and Squires: 13 and up), writing contests, conferences, critique service, writers resource books, monthly newsletter, and more. Critique service accepts prose samples of 1-15 pages. Professional writing assessment covers proper language usage, pacing, presentation, purpose, and persuasiveness. Call for pricing structure. Members receive 10 percent off.

NATIONAL ASSN. OF WOMEN WRITERS. General. Contact: Sheri McConnell, 24165 IH-10 W., Ste. 217-637, San Antonio TX 78257. Toll-free phone/fax (866) 821-5829. E-mail: info@naww .org. Website: www.naww.org. Over 40 chapters across the U.S. (see Website for list of locations). Membership (3,000+) open. Sponsors regional events across the U.S. and national TeleSummits.

PEN-SOULS (prayer and support group, not a critique group). Conducted entirely by e-mail. Contact: Janet Ann Collins, 632 Pelton Way, Grass Valley CA 95945. (530) 272-4905. E-mail: jan@ janetanncollins.com. Membership (12) open.

THE WRITING ACADEMY. Contact: Inez Schneider, new member coordinator, 4010 Singleton Rd., Rockford IL 61114. (815) 877-9675. Website: www.wams.org. Membership (75) open. Sponsors year-round correspondence writing program and annual seminar in August held in Minneapolis.

12

Editorial Services

The following listing is included because so many writers contact me looking for experienced/qualified editors who can critique or evaluate their manuscripts. These people from all over the country offer this kind of service. I cannot personally guarantee the work of any of those listed, so you may want to ask for references or samples of their work.

The following abbreviations indicate what kinds of work they are qualified to do:

GE general editing/manuscript evaluation
LC line editing or copyediting
GH ghostwriting

CA coauthoring
B brochures
NL newsletters
SP special projects

BCE book contract evaluation
WS Website development
PP PowerPoint

The following abbreviations indicate the types of material the editors evaluate:

A articles
SS short stories
P poetry
F fillers
N novels
NB nonfiction books

BP book proposals
JN juvenile novels
PB picture books
QL query letter
BS Bible studies

GB gift books
TM technical material
E essays
D devotionals
S scripts

Always send a copy the editors can write on and an SASE for return of your material.

+ Indicates new listing

ALABAMA

WRITE INTEGRITY EDITORIAL SERVICES/TRACY RUCKMAN, 198 Lake Berry Ln., Lowndesboro AL 36752. E-mail: editor@writeintegrity.com. Website: www.writeintegrity.com. E-mail/mail. GE/LC/GH/B/NL/SP/WS. Edits A/BP/E/D/F/GB/N/NB/QL/SS/Web content. Web design, image-building packages, blog tours, graphic design and layout for print or e-mail newsletters, brochures, one-sheets, display advertising. Charges by standard formatted page. Rates, references, and services on Website.

ARIZONA

CARLA'S MANUSCRIPT SERVICE/CARLA BRUCE, 10229 W. Andover Ave., Sun City AZ 85351-4509. Phone/fax (623) 876-4648. E-mail: Carlaabruce@cox.net. Call/e-mail. GE/LC/GH/typesetting/PDF files for publishers. Edits A/SS/P/F/N/NB/BP/QL/BS/GB/TM/E/D. Charges $25/hr. or gives a project estimate after evaluation. Does ghostwriting for pastors and teachers; professional typesetting. Twenty-four years ghostwriting/editing; 13 years typesetting.

+ **CHRISTIANMANUSCRIPTSUBMISSIONS.COM**, 9633 S. 48th St., Ste. 140, Phoenix AZ 85044. (480) 966-1944. Website: wwwChristianManuscriptSubmissions.com. Now offering writers an optional professional literary critique or a critique & edit of their manuscript. Details on Website.

KATHY WILLIAMSON MINISTRIES/KATHY WILLIAMSON, PO Box 11660, Prescott AZ 86304-1660. (928) 925-5410. E-mail: kathy@christiancopywriter.org. Website: www.ChristianCopywriter.org. E-mail contact. GE/LC/GH/writing coach. Edits A/NB/BP/QL/BS/D. Also Internet marketing, digital transcription, Website sales letters, formats books for self-publishing. Writer for 14 years; self-published a nonfiction book; led critique groups. Free estimate for each project.

ARKANSAS

+ TONJA TAYLOR, 1302 E. 30th Ave., Apt. A, Texarkana AR 71854. (870) 216-2243. Fax (870) 216-2243. E-mail: tonja@tonjataylor.com. Website: www.truthtreasures.com. E-mail contact. GE/ LC/ GH/CA/NL/PP/SP/WS writing coach. Edits: A/SS/P/F/N/NB/ BP/QL/BS/GB/TM/E/D. 20+ years' experience in writing, editing, and publishing. If you mention you saw her listing in this guide, charges $1.25/pg. for copy/line editing; $1/pg. for typing/word processing; $25/hr. with $25 min. and half up front for coaching/consulting (includes marketing advice and promotion), critiques, Websites, special projects, newsletters.

CALIFORNIA

CHRISTIAN COMMUNICATOR MANUSCRIPT CRITIQUE SERVICE/SUSAN TITUS OSBORN, 3133 Puente St., Fullerton CA 92835-1952. Toll-free (877) 428-7992. (714) 990-1532. Fax (714) 990-0310. E-mail: Susanosb@aol.com. Website: www.christiancommunicator.com. Call/ e-mail/write. For book, send material with $160 deposit. Staff of 18 editors. GE/LC/GH/CA/SP/ BCE. Edits A/SS/P/F/N/NB/BP/JN/PB/QL/BS/GB/TM/E/D/S. $100 for short pieces/picture books. Three-chapter book proposal $160 (up to 40 pgs.). Additional editing $40/hr. Over thirty years' experience.

CITY BOY EDITORIAL SERVICE/STEVEN HUTSON, 5022 Avenue N, Ste. 102-128, Palmdale CA 93551. (661) 722-4896. Toll-free fax (866) 501-4280. E-mail: steve@hutsonbooks.com. Website: www .hutsonbooks.com/editorial. Call/e-mail. Edits any genre or type of material. Published author; director of Antelope Valley Christian Writers Conference. Proofreading $1.25/pg.; copyediting $2.25/pg.; 3-chapter critique $125 (up to 100 pgs.). Other projects at $30/hr., or upon discussion with client.

EDITORIAL, BOOK DESIGN, AND PRODUCTION SERVICES/DESTA GARRETT, dg-ink Book Design, PO Box 1182, Daly City CA 94017-1182. (650) 994-2662. Fax (650) 991-3050. E-mail: info@dg-ink.net. Website: www.dg-ink.net, includes work samples. Write/call/e-mail. GE/LC/B/NL/ SP. Complete editing and production for author, including for self-publishing using Adobe InDesign Creative Suite. Edits A/SS/NB/BS/TM/E/D/educational material. Has 20 years' experience doing all aspects of editing, production, and publishing of all types of material for nonprofit Christian foundation, up to large, illustrated, indexed research books. Charges $50/hr.; $40/hr. for Christian authors with Christian material.

V. L. HESTERMAN, PO Box 6788, San Diego CA 92166. E-mail: vhes@mac.com. E-mail or mail only; will follow-up within 1-2 days with phone call if requested. GE/LC/GH/CA/SP. Edits A/SS/F/N/NB/BP/ QL/JN/PB/BS/GB/TM/E/D/photo books, memoirs. 25 years experience. Cost competitive, depends on scope and condition of project. Send or e-mail letter explaining project, with several sample pages, for binding quote of cost. Edits/develops nonfiction material, including editorials; works with book and article writers and publishers as coauthor, line editor, or in editorial development. Book editor, book author, university writing professor, newspaper reporter, writing curriculum development, documentary photography.

DARLENE HOFFA, 512 Juniper St., Brea CA 92821. (714) 990-5980. E-mail: jack.darlene.hoffa@ roadrunner.com. E-mail contact. GE. Edits A/F/NB/BP/D. Nineteen years' experience; author of 11 books. Charges $20/hr. or $2/ms pg.

KATHY IDE/EDITORIAL SERVICES, 203 Panorama Ct., Brea CA 92821. E-mail: Kathy@kathyide .com. Website: www.KathyIde.com. GE/LC/GH/CA/B/NL/SP/WS, writing coach. Edits A/SS/F/N/NB/BP/ QL/JN/BS/GB/D/S. Charges by the hour (mention this listing and get a $5/hr. discount). Freelance author, editor (full time since 1998), and speaker. Has done proofreading and editing for Moody, Thomas Nelson, Barbour/Heartsong, and WinePress.

+ **SUSANNE LAKIN**, 219 Double Bogey Dr., Boulder Creek CA 95006. (530) 200-5466. Fax (413) 812-7929. E-mail: sulakin@comcast.net. Website: www.cslakin.com. E-mail contact. GE/LC/writing coach. Edits: N/NB/BP/QL/JN/BS/GB. Has years of editing experience; member of Christian PEN and CEN (Christian Editor Network); novelist. Specializes in contemporary fiction, fantasy, and nonfiction books related to theology, eschatology, and biblical topics. Charges by the hour or the page. Offers a free sample edit of 5-10 pages before taking on larger project.

KMB COMMUNICATIONS INC./LAURAINE SNELLING, PO Box 1530, Tehachapi CA 93581. (661) 823-0669. Fax (661) 823-9427. E-mail: TLsnelling@yahoo.com. Website: www.LauraineSnelling .com. E-mail contact. GE. Edits SS/N/JN. Charges $50/hr. with $100 deposit, or by the project after discussion with client. Award-winning author of 63 books (YA and adult fiction, 2 nonfiction); teacher at writing conferences.

LIGHTHOUSE EDITING/DR. LON ACKELSON, 13326 Community Rd., #11, Poway CA 92064-4754. (858) 748-9258. Fax (858) 748-7431. E-mail: Isaiah68LA@sbcglobal.net. Website: www .lighthouseedit.com. E-mail/write. GE/LC/GH/CA/B/NL/BCE. Edits A/SS/N/NB/BP/QL/BS/E/D. Charges $35 for article/short story critique; $60 for 3-chapter book proposal. Send SASE for full list of fees. Editor since 1981; senior editor 1984-2002.

B. K. NELSON LITERARY/EDITORIAL SERVICES, 2698 Desert Breeze Way, Palm Springs CA 92262. (760) 778-8800. Fax (760) 778-0034. E-mail: bknelson4@cs.com. Website: www.bknelson .com. John W. Benson, ed. dir. E-mail contact. GE/LC/GH/CA/B/NL/SP/WS/BCE. Edits A/SS/P/F/N/NB/ BP/QL/JN/PB/BS/GB/TM/E/D/S. Has been a literary agent for 22 years and has sold more than 3,000 books to major publishers. Contact for rates.

KAREN O'CONNOR COMMUNICATIONS/KAREN O'CONNOR, 10 Pajaro Vista Ct., Watsonville CA 95076. E-mail: karen@karenoconnor.com. Website: www.karenoconnor.com. E-mail. GE/LC. Book proposal commentary/editing. Edits A/F/NB/BP/QL/D. One-hour free evaluation; $90/hr. or flat fee depending on project. Has 32 years of writing/editing; 25+ years teaching writing; 55 published books and hundreds of magazine articles.

SHIRL'S EDITING SERVICES/SHIRL THOMAS, 9379 Tanager Ave., Fountain Valley CA 92708-6557. (714) 968-5726. E-mail: Shirlth@verizon.net. E-mail (preferred)/write and send material with $100 deposit. GE/LC/GH/SP/rewriting/analysis. Edits A/SS/P/F/N/NB/BP/QL/GB/D/greeting cards/ synopses. Consultation, $75/hr.; evaluation/critique, $75/hr.; mechanical editing $65/hr.; content editing/rewriting $75/hr.

THE STRONG WORD COMMUNICATION SERVICES/ANITA K. PALMER, 5800 Lake Murray Blvd., Unit 14, La Mesa CA 91942-2500. (619) 208-7202. Fax (619) 697-1823 (call ahead). E-mail: anita@thestrongword.com. Website: www.thestrongword.com. E-mail contact. GE/LC/GH/CA/B/NL/ SP/WS. Edits A/SS/N/NB/BP/E/D/memoirs. Published author. Former newspaper and magazine editor with 25 years' experience; experienced in media relations and marketing. Has freelanced for most of the major Christian publishing houses and some general houses. Quick, trustworthy, and reliable. Competitive rates; happy to negotiate: per project, per hour, or per page.

+ **THARSEO PUBLISHING & EDITORIAL SERVICES**, 215 Lake Blvd. #515, Redding CA 96003. (530) 209-3225. E-mail: julialoren@yahoo.com. Website: www.divineinterventionbooks.com. Offers writing workshops, mentoring of authors, content editing, manuscript preparation, consulting on publishing options, project development, and marketing.

THE WORD WORKS/SONJA L. STRUTHERS, 40960 California Oaks Rd., Ste. 369, Murrieta CA 92562-4615. Phone/fax (951) 696-5631. E-mail: info@mywriter.net. Website: www.mywriter.net. Call/e-mail. GE/LC/GH/B/NL/SP/WS/writing coach. Edits A/SS/F/NB/BP/QL/TM/E. Graduate of Irvine College Writing Program; award-winning editor & publisher for Inland Empire Mensa. Offers quote upon review of project only.

WRITINGCOACH.ME/ERICA MONGE, PO Box 727, Orange CA 92856. (714) 606-0130. Fax (866) 520-3072. E-mail: em@writingcoach.me. Website: www.writingcoach.me. E-mail contact; send material for review or critique with $100 deposit. GE/LC/B/NL/SP/WS/PP/press releases/writing coach. Edits A/SS/P/F/N/NB/BP/QL/JN/PB/BS/GB/TM/E/D/S. Fifteen year's experience as published writer/ editor. Exec. editor of a Christian publication. Specializes as a writing coach, helping writers take their ideas to the next level, and get paid for publication. Has a BA & MA. Send manuscript or sample writings and $100 deposit. Will return a written proposal and $100. Projects typically estimate at $75/hr.

COLORADO

ALPHA TRANSCRIPTION/CHERYL A. COLCHIN, 1832 S. Lee St., Unit G, Lakewood CO 80232-6255. (303) 978-0880. Fax (303) 989-9596. E-mail: alphatranscription@juno.com. Call/e-mail. Typing for authors, preferably from cassette tapes, but will consider legible longhand material. Rate determined after discussion with client. Has worked with Dr. Larry Crabb, David Wilkerson, literary agents, and authors since 1988.

EDIT EXPRESS/BRAD LEWIS & OTHER EDITORS, Colorado Springs CO. (719) 649-4478. Fax (866) 542-5165. E-mail: customer.service@editexpress.net. Website: www.editexpress.net. Submit through Website (preferred) or by e-mail. Line editing/substantive editing for nonfiction books or individual chapters (in preparation for submitting to editors). A place where authors and publishers' representatives can submit manuscripts online and know the charges will be based on the speed with which they need substantive editing completed and on the length of the manuscript.

EDIT RESOURCE LLC/ERIC & ELISA STANFORD, 7645 N. Union Blvd., PMB 235, Colorado Springs CO 80920. (719) 599-7808. E-mail: info@editresource.com. Websites: www.editresource .com, www.inspirationalghostwriting.com, www.bookproposals.net. E-mail contact. GE/LC/GH/CA/ NL/SP/copywriting/proposal development. Edits A/F/N/NB/BP/QL/BS/GB/E/D/book doctoring. Rates determined after discussion with client. Combined 35 years of professional editing experience.

SUSAN MARTINS MILLER WRITING & EDITORIAL INC., 3042 Montebello Dr. W., Colorado Springs CO 80918. (719) 659-2426. E-mail: susan@susanmartinsmiller.com. Website: www.susan martinsmiller.com. E-mail contact. GE/LC/GH/CA/SP. Edits A/N/NB/JN/BS/D/book rewrites. Rates determined after discussion with client. 20+ years' writing experience.

OMEGA EDITING/MICHAEL P. COLCHIN, 1832 S. Lee St., Unit G, Lakewood CO 80232-6255. (303) 978-0880. Fax (303) 989-9596. E-mail: omegaediting@juno.com. Write/call/e-mail. GE/ LC/GH/CA/B/NL/SP. Edits A/SS/NB/BP/QL/BS/TM/D. Charges $45 & up, or by the project after discussion with client. Works in partnership with authors and publishers as ghostwriter, coauthor, editor or in editorial development. Published book and article author; 14 years' experience as freelance editor.

+ **PAPYRUS PROOF/KATE JESSE**, 25587 Conifer Rd., Ste. 105 #151. (303) 697-4343. E-mail: ksjpublish@aol.com. Website: www.jesse.us.com/papyrus.html. E-mail contact. GE/LC/B/NL/SP/WS. Edits A/SS/F/NB/BS/GB/TM/E/D/indexing/transcribing. Charges $20-55/hr. depending on type of work. Offers 25 percent discount on first projects for new clients.

THE PERFECT PAPER/PATRICIA UNGER, 16695 Von Neuman Dr., Monument CO 80132. Phone/ fax (719) 481-4688. (719) 481-0437. E-mail: dpunger@comcast.net. Websites: www.theperfect paper.biz, www.aperfectsolutionva.com. Call/e-mail/send with $25 deposit. GE/LC/GH/B/NL/SP/ BCE/PP/transcription. Edits A/SS/P/F/N/NB/BP/ JN/QL/E/D/S. Twenty years' experience transcribing, proofreading, and copyediting. Charges $35/hr. for transcription. Will work with any budget for editing and proofreading.

SCRIBBLE COMMUNICATIONS/BRAD LEWIS, Colorado Springs CO. (719) 649-4478. Fax (866) 542-5165. E-mail: brad.lewis@scribblecommunications.com. Website: www.scribblecom munications.com. E-mail contact. GE/LC/GH/substantive editing/developmental editing. Edits A/NB/ BP/QL/BS/D/Website content. Edited nearly 100 nonfiction books; senior editor of the *New Men's Devotional Bible* (Zondervan); content editor for *New Living Translation Study Bible* (Tyndale). Charges by project, mutually agreed upon with publisher, and stated in editor/author agreement.

SHEVET WRITING SERVICES/MARJORIE VAWTER, 3605 W. 94th Ave., Westminster CO 80031-3156. Phone/fax (720) 540-9516 (call ahead for fax). E-mail: shevetwrite@pcisys.net. Website: www.shevetwritingservices.com. E-mail contact. GE/LC. Edits N/NB/BP. Has been editing/proofreading since 2000. Testimonials and endorsements on Website.

A WAY WITH WORDS/RENEE GRAY-WILBURN, 1820 Smoke Ridge Dr., Colorado Springs CO 80919. (719) 646-4877. E-mail: waywords@earthlink.net. E-mail contact. GE/LC/GH/CA/B/NL/SP. Edits A/SS/F/N/NB/PB/JN/QL/BS/GB/TM/E/D. Line editing/copyediting: $15-25/hr. & up. Project prices negotiable. 12+ years' experience. Provides editorial services for independent authors, Christian publishers, ministries, and small businesses. Open to coauthoring opportunities. Specializes in children's and nonfiction.

FLORIDA

EDITORIAL SERVICES/SHARON LEE ROBERTS, 240 San Marco Dr., Venice FL 34285. (941) 484-0773. Fax (941) 488-0847. E-mail: prose-and-poetry@peoplepc.com. Call/e-mail/fax/write. GE/LC. Edits A/SS/P/F/PB/D. Charges $25/hr. for critique/evaluation/line editing/copyediting ($25 minimum) or $2.50/pg., or negotiable fee for project. Published author of 3 children's storybooks and hundreds of articles, short stories, and poems for children and adults. Former editorial assistant for *Living Streams*, a Christian writer's magazine.

EDITORIAL SERVICES/DIANE E. ROBERTSON, Venice FL. (941) 928-5302. E-mail: pswriter1@ netzero.net. Website: www.freelancewritingbydiane.com. E-mail or call. GE/LC/GH/SP/writing coach. Edits A/SS/P/F/N/NB/BP/JN/PB/QL/BS/TM/E/D/S. Has written 2 novels, 1 book on all types of creative writing, 2 children's books, 200+ articles, short stories, and children's stories; previously served as associate editor of 2 magazines; presently teaches Short Story, Novel Writing, Magazine Writing, and Nonfiction Creative Writing classes at a community college. Charges $23/hr.

EDITORIAL SERVICES/LESLIE SANTAMARIA, Winter Springs FL. E-mail: santamaria@mpinet .net. E-mail first. GE/LC. Edits A/SS/N/NB/BP/JN/PB/QL/E/D/S. Critiques: $65 for short pieces/picture books; $100 for 3-chapter book proposals. Editing services: By the page based on $35/hr. Published author and book reviewer with extensive book and magazine editing experience and a BA in English. Specializes in children's, poetry, and devotions.

LIGHTPOST COMMUNICATIONS/SEAN FOWLDS, 305 Pinecrest Rd., Mount Dora FL 32757-5929. (352) 383-2485. E-mail: sfowlds@earthlink.net. Website: www.seanfowlds.com. E-mail contact. GE/ LC/B/NL/SP/copy for Websites. Edits A/SS/P/F/NB/BP/QL/PB/BS/GB/TM/E/D/S. Offers coaching, writing, and editing services. Negotiated sliding scale starting at $35/hr. Former editor of a national publication.

+ **SIGHT HOUND PRODUCTIONS LLC/ALAN WILSON**, 974 N.W. 126th Ave., Coral Springs FL 33071-4444. (954) 829-3211. Fax (954) 345-6036. E-mail: contacts08@aol.com. E-mail/write. GE/CA/NL/SP. Edits A/SS/N/NB/QL/BS/E/D. Author of 2 books, with more than 13 years of corporate experience; offering precise editing experience. Charges $1.50/double-spaced pg. (no more than 500 pgs.).

GEORGIA

FAITHWORKS EDITORIAL & WRITING, INC./NANETTE THORSEN-SNIPES, PO Box 1596, Buford GA 30515. Phone/fax (770) 945-3093. E-mail: nsnipes@bellsouth.net. Website: www.faith workseditorial.com. E-mail contact. Freelance editor, book doctor, copyeditor/line editor, proofreader, work-for-hire projects. Edits juvenile fiction/short stories; juvenile or adult nonfiction/articles/business/humor. Author of more than 500 articles/stories; has stories in more than 50 compilation books. Member: The Christian PEN (Proofreaders & Editors Network) and CEN (Christian Editors Network). Currently editing and proofreading *Cross & Quill* newsletter (CWFI), as well as corporate newsletters.

BONNIE C. HARVEY, PhD, 5579B Chamblee Dunwoody Rd., Ste. 357, Atlanta GA 30038. (404) 299-6149. Cell (404) 580-9431. Fax (404) 297-6651. E-mail: BoncaH@aol.com. Website: www.bookimprove.com. Call/e-mail/write to discuss terms & payment. GE/LC/GH/CA/SP/theology. Edits A/SS/P/N/NB/JN/QL/BS/GB/E/D/S/theological and academic articles. Does critiquing, editing, book consulting, book proposals, and rewriting. Charges $20/hr. for reading/critiquing; $20/hr. for proofreading; $25/hr. for editing, $45-75/hr. for rewriting. Has PhD in English; 14 years teaching college-level English; teaches English and writing classes at Kennesaw University; more than 27 years' experience as editor; has ghostwritten books and authored 22 books.

ON-TIME EDITORIAL SERVICES/LEIGH DELOZIER, 73 Price Quarters Rd., Ste. 124, McDonough GA 30253. (770) 851-7273. Fax (866) 321-9914. E-mail: leighdelozier@bellsouth.net. Website: www.leighdelozier.com, or www.leighdelozier.net. Call/e-mail. GE/LC/B/NL/SP/Sunday school curriculum. Edits A/BP/JN/QL/GB//D. Also helps create press releases, media kits, and other promotional materials. BS in Journalism; 20 years' experience in publishing and public relations; multipublished author in Christian and corporate markets. Fees by the hour, page, or project, depending on the work. Basic proofreading $25/hr.; editing/rewriting $35-60/hr. Per-page fee for novel editing is at www.leighdelozier.com.

WRITE AVENUE/JILL COX-CORDOVA, 1310 Shiloh Trail East N.W., Kennesaw GA 30144. (678) 521-0899. E-mail: jcoxwritemind@aol.com. Website: www.writeavenue.com. E-mail contact. GE/LC/media résumés/writing coach. Edits A/SS/N/NB/BP/QL/BS/GB/E. Offers a variety of other services. CNN.com Live sr. producer; journalist for 18 yrs in both print and broadcast; media-studies professor for 3 yrs. See Website for list of services and charges.

WRITTEN BY A PRO/SHARLA TAYLOR, 3745 Hwy 17, Ste. 500, PMB 178, Richmond Hill GA 31324. (912) 656-6857. E-mail: writtenbyapro@msn.com. Website: www.writtenbyapro.com. E-mail contact. GE/LC/GH/CA/SP/author assistance for ms preparation/SAT help for college-bound/writing coach. Edits A/SS/N/NB/BP/JN/QL/BS/GB/TM/E/D. Operates an online writing/editing service for authors & job seekers; tutors college-bound students, and teaches writing to middle school and high school students. E-mail or see Website for rates.

IDAHO

WRITE WORDS EDITING/SUSAN LOHRER, PO Box 702, Porthill ID 83853-0702. E-mail: susan@inspirationaleditor.com. Website: www.InspirationalEditor.com. E-mail contact. GE/LC/writing coach. Edits A/SS/N/BP/QL. Specializes in editing women's fiction and romance. Member of Christian Editor Network, Christian Proofreaders and Editors Network, and Romance Writers of America (clients have received multiple book contracts and writing awards). Charges hourly, per-page, or flat rates depending on project and author's needs.

ILLINOIS

ALICE 'N INK/ALICE PEPPLER, 1285 Luther Ln., Apt. 173, Arlington Hts. IL 60004-8176. (847) 749-0582. E-mail: apeppler@aol.com. Website: www.apeppler.com. Call/e-mail/write. GE/LC/B/NL. Edits A/SS/P/F/N/NB/BP/JN/PB/QL/BS/GB/E/D. ($30/hr.). Three-chapter book edit/critique, including market analysis $125; additional editing $30/hr. Publishing experience of 25 years. Published author of Christian books, articles, poetry, monographs. Quality work; quick turnaround.

AMY BADOWSKI'S EDITING SERVICE, 649 Frances Ave., Loves Park IL 61111-5910. E-mail: Amy .Badowski@gmail.com. GE/LC. Edits A/SS/N/NB/BP/JN/E/D. BA English Studies, magna cum laude. Pursuing MA. Teaching. Charges $40-100 for articles; $250-750 for books.

EDITORIAL SERVICES/MELISSA JUVINALL, 206 Ambrose Way, Normal IL 61761. (309) 452-8917. E-mail: kangaj1@hotmail.com. Website: www.bearla.com. E-mail contact. GE/LC. Edits N/NB/JN/PB/ BS/GB/TM. Has a BA & MA in English; specializes in children's lit; 7 year's editing experience; judge for Christy Awards. Charges by the page for proofreading and copyediting; by the hour for critiquing.

THE WRITER'S EDGE, PO Box 1266, Wheaton IL 60187. E-mail: info@writersedgeservice.com. Website: www.WritersEdgeService.com. No phone calls. A manuscript screening service for 90 cooperating Christian publishers. Charges $95 to evaluate a book proposal and, if publishable, will send a synopsis of it to 90 publishers who might be interested. If not publishable, will tell how to improve it. If interested, request a Book Information Form via e-mail or copy from Website. Self-published books considered like new manuscripts. Reviews novels, nonfiction books, juvenile novels, Bible studies, devotionals, biography, and theology but no poetry. See Website for details.

INDIANA

DENEHEN INC./DR. DENNIS E. HENSLEY, 6824 Kanata Ct., Fort Wayne IN 46815-6388. Phone/ fax (260) 485-9891. E-mail: dnhensley@hotmail.com. E-mail/write. GE/LC/GH. Edits A/SS/P/F/N/ NB/BP/JN/QL/BS/E/D/comedy/academic articles/editorials/Op-Ed pieces/Columns/speeches/interviews. Rate sheet for an SASE. Author of 51 books & 3,000 articles and short stories; PhD in English; University English professor; columnist for *Writer's Journal* and *Advanced Christian Writer*.

EDITORIAL SERVICES/APRIL FRAZIER, 7768 N. 100 E., Ossian IN 46777-9360. (260) 402-1883. E-mail: april_lynn@mac.com. E-mail/write. GE/LC/CA. Edits A/SS/F/N/NB/BP/QL/BS/GB/E/D. Charges $25/hr. for proofreading/copyediting; $30/hr. for line editing, and $250 and up for manuscript evaluation. Send an SASE or e-mail for rate sheet. BA in English, AA in Writing, BA in Biblical Studies; ThM in Christian Education and Bible Exposition; published writer.

EDITORIAL SERVICES/JAMES HENDRIX, 107 W. Sherwood Ter., Fort Wayne IN 46807-2846. (260) 458-9236. E-mail: JHendrix@verizon.net. E-mail contact. GE/B/NL/SP/BCE/writing coach. Edits A/SS/F/BP/QL/BS/E/D. Professional freelance writer for 10 years; excellent research skills (PhD in higher education administration). Charges $60/hr.

MENTOR'S PEN EDITORIAL SERVICES/CHRISTINA MILLER, 7084 S. 585 W., Huntingburg IN 47542. (812) 536-3549. E-mail: Christina@mentorspen.com. Website: www.mentorspen.com. E-mail contact. GE/LC/writing coach. Edits N/NB/BP/QL. Published writer, 6 years' experience editing and critiquing, fiction contest judge. Offers free 5-page sample edit.

TYPING/EDITORIAL SERVICES/BARBARA BUIS, 4978 S. County Rd. 75 West, Greencastle IN 46135. (765) 653-4497. E-mail: truk4jsuschrst@yahoo.com. Call/e-mail. LC/transcription from tapes. Edits A/ SS/N/BS/D (anything). Has typed 4 books and helped edit 3 books. Charges $1.50/pg.

XARISCOM/JAMES WATKINS, 318 N. Lenfesty Ave., Marion IN 46952. E-mail: jim@jameswatkins .com. Website: www.jameswatkins.com. E-mail contact. GE/LC/GH/WS. Edits A/NB/BP/QL/BS/D/S. Award-winning author of 14 books & 2,000+ articles & an editor; winner of four editing and 2 book awards. 20+ years' experience. Charge $50 for 2,000 words of critique, editing, market suggestions; $5/pg. for content editing; $15/pg. for rewriting/ghosting; $50/hr. for Website evaluation/consulting.

KANSAS

AFFORDABLE NOVEL CRITIQUE SERVICE/SALLY BRADLEY, 239 N. 4th Ter., Louisburg KS 66053-4179. E-mail: sally@sallysbradley.com. Website: www.sallybradley.com. E-mail contact. GE/ LC/B/SP. Edits SS/N/BP/QL. BA in English, former editor for Christian publishers, contest judge, member of The Christian PEN (Proofreaders and Editors Network) and the Christian Editor Network. Services, prices, and client referrals on Website. Will tailor services to fit your needs.

KENTUCKY

EDITORIAL SERVICES/MARILYN A. ANDERSON, 127 Sycamore Dr., Louisville KY 40223-2956. (502) 244-0751. Fax (502) 452-9260. E-mail: shelle12@aol.com. Call/e-mail. GE/LC. Edits A/F/ NB/BS/TM/E/D. Charges $15-20/hr. for proofreading; $25/hr. for extensive editing; or negotiable by the job or project. Holds an MA and BA in English; former high school English teacher; freelance consultant since 1993. References available. Contributing member of The Christian PEN.

EDITORIAL SERVICES/BETTY L. WHITWORTH, 11740 S. Hwy 259, Leitchfield KY 42754. (270) 257-2461. E-mail: Blwhit@bbtel.com. Call/e-mail; send with $50 deposit. GE. Edits A/SS/N/NB/JN. Typing fees based on project (reasonable). Editing for novels and nonfiction books: fee based on amount of work. Retired English teacher, currently working as a newspaper columnist/journalist and independent editor. Will give estimate with 30 pages. Short manuscripts edited at $10/hr.

MARYLAND

OPINARI BOOK ANALYSIS. (443) 745-1004. E-mail: info@opinebooks.com. Website: www.opine books.com. E-mail contact. Book developer, 2 nonfiction book editors, and book designers analyze and improve nonfiction book manuscripts. Every nonfiction book must have clarity as well as a good message and good writing. Reach your book's audience. Have confidence in your nonfiction manuscript. Invest in its professional presentation. Quality feedback. Detailed recommendations in writing. Two targeted, free phone calls for U.S. clients. Reasonable rates. Fast turnaround. We will work to build quality into Christian nonfiction books!

MASSACHUSETTS

WORD PRO/BARBARA A. ROBIDOUX, 127 Gelinas Dr., Chicopee MA 01020-4813. (413) 592-4386. Fax (413) 594-8375. E-mail: Ebwordpro@aol.com. Call/e-mail. GE/LC/writing coach. Edits A/SS/F/NB/BP/QL/TM/E/D. Fee quoted upon request. BA in English; 18 years as freelancer; book reviewer; on staff of TCC Manuscript Critique Service.

MICHIGAN

+ BLUE WATER INK/JULIE ACKERMAN-LINK, 8816 Eastern Ave. S.E., Byron Center MI 49315. (616) 827-7880. E-mail: BlueWaterInk@gmail.com. Blog: www.bluewaterink.com. Call/e-mail. CA/GE/LC/SP. Edits BP/BS/D/NB/QL. Full-service book-packaging company and publishing consultant. Handles everything from manuscript through printer-ready files, including editing (all levels), designing, and typesetting. Flat-fee bids. Member of the Academy of Christian Editors; author and contributor to the popular devotional Our Daily Bread.

EDITORIAL DRAGON/MICHELLE HUEGEL, 1950 S. 13th St., Lot 277, Niles MI 49120. (269) 591-0672. E-mail: editorialdragon@gmail.com. Blog: www.editorialdragon.wordpress.com. E-mail contact. GE/LC/B/NL/SP/PP/scholarly work/dissertations/transcription. Edits A/SS/P/F/N/NB/JN/BS/GB/TM/E/D/academic writing. Bachelor of Arts in English with a writing concentration. Editor for local Christian newspaper, published articles, writing tutor at Bethel College Writing Center. Charges depend on type and length of project.

EDITORIAL SERVICES/ADAM BLUMER, 719 East H St., Iron Mountain MI 49801. (906) 774-9576. E-mail: adam@blumer.org. Website: www.blumer.org/adam. E-mail contact. GE/LC/GH/BCE. Edits A/SS/F/N/NB/BP/QL/JN/PB/BS/GB/D. More than 17 years' experience in writing, editing, proof-reading; and 8 years of Website updating experience. Employed as full-time editor for 14 years; B.A. in print journalism.

+ **EDITORIAL SERVICES/ASHLEY BARRETT**, 705 N. Rosebud Trl., Buchanan MI 49107. (269) 282-9341. E-mail: LizaSnodgrass@gmail.com. Website: www.ashleyink.com. E-mail contact. GE/GH/CA/B/NL/SP/PP. Edits A/SS/P/F/N/NB/BP/JN/BS/E/D. Has a B.A. in English; Associate of Arts in Professional Writing. Charges $12/hr.

LEAVES OF GOLD CONSULTING LLC/MARY EDWARDS, PO Box 48365, Oak Park MI 48237. (313) 523-5886. E-mail: Edwardsmd@sbcglobal.net. E-mail contact. GE/LC/CA/writing coach. Edits A/SS/F/N/NB/BS/GB/TM/E/D/gospel tracts. Thirty years' experience writing/editing/coaching. Founder of the Called & Ready Writers. Has written for Chicken Soup for the Soul. Provides monthly "how-to" workshops for writers. Fees negotiable depending on writer's level of experience.

WALLIS EDITORIAL SERVICES/DIANA WALLIS, 547 Cherry St. S.E., #6C, Grand Rapids MI 49503-4755. (616) 459-8836. E-mail: WallisEdit@sirus.com. Call/e-mail. GE/LC/SP/WS/proofreading. Edits A/N/NB/JN/BS/TM/D/advertising and promotional copy, Website content, educational materials for students and parents/teachers, catalog copy. Rates per project rather than per hour. Calvin College graduate, 15 years freelancing for publishers, corporations, and ad agencies; details on request.

WRITER'S NUDGE/MARY BUSHA, 1201 Charter Oaks Dr., Davison MI 48423. (810) 653-4218. Email: marybusha@writersnudge.com. Website: www.writersnudge.com. E-mail contact. GE/LC/CA/BCE/writing coach. Edits A/SS/N/NB/BP/JN/PB/QL/BS/GB/E/D. Offers workshops/seminars. Over 30 years of editorial and writing experience. Evaluates your projects and bids on the project.

THE WRITE SPOT/ARLENE KNICKERBOCKER, "Quality and Economy Unite at the Write Spot," PO Box 424, Davison MI 48423-9318. (810) 793-0316. E-mail: writer@thewritespot.org. Website: www.thewritespot.org. E-mail/write. GE/LC/GH/CA/B/NL/classes and speaking/writing coach. Edits A/SS/P/NB/BP/QL/BS/D. Published credits since 1996; references available. Prices on Website.

WRITINGCAREERCOACH.COM/TIFFANYCOLTER, Michigan. E-mail: Tiffany@WritingCareerCoach .com. Website: www.writingcareercoach.com. E-mail contact. GE/GH/SP/NL/WS/PP/writing coach/writing career coaching/business planning. Edits N/NB/BP/QL. BA; Daphne Award–winning writer; multiple articles published; regular contributor to Toledo Business Journal; feature writer/colum-nist. Charges $20/hr. for content editing and career coaching. Offers a discounted coaching package $30/mo. See Website for other services.

MINNESOTA

+ **MY BOOK THERAPY/SUSAN MAY WARREN/RACHEL HAUCK**, PO Box 1290, Grand Marais MN 55604. (218) 370-8395. E-mail: info@mybooktherapy.com. Website: www.mybooktherapy.com. E-mail contact. GE/brainstorming/writing coach. Edits book proposals/crafts synopses. Award-winning, best-selling authors with nearly 40 books in the market. Acclaimed craft instructors from national writing conferences. Warren has been a multiple Christy nominee and a RITA winner. Hauck has been a RITA nominee and an ACFW Book of the Year winner. Price list on Website.

NOBLE CREATIVE, LLC/SCOTT NOBLE, PO Box 131402, St. Paul MN 55113. (651) 494-4169. E-mail: snoble@noblecreative.com. Website: www.noblecreative.com. E-mail contact. GE/LC/GH/B/NL/SP/WS. Edits A/SS/F/N/NB/BP/QL/BS/GB/TM/E/D. More than a decade of experience, including several years as asst. ed. at Decision Magazine. Masters degree in Theological Studies. Charges by the hour or the project.

NORTH COUNTRY TRANSCRIPTION (PSALM 96:12): Writing, Editing and Secretarial Services/CONNIE PETTERSEN. (218) 927-6176. E-mail: cardinals4connie@gmail.com. Call/e-mail. Manuscript typing; edit for punctuation/spelling/grammar. Experienced published author of short fiction; journalist with over 350 articles published; 30 years' secretarial/transcription experience. Types novels/nonfiction mss, résumés, family memoirs. Also does digital recording, editing/writing memoirs for publication or personal use. Transcription by digital voice or cassette tape. Fees: hourly rate or by a 65-character, computer-counted line, plus postage/mileage. Free estimates. Confidentiality guaranteed. References.

+ **A WRITE START COMMUNICATIONS/TAMA WESTMAN/LEE WARREN**, 6673—99th St. S., Cottage Grove MN 55016. (952) 334-2088. Fax (310) 388-5918. E-mail: tama@awritestart.com or lee@awritestart.com. Website: www.awritestart.com. E-mail contact. GE/LC/GH/CA/B/NL/SP/WS/blogs/writing coach. Edits A/SS/P/F/N/NB/BP/QL/JN/PB/BS/GB/TM/E/D/S/promotional material. Freelance writers, award winners, and former editors. Charges $40/hr. and requires a 3-hour minimum payment up front; coaching fee is $75/hr.

MISSISSIPPI

+ **NEXT LEVEL CRITIQUES/SUSAN E. RICHARDSON**, 106 Fox Run Way, Clinton MS 39056. (601) 924-7821. E-mail: nextlevelcritiques@bellsouth.net. Website: www.nextlevelcritiques.com. E-mail contact. GE/writing coach. Edits N/NB/BP/QL/JN/BS. Critique reader for Steeple Hill, former first reader for Angela Hunt, published author, columnist, 19 years in publishing industry, including many years in Christian retailing. Charges by the page. Rate charts on Website.

MISSOURI

BLUE MOUNTAIN EDITORIAL SERVICE/BARBARA WARREN, 4721 Farm Road 2165, Exeter MO 65647. (417) 835-3235. E-mail: barbarawarren@mo-net.com. Website: www.barbarawarrenblue mountainedit.com. E-mail contact. GE/LC/content editor/writing coach. Edits N/NB. Charges $20/hr. Twenty years' experience.

EDITORIAL SERVICES/JUDI LUDWIG, 6204 Clifton Ave., St. Louis MO 63109-3426. (314) 457-0026. E-mail: tludwig4@sbcglobal.net. E-mail contact. GE/LC. Edits A/SS/N/NB/BP/QL/JN/BS/GB/TM/E/D/S. Charges $2/12 pt., double-spaced page, plus postage. Has M.A. in Media Communications; editor for Christian book publisher; book author.

THERE'S AN ANGEL IN YOUR INKWELL/CAROL NEWMAN, PO Box 480835, Kansas City MO 64148-0835. (913) 681-1168. Fax (913) 681-1173. E-mail: carol@angelinyourinkwell.com. Website: www.angelinyourinkwell.com. E-mail contact. GE/GH. Edits A/SS/P/F/NB/BP/QL/E/D. Variable rates according to project; average $40/hr.; 1/2 hr. free consultation. Twenty years national inspirational writer, teacher, and writing coach.

MONTANA

+ **APPRAISING YOUR NOVEL/JAMES L. COTTON**, 652 Treece Gulch Rd., Stevensville MT 59870. (406) 777-5191. E-mail: noveledit2003@yahoo.com. Website: www.appraisingyournovel.com. Call/

e-mail/write. GE. Edits novels. Has 20 years' experience as a newspaper and national magazine editor and associate publisher. Began editing service in 2000. Charges $1/ms pg.

THE WRITE EDITOR/ERIN K. BROWN, Corvallis. E-mail: thewriteeditor@gmail.com. Website: www.writeeditor.net. E-mail contact. GE/LC. Edits A/SS/F/N/NB/BP/QL/JN/BS/E/D/NL/B. Has a certificate in Editorials Practices: Graduate School, USDA, Washington DC; Christy Award judge 2006-2009; member of Editorial Freelancers Assn.; The Christian PEN; coauthor of The Lost Coin.

NEVADA

EDITORIAL SERVICES/JEANETTE HANSCOME, 3201 Heights Dr., Reno NV 89503. (775) 787-1263. E-mail: jeanettehanscome@sbcglobal.net. Website: www.jeanettehanscome.com. E-mail contact. GE/CA/SP/writing coach. Edits A/SS/F/N/NB/BP/QL/JN/E/D/S/YA novels & nonfiction. Author of 3 teen books with Focus on the Family; editor for 4 years; 300+ published articles; leads a critique group; teaches and critiques at writers' conferences. Charges $25-30/hr; flat fees negotiable.

NEW HAMPSHIRE

AMGD ENTERPRISES/SALLY WILKINS, PO Box 273, Amherst NH 03031-0273. (603) 673-9331. E-mail: SEDWilkins@aol.com. E-mail contact. GE/LC/B/NL. Website: www.sallywilkins.com. Edits A/F/NB/BP/QL. Published nonfiction adult and juvenile books and articles; edited 2 successful book proposals; experienced critiquer. Rate sheet for SASE.

NEW JERSEY

TOPNOTCH WRITING SOLUTIONS/MARYANN DIORIO PHD, 1216 Forest Dr., Millville NJ 08332-2597. (856) 327-1231. Fax (856) 327-0291. E-mail: DrMaryAnn@TopNotchWritingSolutions.com. Website: www.TopNotchWritingSolutions.com. E-mail contact. GE/NL/SP/WS/writing coach (www.Top NotchLifeandCareerCoaching.com). Edits A/SS/P/F/BP/QL. 25+ years' experience; award winner; 4 published books; hundreds of published articles, short stories, and poems. Rate sheet available on request.

WRITER'S RELIEF, INC./RONNIE L. SMITH, 409 S. River St., Hackensack NJ 07601. (866) 405-3003. Fax (201) 641-1253. E-mail: Ronnie@wrelief.com. Website: www.writersrelief.com. Call or e-mail. LC/NL/targeting submissions. Proofs A/SS/P/F/N/NB/JN/E. Fifteen years' experience as an author's submission service. Free monthly newsletter for writers contains date-driven list of markets. Contact for rates.

NEW YORK

EDITORIAL SERVICES/STERLING DIMMICK, 311 Chemung St., Apt. 5, Waverly NY 14892-1463. (607) 565-4247. E-mail: sterlingdimmick@hotmail.com. Call. GE/LC/GH/CA/SP. Edits A/SS/P/F/N/NB/BP/JN/PB/QL/BS/GB/TM/E/D/S. Has an AAS in Journalism; BA in Communication Studies. Charges $20/hr. or by the project.

EDITORIAL SERVICES/LAURIE GRAZIANO, 658 E. 34th St., Brooklyn NY 11203-6102. E-mail: grazianolau@yahoo.com. E-mail/write. Research/market. Columns/interviews/instructional. Will write A/P/F/D/greeting card copy. Experienced writer, contributing editor, staff writer, regular columnist. Charges $15-75/hr. or by the project.

EDITORIAL SERVICES/DENISE SYED, 7681 Whispers Ln., Ontario NY 14519. (585) 747-1923. Fax (315) 524-8848. Call. GE/LC/GH/CA/B/NL/SP/WS/BCE/PP. Edits A/SS/F/NB/BP/JN/PB/BS/GB/TM/E/D/legal writing. Retired lawyer with experience in legal writing, technical writing, and writing pertaining to the arts. Loves nonfiction. Encourages writers to be thorough in theology and application, and literary in tone.

NORTH CAROLINA

EDITORIAL SERVICES/MIKE & JASMIN MORRELL, Raleigh NC. (770) 313-1718. E-mail: jasmin is@gmail.com. E-mail contact. GE/LC/B/NL/SP/WS. Edits A/SS/F/N/NB/BP/ JN/PB/QL/BS/GB/E/D. Has edited for Christian publishers and mainstream curriculum publishers. Developmental editing: $8/pg.; copy editing $6/pg. Requires 50 percent of fee up front. Requested revisions included in original fee.

ANNA W. FISHEL, 3416 Hunting Creek Dr., Pfafftown NC 27040. (336) 924-5880. E-mail: awfishel@ triad.rr.com. Call/write/e-mail. GE/CA/SP. Edits A/SS/P/N/NB/JN/E/D. Two decades of professional editing experience; editor with major Christian publishing house for over 10 years; published author of 6 children's books. Charges by the hour. Estimates offered.

PREP PUBLISHING/PATTY SLEEM, 1110 1/2 Hay St., Fayetteville NC 28305. (910) 483-6611. Fax (910) 483-2439. E-mail: preppub@aol.com. Website: www.prep-pub.com. Write. GE/LC/SP. Edits N/ NB. BA in English, MBA from Harvard, author of more than 25 books. Project price based on written query and initial free telephone consultation.

OHIO

IZZY'S OFFICE/DIANE STORTZ, PO Box 31239, Cincinnati OH 45231. (513) 602-6720. E-mail: diane@izzysoffice.com. Website: www.izzysoffice.com. E-mail contact. GE/LC/GH/CA. Edits A/NB/BP/ JN/PB/BS/GB/E/D. Former editorial director for a Christian publisher (10 yrs.); published author; experience as children's editor and magazine copy editor. See Website for client list and list of projects. Copyediting or substantive editing by the hour or per-project basis; book proposal package $750; evaluation and 2-chapter critique $350. Half payment amount due before work begins.

OKLAHOMA

EDITORIAL SERVICES/RICHARD W. RUNDELL, PO Box 983, Haskell OK 74436-0983. (918) 482-5066. E-mail: rwrundell@windstream.net. E-mail contact. GE/LC. Edits A/NB/BS/D. Over 20 years' editing experience; author of books, articles, booklets, devotionals, and book reviews. Rates negotiable.

EPISTLEWORKS CREATIONS/JOANN RENO WRAY, Helping Writers Reach Their High Call, 8409 S. Elder Ave., Broken Arrow, OK 74011-8286. (918) 451-4017 or cell (918) 695-4528. E-mail: epedit@epistleworks.com. Website: http://epistleworks.com. Call/write/e-mail (preferred). GE/LC/ GH/CA/B/NL/SP/Research. Edits A/SS/P/F/N/NB/BP/D. Creates graphic art such as covers and logos; Website design and content; PR materials such as fliers, brochures, booklets, and Web ads including animated. Uses signed contracts with clients. Experienced writer, editor, and artist since 1974. Includes work as editor for a Tulsa monthly Christian newspaper; publishing an online magazine; columnist; editing work of clients, pastors, and ministers, including books; speaking and teaching at national Christian writers' conferences; over 3,000 articles published; and much more. Charges start at $30/hr. with required $45 nonrefundable consulting fee (deducted from total bill). Discounts for churches and ministries. Accepts checks, money orders, or PayPal. See Website for detail on services. Gives binding estimates. Gives detailed time clock report. Mentoring services and e-mail writing classes available. Speaker and teacher.

TWEEN WATERS EDITORIAL SERVICES/TERRI KALFAS, PO Box 1233, Broken Arrow OK 74013-1233. (918) 346-7960. E-mail: tlkalfas@cox.net. E-mail contact. GE/LC/GH/CA/B/SP/BCE. Edits A/N/NB/BP/QL/BS/TM/D/project management/book doctoring. Multiple editorial and freelance writing services. Over 25 years' writing and publishing experience. Equally skilled in copywriting for catalogs, direct marketing, and fund-raising. Writing instructor. Award-winning fiction writer. Available as conference speaker and workshop teacher. Charges $3 per pg./$25 per hr./negotiable on special projects.

WINGS UNLIMITED/CRISTINE BOLLEY, 712 N. Sweetgum Ave., Broken Arrow OK 74012-2156. (918) 250-9239. Fax (918) 250-9597. E-mail: WingsUnlimited@aol.com. Website: www.wingsun limited.com. E-mail contact. GE/LC/GH/CA/SP. Edits NB/BP/D. Specializes in turning sermon series into books for classic libraries. Author/coauthor/ghostwriter of 30+ titles. Over 25 years' experience in development of best-selling titles for major Christian publishing houses. All fees negotiated in advance: developmental edits (format/house style/clarity) range from $1,500-$3,000/100-250 pgs.; substantive rewrite averages $5,000/250 pgs.

OREGON

EDITING GALLERY LLC/CAROL L. CRAIG, 2622 Willona Dr., Eugene OR 97408. (541) 342-7300. E-mail: carollcraig@comcast.net. Website: www.editinggallery.com. Call/e-mail. GE/LC/synopses/writing coach. Edits N/Fiction BP/QL/memoirs. English major; 15+ years' experience. Charges $75/hr.

EDITORIAL SERVICES/FLORENCE C. BLAKE, 4865 Hwy. 234, #176, White City OR 97503. E-mail: florblake@ccountry.net (put "Edit Service" in subject line). E-mail contact. GE/LC/B/NL/SP. Edits A/SS/F/NB/E/D/Christian tracts. Freelance writers since 1999 with over 700 sales, community college writing teacher, senior contributing editor for general publication. Charges $2/double-spaced page.

HONEST EDITING, Bill Carmichael & editing team. E-mail: bill@booksandmanuscripts.com. Website: www.honestediting.com. E-mail contact. GE/LC/SP. Edits N/NB/BP/JN. Check Website for full list of services and instructions.

+ D. C. JACOBSON & ASSOCIATES/DON JACOBSON, 473 West Hood Ave., Ste. 105, Sisters OR 97759. (541) 549-3585. Fax (541) 549-1785. E-mail: query@dcjacobson.com. Website: www.dc jacobson.com. Website submissions only. GE/LC/CA/literary consulting/writing coach. Edits N/NB/BP/JN/QL/BS/GB/D. Thirty+ years' combined experience in publishing, marketing, sales, editorial, and more than 1,000 titles published as former president of a major Christian publisher. Provides editing services to non–literary agent clients, specializing in concept development, crafting salable proposals and queries, and providing ongoing coaching depending on writer's needs (self-publishing, editorial, etc.). Package rates detailed on Website.

PICKY, PICKY INK/SUE MIHOLER, 1075 Willow Lake Road N., Keizer OR 97303-5790. (503) 393-3356. E-mail: suemiholer@comcast.net. E-mail contact. LC. Edits A/NB/BP/QL/BS/D. Freelance editor for several book publishers since 1998. Will help you get your manuscript ready to submit. Charges $30 an hour or $50 for first 10 pages of a longer work; writer will receive a firm completed-job quote based on the first 10 pages.

+ EDITORIAL SERVICES/ROSE ENGLISH, 94760 Oaklea Dr., Junction City OR 97448-9314. Phone/fax (541) 998-3959. E-mail: rose9265@comcast.net. Call/e-mail. GE/LC/B/NL/SP. Edits A/SS/N/NB/JN/PB/BS/E/D. Manuscript editing, freelance graphic design, print shop and ad agency experience. Fee based on project.

SALLY STUART, 1647 S.W. Pheasant Dr., Aloha OR 97006. (503) 642-9844. Fax (503) 848-3658. E-mail: stuartcwmg@aol.com. Website: www.stuartmarket.com. Blog: www.stuartmarket.blogspot .com. Call/e-mail. GE/BCE/agent contracts. Edits A/SS/N/NB/BP/JN/GB. No poetry or picture books. Author of 37 books (including the Christian Writers' Market Guide) and 40+ years' experience as a writer, teacher, marketing expert. Contact for availability (not available December-April).

For books, send copy of book proposal: cover letter, chapter-by-chapter synopsis for nonfiction (5-page overall synopsis for fiction), and first three chapters, double-spaced. Charges $40/hr. for critique; $45/hr. for phone/personal consultations. Comprehensive publishing contract evaluation $80-150.

PENNSYLVANIA

ANGAH CREATIVE SERVICES/DANIELLE CAMPBELL-ANGAH, 961 Taylor Dr., Folcroft PA 19032. (610) 457-8300. E-mail: blessingsofgod77@verizon.net. Website: www.angahcreative.com. Ten years' writing experience; 5 years' editing experience.

REBECCA CARANFA EDITORIAL SERVICES, 502 Idaho Ave., Verona PA 15147-2910. Phone/fax (412) 795-7711. E-mail: BlessingsofGod77@comcast.net. GE/B/NL/SP. Edits A/SS/P/N/NB/JN/GB/TM/E/D. 20 years' experience. Teaching background. Charges $25/hr. or estimate after evaluation of material.

MICHELE T. HUEY EDITORIAL SERVICES, 121 Homestead Ln., Glen Campbell PA 15742-8404. (814) 845-7683. E-mail: writeon4writers@yahoo.com. Website: www.michelehuey.com. E-mail contact. GE/LC/writing coach. Edits A/SS/N/NB/QL/D. English/composition/journalism teacher for 20 yrs.; newspaper reporter, feature writer, former editor, columnist for 12 yrs.; writing mentor for 3 writing organizations. Provide the total number of words and a sample page or two of your manuscript. Charges $30/hr. or $5/pg. Follows rates suggested at www.writersmarket.com/content/howmuch3.asp.

STRONG TOWER PUBLISHING/HEIDI NIGRO, PO Box 973, Milesburg PA 16853-0973. E-mail: strongtowerpubs@aol.com. Website: www.strongtowerpublishing.com. E-mail contact. GE/LC/NL/WS/PP/rewriting/developmental editing/writing coach. Edits A/SS/P/F/N/NB/BS/GB/TM/E/D. Specializes in general theological and eschatological mss. Twenty years' editing experience in book and magazine publishing. Manuscript evaluation, $59-109; proofing, $2 per 250-word page; copyediting, $4/250-word page; developmental editing and book development $40/hr. or by project. Other projects negotiable. Provides free 5-page sample edit. Theological manuscripts must be consistent with basic statement of faith.

WORDS FOR ALL REASONS/ELIZABETH ROSIAN, 108 Deerfield Ln., Johnstown PA 15905-5703. (814) 255-4351. E-mail: wordsforallreasons@atlanticbb.net. Website: www.101steps.zoomshare.com. E-mail contact. GE/LC/GH/CA. Edits A/SS/P/F/N/NB/BP/QL/BS/GB/E/D. More than 35 years' experience writing, teaching, and editing; more than 1,000 published works, plus inspirational novel, how-to book, and 6 chapbooks. Rate sheet on Website.

WRITE HIS ANSWER MINISTRIES/MARLENE BAGNULL, LittD, 316 Blanchard Rd., Drexel Hill PA 19026-3507. Phone/fax (610) 626-6833. E-mail: mbagnull@aol.com. Website: www.writehisanswer.com. Call/write. GE/LC/typesetting. Edits A/SS/N/NB/BP/JN/BS/D. Author of 5 books; compiler/editor of 3 books; more than 1,000 sales to Christian periodicals. Call or write for information on At-Home Writing Workshops, a correspondence study program. Charges $35/hr.; estimates given.

WRITE NOW SERVICES/KAREN APPOLD, 2012 Foxmeadow Cir., Royersford PA 19468. (610) 948-1961. Fax (610) 672-9960. E-mail: KarenAppold@comcast.net. Website: www.writenowservices.com. Call/e-mail. GE/LC/GH/B/NL/SP/WS. Edits A/SS/F/QL/E. Professional editor, writer, consultant since 1993 for magazines, journals, newsletters, and newspapers. Hundreds of published articles and extensive magazine and newspaper editing. Rates determined after free evaluation of project.

SOUTH CAROLINA

EDITORIAL SERVICES/LINDA J. LEE, 108 Quail Creek Dr., West Columbia SC 29169-3434. (803) 939-9713. E-mail: ljlee@bellsouth.net. E-mail contact. GE/LC/B/NL/SP/writing coach. Edits A/

SS/P/N/NB/BP/JN/PB/QL/BS/GB/TM/E/D/S. Contributing editor for P31 Woman magazine; has edited books; has private-tutored for 15 years; writing tutor at college level for 8 years. Charges by the page or as negotiated.

TENNESSEE

CHRISTIAN WRITERS INSTITUTE MANUSCRIPT CRITIQUE SERVICE. PO Box 110390, Nashville TN 37222. Toll-free (800) 21-WRITE. E-mail: ACWriters@aol.com. Website: www.ACWriters.com. Call/write. GE/LC/GH/CA/SP/BCE. Edits A/SS/P/F/N/NB/BP/JN/PB/BS/TM/E/D/S. Send SASE for rate sheet and submission slip.

+ **EDITORIAL SERVICES/KIM PETERSON**, 1114 Buxton Dr., Knoxville TN 37922. E-mail: petersk@BethelCollege.edu. Write/e-mail. GE/LC/GH/CA/B/NL/SP/PP/mentoring/writing coach. Edits A/P/F/N/NB/BP/QL/JN/PB/GB/TM/E/D. Freelance writer; college-level writing instructor; freelance editor; conference speaker. Charges $25-30/hr.

WRITING COACH/LINDA WINN, 138 Bluff Dr., Winchester TN 37398. (931) 962-8801. E-mail: lhwinn@comcast.net. Writing coach.

TEXAS

ASSURANCE EDITING SERVICES/MAUREEN B. MCCLAIN, PO Box 1051, Sanger TX 76266-1051. (940) 458-3814. E-mail: Assuranceedit@juno.com. E-mail/write. LC. Edits A/SS/P/F/N/NB/BP/JN/QL/BS/GB/E/D. Published book and devotional writer; freelancer for 10+ years. E-mail for prices.

+ **B & B WRITING SERVICE/BEVERLY OSTROWSKI**, Texas. E-mail: bandbwrite@gmail.com. Writer for 20 yrs.; screenwriter for 10 yrs.; line editor for more than 10 yrs.

EDITORIAL SERVICES/KELLEY MATHEWS, ThM, 216 Birdbrook Dr., Anna TX 75409. (214) 769-1829. E-mail: kmathews@newdoors.info. Website: www.newdoors.info. E-mail contact. GE/LC/CA/NL/SP. Edits A/NB/BP/PB/BS/GB/TM/D. Has 13 years' experience in editing/proofreading; coauthored 4 books; authored numerous articles. Specializes in theological and women's issues. Charges $30/hr. for proofreading; $50/hr. for copy editing; negotiable flat fee for large book projects.

FACETS BUSINESS COMMUNICATIONS/GEM SMITH, PO Box 79216, Houston TX 77279. (713) 465-8284. Website: www.facetscom.com. Call. GE/B/NL/SP/WS/content development. Edits A/SS/N/NB/BP/QL/BS/GB/TM/E/D/S. Published freelance writer/editor/speaker for 30 years. Has worked with technical/scientific/theological material and authors with English as a second language; also newsletters, manual, and training scripts. Works by the hour with deposit, after discussing project with client. Average is $35-50/hr.

PWC EDITING/PAUL W. CONANT, 527 Bayshore Pl., Dallas TX 75217-7755. (972) 913-9123. Fax (972) 557-7558. E-mail: pwcediting@gmail.com. Website: www.pwc-editing.com. E-mail contact. LC/NL/SP. Edits A/N/NB/BS/TM/E/D/S/dissertations/textbooks/Web pages. Writer, editor; proofreader for book publishers and magazines. Dissertations, $18/hr.; short works, $25/hr.; negotiable terms for long works. Charges publishers up to $25/hr. Prefers to work up a page rate based on a minimum 10-page sample, giving new clients between 1 and 2 hours of free editing.

RENAISSANCE LITERARY SERVICES/JO REAVES, PO Box 248, Trenton TX 75490-7270. Phone/fax (903) 989-2815. E-mail: editor@renaissanceliteraryservices.com. Website: www.renaissance literaryservices.com. E-mail contact. GE/LC/B/NL/SP/WS/PowerPoint/interior layout & design/audio transcription. Edits A/SS/P/F/N/NB/BP/JN/PB/QL/BS/GB/TM/E/D/S. Undergraduate and graduate work in languages and linguistics; managing editor of 3 newspapers; university professor (communications); 23 years' experience as professional editor; published author of 3 books. Charges $3-4/pg., depending on level of editing; additional rates on Website.

SPREAD THE WORD COMMERCIAL WRITING/KATHERINE SWARTS, Houston TX. (832) 573-9501. E-mail: katherine@spreadthewordcommercialwriting.com. Website: www.spreadthe wordcommercialwriting.com. Blog: http://newsongsfromtheheart.blogspot.com. E-mail contact preferred. Copyrighting/editing for newsletters/B/SP/WS. MA in written communication from Wheaton College; over 100 published articles, poems, and other material. Charges up to $80/hr.

THE WRITE WAY EDITORIAL SERVICES/JANET K. CREWS/B. KAY COULTER, 806 Hopi Trl., Temple TX 76504-5008. (254) 778-6490 or (254) 939-1770. E-mails: janetcrews@sbcglobal.net or bkcoulter@sbcglobal.net. Website: www.writewayeditorial.com. Call/e-mail. GE/LC/GH/CA/B/NL/SP/scan to Word document/voice to Word document/graphics. Edits A/SS/N/NB/BP/JN/QL/BS/GB/D. Published author of 3 books; contributor to 2 books; 12 years' combined experience; certified copyeditor. Free estimate; 50 percent of estimate as a deposit; $30/hr. Contact for additional details.

+ **THE WRITING SPA/MARY DEMUTH**, PO Box 1503, Rockwall TX 75087. (214) 475-9083. E-mail: maryedemuth@sbcglobal.net. Website: www.thewritingspa.com. E-mail contact with a $75 deposit. GE/LC/NL/SP/writing coach. Edits A/SS/F/N/NB/BP/QL. "As a published fiction and nonfiction author who teaches at writers' conferences around the nation, I know how to come alongside would-be, aspiring authors." Initial consultation: 5 pgs., double-spaced $75. Writing coach: $75/hr. E-mail for additional package prices.

UTAH

THE WHAT IF GIRL/KATHLEEN WRIGHT, Sandy UT. E-mail: the_whatif_girl@yahoo.com. Blog: www.whatifgirl.wordpress.com. E-mail contact. GE/fiction coaching. Edits N/QL/fiction synopsis. Also a writing coach. BA in journalism, 20+ years' editing/writing experience. Clients include beginning writers through multipublished award winners. Charges by the hour; e-mail for current rate.

VIRGINIA

EDITOR FOR YOU/MELANIE RIGNEY, 4201 Wilson Blvd., #110328, Arlington VA 22203-1859. (703) 863-3940. E-mail: editor@editorforyou.com. Website: www.editorforyou.com. E-mail contact. GE/LC/writing coach. Edits SS/N/NB/BP/QL/E/D. Editor of Writer's Digest magazine for 5 years; book editor/manager of Writer's Digest Books for 1 year; 3.5 years with Macmillan Computer Publishing and Thomsen Financial Publishing in books; 30 years' editing experience; frequent conference speaker/contest judge. Charges $65/hr. for content editing & coaching (provides a binding ceiling on number of hours); fees vary for ms evaluation.

EDITORIAL SERVICES/SKYLAR HAMILTON BURRIS, PO Box 7505, Fairfax Station VA 22039. (703) 944-1530. E-mail: SSburris@cox.net. Website: www.editorskylar.com. E-mail contact. LC/NL/WS. Edits A/SS/P/F/N/NB/JN/BS/GB/TM/E/D/S. Primarily works with authors who are planning either to self-publish or to submit their work to traditional publishing houses and who have completed books that require line-by-line copyediting prior to final proofreading and publication. BA and MA in English. Eight years as a magazine editor; 10+ years' newsletter editing and design. Charges authors $2/double-spaced page for editing. Charges $35/hr. for copyediting books; or $2-$3.50/double-spaced page (depending on difficulty level). Charges $35/hr. for newsletter editing, writing, and design. Free sample edit of 2 pages.

WASHINGTON

BY BRENDA: WRITER & DESIGNER/BRENDA WILBEE, 7463 Leeside Dr., Blaine WA 98230. (360) 746-0308. E-mail: BeeWilbee@gmail.com. Website: www.BrendaWilbee.com. E-mail contact. Offers design services for brochures, newsletter, Websites, and PowerPoint. Has MA in Professional Writing; AA in Graphic Design; author of 9 CBA books and over 100 articles; longtime contributor to Daily Guideposts; and has freelanced as both a writer and designer. Charges are available on Website and can be discussed via e-mail.

DOCUMENT DRIVEN/JANICE HUSSEIN, 16420 S.E. McGillivray, #103—103, Vancouver WA 98683. (503) 789-6245. E-mail: Janice@documentdriven.com. Website: www.documentdriven.com. Call/ e-mail. GE/LC/SP/WS/writing coach. Edits A/N/NB/BP/JN/QL/E/synopsis; submission & manuscript critiques. MS in Writing/Publishing; MBA; 9-years' experience copyediting; 5 years' experience editing. Fee scale on Website; charges by project.

EDITORIAL SERVICES/MARION DUCKWORTH, 15917 N.E. 41st St., Vancouver WA 98682-7473. (360) 896-8599. E-mail: mjduck@comcast.net. Website: www.MarionDuckworthMinistries.com. E-mail/write. GE/Writing Coach. Edits A/NB/BP/QL/BS; also does consultations. Author (for over 25 years) of 17 books and 300 articles; writing teacher for over 25 years; extensive experience in general editing and manuscript evaluation. Charges $25/hr. for critique or consultation. Negotiates on longer projects.

FICTION FIX-IT SHOP/MEREDITH EFKEN, 93 S. Jackson St. #77543, Seattle WA 98104-2818. (402) 445-2529. E-mail: editor@fictionfixitshop.com. Website: www.fictionfixitshop.com. E-mail contact. GE/LC/writing coach. Edits N/BP/YA novels. All editors and coaches (except copy editors) are published novelists. FFS is a member of The Christian PEN and Editorial Freelancers Assn. Rates listed on Website. Editing is hourly; coaching rated by package on a monthly basis.

KALEIDOSCOPE PRESS/PENNY LENT, 2507—94th Ave. E., Edgewood WA 98371-2203. (253) 848-1116. E-mail: K.press@earthlink.net. Call/e-mail/write; agreeable contract & deposit. GE/LC/ GH/CA/B/NL/SP/BCE. Edits A/SS/P/F/N/NB/BP/JN/PB/QL/BS/GB/TM/E/D/S. Also market analysis, newsletters, brochures (graphic design & layout). During 38 years, published in radio, magazines, newspapers. Author/contributor/ghost writer of 12 books. Editor for 7 publishers. All editing negotiated. Discount on larger projects.

LOGOS WORD DESIGNS INC./LINDA L. NATHAN, PO Box 735, Maple Falls WA 98266-0735. (360) 599-3429. Fax (360) 392-0216. E-mail: linda@logosword.com. Website: www.logosword.com. Call/ e-mail. GE/LC/GH/CA/B/NL/SP/résumés/publishing consultations/writing assistance/writes proposals manuscript submission services. Edits A/SS/F/N/NB/BP/JN/PB/QL/BS/TM/E/D/academic/legal/apologetics/conservative political. Over 30 years' experience in wide variety of areas, including publicity, postdoctoral; BA Psychology/some MA. Member: Editorial Freelance Assn.; American Christian Fiction Writers; and N.W. Indiana Editors' Guild. Quote per project. See Website for rates.

WISCONSIN

MARGARET HOUK: EDITING SERVICES, West 2355 Valleywood Ln., Appleton WI 54915-8712. (920) 687-0559. Fax (920) 687-0259. E-mail: marghouk@juno.com. Call/write. GE/LC. Edits A/F/ NB/BP/QL/E/D (all for teens or adults). Author of 5 books and 700 articles; has taught writing and manuscript marketing for many years. Will quote fee based on free phone interview and writing sample.

+ STONE COTTAGE LITERARY SERVICES/JONATHAN RICE, 404 Meadow View Ln., DeForest WI 53532. (608) 842-0156. E-mail: jjrice@charter.net. Write/e-mail. GE/LC/GH/CA/B/SP. Edits A/SS/N/ NB/BS/E/D. ProfessIonally employed editor/writer with national Christian ministry; BA Religious

Studies, MA Creative Writing (fiction), MDiv Pastoral Studies, DMin Homiletics/Narrative Theology. Contact for hourly rates or full project fee estimates.

CANADIAN/FOREIGN

AOTEAROA EDITORIAL SERVICES/VENNESSA NG, PO Box 228, Oamaru 9444, New Zealand. Tel. +64210605477. (A U.S. based number is available to clients). E-mail: editor@aotearoaeditorial .com. Website: www.aotearoaeditorial.com. E-mail contact. GE/LC. Edits SS/N/BP. Seven years' critiquing experience. Page rates vary depending on project: start from $1.50/critique, $1/basic proofread, and $3.00/Copyedit. (Rates are in U.S. dollars and can be paid by PayPal or Western Union.)

BERYL HENNE, #1405 77 University Cres., Winnipeg MB R3T 3N8, Canada. (204) 275-1799. E-mail: bhenne@mts.net. Write or e-mail. GE/LC/SP. Edits A/NB/E/D. Has over 25 years' experience in book and magazine editing, and has worked with many self-publishing authors. Charges $25/hr. for copyediting; $32/hr. for content editing; will negotiate on larger projects.

DORSCH EDITORIAL/AUDREY DORSCH, 1275 Markham Rd., #305, Toronto ON M1H 3A2, Canada. (416) 439-4320. Fax (416) 439-5089. E-mail: audrey@dorschedit.ca. Website: www.dorsch edit.ca. Audrey Dorsch, ed. Editorial services: substantive editing, copyediting, indexing, proofreading, layout.

+ EDITORIAL SERVICES/DARLENE OAKLEY, 629 Van Buren St., RR3, Kemptville ON K0G 1J0, Canada. (613) 258-9883. E-mail: darlene@darscorrections.com. Website: www.darscorrections .com. E-mail contact. GE/LC/GH/B/NL/SP/WS/PP/reviews/critiques/Web copy. Edits A/SS/N/NB/QL/BP/ BS/GB/E/D/synopses/Web copy. Editor/proofreader with Lachesis Publishing & Glasshouse Publishing; member of the Editors' Assn. of Canada and The Word Guild. Detailed edit $3-5/pg. or .012-.02/wd. Proofread: $2/pg or .008/wd. Manuscript critique: $25 up to 50 pgs.; $50 for 50-100 pgs.; $75 for 100 pgs. or more. See Website for details.

WENDY M. MCNEICE, PO Box 656, Capalaba QLD 4157, Australia. Phone 042 787 0330. Fax 07 32072263 (call first, Eastern Standard Time). E-mail: scribe@scribeofspirit.com. Website: www .scribeofspirit.com. E-mail contact. GH/CA/writing coach. Multi-award-winning writer, columnist in international magazine; BA; Graduate Diploma Info Services; Graduate Diploma Ed.

WENDY SARGEANT, PO Box 656, Capalaba, QLD 4157, Australia. Tel. 0427 870 330. E-mail: word fisher52@gmail.com. Website: www.editorsqld.com/freelance/Wendy_Sargeant.htm. E-mail contact. GE/LC/GH/CA/B/NL/SP/WS (writing & evaluation)/PP/instructional design/writing coach. Edits A/SS/F/ N/NB/BP/JN/PB/QL/BS/GB/TM/E/D/S/copywriting. Special interests: technical material, business humor, children's books, educational books (primary, secondary, tertiary, and above), fiction, history, legal. Manuscript assessor and instructional designer with The Writing School. Award-winning author published in major newspapers and magazines. Editing educational manuals. Project officer and instructional designer for Global Education Project, United Nationals Assoc. Information specialist for Australian National University. Charges $55/hr for articles/short stories; .02/wd. for copywriting; $300-400+ for book assessment.

13

Christian Literary Agents

The references in these listings to "published authors" refer to those who have had one or more books published by royalty publishers or who have been published regularly in periodicals. If a listing indicates that the agent is "recognized in the industry," it means he or she has worked with the Christian publishers long enough to be recognized by editors as credible agents.

Do not assume that because an agent is listed below, I can personally vouch for him or her. I am not able to check out each one as thoroughly as you need to. Asking editors and other writers at writers' conferences is a great way to find a good, reliable agent. You might also want to visit www.agentresearch.com and www.sfwa.org/beware/agents.html for tips on finding an agent. For a database of more than 500 agencies, go to www.literaryagent.com.

Finally, at the site for the Association of Authors' Representatives, www.aaronline.org, you will find a list of agents who don't charge fees, except for office expenses. Their Website will also provide information on how to receive a list of approved agents. Some of the listings below indicate which agents belong to the Association of Authors' Representatives, Inc. Those members have subscribed to a set code of ethics. Lack of such a designation, however, does not indicate the agent is unethical; most Christian agents are not members. If they do happen to be members, it should give you an extra measure of confidence.

+ Indicates a new listing

AGENT RESEARCH & EVALUATION INC., 425 N. 20th St., Philadelphia PA 19130. (215) 563-1867. Fax (215) 563-6797. E-mail: info@agentresearch.com. Website: www.agentresearch.info. This is not an agency but a service that tracks the public record of literary agents and helps authors use the data to obtain effective literary representation. Charges fee for this service. Offers a free "agent verification" service at the site. (Answers the question of whether or not the agent has created a public record of sales.) Also offers a newsletter, *Talking Agents* e-zine, free if you send your e-mail address. See Jerry Jenkins's comments on this service on their Website, in the "Story So Far" section.

ALIVE COMMUNICATIONS, 7680 Goddard St., Ste. 200, Colorado Springs CO 80920. (719) 260-7080. Fax (719) 260-8223. E-mail: submissions@alivecom.com. Website: www.alivecom.com. Agents: Rick Christian, president; Lee Hough, Joel Kneedler. Well known in the industry. Estab. 1989. Represents 100+ clients. New clients on referral only. Handles adult & teen novels and nonfiction, gift books, crossover and general-market books. Deals in both Christian (70 percent) and general market (30 percent). Member Author's Guild & AAR.
> **Contact:** E-mail to: submissions@alivecom.com. Responds in 6 wks. to referrals; may not respond to unsolicited submissions.
> **Commission:** 15 percent.
> **Fees:** Only extraordinary costs with client's pre-approval; no review/reading fee.
> **Tips:** If you have a referral, send material by mail, and be sure to mark envelope "Requested Material." Unable to return unsolicited materials.

AMBASSADOR AGENCY, PO Box 50358, Nashville TN 37205. (615) 370-4700, ext. 230. E-mail: Wes@AmbassadorAgency.com. Website: www.AmbassadorAgency.com. Agent: Wes Yoder. Estab. 1973. Recognized in the industry. Represents 25 clients. Open to unpublished authors and new clients. Handles adult nonfiction, crossover books. Also has a Speakers Bureau.

Contact: E-mail.

AUTHORCOACHING.COM, PO Box 428, Newburg PA 17240. (717) 423-6621. Fax (717) 423-6944. E-mail: keith@authorcoaching.com. Website: www.AuthorCoaching.com. Coach: Keith Carroll. Estab. 2000. An agent/coaching service. Works with all inspirational authors.

Contact: By letter, fax, phone, e-mail.

Fees: Visit Website for detailed description of fees.

BENREY LITERARY, PO Box 12721, New Bern NC 28561. (252) 638-5787. E-mail: janet@benrey literary.com. Website: www.BenreyLiterary.com. Agents: Ron & Janet Benrey. Estab. 2006. Recognized in the industry. Represents 30+ clients. Prefers referrals from current clients, or to meet writers at writers' conferences. Handles adult religious/inspirational novels (romance, contemporary women's, mystery, true crime); nonfiction (Christian living); general (thriller or cozy).

Contact: Requires e-queries.

Commission: 15 percent; foreign 20 percent.

BOOKS & SUCH/JANET KOBOBEL GRANT, 52 Mission Circle, Ste. 122, PMB 170, Santa Rosa CA 95409-5370. (707) 538-4184. E-mail: representation@booksandsuch.biz. Website: www.books andsuch.biz. Agents: Janet Kobobel Grant, Wendy Lawton, Etta Wilson, Rachel Zurakowski. Well recognized in industry. Estab. 1997. Member of AAR. Represents 150 clients. Open to new or unpublished authors (with recommendation only). Handles fiction and nonfiction for all ages, picture books, gift books, crossover, and general books.

Contact: E-mail query (no attachments); no phone query. Accepts simultaneous submissions. Responds in 6-8 wks.

Commission: 15 percent.

Fees: No fees.

Tips: "Especially looking for nonfiction. Also historical fiction for adults."

CURTIS BROWN LTD., 10 Astor Pl., New York NY 10003-6935. (212) 473-5400. Agents: Maureen Walters, Laura Blake Peterson, and Ginger Knowlton. Member AAR. General agent; handles religious/inspirational novels for all ages, adult nonfiction, and crossover books.

Contact: Query with SASE; no fax/e-query. Submit outline or sample chapters. Responds in 4 wks. to query; 8 wks. to ms.

Fees: Charges for photocopying & some postage.

BROWNE & MILLER LITERARY ASSOCIATES, 410 S. Michigan Ave., Ste. 460, Chicago IL 60605. (312) 922-3063. Fax (312) 922-1905. E-mail: mail@browneandmiller.com. Website: www.browne andmiller.com. Agent: Danielle Egan-Miller. Estab. 1971. Recognized in the industry. Represents 75+ clients, mostly general, but also select Christian fiction writers. Open to new clients and talented unpublished authors, but most interested in experienced novelists looking for highly professional, full-service representation including rights management. Handles teen and adult fiction, adult nonfiction, and gift books for the general market; adult Christian fiction only. Member AAR, RWA, MWA, and The Author's Guild.

Contact: E-query to mail@browneandmiller.com, or mailed query letter/SASE.

Commission: 15 percent, foreign 20 percent.

PEMA BROWNE LTD., 11 Tena Pl., Valley Cottage NY 10989-2215. (845) 268-0029. E-mail: ppbltd@ optonline.net. Website: www.pemabrowneltd.com. Agent: Pema Browne. Recognized in industry. Estab. 1966. Represents 20 clients (2 religious). Open to unpublished authors; very few new clients at this time. Handles novels and nonfiction for all ages; picture books/novelty books, gift books, crossover books. Only accepts mss not previously sent to publishers; no simultaneous submissions. Responds in 6-8 wks.

Contact: Letter query with credentials; no phone, fax, or e-query. Must include SASE. No simultaneous submissions. No attachments.

Commission: 20 percent U.S. & foreign; illustrators 30 percent.

Fees: None.

Tips: "Check at the library in reference section, in Books in Print, for books similar to yours. Have good literary skills, neat presentation. Know what has been published and research the genre that interests you."

CASTIGLIA LITERARY AGENCY, 1155 Camino del Mar, Ste. 510, Del Mar CA 92014. (858) 755-8761. Fax (858) 755-7063. E-mail: JacLAgency@aol.com. Agents: Julie Castiglia and Sally Van Haitsma. Estab. 1993. Recognized in the industry. Represents 50 clients. Open to unpublished authors (with credentials) and selected new clients by referrals from editors, clients, or published professionals. Handles adult spiritual/inspirational nonfiction, Christian fiction, gift books, and general books. Member AAR.

Contact: Letter only/SASE. No phone/fax/e-query.

Commission: 15 percent; 25 percent foreign.

Fees: For excessive postage and copying, FedEx or messenger service.

Tips: "I do not look at unsolicited manuscripts. We represent books which appeal to the Christian book audience, but we don't specialize in the Christian book market."

DONNA COFFEN, LITERARY AGENT/PUBLICIST, PO Box 822, Huntsville TX 77342. (936) 291-2220. E-mail: admin@literaryagentpublicist.com. Website: www.literaryagentpublicist.com. Agent: Donna Coffen. Estab. 2006. Represents 3 clients. Open to unpublished authors and new clients (in Texas only). Handles novels & nonfiction for all ages, picture books, poetry books, articles, short stories, poetry.

Contact: By letter, phone, or e-mail. Accepts simultaneous submissions. Responds in 4 wks.

Commission: 15 percent; foreign 20 percent.

Fees: Charges a $35 reading fee.

Note: Currently only accepting Texas-based authors.

THE BLYTHE DANIEL AGENCY INC., PO Box 64197, Colorado Springs CO 80962-4197. (719) 213-3427. E-mail: blythe@theblythedanielagency.com. Website: www.theblythedanielagency.com. Agent: Blythe Daniel. Recognized in the industry. Estab. 2005. Represents 20 clients. Open to unpublished authors with a platform and previously published authors. Handles adult religious/inspirational novels, adult nonfiction, limited children's books, and crossover books.

Contact: By e-mail or mail. Accepts simultaneous submissions. Responds in 3 weeks.

Commission: 15 percent; foreign 20 percent.

Fees: Agreed-upon expenses outside normal expenses.

Also: Provides publicity and marketing campaigns to clients as a separate service from literary representation.

Tips: "Preferences are authors who have a solid proposal on the topic of their book, including research on their audience, comparison to competitor's books, why they want to write on the topic, and what the author uniquely brings to the topic. Authors need to have a marketing plan to promote their book and the ability to promote their own book. Currently only handling a minimal number of new clients."

DANIEL LITERARY GROUP, 1701 Kingsbury Dr., Ste. 100, Nashville TN 37215. (615) 730-8207. E-mail: greg@danielliterarygroup.com. Website: www.danielliterarygroup.com. Agent: Greg Daniel. Estab. 2007. Recognized in the Industry. Represents 35 clients. Open to unpublished authors and new clients. Handles adult religious/inspirational novels & nonfiction, crossover & secular books.

Contact: E-mail only. Accepts simultaneous submissions. Responds in 3 wks.

Commission: 15 percent; foreign 20 percent.

Fees: None.

JAN DENNIS LITERARY SERVICES, 19350 Glen Hollow Cir., Monument CO 80132. (719) 559-1711. E-mail: jpdennislit@msn.com. Agent: Jan Dennis. Estab. 1995. Represents 20 clients. Open to unpublished authors and new clients. Handles teen/YA & adult religious/inspirational novels, adult nonfiction, crossover, and general books.

DYSTEL & GODERICH LITERARY MANAGEMENT INC., 1 Union Square W., Ste. 904, New York NY 10003. (212) 627-9100. Fax (212) 627-9313. E-mail: Miriam@dystel.com. Website: www.dystel .com. Agents: Jane Dystel, Miriam Goderich, Stacey Glick, Michael Bourret, Jim McCarthy, and Lauren Abramo. Estab. 1994. Recognized in the industry. Represents 5-10 religious book clients. Open to unpublished authors and new clients. Handles fiction and nonfiction for adults, gift books, general books, crossover books. Member AAR.

Contact: Query letter with bio. Brief e-query; no simultaneous queries. Responds to queries in 3-5 wks.; submissions in 2 mos.

Commission: 15 percent; foreign 19 percent.

Fees: Photocopying is author's responsibility.

Tips: "Send a professional, well-written query to a specific agent."

EAMES LITERARY SERVICES, 4117 Hillsboro Rd., Ste. 251, Nashville TN 37215. (615) 403-3550. Fax (615) 463-9361. E-mail: info@eamesliterary.com. Website: www.eamesliterary.com. Agents: John Eames (John@eamesliterary.com). Open to unpublished authors and new clients. Handles adult & teen religious/inspirational novels & adult nonfiction. Guidelines on Website.

Contact: By e-mail.

Commission: 15 percent.

Fees: None.

EPIC LITERARY AGENCY. 7107 S. Yale Ave., #327, Tulsa OK 74136. (918) 267-3248. E-mail: KevinD@EpicLiterary.com, or info@EpicLiterary.com. Website: www.EpicLiterary.com. Agent: Kevin D. Decker. Estab. 1996. Represents up to 12 clients. Not currently open to unpublished authors; possibly open to new clients. Handles children's novels & nonfiction, picture books, screenplays, TV/movie scripts, gift books, crossover books.

Contact: Submissions by invitation only.

Commission: 15 percent; foreign 20 percent.

Fees: Charges only for special travel or out-of-ordinary expenses.

Tips: "Please query first; we do not accept unsolicited manuscripts."

FINE PRINT LITERARY MANAGEMENT, 240 W. 35th St., Ste. 500, New York NY 10001. (212) 279-1282. Fax (212) 279-0927. E-mail: peter@fineprintlit.com. Website: www.fineprintlit.com. Agent: Peter Rubie and 7 other agents. Open to unpublished authors and new clients. General agent. Handles adult religion/spirituality nonfiction for teens & adults.

Contact: Query/SASE; accepts e-query. Responds in 2-3 mos.

Commission: 15 percent; foreign 20 percent.

SAMUEL FRENCH INC., 45 W. 25th St., New York NY 10010-2751. (212) 206-8990. Fax (212) 206-1429. E-mail: publications@samuelfrench.com. Website: www.samuelfrench.com, www.bakers plays.com. Agent: Roxane Heinze-Bradshaw. Estab. 1830. Open to new clients. Handles rights to some religious/inspirational stage plays. Owns a subsidiary company that also publishes religious plays.

Contact: Query online or by mail. See Website for full submission information. Accepts simultaneous submissions; responds in 10 wks.
Commission: Varies.
Fees: None.

+ GLOBAL TALENT REPS, INC./NATIONAL WRITERS LITERARY AGENCY, 3140 S. Peoria St. #295, Aurora CO 80014. (720) 851-1959. E-mail: a.whelchel@globaltalentreps.com. Website: www .globaltalentreps.com. Agent: Andrew J. Whelchel III. Estab. 1982. Recognized in the industry. Open to unpublished authors and new clients. Handles religious/inspirational novels for all ages, nonfiction for teens & adults, screenplays, movie scripts, gift books, and crossover/secular books.
Contact: Query by e-mail. Accepts simultaneous submissions; responds in 8 wks.
Commission: 10% film; 15% books; 5% scouting.
Fees: Postage charged to new, unknown authors.

SANFORD J. GREENBURGER ASSOCIATES INC., 55 Fifth Ave., New York NY 10003. (212) 206-5600. Fax (212) 463-8718. Website: www.greenburger.com. Agents: Heide Lange, Dan Mandel, Matthew Bialer, Jeremy Katz, Tricia Davey, Courtney Miller-Callihan. Estab. 1945. Represents 500 clients. Open to unpublished authors and new clients. General agent; handles adult religious/inspirational nonfiction. Member of AAR.
Contact: Query/proposal/3 sample chapters to Heide Lange by mail with SASE, or by fax; no e-query. Accepts simultaneous queries. Responds in 6-8 wks. to query; 2 mos. to ms.
Commission: 15 percent; foreign 20 percent.
Fees: Charges for photocopying and foreign submissions.

HARTLINE LITERARY AGENCY, 123 Queenston Dr., Pittsburgh PA 15235. (412) 829-2483. Fax (888) 279-6007. E-mail: joyce@hartlineliterary.com. Website: www.hartlineliterary.com. Agents: Joyce A. Hart, adult novels (romance, mystery/suspense, women's fiction) & nonfiction; Tamela Hancock Murray, adult fiction (romance, mystery/suspense, women's) and nonfiction, tamela@ hartlineliterary.com; Terry Burns, adult fiction & nonfiction, YA, terry@hartlineliterary.com; Diana Flegal, adult novels & nonfiction, diana@hartlineliterary.com. Recognized in industry. Estab. 1992. Represents 150+ clients. Open to new clients. Handles teen/young-adult novels, adult nonfiction, gift books. No poetry.
Contact: E-mail/phone/letter; e-mail preferred. Accepts simultaneous submissions; responds in 6-8 wks.
Commission: 15 percent; foreign 20 percent; films 20 percent & 25 percent.
Fees: Office expenses (very few); no reading fee.
Tips: "Please look at our Website before submitting. Guidelines are listed, along with detailed information about each agent. Be sure to include your biography and publishing history with your proposal. The author/agent relationship is a team effort. Working together we can make sure your manuscript gets the exposure and attention it deserves."

JEFF HERMAN AGENCY, PO Box 1522, Stockbridge MA 01262. (413) 298-0077. Fax (413) 298-8188. E-mail: Jeff@jeffherman.com. Website: www.jeffherman.com. Agents: Jeff Herman and Deborah Herman. Estab. 1987. Recognized in the industry. Represents 20+ clients with religious books. Open to unpublished authors and new clients. Handles adult nonfiction (recovery/healing, spirituality), gift books, general books, crossover.
Contact: Query by mail/SASE, or by e-mail or fax. Accepts simultaneous submissions & e-queries.
Commission: 15 percent; foreign 10 percent.
Fees: No reading or management fees; just copying and shipping.
Tips: "I love a good book from the heart. Have faith that you will accomplish what has been appointed to you."

HIDDEN VALUE GROUP, 1240 E. Ontario Ave., Ste. 102-148, Corona CA 92881. Phone/fax (951) 549-8891. E-mail: bookquery@hiddenvaluegroup.com. Website: www.HiddenValueGroup.com. Agents: Jeff Jernigan & Nancy Jernigan. Estab. 2001. Recognized in the industry. Represents 20+ clients with religious books. Open to previously published authors only. Handles adult novels & nonfiction, gift books, and crossover books. No poetry, articles, or short stories.

  Contact: Letter or e-mail. Accepts simultaneous submissions. Responds in 3-4 wks.
  Commission: 15 percent; foreign 15 percent.
  Fees: None.
  Tips: "Women's nonfiction is of great interest. Make sure the proposal includes author bio, 2 sample chapters, and manuscript summary."

HORNFISCHER LITERARY MANAGEMENT, PO Box 50544, Austin TX 78763. E-mail: queries@ hornfischerlit.com or jim@hornfischerlit.com. Website: www.hornfischerlit.com. Agent: James D. Hornfischer. Estab. 2001. Represents 45 clients. Open to unpublished authors and new clients (with referrals from clients). Considers simultaneous submissions. Responds in 1 mo. General agent; handles adult religious/inspirational nonfiction.

  Contact: E-query only for fiction; query or proposal for nonfiction (proposal package, outline, and 2 sample chapters). Considers simultaneous queries. Responds to queries in 5-6 wks.
  Commission: 15 percent; foreign 25 percent.

ANDREA HURST LITERARY MANAGEMENT, 5050 Laguna Blvd., Ste. 112-330, Elk Grove CA 95758. (916) 686-1995. E-mail: judy@andreahurst.com. Website: www.andreahurst.com. Agent: Judy Mikalonis. Handles adult nonfiction (Christian and mainstream), YA fiction (Christian & mainstream), adult fiction (Christian & contemporary only). No end-times, romance, historical, science fiction, or demon/vampire-centered fiction.

  Contact: E-mail queries only.
  Commission: 15 percent.
  Tips: "Fiction authors must be previously published in the traditional market to be considered. Nonfiction authors must have a strong platform."

+ D. C. JACOBSON & ASSOCIATES, 473 West Hood Ave., Ste. 105, Sisters OR 97759. (541) 549-3585. Fax (541) 549-1785. E-mail: query@dcjacobson.com. Website: www.dcjacobson.com. Agents: Don Jacobson & Jenni Burke. Estab. 2006. Represents 20+ clients. Recognized in the industry (former owner of Multnomah Publishers). Open to unpublished authors & new clients. Handles adult & teen religious/inspirational novels & nonfiction, crossover books.

  Contact: Submissions & queries through Website form only. Accepts simultaneous submissions; responds in 2-5 wks.
  Commission: 15 percent.
  Fees: No reading fees.
  Services: Offers literary consulting services on a fee basis to nonrepresented clients.
  Tips: "Looking for fresh messages to renew the church and redeem the culture for Christ. Please review our Website thoroughly before using our submission form."

WILLIAM K. JENSEN LITERARY AGENCY, 119 Bampton Ct., Eugene OR 97404. Phone/fax (541) 688-1612. E-mail: queries@wkjagency.com. Website: www.wkjagency.com. Agent: William K. Jensen. Estab. 2005. Recognized in the industry. Represents 38 clients. Open to unpublished authors and new clients. Handles adult fiction (no science fiction or fantasy), nonfiction for all ages, picture books, gift books, crossover books.

  Contact: E-mail only. Accepts simultaneous submissions. Responds in 12 wks.
  Commission: 15 percent.
  Fees: No fees.

NATASHA KERN LITERARY AGENCY INC., PO Box 1069, White Salmon WA 98672. Website: www .natashakern.com. Agent: Natasha Kern. Well-recognized member of Author's Guild, ACFW, RWA. Estab. 1987. Represents 36 religious clients. Open to unpublished authors and new clients. Handles adult religious/inspirational fiction (romance, romantic suspense, women's fiction, historical fiction, mystery, suspense, thrillers, & general market novels).

Contact: Accepts e-queries at: queries@natashakern.com only; 3-pg. synopsis & 1 chapter. Responds in 2-4 wks. to queries. Also meets at conferences or through current clients.

Commission: 15 percent; 20 percent foreign (includes foreign-agent commission).

Fees: No reading fee.

Tips: "I have personally sold over 900 books, many of them bestsellers and award winners. See submission guidelines on our Website before sending a query—we read everyone."

K J LITERARY SERVICES, LLC, 1540 Margaret Ave., Grand Rapids MI 49507. (616) 551-9797. E-mail: kim@kjliteraryservices.com. Website: www.kjliteraryservices.com. Agent: Kim Zeilstra.

Contact: E-query preferred; phone query OK.

Commission: 15 percent.

Tips: "Taking new authors by referral only."

THE STEVE LAUBE AGENCY, 5025 N. Central Ave., #635, Phoenix AZ 85012-1502. (602) 336-8910. E-mail: info@stevelaube.com. Website: www.stevelaube.com. Agent: Steve Laube. Estab. 2004. Well recognized in the industry. Represents 60+ clients. Open to new and unpublished authors. Handles adult Christian fiction and nonfiction, history, theology, how-to, health, Christian living. No YA, children's books, or poetry. Accepts simultaneous submissions. Responds in 6-8 wks.

Contact: Letter with proposal and sample chapters by mail is preferred; use guidelines on Website. No e-queries.

Commission: 15 percent; foreign 20 percent.

Fees: No fees.

Tips: "Looking for fresh and innovative ideas. Make sure your proposal contains an excellent presentation."

LEVINE GREENBERG LITERARY AGENCY INC., 307—7th Ave., Ste. 2407, New York NY 10001. (212) 337-0934. Fax (212) 337-0948. Website: www.levinegreenberg.com. Agent: James Levine. Agent: Arielle Eckstut. Estab. 1989. Represents 250 clients. Open to unpublished authors and new clients. General agent; handles adult religious/inspirational nonfiction. Member AAR.

Contact: See guidelines/submission form on Website; prefers e-query.

Commission: 15 percent; foreign 20 percent.

Fees: Office expenses.

Tips: "Our specialties include spirituality and religion."

THE LITERARY GROUP INTL., The Stanford Bldg., 51 E. 25th St., Ste., 401, New York NY 10010. (212) 274-1616. Fax (212) 274-9876. E-mail: js@theliterarygroup.com. Website: www.theliterary group.com. Agent: Frank Weimann. Recognized in the industry. Estab. 1986. Represents 300 clients (120 for religious books). Open to new clients and unpublished authors. Handles fiction and non-fiction for all ages, picture books, general, and crossover.

Contact: Letter.

Commission: 15 percent; foreign 20 percent.

Fees: No fees.

Tips: "Looking for fresh, original spiritual fiction and nonfiction. We offer a written contract which may be canceled after 30 days."

LITERARY MANAGEMENT GROUP, LLC, PO Box 40965, Nashville TN 37204. (615) 812-4445. E-mail: brucebarbour@literarymanagementgroup.com. Website: www.literarymanagementgroup .com. Agents: Bruce R. Barbour & Margaret Langstaff. Estab. 1995. Well recognized in the industry.

Represents 100+ clients. Open to published authors who have a platform and a compelling story or idea. Handles nonfiction only. Other services offered: book packaging and consulting.

Contact: E-mail preferred. Will review proposals, no unsolicited mss.

Commission: 15 percent; foreign 20 percent.

Fees: No fees or expenses on agented books.

Tips: "Follow guidelines, proposal outline, and submissions format on Website. Use Microsoft Word. Study the market and know where your book will fit in."

+ **LIVING WORD LITERARY AGENCY**, PO Box 40974, Eugene OR 97404. phone: 541.683.6567. E-mail: livingwordliterary@gmail.com. Blog: www.livingwordliterary.wordpress.com; Agent: Kimberly Shumate. Estab. 2009. 12 years of publishing experience in sales and editorial. Open to new and unpublished authors. Handles adult fiction (no science fiction or fantasy), YA fiction, Christian living, marriage, parenting, self-help, apologetics, health, inspirational, environmental, social issues, pop-culture, women's issues, and men's issues. No cookbooks, children's books, memoirs, or poetry, please.

Contact: Accepts simultaneous submissions. Responds in 1-2 weeks. Initial email query only. No phone calls or snail mail. See guidelines on Website.

Commission: 15 percent; foreign 20 percent.

Fees: No fees.

Tips: 'Looking for creative, relevant material. I'm all about the underdog, so don't be shy."

STERLING LORD LITERISTIC, INC., 65 Bleecker St., New York NY 10012. (213) 780-6050. Fax (212) 780-6095. E-mail: claudia@sll.com, or info@sll.com. Website: www.sll.com. Agent: Claudia Cross. Recognized in the industry. Represents 10 clients with religious books. Open to unpublished clients with referrals and to new clients. Handles adult and teen Christian fiction, spiritual adult nonfiction, gift books, crossover books, general books.

Contact: Letter, fax or (e-query with referral only). Accepts simultaneous submissions, if informed. Responds in 4-6 wks.

Commission: 15 percent; foreign 20 percent.

Fees: "We charge for photocopy costs for mss or any costs above and beyond the usual cost of doing business."

MACGREGOR LITERARY, 2373 N.W. 185th Ave., Ste. 165, Hillsboro OR 97124. Website: www .MacGregorLiterary.com. Agents: Chip MacGregor & Sandra Bishop. Estab. 2006. Recognized in the industry. Represents 60 clients. Open to unpublished authors and new clients with referral from current client. Handles adult religious/inspirational novels, nonfiction, & crossover books.

Contact: E-mail query to: submissions@macgregorliterary.com. Accepts simultaneous submissions. Responds in 4 wks.

Commission: 15 percent; foreign 20 percent.

Fees: No fees or expenses.

Tips: "We represent books that make a difference. Working with a list of established authors, we are always looking for strong nonfiction projects in a variety of genres. Please check the Website before submitting."

MANUS & ASSOCIATES LITERARY AGENCY, 425 Sherman Ave., Ste. 200, Palo Alto CA 94306. (650) 470-5151. Fax (650) 470-5159. E-mail: manuslit@manuslit.com. Website: www.manuslit .com. Agents: Jillian Manus, Penny Nelson, Dena Fischer, and Jandy Nelson. Members AAR. Estab. 1994. Open to unpublished authors and new clients. Handles adult religious/inspirational novels & nonfiction, gift books, crossover/secular books.

Contact: Query by mail/fax/e-query (no attachments). For fiction, send first 30 pages, bio, and SASE. For nonfiction, send proposal/sample chapters. Responds in 12 weeks. Will respond only when interested.

Commission: 15 percent; foreign 20-25 percent.

WILLIAM MORRIS LITERARY AGENCY, 1325 Avenue of the Americas, New York NY 10019. (212) 586-5100. Fax (212) 246-3583. E-mail: vs@wma.com. Website: www.wma.com. Agent: Valerie Summers. Recognized in the industry. Estab. 1898. Hundreds of clients with religious books. Not open to unpublished authors or new clients. Handles all types of material. Member AAR.

> **Contact:** Send query/synopsis, publication history by mail/SASE. No fax/e-query. No unsolicited mss.
> **Commission:** 15 percent; foreign 20 percent.
> **Fees:** None.

NAPPALAND LITERARY AGENCY, PO Box 1674, Loveland CO 80539. (970) 635-0641. Fax (970) 635-9869. E-mail: literary@nappaland.com. Website: www.nappaland.com/literary. Division of Nappaland Communications Inc. Agent: Mike Nappa. Estab. 1995. Recognized in the industry. Represents 10 clients. Not open to unpublished authors; open to new clients only by referral from a current Nappaland author. Handles literary nonfiction, cultural concerns, Christian living, women's issues, suspense fiction, and women's fiction.

> **Contact:** By e-mail. Accepts simultaneous submissions; responds in 8-10 wks. Unsolicited queries are automatically rejected.
> **Commission:** 15 percent.
> **Fees:** None.
> **Tips:** "Cold queries just don't work—so don't send them. The only way we will consider a new author is if that person is somehow associated with—and recommended by—a current Nappaland author."

+ NASHVILLE AGENCY, PO Box 110909, Nashville TN 37222. Toll-free (866) 333-8663. (615) 263-4143. E-mail: submissions@thenashvilleagency.com. Website: www.thenashvilleagency.com. Agent: Jonathan Clements. Handles adult inspirational novels & nonfiction.

> **Contact:** E-mail query. Responds in 6 wks.

NUNN COMMUNICATIONS INC., 1612 Ginger Dr., Carrollton TX 75007. (972) 394-NUNN (6866). E-mail: info@nunncommunications.com. Website: www.nunncommunications.com. Agent: Leslie Nunn Reed. Estab. 1995. Represents 20 clients. Recognized in the industry. Not open to unpublished authors. Handles adult nonfiction, gift books, crossover books, and general books.

> **Contact:** By e-mail. Responds in 4-6 wks.
> **Commission:** 15 percent.
> **Fees:** Charges office expenses if over $100.

ALLEN O'SHEA LITERARY AGENCY, LLC., 615 Westover Rd., Stamford CT 06902. (203) 359-9965. E-mail: Marilyn@allenoshea.com. Website: www.allenoshea.com. Agents: Marilyn Allen and Coleen O'Shea. Estab. 2003. Represents 4 clients with religious books. Recognized in the industry. Open to unpublished authors (with credentials & platform) and new clients. Handles adult nonfiction.

> **Contact:** Query by mail or e-mail. No simultaneous submissions. Responds in 4 wks.
> **Commission:** 15 percent; foreign 15-25 percent.
> **Fees:** For overseas mailing.
> **Tips:** "We specifically like practical nonfiction."

KATHI J. PATON LITERARY AGENCY, PO Box 2240, New York NY 10101-2240. (212) 265-6586. E-mail: KJPLitBiz@optonline.net. Website: www.PatonLiterary.com. Agent: Kathi Paton. Estab. 1987. Handles adult nonfiction Christian life and issues.

> **Contact:** Prefers e-mail query.
> **Commission:** 15 percent; foreign 20 percent.
> **Fees:** For photocopying & postal submissions.

PATRICK-MEDBERRY ASSOCIATES, 25379 Wayne Mills Pl., #155, Valencia CA 91355. (661) 251-4428. E-mail: patrickmedberry@sbcglobal.net. Agents: Peggy Patrick & C. J. Medberry. Estab. 2005. Management & production company specializing in Christian writers, directors, and producers, as well as religious and inspirational novels, screenplays, TV/movie scripts, crossover books, general books, and screenplays. Open to unpublished authors and new clients.

Contact: Query by letter, fax, or e-mail; no calls.
Commission: 10 percent.
Fees: None.

+ PELHAM LITERARY AGENCY, PMB 315, 2650 Jamacha Rd., Ste. 147, El Cajon CA 92019. (619) 447-4468. E-mail: jmeals@pelhamliterary.com. Website: www.pelhamliterary.com. Agents: Howard Pelham and Jim Meals. Recognized in the industry. Estab. 1993. Open to unpublished authors and new clients. Handles adult and teen religious/inspirational novels & nonfiction, crossover books.

Contact: Brief query letter; e-query OK. Provides a list of published clients and titles. Accepts simultaneous submissions. Responds in 6 wks.
Commission: 15%; foreign 20%.
Fees: Charges for postage and copying only. Offers an optional extensive critique for $200. Information on Website.
Tips: We are actively seeking writers for Christian fiction market, but also open to nonfiction. We specialize in genre fiction and enjoy working with new authors."

+ THE QUADRIVIUM GROUP, 7512 Dr. Phillips Blvd., Ste. 50-229, Orlando FL 32819. (407) 516-1857. Website: www.TheQuadriviumGroup.com. Agents: Steve Blount (SteveBlount@TheQuadrivium Group.com); Susan Blount (SusanBlount@TheQuadriviumGroup.com). Estab. 2006. Represents 20-30 clients. Recognized in the industry. Open to a limited number of unpublished authors (with credentials, platform, compelling story/idea), and to new clients (mostly by referral). General agent. Handles Christian and general fiction and nonfiction for all ages, gift books, crossover books. Other services offered: consulting on book sales and distribution.

Contact: E-mail preferred; responds in 2-4 wks.
Commission: 15 percent; foreign 20 percent.
Fees: Only extraordinary costs with client's permission.

+ RED WRITING HOOD INK, 2075 Attala Rd. 1990, Kosciusko MS 39090. (662) 674-0636. Fax (209) 653-0636. E-mail: rwhi@bellsouth.net. Website: www.redwritinghoodink.net. Agent: Sheri Ables. Estab. 1997. Represents 4 clients with religious books. Recognized in the industry. Open to unpublished authors with strong platform; open to new clients. Handles novels & nonfiction for teens/young adults/adults; gift books; crossover books; some general titles.

Contact: No simultaneous submissions; responds in 3-4 weeks to e-mail; 1-6 months for postal, depending on backlog.
Commission: 15 percent; foreign 20 percent.

RLR ASSOCIATES, LTD., Literary Dept., 7 W. 51st St., New York NY 10019. (212) 541-8641. Fax (212) 541-6052. Also has a California office. E-mail: sgould@rlrassociates.net. Website: www.rlr literary.net. Scott Gould, literary assoc. Estab. 1972. Represents 50+ clients. Open to unpublished authors and new clients. General agency; handles adult religious/inspirational nonfiction.

Contact: Query with SASE. Considers simultaneous submissions. Responds in 5 wks.
Commission: 15 percent; foreign 20 percent.

ROSENBAUM & ASSOCIATES LITERARY AGENCY, PO Box 277, Brentwood TN 37024-0277. (615) 834-8564. Fax (615) 834-8560. E-mail: bucky@rosenbaumagency.com. Website: www.rosen baumagency.com. Agent: Bucky Rosenbaum. Estab. 2006. Well recognized in the industry. Represents 30-40 clients. Open to a limited number of new clients and unpublished authors by referral only. Handles mostly adult nonfiction and some general books, crossover books.

Contact: Unpublished query by mail/SASE; published authors by phone or e-mail. No simultaneous submissions; responds in 6-8 wks.
Commission: 15 percent; foreign 10 percent, plus subagent commission.
Fees: Only extraordinary costs with client's permission; no reading fees.
Tips: "Request a product proposal template by e-mail."

GAIL ROSS LITERARY AGENCY, 1666 Connecticut Ave. N.W., #500, Washington DC 20009. (202) 328-3282. Fax (202) 328-9162. E-mail: jennifer@gailross.com. Website: www.gailross.com. Contact: Jennifer Manguera. Estab. 1988. Represents 200 clients. Open to unpublished authors and new clients (mostly through referrals). General agent; handles adult religious/inspirational nonfiction, history, health, and business books.
Contact: Query with outline, sample pages, résumé/SASE; no e-query. Accepts simultaneous queries.
Commission: 15 percent; foreign 25 percent.
Fees: Office expenses.

CAROL SUSAN ROTH LITERARY & CREATIVE, PO Box 620337, Woodside CA 94062. (650) 323-3795. E-mail: carol@authorsbest.com. Website: www.AuthorsBest.com. Agent: Carol Susan Roth. Recognized in the industry. Estab. 1996. Represents 75 clients. Open to unpublished authors and new clients. Handles adult religious/inspirational nonfiction, gift books, crossover, general, health, science & spirit (no fiction or memoirs).
Contact: Query by e-mail with your pitch, author bio, and platform (no attachments).
Commission: 15 percent.
Fees: None. "I do make referrals out to ghostwriters and publicists upon request."
Tips: "We are interested in working with experts who are interested in developing many books. One of my first-time authors has sold 150,000 copies of *Glimpses of Heaven*."

DAMARIS ROWLAND AGENCY, 420 E. 23rd St., Apt. 6F, New York NY 10010-5040. (212) 475-8942. Cell (917) 538-3916. Fax (212) 358-9411. Agent: Damaris Rowland. Estab. 1994. Represents 40 clients. Open to unpublished authors and new clients. No New Age material. Very selective.
Contact: Query letter.
Commission: 15 percent; foreign 20 percent.
Fees: Some office expenses.

SCHIAVONE LITERARY AGENCY INC., 236 Trails End, West Palm Beach FL 33413-2135. Phone/fax (561) 966-9294. E-mail: profschia@aol.com. Website: www.publishersmarketplace.com/members/profschia. Agent: James Schiavone, EdD. Recognized in the industry. Estab. 1997. Represents 6 clients. Open to unpublished and new clients. Handles adult, teen, and children's fiction and nonfiction; celebrity biography; general books; crossover books.
Contact: Query letter/SASE; one-page e-mail query (no attachments).
Commission: 15 percent, foreign 20 percent.
Fees: No reading fees; authors pay postage only.
Tips: Works primarily with published authors; will consider first-time authors with excellent material. Actively seeking books on spirituality, major religions, and alternative health. Very selective on first novels.

SERENDIPITY LITERARY AGENCY, LLC, 305 Gates Ave., Brooklyn NY 11216. (718) 230-7689. Fax (718) 230-7829. E-mail: rbrooks@serendipitylit.com. Website: www.serendipitylit.com. Agent: Regina Brooks. Member AAR. Estab. 2000. Represents 50 clients; 3 with religious books. Recognized in the industry. Open to unpublished authors and new clients. General agent; handles fiction & nonfiction for all ages, gift books, crossover books, general books. No science fiction. No picture books for now.
Contact: By e-mail or letter; no faxes. Accepts simultaneous submissions. Responds in 8-12 wks.

Commission: 15 percent; foreign 20 percent.
Fees: None.

THE SEYMOUR AGENCY, 475 Miner Street Rd., Canton NY 13617. (315) 386-1831. E-mail: mary sue@twcny.rr.com. Website: www.theseymouragency.com. Agent: Mary Sue Seymour. Member AAR. Estab. 1992. Represents 35 religious clients. Open to unpublished authors and new clients (prefers published authors). Handles romance novels, Christian chick lit, Christian historical romance, and nonfiction for all ages, general books, crossover books.
  Contact: Query letter or e-mail with first 50 pages of ms; no fax query. For nonfiction, send proposal with chapter 1. Simultaneous query OK. Responds in 1 mo. for queries and 2-3 mos. for mss.
  Commission: 15 percent for unpublished authors; 12.5 percent for published authors; foreign 20 percent.
  Fees: None.
  Tips: "We have multibook sales to Zondervan, Thomas Nelson, Harvest House, and Cook Communications."

THE SHEPARD AGENCY, 73 Kingswood Dr., Bethel CT 06801. (203) 790-4230. Fax (203) 798-2924. E-mail: shepardagcy@mindspring.com. Agent: Jean Shepard. Recognized in the industry. Estab. 1987. Represents 11 clients. Open to unpublished authors; no new clients at this time. Handles fiction and nonfiction for all ages; no picture books; especially business, reference, professional, self-help, cooking, and crafts. Books only.
  Contact: By e-mail.
  Commission: 15 percent; foreign variable.
  Fees: None except long-distance calls and copying.

KEN SHERMAN & ASSOCIATES, 9507 Santa Monica Blvd., Beverly Hills CA 90210. (310) 273-3840. Fax (310) 271-2875. E-mail: ken@kenshermanassociates.com. Agent: Ken Sherman. Estab. 1989. Represents 50 clients. Open to unpublished authors and new clients. Handles adult religious/inspirational novels, nonfiction, screenplays and TV/movie scripts.
  Contact: By referral only. Responds in 1 mo.
  Commission: 15 percent; foreign 20 percent; dramatic rts. 15 percent.
  Fees: Charges office expenses and other negotiable expenses.

WENDY SHERMAN ASSOCIATES, 450 Seventh Ave., Ste. 2307, New York NY 10123. (212) 279-9027. Fax (212) 279-8863. Website: www.wsherman.com. Agents: Wendy Sherman, Michelle Brower. Open to unpublished authors and new clients. General agents. Handle adult religious nonfiction.
  Contact: Query by mail/SASE or send proposal/1 chapter. No phone/fax/e-query. Guidelines on Website.
  Commission: 15 percent; foreign 20 percent.

SIMENAUER & GREENE LITERARY AGENCY, PO Box 770968, Naples FL 34107-0968. (239) 594-1484, or (239) 597-9877. E-mail: jsliteraryagent@gmail.com, and cjgliteraryagent@gmail.com. Website: www.jsimenaur.com. Agents: Jackie Simenaur and Carole J. Greene. Open to unpublished authors and new clients. Handles spiritual fiction & nonfiction.
  Contact: For fiction, query with first 3 chapters, synopsis, bio, and SASE. For nonfiction, send query with SASE. Simultaneous OK; e-query preferred. Responds in 3-5 wks.
  Commission: 15 percent; foreign 20 percent.
  Fees: Charges only postage/shipping and long-distance (foreign) calls.

MICHAEL SNELL LITERARY AGENCY, PO Box 1206, Truro MA 02666-1206. (508) 349-3718. Agent: Michael Snell. Estab. 1978. Represents 200 clients. Open to unpublished authors and new clients. General agent: handles adult religious/inspirational nonfiction.

Contact: Query with SASE. No simultaneous submissions. Responds in 1-2 wks.
Commission: 15 percent; foreign 15 percent.

SPENCERHILL ASSOCIATES, LTD./KAREN SOLEM, PO Box 374, Chatham NY 12037. (518) 392-9293. Fax (518) 392-9554. E-mail: ksolem@klsbooks.com. Agent: Karen Solem. Member of AAR. Recognized in the industry. Estab. 2001. Represents 14 clients with religious books. Not currently open to unpublished authors; very selective of new clients. Primarily handles adult Christian fiction; no YA, children's, or nonfiction.
Commission: 15 percent; foreign 20 percent.
Fees: Photocopying and Express Mail charges only.

STEELE-PERKINS LITERARY AGENCY, 26 Island Ln., Canandaigua NY 14424. (585) 396-9290. Fax (585) 396-3579. E-mail: pattiesp@aol.com. Agent: Pattie Steele-Perkins. Member AAR. Handles inspirational romance novels.
Contact: Proposal/3 chapters. Considers simultaneous submissions. Responds in 6 weeks. E-mail instead of calling.
Commission: 15 percent.

LESLIE H. STOBBE, 300 Doubleday Rd., Tryon NC 28782. (828) 808-7127. Fax (978) 945-0517. E-mail: lstobbe@alltel.net. Well recognized in the industry. Estab. 1993. Represents 75 clients. Open to new clients. Handles adult fiction and nonfiction.
Contact: By e-mail.
Commission: 15 percent.
Fees: None.
Tips: "I will not accept clients whose theological positions in their book differ significantly from mine."

STONE MANNERS AGENCY, 9911 W. Pico Blvd., Ste. 1400, Los Angeles CA 90035-2715. (323) 655-1313. Fax (323) 655-7676. Agent: Michael Sheehy. Handles religious/inspirational TV/film screenplays as well as general screenplays.
Contact: Queries only.

SUITE A MANAGEMENT TALENT & LITERARY AGENCY, 120 El Camino Dr., Ste. 202, Beverly Hills CA 90212. (310) 278-0801. Fax (310) 278-0807. E-mail: suite-A@juno.com. Agent: Lloyd D. Robinson. Recognized in the industry. Estab. 2001. Several clients. Open to new and unpublished clients (if published in other media). Specializes in screenplays and novels for adaptation to TV movies.
Contact: By mail or fax only. For consideration of representation, send current bio, and for each screenplay, your WGA registration number, log line, and 2 paragraph synopsis only. Complete scripts or e-mail submissions are not read; attachments are deleted. Responds only if interested.
Commission: 10 percent.
Comments: Representation limited to adaptation of novels and true-life stories for film and television development. Work must have been published for consideration.

MARK SWEENEY & ASSOCIATES, 28540 Altessa Way, Ste. 201, Bonita Springs FL 34135. (239) 594-1957. Fax (239) 594-1935. E-mail: sweeney2@comcast.net. Agents: Mark Sweeney; Janet Sweeney. Recognized in the industry. Estab. 2003. Open to unpublished authors and new clients on a restricted basis. Handles adult religious/inspirational nonfiction, crossover books, general books. No new fiction at this time.
Contact: E-mail.
Commission: 15 percent; foreign 15 percent.
Fees: None.

TALCOTT NOTCH LITERARY SERVICES, 276 Forest Rd., Milford CT 06461. (203) 877-1146. Fax (203) 876-9517. E-mail: gpanettieri@talcottnotch.net. Website: www.talcottnotch.net. Agent: Gina Panettieri. Not yet recognized in the industry; building a Christian presence. Estab. 2003. Represents 25 clients (3 with religious books). Open to unpublished authors and new clients. Handles nonfiction & fiction, crossover & general market books for all ages.

> **Contact:** By e-mail (editorial@talcottnotch.net). Accepts simultaneous submissions; responds in 8 wks.
>
> **Commission:** 15 percent; foreign or with co-agent 20 percent.
>
> **Fees:** None.
>
> **Tips:** "While Christian and religious books are not our main focus, we are open to unique and thought-provoking works from all writers. We specifically seek nonfiction in areas of parenting, health, women's issues, arts & crafts, self-help, and current events. We are open to academic/scholarly work as well as commercial projects."

3 SEAS LITERARY AGENCY, PO Box 8571, Madison WI 53708. (608) 221-4306. E-mail: three seaslit@aol.com. Website: www.threeseaslit.com. Agent: Michelle Grajkowski. Estab. 2000. Represents 40 clients. Open to unpublished authors and new clients. General agent; handles adult religious/inspirational novels & nonfiction.

> **Contact:** E-query only with synopsis & 1 chapter (queries@threeseaslit.com). Considers simultaneous submissions. Responds in 2-3 mos.
>
> **Commission:** 15 percent; foreign 20 percent.

TRIDENT MEDIA GROUP, LLC., 41 Madison Ave., 36th Fl., New York NY 10010. (212) 262-4810. Fax (212) 262-4849. E-mail: pfedorko@tridentmediagroup.com. Website: www.tridentmediagroup .com. Agent: Paul Fedorko. Open to unpublished authors and new clients. General agent. Handles adult religious nonfiction.

> **Contact:** No unsolicited mss. Query/SASE first; send outline and sample chapters on request. Responds to queries in 3 wks.; mss in 6 wks.

VAN DIEST LITERARY AGENCY, PO Box 1482, Sisters OR 97759. (541) 549-0477. Fax (541) 549-1213. E-mail through Website: www.ChristianLiteraryAgency.com. Agents: David & Sarah Van Diest. Estab. 2004. Represents 20 clients. Open to unpublished authors and new clients. Recognized in the industry. Handles teen & adult novels, nonfiction for all ages, crossover books.

> **Contact:** By e-mail. Responds in 4 wks.
>
> **Commission:** 15 percent; 25 percent for first-time authors.

VERITAS LITERARY AGENCY, 601 Van Ness Ave., Opera Plaza Ste. E, San Francisco CA 94102. E-mail: submissions@veritasliterary.com. Website: www.veritasliterary.com. Agent: Katherine Boyle (kboyle@veritasliterary.com). Member AAR. Handles serious religious nonfiction (no New Age).

> **Contact:** Query with SASE; e-query OK (no attachments); no fax queries.

WATERSIDE PRODUCTIONS INC., 2376 Oxford Ave., Cardiff-by-the-Sea CA 92007. (760) 632-9190. Fax (760) 632-9295. E-mail: admin@waterside.com. Website: www.waterside.com. Agent: William E. Brown (webrown@waterside.com). Christian agent in a highly regarded general agency. Interested in handling Christian books, or books which otherwise challenge and engage readers from a Judeo-Christian perspective. Prefers nonfiction, but will look at fiction (the bar is very high). In addition to spiritually oriented books, devotions, theology, chick lit and mom lit, list includes business books: leadership, marketing, sales, business development.

> **Contact:** Query via online form (see Website). Considers simultaneous submissions.
>
> **Commission:** 15 percent; foreign 25 percent.

WOLGEMUTH&ASSOCIATESINC.,8600CrestgateCir.,OrlandoFL32819.(407)909-9445.Fax(407) 909-9446. E-mail: rwolgemuth@wolgemuthandassociates.com. Agent: Robert D. Wolgemuth; Andrew

D. Wolgemuth (awolgemuth@wolgemuthandassociates.com); Erik S. Wolgemuth (ewolgemuth@ wolgemuthandassociates.com). Member AAR. Well recognized in the industry. Estab. 1992. Represents 55 clients. No new clients or unpublished authors. Handles mostly adult nonfiction; most other types of books handled only for current clients.

> **Contact:** By letter.
> **Commission:** 15 percent.
> **Fees:** None.
> **Tips:** "We work with authors who are either best-selling authors or potentially best-selling authors. Consequently, we want to represent clients with broad market appeal."

WORDSERVE LITERARY GROUP, 10152 S. Knoll Cir., Highlands Ranch CO 80130. (303) 471-6675. Website: www.wordserveliterary.com. Agents: Greg Johnson and Rachelle Gardner. Estab. 2003. Represents 80 clients. Recognized in the industry. Open to new clients. Handles novels & nonfiction for all ages, gift books, crossover books, general books (memoir, military, self-help, adult fiction).

> **Contact:** By e-mail. Visit Website for submission guidelines. Responds in 4-8 wks.
> **Commission:** 15 percent; foreign 15-20 percent.
> **Fees:** None.
> **Tips:** "**Nonfiction:** First impressions count. Make sure your proposal answers all the questions on competition, outline, audience, felt need, etc. **Fiction:** Make sure your novel is completed before you submit a proposal (synopsis, plus 5 chapters)."

THE WRITER'S EDGE, See listing under Editorial Services—Illinois.

WRITERS HOUSE, 21 W. 26th St., New York NY 10010. (212) 685-2400. Fax (212) 685-1781. E-mail: azuckerman@writerhouse.com. Website: www.writershouse.com. Agent: Albert Zuckerman. Estab. 1974. Represents 440 clients. General agency; handles adult religious/inspirational fiction. Member of AAR.

> **Contact:** One-page query by mail/SASE. No e-mail/fax queries. Responds in 1 mo. to query.
> **Commission:** 15 percent; foreign 20 percent.
> **Fees:** No fees.
> **Tips:** "See Website for details. Write a compelling query so we'll ask to see your manuscript."

YATES & YATES, 1100 W. Town and Country Rd., Ste. 1300, Orange CA 92868-4654. (714) 480-4000. Fax (714) 480-4001. E-mail: email@yates2.com. Website: www.yates2.com. Estab. 1989. Recognized in the industry. Represents 50+ clients. Not currently open to unpublished authors or new clients. Handles adult novels, nonfiction for adults and teens, TV/movie scripts, general books, crossover books.

> **Contact:** E-mail.
> **Commission:** Negotiable.
> **Fees:** Negotiable.

ZACHARY SHUSTER HARMSWORTH LITERARY AND ENTERTAINMENT AGENCY, 1776 Broadway, Ste. 1405, New York NY 10019. (212) 765-6900. Fax (212) 765-6490; and 535 Boylston St., Ste. 1103, Boston MA 02116. (617) 262-2400. Fax (617) 262-2468. E-mail: mchappell@zsh literary.com. Website: www.zshliterary.com. Agent: Mary Beth Chappell (Boston office). Recognized in the industry. Represents 15-30 religious clients. Open to unpublished authors and new clients. Handles adult religious/inspirational novels & adult nonfiction, crossover books, general books.

> **Contact:** E-mail query letter. Accepts simultaneous submissions. Responds in 2 wks. on queries, 8 wks. on full mss.
> **Commission:** 15 percent; foreign & film 20 percent.
> **Fees:** Office expenses only.

Tips: "We are looking for inspirational fiction, Christian nonfiction, especially that which focuses on the emerging/emergent church or that which would appeal to readers in their 20s and 30s, and teen/YA series."

14

Contests

Below is a listing of some of the contests mentioned throughout this guide, plus additional contests that will be of interest. Some are sponsored by book publishers or magazines, some by conferences or writers' groups, some by independent groups. The contests are arranged by genre or type of material they are looking for, such as poetry, fiction, nonfiction, etc. Send an SASE to each one you are interested in to obtain a copy of their complete contest rules and guidelines, or check out their Website. (This is particularly important because many contests had not set deadlines and final details for their 2010 contests when this guide was written and so some details may change.) A listing here does not guarantee the legitimacy of a contest. For guidelines on evaluating contests and to determine if a contest is legitimate, go to: www.sfwa.org/beware/contests.html.

+ Indicates a new listing

CHILDREN/YOUNG-ADULT CONTESTS, WRITING FOR

THE CHILDREN'S WRITER CONTESTS. Offers a number of contests for children's writers. Website: www.childrenswriter.com.

DELACORTE DELL YEARLING CONTEST FOR FIRST MIDDLE-GRADE NOVEL, Random House Inc., 1745 Broadway, 9th Fl., New York NY 10019. Website: www.randomhouse.com/kids/writing contests/index.html#middlegrade. Contemporary and historical fiction manuscripts, 96-160 pgs., for ages 9-12. Submit between April 1 and June 30. Prizes: $1,500, book contract, and $7,500 advance.

DELACORTE DELL YEARLING CONTEST FOR FIRST YOUNG ADULT NOVEL, Random House Inc., 1745 Broadway, 9th Fl., New York NY 10019. Website: www.randomhouse.com/kids/writing contests/index.html#youngadult. Contemporary and historical fiction manuscripts, 100-224 pgs., for ages 12-18. Submit between October 1 and December 31. Prizes: $1,500, book contract, and $7,500 advance.

HIGHLIGHTS FOR CHILDREN FICTION CONTEST, 803 Church St., Honesdale PA 18431. (570) 253-1080. Website: www.highlights.com. Offers 3 prizes of $1,000 each for stories up to 800 words for children; for beginning readers to 500 words. See Website for guidelines and current topic. No crime, violence, or derogatory humor. No entry fee or form required. Entries must be postmarked between January 1 and January 31.

CORETTA SCOTT KING BOOK AWARD, Coretta Scott King Task Force, American Library Assn., 50 E. Huron St., Chicago IL 60611. Toll-free (800) 545-2433. E-mail: olos@ala.org. Website: www.ala .org. Annual award for children's books by African American authors and/or illustrators published the previous year. Books must fit one of these categories: preschool to grade 4; grades 5-8; grades 9-12. Deadline: December 1 each year. Guidelines on Website. Prizes: a plaque, a set of encyclopedias, and $1,000 cash. Recipients are authors and illustrators of African descent whose distinguished books promote an understanding and appreciation of the "American Dream."

LEE & LOW BOOKS NEW VOICES AWARD, 95 Madison Ave., New York NY 10016. E-mail: info@lee andlow.com. Website: www.leeandlow.com. Annual award for a children's fiction or nonfiction picture book story by a writer of color; to 1,500 words. Deadline: between May 1 and October 31. Prizes: $1,000 plus publication contract for winner; $500 for Honor Award Winner. Guidelines on Website.

MILKWEED PRIZE FOR CHILDREN'S LITERATURE, Milkweed Editions, 1011 Washington Ave. S., Ste. 300, Minneapolis MN 55415. (612) 332-3192. E-mail: editor@milkweed.org. Website: www .milkweed.org. Annual prize for unpublished novel intended for readers 8-13; 90-200 pgs. Prize: $10,000 advance against royalties and publication. Guidelines on Website.

POCKETS WRITING CONTEST, PO Box 340004, Nashville TN 37203-0004. (615) 340-7333. Fax (615) 340-7267. E-mail: pockets@upperroom.org. Website: www.pockets.org. United Methodist. Lynn W. Gilliam, ed. Devotional magazine for children (6-11 yrs.). Fiction-writing contest; submit between March 1 and August 15 every yr. Prize: $1,000 and publication in *Pockets*. Length: 1,000-1,600 words. Must be unpublished and not historical fiction. Previous winners not eligible. Send to Pockets Writing Contest at above address, designating "Fiction Contest" on outside of envelope. Send SASE for return and response.

SKIPPING STONES YOUTH HONOR AWARDS, PO Box 3939, Eugene OR 97403. (541) 342-4956. E-mail: editor@skippingstones.org. Website: www.skippingstones.org. Interfaith/multicultural. Arun N. Toké, exec. ed.; Nina Forsberg, asst. ed. A multicultural awareness and nature appreciation magazine for young people 7-17, worldwide. Annual Youth Honor Awards for students 7-17. Deadline June 25. Send SASE for guidelines.

SOCIETY OF CHILDREN'S BOOK WRITERS & ILLUSTRATORS GOLDEN KITE AWARDS. Offers $2,500 in cash awards. Website: www.scbwi.org.

FICTION CONTESTS

AMAZON BREAKTHROUGH NOVEL AWARD. In cooperation with Penguin and Hewlett-Packard. Penguin will publish winning novel with a $25,000 advance. Details: www.amazon.com/Breakthrough-Novel-Award-Books/b?ie-UTF8&node-332264011. May deadline.

AMERICAN CHRISTIAN FICTION WRITERS CONTESTS. President; PO Box 101066, Palm Bay FL 32910-1066. Phone/fax (321) 984-4018. E-mail: genesis@ACFW.com. Website: www.ACFW.com. Sponsors a fiction contest and others. See Website for current contests and rules.

BARD FICTION PRIZE. Awarded annually to a promising, emerging young writer of fiction, aged 39 years or younger. Entries must be previously published. Deadline: July 15. No entry fee. Prizes: $30,000 and appointment as writer in residence for one semester at Bard College, Annandale-on-Hudson NY. E-mail: bfp@bard.edu. Website: www.bard.edu/bfp.

BOSTON REVIEW SHORT STORY CONTEST, Boston Review, 35 Medford St., Ste. 302, Somerville MA 02143. Website: www.bostonreview.net. Prize: $1,500 (plus publication) for an unpublished short story to 4,000 words. Entry fee: $20. Deadline: October 1. Details on Website.

BULWER-LYTTON FICTION CONTEST. For the worst opening line to a novel. Deadline: April 15. Website: www.bulwer-lytton.com. Rules on Website.

CANADIAN WRITER'S JOURNAL SHORT FICTION CONTEST, White Mountain Publications, Box 1178, New Liskeard ON P0J 1P0, Canada. (705) 647-5424. Canada-wide toll-free (800) 258-5451. Website: www.cwj.ca. Sponsors semiannual short fiction contests. Deadline: April 30 (may vary). Length: to 1,500 words. Entry fee: $5. Prizes: $150, $100, $50. All fiction needs for CWJ are filled by this contest. E-mail: cwc-calendar@cwj.ca.

ALEXANDER PATTERSON CAPON PRIZE FOR FICTION, New Letters, UMKC, University House, 5101 Rockhill Rd., Kansas City MO 64110. (816) 235-1168. E-mail: newletters@umkc.edu. Website: www.newletters.org. Deadline: May 18. Entry fee: $15. Prize: $1,500.

THE CHRISTY AWARDS, 1571 Glastonbury Rd., Ann Arbor MI 48103. Phone/fax (734) 663-7931. E-mail: CA2000DK@aol.com. Website: www.christyawards.com. Awards in 9 fiction genres for excellence in Christian fiction. Nominations made by publishers, not authors. For submission guidelines and other information, see Website. Awards are presented at an annual Christy Awards banquet held Friday prior to the annual ICRS convention in July.

GLIMMER TRAIN PRESS FICTION CONTESTS. Glimmer Train Press, 1211 N.W. Glisan St., #207, Portland OR 97209. (503) 221-0836. Website: www.glimmertrain.com. Check Website for current contests.

+ JAMES JONES FIRST NOVEL FELLOWSHIP, c/o MA/MFA in Creative Writing, Wilkes University, 84 W. South St., Wilkes-Barre PA 18766. (570) 408-4534. E-mail: jamesjonesfirstnovel@wilkes.edu. Website: www.wilkes.edu/pages/1159.asp. Deadline: March 1. Entry fee: $25. Prizes: $10,000 first prize; $750 for two runners-up. Submit a 2-page outline and the first 50 pages of an unpublished novel.

SERENA MCDONALD KENNEDY AWARD, Snake Nation Press. Website: www.snakenationpress .org. Novellas to 50,000 words, or short story collection to 200 pgs. (published or unpublished). Deadline: check Website. Entry fee: $25. Prize: $1,000 and publication. Guidelines on Website. May not be held every year.

C. S. LEWIS CONTESTS. Check Website for current contests: www.cslewis.com.

THE MARY MCCARTHY PRIZE IN SHORT FICTION, PO Box 4456, Louisville KY 40204. (502) 458-4028. E-mail: sarabandeb@aol.com. Website: www.sarabandebooks.org. Prize: $2,000 and publication of a collection of short stories, novellas, or a short novel (150-250 pgs.), plus a standard royalty contract. Deadline: between January 1 and February 15. Entry fee: $25.

NATIONAL WRITERS ASSOCIATION NOVEL-WRITING CONTEST. The National Writers Assn., 3140 S. Peoria, #295, Aurora CO 80014. (303) 841-0246. Website: www.nationalwriters.com. Check Website for current contests and guidelines.

NATIONAL WRITERS ASSOCIATION SHORT-STORY CONTEST. The National Writers Assn., 10940 S. Parker Rd., #508, Parker CO 80134. (303) 841-0246. Website: www.nationalwriters.com. Check Website for current contests and guidelines.

THE FLANNERY O'CONNOR AWARD FOR SHORT FICTION. University of Georgia Press, 330 Research Dr., Athens GA 30602. Website: www.ugapress.uga.edu. For collections of short fiction, 50,000-75,000 words. Prize: $1,000, plus publication under royalty book contract. Entry fee: $25. Deadline: between April 1 and May 31 (postmark). Guidelines on Website.

OPERATION FIRST NOVEL. Sponsored by the Jerry B. Jenkins Christian Writers Guild, 5525 N. Union Blvd., Ste. 200, Colorado Springs CO 80918. For unpublished novelists who are students or annual members of the Christian Writers Guild. Winner receives $20,000 and a book contract with a major CBA publisher. Length: 75,000-100,000 words. No entry fee. Deadline: October 1 (may vary). For contest rules, go to www.ChristianWritersGuild.com/contest.asp.

KATHERINE ANNE PORTER PRIZE FOR FICTION. Literary Contest/Fiction, *Nimrod* journal, University of Tulsa, 800 S. Tucker Dr., Tulsa OK 74104. (918) 631-3080. E-mail: nimrod@utulsa.edu. Website: www.utulsa.edu/nimrod/awards.html. Quality prose and fiction by emerging writers of contemporary literature, unpublished. Prizes: $2,000 and publication; $1,000 and publication. Entry fee: $20. Deadline: between January 1 and April 30.

TAMARAK AWARD. Website: www.minnesotamonthly.com. For residents of Minnesota, North Dakota, South Dakota, Iowa, Wisconsin, and Michigan only. Prize: $10,000. Winning story to be published in the fall issue of *Minnesota Monthly*. Short fiction to 4,000 words. Spring deadline. Details on Website.

TOBIAS WOLFF AWARD IN FICTION. Western Washington University, Bellingham WA. E-mail: bhreview@cc.wwu.edu. Website: www.wwu.edu/~bhreview. Prize: $1,000, plus publication. Short story or novel excerpt to 8,000 words. Entry fee: $18 for first story/chapter; $10 each additional. Deadline: postmarked between December 1 and March 15. Details on Website.

WORD SMITTEN'S TENTEN FICTION COMPETITION. Word Smitten LLP, PO Box 5067, St. Petersburg FL 33737. E-mail: award@wordsmitten.com. Website: www.wordsmitten.com. Annual contest for a short story of exactly 1,010 words. Deadline: July 1. Entry fee: $18. Prize: $1,010, plus publication.

WRITER'S JOURNAL ANNUAL FICTION CONTEST, Val-Tech Media, PO Box 394, Perham MN 56573. E-mail: writersjournal@writersjournal.com. Website: www.writersjournal.com. Prizes: $500, $200, $100, plus publication. Maximum 5,000 words. Entry fee: $15. Deadline: January 30. Sponsors several contests; see Website.

NONFICTION CONTESTS

AMY WRITING AWARDS. A call to present spiritual truth reinforced with biblical references in general, nonreligious publications. To be eligible, submitted articles must be published in a general, nonreligious publication and must be reinforced with at least one passage of Scripture. First prize is $10,000, with a total of $34,000 given annually. Deadline is January 31 of following year. For details and a copy of last year's winning entries, contact: The Amy Foundation, PO Box 16091, Lansing MI 48901-6091. (517) 323-6233. E-mail: amyfoundtn@aol.com. Website: www.amy found.org.

AWP CREATIVE NONFICTION PRIZE, Assoc. of Writers and Writing programs, George Mason University, Fairfax VA. E-mail: awp@awpwriter.org. Website: www.awpwriter.org. For authors of book-length manuscripts; submit only 150-300 pgs. Prize: $2,000. Entry fee: $10 for members; $25 for nonmembers. Deadline: February 28 (may vary). Guidelines on Website.

THE BECHTEL PRIZE. *Teachers and Writers* magazine contest. E-mail: info@twc.org. Website: www.twc.org/publications/bechtel-prize. Prize: $1,500, plus publication. Contemporary writing articles (unpublished) to 5,000 words. Entry fee: $20. Deadline: June 30 (varies).

ERMA BOMBECK WRITING COMPETITION. Website: www.wcpl.lib.oh.us/adults/erma.html. Personal essay (humor or human interest), 450 words. Prizes: $100 prize in each category and free registration in writers' conference. Entry fee: none. Deadline: January or February (varies). Use online entry form.

THE BROSE PRIZE. The Brose Foundation, Lake Forest College, 555 N. Sheridan, Lake Forest IL 60045. (847) 735-5175. Fax (847) 735-6192. E-mail: rmiller@lfc.edu. Offered only every 10 years for unpublished work. Open to a book or treatise on the relationship between any discipline or topic and the Christian religion. Prizes: $4,000-$15,000. Next contest deadline: September 1, 2010. Entries become the property of the college. Send SASE for guidelines.

DOROTHY CHURCHILL CAPON PRIZE FOR ESSAY. New Letters, UMKC, University House, 5101 Rockhill Rd., Kansas City MO 64110. (816) 235-1168. E-mail: newletters@umkc.edu. Website: www.newletters.org. Prize: $1,500. Entry fee: $15. Deadline: May 18.

ANNIE DILLARD AWARD IN CREATIVE NONFICTION. Essays on any subject to 8,000 words. Unpublished works only. First prize: $1,000. Entry fee: $18 for first; $10 each additional. Deadline: between December 1 and March 15. Manuscripts to: Bellingham Review, Mail Stop 9053, Western Washington University, Bellingham WA 98225. (360) 650-4863. E-mail: bhreview@cc.wwu.edu. Website: www.wwu.edu/~bhreview. Details on Website.

EUREKA STREET/READER'S FEAST AWARD. PO Box 553, Richmond VIC 3121, Australia. +613 9421 9600. Fax +613 9421 9600. E-mail: eureka@eureksstreet.com.au. Website: www .crimeandjusticefestival.com/eureka. For unpublished essays on social justice and human rights up to 1,500 words. $5,000 award to an Australian writer. Deadline: mid-June. E-mail submissions only. Details on Website.

EVENT CREATIVE NONFICTION CONTEST. The Douglas College Review, PO Box 2503, New Westminster BC V3L 5B2, Canada. 604 527-5293. E-mail: event@douglas.bc.ca. Website: http:// event.douglas.bc.ca. Previously unpublished creative nonfiction to 5,000 words. Prizes: Three $500 prizes and publication in Event. Entry fee; $29.95. Deadline: April 15.

GRAYWOLF PRESS NONFICTION PRIZE. 2402 University Ave., Ste. 203, St. Paul MN 55114. (651) 641-0036. Website: www.graywolfpress.org/Company_Info/Submission_Guidelines/Graywolf_Press_ Nonfiction_Prize_Submission_Guidelines. For the best literary nonfiction book by a writer not yet established in the genre. Prize: $12,000 advance and publication. Entry fee: none. Deadline: between September 1 and October 1.

GUIDEPOSTS CONTEST. 16 E. 34th St., New York NY 10016. (212) 251-8100. Website: www .guideposts.org. Interfaith. Writers Workshop Contest held on even years, with a late June deadline. True, first-person stories (yours or someone else's), 1,500 words. Needs one spiritual message, with scenes, drama, and characters. Winners attend a week-long seminar (all expenses paid) on how to write for *Guideposts*.

JEBAIRE YOUTH ESSAY CONTEST. Stand Up and Be Counted. Website: www.jebairepublishing .com. Sponsors an annual contest for youth, ages 9-16. Essays 700-1,200 words on specific topics. Guidelines available by e-mail (info@jebairepublishing.com).

CORETTA SCOTT KING AWARDS. American Library Assn. Toll-free (800) 545-2433, ext. 4294. E-mail: olos@ala.org. Website: www.ala.org. Offered annually to an African American author and illustrator to promote understanding and appreciation of culture and the contributions of all people. Prize: $1,000, plus a set of encyclopedias. Guidelines on Website.

RICHARD J. MARGOLIS AWARD. Blue Mountain Center, c/o Margolis & Assocs., 533 Boyston St., 8th Fl., Boston MA 02116. E-mail: hwsm@margolis.com. Website: www.margolis.com/ award. Given annually to a promising young journalist or essayist whose work combines warmth, humor, wisdom, and concern with social justice. Prize: $5,000. Deadline: July 1. Guidelines on Website.

OPERATION FIRST BOOK (nonfiction). Sponsored by the Jerry B. Jenkins Christian Writers Guild, 5525 N. Union Blvd., Ste. 200, Colorado Springs CO 80918. For unpublished authors who are students or annual members of the Christian Writers Guild. Length: 75,000-100,000 words. Winner receives $10,000 and their proposal is considered by a major Christian publisher. Entry fee: none. Deadline: September 2010 (check Website for exact date). For contest rules, go to www .ChristianWritersGuild.com and click on "Contests."

+ THE UNRECOGNIZED WOMAN ESSAY CONTEST. Website: www.theunrecognizedwoman.com. Essay contest for teen girls to write about a woman who has impacted her life—and what it has inspired her to do to impact the lives of others.

LAMAR YORK PRIZE FOR NONFICTION. *The Chattahoochee Review*, George Perimeter College, 2101 Womack Rd., Dunwoody GA 30338. Website: www.gpc.edu/~gpccr. Essays up to 5,000 words. Prize: $1,000 and publication in *The Chattahoochee Review*. Entry fee: $12. Deadline: between October 1 and January 31. Guidelines on Website.

PLAY/SCRIPTWRITING/SCREENWRITING CONTESTS

AMBASSADOR SCREENWRITING AWARD. E-mail: info@ambassadorcommunications.biz. Website: www.ambassadorcommunications.biz/faithandvalues.html. Honors the best in faith-based TV-series pilots and feature-length screenplays. Claire Hutchinson, contest coordinator. Monetary prizes. Check Website for details and current status of this contest.

ANNUAL SCRIPTAPALOOZA SCREENPLAY COMPETITION. (323) 654-5809. E-mail: info@ scriptapalooza.com. Website: www.scriptapalooza.com. Prize: $10,000. Entry fee: $50. Deadline: April 15 (varies). Details on Website.

AUSTIN FILM FESTIVAL SCREENWRITERS COMPETITION, 1145 W. 5th St., Ste. 210, Austin TX 78703. (512) 478-4795. E-mail: info@austinfilmfestival.com. Website: www.austinfilmfestival.com. Offers a number of contest categories for screenplays. See current details on Website.

BAKER'S PLAYS HIGH SCHOOL PLAYWRITING COMPETITION. Plays may be about any subject and any length as long as the play can be reasonably produced by high school students on a high school stage. Deadline: January 30 (may vary). Prizes: $500, $250, and $100. Guidelines on Website: www.bakersplays.com.

CITA PLAY & SKETCH CONTEST, PO Box 26471, Greenville SC 29616. E-mail: admin@cita.org. Website: www.CITA.org. (click on "Services"). To encourage Christian playwrights and the writing of new plays/musicals that are informed by a biblical worldview in influencing our culture and furthering the Kingdom of God. Info on upcoming competitions will be listed on Website as available.

KAIROS PRIZE FOR SPIRITUALLY UPLIFTING SCREENPLAYS. John Templeton Foundation. E-mail: contact@kairosprize.com. Website: www.kairosprize.com. Biannual. For first-time screenwriters with a religious message. Prizes: $25,000, $15,000, $10,000. Guidelines on Website.

MOONDANCE INTERNATIONAL FILM FESTIVAL COMPETITION, 970—9th St., Boulder CO 80302. E-mail: director@moondancefilmfestival.com. Website: www.moondancefilmfestival.com. Open to films, screenplays, and features. Deadline: May 15. Entry Fees: $25-75. Prize: winning entries screened at festival. Details on Website.

NATIONAL CHILDREN'S THEATRE FESTIVAL, Actor's Playhouse at the Miracle Theatre, Coral Gables FL. E-mail: maulding@actorsplayhouse.org. Website: www.actorsplayhouse.org. Annual playwriting prize offering $500 and full production of winning musical, and author's transportation and lodging at the festival. Deadline: April 1. Entry fee: $10 (entry form on Website). Earl Maulding, festival dir. Details on Website.

NICHOLL FELLOWSHIPS IN SCREENWRITING, 1313 N. Vine St, Hollywood CA 90028-8107. (310) 247-3010. E-mail: nicholl@oscars.org. Website: www.oscars.org/nicholl/index.html. International contest held annually, open to any writer who has not optioned or sold a treatment, teleplay, or screenplay for more than $5,000. Up to five $30,000 fellowships offered each year to promising authors. Guidelines/required application form on Website.

MILDRED & ALBERT PANOWSKI PLAYWRITING AWARD, Award Coordinator, Forest Roberts Theatre, Northern Michigan University, Marquette MI 49855-5364. Website: www.nmu.edu/theatre. Unpublished, unproduced, full-length plays. Deadline: October 31. Prizes: $2,000, a summer workshop, a fully mounted production, and transportation to Marquette. Guidelines on Website.

THE WRITERS NETWORK ANNUAL SCREENPLAY & FICTION COMPETITION. Fade In Magazine, 287 S. Robertson Blvd., #467, Beverly Hills CA 90211. (310) 275-0287. E-mail: writers net@aol.com. Website: www.fadeinonline.com. Deadline: May 31. Must submit online. Over $10,000 in cash prizes. Guidelines on Website.

POETRY CONTESTS

ANHINGA PRIZE FOR POETRY, E-mail: info@anhinga.org. Website: www.anhinga.org. A $2,000 prize for original poetry book in English. Winning manuscript published by Anhinga Press. For poets trying to publish a first or second book of poetry. Submissions: 48-80 pgs. Number pages and include $25 reading fee. Deadline: between February 15 and May 1 each year. Details on Website.

ANNUAL CAVE CANEM POETRY PRIZE. Supports the work of African American poets with excellent manuscripts who have not found a publisher for their first book. Deadline: May 16 (varies). Prize: $1,000, publication by a national press, and 15 copies of the book. Details on Website: www.cave canempoets.org. E-mail: ccpoets@verizon.net.

MURIEL CRAFT BAILEY MEMORIAL POETRY AWARD, CWG Poetry Contest 2010, 4956 St. John Dr., Syracuse NY 13215. E-mail: poetry@comstockreview.org. Awarded annually. Deadline: July 1. Prizes: $100 to $1,000. Finalists published in the Comstock Review. Unpublished poems to 40 lines. Entry fee: $5 for each poem (no limit on number of submissions). Details on Website: www.comstock review.org.

BALTIMORE REVIEW POETRY CONTEST. All styles and forms of poetry. April 1-July 1. Entry fee: $10. Prizes: $300 & publication; $150; $50. Details on Website: www.baltimorereview.org. Click on "Contests."

BLUE MOUNTAIN ARTS/SPS STUDIOS POETRY CARD CONTEST, PO Box 1007, Boulder CO 80306. (303) 449-0536. E-mail: poetrycontest@sps.com. Website: www.sps.com. Biannual contest (even years). Deadline: June 30. Rhymed or unrhymed original poetry (unrhymed preferred). Poems also considered for greeting cards or anthologies. Prizes: $300, $150, $50. Details on Website.

BOSTON REVIEW ANNUAL POETRY CONTEST. Deadline: June 1. First prize: $1,500, plus publication. Submit up to 5 unpublished poems. Entry fee: $20 (includes a subscription to Boston Review). Submit manuscripts in duplicate with cover note. Send manuscript and fee to: Poetry Contest, Boston Review, 35 Medford St., Ste. 302, Somerville MA 02143. Website: www.bostonreview .net. Details on Website.

49TH PARALLEL POETRY AWARD, Mail Stop 9053, Western Washington University, Bellingham WA 98225. (360) 650-4863. E-mail: bhreview@cc.wwu.edu. Website: www.wwu.edu/bhreview. Poems in any style or on any subject. Deadline: between December 1 and March 15. Entry fee: $18 for first entry; $10 for each additional entry. First prize: $1,000 and publication. Details on Website.

GRIFFIN POETRY PRIZE. Contact: Ruth Smith, mngr., The Griffin Trust for Excellence in Poetry, 363 Parkridge Crescent, Oakville ON L6M 1A8, Canada. (905) 565-5993. E-mail: info@griffinpoetryprize .com. Website: www.griffinpoetryprize.com. Prizes: two $50,000 awards (one to a Canadian and one to a poet from anywhere in the world) for a collection of poetry published in English during the preceding year. All submissions must come from publishers. Deadline: December 31. Details on Website.

SARA HENDERSON HAY PRIZE, The Pittsburgh Quarterly, 6336 Crombie St., Pittsburgh PA 15217. Enter up to 3 poems, no more than 100 lines each. Deadline: July 1. Prize: $600. Entry fee: $10. Details: www.city-net.com/~tpq.

TOM HOWARD/JOHN H. REID POETRY CONTEST, 351 Pleasant St., PMB 222, Northampton MA 01060. Website: www.winningwriters.com/tompoetry.htm. Deadline: between December 15 and September 30. Poetry in any style or genre. Published poetry accepted. Entry fee: $7 for every 25 lines. Prizes: $2,000 first prize; total of $5,250 in cash prizes. Details on Website.

+ KDGOSPEL MEDIA POETRY CONTEST. Website: www.kdgmmag.com. Sponsors an annual poetry contest from January 1 through August 30. Winners will be included in their October issue.

BARBARA MANDIGO KELLY PEACE POETRY AWARDS, Nuclear Age Peace Foundation, PMB 121, 1187 Coast Village Rd., Ste. 1, Santa Barbara CA 93108-2794. (805) 965-3443. E-mail: waging peace@napf.org. Website: www.wagingpeace.org. Annual series of awards to encourage poets to explore and illuminate positive visions of peace and the human spirit. Deadline: July 1. Prizes: $1,000 for Adult; $200 for Youth 13-18 years; and $200 for Youth ages 12 and under. Adult entry fee: $15 for up to 3 poems (no youth fee).

THOMAS MERTON POETRY OF THE SACRED CONTEST. Poetry that expresses, directly or indirectly, a sense of the holy or that, by mode of expression, evokes the sacred. The tone may be religious, prophetic, or contemplative. Deadline: December 31. First prize: $500; three honorable mentions, $100 each. Submit 1 poem. Entry fee: none. Submit to: The Thomas Merton Prize, The Thomas Merton Foundation, 2117 Payne St., Louisville KY 40206-2011, or e-mail to: vhurst@mertonfoundation.org. For details call (502) 899-1991 or visit Website: www.merton foundation.org.

KATHRYN A. MORTON PRIZE IN POETRY, Sarabande Books, PO Box 4456, Louisville KY 40204. (502) 458-4028. E-mail: info@sarabandebooks.org. Website: www.sarabandebooks.org. Prize: $2,000, plus publication of a book of poetry. Submit: minimum of 48 pages of poetry. Entry fee: $25. Deadline: January 1 through February 15 (postmark).

NEW LETTERS PRIZE FOR POETRY, New Letters, UMKC, University House, 5101 Rockhill Rd., Kansas City MO 64110. (816) 235-1168. E-mail: newletters@umkc.edu. Website: www.newletters .org. Deadline: May 18. Entry fee: $15. Prize: $1,500 for best group of 3 to 6 poems.

JESSE BRYCE NILES CHAPBOOK CONTEST. Submit 25-34 pages of poetry. August 1-September 30. Entry fee: $25. Prizes: $1,000, plus 50 copies of chapbook. Details on Website: www.comstock review.org.

+ PEARL POETRY PRIZE, Pearl Editions, 3030 E. Second St., Long Beach CA 90803. Website: www.pearlmag.com. Submit: May 1-July 15. Entry fee: $20. Prizes: $1,000 and publication in Pearl Editions.

POETRY SOCIETY OF VIRGINIA POETRY CONTESTS, PO Box 1019, Lynchburg VA 24505 (address for adult submissions). See Website for addresses for other contests. Website: www.poetry societyofvirginia.org. Categories for adults and students. Prizes: $10-100. Entry fee per poem for nonmembers: $3. Deadline: January 21. List of contests on Website.

SILVER WINGS CONTEST, PO Box 2340, Clovis CA 93613-2340. (559) 347-0194. E-mail: clovis wings@aol.com. Jackson Wilcox, ed. Annual poetry contest on a theme. Deadline: December 31. Send SASE for details. Winners published in March issue. $325 in prizes. Entry fee: $3 entry fee.

SLIPSTREAM ANNUAL POETRY CHAPBOOK COMPETITION, Dept. W-1, Box 2071, Niagara Falls NY 14301. Website: www.slipstreampress.org/contest.html. Prize: $1,000, plus 50 copies of chapbook. Deadline: December 1. Send up to 40 pages of poetry. Reading fee: $20.

SOUL-MAKING LITERARY COMPETITION, National League of American Pen Women, Nob Hill, San Francisco Branch, 1544 Sweetwood Dr., Broadmoor Village CA 94015-2029. E-mail: pennobhill@aol.com. Website: www.soulmakingcontest.us. One-page poems only (single- or double-spaced). Up to 3 poems/entry. Deadline: November 30. Entry fee: $5. Prizes $25, $50, $100.

HOLLIS SUMMERS POETRY PRIZE, Ohio University Press, 19 Circle Dr., The Ridges, Athens OH 45701. (740) 593-1155. E-mail: oupress@ohio.edu. For unpublished collection of original poems, 60-95 pgs. Entry fee: $20. Deadline: October 31. Prize: $1,000, plus publication in book form. Details on Website: www.ohiou.edu/oupress/poetryprize.htm.

THE MAY SWENSON POETRY AWARD, Utah State University Press, 7800 Old Main Hill, Logan UT 84322-7800. (435) 797-1362. Website: www.usu.edu/usupress. Collections of original poetry, 50-100 pgs. Deadline: September 30. Prize: $1,000, publication, and royalties. Reading fee: $25. Details on Website.

TIME OF SINGING POETRY CONTESTS, PO Box 149, Conneaut Lake PA 16316. E-mail: timesing@ zoominternet.net. Website: www.timeofsinging.com. Lora Zill, ed. Sponsors 1-2 annual poetry contests on specific themes or forms. Entry fee: $2/poem. Cash prizes. Details on Website.

KATE TUFTS DISCOVERY AWARD, Claremont Graduate University, 150 E. 10th St., Harper East B7, Claremont CA 91711-6165. (909) 621-8974. E-mail: tufts@cgu.edu. Presented annually for a first or very early work by a poet of genuine promise. Prize: $10,000. Deadline: September 15. Details and entry form on Website: www.cgu.edu/tufts.

UTMOST NOVICE CHRISTIAN POETRY CONTEST. Utmost Christian Writers Foundation, 121 Morin Maze, Edmonton AB T6K 1V1, Canada. E-mail: nnharms@telusplanet.net. Website: www.utmost christianwriters.com/poetry-contest/poetry-contest-rules.php. Nathan Harms. Prizes: $500, $300, $200; Best Rhyming Poem $250. Entry fee: $10/poem. Deadline: August 31. Details and entry form on Website.

WAR POETRY CONTEST. 351 Pleasant St., PMB 222, Northhampton MA 01060. E-mail: warcontest@ winningwriters.com. Website: www.winningwriters.com/annualcontest.htm. Sponsored by Winning Writers. Submit 1-3 unpublished poems on the theme of war, up to 500 lines total. Prizes: $2,000 first prize; $5,000 in total prizes. Entry fee: $15. Deadline: between November 15 and May 31.

+ ROBERT E. LEE WILSON & RUTH I. WILSON POETRY BOOK AWARD. PO Box 250, Chesterfield MO 63006. E-mail: margiereviewW@aol.com. Website: www.margiereview.com. Entry fee: $25. Deadline: March 14. Submit an unpublished book of 48-64 pages of poetry.

WINNING WRITERS. Variety of poetry contests. Website: www.winningwriter.com.

YALE SERIES OF YOUNGER POETS COMPETITION. PO Box 209040, New Haven CT 06520. (203) 432-0960. Fax (203) 432-0948. E-mail: robert.flynn@yale.edu. Website: www.yale.edu/ yup. Robert Flynn, ed./religion. Open to poets under 40 who have not had a book of poetry published. Submit complete manuscripts of 48-64 pgs. Entry fee: $15. Deadline: between October 1 and November 15. Publishes one book each year. Details on Website.

MULTIPLE-GENRE CONTESTS

AMERICAN LITERARY REVIEW CONTESTS. PO Box 311307, University of North Texas, Denton TX 76203. E-mail: americanliteraryreview@yahoo.com. Website: www.engl.unt.edu/alr. Now sponsors three contests: short fiction, creative nonfiction, and poetry. Prize: $1,000 and publication in fall issue of the magazine. Entry fee: $15. Deadline: between June 1 and September 1. Details on Website.

BAKELESS LITERARY PUBLICATION PRIZES. Bread Loaf Writers' Conference, Middlebury College, Middlebury VT 05753. E-mail: bakelessprize@middlebury.edu. Website: www.bakeless prize.org. Book series competition for new authors of literary works of poetry, fiction, and nonfiction. Entry fee: $10. Deadline: between September 15 and November 1. Details on Website.

BEST NEW CANADIAN CHRISTIAN AUTHOR CONTEST. The Word Guild, Box 34, Port Perry ON L9L 1A2, Canada. E-mail: admin@thewordguild.com. Website: www.thewordguild.com. Appears to be looking for sponsors for their contest. Check Website for any current contests.

BYLINE CONTESTS. PO Box 111, Albion NY 14411-0111. (585) 355-8172. E-mail: Robbi@ bylinemag.com. Website: www.BylineMag.com. General market. Robbi Hess, ed. Sponsors many contests year round; details on Website; click on "Contest" button. Note that this magazine is suspended at this time, but they are still sponsoring monthly contests.

CANTICLE WRITING CONTEST. Blog: http://heidihesssaxton.blogspot.com. Heidi Saxton, ed. Check blog for details on current contest. Winners published in Canticle magazine.

CHICKEN SOUP FOR THE SOUL CONTESTS. Website: www.chickensoup.com. See Website for list of current contests.

CHRISTIAN SMALL PUBLISHER BOOK OF THE YEAR. Website: www.christianpublishers.net. Honors books produced by small publishers each year for outstanding contributions to Christian life. Categories: nonfiction, fiction, children's. Books need to have been published this year or last. Deadline: November 15. Eligible small publisher must have annual revenues of $350,000 or less. Details and nomination form on Website.

COLUMBIA FICTION/POETRY/NONFICTION CONTEST. 415 Dodge Hall, 2960 Broadway, New York NY 10027. Website: www.columbiajournal.org/contests.htm. Length: 20 double-spaced pgs. or up to 5 poems. Prize: $500 in each category, plus publication. Deadline: January 15 (varies). Details on Website.

ECPA CHRISTIAN BOOK AWARDS. 9633 S. 48th St., Ste. 140, Phoenix AZ 85044. (480) 966-3998. E-mail: info@ecpa.org. Website: www.ECPA.org. Presented annually to the best books in Christian publishing. Awards recognize books in 6 categories: Bibles, Fiction, Children & Youth, Inspiration & Gift, Bible Reference & Study, and Christian Life. Only ECPA members in good standing can nominate products. Deadline: January each year. Awards are presented annually at the International Christian Retail Show.

EVANGELICAL PRESS ASSOCIATION ANNUAL CONTEST. PO Box 28129, Crystal MN 55428. (763) 535-4793. E-mail: director@epassoc.org. Website: www.epassoc.org. Sponsors annual contest for member publications.

FAULKNER-WISDOM CREATIVE WRITING COMPETITION. Faulkner House, 624 Pirate's Alley, New Orleans LA 70116. (504) 586-1609. E-mail: Faulkhouse@aol.com. Website: www.wordsand music.org. Unpublished novels, novellas, short stories, essays, and poetry. Prizes: $750-7,500. Entry Fees: $25-40. Deadline: between January 15 and May 1 (postmark). Guidelines on Website.

FREELANCE WRITER'S REPORT CONTEST. 45 Main St., PO Box A, North Stratford NH 03590-0167. (603) 922-8383. E-mail: editor@writers-editors.com. Website: www.writers-editors.com. Dana K. Cassell, ed. Open to all writers. Nonfiction, fiction, children's, poetry. Prizes: $100, $75, $50. Deadline: March 15. Details on Website.

GOD USES INK NOVICE CONTEST. The Word Guild, 698A Highpoint Ave., Waterloo ON N2V 1G9, Canada. (519) 886-4196. E-mail: info@thewordguild.com. Website: www.thewordguild.com. Prizes: Free registration to the next Write! Canada Writers' Conference (a nearly $400 value), plus other cash prizes. Open to everyone who has never been paid for their writing. Three age categories: 14-19, 20-29, and 30+. Deadline: March 31 (may vary).

ERIC HOFFER AWARD. PO Box 11, Titusville NJ 08560. E-mail: editor@hopepubs.com. Website: www.bestnewwriting.com. Submit books via mail; no queries. The prose category is for creative fiction and nonfiction less than 10,000 words. Annual award for books features 14 categories. Pays $500 for winning prose; $1,500 for winning book. Guidelines at www.HofferAward.com.

INSCRIBE CHRISTIAN WRITERS' CONTEST. Edmonton AB, Canada. Contact: Eunice Matchett, 4304—45th St., Drayton Valley AB T7A 1G7, Canada. (780) 542-7950. Fax (780) 514-3702. E-mail: query@inscribe.org. Website: www.inscribe.org. Sponsors a fall contest open to nonmembers; details on Website.

INSIGHT WRITING CONTEST. 55 W. Oak Ridge Dr., Hagerstown MD 21740-7301. (301) 393-4038. Fax (301) 393-4055. E-mail: insight@rhpa.org. Website: www.insightmagazine.org. Review and Herald/Seventh-day Adventist. Dwain N. Esmond, ed. A magazine of positive Christian living for Seventh-day Adventist high schoolers. Sponsors short story and poetry contests; includes a category for students 22 or under. Submit by e-mail. Prizes: $50-$250. Deadline: June 1. Details on Website.

INSPIRATIONAL WRITERS ALIVE! OPEN COMPETITION 2010. c/o Winonna Peveto, PO Box 55363, Houston TX 77255-5363. E-mail: marthalrogers@sbcglobal.net. Categories: adult short story, juvenile short story, articles, poetry, book proposals (child & adult), drama. Prizes: $30, $20, $15. Entry fees: $10 nonmembers, $5 members for all categories except proposals; proposals $15/$7. Deadline May 15. E-mail for complete guidelines.

INTERNATIONAL LIBRARY OF PHOTOGRAPHY FREE PHOTO CONTEST. 3600 Crondall Ln., Ste. 101, Owings Mills MD 21117. Website: www.picture.com/contest/enter.asp. Ongoing contest. Prize: $100,000 in prizes to amateur photographers. Submit photos electronically on Website. Details on Website.

MINISTRY & LITURGY VISUAL ARTS AWARDS. 160 E. Virginia St., #290, San Jose CA 95112. (408) 286-8505. Fax (408) 287-8748. E-mail: mleditor@rpinet.com. Website: www.rpinet.com/vaaentry.pdf. Visual Arts Awards held in 5 categories throughout the year. Best in each category wins $100. Entry fee: $30. Different deadline for each category; see Website.

MISSISSIPPI REVIEW PRIZE. 118 College Dr., #5144, Hattiesburg MS 39406-0001. (601) 266-4321. E-mail: rief@mississippireview.com. Website: www.mississippireview.com/contest.html. Fiction & poetry. Prize: $1,000 in each category. Entry fee: $15. Deadline: April 2 to October 1 (may vary).

MOM'S CHOICE AWARDS. The Just For Mom Foundation. Website: www.momschoiceawards.org. Various award categories. Details on Website.

NEW MILLENNIUM AWARDS. Website: www.newmillenniumwritings.com/awards.html. Prizes: $1,000 award for each category. Best Poem, Best Fiction, Best Nonfiction, Best Short-Short Fiction (fiction and nonfiction 6,000 words; short-short fiction to 1,000 words; 3 poems to 5 pgs. total). Entry fee: $17 each. Deadline: June 17. Guidelines on Website. Enter online or off.

ONCE WRITTEN CONTESTS. Fiction and poetry contests. Website: www.oncewritten.com.

POWER AWARDS. E-mail: info@penofthewriter.com. Website: www.penofthewriter.com/awards. Established to assist self-published authors obtain industry recognition. Online voting in 5 genres: fiction, nonfiction, anthology, poetry, and children's. Winners receive stickers for books, framed certificates, online promotion, and one-year posting on Pen of the Writer Website. Deadline: August 15.

RUMINATE POETRY AND FICTION CONTEST. 140 N. Roosevelt Ave., Fort Collins CO 80521. (970) 449-2726. E-mail: editor@ruminatemagazine.com. Website: www.ruminatemagazine.com. An intimate and hip publication of faith literature and art. Annual poetry contest deadline May 15; annual fiction contest deadline November 15. Entry fee: $15. Prizes: $300 1st prize; $150 to runner-up. Details on Website.

MONA SCHREIBER PRIZE FOR HUMOROUS FICTION AND NONFICTION. 15442 Vista Haven Pl., Sherman Oaks CA 91403. E-mail: brashcyber@pcmagic.net. Website: www.brashcyber.com. Humorous fiction and nonfiction to 750 words. Prizes: $500, $250, and $100. Entry fee: $5. Deadline: December 1.

SOUL-MAKING LITERARY COMPETITION. Webhallow House, 1544 Sweetwood Dr., Colma CA 94015-2029. E-mail: PenNobHill@aol.com. Website: www.SoulMakingContest.us/page3.html. Lists various competitions: prose and poetry. Prizes: up to $100. Entry fee: $5. Guidelines on Website.

THE STORYTELLER CONTESTS, 2441 Washington Rd., Maynard AR 72444. (870) 647-2137. Fax (870) 647-2454. E-mail: storyteller1@hightowercom.com. Contest Website: www.thestoryteller magazine.com. Fossil Creek Publishing. Regina Cook Williams, ed./pub. Family audience. Offers 1 or 2 paying contest/yr., along with People's Choice Awards, and Pushcart Prize nominations.

TICKLED BY THUNDER CONTESTS. 14076—86A Ave., Surrey BC V3W 0V9, Canada. (604) 591-6095. E-mail: info@tickledbythunder.com. Website: www.tickledbythunder.com. Larry Lindner, ed. Sponsors several writing contests each year in various genres. Entry fee $10 for nonsubscribers. Prizes: $5-150 Cdn. Details on Website or by mail.

+ TWEENER TIME COMPETITIONS. Tweener Ministries Inc., PO Box 1284, Warsaw IN 46581-1284. (574) 269-6100. E-mail: info@tweenerministries.org. Website: www.tweenerministries .org. Sponsors contests for tweens: Songwriting Competition, Creative Competitions, Chapter Book Competition, and Cover Art Competition.

WORD GUILD CANADIAN CHRISTIAN WRITING AWARDS. The Word Guild, 698A Highpoint Ave., Waterloo ON N2V 1G9, Canada. (519) 886-4196. E-mail: info@thewordguild.com. Website: www.thewordguild.com. The following may be entered by author, writer, or publisher: fiction and nonfiction books, articles, columns, reviews, poems, song lyrics, scripts/screenplays published in the last year. Prizes: Cash and recognition. Deadline: Round One October; Round Two January.

THE WRITER CONTESTS. 21027 Crossroads Cir., Waukesha WI 53189. (262) 796-8776. E-mail: editor@writermag.com. Website: www.writermag.com. General. How-to for writers. Occasionally sponsors a contest. Check Website.

WRITER'S DIGEST. 4700 E. Galbraith Rd., Cincinnati OH 45207. (513) 531-2690, ext. 1483. Fax (513) 531-1843. E-mail: wdsubmissions@fwpubs.com. Website: www.writersdigest.com. Sponsors annual contests for articles, short stories, poetry, children's fiction, self-published books, and scripts (categories vary). Deadlines: vary according to contest. Prizes: $25,000 or more for each contest. See Website for list of current contests and rules.

+ WRITERS-EDITORS NETWORK ANNUAL INTL. WRITING COMPETITION. PO Box A, North Stratford NH 03590. Fax (603) 922-8339. Website: www.writers-editors.com. Deadline: March 15 (may vary). Prizes: $50-100. Categories: Nonfiction, fiction, children's literature, and poetry. Entry Fees: $3-10.

WRITERS' JOURNAL CONTESTS. PO Box 394, Perham MN 56573-0394. (218) 346-7921. Fax (218) 346-7924. E-mail: writersjournal@writersjournal.com. Website: www.writersjournal.com. Leon Ogroske, ed. Runs several contests each year. Prizes: $10- 500. Variety of categories. Different starter lines and deadlines for each category. Details on Website, or send SASE.

WRITERS' UNION OF CANADA AWARDS & COMPETITIONS. 90 Richmond St. E., Ste. 200, Toronto ON M5C 1P1, Canada. (416) 703-8982. Fax (416) 504-9090. E-mail: info@writersunion.ca. Website: www.writersunion.ca. Various competitions. Prizes: $500-10,000. Details on Website.

YOUNG SALVATIONIST CONTEST. PO Box 269, Alexandria VA 22313-0269. (703) 684-5500. Fax (703) 684-5539. E-mail: ys@usn.salvationarmy.org. Website: http://publications.salvationarmyusa.org. Sponsors a contest for fiction, nonfiction, poetry, original art, and photography. Send SASE for details.

CONTESTS SPONSORED BY WRITERS' CONFERENCES/GROUPS
(This list includes only those contests that are open to nonmembers of the groups or nonattendees at the conferences.)

ANNUAL GREEN LAKE WRITERS CONTEST. Green Lake Conference Center, Attn: Program, W2511 State Rd. 23, Green Lake WI 54941. Poetry, fiction, nonfiction, and general inspiration. Deadline:

June 4. Prizes: $50, $25, and $15 in each category. You do not have to be present or attend conference to enter. Entry fee: $5 (for poetry) or $10 (other genres) for each entry.

OZARK CREATIVE WRITERS CONTESTS. Contact: Sheila P. Smith, 223 Sycamore Dr., Bluff City TN 37618. E-mail submissions only: ozarkcreativewriters@earthlink.net. Website: www.ozarkcreative writers.org. Contest details on Website.

SOUTHWEST WRITERS ANNUAL CONTEST. 3721 Morris N.E., Ste. A, Albuquerque NM 87111-3611. (505) 265-9485. E-mail: swriters@juno.com. Website: www.southwestwriters.org. Novels, short stories, short nonfiction, and others. Includes inspirational/spiritual novels. Deadline: May 1; late deadline May 15 (Include a $5 extra fee). Prizes: Cash prizes in each category of $150, $100, $50, plus a $1,000 Storyteller Award selected from the first-place winners. Guidelines on Website or by mail.

RESOURCES FOR CONTESTS

ADDITIONAL CONTESTS. You will find some additional contests sponsored by local groups and conferences that are open to nonmembers. See individual listings in those sections.

BYLINE MAGAZINE CONTEST LISTINGS. Website: www.bylinemag.com. Click on "Contests."

CHECK FOR LITERARY SCAMS. For help in determining if a contest is legitimate or not, go to www.windpub.com/literary.scams.

FREELANCE WRITING: WEBSITE FOR TODAY'S WORKING WRITER. Website: www.freelance writing.com/writingcontests.php.

KIMN SWENSON GOLLNICK'S WEBSITE. Contest listings. Website: www.KIMN.net/contests.htm.

MAJOR LITERARY AWARDS

AUDIES: www.audiopub.org

CALDECOTT MEDAL: www.ala.org

EDGAR: www.mysterywriters.org

HEMINGWAY FOUNDATION/PEN AWARD: www.pen-ne.org

HUGO: http://worldcon.org/hugos.html

NATIONAL BOOK AWARD: www.nationalbook.org

NATIONAL BOOK CRITICS CIRCLE AWARD: www.bookcritics.org

NEBULA: http://dpsinfo.com/awardweb/nebulas

NEWBERY: www.ala.org

NOBEL PRIZE FOR LITERATURE: www.nobelprize.org

PEN/FAULKNER AWARD: www.penfaulkner.org

PINNACLE AWARD/ECPA: www.ECPA.org

PULITZER PRIZE: www.pulitzer.org

RITA: www.rwanational.org/cs/contests_and_awards

15

Denominational Listing of
Book Publishers and Periodicals

An attempt has been made to divide publishers into appropriate denominational groups. However, due to the extensive number of denominations included, and sometimes incomplete denominational information, some publishers may inadvertently have been included in the wrong list. Additions and corrections are welcome.

**ANTIOCHIAN
ORTHODOX**
Book Publisher:
Conciliar Press

Periodicals:
AGAIN Magazine
The Handmaiden

ASSEMBLIES OF GOD
Book Publisher:
Gospel Publishing House

Periodicals:
Enrichment Journal
Live
Men.ag.org
Testimony
Today's Pentecostal Evangel
WT Online

BAPTIST, FREE WILL
Book Publishers:
Randall House
Randall House Digital

Periodicals:
Together with God

BAPTIST, SOUTHERN
Book Publishers:
B & H Publishing
Baptist Press
Baylor Univ. Press
Founders Press
New Hope Publishers

Periodicals:
Founders Journal
Journey
Let's Worship
Louisiana Baptist Messenger
Mature Living
On Mission
ParentLife
The Pathway

BAPTIST (OTHER)
Book Publishers:
Judson Press (American)
Mercer Univ. Press

Periodicals:
African-American Pulpit
  (American)
Faith Detectives (Regular)
Florida Baptist Witness
Friends Journal
God's Explorers (Regular)
Link & Visitor
Living My Faith (Regular)
Point
Real Faith in Life (Regular)
Secret Place (American)
Sword of the Lord
  (Independent)
Truth Travelers (Regular)

CATHOLIC
Book Publishers:
ACTA Publications
Alba House

American Catholic Press
Canticle Books
Catholic Book Publishing
Catholic Univ./
  America Press
Cistercian Publications
HarperOne (Cath. bks.)
Libros Liguori
Liguori Publications
Liturgical Press
Loyola Press
Oregon Catholic Press
Our Sunday Visitor
Pauline Books
Pauline Kids
Paulist Press
Pflaum Publishing
Regnery Publishing
St. Anthony Messenger
St. Catherine of Siena Press
Tau Publishing

Periodicals:
America
Angel Face
Annals of St. Anne
Arkansas Catholic
Arlington Catholic Herald
Atlantic Catholic
Australian Catholics
Bread of Life
Canticle
Catechist
Catechumenate
Catholic Digest

Catholic Forester
Catholic Insight
Catholic Library World
Catholic New York
Catholic Peace Voice
Catholic Register
Catholic Sentinel
Catholic Servant
Catholic Telegraph
Catholic Yearbook
CGA World
Columbia
Commonweal
Culture Wars
Desert Call
Diocesan Dialogue
Emmanuel
Faith & Family
Family Digest
Interim
Island Catholic News
Koinonia
Leaves
Liguorian
Marian Helper
Messenger/Sacred Heart
Messenger/St. Anthony
Miraculous Medal
Montana Catholic
National Catholic Reporter
One
Our Sunday Visitor
Parish Liturgy
Prairie Messenger
Priest
Promise
Review for Religious
RTJ
Seeds
Share
Social Justice Review
Spirit
Spiritual Life
St. Anthony Messenger
St. Joseph's Messenger
Today's Catholic Teacher
Today's Parish
TG! (True Girl)
U.S. Catholic
Venture

Visions
Way of St. Francis

CHRISTIAN CHURCH/
CHURCH OF CHRIST
Book Publishers:
Chalice Press (Disciples of
    Christ)
College Press (Church of Christ)
CrossLink Publishing
Star Bible

Periodical:
DisciplesWorld (Disciples of
    Christ)

CHURCH OF GOD
(CLEVELAND, TN)
Book Publisher:
Pathway Press

Periodical:
Youth and CE Leadership

CHURCH OF GOD
(HOLINESS)
Periodicals:
Beginner's Friend
Church Herald and Holiness
    Banner
Gems of Truth
Junior Companion
Primary Pal (KS)
Youth Compass

CHURCH OF GOD
(OTHER)

Periodicals:
Bible Advocate
    (Seventh-day)
Gem
Now What? (Seventh-day)

CHURCH OF THE
NAZARENE
Book Publishers:
Beacon Hill Press
Lillenas (music)

Periodicals:
Adventures

Celebrate
Credo
Kid Zone
Mission Connection
Passport

EPISCOPAL/ANGLICAN
Book Publishers:
Forward Movement
Latimer Press
Morehouse Publishing

Periodicals:
Central Florida Episcopalian
Episcopal Life
Interchange
Living Church
Sewanee Theological
    Review

EVANGELICAL
COVENANT CHURCH
Periodicals:
Covenant Companion
inSpirit Magazine

LUTHERAN
Book Publishers:
Augsburg Fortress
Augsburg/Worship & Music
Concordia
Concordia Academic
Congregational Life &
    Learning
Langmarc Publishing
Lutheran University Press
Lutheran Voices
Northwestern Publishing

Periodicals:
Canada Lutheran (ELCC)
Canadian Lutheran
Cresset
Esprit (ELCC)
Lutheran Digest
Lutheran Forum
Lutheran Journal
Lutheran Partners (ELCA)
Lutheran Witness
Lutheran Woman's Quarterly
    (MO Synod)

Word & World (ELCA)

MENNONITE
Book Publisher:
Kindred Books

Periodicals:
Canadian Mennonite
Evangel (OR)
Mennonite Historian
The Messenger
Partners
Purpose
Rejoice!
Story Mates

METHODIST, FREE
Periodicals:
Evangel
Light and Life

METHODIST, UNITED
Book Publishers:
Abingdon Press
Dimensions for Living
United Methodist Publishing
    House

Periodicals:
Alive Now
Good News (KY)
Interpreter
Mature Years
Methodist History
New World Outlook
Pockets
Upper Room

PRESBYTERIAN
Book Publisher:
P & R Publishing

Periodicals:
Channels (PCC)
Glad Tidings
*Horizons/*women (USA)

Layman (USA)
Presbyterian Outlook (USA)
Presbyterians Today

QUAKER/FRIENDS
Book Publishers:
Barclay Press
Friends United Press

Periodicals:
Fruit of the Vine
Quaker Life

REFORMED
Periodicals:
Perspectives
Reformed Worship
Vision (MI)

SEVENTH-DAY ADVENTIST
Book Publishers:
Pacific Press
Review and Herald

Periodicals:
Connected
Cornerstone Youth Resources
Guide Magazine
Insight (MD)
Journal/Adventist Education
Kids' Ministry Ideas
Liberty
Message
Our Little Friend
Primary Treasure
Sabbath School Leadership
Vibrant Life

UNITED CHURCH OF CANADA
Book Publisher:
United Church Publishing House

Periodicals:
Aujourd'hui Credo

Fellowship Magazine
Theological Digest & Outlook
United Church Observer

UNITED CHURCH OF CHRIST
Book Publishers:
Pilgrim Press
UCC Press

WESLEYAN CHURCH
Book Publisher:
Wesleyan Publishing House

Periodicals:
Light from the Word
Vista
Wesleyan Life

MISCELLANEOUS DENOMINATIONS

Church of God (Anderson IN): *Warner Press*

Evangelical Free Church: *EFCA Today*

Foursquare Church: *Advance*

Grace Brethren Churches: *BMH Books*

Open Bible Standard Churches: *MESSAGE of the Open Bible*

Orthodox Church in America: *Divine Ascent*

Pentecostal Holiness Church: *IPHC Experience*

Pentecostal, United: *Vision (adult)*

Plymouth Brethren:
Chapter Two (books)

16

Book Publishers and Periodicals
by Corporate Group

This chapter contains a list of book publishers, followed by a list of periodicals, that belong to the same group, or family, of publications.

BARBOUR PUBLISHING, INC.
Barbour Publishing
Heartsong Presents
Heartsong Presents Mysteries

BRENTWOOD CHRISTIAN PRESS
Poems by Me
Poet's Cove
Self Publish Press
Sermon Select Press
Southern Baptist Press

CHRISTIANITY TODAY INTERNATIONAL
Books & Culture
Christian History
Christianity Today
Christianity Today Movies
Christian Music Today
Leadership
Men of Integrity
PreachingToday.com
SmallGroups.com
Today's Christian Woman
Your Church

CHRISTIAN MEDIA NETWORK
The Apocalypse Chronicles
Christian Media
Sound Body

DAVID C. COOK
Lion Publishing (books)
Scripture Press

Victor Books
Power for Living
Quiet Hour

FOCUS ON THE FAMILY
Focus on the Family (books)
Boundless Webzine
Clubhouse
Clubhouse Jr.
Focus on the Family
Plugged In

BILLY GRAHAM EVANGELISTIC ASSOCIATION
Decision
Decision Online

GROUP PUBLICATIONS INC.
Group Publishing
Children's Ministry
Group magazine
Rev. magazine

GUIDEPOSTS
Guideposts Books
Ideals Children's Books
Ideals Publications
Angels on Earth
Guideposts
Ideals magazine
Positive Thinking

HARPERCOLLINS
Avon Inspire
HarperOne

ZonderKidz
Zondervan

THOMAS NELSON PUBLISHERS
J. Countryman
Editorial Betania
Editorial Caribe
Editorial Catolica
Editorial Diez Puntos
Grupo Nelson
Leader Latino
Nelson Fiction, Thomas
Tommy Nelson
W Publishing Group

RANDALL HOUSE PUBLICATIONS
Direction Student
Horizon Student

RANDOM HOUSE
Multnomah Books
WaterBrook Press

THE SALVATION ARMY
Faith & Friends
Good News!
New Frontier
Priority!
War Cry
Young Salvationist

STANDARD PUBLISHING
Standard Publishing (books)
Christian Standard

Devotions
The Lookout
Seek

**STRANG
COMMUNICATIONS**
Charisma
Charisma House (books)
Charisma Kids (books)
Creation House
   (copublishing)
FrontLine (books)
Publicaciones Casa (books)

Realms (books)
Siloam (books)
Christian Retailing
Ministry Today
SpiritLed Woman

THE UPPER ROOM
Fresh Air Books
Upper Room Books
Alive Now
Devo'zine
The Upper Room
Weavings

URBAN MINISTRIES, INC.
Direction
InTeen
J.A.M.: Jesus and Me
Juniorway
Precepts for Living
Preschool Playhouse
Primary Street
Young Adult Today

GLOSSARY OF TERMS

Note: This glossary is not intended to be exhaustive. It includes primarily terms found in this market guide.

Advance: Amount of money a publisher pays to an author up front, against future royalties. The amount varies greatly from publisher to publisher, and is often paid in two or three installments (on signing contract, on delivery of manuscript, and on publication).

All rights: An outright sale of your material. Author has no further control over it.

Anecdote: A short, poignant, real-life story, usually used to illustrate a single thought.

Assignment: When an editor asks a writer to write a specific piece for an agreed-upon price.

As-told-to story: A true story you write as a first-person account, but about someone else.

Audio books: Books available on CDs.

Avant-garde: Experimental; ahead of the times.

Backlist: A publisher's previously published books that are still in print a year after publication.

B & W: Abbreviation for a black and white photograph.

Bar code: Identification code and price on the back of a book read by a scanner at checkout counters.

Bible versions: AMP—Amplified Bible; ASV—American Standard Version; CEV—Contemporary English Version; ESV—English Standard Version; GNB—Good News Bible; HCSB—Holman Christian Standard Bible; ICB—International Children's Bible; KJV—King James Version; MSG—The Message; NAB—New American Bible; NAS—New American Standard; NEB—New English Bible; NIrV—New International Reader's Version; NIV—New International Version; NJB—New Jerusalem Bible; NKJV—New King James Version; NLT—New Living Translation; NRSV—New Revised Standard Version; RSV—Revised Standard Version; TLB—*The Living Bible*; TNIV—Today's New International Version.

Bimonthly: Every two months.

Bio sketch: Information on the author.

Biweekly: Every two weeks.

Bluelines: Printer's proofs used to catch errors before a book is printed.

Book proposal: Submission of a book idea to an editor; usually includes a cover letter, thesis statement, chapter-by-chapter synopsis, market survey, and 1-3 sample chapters.

Byline: Author's name printed just below the title of a story, article, etc.

Camera-ready copy: The text and artwork for a book that are ready for the press.

Chapbook: A small book or pamphlet containing poetry, religious readings, etc.

Circulation: The number of copies sold or distributed of each issue of a publication.

Clips: See "Published clips."

Column: A regularly appearing feature, section, or department in a periodical using the same heading; written by the same person or a different freelancer each time.

Concept statement: A 50-150 word summary of your proposed book.

Contributor's copy: Copy of an issue of a periodical sent to the author whose work appears in it.

Copyright: Legal protection of an author's work.

Cover letter: A letter that accompanies some manuscript submissions. Usually needed only if you have to tell the editor something specific or to give your credentials for writing a piece of a technical nature. Also used to remind the editor that a manuscript was requested or expected.

Credits, list of: A listing of your previously published works.

Critique: An evaluation of a piece of writing.

Defamation: A written or spoken injury to the reputation of a living person or organization. If what is said is true, it cannot be defamatory.

Derivative work: A work derived from another work, such as a condensation or abridgement. Contact copyright owner for permission before doing the abridgement and be prepared to pay that owner a fee or royalty.

Devotional: A short piece that shares a personal spiritual discovery, inspires to worship, challenges to commitment or action, or encourages.

Editorial guidelines: See "Writer's guidelines."

Electronic submission: The submission of a proposal or article to an editor by electronic means, such as by e-mail or on disk.

Endorsements: Flattering comments about a book; usually carried on the back cover or in promotional material.

EPA/Evangelical Press Assn: A professional trade organization for periodical publishers and associate members.

E-proposals: Proposals sent via e-mail.

E-queries: Queries sent via e-mail.

Eschatology: The branch of theology that is concerned with the last things, such as death, judgment, heaven, and hell.

Essay: A short composition usually expressing the author's opinion on a specific subject.

Evangelical: A person who believes that one receives God's forgiveness for sins through Jesus Christ, and believes the Bible is an authoritative guide for daily living.

Exegesis: Interpretation of the Scripture.

Feature article: In-depth coverage of a subject, usually focusing on a person, an event, a process, an organization, a movement, a trend or issue; written to explain, encourage, help, analyze, challenge, motivate, warn, or entertain as well as to inform.

Filler: A short item used to "fill" out the page of a periodical. It could be a timeless news item, joke, anecdote, light verse or short humor, puzzle, game, etc.

First rights: Editor buys the right to publish your piece for the first time.

Foreign rights: Selling or giving permission to translate or reprint published material in a foreign country.

Foreword: Opening remarks in a book introducing the book and its author.

Freelance: As in 50 percent freelance: means that 50 percent of the material printed in the publication is supplied by freelance writers.

Freelancer or freelance writer: A writer who is not on salary but sells his material to a number of different publishers.

Free verse: Poetry that flows without any set pattern.

Galley proof: A typeset copy of a book manuscript used to detect and correct errors before the final print run.

Genre: Refers to type or classification, as in fiction or poetry. Such types as westerns, romances, mysteries, etc., are referred to as genre fiction.

Glossy: A black-and-white photo with a shiny, rather than matte, finish.

Go-ahead: When a publisher tells you to go ahead and write up or send your article idea.

Haiku: A Japanese lyric poem of a fixed 17-syllable form.

Hard copy: A typed manuscript, as opposed to one on disk or in an e-mail.

Holiday/seasonal: A story, article, filler, etc., that has to do with a specific holiday or season. This material must reach the publisher the stated number of months prior to the holiday/ season.

Homiletics: The art of preaching.

Honorarium: If a publisher indicates they pay an honorarium, it means they pay a small flat fee, as opposed to a set amount per word.

Humor: The amusing or comical aspects of life that add warmth and color to an article or story.

Interdenominational: Distributed to a number of different denominations.

International Postal Reply Coupon: See "IRC."

Interview article: An article based on an interview with a person of interest to a specific readership.

IRC or IPRC: International Postal Reply Coupon: can be purchased at your local post office and should be enclosed with a manuscript sent to a foreign publisher.

ISBN: International Standard Book Number; an identification code needed for every book.

Journal: A periodical presenting news in a particular area.

Kill fee: A fee paid for a completed article done on assignment that is subsequently not published. Amount is usually 25-50 percent of original payment.

Libel: To defame someone by an opinion or a misquote and put his or her reputation in jeopardy.

Light verse: Simple, lighthearted poetry.

Little/Literary: Small circulation publications whose focus is providing a forum for the literary writer, rather than on making money. Often do not pay, or pay in copies.

Mainstream fiction: Other than genre fiction, such as romance, mystery, or science fiction. Stories of people and their conflicts handled on a deeper level.

Mass market: Books intended for a wide, general market, rather than a specialized market. These books are produced in a smaller format, usually with smaller type, and are sold at a lower price. The expectation is that their sales will be higher.

Ms: Abbreviation for manuscript.

Mss: Abbreviation for more than one manuscript.

Multiple submissions: Submitting more than one piece at a time to the same publisher, usually reserved for poetry, greeting cards, or fillers, not articles. Also see "Simultaneous submissions."

NASR: Abbreviation for North American serial rights.

Newsbreak: A newsworthy event or item sent to a publisher who might be interested in publishing it because it would be of interest to his particular readership.

Nondenominational: Not associated with a particular denomination.

Not copyrighted: Publication of your piece in such a publication will put it into public domain and it is not then protected. Ask that the publisher carry your copyright notice on your piece when it is printed.

Novella: A short novel starting at 20,000 words—35,000 words maximum. Length varies from publisher to publisher.

On acceptance: Periodical or publisher pays a writer at the time manuscript is accepted for publication.

On assignment: Writing something at the specific request of an editor.

Onetime rights: Selling the right to publish a story one time to any number of publications (usually refers to publishing for a nonoverlapping readership).

On publication: Publisher pays a writer when his/her manuscript is published.

On speculation/On spec: Writing something for an editor with the agreement that he will buy it only if he likes it.

Overrun: The extra copies of a book printed during the initial print run.

Over the transom: Unsolicited articles that arrive at a publisher's office.

Payment on acceptance: See "On acceptance."

Payment on publication: See "On publication."

Pen name/pseudonym: Using a name other than your legal name on an article or book in order to protect your identity or the identity of people included, or when the author wishes to remain anonymous. Put the pen name in the byline under the title, and your real name in the upper, left-hand corner.

Permissions: Asking permission to use the text or art from a copyrighted source.

Personal experience story: A story based on a real-life experience.

Personality profile: A feature article that highlights a specific person's life or accomplishments.

Photocopied submission: Sending an editor a photocopy of your manuscript, rather than an original. Some editors prefer an original.

Piracy: To take the writings of others just as they were written and put your name on them as the author.

Plagiarism: To steal and use the ideas or writings of another as your own, rewriting them to make them sound like your own.

Press kit: A compilation of promotional materials on a particular book or author, usually organized in a folder, used to publicize a book.

Print-on-demand (POD): A printing process where books are printed one at a time instead of in quantity. The production cost per book is higher, but no warehousing is necessary. Bookstores typically will not carry POD books.

Public domain: Work that has never been copyrighted, or on which the copyright has expired. Subtract 75 from the current year, and anything copyrighted prior to that is in public domain.

Published clips: Copies of actual articles you have had published, from newspapers or magazines.

Quarterly: Every three months.

Query letter: A letter sent to an editor telling about an article you propose to write and asking if he or she is interested in seeing it.

Reporting time: The number of weeks or months it takes an editor to get back to you about a query or manuscript you have sent in.

Reprint rights: Selling the right to reprint an article that has already been published elsewhere. You must have sold only first or onetime rights originally, and wait until it has been published the first time.

Review copies: Books given to book reviewers or buyers for chains.

Royalty: The percentage an author is paid by a publisher on the sale of each copy of a book.

SAE: Self-addressed envelope (without stamps).

SAN: Standard Account Number, used to identify libraries, book dealers, or schools.

SASE: Self-addressed, stamped envelope. Should always be sent with a manuscript or query letter.

SASP: Self-addressed, stamped postcard. May be sent with a manuscript submission to be returned by publisher indicating it arrived safely.

Satire: Ridicule that aims at reform.

Second serial rights: See "Reprint rights."

Semiannual: Issued twice a year.

Serial: Refers to publication in a periodical (such as first serial rights).

Sidebar: A short feature that accompanies an article and either elaborates on the human interest side of the story or gives additional information on the topic. It is often set apart by appearing within a box or border.

Simultaneous rights: Selling the rights to the same piece to several publishers simultaneously. Be sure everyone is aware that you are doing so.

Simultaneous submissions: Sending the same manuscript to more than one publisher at the same time. Usually done with nonoverlapping markets (such as denominational or newspapers) or when you are writing on a timely subject. Be sure to state in a cover letter that it is a simultaneous submission and why.

Slander: The verbal act of defamation.

Slanting: Writing an article so that it meets the needs of a particular market.

Slush pile: The stack of unsolicited manuscripts that have arrived at a publisher's office.

Speculation: See "On speculation."

Staff-written material: Material written by the members of a magazine staff.

Subsidiary rights: All those rights, other than book rights, included in a book contract such as paperback, book club, movie, etc.

Subsidy publisher: A book publisher who charges the author to publish his book, as opposed to a royalty publisher who pays the author.

Synopsis: A brief summary of work from one paragraph to several pages long.

Tabloid: A newspaper-format publication about half the size of a regular newspaper.

Take-home paper: A periodical sent home from Sunday school each week (usually) with Sunday school students, children through adults.

Think piece: A magazine article that has an intellectual, philosophical, or provocative approach to a subject.

Third world: Reference to underdeveloped countries of Asia and Africa.

Trade magazine: A magazine whose audience is in a particular trade or business.

Traditional verse: One or more verses with an established pattern that is repeated throughout the poem.

Transparencies: Positive color slides, not color prints.

Unsolicited manuscript: A manuscript an editor didn't specifically ask to see.

Vanity publisher: See "Subsidy publisher."

Vignette: A short, descriptive literary sketch or a brief scene or incident.

Vitae/Vita: An outline of one's personal history and experience.

Work-for-hire: Signing a contract with a publisher stating that a particular piece of writing you are doing for him is work-for-hire. In the agreement you give the publisher full ownership and control of the material.

Writers' guidelines: An information sheet provided by a publisher that gives specific guidelines for writing for the publication. Always send an SASE with your request for guidelines.

GENERAL INDEX

This index includes periodicals, books, distributors, greeting cards/specialty markets, and agents, as well as some of the organizations/resources and specialty lists or areas you may need to find quickly. Conferences, groups, and editorial services are listed alphabetically by state in those sections (not in the index). Check the table of contents for the location of supplementary listings.

Note: Because of the many changes in the market, and to help you determine the current status of any publisher you might be looking for, all markets (past and present) will be listed in this index. If they are not viable markets, their current status will be indicated here. The following codes will be used:

(ABD) asked to be deleted
(BA) bad address or contact information
(ED) editorial decision
(NF) no freelance
(NR) no recent response
(OB) out of business
(UTC) unable to contact

These changes will be noted in this listing for five years before being dropped altogether.

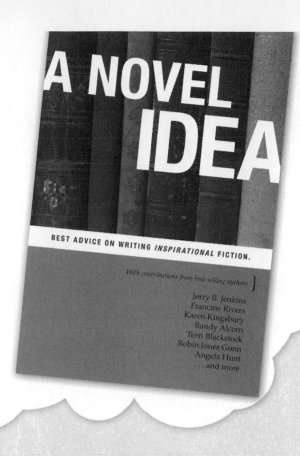

A NOVEL IDEA

BEST ADVICE ON WRITING *INSPIRATIONAL* FICTION.

With contributions from best-selling authors }

Jerry B. Jenkins
Francine Rivers
Karen Kingsbury
Randy Alcorn
Terri Blackstock
Robin Jones Gunn
Angela Hunt
. . . and more

Expert advice from successful fiction writers who have published thousands of novels, with more than 70 million copies sold.

Whether you're a novice or have been writing for years, learn the best ways to plan, perfect, and promote your writing. Discover what makes a novel Christian, and master the art of writing about tough topics.

This valuable guide contains tips on

> plotting,
> dialogue,
> point of view,
> characterization,

> marketing,
> social networking,
> and more. . . .

For the first time, best-selling Christian novelists have joined together to bring you this comprehensive guide on the craft of writing. If you've always wanted to write the next great novel or felt compelled to tell the story that's burning inside you, *A Novel Idea* will give you the tools you need.

CP0373

WE TRAIN WRITERS

Mentor-Guided Email Courses For Youth And Adults

Courses • Conferences
Contests • Critiques

JERRY B. JENKINS
CHRISTIAN
WRITERS
G U I L D

ChristianWritersGuild.com
ContactUs@ChristianWritersGuild.com
Toll-Free (866)495-5177